HALSBURY'S

Laws of England

ANNUAL ABRIDGMENT

1979

HALSBURY'S
Laws of England
ANNUAL ABRIDGMENT
1979

EDITOR

KENNETH MUGFORD

of Lincoln's Inn, Barrister

ASSISTANT EDITOR

GILLIAN MATHER LLB

BUTTERWORTHS

LONDON

ENGLAND	Butterworth & Co (Publishers) Ltd 88 Kingsway, London WC2B 6AB
AUSTRALIA	Butterworth Pty Ltd 586 Pacific Highway, Chatswood, Sydney, NSW 2067 Also at Melbourne, Brisbane, Adelaide and Perth
CANADA	Butterworth & Co (Canada) Ltd 2265 Midland Avenue, Scarborough, Toronto M1P 4S1
NEW ZEALAND	Butterworths of New Zealand Ltd T. & W. Young Building, 77–85 Customhouse Quay, Wellington
SOUTH AFRICA	Butterworth & Co (South Africa) (Pty) Ltd 152–154 Gale Street, Durban
USA	Butterworth & Co (Publishers) Inc 10 Tower Office Park, Woburn, Boston, Mass 01801

Editorial Staff

JANE RUDDICK LLB
of Gray's Inn, Barrister

WENDY SPILLING LLB

GOURI PREECE BA
of Gray's Inn, Barrister

SHEILA SELLARS BA

MADELEINE JONES LLB
Solicitor

ANNE RADFORD BA

Indexer

DAVID ROBERTS

Administrative Manager

PHYLLIS BUCK

ISBN 0 406 03365 x

Typeset by CCC in Great Britain by William Clowes (Beccles) Limited, Beccles and
London

PUBLISHERS' NOTE

This is the sixth Annual Abridgment and covers the year 1979. The Abridgment constitutes year by year a comprehensive survey of English case law, statute law and subordinate legislation. European Community law and decisions of Commonwealth courts are given attention commensurate with their importance. Further, the Abridgment chronicles and tabulates topics which may be of interest to lawyers. Such topics are derived from government papers, reports of committees, the EEC official journal, legal periodicals and the daily press.

Each Annual Abridgment is complete without any recourse to any other publication.

The alphabetical arrangement, the comprehensive tables and index and the inclusion of destination and derivation tables of consolidation legislation make the work an ideal aid in research. At the same time, the typography and presentation have been so designed that the Abridgment is suitable for independent study. A section entitled "In Brief", which immediately follows the table of contents, shows at a glance the year's main developments.

When referring to this volume reference should be made to both the year and the relevant paragraph number: e.g. "1979 Halsbury's Abridgment para. 2039".

This volume covers the law made in 1979 and is compiled from sources available in London on 31st December 1979.

BUTTERWORTH LAW PUBLISHERS LTD

TABLE OF CONTENTS

Text of this Work arranged under Titles as follows:

IN BRIEF

A summary of the year's main developments

Agriculture
An occupier of a commercial unit, despite not being the sole occupier, cannot apply for succession to an agricultural tenancy: *Jackson v Hall*; *Williamson v Thompson*, para. 47.

Arbitration
The Arbitration Act 1979 amends in several respects the law relating to arbitrations, including the provision of a limited right of appeal to the High Court in place of the special case procedure: para. 135.

A court can dismiss a claim in arbitration for want of prosecution: *Bremer Vulkan Schiffbau und Maschinenfabrik v South India Shipping Corpn, Gregg v Raytheon Ltd*, para. 162.

Banking
The Banking Act 1979 provides for the authorisation and supervision by the Bank of England of institutions which take deposits from the public: para. 192.

Commonwealth and dependencies
The Crown Agents Act 1979 establishes a corporate body to be called the Crown Agents for Overseas Governments and Administrations in place of the existing Crown Agents: para. 318.

Companies
Where, consequent upon the winding up of a company, the company's property is sold at a profit, the liquidator will be liable to pay corporation tax in respect of the chargeable gain realised: *Re Mesco Properties Ltd*, para. 381.

The court has an unfettered discretion whether or not to make a compulsory winding up order and is not compelled to give effect to the views of the majority creditors in value: *Re Southard and Co Ltd*, para. 387.

Conflict of laws
A properly executed Moslem "talaq" divorce obtained overseas will be recognised in the United Kingdom: *Quazi v Quazi*, para. 429.

Constitutional law
The Crown has no legal duty to protect a subject from unlawful arrest and imprisonment: *Mutasa v Attorney-General*, para. 443.

Contempt of court
The publication of the name of a witness granted anonymity may amount to contempt of court where such publication constitutes interference with the administration of justice: *Attorney General v Leveller Magazine Ltd*, para. 469.

Contract

The High Court has laid down principles for the making of awards under the Law Reform (Frustrated Contracts) Act 1943: *B.P. Exploration Co (Libya) Ltd v Hunt (No. 2)*, para. 502.

A doctor will be in breach of contract if he fails to exercise reasonable skill and care in performing an operation for a legal abortion, with the result that he fails to abort the woman: *Sciuriaga v Powell*, para. 471.

Courts

The Court of Appeal has outlined the characteristics of a court: *Attorney General v BBC*, para. 467.

Criminal law

There is no property in confidential information capable of being the subject of a charge of theft: *Oxford v Moss*, para. 642.

The House of Lords has affirmed that subjective intent is not an essential element of the offence of blasphemous libel: *R v Lemon*, para. 583.

A person who enters a building as a trespasser intending to steal anything he might find may be convicted of burglary notwithstanding that he finds nothing worth stealing: *Attorney-General's References (Nos. 1 and 2 of 1979)*, para. 584.

The offence of misconduct in a public office does not necessarily involve an element of corruption: *R v Dytham*, para. 634.

Criminal procedure

The Criminal Evidence Act 1979 allows defendants to be asked questions tending to show that they have committed an offence where they have given evidence against another person charged in the same proceedings: para. 670.

The Court of Appeal has considered the principles applying to the admissibility of statements made by a defendant: *R v Pearce*, para. 672.

A judge cannot exclude evidence merely because it could not have been obtained but for the activities of an agent provocateur: *R v Sang*, para. 689.

Damages and compensation

The Vaccine Damage Payments Act 1979 makes provision for the payment of compensation to those damaged as a result of routine vaccination or through contact with a person so vaccinated: para. 1947.

The House of Lords has affirmed that an award of damages to a person who is unconscious or insensible should include a sum for loss of future earnings: *Lim Poh Choo v Camden and Islington Area Health Authority*, para. 805.

Deeds

Rectification of a deed may be ordered to give effect to the common intention of the parties notwithstanding that the intention is the legitimate avoidance of tax: *Re Slocock's Will Trusts*, para. 1891.

Discovery

For a document to be protected from discovery on the ground of legal professional privilege, its dominant purpose must be that of preparation for litigation: *Waugh v British Railways Board*, para. 916.

Where the Crown alleges that disclosure of documents would be injurious to the public interest the court has a discretion to review such a claim: *Burmah Oil Co Ltd v Bank of England*, para. 915.

In cases of alleged discrimination an industrial tribunal has a discretion to order discovery of confidential reports on employees: *Science Research Council v Nasse; BL Cars Ltd (formerly Leyland Cars) v Vyas*, para. 913.

Divorce

A custody order made in respect of a child does not preclude a denial that the child is a child of the family in subsequent proceedings: *Rowe v Rowe*, para. 947.

A properly executed Moslem "talaq" divorce obtained overseas will be recognised in the United Kingdom: *Quazi v Quazi*, para. 429.

Easements

There is a rule of public policy that a transaction is not, without good reason, to be treated as depriving land of a suitable means of access: *Nickerson v Barraclough*, para. 984.

Education

The Education Act 1979 abolishes the duty to give effect to the comprehensive principle in education: para. 998.

Employment

An employer is not entitled to a redundancy rebate unless he is under a statutory obligation to make a redundancy payment: *Secretary of State for Employment v Globe Elastic Thread Co Ltd*, para. 1098.

In cases of alleged discrimination an industrial tribunal has a discretion to order discovery of confidential reports on employees: *Science Research Council v Nasse; BL Cars Ltd (formerly Leyland Cars) v Vyas*, para. 913.

Evidence

No party in a case has any property in the evidence of an expert witness, and such a witness can be compelled by the court to give evidence: *Harmony Shipping Co SA v Davis and Saudi Europe Line Ltd*, para. 1256.

Execution

The Charging Orders Act 1979 makes provision for the imposition of charges to secure payment of money due or to become due under judgments or court orders: para. 1263.

Executors and administrators

The widow of an intestate may require appropriation of the matrimonial home in satisfaction of her interest in the estate, notwithstanding that the home's value is greater than her interest: *Re Phelps (deceased), Wells v Phelps*, para. 1271.

Gift and estate taxation

Rectification of a deed may be ordered to give effect to the common intention of the parties notwithstanding that the intention is the legitimate avoidance of tax: *Re Slocock's Will Trusts*, para. 1891.

Housing

Homeless persons can sue local authorities in damages for breach of the statutory duty to house: *Thornton v Kirklees Metropolitan Borough Council*, para. 1432.

Human rights

The European Commission of Human Rights has no jurisdiction to consider allegations of violation of the European Convention on Human Rights made against the European Communities: *Confederation Francaise Democratique du Travail v European Communities*, para. 1446.

The European Court of Human Rights has held that prohibitive legal costs amounted to a denial of access to a court: *Airey's case*, para. 1451.

Husband and wife

A husband and wife are not immune from liability in tort for conspiracy: *Midland Bank Trust Co Ltd v Green (No. 3)*, para. 1646.

Income taxation

The House of Lords has examined the extent of the Inland Revenue's powers of search and seizure in cases of suspected tax fraud: *Inland Revenue Comrs v Rossminster Ltd*, para. 1532.

Where, consequent upon the winding up of a company, the company's property is sold at a profit, the liquidator will be liable to pay corporation tax in respect of the chargeable gain realised: *Re Mesco Properties Ltd*, para. 381.

Industrial and provident societies

The Credit Unions Act 1979 establishes a legal framework for credit unions in Great Britain: para. 1579.

Injunctions

The Court of Appeal has set out guidelines as to what is required of a party seeking a Mareva injunction: *Third Chandris Shipping Corpn, Western Sealane Corpn, Aggelikai Ptera Compania Maritima SA v Unimarine SA*, para. 1594.

Insurance

A broker's knowledge of facts about an insured person is to be imputed to the insurer, and the insurer is entitled to be indemnified by the broker for liability arising as a result of the broker's failure to inform the insurer of the facts: *Woolcott v Excess Insurance Co Ltd*, para. 1629.

Land charges

The Court of Appeal has considered the meaning of "purchaser for money or money's worth" in relation to the registration of land charges: *Midland Bank Trust Co Ltd v Green*, para. 1657.

Land registration

A wife's unregistered interest in the matrimonial home is an overriding interest within the Land Registration Act 1925: *Williams and Glyn's Bank v Boland*, para. 1934.

Landlord and tenant

A proviso in a lease that before the tenant applies for the landlord's consent to assignment he must offer to surrender the lease is valid: *Bocardo SA v S & M Hotels Ltd*, para. 1687.

An adult who lives platonically with a person not related to him can never establish the required familial nexus to succeed to a statutory tenancy: *Carega Properties SA v Sharratt*, para. 1709.

Where a lessee assigns a lease in breach of covenant, notice of forfeiture of the lease should be served on the assignee, not the lessee: *Old Grovebury Manor Farm Ltd v W Seymour Plant Sales and Hire Ltd (No. 2)*, para. 1691.

Leasehold enfranchisement or extension

The Leasehold Reform Act 1979 gives a tenant in possession claiming to acquire the freehold under the Leasehold Reform Act 1967, further protection against artificial inflation of the price he has to pay: para. 1725.

Legal aid and advice

The Legal Aid Act 1979 makes various amendments to the existing provisions for legal aid, advice and assistance, including the extension of the scope of advice and assistance: para. 1737.

A legal aid order made by the Crown Court does not extend to expenses incurred by a solicitor in respect of work done prior to the making of the order: *R v Rogers*, para. 1730.

Libraries

The Public Lending Right Act 1979 confers a public lending right on authors entitling them to payment in respect of loans of their works from public libraries: para. 1754.

Local government

The Local Government Boundary Commission should fix the number of councillors for a borough in accordance with the interests of effective and convenient local government; electoral equality is a secondary consideration only: *London Borough of Enfield v Local Government Boundary Commission for England*, para. 1763.

Medicine

The Nurses, Midwives and Health Visitors Act 1979 establishes a United Kingdom Central Council for Nursing, Midwivery and Health Visiting and four National Boards, and it contains provisions as to education and training requirements: para. 1832.

Minors

A custody order made in respect of a child does not preclude a denial that the child is a child of the family in subsequent proceedings: *Rowe v Rowe*, para. 947.

A child does not cease to be in the care of a local authority immediately upon receipt of the parent's notice of his intention to resume care: *London Borough of Lewisham v Lewisham Juvenile Court Justices*, para. 1863.

Mistake

Rectification of a deed may be ordered to give effect to the common intention of the parties notwithstanding that the intention is the legitimate avoidance of tax: *Re Slocock's Will Trusts*, para. 1891.

Mortgage

A wife's unregistered interest in the matrimonial home is an overriding interest within the Land Registration Act 1925: *Williams and Glyn's Bank v Boland*, para. 1934.

Nuisance

An occupier is under a duty of care in respect of hazards arising from natural causes on his own property which encroach on adjoining land and cause damage: *Leakey v National Trust*, para. 1999.

Nuisance

An occupier is under a duty of care in respect of hazards arising from natural causes on his own property which encroach onto adjoining land and cause damage: *Leakey v National Trust*, para. 1999.

Police

The courts have no power to prevent the interruption of telephone conversations by the Post Office on behalf of the police: *Malone v Metropolitan Police Commissioner*, para. 2093.

Practice and procedure

The Rules of the Supreme Court have been amended to allow service by post in many cases in which personal service was previously required: para. 2155.

A defendant's right not to have to disclose his case prior to a criminal hearing does not necessarily extend to concurrent civil proceedings: *Jefferson Ltd v Bhetcha*, para. 2137.

The dismissal of an action for want of prosecution is not appropriate where the plaintiff has an indefeasible right to bring another action within the limitation period: *Tolley v Morris*, para. 2169.

Prisons

The High Court has outlined certain principles which should be observed when a prison board of visitors is adjudicating under the prison disciplinary procedure: *R v Hull Prison Board of Visitors, ex parte St. Germain (No. 2)*, para. 2175.

Sale of land

The Estate Agents Act 1979 regulates certain activities of estate agents in relation to the acquisition or disposal of interests in land, with the object of protecting users of their services: para. 2367.

There is a rule of public policy that a transaction is not, without good reason, to be treated as depriving land of a suitable means of access: *Nickerson v Barraclough*, para. 984.

The widow of an intestate may require appropriation of the matrimonial home in satisfaction of her interest in the estate, notwithstanding that the home's value is greater than her interest: *Re Phelps (deceased), Wells v Phelps*, para. 1271.

With respect to the sale of land, a solicitor has ostensible authority to effect an exchange of contracts by telephone: *Domb v Isoz*, para. 2355.

Sex discrimination

The Court of Appeal has considered the meaning of "provision in relation to retirement" in sex discrimination legislation: *Roberts v Cleveland Area Health Authority*; *Garland v British Rail Engineering Ltd*; *Turton v MacGregor Wallcoverings Ltd*, para. 2507.

Shipping and navigation

The Merchant Shipping Act 1979 amends the law of pilotage, carriage by sea, shipowners' and salvors' liability and pollution from ships: para. 2567.

Solicitors

A solicitor who is instructed by his client to carry out a transaction conferring a benefit on a third party owes a duty of care to the third party: *Ross v Caunters*, para. 2698.

The Court of Appeal has examined the extent of a solicitor's duty to inform his client of his rights in relation to the payment of a bill of costs: *Clement-Davis v Inter GSA*, para. 2695.

Telecommunications

The courts have no power to prevent the interception of telephone conversations by the Post Office on behalf of the police: *Malone v Metropolitan Police Commissioner*, para. 2093.

Tort

A husband and wife are not immune from liability in tort for conspiracy: *Midland Bank Trust Co Ltd v Green (No 3)*, para. 1646.

Town and country planning

Control of office development has been terminated: para. 2754.

Trade unions

The House of Lords has considered the granting of interlocutory injunctions preventing trade unions from blacking firms where such action is claimed to be in furtherance of a trade dispute: *NWL Ltd v Woods, NWL Ltd v Nelson*, para. 2831; *Express Newspapers Ltd v MacShane*, para. 2828.

Unfair dismissal

The qualifying period for complaints of unfair dismissal is now fifty-two weeks: para. 2917.

Weights and measures

The Weights and Measures Act 1979 makes new provisions relating to packaged goods and amends existing legislation: para. 3089.

REFERENCES AND ABBREVIATIONS

ACTR	Australian Capital Territory Reports
All ER	All England Law Reports
ALJ	Australian Law Journal
ALJR	Australian Law Journal Reports
ALR	Australian Law Reports
ATC	Annotated Tax Cases
BJAL	British Journal of Administrative Law
Brit J Criminol	British Journal of Criminology
BTR	British Tax Review
CCC	Canadian Criminal Cases
CLJ	Cambridge Law Journal
CLR	Commonwealth Law Reports (Australia)
CMLR	Common Market Law Reports
CML Review	Common Market Law Review
Conv	Conveyancer
Conv (NS)	Conveyancer and Property Lawyer
Cr App Rep	Criminal Appeal Reports
Crim LR	Criminal Law Review
DLR	Dominion Law Reports (Canada)
EA	East Africa Law Reports
ECR	European Court Reports
EHRR	European Human Rights Reports
FR	Federal Court Reports (Canada)
FSR	Fleet Street Reports
ICLQ	International and Comparative Law Quarterly
ICR	Industrial Cases Reports
IJR	Irish Jurist Reports
ILJ	Industrial Law Journal
ILT	Irish Law Times
ILTR	Irish Law Times Reports
Imm AR	Immigration Appeals
IR	Irish Reports
IRLR	Industrial Relations Law Reports
ITR	Industrial Tribunal Reports
JBL	Journal of Business Law
JCL	Journal of Criminal Law
JP	Justice of the Peace Reports
JP Jo	Justice of the Peace Journal
JPL	Journal of Planning and Environmental Law
JR	Juridical Review
JSPTL	Journal of the Society of Public Teachers of Law
KIR	Knight's Industrial Reports
LE	Legal Executive
LG	Law Guardian
LGC	Local Government Chronicle
LGR	Local Government Reports
Lloyd's Rep	Lloyd's Reports
LMCLQ	Lloyd's Maritime and Commercial Law Quarterly
LQR	Law Quarterly Review
LS Gaz	Law Society Gazette

LS Gaz R	Law Society Gazette Reports
L(TC)	Income Tax Leaflets
Med Sci & Law	Medicine Science & The Law
MLR	Modern Law Review
NI	Northern Ireland Reports
NILQ	Northern Ireland Law Quarterly
NLJ	New Law Journal
NSWLR	New South Wales Law Reports
NZLR	New Zealand Law Reports
OJC	Official Journal of the European Communities—communications and information series
OJL	Official Journal of the European Communities—legislation series
OR	Ontario Reports
PL	Public Law
P & CR	Property and Compensation Reports
RA	Rating Appeals
RPC	Reports of Patent Etc. Cases
RRC	Ryde's Rating Cases
RTR	Road Traffic Reports
RVR	Rating and Valuation Reporter
SASR	South Australian State Reports
SC	Session Cases
SCR	Supreme Court Reports (Canada)
SLG	Scottish Law Gazette
SLT	Scots Law Times
Sol Jo	Solicitors' Journal
STC	Simon's Tax Cases
TC	Tax Cases
TR	Taxation Reports
Traff Cas	Traffic Cases
VR	Victorian Reports
WAR	Western Australian Reports
WIR	West Indian Reports
WLR	Weekly Law Reports
WWR	Western Weekly Reports (Canada)

TABLE OF STATUTES

TABLE OF STATUTORY INSTRUMENTS

TABLE OF SECONDARY LEGISLATION OF THE EUROPEAN COMMUNITIES

TABLE OF CASES

Decisions of the European Court of Justice are listed both alphabetically and numerically. The numerical table follows the alphabetical.

41

HALSBURY'S
Annual Abridgment 1979

ADMINISTRATIVE LAW

Halsbury's Laws of England (4th edn.), Vol. 1, paras. 1–215

1 **Articles**

Damages As a Remedy for Unlawful Administrative Action, Jeremy McBride: [1979] CLJ 323.

Judicial Review by Certiorari, W. T. West: 123 Sol Jo 760.

Public Policy and the Wrongdoer, F. Graham Glover (when a plaintiff, who has acted in breach of the law, will be denied relief on grounds of public policy): 129 NLJ 37.

2 **Certiorari—availability—presence of hostile superior officer at disciplinary hearing—application to quash committee's decision**

A fire officer was charged with disobeying a lawful order without sufficient cause. The matter, which would normally have been heard by the Chief Fire Officer ('CFO'), was referred to a disciplinary committee because of hostile relationships between the two men. The committee found the officer guilty, and, on retiring to consider sentence, requested the assistance of the CFO who had been present throughout the hearing. The officer was subsequently sentenced to a reduction in rank. When he protested about the CFO's presence during the committee's deliberations, he was informed that the decision on sentence had been made entirely by the members of the committee. An application was made for an order of certiorari to quash the committee's decision on the ground of breach of natural justice. *Held*, while all the CFO had done was to advise the committee on the various sentences and in actual fact the officer had not been unjustly treated, the principle that justice must always be manifestly seen to have been done applied to quasi-judicial bodies. The officer's obvious hostility to the CFO rendered it imperative that that rule be applied; the committee's assurance in response to the officer's protest was insufficient to rectify the matter and accordingly the application should be granted.

R v LEICESTER FIRE AUTHORITY, EX PARTE THOMPSON [1978] LS Gaz R 1234 (Queen's Bench Division: LORD WIDGERY CJ, GRIFFITHS and GIBSON JJ). *Ward v Bradford Corpn* (1971) 115 Sol Jo 606, CA applied.

3 **—— —— taxpayer's allegations that proceedings before Commissioners a nullity**

See *Dutta v Doig (Inspector of Taxes)*, para. 1497.

4 **Issue of certificate by statutory authority—certificate invalid—whether void or voidable**

See *London and Clydeside Estates Ltd v Aberdeen District Council*, para. 409.

5 Judicial control of administrative action—abuse of discretion—directions by Secretary of State concerning reimbursement of wages of doctors' staff

See *Glanvill v Secretary of State for Social Services*, para. 1945.

6 Mandamus—law against obscene publications—application to compel enforcement of that law

See *R v Metropolitan Police Commissioner, ex parte Blackburn*, para. 2084.

7 Natural justice—breach—appeal—jurisdiction to hear appeal—whether defects curable on appeal

Australia

A racehorse owner was disqualified for one year and his membership of the Australian Jockey Club was forfeited after a stewards' inquiry. The owner's appeal to the committee of the club was dismissed. He brought an action for a declaration that his disqualification and the dismissal of his appeal were void on the grounds that the stewards had failed to observe the rules of natural justice and their decision was therefore invalid and accordingly the committee had no jurisdiction to hear or determine the appeal from it. The trial judge held that although there had been a breach of natural justice, the proceedings before the committee constituted a hearing de novo and the defects in the stewards' inquiry were thereby cured. The owner appealed to the Privy Council. *Held*, a decision reached in breach of natural justice was void, not voidable, but until declared void by a competent body, it was of some effect or existence in law. Assuming the stewards' decision to be void, it was still a decision for the purposes of an appeal and the committee therefore had jurisdiction to entertain the appeal. There was no absolute rule that defects in natural justice could or could not be cured by appeal proceedings. However, where a member of a body was deemed by its rules to have agreed to accept what in the end was a fair decision, the court had to decide whether at the end of the proceedings there had been a fair result reached by fair methods which the member should fairly be taken to have accepted. On the facts, the owner's case had received overall full and fair consideration and there was no basis on which the court should interfere. The appeal would be dismissed.

CALVIN V CARR [1979] 2 All ER 440 (Privy Council: LORD WILBERFORCE, VISCOUNT DILHORNE, LORD HAILSHAM OF ST MARYLEBONE, LORD KEITH OF KINKEL and LORD SCARMAN). *Crane v Director of Public Prosecutions* [1921] All ER Rep 19 applied.

8 —— —— disclosure to parties of information before court—wardship proceedings

See *B v W (Wardship: Appeal)*, para. 1877.

9 —— disciplinary hearing—presence of hostile superior officer at disciplinary hearing

See *R v Leicester Fire Authority, ex parte Thompson*, para. 2.

10 —— —— prior notice of hearing—adequacy of notice

See *R v Gaming Club for Great Britain, ex parte Fenton, Mills and Wood*, para. 312.

11 —— domestic inquiry—employee's right to know case against him

See *Bentley Engineering Co Ltd v Mistry*, para. 2904.

12 —— opportunity to be heard—arbitration hearing

See *Thos. P. Gonzalez Corpn v Muller's Muhle, Muller GmbH & Co KG*, para. 140.

13   —— —— **disciplinary hearing before prison board of visitors**

See *R v Hull Prison Board of Visitors, ex parte St Germain (No. 2)*, para. 2175.

14   —— —— **public inquiry—decision based on issue not raised at inquiry**

See *Charles Church Ltd v Secretary of State for the Environment*, para. 2749.

15   —— —— —— **right of cross-examination**

A public inquiry was held into two motorway schemes. At the inquiry, the inspector refused to allow cross-examination of a witness concerning evidence of future traffic predictions given on behalf of the Department of the Environment. The inspector recommended that both schemes proceed. Objectors to the scheme requested that the inquiry be re-opened in the light of new evidence, but the minister refused, stating that he was satisfied that the evidence did not affect the inspector's recommendation. The objectors unsuccessfully appealed for an order to quash the minister's decision. The objectors further appealed, contending that the inspector was wrong to disallow cross-examination, and that they should have had an opportunity of commenting on the undisclosed new evidence that the minister had considered after the inquiry. *Held*, TEMPLEMAN LJ dissenting, the courts should ensure that public inquiries were conducted in accordance with the requirements of natural justice. Cross-examination should be allowed in a proper case. The instant case was such a case, as traffic forecasts were not governmental policy. Natural justice required that the objectors should also have had an opportunity of dealing with the new evidence. The appeal would be allowed.

BUSHELL v SECRETARY OF STATE FOR THE ENVIRONMENT (1979) 123 Sol Jo 605 (Court of Appeal: LORD DENNING MR, SHAW and TEMPLEMAN LJJ). Decision of Sir Douglas Frank QC sitting as a deputy High Court judge (1977) 122 Sol Jo 110, 1977 Halsbury's Abridgment para. 14 reversed. *Re Trunk Roads Act 1936, Re London–Portsmouth Trunk Road (Surrey) Compulsory Purchase Order (No. 2) 1938* [1939] 2 All ER 464, DC, distinguished.

This decision has been reversed by the House of Lords; see Times, 12th February 1980.

16   —— **power of Inland Revenue to seize documents—nature of power**

See *Inland Revenue Comrs v Rossminster Ltd*, para. 1532.

17   **Parliamentary Commissioner—investigation into delay in issuing documentation for purposes of claiming social security benefit in EEC member states**

See *Re Medical Treatment in Germany*, para. 1235.

18   —— **jurisdiction**

The government has made observations on the views of the Select Committee on the Parliamentary Commissioner (fourth report) (session 1977–78). The government has stated, inter alia, that it agrees with the Select Committee that there is no need for direct access to the Parliamentary Commissioner and welcomes the committee's conclusion that the parliamentary convention which inhibits members from taking up their colleagues' constituency cases shoud be interpreted flexibly where the reference of cases to the Parliamentary Commissioner is concerned. The government will accede to the committee's wishes and extend the jurisdiction of the Parliamentary Commissioner to include both the non-statutory and the statutory duties of career consular officers overseas. The government, however, has stated that it will not extend the jurisdiction to the commercial activities of government departments, nor to personnel matters relating to the Civil Service, retired Civil Servants nor to applicants for Civil Service posts. The government has also declined to give the Parliamentary Commissioner a right of access to Cabinet papers, stating that the cases where such access might be necessary would be very rare and that there is no evidence that present arrangements would give rise to any difficulties in the discharge of the Parliamentary Commissioner's responsibilities. See *Observations by the Government on the Fourth Report from the Select Committee on the Parliamentary Commissioner for Administration (Session 1977–78)* Cmnd. 7449.

19   —— —— Northern Ireland

The Parliamentary Commissioner (No. 2) Order 1979, S.I. 1979 No. 1705 (in force on 24th January 1980), adds the Northern Ireland Court Service to the list of departments and authorities which are subject to investigation by the Parliamentary Commissioner for Administration.

20   —— maladministration—remedies

Following an increase in vehicle excise duty in 1977 complaints were made to the Parliamentary Commissioner that persons had been misled by an ambiguously worded notice on the documents sent to them in connection with the renewal of their licences in March 1977 and, in consequence, they had delayed renewal until after budget day and subsequently had to pay a higher rate for the renewal (usually £10) than if they had renewed their licences before the budget. The Parliamentary Commissioner upheld the complaints and the Department of Transport instituted a scheme to make repayments in appropriate instances. The repayments were said to be made ex gratia; claims had to be made on forms available from the Driver and Vehicle Licensing Centre; claims had to be submitted by a specified date; and the scheme was advertised in the national press. Repayments were made in 102,500 instances, totalling £1.18 million. Subsequently, further complaints were made to the Parliamentary Commissioner by persons who had failed to receive repayments. In respect of these claims, the commissioner found that the repayments scheme was a discretionary act of policy and (subject to any decision by the courts) that there was no legal obligation to make any payment. Further, that there was no maladministration in the decision to require prospective claimants to submit claims. The commissioner also upheld the decision not to advertise the scheme even more widely, finding that the decision was reached with regard to cost-effectiveness in public expenditure and in the light of experienced professional advice from the Central Office of Information. The decision to require claims to be made within fifty days (and the acceptance for consideration of all claims made during the subsequent fortnight) was regarded as reasonable in the circumstances, as was the restriction of the scheme to the actual recipients of the ambiguously worded form in March 1977. See Parliamentary Commissioner for Administration, Third Report for Session 1978–79, Investigation of complaints about a Department of Transport scheme for partial repayment of vehicle excise duty incurred by certain individuals in 1977 (HC 247).

21   —— —— report

Two cases in the Fourth Report of the Parliamentary Commissioner for Administration for the Session 1978–79 (H of C Paper No. 302) concern the failure of the Department of Health and Social Security to bring the availability of social security benefits adequately to the attention of potential claimants, although it may be the department's usual practice to do so. In *Case 3A/343/78* the complaint concerned the failure to invite a person to apply for a retirement pension and in *Case 5/590/78* a complaint was made concerning industrial disablement benefit. The Commissioner dismissed both complaints on the ground that the onus was on the individual to make the application. He found injustice, however, where a tax office had given mistaken advice which had been acted upon to the detriment of the tax payer (in relation to top slicing relief). The result of his investigation of that complaint (*Case 1A/18/78*) was an apology and an offer of compensation of £1243; this the Commissioner regarded as a satisfactory remedy.

22   —— matters excluded from investigation

The Parliamentary Commissioner Order 1979, S.I. 1979 No. 915 (in force on 25th

August 1979), narrows the exception to the Parliamentary Commissioner's jurisdiction provided by the Parliamentary Commissioner Act 1967, Sch. 3, para. 2 (which relates to action taken by United Kingdom Government officials outside the United Kingdom) by excluding from it action taken by career consular officers in relation to United Kingdom citizens with a right of abode in the United Kingdom.

23   Tribunal—vaccine damage tribunals

The Tribunals and Inquiries (Vaccine Damage Tribunals) Order 1979, S.I. 1979 No. 659 (in force on 12th July 1979), brings under the supervision of the Council on Tribunals, tribunals constituted under the Vaccine Damage Payments Act 1979, para. 1947. The Order also provides for the selection of the chairman of the tribunals from a panel appointed by the Lord Chancellor, the Lord President of the Court of Session or the Lord Chief Justice of Northern Ireland, as the case may be.

ADMIRALTY

Halsbury's Laws of England (4th edn.), Vol. 1, paras. 301–568

24   Article

The Sister Ship Action in Rem, D. Rhidian Thomas (Administration of Justice Act 1956, s. 3(4) and the legal problems which have emerged): [1979] 2 LMCLQ 158.

25   Action in rem—commencement of action by issue of writ prior to winding up order—creditor's right to continue claim against company in liquidation

See *Re Aro Co Ltd*, para. 384.

26   Commencement of actions—procedure

See para. 2102.

27   Limitation of liability—entitlement to decree—single claim against plaintiffs

In arbitration proceedings, shipowners were held liable to cargo-owners for damage to cargo. The shipowners subsequently sought to limit their liability under the Merchant Shipping Act 1894, s. 503. The cargo-owners unsuccessfully contended that, as s. 504 (which provided for distribution of the amount for which the shipowner was liable between several claimants) did not apply because only one claim had been made, the shipowners should have raised the issue of limitation under s. 503 by their defence in the arbitration and that they could not subsequently do so. The cargo-owners appealed. *Held*, BRANDON LJ dissenting in part, it was sensible to deal with the question of liability first and limitation afterwards as a separate and distinct issue. This was not a case where the defence was one which not only could have been raised in the previous proceedings but should have been so raised, and res judicata did not therefore apply. Accordingly, the appeal would be dismissed.

THE PENELOPE II, AFROMAR INC v GREEK ATLANTIC COD FISHING CO (1979) Times, 21st November (Court of Appeal: LORD DENNING MR, BRANDON and BRIGHTMAN LJJ). Decision of Sheen J [1979] 2 Lloyd's Rep 42 affirmed.

28   Pilotage—Pilotage Commission—establishment

See Merchant Shipping Act 1979, para. 2567.

29   Practice—stay of proceedings—considerations governing grant

See *The Vishva Prabha*, para. 424.

30   Salvage—limitation of salvor's liability

See Merchant Shipping Act 1979, para. 2567.

AFFILIATION AND LEGITIMATION

Halsbury's Laws of England (4th edn.), Vol. 1, paras. 601–694

31   Affiliation order—enforcement

As some doubts have been expressed whether the table listing maximum periods of imprisonment in the Magistrates' Courts Act 1952, Sch. 3, para. 1 (as substituted by the Criminal Law Act 1977, s. 59) applies in respect of sums due under affiliation orders and orders enforceable as affiliation orders, the Home Secretary has stated his opinion that the table applies in respect of such payments, subject to the proviso that the maximum period of imprisonment which may be imposed is six weeks. The effect of the 1977 amendments is to raise the amount of arrears that must be outstanding relative to the period of imprisonment which may be imposed; as a result there may now be a number of cases where the period of imprisonment which may be imposed for arrears is governed by the table rather than the overall maximum of six weeks. See Home Office circular 31/1979.

32   —— paternity—blood tests

The Blood Tests (Evidence of Paternity) (Amendment) Regulations 1979, S.I. 1979 No. 1226 (in force on 1st November 1979), increase the fees payable under the Blood Tests (Evidence of Paternity) Regulations 1971 in respect of blood tests carried out for the purpose of determining paternity in civil proceedings.

AGENCY

Halsbury's Laws of England (4th edn.), Vol. 1, paras. 701–877

33   Articles

Estate Agents Act 1979 (para. 2367), Catherine M. Douglas and Robert G. Lee: 123 Sol Jo 478.

Payments to Accommodation Agencies, Ian R. Cartwright (on whether certain payments may be affected by the Rent Act 1977, 1977 Halsbury's Abridgment para. 1671): 123 Sol Jo 577.

34   Agent—authority—apparent authority—reliance by third party on representation by principal

Canada

In a case concerning the purported sale of sulphur by an employee of a company without the approval of that company, *held*, where an agent exceeded his actual authority and the third party dealing with the agent sought to bind the principal on the basis of the agent's apparent authority, the third party had to show that he had relied on a representation, express or implied, of the principal himself. The company would not therefore, in the absence of any representation by the management, be bound where an employee agreed on behalf of the company to an exceptional kind of transaction in circumstances where ordinarily approval by a superior would have been expected.

ROCKLAND INDUSTRIES INC V AMERADA MINERALS CORPN OF CANADA LTD (1978) 95 DLR (3d) 64 (Supreme Court of Alberta).

35   —— —— **contract for sale of goods—authority of buyer's representative to vary contract**

See *Toepfer v Warinco AG*, para. 2332.

36   —— —— **copyright agent—authority to bring ex parte application on behalf of copyright owners**

See *Carlin Music Corpn v Collins*, para. 520.

37   —— —— **solicitor—authority to exchange contracts**

See *Domb v Isoz*, para. 2355.

38   —— **estate agent**

See Estate Agents Act 1979, para. 2367.

39   —— —— **introduction to property—negotiation of lease through second agent—entitlement to commission**

The plaintiff was one of a number of estate agents employed by a company to find office accommodation, on terms that if he negotiated a lease on property for which he was not retained by the lessors he would look to the company for his commission. He later introduced the company to certain property, but the company, without telling him, negotiated the lease through the lessor's agents. The plaintiff claimed commission in respect of the negotiation. *Held*, it was plain that the plaintiff had introduced the property to the company and had carried out some negotiations which had ceased when he received no further instructions. As he was willing to carry out negotiations and the company had dealt through other agents without informing him, the plaintiff was entitled to treat the work which he had done as abortive and could therefore claim compensation on a quantum meruit basis.

SINCLAIR GOLDSMITH V MINERO PERU COMERCIAL (1978) 248 Estates Gazette 1015 (Queen's Bench Division: O'CONNOR J).

40   —— **insurance agent—imputation of knowledge to insurers—liability to indemnify insurer**

See *Woolcott v Excess Insurance Co Ltd*, para. 1628.

41   —— **right of set-off—right to set loss of profit against freight charges owed to principal**

See *James & Co Scheepvaarten Handelmij BV v Chinecrest Ltd*, para. 2547.

42   **Creation—whether party to contract principal or agent**

A member of the London Cocoa Terminal Market Clearing House agreed to act as broker for clients who could not go into the Market. The clients granted certain call options, which the broker exercised, but due to administrative difficulties the exercise was not notified to the clients until after the date specified in the contract. The clients alleged that under the contract the broker was obliged to notify them of the exercise or the options would be abandoned, and accordingly claimed damages to compensate for trading differences between the date specified in the contract and the actual date of notification. The broker contended that he had been acting as the clients' agent and the loss which the clients had suffered as a result of breach of the agency contract was nil. The court upheld the arbitrators' award in favour of the clients which was made on the ground that, according to market practice, both parties to brokerage contracts were principals. On appeal, *held*, in so far as the broker had undertaken to use the clearing house on his clients' behalf and had received a commission for that service he was an agent. However, market practice assigned the rights and liabilities attached to the option to him and regarded him as a principal to the brokerage contract. The law therefore obliged him to give his clients notice of the exercise of the options and the award would be upheld.

LIMAKO BV v H. HENTZ & CO INC [1979] 2 Lloyd's Rep 23 (Court of Appeal: MEGAW, ROSKILL and LAWTON LJJ).

43   Estate Agents Act 1979

See para. 2367.

44   Principal—liability—liability for agent's negligence—whether agent acting within authority

The plaintiff, a car dealer, took the defendant for a demonstration ride and gave him the telephone number of a third party who would hand over the vehicle should the defendant wish to buy it. The defendant telephoned the third party and arranged to collect the car. On receipt of the defendant's cheque the documents to the car were handed over. During a demonstration by the third party the car suddenly accelerated forwards, colliding with another car before hitting a tree, as a result of which the car had to be wholly written off. The defendant stopped the cheque and the plaintiff brought an action against him. The defendant counter-claimed for the value of the car on the ground that the third party was the plaintiff's agent and therefore the plaintiff was responsible for his negligence; alternatively, the plaintiff had failed to show that he had taken due care of the car and the damage caused was while the plaintiff was still a bailee of the car. *Held*, on the sale of a second-hand car where authority had been given by the seller to another person to hand over the car, the authority extended to a demonstration of the controls and if the person acted negligently, the seller was responsible for that negligence. Where an agent was appointed the seller remained the bailee of the car even though the property had passed to the buyer. The seller was therefore under a duty to take some care of the car and had failed to do so.

NELSON v RAPHAEL [1979] RTR 437 (Court of Appeal: MEGAW and BRIDGE LJJ and DUNN J).

45   Termination of agency—appointment of receiver and winding up order

See *Re Peek Winch & Tod Ltd*, para. 385.

AGRICULTURE

Halsbury's Laws of England (4th edn.), Vol. 1, paras. 1001–1853

46   Agricultural holding—application for succession to tenancy of deceased tenant—Agricultural Land Tribunal decision

DAGG v LOVETT (1979) 251 Estates Gazette 75: L. K. Brownson (application under Agriculture (Miscellaneous Provisions) Act 1976, s. 20, by widow of deceased tenant for tribunal's direction entitling her to tenancy; application by landlord for consent to notice to quit; widow's ineligibility under s. 18 (1) (b) waived as she had satisfied the requirement to a "material" extent within meaning of s. 21 (1) (b); her involvement in management substantial for five years before husband's death; application dismissed, however, as widow not suitable under s. 20 to farm the holding satisfactorily and profitably due to lack of experience; no decision necessary on landlord's application).

47   —— —— **eligibility—joint occupier of commercial unit**

In two cases which were heard together before the House of Lords, the questions for the court were (i) whether an applicant for a new tenancy under the Agriculture (Miscellaneous Provisions) Act 1976 was rendered ineligible by the fact that he was an occupier of a commercial unit under s. 18 (2) (c) notwithstanding that he was not the sole occupier; (ii) if a joint occupier of a such a unit at the time of the death of the tenant of the holding in respect of which a direction was sought was ineligible, whether he could make himself eligible by divesting himself of that occupation before he applied for a direction.

In the first case a farmer farmed two neighbouring holdings, the first of which he owned and was a commercial unit within the Agriculture Act 1967, s. 40, and the second of which he rented. Upon his death the first farm passed to his two sons. One son then assigned his interest in the first farm and made an application for a direction entitling him to succeed to the tenancy of the second farm. He claimed to be eligible since at the date of the application he was not the occupier of a commercial unit. The Court of Appeal had held that the date at which a person had to be an eligible person within the meaning of the 1976 Act, s. 18 was the date of the application and that he was thus eligible to apply.

In the second case, following the death of a tenant farmer, his son applied for a direction under the 1976 Act. He already owned a commercial unit in partnership with his brother and the High Court held that he was not entitled to succeed as he was the occupier of a commercial unit for the purposes of s. 18 (2) (c), that provision disqualifying joint occupiers as well as sole occupiers. *Held*; (i) LORD RUSSELL OF KILLOWEN dissenting, the 1976 Act intended to give a person who could show that he had derived his livelihood either entirely or principally from work on the relevant holding, the right to apply for a new tenancy provided that he did not occupy a viable farm. Parliament had not intended to give each of two joint occupiers of a commercial unit, which might have been of such a size and character as to provide them with a good living, the right to apply; (ii) eligibility was to be determined at the time of the death of the tenant. Parliament had not intended that a person, who at the date of death was ineligible, could bring himself within the class of eligible persons by divesting himself of that occupation.

Thus in the first case the appeal would be allowed as the son was not an eligible person at the time of the death of his father. In the second case the appeal would be dismissed as the applicant was the joint owner of a commercial unit.

JACKSON v HALL; WILLIAMSON v THOMPSON [1980] 1 All ER 177 (House of Lords: VISCOUNT DILHORNE, LORD EDMUND-DAVIES, LORD FRASER OF TULLYBELTON, LORD RUSSELL OF KILLOWEN and LORD LANE). Decision of Court of Appeal in *Jackson v Hall* [1979] 1 All ER 449, reversed, decision of Michael Kempster QC, sitting as a deputy High Court judge in *Williamson v Thompson* (1979) 251 Estates Gazette 955 affirmed.

48   —— **compulsory acquisition—compensation**

See *Wakerley v St Edmundsbury Borough Council*, para. 396.

49   —— **tenancy from year to year—licence to occupy agricultural land—whether effective as tenancy from year to year**

Every year from 1964, the plaintiff had made "grass keep" agreements in respect of a piece of land with its original owner, whereby he had a licence to pasture his animals on the land and to mow and take away the grass. Each agreement was for less than a year. In 1972, the plaintiff transferred the unexpired portion of the grass keep agreement for that year to the defendant. There was evidence of arrangements made between the defendant and the original owner for his use of the land in subsequent years. The original owner died in 1974 and left the land in her will to the plaintiff, who sought possession of it from the defendant. The defendant refused on the ground that he was entitled to possession under the Agricultural Holdings Act 1948, s. 2 (1), as a deemed tenant from year to year. The plaintiff contended that the case fell within the proviso to s. 2 (1), since the defendant had a licence to occupy land made "in contemplation of the use of the land only for grazing or mowing during some specified period of the year". *Held*, there was ample evidence to support a finding that the agreements between the defendant and the original owner were on the same terms as the agreement which the defendant had taken over from the plaintiff. These licences only extended over part of a year and thus fell within the proviso to s. 2 (1). An order for possession would accordingly be made.

LUTON V TINSEY (1978) 249 Estates Gazette 239 (Court of Appeal: MEGAW, BROWNE and WALLER LJJ).

50 —— —— **series of agreements for occupation of agricultural land—whether effective as tenancy from year to year**

The plaintiffs bought a farm with the intention of building on it at some time in the future. They agreed that a local farmer could use the land to graze cattle for several years under a series of agreements, each covering a period of six months. Thirteen years later the plaintiffs wanted to sell and, when the next six month agreement was signed, they required the farmer to promise vacant possession at the end of the period. The court rejected the farmer's claim that he had become a tenant from year to year under the Agricultural Holdings Act 1948. On appeal, *held*, when the original agreement was made it was intended that the farmer would hold the land under a series of six month agreements for at least three years, since that was the shortest duration which could be described by the word several. After the three years he would have further six month periods until he received reasonable notice, which should have been given at least six months before the final agreement was signed. Such notice had not been given and therefore the final agreement could not amount to surrender by operation of law. The farmer would accordingly remain as a tenant from year to year.

SHORT BROS (PLANT) LTD V EDWARDS (1978) 249 Estates Gazette 539 (Court of Appeal: STEPHENSON, GEOFFREY LANE and BRANDON LJJ).

51 **Agricultural levy—reliefs**

The Agricultural Levy Reliefs (Frozen Beef and Veal) Order 1979, S.I. 1979 No. 121 (in force on 15th February 1979), requires the Minister of Agriculture, Fisheries and Food to allocate the United Kingdom's share of a quota for the levy-free import of frozen beef and veal under the provisions of Council Regulation (EEC) 3063/78. Entitlement to relief is determined by the issue of licences.

52 **Agricultural Statistics Act 1979**

The Agricultural Statistics Act 1979 consolidates the Agriculture Act 1947, ss. 78–81 and other enactments relating to agricultural statistics. The Act received the royal assent on 22nd March 1979 and came into force on 22nd April 1979.

Derivation and destination tables appear on p. 11 following.

DESTINATION TABLE

This Table shows in column (1) the enactments repealed by the Agricultural Statistics Act 1979 and in column (2) the provisions of that Act corresponding thereto.

In certain cases, the enactment in column (1), though having a corresponding provision in column (2), is not wholly repealed as it is still partly required for the purposes of other legislation.

(1)	(2)	(1)	(2)
Agriculture Act 1947 (c. 48)	Agricultural Statistics Act 1979 (c. 13)	Agriculture (Miscellaneous Provisions) Act 1972 (c. 62)	Agricultural Statistics Act 1979 (c. 13)
s. 78 (1) (1A) (2)–(4) (5) (6) 79 80 81	s. 1 (1) 6 (1) 1 (2)–(4) 5 (6) 6 (1) 2 (1) 3 4	s. 18	s. 1 (1)
		Agriculture (Miscellaneous Provisions) Act 1976 (c. 55)	
		s. 6, Sch. 2	ss. 1 (1), 6 (1)

DERIVATION TABLE

The following table shows in the right hand column the legislative source from which the sections of the 1979 Act in the left hand column have been derived. In the table the following abbreviations are used:

1947	=	The Agriculture Act 1947 (10 & 11 Geo. 6. c. 48)
1972	=	The Agriculture (Miscellaneous Provisions) Act 1972 (1972 c. 62)
1976	=	The Agriculture (Miscellaneous Provisions) Act 1976 (1976 c. 55)
1977	=	The Criminal Law Act 1977 (1977 c. 45)
1978 (1)	=	The Interpretation Act 1978 (1978 c. 30)
1978 (2)	=	The Transfer of Functions (Wales) (No. 1) Order 1978 (S.I. 1978 No. 272)

Section of Act	Derivation
1 (1)	1947 s. 78 (1); 1972 s. 18; 1976 s. 6 (1) (a); 1978 (2) Art 2 (1), Sch. 1.
(2)	1947 s. 78 (2); 1978 (2) Art. 2 (1), Sch. 1.
(3), (4)	1947 s. 78 (3), (4)
(5)	See 1947 s. 106.
2 (1)	1947 s. 79; 1978 (2) Art. 2 (1), Sch. 1.
(2)	1947 s. 108 (1).
3	1947 s. 80; Industrial Training Act 1964 s. 2B; European Communities Act 1972, s. 12; 1978 (2) Art. 2 (1), Sch. 1.
4 (1)	1947 s. 81 (1).
(2)	1947 s. 81 (2); 1977 ss. 28 (2), 32 (1).
5 (1)–(5)	1947 s. 107.
(6)	1947 s. 78 (5).
6 (1)	1978 (2), Art. 2 (1), Sch. 1 (definition of "the appropriate Minister"); 1978 (1), s. 22 (1), Sch. 2 para. 5 (b) (definition of "land"); 1947 s, 781 (1A); 1976 s. 6 (1) (b) (definition of "livestock"); 1947 s. 78 (6) (definition of "owner"); 1947 s. 81 (2); 1977 s. 28 (7) (definition of "the prescribed sum"); 1947 s. 81 (2); 1976 s. 6 (1) b) (definition of "relevant land").
(2)	1947 ss. 78 (1A), 109; 1976 s. 6 (1) (b).
7	[Amendments and repeals.]
8	[Citation etc.]
Sch. 1	[Consequential amendments.]
Sch. 2	[Enactments repealed.]

53   Agricultural worker—accommodation provided by employer—security of tenure—meaning of agricultural work

A gamekeeper on an estate whose job was to rear pheasants for his employer's shoot appealed against a decision upholding an order granting possession of his cottage on the estate to his employer. He contended that he was entitled to security of tenure as an agricultural worker under the Rent (Agriculture) Act 1976. Section 1 of the Act defines agriculture as including the keeping and breeding of livestock which in turn includes any animal kept for the production of food. The gamekeeper argued that the pheasants were kept for the production of food, as the great majority of the birds shot were sold to butchers and game dealers. *Held*, the purpose of shooting pheasants was sport; it was no part of food production or the keeping of livestock. On the authorities, pheasants were not "livestock" within the meaning of s. 1, as the rearing and keeping of pheasants for sport was not an agricultural occupation and pheasants so kept and reared were not "livestock" in an agricultural context. The gamekeeper was not, therefore, employed in agriculture and the appeal would accordingly be dismissed.

EARL OF NORMANTON v GILES [1980] 1 All ER 106 (House of Lords: LORD WILBERFORCE, VISCOUNT DILHORNE, LORD DIPLOCK, LORD SALMON and LORD RUSSELL OF KILLOWEN). Decision of the Court of Appeal (1978) 248 Estates Gazette 869, 1978 Halsbury's Abridgment para. 49 affirmed. *Lord Glendyne v Rapley* [1978] 2 All ER 110, CA, 1978 Halsbury's Abridgment para. 48 applied.

54   ———— ———— ———— transitional provisions

The defendant and her husband, a farm worker, occupied a cottage owned by the husband's employer rent-free. In 1968 the husband fell ill and in 1969 his employment was terminated, but he and the defendant were allowed to remain in the cottage. In 1972 the cottage was sold to the plaintiff, who agreed that the defendant and her husband should remain in occupation. In 1973 the husband died and the defendant continued to live in the cottage rent-free until May 1977, when the plaintiff served notice to quit on her. An order was made for possession and the defendant appealed. *Held*, EVELEIGH LJ dissenting, the question was whether the defendant was given security of tenure by the Rent (Agriculture) Act 1976, which came into force on 1st January 1977. Schedule 9, para. 3 of the Act provided that a person who was occupying a dwelling-house as his residence on the operative date (namely, 1st January 1977) should become the statutory tenant if, on the assumption that the Act was in force at all material times before that date, he would be a statutory tenant on that date. Assuming the Act could be deemed to have been in force since 1968, at that time the husband would have been "a protected occupier in his own right" under s. 2 (1) and thus had security of tenure. After his employment was terminated, he would have continued as a protected occupier under s. 2 (2) or (3). The change of ownership of the cottage would not have affected his status. On his death, the defendant would have become a statutory tenant by virtue of s. 4 (2) and (3) and remained so at the date of the notice to quit.

The question then arose as to what were "all material times" in para. 3, and how far back the Act could be assumed to have been in force. The phrase meant at all times when any fact existed or event occurred which, if the Act had been in force at that time and thereafter, would have been relevant for the decision of the question with which the paragraph was concerned; namely, whether on and after 1st January 1977 the defendant was a statutory tenant. Thus the Act could be deemed to have been in force throughout the whole period from 1968. On that assumption, the defendant was the statutory tenant, and could not be given notice to quit without compliance with the provisions of the Act. The appeal would be allowed and the order for possession revoked.

SKINNER v COOPER [1979] 2 All ER 836 (Court of Appeal: MEGAW, WALLER and EVELEIGH LJJ).

55   Agriculture (Miscellaneous Provisions) Act 1968—amendment

The Agriculture (Miscellaneous Provisions) Act 1968 (Amendment) Regulations 1979, S.I. 1979 No. 25 (in force on 9th February 1979), amend the 1968 Act by substituting references to "area" and "areas" for references to "acreage" and "acreages" in s. 40 (3) (c), which provides for specifying the minimum amount of crop in respect of which payments may be made, and the manner in which the amounts of crop are to be determined for the purposes of a scheme made under s. 40 (1), (2).

56   Cereals Marketing Act 1965—amendment

The Cereals Marketing Act 1965 (Amendment) Regulations 1979, S.I. 1979 No. 26 (in force on 9th February 1979), further amend the Cereals Marketing Act 1965 by substituting references to "area" for references to "acreage" in ss. 13 (4), 15 (1) and 16 (6) (a), which provide for the specification of a rate of levy and its imposition.

57   Common agricultural policy—agriculture—agricultural producer—definition

In the course of national proceedings a German court asked the European Court of Justice to define the concept "agricultural producer" in the context of the EEC Treaty. *Held*, although EEC Treaty, art. 38 and related provisions allowed the scope of the agricultural provisions of the Treaty to be determined, there was no precise definition of the concept of "agriculture". Consequently, for the purposes of the agricultural rules derived from the Treaty, it was for the relevant competent authorities to define the scope of such rules, in relation both to persons and subject-matter.

Case 139/77: DENKAVIT FUTTERMITTEL GmbH v FINANZAMT WARENDORF [1978] ECR 1317 (European Court of Justice).

58   —— beef and veal—imports from non-member states—charges for veterinary and public health inspections

See *Simmenthal SpA v Amministrazione delle Finanze dello Stato*, para. 1207.

59   —— butter—subsidy

The Butter Subsidy (Protection of Community Arrangements) Regulations 1979, S.I. 1979 No. 586 (in force on 25th May 1979), consolidate with amendments the provisions previously made enabling the recovery of butter subsidies in certain circumstances, prohibiting the use of subsidised butter for manufacture and requiring records to be kept and information to be furnished about exports of butter.

60

The Butter Subsidy (Protection of Community Arrangements) (Amendment) Regulations 1979, S.I. 1979 No. 1175 (in force on 27th September 1979) amend the principal Regulations, supra., by re-defining "subsidy payment" and by amending the regulation relating to the recovery of a subsidy payment.

61   —— common organisation of markets—principle of non-discrimination

In proceedings before the English Commercial Court the plaintiffs, manufacturers of isoglucose, maintained that the British Government was not entitled to implement Regulation 1862/76 on the abolition of production refunds for starch used in the manufacture of isoglucose and the provisions of Regulation 1111/77 imposing production levies on isoglucose manufacturers. The court stayed the proceedings and referred to the European Court certain questions on the validity of those regulations. *Held*, the abolition of the refunds did not discriminate between manufacturers of isoglucose and manufacturers of other starch products since isoglucose, on account of its characteristics and properties, was not in competition with such other products and, moreover, as isoglucose was at least partially interchangeable with sugar, the maintenance of the refunds could have constituted discrimination against sugar manufacturers. However, although isoglucose was a direct substitute for, and as such in direct competition with liquid sugar, isoglucose and sugar manufacturers were treated differently as regards the imposition of production levies under Regulation 3330/74, art. 27 and Regulation 1111/77, arts. 8 and 9 respectively. Accordingly, to the extent that the latter imposed on isoglucose manufacturers a production levy which was manifestly unequal to that imposed on sugar manufacturers, those provisions were contrary to the prohibition on discrimination laid down in EEC Treaty art. 40 (3) and as such were invalid.

Joined Cases 103 and 145/77: ROYAL SCHOLTEN-HONIG (HOLDINGS) LTD v INTERVENTION BOARD FOR AGRICULTURAL PRODUCE [1978] ECR 2037 (European Court of Justice).

In implementation of this decision Council Regulation (EEC) 1293/79 (OJ No. L162, 30.6.79) amended Regulation 1111/77 by applying to isoglucose production rules analogous to those applied to sugar production.

62   —— —— **supremacy of community legislation**

In the course of the prosecution of a Northern Irish pig producer for offences in connection with the transport of pigs, the Resident Magistrate of Armagh referred to the European Court questions as to the classification of the Pigs Marketing Scheme in the context of the EEC Treaty and the effect on its practices of certain provisions of Community law. The Scheme, administered by the Pigs Marketing Board, was set up by Northern Ireland legislation to govern the marketing of bacon pigs by conferring on the Board the sole right to market such pigs, thus prohibiting sales by producers otherwise than to or through the agency of the Board, and the power to determine wholesale prices. *Held*, the effect of EEC Treaty, art. 38 (2) was that Treaty provisions relating to the common agricultural policy were to prevail over any other rules relating to the establishment of the common market and accordingly, the effect of the Scheme, which concerned a sector of economic activity, namely bacon pigs, covered by the common organisation of the market in pigmeat under Council Regulation (EEC) 2759/75, could not be justified or exempted under any other Treaty provision. Further, in accordance with the concept on which the common organisation of markets were based, namely, an open market to which every producer had free access, once such an organisation of the market had been established in a given sector pursuant to art. 40, member states were under an obligation to refrain from taking any measure which might undermine it in any way. Therefore, a national system such as the one operated under the Pigs Marketing Scheme was to be regarded as incompatible with Community legislation on the common organisation of the market in pigmeat.

The court pointed out that arts. 30 and 34 on the abolition of quantitative restrictions on imports and exports between member states were, in accordance with current practice relating to consolidating agricultural regulations, an integral part of Regulation 2759/75, and that all three provisions, being directly applicable, conferred on individuals rights which were to be protected by national courts.

Case 83/78: PIGS MARKETING BOARD (NORTHERN IRELAND) v REDMOND [1979] 1 CMLR 177 (European Court of Justice). Case 111/76: *Officier Van Justitie v Van Den Hazel* [1977] ECR 901, ECJ referred to.

63   —— **eggs—marketing standards—cost of national supervision of system**

Under Italian law the preparation and distribution of labels to be affixed to egg packs was reserved to the Ministry of Agriculture and Forestry, in implementation of Regulation 2772/75 on marketing standards for eggs. That regulation provides that all egg packs are to carry an official label, such labels to be issued by or under the supervision of certain national official agencies designated by member states. In proceedings before an Italian court the operator of an authorised packing centre sought reimbursement of substantial sums paid to the Ministry in return for the issue of the necessary labels, on the grounds that they had been wrongly charged. The court stayed the proceedings and referred to the European Court certain questions on the interpretation of Regulation 2772/75 in relation to the validity of the charges. *Held*, since the regulation contained no provision relating to the selling price of labels or the method of financing the costs of supervising the system laid down by the regulation, member states were free to determine the means of financing the system themselves, providing that the method chosen did not jeopardise the objectives of that system. In the present case the Italian method of financing the system, namely to make the issue of the labels conditional on payment of a sum representing both the actual cost of the labels and a contribution to the cost of operating the system, was permissible: the introduction of additional conditions in consequence of the national implementation of provisions of a regulation did not affect its directly applicable nature, provided that such conditions complied with the aim and objectives of the regulation in question. Further, since the relevant Italian provisions were applicable on the basis of the location of the packing centres rather than the nationality of the traders, the principle on which they were based did not constitute discrimination on the grounds of nationality as prohibited by EEC Treaty, art. 7. Therefore, providing that the charges made in respect of the issue of the labels did not exceed the real cost of supervising the system, a question to be determined by the national court concerned, such charges were permissible.

Case 31/78: Bussone v Italian Ministry for Agriculture and Forestry [1978] ECR 2429 (European Court of Justice).

64   —— impact of European Monetary System

Council Regulation (EEC) 652/79 (OJ No. L84, 4.4.79) introduced the European Currency Unit (ECU) into the common agricultural policy. Commission Regulation (EEC) 706/79 (OJ No. L89, 9.4.79) lays down detailed rules for its application and contains transitional provisions to facilitate the changeover to the new monetary system.

65   —— meat—imports from non-member states—customs duties—charges having equivalent effect—scope of exemption from prohibition

Two German undertakings imported into Germany from third countries quantities of game and tinned beef respectively. In accordance with German legislation both consignments were subjected to health inspections the charges for which the importers refused to pay on the grounds that they were charges having an effect equivalent to customs duties and as such were prohibited under certain provisions of Community law. The German customs authorities claimed, however, that EEC Council Directive 72/462, authorising the levying of charges for health inspections carried out on fresh meat imported from third countries should be extended by analogy to inspections of other imported meat. The German courts referred questions on the interpretation of the directive to the European Court. *Held*, the imported goods were covered by Council Regulations (EEC) 827/68 and 805/68, which established a common organisation of the markets in certain types of meat and beef and veal respectively, and accordingly were subject to the prohibition on the levying of any charges having an effect equivalent to customs duties under art. 2 (2) and art. 20 (2) of those regulations respectively. Further, although those articles provided for derogations from the prohibitions in certain cases and the court had already decided that Directive 72/462 constituted such a valid derogation, since the conditions for the implementation of that directive had not yet been fulfilled it could not yet be applied to justify the imposition of the charges. Additionally, even were the directive to be regarded as being applicable at the date of the imports in question, it was not to be extended beyond the defined scope of its application: it was not a particular application of a general principle of Community law.

Case 137/77: City of Frankfurt-am-Main v Firma Max Neumann; Case 138/77: Firma Herman Ludwig v Free and Hanseatic City of Hamburg [1978] ECR 1623, 1645 (European Court of Justice). Case 70/77: *Simmenthal SpA v Amministrazione delle Finanze delle Stato* [1978] ECR 1453, ECJ, para. 1207 referred to.

66   —— —— protection of Community arrangements

The Common Agricultural Policy (Agricultural Produce) (Protection of Community Arrangements) (Amendment) Order 1979, S.I. 1979 No. 1541 (in force on 6th

December 1979), amends the Common Agricultural Policy (Agricultural Produce) (Protection of Community Arrangements) (No. 2) Order 1973 by extending the powers for the protection of the Community support system to cover Community arrangements in respect of pure-bred breeding animals of the domestic bovine species bought into the common organization of the market in beef and veal under Council Regulation (EEC) 425/77.

67   —— pigmeat—common price system—power of member states to take unilateral measures to control prices

A Belgian pork-butcher was charged with failing to observe the retail selling prices of pigmeat laid down under Belgian law. His defence was that the Belgian provisions were incompatible with EEC Council Regulation 121/67 on the common organisation of the market in pigmeat. The Belgian court referred to the European Court the question whether the relevant national provisions involved an infringement of the regulation. *Held*, in proceedings under EEC Treaty, art. 177 the Court was unable to give a ruling on the compatibility of rules of national law with provisions of community law and it would therefore answer the question in terms of the extent to which the regulation allowed member states to regulate internally the retail selling prices of pigmeat. It was clear that in sectors covered by a common organisation of the market and particularly so where that organisation was based on a common price system, member states could no longer take action in relation to prices so fixed. However, where that price system applied at the production and wholesale stages, as in the case of pigmeat, member states remained free to take appropriate measures in fixing prices at the retail and consumption stages, providing that the maximum profit margin laid down was calculated essentially on purchase prices charged at the production and wholesale stages and was fixed at a level which did not impede intra-community trade.

Case 154/77: PROCUREUR DU ROI v DECHMANN [1978] ECR 1573 (European Court of Justice).

68   ———— effect of common organisation of market on national system

See Case 83/78: *Pigs Marketing Board v Redmond*, para. 62.

69   —— sugar—common organisation of the market—derogation from provisions as to basic quotas—validity

See *Société des Usines de Beauport v EC Council*, para. 1171.

70   ———— power of member state to intervene

The common organisation of the market in sugar is governed by Council Regulation (EEC) 3330/74, which fixes production quantities for each member state and determines quotas for sugar manufacturers. A Danish producer and processor of sugar beet did not produce enough beet for its requirements, and therefore purchased beet for processing from other producers. The production quantity allotted to Denmark on its accession to the Community exceeded previous quantities fixed by national legislation. Difficulties arose between the producer and the other producers concerning allocation of the quantities to be supplied within the producer's increased quota. The Danish government intervened and made an order under Council Regulation (EEC) 741/75, whereby, failing an agreement as to how the quantity of beet should be allocated, the member state concerned may lay down special rules for such allocation. The producer contested the legality of the order before the national courts, which requested a preliminary ruling from the European Court of Justice on the interpretation of Regulation 741/75. *Held*, since the common organisation of the market in sugar covered relations between sugar manufacturers and beet growers, such relations fell exclusively within the competence of the Community, so that member states were no longer in a position to adopt unilateral measures. In view of possible difficulties in the conclusion of agreements, Regulation 741/75 was intended to remove that disability and enable member states to intervene in certain cases. Hence the regulation was intended to empower member states, having regard to impediments which might result from Community powers, to proceed in conformity with their national law to allocate delivery rights for beet within the basic quota limits of the sugar manufacturer concerned.

Case 151/78: SUKKERFABRIKEN NYKØBING LIMITERET v MINISTRY OF AGRICULTURE [1979] ECR 1 (European Court of Justice).

71   —— transitional period—accession compensatory amounts—application in cases of force majeure

In 1975 a ship carrying a quantity of wheat from Germany to the United Kingdom sank and the French exporter applied to the German customs authorities for the payment of "accession" compensatory amounts under EEC Commission Regulation 269/73. That regulation established a system of "accession" compensatory amounts during the transitional period following the accession of the United Kingdom, Eire and Denmark in order to compensate the differences in price levels between original and new member states. Article 5 (2) provided for the payment of such amounts upon proof of the completion of the import formalities of the member state of destination. The German authorities refused to make the payment on the grounds that the exporter had no such proof. Proceedings were brought in Germany and the national court referred the question of interpretation of art. 5 (2) to the European Court. *Held*, there was an omission in Regulation 269/73 in that it failed to provide for cases of force majeure. That omission should be made good by applying by analogy the provisions of EEC Commission Regulation 192/75 on the payment of export refunds in respect of agricultural products: art. 6 (1) of that regulation exempted exporters from the requirement of proof of importation into a third country where the product had perished in transit as a result of force majeure. Accordingly, Regulation 269/73, art. 5 (2) was to be interpreted as meaning that where goods exported from an old member state to a new member state perished in transit as a result of force majeure the exporter was entitled to the same compensatory amounts as if the goods had reached their destination and import formalities had been completed.

Case 6/78: UNION FRANÇAISE DE CEREALES v HAUPTZOLLAMT HAMBURG-JONAS [1978] ECR 1675 (European Court of Justice).

72   ————— products not subject to common organisation of market—retention of national restriction on imports—validity of restriction

In August 1977 the Department of Trade introduced a ban on the import into the United Kingdom of main-crop potatoes. The European Commission then notified the United Kingdom government of the need to lift the restriction by the end of 1977, the date on which, under the Act of Accession, art. 9 (2), the application of transitional measures provided for by the Act was to terminate. The ban was continued, however, the United Kingdom claiming that art. 60 (2), which provided for the retention of restrictions forming part of a national market organisation pending the implementation of a common organisation of the market for the product in question, constituted a special provision under art. 9 (2), and that it was therefore entitled to maintain the restriction in question until the establishment of a common organisation of the market for potatoes. The Commission therefore instituted proceedings before the European Court, seeking a declaration under EEC Treaty, art. 169 that the United Kingdom, by failing to lift the ban, had failed to fulfil an obligation under EEC Treaty, art. 30. *Held*, the provisions of the Act of Accession were to be interpreted with regard to the foundations and system of the Community as established by the Treaty. At the date of the accession of the new member states the Treaty was already fully operative and art. 9 of the Act, in providing for derogations from the immediate application of Community rules in order to facilitate the integration of those states, was to be given a restrictive interpretation. Accordingly, in view of the fact that all quantitative restrictions and measures having equivalent effect had been completely eliminated as between the original member states, art. 60 (2) could not constitute a special provision within the meaning of art. 9 (2), which was to be interpreted as referring to clearly delimited provisions determined as to time, rather than a provision such as art. 60 (2) referring to an uncertain future event, namely, the implementation of the common organisation of a market. Therefore, by failing to abolish the restriction on imports of potatoes by the end of 1977, the United Kingdom had failed to fulfil an obligation under the Treaty.

In his opinion the Advocate General considered that art. 60 (2) constituted a special provision within the meaning of art. 9 (2) and that the action should therefore be dismissed.

Case 231/78: Re IMPORT OF POTATOES: EC COMMISSION v UNITED KINGDOM [1979] 2 CMLR 427 (European Court of Justice). Case 48/74: *Charmasson v Minister for Economic Affairs* [1974] ECR 1383, 1975 Halsbury's Abridgment para. 75 referred to.

In a Press Release dated 9th April 1979 the Ministry of Agriculture Fisheries and Food announced that, following the ruling of the European Court, the ban on the import of potatoes would be lifted with effect from that date.

73   In proceedings in the High Court a Dutch exporter of potatoes, who in 1978 had been refused permission to export potatoes into the United Kingdom, sought a declaration that the United Kingdom was no longer entitled to restrict the importation of potatoes from other member states. The court stayed the proceedings and referred to the European Court the question of the validity of the restriction in the light of the Act of Accession, art. 60 (2). *Held*, adopting the judgment given in Case 231/78, para. 72, art. 60 (2) could not be regarded as a special provision within the meaning of art. 9 (2), and accordingly its application terminated at the end of 1977.

Case 118/78: CJ MEIJER BV v DEPARTMENT OF TRADE, MINISTRY OF AGRICULTURE, FISHERIES AND FOOD AND COMMISSIONERS OF CUSTOMS AND EXCISE [1979] 2 CMLR 398 (European Court of Justice).

For the proceedings in which the reference was made see [1978] 2 CMLR 563, 1978 Halsbury's Abridgment para. 86.

74   —— **wine**

Council Regulation (EEC) 337/79 (OJ No. L 54 5.3.79) consolidates earlier provisions concerning the common organisation of the market in wine. Regulations No. 24, 816/70 and 2506/75, as amended, are repealed.

75   The Common Agricultural Policy (Wine) Regulations 1979, S.I. 1979 No. 1094 (in force on 18th October 1979), provide for the enforcement throughout the United Kingdom of specified EEC Regulations concerned with the production and marketing of wine and related products. The Regulations designate enforcement authorities, exempt certain products from provisions relating to information required on labels, prescribe offences and a penalty and provide for specified defences, and largely re-enact, with amendments, the Common Agricultural Policy (Wine) Regulations 1978, 1978 Halsbury's Abridgment para. 87.

76   —— **monetary compensatory amounts—publication of regulations**

See Case 98/78: *Firma A. Racke v Hauptzollamt Mainz*; Case 99/78: *Weingut Gustav Decker KG v Hauptzollamt Landau*, para. 1169.

77   **Corn Sales Act 1921—metrication**

The Corn Sales Act 1921 (Amendment) Regulations 1979, S.I. 1979 No. 357 (in force on 1st May 1979), amend the Corn Sales Act 1921, s. 5 (1), (2), by substituting references to kilograms for references to imperial pounds.

78   Dutch elm disease

The Dutch Elm Disease (Local Authorities) (Amendment) Order 1979, S.I. 1979 No. 638 (in force on 11th July 1979), amends the Dutch Elm Disease (Local Authorities) Order 1977, 1977 Halsbury's Abridgment para. 89, by adding provisions governing the procedure for serving notices under that Order in the case of a body corporate or partnership, or in cases where the occupier of premises is unknown. Where a notice is served in a case where the occupier of premises is unknown, failure to comply with the notice will not constitute an offence. Certain local authorities are removed from the list of authorities empowered to take steps to prevent the spread of Dutch elm disease.

79

The Dutch Elm Disease (Restriction on Movement of Elms) (Amendment) Order 1979, S.I. 1979 No. 639 (in force on 11th July 1979), amends the Dutch Elm Disease (Restriction on Movement of Elms) Order 1977, 1977 Halsbury's Abridgment para. 90, by adding provisions governing the procedure for serving notices under that Order in the case of a body corporate or partnership, or in cases where the owner or person in charge of an elm is unknown. Where a notice is served in a case where the owner or person in charge of an elm is unknown, failure to comply with the notice will not constitute an offence. Certain areas are added to the list of areas from which the movement of elm is restricted.

80   Eggs—grading machines

See para. 3070.

81   —— levy

The Eggs Authority (Rates of Levy) Order 1979, S.I. 1979 No. 257 (in force on 1st April 1979), specifies the rate of levy to be raised in respect of the accounting period beginning 1st April 1979 and ending 31st March 1980 to meet the aggregate of the amounts determined for financing the functions of the Eggs Authority.

82   Fertilisers and feeding stuffs

The Fertilisers and Feeding Stuffs (Amendment) Regulations 1979, S.I. 1979 No. 1617 (in force on 4th January 1980), further amend the Feeding Stuffs Regulations 1973, Sch. 3 in order to implement the provisions of certain Commission Directives (EEC) so as to restrict the use of certain substances in feeding stuffs and silage and to extend the list of permitted preservatives and emulsifiers. These regulations consolidate the Fertilisers and Feedings Stuffs (Amendment) Regulations 1976, 1976 Halsbury's Abridgment para. 131 and the 1977 Amendment Regulations, 1977 Halsbury's Abridgment para. 92, which are revoked.

83   Grants for guarantees of bank loans—extension of period

The Grants for Guarantees of Bank Loans (Extension of Period) Order 1979, S.I. 1979 No. 323 (in force on 1st April 1979), extends the provisions of the Agriculture Act 1967, s. 64 to guarantees given during the five years beginning on 1st April 1969.

84   Hill livestock—compensatory allowances

The Hill Livestock (Compensatory Allowances) (Amendment) Regulations 1979, S.I. 1979 No. 941 (in force on 27th July 1979), amend the Hill Livestock (Compensatory Allowances) Regulations 1975, 1975 Halsbury's Abridgment para. 93, by raising the overall limit on payments per hectare of eligible land and by amending references to the maximum permitted headage payments for cattle and sheep in accordance with Commission Regulation (EEC) 1054/78. An increase in the amount of compensatory allowance payable in respect of certain ewes for the year 1979 is also provided for by the Regulations.

These regualations have been consolidated; see para. 85.

85　　The Hill Livestock (Compensatory Allowances) Regulations 1979, S.I. 1979 No. 1748 (in force on 1st January 1980), consolidate the Hill Livestock (Compensatory Allowances) Regulations 1975, 1975 Halsbury's Abridgment para. 93, as amended, which implemented part of Council Directive (EEC) 75/268. The Regulations increase the compensatory allowance payable for cattle and increase the overall limit on payments for each hectare of eligible land in accordance with Commission Regulation (EEC) 2141/79.

86　　—— subsidy—replacement of slaughtered cattle under brucellosis eradication scheme—effect on subsidy on breeding herd

Decision of Parliamentary Commissioner for Administration:

Case 3B/659/78: RE SLAUGHTER OF HILL CATTLE IN SCOTLAND [1979] 2 CMLR 505 (hill land farmer entitled to claim subsidy on each breeding cow on certain qualifying date provided cow had been in herd throughout preceding year under Hill Livestock (Compensatory Allowances) Regulations 1975, S.I. 1975 No. 2210, implementing Council Directive (EEC) 75/268, 1975 Halsbury's Abridgment paras. 93, 72, respectively; part of herd slaughtered under brucellosis eradication scheme; farmer entitled to claim subsidy in respect of slaughtered cattle provided replaced within reasonable time; supply difficulties so farmer obtained permission to restock with, inter alia, in-calf heifers and bulling heifers, which he then resold before they calved; Department of Agriculture and Fisheries for Scotland claimed repayment of subsidy on ground that farmer had not replaced losses in accordance with regulations; farmer complained to Parliamentary Commissioner for Administration on ground, inter alia, that he had not been made sufficiently aware of conditions under which losses were to be replaced to qualify for subsidy and that he had offered to replace bulling heifers so he could retain payments; subsidy payable only in relation to breeding cows; approval of in-calf heifers and bulling heifers permitted only subject to understanding that would be kept on to become breeding cows in the herd; Department's correspondence and explanatory notes clearly explained this; further, time for replacement had long passed, eighteen months since herd was declared brucellosis free, and no grounds to justify extension; therefore complaint dismissed).

87　　Home-Grown Cereals Authority—levy scheme

The Home-Grown Cereals Authority (Rate of Levy) Order 1979, S.I. 1979 No. 782 (in force on 1st August 1979) specifies in respect of home-grown wheat, barley and oats the rate of levy to be raised for the year beginning 1st August 1979 to meet the amounts apportioned by the Ministers to these kinds of home-grown cereals to finance the Home-Grown Cereals Authority in the performance of their non-trading functions under Part I of the Cereals Marketing Act 1965. The Order also includes provisions as to the quantity of such cereals in respect of which levy is to be imposed. The levy will be recovered in accordance with the provisions of a scheme under s. 16 of the 1965 Act.

88　　Hops—certification

The Hops Certification Regulations 1979, S.I. 1979 No. 1095 (in force on 1st October 1979), provide for the implementation in the United Kingdom of the European Economic Community hop certification system set up under Community legislation. Regulation 13 repeals the Hop Trade Act 1814 and the Hop (Prevention of Frauds) Act 1866 and revokes the Hops (Import Regulation) Order 1961.

89　　—— delegation of intervention functions

The Intervention Functions (Delegation) (Hops) Regulations 1979, S.I. 1979 No. 433 (in force on 27th April 1979), empower the Hops Marketing Board to act for the Intervention Board for Agricultural Produce by carrying out in England functions which the Intervention Board may delegate to it with respect to hops.

90 ## Horticulture—development

The Farm and Horticulture Development (Amendment) Regulations 1979, S.I. 1979 No. 1559 (in force on 31st December 1979), apply to the whole of the United Kingdom and are made under the European Communities Act 1972, s. 2 (2). They amend the 1978 Regulations, 1978 Halsbury's Abridgment para. 97, in order to express the guidance premia in sterling terms to take account of Council Directive (EEC) 78/1017.

91 ## Horticulture Capital Grant Scheme—plums

The Fruiting Plum Tree (Planting Grants) Scheme 1979, S.I. 1979 No. 876 (in force on 1st August 1979), authorises the payment of grants towards the cost of purchasing and planting fruiting plum trees in connection with a plum production business. Application for a grant must be made by 31st July 1986.

92 The Plum Material and Clearance Grants Scheme 1979, S.I. 1979 No. 877 (in force on 1st August 1979), authorises the payment of grants towards capital expenditure in connection with a plum material business. Application for a grant must be made by 31st July 1986.

93 ## Meat and Livestock Commission levy scheme

The Meat and Livestock Commission Levy Scheme (Confirmation) Order 1979, S.I. 1979 No. 393 (in force on 30th March 1979), confirms the Scheme which revokes and replaces the Meat and Livestock Commission Levy Scheme 1968, as varied. The new Scheme imposes charges, to meet the Commission's expenses, on slaughterers by reference to livestock slaughtered by them and on exporters by reference to livestock exported by them. There are provisions enabling slaughterers to avoid the payment of charges where livestock are slaughtered because of disease, to recover part of any payment made in respect of livestock purchased from another party and to recover all of any payment made in respect of livestock slaughtered by the slaughterer but not purchased by him. The Scheme also provides for the registration of slaughterers and exporters, for the keeping of appropriate records by them and for the making of returns to the Commission.

94 ## Milk Marketing Scheme—amendment

The Milk Marketing Scheme (Amendment) Regulations 1979, S.I. 1979 No. 249 (in force on 4th April 1979), replace the Milk Marketing Scheme 1933, para. 66, as amended, which provides for consultation by the Milk Marketing Board with the Dairy Trade Federation as to the Board's selling prices and related matters. The amendments made to para. 66 are made for the purpose of putting the Board and their milk purchasers on an equal footing when negotiating such prices. This is a requirement of Council Regulation (EEC) 1422/78 concerning the granting of certain special rights to milk producer organisations in the United Kingdom.

95 ## Seed potatoes—fees

The Seed Potatoes (Fees) Regulations 1979, S.I. 1979 No. 366 (in force on 24th April 1979), prescribe fees in respect of matters arising under the Seed Potatoes Regulations 1978, 1978 Halsbury's Abridgment para. 110. The Seed Potatoes (Fees) Regulations 1978, 1978 Halsbury's Abridgment para. 111, are revoked.

96 ## Seeds—beet

The Beet Seeds (Amendment) Regulations 1979, S.I. 1979 No. 1004 (in force on 10th September 1979), amend the Beet Seeds Regulations 1976, 1976 Halsbury's Abridgment para. 92, requiring certain alternatives in labelling requirements and making changes to definitions, to references to other statutory instruments and to provisions relating to general licences and the sampling and testing of seeds. The amendments give effect to Council Directive (EEC) 78/692.

97   —— cereal

The Cereal Seeds (Amendment) Regulations 1979, S.I. 1979 No. 1003 (in force on 10th September 1979), amend the Cereal Seeds Regulations 1976, 1976 Halsbury's Abridgment para. 93, by prescribing certain alterations in labelling requirements and making changes to definitions, to references to other statutory instruments and to provisions relating to general licences and the sampling and testing of seeds. The amendments give effect to Council Directives (EEC) 78/55 and 78/692.

98   —— fees

The Seeds (Fees) Regulations 1979, S.I. 1979 No. 888 (in force on 1st August 1979), supersede the 1978 Regulations, 1978 Halsbury's Abridgment para. 113.

The Regulations prescribe fees in respect of matters arising under the Vegetable Seeds Regulations 1979, para. 101, the Cereal Seeds Regulations 1976, the Fodder Plant Seeds Regulations 1976, the Beet Seeds Regulations 1976, the Oil and Fibre Plant Seeds Regulations 1976, 1976 Halsbury's Abridgment paras. 92, 93, 95 respectively and the Seeds (Registration and Licensing) Regulations 1974, 1974 Halsbury's Abridgment para. 106 or any regulations amending or superseding any of those Regulations.

99   —— oil and fibre plants

The Oil and Fibre Plant Seeds Regulations 1979, S.I. 1979 No. 1005 (in force on 10th September 1979), regulate the marketing in Great Britain of seeds of oil and fibre plants, but exclude seeds used for research, experiment or selection processes, and uncleaned seeds marketed with a view to processing or other treatment. The Oil and Fibre Plant Seeds Regulations 1976, 1976 Halsbury's Abridgment para. 95, are revoked. The Regulations give effect to Council Directive (EEC) 66/402, as amended.

100   —— plant varieties—National Lists

The Seeds (National Lists of Varieties) Regulations 1979, S.I. 1979 No. 133 (in force on 12th March 1979) supersede the Seeds (National Lists of Varieties) Regulations 1973 and implement EEC Council Directives relating to the common catalogue of agricultural plant species and the marketing of vegetable seed. The Regulations require the Minister of Agriculture, Fisheries and Food and the Secretaries of State for Scotland, Wales and Northern Ireland jointly to prepare and publish National Lists of varieties of specified kinds of agricultural and vegetable crops, and specify the criteria to be met and the procedure to be followed before a variety can be entered in the Lists.

101   —— vegetable seeds

The Vegetable Seeds Regulations 1979, S.I. 1979 No. 774 (in force on 1st August 1979), re-enact, with modifications, the Vegetable Seeds Regulations 1975, 1975 Halsbury's Abridgment para. 105, which are revoked. The Regulations restrict the marketing of vegetable seeds to specified grades and require them to be sold in sealed packages, labelled or marked with prescribed particulars. Provision is made for the taking of samples for the enforcement of the obligations imposed by the Regulations and of the civil rights of a purchaser.

102   Sugar beet—research and education

The Sugar Beet (Research and Education) Order 1979, S.I. 1979 No. 222 (in force on 1st April 1979), provides for the assessment and collection of contributions towards the cost of research and education projects for the year beginning 1st April 1979, from the British Sugar Corporation Ltd and growers of home-grown beet.

103   Tractors—approval of agricultural or forestry tractors

The Agricultural or Forestry Tractors and Tractor Components (Type Approval)

Regulations 1979, S.I. 1979 No. 221 (in force on 3rd April 1979) consolidate the provisions of the Agricultural or Forestry Tractors (Type Approval) Regulations 1975, Halsbury's Abridgment 1975, para. 108, as amended. The new regulations include provisions which are in accordance with various EEC Council Directives.

104   —— —— **fees**

The Agricultural or Forestry Tractors and Tractor Components (Type Approval) (Fees) Regulations 1979, S.I. 1979 No. 1376 (in force on 28th November 1979), re-enact, with alterations, the Agricultural or Forestry Tractors (Type Approval) (Fees) Regulations 1976, 1976 Halsbury's Abridgment para. 100. They prescribe the fees payable for the testing of agricultural or forestry tractors and their components and the issue of documents in connection with the type or component type approval of such tractors and their components for the purposes of certain EEC directives. The alterations include the addition of five new directives relating to driver-perceived noise, roll-over protection structures, emission of pollutants, driver's seat and lights and light signalling.

ANIMALS

Halsbury's Laws of England (4th edn.), Vol. 2, paras. 201–497

105   **Badgers—special protection**

The Badgers (Areas of Special Protection) Order 1979, S.I. 1979 No. 1249 (in force on 1st December 1979) declares the county of West Yorkshire to be an area of special protection for badgers for the purposes of the Badgers Act 1973.

106   **Bees—importation restrictions**

The Importation of Bees (Prohibition) Order 1979, S.I. 1979 No. 587 (in force on 25th May 1979) prohibits the importation of bees into Great Britain from any of the countries or parts of countries named in the Schedule, and from other countries or parts of countries unless the order's requirements are otherwise complied with.

This Order has been amended; see para. 107.

107   The Importation of Bees (Prohibition) (Amendment) Order 1979, S.I. 1979 No. 1588 (in force on 31st December 1979), amends the 1979 Order, para. 106 by continuing it in operation until 30th June 1980 and adding certain countries to the list of countries from which the importation of bees into Great Britain is prohibited.

108   **Carriage of animals—carriage by air—liability of carrier—offence committed in foreign territory**

A cargo of birds was carried by an Indian airline from Bombay to London. Delays occurred en route due to engine trouble and in consequence most of the birds were dead on arrival. It was clear that the deaths had occurred before the aeroplane entered English air space. The airline was charged with an offence under the Diseases of Animals Act 1950 in that it had carried the birds by air in a way likely to cause them injury or unnecessary suffering. The airline contended that no proceedings could be brought in England against it because it was a foreign national and the offence had been committed outside English air space. *Held*, the relevant provisions were contained in the Transit of Animals (General) Order 1973, art. 3 (3) of which provided that in relation to carriage by sea or air, the provisions of the order applied to animals carried on any vessel or aircraft to or from a port or airport in Great Britain, whether or not such animals were loaded or unloaded at such port or airport. This provision clearly extended to flights outside the territorial limits of

Great Britain. Hence the provisions of the 1973 Order applied notwithstanding that the acts were done by a foreign national in foreign territory.

AIR INDIA V WIGGINS [1980] 1 All ER 192 (Queen's Bench Division: LORD WIDGERY CJ, EVELEIGH LJ and KILNER BROWN J).

109   —— carriage by road and rail—welfare of animals

The Transit of Animals (Road and Rail) (Amendment) Order 1979, S.I. 1979 No. 1013 (in force on 1st September 1979) makes a number of minor amendments to the Transit of Animals (Road and Rail) Order 1975, which laid down detailed requirements with regard to the construction and maintenance of vehicles and receptacles used for transporting animals and prescribed measures designed to safeguard the welfare of animals during loading, unloading and carriage.

110   Conservation of wild creatures and wild plants—Essex Emerald Moth

The Conservation of Wild Creatures and Wild Plants (Essex Emerald Moth) Order 1979, S.I. 1979 No. 353 (in force on 26th March 1979), adds the Essex Emerald Moth to the wild creatures which are protected under the Conservation of Wild Creatures and Wild Plants Act 1975, 1975 Halsbury's Abridgment para. 113.

111   Coypus—licence fees

The Coypus (Keeping) (Amendment) Regulations 1979, S.I. 1979 No. 1668 (in force on 1st January 1980), further amend the Coypus (Keeping) Regulations 1967 by increasing the fee for a licence to keep coypus.

112   Diseases of animals—Aujeszky's disease of swine

The Aujeszky's Disease of Swine Order 1979, S.I. 1979 No. 815 (in force on 1st August 1979) extends the Diseases of Animals Act 1950 to include Aujeszky's disease for all purposes of the Act. A duty is also imposed upon all persons knowing or suspecting that any swine or carcase of swine in his possession or charge is affected with Aujeszky's disease to notify the fact to the relevant authorities.

113   —— cattle—brucellosis

The Brucellosis (England and Wales) Order 1979, S.I. 1979 No. 1288 (in force on 1st November 1979), amends the 1978 Order, 1978 Halsbury's Abridgment, para. 119. The Order adds new livestock markets to the eradication areas in Sch. 1 and certain areas to the attested areas in Sch. 2.

114   —— —— —— replacement of herd—effect on hill farming subsidy

See *Re Slaughter of Hill Cattle in Scotland*, para. 86.

115   —— —— epizootic abortion

The Epizootic Abortion (Revocation) Order 1979, S.I. 1979 No. 1365 (in force on 1st November 1979) revokes the Epizootic Abortion Order 1922. Epizootic abortion is now referred to as brucellosis in cattle. The Brucellosis (England and Wales) Order 1978, 1978 Halsbury's Abridgment para. 119 and the Brucellosis (Scotland) Order 1978 provide control measures which meet the objectives of the 1922 Order.

116   —— disinfectants

The Diseases of Animals (Approved Disinfectants) (Amendment) Order 1979, S.I. 1979 No. 37 (in force on 31st January 1979), further amends the Diseases of Animals (Approved Disinfectants) Order 1978, 1978 Halsbury's Abridgment para. 126, by adding to the list of approved disinfectants specified newly approved disinfectants and by deleting certain disinfectants from the list.

117   The Diseases of Animals (Approved Disinfectants) (Amendment) (No. 2) Order 1979, S.I. 1979 No. 773 (in force on 17th July 1979), further amends the Diseases of Animals (Approved Disinfectants) Order 1978, 1978 Halsbury's Abridgment para. 126, by adding to the list of approved disinfectants specified newly approved disinfectants and by deleting certain disinfectants from the list.

118   The Diseases of Animals (Fees for the Testing of Disinfectants) Order 1979, S.I. 1979 No. 751 (in force on 27th July 1979), revokes the Diseases of Animals (Fees for the Testing of Disinfectants) Order 1978, 1978 Halsbury's Abridgment, para. 128. The Order prescribes revised fees payable for the testing of disinfectants for the purpose of determining their suitability for listing as approved disinfectants in the Diseases of Animals (Approved Disinfectants) Order 1978, 1978 Halsbury's Abridgment, para. 126.

119   —— **fees**

The Diseases of Animals (Miscellaneous Fees) (Revocation) Order 1979, S.I. 1979 No. 1281 (in force on 8th November 1979), revokes the 1978 Regulations, 1978 Halsbury's Abridgment para. 131.

120   —— **importation of hay and straw**

The Importation of Hay and Straw Order 1979, S.I. 1979 No. 1703 (in force on 1st February 1980), prohibits the landing in Great Britain of any hay or straw from abroad except under the authority of a licence. Inspectors appointed under the Diseases of Animals Act 1950 will have the power to ensure that all hay or straw landed in contravention of the Order is destroyed. Deliberate contravention of the Order is an indictable offence.

The Importation of Hay, Straw and Dried Grass Order 1961 is revoked.

121   —— **rabies—control**

The Rabies Virus Order 1979, S.I. 1979 No. 135 (in force on 13th March 1979), prohibits the importation, keeping or deliberate introduction into animals of rabies virus except under the authority of a licence and in accordance with the conditions of that licence. The Order has no application to such importation etc. of any virus contained in a medicinal product as is permitted under the Medicines Act 1968. It further provides powers of seizure and destruction, without compensation, of any rabies virus imported or kept in contravention of the Order or in breach of any licence conditions. Powers for requiring cleaning and disinfection of places and vehicles where the virus is, or has been, present are also provided. Intentional contravention of import controls is now an indictable offence and the maximum fine for summary offences for contravention is increased to £1,000. Conviction on indictment renders a person liable to imprisonment for up to twelve months or to an unlimited fine or both.

The Order applies to Great Britain.

122   **Endangered Species (Import and Export) Act 1976—modification**

The Endangered Species (Import and Export) Act 1976 (Modification) Order 1979, S.I. 1979 No. 1054 (in force on 19th September 1979), modifies two Schedules to the Endangered Species (Import and Export) Act 1976, 1976 Halsbury's Abridgment para. 127, by adding certain other plants to the scope of the Act, and by bringing under its control certain products derived from dolphins and porpoises. Other products derived from whales, namely sperm oil, spermaceti wax and ambergris, are also brought under control, as are animal teeth.

123   **Equine animals—importation**

The Importation of Equine Animals Order 1979, S.I. 1979 No. 1701 (in force on 1st February 1980), prohibits the landing in Great Britain of equine animals from abroad, unless under the authority of a licence, and gives power to veterinary inspectors to deal with disease amongst equine animals landed in Great Britain and to take action in the case of contravention of the Order.

The Equine Animals (Importation) Order 1973 is revoked.

124　Mink—licence fees

The Mink (Keeping) (Amendment) Regulations 1979, S.I. 1979 No. 1669 (in force on 1st January 1980), further amend the Mink (Keeping) Regulations 1975, 1975 Halsbury's Abridgment para. 129, by increasing the fee for a licence to keep mink.

125　Poultry, hatching eggs and captive birds—importation

The Importation of Birds, Poultry and Hatching Eggs Order 1979, S.I. 1979 No. 1702 (in force on 1st February 1980), supersedes previous Orders and prohibits the importation of poultry, hatching eggs and captive birds into Great Britain without a licence.　The Order contains provisions relating to quarantine and hygiene and confers powers on veterinary inspectors to deal with any suspected disease or any other contravention of the Order.　Any intentional contravention of the Order is an indictable offence.

The following Orders are revoked: the Poultry and Hatching Eggs (Importation) Order 1972 as amended and the Importation of Captive Birds Order 1976, 1976 Halsbury's Abridgment para. 133.

126　Wild birds—importation

The Wild Birds (Importation) Order 1979, S.I. 1979 No. 1007 (in force on 13th August 1979) prohibits the importation of birds of prey (whether live or dead) or their eggs, unless authorised by a licence granted under section 10 of the Protection of Birds Act 1954.

127　—— protection

Council Directive (EEC) 79/409 lays down rules for the protection, management, control and exploitation of wild birds within the territory of member states, and requires member states to implement those rules within two years.　(OJ No. L103, 25.4.79.)

128

The Wild Birds (Dunsfold Aerodrome) Order 1979, S.I. 1979 No. 437 (in force on 5th April 1979), amends the Protection of Birds Act 1954 by adding lapwings found within the area of Dunsfold Aerodrome, Godalming, Surrey to Schedule 2 (wild birds which may be killed or taken by authorised persons).

129

The Wild Birds (Lapland Bunting) Order 1979, S.I. 1979 No. 423 (in force on 30th March 1979) adds the Lapland Bunting to Schedule 1, Part 1 of the Protection of Birds Act 1954 which confers protection by special penalties at all times.

130

The Wild Birds (Special Protection in Severe Weather) Order 1979, S.I. 1979 No. 70 (in force on 26th January 1979), created periods of special protection for all wild birds listed in Schedule 3 to the Protection of Birds Act 1954 during which they were protected in the same manner as they are during the close season.　The protection lasted for the short anticipated period of severe weather.

131

The Wild Birds (Various Species) Order 1979, S.I. 1979 No. 438 (in force on 5th April 1979), amends the Protection of Birds Act 1954 by adding twenty new species of wild birds to Schedule 4 (wild birds which may not be sold alive unless close-ringed and bred in captivity).

ARBITRATION

Halsbury's Laws of England (4th edn.), Vol. 2, paras. 501–653

132   Articles

Arbitration Act 1979, John A. Franks (a look at the provisions of the new Act, para. 135): 123 Sol Jo 359.

Arbitration Act 1979—A Pragmatic Compromise, Christopher Staughton (a review of the legal obstacles which the Act, para. 135, purports to remove, together with a forecast of how it will operate in practice): 129 NLJ 920.

Reviewing the Law of Arbitration, David Lyons: 128 NLJ 1188.

133   Application to compel statement of special case—issue of repudiation of contract—question of law

Sub-contractors agreed to execute certain sub-contract works for main contractors. The contract provided that the price should remain fixed until 3rd June 1975 and that the price of any work to be carried out after that date was "to be negotiated". A substantial amount of work remained uncompleted on 3rd June 1975, and a dispute arose between the parties as to the meaning of "to be negotiated". The main contractors repeatedly refused to accept a schedule of terms embodying the sub-contractors' interpretation of the contract and the sub-contractors finally accepted that refusal as a repudiation of the contract and withdrew from site. The dispute was referred to arbitration on the issues of construction and repudiation. The arbitrator was requested to express his conclusion on the repudiation issue so that the parties could decide whether to take the issue of construction to the High Court. The arbitrator found that the main contractors had repudiated the contract and stated his award in the form of a consultative case on the issue of construction alone. The main contractors requested the arbitrator to state a special case on the issue of repudiation, but the arbitrator refused. The main contractors applied for an order pursuant to the Arbitration Act 1950, s. 21 (1) that the arbitrator should state his award in the form of a special case on the question of law whether the main contractors had repudiated the contract. The sub-contractors contended that the question disclosed no issue of law. *Held*, a question as to repudiation was not one which always fell within the provisions of s. 21 (1) as there was no exact analogy between repudiation and the question of frustration (on which the court always had power to order a special case); there might be cases of repudiation where the principles of law were so clearly established that the arbitrator need only make a decision on the facts. However, since the essential issue in the instant case was whether the main contractors' conduct went to the root of the contract and this closely resembled the issue of commercial frustration, it would be artificial to draw a distinction between the two for the purposes of s. 21 (1). Further, the question of the extent to which a party holding an honest if misplaced view of his contractual rights and duties could act on that view before actually repudiating the contract was a legal issue appropriate for a decision of the High Court. The order would accordingly be granted and the arbitrator ordered to state a case.

PETER LIND AND CO LTD v CONSTABLE HART AND CO LTD [1979] 2 Lloyd's Rep 248 (Queen's Bench Division: MUSTILL J).

The procedure for making an award in the form of a special case under the 1950 Act, s. 21 has ceased to have effect: Arbitration Act 1979, s. 1 (1). There is now a right of appeal to the High Court on any question of law arising out of an award made under an arbitration agreement: 1979 Act, s. 1 (2).

134   Arbitration Act 1975—parties to convention

The Arbitration (Foreign Awards) Order 1979, S.I. 1979 No. 304 (in force on 12th April 1979), specifies the states which are parties to the 1958 New York Convention on the Recognition and Enforcement of Foreign Arbitral Awards. Under the Arbitration Act 1975, 1975 Halsbury's Abridgment para. 137, arbitral awards made in such states are enforceable in the United Kingdom. The Order also specifies

Grenada as a state which is party to the 1927 Geneva Convention on the Execution of Foreign Arbitral Awards.

The Arbitration (Foreign Awards) Order 1975, 1975 Halsbury's Abridgment para. 138 is revoked.

135   Arbitration Act 1979

The Arbitration Act 1979 amends the law relating to arbitrations, implementing provisions of the Report on Arbitration by the Commercial Court Committee (Cmnd. 7284). The Act received the royal assent on 4th April 1979 and came into force on 1st August 1979, S.I. 1979 No. 750.

Section 1 provides a new procedure for judicial review of arbitration awards. The procedures under the Arbitration Act 1950, s. 21, for statement of a case for a decision of the High Court and under which the court may set aside or remit awards on the grounds of errors of fact or law on the face of the award, are replaced by a limited right of appeal to the High Court on questions of law. The High Court is also empowered to order arbitrators to state the reasons for the award in greater detail. The right of appeal from the High Court to the Court of Appeal is limited.

Section 2 gives the High Court jurisdiction to determine preliminary points of law arising in the course of references to arbitration. The right of appeal from such a decision is limited.

Section 3 enables parties to arbitrations, other than statutory arbitrations, to exclude by agreement in writing the right of appeal under s. 1 or determination of questions of law under s. 2. Exclusion agreements only have effect in relation to domestic arbitration agreements if they are entered into after the commencement of the arbitration. Similarly, under s. 4, such agreements only have effect in relation to arbitrations concerned with maritime matters, insurance or commodity dealing, if they are entered into after the commencement of the arbitration or the award or question relates to a contract expressed to be governed by a law other than the law of England or Wales. Power is conferred on the Secretary of State to provide by order that the provisions relating to maritime, insurance and commodity arbitrations are to cease to have effect.

Under s. 5, where a party fails to comply with an order given by the arbitrator or umpire, the High Court may authorise the arbitrator or umpire to proceed with the arbitration in default of appearance or any other act by the party.

Section 6 contains minor amendments relating to arbitration awards and appointment of arbitrators or umpires. Section 7 applies to the Act certain provisions of the Arbitration Act 1950, Part I, and s. 8 contains the short title, commencement and repeals. The Act forms part of the law of England and Wales only.

136   Arbitration clause—breach—appropriate remedy

A contract for the sale of soya meal contained an arbitration clause providing that any dispute arising out of the contract should be settled by arbitration in London and that neither party should bring any action or other legal proceedings in respect of any such dispute until it had been heard and determined by the arbitrators. A dispute arose, the matter was referred to arbitration and an award was made in favour of the sellers. The buyers appealed to the Board of Appeal of GAFTA. At the same time, the sellers brought proceedings in the Italian courts to obtain security for damages awarded in the arbitration, and an order was made for the attachment of property belonging to the buyers. The Board of Appeal upheld the award in favour of the sellers and also awarded the buyers a sum in respect of a counter-claim for the sellers' breach of the arbitration clause by taking proceedings in Italy. On appeal, the awards were upheld. Both parties appealed further and, while the appeals were pending, the buyers issued a writ seeking a declaration that the arbitration clause was of no effect and that they should be at liberty to revoke the authority to make awards. The officers of the Court of Appeal were not notified of the issue and service of the writ. *Held*, on the buyers' appeal, it was intolerable for them to ask the court to determine an appeal when they had started proceedings in another court claiming that all the proceedings in this country were without jurisdiction. The appeal would be dismissed as being an abuse of the processes of the court.

On the sellers' cross-appeal, the proceedings in Italy clearly fell within the scope of the clause prohibiting "other legal proceedings". The sellers were in breach of that clause, but contended that the buyers were not entitled to damages because the appropriate remedy for breach of an arbitration agreement was not damages but enforcement of the agreement. However, loss could arise in such circumstances since, if a foreign court ordered sequestration, that order might cause the party subject to it financial loss. Damage had been proved in the present case and the cross-appeal would be dismissed.

MANTOVANI v CARAPELLI SpA (1979) 123 Sol Jo 568 (Court of Appeal: MEGAW, LAWTON and BROWNE LJJ). Decision of Donaldson J [1978] 2 Lloyd's Rep 63, 1978 Halsbury's Abridgment para. 2416 affirmed.

137　　——— guarantee—whether guarantor bound by award

See *The Vasso*, para. 1401.

138　　——— right of party to bring action without going to arbitration—whether action should be stayed

Canada
An arbitration clause compelling the parties to a contract to refer any question, dispute or difference arising between them to arbitration is not a *Scott v Avery* clause and consequently reference to arbitration is not a condition precedent to the bringing of any action on the contract. However, an action brought on the facts alone should be stayed, thus leaving the parties to their contractual rights of arbitration.

IRVING PULP AND PAPER LTD v BABCOCK AND WILCOX LTD (1978) 93 DLR (3rd) 407 (Supreme Court of New Brunswick). *Collins v Locke* (1879) 4 App Cas 674, PC and *Heyman v Darwins Ltd* [1942] AC 356, HL applied.

139　　——— time limit—application for extension of time

The plaintiffs entered into a contract of affreightment with the defendants to provide vessels to carry cargoes of grain from the United States to Japan. The contract gave the plaintiffs freedom to nominate vessels and also contained an arbitration clause which provided a nine month time limit from final discharge. One of the vessels nominated by the plaintiffs was one which they had time chartered from a third party and that nomination was accepted by the defendants. However, no similar arbitration clause existed in the charter between the plaintiffs and the third party. The vessel grounded in mud whilst loading in the United States, but was successfully freed and delivered her cargo in Japan on 21st April 1977. In March 1978, the third party amended an existing claim against the plaintiffs to include a claim for damages for unsafe berth damage caused when the vessel ran aground. After an unexplained delay, the plaintiffs, on 20th July 1978, asked the defendants for an indemnity should they be found liable to the third party on the amended claim. The defendants argued that the plaintiffs' claim was time barred under the arbitration clause. The plaintiffs applied under the Arbitration Act 1950, s. 27 for an extension of time for the commencement of arbitration proceedings. The application was refused on the grounds that the case being made by the third party was, on the face of it, without foundation; the plaintiffs had failed to obtain a similar arbitration clause from the third party; the delay between the date when the plaintiffs knew of the third party's amended claim and the date when they communicated that knowledge to the defendants was unexplained; no undue hardship would be caused to the plaintiffs if the application was refused. The plaintiffs appealed. *Held*, on the unusual facts of the case, there were no grounds on which the court would be justified in interfering with the judge's decision. Accordingly, the appeal would be dismissed.

SANKO STEAMSHIP CO LTD v TRADAX EXPORT SA [1979] 2 Lloyds Rep 273 (Court of Appeal: STEPHENSON and GEOFFREY LANE LJJ).

140   Arbitration hearing—opportunity to be heard—request for adjournment to prepare case

Under a contract for the sale of lentils shipments were to be made in July and August 1977 and the sellers guaranteed an export licence. Due to a crop failure, the authorities refused additional export licences so the sellers were unable to make any large shipments before December 1977. On 2nd September 1977 the buyers declared that the sellers were in default and nominated an arbitrator under the GAFTA rules. The sellers took no action until 14th October when GAFTA informed them by letter that the hearing would be on 25th October and that an arbitrator had been appointed for them. The sellers instructed solicitors who obtained an adjournment of the hearing until 8th November; they received the sellers' papers on 2nd November but their request for a further adjournment was refused. The arbitrators awarded damages against the sellers who then applied for the award to be set aside. *Held*, although arbitrations were intended to be quick, both parties must have a reasonable opportunity of dealing with the case against them. The sellers were aware of the issues involved and had ample opportunity to prepare and present their case but chose not to. Accordingly the arbitrators were entitled to reach a decision without giving the sellers more time in which to put forward a defence. There was no injustice in allowing the award to stand, taking account of the sellers' right of appeal. The application would be refused.

THOS P. GONZALEZ CORPN v MULLER'S MUHLE, MULLER GmbH & Co KG [1978] 2 Lloyd's Rep 541 (Queen's Bench Division: DONALDSON J).

141   Arbitrator—appointment—failure to appoint umpire—jurisdiction to make award

The terms of a charterparty provided that disputes should be laid before a board comprised of two arbitrators, one chosen by each of the parties, and an umpire to be chosen by the arbitrators themselves. A dispute arose and two arbitrators made an award in favour of the shipowners. The charterers appealed, contending that the arbitrators had no jurisdiction to act without appointing an umpire. *Held*, the arbitrators should have appointed an umpire, as this would have saved time and money in the event of their disagreeing. However, their failure to appoint an umpire did not deprive them of jurisdiction, and as they had agreed on their decision the award would be upheld.

TERMAREA SRL v REDERIAKTIEBOLAGET SALLY [1979] 2 All ER 989 (Queen's Bench Division: MOCATTA J).

Now, unless the contrary intention is expressed in the arbitration agreement, in any case where there is a reference to three arbitrators, the award of any two of them is binding: see Arbitration Act 1979, para. 135, s. 6 (2).

142   —— —— time for appointment—discretion of court to extend time

Buyers of soya bean meal whose goods were only partially delivered owing to a United States export embargo appointed an arbitrator on October 31st 1973 to adjudicate a claim arising out of a shipment due to have been delivered in July 1973. The contract was subject to the GAFTA arbitration rules, which at the date of the contract specified a period of three calendar months for such an appointment. In October 1973 the rules were changed to allow a fixed ninety day period. The questions therefore arose, inter alia, whether the original or amended rules applied to the buyers' appointment, whether their claim was consequently time-barred or whether they could be granted a retrospective extension of time to allow the appointment. *Held*, there was a distinction to be drawn between substantive and procedural provisions, with reference to deciding which rules applied; substantive provisions had to be taken as found at the date a contract was made, procedural ones as they existed on the date they were invoked. The provisions relating to arbitrators were procedural and thus took effect as amended. On that basis the appointment of the arbitrator had been out of time, although for the purpose of disputes arising out of shipments delivered in the August and September it was valid. Under the Arbitration Act 1950, s. 27, however, the court had a discretion to extend the time for appointment of arbitrators, and that discretion would be exercised to validate the buyers' appointment out of time for July.

BUNGE SA v KRUSE [1979] 1 Lloyd's Rep 279 (Queen's Bench Division: BRANDON J). *Offshore International SA v Banco Central SA* [1976] 3 All ER 749, 1976 Halsbury's Abridgment para. 408 applied.

143   Claimants unsuccessfully applied for an extension of time under the Arbitration Act 1950, s. 27 for the appointment of an arbitrator under a charterparty. The claimants appealed, contending that the judge had wrongly exercised his discretion in view of the considerable amount involved in the claim; that the substantial delay beyond the contractual time in appointing an arbitrator was excused by a substantial number of factors; and that the delay had not caused prejudice to the respondents. *Held*, having given all due weight to the claimants' various submissions, it had not been shown that the judge's exercise of his discretion on the material before him was wrong. Accordingly, the appeal would be dismissed.

THE HELLAS IN ETERNITY, CAST SHIPPING LTD V TRADAX EXPORT SA [1979] 2 Lloyd's Rep 280 (Court of Appeal: MEGAW and BROWNE LJJ).

144   —— —— **validity of appointment**

A dispute arose between the disponent owners and the charterers of two vessels. The registered owners purported to appoint an arbitrator and wrote to the charterers notifying them that an appointment had been made by the "owners". The charterers contended that the appointment was invalid because the registered owners were not parties to the dispute, that the disponent owners had never appointed an arbitrator and that they could not do so now because they were out of time. The trial judge found that, on its true construction, the letter nominated the arbitrator on behalf of the disponent owners. The charterers appealed. *Held*, where a charterparty was made by disponent owners on their own behalf and not as agents for the registered owners, the question of whether the word "owners" used in any document relating to the charterparty meant the disponent owners or the registered owners depended on the context in which the word was used. When the word "owner" was used in letters headed with a reference to the charterparty, the letters being concerned with the appointment of an owner's arbitrator in disputes under the charterparty, the only sensible meaning to give the word was "those who in the capacity of owners are making a claim under the charterparty"; the disponent owners. Accordingly, the appeal would be dismissed.

THE DELIAN LETO AND THE DELIAN SPIRIT, CARRAS SHIPPING CO LTD V THE FOOD CORPORATION OF INDIA [1979] 2 Lloyd's Rep 179 (Court of Appeal: ROSKILL and BRANDON LJJ and SIR DAVID CAIRNS). Decision of Lloyd J [1978] 2 Lloyd's Rep 433 affirmed.

145   —— **jurisdiction—power to award interest on sum already paid**

A freight contract was concluded between shipowners and charterers for the carriage of cement. The contract provided for an amended charterparty to be incorporated into the contract and issued for each vessel carrying cement under the contract. Twelve voyages were performed and disputes arose between the owners and the charterers as to the payment of demurrage. The disputes were submitted to arbitration as provided for under the contract. The owners sought to recover interest on demurrage which had been paid late in breach of an express term of the contract. They also claimed further interest upon such interest if any were to be awarded in respect of the period between the due date of payment and the actual date of payment. The arbitrator rejected the owners' claims and they sought to set aside or remit the award for error of law on the face of it, on the grounds that the arbitrator had jurisdiction to award the interest claimed. *Held*, (i) interest was not payable as damages for late payment under common law unless there was an express or implied term in the contract to this effect; (ii) in so far as the Admiralty court had no power to award interest otherwise than as an adjunct to a judgment for the principal sum, neither the Commercial court nor an arbitrator had such a power; (iii) the general practice was to award interest "on the amount found due" and the arbitrator did not have the power to award interest on sums not due because paid, albeit late. Accordingly, the claims for interest and interest upon interest would fail.

TEHNO-IMPEX v GEBR VAN WEELDE SCHEEPVAARTKANTOOR BV (1979) 5th November (unreported) (Queen's Bench Division: PARKER J). *The Medina Princess* [1962] 2 Lloyd's Rep 17 followed.

146   —— —— power to impose conditions for statement of special case

A dispute between charterers and owners as to liability under a charterparty was referred to arbitration and the umpire's decision that the charterers were liable in damages to the owner was upheld on a case stated. A dispute then arose as to the basis for the calculation of the damages. On a further reference to arbitration the arbitrators, finding that in any event the charterers were liable for a substantial amount, ordered that the award would be stated in the form of a special case only on condition that the charterers first paid that amount into a joint account, since the point of law in issue involved a considerably smaller sum. On the charterers' summons the judge upheld the decision of the arbitrators and ordered them to state a special case provided that the charterers paid the undisputed amount into a joint account. The charterers appealed, claiming that neither the arbitrators nor the judge had jurisdiction to make such a conditional order. *Held*, the Arbitration Act 1950, s. 21 (1) gave the arbitrators an unfettered discretion to make an award in the form of a special case. Further, s. 28, in providing that any order made under s. 21 could be made on such terms as to costs or otherwise as the authority making the order thought just, clearly conferred a discretion, by means of the word "otherwise", to impose conditions such as the one in issue. Accordingly, both the arbitrators and the judge had jurisdiction to make the order in question and the appeal would be dismissed.

THE FURNESS BRIDGE, ANTCO SHIPPING LTD v SEABRIDGE SHIPPING LTD [1979] 3 All ER 186 (Court of Appeal: LORD DENNING MR, LAWTON and GEOFFREY LANE LJJ). For proceedings as to liability see 1977 Halsbury's Abridgment para. 2579.

The procedure for making an award in the form of a special case under the Arbitration Act 1950, s. 21 has ceased to have effect: Arbitration Act 1979, s. 1 (1). There is now a right of appeal to the High Court on any question of law arising out of an award made under an arbitration agreement: Arbitration Act 1979, s. 1 (2). For a summary of the 1979 Act see para. 135.

147   Award—appeal—evidence—admissibility of letter written "without prejudice"

The applicants, who were suppliers of seed, entered into a contract to supply certain seeds to the respondent farmers. The farmers alleged that the seed was not of the type specified and claimed compensation for loss of profits. The suppliers disputed liability and in the course of correspondence between the parties, letters were written "without prejudice". In arbitration proceedings, the arbitrators received and admitted these letters as evidence. The farmers were awarded damages and the suppliers appealed on the grounds that the letters ought not to have been admitted. *Held*, as a matter of public policy it was highly undesirable that "without prejudice" letters should come before the courts or more especially arbitrators who were lay arbitrators and not lawyers. The appeal would be allowed and the order set aside.

FINNERY LOCK SEEDS LTD v GEORGE MITCHELL (CHESTERHALL) LTD [1979] 2 Lloyd's Rep 301 (Queen's Bench Division: SIR DOUGLAS FRANK QC sitting as a deputy High Court judge).

148   —— enforcement of award—alternative procedures—public health

See *Leonidis v Thames Water Authority*, para. 2497.

149   —— grounds for setting aside—error of law on face of award

A firm of contractors agreed to construct an oil terminal for property owners. The contractors' designs were accepted on the basis that the full detailed designs would comply with sound engineering practice. In March 1973 the contractors submitted detailed designs which the owners rejected as being incomplete. Under the contract, any design could be varied by a written order given to the contractors by a firm of engineers. In May 1973 the engineers gave an oral order to change the design of part of the terminal; in August 1974 the contractors notified the owners of their intention to claim an extra payment for the additional work involved. The owners contested the claim. The disputes concerning the designs and the extra payment were referred to an arbitrator who found in favour of the owners. The contractors applied for the award to be set aside on the ground that the arbitrator had erred in law. *Held*, (i) the drawings and calculations submitted by the contractors in March 1973 were contradictory. As the contractors had not explained the discrepancy to the owners, the arbitrator had not erred in law in finding that the designs were incomplete and did not comply with sound engineering practice. (ii) The fact that the engineers' order was oral not written did not prevent the contractors from claiming an extra payment. However, the contract required them to notify the owners of their intended claim. The arbitrator had not erred in law in finding that their notice in August 1974 was too late as it had not been given as soon as practicable after May 1973, the date of the engineers' order. Accordingly the application to set aside the award would be refused.

HERSENT OFFSHORE SA AND AMSTERDAMSE BALLAST BETON-EN WATERBOUW BV v BURMAH OIL TANKERS LTD [1978] 2 Lloyd's Rep 565 (Queen's Bench Division: THOMPSON J).

150 ————— **misconduct of arbitrator or umpire**

Buyers had not fulfilled their obligations under contracts for the sale of soya bean meal, which were on GAFTA terms. When the matter had originally been referred to arbitration the buyers' only defence had been frustration of the contracts due to changes in policy by the Government of Portugal. The buyers had maintained firstly that they intended that the goods should be received in Rotterdam from the United States and then transhipped to Lisbon, but this became impossible because the Portuguese Government gave the exclusive right to import such products to a state trading body. Secondly, the buyers had claimed that they had intended to pay in foreign currency, but that such payment had become illegal following a change in government policy regarding remittances of funds from Portugal. However, at the hearing before the Board of Appeal of GAFTA the buyers also sought to raise the defence that five out of the eighteen notices of appropriation tendered by the sellers were non-contractual under GAFTA terms and thus, in any event, the buyers were not in default in refusing to take up and pay for the bills of lading referred to in these notices. The Board ruled that such a defence was not open to the buyers, but stated their award in the form of a special case, the only question for the High Court being that of frustration. The buyers, by notice of motion, applied to have the award set aside or remitted to the Board for further consideration. On the question of frustration the court held that the contracts had not been frustrated. If the buyers had ever intended to tranship the goods to Lisbon, this intention was never communicated to the sellers. Furthermore the fact that the buyers were unable to fulfil this intention should not have prevented performance of the contract, because delivery could still have been taken at Rotterdam and the goods resold elsewhere. Performance was not rendered illegal by the change in policy regarding remittances of funds from Portugal either. It would have been legal to have paid with funds from outside Portugal, but the buyers were unable to do so because they had unexpectedly run out of foreign currency. This was not sufficient to amount to frustration, particularly as they had not used reasonable endeavours to obtain more funds. But on the notice of motion the court held that the Board had been guilty of misconduct in not allowing the buyers to raise their second defence and the award should be set aside and the matter remitted to the Board for consideration of the buyers' second defence; the Board to make an interim award of damages to the sellers in respect of all the shipments other than the five in dispute. The buyers appealed against the conditions imposed by the High Court in remitting the case, and the sellers cross-appealed on the ground that the Board had been right in refusing to allow the buyers to put forward a new defence at such a late date. *Held*, dismissing the appeal and allowing the cross-appeal, the Board were justified in refusing to allow the defence to be put forward. The Board, as experienced businessmen, were familiar with the general way in which contracts of this sort would have been administered and were free to use their own knowledge in coming to the conclusion that it would not be fair to allow the defence to be put.

CONGIMEX SARL (LISBON) v CONTINENTAL GRAIN EXPORT CORPN (NEW YORK) [1979] 2 Lloyd's Rep 346 (Court of Appeal: LORD DENNING MR, WALLER and CUMMING-BRUCE LJJ).

151 —— remission—application for remission on basis of new evidence—circumstances in which award will be remitted

A dispute under a charterparty was referred to arbitration. The charterers were represented at the proceedings by their solicitor and counsel and an expert witness. At no stage in the proceedings was an adjournment requested on behalf of the charterers, nor did they apply during the six weeks which elapsed between the end of the hearing and the publication of the award for the award to be delayed. However, they subsequently applied by notice of motion for the award to be remitted to the arbitrators for consideration of new evidence, on the grounds that they had been taken by surprise by certain evidence of the owners and that the charterers' expert had had further thoughts on one of the issues. *Held*, a party applying for the remission of an award had to show: (i) that the evidence they now sought to adduce had not been available at the time of the arbitration; (ii) that they could not have obtained it by that time by the exercise of due diligence; (iii) that had they had such evidence it would have been likely to have had a substantial effect upon the result of the arbitration; and (iv) that they had had no opportunity of seeking a delay in the issue of the award while they tried to obtain the new evidence. In the present case, the fresh evidence in question had been available to the charterers, in the shape of their expert witness, at the hearing and, further, it had been open to them, either during the hearing or the following six weeks, to request the arbitrators to receive further evidence. There were therefore no grounds for allowing the charterers now to adduce further evidence and the application would be dismissed.

THE STAINLESS PATRIOT, WHITEHALL SHIPPING CO LTD v KOMPASS SCHIFFAHRTS-KONTOR GmbH [1979] 1 Lloyd's Rep 589 (Queen's Bench Division: DONALDSON J).

152 ——— award in form of special case—remission for further findings of fact

A dispute arose between charterers and carriers concerning damage to certain cargoes. The real claimants were the underwriters seeking to exercise subrogation rights and for that purpose using the name of the charterers. The dispute was referred to arbitration and, the arbitrators being unable to agree, the umpire entered upon the reference. His award stated that he could not decide whether property in the goods had passed to the consignee because of the terms of payment and the absence of bills of lading. He found, however, that the charterers had a right to sue the carriers. The underwriters, in the name of the charterers, sought to remit the award in order that they might call further evidence to determine when the property in the cargo had passed. *Held*, as neither party had made all the relevant information available to the tribunal, the necessity for justice to be done on the basis of the full facts far outweighed the necessity to treat the facts found as being sacrosanct. The award would, therefore, be remitted to the umpire for the consideration of any further evidence adduced by either party relevant to the right to sue.

THE GAMMA, BJORN-JENSEN & CO v LYSAGHT (AUSTRALIA) LTD [1979] 1 Lloyd's Rep 494 (Queen's Bench Division: DONALDSON J).

The special case procedure under the Arbitration Act 1950, s. 21, has ceased to have effect: Arbitration Act 1979, s. 1 (1). There is now a right of appeal to the High Court on any question of law arising out of an award: s. 1 (2). For a summary of the 1979 Act, see para. 135.

153   —— —— **time limit for applying for remission—time when award executed and published**

See *The Archipelagos and Delfi, Bulk Transport Corpn v Sissy Steamship Co Ltd, Bulk Transport Corpn v Ifled Shipping Corpn*, para. 2525.

154   —— **salvage award—appeal—jurisdiction of arbitrator**

See *The Geestland*, para. 2579.

155   —— **special case—application to compel statement of special case—whether questions of law disclosed**

Buyers of grain refused to accept delivery on the grounds that it was infested with insects and that no shipping documents had been supplied to them at the time of delivery as stipulated by the contract. The Board of Appeal of GAFTA declined to state their award in the sellers' favour as a special case on the ground that the matter was entirely within its competence. On the buyers' application under the Arbitration Act 1950, s. 21 (1) for an order directing the board to state a special case, *held*, the question of the tendering of shipping documents was clearly one of law and an ideal subject for referral as a special case; it was an issue both clear-cut and substantial. The sellers' contention that the buyers had waived their right to complain by not complaining about the absence of documents at the time was likewise a question of law suitable for determination by the court. Accordingly, the board would be directed to state its award in the form of a special case.

THE EUROMETAL, CEREALMANGIMI SpA v TOEPFER [1979] 2 Lloyd's Rep 72 (Queen's Bench Division: LLOYD J). *The Lysland, Halfdan Greig & Co A/S v Sterling Coal and Navigation Corpn* [1973] QB 843, CA applied.

The special case procedure under 1950 Act, s. 21 has ceased to have effect: Arbitration Act 1979, s. 1 (1). There is now a right of appeal to the High Court on any question of law arising out of an award: s. 1 (2). For a summary of the 1979 Act, see para. 135.

156   —— —— **imposition of conditions for stating of special case—validity of conditions**

See *Antco Shipping Ltd v Seabridge Shipping Ltd*, para. 86.

157   **Commodity contracts**

The Arbitration (Commodity Contracts) Order 1979, S.I. 1979 No. 754 (in force on 1st August 1979), specifies commodity markets or exchanges in England and Wales and descriptions of contracts for the purpose of the Arbitration Act 1979, s. 4, para. 135, which defines "commodity contract" for the purposes of agreements excluding the right of appeal under s. 1 or determination of questions of law under s. 2.

158   **Costs of arbitration—order for costs against main beneficiaries**

A dispute arising out of a contract for the sale of soya bean meal was referred to arbitration. The arbitrators found that the buyers were in default and awarded the sellers damages and a sum as carrying charges together with interest and costs. The buyers appealed to the Board of Appeal of GAFTA. The Board found in favour of the buyers on the issue of damages, awarding them $10,000. It was conceded that the sellers were entitled to $31,000 as carrying charges, and the Board awarded interest on part only of the claim. The Board additionally awarded that the sellers should pay the appeal fees and all but £5 of the original arbitration fees. The sellers sought the remission of the award to the Board on the ground that the Board had been guilty of technical misconduct in failing to award interest in respect of part of the claim and in failing to award the sellers the cost of the arbitration proceedings, arguing that it was unusual that they, as main beneficiaries, should be expected to pay costs. *Held*, (i) if an order as to costs was unusual on its face, there was a rebuttable presumption that the arbitrators were wrong. In the instant case, the award was unusual on its face, and it was for the buyers to show the factors which, in exercise of a judicial discretion, the arbitrators could have relied upon as justifying their award. However, in considering whether or not to remit an award, the court was solely concerned with whether there was material upon which the arbitrators could have justified their order; since the Board could have justified its order as to costs in this instance, the court was not entitled to interfere. (ii) On the assumption that the award of $31,000 in respect of carrying charges was right, there was no possible justification for the Board denying the sellers interest on that award; interest had to go on until the date of payment. Accordingly, the award would be remitted to the Board to reconsider the question of interest in relation to the carrying charges claim.

WARINCO AG v ANDRE & CIE SA [1979] 2 Lloyd's Rep 298 (Queen's Bench Division: DONALDSON J). *Dineen v Walpole* [1969] 1 Lloyd's Rep 261 applied.

159 ——**order for each party to bear half the costs of award— correctness of order**

On a reference to arbitration the umpire found that the owners of a ship let under a charterparty were entitled to recover damages in respect of only part of the damage suffered by the ship as a result of the alleged fault of the charterers. In view of this finding he considered that the costs of the award should be apportioned to reflect the degree of success of the owners in their claim. However, in the absence of details of the damage sustained, he was unable to make such an apportionment and he therefore ordered that each party was to bear half the costs of the award. On an application to set aside the award as to costs on the ground of technical misconduct, *held*, the umpire had failed to proceed in accordance with the clearly established principle that costs follow the event and the award would therefore be remitted for further consideration.

The court pointed out that although the general principle as to the award of costs could be departed from in certain cases, only special circumstances could justify such a departure.

THE AGHIOS NICOLAOS, BLUE HORIZON SHIPPING CO SA v ED AND F. MAN LTD [1979] 1 Lloyd's Rep 475 (Queen's Bench Division: PARKER J).

160 **International investment disputes—Jersey**

The Arbitration (International Investment Disputes) (Jersey) Order 1979, S.I. 1979 No. 572 (in force on 1st July 1979) extends with certain exceptions, adaptations and modifications, the provisions of the Arbitration (International Investment Disputes) Act 1966 to the Bailiwick of Jersey.

161 **Notice of arbitration—service of notice—service by telex—date of service**

On 9th January 1971 a vessel subject to a charterparty was damaged whilst discharging her cargo. On Friday 7th January 1977 the shipowners telexed a purported notice of arbitration to the Tokyo office of the charterers. It was received by the charterers after office hours and was only seen by a responsible member of staff on 10th January 1977. The owners claimed damages for breach of the charter. The charterers contended that the claim was time-barred since it had not been referred to arbitration within the six-year period from the date on which the cause of the arbitration occurred, as the period expired on 8th or 9th January 1977. The question was whether the notice of arbitration had been served on 7th or 10th January 1977. *Held*, a claimant in an arbitration had to serve a notice on his opponent but a valid notice might be sent by telex. In the case of an English registered company a telex notice served under the Limitation Act 1939, s. 27 (3) was served when it was received at the company's registered office whether that was within normal working hours or not. The telex was received by the charterers on

7th January and the notice of arbitration had therefore been served within the six-year period and a claim for damages could be brought.

NV STOOMV MAATS "DE MAAS" v NIPPON YUSEN KAISHA (1979) Times, 8th December (Queen's Bench Division: PARKER J).

See also Times, 8th December 1979.

162   Reference to arbitration—injunction restraining arbitration proceedings—power of court to dismiss claim for want of prosecution

The respondents in two separate arbitration disputes successfully contended that the claimants were responsible for several years' delay in the arbitration proceedings. Both respondents were granted injunctions restraining the claimants from taking any further action. The claimants appealed, contending that the court had no jurisdiction to restrain the proceedings for want of prosecution. *Held*, although arbitrators had no power to dismiss an arbitration for want of prosecution, the court had an inherent jurisdiction to restrain arbitration proceedings when it would be right and just to do so. The claimants in both disputes were guilty of such delay that both respondents had been seriously prejudiced and a fair hearing would be impossible. Moreover, the claimants' delay had amounted to a repudiation of the arbitration agreement between the parties thereby entitling the respondents to rescind it and apply for an injunction. The court could dismiss a claim in arbitration for want of prosecution in the same way that it could dismiss a plaintiff's claim in litigation for the same reason. Accordingly the appeals would be dismissed.

BREMER VULKAN SCHIFFBAU UND MASCHINENFABRIK v SOUTH INDIA SHIPPING CORPN; GREGG v RAYTHEON LTD [1980] 1 All ER 420 (Court of Appeal: LORD DENNING MR, ROSKILL and CUMMING-BRUCE LJJ). Decision of Donaldson J [1979] 3 All ER 194 affirmed on other grounds.

In relation to arbitrations commenced after 1st August 1979, some remedy for delay is provided by the Arbitration Act 1979, s. 5, para. 135.

163   Stay of proceedings—allegation of fraud—jurisdiction of court to grant stay—non-domestic arbitration agreement

The plaintiff supplied the defendants with information on the manufacture of machines for making air-gun pellets. Their agreement contained an arbitration clause to operate in respect of any dispute arising out of the agreement. A dispute arose and payment of royalties to the plaintiff ceased. He claimed damages for breach of contract and an injunction to restrain the defendants from continuing to use confidential information. The defendants sought a stay of proceedings under the Arbitration Act 1975, s. 1. The plaintiff contended that the defendant's allegation that he had obtained the confidential information from his previous employers amounted to an allegation of fraud and that the arbitration agreement should consequently be set aside under the Arbitration Act 1950, s. 24 (2). The defendants denied that they were alleging fraud. *Held*, the plaintiff's allegation of misuse of confidential information was a matter capable of being dealt with under the arbitration agreement; prima facie the court had no power to set aside a non-domestic arbitration agreement whether fraud was alleged or not because the 1975 Act, s. 1 overrode the 1950 Act, s. 24 (2). In any event it was not clear that fraud had been alleged and if the court had a discretion it would exercise it against the plaintiff. The proceedings would accordingly be stayed.

PACZY v HAENDLER AND NATERMANN GmbH [1979] FSR 420 (Chancery Division: WHITFORD J).

164   —— conditions for obtaining stay—existence of arbitration agreement—whether a domestic agreement

Shippers sought a stay of an action brought in respect of goods destroyed by fire while in their care. They claimed that their standard business conditions, which contained an arbitration clause, applied to the contract and that the matter should go to arbitration under the Arbitration Act 1950, s. 4 (now Arbitration Act 1975, s. 1 (1)). The owner of the goods contended that the shippers' standard conditions did not apply to the contract and that accordingly there was no justification for granting a stay. *Held*, where it was unclear whether an effective arbitration agreement even existed, a stay could not be granted. In any event, a stay could only be granted under s. 1 where an arbitration agreement was not a domestic one as defined in s. 1 (4). If an agreement existed in the instant case it was highly likely that it was a domestic one and thus the section would be inapplicable. The action would therefore be allowed to proceed.

WILLCOCK V PICKFORDS REMOVALS LTD [1979] 1 Lloyd's Rep 244 (Court of Appeal: ROSKILL, ORMROD and BROWNE LJJ).

AVIATION

Halsbury's Laws of England (4th edn.), Vol. 2, paras. 801–1423

165   Air and air traffic control—general regulations

The Rules of the Air and Air Traffic Control (Fifth Amendment) Regulations 1979, S.I. 1979 No. 1417 (in force on 1st December 1979), further amend the Rules of the Air and Air Traffic Control Regulations 1976, 1976 Halsbury's Abridgment para. 180. Gliders must now comply with specified rules with respect to Birmingham Airport, special rules are now made for Sumburgh Airport and further special rules are substituted with regard to cross-channel air traffic.

166   Air navigation—general regulations

The Air Navigation (Fifth Amendment) Order 1979, S.I. 1979 No. 1318 (in force on 19th November 1979, except art. 2 (6) a (ii) (iii), (b) for which the date is 1st January 1981), further amends the Air Navigation Order 1976, 1976 Halsbury's Abridgment para. 158. The changes include provisions that certain aeroplanes and all helicopters (in the case of technical logs) may now carry both copies of the technical log and the load sheet in the aircraft if it is not reasonably practicable for one copy of each to be kept on the ground. Further, certain turbo-jet aeroplanes, aeroplanes, helicopters and gyroplanes are now required to be equipped with both internal and external emergency lighting to facilitate the evacuation of passengers.

167   —— Isle of Man

The Air Navigation (General) (Isle of Man) Regulations 1979, S.I. 1979 No. 1184 (in force on 12th October 1979), provide that the Air Navigation (General) Regulations 1976, 1976 Halsbury's Abridgment para. 154, suitably adapted, are to have effect in the Isle of Man.

168

The Air Navigation (Isle of Man) Order 1979, S.I. 1979 No. 929 (in force on 1st September 1979), provides that the Air Navigation Order 1976, 1976 Halsbury's Abridgment para. 158, as amended, is to apply to the Isle of Man, with certain modifications. This Order revokes the Air Navigation (Isle of Man) Order 1972.

169   —— noise certification

The Air Navigation (Noise Certification) Order 1979, S.I. 1979 No. 930 (in force on 1st August 1979), revokes and replaces the Air Navigation (Noise Certification) Order 1970, S.I. 1970 No. 823 as amended. The order prohibits an aeroplane to which it applies, wherever registered, from landing or taking off unless it has a noise certificate issued, by the Civil Aviation Authority or other competent authorities of prescribed countries, or in pursuance of the Chicago Convention. The Order also makes provision for the issue of the certificates, specifies standards to which an aeroplane must comply to obtain them and contains other ancillary provisions concerning offences in relation to noise certificates.

170 —— services—joint financing

The Civil Aviation (Joint Financing) (Second Amendment) Regulations 1979, S.I. 1979 No. 1599 (in force on 1st January 1980), further amend the Civil Aviation (Joint Financing) Regulations 1978, 1978 Halsbury's Abridgment para. 172, by altering the charge payable by aircraft operators to the Civil Aviation Authority in respect of crossings between Europe and North America. The charges altered are those attributable to the Danish and Icelandic air navigation services and are payable in pursuance of the 1956 Agreements on the Joint Financing of certain Air Navigation Services.

171 Air travel organisers—licensing

The Civil Aviation (Air Travel Organisers' Licensing) (Third Amendment) Regulations 1979, S.I. 1979 No. 5 (in force on 1st April 1979), further amend the Civil Aviation (Air Travel Organisers' Licensing) Regulations 1972. They provide that where the holder of a current licence applies for the grant of another licence three months before the current licence expires, the application will no longer keep the current licence in force after its expiry date unless it is accompanied by the appropriate fee and by such particulars as the Civil Aviation Authority may have specified in a notice in writing served not less than four months before the expiration of the term of the current licence.

172 Aviation Security Fund—contributions to fund—prescribed aerodromes

The Aviation Security Fund (Amendment) Regulations 1979, S.I. 1979 No. 145 (in force on 1st April 1979), amend the Aviation Security Fund Regulations 1978, 1978 Halsbury's Abridgment para. 177. The sum which, multiplied by the number of passengers in excess of 2,000 who during each period of one month arrive by air at the aerodrome, is equal to the contribution payable in respect of the aerodrome for that month, is increased from 80p to 85p. The weight limit for aircraft whose passengers are excluded from the number of passengers used in this calculation is raised from 5 tonnes to 10 tonnes. Certain words in the definition of "aerodrome" are updated, but the list of aerodromes in respect of which contributions are required to be made is unchanged. The increased contributions are payable in respect of any period beginning on or after 1st April 1979.

173 British Airports Authority—statutory powers—power to ban minicabs—validity of banning notice

See *Cinnamond v British Airports Authority*, para. 2177.

174 Carriage by air—limitation of liability—sterling equivalents

The Carriage by Air (Sterling Equivalents) Order 1979, S.I. 1979 No. 765 (in force on 1st August 1979), supersedes the Carriage by Air (Sterling Equivalents) Order 1978, 1978 Halsbury's Abridgment para. 178, by specifying new sterling equivalents of amounts expressed in gold francs as the limit of the air carrier's liability under the Warsaw Convention of 1929, and under that Convention as amended by the Hague Protocol of 1929, as well as corresponding provisions applying to carriage by air to which the Convention and Protocol do not apply.

175 —— —— substitution of unit of liability

The Carriage by Air Acts (Application of Provisions) (Second Amendment) Order 1979, S.I. 1979 No. 931 (in force on 1st August 1979) further amends the Carriage by Air Acts (Application of Provisions) Order 1967. In consequence of the coming into force of the amended Articles of Agreement of the International Monetary Fund, the Order substitutes special drawing rights for gold francs as the unit in which the limits of the air carrier's liability are expressed for the purposes of non-international carriage, but does not make any change in those limits.

176   —— successive carriers—actions between carriers—joint and several liability—limitation period

Canada

The plaintiff consigned polio vaccine to the defendant airline for carriage from Canada to Ecuador. The vaccine had to be kept frozen throughout. The defendant engaged a third party airline to carry the vaccine for the second half of the journey, during which it thawed owing to delay. It subsequently had to be destroyed. The plaintiff claimed damages from the defendant who claimed in turn against the third party. The latter contended that the complaint had not been served on it within the time limit prescribed by the Warsaw Convention, art. 26 (2) and that third party proceedings had become time-barred under art. 29 (1) because more than two years had passed since the damage occurred. *Held*, the defences would fail, (i) because the third party had known of the damage almost immediately it had been discovered and in any event service of notice on one carrier applied equally to a successive carrier as they were jointly and severally liable; (ii) because art. 29 applied only to actions between passengers or cargo-owners and carriers, not to actions between carriers. Accordingly the defendant was liable to the plaintiff and the third party to the defendant.

CONNAUGHT LABORATORIES LTD v AIR CANADA; AEROLINEAS NACIONALES DEL ECUADOR SA (THIRD PARTY) (1978) 94 DLR (3d) 586 (High Court of Ontario).

177   Carriage by Air and Road Act 1979

See para. 289.

178   Civil Aviation Authority—charges payable to Authority—navigation services

The Civil Aviation (Navigation Services Charges) (Second Amendment) Regulations 1979, S.I. 1979 No. 267 (in force on 1st April 1979), amend the Civil Aviation (Navigation Services Charges) Regulations 1977, 1977 Halsbury's Abridgment para. 200. Charges are no longer payable in respect of the domestic part of an international flight, or in respect of navigation services provided in connection with the use of Birmingham, Bournemouth (Hurn), Liverpool and Manchester aerodromes. The charge payable for a helicopter flight from the United Kingdom to an offshore installation in the area specified in reg. 6A is increased to £25.

179   The Civil Aviation (Navigation Services Charges) (Third Amendment) Regulations 1979, S.I. 1979 No. 1274 (in force on 1st November 1979), further amend the Civil Aviation (Navigation Services Charges) Regulations, 1977 Halsbury's Abridgment para. 200. Charges payable to the Authority for navigation services provided in connection with the use of certain specified aerodromes are increased and the charge payable by an aircraft operator in respect of a communicated flight plan within the Stanwick Oceanic Control Area is also increased.

180   ———— Canada

The Civil Aviation (Canadian Navigation Services) (Second Amendment) Regulations 1979, S.I. 1979 No. 237 (in force on 1st April 1979), further amend the Civil Aviation (Canadian Navigation Services) Regulations 1977, 1977 Halsbury's Abridgment para. 202, by increasing the charge for air navigation services provided by the Government of Canada in the Gander Flight Information Region.

181   ———— route charges

The Civil Aviation (Route Charges for Navigation Services) (Second Amendment) Regulations 1979, S.I. 1979 No. 154 (in force on 1st April 1979), further amend the Civil Aviation (Route Charges for Navigation Services) Regulations 1978, 1978 Halsbury's Abridgment para. 185. They give effect to a new tariff in relation to flights which enter the airspace defined in the Regulations where the United Kingdom provides air navigation services.

182 —— functions

The Civil Aviation Authority (Fifth Amendment) Regulations 1979, S.I. 1979 No. 514 (in force on 30th May 1979), further amend the Civil Aviation Authority Regulations 1972. The amendments relate to the granting, revocation, suspension and variation of air transport licences and the procedure in air transport licensing cases.

183 International carriage—limitation of liability—wilful misconduct of carrier's servant

The plaintiffs were owners of a box of platinum which was carried to London (Heathrow) Airport by the first defendants, where the plaintiff transferred it to the second defendants' warehouse ready for export. The box disappeared from the warehouse while security was lax. The plaintiffs claimed the value of the platinum from both defendants. The second defendants authorised the first defendants to send the plaintiffs a cheque for a small amount which they claimed represented the total extent of their liability because no value had been declared for the platinum on the air waybill. The plaintiffs signed a receipt for the cheque but subsequently returned it because their investigations in London had not been completed. The second defendants claimed both that signing the receipt amounted to an acceptance of the small sum by the plaintiffs in full and final settlement of their claim, and that they were exempted from liability by certain articles of the Warsaw Convention. The plaintiffs relied on art. 25 of the Convention, which bars reliance on exemption clauses by those who were guilty of wilful misconduct or by those whose servants had caused the loss in the course of their employment. *Held*, the defendants could not claim that the cheque had been accepted in full and final settlement of the claim, because any intention on the plaintiffs' part to do so should have been clearly expressed. They were also barred from claiming any exemption under the Convention because the evidence showed that the theft had been deliberately facilitated by one of their servants who was therefore guilty of wilful misconduct.

RUSTENBURG PLATINUM MINES LTD v SOUTH AFRICAN AIRWAYS AND PAN AMERICAN WORLD AIRWAYS INC [1979] 1 Lloyd's Rep 19 (Court of Appeal: LORD DENNING MR, EVELEIGH LJ and SIR DAVID CAIRNS). Decision of Ackner J [1977] 1 Lloyd's Rep 564, 1977 Halsbury's Abridgment para. 209 affirmed.

184 —— loss of baggage contents—time limit for complaint

The plaintiff discovered that his suitcase was torn on arrival, after travelling on an aircraft owned by the defendant. He immediately reported the damage to the defendant, but later found that some of the contents were missing. He claimed that the defendant was liable both for the damage and the loss of contents. The defendant admitted liability for damage to the suitcase, but argued that the loss of contents came within the meaning of "damage" in art. 26 (2) of the Warsaw Convention, as amended and set out in the Carriage by Air Act 1961, Sch. 1. If art. 26 (2) applied, the loss of contents should have been reported within seven days of receipt of the suitcase. The trial judge held that "damage" in art. 26 (2) meant physical injury to the suitcase, and that the loss of contents did not, therefore, have to be reported within seven days. The defendant appealed. *Held*, LORD DENNING MR dissenting, "damage" in art. 26 (2) was confined to physical injury and did not include partial loss of contents. The appeal would be dismissed.

LORD DENNING MR was of the opinion that "damage" in art. 26 (2) included partial loss of contents, but dismissed the appeal on the ground that the initial complaint of damage, made within seven days of receipt, was sufficient to satisfy art. 26 (2) in respect of both the damage and the loss of contents.

FOTHERGILL v MONARCH AIRLINES LTD [1979] 3 All ER 445 (Court of Appeal: LORD DENNING MR, BROWNE and GEOFFREY LANE LJJ). Decision of Kerr J [1977] 3 All ER 616, 1977 Halsbury's Abridgment para. 210 affirmed.

Article 26 (2) has now been modified to include instances involving loss of part of the baggage: Carriage by Air and Road Act 1979, para. 289, s. 2.

185   Limitation of liability—right of carrier—claims in respect of death of passenger and loss of luggage

Canada

The plaintiff's husband was killed when the defendants' aircraft, in which he was travelling as a passenger, crashed. The plaintiff brought an action claiming damages for the death of her husband and the loss of his baggage. The defendants admitted liability, but successfully contended that they were entitled to limit their liability under the Warsaw Convention, arts. 3 and 4. The plaintiff appealed. *Held*, article 3 provided that the absence, irregularity or loss of a passenger ticket would not affect the existence or validity of the contract of carriage, and the benefit of the limitation would only be lost where no ticket was delivered; the defendants had delivered a ticket and their right to the limitation on the claim for damages for the death of the plaintiff's husband was therefore preserved. Article 4, which governed baggage claims, provided that the luggage ticket should contain certain particulars; the ticket was of a type legible by an ordinary person using ordinary diligence and its content was adequate to meet the requirements of the Convention. Accordingly, the appeal would be dismissed.

LUDECKE v CANADIAN PACIFIC AIRLINES LTD [1979] 2 Lloyd's Rep 260 (Supreme Court of Canada). Decision of Quebec Court of Appeal [1975] 2 Lloyds' Rep 87, 1975 Halsbury's Abridgment para. 186 affirmed. *Montreal Trust Co and Stampleman v Canadian Pacific Airlines Ltd* [1977] 2 Lloyd's Rep 80 distinguished.

186   Noise insulation—grants—schools

The Heathrow Airport-London Noise Insulation Grants (Schools) (Amendment) Scheme 1979, S.I. 1979 No. 414 (in force on 1st May 1979), varies the Heathrow Airport–London Noise Insulation Grants (Schools) Scheme 1977, 1977 Halsbury's Abridgment, para. 215, by increasing the total maximum grant payable from £220,000 to £230,000.

BAILMENT

Halsbury's Laws of England (4th edn.), Vol. 2, paras. 1501–1589

187   Bailee—duty of care—duty of care when property in goods passed to purchaser

See *Nelson v Raphael*, para. 44.

188   Bailee and bailor—duty of care—dangerous machinery

See *Pivovaroff v Chernabaeff*, para. 1957.

BANKING

Halsbury's Laws of England (4th edn.), Vol. 3, paras. 1–182

189   Articles

The Need for Banking Law Reform, Derek Wheatley: 129 NLJ 872.

New Rules for Bankers, Patricia A. Bickerton (examination of the legislation contained in the Banking Act 1979, para. 192): [1979] LS Gaz 672.

Supervising the Banks, T. Michael Ashe (the Banking Act 1979, para. 192): 129 NLJ 1160.

190 **Bank—relationship with customer—transfer of liability for debt— undue influence**

Canada
A widow was asked to sign a promissory note which transferred liability for her husband's debts to her. She claimed that she had had no knowledge of what was contained in the note but had placed reliance on the bank in signing whatever papers were placed before her. *Held*, the bank had an obligation to ensure that the widow had full knowledge of the possible consequences of signing, and should have told her that she was not obliged to sign. She should also have been advised to seek an independent opinion, since the bank might otherwise have been thought to have exerted undue influence. As she had never received this advice the note was not enforceable.

ROYAL BANK OF CANADA v HINDS (1978) 20 OR (2d) 613 (High Court of Ontario).

191 **Bank manager—duty of care—liability of bank for negligent misstatement**

See *Box v Midland Bank Ltd*, para. 1958.

192 **Banking Act 1979**

The Banking Act 1979, which implements Council Directive (EEC) 77/780, OJ No. L322, 17.2.1979, provides for the authorisation and supervision by the Bank of England of institutions which take deposits from the public. The Act received the royal assent on 4th April 1979. Sections 1–20, 34–38, 40–50, Schs. 1–4 came into force on 1st October 1979, S.I. 1979 No. 938. The remaining provisions come into force on days to be appointed: s. 49 (3).

Part I: Control of Deposit-taking
Section 1 imposes a general prohibition on the acceptance of deposits in the course of carrying on a deposit-taking business and defines "deposit". Section 2 exempts from the prohibition institutions recognised and licensed under the Act, the Bank of England and the bodies listed in Sch. 1. The criteria of recognition and licensing of banks by the Bank of England are set out in s. 3 and Sch. 2; s. 3 also introduces Sch. 3 which relates to transitional licences. Section 4 requires the Bank to make an annual report and list of recognised and licensed institutions. The procedure for applying for recognition and licences is contained in s. 5. The grounds for revocation of recognition or licence and the Bank's powers and procedure with respect to revocation are contained in ss. 6, 7 and Sch. 4. Section 8 empowers the Bank to give directions in connection with the termination of deposit-taking authority, and s. 9 governs the duration of such directions and direction-making power. Section 10 deals with conditional licences. Sections 11, 12 provide for an appeals procedure to the Chancellor of the Exchequer. Appeals on points of law may be made to the courts: s. 13. Sections 14, 15 are concerned with the duties of licensed institutions. The Bank is empowered to obtain information and require production of documents from licensed institutions which have had their authorisation revoked: s. 16. Section 17 deals with the Bank's powers of investigation into the affairs of a recognised bank or licensed institution and s. 18 provides for their winding up on petition by the Bank. Restrictions on the disclosure of information by the Bank are contained in s. 19. Section 20 is concerned with disclosure to the Bank of information obtained under the Companies Acts.

Part II: The Deposit Protection Scheme
Section 21 and Sch. 5 provide for the setting up of the Deposit Protection Board which is to manage the Deposit Protection Fund. The resources, investments and payments of the Fund are covered by s. 22. Section 23 defines contributory institutions and makes general provisions as to contributions. Initial, further and special contributions to the Fund and the Board's power to borrow are contained in ss. 24–26. Section 27 provides for maximum and minimum contributions. When institutions become insolvent, payments may be made to depositors with protected

deposits: s. 28. Protected deposits are defined in s. 29. Section 30 makes provisions with respect to joint deposits and trustee deposits. Section 31 deals with the liability of insolvent institutions in respect of payments made by the Board. Provision for repayment to institutions in respect of contributions is made by s. 32. Section 33 deals with the tax treatment of contributions and repayments.

Part III: Advertisements and Banking Names
Section 34 deals with the Treasury's control over advertisements for deposits. The Bank may give a specific direction to a licensed institution if it considers that an advertisement is misleading: s. 35. Section 36 puts a restriction on the use of certain banking names and descriptions and s. 37 provides transitory exceptions from s. 36.

Part IV: Miscellaneous and General
Amendments to Consumer Credit Act 1974, 1974 Halsbury's Abridgment para. 1597 are contained in s. 38. Section 39 makes fraudulent inducement to make a deposit an offence and s. 40 is concerned with representative offices of overseas deposit-taking institutions. Sections 41, 42 contain provisions with respect to offences committed under the Act. Directors, managers and controllers of deposit-taking institutions are excluded from certain provisions relating to the rehabilitation of offenders: s. 43. Section 44 is concerned with evidence as to the recognition or licensing of an institution under the Act. Section 45 regulates the service of notices under the Act. Certain obsolete enactments are repealed by s. 46. Section 47 provides for a defence of contributory negligence for bankers, notwithstanding the provisions of Torts (Interference with Goods) Act 1977, s. 11 (1), 1977 Halsbury's Abridgment para. 2912. Section 48 defines and deals with municipal banks and s. 49 defines director, controller and manager for the purposes of the Act. Other expressions used in the Act are interpreted in s. 50. Consequential amendments and repeals are contained in s. 51, Schs. 6, 7 and s. 52 deals with short title, commencement and extent.

193   —— exempt transactions

The Banking Act 1979 (Exempt Transactions) Regulations 1979, S.I. 1979 No. 1204 (in force on 1st October 1979), exempt deposits taken by certain institutions from the prohibition on deposit-taking. The institutions are: charities; the Central Board of Finance of the Church of England; the Central Finance Board of the Methodist Church; industrial and provident societies; the British Railways Savings Bank; solicitors; estate agents.

194   —— implementation

The Bank of England is issuing a handbook entitled "Handbook of Banking Supervision". The handbook is to be divided into four parts: Part A, summarising the provisions of the 1979 Act; Part B, the implementation of the 1979 Act; Part C, the principles of supervision and Part D, a list of recognised banks and licensed Institutions. Parts A and B have now been published.

Part B is divided into eight sections; I. Institutions covered by the 1979 Act; II. Application for recognition or a licence (no form of application for recognition or a licence is prescribed but applicants are required to complete a questionnaire in the appropriate form prescribed in Annexes A, B, and C); III. Application of the criteria (the principles underlying the statutory criteria for recognition and licences and the manner in which the Bank will administer them); IV. Notification (no notifications are expected to be made until near the end of the six-month period which commenced on 1st October 1979. Lists of successful applicants will be published in the London Gazette); V. Representative offices of overseas deposit-taking institutions; VI Deposit Protection Fund (when the whole of Part II of the Act is in force the Bank of England will call for details of deposit bases. Initial deposits to the Deposit Protection Fund will be geared to yield an initial fund of between £5 and 6 million by contributions of between £300,000 and £2,500); VII. Additional requirements for recognised banks and licensed institutions; VIII. Powers of the Bank of England.

195   Community legislation—implementation

Council Directive (EEC) 77/780, OJ No. L322, 17.2.1979, requires member states to introduce a system of authorisation for credit institutions by December 1979. The Directive was implemented in the United Kingdom by the Banking Act 1979, para. 192, subject to certain defined exceptions including building societies, in respect of which an application was made, under art. 2 (5) of the directive, to defer the application of the directive for a period of five years: see the Report of the Chief Registrar of Friendly Societies for the Year 1978; Part 2, Building Societies, p. 23.

196   Following money in equity—money paid to bank under mistake of fact—right to recover

See *Chase Manhattan Bank NA v Israel-British Bank (London) Ltd*, para. 1136.

197   Letter of credit—irrevocable letter of credit—delay in bank paying under the credit—damages

The plaintiffs, an export company, agreed to sell certain machinery to a Nigerian company for U.S. $126,000. Payment was to be made by irrevocable letter of credit valid for six months and issued by the defendants, the London branch of a Nigerian bank. The appropriate documents were presented to the defendants, through the plaintiffs' bank, within the six month period and payment should have been made on 5th October 1977. In fact, despite repeated complaints by the plaintiffs' bank, payment was not made until 12th December 1977. In an action for damages the plaintiffs contended that the defendants were liable for all losses reasonably foreseen as a result of the breach, and accordingly claimed (i) £3,000 being the loss consequential upon a change in the dollar–sterling exchange rate between 5th October and 12th December; (ii) interest on the sterling equivalent of $126,000 between those dates; (iii) the fees of the plaintiffs' bank for their services in seeking payment. *Held*, (i) although the price of the goods was agreed to be paid in dollars, the plaintiffs' loss was incurred in sterling and was a foreseeable loss. The value of foreign currency to an English company engaged in the export trade was the amount of sterling which that currency would buy, and that amount had decreased by £3,000 between October and December; (ii) they were entitled to interest on the $126,000 at 7½ per cent, the rate at which they were able to borrow; (iii) it was also foreseeable that the plaintiffs would incur expenses in seeking to obtain payment and were entitled to recover those expenses plus interest.

OZALID GROUP (EXPORT) LTD v AFRICAN CONTINENTAL BANK LTD [1979] 2 Lloyd's Rep 231 (Queen's Bench Division: DONALDSON J). *Miliangos v George Frank (Textiles) Ltd* [1976] 1 Lloyd's Rep 201, HL, 1975 Halsbury's Abridgment para. 1916 applied.

198   Payment of cheques—payment of cheque previously stopped by drawer—recovery from payee of money paid under mistake of fact

See *Barclays Bank Ltd v W J Simms Son & Cooke (Southern) Ltd*, para. 1888.

199   Savings Banks—Registrar's fees—amendment

The Savings Banks (Registrar's Fees) (Amendment) Warrant 1979, S.I. 1979 No. 258 (in force on 16th March 1979), amends the Savings Banks (Registrar's Fees) Warrant 1976, 1976 Halsbury's Abridgment para. 196 by increasing the fees to be paid for certificates given by the Registrar of Friendly Societies as to the rules of trustee savings banks.

200   The Savings Banks (Registrar's Fees) (Amendment) Warrant 1979, S.I. 1979 No. 1761 (in force on 1st January 1980), further amends the Savings Banks (Registrar's Fees) Warrant 1976, 1976 Halsbury's Abridgment para. 196 and increases the fees to be paid for certificates given by the Registrar of Friendly Societies as to the rules of trustee savings banks.

201   Trustee savings banks

The Trustees Savings Banks (Amendment) Regulations 1979, S.I. 1979 No. 259 (in force on 16th March 1979), amend the Trustees Savings Banks Regulations 1972. The provisions relating to the declaration to be made by a depositor in connection with other accounts held by him in trustee savings banks have been removed. A new definition of current account deposit has been provided. The Regulations also remove the restrictions on the repayment of deposits on death without the necessity for proof from the Inland Revenue Commissioners that any death duties or capital transfer tax payable on the death of the depositor have been paid or that none are payable. As from 1st May 1979 a depositor no longer has the power to make a nomination.

202   —— Fund for the Banks for Savings

The Trustee Savings Banks (Fund for the Banks for Savings) Order 1979, S.I. 1979 No. 551 (in force on 21st May 1979), specified the limits of the sums which a trustee savings bank might withdraw from the amounts standing to its credit in the Fund for the Banks for Savings during the half year ending on 20th November 1979. The specified limit was either the amount by which the sum in credit to the trustee savings bank in the Fund exceeded the figure in column (2) of the Schedule to the Order or £10,000, whichever was the greater.

This Order has been revoked; see para. 203.

203   The Trustee Savings Banks (Fund for the Banks for Savings) (No. 2) Order 1979, S.I. 1979 No. 1183 (in force on 25th September 1979), revokes the Trustee Savings Banks (Fund for the Banks for Savings) Order 1979, para. 202. The Order specifies revised limits on the sums which a trustee savings bank may withdraw from the amounts standing to its credit in the Fund for the Banks for Savings during the half year ending on 20th November 1979. The specified limit is either the amount by which the sum standing to the credit of the trustee savings bank in the Fund exceeds the figure in column (2) of Schedule 1 to the Order or £10,000, whichever is the greater. The Order also provides the limit on withdrawals from the Fund during the half years falling within the period from 20th November 1979 to 20th May 1986. In addition to the specified limit, the trustee savings bank may withdraw the sum credited to it as interest earned on the amount which stood to its credit in the Fund in the immediately preceding half year.

204   —— life annuities

The Trustee Savings Banks Life Annuity (Amendment) Regulations 1979, S.I. 1979 No. 552 (in force on 21st May 1979), amend the Trustee Savings Bank Life Annuity Regulations 1930 by providing that future commission and annuity payments will be paid by the National Debt Commissioners to the relevant trustee savings banks.

205   —— post office register

The Post Office Register (Trustee Savings Banks) (Amendment) Regulations 1979, S.I. 1979 No. 553 (in force on 21st May 1979), amend the Post Office Register (Trustee Savings Banks) Regulations 1930 by providing that in future the proceeds of sale of government stock and any dividends received on such stock will be paid by the National Debt Commissioners to the trustees of the relevant trustee savings bank and will no longer be credited to the trustee's account in the Fund for the Banks for Savings. The Commissioners will also receive payments from and make payments to the trustees in respect of unclaimed redemption moneys without making use of the Fund for the Banks for Savings for these transactions.

206   Trustee Savings Banks Act 1976—commencement

The Trustee Savings Banks Act 1976 (Commencement No. 7) Order 1979, S.I. 1979 No. 1475, brings into force on 21st November 1979, for certain limited purposes, the following provisions of the Act, 1976 Halsbury's Abridgment, para, 198: s. 36

(1), (2), Sch. 5, paras. 8 (1) (a), 15 (a) and Sch. 6. The effect is to repeal certain provisions in the Trustee Savings Banks Act 1969 and the Trustee Savings Banks Act 1976 relating to the statutory requirements for ordinary deposits with trustee savings banks and to repeal the references to ordinary deposits in the Trustee Investments Act 1961, Sch. 1. Certain other minor provisions of the 1969 Act are repealed.

BANKRUPTCY AND INSOLVENCY

Halsbury's Laws of England (4th edn.), Vol. 3, paras. 201–1062

207　Article

Criminal Bankruptcy Reconsidered, A. N. Khan (in the light of the House of Lords decision in *Anderson v Director of Public Prosecutions* [1978] 2 WLR 994, 1978 Halsbury's Abridgment para. 225): 123 Sol Jo 195.

208　Bankruptcy notice—application to set aside—when application heard

A company served a bankruptcy notice on a debtor based on an unsatisfied judgment. The debtor's application to set aside the bankruptcy notice was refused and he gave notice of appeal against the refusal. Before the appeal was heard, the company's petition for a receiving order based on failure to comply with the bankruptcy notice was granted by the registrar. The debtor appealed against the receiving order, relying on the Bankruptcy Rules 1952, r. 179, which provides that where the act of bankruptcy alleged in the petition is non-compliance with the requirements of a bankruptcy notice, no receiving order is to be made against the debtor until the application has been heard. He contended that the application to set aside the bankruptcy notice had not been "heard" within the meaning of r. 179 so long as an appeal against the registrar's decision was outstanding. *Held*, there was authority for the proposition that, for the purposes of r. 139, where there had been an actual hearing by the registrar of an application to set aside a bankruptcy notice, that application was "heard" at the date of the registrar's decision. Although the present case concerned a different rule, the same words appearing in the same set of rules and dealing with the same subject-matter should be given the same meaning. Hence r. 179 did not preclude the making of a receiving order once the hearing by the registrar of the application to set aside the bankruptcy notice was completed, notwithstanding that there was an appeal outstanding. In the ordinary course of events, a court dealing with an application to make a receiving order would stand over the application until the appeal against the refusal to set aside the bankruptcy notice was finally dealt with, but only if there was a bona fide appeal being pursued with due diligence. In this case, the appeal had not been pursued with due diligence and there were no grounds for overturning the receiving order. The appeal would be dismissed.

Re A Debtor (No. 44 of 1978); Wolsey-Neech v Chantry Mount and Hawthorns Ltd [1979] 3 All ER 265 (Chancery Division: Fox and Browne-Wilkinson JJ). *Re A Debtor (No. 10 of 1953), ex parte The Debtor v Ampthill RDC* [1953] 2 All ER 561, DC applied.

209　Bankruptcy order—time for compliance—extension of time

Following the issue of a bankruptcy notice against him, the debtor made an application to set aside the notice on the ground, inter alia, that it was founded upon fraud. His application was heard and dismissed by the registrar after the date on which the bankruptcy notice expired. A receiving order was made on the basis that the act of bankruptcy had been completed and no extension of time for compliance with the notice had been granted. The debtor appealed against the order, contending that there had been an extension of time under either (i) the Bankruptcy Rules 1952, r. 139 (2), which provided that if an application could not be heard within the time specified in the notice, the registrar would grant an extension. Rule 139 (1) provided that the filing of an affidavit under r. 137 (relating to counterclaim, set-off and cross demand) operated as an application to set aside the bankruptcy notice; or (ii) the Bankruptcy Act 1914, s. 109 (4), giving the court a general discretion to extend time where it thought fit. *Held*, (i) the debtor's application was not made under r. 137 but under r. 31 which provided that every application to the courts was to be made by motion supported by affidavit. The word "application" in r. 139 (2) was restricted to an application made by filing an affidavit under r. 137, and not by motion under r. 31. (ii) The registrar made no conscious statement relating to the extension of time, and the court would reject the debtor's contention that by certain words and phrases the registrar had intimated that he would use his discretion and extend the time for compliance.

However, the registrar had misdirected himself in law by not inquiring into the consideration for the debt despite the allegation of fraud. The appeal would be allowed on that basis and the bankruptcy notice set aside.

RE LINDSEY (A DEBTOR) (1979) 25th January (unreported) (Chancery Division: GOULDING and FOX JJ).

210   Department of Trade—annual report

The Department of Trade in its annual report for 1978 (HMSO) has disclosed that there were 3,540 bankruptcy cases in 1978, compared with 4,095 in 1977, and that there were seventy deeds of arrangement compared with 82 in 1977. The estimated liabilities in these failures totalled £217 million, an increase of 89 per cent over 1977. Of the 733 applications for discharge under the Bankruptcy Act 1914, s. 26 about 15 per cent were refused or adjourned generally. There were 2,571 applications under the Insolvency Act 1976, s. 8, of which approximately 32 per cent were refused. During 1978 there were 103 prosecutions for offences under the Bankruptcy Acts which resulted in ninty-nine convictions.

211   Discharge from bankruptcy—order for automatic discharge— discretion of court to make order

After being adjudicated bankrupt, a debtor applied for an order under the Insolvency Act 1976, s. 7 that he should be automatically discharged five years after the adjudication. The registrar indicated before hearing the debtor's submission, that he did not think it a suitable case for automatic discharge and, after hearing the submission, refused the order. The debtor appealed claiming that the registrar had not given him an open-minded hearing and had not given sufficient weight to certain facts which were in the debtor's favour. *Held*, the ordinary machinery of discharge was designed to protect creditors and members of the public, and it should not be dispensed with in favour of an automatic discharge where the registrar had real doubts about the wisdom of doing so. The court's duty, when considering an application under s. 7, was to consider all the circumstances of the case and there was nothing to suggest that the registrar in question had not done so. It was for the registrar to decide to which facts he attached the most importance, and the appellate court could only reverse his decision where he had been wrong in law, or had considered irrelevant facts or had failed to consider pertinent facts. The appeal would be dismissed.

RE REED (A DEBTOR) [1979] 2 All ER 22 (Chancery Division: GOULDING and FOX JJ).

212   —— suspended discharge granted subject to subsequent condi- tions—entitlement to automatic discharge

See *Re a Debtor (No. 13 of 1964), ex parte Official Receiver and Trustee v The Debtor*, para 213.

213   —— —— whether conditional discharge

A debtor was adjudicated bankrupt in 1964. In May 1968, he was granted a discharge which was suspended for six months on condition that he continued to be liable to pay his creditors a certain sum by instalments. In 1978, the debtor had almost £7000 left to pay under the 1968 order. He then claimed that by reason of the Insolvency Act 1976, s. 7 (4), he had been absolutely discharged and was no longer under any liability to pay the outstanding balance. Section 7 (4) of the 1976 Act provides that a person adjudicated bankrupt before 1st October 1972 and not discharged by 1st October 1977 is in the same position as if he had been granted an absolute discharge on that date. Section 7 (5) of the Act provides that reference to discharge in s. 7 (4) includes conditional orders of discharge. The Official Receiver's application for a review of the 1968 order was dismissed by the judge who held, without considering the circumstances of the case, that the debtor had been absolutely discharged under s. 7 (4). The Official Receiver appealed. *Held*, the question was whether, for the purposes of s. 7, the order of May 1968 discharged the debtor six months later, or whether he remained undischarged on 1st October 1977, the condition as to payment of the debt not being fully satisfied by that date. On the true construction of s. 7 (5) a conditional order was an order which imposed conditions precedent to the discharge and did not include an order which imposed conditions subsequent to discharge. The conditions imposed by the 1968 order were conditions subsequent, the debtor having been discharged subject to those conditions in November 1968, that is, on the expiry of the six month period provided for. Therefore, as he had not been absolutely discharged on 1st October 1977, by virtue of s. 7 (4), the 1968 order was still open to review. Accordingly, the appeal would be allowed and the Official Receiver's application remitted to the county court for consideration on its merits.

RE A DEBTOR (NO 13 OF 1964), EX PARTE OFFICIAL RECEIVER AND TRUSTEE V THE DEBTOR [1979] 3 All ER 15 (Chancery Division: FOX and BROWNE-WILKINSON JJ). *Re a Debtor (No. 946 of 1926)* [1939] 1 All ER 735 and *Re Tabrisky* [1947] 2 All ER 182, applied.

214   **Evidence—debtor abroad—admissibility of affidavit evidence in absence of debtor from proceedings—application to give evidence abroad**

In November 1976 the creditor presented a petition in bankruptcy against the debtor, who disputed the court's jurisdiction contending that he had acquired a domicile of choice in Spain. Affidavits were filed and the debtor applied for leave to give his evidence in Spain, as warrants for his arrest on charges of corrupt practices were outstanding in England. The registrar dismissed the application. An application to the registrar by the creditor for a direction that the debtor's affidavits would not be admitted in evidence unless he attended for cross-examination was refused as being too premature. Both parties appealed. *Held*, the warrants for the debtor's arrest were relevant factors to take into account in deciding whether or not to make an order for examination abroad. This was not conclusive however; cost, delay and the possibility of injustice to the creditor were also to be considered. The registrar had exercised his discretion according to these principles and the court would not interfere with that decision. Further, a debtor who did not attend for cross-examination would run the risk that his evidence would not be admitted. This was a question for the trial judge to decide if the debtor did not appear at the hearing. The registrar was correct in refusing the application for a direction by the creditor. Both appeals would therefore be dismissed.

RE A DEBTOR (NO. 2283 OF 1976), EX PARTE DEBTOR V HILL SAMUEL & CO LTD [1979] 1 All ER 434 (Court of Appeal: BUCKLEY and BRIDGE LJJ and SIR DAVID CAIRNS).

215   **Fees**

The Bankruptcy Fees (Amendment) Order 1979, S.I. 1979 No. 780 (in force on 23rd July 1979) increases from £3.75 to £5.75 the fee payable for insertion in the London Gazette of notices in bankruptcy proceedings.

216   The Bankruptcy Fees (Amendment No. 2) Order 1979, S.I. 1979 No. 1589 (in force on 1st January 1980), further amends the Bankruptcy Fees Order 1975, 1975

Halsbury's Abridgment para. 222. The order abolishes the use of adhesive stamps and the separate fee payable for the insertion in the London Gazette of notices authorised by the Bankruptcy Act 1914 or Bankruptcy Rules 1952. From 1st January 1980 an element for Gazette notices is included within an increased stationery fee. In cases where the receiving order was made before 1st January 1980 a flat fee is charged to cover all future Gazette notices. The order also abolishes the procedure by which the Lord Chancellor's directions may be obtained where payment of a fee is disputed.

217   The Bankruptcy (Amendment) Rules 1979, S.I. 1979 No. 1590 (in force on 1st January 1980) amend the Bankruptcy Rules 1952 so as to take account of the Bankruptcy Fees (Amendment No. 2) Order 1979, see para. 216, which abolishes the use of adhesive stamps for the payment of fees and the separate fee for the insertion of notices in the London Gazette.

218   Proof of debts—set-off—mutual dealings not arising out of contract

An order was made for the compulsory winding up of a company in February 1975. A liquidator was appointed. Among the company's creditors were the Inland Revenue and the Department of Health and Social Security. The Customs and Excise Commissioners owed the company a balance in respect of input tax. In September 1976, the commissioners by mistake sent a cheque to the liquidator in part settlement of the sum owed by them to the company. The commissioners subsequently sought to set off the debts owed to the Inland Revenue and the Department of Health and Social Security against their obligation to repay input tax, by virtue of the Bankruptcy Act 1914, s. 31. The commissioners commenced proceedings to recover the sum which they had inadvertently paid to the liquidator. The liquidator contended that s. 31 did not require the commissioners to set off the input tax, and that even if they were required to do so, s. 31 ceased to apply when the commissioners paid the sum in part settlement. *Held*, (i) on its true construction, s. 31 applied to debts due to and from the Crown; (ii) the provisions of s. 31 were mandatory and could not be excluded. Since the debt due from the commissioners had fallen to be set off against the debts due from the company immediately before the commencement of the winding up the Crown was under no liability to pay anything to the liquidator. The sum paid in error was recoverable at law, being moneys paid under a mistake.

RE CUSHLA LTD [1979] STC 615 (Chancery Division: VINELOTT J). *Re D. H. Curtis (Builders) Ltd* [1978] 2 All ER 183, 1978 Halsbury's Abridgment para. 254 followed. *National Westminster Bank Ltd v Halesowen Presswork and Assemblies Ltd* [1972] 1 All ER 641, HL applied.

219   Property available for distribution—matrimonial home—husband and wife joint tenants—mortgage secured on house

New Zealand

A husband and wife were joint tenants of the matrimonial home in unequal shares, the wife's share being seventy-five per cent, the husband's twenty-five per cent. In 1973 they opened a joint bank account. In 1974 the husband's business ran into financial difficulties and overdraft facilities were arranged secured by a mortgage to the bank executed by the husband and wife. As the account became overdrawn in excess of the credit limit, a loan was arranged from a solicitor's nominee company and another mortgage was executed by the husband and wife in favour of the company. The loan was paid into the joint bank account. On the bankruptcy of the husband, the official receiver sold the house and directed that the mortgages should be discharged from both the husband's and wife's shares of the proceeds of sale. The wife brought an action contending that the mortgages had been raised solely for the purpose of the husband's business and should be discharged only from his share of the proceeds of sale. She was successful at first instance and the official receiver appealed. *Held*, the principle of exoneration, whereby a person who charged his property to secure the debt of another was in the position of a surety and entitled to be indemnified by the principal debtor to the exoneration of his own estate, did not apply in this case. There was no evidence of any agreement that the husband should be the principal debtor and the husband and wife were at all times co-debtors of the bank and the nominee company. The official receiver did not therefore take the husband's interest in the property subject to any equity in favour of the wife and the appeal would be allowed.

RE BERRY (A BANKRUPT) [1978] 2 NZLR 373 (Court of Appeal).

220　Receiving order—jurisdiction to make order—reduction of debt below minimum sum to found petition—effect of payment by debtor to sheriff

A creditor obtained judgment against the debtor for £1,417·95 and subsequently served a bankruptcy notice based on that debt on the debtor. As the debtor did not comply with the notice, the judgment creditor then filed a bankruptcy petition. Before the hearing, he levied execution and on 23rd May 1977 the debtor paid £1,400 to the sheriff, who appropriated £70·63 towards the claim of a prior creditor and £1,329·37 towards that of the judgment creditor. On 31st May 1977, a receiving order was made against the debtor. The debtor applied for rescission of the receiving order on the ground that the registrar had no jurisdiction to make it because the Bankruptcy Act 1914, s. 4 (1) (a) provided that the minimum sum on which a creditor's petition could be founded was £200, and the debt owed to the judgment creditor had been reduced to £88·58 prior to the making of the order, since payment to the sheriff constituted payment to the judgment creditor. *Held*, payment to the sheriff did not satisfy the judgment creditor's claim, since the claim could only be satisfied when the judgment creditor was in a position to maintain an action against the sheriff for money had and received. The judgment creditor could only do so if the fourteen-day period prescribed by the 1914 Act, s. 41, had elapsed without the occurrence of specified events upon which the sheriff had to pay the money to the Official Receiver or the trustee in bankruptcy; thus the judgment creditor could not on the date the order was made be described as having a vested interest in the money liable to be divested. The registrar had jurisdiction to make the order and the application would be refused.

RE A DEBTOR (NO. 2 OF 1977), EX PARTE THE DEBTOR V GOACHER [1979] 1 All ER 870 (Chancery Division: WALTON and FOX JJ).

221　—— restriction on making order—application to set aside bankruptcy notice pending

See *Re A Debtor (No. 44 of 1978), Wolsey-Neech v Chantry Mount and Hawthorns Ltd*, para. 208.

BARRISTERS

Halsbury's Laws of England (4th edn.), Vol. 3, paras. 1101–1221

222　Article

Should the Silk System Continue?, Oliver Thorold (the advantages and disadvantages of the system): 129 NLJ 555.

223　Chambers—names of barristers

The Bar Council has approved a ruling that, in addition to the names of barristers practising primarily from a set of chambers, the names of any other barristers who are prepared to work and attend conferences in those chambers (whilst practising primarily from another set) must also be included on the notice outside the chambers. No barrister's name, however, may appear on any such notice unless he is a member of the circuit in which the chambers are situate; but this does not apply to chambers in London or (if the barrister specialises in Chancery, patent, local government, planning or Revenue matters and has the consent of the leader of the circuit) to provincial chambers. No barrister's name (except with the prior approval of the Bar Council and, in the case of provincial chambers, of the leader of the circuit) may appear on more than one notice outside a set of chambers in addition to the set from which he practises primarily. Where, under this ruling, a barrister's name appears outside more than one set of chambers his notepaper may state this. See the Annual Statement of the Inns of Court and the Bar 1978–79, p. 33.

224 Complaints against counsel—procedure

Arrangements have been made following correspondence between the Chairman of the Bar and the Registrar of the Court of Appeal (Criminal Division) and with the agreement of the Lord Chief Justice, for handling complaints against counsel which are contained in notices of application for leave to appeal and for the procedure to be followed when counsel is asked to attend before the Court of Appeal (Criminal Division) to give evidence.

In relation to specific factual complaints where the applicant has waived privilege or no question of privilege appears to arise, the Criminal Appeal office may ask by letter for information from counsel in relation to the facts. Counsel will be sent a copy of the document in which the complaint is made and asked whether he can give any information which might assist the court. Other than in exceptional circumstances, counsel's letter will be sent to the complainant shortly after it has been received. If oral evidence is to be given to the Court of Appeal, counsel should be called as a witness either by the Crown or by the appellant; he should not be called by the court itself. A full proof should be obtained from counsel who will if possible first have the opportunity of seeing the original brief and other relevant documents. Counsel who is giving evidence should be regarded in material respects as being in the same position as any other witness as to fact (including any claim for expenses). The procedure is set out in the *Guardian Gazette*, 26th September 1979.

225 Conduct of case—offensive behaviour of client—circumstances justifying withdrawal from case

The Bar Council has ruled that, where a lay client behaves in an offensive manner, his counsel should nevertheless continue to act except in two situations. These are: (i) where the behaviour is such that counsel is justified in assuming that his instructions have been withdrawn (in such circumstances the Bar Council advises that counsel should discuss the position with his instructing solicitors before withdrawing from the case); and (ii) where counsel finds that his professional conduct is being, or is likely to be, impugned (in such circumstances the Bar Council advises that counsel ought not to continue to appear unless in his opinion he cannot withdraw from the case at that stage without jeopardising the interests of the lay client). The Bar Council in its ruling adds that when counsel decides to continue in a case after the lay client has behaved in an offensive manner it is advisable that he should ask the lay client for a statement in writing that he is satisfied with counsel's conduct of the case and has no complaint to make about it.

See the Annual Statement of the Inns of Court and the Bar 1978–79, p. 29.

226 Defending counsel—duty to ensure representation of client

The Bar Council has re-iterated the principle that it is the paramount duty of defending counsel to ensure that an accused person is never left unrepresented at any stage of his trial. The Bar Council has approved a further ruling in relation to lengthy trials involving numerous defendants. Where, after the conclusion of the opening speech by the prosecution, defending counsel is satisfied that during a specific part of the trial there is no serious possibility that events will occur which relate to his client, he may with the consent of (*a*) his solicitor (or his representative), and (*b*) his client, absent himself for that part of the trial. He should also inform the judge. In this event it is his duty (*a*) to arrange for other defending counsel to guard the interests of such client, (*b*) to keep himself informed throughout of the progress of the trial and in particular of any development which could affect his client, and (c) not to accept other commitments which would render it impracticable for him to make himself available at reasonable notice if the interests of his client so require. See the Annual Statement of the Inns of Court and the Bar 1978–79, p. 35.

In a separate ruling, the Bar Council has stated that if during the course of a criminal trial (and prior to final sentence) the defendant voluntarily absconds and the defending counsels instructing solicitor withdraws from the case, counsel too should withdraw. If counsel is instructed under a legal aid certificate he must apply to the court under s. 31 (2) of the Legal Aid Act 1974. If the judge requests counsel to continue in the case, counsel has an absolute discretion whether or not to do so. See the Annual Statement of the Inns of Court and the Bar 1978–79, p. 36.

227 Directorships—compatibility with practice

The Bar Council has issued a statement for the guidance of practising barristers who are also directors of companies or may become directors. A practising barrister may be a director of a public or private company provided that his duties do not prevent the Bar from being his primary occupation and that his association with the company would not adversely affect the reputation of the Bar. Except in the case of a small family company, with the consent of the Bar Council, a practising barrister may not be an executive director of a company; nor may he do work for the company normally done by an executive director. Nor may he undertake legal work for the company which, as a barrister, he could only undertake if instructed by a solicitor. He may, however, give advice to the company on matters of general policy and general legal principles provided that it is compatible with his position as a director and is not of a kind which he would give as a barrister advising a client. Where he advises the company in relation to a specific problem, either in a general way or as a matter of urgency, he should ensure that the company consults its solicitors as soon as the matter reaches the appropriate point. See the Annual Statement of the Inns of Court and the Bar 1978–79, p. 31.

228 Employment—barrister employed by company—right to advise company

The Bar Council has ruled that it is not contrary to existing rules for a barrister employed or exclusively retained by a company to advise that company or an associated company on the registration of trade agreements under the provisions of European Community legislation. See the Annual Statement of the Inns of Court and the Bar 1978–79, p. 36.

229 Fees—interlocutory matters

See para. 2121.

230 Law Centres and legal advice centres

The Rules for Law Centres have been replaced by the Rules for Law Centres and Legal Advice Centres dated 23rd July 1979; see the *Guardian Gazette*, 26th September 1979, p. 925.

A barrister may accept full-time or part-time employment at (i) a law centre which employs, or has the services of, one or more solicitors to whom the Law Society has granted a waiver; (ii) any other centre at which legal advice is habitually given to members of the public without fee or at a nominal fee and which has been designated by the Bar Council as suitable for the employment of barristers. Separate rules relate to barristers employed at law centres (rr. 2–14), barristers employed at legal advice centres (rr. 15–20) and barristers attending at law centres and legal advice centres (rr. 21–24). In particular, the rules relate to barristers acting without instructions from a solicitor: interviewing clients, writing letters, negotiating on behalf of clients and drafting pleadings (see rr. 3, 16 and 22). Barristers are not permitted to sue out any writ or process, instruct counsel or carry on conveyancing work (see rr. 4, 17 and 23). Barristers attending law centres and barristers employed at or attending legal advice centres may not appear as advocates in courts or tribunals in the course of such work (see rr. 17 and 23).

231   Negligence—advice given to solicitor by counsel—extent of counsel's duty towards solicitor

See *Smith v McInnis*, para. 2703.

232   Possession of documents—etiquette

The Bar Council has approved a ruling relating to the use of documents belonging to the other side. If, before or during a case, a document belonging to the other side should come into the possession of counsel, he should (if he intends to make any use of it) inform his opponent that it has come into his possession. This information should be communicated in sufficient time for the opponent to raise an objection to the use of the document if he so wishes. See The Law Society Gazette, 27th June 1979, p. 639.

233   Professional misconduct

The Bar Council has stated that the failure of a barrister to respond to a request from the Professional Conduct Committee for comments or information on a complaint should be dealt with as professional misconduct. The failure of a barrister to attend disciplinary tribunal proceedings when so requested on behalf of the Senate should be similarly dealt with. See the Annual Statement of the Inns of Court and the Bar 1978–79, p. 28.

234   Right of audience—Court of Appeal and High Court—whether right exclusive

See *Engineers' and Managers' Association v Advisory, Conciliation and Arbitration Service*, para. 574.

235   Royal Commission on Legal Services—recommendations

See para. 1720.

236   Training—overseas applicants—discrimination on racial grounds

See *Ghaffar v Council of Legal Education*, para. 2195.

BETTING, GAMING AND LOTTERIES

Halsbury's Laws of England (4th edn.), Vol. 4, paras. 1–190

237   Article

The Great Gamble, G. N. Benson (Gaming Act 1845, s. 18 in relation to the law of contract): 122 Sol Jo 853.

238   Bingo club—entertainment charge—whether value added tax payable

See *Tynewydd Labour Working Men's Club and Institute v Customs and Excise Comrs*, para. 2972.

239   Gaming Board for Great Britain—breach of rules of natural justice

See *R v Gaming Board for Great Britain, ex parte Fenton, Mills and Wood*, para. 312.

240   —— report

See para. 311

241   Gaming machines—value of supply for value added tax purposes

See *Townville (Wheldale) Miners Sports and Recreation Club and Institute v Customs and Excise Comrs*, para. 3034.

242   Lottery—definition—contribution—declaration as to legality of scheme subject of criminal proceedings

Cigarette manufacturers adopted a sales promotion scheme whereby each packet of cigarettes contained a ticket, some of which entitled the holder to a prize. The Director of Public Prosecutions commenced criminal proceedings against the manufacturers, alleging that they were holding unlawful lotteries and competitions. The manufacturers sought a declaration from the Commercial Court as to the legality of the scheme. The court declared the scheme to be unlawful and the manufacturers appealed. *Held*, the Lotteries and Amusements Act 1976, s. 1, provided that all lotteries which did not constitute gaming were unlawful except as provided by the Act. The manufacturers' contention was that the scheme was not a lottery. An essential element of a lottery was that there had to be some actual contribution made by the participants in return for their obtaining a chance to take part in it. The cost of the cigarettes was unaffected by the scheme and there was no charge for participation in the scheme above and beyond the price of the cigarettes. The chance to take part was freely given and the scheme was not therefore a lottery. Under the 1976 Act, s. 14, it was unlawful to conduct a competition in which success did not depend to a substantial degree on the exercise of skill, if this was done in connection with any trade or business or the sale of any article to the public. The mischief aimed at in the 1976 Act was to prevent people evading the law against lotteries by introducing a small element of skill. Section 14 was not intended to catch innocent schemes, and did not include the benefit of a chance of a prize which was given free by the promoters. The scheme was not an illegal competition.

Finally, the court had to decide whether it should exercise its discretion to grant a declaration in respect of the scheme which was the subject of criminal proceedings. The alleged offences involved minimal criminality, the sole issue in both proceedings was a point of law and it was desirable that an authoritative ruling was speedily obtained. The court would therefore exercise its discretion to grant a declaration that the scheme was lawful. The appeal woud be allowed.

IMPERIAL TOBACCO LTD v ATTORNEY GENERAL [1979] 2 All ER 592 (Court of Appeal: LORD DENNING MR, ORMROD and BROWNE LJJ). *Whitbread & Co Ltd v Bell* [1970] 2 All ER 64, *Readers Digest Association Ltd v Williams* [1976] 3 All ER 737, DC, 1976 Halsbury's Abridgment para. 238 and *Douglas v Valente* 1968 SLT 85 applied. *Taylor v Swetten* (1883) 11 QBD 207, *Hall v McWilliam* (1901) 17 TLR 561, *Willis v Young and Stembridge* [1907] 1 KB 448, *Bartlett v Parker* [1912] 2 KB 497, *Minty v Sylvester* (1915) 85 LJKB 1982, *Kerslake v Knight* [1925] All ER Rep 679, *Howgate v Ralph* (1929) 93 JP 163, *DPP v Bradfute* [1967] 1 All ER 112 overruled.

This decision has been reversed by the House of Lords; see Times, 7th March 1980.

243   Pools Competitions Act 1971—continuation

The Pools Competitions Act 1971 (Continuance) Order 1979, S.I. 1979 No. 763 (in force on 26th July 1979), continues in force the Pools Competitions Act 1971 until, and including, 26th July 1980.

244   Royal Commission on Gambling—recommendations—proposed legislation

In the course of a debate in the House of Commons on the report of the Royal Commission on Gambling, 1978 Halsbury's Abridgment, para. 251, the Home Secretary gave an indication of the government's attitude to some of the proposals made in the report (see the Financial Times, 30th October 1979). Legislation would be introduced to enable the Gaming Board to penetrate the corporate veil surrounding casinos to enable it to find out who actually controls them. Further, casinos and bingo clubs would be required to submit audited accounts to the Gaming

Board at regular intervals. In response to the Royal Commission's call for the prevention of commercial exploitation and improved control over lotteries, new regulations would be introduced enabling a tighter control to be maintained over local lotteries. The proposal to abolish the "spot-the-ball" competition run by the Pools Promoters' Association and similar contests has been rejected by the government.

BILLS OF EXCHANGE AND OTHER NEGOTIABLE INSTRUMENTS

Halsbury's Laws of England (4th edn.), Vol. 4, paras. 301–523

245 Assignment—previous charge over book debts in favour of third party—priority over proceeds of bills

The plaintiffs brought an action against a bank claiming the proceeds received by the bank upon collection of amounts due under certain bills of exchange and a letter of credit. The bills of exchange and the letter of credit had been assigned to the plaintiffs by a company in settlement of an amount owed by the company to the plaintiffs. The company had, however, previously executed a debenture in favour of the bank by way of first fixed charge on all book debts which prohibited the company from purporting to assign book debts without the written consent of the bank. The bank claimed that it was entitled to the proceeds of the bills by reason of its fixed charge on book debts in the debenture. *Held*, the relevant bills constituted book debts within the meaning of the debenture. On its true construction, the debenture conferred on the bank a specific charge in equity on all future book debts owed to the company; subject to any rights of the plaintiffs as assignees of the bills, the rights of the bank as specific chargee attached in equity to the proceeds of the book debts as soon as they were paid. Although at the date of assignment the plaintiffs had actual knowledge of the existence of a charge on the bills, they had no actual or constructive knowledge of the provision containing restrictions on assignment. The plaintiffs were therefore entitled to assume that the company had an equity of redemption in the bills capable of being disposed of in the ordinary way. Thus the plaintiffs were entitled to priority over the bank in respect of the sums due under the bills, and their claim would succeed.

SIEBE GORMAN & CO LTD V BARCLAYS BANK LTD [1979] 2 Lloyd's Rep 142 (Chancery Division: SLADE J). *Deeley v Lloyds Bank Ltd* [1912] AC 756, HL and *Devaynes v Noble, Clayton's Case* (1816) 1 Mer 529, 572 applied.

246 Bill of exchange—dishonour—indorsement—transfer of liability to indorser

The managing director of a company that had accepted two bills of exchange, indorsed the bills by signing them "for and on behalf of the company". Subsequently, the bills were dishonoured, but neither the director nor the company paid the amount of the bills. The plaintiffs who were the holders of the bills which had been drawn in their favour, claimed the amount against the director. *Held*, an indorsement of a bill amounted to a warrant that the bill would be honoured and imposed, in certain circumstances, a transfer of liability to the indorser. As liability could not be transferred to oneself, the only way in which validity could be given to the present indorsement was to construe it as binding someone other than the acceptor. The director's signature made him personally liable on the bills and the words "for and on behalf of the company" did not vary or amend his agreement to assume liability for the default of the company. The plaintiffs' claim would be allowed.

ROLFE, LUBELL & CO V KEITH [1979] 1 All ER 860 (Queen's Bench Division: KILNER BROWN J).

247   —— —— partial failure of consideration

The plaintiffs, a manufacturing company incorporated outside the United Kingdom, had supplied fire hoses to the defendants, an English company, for some eight or nine years.   From time to time, the hoses supplied by the plaintiffs had not been up to standard and the defendants had called upon the plaintiffs to replace the defective hoses free of charge.   By the end of 1977, the position of the accounts between the two parties were in a state of confusion.   In January 1978, the defendants agreed to accept a bill of exchange in the sum of one million Austrian schillings payable in October 1978, and to pay to the plaintiffs £3,000 per month commencing in February 1978 on account of their indebtedness to the plaintiffs.   The defendants made payments in February and March, but subsequently stopped the payments because defective hoses were again supplied by the plaintiffs.   The defendants claimed that they were entitled to a refund of £11,000 in respect of the defective hoses.   The plaintiffs presented the bill of exchange in due course and the bill was dishonoured.   In an action by the plaintiffs, summary judgment for the whole amount of the bill was granted.   The defendants appealed, contending that it was arguable that there was an initial failure of consideration for the bill in that the amount shown by the invoices to have been due from the defendants to the plaintiffs was not one million schillings but 400,897 schillings.   The defendants also applied for a stay of execution of judgment under RSC Ord. 14, r. 3.   *Held*, on the available information, there was an arguable case for a defence in respect of part of the one million schillings due on the bill as there was a possibility that the indebtedness of the defendants to the plaintiffs would be discovered to be no more than 400,897 schillings.   It was therefore arguable that there was no consideration for the bill except to the extent of 400,897 schillings.   This was not a case in which it would be right to exercise the discretion to stay execution of the judgment and the order would stand to the extent of the sum of 400,897 schillings.   The appeal would, accordingly, be allowed.

THONI GmbH & Co KG v RTP EQUIPMENT LTD [1979] 2 Lloyd's Rep 282 (Court of Appeal: BUCKLEY, BRIDGE and WALLER LJJ).   *Forman v Wright* (1851) 11 CB 481 applied.

248   —— —— plaintiff obtaining judgment—appropriateness of Mareva injuction pending defendant's counterclaim

See *Montecchi v Shimco (UK) Ltd; Navone v Shimco (UK) Ltd*, para. 1598.

249   —— —— —— appropriateness of stay of execution pending defendant's counterclaim

See *Montecchi v Shimco (UK) Ltd; Navone v Shimco (UK) Ltd*, para. 1598.

250   —— formal requirements—date of maturity—whether payable at fixed or determinable future time

On a claim for money due under a bill of exchange, the defendants claimed that the words "at ninety days D/A sight of this first bill of exchange pay" on the face of the bill did not disclose a fixed date for payment and that therefore the bill was defective in form.   The court considered that "D/A" meant days after acceptance and therefore the bill was good.   On appeal, *held*, the bill lacked sufficient clarity because, even if D/A meant days after acceptance, there were no provisions as to the date of maturity in the event of non-acceptance.   As it was not expressed to be payable at a fixed or determinable future time, the bill was defective.

KOREA EXCHANGE BANK v DEBENHAMS (CENTRAL BUYING) LTD (1979) 123 Sol Jo 163 (Court of Appeal: MEGAW, WALLER and EVELEIGH LJJ).

251   —— incorrect company name on face of bill—personal liability of company director

See *Maxform SpA v B. Mariani and Goodville Ltd*, para. 365.

252　Cheque—cheque signed by director on behalf of company— company name incorrectly stated—liability of director

See *British Airways Board v Parish*, para. 364.

253　Promissory note—form—payment of sum certain—interest payable from date of advance

Canada

The respondent signed an instrument promising to pay the appellant company a certain sum of money with interest by instalments "from the date of advance". He made two payments, then defaulted and the whole balance became due. The appellant sued on the instrument, alleging it to be a promissory note. The respondent successfully contended that the promise in the instrument was not a promise to pay a "sum certain" within the definition of a promissory note in the relevant legislation. On appeal, *held*, the instrument specified the date of advance as the date from which interest was to be calculated, but that date was inherently uncertain without the aid of inadmissible extrinsic evidence. Hence the promise to pay a certain sum with interest "from the date of advance" was not a promise to pay a sum certain and the instrument was not, therefore, a promissory note. The appeal would be dismissed.

MACLEOD SAVINGS AND CREDIT UNION LTD v PERRET (1978) 91 DLR (3d) 612 (Supreme Court of Alberta).

BRITISH NATIONALITY AND ALIENAGE

Halsbury's Laws of England (4th edn.), Vol. 4, paras. 901–973

254　Citizenship—fees

The British Nationality (Amendment) Regulations 1979, S.I. 1979 No. 240 (in force on 4th April 1979), further amend the British Nationality Regulations 1975, 1975 Halsbury's Abridgment para. 260, by increasing certain fees payable in respect of the conferment of citizenship of the United Kingdom and Colonies by registration or naturalisation.

255　Immigration

See IMMIGRATION.

256　Race relations

See RACE RELATIONS.

BUILDING CONTRACTS, ARCHITECTS AND ENGINEERS

Halsbury's Laws of England (4th edn.), Vol. 4, paras. 1101–1369

257　Articles

Building Defects: Caveat Builder, M. J. Gidden: 123 Sol Jo 795.

The 1979 NHBC Agreement, H. W. Wilkinson (review of the National House-Building Council's agreement): 129 NLJ 1239.

258   Architect—duty of care—duty to advise clients of planning permission requirements

An architect was instructed to design a building which did not require an office development permit. Such a permit was required for office buildings over 10,000 square feet. The architect designed a building consisting of offices, the area of which was under 10,000 square feet, plus a car park and caretaker's flat, having been told by the local planning officer that the car park and flat would be excluded from the computation of office space. Planning permission was granted and the building erected. However, the owners were unable to let it due to the absence of an office development permit. In an action for damages, it was held that the planning permission was of no effect since an office development permit had not been obtained and that the architect had been negligent in failing to warn the owners that the planning permission might be void. On appeal, *held*, it was not necessary to decide whether the judge was right or wrong in his construction of the office development permit provisions. The question was whether the architect had been negligent in failing to warn the owners that the planning permission might be invalid. He could not be said to have been negligent as he had considered that the final decision would be made by the planning committee, which decision would be conclusive. Nor could he be said to have been negligent in failing to warn the owners after the planning permission was granted, since he had regarded it as conclusive and had never experienced a situation where a planning permission, once granted, had become ineffective. It did not matter whether he was right or wrong in law; he had not been negligent and the appeal would be allowed.

BL HOLDINGS LTD v ROBERT J. WOOD AND PARTNERS (1979) 123 Sol Jo 570 (Court of Appeal: MEGAW, LAWTON and BROWNE LJJ). Decision of Gibson J (1978) 122 Sol Jo 525, 1978 Halsbury's Abridgment para. 267 reversed.

259   Builder—duty of care—duty to build dwellings fit for habitation—excluded cases—approved scheme

The House-Building Standards (Approved Scheme etc.) Order 1979, S.I. 1979 No. 381 (in force on 18th April 1979), is made under the Defective Premises Act 1972, s. 2. In it, the Secretary of State approves the Scheme to be operated from 18th April 1979 by the National House-Building Council, and the forms of Notice of Insurance Cover issued by the Council in relation to dwellings erected pursuant to the Scheme. In relation to any dwelling falling within the approved Scheme and in respect of which a Standard or Common Parts Notice of Insurance Cover is issued, no action can be brought by any person having or acquiring an interest in the dwelling for breach of the duty imposed by the 1972 Act, s. 1, relating to building standards. The Scheme applies to dwellings erected by house-builders and developers whose names are on the Council's register. Under the Scheme, purchasers of dwellings enter into agreements in the appropriate form with house-builders or developers, and are insured against defects in the state of the dwellings.

260   —— —— liability of amateur builder as vendor

See *Hone v Benson*, para. 1959.

261   —— —— work taken on before statutory duty imposed—whether duty applied

See *Alexander v Mercouris*, para. 2719.

262   Building contract—whether agreement building contract or partnership

See *Walker West Developments Ltd v F. J. Emmett Ltd*, para. 2009.

BUILDING SOCIETIES

Halsbury's Laws of England (4th edn.), Vol. 4, paras. 1501–1723

263   Advance—illegal advance on second mortgage—rights of building society under mortgage

A building society made an advance on a mortgage, intending that it should acquire a first legal charge. However, the society had overlooked the fact that the purchaser of the house had already obtained a bridging loan for the initial purchase, and that the company providing the loan had a prior equitable charge on the property. The purchaser sought vacation of the registration of the land charge in respect of the purported mortgage deed, claiming that it was void under the Building Societies Act 1962 s. 32, which prohibits building societies from making any advance which is not on first mortgage. *Held*, the purpose of s. 32 was to protect the members and outside creditors of the building society so that its funds should not be advanced on security that might be inadequate to meet the loan. It could not be argued that the section should be used to deny the building society its rights under the registered mortgage. The vacation of the register would not therefore be granted.

NASH v HALIFAX BUILDING SOCIETY [1979] 2 All ER 19 (Chancery Division: BROWNE-WILKINSON J). Dictum of Clauson J in *Hayes Bridge Estate v Portman Building Society* [1936] 2 All ER 1400 at 1407 applied.

264   Authorised investments

The Building Societies (Authorised Investments) (Amendment) Order 1979, S.I. 1979 No. 1301 (in force on 3rd December 1979), amends the Building Societies (Authorised Investments) (No. 2) Order 1977, 1977 Halsbury's Abridgment para. 287 by adding to the classes of investments in which building societies may place funds not immediately required for their purposes. The additions are investments in sterling certificates of deposit issued by certain banks, and in Passenger Transport Executives. This Order further amends the 1977 Order by permitting societies to hold their investments in the names of specified nominees.

265   Fees

The Building Societies (Fees) Regulations 1979, S.I. 1979 No. 1550 (in force on 1st January 1980), supersede the Building Societies (Fees) Regulations 1978, 1978 Halsbury's Abridgment para. 273 and increase the fees payable under the Building Societies Act 1962. The fee payable on an application for the right to obtain names and addresses from the register of members of a building society is reduced.

266   Mortgage deed—form

The Chief Registrar of Friendly Societies in his report for the year 1978 (Part 2, Building Societies) refers to a society which sought to effect a variation in mortgage deeds by giving notice to call in the mortgage unless the borrower agreed to the abolition of the existing twenty-eight-day period of notice needed to effect a change in interest rates. Although the society concerned did not intend to implement the notice if the borrower persisted in his objection to the variation, the registry regarded the notice as unacceptable and wholly inconsistent with the nature of a building society mortgage that the power to call in be exercised where a borrower had refused to agree to a variation in his mortgage deed. In the light of this view the building society withdrew the notice. See pp. 21, 22 of the report.

267   Special advances

The Building Societies (Special Advances) Order 1979, S.I. 1979 No. 1639 (in force on 6th December 1979) increases to £25,000 the limit beyond which an advance made by a building society to an individual is to be treated as a special advance for the purposes of the Building Societies Act 1962.

The Building Societies (Special Advances) Order 1975, 1975 Halsbury's Abridgment para. 304 is revoked.

268   **Transfer of engagements—transfer without consent of members—factors to be taken into account**

Where a society applies to the central office to confirm a union of societies or transfer of engagements notwithstanding the absence of the consent in writing of the holders of two-thirds of the number of shares, the registrar exercises his discretion under the Building Societies Act 1962, s. 20 (4), by considering whether or not (in the light of all information available to him, including its effect upon the interests of members of both societies) the merger is likely to command the assent of a substantial majority of members in each society. He does not seek to substitute his judgment for that of the members but rather to give effect to their judgment so far as it can reasonably be assessed. See Report of the Chief Registrar of Friendly Societies for the year 1978: Part 2, Building Societies, App. 1 (application to the central office under s. 20 (4) of the Building Societies Act 1962 by the Anglia Building Society and the Hastings and Thanet Building Society for confirmation of transfer of engagements).

CAPITAL GAINS TAXATION

Halsbury's Laws of England (4th edn.), Vol. 5, paras. 1–247

269   **Articles**

Capital Gains Tax Avoidance—End of an Era?, R. S. Evans (the effect of the decision in *Eilbeck v Rawling* [1979] STC 16, para. 271 if it is sanctioned on appeal): 129 NLJ 990.

Conditional Contracts and the Development Land Tax Act 1976, Victor Callender (1976 Halsbury's Abridgment para. 287): [1979] Conv 285.

Inflation Gains Tax, T. Michael Ashe (criticism of capital gains tax in its failure to adjust to take account of inflation): 129 NLJ 9.

The Legal Effect of Transactions Infected by "An Understanding", Louis Blom-Cooper (discussion on *Chinn v Hochstrasser (Inspector of Taxes)*; *Chinn v Collins (Inspector of Taxes)* [1979] 2 All ER 529, CA, para. 285): [1979] BTR 301.

Tax Avoidance and Legal Personality, T. Flanagan (examination of *Floor v Davis* [1978] 2 All ER, CA, 1978 Halsbury's Abridgment para. 280, as it illustrates the circumstances in which the courts may disregard legal personality in order to defeat an exercise in tax avoidance): [1979] Conv 195.

270   **Capital Gains Tax Act 1979**

The Capital Gains Tax Act 1979 consolidates the Finance Act 1965, Part III with related provisions in that and subsequent Acts. The Act received the royal assent on 22nd March 1979 and provisions authorising the making of any order or other instrument, together with provisions conferring any power or improving any duty which operates or could operate in relation to tax for more than one chargeable period (except where the tax is all tax for chargeable periods to which the Act does not apply), came into force on 6th April 1979. Otherwise the Act applies in relation to tax payable for the years 1979–1980 onwards, and to tax for other chargeable periods beginning after 5th April 1979.

Destination and derivation tables appear on pp. 62–79 following.

DESTINATION TABLE

This table shows in column (1) the enactments repealed by the Capital Gains Tax Act 1979 and in column (2) the provisions of that Act corresponding to the repealed provisions.

In certain cases the enactment in column (1), though having a corresponding provision in column (2), is not, or is not wholly, repealed, as it is still required, or partly required, for the purposes of other legislation.

(1)	(2)	(1)	(2)
Interpretation Act 1978 (c. 30)	Capital Gains Tax Act 1979 (c. 14)	Finance Act 1965 (c. 25)	Capital Gains Tax Act 1979 (c. 14)
Sch. 2, para. 5 (*b*)★	s. 155 (1)	s. 25 (10)	s. 55 (4)
		(11)	52 (3)
Finance Act 1965 (c. 25)		(12)	55 (6)
		(13)	Rep., 1971 c. 68, ss. 59 (1), 69 (7), Sch. 14, Part V
s. 19	1		
20 (1)	2 (1)	25A	Sch. 6, para. 15
(2)	12 (1), (2)	26	s. 153; see also Sch. 6, para. 9
(3)	3		
(4), (5)	4	27 (1)	130
(6)	7	(2)	6
(7)	ss. 14 (1), 29 (4)	(3)	Rep., 1975 c. 45, s. 75 (5), Sch. 14, Part IV
21	Rep., 1978 c. 42, ss. 44 (7), 80 (5), Sch. 13, Part IV		
22 (1), (2)	s. 19 (1), (2)	(4)	s. 71 (1)
(3)	20 (1)	(5)	133
(4)	19 (3)	(6)	131
(5)	46 (1)	(7), (8)	19 (4), (5)
(6)–(8)	23	(9)	71 (2)
(9)	ss. 20 (3), 28 (1), 106	(10)	ss. 19 (4), 71 (1), 130
(10)	28 (2), (3)	28 (1), (2)	s. 143 (1), (2)
23 (1), (2)	29 (1), (2)	(3)	(3), (4)
(3)–(5)	22	29 (1)	101 (1)–(4)
(6)	29 (3)	(2)–(4)	102 (1)–(3)
(7)	(5)	(4A)	101 (8)
24 (1)	49 (1)	(5), (6)	103 (1), (2)
(2)–(4)	Rep., 1971 c. 68, ss. 59 (1), 69 (7), Sch. 14, Part V	(7)	101 (5)
		(8)	(6), (7)
(5)–(7)	s. 49 (2)–(4)	29 (9)	104
(8)	Rep., 1969 c. 32, ss. 42, 61 (6), Sch. 19, para. 5 (4), (6), Sch. 21, Part VI	(10)	105
		(11)	Rep., 1968 c. 44, s. 61 (10), Sch. 20, Part III
(9)	s. 49 (10)	(12)	s. 101 (9)
(10)	Rep., 1968 c. 44, s. 61 (10), Sch. 20, Part III	(13)	ss. 101 (7), 102 (4)
		30	s. 128
(11)–(14)	s. 49 (6)–(9)	31	147
24A	Rep., 1971 c. 68, ss. 59 (1), 69 (7), Sch. 14, Part V	33 (1)	115 (1)
		(2)	116 (1)
		(3)	115 (3)
		(4)	Rep., 1971 c. 68, ss. 60, 69 (7), Sch. 14, Part VII
25 (1)	s. 52 (1), (2)		
(2)	53	(5)	s. 115 (4)
(3)	54 (1)	(6)	ss. 118, 119 (1), (2)
(4)	55 (1)	(7)–(9)	s. 115 (5)–(7)
(4A)	Rep., 1975 c. 7, ss. 52 (2), 59 (5), Sch. 13, Part I	(9A)	120
		(10)	121 (1), (2)
		(11), (12)	115 (8), (9)
(5), (5A), (6), (7)	Rep., 1971 c. 68, ss. 59 (1), 69 (7), Sch. 14, Part V	34 (1)	124 (1)
		(1A), (1B)	(2), (3)
		(2)–(6)	(5)–(8)
(8)	s. 54 (2)	35 (1), (2)	145
(9)	52 (4)	(3)–(5)	Rep., 1970 c. 10, s. 538 (1), Sch. 16

★ Not repealed.

(1)	(2)	(1)	(2)
Finance Act 1965 (c. 25)	Capital Gains Tax Act 1979 (c. 14)	Finance Act 1965 (c. 25)	Capital Gains Tax Act 1979 (c. 14)
s. 36	Rep., 1970 c. 10, s. 538 (1), Sch. 16	para. 4	s. 32 (1)–(3)
37 (1)	Rep., 1972 c. 41, ss. 112 (11), 134 (7), Sch. 28, Part X	paras. 5, 6	ss. 33, 34
		para. 7	s. 35 (1)–(4)
(2)–(4)	Rep., 1970 c. 10, s. 538 (1), Sch. 16	paras. 8–11	ss. 36–39
38 (1)	ss. 92 (a), 96	para. 12	s. 141
(2)	92 (a), 97 (1), (2)	13 (1)	21 (1)
39	s. 10	(2), (3)	(3), (4)
40 (1)	13 (1), (3)	(4), (5)	(5), (7)
(2)	(1), (2)	Sch. 6,	
(3)	(5), (6)	para. 14 (1)	s. 40 (1)
41	15 (1)–(9)	(2)–(4)	Rep., 1972 c. 41, 116, 134 (7), Sch. 28, Part XII
42	17		
43 (1)	18 (1)		
(2), (3)	(3), (4)	(5)	s. 40 (2)
44 (1)	150 (1), Sch. 6, para. 2 (1)	(6)	———
		15	41
(2)	150 (2), Sch. 6, para. 2 (2)	16 (1)	Rep., 1971 c. 68, ss. 59 (1), 69 (7), Sch. 14, Part V
(3)	150 (3), Sch. 6, para. 2 (3)		
(4)	150 (4), Sch. 6, para. 2 (4)	(2)	s. 47 (1)
		17	42
(5)	150 (5), Sch. 6, para. 2 (5)	18	74
		19 (1)	113 (1), (2)
(6)–(8)	Rep., 1970 c. 10, s. 538 (1), Sch. 16	(2)–(4)	(3)–(5)
		20	11
45 (1)	ss. 12 (3), 47 (2), (3), 51, 64, 155 (1), Sch. 3, para. 10 (1)	21 (1)–(3)	43 (1)–(3)
		(4)	43 (4), Sch. 6, para. 12 (4)
(2)	Rep., 1968 c. 3, s. 96 (3), Sch. 11	(5)	43 (5)
(3)	s. 155 (2)	22 (1), (2)	Sch. 5, para. 1 (1), (2)
(4)	24	(3)	Sch. 6, para. 3
(5)	20 (2)	(4)	Sch. 5, para. 2 (1)
(6)	14 (2)	(5)	1 (3)
(7)	60	(6)	2 (2)
(8)	ss. 92 (a), (b), 93	23	9
(9)	s. 32 (4)	24	11
(10)	155 (5)	25 (1), (2)	12 (1), (2)
(11)	Rep., 1970 c. 10, s. 538 (1), Sch. 16	(3), (4)	(4), (5)
94 (1)	s. 99 (1)	26 (1)–(3)	13 (1)–(3)
(2)	Rep., 1972 c. 41, ss. 112 (11), 134 (7), Sch. 28, Part X	(4)	(5)
		(5)	Rep., 1971 c. 68, s. 56 (3), 69 (7), Sch. 14, Part IV
(3)	ss. 92 (d), 99 (2)		
(4)–(8)	Rep., 1970 c. 10, s. 538 (1), Sch. 16	(6)	Sch. 5, para. 13 (6)
		paras. 27, 28	paras. 14, 15
(9)	s. 99 (3)	para. 29 (1)–(3)	para. 16
Sch. 6,		(4)	Rep., 1970 c. 10, s. 538 (1), Sch. 16
para. 1	30		
2	31	30	Sch. 5, para. 17
3 (1)–(4)	Rep., 1971 c. 68, ss. 56 (3), 69 (7), Sch. 14, Part IV	31	See Sch. 16, para. 10 (2) (b)
		Sch. 7,	
		para. 1	s. 122
(5)	Sch. 16, para. 12 (2)	2 (1)	65 (2), (7)
(6)	Rep., 1971 c. 68, ss. 56 (3), 69 (7), Sch. 14, Part IV	(2), (3)	(3), (4)
		(4)	Rep., 1971 c. 68, ss. 56 (3), 69 (7), Sch. 14, Part IV
(7)	Sch. 6, para. 12 (3)	(5)–(7)	s. 65 (5)–(7)
(8)	(1)	(8)	(4), (7)

(1)	(2)	(1)	(2)
Finance Act 1965 (c. 25)	Capital Gains Tax Act 1979 (c. 14)	Finance Act 1965 (c. 25)	Capital Gains Tax Act 1979 (c. 14)
para. 3 (1)	s. 72 (1)	para. 12 (1), (2)	Rep., 1975 c. 45, s. 75 (5), Sch. 14, Part IV
(2)	(2), (5)		
(3)	(3)	Sch. 10,	
(4)	(5)	paras. 1, 2	Rep., 1970 c. 10, s. 538 (1), Sch. 16
4 (1)	77 (1), (2)		
(2)	78	para. 3	s. 45
(3), (4)	79 (1), (2)	4 (1)	8 (1), (2)
(5)	ss. 79 (3), 80 (1)	(2), (3)	(3), (4)
(6)	Rep., 1966 c. 18, ss. 43, 53 (7), Sch. 10, para. 8 (4), Sch. 13, Part VI	paras. 5–11	Rep., 1970 c. 10, s. 538 (1), Sch. 16
		para. 12 (1), (2)	s. 48
(7)	s. 77 (3)	(3)	Rep., 1971 c. 68, ss. 59 (1), 69 (7), Sch. 14, Part V
5 (1)	82 (1)		
(2)	Rep., 1977 c. 36, s. 59 (5), Sch. 9, Part VI	13	s. 154
		14	Rep., 1970 c. 10, s. 538 (1), Sch. 16
(3)	s. 82 (3)		
6 (1)	85 (1), (3)	paras. 16–18	Rep., 1970 c. 10, s. 538 (1), Sch. 16
(2), (3)	(1)		
7 (1)	ss. 85 (2), (3), 86 (1)		
(2)	Rep., 1970 c. 10, s. 538 (1), Sch. 16	**Finance Act 1966 (c. 18)**	
(3)	s. 86 (2)		
8	Rep., 1969 c. 32, ss. 42, 61 (6), Sch. 19, para. 15 (6), Sch. 21, Part VI	s. 43 Sch. 10,	———
9	s. 142	para. 1	s. 55 (2)–(5)
10	140	2 (1), (2)	125
11	134 (1)–(4)	(3)	Rep., 1978 c. 42, s. 80 (5), Sch. 13, Part IV
11A (1), (2), (3)	135		
		3	Rep., 1970 c. 10, s. 538 (1), Sch. 16
12	144		
13	58	4	s. 108
14 (1), (2)	137 (1), (2)	5	Rep., 1971 c. 68, ss. 59 (1), 69 (7), Sch. 14, Part V
(3)	(3), (4)		
(4)	138 (2)–(4)	6 (1)	Sch. 5, para. 14 (1)
(5)	137 (5)	(2)	
(6)	ss. 137 (6), 138 (2)	7 (1)	s. 81 (1)
(7)	137 (7), 138 (2)	(2)	ss. 80 (2), 81 (2)
(8)	s. 137 (8)	(3)	77 (1), 82 (1), 85 (3)
15 (1), (2)	25 (1), (2)		
(3), (4)	(4), (5)	(4)	s. 81 (3)
16	151	(5)	
17 (1)–(4)	62 (1)–(4)	8 (1)–(3)	s. 73
(5)	(5), (6)	(4)	
18	75 (1)–(3)	9	ss. 21 (2), 72 (4), 83 (4), (5), 109
19	59		
20	44	10 (1)–(3)	s. 61 (1)–(3)
21	63	(4)	Rep., 1971 c. 68, ss. 59 (1), 69 (7), Sch. 14, Part V
Sch. 8, paras. 1–4	Sch. 3, paras. 1–4		
para. 5 (1), (2)	para. 5 (1), (2)	(5), (6)	s. 61 (4), (5)
(3)	Rep., 1972 c. 41, s. 134 (7), Sch. 28, Part XII	paras. 11–13	
		14, 15	Rep., 1970 c. 10, s. 538 (1), Sch. 16
(4)–(6)	Sch. 3, para. 5 (3)–(5)		
paras. 6, 7	paras. 6, 7	**Finance Act 1967 (c. 54)**	
para. 8	Rep., 1968 c. 44, ss. 34, 61 (10), Sch. 12, para. 7 (7), Sch. 20, Part III		
		s. 32	———
9	Sch. 3, para. 9	35 (1)	Rep., 1970 c. 10, s. 538 (1), Sch. 16
10	10 (2), (3)		

(1)	(2)	(1)	(2)
Finance Act 1967 (c. 54)	Capital Gains Tax Act 1979 (c. 14)	Finance Act 1968 (c. 44)	Capital Gains Tax Act 1979 (c. 14)
s. 35 (2)	s. 143 (3)	para. 4 (1), (2)	50
(3)	———	(3)–(7)	Rep., 1971 c. 68, ss. 59 (1), 69 (7), Sch. 12, para. 17, Sch. 14, Part V
(4)	Rep., 1970 c. 10, s. 538 (1), Sch. 16		
37	s. 112	5 (1)	Sch. 5, para. 12 (3)
45 (3) (h)	———	(2), (3)	
Sch. 13, para. 1	ss. 115 (2), 116 (1)	6	Rep., 1971 c. 68, ss. 55 (1), 69 (7), Sch. 14, Part III
2 (1)	116 (2), 121 (3)		
(2)		7 (1)–(6)	Sch. 3, para. 8
(3)	———	(7)	9 (1)
3 (1)	s. 21 (6), Sch. 5, para. 18	8 (1)	
(2)	———	(2)	s. 134 (1), (4)
4 (1)	s. 83 (1)		(5)
(2)	ss. 82 (2), 83 (2)	9	
(3)	s. 83 (3), (4)	paras. 10–12	Rep., 1971 c. 68, ss. 56 (3), 69 (7), Sch. 14, Part IV
(5)	82 (3)		
(6)	———	para. 13	Rep., 1970 c. 10, s. 538 (1), Sch. 16
5 (1)	75 (4)		
(2)	———	14	———
6	35 (5)	15 (1), (2)	s. 86 (3)
7	Rep., 1970 c. 10, s. 538 (1), Sch. 16	(3)	Rep., 1970 c. 10, s. 538 (1), Sch. 16
8	Sch. 3, para. 5 (1)	paras. 16, 17	Rep., 1969 c. 32, s. 61 (6), Sch. 21, Part VI
9	———		
10 (1)	s. 15 (10)	18–21	Rep., 1970 c. 10, s. 538 (1), Sch. 16
(2)	———		
11	Rep., 1969 c. 32, ss. 42, 61 (6), Sch. 19, para. 3 (3), Sch. 21, Part VI	para. 22 (1)–(3)	s. 16 (1)–(3)
		(4)	
12	Rep., 1970 c. 10, s. 538 (1), Sch. 16	23 (1)	s. 16 (4)
		(2)–(6)	Rep., 1970 c. 10, s. 538 (1), Sch. 16
Finance Act 1968 (c. 44)		Finance Act 1969 (c. 32)	
s. 32 (1), (2)	Sch. 5, para. 3 (1)	s. 41 (1)	s. 67 (1)
(3)		(2)	64 (1), Sch. 2, Part I, paras. 1, 2
(4), (5)	Sch. 5, para. 3 (2), (3)		
(6)	8	(3)	———
(7)	4 (1)	(4)–(6)	Rep., 1970 c. 10, s. 538 (1), Sch. 16
34	———		
61 (5)	———	(7)	Rep., 1977 c. 36, s. 59 (5), Sch. 9, Part VI
Sch. 11, para. 1 (1)	Sch. 5, para. 4 (1)		
(2)		(8)	Rep., 1975 c. 45, s. 75 (5), Sch. 14, Part IV
(3)–(7)	Sch. 5, para. 4 (2)–(6)		
(8)	Rep., 1971 c. 68, ss. 56 (3), 69 (7), Sch. 14, Part IV	42	
		61 (3) (e)	———
(9)	Sch. 5, para. 4 (7)	Sch. 18, Part I	Sch. 2, Part II
paras. 2–4	paras. 5–7	II	Rep., 1970 c. 10, s. 538 (1), Sch. 16
Sch. 12, para. 1 (1)–(4)	s. 127 (1)–(4)	III	Rep., 1971 c. 68, ss. 56 (3), 69 (7), Sch. 14, Part IV
(5)	Sch. 5, para. 15		
(6)	s. 127 (5)	Sch. 19, para. 1 (1)–(4)	Sch. 6, para. 17
2 (1)	s. 103 (3)	1 (5)	———
(2)	———		
3 (1)	119 (1)		
(2), (3)	(3), (4)		

(1)	(2)	(1)	(2)
Finance Act 1969 (c. 32)	Capital Gains Tax Act 1979 (c. 14)	Finance Act 1969 (c. 32)	Capital Gains Tax Act 1979 (c. 14)
Sch. 19,		para. 22 (3), (4)	s. 98
para. 2 (1), (2)	Sch. 6, para. 18	(5)	86 (3)
(3)	—	23	Rep., 1971 c. 68, ss. 55 (1), 69 (7), Sch. 14, Part III
3 (1)	s. 135		
(2)	Rep., 1970 c. 10, s. 538 (1), Sch. 16	**Taxes Management Act 1970 (c. 9)**	
(3)	—	s. 47 (4)	—
4	s. 15 (5)	57 (3) (c)†	—
5	Rep., 1971 c. 68, ss. 59 (1), 69 (7), Sch. 14, Part V	**Income and Corporation Taxes Act 1970 (c. 10)**	
6 (1)	s. 47 (3)	Sch. 15,	
(2)	—	para. 6 (1)	s. 10
7 (1)	101 (7) (b)	(2)	155 (1)
(2)	—	(3)	32 (3)
8 (1), (2)	Rep., 1971 c. 68, ss. 59 (1), 69 (7), Sch. 14, Part V	(4)	35 (5)
		(5)	16 (4)
(3)	s. 52 (2)	(6)	98 (1)
(4)	—	7	18 (2)
9	46 (2)	11†	See against enactments amended
10 (1)–(4)	107 (1)–(4)	12 (1) (a)	s. 31 (2)
(5)	109 (1)	(b), (c)	34 (3), (4)
(6)	107 (5)	(d)	(6)
(7)	Rep., 1971 c. 68, ss. 55 (1), 69 (7), Sch. 14, Part III	**Finance Act 1970 (c. 24)**	
(8), (9)	s. 107 (6), (7)	s. 28 (1)†	—
11 (1)	110 (1)		
(2)	Rep., 1970 c. 10, s. 538 (1), Sch. 16	**Finance Act 1971 (c. 68)**	
(3)	s. 110 (2)	s. 55 (1), (4)	—
(4)	Rep., 1971 c. 68, ss. 55 (1), 69 (7), Sch. 14, Part III	(6)	—
		56	—
12	s. 63 (3)	58 (1)	ss. 137 (4), (9), 139
13	Rep., 1970 c. 10, s. 538 (1), Sch. 16	(2)	s. 137 (4)
14 (1)	s. 122 (1), (3)	(3)	138 (1), (2)
(2)	(2)	(4)	ss. 137 (9), 138 (4), 139
(3)	—	ss. 59, 60	—
15 (1)–(4)	123 (1)–(4)	s. 69 (3)†	
(4A)	Sch. 6, para. 23	Sch. 3,	
(5)	Rep., 1971 c. 68, ss. 55 (1), 69 (7), Sch. 14, Part III	para. 10	s. 97 (1)
		Sch. 6,	
(6)	—	para. 91	74 (1)–(3)
(7)	s. 123 (2)	Sch. 8,	
(8)	(5)	para. 16 (1)	34 (4), (7)
(9)	—	Sch. 9,	
16 (1)–	117 (1)–(5)	paras. 1, 2	—
(5)		para. 3	Sch. 6, para. 22 (3)
(6)	Rep., 1970 c. 10, s. 538 (1), Sch. 16	5	Sch. 6, para. 21; see also Sch. 5, para. 10
(7)	s. 117 (6)		
(8)	—	Sch. 10,	
(9)	121 (3)	para. 1 (1)	s. 66 (4), Sch. 6, para. 13
17	118		
paras. 18–21	Rep., 1970 c. 10, s. 538 (1), Sch. 16		
para. 22 (1), (2)	Rep., 1970 c. 10, s. 538 (1), Sch. 16		

† Repealed in part.

(1)	(2)
Finance Act 1971 (c. 68)	Capital Gains Tax Act 1979 (c. 14)
Sch. 10,	
para. 1 (2)	66 (3)
2	Sch. 6, para. 13
3	Rep., 1977 c. 36, s. 59 (5), Sch. 9, Part VI
4	s. 67
5	65 (1), Sch. 5, paras. 2 (3), 13 (4)
6 (1)	66 (1)
(2)	(2), (4)
7 (1)	68 (1), (4)
(2), (3)	68 (2), (3)
8	69
9 (1)	70 (1), (7)
(2)	(2), (7)
(3)	(4)
10	27
11	111
12	Sch. 7, para. 2 (3)
13	Rep., 1977 c. 36, s. 59 (5), Sch. 9, Part VI
para. 1	s. 49 (1)
2	(10)
3	(5)
4	47 (2)
5	44 (2)
6	56 (1)
paras. 7, 8	55 (1)
para. 9	56 (2)
10	57
11	Sch. 6, para. 16
12	Rep., 1975 c. 7, ss. 52 (2), 59 (5), Sch. 13, Part I
13	s. 147 (3)
14	Rep., 1975 c. 7, ss. 52 (2), 59 (5), Sch. 13, Part I
15	Sch. 6, para. 9
16	s. 61 (2)
17 (a)	50 (1)
(b), (c)	
18	Sch. 6, para. 9 (1)
Finance Act 1972 (c. 41)	
s. 112 (1)	ss. 92 (d), 94 (1)
(2)–(10)	94 (2)–(10)
(11)	
(12)	94 (11)
(13)	92 (b), (c)
113	ss. 92 (d), 97 (3), 100
114 (1)	s. 95
(2)	150 (4), Sch. 5, para. 1 (1), Sch. 6, para. 2 (4)
115	76
116 (1)	40 (1)
(2)–(4)	40 (1)
117	8

(1)	(2)
Finance Act 1972 (c. 41)	Capital Gains Tax Act 1979 (c. 14)
s. 118	s. 121 (1) (d)
119	146
124 (2)†	13 (4)
134 (3) (c)	
Sch. 24, para. 1	s. 124 (8)
2	74 (1), (2), (5)
Finance Act 1973 (c. 51)	
s. 37	115 (3)
51 (1)–(3)	152
(4)	Sch. 6, para. 5
(5)	
54 (1)†	s. 155 (3), Sch. 6, para. 4
Sch. 16, para. 15 (1)	142 (2), (4)
(2)	
20, para. 1	Rep., 1975 c. 7, ss. 52 (2), 59 (5), Sch. 13, Part I
2	
3	
paras. 4–6	Sch. 6, paras. 6–8
para. 7	
8	Rep., 1975 c. 7, ss. 52 (2), 59 (5), Sch. 13, Part I
21, para. 4	s. 150 (3), Sch. 6, para. 4
Finance Act 1974 (c. 30)	
s. 8 (8)	
31	s. 121 (1) (e)
ss. 32, 33	
48	Sch. 5, para. 9 (1), (2), (5)
57 (3) (b)†	
Sch. 8, para. 6	Sch. 6, para. 23
Finance Act 1975 (c. 7)	
s. 39 (6)★	s. 149 (8)
53	146 (1), (3)
Sch. 12, para. 12	Sch. 6, para. 15
13	s. 153
17	Sch. 6, para. 16
Finance (No. 2) Act 1975 (c. 45)	
s. 44 (4)	s. 7
57 (1)	8 (3)
(2)–(5)	9
(6)	Sch. 7, para. 9
(7)	
59 (1), (2)	s. 70 (3)
(3)–(6)	(4)–(7)
(7)	

† Repealed in part.   ★ Not repealed.

(1)	(2)	(1)	(2)
Finance (No. 2) Act 1975 (c. 45)	Capital Gains Tax Act 1979 (c. 14)	Finance Act 1977 (c. 36)	Capital Gains Tax Act 1979 (c. 14)
s. 60 (1)	s. 25 (3)	s. 40 (10)	Sch. 7, para. 2 (4)
60 (2)	——	43 (1)–(8)	s. 26
61 (1)	140 (1)	(9)	Sch. 6, para. 11
(2)	——	59 (3) (c)†	——
62 (1)	90		
(2)	——	Finance Act 1978 (c. 42)	
ss. 63, 64	——		
s. 75 (3) (c)†	——		
Sch. 8, para. 5	89	s. 44 (1)–(6)	s. 5
		(7)	——
Finance Act 1976 (c. 40)		(8)	ss. 94 (3), 97 (3), 100
		(9)	
s. 52 (1)	——	45 (1)	s. 128 (1), (3), (5)
(2)	Rep., 1978 c. 42, s. 80 (5), Sch. 13, Part IV	(2)	(2)
		(3), (4)	(4), (5)
		(6)†	——
(3)	s. 45 (1)	46	126
(4)	Rep., 1978 c. 42, s. 80 (5), Sch. 13, Part IV	47 (1)	115 (7)
		(2)	120
		(3)	——
53 (1)–(7)	s. 84 (1)–(7)	48 (1)	124 (1)–(3)
(8)	Sch. 6, para. 20 (4)	(2), (3)	(5), (6)
55	s. 148	48 (4)	124 (8)
56 (1)	149 (1), (8)	(5)	——
(2)–(7)	(2)–(7)	49	136
90 (5)*	149 (8)	50	101 (8)
Sch. 11, para. 1 (1)	147	51 (1)	107 (3)
(2)	Sch. 6, para. 24	(2)	——
6	——	52 (1)	49 (6)–(9)
		(2)	——
Finance Act 1977 (c. 36)		80 (3) (c)†	——
		Sch. 7	Sch. 1
		8, para. 1	4, paras. 1, 3
s. 40 (1)	s. 85 (1)	2	2, 3
(2)	87 (1)	paras. 3–7	4–8
(3)	ss. 87 (2), 88 (1)	11, para. 2 (1)	s. 149 (1), (8)
(4)–(7)	s. 88 (2)–(5)	(2)	(6)
(8)	87 (4)	(3)	——
(9)	ss. 87 (3), (5), 139		

† Repealed in part.   * Not repealed.

TABLE OF DERIVATIONS

This table shows in the right hand column the legislative source from which the sections of the Capital Gains Tax Act 1979 in the left hand column have been derived. In the table the following abbreviations are used:

1965	= The Finance Act 1965, and so on as respects subsequent years except 1970.
1970	= The Income and Corporation Taxes Act 1970.
1970(F)	= The Finance Act 1970.
1975 (No. 2)	= The Finance (No. 2) Act 1975.

Section of Act	Derivation
1	1965 s. 19.
2 (1)	1965 s. 20 (1).
(2)	Drafting.
3	1965 s. 20 (3).
4 (1)	1965 s. 20 (4).
(2)	1965 s. 20 (5).
5	1978 s. 44 (1)–(6)
6	1965 s. 27 (2).
7	1965 s. 20 (6); 1975 (No. 2) s. 44 (4).
8 (1)	1965 Sch. X 4 (1); 1972 s. 117.
(2)	1965 Sch. X 4 (1); 1972 s. 117; 1975 (No. 2) s. 57 (2).
(3)	1965 Sch. X 4 (2); 1972 s. 117; 1975 (No. 2) s. 57 (1).
(4)	1965 Sch. X 4 (3); 1972 s. 117.
9 (1)	1975 (No. 2) s. 57 (2).
(2)	1975 (No. 2) s. 57 (3).
(3)	1975 (No. 2) s. 57 (4).
(4)	1975 (No. 2) s. 57 (5).
10	1965 s. 39; 1970 Sch. XV 6 (1).
11	1965 Sch. VI 20.
12 (1)	1965 s. 20 (2).
(2)	1965 s. 20 (2); 1970 Sch. XV 11.
(3)	1965 s. 45 (1); 1970 Sch. XV 11.
13 (1)	1965 s. 40 (1), (2) (a).
(2)	1965 s. 40 (2).
(3)	1965 s. 40 (1).
(4)	1972 s. 124 (2).
(5)	1965 s. 40 (3).
(6)	1965 s. 40 (4).
14 (1)	1965 s. 20 (7).
(2)	1965 s. 45 (6); 1970 Sch. XV 11.
15 (1)	1965 s. 41 (1).
(2)	1965 s. 41 (2).
(3)	1965 s. 41 (3).
(4)	1965 s. 41 (4).
(5)	1965 s. 41 (5); 1969 Sch. XIX 4; 1970 Sch. XV 11.
(6)	1965 s. 41 (6).
(7)	1965 s. 41 (7).
(8)	1965 s. 41 (8).
(9)	1965 s. 41 (9).
(10)	1967 Sch. XIII 10 (1).
16 (1)	1968 Sch. XII 22 (1).

Section of Act	Derivation
16 (2)	1968 Sch. XII 22 (2); 1970 Sch. XV 11.
(3)	1968 Sch. XII 22 (3); 1970 Sch. XV 11.
(4)	1968 Sch. XII 23 (1); 1970 Sch. XV 6 (5).
17	1965 s. 42; 1970 Sch. XV 11.
18 (1)	1965 s. 43 (1).
(2)	1970 Sch. XV 7.
(3)	1965 s. 43 (2).
(4)	1965 s. 43 (3).
19 (1)	1965 s. 22 (1).
(2)	1965 s. 22 (2).
(3)	1965 s. 22 (4).
(4)	1965 s. 27 (7), (10).
(5)	1965 s. 27 (8).
20 (1)	1965 s. 22 (3).
(2)	1965 s. 45 (5).
(3)	1965 s. 22 (9).
21 (1)	1965 Sch. VI 13 (1).
(2)	1966 Sch. X 9.
(3)	1965 Sch. VI 13 (2).
(4)	1965 Sch. VI 13 (3).
(5)	1965 Sch. VI 13 (4).
(6)	1967 Sch. XIII 3.
(7)	1965 Sch. VI 13 (5).
22 (1)	1965 s. 23 (3).
(2)	1965 s. 23 (4).
(3)	1965 s. 23 (5).
23 (1)	1965 s. 22 (6).
(2)	1965 s. 22 (7).
(3)	1965 s. 22 (8).
24	1965 s. 45 (4).
25 (1)	1965 Sch. VII 15 (1).
(2)	1965 Sch. VII 15 (2).
(3)	1975 (No. 2) s. 60.
(4)	1965 Sch. VII 15 (3).
(5)	1965 Sch. VII 15 (4).
26	1977 s. 43 (1)–(8).
27	1971 Sch. X 10.
28 (1)	1965 s. 22 (9).
(2)	1965 s. 22 (10).
(3)	1965 s. 22 (10).
29 (1)	1965 s. 23 (1).
(2)	1965 s. 23 (2).
(3)	1965 s. 23 (6).
(4)	1965 s. 20 (7).
(5)	1965 s. 23 (7).
30	1965 Sch. VI 1.
31 (1)	1965 Sch. VI 2 (1).
(2)	1965 Sch. VI 2 (2); 1970 Sch. XV 12 (1) (a).
(3)	1965 Sch. VI 2 (3).
32 (1)	1965 Sch. VI 4 (1).
(2)	1965 Sch. VI 4 (2).

Section of Act	Derivation
32 (3)	1970 Sch. XV 6 (3).
(4)	1965 s. 45 (9).
33	1965 Sch. VI 5.
34 (1)	1965 Sch. VI 6 (1).
(2)	1965 Sch. VI 6 (2).
(3)	1965 Sch. VI 6 (3); 1970 Sch. XV 12 (b).
(4)	1965 Sch. VI 6 (4); 1970 Sch. XV 11, 12 (c); 1971 Sch. VIII 16 (1).
(5)	1965 Sch. VI 6 (5).
(6)	1965 Sch. VI 6 (6); 1970 Sch. XV 12 (d).
(7)	1971 Sch. VIII 16 (1).
35 (1)	1965 Sch. VI 7 (1).
(2)	1965 Sch. VI 7 (2).
(3)	1965 Sch. VI 7 (3).
(4)	1965 Sch. VI 7 (4).
(5)	1967 Sch. XIII 6; 1970 Sch. XV 6 (4).
36	1965 Sch. VI 8.
37	1965 Sch. VI 9.
38	1965 Sch. VI 10.
39	1965 Sch. VI 11.
40 (1)	1965 Sch. VI 14 (1); 1972 s. 116 (1).
(2)	1965 Sch. VI 14 (5).
41	1965 Sch. VI 15.
42	1965 Sch. VI 17.
43	1965 Sch. VI 21.
44 (1)	1969 Sch. VII 20 (1).
(2)	1965 Sch. VII 20 (2); 1971 Sch. XII 5.
45 (1)	1965 Sch. X 3 (1); 1976 s. 52 (3).
(2)	1965 Sch. X 3 (2).
(3)	1965 Sch. X 3 (3); 1970 Sch. XV 11.
(4)	1965 Sch. X 3 (4); 1970 Sch. XV 11.
(5)	1965 Sch. X 3 (5).
46 (1)	1965 s. 22 (5).
(2)	1969 Sch. XIX 9.
47 (1)	1965 Sch. VI 16 (2).
(2)	1965 s. 45 (1); 1971 Sch. XII 4.
(3)	1965 s. 45 (1); 1969 Sch. XIX 6.
48	1965 Sch. X 12.
49 (1)	1965 s. 24 (1); 1971 Sch. XII 1.
(2)	1965 s. 24 (5).
(3)	1965 s. 24 (6).
(4)	1965 s. 24 (7).
(5)	1971 Sch. XII 3.
(6)	1965 s. 24 (11); 1978 s. 52 (1).
(7)	1978 s. 52 (1).
(8)	1978 s. 52 (1).
(9)	1978 s. 52 (1).
(10)	1965 s. 24 (9); 1971 Sch. XII 2.
50 (1)	1968 Sch. XII 4 (1); 1971 Sch. XII 17 (a).
(2)	1968 Sch. XII 4 (2).
51	1965 s. 45 (1).

Section of Act	Derivation
52 (1)	1965 s. 25 (1).
(2)	1965 s. 25 (1); 1969 Sch. XIX 8 (3).
(3)	1965 s. 25 (1).
(4)	1965 s. 25 (9).
53	1965 s. 25 (2).
54 (1)	1965 s. 25 (3).
(2)	1965 s. 25 (8).
55 (1)	1965 s. 25 (4); 1971 Sch. XII 7, 8.
(2)	1966 Sch. X 1 (1).
(3)	1966 Sch. X 1 (2).
(4)	1965 s. 25 (10); 1966 Sch. X 1 (3).
(5)	1966 Sch. X 1 (4).
(6)	1965 s. 25 (12).
56 (1)	1971 Sch. XII 6.
(2)	1971 Sch. XII 9.
57	1971 Sch. XII 10.
58	1965 Sch. VII 13.
59	1965 Sch. VII 19.
60	1969 s. 45 (7); 1970 Sch. XV 11.
61 (1)	1966 Sch. X 10 (1).
(2)	1966 Sch. X 10 (2); 1971 Sch. XII 16.
(3)	1966 Sch. X 10 (3).
(4)	1966 Sch. X 10 (5).
(5)	1966 Sch. X 10 (6).
62 (1)	1965 Sch. VII 17 (1).
(2)	1965 Sch. VII 17 (2).
(3)	1965 Sch. VII 17 (3); 1969 Sch. XIX 12.
(4)	1965 Sch. VII 17 (4).
(5)	1965 Sch. VII 17 (5).
(6)	1965 Sch. VII 17 (5).
63 (1)	1965 Sch. VII 21 (1).
(2)	1965 Sch. VII 21 (2).
(3)	1965 Sch. VII 21 (3); 1970 Sch. XV 11.
(4)	1965 Sch. VII 21 (4).
(5)	1965 Sch. VII 21 (5).
(6)	1965 Sch. VII 21 (6).
(7)	1965 Sch. VII 21 (7).
(8)	1965 Sch. VII 21 (8).
64	1965 s. 45 (1); 1969 s. 41.
65 (1)	1971 Sch. X 5.
(2)	1965 Sch. VII 2 (1).
(3)	1965 Sch. VII 2 (2).
(4)	1965 Sch. VII 2 (3) (8).
(5)	1965 Sch. VII 2 (5).
(6)	1965 Sch. VII 2 (6).
(7)	1965 Sch. VII 2 (1) (7) (8).
66 (1)	1971 Sch. X 6 (1).
(2)	1971 Sch. X 6 (2).
(3)	1971 Sch. X 1 (2).
(4)	1971 Sch. X 1 (1), 6 (2).
67 (1)	1969 a. 41 (1); 1971 Sch. X 4 (1).
(2)	1971 Sch. X 4 (2).

Section of Act	Derivation
67 (3)	1971 Sch. X 4 (3).
68	1971 Sch. X 7.
69	1971 Sch. X 8.
70 (1)	1971 Sch. X 9 (1).
(2)	1971 Sch. X 9 (2).
(3)	1975 (No. 2) s. 59 (1) (2).
(4)	1971 Sch. X 9 (3); 1975 (No. 2) s. 59 (3).
(5)	1975 (No. 2) s. 59 (4).
(6)	1975 (No. 2) s. 59 (5).
(7)	1971 Sch. X 9 (1) (1); 1975 (No. 2) s. 59 (6).
71	1965 s. 27 (4) (9) (10).
72 (1)	1965 Sch. VII 3 (1).
(2)	1965 Sch. VII 3 (2).
(3)	1965 Sch. VII 3 (3).
(4)	1966 Sch. X 9.
(5)	1965 Sch. VII 3 (2) (4).
73	1966 Sch. X 8, 9.
74	1965 Sch. VI 18; 1971 Sch. VI 91; 1972 Sch. XXIV 2.
75 (1)	1965 Sch. VII 18 (1).
(2)	1965 Sch. VII 18 (2).
(3)	1965 Sch. VII 18 (3).
(4)	1967 Sch. XIII 5.
76	1972 s. 115.
77 (1)	1965 Sch. VII 4 (1); 1966 Sch. X 7 (3).
(2)	1965 Sch. VII 4 (1) (a).
(3)	1965 Sch. VII 4 (7).
78	1965 Sch. VII 4 (2).
79 (1)	1965 Sch. VII 4 (3).
(2)	1965 Sch. VII 4 (4).
(3)	1966 Sch. VII 4 (5).
80 (1)	1965 Sch. VII 4 (5).
(2)	1966 Sch. X 7 (2).
81 (1)	1966 Sch. X 7 (1).
(2)	1966 Sch. X 7 (2).
(3)	1966 Sch. X 7 (4).
82 (1)	1965 Sch. VII 5 (1); 1966 Sch. X 7 (3).
(2)	1967 Sch. XIII 4 (2).
(3)	1965 Sch. VII 5 (3); 1967 Sch. XIII 4 (5).
83 (1)	1967 Sch. XIII 4 (1).
(2)	1967 Sch. XIII 4 (2).
(3)	1967 Sch. XIII 4 (3).
(4)	1966 Sch. X 9; 1967 Sch. XIII 4 (4).
(5)	1966 Sch. X 9 (2).
84	1976 s. 53.
85 (1)	1965 Sch. VII 6; 1977 s. 40 (1).
(2)	1965 Sch. VII 7.
(3)	1965 Sch. VII 6 (1), 7 (1); 1966 Sch. X 7 (3).
86 (1)	1965 Sch. VII 7 (1).
(2)	1965 Sch. VII 7 (3).
(3)	1968 Sch. XII 15 (1) (2); 1969 Sch. XIX 22 (5).

Section of Act	Derivation
87 (1)	1977 s. 40 (2).
(2)	1077 s. 40 (3) (*a*).
(3)	1977 s. 40 (9).
(4)	1977 s. 40 (8).
(5)	1977 s. 40 (9).
88 (1)	1977 s. 40 (3) (*b*).
(2)	1977 s. 40 (4).
(3)	1977 s. 40 (5).
(4)	1977 s. 40 (6).
(5)	1977 s. 40 (7).
89 (1)	1975 (No. 2) s. 34 (7); Sch. VIII 1, 5.
(2)	1975 (No. 2) Sch. VIII 5.
90	1975 (No. 2) s. 62.
91	Drafting
92 (*a*)	1965 s. 38 (1), (2), 45 (8).
(*b*)	1965 s. 45 (8); 1972 s. 112 (13).
(*c*)	1972 s. 112 (13).
(*d*)	1965 s. 94 (3); 1972 ss. 112 (1), 113.
93	1965 s. 45 (8); 1970 Sch. XV 11.
94 (1)	1972 s. 112 (1).
(2)	1972 s. 112 (2).
(3)	1972 s. 112 (3); 1978 s. 44 (8) (*a*).
(4)	1972 s. 112 (4).
(5)	1972 s. 112 (5).
(6)	1972 s. 112 (6).
(7)	1972 s. 112 (7).
(8)	1972 s. 112 (8).
(9)	1972 s. 112 (9).
(10)	1972 s. 112 (10).
(11)	1972 s. 112 (12).
95	1972 s. 114 (1).
96	1965 s. 38 (1).
97 (1)	1965 s. 38 (2); 1070 Sch. XV 11; 1971 Sch. III 10.
(2)	1965 s. 38 (2).
(3)	1972 s. 113; 1978 s. 44 (8) (*b*).
98 (1)	1969 Sch. XIX 22 (3); 1970 Sch. XV 6 (6).
(2)	1969 Sch. XIX 22 (4).
99 (1)	1965 s. 94 (1).
(2)	1965 s. 94 (3).
(3)	1965 s. 94 (9).
100	1972 s. 113; 1978 s. 44 (8) (*b*).
101 (1)	1965 s. 29 (1).
(2)	1965 s. 29 (1).
(3)	1965 s. 29 (1).
(4)	1965 s. 29 (1).
(5)	1965 s. 29 (7).
(6)	1965 s. 29 (8) (*a*) (*c*).
(7)	1965 s. 29 (8) (*b*) (*bb*), (13) (*a*); 1969 Sch. XIX 7.
(8)	1978 s. 50.
(9)	1965 s. 29 (12).
102 (1)	1965 s. 29 (2).
(2)	1965 s. 29 (3).

Section of Act	Derivation
102 (3)	1965 s. 29 (4).
(4)	1965 s. 29 (13) (b).
103 (1)	1965 s. 29 (5).
(2)	1965 s. 29 (6).
(3)	1968 Sch. XII 2 (1).
104	1965 s. 29 (9).
105	1965 s. 29 (10).
106	1965 s. 22 (9).
107 (1)	1969 Sch. XIX 10 (1); 1970 Sch. XV 11.
(2)	1969 Sch. XIX 10 (2).
(3)	1969 Sch. XIX 10 (3); 1978 s. 51 (1).
(4)	1969 Sch. XIX 10 (4).
(5)	1969 Sch. XIX 10 (6).
(6)	1969 Sch. XIX 10 (8).
(7)	1969 Sch. XIX 10 (9).
108	1966 Sch. X 4.
109 (1)	1966 Sch. X 9; 1969 Sch. XIX 10 (5).
(2)	1966 Sch. X 9 (2).
110	1969 Sch. XIX 11.
111	1971 Sch. X 11.
112	1967 s. 37.
113 (1)	1965 Sch. VI 19 (1).
(2)	1965 Sch. VI 19 (1) (b).
(3)	1965 Sch. VI 19 (2).
(4)	1965 Sch. VI 19 (3).
(5)	1965 Sch. VI 19 (4).
114	Drafting.
115 (1)	1965 s. 33 (1).
(2)	1967 Sch. XIII 2 (1).
(3)	1965 s. 33 (3); 1973 s. 37.
(4)	1965 s. 33 (5).
(5)	1965 s. 33 (7).
(6)	1965 s. 33 (8).
(7)	1965 s. 33 (9); 1978 s. 47 (1).
(8)	1965 s. 33 (11).
(9)	1965 s. 33 (12).
116 (1)	1965 s. 33 (2); 1967 Sch. XIII 2 (1).
(2)	1965 s. 33.
117	1969 Sch. XIX 16 (1)–(5), (7).
118	1965 s. 33 (6); 1969 Sch. XIX 17.
119 (1)	1965 s. 33 (6); 1968 Sch. XII 3 (1).
(2)	1965 s. 33 (6).
(3)	1968 Sch. XII 3 (2).
(4)	1968 Sch. XII 3 (3); 1970 Sch. XV 11.
120	1978 s. 47 (2).
121 (1)	1965 s. 33 (10); 1972 s. 118; 1974 s. 31.
(2)	1965 s. 33 (10).
(3)	1965 s. 33; 1967 Sch. XIII 2 (2); 1969 Sch. XIX 16 (9); 1978 s. 47 (2).
122 (1)	1965 Sch. VII 1 (1); 1969 Sch. XIX 14 (1).

Section of Act	Derivation
122 (2)	1965 Sch. VII 1 (2); 1969 Sch. XIX 14 (2).
(3)	1965 Sch. VII 1 (3); 1969 Sch. XIX 14 (1).
123 (1)	1969 Sch. XIX 15 (1).
(2)	1969 Sch. XIX 15 (2) (7).
(3)	1969 Sch. XIX 15 (3).
(4)	1969 Sch. XIX 15 (4).
(5)	1969 Sch. XIX 15 (8).
124 (1)	1965 s. 34 (1); 1978 s. 48 (1).
(2)	1978 s. 48 (1).
(3)	1978 s. 48 (1).
(4)	1965 s. 34 (2).
(5)	1965 s. 34 (3); 1978 s. 48 (2).
(6)	1965 s. 34 (4); 1978 s. 48 (3).
(7)	1965 s. 34 (5).
(8)	1965 s. 34 (6); 1972 Sch. XXIV 1; 1978 s. 48 (4).
125 (1)	1966 Sch. X 2 (1).
(2)	1966 Sch. X 2 (2).
126	1978 s. 46.
127 (1)–(4), (5).	1968 Sch. XII 1 (1)–(4), (6).
128 (1)	1965 s. 30 (1); 1978 s. 45 (1).
(2)	1965 s. 30 (2); 1978 s. 45 (2).
(3)	1965 s. 30 (3); 1978 s. 45 (1).
(4)	1965 s. 30 (4); 1978 s. 45 (3).
(5)	1965 s. 30 (5); 1978 s. 45 (1) (4).
(6)	1965 s. 30 (6).
129	Drafting.
130	1965 s. 27 (1) (10).
131	1965 s. 27 (6).
132	Drafting.
133	1965 s. 27 (5).
134 (1)	1965 Sch. VII 11 (1); 1968 Sch. XII 8 (1).
(2)	1965 Sch. VII 11 (2).
(3)	1965 Sch. VII 11 (3).
(4)	1965 Sch. VII 11 (4); 1968 Sch. XII 8 (1).
(5)	1968 Sch. XII 8 (2).
135	1969 Sch. XIX 3 (1).
136	1978 s. 49.
137 (1)	1965 Sch. VII 14 (1).
(2)	1965 Sch. VII 14 (2).
(3)	1965 Sch. VII 14 (3).
(4)	1965 Sch. VII 14 (3); 1971 s. 58 (1) (2).
(5)	1965 Sch. VII 14 (5).
(6)	1965 Sch. VII 14 (6).
(7)	1965 Sch. VII 14 (7).
(8)	1965 Sch. VII 14 (8).
(9)	1971 s. 58 (1) (4).
138 (1)	1971 s. 58 (3).
(2)	1965 Sch. VII 14 (4) (6); 1971 s. 58 (3).
(3)	1965 Sch. VII 14 (4).
(4)	1965 Sch. VII 14 (4); 1971 s. 58 (4).
139	1971 s. 58 (1) (4); 1977 s. 40 (9).

Section of Act	Derivation
140 (1)	1965 Sch. VII 10 (1); 1975 (No. 2) s. 61 (1).
(2)	1965 Sch. VII 10 (2).
(3)	1965 Sch. VII 10 (3).
141	1965 Sch. VI 12.
142 (1)	1965 Sch. VII 9 (1).
(2)	1965 Sch. VII 9 (2); 1973 Sch. XVI 15 (1).
(3)	1965 Sch. VII 9 (3).
(4)	1973 Sch. XVI 15 (1).
143 (1)	1965 s. 28 (1).
(2)	1965 s. 28 (2).
(3)	1965 s. 28 (3); 1967 s. 35 (2).
(4)	1965 s. 28 (3).
144	1965 Sch. VII 12.
145	1965 s. 35.
146 (1)	1972 s. 119 (1); 1975 s. 53.
(2)	1972 s. 119 (2).
(3)	1972 s. 119 (3); 1975 s. 53.
147 (1)	1965 s. 31 (1); 1976 Sch. XI 1.
(2)	1965 s. 31 (2).
(3)	1965 s. 31 (3); 1971 Sch. XII 13.
(4)	1965 s. 31 (4).
(5)	1965 s. 31 (5).
(6)	1965 s. 31 (6).
(7)	1965 s. 31 (7).
(8)	1965 s. 31 (8).
(9)	1965 s. 31 (9).
148	1976 s. 55.
149 (1)	1976 s. 56 (1); 1978 Sch. XI 2 (1).
(2)	1976 s. 56 (2).
(3)	1976 s. 56 (3).
(4)	1976 s. 56 (4).
(5)	1976 s. 56 (5).
(6)	1976 s. 56 (6); 1978 Sch. XI 2 (2).
(7)	1976 s. 56 (7).
(8)	1975 s. 39; 1976 ss, 56 (1), 90.
150 (1)	1965 s. 44 (1).
(2)	1965 s. 44 (2)
(3)	1965 s. 44 (3); 1973 Sch. XXI 4.
(4)	1965 s. 44 (4); 1972 s. 114 (2).
(5)	1965 s. 44 (5).
(6)	Drafting.
151	1965 Sch. VII 16.
152	1973 s. 51 (1)–(3).
153	1965 s. 26; 1975 Sch. XII 2, 13.
154	1965 Sch. X 13.
155 (1) "chargeable period" "close company"	Drafting for part IX.
"land"	1970 Sch. XV 6 (2).
other	Interpretation Act 1978 Sch. II 5 (*b*).
definitions	1965 s. 45 (1); 1970 Sch. XV 6 (2), 11.

Section of Act	Derivation
155 (2)	1965 s. 45 (3); 1970 Sch. XV 11.
(3)	1973 s. 54 (1) (*b*).
(4)	Drafting.
(5)	1965 s. 45 (10).
156–160	
Sch. 1.	1978 Sch. VII.
Sch. 2	1969 s. 41 (2), Sch. XVIII Part I; existing orders under 1969 s. 41 (2).
Sch. 3	
para. 1	1965 Sch. VIII 1.
2	1965 Sch. VIII 2.
3	1965 Sch. VIII 3.
4	1965 Sch. VIII 4.
5 (1)	1965 Sch. VIII 5 (1); 1967 Sch. XIII 8; 1970 Sch. XV 11.
(2)	1965 Sch. VIII 5 (2); 1970 Sch. XV 11.
(3)	1965 Sch. VIII 5 (4); 1970 Sch. XV 11.
(4)	1965 Sch. VIII 5 (5); 1970 Sch. XV 11.
(5)	1965 Sch. VIII 5 (6); 1970 Sch. XV 11.
6	1965 Sch. VIII 6; 1970 Sch. XV 11.
7	1965 Sch. VIII 7; 1970 Sch. XV 11.
8	1968 Sch. XII 7 (1)–(6).
9	1965 Sch. VIII 9; 1968 Sch. XII 7 (7); 1970 Sch. XV 11.
10 (1)	1965 s. 45 (1).
(2)	1965 Sch. VIII 10 (1).
(3)	1965 Sch. VIII 10 (2).
Sch. 4	
para. 1	1978 Sch. VIII 1.
2	1978 Sch. VIII 2 (1) (2) (3).
3	1978 Sch. VIII 1, 2 (4).
4–8	1978 Sch. VIII 3–7.
Sch. 5	
para. 1 (1)	1965 Sch. VI 22 (1); 1972 s. 114 (2).
(2)	1965 Sch. VI 22 (2).
(3)	1965 Sch. VI 22 (5).
2 (1)	1965 Sch. VI 22 (4).
(2)	1965 Sch. VI 22 (6).
(3)	1971 Sch. X 5.
3 (1)	1968 s. 32 (1) (2) (6).
(2)	1968 s. 32 (4) (6).
(3)	1968 s. 32 (5).
4 (1)	1968 z. 32 (7), Sch. XI 1 (1).
(2)	1968 Sch. XI 1 (3).
(3)	1968 Sch. XI 1 (4); 1970 Sch. XV 11.
(4)	1968 Sch. XI 1 (5).
(5)	1968 Sch. XI 1 (6).
(6)	1968 Sch. XI 1 (7).
(7)	1968 Sch. XI 1 (9).
5	1968 Sch. XI 2; 1970 Sch. XV 11.
6	1968 Sch. XI 3.
7	1968 Sch. XI 4.
8 (1)	1968 s. 32 (6).
(2)	1972 Sch. XXVIII Part VI Note 3.
9 (1)	1965 Sch. VI 23 (1); 1974 s. 48 (2) (3).
(2)	1965 Sch. VI 23 (2); 1974 s. 48 (2).
(3)	1965 Sch. VI 23 (3).
(4)	1965 Sch. VI 23 (4).
(5)	1965 Sch. VI 23 (5); 1974 s. 48 (4).
10	Drafting.

Section of Act	Derivation
Sch. 5	
para. 11	1965 Sch. VI 24.
12 (1)	1965 Sch. VI 25 (1).
(2)	1965 Sch. VI 25 (2).
(3)	1968 Sch. XII 5 (1).
(4)	1965 Sch. VI 25 (3).
(5)	1965 Sch. VI 25 (4).
13 (1)	1965 Sch. VI 26 (1).
(2)	1965 Sch. VI 26 (2).
(3)	1965 Sch. VI 26 (3).
(4)	1971 Sch. X 5.
(5)	1965 Sch. VI 26 (4).
(6)	1965 Sch. VI 26 (6).
14 (1)	1965 Sch. VI 27 (1); 1966 Sch. X 6 (1).
(2)	1965 Sch. VI 27 (2).
(3)	1965 Sch. VI 27 (3).
15	1965 Sch. VI 28; 1968 Sch. XII 1 (5).
16	1965 Sch. VI 29.
17	1965 Sch. VI 30.
18	1967 Sch. XIII 3.
Sch. 6	
para. 1	Drafting.
2 (1)	1965 s. 44 (1).
(2)	1965 s. 44 (2); 1971 Sch. XIV Part V.
(3)	1965 s. 44 (3).
(4)	1965 s. 44 (4); 1972 s. 114 (2).
(5)	1965 s. 44 (5).
(6)	Drafting.
3	1965 Sch. VI 22 (3).
4	1973 s. 54, Sch. XXI 4.
5	1973 s. 51 (4).
6	1973 Sch. XX 4.
7	1973 Sch. XX 5.
8	1973 Sch. XX 6.
9	1971 s. 59 (1), Sch. XII 15, 18.
10	Drafting.
11	1977 s. 43 (9).
12 (1)	1965 Sch. VI 3 (8).
(2)	1965 Sch. VI 3 (5).
(3)	1965 Sch. VI 3 (7); 1970 Sch. XV 11.
(4)	1965 Sch. VI 21 (4).
13	1971 Sch. X 1 (1), 2.
14	Drafting.
15	1965 s. 25A; 1975 Sch. XII 12.
16	1971 Sch. XII 11; 1975 Sch. XII 17.
17	1969 Sch. XIX 1 (1)–(4).
18	1969 Sch. XIX 2 (1) (2).
19	Drafting.
20 (1)–(3)	Drafting.
(4)	1976 s. 53 (8).
21	1971 Sch. IX 5.
22 (1)	Drafting.
(2)	Drafting.
(3)	1971 Sch. IX 3.
23	1974 Sch. VIII 6.
24	1976 Sch. XI 1 (2).
25–29	Drafting.
Sch. 7	
para. 2 (4)	1977 s. 40 (10).

271   Deductions—cost of acquisition of asset—consideration for acquisition—whether consideration wholly and exclusively for asset

A taxpayer paid a Jersey company to arrange a tax avoidance scheme by which he could reduce his liability to capital gains tax in respect of a sale of shares. Firstly a settlement was created in Jersey with the taxpayer as beneficiary in the reversionary interest. Secondly he borrowed money from the company to purchase the reversionary interest in a Gibraltar settlement which he later sold at a loss. He used the combined proceeds of sale of his interests in both settlements to repay the loan from the company. The Revenue refused to accept his claim that the loss on the Gibraltar settlement should be set off against his assessment to tax on the grounds that (i) the payments made under the scheme were circular, and this demanded that the transactions be viewed as a whole and not separately, and (ii) the money paid by the taxpayer for the Gibraltar settlement was not a consideration given wholly or exclusively for the purchase of the asset. *Held*, the circularity of payments was to be ignored because there was no underlying purpose of concealing the nature of the transactions. To regard the series of transactions as one because there was no ultimate loss would be incorrect, since each transaction was complete in itself. However the payments for the Gibraltar settlement were not made wholly or exclusively for the asset, but also to pay the company to continue the scheme and therefore the loss could not be set off against the taxpayer's assessment.

EILBECK (INSPECTOR OF TAXES) v RAWLING [1979] STC 16 (Chancery Division: SLADE J).

272   Disposal of assets—deemed disposals—capital sum derived from assets—deferred consideration for shares

In 1970 the taxpayers agreed to sell shares in a private company. The consideration was partly a fixed sum per share to be paid immediately and partly a deferred payment to be calculated in accordance with the agreement. The relevant date for calculating the amount of the deferred consideration was 5th December 1972. On the question of capital gains tax liability the Revenue contended that the right to receive the deferred consideration was an asset from which a capital sum was derived when the right matured on 5th December 1972 and that accordingly there was a deemed disposal under Finance Act 1965, s. 22 (3). *Held*, although s. 22 (3) was confined to cases where no asset was acquired by the person paying the capital sum, in the present case the purchasers did not acquire any assets in 1972 when they made the payments. The capital sum was derived from the rights to the deferred consideration given to the taxpayers in 1970 and not from the shares. There was a deemed disposal in 1972 and chargeable gains arose.

MARREN (INSPECTOR OF TAXES) v INGLES [1979] 1 WLR 1131 (Court of Appeal: ORMROD and TEMPLEMAN LJJ and SIR DAVID CAIRNS). Decision of Slade J [1979] STC 58, 1978 Halsbury's Abridgment para. 278 reversed.

Finance Act 1965, s. 22, now Capital Gains Tax Act 1979, s. 20.

273   —— disposal of shares—transfer of value in shares—control of company

The taxpayer and his two sons-in-law had a substantial shareholding in an electronics company which they agreed to sell, subject to contract, to an American company. With the object of reducing liability to capital gains tax on the proceeds of the sale they devised a scheme whereby a new company was incorporated, with share capital divided into preferred and ordinary shares, having equal voting rights but the latter conferring superior rights as to the return of capital on a winding up. Pursuant to an agreement the taxpayer and his sons-in-law transferred their shares in the electronics company to the new company in return for the allotment and issue to them of 100,000 preferred shares in the new company, in the proportions 44 per cent, 34 per cent and 22 per cent respectively, no other shares having been issued. That company then sold the shares in the electronics company to the American company. Shortly afterwards a further 100 preferred shares were sold to a company registered in the Cayman Islands, which later became the only shareholder to accept a rights issue of ordinary shares offered to preferred shareholders. An extraordinary general meeting was then held, at which the taxpayer and one of his sons-in-law were not present, where a resolution was passed to wind up the company. Thus the greater part of the company's capital, namely the proceeds of the sale of shares to the American company, passed to the Cayman Islands company by virtue of its ordinary shareholding.

The taxpayer was assessed to capital gains tax under the Finance Act 1965, s. 19 (1), on the ground, inter alia, that there had been a part disposal of his shares within the meaning of Sch. 7, para. 15 (2), which provides that where a person having control over a company exercises that control so that value passes from his shares into the shares of others there is a disposal of the shares out of which value passed. The Special Commissioners upheld the assessment but Goulding J allowed the taxpayer's appeal on the grounds that para. 15 (2) did not apply where control of a company was exercised by a group of persons. The Court of Appeal reversed that decision and the taxpayer appealed. *Held*, LORD WILBERFORCE and LORD KEITH dissenting, para. 15 (2) was to be construed as including the exercise by two or more persons of control of a company. First, there was no evidence of an intention to exclude the application of the Interpretation Act 1889, s. 1 (1) (b) to para. 15 (2): the effect of reading the words in the singular as including the plural was merely to treat as a disposal acts done by two or more persons which, had they been done by only one person, would have constituted a disposal. Secondly, Sch. 18, para. 3, which defined "control", provided that, unless the context otherwise required, where two or more persons satisfied one of the conditions for control, they were deemed to have control of the company, and there was nothing in para. 15 (2) which rendered its application inappropriate to that provision. Thus, the taxpayer and his sons-in-law were persons having control within the meaning of the provision. They had collectively exercised this control in passing the resolution to wind up the company which had resulted in the disposal in question. The appeal would be dismissed.

FLOOR v DAVIS (INSPECTOR OF TAXES) [1979] STC 379 (House of Lords: LORD WILBERFORCE, LORD DIPLOCK, VISCOUNT DILHORNE, LORD EDMUND-DAVIES and LORD KEITH OF KINKEL). *Blue Metal Industries Ltd v R W Dilley* [1969] 3 All ER 437, PC distinguished. Decision of Court of Appeal [1978] 2 All ER 1079, 1978 Halsbury's Abridgment, para. 280 affirmed.

Interpretation Act 1889, s. 1 (1) (b) now Interpretation Act 1978, s. 6 (c). Finance Act 1965, s. 19 (1) and Sch. 7, para. 15 (2) now Capital Gains Tax Act 1979, ss. 1 (1) and 25 (2) respectively. Finance Act 1965, Sch. 18, para. 3 now Income and Corporation Taxes Act 1970, s. 302.

274   —— **surrender of rights—payment for release from service agreement**

A sales director was released from his service contract with the taxpayer company in consideration of a payment from him of £50,000. The company was assessed to corporation tax on the amount, on the basis that the company's rights under the service contract were assets within the Finance Act 1965, s. 22 (1), and that the release of those rights in return for consideration received was a disposal of assets under s. 22 (3). The Court of Appeal allowed an appeal by the company, holding that the company's rights were not an asset within s. 22 (1) because such an asset consisted of property for which a market value could be ascertained and a right to personal services under a service contract, not being assignable, could not have a market value. On appeal, *held*, if an employer was able to exact from an employee a substantial sum as a term of releasing him from his obligations to serve, the rights of the employer bore quite sufficiently the mark of an asset, within s. 22 (1), (3), as something he could turn to account, notwithstanding that his ability to do so was by a type of disposal limited by its nature. It was erroneous to deduce from the language of s. 22 (4) of the Act, which introduced the concept of market value for certain purposes, that there was a principle of general application for the purposes of capital gains tax that an asset must have a market value. Accordingly, the sum of £50,000 paid by the director to secure his release from the contract constituted a chargeable gain in the hands of the company. The appeal would be allowed.

O'BRIEN (INSPECTOR OF TAXES) v BENSON'S HOSIERY (HOLDINGS) LTD [1979] STC

735 (House of Lords: LORD DIPLOCK, VISCOUNT DILHORNE, LORD SIMON OF GLAISDALE, LORD FRASER OF TULLYBELTON and LORD RUSSELL OF KILLOWEN). Decision of the Court of Appeal [1978] STC 549, 1978 Halsbury's Abridgment para. 281 reversed.

Finance Act 1965, s. 22 (1), (3), (4) now Capital Gains Tax Act 1979, s. 19.

275   **Exemptions and reliefs—annual payments due under a covenant**

The taxpayer company assigned, by agreements executed under seal, certain patents and other rights to another company, for which the taxpayer received royalties. The taxpayer decided to pay its shareholders a dividend by distributing in specie its rights to receive the payments. The question arose as to whether this was a chargeable gain arising on the disposal of an asset which, pursuant to the Income and Corporation Tax Act 1970 s. 265, would result in liability to corporation tax. Under the Finance Act 1965, Sch. 7, para. 12 (c) no chargeable gain accrues on the disposal of a right to annual payments due under a covenant. The point at issue was whether the payments were due under a "covenant". *Held*, para. 12 (c) applied only to cases where there was a gratuitous promise to make the payments, which was enforceable only because of the form in which it was evidenced, i.e. under English law in a document under seal and under Scottish law by the writ or oath of the undertaker. The agreements in the instant case would have been enforceable even if they had not been under seal because they were bilateral, in that the payments were consideration for the obligation undertaken by the taxpayer in assigning its rights. Hence the agreements did not fall within the exemption provided by para. 12 (c).

RANK XEROX LTD v LANE (INSPECTOR OF TAXES) [1979] STC 740 (House of Lords: LORD WILBERFORCE, VISCOUNT DILHORNE, LORD SALMON, LORD RUSSELL OF KILLOWEN and LORD KEITH OF KINKEL). Decision of the Court of Appeal [1978] 2 All ER 1124, 1978 Halsbury's Abridgment para. 283 reversed.

Finance Act 1965, Sch. 7, para. 12 now Capital Gains Tax Act 1979, s. 144.

276   **—— gilt-edged securities**

The Capital Gains Tax (Gilt-edged Securities) (No. 1) Order 1979, S.I. 1979 No. 1231 (made on 27th September 1979), adds 12 per cent Treasury Loan 1983 "A", Variable Rate Treasury Stock 1983, 13¾ per cent Treasury Stock 2000–2003, 13¼ per cent Exchequer Stock 1987, 12¼ per cent Exchequer Stock 1999, 11 per cent Exchequer Stock 1991 to the category of stocks and bonds which are exempt from tax on capital gains if held for more than twelve months.

277   The Capital Gains Tax (Gilt-edged Securities) (No. 2) Order 1979, S.I. 1979 No. 1676 (made on 7th December 1979) adds 11½ per cent Treasury Stock 2001–2004, 12 per cent Treasury Stock 1984, 12¼ per cent Exchequer Stock 1999"A", 3 per cent Exchequer Stock 1984, 11¾ Treasury Stock 2003–2007, 11¼ per cent Exchequer Stock 1984, 11½ per cent Treasury Stock 1989 and 12 per cent Exchequer Stock 1999–2002"A" to the category of stocks and bonds which are exempt from tax on capital gains if held for more than twelve months.

278   **—— private residences**

In 1974 it was recognised that many owner-occupiers had difficulty in selling their houses when they were obliged to move elsewhere, perhaps because of their employment. As a result it was announced on 12th February 1975 that the Inland Revenue would, as a temporary measure, allow a modest extension of the statutory period prescribed by the Finance Act 1965, s. 29 (2) (where a dwelling house which has been the owner's only or main residence, the last 12 months of ownership automatically qualifies for exemption from capital gains tax whether or not he lives there in that period), provided that there was a continuing intention to sell. An Inland Revenue Press Release dated 11th January 1977 set out the Revenue's practice in such cases and stated that if the residence were not sold within 24 months the statutory rules would apply. Two complaints were made to the Parliamentary Commissioner that the Inland Revenue practice of restricting the promised "modest extension" of the 12-month period to a maximum of 24 months constituted maladministration. The Revenue stated that it would not have been reasonable for them to have examined the merits of individual cases where there had been delay in disposing of residences and the Parliamentary Commissioner ruled in each case that the Revenue's unwillingness to examine the merits (and consequential strict application of the concession) did not constitute maladministration. See Case IB/656/77 and Case IB/685/77 in Parliamentary Commissioner for Administration: Investigations Completed—May–July 1978 (HC 664).

Finance Act 1965, s. 29 (2) now Capital Gains Tax Act 1979, s. 102.

279   —— retirement relief—disposal of business—extra-statutory concessions

The Inland Revenue have issued a Press Release dated 30th March 1979 announcing a new extra-statutory concession and the revision of existing concessions relating to retirement relief under the Finance Act 1965, s. 34, which is consolidated as from 6th April 1979 in the Capital Gains Tax Act 1979, s. 124.

The new extra-statutory concession provides relief where an asset is owned by a director and used by his family company. The concession applies to future disposals and to past disposals where the tax liability has not yet been settled. The 1965 Act, s. 34 (1) (b) (1979 Act, s. 124 (1) (b)), provides relief on the disposal by an individual of shares in a company of which he is a full-time working director, if it is his family trading company. If he makes a disposal of an asset which he owns and (i) it has throughout the period of ownership been used rent-free for the purposes of a trade carried on by the company, (ii) throughout his period of ownership he has been a full-time working director of the company and the company has been his family trading company, and (iii) the disposal is associated with a disposal of shares in that company by him which qualifies for relief under s. 34 (1) (b) (s. 124 (1) (b)), then the disposal of the asset will be regarded as qualifying for that relief. Where the conditions in (i) and (ii) are satisfied at the time of disposal but were not satisfied at some earlier time then only a proportion of the gain will be eligible for relief. Where the company has paid rent for the asset no relief will be given unless the rent was clearly less than market rent, when a proportion of the gain will qualify.

Three existing extra-statutory concessions have been altered to make them conform with the changes to retirement relief effected by the Finance Act 1978, s. 48. The revised concessions apply to disposals made after 11th April 1978 where the tax liability has not yet been settled. The altered concessions are:

(i) ESC D7 Retirement Relief: business passing to spouse;
(ii) ESC D8 Retirement Relief: change in business during ten years before disposal;
(iii) ESC D9 Retirement Relief: directors of groups of companies.

280   —— —— —— statements of practice

The Inland Revenue have issued a Press Release dated 30th March 1979 stating that they have altered the wording of two statements of practice to make them conform with the changes to retirement relief effected by the Finance Act 1978, s. 48.

(i) SP5/79: Family company: sale of assets in anticipation of liquidation (first issued on 4th January 1973). Where a company's chargeable assets are sold as a preliminary to liquidation, Finance Act 1965, s. 34 (3) (b), as amended by Finance Act 1978, s. 48, which limits the relief by reference to those assets may prevent relief on the subsequent disposal of shares in the winding up. In such cases the Board are prepared to consider the granting of concessional relief on request.

(ii) SP6/79: Closure of business followed by sale of assets on liquidation of company (first issued on 9th August 1976 headed "Delay in sale of business on completion of liquidation", see 1976 Halsbury's Abridgment para. 280). This statement of practice meets the case where there is an interval between the time when a business is closed down and the time when the business assets are sold or, in the case of a company liquidation, a capital distribution is received by the shareholder.

One of the conditions for relief under the Finance Act 1965, s. 34 (as amended by the Finance Act 1978, s. 48) in respect of gains accruing to an individual on the disposal by way of sale or gift of a business (or part of a business) is that he has owned the business throughout the qualifying period of at least one year ending with the disposal. For an individual who receives a capital distribution on the liquidation of a company the test is that it has been his family trading company and he has been a full time working director of it throughout the qualifying period of at least one year ending with the date of distribution.

Neither the individual owner of a business nor the shareholder in a family trading company can satisfy in strictness the qualifying period of ownership test where there is a gap between the date on which the business is closed down and the date of disposal or capital distribution.

The Inland Revenue will in practice be prepared to apply that test by reference to the period ending with the permanent closing down of the business, provided that:

(a) in the case of an individual owner the business assets are disposed of within three years of the closure; or

(b) in the case of an individual shareholder the capital distribution is received within three years of the closure;

(c) the business assets belonging to the individual in (a) or to the company of which the shareholder in (b) is a member are not used or leased for any purpose in the period from the closure of the business to the disposal.

In each case the amount of relief will be calculated by reference to the age of the taxpayer at the date of the closure.

Finance Act 1965, s. 34, as amended, now Capital Gains Tax Act 1979, s. 124.

281　Finance (No. 2) Act 1979

See para. 2247.

282　Gain—computation—assets held on 6th April 1965—new holding arising after 5th April 1965

Scotland

Prior to 6th April 1965 the taxpayer's wife held shares in a private company. It was taken over by another company, L Ltd, whose articles of association placed no restriction on the transfer of its shares, and on 2nd September 1967 the shares held by the taxpayer's wife were exchanged for shares in L Ltd. On 11th March 1974 she sold a proportion of these shares, their market value having dropped considerably since 2nd September 1967. The question arose as to whether this loss was an allowable loss which could be deducted from the gain made prior to 2nd September 1967, as provided by the Finance Act 1965, Sch. 6, para. 27 (2). The Crown contended that the gain or loss accruing on the disposal of the wife's shares fell to be apportioned by the method prescribed by para. 24, by virtue of para. 27 (3), which provides that the rest of para. 27 does not apply " . . . in relation to a reorganisation of a company's share capital, if the new holding differs only from the original shares in being a different number . . . of shares of the same class as the original shares". *Held*, the original shares, being subject to restriction on the right of transfer, were not of the same class as the shares in L Ltd, which were freely transferable. Thus para. 27 (3) had no application. The court also considered that the phrase "reorganisation of a company's share capital" was to be construed as not including an amalgamation of two companies.

INLAND REVENUE COMRS v BEVERIDGE [1979] STC 592 (Inner House).

Finance Act 1965, Sch. 6, para. 27 now Capital Gains Tax Act 1979, Sch. 5, para. 14.

The Inland Revenue have since changed their practice in the light of the decision in this case, such that para. 14 (3) of the 1979 Act (previously para. 27 (3) of the 1965 Act) no longer applies where the shares comprised in the new holding are shares in a different company from the old shares; see Statement of Practice SP 14/79.

283　——— sale of land reflecting development value

The taxpayer sold some farming land at a price which reflected the expectation of planning permission being granted for residential development. Permission was not granted. He was assessed to capital gains tax under the Finance Act 1965, Sch. 6, para. 23, which provided that in certain circumstances the gain was to be computed by reference to the extent to which the consideration for the disposal exceeded what the market value would have been if immediately before disposal it had become unlawful to carry out any development. The taxpayer contended that the requirements of para. 23 were not satisfied since the statutory hypothesis that development had "become" unlawful was not capable of application as it was already unlawful to carry out development in the absence of planning permission. The assessment was upheld. On appeal, *held*, the assumption to be made for the purposes of para. 23 was that the land was incapable of development, not merely that for the time in question it was without benefit of planning permission. The effect of para. 23 was to cause an assumed transition from a situation where such permission was possible, to one where it was unlawful; the assumption was that there had been a change, not in the circumstances of the land, but in the law. Accordingly, despite the fact that at the time of disposal there was no planning permission to develop the land, para. 23 was capable of applying to the taxpayer's land. The appeal would be dismissed.

WATKINS v KIDSON (INSPECTOR OF TAXES) [1979] STC 464 (House of Lords: LORD WILBERFORCE, VISCOUNT DILHORNE, LORD SALMON, LORD KEITH OF KINKEL and LORD SCARMAN). Decision of Court of Appeal [1978] 2 All ER 785, 1978 Halsbury's Abridgment para. 292 affirmed.

Finance Act 1965, Sch. 6, para. 23 as amended now Capital Gains Tax Act 1979, Sch. 5, para. 9.

284   —— **gain arising from sale of loan—whether loan a debt on a security—whether gain chargeable**

The taxpayer company devised a capital loss scheme with the intention of accruing an artificial loss to set off against a chargeable gain made on the sale of a farm. The question arose whether profits made on the sale to a finance company of a loan made by the taxpayer company to an investment company created especially for the purposes of the scheme was a chargeable gain as being a debt on a security within the Finance Act 1965, Sch. 7, para. 11. *Held*, to be a debt on a security a loan had to be similar to, but not necessarily identical with, loan stock. The loan had all the characteristics of loan stock although it had been evidenced by a statutory declaration rather than by a loan certificate. It was therefore a debt on a security within para. 11 and a chargeable gain had accrued to the taxpayer company at its disposal.

W. T. RAMSAY LTD v INLAND REVENUE COMRS [1979] 1 WLR 974 (Court of Appeal: LORD SCARMAN, ORMROD and TEMPLEMAN LJJ). Dicta of Lords Wilberforce and Russell in *Aberdeen Construction Group Ltd v IRC* [1978] AC 885 at 895, 903, HL, 1978 Halsbury's Abridgment para. 276 applied. Decision of Goulding J [1978] 2 All ER 321, 1978 Halsbury's Abridgment para. 284 reversed.

Finance Act 1965, Sch. 7, para. 11 now Capital Gains Tax Act 1979, s. 134.

285   **Settled property—persons becoming absolutely entitled—tax avoidance scheme**

In 1960 a settlor settled shares on discretionary trusts for the benefit of his two sons, the taxpayers. In 1969 he set up a scheme to mitigate capital gains tax. In March 1969, non-resident trustees were appointed. On 28th October 1969, the trustees appointed to each taxpayer an interest in half the settled shares contingent on each taxpayer surviving until 1st November 1969. On the same day, the taxpayers assigned their contingent interests to a Jersey company for a consideration. At the same time, a contract was entered into for each taxpayer to purchase the same number of shares from the company. On the completion of these transactions, the taxpayers were assessed to capital gains tax. Their appeal was dismissed and they appealed further. *Held*, capital gains tax was imposed under the Finance Act 1965, s. 25 (3), when a person became absolutely entitled to any settled property as against the trustee. Under s. 42 (2), where the trustees were non-resident, as in this case, tax could be recovered from the beneficiaries if they were resident in the United Kingdom. The object of this scheme was to ensure that it was the non-resident Jersey company, and not the taxpayers, who were resident, who became absolutely entitled as against the trustees.

Whether the scheme succeeded depended on ascertaining the true legal effect of the transactions without regard to the fiscal consequences. Properly construed, the share sale agreement was not for the sale of the specified settlement shares but of unspecified shares in the same company. Accordingly, the Jersey company was not just a conduit through which the settlement shares passed from the trustees to the taxpayers, and it was the Jersey company who became "absolutely entitled" to the settlement shares as against the trustees. Thus s. 42 (2) did not apply to make the taxpayers liable to tax. However, even if the sale agreement was a contract to sell particular shares, the remedy of specific performance would not be available to the taxpayers in the event of a breach, as damages would be an adequate remedy. Thus they did not have any equitable interest in the settlement shares, so they could not be regarded as having beneficial interests under the settlement on 1st November 1969, with the consequence that s. 42 (2) did not apply.

The Crown's other contention, that the scheme constituted a "settlement" within the 1965 Act, s. 42 (7), of which the taxpayers were beneficiaries and thus liable to tax arising on the disposal of the shares, was incorrect. An arrangement would not fall within the definition of a settlement unless there was an act of bounty by the settlor in favour of others. At the time the arrangement was commenced in March 1969, the settlor was no longer in a position to confer bounty on the taxpayers, having parted with all his interest in the trust fund comprised in the 1960 settlement at the time it was made. Thus the scheme did not constitute a settlement on which any liability to tax would accrue. The appeal would be allowed.

CHINN V HOCHSTRASSER (INSPECTOR OF TAXES); CHINN V COLLINS (INSPECTOR OF TAXES) [1979] 2 All ER 529 (Court of Appeal: BUCKLEY, SHAW and GOFF LJJ). Decision of Templeman J [1978] 1 All ER 65, 1977 Halsbury's Abridgment para. 308 reversed.

Finance Act 1965, Part III, now Capital Gains Tax Act 1979.

286   —— separate funds—beneficiaries becoming absolutely entitled to one fund—liability of trustees of other fund to tax

A marriage settlement made in 1944 reserved certain powers of appointment to the husband and wife. In 1955 by a deed of appointment and release, part of the settlement was appointed on trust for a daughter of the marriage absolutely, contingently on her attaining the age of twenty-five. In 1972 an arrangement was made whereby the remainder of the fund subject to the 1944 settlement was held on trust by the original trustees for the wife for life with remainder to her husband for his life, with remainder to their two daughters in equal shares absolutely. The life tenants and the remainderman then assigned their respective interests in the main fund to two companies in the Cayman Islands, for a financial consideration. New trustees, resident in the Cayman Islands, were appointed and the company holding the beneficial interests in the remainder subsequently assigned those interests to the company already holding the life interests, thus making that company absolutely and beneficially entitled to the fund as against the Cayman Island trustees. The Inland Revenue therefore made an assessment to capital gains tax on the chargeable gain thus arising under the Finance Act 1965, s. 25 (3). However in view of the absence abroad of the trustees, the assessment was made on the trustees of the 1955 fund on the basis of s. 25 (1), (11) and Sch. 10, para. 12. The assessment and liability were upheld by the Special Commissioners and the trustees appealed. At first instance the appeal was allowed on the ground that, notwithstanding that the original fund and the 1955 fund constituted a single settlement and the trustees of both funds were to be treated as a single body for the purposes of s. 25, tax could not be recovered from the trustees of the 1955 fund as Sch. 10, para. 12 did not make persons having no control over assets, liable for any tax arising on their disposal. On appeal by the Crown, *held*, the court would dismiss the appeal and affirm the judge's decision but on different grounds. For tax purposes, where a settlement originally or as a result of an appointment created different trusts of different properties then there were different states of affairs that thus created different settlements. The 1955 appointment resulted in there being two settlements and tax had to be calculated and charged separately on the two funds. The trustees of the 1955 fund ceased to be the trustees of the main fund when new non-resident trustees were appointed and were not therefore liable to tax in respect of it.

The Crown had contended that if the 1955 appointment had created a separate settlement, the trustees of the 1955 fund became absolutely entitled against the main fund trustees, and, had the appointment been made after the introduction of the 1965 Act, tax would have been immediately payable, there being a deemed disposal under s. 25 (3). The Court rejected that contention on the ground that some of the 1944 settlement trusts and powers remained effective in relation to the 1955 fund so the trustees did not become absolutely entitled against the main fund trustees. It did not necessarily follow that a separate settlement created by an appointment, made someone absolutely entitled to the appointed fund so as to make tax payable under s. 25 (3). It would only do so if the circumstances of the appointment made some person absolutely entitled to the appointed fund as against the trustees of the original fund.

ROOME v EDWARDS (INSPECTOR OF TAXES) [1980] 2 WLR 156 (Court of Appeal: BUCKLEY, BRIDGE and TEMPLEMAN LJJ). Decision of Brightman J [1979] 1 WLR 860 affirmed on different grounds.

Finance Act 1965, s. 25 (1), (11), (3), Sch. 10, para. 12 now Capital Gains Tax Act 1979, ss. 52, 48.

CARRIERS

Halsbury's Laws of England (4th edn.), Vol. 5, paras. 301–484

287   Articles

Aspects of the Limitation of Actions under CMR, A. C. Hardingham (commentary on the decisions in *Moto Vespa SA v MAT (Britannia Express) Ltd* [1979] 1 Lloyd's Rep 175, para. 296, and *Muller Batavier Limited v Laurent Transport Co Ltd* [1977] 1 Lloyd's Rep 411, 1977 Halsbury's Abridgment para. 317): [1979] LCMLQ 362.

The Delay Provisions of the CMR, A. C. Hardingham (an analysis of the delay provisions of the Convention on the Contract for the International Carriage of Goods by Road): [1979] 2 LMCLQ 193.

The time bar regulations in the CMR Convention, Johan Wetter (problems associated with the taking of proceedings for a claim under the Convention on the Contract for the International Carriage of Goods by Road): [1979] LMCLQ 504.

288   Carriage by air

See AVIATION.

289   Carriage by Air and Road Act 1979

The Carriage by Air and Road Act 1979 enables effect to be given to the provisions of certain protocols signed at Montreal on 25th September 1975 which amend the Warsaw Convention. The Act also modifies art. 26 (2) of the Convention and certain Acts relating to carriage by air and road. It received the royal assent on 4th April 1979; s. 2 came into force on that date, the remainder comes into force on days to be appointed.

Section 1 and Sch. 1 replace the Carriage by Air Act 1961, Sch. 1 (containing the text of the Warsaw Convention) with a new schedule containing the Convention as amended in Montreal in 1975. Schedule 2 of the 1979 Act makes the necessary consequential amendments. Section 2 modifies art. 26 (2) of the carriage by air Convention by adding s. 4A to the 1961 Act: "damage" to baggage or cargo now includes partial loss. Section 3 makes consequential amendments to the 1961 Act, the Carriage by Air (Supplementary Provisions) Act 1962, the Carriage of Goods by Road Act 1965 and the Carriage of Passengers by Road Act 1974. The financial extent of carriers' liability for damage or loss is now expressed by reference to special drawing rights instead of to gold francs: s. 4. Section 5 provides that the sterling equivalent of the special drawing rights is to be determined by reference to the rate fixed for the date in question by the International Monetary Fund. A Treasury certificate affirming the rate is conclusive evidence in any proceedings. Sections 6, 7 contain supplementary provisions.

290   Carriage by rail

See RAILWAYS.

291   Carriage by sea

See SHIPPING.

292   Carriage of animals—carriage by air—liability of carrier—offence committed in foreign territory

See *Air India v Wiggins*, para. 108.

293   ——carriage by road and rail—welfare of animals

See para. 2239.

294   Carriage of passengers by road—unlicensed hire car—power of airport authority to prohibit

See *Cinnamond v British Airports Authority*, para. 2177.

295   Carrier of patented product—infringement—whether carrier an infringer

See *Smith Kline and French Laboratories v R D Harbottle (Mercantile) Ltd*, para. 2023.

296   Contract of carriage—contract between agents and carriers—right of agents' principals to bring action—whether action time-barred

The plaintiffs' agents made a contract with the defendant carriers for the carriage of two lathes from Birmingham to Madrid via Barcelona, to which the Convention in the Schedule to the Carriage of Goods by Road Act 1965 applied. The carriers knew that the agents often acted for the plaintiffs, but on this occasion the agents did not disclose their principals' identity. Following an accident near Madrid the lathes were damaged and the plaintiffs refused delivery and claimed damages from the carriers. The carriers contended that (i) there was no privity of contract between themselves and the plaintiffs as undisclosed principals; (ii) there were two separate contracts of carriage, one between Birmingham and Barcelona and one between Barcelona and Madrid, and that under Spanish law the Convention did not apply to the latter; (iii) the action was time-barred by art. 32 of the Convention; (iv) under art. 31 the court did not have jurisdiction to hear the action. *Held*, (i) the agents had acted as forwarding agents throughout and the mere fact that they had not disclosed the plaintiffs' existence did not prevent the latter taking action; (ii) on the evidence there was only one contract of carriage and therefore the Convention was applicable; (iii) art. 32 did not apply because there had been no delivery of the goods, but, had there been, there had been a written claim which suspended the limitation period until it was rejected; (iv) the court had jurisdiction to hear the action because the goods had been taken over by the carriers in England.

MOTO VESPA SA v MAT (BRITANNIA EXPRESS) LTD; MOTO VESPA SA v MATEU AND MATEU SA [1979] 1 Lloyd's Rep 175 (Queen's Bench Division: MOCATTA J).

297 —— date of contract—whether contract formed when passage booked or ticket received—validity of exemption clause printed on ticket

A housewife was seriously injured when a mooring cable on a cross-channel ferry lashed her shoulder when the vessel was casting off. The ferry operators claimed that they were protected from liability in negligence by an exclusion clause contained in the ticket. The passenger contended that the contract ran from the date of booking the ticket and that as the booking had been accepted with no mention of any conditions of carriage none could apply. The ticket had subsequently arrived by post. *Held*, the operators had unquestionably been negligent in allowing the passenger to be in the position she was in when she was injured. No warning had been given that potential danger existed and no attempt had been made to cordon off the danger area although it was normal practice to do so. The contract had to be taken as being effective from the date the booking was accepted, at which time no conditions had been brought to the passenger's attention. Conditions could not be incorporated subsequently and accordingly the operators were not protected by the exclusion clause. As to the quantum of damages, a housewife was entitled to be compensated for her loss in the same way as an employed earner and therefore she would be awarded damages reflecting the cost of employing someone to perform the domestic functions she was no longer capable of performing herself.

THE DRAGON, DALY v GENERAL STEAM NAVIGATION CO LTD [1979] 1 Lloyd's Rep 257 (Queen's Bench Division: BRANDON J). *The Eagle* [1977] 2 Lloyd's Rep 70, 1977 Halsbury's Abridgment para. 502 applied.

Liability for death or personal injury cannot now be excluded: Unfair Contract Terms Act 1977, s. 1, see 1977 Halsbury's Abridgment para. 540.

298 International carriage of goods—carriage by road—dangerous goods

A revised edition of the European Agreement concerning the International Carriage of Dangerous Goods by Road (ADR) (4th edn. 1978), has been published which includes Annexes A and B and all amendments made up to and including that dated 1st October 1978. The purpose of the agreement is to ensure that dangerous goods arriving at a frontier by road have been safely packed and are being carried safely. The parties to the agreement (Austria, Belgium, East Germany, France, Italy, Luxembourg, the Netherlands, Norway, Poland, Portugal, Spain, Sweden, Switzerland, the United Kingdom, West Germany and Yugoslavia, as at April 1976) undertake that the transport by road of dangerous goods which are packed and labelled in accordance with Annex A, and are carried in vehicles complying with the provisions of Annex B, will be permitted through their territories. A special appendix dealing with the road-sea carriage of dangerous goods to or from the United Kingdom is currently being prepared.

The revised text of the ADR, together with Annexes A and B, is available from H. M. Stationery Office.

299 —— —— fees

The International Carriage of Perishable Foodstuffs (Fees) Regulations 1979, S.I. 1979 No. 416 (in force on 1st October 1979), prescribe the fees payable for tests, type approval examinations and certification of transport equipment used or intended to be used for the international carriage of perishable foodstuffs. The Regulations are made in accordance with powers contained in International Carriage of Perishable Foodstuffs Act 1976, 1976 Halsbury's Abridgment para. 298.

300 —— safe containers

The government has ratified the International Convention for Safe Containers (CSC) signed at Geneva in 1972 and the convention entered into force on 8th March 1979. For the text of the convention, see Cmnd. 7535. For the purposes of the convention a "container" is an article of transport equipment which, inter alia, is specially designed to facilitate the transport of goods, by one or more modes of transport, without intermediate reloading; the definition excludes vehicles and packaging but includes containers carried on a chassis. Some of the requirements of the convention will be implemented by regulations but arrangements for the approval of containers and examination schemes are to be dealt with by the Health and Safety Executive by administrative action. The executive have published a document "Initial Arrangements in GB for the approval of containers" which is available from HM Stationery Office. Part 1 explains that the Health and Safety Executive will authorise suitable organisations to carry out the functions of approving containers and lays down the conditions that organisations will be expected to meet before being eligible for appointment. Part 2 gives details of the method by which manufacturers and owners of containers may make application for the approval of containers and the procedure to be adopted by the authorised organisations in considering such applications. Owners may apply for interim approval of their examination arrangements pending publication by the Health and Safety Executive of details of the procedure for the approval of examination schemes.

301   International Carriage of Perishable Foodstuffs Act 1976—commencement

The International Carriage of Perishable Foodstuffs Act 1976 (Commencement) Order 1979, S.I. 1979 No. 413, brought the whole of the International Carriage of Perishable Foodstuffs Act 1976, 1976 Halsbury's Abridgment para. 298, into force on 1st October 1979.

302   —— regulations

The International Carriage of Perishable Foodstuffs Regulations 1979, S.I. 1979 No. 415 (in force on 1st October 1979), make provisions in accordance with International Carriage of Perishable Foodstuffs Act 1976, 1976 Halsbury's Abridgment para. 298. They prescribe those foodstuffs to be regarded as perishable, temperature conditions for the international carriage of the prescribed foodstuffs and the standards of thermal efficiency for transport equipmemt. They also make provision as to the testing and certification of transport equipment.

303   Negligence—duty of care owed to passengers

See *McCready v Miller*, para. 1963.

CHARITIES

Halsbury's Laws of England (4th edn.), Vol. 5, paras. 501–985

304   Article

Charity Law on the Football Field, Michael Bryan (deficiencies in the law of charitable trusts and the difficulties hindering reform): 129 NLJ 86.

305   Charitable trust—charitable purposes—trust for promotion of sport

In 1972 the Football Association Youth Trust was set up, the objects of which were, under clause 3 of the trust deed, to encourage the sport of association football and other games and sports with a view to promoting the physical education and development of pupils of schools and universities. The trust was registered as a charity by the Charity Commissioners but the appeal of the Inland Revenue Commissioners against that decision was allowed on the grounds that the objects of the trust were not exclusively legally charitable. The trustees appealed. *Held*, BRIDGE LJ dissenting, the trust could not be classed as an educational charity since the elusive phrase "physical education and development" did not denote anything having anything to do with education in the context of the law of charities, and it was clear that a trust merely for the encouragement of sport was not charitable. Further, a trust not otherwise charitable could not be converted simply by limiting the beneficiaries of the trust to pupils of schools and universities. The submission that the trust was charitable in that it was for purposes beneficial to the community also failed: while a trust to provide facilities for exercise and physical recreation, being for objects beneficial to the community, was prima facie charitable, on a true construction of clause 3 the trust fund in question was applicable equally to non-charitable purposes, in the form of certain types of sport which did not involve exercise and physical recreation. Although the trust satisfied the requirements of recreation and public benefit under the Recreational Charities Act 1958, s. 1, it was not charitable by virtue of that section since the fund potentially could be applied for the provision of facilities for sports which could not be said to be in the interests of social welfare. Accordingly, the trust in question was not charitable and the appeal would be dismissed.

BRIDGE LJ held that on a true construction of clause 3 a valid charitable trust had been created for exclusively educational purposes.

INLAND REVENUE COMRS v MCMULLEN [1979] 1 All ER 588 (Court of Appeal: STAMP, ORR and BRIDGE LJJ). *Re Nottage* [1895] Ch 649, CA and *Dunne v Byrne* [1912] AC 407, PC applied. Decision of Walton J [1978] 1 All ER 230, 1977 Halsbury's Abridgment para. 326 affirmed.

This decision has been reversed by the House of Lords; see Times, 7th March 1980.

306   **Charity Commissioners—annual report**

In the Report of the Charity Commissioners for England and Wales for 1978 (HC 94) the commissioners state that in their view any provision in the governing instrument of purported charity which allows funds to be applied for non-charitable purposes such as the remuneration of trustees, directors, etc., may be open to question on the ground that the expenditure is not for charitable purposes. Following the principle in *Re Duke of Norfolk's Settlement Trust* [1978] 3 WLR 655, 1978 Halsbury's Abridgment para. 2912, they would agree to register an institution containing such provisions as a charity only in very special cases. They also emphasise the importance for trustees to ensure that books and statements of account, including cash balances, are checked by at least one trustee or are audited professionally or by a competent independent person with suitable financial experience.

During 1978 3,506 charities were registered (92 fewer than in 1977) and 202 charities were removed from the register. The number of registered charities stands at 129,212. The report includes, as appendices, newly revised guidance notes suggesting the ways in which the income of charities for the relief of poverty and for the relief of sickness might be applied in present-day circumstances. Another appendix to the report sets out the text of a booklet produced by the official custodian offering guidance to trustees in the selection and management of investments.

307   **Visitor—jurisdiction—dispute as to membership of corporation**

See *Patel v University of Bradford Senate*, para. 1010.

CHOSES IN ACTION

Halsbury's Laws of England (4th edn.), Vol. 6, paras. 1–89

308   **Assignment—equitable assignment—whether absolute or by way of charge**

See *Lloyds and Scottish Finance Ltd v Cyril Lord Carpets Sales Ltd,* para. 376.

309   **—— existence of previous charge over chose—priority between assignees**

See *Siebe Gorman & Co Ltd v Barclays Bank Ltd,* para. 245.

CLUBS

Halsbury's Laws of England (4th edn.), Vol. 6, paras. 201–411

310　Amateur athletics federation—one member from each country— Chinese association elected to represent China and Taiwan— whether Taiwan a separate country for purposes of federation rules

The International Amateur Athletic Federation was an unincorporated association whose members were national associations which controlled athletics in their respective countries. In 1954 the association controlling athletics in mainland China was admitted, but in 1956 when the association controlling athletics in Taiwan was also admitted, it resigned as a protest. The governments of both mainland China and Taiwan each claimed that it was the sole government of China which included the mainland and Taiwan. In 1978, as the United Nations and many nations had recognised the mainland government as the government of the whole of China, the federation adopted a resolution that the mainland association be made a member of the federation, as representing mainland China and Taiwan. By rule 1 of the federation's rules only one member from each country could be affiliated and the Taiwan association was therefore no longer considered a member of the federation. The Taiwan association sought a declaration that it was, and remained, a member. *Held*, rule 1 did not preclude the Taiwan association from being a member. The rule had been introduced to control the situation where rival associations claimed to be in control of athletics in the same areas and did not intend to include the political aspirations of a nation. Taiwan was a separate geographical entity and the Taiwan association had been found, as a question of fact, to control athletics in that area. In the alternative, as the Taiwan association had been treated as a member, had paid its subscriptions and entered competitions without serious challenge from members, it had established an estoppel by representation so as to preclude the federation from challenging the validity of its membership. Further, in electing both the mainland China and Taiwan associations, the federation had made a representation of fact as to the meaning of "country" in rule 1 and were estopped from denying that Taiwan was not a country within the meaning of the rule. The declarations would therefore be granted.

REEL v HOLDER [1979] 1 WLR 1252 (Queen's Bench Division: FORBES J).

311　Gaming Board for Great Britain—report

The Report of the Gaming Board for Great Britain 1978 (HC11) discloses that there were 127 clubs licensed for gaming other than bingo, bridge or whist (casino gaming) operating at the end of 1978 and that their "estimated drop" (i.e. money changed into chips) in 1977/78 was £727 million (7 per cent increase over 1976/77). The 53 localities in which such clubs may be licensed are set out in Appendix 1 to the report. At the end of 1978 there were 1,530 clubs in England and Wales licensed for bingo (this represented a small decrease compared with 1977; but the number of clubs actually operating increased slightly). The board draws attention of licence holders to their continuing responsibility for the conduct of bingo in clubs where the licence is in the process of being transferred. The board also states that if a licence holder wishes to dispose of his licence but retain management responsibility and a financial interest, a lack of clarity as to who is in actual control may result; and the board cannot accept a situation where someone other than the licence holder has responsibility for compliance with the Gaming Act 1968, Sch. 2. At 30th June 1978 966 clubs in England and Wales were registered under Part II of the 1968 Act and 17,545 clubs under Part III. Seven pool promoters renewed their licences under the Pool Competitions Act 1971 during 1978 (ten in 1977). By the end of 1978, 347 local authorities (149 in 1977) and 804 societies (162 in 1977) had registered lottery schemes under the Lotteries and Amusements Act 1976. The board stated, in relation to the certification of employees under the Gaming Act 1968, s. 19, that a decision by it to revoke a certificate or to refuse an initial application did not constitute a ban for life; each application was considered on its merits.   Where the board was minded to refuse an application or revoke a certificate, it invited representations from the person concerned.

312   —— **revocation of certificate of approval—application of principles of natural justice**

The applicants held managers' certificates under the Gaming Act 1968, s. 19.   A former employee made allegations to the Gaming Board of breaches of the 1968 Act and the Exchange Control Act 1947 by the applicants.   There was a hearing before the Board, as a result of which the applicants' certificates were revoked.   They applied for an order of certiorari to quash that decision on the ground that there was a breach of the rules of natural justice.   *Held*, the first principle to be applied to cases of this sort was that the Board ought to have given prior notice indicating clearly the areas of complaint.   Secondly, the proceedings should be so conducted that justice should not only be done but be seen to be done.   Thirdly, the court should not in deciding whether the foregoing principles had been obeyed use as the foundation for its judgment even the honest assertion on affidavit of the Board itself that no irregularity had occurred.   In this case, insufficient notice of the charges was given to the applicants.   Nor was justice seen to be done in that matters were raised by the Board which were outside the letters of complaint.   While accepting the contents of the chairman's affidavit, it would be wrong to conclude that there was no appearance of injustice.   The relief sought would be granted.

R v GAMING BOARD FOR GREAT BRITAIN, EX PARTE FENTON, MILLS AND WOOD (1979) (unreported) (Divisional Court of the Queen's Bench Division).

COMMONWEALTH AND DEPENDENCIES

Halsbury's Laws of England (4th edn.), Vol. 6, paras. 801–1206

313   **Bermuda—constitution**

The Bermuda Constitution (Amendment) Order 1979, S.I. 1979 No. 452 (in force on 28th May 1979) amends the Constitution of Bermuda with respect to the composition of the Constituency Boundaries Commission.

314   The Bermuda Constitution (Amendment) (No. 2) Order 1979, S.I. 1979 No. 1310 (in force on 1st December 1979), further amends the Constitution of Bermuda in respect of matters other than the Constituency Boundaries Commission.

315   **Cayman Islands—appeal to Privy Council—time limit for dispatch of records**

In a case on the interpretation of the Cayman Islands (Appeal to Privy Council) Order 1965, s. 5, regarding the possible extension of the time period for the dispatch of the records of the appeal to England, it was held that the length of the period accorded an appellant under s. 5 (b) to take steps for the dispatch of records was at the discretion of that court and once determined could be extended, either expressly or by implication.

ROULSTONE v PANTON [1979] 1 WLR 1465 (Privy Council: LORD HAILSHAM OF ST MARYLEBONE LC, VISCOUNT DILHORNE, LORD RUSSELL OF KILLOWEN, LORD KEITH OF KINKEL and SIR CLIFFORD RICHMOND).

316   **Commonwealth   Development   Corporation—appointment   of members**

The Commonwealth Development Corporation Regulations 1979, S.I. 1979 No. 495 (in force on 1st June 1979) deal with the terms of appointment and conditions of tenure of members of the Commonwealth Development Corporation and with its proceedings.   The Commonwealth Development Corporation Regulations 1977, 1977 Halsbury's Abridgment para. 338 are revoked.

317   Crown Agents—accounting year

The Crown Agents (First Accounting Year) Order 1979, S.I. 1979 No. 1673 (made on 11th December 1979) prescribes 1st January 1980 as the date on which the first accounting year shall begin for the purposes of the Crown Agents Act 1979; para. 318.

318   Crown Agents Act 1979

The Crown Agents Act 1979 establishes a statutory corporate body to be called the Crown Agents for Oversea Governments and Administrations in place of the existing Crown Agents, and sets up a further body corporate, the Crown Agents Holding and Realisation Board, for the purpose of managing and realising certain assets and discharging certain liabilities of the existing Crown Agents. The Act defines the functions, powers and duties of each body and confers wide powers of control on the Minister of Overseas Development. The Act received the royal assent on 4th April 1979 and came into force on that day.

Crown Agents for Oversea Governments and Administrations
Section 1 provides that on a day to be appointed by the Minister the term of office of each of the existing Crown Agents shall expire and there shall come into being a body corporate called the Crown Agents for Oversea Governments and Administrations in accordance with the provisions of Schedule 1. Under s. 2 on the same day all rights, liabilities and obligations of and all property held by the pre-existing Agents will vest in the new body as provided by Schedule 2, subject to the provisions of Schedule 5, para. 7. Section 3 confers a general power on the Crown Agents to perform their functions under the Act, both as agents of any body or authority as defined in Sch. 3, and in their own right.
   Section 4 authorises the Crown Agents to carry out the agency activities defined in Sch. 4 and s. 5 sets out authorised activities which may be performed by them in their own right. In both instances additional activities may be authorised by the Minister by order. Incidental and consequential activities are authorised by s. 6 and s. 7 provides that the Agents are under a duty to act as agents of certain bodies when so required by the Minister. The financing of agency activities is dealt with by s. 8. Section 9 provides that at the request of the Minister the Crown Agents are to undertake a review of their affairs with a view to the efficient management of their activities, and under s. 10 the Minister may at any time require the Agents to provide information regarding any aspect of their activities. Section 11 requires the Agents to make annual reports to the Minister on the performance of their functions and on their policies, programmes and plans. Under s. 12 any subsidiary of the agents is subject to their control.

Financial provisions
Section 13 sets out the general financial duties of the Crown Agents and provides that the Minister may determine an appropriate overall rate of return for any specified period, during which period the Agents are to organise their activities with the object of achieving that return. Under s. 14 the Minister is empowered to give directions as to the holding and allocation of the reserves of the Agents and any wholly owned subsidiaries, and s. 15 provides for the management of any liquid assets held by the same. The Minister may direct that any annual revenue surplus of the Agents be paid to him: s. 16. Section 17 provides that the transfer of assets to the Agents under s. 2 shall have the effect of creating a commencing capital debt owed to the Minister by the Agents, repayable as the Minister may determine. Section 18 authorises the Agents to borrow money only as provided by that section. Under s. 19 certain liabilities of the Agents and their subsidiaries are limited, and s. 20 authorises the Minister to make certain grants and loans to them. Any sums borrowed by the agents other than from the Minister may be guaranteed by the Treasury: s. 21. Section 22 requires the Agents to keep proper accounts and records and to prepare annual statements of accounts, and by s. 23 the Minister is empowered to give directions with respect to any aspect of the financial affairs of the Agents. The Agents are under a duty to insure against any insurable financial risks arising from their activities: s. 24.

Crown Agents Holding and Realisation Board
Section 25 establishes the Board as a corporate body, to be composed of the members of the Crown Agents. The primary duty of the Board is to realise the assets and discharge the liabilities vested in it by virtue of Schedule 5, which defines its powers. Section 26 provides that the liability of the pre-existing Agents to repay grants made to them shall cease and not become the liability of the Agents or the Board.

Miscellaneous and General
Section 27 exempts the Board and any wholly owned subsidiary from corporation tax and provides that the provisions of the Moneylenders Acts 1900 to 1927 shall not apply to the Crown Agents or the Board. The position as to the revenues of and alienations by the former Agents is dealt with by s. 28. Any administrative expenses incurred by the Minister in connection with the Act are payable out of Parliamentary funds: s. 29. Section 30 lays down the procedure for the making of orders and regulations and the giving of consents under the Act. Section 31 deals with interpretation, s. 32 with amendments, transitional provisions and repeals as set out in Schedules 6 and 7, and s. 33 with citation and extent.

319   **—— appointed day**

The Crown Agents Act 1979,(Appointed Day) Order 1979, S.I. 1979 No. 1672 (made on 11th December 1979), appoints 1st January 1980 as the day on which bodies corporate named the Crown Agents for Oversea Governments and Administrations and the Crown Agents Holding and Realisation Board are to come into being, to function under and in accordance with the Crown Agents Act 1979, para. 318.

320   **Kiribati Act 1979**

The Kiribati Act 1979 provides for the independence of Kiribati, formerly the Gilbert Islands, within the Commonwealth and for various connected matters, including nationality. The Act received the royal assent on 19th June 1979 and came into force on that date.

    Section 1 provides that the government of the United Kingdom ceased to be responsible for the government of Kiribati on 12th July 1979 and that no Act of the United Kingdom parliament passed on or after that date shall extend to Kiribati as part of its law, although any pre-existing rule of law or Act of the United Kingdom Parliament shall continue to have effect: s. 3. Kiribati may be constituted as a Republic by an Order in Council: s. 2. Section 5 provides for the retention of United Kingdom citizenship by certain citizens of Kiribati, including those having a close connection with the United Kingdom. Supplementary provisions are contained in ss. 4, 6–8 and the Schedule.

321   **Kiribati—appeal to Privy Council**

The Kiribati Appeals to Judicial Committee Order 1979, S.I. 1979 No. 720 (in force on 12th July 1979), makes provision in respect of appeals from the High Court of Kiribati to the Judicial Committee of the Privy Council.

322   **—— constitution**

The Kiribati Independence Order 1979, S.I. 1979 No. 719 (in force on 12th July 1979), provides for the constitution of the Gilbert Islands as an independent republic under the name Kiribati. The constitution provides for an elected legislature, an elected president and a Cabinet responsible to the legislature, and an independent judiciary and public service. It also makes provision for the protection of the fundamental rights and freedoms of the individual, for citizenship and for finance, and contains a chapter dealing with Banaba and the Banabans.

323   Malaysia—appeal to Privy Council

Malaysia

In a case concerning the procedure of criminal appeals to the Malaysian Federal Court and the monarch under the Courts of Judicature Act 1964, as amended by the Courts of Judicature (Amendment) Act 1976, it was held that where on 1st January 1978 (the date of commencement of the 1976 Act), there was no appeal to the monarch pending, there was no right to a special appeal.

LEE CHOW MENG V PUBLIC PROSECUTOR, MALAYSIA [1979] 1 WLR 1463 (Privy Council: LORD WILBERFORCE, LORD RUSSELL OF KILLOWEN and LORD KEITH OF KINKEL).

324   St. Christopher, Nevis and Anguilla—emergency legislation—detention of subject without reasons—damages

The plaintiff was imprisoned without trial under emergency legislation. No evidence was offered against him and he was subsequently released. He claimed damages for false imprisonment and compensation for his unlawful arrest and detention. He was awarded substantial damages by the West Indies Associated States Court of Appeal, including an unspecified small sum as exemplary damages, on the ground that the regulations under which he had been detained were unlawful. The appeal court felt bound to follow two of its previous decisions. The state appealed, contending that his imprisonment had been lawful and further that unquantified exemplary damages could not be awarded. *Held*, the emergency regulations were not themselves invalid, but the plaintiff's detention had been as no justification had been given for it. Exemplary damages did not have to be specified as a separate sum from any compensatory damages awarded. The appeal would accordingly be dismissed.

The court considered the West Indian court correct in considering itself bound by its previous decisions, as did the English Court of Appeal. Provided further appeal was possible, courts of appeal should follow their own decisions on points of law and leave it to the final court to correct any errors as to the law.

ATTORNEY-GENERAL OF ST CHRISTOPHER, NEVIS AND ANGUILLA V REYNOLDS [1979] 3 All ER 129 (Privy Council: LORD SALMON, LORD SIMON OF GLAISDALE, LORD FRASER OF TULLYBELTON, LORD RUSSELL OF KILLOWEN and LORD SCARMAN).

325   Saint Vincent—constitution

The Saint Vincent Constitution Order 1979, S.I. 1979 No. 916 (in force on 27th October 1979), provides a new constitution for Saint Vincent upon its attainment of fully responsible government within the Commonwealth with the style of Saint Vincent and the Grenadines at the termination of the status of association with the United Kingdom.

326   —— modification of enactments

The Saint Vincent Modification of Enactments Order 1979, S.I. 1979 No. 917 (in force on 27th October 1979), amends and modifies certain enactments, pursuant to the termination of association between the United Kingdom and Saint Vincent.

327   —— termination of association

The Saint Vincent Termination of Association Order 1979, S.I. 1979 No. 918 (in force on 27th October 1979), terminates the status of association of Saint Vincent with the United Kingdom, with effect from 27th October 1979.

328   Southern Rhodesia Act 1979

The Southern Rhodesia Act 1979 enables provision to be made, by Order in Council, for an independent constitution for Zimbabwe. The constitution will come into force on the attainment by Southern Rhodesia, in accordance with an Act of Parliament passed after this Act, of independence as the Republic of Zimbabwe.

The Act also enables provision to be made for the holding of elections prior to Southern Rhodesia attaining independence and in relation to the government of Southern Rhodesia in the period prior to independence. The Act received the royal assent on 14th November 1979, and came into force on that date.

Section 1 empowers Her Majesty to provide a constitution by Order in Council (which is required to be laid before Parliament after being made), and provides for the revocation of the Constitution of Southern Rhodesia 1961 (which is still in force although largely suspended).

Section 2 enables particular provisions of the new constitution to be brought into operation before independence, in order that the constitution can function from the date of independence (s. 2 (1), (2)). Orders under this section are required to be laid before Parliament, and expire at the end of twenty-eight days unless approved by resolution of each House (s. 2 (3)).

Section 3 provides for the making of Orders in Council for the government of Southern Rhodesia during the period up to independence (s. 3 (1)), including making provision for conferring power to make laws for the peace, order and good government of Southern Rhodesia, including laws having extra-territorial operation (s. 3 (3)). There is also power to deal with the consequences of the expiry of any provisions relating to sanctions, whether made under the Southern Rhodesia Act 1965, s. 2 or otherwise (s. 3 (2)). Certain Orders made under the 1965 Act (except those relating to sanctions) are carried forward notwithstanding that the authority for the making of those Orders may have expired (s. 3 (4)).

329 Southern Rhodesia—Commonwealth forces—jurisdiction

The Southern Rhodesia (Commonwealth Forces) (Jurisdiction) Order 1979, S.I. 1979 No. 1653 (in force on 12th December 1979), makes provision in relation to Commonwealth forces stationed in Southern Rhodesia. Such forces are to be subject to the service law of the Commonwealth country to which they belong and are to be exempt from criminal and civil process (but not arrest) under the law of Southern Rhodesia. There are also provisions for exempting Commonwealth forces in Southern Rhodesia from certain duties in Southern Rhodesia.

330 —— constitution—temporary provisions

The Southern Rhodesia Constitution (Interim Provisions) Order 1979, S.I. 1979 No. 1571 (ss. 1, 3 in force on 4th December 1979, the remainder in force on a day to be appointed), makes temporary provision for the government of Southern Rhodesia. The legislative and executive powers, and the prerogative of mercy, are, by the Order, vested in a Governor and he may give directions as to the authorities by whom executive powers may be exercised. All authorities in Southern Rhodesia are required to comply with the Governor's directions.

The Order also makes provision for the revocation or suspension of a number of earlier constitutional provisions and for the suspension of appeals to Her Majesty in Council.

331 —— consultations for constitutional settlement

The Southern Rhodesia (Immunity for Persons attending Meetings and Consultations) Order 1979, S.I. 1979 No. 820 (in force on 13th July 1979), confers upon persons present in the United Kingdom to attend meetings and consultations to achieve a constitutional settlement in Southern Rhodesia, immunity from suit and legal process and personal inviolability.

332

The Southern Rhodesia (Immunity for Persons attending Meetings and Consultations) (No. 2) Order 1979, S.I. 1979 No. 1374 (in force on 30th October 1979), confers upon persons present in the United Kingdom to attend meetings and consultations to achieve a constitutional settlement in Southern Rhodesia, immunity from suit and legal process and personal inviolability.

333   —— expiry of orders—consequential provisions

The Southern Rhodesia (Legal Proceedings and Public Liabilities) Order 1979, S.I. 1979 No. 1601 (in force on 7th December), revokes and replaces, in substantially the same terms, the Southern Rhodesia (Expiring Orders) (Consequential Provisions) Order 1979, S.I. 1979 No. 1445 (in force on 16th November, the date of expiry of the Southern Rhodesia Act 1965, s. 2).   The Order is designed to make provision consequential upon the lapse of certain Orders made under the Southern Rhodesia Act 1965, s. 2, and to ameliorate, and provide for, certain consequences of unconstitutional action in Southern Rhodesia.

The Order contains provisions relating to the Reserve Bank of Rhodesia Orders 1965 and 1967, to proceedings against and liabilities of, the Government of Southern Rhodesia, to the liability of the registrar and trustees of the sinking fund of any stock issued by that Government or for which that Government is responsible and to the records relating to such stock.

334   —— export of goods—removal of prohibition

See para. 768.

335   —— liability of Crown for acts of illegal regime—detention of Southern Rhodesian citizen

See *Mutasa v Attorney General*, para. 443.

336   —— sanctions

The Southern Rhodesia (United Nations Sanctions: Islands and Overseas Territories) (Revocations) Order 1979, S.I. 1979 No. 1655 (in force on 12th December 1979), revokes five Orders which were made under the United Nations Act 1946, s. 1 relating to sanctions, in order to give effect to the resolutions of the Security Council of the United Nations.

337   —— Zimbabwe

See paras. 342, 343, 344.

338   Statute Law (Repeals) Act 1976—extension to colonies

The Statute Law (Repeals) Act 1976 (Colonies) Order 1979, S.I. 1979 No. 111 (in force on 27th February 1979), provides for the extension of the repeals of certain specified enactments to the colonies mentioned in the Order.

339   Trinidad and Tobago—constitution—alleged infringement of human rights—failure to apply for statutory review—appropriate course of action

See *Harriksoon v A-G of Trinidad and Tobago*, para. 1449.

340   Turks and Caicos Islands—constitution

The Turks and Caicos Islands (Constitution) (Amendment) Order 1979, S.I. 1979 No. 919 (in force on 24th August 1979), amends the Turks and Caicos Islands (Constitution) Order 1976, 1976 Halsbury's Abridgment para. 338 by providing for the appointment of not more than two Parliamentary Secretaries.

341   Virgin Islands—constitution

The Virgin Islands (Constitution) (Amendment) Order 1979, S.I. 1979 No. 1603 (in force on a day to be appointed), amends the Virgin Islands (Constitution) Order 1976, 1976 Halsbury's Abridgment para. 340, providing for the possibility of the appointment of a third Minister to the Executive Council of the Virgin Islands.

342   Zimbabwe Act 1979

The Zimbabwe Act 1979 makes provision for the attainment by Southern Rhodesia of fully responsible status as a republic under the name of Zimbabwe and for connected matters, including the grant of an amnesty. The Act received the royal assent on 20th December 1979 and came into force on that date.

Section 1 provides for the establishment of the independent Republic of Zimbabwe and, in consequence for the cessation of the responsibility for Southern Rhodesia of the Parliament and Government of the United Kingdom. The date of independence is to be set by an Order in Council to be laid before Parliament after being made.

Section 2 and Sch. 1 make provision relating to nationality. By s. 2 the British Nationality Act 1948 is amended to remove Southern Rhodesia from the list of countries whose citizens are also British subjects or Commonwealth citizens. Schedule 1 saves for a limited period, the right of certain categories of persons to be registered as citizens of the United Kingdom and Colonies, notwithstanding that they will have ceased to have Commonwealth citizenship on the independence of Zimbabwe. (There is a consequential provision modifying the law relating to deportation in Sch. 2.)

Section 3 provides for an amnesty in the law of the United Kingdom, including immunity from action in tort or reparation, in respect of certain acts. These include the purported declaration of independence on 11th November 1965, the making of purported constitution for Southern Rhodesia, and acts done in the conduct or on the orders of organisations opposed to the successive administrations which purported to be the government of Southern Rhodesia or Zimbabwe Rhodesia, or by persons resisting such organisations.

Section 4 enables Her Majesty by Order in Council to modify enactments of the United Kingdom Parliament, or any instrument made under such an enactment, in consequence of Zimbabwe becoming independent as a republic or of the provisions about nationality in s. 2 (1). Provision may also be made for regulating the payment of claims against the Government of Zimbabwe out of assets in the United Kingdom.

Section 5 makes provisions for modifying any law in the event of Zimbabwe subsequently becoming a member of the Commonwealth. Orders under ss. 4 and 5 are required to be laid in draft before both Houses of Parliament and approved by resolution of both Houses before being made (ss. 4 (7), 5 (4)).

Section 6 and Sch. 2 provide for the continuance, after independence, of certain laws relating to persons and things connected with Zimbabwe, notwithstanding its change in status, and s. 6 and Sch. 3 repeal a number of measures and provisions relating to Southern Rhodesia in consequence of the change in its status.

Section 7 contains citation and definitions.

343   Zimbabwe—constitution

The Zimbabwe Constitution Order 1979, S.I. 1979 No. 1600 (in force on the day on which Southern Rhodesia becomes independent as a republic under the name of Zimbabwe), provides for the Constitution of Zimbabwe. The Constitution provides for a Parliament, a President and a Prime Minister and Cabinet responsible to the Parliament, as well as for the judiciary, the Public Service, the Prison Service, the Police Force and the Defence Forces. The Constitution also provides for the protection of the fundamental rights and freedoms of the individual, for citizenship and for finance. Transitional and interim provisions will be made by further Orders.

344   —— —— elections and appointments

The Southern Rhodesia (Constitution of Zimbabwe) (Elections and Appointments) Order 1979, S.I. 1979 No. 1654 (sections 3 (2), 4, 5, 6 (2), 7 in force on a date to be appointed, the remainder in force on 13th December 1979), makes provision for the holding of elections and the making of certain appointments in Southern Rhodesia for the purpose of enabling the Independent Constitution of Zimbabwe to function from Independence Day.

The Governor is required to make arrangements for the holding of elections to the House of Assembly and to the Senate and he is further authorised to appoint certain Senators. Provision is also made for the appointment of a Prime Minister and other Ministers and for the election of a President-elect.

COMPANIES

Halsbury's Laws of England (4th edn.), Vol. 7

345   Articles

Actions Against Limited Companies: Is the Rule in *Foss v Harbottle* Still Viable?, Ralph J. Henham: [1979] L S Gaz 1006.

A Gift Horse's Mouth, Barry McCutcheon (examination of reliefs introduced by the Finance Act 1978, 1978 Halsbury's Abridgment para. 2312, where the assets disposed of are shares in a family company): [1979] BTR 161.

Corporate Unveiling: Judicial Attitudes—1, Henry E. Markson: 123 Sol Jo 831

Department of Trade Investigations, John Hull (a review of the investigatory system of company inspectors): 129 NLJ 825.

Derivative Action in Company Law, D. W. Fox, A. N. Khan and M. L. Bowen (the case of *Daniels v Daniels* [1978] 2 WLR 73, 1977 Halsbury's Abridgment para. 381, as it extends the law propounded in *Foss v Harbottle*): 123 Sol Jo 429.

Directors' Disqualification Orders, A. N. Khan (courts' powers under Companies Act 1976, ss. 28, 29 to make a disqualification order against a person in default of the companies legislation): 122 Sol Jo 819.

Directors' Duties, Henry E. Markson (in the light of *Abbey Glen Property Corp v Stumborg* (1978) 85 DLR (3d) 35, para. 362): 129 NLJ 559.

Directors' Right to Inspect Books: Public Wrong or Private Right?, A. N. Khan (analysis of present law on company directors' right to inspect the books of their company): 123 Sol Jo 57.

Exempting the Directors, E. J. Rule and H. S. Brar (consideration of whether company director can contract with the company of which he is director): 129 NLJ 6.

Foreign Companies' Compliance with Company Law, David Milman (issues raised by the provisions of s. 106 of the Companies Act 1948 in the light of *Luckins v Highway Motel Pty Ltd* (1975) 50 ALJR 309); 123 Sol Jo 560.

Industrial Democracy—Participation or Control?, D. B. Broadbent (discussion on meaning of industrial democracy): 128 NLJ 1227.

Lending in the "Ordinary Course of Business", Keith Walmsley (with reference to *Fowlie v Slater* (1979) (unreported), para. 379 and *Steen v Law* [1964] AC 287): 129 NLJ 801.

Personal Liability on Company Cheques, Henry E. Markson (circumstances in which signatories of company cheques may incur personal liability): 122 Sol Jo 851.

Pooling Agreements under English Company Law, Stephen Kruger (a consideration of the contemporary situation with reference to New York Business Corporation Law): (1978) 94 LQR 557.

Powers of Directors and Receivers, James R. Campbell (the difference between English and Scots law on company receivers): 129 NLJ 261.

Proper Purpose Doctrine and the Companies Bill, Kenneth C. K. Chow (criticisms of the Companies Bill in relation to the proper purpose doctrine): 129 NLJ 123.

Section 54: The Slater Case and Proviso (a), R.C.B. Hopkins (discussion of *Fowlie v Slater* (1979) (unreported), para. 379 and its effect on scope of Companies Act 1948, s. 54 (1) (a)): 129 NLJ 1089.

Tax and Company Unveiling, Henry E. Markson (in the light of *Kinookimaw Beach Association v Board of Review Comrs* [1978] 6 WWR 749, para. 371): 129 NLJ 968.

346   **Accounts**

The Companies (Accounts) Regulations 1979, S.I. 1979 No. 1618 (in force on 31st December 1979) amend the requirements of the Companies Acts 1948 and 1967 regarding matters to be stated in the company's accounts. The changes relate to (i) the bands by reference to which the amount of directors' emoluments are to be shown which are increased to £5,000; (ii) thresholds for the stating of independent companies' turnover which are increased to £1,000,000; (iii) thresholds for the stating of the emoluments of directors of independent companies which are increased to £40,000. In the case of any company the threshold is increased to £10,000 and £5,000.

The Companies (Accounts) Regulations 1971 are revoked.

347   —— **negligent error in certified accounts—liability of auditors to third party**

New Zealand

A company relied, inter alia, on the consolidated accounts of a holding company and its subsidiaries in making a takeover offer for the shares in the holding company. The assets of the holding company were overstated because certain items had been included twice. The same error had been made in previous years and the holding company's auditors, although aware of some discrepancy, did not investigate and gave an unqualified certificate upon the accounts. The nature and extent of the error was discovered after the takeover was completed. The acquiring company, in reliance upon the principles enunciated in *Hedley Byrne and Co. Ltd v Heller and Partners Ltd* [1963] 3 All ER 575, brought an action against the auditors in negligence. *Held,* the test was whether the nature of the relationship between the parties was such that one party could fairly have been held to have assumed a responsibility to the other as regards the reliability of the advice or information. The annual accounts of a company were used for many purposes and auditors did not assume responsibility to all persons dealing with the company merely because it was reasonably foreseeable, in a general way, that a transaction of this nature might take place. The auditors did not know that the accounts were required as a basis for a takeover bid and were not liable to the acquiring company for negligent misstatement.

Scott Group Ltd v McFarlane [1978] 1 NZLR 553 (Supreme Court).

348   **Action by shareholder—representative action—action in tort— whether representative action should be permitted**

See *Prudential Assurance Co Ltd v Newman Industries Ltd,* para. 2152.

349   **Articles of association—provisions for remuneration of directors**

The Investment Protection Committee of the British Insurance Association has expressed concern at the practice of including in articles of association provisions under which the amount payable to directors by way of fees would not require the approval of the shareholders. The committee has indicated that insurance companies, as investors, would regard articles as acceptable if they provided either that directors might receive such amounts as were determined by the company in general meeting, or that the directors should be paid such amount as they themselves decided within a prescribed aggregate amount. See the Law Society Gazette, 24th October 1979, p. 1034.

350   **Auditors—financial involvement with client—disqualification**

The Institute of Chartered Accountants has issued its own Introductory Notes to the Explanatory Notes to Statement 1—Professional Independence, issued by the six CCAB bodies. The Explanatory Notes, which are common to all bodies, warn that financial involvement with a client may affect objectivity (note 7) and state that a practice should not have as an audit client a company in which a partner in the practice (or spouse or minor child) is the beneficial holder of shares, nor should it employ on the audit any member of staff who is a beneficial holder of such shares (note 8, to which there are limited exceptions). Similar restrictions are imposed on the audit of public companies if a partner is a trustee of a trust holding more than 10 per cent of its shares (note 12). Where shares are held in an audit company they should not be voted at a general meeting in relation to the appointment and remuneration of auditors (note 15). The full text of the statement with explanatory notes and introductory notes is set out in Accountancy, May 1979, pp. 45–47.

351   Business names—incorrect name on face of bill of exchange—bill signed by director—personal liability of director for sum owed

See *Maxform SpA v B. Mariani and Goodville Ltd*, para. 365.

352   Companies Act 1976—commencement

The Companies Act 1976 (Commencement No. 6) Order 1979, S.I. 1979 No. 1544 brought into force on 28th November 1979 s. 34 (1) and Sch. 1 of the Act so far as they were not already in operation.

353   Companies Court—applications and orders heard by registrar—exercise of functions by chief clerk

See para. 2113.

354   —— jurisdiction—order for possession—premises let to company being wound up

An order was made by the Companies Court for the winding up of a company which was the tenant of certain premises. The landlord applied to the Companies Court for an order for possession or alternatively for leave to commence an action for possession in the Queen's Bench Division. The registrar refused to make an order on the ground that it might affect third parties such as subtenants or mortgagees. Leave to commence an action in the Queen's Bench Division was given. The landlord sought a variation of the order. *Held*, an order for possession would not itself disturb the possession of third parties, but would merely cause the company to forfeit the lease. The point at which the rights of third parties might come into question was if the landlord were to seek to enforce the order by means of a writ of possession. If he were to do so, any third parties affected would have to apply for relief under the Law of Property Act 1925, s. 146 and the Rent Act 1977, s. 137, which enabled any such person to apply for relief in the action of the landlord, if any, or otherwise by action of his own. A winding up proceeding was not an "action" and therefore third parties could not apply for relief in the winding up but would have to do so in separate proceedings. Since an order for possession would thus not delay the winding up, such an order would be made.

RE BLUE JEANS SALES LTD [1979] 1 All ER 641 (Chancery Division: OLIVER J). *General Share and Trust Co v Wetley Brick and Pottery Co* (1882) 20 Ch D 260 applied.

355   —— proceedings in chambers—transaction of business by post

See para. 2114.

356   Company accounting and disclosure—EEC requirements—adoption

The government has stated that reform of the law relating to company accounting and disclosure is overdue. The existing requirements are no longer appropriate for large public companies and there is concern at the amount of detailed financial information at present required from small private companies. The existing law will have to be recast completely following the adoption in July 1978 of the EEC Fourth Directive on Company Law (EEC Directive 78/660). This change will be effected by a comprehensive statement of accounting requirements in place of the Companies Act 1948, Sch. 8. Less onerous requirements will be placed on small companies than on large ones. The government has issued a consultative document (Companies Accounting and Disclosure, Cmnd. 7654) in Part A of which it deals with its broad approach to company accounting and disclosure and covers a number of matters not directly linked to the EEC Fourth Directive. Part B of the document sets out the manner in which it proposes to incorporate the requirements of the Directive into English law. The text of the EEC Fourth Directive is set out in an Annex.

357   Debenture—appointment of receiver—collection of value added tax—discretion to pay tax to debenture holder

A bank, as the holder of a debenture issued by a company to secure its debts, appointed a receiver and manager of the company's property. The company carried on trading, and so continued to be a taxable person for the purpose of value added tax. The receiver issued a summons to determine whether he was entitled to collect the tax and apply the money in discharge of the moneys due under the debenture. *Held*, under Law of Property Act 1925, s. 109 (8), a receiver appeared to have a discretion in relation to a debenture holder as to whether or not to pay value added tax, since the debenture holder could not prevent him from paying but the Customs and Excise Commissioners could not sue him if he did not. However, it was not a true discretion because if the receiver did not pay the tax he would cause the company to commit a criminal offence.

RE JOHN WILLMENT (ASHFORD) LTD [1979] STC 286 (Chancery Division: BRIGHTMAN J).

358   —— —— receiver acting as company's agent—duty to account—detail required

A company executed a debenture in favour of a bank to secure an overdraft. Clause 4 of the debenture gave the bank power to appoint a receiver and manager who was deemed to be the company's agent. The bank called in the overdraft and, under the debenture, appointed the defendant as receiver. He continued to act until the debt to the bank was discharged and his receivership terminated. The company thereafter continued in business. In accordance with the Companies Act 1948, s. 372 (2) the defendant prepared two abstracts of his receipts and payments for the period of his receivership and sent them to the company. The company was, dissatisfied with the figures supplied and requested more information for the purpose of producing its audited accounts. The defendant refused to elaborate on the figures given on the ground that he had done all that he was required to do under s. 372 (2). The company brought proceedings against him claiming an account of receipts and payments during his receivership and an account of the calculation of his remuneration or a general account. The registrar adjourned the proceedings to the court for determination of a preliminary issue whether the defendant was under a duty to account to the company in more detail than that required under s. 372 (2). The defendant contended that, where a company was a borrower under a debenture governed by the Companies Acts, it had no equitable right to call on the receiver as an agent account to it, because the duty imposed on the directors of the company under the Companies Act 1976, s. 12 to keep accounts, coupled with the receiver's duty under s. 372 (2), replaced any equitable right the company might have had to call on the receiver to account. This was emphasised by s. 375 of the 1948 Act which provided a summary remedy to a member, creditor or registrar of companies, but not to the company itself where the receiver had failed in his duty laid down in s. 372 (2). *Held*, a receiver appointed under a debenture stating him to be an agent in practice ran the company on behalf of the directors. He was therefore answerable to the company for the conduct of its affairs and under a duty to keep a more detailed account than that required under s. 372 (2), producing it to the company when so required. To enforce such a right the company needed a remedy beyond that provided in s. 375. The receiver would be treated as an accounting party to the company.

SMITHS LTD V MIDDLETON [1979] 3 All ER 842 (Chancery Division at Manchester: BLACKETT-ORD V-C, VICE-CHANCELLOR OF THE COUNTY PALATINE OF LANCASTER). Dicta of Jenkins LJ in *Re B Johnson & Co (Builders) Ltd* [1955] 2 All ER 775 at 790 and Phillimore J in *R v Board of Trade, ex parte St Martin Preserving Co Ltd* [1964] 2 All ER 561 at 566 applied.

359   Department of Trade—annual report to Parliament

The Department of Trade in its Annual Report for 1978 (HMSO) has disclosed that at the end of 1978 there were 15,825 public companies on the register in Great Britain and 676,357 private companies; the corresponding figures for 1977 were 15,635 and 611,560. The figures exclude companies in liquidation or in the course of removal from the register. In 1978, 25,123 companies were removed from the register, including 17,841 which were struck off as defunct under the Companies Act 1948, s. 353, and 7,686 which were wound up voluntarily or under the supervision of the court; in 1977, 40,113 companies were removed from the register. During 1978, 2,245 summonses were issued for failure to forward annual returns (contrary to s. 126 of the 1948 Act) and there were 1,251 convictions for this offence. Appendix C of the report lists the companies treated as banking or discount companies for the purposes of the Protection of Depositors Act 1963 and for the purposes of the Companies Act 1948, Sch 8. Appendix D lists the accountants recognised by the department for the purposes of the 1948 Act, s. 161 (1) (a).

360   Director—commission of criminal offence under statute—meaning of "director" for purposes of statute

Australia
A man alleged to be a company director was convicted of acting dishonestly and not using reasonable diligence in the discharge of the duties of his office under Australian company legislation. On appeal from his conviction the question arose as to whether he was a director at the time of the alleged commission of the offences; for he had previously been properly appointed as a director, but had not been re-appointed in accordance with the company's articles, although he had continued to act as a director. Held, the legislation applied not only to properly appointed directors, but also to de facto directors who held over after their appointments had terminated, and the man was therefore a director within the meaning of the legislation at the time of the alleged offences.

CORPORATE AFFAIRS COMMISSION V DRYSDALE (1978) 22 ALR 161 (High Court of Australia).

361   —— disclosure of confidential information—covenant to restrict

See *Greer v Sketchly*, para. 2806.

362   —— fiduciary duties—dealings of directors with third party—liability to account for profit

Canada
The defendants had been directors of a land development company and as such had negotiated with a third party with a view to a joint undertaking between the two parties. The third party then refused to do business with the company and certain land transactions were therefore conducted between the third party and the directors personally. Between the date of the alleged breach of duty and the date of the action there was a complete change of shareholders and the successor to the company brought an action against the former directors for breach of fiduciary duty. Held, the defendants were liable to account for all the profits derived from the transaction. It was irrelevant that the third party had refused to deal with the company. Further, the court would reject the argument that the new shareholders would be unjustly

enriched if the directors were compelled to account to them. A change in the shareholders did not diminish the rigours of the obligation to account to the company, which remained unchanged in its character of a corporate entity.

ABBEY GLEN PROPERTY CORP v STUMBORG (1978) 85 DLR (3d) 35 (Supreme Court of Alberta). *Regal (Hastings) Ltd v Gulliver* [1942] 1 All ER 378, HL applied.

363 —— —— **director a shareholder in another company—duty to disclose interest**

Canada

The plaintiff, a shareholder and former director of the defendant company engaged in land development and construction business, brought an action against a director of that company under a Canadian provision corresponding to the Companies Act 1948, s. 199 relating to the duty of directors to disclose an interest in a contract. The director had personally accepted shares in another company which had been established to purchase land which the defendant company would then develop. *Held*, a director of a company who took a substantial personal interest in another company having important dealings with the former company was in breach of his fiduciary duty to the former company and, unless he made a disclosure to and secured the consent of the company, he would be liable to account to the company for the profits. The director was accordingly liable to account for his profits as no disclosure had taken place.

REDEKOP v ROBCO CONSTRUCTION LTD (1978) 89 DLR (3d) 507 (Supreme Court of British Columbia). *Regal (Hastings) Ltd v Gulliver* [1942] 1 All ER 378, HL and *Abbey Glen Property Corp v Stumborg* (1978) 85 DLR (3d) 35, para. 362, applied.

364 —— **personal liability—bill of exchange—cheque signed by director in name of company—company name incorrectly stated**

The managing director of a company drew a cheque on the company's account in favour of the plaintiff board to whom the company owed money. The cheque was signed by the director but did not contain the full name of the company. The cheque was therefore in breach of the Companies Act 1948, s. 108, which provides that directors of a company are personally liable on a bill of exchange or similar document if the name of the company is not mentioned in the document in legible characters and the company fails to pay it. The cheque was dishonoured, but the director agreed that he would pay the amount in instalments. When the company subsequently went into liquidation the board obtained summary judgment for the amount outstanding, The director's appeal was dismissed and he further appealed, contending that the liability of a person signing a cheque in contravention of s. 108 was analogous to the contractual liability of a surety. *Held*, there was no justification for the proposition that a person who was under the statutory liability created by s. 108 (4) was in the position of a surety which was a purely contractual liability. Section 108 imposed personal liability upon the signatory of a cheque for breach of statutory duty. The appeal would be dismissed accordingly.

BRITISH AIRWAYS BOARD v PARISH [1979] 2 Lloyd's Rep 361 (Court of Appeal: MEGAW and BRIDGE LJJ).

365 —— —— —— **incorrect company name on face of bill—bill signed by director**

Judgment was given against a company in respect of money owed on certain bills of exchange signed by its director, although the name given for the company on the face of the bill was its trading name, not its registered name. When the company did not pay the money owed, the holder of the bill sought to recover the money from the director personally under the Companies Act 1948, s. 108. That section provided that every bill of exchange which is purported to be signed on behalf of the company should show the company's name clearly and that if it did not a director who signed the bill would be personally liable for the amount stated to be payable. The director contended that the Registration of Business Names Act 1916 rendered the registered trading name sufficient and avoided the effect of s. 108. *Held*, the

1916 Act and its amendments were passed prior to 1948 and it was reasonable to assume that if Parliament had intended s. 108 to be affected by the 1916 Act it would have made express provision to that effect. The trading name which appeared on the face of the bill was not the name required by the section and therefore the director was personally liable.

MAXFORM SpA v B. MARIANI AND GOODVILLE LTD [1979] 2 Lloyd's Rep 385 (Chancery Division: MOCATTA J).

366 ———— **infringement of patent by company**

See *Mentmore Manufacturing Co Ltd v National Manufacturing Co Inc*, para. 2028.

367 **Forms**

The Companies (Forms) (Revocation) Order 1979, S.I. 1979 No. 1545 (in force on 17th December 1979), revokes the Companies Forms Order 1949, as amended, prescribing the forms required by the Companies Acts 1948-76. For provisions as to new forms see para. 369.

368 The Companies (Forms) (Revocation) Regulations 1979, S.I. 1979 No. 1546 (in force on 17th December 1979), revoke the Companies (Forms) Regulations 1967, which prescribed forms for the purposes of the Companies Act 1967, ss. 43 and 44.

369 The Companies (Forms) Regulations 1979, S.I. 1979 No. 1547 (in force on 17th December 1979), prescribe revised forms for the purposes of the Companies Acts 1948 to 1976. Existing forms may continue to be used until 16th December 1980.

370 **Investigation of company's affairs—disclosure of information to Secretary of State**

See Banking Act 1979, para. 192.

371 **Lifting the corporate veil—company formed by persons exempt from taxation—liability of company for taxation**

Canada
Seven bands of Indians incorporated a company in order to operate a resort providing amenities to the general public; the resort being on Indian land. The company was assessed to tax on the ground that it did not fall within the exemption from taxation on the property of Indians situated on reserves since it was a corporate entity. The company appealed against this assessment. *Held*, allowing the appeal, the corporate veil could be lifted to prevent tax-payers from avoiding tax, therefore it could also be lifted to give those intended to be exempt from tax the benefit of such exemption. The assessment would therefore be set aside.

KINOOKIMAW BEACH ASSOCIATION v BOARD OF REVIEW COMRS [1978] 6 WWR 749 (Court of Queen's Bench of Saskatchewan).

372 **Production of company's books—application for production by Director of Public Prosecutions—exercise of judge's jurisdiction to make order**

The Director of Public Prosecutions made an application under the Companies Act 1948, s. 441 (1) for an order for the production and inspection of a company's books, records, correspondence and papers, on the ground that he had reasonable cause to believe that a subordinate manager, being an officer of the company, had committed an offence in connection with the management of the company's affairs by sending out fraudulent statements containing exaggerated claims for money due to the company. By s. 441 (3) no appeal lay from the decision of the judge. The application was refused on the ground that the subordinate manager was not an officer of the company and an offence in connection with the management of the company's affairs was restricted to the situation where positive requirements relating to the management of a company had not been complied with. On appeal, *held*, s. 441 was designed to protect crimes from being hidden behind the corporate framework of a company, and extended to cases of suspected fraud, and a person exercising a function central to the administration of the company was an officer of the company within the ambit of s. 441. The judge had made an error of law in refusing jurisdiction to make an order under s. 441 and an appeal lay to the court. Therefore, notwithstanding the provision in s. 441 (3), the appeal would be allowed and an order drawn up.

RE A COMPANY [1980] 1 All ER 284 (Court of Appeal: LORD DENNING MR, SHAW and TEMPLEMAN LJJ).

373   Register of members—rectification—unauthorised issue of shares and entry in register—court's jurisdiction to rectify

A company issued 200,000 £1 ordinary shares to its parent company, LACOP, a company resident outside the scheduled territories, in return for sterling investments worth £200,000. LACOP's name was entered in the company register as the holder of the shares. Both companies innocently omitted to obtain Treasury permission for this transaction as required by the Exchange Control Act 1947. When they discovered their mistake the company, with LACOP's consent, applied under the Companies Act 1948, s. 116, for rectification of the register by striking out LACOP's name as the holder of the shares. The company intended to repay £150,000 to LACOP. *Held*, the court had jurisdiction to order rectification because, first, the issue of shares was void under ss. 8 (1) and 18 (1) of the 1947 Act. Secondly, the company was prohibited from entering LACOP's name in the register under s. 13 (*a*). Thus LACOP's name had been entered without sufficient cause within s. 116 of the 1948 Act. Although the order would appear to effect a reduction in the company's capital without the appropriate protection provided by the 1948 Act, in reality, because the shares in question were invalid, the company's issued capital was £200,000 less than it appeared. Furthermore the order would not contain an approval of the intention to repay the £150,000 and would not therefore affect any remedies the creditors might seek in respect of the repayment.

RE TRANSATLANTIC LIFE ASSURANCE CO LTD [1979] 3 All ER 352 (Chancery Division: SLADE J).

374   Registers and other records—use of computers

The Companies (Registers and other Records) Regulations 1979, S.I. 1979 No. 53 (in force on 12th February 1979), make provision with respect to registers and other records provided for under the Companies Acts 1948–76 which are kept by recording the matters in question otherwise than in a legible form. They stipulate the place where the duty provided for in the Stock Exchange (Completion of Bargains) Act 1976, s. 3 (3), to allow inspection of and to furnish reproductions of such registers and other records, is to be performed. They also make provision for the giving of notice of the place for inspection of such registers and modify the provisions of the Companies Acts relating to them.

375   Registration of charges—floating equitable charge—creation— retention of title clause in contract

See *Re Bond Worth Ltd*, para. 1137; *Borden (U.K.) Ltd v Scottish Timber Products Ltd*, para. 1138.

376   —— whether transactions assignments or charges

Under a provision in the Northern Ireland Companies Act 1960 corresponding to the Companies Act 1948, s. 25, a charge on book debts of a company is void against the liquidator unless it has been duly registered. A block discounting agreement under which the plaintiffs made advances to the defendant company, which had later gone into liquidation, in respect of blocks of credit sale agreements, provided for the absolute assignment of the company's customers' debts to the plaintiffs. The assignments were not registered. In practice however, the parties departed from the terms of the agreement and the liquidator contended that the true effect of the transactions had been to create charges on the book debts, which were invalid against the liquidator. This contention was rejected by the Court of Appeal; on appeal against its decision, *held*, the agreement was an essential element of the parties' contractual intentions and the assignments were made under it. To suppose that the assignments were not made by way of sale, but by way of security, would have been to impose a totally different form of transaction from that which the parties had selected. There was no agreement to abandon the agreement nor to alter its terms. Accordingly the transactions were absolute assignments and the appeal would be dismissed.

LLOYDS AND SCOTTISH FINANCE LTD v CYRIL LORD CARPETS SALES LTD (1979) (unreported) (House of Lords: LORD WILBERFORCE, VISCOUNT DILHORNE, LORD SALMON, LORD KEITH OF KINKEL and LORD SCARMAN). Decision of the Court of Appeal, sub nom *Lloyds and Scottish Finance Ltd v Prentice* (1977) Times 3rd November, 1977 Halsbury's Abridgment para. 384 affirmed. *Olds Discount Co Ltd v Playfair Ltd* [1938] 3 All ER 275 followed.

377   **Resolution—special resolution—notice specifying intention to propose resolution—validity**

On 2nd April 1979 a company sent notices to its shareholders convening an extraordinary general meeting at which a special resolution was to be proposed that the company's share premium account be cancelled. At the meeting, on 26th April, an amended special resolution was passed that the premium be reduced instead of cancelled. A petition was presented for confirmation of the reduction. *Held*, under the Companies Act 1948, s. 141 (2), a special resolution had to be passed at a general meeting of which not less than twenty-one days' notice specifying the intention to propose the resolution as a special resolution had been duly given. The resolution passed had to be the same as that specified. The resolution passed in this case differed from that specified, both in form and in substance. The notices had not specified the text of the resolution passed or its substance and hence were invalid. Although grammatical or clerical errors could be corrected, or words reduced to more formal language, the substance had to be identical. Accordingly the court had no jurisdiction to confirm the reduction and the petition would be dismissed.

RE MOORGATE MERCANTILE HOLDINGS LTD [1980] 1 All ER 40 (Chancery Division: SLADE J).

378   **Shares—issue of redeemable preference shares not in accordance with company's articles—validity of issue**

A company brought an action claiming that a purported issue of its preference shares was ultra vires. The articles of association incorporated the Table A articles, Part I, arts. 2 and 3. Article 2 provided that preference shares could be issued on the passing of an ordinary resolution. Article 3 provided that where redeemable preference shares were sanctioned by the passing of an ordinary resolution, the terms upon which they could be redeemed should be determined by special resolution. An extraordinary general meeting of the company passed a special resolution sanctioning the issue of forty eight thousand redeemable preference shares; however the terms of redemption were not stated in the resolution, but in a statement made after the purported issue of the shares. *Held*, the purported issue was ultra vires, as a further special resolution should have been passed in accordance with article 3, fixing the terms upon which the shares were to be redeemed.

E. PEARSE & CO LTD v OLIVER (1979) 7th February (unreported) (Chancery Division: OLIVER J).

379   **—— purchase of shares—loan to purchase holding company's shares—whether lending money in ordinary course of business**

Company A lent a total of three million pounds to company B, who then used the money to purchase shares in company C, the parent company of company A.

Under the Companies Act 1948, s. 54(1) it is unlawful to grant loans to assist in the purchase of the holding company's shares, and the defendant, as an officer of company A, was charged with authorising such a loan. By a proviso in s. 54(1) there is no prohibition on the lending of the money by the company in the ordinary course of business, if lending money is part of the ordinary course of business, and the defendant sought to rely on this proviso. Company A was in fact an investment bank and a major part of its loan business consisted of making large loans to individual borrowers. Company B was a share dealing company, and although it was not a subsidiary of company C its directors were also employees of company C and it was under the de facto control of company C. It was found that the loans to company B were for the specific purpose of projected deals which would have ultimately benefited company C. The magistrates upheld the defendant's contention and on appeal, *held*, the loan to company B was normal in the context of company A's ordinary business. However, the proviso was not to be read as exempting particular loan transactions made for identifiable purposes. The proviso did not therefore apply and the appeal would be allowed.

FOWLIE V SLATER (1979) 23rd March (unreported) (Queen's Bench Division: LORD WIDGERY CJ, MICHAEL DAVIES and NEILL JJ). *Steen v Law* [1963] 3 All ER 770, PC followed.

380   **Winding up—distribution of assets—overpayment to share-holders by liquidator—whether overpayment recoverable**

Scotland

A private company went into members' voluntary liquidation and a liquidator was appointed. He died before the winding up was complete and it was discovered that he had underestimated the amount of tax due and had overpaid the shareholders. His successor as liquidator brought an action against the trustees of the principal shareholder claiming repayment of the money which was paid to them in excess of what was due, contending that the error was not one of law but of fact, in that his predecessor had miscalculated the money which he had available for distribution. *Held*, the error was an error of law, being a misinterpretation of a public taxing statute, the provisions of which the liquidator was under a statutory duty to take into account. Although there were exceptions to the general rule that an error of law was a bar to such a claim, this was not one of them and the claim would be dismissed.

TAYLOR V WILSON'S TRUSTEES (1975) 1979 SLT 105 (Inner House).

381   —— —— **priority of payments—corporation tax on chargeable gain**

Following the commencement of winding up proceedings certain properties of the company were sold, realising a profit, and consequently rendering the company liable for corporation tax in respect of the chargeable gains realised. The liquidator sought the court's determination whether the corporation tax was part of the "fees or other expenses properly incurred in preserving, realising or getting in the assets" of the company within the meaning of the Companies (Winding Up) Rules 1949, r. 195 (1), or a "necessary disbursement" of the liquidator within the meaning of that rule, or whether in any event the liability for the tax was part of the "costs, charges or expenses incurred in the winding up" within the meaning of the Companies Act 1948, s. 267. *Held*, (i) the company was bound to pay the tax and the liquidator was the proper officer to pay it. The liability to tax was therefore a "necessary disbursement" of the liquidator within r. 195 (1) but not an "expense incurred in . . . realising . . . the asset" since it was not a direct consequence of the realisation of the company's assets. (ii) The discharge of the liability for tax was a "charge or expense incurred" in the winding up within the Companies Act 1948, s. 267.

RE MESCO PROPERTIES LTD [1979] STC 778 (Court of Appeal: BUCKLEY, BRIDGE and TEMPLEMAN LJJ). Decision of Brightman J [1979] STC 11, 1978 Halsbury's Abridgment para. 372 affirmed.

382   —— fees

The Companies (Department of Trade) Fees (Amendment) Order 1979, S.I. 1979 No. 779 (in force on 23rd July 1979) increases from £3.75 to £5.75 the fee payable for insertion in the London Gazette of notices relating to companies in compulsory winding up.

383   The Companies (Department of Trade) Fees (Amendment No. 2) Order 1979, S.I. 1979 No. 1591 (in force on 1st January 1980), amends the Companies (Department of Trade) Fees Order 1975, 1975 Halsbury's Abridgment para. 397. The order abolishes the use of adhesive stamps, and the individual fees payable for the insertion in the London Gazette of notices relating to companies being wound up by the court. From 1st January 1980 an element for Gazette notices is included within an increased stationery fee. In cases where the winding up order was made before 1st January 1980 a flat fee is charged to cover all future Gazette notices.

384   —— issue of writ by creditor prior to winding-up—subsequent application for leave to continue action—exercise of court's discretion

The plaintiff creditors issued a writ in rem in respect of damages against a ship before its owners went into liquidation. The ship had already been arrested by another set of creditors. The plaintiffs did not serve the writ or arrest the vessel but merely entered a caveat in the Admiralty register. After the winding-up order was made against the owners, the plaintiffs applied under the Companies Act 1948, s. 231, for the court's leave to continue the action started before the winding-up. Leave was refused on the grounds that the plaintiffs had not served the writ or arrested the vessel and were therefore not secured creditors who would be entitled to priority over other unsecured creditors. The plaintiffs appealed. *Held*, the question was whether the plaintiffs had become secured creditors when they issued the writ and had thereby acquired a charge or lien. If they had, it was unarguable that they should have been given leave under s. 231 to proceed with the action and establish their claim. The discretion under s. 231 gave the court freedom to do what was right and fair in the circumstances. There was no virtue in confining relief under the section to a claimant who had served a writ on the ship as distinct from a claimant who had issued a writ but not served it. Leave ought to have been granted to the plaintiffs under s. 231 even if it was incorrect to regard them as secured creditors at the commencement of the winding up and accordingly the appeal would be allowed.

RE ARO CO LTD (1979) Times, 30th November (Court of Appeal: STEPHENSON, BRANDON and BRIGHTMAN LJJ). Decision of Oliver J [1979] 1 All ER 32, 1978 Halsbury's Abridgment para. 368, reversed.

385   —— order—effect upon authority of company's agent

In a contract for the sale of certain businesses, it was provided that an audited profit and loss account of the businesses should be delivered to the sellers by a specified date. Before such delivery took place, a petition was presented for the compulsory winding up of the sellers' company. A receiver was appointed and a winding up order made. Subsequently an audited profit and loss account was received by the sellers' solicitors. The receiver contended that the contract had not been completed as delivery of the profit and loss account to the solicitors did not amount to delivery to the sellers. *Held*, on the true construction of the contract, "seller" meant the seller acting through its officers and servants or any other duly authorised agent. In the agreement, the sellers had held out the solicitors to be their solicitors for all purposes connected with the agreement. The solicitors had either express or ostensible authority to accept delivery of the profit and loss account on the sellers' behalf.

The next question was what effect the appointment of the receiver and the winding up order had upon the solicitors' authority. Although the appointment of a receiver out of court did not operate to dismiss the company's servants or terminate its agents' authority, the making of a compulsory winding up order did so. Thereafter the solicitors had no actual authority, but still had ostensible authority until the buyer had actual or constructive notice of some event which rendered the sellers' representation no longer one upon which the buyer was entitled to rely. No such notice was received until after the delivery of the profit and loss account. Hence the delivery was good. Finally, the sellers were bound by the European Communities Act 1972, s. 9 (4), so that they were incapable of saying that by reason of the winding up order the solicitors were not their agents for the purpose of the receipt of the account, and the receiver could stand in no better position.

Re Peek Winch and Tod Ltd (1979) 130 NLJ 116 (Court of Appeal: Buckley, Shaw and Brandon LJJ).

386 —— petition—petition by creditor—petition opposed by contributory—exercise of court's discretion to grant adjournment

The creditor of a company presented a petition for winding up the company. The company was unable to pay its debts under the Companies Act 1948, ss. 222 (e) and 223 (d). A director, who was also a contributory of the company, opposed the petition and applied for its adjournment, alleging that the company's inability to pay its debts was the fault of its other director-contributory, and if it was allowed to continue operating it could become solvent again. The creditor opposed the adjournment and sought an immediate winding up order. *Held*, where a winding up petition was presented by a creditor who proved that he was unpaid and that the company was unable to pay its debts, he was prima facie entitled to a winding up order. The court had a discretion under ss. 225 (1) and 346 (1) of the 1948 Act to consider the wishes of contributories but far less weight would be attached to those wishes as compared with those of an unpaid creditor. On the facts in the instant case the petition should not be adjourned.

Re Camburn Petroleum Products Ltd [1979] 3 All ER 297 (Chancery Division: Slade J).

387 —— —— —— voluntary liquidation already in existence—exercise of court's discretion

A wholly owned subsidiary company was placed in voluntary liquidation by the parent company which then, in its capacity as an unsecured creditor, presented a petition to wind up compulsorily, on the grounds that a compulsory liquidation would realise the assets of the insolvent company more quickly and economically. The petition was supported by an associated company, which was also an unsecured creditor, but was opposed by seven independent creditors who wished the voluntary liquidation to continue but whose total unsecured indebtedness was far less than that of either the petitioning or supporting company. At first instance the petition was dismissed, the judge taking the view that the voluntary liquidation should continue. On appeal it was contended that an unpaid creditor in respect of an undisputed debt was prima facie entitled as of right to a winding up order and if the creditors disagreed amongst themselves, when exercising its discretion under the Companies Act 1948, s. 346, the court had to give effect to the views of the majority in value unless there were exceptional circumstances. *Held*, under s. 346 the court had an unfettered discretion whether or not to make a compulsory winding up order on a petition by an undisputed creditor. Although the views of the majority of creditors in value was a factor to be taken into account, it was not decisive and the court had to consider the interests of the other creditors. Under the circumstances, particularly in view of the relationship between the petitioning creditor, the supporting creditor and the debtor, the judge had been justified in taking into account all the considerations he did and had not left out of account any relevant matter. He had thus properly exercised his discretion.

Re Southard and Co Ltd [1979] 3 All ER 556 (Court of Appeal: Buckley, Bridge and Templeman LJJ). Decision of Brightman J [1979] 1 All ER 582 affirmed.

388   —— —— petition by receiver—locus standi to present petition

A company executed a debenture in favour of a bank; under it the bank was empowered to appoint a receiver at any time after repayment had been demanded, such receiver to be the agent of the company. The articles of the company incorporated Table A, art. 80, stipulating that the company should be managed by the directors, who could exercise all the powers of the company except those required by statute or the articles to be exercised by the company in general meeting. A receiver was appointed by the bank and he presented a petition for compulsory winding up of the company. The petition was later amended to be the petition of the company by the agency of the receiver. On a question of whether the receiver was entitled to present the petition, *held*, art. 80 did not confer power on the directors to present a winding up petition; a petition could only be presented if their decision had been ratified in general meeting. However, whilst the receiver could not present a petition by reason of the directors' powers being vested in him, the presentation of the petition was incidental and conducive to the powers conferred on him under the debenture. The protection and preservation of the assets of the company were incidental to his power to take possession of them. The court would exercise its discretion and make a winding up order.

RE EMMADART LTD [1979] 1 All ER 599 (Chancery Division: BRIGHTMAN J).

389   —— —— presentation   by   unauthorised   person—whether petition capable of ratification in general meeting

The articles of a company stated that the quorum for a directors' meeting was two, and that one could act alone only if there was no other director for the time being. One of the two original directors made an invalid appointment of a solicitor as company secretary, and the latter then issued notice of an extraordinary general meeting to remove the other director from office, and presented a winding up petition on the company's behalf. The second director challenged this because the solicitor had no right to act in the company's name, and accordingly the first director purported to make another appointment to the board, to issue himself with a majority of the company's shares and to ratify both the solicitor's appointment as company secretary and the presentation of the winding up petition. The second director sought to prevent prosecution of the petition on the ground that it was an abuse of the process of the court. *Held*, the court would be entitled to continue the hearing if it considered the company in general meeting would authorise the petition, and would do so if it was clear the petitioner had control of the voting power. However, this would only apply if authorisation could be sought and was certain to be given. In this case there was no time to call a general meeting and as such a meeting would not give authorisation the petition was an abuse of the process of the court.

RE BUSHEY MOTORS LTD (1979) 16th January (unreported) (Chancery Division: OLIVER J).

390   —— property available for distribution—discovery of property— court's power to order private examination

A company executed charges in favour of certain banks. It was subsequently compulsorily wound up and a liquidator was appointed. He considered that the charges constituted fraudulent preference and were void, having been executed at a time when the company was unable to pay its debts. He told the banks that he was instructing solicitors to take proceedings and that papers were with counsel. However, he did not commence proceedings and requested further information from the banks concerning the charges. The banks refused to give the information and the liquidator applied for an order under the Companies Act 1948, s. 268, to examine the bank officials and for production of documents in their custody. The order was granted and the banks sought its discharge or variation on the ground that before he made the application the liquidator had decided to issue proceedings against the banks and to grant the order would afford him a special advantage by way of early discovery not available to an ordinary litigant. *Held*, when a liquidator had already commenced litigation or made a firm decision to do so, an order would normally be refused if his purpose was to achieve an advantage beyond that available to an ordinary litigant. However, where his object was merely to elicit information to enable him to decide whether there was a valid claim, the court would approach the application without any predisposition to refuse it. The evidence showed that following counsel's advice the liquidator had decided to defer proceedings until he obtained further information. His application came clearly within the purpose and intention of s. 268 and any potential hardship to the banks was outweighed by the public interest in the completion of the liquidation. The banks' motion would be dismissed.

RE CASTLE NEW HOMES LTD (IN LIQUIDATION) [1979] 2 All ER 775 (Chancery Division: SLADE J). *Re North Australian Territory Co* (1890) 45 Ch D 87 and dicta of Buckley J in *Re Rolls Razor Ltd* [1968] 3 All ER 698 at 700 applied.

391   In April 1970, a company which had just paid a substantial interim dividend was having serious liquidity problems. On 1st May, its merchant bankers agreed to underwrite an issue of ordinary shares and on 13th May its auditors produced a report. On 15th May the merchant bankers refused to underwrite the issue. The company then collapsed; an order was made for its compulsory winding up and a liquidator was appointed. In 1974 the liquidator applied for an order under the Companies Act 1948, s. 268, for the examination of a partner in the firm of auditors and for production of certain documents relating to the company. The order was made and the partner moved to discharge it on the ground that it would be unfair and oppressive to make it since it was clear that the liquidator was contemplating bringing an action against him. *Held*, in deciding whether to make an order for examination of a person under s. 268, the court should consider not whether proceedings against him were imminent but the reason why the liquidator was seeking the order. An order would not be granted where it was apparent that s. 268 was being used in an unfair, oppressive or vexatious way; for example, by improving the liquidator's position as a litigant in subsisting litigation. However, an order would normally be made where no writ had been issued and the order was fairly required by the liquidator to assist him in the discharge of his duties, one of which was to decide whether, and against whom, an action should be brought. In the circumstances, there were no grounds for discharging the order and the motion would be dismissed.

RE SPIRAFLITE LTD (1974) [1979] 2 All ER 766 (Chancery Division: MEGARRY J).

392   ——**rules**

The Companies (Winding-up) (Amendment) Rules 1979, S.I. 1979 No. 209 (in force on 1st April 1979), amend the Companies (Winding Up) Rules 1949 in several respects, including those rules relating to the advertisements of petitions. Such advertisements can now be confined to the London Gazette and can be restrained until after service. Provision is made for a shorter form of advertisement.

393   The Companies (Winding-up) (Amendment No. 2) Rules 1979, S.I. 1979 No. 1592 (in force on 1st January 1980), amend the Companies (Winding-up) Rules 1949 so as to take account of the Companies (Department of Trade) Fees (Amendment No. 2) Order 1979, see para. 383, which abolishes the use of adhesive stamps for the payment of fees and the separate fee for the insertion of notices in the London Gazette.

394   ——**voluntary winding up—stock issued at discount—creditor's right to recover stock with unpaid interest—application of bankruptcy rules**

In 1972 a company made an issue of Unsecured Loan Stock at 7 per cent discount, with interest at $9\frac{3}{4}$ per cent per annum. The stock was constituted by a trust deed between the company and the appellants, trustees of the stock, which provided for further issues of stock on identical terms, to rank pari passu and to form a single series with the first issue. A further issue was subsequently made at par with interest at the contractual rate. In January 1976 the company went into creditor's voluntary liquidation and the trustees claimed unpaid interest on the whole stock from December 1974 to the date of the commencement of the winding up and repayment of the outstanding principal, with no reduction in respect of the 7 per cent discount given on the first issue of stock. Under the Companies Act 1948, s. 317 the rules of the law of bankruptcy as to the estates of bankrupts apply to the rights of creditors and debts provable on the winding up of an insolvent company. The Bankruptcy Act 1914, s. 66 (1) provides that where a debt is proved and includes interest or any pecuniary consideration in lieu of interest the interest is to be calculated at a rate not exceeding 5 per cent. Relying on s. 66 (1) the liquidator thus rejected the claim for interest, on the grounds that the interest actually paid until December 1974 averaged out at a rate in excess of 5 per cent in respect of the period in which no interest had been paid. He further maintained that the discount on the first issue constituted a pecuniary consideration in lieu of interest, and he therefore required the trustees to identify, at their own expense, the outstanding stock of the first issue in order to make the necessary reduction. At first instance the judge dismissed the claim for interest but held that the trustees were entitled to recover the full amount of the outstanding stock. The trustees appealed as to interest and the liquidator cross-appealed as to the principal. *Held*, (i), s. 66, being a general rule in force under the law of bankruptcy relating to debts provable in bankruptcy, applied to the present case by virtue of s. 317, with the result that a debt with interest was provable but inferior to other debts; (ii), the trustees were entitled to interest at 5 per cent in respect of their claim for unpaid interest, the balance being deferred: nothing received by the creditor prior to the period in question was relevant; and (iii), the discount allowed on the first issue was merely an inducement, taking effect as a condition of the issue of the stock that interest would be calculated on the full nominal value of the stock, rather than the 93 per cent actually advanced: the trustees were therefore entitled to the full nominal value of the outstanding stock. The appeal would be allowed in part and the cross-appeal dismissed.

RE JESSEL SECURITIES LTD (1978) 21st December (unreported) (Court of Appeal: BUCKLEY, GOFF and EVELEIGH LJJ).

COMPULSORY ACQUISITION OF LAND

Halsbury's Laws of England (4th edn.), Vol. 8, paras. 1–400

395   Articles

Boundaries of Equivalent Reinstatement, H. W. Wilkinson (whether compensation for compulsory purchase should be on market value basis or equivalent reinstatement basis): 129 NLJ 1043.

Challenging a Compulsory Purchase Order, Alec Samuels (possibilities of effectively challenging a compulsory purchase order): [1979] JPL 72.

396   Compensation—assessment—agricultural holding—licence to farm surrendered land—reduction of compensation

A yearly agricultural tenancy was surrendered to the acquiring authority on the compulsory acquisition of the land subject to the tenancy. The surrender agreement expressly incorporated the Land Compensation Act 1973, s. 48, concerning compensation. It made an additional provision that the tenants were to be granted a gratuitous licence for three years and three months to farm part of the land surrendered. The question arose whether the benefit of the licence should be set off against the compensation payable to the tenants. The Lands Tribunal held that it should be set off, and the tenants appealed. *Held*, SIR DAVID CAIRNS dissenting, the clause concerning the surrender was expressed to contain various benefits which the authority promised to grant to the tenants as a reward for the voluntary surrender, including payment of compensation to which they were entitled under s. 48 and the grant of the licence. Hence it was clear that the clause was intended to convey a benefit and not a detriment, and should be read as giving the tenants, and not the council, any profit which might accrue from the farming activities under the licence. The appeal would be allowed and the compensation increased accordingly.

WAKERLEY v ST EDMUNDSBURY BOROUGH COUNCIL (1978) 249 Estates Gazette 639 (Court of Appeal: ROSKILL and GEOFFREY LANE LJJ and SIR DAVID CAIRNS). Decision of the Lands Tribunal (1977) 33 P & CR 497, 1977 Halsbury's Abridgment para. 419 reversed.

397   —— —— Lands Tribunal decisions

ALI v NOTTINGHAM CITY COUNCIL (1979) 249 Estates Gazette 1284: Sir Douglas Frank QC (compulsory purchase order made in respect of unfit house bought by claimant less than two years before making of order; claim for owner-occupier's supplement under Housing Act 1969, Sch. 5; acquiring authority submitted Lands Tribunal had no jurisdiction in the matter as Sch. 5, para. 1 (2) (a) provided that supplement was payable "if the authority are satisfied" that claimant had made all reasonable inquiries about likelihood of compulsory purchase order, and in this case the authority were not so satisfied; submission upheld; court would not interfere unless authority acted perversely, which it had not).

398   DAWSON v NORWICH CITY COUNCIL (1978) 250 Estates Gazette 1297: V. G. Wellings QC (local authority with compulsory purchase powers bought agricultural holding from landlord and gave tenant notice to quit on ground land required for non-agricultural use; tenant elected to claim compensation from acquiring authority under the Land Compensation Act 1973, s. 59 which applies when notice to quit served after authority has agreed to purchase landlord's holding; authority contended election ineffective as s. 59 applied only when notice to quit served by private landlord not authority; tenant also claimed compensation to be assessed taking account of power landlord would have had to determine tenancy on ground of requirement for non-agricultural use; s. 59 applied whether notice served by landlord or authority; when assessing compensation, tenant entitled to his true loss only and assessor not bound to consider landlord's power to determine tenancy).

399   DICCONSON HOLDINGS LTD v ST HELENS METROPOLITAN BOROUGH COUNCIL [1979] RVR 69: V. G. Wellings QC (plaintiffs sought compensation in respect of the compulsory purchase of their land, which they claimed would provide the best access to certain agricultural land ripe for residential development; local authority accepted that the plaintiffs were entitled to compensation in respect of the probable grant of planning permission for their own land, but contended that the agricultural land was not likely to be developed and that the plaintiffs' land would not provide reasonable access; tribunal upheld plaintiffs' claim).

400   EVANS v GLASGOW DISTRICT COUNCIL [1979] RVR 258: W. A. Elliott QC (compulsory purchase of premises in which claimant carried on printing business as yearly tenant in 1967; claimant allowed to remain; final notice to quit given in 1975; claim for disturbance payment for removal expenses and temporary loss of profits until business sold, due to financial difficulties, in 1977; authority contended that claimant should have closed down business and avoided removal expenses, having regard to his age (sixty years) and financial position of business; claimant had acted reasonably in deciding to carry on business at new premises; sum for temporary loss of profits reduced as certain other factors (flood damage, loss of custom of associated company, additional borrowed capital) had contributed to losses and were not attributable to displacement; promised gratuities to staff were not part of reasonable expenses of removal).

401   KHAN v BIRMINGHAM CITY COUNCIL [1978] RVR 231: E. C. Strathon FRICS (compulsory purchase of freehold interest in house; one room in house owner-occupied, remainder let to weekly tenants; claimant entitled to owner-occupier's supplement in respect of his own room only; full compulsory purchase value was not to be assessed on the basis of vacant possession, but on the basis of subsisting tenancies).

402   MIT SINGH V DERBY COUNTY COUNCIL (1979) 37 P & CR 527: W. H. Rees FRICS (claim for owner-occupier compensation after compulsory acquisition of house; house let to tenant during qualifying period subject to arrangement that claimant's son should sleep in back-bedroom; parties reached agreement on price for value of owner-occupier's compensation; council contended that as value had been agreed tribunal had no jurisdiction; if tribunal had jurisdiction, council contended that claimant did not qualify for compensation as had not been in occupation of house for whole of qualifying period; tribunal had jurisdiction as agreement for amount of compensation was conditional agreement only; tenant had had real control over whole house during qualifying period; son's position was similar to that of lodger; the owner's claim would fail).

403   SADIK AND SADIK V LONDON BOROUGH OF HARINGEY (1979) 37 P & CR 120: J. D. Russell-Davies FRICS (in assessing compensation for the compulsory purchase of a house owned by Turkish Cypriots with no knowledge of English, a tribunal accepted that the assessment should include the sum paid for the services of an interpreter, but warned that each claim under that head should be carefully assessed).

404   WATERWORTH V BOLTON METROPOLITAN BOROUGH COUNCIL (1979) 37 P & CR 104: E. C. Strathon FRICS (claimant sold part of land to local authority in 1972; he wanted to sell the remainder to a property company for residential development but the authority refused planning permission because it considered that the land should be maintained as an open space; an appeal to the Secretary of State failed because there was no easy access to the land; in 1975 claimant sold land to another company which was developing neighbouring land for residential use and therefore had no access problem; company obtained planning permission in 1976; in claiming compensation for severance of the land in 1972, the claimants alleged that the planning permission was irrelevant, because it was the authority which had prevented a claim being made at the date of severance; tribunal upheld authority's contention that the assessment should be based on the loss caused to the claimant by severance, not the value of the land on that date; deferment of the planning permission was acceptable in the circumstances and the assessment would be made on that basis).

405   WILKINSON V MIDDLESBROUGH BOROUGH COUNCIL (1979) 63/1978 (unreported) (compulsory purchase of land comprising large multi-partnered veterinary practice; claimants contended that compensation was payable on reinstatement value; one of the criteria to be satisfied was that land was devoted to a purpose of such a nature that there was no demand or market for land for that purpose; it was the custom in the area in question not to sell or buy practices on the open market but to enlarge practices by increasing the numbers of partners; thus although there was no market in respect of multi-partnered practices this was caused by the system; the tribunal considered that but for such a system there would be a market; compensation would therefore be assessed on the open market value and not on the basis of reasonable cost of equivalent reinstatement).

406   **—— —— leasehold interest—uncertain freeholder**

A local authority compulsorily purchased a leasehold interest in land with uncertain freehold title. On the question of compensation, deductions from the agreed freehold value of the land were made by the Lands Tribunal in respect of the cost of a lay-by constructed by the council, legal fees and insurance premiums for an indemnity against a third party claiming the freehold title. In addition, the freeholder with uncertain title was deemed to accept a fixed sum and not claim a half interest and a deduction was made of this fixed sum. On appeal by the council, *held*, the council's contention that the Tribunal had failed to decide whether the reputed freeholder was in the market as a purchaser, was incorrect. There was no reason to suppose that the reputed freeholder had abandoned all interest in the development of the land. Evidence could be adduced to show that he had kept his position open, the decision relating to his own compensation having been adjourned until the outcome of this decision. The appeal would be dismissed.

HONISETT v ROTHER DISTRICT COUNCIL [1978] RVR 228 (Court of Appeal: STEPHENSON, ROSKILL and GEOFFREY LANE LJJ).

407 ———— **market value—exclusion of purchasers wanting land for special purposes**

See *Blandrent Investment Developments Ltd v British Gas Corpn*, para. 982.

408 ———— **potential use of land—scheme underlying acquisition**

A district council compulsorily acquired the plaintiff's land for the purpose of securing its development as a whole for industry. In assessing compensation the question raised was on the applicability of the *Pointe Gourde* principle, that compensation cannot include an increase in value which is entirely due to the scheme underlying the acquisition. Before the confirmation of the compulsory purchase order, the county council issued a report which included a scheme for industrial development of the plaintiff's land. The scheme outlined in the report did not itself provide for compulsory acquisition. The question to be decided was whether the scheme underlying the acquisition was the district council's scheme or the county council's scheme. *Held*, although the county council's scheme had originally been a scheme by an authority different from the acquiring authority, the two schemes had merged to become a scheme to which the acquiring authority was a party. It was not necessary for the scheme to provide for the acquisition; it was enough if it formed the basis of the acquisition. The county council's scheme would be taken into consideration in assessing compensation.

BIRD v WAKEFIELD METROPOLITAN DISTRICT COUNCIL (1978) 248 Estates Gazette 499 (Court of Appeal: MEGAW, BROWNE and SHAW LJJ). Decision of the Lands Tribunal (1976) 243 Estates Gazette 755, 1977 Halsbury's Abr para. 410 affirmed.

409 ———— **certificate of alternative development—statement of rights of appeal not included—validity of certificate**

Scotland

A company, which owned land which a local authority proposed to acquire compulsorily, applied for a certificate of alternative development. A certificate was issued by the local planning authority, but it did not include a statement of rights of appeal, as required by the Scottish equivalent of the Land Compensation Development Order 1974, art. 3 (3). The company brought an action against the local planning authority contending that the certificate was invalid and that the local planning authority was bound to issue a fresh certificate complying with the requirements of the order. *Held*, the certificate was invalid because the requirement to include a statement of the rights of appeal was mandatory and had not been complied with. It was not possible to treat the certificate as consisting of two parts, i.e. the actual certificate and the statement of rights of appeal, which were capable of being severed from each other. The position however was not the same as if no certificate had been issued since an invalid certificate was not a complete nullity but had some legal effect until set aside. Hence there could be no deemed issue of a certificate under the Scottish equivalent of the Land Compensation Act 1961, s. 18 (4), since that section only applied where no certificate had been issued at all. The obligation to issue a valid certificate was a continuing one notwithstanding that the Land Compensation Development Order 1974, art. 3 (2) provided that the certificate should be issued not later than two months after receipt of the application. A certificate could be issued outside the two month period and in the circumstances the issue of a fresh certificate was the appropriate remedy.

LORD HAILSHAM OF ST MARYLEBONE LC and LORD KEITH OF KINKEL considered the usage of the terms "void" and "voidable" in relation to the effect of non-compliance by a statutory authority with the statutory requirements affecting the discharge of one of its functions and found them to be misleading and tending towards the rigid classification of facts, which should not be encouraged in administrative law.

LONDON AND CLYDESIDE ESTATES LTD v ABERDEEN DISTRICT COUNCIL [1979] 3 All ER 876 (House of Lords: LORD HAILSHAM OF ST MARYLEBONE LC, LORD WILBERFORCE, LORD FRASER OF TULLYBELTON, LORD RUSSELL OF KILLOWEN and LORD KEITH OF KINKEL). *Calvin v Carr* [1979] 2 All ER 440, para. 7 applied.

410   —— disturbance—assessment—Lands Tribunal decision

RAKUSEN PROPERTIES LTD v LEEDS CITY COUNCIL (1979) 38 P & CR 352: V. G. Wellings QC (fee simple of a factory was owned by a property company which issued a purchase order because the premises were no longer capable of reasonably beneficial use; the factory's trade was carried on by a wholly owned subsidiary company; both claimed compensation from the local authority for disturbance caused by the acquisition; trading company asked that the corporate veil should be lifted to allow it to claim; before the purchase order was confirmed by the Secretary of State, the factory was destroyed by fire; the tribunal found it unnecessary to lift the corporate veil because it was impossible to say whether the purchase or fire had caused the trading company's loss; property company could not say that it had lost by the acquisition because it had not attempted to prevent confirmation of the order; neither company was entitled to claim compensation for the disturbance).

411   —— —— —— whether interest charges recoverable

The claimants agreed to sell their factory to the council. As they were unable to find suitable alternative premises ready for occupation, the claimants purchased an empty site on which they built and equipped a new factory with the aid of a bank overdraft. In addition to agreed compensation, the claimants were awarded compensation for bank charges and interest payable on the overdraft on the ground that such expenditure was a direct result of the acquisition of their factory. On appeal by the council, *held*, there was a rebuttable presumption that the purchase price of new premises was something for which a claimant received value for money and therefore no compensation was payable. The bank charges and interest were costs incurred in acquiring a new factory, not in moving from the old one, and were therefore part of the purchase price. The presumption of value for money applied and as there was no evidence for rebuttal, the claimants were not prima facie entitled to the compensation. The appeal would be allowed.

SERVICE WELDING LTD v TYNE AND WEAR COUNTY COUNCIL (1979) 250 Estates Gazette 1291 (Court of Appeal: MEGAW, BRIDGE and TEMPLEMAN LJJ). Decision of Lands Tribunal (1977) 34 P & CR 228, 1977 Halsbury's Abridgment para. 416 reversed.

412   —— —— increase in operating costs following move to new premises

When the head office of a group of companies was compulsorily acquired they took a lease of a new office building nearby. They put forward a claim for additional compensation in respect of disturbance, which included a sum for increased operating costs consequent on taking a lease of the whole of the new building. Their claim in respect of increased operating costs was rejected by the Lands Tribunal on the ground that taking a lease of the whole building was unreasonable as only two floors were necessary. On appeal, *held*, increased operating costs were a possible head of claim but such a claim would succeed only where there was no alternative to increasing the costs and the claimants were in no better position than they were previously. The Lands Tribunal had been entitled to conclude that the claimants had derived benefit from the increased expenditure and had suffered no loss.

J. BIBBY & SONS LTD v MERSEYSIDE COUNTY COUNCIL (1979) 251 Estates Gazette 757 (Court of Appeal: MEGAW, EVELEIGH and BRANDON LJJ). Decision of Lands Tribunal (1977) 243 Estates Gazette 467, 1977 Halsbury's Abridgment para. 409 affirmed.

413   —— —— **loss of profit—agreed gross amount—whether corporation tax deductible**

See *Stoke on Trent County Council v Wood, Mitchell & Co Ltd*, para. 1515 and para. 1516.

414   —— **notice of claim—particulars required**

See *Methodist Church Trustees v North Tyneside Borough Council*, para. 421.

415   —— **time limit for claim**

Following criticism by the Parliamentary Commissioner for Administration, supported by a Select Committee of the House of Commons, the Minister of Transport, in a written parliamentary reply, has stated that the Department of Transport in 1975 had failed to take all the proper steps to ensure that householders affected by a road improvement scheme (the Rochester Way) were aware of their rights to compensation. The Minister said that legislation would be introduced to allow payments to be made to persons who had submitted late claims. In addition, the government would amend the Land Compensation Act 1973 to remove the time limit for future compensation claims. See the Financial Times, 23rd October 1979.

416   **Compulsory purchase order—confirmation by confirming authority—consideration of alternative schemes—effect of failure to refer to minor scheme in decision**

The plaintiffs objected to a compulsory purchase order being made in respect of their property. An inquiry was held and the plaintiffs put forward alternative schemes: a major scheme involving the whole site and a minor scheme affecting only three houses. The inspector's report noted both schemes but the Secretary of State's decision letter contained no reference to the minor scheme. On an application by the plaintiffs to quash the decision, *held*, the Secretary of State was entitled not to mention a point if he thought it too trivial and insubstantial. However he was bound to deal with all material matters. Despite the fact that the minor scheme was merely the alternative to the major scheme he ought to have mentioned it. His decision would therefore be quashed.

LONDON WELSH ASSOCIATION LTD v SECRETARY OF STATE FOR THE ENVIRONMENT (1979) 252 Estates Gazette 378 (Queen's Bench Division: FORBES J).

417   —— **service of notice of order—failure to serve notice on joint owner—whether substantial prejudice**

A husband and wife were joint owners of a house which they allowed to become overcrowded and to fall into disrepair. As a result the council decided to issue a compulsory purchase order, but failed to serve a notice on the wife. The husband contested the order, but the Secretary of State confirmed it, whereupon the wife sought to quash the confirmation on the ground that as she had not received notice there had been a breach of natural justice. She swore several affidavits, which contained conflicting evidence, but the court, after allowing her to be cross-examined as to the contents of the affidavits, decided that the failure to serve notice had deprived her of the chance to object to the order and upheld her claim. On appeal *held*, there could be no such thing as a technical breach of natural justice, and as the wife had not proved on affidavit that she had been prejudiced by the council's failure to serve the notice the order would not be quashed. In general cross-examination on affidavits in proceedings for judicial review, prerogative writ proceedings and applications for compulsory purchase orders should not be necessary, and it should not have been permitted in this case because it was plain from the affidavits that the wife's evidence was unreliable.

GEORGE v SECRETARY OF STATE FOR THE ENVIRONMENT (1979) 250 Estates Gazette 339 (Court of Appeal: LORD DENNING MR, ROSKILL and CUMMING-BRUCE LJJ). Decision of Sir Douglas Frank QC, sitting as a deputy High Court judge, (1978) 248 Estates Gazette 49, 1978 Halsbury's Abridgment para. 408 reversed.

418   Entry onto land—entry before completion—rate of interest after entry

The Acquisition of Land (Rate of Interest after Entry) Regulations 1979, S.I. 1979 No. 616 (in force on 5th July 1979) decrease from 14 per cent to 13 per cent the annual rate of interest payable where entry is made, before payment of compensation, on land in England and Wales which is being purchased compulsorily. The Acquisition of Land (Rate of Interest) (No. 3) Regulations 1978, 1978 Halsbury's Abridgment para. 404 are revoked.

These regulations have been revoked; see para. 419.

419   The Acquisition of Land (Rate of Interest After Entry) (No. 2) Regulations 1979, S.I. 1979 No. 1166 (in force on 16th October 1979) increase from 13 per cent to 14 per cent the annual rate of interest payable where entry is made before payment of compensation, on land in England and Wales which is being purchased compulsorily. The Acquisition of Land (Rate of Interest) Regulations 1979, para. 418 are revoked.

These regulations have been revoked; see para. 420.

420   The Acquisition of Land (Rate of Interest after Entry) (No. 3) Regulations 1979, S.I. 1979 No. 1743 (in force on 25th January 1980), increase from 14 per cent to 17 per cent the annual rate of interest payable, where entry is made before payment of compensation, on land in England and Wales which is being acquired compulsorily. The Acquisition of Land (Rate of Interest after Entry) (No. 2) Regulations 1979, para. 419, are revoked.

421   Notice to treat—withdrawal—claimant's failure to deliver proper notice of claim

A compulsory purchase order was made in respect of a church and a notice to treat was served on the church trustees, who subsequently served a notice of claim. The acquiring authority then decided it did not wish to acquire the church and sought to withdraw the notice to treat under the Land Compensation Act 1961, s. 31, on the ground that the trustees had failed to serve a proper notice of claim under the 1961 Act, s. 4, contending that as the notice of claim did not quantify the amount claimed, it did not comply with the provisions of s. 4. The trustees conceded that this was the literal meaning of the section, but argued that the court was entitled to depart from the literal meaning, because to give the words their literal effect would either (i) require them to do the impossible, or (ii) produce anomalies which Parliament could not have intended. *Held*, (i) the legislation did not impose a duty on the claimants to do something which was impossible. They were under no obligation to make a claim for compensation; the Act merely provided that certain consequences would follow if no claim were made. Their contention that it was impossible for them to quantify the claim because the compensation was to be assessed at prices current at a future date, when the work of reinstatement could reasonably be started, was incorrect. The claim could be stated at values current at the date of claim, with a statement that the claim would be adjusted to take account of changes in prices and values between the dates of claim and of assessment. Therefore there was no reason to depart from the literal meaning of s. 4 on the ground that it required the claimants to do the impossible. (ii) Since Parliament appeared in s. 31 to have intended the authority to have the right to withdraw at any time up to the moment when there was a quantified claim, the possible unfairness and disruption to the claimants did not justify saying that the literal construction defeated the intention of the Act. Therefore since a notice complying with s. 4 had not yet been served, the authority still had the right to withdraw the notice to treat under s. 31.

METHODIST CHURCH TRUSTEES v NORTH TYNESIDE BOROUGH COUNCIL (1979) 38 P & CR 665 (Chancery Division: BROWNE-WILKINSON J).

422   Planning blight—notice—Lands Tribunal decision

BARRETT v SECRETARY OF STATE FOR TRANSPORT (1979) 184/1978 (unreported) (applicant served blight notice in respect of premises; contended that land was on or adjacent to line of proposed highway as indicated in an order or scheme under Town and Country Planning Act 1971, s. 192 (1) (d); authority served counter-notice on grounds that it did not propose to acquire the premises, nor was there an order or scheme which had come into operation; document entitled "choice of route" did not constitute an order or scheme; further, proposed road did not come near to subject premises; counter notice therefore upheld).

CONFLICT OF LAWS

Halsbury's Laws of England (4th edn.), Vol. 8, paras. 401–795

423   **Articles**

Jurisdiction and the Territorial Element, Gavin McFarlane (authorities on the territorial element in the jurisdiction of English courts): 143 JP Jo 3.

Place of the Tort: A Legal Change of Scene, Allan C. Hutchinson: 129 NLJ 1067.

Recognition of Foreign Divorce Decrees, F. Graham Glover: 9 Fam Law 78.

424   **Contract—foreign jurisdiction clause—application for stay of proceedings—considerations governing grant**

The plaintiffs shipped a quantity of hessian goods at Calcutta for Rotterdam on the defendants' vessel. The bills of lading provided that the contract should be governed either by the law of the place where the defendants' principal business was situated or by the law of the port of destination, at the defendants' option. On delivery at Rotterdam, the goods were found to be severely damaged by fuel oil which had passed into the hold through a hole in the bulkhead. The hole could quite easily have been seen on any normal inspection of the hold. The plaintiffs claimed damages and contended that the defendants had no defence as the facts showed beyond doubt that the hole must have been there before the cargo was loaded. The defendants applied for a stay of proceedings on the ground that the plaintiffs had agreed that disputes between the parties should be decided in the place where the defendants had their principal place of business, Bombay. *Held*, (i) on the facts, it was abundantly clear that the hole in the bulkhead must have been present before the goods were loaded and, as the defendants had not suggested any defence to the claim, there was no dispute at all on the question of liability which ought to be submitted to the Court of India. (ii) A stay would be refused on the grounds that, on the matters of title to sue and quantum, which might be in dispute, there was no multiplicity of proceedings; there was no difference in the relevant law wherever the proceedings were heard as the bills of lading incorporated the Hague Rules; all the relevant evidence, which was documentary evidence, was in Europe; if a stay were to be granted, the proceedings in India would be time-barred. Accordingly, the defendants' application would be dismissed.

THE VISHVA PRABHA [1979] 2 Lloyd's Rep 286 (Queen's Bench Division: SHEEN J).

425   —— —— **subsequent change in nature of court—effect of clause**

By a contract made in 1973 the defendant company, registered in England but carrying on business entirely in Angola, agreed to purchase shares from the plaintiff, an Angolan resident, the price to be paid by instalments. The contract provided that the District Court of Luanda was to have exclusive jurisdiction over any dispute arising under the contract. In 1977 the plaintiff, having left Angola in 1975 following the outbreak of civil war, commenced proceedings in England to recover the last instalment of the purchase price. The defendant company's application for a stay of the proceedings was refused, either as a matter of construction of the jurisdiction clause or as a matter of discretion. The company appealed. *Held*, as a result of events in Angola in 1975, culminating in its independence and the drawing up of a new constitution, the court on which the contract conferred jurisdiction was no longer the same as that contemplated by the parties in 1973: the new constitution introduced a new method of selection and appointment of judges and provided for the application of Angolan law which, although for the present resembled Portuguese law as applied in Angola until 1975, was clearly susceptible to change at any time. Accordingly, the plaintiff was not bound by the clause. Further, although it was therefore unnecessary to review the lower court's exercise of its discretion in refusing to stay the proceedings, it was clear that the plaintiff had proved that on the facts of the case, including the fact that he was justified in fearing for his life were he to return to Angola, it was just and proper to allow the action to continue in England. The appeal would be dismissed.

CARVALHO v HULL BLYTH (ANGOLA) LTD [1979] 3 All ER 280 (Court of Appeal: BROWNE and GEOFFREY LANE LJJ). Dicta of Willmer J in *The Fehmarn* [1957] 2 All ER 707 at 709 applied.

426 —— illegality under law of place of performance

See *Toprak Mahsulleri Ofisi v Finagrain Compagnie Commerciale Agricole et Financiere SA*, para. 504.

427 —— proper law—alleged agency agreement—revocation of agreement—whether breach committed within jurisdiction

The plaintiffs, who were a company incorporated in the British Virgin Islands, entered into a purported contract with the defendants, an insurance company incorporated in Italy, by which the plaintiffs were to act as the defendants' underwriting agents. The contract provided, inter alia, for disputes to be settled under the International Chamber of Commerce Rules in Geneva, and for all correspondence to the plaintiffs to be sent to their solicitors in the Channel Islands. On March 13th 1977, the defendants informed the plaintiffs' London solicitors, by telex, that there was no concluded agreement between the parties and asked for confirmation that the underwriting would cease. On March 14th the defendants agreed to postpone their instruction to terminate the underwriting until the conclusion of a meeting to be convened in Milan. As a result of that meeting in April the defendants terminated the purported underwriting agreement by telex to the plaintiffs' Channel Islands solicitors (not to London), on April 20th. The plaintiffs sought damages for breach of contract and were given leave to serve notice of writ on the defendants out of the jurisdiction. On appeal to set aside the service under RSC Ord. 11, the defendants contended (i) the agreement was not governed by English law and (ii) nor was the breach committed within the jurisdiction. *Held*, (i) the agreement was governed by Italian law and not by English law, as the defendants were resident in Italy and had negotiated and signed the contract in Milan. Alternatively, the proper law was the law of the Canton of Geneva as the law of the place where arbitration was to have taken place. (ii) The telex of March 13th was a repudiation of a kind which required acceptance and did not operate automatically to terminate the contract irrespective of any election on the part of the plaintiffs. In any event, the agreement to meet in Milan was a waiver of the alleged breach. The relevant breach occurred when the defendants sent their telegram of April 20th from Milan and thus the only relevant breach was committed in Italy and not within the jurisdiction. The plaintiffs had failed to establish either of the grounds upon which they sought to bring their case within Ord. 11 and the defendants' appeal would be allowed.

ATLANTIC UNDERWRITING AGENCIES LTD v COMPAGNIA DI ASSICURAZIONE DI MILANO SpA [1979] 2 Lloyd's Rep 240 (Queen's Bench Division: LLOYD J).

428 Divorce and nullity—recognition of foreign proceedings—change of status by one party

The parties were married in Ceylon and subsequently moved to Malaysia and became Malaysian citizens. The wife later made her home in England with her children while they were completing their education. In 1976 the husband, who was still living in Malaysia, became a Muslim. His wife subsequently obtained a divorce in England due to her husband's previous unreasonable behaviour. He appealed against the decree on the ground that his religious conversion in 1976 had automatically ended their marriage. *Held*, the marriage had ended in 1976 since the law of Malaysia, where the parties had a common domicile at that time, regarded it as doing so. However, the court would not recognise the marriage as ended under the Recognition of Divorces and Legal Separations Act 1971 since the manner in which the marriage ended was not a divorce or legal separation within the meaning of the Act, nor had there been any formal proceedings. Moreover, the husband's changed status under Malaysian law could not be recognised at common law as a foreign decree of nullity since such action would be contrary to natural justice: his wife was unaware of his religious conversion and had no opportunity of taking legal advice in Malaysia. Accordingly she was still married when she petitioned for divorce and the appeal would be dismissed.

VISWALINGHAM v VISWALINGHAM (1979) 123 Sol Jo 604 (Court of Appeal: ROSKILL and ORMROD LJJ and SIR DAVID CAIRNS). *Salvesen (or Von Lorang) v Administrator of Austrian Property* [1927] AC 641, HL applied.

429   —— —— divorce by talaq

The parties married in 1963 according to Islamic law. In 1968 they effected a khula divorce in Thailand where they had been living for three years. In 1969 the husband moved to Pakistan and in 1974 he pronounced talaq there, which took effect automatically after ninety days. The husband, who had been living in England since 1973, sought a declaration that either the khula or talaq was valid by English law. At first instance the khula was recognised under the common law provisions referred to in the Recognition of Divorces and Legal Separations Act 1971, s. 6 and the talaq under s. 3 of the same Act as being within the meaning of "other proceedings" in s. 2 (a). The Court of Appeal held that neither the khula nor the talaq could be recognised under s. 6 as at the time of the khula the parties were domiciled in Thailand, and the husband had failed to prove that it was a valid and effective divorce by Thai law, and at the time of the talaq the husband had acquired a domicile of choice in England. Nor could either form of divorce be recognised under s. 2 (a) as the khula required no intervention by the state in any form and the talaq, although registered in Pakistan, was effected simply by the unilateral act of the husband. On appeal it was not disputed that the parties were Pakistan nationals, nor that if the procedural requirements were satisfied the divorce would be recognised in Pakistan. The sole question for the court was whether the divorce was obtained by "judicial or other proceedings", which took place in Pakistan, within the meaning of s. 2 (a). *Held*, the purpose of the 1972 Act was to give effect to the Hague Convention on the Recognition of Divorces and Legal Separations of 1970, which was designed to prevent the situation where a marriage was recognised as having been dissolved in some jurisdictions but as subsisting in others. Article 1 specifically provided that the Convention would apply to the "recognition in one contracting state of divorces and legal separations obtained in another contracting country which follow judicial or other proceedings officially recognised in that state and which are legally effective there." The word "other" in the 1972 Act, s. 2 (a) was not to be construed ejusdem generis with "judicial" but in the light of the 1970 Convention. The 1972 Act was passed to enable the United Kingdom to ratify the Convention and the latter was a legitimate aid to construing the provisions of the Act. Hence the words "other proceedings" included all proceedings for divorce, other than judicial proceedings, which were legally effective in the country where they were taken.

The pronouncement of the talaq was required by Pakistan law to be notified to a public authority (and to the wife) which was in turn required to constitute an arbitration council for the purposes of conciliation and to invite each spouse to nominate a representative. These proceedings were enforced by penal sanctions and the talaq was not effective until ninety days after the commencement of proceedings. The talaq was therefore within the meaning of "other proceedings" under s. 2 (a).

LORD SCARMAN AND VISCOUNT DILHORNE recommended that the law should be altered so that a resident in the United Kingdom whose divorce or legal separation abroad was recognised in the United Kingdom as valid, should not be debarred from the protection afforded by the Matrimonial Act 1973 by the fact that a divorce or legal separation was not granted in the English courts.

QUAZI V QUAZI [1979] 3 All ER 897 (House of Lords: LORD DIPLOCK, VISCOUNT DILHORNE, LORD SALMON, LORD FRASER OF TULLYBELTON, LORD SCARMAN). Decision of Court of Appeal [1979] 3 All ER 424 reversed.

430   —— —— nullity of marriage

In 1957, the respondent, an Italian domiciled in Italy, married an American woman in Italy. She immediately returned to the United States and in 1961 obtained a decree of nullity there. The court's jurisdiction was based on six months' residence but in fact she had resided there for the three years preceding her application. The decree of nullity could not have been recognised in Italy. In 1967, the respondent married the petitioner, an English woman, in London. They lived in England until 1971 when they separated and the petitioner brought a petition for nullity on the ground that the respondent's previous marriage was valid and subsisting. *Held*, although the respondent was incapable of marrying the petitioner by the law of his domicile, a foreign decree of nullity based on residence of sufficient quality would be recognised by the English courts although it would not be recognised in Italy. Although the American decree was based on six months' residence, the former wife's actual residence was of sufficient quality and length for the court to recognise the decree as valid. Therefore there had been no bar to the petitioner and the respondent marrying in England.

PERRINI V PERRINI [1979] 2 All ER 323 (Family Division: SIR GEORGE BAKER P). *Indyka v Indyka* [1969] 1 AC 33, HL, *Robinson-Scott v Robinson-Scott* [1958] P 71 and *Law v Gustin (formerly Law)* [1976] Fam 155, 1975 Halsbury's Abridgment para. 1145 applied.

431   —— —— spouse unrepresented in foreign proceedings

A wife had been granted a maintenance order in England against her husband, who was in arrears with his payments. He filed a petition for divorce in Quebec and, upon being served with the petition, the wife's solicitors wrote to the registrar of the Quebec court informing him of the maintenance order, the arrears and the wife's intention to contest the petition. The solicitors also sought legal aid for the wife from the Legal Services Commission in Quebec. A decree nisi was granted by a Canadian judge without the wife being represented, and the solicitors received notice of the decree still without having received any reply to their letters to the registrar or their application for legal aid. The Quebec court would not enforce the English maintenance order, and the wife could only make a claim for maintenance before a Canadian court if she was physically present in the court, and she could not get legal aid to travel to Canada. The wife filed a divorce petition in England, the husband replying that the Canadian decree had already dissolved the marriage; indeed he had already remarried. The wife asked that, pursuant to the Recognition of Divorces and Legal Separations Act 1971, s. 8 (2) (a) (ii), the Canadian decree should not be recognised by the English Court, as it had been obtained without her having been given such opportunity to take part in the proceedings as should reasonably have been given. *Held*, on the evidence the wife had not had an adequate and effective opportunity of presenting her views to the Canadian court, and after balancing the interests of all the parties, the court would exercise its discretion under s. 8 (2) (a) (ii) and refuse recognition of the Canadian decree. Recognition would result in particular disadvantage to the wife and children, in that it would oust the English courts' jurisdiction to deal with the matrimonial home and financial relief for the wife and thus, in view of the wife's difficulties in getting protection from the Canadian courts, recognition should not be granted. Furthermore in the particular circumstances of the case it would be against public policy to recognise the decree.

JOYCE V JOYCE [1979] 2 All ER 156 (Family Division: LANE J).

432 **Evidence—proof of foreign law—whether court entitled to consider developments in interpretation of foreign law**

Canada
The owners of a Japanese ship entered into a deed of mortgage with the plaintiff to secure payments of the instalments payable on the ship. The instalments were not paid and the plaintiff brought an action in rem to enforce the mortgage. The jurisdiction of the Canadian court was not contested. However, under the Corporate Reorganisation Laws of Japan, a device available for the liquidation or rehabilitation of a company in financial difficulties, the owners were unable to make payments of debts owed by them. The plaintiff contended that the Japanese law was effective only in regard to property of a debtor company existing within Japanese territory. *Held,* Japanese law clearly stated that reorganisation proceedings were effective only in respect to properties in Japan. Despite the unsatisfactory result of such a law in a case where considerable foreign assets were involved, the Canadian court was bound to adhere to it and could not speculate as to desirable future developments in that law.

ORIENT LEASING CO LTD v THE SHIP "KOSEI MARU" (1978) 94 DLR (3d) 658 (Federal Court of Canada).

433 **International carriage of goods by road—jurisdiction of court**

See *Moto Vespa SA v MAT (Britannia Express) Ltd,* para. 296.

434 **Jurisdiction—contract conferring exclusive jurisdiction on foreign court—subsequent change in nature of court—effect of jurisdiction clause**

See *Carvalho v Hull Blyth (Angola) Ltd,* para. 425.

435 **Maintenance orders—reciprocal enforcement**

The Maintenance Orders (Facilities for Enforcement) (Revocation) Order 1979, S.I. 1979 No. 116 (in force on 1st April 1979), revokes the Maintenance Orders (Facilities for Enforcement) Order 1959 in so far as it extends the Maintenance Orders (Facilities for Enforcement) Act 1920 to Alberta, Fiji, Hong Kong, Norfolk Island, Saskatchewan, Singapore, Turks and Caicos Islands and Western Australia. The Order also revokes the Maintenance Orders (Facilities for Enforcement) (Tanganyika) Order 1964 which extended the 1920 Act to Tanganyika.

436 The Reciprocal Enforcement of Maintenance Orders (Designation of Reciprocating Countries) Order 1979, S.I. 1979 No. 115 (in force on 1st April 1979) designates Alberta, Fiji, Hong Kong, Norfolk Island, Saskatchewan, Singapore, Turks and Caicos Islands, the United Republic of Tanzania (except Zanzibar) and Western Australia as reciprocating countries for the purposes of the Maintenance Orders (Reciprocal Enforcement) Act 1972, Part I. The Order also varies the Reciprocal Enforcement of Maintenance Orders (Designation of Reciprocating Countries) Order 1974, Halsbury's Abridgment 1974 para. 1078 in relation to certain named Australian States and territories and Ontario.

437 The Magistrates' Courts (Reciprocal Enforcement of Maintenance Orders) (Amendment) Rules 1979, S.I. 1979 No. 170 (in force on 1st April 1979), amend the 1974 Rules. Rule 9 (1) of the 1974 Regulations is amended so as to allow the Secretary of State, in those cases where sums would normally be sent to the Crown Agents for transmission, to direct that other arrangements for payment should be made. Additions are made to those countries and territories which are designated as reciprocating countries for the purposes of the Maintenance Orders (Reciprocal Enforcement) Act 1972, Part I.

438   —— —— Hague Convention countries

The Reciprocal Enforcement of Maintenance Orders (Hague Convention Countries) Order 1979, S.I. 1979 No. 1317 (in force on 1st March 1980), provides that the Maintenance Orders (Reciprocal Enforcement) Act 1972, Part I is to apply in relation to Czechoslovakia, France, Norway, Portugal, Sweden and Switzerland (the 'Convention countries') as it applies to reciprocating countries designated under s. 1 of the Act, subject to certain exceptions, adaptations and modifications. Schedule 3 to the order sets out in full the provisions of Part I as they apply to the Convention countries.

439   —— —— recovery of maintenance—American states

The Recovery of Maintenance (United States of America) Order 1979, S.I. 1979 No. 1314 (in force on 1st January 1980), applies the provisions of the Maintenance Orders (Reciprocal Enforcement) Act 1972, Part II to certain American states subject to a specified modification.

440   —— —— —— procedure

The Magistrates' Courts (Recovery Abroad of Maintenance) (Amendment) Rules 1979, S.I. 1979 No. 1561 (in force on 1st January 1980), apply, subject to a modification, the provisions of the Magistrates' Courts (Recovery Abroad of Maintenance) Rules 1975, 1975 Halsbury's Abridgment para. 1132, to the American states specified in the Recovery of Maintenance (United States of America) Order 1979, see para. 439.

441   Practice—infringement of patent—application for stay pending determination of foreign action

In an action for the alleged infringement of two letters patent, the defendants denied the validity of the patents, and denied infringement. The defendants unsuccessfully applied for an order that the proceedings be stayed pending the outcome of an action in the United States between the plaintiffs and the defendants' suppliers. The plaintiffs' application to have a paragraph of the defence which raised issues concerning anti-trust laws in the United States struck out was granted. The defendants appealed, contending that if the defences raised by their suppliers in the United States action should be established the plaintiffs would, as a result be restrained by an order of the United States court from proceeding with the English action. *Held*, (i) the view of the United States court as to the grant or refusal of an interlocutory injunction restraining the plaintiffs from pursuing their English action was properly a relevant factor in the matter of discretion. However, there was nothing to suggest that the judge had applied a wrong principle in exercising his discretion or that he had taken into account any material factor which he should not have considered. This was not a case in which a stay of proceedings should be ordered. (ii) The paragraph of the statement of claim should be struck out because, if all the issues of fact and United States law were to be argued in the English action, the resulting increase in the length and complexity of the English proceedings would be likely to take up most of the remaining life of the patents. The appeal would, accordingly be dismissed.

WESTERN ELECTRIC CO INC v RACAL-MILGO LTD [1979] RPC 501 (Court of Appeal, MEGAW, LAWTON and CUMMING-BRUCE LJJ).

CONSTITUTIONAL LAW

Halsbury's Laws of England (4th edn.), Vol. 8, paras. 801–1647

442   Article

Judicial Immunity Reconsidered, Henry E. Markson: 123 Sol Jo 712.

443 Civil proceedings against Crown—liability of Crown for acts of illegal regime in Rhodesia

The plaintiff, a citizen of Southern Rhodesia, was arrested and detained in prison without trial by the illegal regime; the United Kingdom government was unable to obtain his release. He was eventually released on condition that he left the country. He came to the United Kingdom, where he commenced an action against the Attorney-General, seeking a declaration that the United Kingdom government had failed in its duty to protect him from unlawful arrest and detention or to secure his early release. *Held*, the Crown was under no legal duty to protect a subject from unlawful arrest and imprisonment. Furthermore under the Crown Proceedings Act 1947, s. 40 (2) (b) the Crown was protected from suit in respect of any alleged liability arising otherwise than in respect of Her Majesty's Government in the United Kingdom. By the Southern Rhodesia Act 1965, s. 1, the Rhodesian constitution existing prior to 1965 continued in force, thus the United Kingdom government had not taken over the government of Rhodesia but continued to have only the limited responsibilities it had prior to 1965. As a consequence the alleged liability arose otherwise than in respect of Her Majesty's Government in the United Kingdom. The declaration sought would not be granted.

MUTASA v ATTORNEY-GENERAL [1979] 3 All ER 257 (Queen's Bench Division: BOREHAM J).

444 Consular fees

The Consular Fees Regulations 1979, S.I. 1979 No. 875 (in force on 6th August 1979), prescribe the manner in which consular officers and certain public officers should carry out the duties imposed on them by the Consular Salaries and Fees Act 1891, s. 2 (2) and the Fees (Increase) Act 1923, s. 8 (2). The Consular Fees Regulations 1978, 1978 Halsbury's Abridgment para. 432 are revoked.

445 Emergency controls

See EMERGENCY CONTROLS.

446 Foreign compensation—financial provisions

The Foreign Compensation (Financial Provisions) Order 1979, S.I. 1979 No. 109 (in force on 20th March 1979) directs the Foreign Compensation Commission to pay into the Exchequer, out of the funds paid to the Commission for the purpose of being distributed under the Foreign Compensation Acts 1950 and 1962, amounts in respect of the Commission's expenses during the period 1st October 1977 to 30th September 1978 in relation to the distribution of those funds.

447 Imposition of levy—interference with enjoyment of property— whether imposition unconstitutional

See *Mootoo v A-G of Trinidad and Tobago*, para. 1450.

448 Judicial pensions

See PENSIONS.

449 Ministers—salaries

The Ministerial and Other Salaries and Pensions Order 1979, S.I. 1979 No. 905 (in force on 26th July 1979), increases the salaries payable to Ministers, Members of the Opposition and the Speaker of the House of Commons under the Ministerial and Other Salaries Act 1975, 1975 Halsbury's Abridgment para. 474. The Order also provides that those salaries and the salaries of certain other office holders should be treated as being payable at higher levels for pension purposes. The Ministerial and Other Salaries Order 1978, 1978 Halsbury's Abridgment para. 435 is revoked.

450   Ministry of Overseas Development—dissolution

The Ministry of Overseas Development (Dissolution) Order 1979, S.I. 1979 No. 1451 (in force on 21st November 1979), provides for the dissolution of the Ministry of Overseas Development and for the transfer to the Secretary of State or, in the case of functions relating to certain bodies, to the Secretary of State for Foreign and Commonwealth Affairs of all the functions of the Minister of Overseas Development.

451   Northern Ireland

See NORTHERN IRELAND.

452   Rights of subject—rights to privacy—claim for declaration that telephone tapping unlawful

See *Malone v Metropolitan Police Commissioner*, para. 2093.

453   Scotland Act 1978—repeal

The Scotland Act 1978 (Repeal) Order 1979, S.I. 1979 No. 928 (in force on 26th July 1979), repeals the Scotland Act 1978, 1978 Halsbury's Abridgment para. 437.

454   Secretary of State—transfer of functions—education and science

The Transfer of Functions (Arts and Libraries) Order 1979, S.I. 1979 No. 907 (in force on 1st September 1979), transfer to the Chancellor of the Duchy of Lancaster certain functions exercised by the Secretary of State for Education and Science under various Acts and in relation to specified institutions.

455   —— —— prices and consumer protection

The Secretary of State for Trade Order 1979, S.I. 1979 No. 578 (in force on 1st June 1979) transfers to the Secretary of State for Trade the remaining statutory function of the Secretary of State for Prices and Consumer Protection. It also provides for the conversion of certain references to the Secretary of State for Prices and Consumer Protection and his department and officers, following the transfer of his functions to the Secretary of State for Trade.

456   —— —— transport

The Minister of Transport Order 1979, S.I. 1979 No. 571 (in force on 24th May 1979), transfers to the Minister of Transport the functions previously exercised by the Secretary of State for Transport.

457   Wales Act 1978—repeal

The Wales Act 1978 (Repeal) Order 1979, S.I. 1979 No. 933 (in force on 26th July 1979), repeals the Wales Act 1978, 1978 Halsbury's Abridgment para. 442.

CONSUMER PROTECTION AND FAIR TRADING

Halsbury's Laws of England (3rd edn.), Vol. 38, paras. 94–185

458   Articles

Consumer Safety Act 1978, Gayle M. Plummer: 128 NLJ 1184.
Practical Problems Arising from the Price Marking (Bargain Offers) Order 1979, para. 461, M. Carlisle: 129 NLJ 815.

459   Oil lamps—safety

The Oil Lamps (Safety) Regulations 1979, S.I. 1979 No. 1125 (in operation except for reg. 9, in relation to the sale or possession for the purpose of sale of goods and component parts by the manufacturer or importer thereof into Great Britain on 1st March 1980, in any other case, on 31st December 1980 and reg. 9, on 31st December 1980), impose safety requirements for indoor oil lamps based on the provisions of British Standard BS 2049:1976, as amended. The regulations provide for, inter alia, the construction, design and performance of oil lamps including provisions relating to resistance of fuel containers to corrosion, emission of carbon monoxide and smoke, safety on overturning, stability, surface temperature and performance in a draught.

460   Price control

See EMERGENCY CONTROLS.

461   Price marking—bargain offers

The Price Marking (Bargain Offers) Order 1979, S.I. 1979 No. 364 (in force on 2nd July 1979), prohibits the indication of a price for the retail sale of goods or a charge for the provision of services to non-business users which includes an express or implied statement that the price or charge in question is lower than another price or charge for, or a value ascribed to, goods or services of the same description. The prohibition does not apply to comparisons between the indicated price or charge and, inter alia, prices or charges which have been charged in the ordinary course of business by the person giving the price indication or by another identified person, prices or charges which the person giving the price indication proposes to charge from a specified future time, and prices or charges for goods or services of the same description in a different condition or quantity, or in different circumstances, or on different terms. The Indication of Prices (Beds) Order 1978, 1978 Halsbury's Abridgment para. 458 is revoked in part.

462   The Price Marking (Bargain Offers) (Amendment) Order 1979, S.I. 1979 No. 633 (in force on 2nd July 1979) amends the Price Marking (Bargain Offers) Order 1979, supra. The Order substitutes fresh provisions for those relating to the comparison of an indicated price with a recommended or suggested price which would otherwise be prohibited. Comparison will be permitted with a price recommended or suggested by any person in the course of business.

463   The Price Marking (Bargain Offers) (Amendment No. 2) Order 1979, S.I. 1979 No. 1124 (in force on 10th December 1979), further amends the Price Marking (Bargain Offers) Order 1979 supra by extending the prohibition imposed on comparisons with recommended or suggested prices to four additional sectors, namely domestic electrical applicances and similar appliances powered by other fuels, consumer electronic goods, carpets and furniture.

464   Tear-gas capsules—prohibition of sale

The Tear-Gas Capsules (Safety) Order 1979, S.I. 1979 No. 887 (in force on 20th August 1979), prohibits persons from supplying, offering to supply, agreeing to supply, exposing for supply or possessing for supply any injurious tear-gas capsule.

465   Trade descriptions

See TRADE DESCRIPTIONS.

CONTEMPT OF COURT

Halsbury's Laws of England (4th edn.), Vol. 9, paras. 1–125

466   Committal order—validity—order not in correct form

On 11th April 1979 an order was made committing the defendant to prison for contempt. The defendant's subsequent application to be released on the ground that he had purged his contempt was refused. He appealed, contending that the committal order was invalid because the form used had not been amended as prescribed by the County Court (Amendment No. 4) Rules 1978, 1978 Halsbury's Abridgment para. 533, which took effect on 12th March 1979. *Held*, it was necessary where the liberty of the subject was concerned to ensure that procedural requirements were properly complied with. However, a mere minor error of expression in a form which was not of any conceivable substance was not a matter to which the court was required to give effect. The new form should be used in future but minor insignificant errors such as those in the present case were not a sufficient basis for quashing the order. The appeal would be dismissed.

PALMER v TOWNSEND (1979) 123 Sol Jo 570 (Court of Appeal: MEGAW and GEOFFREY LANE LJJ).

467   Criminal contempt—contempt in connection with proceedings in an inferior court—local valuation court

A religious sect sought to have its premises recognised as a place of public religious worship for the purposes of rate relief. The Attorney General and others sought injunctions restraining the BBC from televising a programme about the sect whilst the case before the local valuation court was still pending. By RSC Ord. 52, r. 1(2) the Divisional Court had the power to make an order in respect of a contempt committed in connection with proceedings in an inferior court. The local valuation court was held to be an 'inferior court' and the BBC appealed against this decision. *Held*, LORD DENNING MR dissenting, the valuation court had all the attributes of a court: it was created by the state; its procedure was conducted in accordance with the rules of natural justice; its procedure involved a public hearing with the power to hear oral evidence, examine witnesses and to hear argument on the issues before it; its decision was final and binding unless it was reversed on appeal; there were at least two parties involved in any case brought before it; its decision was judicial in nature and concerned legal rights. The fact that no legally qualified person presided over the court did not affect its status as a court. The appeal would be dismissed.

A-G v BRITISH BROADCASTING CORPN [1979] 3 All ER 45 (Court of Appeal: LORD DENNING MR, EVELEIGH LJ and SIR STANLEY REES). Decision of the Divisional Court of the Queen's Bench Division [1978] 3 All ER 731, 1978 Halsbury's Abridgment para. 467 affirmed.

468   —— injunction to restrain publication of article on thalidomide— whether amounts to violation of freedom of expression

See para. 1459.

469   —— publication of name of witness granted anonymity—whether amounts to interference with administration of justice

The Attorney General applied for an order against three newspapers for alleged contempt of court. The papers had published the name of an army officer called as a witness in a case concerning the Official Secrets Act 1920 whose name had been withheld in the interests of national security. The papers' contention that they could not be guilty of the contempt alleged because there had been no formal direction or mandatory order not to disclose the witness' identity was rejected. The papers appealed. *Held*, criminal contempt involved an interference with the due administration of justice. Generally, the system of administration of justice required that it be done in public, unless the nature of the proceedings were such that this would interfere with such administration of justice. Where the reason for a ruling which involved departing from the general principle of open justice was that the departure was necessary in the interests of the administration of justice, and it would be apparent to anyone who was aware of the ruling that the result the ruling was designed to achieve would be frustrated by a particular kind of act done outside the courtroom, the doing of such an act could constitute contempt. A warning that such an act might amount to contempt should generally be given by the court, although it should not be implied that there could be no committal for contempt unless there had been some sort of warning. In the present case, no such warning had been given. The application to withhold the name was granted before the witness' evidence was heard, from which his identity could easily be deduced by anyone. Thus there were no longer any grounds for inferring that publication of the witness' name would interfere with the due administration of justice. Where in the interests of the due administration of justice the courts departed from the general principle of open justice, no one should be exposed to penal sanctions for failing to draw an inference as to what it was permissible to publish, unless the inference was so obvious as to speak for itself. The papers were not guilty of contempt of court and the appeal would be allowed.

A-G v LEVELLER MAGAZINE LTD [1979] 1 All ER 745 (House of Lords: LORD DIPLOCK, VISCOUNT DILHORNE, LORD EDMUND-DAVIES, LORD RUSSELL OF KILLOWEN and LORD SCARMAN). Decision of Divisional Court of the Queen's Bench Division [1978] 3 All ER 731, 1978 Halsbury's Abridgment para. 471 reversed.

CONTRACT

Halsbury's Laws of England (4th edn.), Vol. 9, paras. 201–699

470   Articles

Damages in Contract for Mental Distress, P. H. Clarke (examination of cases in which the issue of such damages has been discussed): 52 ALJ 626.

Frustrated Holidaymakers and Frustrated Contracts, A. M. Tettenborn (how the French air traffic controllers' work-to-rule in 1978 affected the development of the doctrine of frustration): 129 NLJ 62.

Liquidated Damages: An Empirical Study in the Travel Industry, Alan Milner (examination of how sensible is the assumption that the liquidated damages clause in a consumer contract is an effective mechanism in the avoidance of dispute): 42 MLR 508.

Long Live the Fundamental Breach, A. N. Khan (circumstances in which party to a contract can avoid his contractual obligation under an exemption clause): 123 Sol Jo 106.

Mitigation of Damage: Recent Developments, R. G. Lawson: 128 NLJ 1185.

Offer and Acceptance in the Supermarket, Bernard S. Jackson (on what constitutes a contract of sale in the supermarket): 129 NLJ 775.

Unfair Computer Contracts, Richard Morgan (an assessment of the effects of the Unfair Contract Terms Act 1977, 1977 Halsbury's Abridgment para. 540, on computer contracts): 129 NLJ 763.

471   Breach of contract—failure properly to perform contract to carry out abortion— right of mother to damages for birth of child

A woman brought an action for breach of contract against a doctor, claiming that he had failed properly to carry out an abortion operation on her, with the result that she gave birth to a child. On the evidence the doctor believed at the time that he had failed to abort her because she had never been pregnant. However he did not inform her of this, but allowed her to believe that she had had an abortion. He made no attempt to see her again, or to make sure her case was followed up by another doctor. Furthermore he had no tests carried out on her or on the material aspirated from her body during the operation. When the woman subsequently discovered that she was still pregnant she attempted to rectify the situation. She was eventually offered another termination when she was twenty-two weeks pregnant, by which time the operation would have involved a far greater degree of risk, and she consequently turned the offer down. *Held*, the doctor had been in breach of contract in that he had failed to exercise reasonable skill and care in carrying out the operation, and had negligently omitted to conduct any tests or see that the case was followed up. There was no evidence to suggest that the woman had allowed the pregnancy to continue because of a desire on her part to keep the child, and her refusal of a termination in the twenty-second week had been reasonable in view of the risk involved. Furthermore it was not against public policy to award damages where there was a failure to carry out a legal abortion, even though it resulted in the birth of a healthy child.

SCIURIAGA V POWELL (1979) 123 Sol Jo 406 (Queen's Bench Division: WATKINS J).

472   —— fundamental breach—goods not in conformity with contract

See *Toepfer v Warinco AG*, para. 2332.

473   —— sale of land—breach caused by fulfillment of condition precedent

See *100 Main Street v W. B. Sullivan Construction Ltd*, para. 2360.

474   —— solicitor—failure to give sound advice to vendor of house— measure of damages

See *Inder Lynch Devoy and Co v Subritzky*, para. 2691.

475   —— waiver of breach—goods not in conformity with contract— loading of goods supervised by buyer's representatives

See *Toepfer v Warinco AG*, para. 2332.

476   —— whether breach committed within jurisdiction

See *Atlantic Underwriting Agencies Ltd v Compagnia Di Assicurazione Di Milano SpA*, para. 427.

477   Building contracts

See BUILDING CONTRACTS.

478   Collateral contract—waiver of covenant in lease—whether cove- nant enforceable by landlord

See *Brikom Investments Ltd v Carr*, para. 1683.

479   Condition—contract of carriage—validity of condition made known after travel booking accepted—effective date of contract

See *The Dragon*, para. 297.

480   —— waiver—agreement conditional upon court's consent

New Zealand

The parties entered an agreement for the sale and purchase of a farm. The agreement was conditional upon the consent of the Administrative Division of the Supreme Court being granted by 26th January. The statutory time limit for filing an application form for the court's consent expired on 24th January. The purchasers had to sign a declaration to accompany the application. Their solicitors, realising that the declaration would not be completed before 24th January, asked the vendor's solicitors to file the application without the declaration, which they agreed to do. The declaration was later sent to the court on 28th January and the court's consent was granted on 12th February. The vendors refused to perform the contract. The Court of Appeal granted the purchasers a decree of specific performance. On appeal by the vendors, *held*, the vendors had waived their right to treat the contract as being at an end by lodging the application with the knowledge of the late delivery of the declaration. The appeal would be dismissed.

NEYLON v DICKENS [1978] 2 NZLR 35 (Privy Council: LORD WILBERFORCE, LORD HAILSHAM OF ST. MARYLEBONE, LORD EDMUND-DAVIES, LORD FRASER OF TULLYBELTON and LORD SCARMAN). Dictum of Lord Wilberforce in *Mardorf Peach v Attica Sea Carriers Corporation of Liberia, The Laconia* [1977] 1 All ER 545, 551, HL, 1977 Halsbury's Abridgment para. 2589 applied.

481   Consideration—adequacy—pre-existing contract—effect of commercial pressure

Hong Kong

The plaintiffs controlled a private company and the defendants were the majority shareholders in a public company. The plaintiffs entered into an agreement (the main agreement) with the public company to sell their shares in the private company, the purchase price to be satisfied by the issue of shares in the public company. In order not to depress the market, the plaintiffs agreed not to sell a percentage of the shares in the public company for a year. To ensure the plaintiffs' protection from a possible drop in the value of the shares during the year a subsidiary agreement between the plaintiffs and the defendants provided for purchase by the defendants at the end of the year at a fixed price. Subsequently realising that they had thus agreed to forgo any advantage from a possible increase in the value of the shares, the plaintiffs refused to carry out the main agreement unless the defendants cancelled the subsidiary agreement and replaced it with a guarantee by way of indemnity. The defendants, under pressure, did so.

The share price dropped and the plaintiffs sought to rely on the guarantee. The defendants refused to indemnify them and they brought an action on the guarantee. The Supreme Court of Hong Kong gave judgment for the plaintiffs but that decision was reversed on appeal. On further appeal to the Privy Council, *held*, the plaintiffs' promise, under the main agreement, not to sell a percentage of the shares for a year was made at the defendants' request and it was recognised that the plaintiffs would be compensated by some form of guarantee against a fall in share prices at that date. The agreed cancellation of the subsidiary agreement had left the plaintiffs unprotected. The consideration for the guarantee included the plaintiffs' promise not to sell the shares for a year and, although antecedent to the guarantee, was good consideration for the defendants' promise of indemnity. It was not merely an invalid past consideration. Further, to secure a party's promise by a threat of repudiation of a pre-existing obligation was not an abuse of a dominant bargaining position, nor was the defendants' consent to the guarantee obtained by duress. There had been commercial pressure brought to bear, but no coercion. The plaintiffs' appeal would be allowed.

PAO ON v LAU YIU [1979] 3 All ER 65 (Privy Council: LORD WILBERFORCE, VISCOUNT DILHORNE, LORD SIMON OF GLAISDALE, LORD SALMON and LORD SCARMAN). *Lampleigh v Brathwaite* (1615) Hob 105 and dictum of Bowen LJ in *Re Casey's Patents, Stewart v Casey* [1892] 1 Ch at 115, 116 applied.

482   Construction—contract for sale of ship—shipping practice

Two parties negotiated the sale of a ship on the basis of a form of agreement under which the ship was to be delivered "class maintained" and with "continuous machinery survey cycle up to date". Certain classification rules provided that if machinery was continuously surveyed, each item had to be surveyed once every five years and in general 20 per cent of all machinery had to be examined each year. The buyer eventually accepted the sellers terms but notified them that they expected about 75 per cent of the ship's machinery to be surveyed by the delivery date. When the ship was delivered, only 25 per cent of its machinery had been surveyed during the three years since the beginning of the relevant five year cycle. The buyers refused delivery contending that (i) their notification regarding a 75 per cent survey was a contractual term which had been broken; (ii) the classification rules required 20 per cent of machinery to be surveyed each year and therefore the continuous machinery survey was not up to date as required by the agreement; (iii) the sellers were in breach of an implied obligation to notify Lloyd's of certain defects which might affect the ship's class. *Held*, (i) the buyers' notification regarding a 75 per cent survey was not a contractual term; the words used merely expressed their hope or anticipation; (ii) the classification rules had to be construed according to shipping practice which showed that the requirement for a 20 per cent survey each year was not a contractual term. Therefore, the words "up to date" in the continuous machinery survey clause meant that everything had to be surveyed once every five years and not that 20 per cent had to be surveyed each year; (iii) there was no implied obligation to notify Lloyd's of defects which might affect maintenance of the ship's class since shipping practice was against notifying such matters. Accordingly the sellers were not in breach of contract.

THE BUENA TRADER, COMPANIA DE NAVEGACION POHING SA V SEA TANKER SHIPPING (PTE) LTD [1978] 2 Lloyd's Rep 325 (Court of Appeal: LORD DENNING MR, GOFF and CUMMING-BRUCE LJJ).

483 —— **variation of contract—breach—payment made on non-contractual document—estoppel**

A contract for the sale of United States wheat provided that the quantity of wheat shipped would be the natural weight indicated by official inspection certificates on loading. Natural weight is expressed in pounds and bushels in the United States and in kilogrammes and hectolitres on the continent. Payment was to be made by letters of credit against presentation of the certificates. It was subsequently agreed that the documents presented at the bank confirming the letters of credit should additionally include a certificate of an official laboratory in respect of natural weight. Shortly after shipment, the sellers notified the buyers of the natural weight which had been shipped. At the same time, the sellers sent official certificates of weight to the confirming bank accompanied by an invoice. The invoice was based upon the natural weight as stated in an unoffical laboratory certificate. The natural weight shown in the laboratory certificate was higher than the mathematical equivalent of the pounds per bushel given in the official certificates. The buyers did not see the documents presented to the bank for several months. The buyers' claim for the amount overpaid against the invoice was rejected by the sellers. In arbitration proceedings, the Board of Appeal of GAFTA found in favour of the buyers, but stated their award in the form of a special case. The sellers contended, inter alia, that the buyers had waived their right to claim damages for breach of contract when the bank made payment against the laboratory certificate, as that certificate was a non-contractual document. *Held*, it was clear from the original contract that the natural weight was a matter of quality which would probably be stated in pounds per bushel as the wheat was of American origin; the laboratory certificate was an optional certificate to indicate the equivalence in kilogrammes of the natural weight in pounds. The agreed operation of the letter of credit was in materially different terms from the original contract, and the original contract had, therefore been amended. However, the sellers had committed a breach of the sale contract, as amended, by their failure to present an official laboratory certificate to the bank. The action of the bank, in making payment against a non-contractual document, could not constitute an unequivocal representation that the buyers would not enforce their right to claim damages, and no equitable estoppel therefore arose in favour of the sellers.

ETS SOULES & CIE V INTERNATIONAL TRADE DEVELOPMENT CO LTD [1979] 2 Lloyd's Rep 122 (Queen's Bench Division: ROBERT GOFF J). *W. J. Alan & Co Ltd v El Nasr Export & Import Co* [1972] 1 Lloyd's Rep 313 applied.

484 **Contract of service—contract with minor—whether beneficial to minor—right of adult party to enforce**

See *Toronto Marlboro Major Junior 'A' Hockey Club v Tonelli*, para. 1870.

485   Contractual discretion—exercise—principles to be applied

See *The Vainqueur José, CVG Siderurgicia del Orinoco SA v London Steamship Owners'
Mutual Insurance Association Ltd*, para. 1614.

**486   Contractual term—excess payment—whether intended as
gratuity**

In 1937 the defendant authority agreed to reimburse the plaintiff company the
reasonable cost of installing a sewerage pipe. The pipe was finally installed in 1971,
whereupon the authority paid the company a substantial sum. The company
claimed a larger amount and the authority offered a further amount "in full and final
settlement" which was accepted on account. The company submitted their claim
for the whole of the larger amount to arbitration. On a case stated by the arbitrator
the court was asked to determine, inter alia, whether the authority was entitled to
recover any sums paid in excess of the amount to which the company was entitled.
Held, since both parties were important and respectable public undertakings, under
a duty to get value for public money, it was inconceivable that the authority would
have given a gratuity to the company. Accordingly, any sums paid in excess of the
amount due could not be construed as voluntary payments and were therefore
recoverable.

MERSEY DOCKS AND HARBOUR CO v NORTH WEST WATER AUTHORITY [1979] LS
Gaz R 101 (Queen's Bench Division: CANTLEY J). Dicta of MacKinnon LJ in
Shirlaw v Southern Foundries [1939] 2 KB 206 at 227, CA applied.

487   —— express term—duty to obtain import licence—nature of duty

See *Coloniale Import-Export v Loumidis Sons*, para. 499.

488   —— implied terms—Law Commission recommendations

The Law Commission has recommended that the implied obligations of a supplier
of goods under a "contract analogous to sale" (e.g. a contract of barter and a contract
for work and materials) should be put into statutory form and should be modelled
on the statutory obligations of the seller. Also, it recommended that implied terms
as to merchantable quality and fitness of purpose should be expanded to include an
obligation on the supplier that the goods should not only be of merchantable quality
or fit for their purpose at the time when the obligation arose but should continue to
be of such quality and fitness as can reasonably be expected at any particular time
thereafter. See *Law of Contract: Terms in Contracts for the Supply of Goods* (Law
Com. No. 95; HC 142).

**489   —— term depriving buyer of right to reject documents—incorpo-
ration of term into contract—effect**

See *S.I.A.T. Di De Ferro v Tradex Overseas SA*, para. 2336.

**490   —— term requiring payment against documents within certain
time—whether obligation mutual**

The sellers bought rapeseed c.i.f. Rotterdam/Europort and resold it to the buyers.
The contract contained a special clause that payment in cash would be against
documents if tendered to them by the seller by telegraphic transfer on the date of the
arrival of the vessel at the port of discharge but not later than twenty days after the
date of the bill of lading. The bill of lading was dated 11th December 1974.
However, the ship grounded on route and its arrival was delayed until April 1975.
The sellers received the bill of lading in January and in February issued delivery
orders to the buyers who rejected them on the ground that the presentation was out
of time, contending that the buyers were in default. It was decided that the
payments clause related to the time of payment and imposed no obligation upon
the sellers to present the documents in the stated time. The buyers appealed and the
decision was reversed. On appeal by the sellers the questions for the court were (i)

whether the clause imposed obligations upon the sellers and (ii) whether those obligations were conditions, warranties or innominate terms. *Held*, (i) it was a general principle of law that where the parties agreed that something would be done, the performance of which depended upon co-operation, each party would be bound to do all that was necessary for the doing of that thing; thus the sellers were under an implied obligation to tender the documents in time for the buyers to take up and pay for them on that date; (ii) terms as to the time of performance by the sellers of their obligations under c.i.f. contracts were generally held to be conditions. Further, on the terms of this contract the buyers were to take delivery when the vessel was ready to discharge and they could only have done that if they had already obtained possession of the documents against payment. It was therefore essential that the sellers acted in a way to enable them to do so and the term was a condition of the contract. Accordingly the appeal would be dismissed.

ALFRED C. TOEPFER (HAMBURG) v LENERSAN-POORTMAN N. V. (ROTTERDAM) ALFRED C. TOEPFER (HAMBURG) v VERHEIJDENS VEERVOEDER COMMISSIEHANDEL (ROTTERDAM) (1979) 25th May (unreported) (Court of Appeal: MEGAW, EVELEIGH and BRANDON LJJ). Decision of Donaldson J [1978] 2 Lloyd's Rep 555, 1978 Halsbury's Abridgment para. 491, affirmed.

491   Exclusion clause—contract of carriage—incorporation of clause—validity

See *The Dragon*, para. 297.

492   —— sale of land—whether effective to exclude liability

See *Hone v Benson*, para. 1959.

493   —— scope of clause—clause limiting liability of carrier—liability for goods damaged in storage pending shipment

See *Captain v Far Eastern Steamship Co*, para. 2520.

494   Force majeure clause—construction—extension of shipment period due to strike

A contract for the sale of United States soya beans provided for shipment between 5th and 25th October. The shipment period could be extended under a force majeure clause if there were strikes at the loading ports, providing notice was given naming the port or ports concerned. On 25th October the sellers notified the buyers that they were claiming an extension under the clause due to strikes at eight specified United States ports. The buyers claimed damages for breach of contract on the ground that the notice was invalid and referred the matter to arbitration. The Board of Appeal of FOSFA found in favour of the sellers but stated their award in the form of a special case. *Held*, the validity of the notice depended on the construction of the force majeure clause. The clause was intended to refer to ports which the sellers had arranged or intended to use before the strikes occurred; it did not require them to prove that any other United States ports were closed. The sellers' notice stated clearly that certain ports which they would have used were closed by strikes. As they could have shipped the cargo from any one or more of those ports within the guaranteed period but for the strikes, their notice was valid and they were entitled to an extension in the shipment period.

SOCIEDAD IBERICA DE MOLTURACION SA v TRADAX EXPORT SA [1978] 2 Lloyd's Rep 545 (Queen's Bench Division: DONALDSON J).

495   —— —— failure to obtain import licence

See *Coloniale Import-Export v Loumidis Sons*, para. 499.

496   Formation of contract—contract of carriage—whether effective from booking of passage or receipt of ticket—validity of conditions of carriage printed on ticket

See *The Dragon*, para. 297.

497   Frustration—act of foreign government—liability of buyer

See *Congimex SARL (Lisbon)* v *Continental Grain Export Corpn (New York)*, para. 150.

498   —— contract for sale of land—purchaser intending to develop land—development prohibited—whether contract frustrated

See *Victoria Wood Development Corpn Inc v Ondrey*, para. 2358.

499   —— force majeure and prohibition clauses—liability of buyer

Under a contract for the sale of coffee c.i.f. Piraeus, non-performance could only be justified by force majeure. The contract also provided that the buyers had the responsibility of obtaining an import licence. They followed the customary procedure for obtaining a licence in good time, but the Greek authorities refused their application. The sellers resold the coffee and claimed damages for breach of contract. The buyers contended that they were entitled to rely on the force majeure clause which prevailed over the clause requiring them to obtain a licence. Arbitrators found in favour of the sellers but stated their award in the form of a special case. *Held*, the contract gave the buyers responsibility for obtaining an import licence but did not express the nature of their obligation. The only term that could be implied was a limited obligation on the part of the buyers to use their best endeavours to obtain a licence, not an absolute warranty to do so. The word "responsibility" on its own was not sufficiently clear to impose an absolute warranty in a commercial contract. Moreover, a limited obligation was more consistent with a force majeure clause in the same contract. Therefore, as the buyers had taken all reasonable steps open to them to obtain a licence, they could justify their inability to perform the contract through force majeure.

COLONIALE IMPORT-EXPORT V LOUMIDIS SONS [1978] 2 Lloyd's Rep 560 (Queen's Bench Division: LLOYD J). *Anglo-Russian Merchant Traders Ltd v John Batt & Co (London) Ltd* [1917] 2 KB 679, CA, applied.

500   —— —— liability of seller

Sellers contracted to sell to buyers 1,000 tonnes of extracted soya bean meal c.i.f. Rotterdam for shipment 500 tonnes each April and May 1973. The contract provided by cl. 9 that the sellers could extend the period of shipment by giving notice. Clause 22, a force majeure clause, also provided for an extension of time. In March and April 1973 flooding in the River Mississippi caused delays in the loading of the soya bean meal. The sellers purported to give notice under both cls. 9 and 22. In July, the buyers called for fulfillment of the April shipment with goods with a bill of lading dated the last day of the period of shipment as extended by cl. 22, failing which they would hold the sellers in default. The sellers never tendered any goods in respect of the April shipment. The dispute was referred to arbitration and the Board of Appeal of GAFTA, holding the sellers liable in damages for breach of contract, stated their award in the form of a special case. The trial judge held that on the question of whether the purported extensions under cls. 9 and 22 were valid (in order to determine the date of default for the purpose of the assessment of damages), the purported notice under cl. 9 was invalid; the buyers, having accepted the notice under cl. 22 as valid although it was prima facie invalid as being out of time, were not also bound to treat as valid the notice under cl. 9. The sellers appealed. *Held*, the burden of proving that the cl. 9 notice was valid was upon the sellers; they had not discharged that burden and the Board, therefore, had been entitled to treat that notice as invalid. It had not been established that the notice under cl. 22 was invalid, and the buyers were therefore entitled to treat it as valid;

the buyers did not have the burden of proving that cl. 22 was valid merely because they were contending that the cl. 9 notice was invalid. The decision of the trial judge would be upheld, the damages being assessed as at the date for shipment as extended by cl. 22 only.

BUNGE GmbH v ALFRED C TOEPFER [1979] 1 Lloyd's Rep 554 (Court of Appeal: MEGAW, WALLER and EVELEIGH LJJ). Decision of Brandon J [1978] 1 Lloyd's Rep 506, 1978 Halsbury's Abridgment para. 500 affirmed.

501   —— —— —— **date of default**

Sellers sold the buyers a quantity of soya bean meal c.i.f. Rotterdam, to be shipped in April 1973. The contract incorporated the terms of GAFTA 100, including prohibition and force majeure clauses. Flooding of the Mississippi river prompted the United States government to restrict the export of soya bean meal not yet loaded on board ship. The sellers were prevented from appropriating the contract goods and invoked the force majeure clause. They adduced no evidence to show whether there were alternative goods available for shipment. The issue of the sellers' liability, and the appropriate date for the assessment of damages if they were liable, came before the court as a special case stated by the Board of Appeal of GAFTA. *Held*, (i) the flooding of the Mississippi came within the scope of the force majeure clause but the sellers could not rely on it because they were unable to show that the flooding had occasioned delay in the shipment of the goods they had intended to appropriate to the contract; they had failed to establish a chain of contracts back from themselves to an affected shipper; (ii) even if they were entitled to rely on their force majeure notices, they had delayed in passing them to the buyers and thus remained liable; (iii) because the force majeure notices were ineffective, the sellers were in default in accordance with the contract on the eleventh day after the goods should have been shipped. Damages had therefore to be assessed as at 11th May 1973. The buyers' contention that the sellers were not liable in damages until July, by which time the price of soya bean meal had greatly increased, was insupportable as that required the force majeure notice to be treated as bad for the purposes of establishing breach of contract and good for the purposes of assessment of damages.

AVIMEX SA v DEWULF AND CIE [1979] 2 Lloyd's Rep 57 (Queen's Bench Division: ROBERT GOFF J).

502   —— **valuable benefit obtained—principles governing award of just sum**

In a case in which a contract for the joint exploration of an oil concession had been frustrated, an action was brought for the award of a just sum under the Law Reform (Frustrated Contracts) Act 1943, s. 1 (3). The court laid down certain principles to be applied in considering whether to make an award and in the assessment of the just sum. It must first be shown that the defendant has, by reason of something done by the plaintiff in, or for the purpose of, the performance of the contract, obtained a valuable benefit (other than a payment of money) before the time of discharge. That benefit must be identified, and valued, and such value forms the upper limit of the award. The benefit could be identified as the end product of the services, but should not be identified as the services themselves. In cases where the defendant has obtained the benefit by reason of work done both by the plaintiff and by himself, that benefit must be apportioned by deciding what proportion is attributable to the work done by the plaintiff. The benefit is to be valued as at the date of frustration. No allowance, however, is to be made for "the time value of money" in circumstances where the defendant has had the use of the product of the plaintiff's contractual performance over a period of time before the frustrating event occurred. Expenditure incurred by the defendant before the time of discharge in, or for the purpose of performance of the contract, should be deducted from the value of the benefit, provided that it is shown that the defendant has suffered a change of position. The effect of the circumstances giving rise to the frustration of the contract must also be taken into account in relation to the benefit.

Having established that the defendant has obtained a valuable benefit, the court has next to assess a just sum to award to the plaintiff in respect of his performance. In cases where the benefit has been requested by the defendant, the basic measure of recovery in restitution is the reasonable value of the plaintiff's performance. If the defendant's actual benefit is less than the just sum which would otherwise be awarded, the award must be reduced to a sum equal to that benefit. The contract consideration is always relevant as providing some evidence of what will be a reasonable sum. In many cases it will be unjust to award more than the contract consideration, or a rateable part of it.

B.P. EXPLORATION CO (LIBYA) LTD v HUNT (No. 2) [1979] 1 WLR 783 (Queen's Bench Division: ROBERT GOFF J). *B.P. Exploration Co (Libya) Ltd v Hunt* [1976] 1 WLR 788, 1976 Halsbury's Abridgment para. 1979 followed.

503   Illegality—contract contrary to Peruvian exchange regulations— enforceability

See *The American Accord, United City Merchants (Investments) Ltd v Royal Bank of Canada*, para. 1904.

504   —— letter of credit—permission required under foreign exchange control—whether contract impossible to perform

Under a contract for the sale of wheat, payment was to be made by a letter of credit to be confirmed by a first class United States or West European bank. The letter of credit was to be opened by 31st March 1975. Exchange control permission was required in order to pay the sellers in foreign currency, but the buyers, a Turkish state organisation, took no steps to obtain the currency until 12th March 1975. Despite demands by the sellers throughout April 1975 that the letter of credit be opened, none was provided. On 30th April 1975, the sellers finally notified the buyers that they were treating them as being in default on the contract. In arbitration proceedings, the buyers contended that it would have been illegal for them to have procured a letter of credit without first obtaining exchange control permission under Turkish law and that the contract was, therefore, impossible to perform. The Board of Appeal of GAFTA found in favour of the sellers and stated their award in the form of a special case. *Held*, the place of performance was not Turkey and illegality under the law of Turkey was, therefore, no defence; the letter of credit had to be confirmed by a United States or West European bank, and the sellers were not concerned with the means by which that letter of credit was provided. The date of default was 30th April and not 31st March (the last date under the contract on which the letter of credit was to be opened) as the conduct of the buyers had led the sellers to believe that the contract was still open in April, and it could be inferred that there was an extension of time until the contract was determined by the sellers.

TOPRAK MAHSULLERI OFISI v FINAGRAIN COMPAGNIE COMMERCIALE AGRICOLE ET FINANCIERE SA [1979] 2 Lloyd's Rep 98 (Court of Appeal: LORD DENNING MR, ROSKILL and CUMMING-BRUCE LJJ). *Kleinwort Sons & Co v Unigarische Baumwolle Industrie Aktiengesellschaft* [1939] 2 KB 678 and *Rickards v Oppenheim* [1950] 1 KB 616 applied.

505   Mistake—undue influence—influence of son over elderly parents—whether transaction voidable

See *Avon Finance Co Ltd v Bridger*, para. 902.

506   —— unilateral mistake as to subject matter of contract—apportionment of loss

See *Haris Al-Afaq Ltd v Cameron Dempsey & Ivy*, para. 1892.

507   Non-delivery—liability of seller—assessment of damages—date of default

The sellers failed to perform a contract for the sale of soya bean meal and were in default. The date of default for the purposes of assessing damages was 31st July, 1st July or the 10th/11th July 1973. Under the terms of the contract a notice of appropriation had to be given within ten days of the bill of lading date which was 30th June. The prima facie date of default was therefore 10th/11th July. The sellers contended however that the buyers' request for an appropriation on 20th July was sent after the time limit for appropriation had passed. The buyers were thus waiving the time limit and the sellers were not in breach until 31st July where the buyers treated the contract as at an end. *Held*, a seller was only *prima facie* in default if he did not give notice of appropriation within ten days. In the case of string contracts with a specified degree of despatch, he would be deemed to have given the notice within the required period. The date of default was not 31st July. The buyers' repudiation of the contract on the 31st July specified that they would settle on the basis that 1st July was the date of default. This offer was not taken up by the sellers and the offer lapsed. The date of default was not the 1st July. On a question of whether the default date was the 10th or 11th July the court would follow a House of Lord's decision on the same question. The date of default was therefore 11th July.

BUNGE CORPN v USINES DE STORDEUR SA (1979) 1st February (unreported) (Queen's Bench Division: DONALDSON J). *Bremer Handelsgesellschaft mbH v Vanden Avenne–Izegem PVBA* [1978] 2 Lloyds Rep 106, HL, 1978 Halsbury's Abridgment para. 499 applied.

508   Novation—incorporation of first contract into second agreement—conduct of parties—whether new contract created

Canada

The plaintiff installed coin-operated washing machines in a block of flats under a contract which gave him the exclusive right to operate the machines for five years. The agreement also covenanted to bind any purchaser of the building to the terms of the contract. Six months later, the building was sold to the defendants under a contract which included a copy of the plaintiff's original installation contract. The defendants allowed the plaintiff to operate the machines for a few months but subsequently replaced them with their own machines. The plaintiff claimed damages from the defendants who argued that they were not a party to the installation contract. *Held*, what had to be considered was whether consent to novation could be inferred from the defendants' conduct. By their acceptance of the sale agreement which incorporated the installation contract and their acquiescence in the plaintiff's initial operation of the machines, the defendants had consented to a novation which created a new contract between the parties. Therefore the defendants were bound by the terms of the contract and the plaintiff's claim would be allowed.

PACIFIC WASH-A-MATIC LTD v R. O. BOOTH HOLDINGS LTD (1978) 88 DLR (3d) 69 (Supreme Court of British Columbia).

509   Offer and acceptance—validity of insurance policy

See *Rust v Abbey Life Assurance Co Ltd*, para. 1631.

510   Oral contract—condition—incorporation of condition into contract—previous course of dealing

Scotland

The owners of a crane damaged while on hire appealed against a decision that the hirers of the crane were not liable for the damage. The crane had been hired by telephone and, shortly after being delivered to the hirers, overbalanced and was damaged. It was the practice of the hiring company after making an oral contract, to send the hirers an acknowledgement of order form. This set out the particular terms of hire and a statement to the effect that the contract of hire was subject to the general conditions for the hiring of plant issued by the Contractors' Plant Association, a copy of which would be sent to the hirer on request. One of these conditions provided that the hirer should make good loss of or damage to the plant. The hirers had hired plant from the owners on twelve occasions during the previous four years and the same procedure had been followed on each occasion. The hirers conceded that a course of dealing had been established, but maintained that the general conditions of the CPA had never been incorporated into the contract. They had never seen a copy of the conditions and not being connected with the plant hire trade were not familiar with the conditions. The owners contended that the conditions were incorporated because by repeatedly referring to the conditions and their availability on request, they had taken sufficient action for incorporation and the hirers, by continuing to enter into oral contracts with the owners without requesting a copy of the conditions, had led the owners to believe that they agreed to the conditions. *Held*, this case differed from other cases involving a course of dealing in that in those cases the term relied upon was contained in a written document given to the contracting party, whereas in the present case there was merely a reference to a term contained in a written document never seen by the hirers. This case was analagous to the "ticket cases" but, as pointed out in *M'Cutcheon v MacBrayne* [1964] I All ER 430 the ticket cases were in a different category and different principles applied. Only one case bore any similarity to the present case, *M'Connell and Reid v Smith* 1911 SC 635, in which it was stated that mere reference was not sufficient to import the term into the contract, it was necessary to show that reasonable means were taken to give the other party notice of the condition. What constituted reasonable and sufficient notice depended upon the nature and scope of the condition and the whole facts and circumstances of the case. In this case the condition was particularly stringent, requiring particularly clear notice. It would have been easy to send a copy of the conditions with the acknowledgement; indeed this was done with other hirers who hired plant under written contracts, which contained a notice drawing particular attention to the condition in question. The owners had not given reasonable and sufficient notice to the hirers and the appeal would be dismissed.

GRAYSTON PLANT LTD V PLEAN PRECAST LTD 1976 SC 206 (Inner House).

511   Part performance—claim on quantum meruit basis—whether contract abandoned

Canada

A painter contracted to paint a woman's house. He completed three-quarters of the work but was unable to continue because he was short of paint. The woman refused to give him an advance, there being no provision in the contract that she should do so. The painter brought an action claiming he was entitled to recover on a quantum meruit for the value of the work completed. The total contract price was $550 and the court awarded him $375. The woman counterclaimed for $335 she had paid to get the house completed. Her counterclaim was dismissed. She appealed on the grounds that the plaintiff's claim on a quantum meruit should never have been allowed because the contract was an entire one and the painter had abandoned it before it was completed or substantially completed. *Held*, dismissing the appeal, the painter had not abandoned the contract but had wished to complete it. The only thing preventing him from doing so was the lack of paint. The woman had refused him an advance to buy more paint and had not been prepared to buy the paint herself and deduct it from the total contract price; thus he had had no alternative but to stop work. The trial judge was therefore right in allowing the painter's claim. The woman had paid an extra $160 above the $550 contract price, in paying someone else to finish the job. Although this would normally be allowed as a counterclaim, in this case the extra expense was caused by the inexperience of the man employed and in his using more paint than was necessary, and was not a genuine extra expense. The counterclaim would not, therefore, be allowed.

KEMP V McWILLIAMS (1978) 87 DLR (3d) 544 (Court of Appeal of Saskatchewan).

512   Privity—agreement conferring benefit on stranger to contract— reliance on agreement by stranger

Canada

An agreement was made between shareholders of a family-owned company whereby upon the death of any one shareholder, the remainder would pay certain benefits to the deceased's widow. The widow tried to enforce this agreement in her personal capacity as beneficiary under the agreement. *Held*, privity of contract prevented her from doing this but she could enforce the agreement as her husband's personal representative and executrix.

GASPARINI V GASPARINI (1978) 87 DLR (3d) 282 (Court of Appeal of Ontario).

513   Repudiation—arbitration—question of fact or law

See *Peter Lind and Co Ltd v Constable Hart and Co Ltd*, para. 133.

514   —— contract for design of plant—implied term as to fitness for purpose—right of one party to repudiate for breach of term

Plaintiffs contracted to design and supply a spray drying plant for use in the manufacture of powdered detergent. The defendants cancelled the supply order on the grounds that the design did not provide sufficient safety precautions and that the detergent produced would not be of a commercially acceptable quality. The plaintiffs alleged that this was a wrongful repudiation and sought damages. *Held*, there was an implied term in the contract that the plant would be reasonably fit for the purpose for which it was intended to be used. According to expert witnesses the plaintiffs were not in breach of that term, but had in fact designed a plant which was superior to those in use elsewhere. Accordingly the defendants had not been entitled to repudiate the contract and were liable in damages.

SPRAY PROCESSES LTD V MANRO PRODUCTS LTD (1979) 12th January (unreported) (Queen's Bench Division: SIR DOUGLAS FRANK QC sitting as a deputy High Court judge).

515   Sale of goods

See SALE OF GOODS.

516   Sale of land

See SALE OF LAND.

517   Waiver—covenant in lease—waiver subsisting over subsequent assignments

See *Brikom Investments Ltd v Carr*, para. 1683.

COPYRIGHT

Halsbury's Laws of England (4th edn.), Vol. 9, paras. 801–970

518   Article

Copyright, M. C. Dobbs (the scope of the Copyright Act 1956): 123 Sol Jo 558.

519   Anton Piller order—application for leave to appeal—no application for discharge of order—order already executed

See *Bestworth Ltd v Wearwell Ltd*, para. 2107.

520   —— application for order for discovery—unlawful interference with business

The Mechanical-Copyright Protection Society (MCPS) acted as agents for over two thousand copyright owners of mechanically reproduced works, by collecting the licence fees payable, in return for which they received a small commission. An inspector found the defendants' warehouse full of imported records and cassettes upon which no fees had been paid. The MCPS and two particular copyright owners made an ex parte application before service of a writ for an Anton Piller order, to restrain the defendants' unlawful dealings and for discovery of any documents and records, on the ground that the defendants had interfered with the MCPS's business by unlawful means. Relief was refused at first instance and on appeal, *held*, importation without a licence was unlawful and interfered with the MCPS's business as agents and affected their commission. Thus the MCPS's business was being unlawfully interfered with by the conduct of the defendants. To obtain relief in the form of an Anton Piller order three conditions had to be satisfied: that there was a strong prima facie case; that the damage, actual or potential, was serious, that there was a strong possibility that the defendants would destroy incriminating evidence once the writ had been issued. All these conditions had been satisfied on the evidence. Thus, the appeal would be allowed and the relief granted.

ORMROD LJ noted that the MCPS would be entitled to sue in their own name as it would be impossible for them to consult their large number of principals before starting litigation of this nature.

CARLIN MUSIC CORPN. V COLLINS [1979] FSR 548 (Court of Appeal: LORD DENNING MR, ORMROD and BROWNE LJJ). *Anton Piller KG v Manufacturing Processes Ltd* [1976] Ch. 55, 1975 Halsbury's Abridgment, para. 2623 followed.

521 Three intending plaintiffs alleged infringement of copyright under the Copyright Act 1956, s. 5 (3). Before the issuing of a writ, they made an ex parte application for, inter alia, an injunction to restrain the intended defendants from unlawfully interfering with the third plaintiff's business (a royalty collection agency) by distributing imported records, the copyright of which was vested in the first and second plaintiffs. They also sought an order for entry into the defendants' premises for the purpose of inspecting and removing articles which infringed the plaintiffs' copyright. The High Court refused to do this, and on appeal *held*, the plaintiffs feared that once a writ was served, the infringing goods would disappear. The intentional employment of unlawful means to injure a person's business was an actionable wrong. The plaintiffs had established that there was a sufficient prima facie unlawful act to justify the application for relief and the injunction would be granted and the order made.

RE M's APPLICATION (1979) 123 Sol Jo 142 (Court of Appeal: LORD DENNING MR, ORMROD and BROWNE LJJ).

552 ### Assignment—assignment of legal and equitable title—formalities

Plaintiffs brought an action for infringement of copyright in three sets of drawings, two of which had been prepared by independent contractors and the third by an employee of a company, the assets of which had been vested in the plaintiffs on incorporation. The court ordered that the action in respect of the first two be struck out because the plaintiffs had failed to show that copyright had passed to them and no amendment would have given them a cause of action at the date of the writ. The action on the third was not struck out because the particulars could be amended to show that the plaintiffs had acquired a beneficial interest in the copyright. On appeal *held*, as the plaintiffs had not established that copyright in the first two sets of drawings had passed to them they had no reasonable cause of action in respect of them and so it was correct to strike out the action. The action in respect of the third should also be struck out because, whether beneficial ownership in the copyright had passed or not, there had been no disposition in writing within Law of Property Act 1925, s. 53 (1) (c) and Copyright Act 1956, s. 36, and therefore the plaintiffs had not had a title on which to sue at the date of the writ.

ROBAN JIG AND TOOL CO LTD V TAYLOR [1979] FSR 130 (Court of Appeal: STAMP, ORMROD and BRIDGE LJJ).

523 ### Infringement—advertisements—interlocutory relief

Interlocutory relief was sought to restrain infringement of copyright in photographs which the defendants had used in advertisements for their blank tapes. There were twenty-four plaintiffs, and although only four had had their copyright infringed, the other twenty were seeking to justify their claim on a *quia timet* basis. The plaintiffs further alleged that the advertisements implied that the plaintiffs' tapes were defective, and incited the public to infringe copyright. The defendants admitted the breach of copyright, but sought, firstly, to have all but the four plaintiffs directly affected, eliminated from the action. Secondly, they applied to have all those parts of the statements of claim relating to allegations other than the infringement of copyright struck out, as they were not reasonable causes of action. *Held*, relief regarding the infringement of copyright would be granted, but only to the four plaintiffs directly involved. The other twenty plaintiffs had failed to show that any future breach of their copyright by the defendants was threatened. The other allegations would be struck out altogether. There was no implication in the advertisements that the tapes were defective, nor was the advertising of blank tapes an incitement to the general public to breach copyright.

A AND M RECORDS INC v AUDIO MAGNETICS INC (UK) LTD [1979] FSR 1 (Chancery Division: FOSTER J).

524   —— application for summary judgment—defence of innocence—whether defence plausible

The defendants published in their newspaper photographs which had been taken by the plaintiff, but which the defendants had purchased for £3000 from a third party, W. The defendants had obtained from W a signed undertaking to the effect that he had copyright in the photographs and had the right to sell them. The plaintiff had never assigned the copyright to W and had not given permission for the photographs to be published. The plaintiff applied for summary judgment under RSC Ord. 14, following the issue of a writ seeking, inter alia, a declaration that the defendants had infringed her copyright in the photographs and had wrongfully converted the infringing copies to their own use, and an inquiry as to damages for the infringement and the conversion. The defendants claimed that they had been unaware of the plaintiff's copyright, and that they had believed and had had reasonable grounds for believing that W owned and was entitled to sell the copyright and that publication would not infringe any copyright. *Held*, the defendants knew from the outset that the plaintiff had taken the photographs and ought therefore to have had a suspicion that she owned the copyright. Any reasonable purchaser, particularly for a sum of £3000, would have made inquiries as to how W obtained the copyright in photographs someone else had taken. The defendants had failed to establish a plausible defence and the plaintiff would be granted the declaration sought, without the matter going to trial. An inquiry would be made as to damages for infringement, including damages for flagrancy. The Copyright Act 1956, s. 18 (2) (b) precluded an award of damages for conversion where there was a defence of innocence. Such a defence could not be determined as part of an inquiry but would have to go to trial, since it went to liability and not quantum. But the defendants could not rely on the defence as they had not shown that they had "reasonable grounds for believing" that the articles were not infringing copies. Thus they were not protected by s. 18 (2) and an inquiry as to damages for conversion would be made.

THE LADY ANNE TENNANT v ASSOCIATED NEWSPAPERS GROUP LTD [1979] FSR 298 (Chancery Division: MEGARRY V-C).

525   —— conversion of second-hand cars—interlocutory relief

The defendants intended to buy second-hand motor cars, manufactured by the plaintiffs, and carry out certain conversions which, the plaintiffs claimed, would infringe their copyright and would constitute passing off. One such conversion had already been carried out and the car sold to the first defendant. The plaintiffs sought interlocutory relief, which was granted by the trial judge because the damage which could be done to the plaintiffs was considerable, since their reputation rested on the faultless engineering and finish of their cars. The first defendant appealed against that part of the injunction which restrained him from using his car. *Held*, use of his car for domestic purposes only would be excluded from the ambit of the injunction.

ROLLS-ROYCE LTD v ZANELLI [1979] RPC 148 (Court of Appeal: BUCKLEY, ORR and GOFF LJJ).

526   **—— discovery of documents in action for infringement—relevance of documents to questions raised in action**

See *British Leyland Motor Corpn v Wyatt Interpart Co Ltd*, para. 919.

527   **—— frames from cinematograph films—use of frames in magazine and poster**

A British publishing company obtained photographs from an American television film series, and published several of them in a magazine, and one in the form of a poster. Some of the prints were bought from an agency with the proviso that they be used for editorial purposes, and others were obtained free of charge from the BBC on condition that they were used to publicise the television series. The makers of the series claimed an infringement of their film copyright within the meaning of the Copyright Act 1956, s. 13 (5), contending that by printing copies of the magazine and poster the defendants had made copies of frames from the plaintiffs' cinematograph films; each frame being part of a film, the prints were therefore copies of the films within the meaning of s. 13 (10) of the Act. *Held*, a single frame from a film could not be construed as 'a substantial part' of the film, and its use in a magazine or poster did not equate with a sequence of moving images which went to make up a film, and therefore the prints were not copies of the films within the meaning of the Act. This being so, the defendants had not infringed the plaintiffs' copyright. However, should an infringement be acknowledged to have taken place in a later holding, the defendants would be liable for conversion damages in respect of those photographs obtained from the BBC, since they should have made inquiry as to the feasibility of their intention to exploit the prints for their own profit. The action would be dismissed.

SPELLING GOLDBERG PRODUCTIONS INC v B.P.C. PUBLISHING [1979] FSR 494 (Chancery Division: MERVYN DAVIES QC sitting as a deputy High Court judge).

528   **—— historical work—permitted degree of copying**

The author of a non-fiction book brought a copyright action against a novelist whom he alleged had copied passages of his book to introduce the subject-matter of a novel and give it credibility. In considering whether the copying had been substantial, *held*, the degree of copying which could be permitted from a historical work was greater than that from a work of fiction, since the author of the former would be presumed to have intended that a reader should use the information contained in the book. However, the non-fiction book in this case was not a historical work for historians but a mixture of facts, recollections and philosophy which was intended as a book for the general reader and was therefore in competition with the novel. The novelist had clearly copied passages from the non-fiction book and was accordingly in breach of copyright.

RAVENSCROFT v HERBERT (1979) 22nd March (unreported) (Chancery Division: BRIGHTMAN J).

529   **—— interlocutory injunction—importation—free trade agreement—whether injunction available**

The defendant imported records and tapes from Portugal, which it sold to record shops in the United Kingdom. It was accepted by all the parties that they were not illegal or "bootleg" records and tapes. The plaintiff issued a writ seeking to restrain the defendant. The defendant accepted that, prima facie, the importation contravened the Copyright Act 1956, s. 16 (2), (3), relating to importation, in that had the records and tapes been made in the United Kingdom, they would have constituted an infringement of copyright. The defendant contended however, that EEC Treaty art. 113, relating to harmonisation of laws, together with Council Regulation (EEC) 2844/72, establishing a Community free trade area with Portugal, constituted a complete defence. The defendant sought an interlocutory injunction to restrain the plaintiff from distributing to the defendant's customers, letters or circulars alleging that the importation of the records and tapes was illegal or unlawful. *Held*, the defendant itself had issued a circular to its customers flatly asserting its right to import, before the plaintiff had issued its own circular as a riposte. It was outside the maxims of equity to allow a defendant, who had enjoyed the benefits of its own type of circular, to halt the plaintiff's use of the same tactics. It was not therefore an appropriate case in which to grant the defendant an interlocutory injuction.

POLYDOR LTD v HARLEQUIN RECORD SHOPS LTD [1979] 3 CMLR 432 (Chancery Division: MEGARRY V-C).

530   —— musical work—performance in public—meaning of "in public"

A society exploited the performing rights in recordings of musical works by taking assignments of the rights and granting licences to persons to play the recordings in public for a fee. The defendants were owners of record shops who refused to obtain licences or pay fees in respect of records which were played over loudspeakers in the shops. The society claimed that this constituted an infringement of its performing rights in the works and sought an injunction restraining the alleged infringement. The defendants contended that playing the records did not constitute performance "in public", and hence was not restricted by the Copyright Act 1956, s. 2 (5). *Held*, the playing of the records in the shops constituted a performance "in public", since a performance given to an audience constituted of persons present in shops which the public at large was permitted and encouraged to enter with a view to purchasing records and increasing the shopowner's profit could only be described as a performance in public. The injunction would be granted.

PERFORMING RIGHT SOCIETY LTD v HARLEQUIN RECORD SHOPS LTD [1979] 2 All ER 828 (Chancery Division: BROWNE-WILKINSON J).

531   —— reproduction of drawings—proof of copying

The plaintiffs brought an action for infringement of artistic copyright in drawings relating to knock-down plastic drawers for the furniture industry. They alleged that the defendants had reproduced the drawings by manufacturing a certain design of drawers. The defendants admitted having had access to the plaintiffs products but contested (i) that they did not copy and (ii) that they were entitled to rely on the defence provided in the Copyright Act 1956, s. 9 (8), that the making of a three-dimensional object could not infringe the copyright in an artistic work, if the object would not appear to non-experts to be a reproduction of that artistic work. These contentions were rejected at first instance but upheld by the Court of Appeal. On appeal by the plaintiffs, *held*, (i) there was a striking similarity between the defendants' drawers and the plaintiffs' drawers, which, combined with proof of access to the plaintiffs productions, establishing a prima facie case of infringement which the defendants had to answer. The defendants had not only failed to demonstrate any alternative to copying or proved that all they had done had been to adopt a concept, but also had, on the evidence, positively supported the charge of copying specific drawings, directly or through components made by them. (ii) Whether an object would or would not appear to a non-expert to be a reproduction of a drawing, or part of it, was an issue of fact to be decided by the judge (as a non-expert) upon a visual comparison of the object with the drawing. A non-expert would, in the present case, have recognised that the defendants' drawer was a reproduction of the plaintiffs' drawing and the defence therefore failed and the defendants were guilty of infringement.

L. B. (PLASTICS) LTD v SWISH PRODUCTS LTD [1979] RPC 551 (House of Lords: LORD WILBERFORCE, LORD HAILSHAM OF ST. MARYLEBONE, LORD SALMON, LORD FRASER OF TULLYBELTON and LORD KEITH OF KINKEL).

Decision of the Court of Appeal [1978] FSR 32, 1978 Halsbury's Abridgment para. 518 reversed.

532   The plaintiff was the manufacturer and patent holder of steel lintels designed for use with cavity walls. The defendant received a brochure illustrating the plaintiff's lintels, and later began to manufacture lintels which differed only in that the rear support member was inclined at a slight angle and there was no flange at the rear lower corner. In an action alleging infringement of the copyright in the plaintiff's drawings and infringement of the patent, the trial judge dismissed the copyright claim, but held that there had been an infringement of the patent. The defendant appealed and the plaintiff cross-appealed. *Held*, (i) the defendant's drawings had been found to be original, and those details which were identical were not sufficient to infringe the copyright as there could be no infringement of copyright by coincidence. (ii) The patent had not been infringed, since although the presence of a back plate was essential to complete the box structure of the lintel, an essential feature of the plaintiff's lintel required that the back plate should be truly vertical, a feature which was absent in the defendant's lintel. Accordingly, the defendant's appeal would be allowed and the plaintiff cross-appeal dismissed.

CATNIC COMPONENTS LTD v HILL AND SMITH LTD [1979] FSR 619 (Court of Appeal: BUCKLEY and WALLER LJJ and SIR DAVID CAIRNS). Decision of Whitford J [1978] FSR 405, 1978 Halsbury's Abridgment para. 521 reversed in part.

533   —— —— **resemblance between products**

The plaintiff company designed and constructed a racing car, the D.N.9. The design drawings were made by their chief designer and his staff. The D.N.9 was seventy per cent complete when the company ran into financial difficulties and the designer gave a number of drawings of the car to the defendants. On leaving the company, he joined the defendants and constructed a modified copy of the D.N.9 using the D.N.9 drawings. The new car, the F.A.1 was, as a result, finished before the D.N.9 and attracted the publicity and the interest of sponsors which would have accrued to the D.N.9. The plaintiffs brought an action for copyright infringement of the D.N.9 plans claiming they were entitled to additional damages under the Copyright Act 1956, s. 17 (3) as there had been flagrant infringement. The defendants contended that (i) if copyright existed, it belonged to the designer as author of the work; (ii) they had a defence under s. 18 (2) of the 1956 Act as they had reasonable grounds for believing that they were not infringing copyright; (iii) that s. 9 (8) of the 1956 Act was applicable, which provided that the making of a three-dimensional object could not infringe the copyright in an artistic work if the object would not appear to non-experts to be a reproduction of the artistic work. *Held*, (i) the drawings were original works under which copyright existed. The designer's contract showed clearly that he was an employee of the plaintiff company and the copyright on the D.N.9 drawings therefore vested in the plaintiffs; (ii) although the defendants believed that the plaintiff company would be wound up and the D.N.9 would never appear on a race track, they did know that the F.A.1 was a modified reproduction of the D.N.9; (iii) the resemblance between the F.A.1 car and the D.N.9 drawings was recognisable to a layman. Further the infringement had been flagrant in view of the benefits received by the F.A.1 and additional damages would be awarded. The F.A.1 was not to be driven using or incorporating any part which was a copy of the D.N.9.

NICHOLS ADVANCED VEHICLE SYSTEMS INC v REES [1979] RPC 127 (Chancery Division: TEMPLEMAN J).

534   —— **sale of infringing article—knowledge of infringement—actual or constructive knowledge**

Australia

The owners of a copyright in a cassette recording sought to restrain the sale in Australia of copies of the cassette, which had been imported from Singapore. There was no challenge to ownership or subsistence of copyright and it was conceded that the offending cassettes had been copied from the plaintiffs' tapes. However, the defendants sought to rely on the provisions in an Australian statute, which are identical in substance to the provisions in the Copyright Act 1956, s. 5 (3), and which provide, inter alia, that the copyright in a musical work is infringed where an imported article is sold without the licence of the copyright owner and the seller knows that if the article had been manufactured in the place into which it was imported it would have constituted an infringement of copyright. The defendants maintained that they had no such knowledge and that, therefore, the copyright had not been infringed. The trial judge, in the absence of proof of any knowledge on the part of the defendants, found for the defendants. The plaintiffs appealed, tendering new evidence in the form of an affidavit, from which it appeared that the shop manager knew at the time of the sale that the tapes were pre-recorded. The plaintiffs further contended that in any event actual knowledge was not required, but only constructive knowledge. *Held*, it was necessary to show actual knowledge, which could be inferred where a person in that line of business ought to have had such knowledge, unless there was evidence leading the court to the contrary conclusion. Thus it could be inferred that the shop-manager knew that he was dealing with infringing cassettes and, as no evidence was produced refuting this, as an employee of the defendants, his knowledge was their knowledge. The defendants had, therefore, infringed the copyright and an injunction would be granted.

RCA CORPN v CUSTOM CLEARED SALES PTY LTD [1978] FSR 576 (Supreme Court of New South Wales).

535   —— trade literature—reproduction of leaflet for sale with product

The plaintiffs, inventors of a herbicide, had carried out most of the research and trials for the use of the herbicide, which they had published in scientific journals. For sale with their own product they had compiled and published a leaflet, giving details of how and when the product should be used. With the expiry of the patent, the defendants started to manufacture the herbicide and produced a leaflet similar to the plaintiffs'. The plaintiffs brought an action for infringement of copyright and sought interlocutory relief, which was refused by the trial judge. On appeal, *held*, it was arguable both that the plaintiffs had a copyright on which they were entitled to sue and that there had been an infringement of that copyright; for although the defendants were entitled to use information in the public domain in compiling their trade literature, they were not entitled to copy the plaintiffs' trade literature, thereby using the plaintiffs' skill and judgment and saving themselves the trouble of compiling and selecting their own information. As damages would not be an adequate remedy for either party, and the balance of convenience was in favour of maintaining the status quo, an interlocutory injunction would be granted.

ELANCO PRODUCTS LTD v MANDOPS (AGROCHEMICAL SPECIALISTS) LTD [1979] FSR 46 (Court of Appeal: BUCKLEY, ROSKILL and GOFF LJJ).

536   —— use of confidential information—order for inspection—plaintiff's employee as inspector

The defendants, two directors of a company which was a subsidiary of the plaintiff American corporation, bought the business from the receiver when it went into liquidation. The plaintiff alleged that the defendants were using confidential information and drawings made during the period when the company had been a subsidiary. The defendants claimed that the drawings had been used to complete orders already under way at the time of liquidation, but that they had since made fresh drawings based on new technology. The plaintiff applied for an order to inspect the drawings to ascertain whether they infringed their copyright and whether use had been made of confidential information in the new drawings. They put forward one of their employees as a competent inspector. The defendants objected on the grounds that the employee could apply the knowledge contained in the drawings for the plaintiff's benefit. *Held*, an order would be made to allow inspection of the drawings without removing or taking copies of them. The defendants' objections to the projected inspector would be overruled since the employee would be unable to store enough information in his mind by examination of the drawings to make him a risk, and further he was the most suitable person since he was familiar with the original drawings and would therefore know what constituted a direct infringement of copyrights held by the plaintiff.

CENTRI-SPRAY CORP v CERA INTERNATIONAL LTD [1979] FSR 175 (Chancery Division: WHITFORD J).

537   International Conventions

The Copyright (International Conventions) (Amendment) Order 1979, S.I. 1979 No. 577 (in force on 21st June 1979) further amends the Copyright (International Conventions) Order 1972 to take account of the accession of El Salvador to the Universal Copyright Convention. The Order extends to dependent countries of the Commonwealth to which the 1972 Order extends.

538

The Copyright (International Conventions) Order 1979, S.I. 1979 No. 1715 (in force on 24th January 1980), supersedes with amendments certain specified orders providing for the protection, in the United Kingdom and the countries to which the Copyright Act 1956 has been extended, of works and other subject matter originating in other countries party to international copyright conventions. The amendments take account of the accession of El Salvador and the Republic of Ireland to the International Convention for the Protection of Performers, Producers of Phonograms and Broadcasting Organisations.

539   Performing Right Tribunal—Hong Kong

The Copyright (Hong Kong) (Amendment) Order 1979, S.I. 1979 No. 910 (in force on 24th August 1979), amends the Copyright (Hong Kong) Order 1972 by extending the provisions of the Copyright Act 1956 so as to establish a Performing Right Tribunal in and for Hong Kong.

540   Reversionary interest—ownership of interest—validity of assignments—works of joint authorship

The Court of Appeal was required to consider the rights of the parties in a complex case involving the ownership of a multitude of reversionary interests under the Copyright Acts 1911 and 1956. Under the 1911 Act the proviso to s. 5 (2) (as preserved by the 1956 Act) provided that the copyright in a work reverted to the author's legal representatives twenty-five years after his death. Section 24 substituted a longer period of copyright for that in the Literary Copyright Act 1842 but provided that, where an author had assigned the whole of his copyright under the 1842 Act, the substituted right would return to the author on the date on which the first right was due to expire. The questions for the court were whether (i) an aptly worded assignment dated before the 1911 Act which assigned the whole term of the copyright in a pre-1912 work could constitute an express agreement within the s. 24 (1) proviso; (ii) an assignment of the copyright in a pre-1912 work made after the 1911 Act was effective to assign the substituted right and, if so, whether the s. 5 (2) proviso applied; (iii) a song in which the music and lyrics were written by different people was a collective work and, if so, whether the s. 5 (2) proviso included the individual copyrights as well as the collective copyright; (iv) a song which was a work of joint authorship was collective. *Held,* (i) the words "express agreement" in s. 24 (1) meant an agreement expressly referring to the substituted right and therefore could not refer to an assignment made before the 1911 Act; (ii) the words could apply to assignments made after the passing of the 1911 Act, although the wording of the assignments in question was not effective to transfer the substituted copyright to the assignee. If it had been, the s. 5 (2) proviso would have applied; (iii) a song in which the music and lyrics were written by different people was a collective work, but the s. 5 (2) proviso only applied to the separate, independent copyright in a collective work, not to the individual copyrights; (iv) a work of joint authorship was not a collective work. There were two separate definitions of joint authorship in the Act and if it had been intended to exclude such works from the s. 5 (2) proviso it would have been done expressly.

REDWOOD MUSIC LTD v B. FELDMAN AND CO LTD [1979] RPC 385 (Court of Appeal: STEPHENSON, BRIDGE and SHAW LJJ).

For earlier proceedings see *Redwood Music Ltd v Francis, Day and Hunter* [1978] RPC 429, 1978 Halsbury's Abridgment para. 525.

CORONERS

Halsbury's Laws of England (4th edn.), Vol. 9, paras. 1001–1200

541　　Article

The Coroner's Jury, Anthony Morris: 129 NLJ 1225.

CORPORATIONS

Halsbury's Laws of England (4th edn.), Vol. 9, paras. 1201–1407

542　　Government of corporations—visitor—jurisdiction—university

See *Patel v University of Bradford Senate*, para. 1010.

COUNTY COURTS

Halsbury's Laws of England (4th edn.), Vol. 10, paras. 1–684

543　　Administration of Justice Act 1977—commencement

The Administration of Justice Act 1977 (Commencement No. 6) Order 1979, S.I. 1979 No. 972, brought into force, on 3rd September 1979, 1977 Act, s. 20, 1977 Halsbury's Abridgment para. 580, which amends County Courts Act 1959, s. 186 so as to allow the service of summonses and other documents to be proved by certificate, instead of by indorsement on a copy of the relevant document.

544　　Adoption proceedings—refusal to perfect order—application for mandamus—availability

The applicants, a married couple, applied to the county court to adopt the wife's niece who had been living with them since the death of her mother. The application had strong support from the guardian ad litem, and the consent of the niece's father, from whom she was estranged. The judge pronounced an adoption order, but subsequently stated that he had reconsidered the case and felt obliged to refuse to perfect the order until he had thoroughly considered the advantages of wardship proceedings. The judge dismissed the applicants' application to perfect the order. The applicants then applied to the High Court for an order of mandamus to compel the judge to perfect his order. *Held*, it was plain from the authorities that a judge might alter or vary an order at any time until the order was perfected, provided that there was a valid reason for so doing. The power vested in the judge was a judicial discretion, and the sole question was whether the judge had exercised his discretion judicially. In the instant case, the judge gave no reason at all to support his conclusion that the niece should be made a ward of court and therefore did not exercise his discretion judicially and was not justified in varying or altering the original order. Accordingly, that order should stand, and the judge would be directed that his original order should be perfected.

R v COLCHESTER AND CLACTON COUNTY COURT, EX PARTE ADW AND BAW (1979) 9 Fam Law 155 (Queen's Bench Division; LORD WIDGERY CJ, BRIDGE LJ and CAULFIELD J).

545　　County Court Rules—amendment

The County Court (Amendment) Rules 1979, S.I. 1979 No. 1045 (in force on 3rd September 1979), further amend the County Court Rules 1936. An adoption order following divorce may now be made by the relevant divorce county court; proof of service of documents by certificate is allowed and a certificate of postal service may be entered on the praecipe rather than on a copy of the summons; summonses sent by post must be sent first class and there is a prescription of service on the seventh day after posting; the requirement that conduct money should not be less than the prescribed minimum is abolished; a person making an affidavit may now in certain circumstances give a "work address" instead of a "home address" and may also apply for permission to omit the address altogether; contribution orders may not be enforced where the claim in the main proceedings is unsatisfied except with the leave of the court; the Rules applicable to summary proceedings for possession of land are amended so that in all cases unnamed respondents are given notice in Form 399 of their right to be heard in the proceedings; interest rates in equity proceedings are brought into line with those applicable in the High Court; the period for service of an application for a new tenancy under the Landlord and Tenant Act 1954, Part II is increased to two months; general directions as to who should be made respondents in guardianship proceedings are given; a solicitor whose client's legal aid certificate has been discharged or revoked need no longer apply to be taken off the court record; the title of Form 138, used in Rent Act cases, is reworded; and a plaintiff may now obtain restitution of premises that have been re-entered wrongfully after the execution of a warrant of possession.

546   The County Court (Amendment No. 2) Rules 1979, S.I. 1979 No. 1488 (in force on 10th December 1979), amend the County Court Rules 1936. The forms of originating application for family provision under the Inheritance (Provision for Family and Dependants) Act 1975, s. 1 and the Matrimonial Causes Act 1973, s. 35 are amended to take account of the increase in the upper limit of county court jurisdiction to £15,000. A court officer is required to inform the police immediately the court varies or discharges an injunction with a power of arrest attached under the Domestic Violence and Matrimonial Proceedings Act 1976, s. 2 or directs that a magistrates' court order with a power of arrest attached is to cease to have effect under the Domestic Proceedings and Magistrates' Courts Act 1978, s. 28; a copy of the variation or discharging order must also be delivered to the police.

547   Fees—amendment

The County Court Fees (Amendment) Order 1979, S.I. 1979 No. 967 (in force on 3rd September 1979), amends the County Court Fees Order 1978, 1978 Halsbury's Abridgment para. 539 by increasing the fees payable for (i) the issue of all proceedings, (ii) bailiff service, (iii) warrants of delivery or of execution against goods, (iv) applications and orders for the attendance of judgment debtors and (v) warrants of possession.

548   The County Court Fees (Amendment No. 2) Order 1979, S.I. 1979 No. 1149 (in force on 24th September 1979) further amends the County Court Fees Order 1978, 1978 Halsbury's Abridgment para. 539 by increasing the fee payable on the commencement of proceedings for any relief or remedy other than for the recovery of a sum of money or for the delivery of goods.

549   Funds in court

The County Court Funds (Amendment) Rules 1979, S.I. 1979 No. 105 (in force on 1st March 1979) amend the County Court Funds Rules 1965, r. 24 (1) by raising the rate of interest allowed on money in a short-term investment account from 10 per cent to 12½ per cent per annum.

550   The County Court Funds (Amendment No. 2) Rules 1979, S.I. 1979 No. 1619 (in force on 1st January 1980), further amend the County Court Funds Rules 1965, r. 24 (1) by raising the rate of interest allowed on money in a short term investment account from 12½ per cent to 15 per cent per annum.

551   Jurisdiction—former jurisdiction of Stannaries Court—summary offence

See *R v East Powder JJ, ex parte Lampshire*, para. 1785.

552   —— power of court to amend application

An originating application was taken out in the name of a tenants' association asking for specific performance of covenants to repair contained in its members' leases. The landlord contended that the association, as an unincorporated body, had no legal right of action and that the proceedings were therefore a nullity. Accordingly, the association applied to have the proceedings amended under the County Court Rules, Ord. 15, r. 1, requesting that one tenant be substituted as plaintiff to pursue the claim for specific performance as set out in the application. At the same time an application was made for an alternative claim for damages for breach of contract to be included in the application. The judge set aside an order by the registrar striking out the proceedings, holding that he had jurisdiction to amend the application under Ord. 5, r. 6 and Ord. 15. On appeal by the landlord, *held*, Ord. 5, r. 6 concerned actions that would have been defeated by reason of misjoinder or non-joinder of parties and did not apply in this instance. Ord. 15, r. 1 gave the court jurisdiction to amend applications. However, in this instance, if the case had been made out, the measure of damage would have been different in the case of virtually every tenant, for a great number of reasons. To allow the substitution of an individual claim for damages by one tenant only would have added to the existing confusion. Accordingly, the appeal would be dismissed.

HERMITAGE COURT OWNERS' ASSOCIATION v CLYFTVILLE PROPERTIES LTD (1979) 251 Estates Gazette 261 (Court of Appeal: EVELEIGH and BRANDON LJJ).

553   Jury—right to trial by jury—action for false imprisonment

The plaintiff brought an action in the county court claiming damages for false imprisonment. He alleged that a ticket collector in an underground station had wrongfully detained him for fifteen minutes at a ticket barrier after he had lost his ticket. The plaintiff applied to have the action tried with a jury pursuant to the County Courts Act 1959, but the judge refused on the ground that there was no genuine claim in issue on the admitted facts, and that on other grounds costs outweighed the merits. The plaintiff appealed. *Held*, it could not be said that the claim for false imprisonment was not in issue, as required under s. 94 (3) of the 1959 Act. The Regulation of Railways Act 1889, s. 5 (2) made detention of a passenger who did not produce a ticket lawful only if he had refused to give his name and address. As there was no allegation by the defendants or admission by the plaintiff that he had failed to do so, there was no basis for saying that there was not a claim for false imprisonment in issue. The judge had erred on the material before her as she was not entitled to form a view that the claim was suspect and so was not in issue. The appeal would be allowed.

HARMSWORTH v LONDON TRANSPORT EXECUTIVE (1979) 123 Sol Jo 825 (Court of Appeal: MEGAW, SHAW and WALLER LJJ).

COURTS

Halsbury's Laws of England (4th edn.), Vol. 10, paras. 701–991

554   Article

Crown Court or Magistrates' Court? Brian Harris (some problems for the practitioner): [1979] LS Gaz 263.

555   Commercial Court—procedure

See para. 2112.

556   Companies Court—applications and orders heard by registrar—exercise of functions by chief clerk

See para. 2113.

557   —— **proceedings in chambers—transaction of business by post**

See para. 2114.

558   **Court of Appeal—application for bail pending appeal against sentence—test to be applied**

See *R v Watton*, para. 659.

559   —— **jurisdiction—criminal appeal—criminal cause or matter**

See *R v Director of Public Prosecutions, ex parte Raymond*, para. 655.

560   **Crown Court—jurisdiction—appeal against conviction allowed— power to direct new charge to be brought**

On appeal against a conviction for dangerous driving contrary to the Road Traffic Act 1972, s. 2, the Crown Court allowed the appeal but charged and found the defendant guilty of the lesser offence of careless driving under s. 3. On appeal, by way of case stated, *held*, the Crown Court had the power under the Courts Act 1971, s. 9 (2) (c) to do anything that the lower court had the power to do. The magistrates had the power under Sch. 4, Part IV, para. 4 of the 1972 Act to allow a lesser charge to be preferred if the charge was not proven and therefore there was no injustice in the Crown Court's doing the same.

KILLINGTON v BUTCHER [1979] Crim LR 458 (Queen's Bench Division: MICHAEL DAVIES and ROBERT GOFF JJ).

561   —— —— **power to revoke community service order**

In March 1978 the appellant, who was subject to two concurrent community service orders made in 1977 in respect of convictions for handling stolen goods and theft, was convicted by the Crown Court of handling and sentenced to imprisonment. In exercise of its jurisdiction under the Powers of Criminal Courts Act 1973, s. 17 (3), as amended by the Criminal Law Act 1977, s. 65 and Sch. 12, the court also revoked the two orders on the basis of the appellant having committed offences since they were made and substituted two consecutive sentences of imprisonment. The appellant appealed against sentence on the ground that the court had no jurisdiction to revoke the orders, which were made prior to the entry into force in May 1977 of Sch. 12. *Held*, there was nothing in s. 65 or Sch. 12 to indicate that the amendment operated retrospectively, and accordingly the court had no jurisdiction to revoke the orders. The substituted sentences would be quashed.

R v ADAIR [1979] LS Gaz R 101 (Court of Appeal: GEOFFREY LANE LJ, ACKNER and WATKINS JJ).

562   —— **power to vary sentence—variation pursuant to breach of undertaking—sentence of imprisonment for suspended sentence**

See *R v Grice*, para. 725.

563   **High Court—Chancery Division—appeal against tax assessment— appeal by way of case stated—jurisdiction**

See *Thomas v Ingram (Inspector of Taxes)*, para. 1498.

564   —— **Family Division—appeal from registrar to judge—lodgment of notes of evidence**

See para. 2130.

565   **House of Lords—petition for leave to appeal—costs**

See para. 2138.

566   —— —— **criminal causes—procedure**

See para. 2139.

567   —— —— **petitions out of time**

See para. 2138.

568   —— —— **procedure**

See para. 2139.

569   **Judicial pensions**

See PENSIONS.

570   **Jurisdiction—application for access—court's responsibility in deciding issue**

See *Mnguni v Mnguni*, para. 1852.

571   —— **jurisdiction to hear action brought under international convention**

See *Malone v Metropolitan Police Commissioner*, para. 2093.

572   **Juvenile courts—constitution**

See para. 1872.

573   **Precedent—courts other than final courts of appeal**

See *Attorney-General of St Christopher, Nevis and Anguilla v Reynolds*, para. 324.

574   **Right of audience—Court of Appeal and High Court—representation of trade union by officer**

In a case in the Court of Appeal concerning a trade union, the question arose whether the union's deputy general secretary had a right of audience to make representations on its behalf. *Held*, although a trade union was not a body corporate, it was a legal entity capable of suing and being sued. Provision was made for any person to represent a party to proceedings before the Employment Appeal Tribunal or in the county court by the Employment Protection (Consolidation) Act 1978, Sch. 11, para. 20, and the County Courts Act 1959, s. 89, respectively. The High Court and the Court of Appeal should not be in a different position. Every court had the power to regulate its own proceedings and incidentally to say whom it would hear as an advocate or representative of a party before it. Thus exceptions could be made to the general rule that only members of the Bar would be heard. As the point to be put was a simple one, the court would in its discretion allow the union to be represented by a duly authorised officer.

ENGINEERS' AND MANAGERS' ASSOCIATION v ADVISORY CONCILIATION AND ARBITRATION SERVICE (No. 1) [1979] 3 All ER 223 (Court of Appeal: LORD DENNING MR, LAWTON and CUMMING-BRUCE LJJ). *Collier v Hicks* (1831) 2 B & Ad 663 considered.

For substantive proceedings in this case, see para. 2833.

CREMATION AND BURIAL

Halsbury's Laws of England (4th edn.), Vol. 10, paras. 1001–1243

575   Cremation—documents

The Cremation Regulations 1979, S.I. 1979 No. 1138 (in force on 1st November 1979), amend the Cremation Regulations 1930 to make new provision for the documents which may be accepted by the medical referee of a cremation authority to enable him to authorise the cremation of the remains of a person who has died outside England and Wales. Regulation 4 provides for the acceptance in England and Wales of applications for cremation, medical certificates and coroners' certificates (or equivalent certificates) in the forms in use in Scotland, Northern Ireland, the Isle of Man and the Channel Islands, and of applications for cremation and medical certificates from other places. Regulation 6 provides that, in the case of the remains of a child still-born outside England and Wales, the medical referee may accept a medical certificate given in the place where the still-birth occurred.

576   Human remains—removal—licence fee

The Human Remains Removal Licence (Prescribed Fee) Order 1979, S.I. 1979 No. 1258 (in force on 1st November 1979), increases from £5 to £6 the prescribed fee for a licence issued under the Burial Act 1857, s. 25 for the removal of human remains interred in a place of burial.

CRIMINAL LAW

Halsbury's Laws of England (4th edn.), Vol. 11, paras. 1–1380

577   Articles

Alibi for a Judge, Alastair M. Darroch (problems concerning Criminal Justice Act 1967, s. 11): 129 NLJ 125.

Blasphemy and Mens Rea, Dr G. F. Orchard: [1979] NZLJ 347.

Burglary and Intent to Steal, G. L. Bennett (the issues raised by the decision in *R v Hussein* [1978] Crim LR 219, CA, 1978 Halsbury's Abridgment para. 663): 129 NLJ 750.

"Clocks, Crooks and the Rolling Lie"—Recent Trends in Trade Descriptions, Eric L. Newsome (examination of the issues raised in cases involving the falsification of odometer readings): 143 JP Jo 588.

Conditional Intent and Attempting the Impossible—Letting the Wicked Escape, Alec Samuels (considerations arising where intention to commit a crime is conditional upon certain circumstances or where the crime attempted is impossible): 143 JP Jo 187.

Counselling and Assisting Homosexuals, A. C. E. Lynch (examination of agencies which give support to homosexuals): [1979] Crim LR 630.

Crime and Personality, Professor H. J. Eysenck (sociological factors affecting criminality): 123 Sol Jo 23.

Criminal Driving, Alec Samuels (judicial thinking on recent cases): 129 NLJ 323.

Defence of Autrefois Acquit, Billy Strachan (on the availability of the plea and its application in practice): 123 Sol Jo 592.

The Defence of "Public Good", David Telling (the Obscene Publications Act 1959, s. 4): 129 NLJ 299.

An Englishperson's Castle of Low Walls, A. N. Khan (facets of the law relating to searches by warrants): 123 Sol Jo 24.

Forcible Eviction and the Criminal Law Act 1977, John Ottaway (the implications of Part 2 of the Act with reference to ss. 6, 7 and 12): 129 NLJ 792.

Implied and Constructive Malice in Murder, R. A. Duff (the definitions of "malice aforethought"): 95 LQR 418.

Inciting the Impossible, Michael Cohen (considerations arising where there is incitement to a crime which is impossible to commit): [1979] Crim. LR 239.

Incomplete Attempts of Crimes, G. Maddison and A. N. Khan (an examination of the unsatisfactory nature of the law with regard to attempts to commit crimes which are impossible to complete): 123 Sol Jo 465.

Intent to Steal and the Impossibility Rule, Glanville Williams, 129 NLJ 1167.

Manslaughter by Fright or Flight—Manslaughter by Putting Victim in Fear and Flight and Causing his Death, Alex Samuels: 143 JP Jo 634.

Mens Rea, Motive, and the Problem of "Dishonesty" in the Law of Theft, Martin Wasik (the notion of dishonesty and its relevance to motive): [1979] Crim LR 543.

Obscenity (a series of articles covering the definition and history of obscenity; the law relating to obscene publications and seizure of the same; children and obscenity; indecency; obscenity in the theatre; and the medical implications of obscenity): Court (Journal of Legal Practice in Magistrates' Courts) Autumn 1979.

Perverting the Course of Justice by Assisting a Suspect to Avoid Arrest, J. Kodwo Bentil: 143 JP Jo 548.

Possession and Section 28 of the Misuse of Drugs Act 1971, Robert Ribeiro and John Perry (effect of s. 28 on the offence of possessing a controlled drug): [1979] Crim LR 90.

Proof that Goods Are Stolen, David Stone (a review of the possible means of proving that goods are stolen): 129 NLJ 1018.

Recovering the Profits of Bribery, Caroline A. Needham: 95 LQR 536.

Resisting Unlawful Police Action, A. Parkin (examination of the court's attitude towards the dilemma faced by anyone confronted by an exercise of police authority which he believes to be unlawful): 129 NLJ 850.

Stealing Information, A. Tettenborn (brief examination of the law in relation to the theft of information): 129 NLJ 967.

Still Scope for Mischief, David Cowley (the common law crime of public mischief): 129 NLJ 485.

Strict Liability Offences: How Strict? M. L. Bowen, D. W. Fox and A. N. Khan (judicial attitudes towards discerning offences of strict liability): 123 Sol Jo 72.

Taking a Conveyance Without Authority, Alec Samuels (a clarification of the law against borrowing motor vehicles): 143 JP Jo 244.

Theft Act 1978, G. Syrota: (1979) 42 MLR 301.

The Theft Act 1978, Jim Treleaven: Law Notes Vol. 98, No. 8, p. 220.

Theft (a series of articles covering theft, robbery, burglary, conveyance taking, criminal deception, blackmail and handling stolen goods): Court (Journal of Proceedings in Magistrates' Courts) Spring 1979.

Theft, Conspiracy and Jurisdiction: Tarling's case, J. C. Smith (a discussion of the criminal liability of company executives involved in share deals): [1979] Crim LR 220.

578 Assault—defence—whether accused acting in self-defence

Following an accident between two cars the defendant's car was pursued by the other and repeatedly overtaken. The two cars stopped and both drivers got out, but on seeing that the defendant was holding a metal steering wheel lock the other driver returned to his car. The defendant hit him several times with the steering wheel lock and smashed his car windscreen. Magistrates acquitted him of charges of assault and criminal damage on the ground that he had acted in self-defence. The prosecution appealed by way of case stated. *Held*, the other driver had ceased to be a threat when he returned to his car and therefore the case would be remitted to the magistrates for a decision on the basis that the defendant could not rely on self-defence.

PRIESTNALL v CORNISH [1979] Crim LR 310 (Queen's Bench Division: LORD WIDGERY CJ, EVELEIGH LJ and STEPHEN BROWN J).

579 —— police officer—execution of duty

The police suspected that the car in which the defendant and others were travelling had been stolen. They were detained for two hours at night whilst inquiries were made. They were then released, no charges were preferred and they received an apology. The police sergeant retained the car keys since the car owner had a provisional driving licence only, although the defendant possessed a full driving licence. The defendant and the car owner insistently demanded the return of the keys, in vain. When they refused to leave the station, the sergeant ejected them. The defendant was charged with assaulting a police officer in the execution of his duty contrary to the Police Act 1964, s. 51. The defendant submitted that he had a right to remain at the station and insist on the return of the keys as the sergeant was acting tortiously in refusing their return; the sergeant was not acting in the execution of his duty in ejecting the defendant, and the defendant was therefore entitled to use reasonable force against the sergeant in self-defence. He was convicted. The defendant unsuccessfully appealed, the judge refusing to state a case on the ground that no point of law arose. The defendant applied for an order of mandamus to require the judge to state a case. *Held*, it was for the sergeant in charge to determine whether a person could be allowed to remain in a police station and there was a limit to a citizen's right to make a complaint or transact business at the station. The evidence was sufficient for the judge to conclude that the sergeant had been justified in asking the defendant to leave and that therefore he had been acting in the execution of his duty. The application would be dismissed.

R v KNIGHTSBRIDGE CROWN COURT, EX PARTE UMEH [1979] Crim LR 727 (Queen's Bench Division: EVELEIGH LJ and WOOLF J).

580   —— —— —— **apprehension of breach of the peace**

See *R v Podger*, para. 658.

581   The defendant was one of a group of youths who had been asked by the police to move on, although none of them had committed an arrestable offence. They were asked again to move, and a constable took hold of the defendant's arm. There was a struggle in which the defendant punched the constable in the stomach and he was charged with assaulting a constable in the execution of his duty. On appeal against his conviction by magistrates, *held*, there was no evidence that the constable had apprehended a breach of the peace and therefore his action was not justified. The appeal would be allowed.

HICKMAN v O'DWYER [1979] Crim LR 309 (Queen's Bench Division: BRIDGE LJ and CAULFIELD J).

582   **Automatism—evidence—admissibility of medical evidence**

See *R v Smith*, para. 696.

583   **Blasphemous libel—intent**

The editor of a newspaper and the newspaper itself were convicted of blasphemous libel. In his summing up the trial judge directed the jury that it was not necessary for the prosecution to prove an intent on the part of the accused to attack the Christian religion. On appeal, *held*, LORD DIPLOCK and LORD EDMUND-DAVIES dissenting, subjective intent was not an essential element of the offence. The creation of the offence was intended to prevent the publication of blasphemous libels and the harm was done by their intentional publication, whether or not the publisher intended to blaspheme. The appeal would be dismissed.

LORD EDMUND-DAVIES considered that with the increasing tendency in the law to move away from strict liability, it would be a step backwards to treat the state of a person's mind as irrelevant in a case of blasphemy.

R v LEMON [1979] 1 All ER 898 (House of Lords: LORD DIPLOCK, VISCOUNT DILHORNE, LORD EDMUND-DAVIES, LORD RUSSELL OF KILLOWEN and LORD SCARMAN). Decision of the Court of Appeal [1978] 3 All ER 175, 1978 Halsbury's Abridgment para. 591 affirmed.

For discussion of this case, see Time to abolish criminal blasphemy, Justinian, Financial Times, 26th February 1979.

584   Burglary—burglary with intent to steal—need to prove intent

The Attorney-General referred to the Court of Appeal two questions on the interpretation of the Theft Act 1968, s. 9 (1) (a). The questions were (i) whether a defendant who had entered a house as a trespasser with the intention of stealing money was entitled to be acquitted of an offence under s. 9 (1) (a) if his intention to steal was conditional upon finding any money in the house, and (ii) whether a defendant who attempted to enter a house as a trespasser with the intention of stealing anything of value he might find in the house was entitled to be acquitted of the offence of attempted burglary on the ground that such an intention was insufficient to amount to "the intention of stealing anything" as required by s. 9. *Held*, on a true construction of the wording of s. 9 (1) (a), where at the moment of entering or attempting to enter a building or a part of a building as a trespasser the defendant intended to steal anything in that building, the fact that there was nothing in the building worth his while stealing was immaterial. Accordingly, both questions would be answered in the negative.

The court pointed out that in some cases it would be undesirable to frame indictments by reference to the theft or attempted theft of specific objects. There was no reason why, where the justice of the case required it, a more imprecise form of criminal pleading should not be adopted, provided that the indictment correctly reflected what the defendant was alleged to have done.

ATTORNEY-GENERAL'S REFERENCES (NOS. 1 AND 2 OF 1979) [1979] 3 All ER 143 (Court of Appeal: ROSKILL LJ, BRISTOW and MICHAEL DAVIES JJ). *R v Walkington* [1979] 2 All ER 716, CA, para. 585 and dicta of Lord Scarman in *Director of Public Prosecutions v Nock* [1978] 2 All ER 654, HL, at 664, 1978 Halsbury's Abridgment para. 598 applied.

585   ——— entering part of a building as a trespasser—whether shop counter part of a building

Whilst in a department store, a customer went behind a counter area which was reserved for staff only, and opened further a partially opened but empty till. He was convicted of burglary by entering as a trespasser part of a building with intent to steal, contrary to the Theft Act 1968, s. 9 (1) (a). He appealed, contending that he had not trespassed because the counter area could not constitute part of a building for the purposes of s. 9 (1) (a). Also he did not have the necessary mens rea for theft, because his intention to steal was conditional upon him finding something worthwhile stealing. *Held*, it was for the jury to decide whether the counter area was part of a building from which the general public were excluded, and there was ample evidence from which to conclude that customers were impliedly prohibited from entering the area and that the accused knew of this prohibition. When a person entered part of a building as a trespasser, intending at the time of entry to steal anything, such an intention was sufficient to found a conviction and it was immaterial that there was in fact nothing worth stealing.

R v WALKINGTON [1979] 2 All ER 716 (Court of Appeal: GEOFFREY LANE LJ, SWANWICK and WIEN JJ).

586   Conspiracy—conspiracy to produce or supply a controlled drug—whether a common law offence

The appellants were convicted of conspiring to contravene the Misuse of Drugs Act 1971, s. 4, relating to the production and supply of a controlled drug. Holding that the conspiracy was an offence under the Act since the substantive crimes were also offences under the Act, the court made an order under s. 4 forfeiting the appellants' property. On appeal, the appellants contended that conspiracy was an offence at common law and not under the Act. *Held*, conspiracy to contravene the Act was also an offence under that Act. The property of persons convicted of the conspiracy was equally subject to forfeiture as that of persons convicted of the substantive offences. The appeal would be dismissed.

R v TODD; R v CUTHBERTSON; R v MCCOY (1979) 69 Cr App Rep 330 (Court of Appeal: ROSKILL LJ, BRISTOW and MICHAEL DAVIES JJ).

587   ——**conspiracy to steal—whether a statutory or common law offence**

The appellants were convicted of conspiracy to steal, contrary to Criminal Law Act 1977, s. 1. They contended that as the common law offence of conspiracy to defraud was expressly preserved by s. 5 of the 1977 Act conspiracy to steal and any other offence which necessarily involved fraud continued to be offences at common law and were not therefore included in the statutory offence. *Held*, conspiracy to steal was no longer an offence under the common law but was an offence under s. 1. It was only conspiracy to defraud simpliciter which continued to be a common law offence. The appellants had been properly charged with conspiracy to steal, contrary to s. 1.

R v DUNCALF [1979] 2 All ER 1116 (Court of Appeal: ROSKILL and ORMROD LJJ and WATKINS J). *R v Quinn* [1978] Crim LR 750, 1978 Halsbury's Abridgment para. 600, and dictum of Lord Widgery CJ in *R v Walters* [1979] RTR 220, CA, para. 704, disapproved.

For the 1977 Act, ss. 1, 5, see 1977 Halsbury's Abridgment, para. 635.

588   ————**power of circuit judge to amend voluntary indictment**

See *R v Walters*, para. 704.

589   **Criminal damage—recklessness**

The defendant was charged with arson under the Criminal Damage Act 1971, s. 1 (1), (3). He had gone to sleep inside a haystack; on feeling cold, he had lit a fire inside the stack. The stack caught fire and extensive damage resulted. A pyschiatrist gave evidence that the defendant had a long history of schizophrenia and might not have had the same ability to foresee or appreciate risk as the mentally normal person. The defendant was convicted on the basis that he was reckless as to whether damage was caused or not. He appealed, contending that the judge had misdirected the jury as to the meaning of "reckless"and in particular had failed to make it clear that the test of recklessness was a subjective one. *Held*, the question was whether the defendant had to be proved actually to have foreseen the risk of some damage resulting from his actions and nevertheless to have run the risk (the subjective test), or whether it was sufficient to prove that the risk of damage resulting would have been obvious to any reasonable person in the defendant's position (the objective test). On the balance of authority, the subjective test was correct. In a case such as this, a man was reckless when he carried out a deliberate act appreciating that there was a risk that damage to property might result from his act; the risk being one which it was in all the circumstances unreasonable for him to take. The defendant's schizophrenia might have prevented the idea of danger entering his mind. This point was not left clearly to the jury and the appeal would be allowed and the conviction quashed.

R v STEPHENSON [1979] 2 All ER 1198 (Court of Appeal: GEOFFREY LANE LJ, ACKNER and WATKINS JJ). *British Railways Board v Herrington* [1972] AC 877, HL applied.

590   **Criminal liability—statutory offence of strict liability—vicarious liability of employer**

See *Swan v Macnab*, para. 1115.

591   **Dangerous drugs—control**

The Misuse of Drugs (Amendment) Regulations 1979, S.I. 1979 No. 326 (in force on 14th May 1979) amend the Misuse of Drugs Regulations 1973 by adding phencyclidine to Schedule 2 of those regulations.

592   The Misuse of Drugs Act 1971 (Modification) Order 1979, S.I. 1979 No. 299 (in force on 14th May 1979) adds phencyclidine to Part I, Sch. 2 of the 1971 Act (which specifies the Class A drugs subject to control).

593   —— forfeiture order—time limit for imposing order

The defendant was charged with fraudulent evasion of the prohibition on the importation of cocaine. At her trial at the Crown Court, she pleaded guilty and was sentenced to a term of imprisonment. Three and a half months later the judge made an order under Misuse of Drugs Act 1971, s. 27, or alternatively under Powers of Criminal Courts Act 1973, s. 43, for forfeiture of money found in her possession which was considered to relate to the offence. On appeal she contended that a forfeiture order was a sentence or other order made by the Crown Court when dealing with an offender under Courts Act 1971, s. 11 (2), and accordingly could not be imposed outside the time limit for variation laid down by that provision. That limit was a period of twenty-eight days from the passing of the original sentence. The appeal was dismissed. On further appeal, *held*, a forfeiture order was in the nature of a penalty and hence was a sentence for the purposes of s. 11 (2) if made against an offender who was being sentenced for other offences. Therefore any variation of a sentence by adding a forfeiture order had to be made within the time limit prescribed. As it had not been, it was invalid and the appeal would be allowed.

R v MENOCAL [1979] 2 All ER 510 (House of Lords: LORD WILBERFORCE, LORD SALMON, LORD EDMUND-DAVIES, LORD FRASER OF TULLYBELTON and LORD KEITH OF KINKEL). Decision of the Court of Appeal [1978] 3 All ER 961, 1978 Halsbury's Abridgment para. 610 reversed.

594   —— licence fees

The Misuse of Drugs (Licence Fees) Regulations 1979, S.I. 1979 No. 218 (in force on 1st April 1979), prescribe the fee payable under the Misuse of Drugs Act 1971, s. 30, in relation to a licence to produce, supply, offer to supply or possess controlled drugs.

595   —— offence by occupier—whether squatter an occupier

Scotland

The appellant, who had been convicted of permitting his house to be used for the purpose of smoking cannabis resin, contended that as he had been squatting in the house with no legal right to be there he was not the occupier within the meaning of Dangerous Drugs Act 1965, s. 5. *Held*, it was not necessary for a person to have a legal right to occupy premises for him to be an occupier under the Act. It was sufficient for him to have possession of the premises to the extent that he controlled them. The appeal would be dismissed.

CHRISTISON v HOGG 1974 SC 55 (High Court of Justiciary). *R v Mogford* [1970] 1 WLR 988 distinguished.

596   —— possession—drug ordered through post—when person ordering drug takes possession

The appellant, the occupier of one bed-sitting room in a house comprised entirely of bed-sitting rooms, received through the post a prohibited drug which he had ordered. On arrival the envelope containing the drug was placed on a table in the hallway, whilst the appellant was in his room and unaware of its arrival. A police officer who arrived with a warrant to search the room, took the envelope up to the appellant, who opened it and gave the contents to the policeman. He was subsequently convicted of unlawful possession of a controlled drug. He appealed, claiming that he had never had possession or control of the drug. *Held*, dismissing the appeal, the stipulations as to the matters to be proved in cases of possession of drugs in a container laid down in *R v Warner*, did not apply in this case, as the facts were different in nature. The appellant had instructed his supplier to send him the drug through the post and had received the drug according to those instructions. Thus following *R v Cavendish*, he was properly to be regarded as having been in possession of the drug from the time it came through the letterbox.

R v PEASTON [1978] LS Gaz R 1201 (Court of Appeal: LORD WIDGERY CJ, BRIDGE LJ AND WIEN J). *R v Cavendish* [1961] 1 WLR 1083, CA applied, *R v Warner* [1969] 2 AC 256, HL distinguished.

597   —— —— possession of cannabis or cannabis resin—duplicity of count

See *R v Best*, para. 705.

598   —— possession and supply—whether conspiracy a common law offence

See *R v Todd; R v Cuthbertson; R v McCoy*, para. 586.

599   —— —— urine sample—discretion to admit as evidence

See *R v Beet*, para. 673.

600   —— unlawful production of controlled drug—failure to produce because of incorrect process—whether attempt to commit impossible act

A man conspired with others to produce amphetamine, but failed because the wrong process was used and an incorrect ingredient included. The man was convicted of conspiring to produce a controlled drug and appealed, claiming that his case fell within the principles of *DPP v Nock*, in that a conspiracy to do something inherently impossible did not constitute a conspiracy to commit an unlawful act. *Held*, if the man and his co-defendants had acquainted themselves with the proper process they would have succeeded in manufacturing the drug. Thus the act was inherently possible, unlike in *DPP v Nock* where the attempted production of cocaine from lignocaine hydrochloride was impossible. The appeal would be dismissed.

R v HARRIS [1979] LS Gaz R 321 (Court of Appeal: SHAW LJ, SMITH and MUSTILL JJ). *DPP v Nock* [1978] 2 All ER 654, HL, 1978 Halsbury's Abridgment para. 598 distinguished.

601   Defence—automatism—medical evidence—admissibility

See *R v Smith*, para. 696.

602   —— diminished responsibility—medical evidence—jury's duty to consider whole of circumstances

See *R v Kiszko*, para. 620.

603   Duress—escape from prison—absence of coercion to commit crime—availability of defence

Australia
The defendant was charged with escaping from prison. He sought to raise defences of duress and necessity on the basis that he feared for his life as a result of threats made against him by other prisoners. The judge directed the jury that the defences were not available to him, and he was convicted. He sought leave to appeal against the judge's ruling. *Held*, the defence of duress was confined to cases where the accused was constrained to commit a particular offence nominated by the person making the threats. It did not apply where, as in the present case, there was no coercion on the accused to commit the offence, but he committed it in order to evade the possible consequences of the threats against him. As to the defence of necessity, it was doubtful whether such a defence was known to the law, but in any event the facts of the present case were not capable of supporting it. The application would be dismissed.

R v DAWSON [1978] VR 536 (Supreme Court of Victoria).

604   —— voluntary submission to possibility of duress—member of terrorist organisation

Northern Ireland
The accused joined the Irish Republican Army, an illegal terrorist organisation. He

later decided to leave the organisation and asked to be released from it; he was threatened with violence and ordered to take part in a robbery. In carrying out the robbery he killed a man. On charges of murder, robbery and belonging to a proscribed organisation, he pleaded duress. *Held*, a person who voluntarily joined an illegal organisation with criminal objectives and coercive methods, thus submitting himself to the possibility of illegal compulsion, could not rely on the duress to which he had voluntarily exposed himself, either as an excuse for the crimes unwillingly committed or in respect of his continued association with the proscribed organisation.

R v FITZPATRICK [1977] NI 20 (Court of Criminal Appeal).

605   Explosive substances—possession—whether substance having pyrotechnic effect explosive

See *R v Wheatley*, para. 1276.

606   False trade description

See TRADE DESCRIPTIONS.

607   Firearms

See FIREARMS.

608   Illegal immigration

See IMMIGRATION.

609   Incitement to crime—incitement to arrange commission of assault—whether criminal offence

On a question of whether it was a crime to incite another to arrange the commission of assault, *held*, it was not a crime to invite someone to do an act which would involve that person in no more than secondary liability for the offence were it committed, and further, an indictment for incitement to assault would be incorrect.

R v BODIN [1979] Crim LR 176 (Crown Court at Lincoln: Judge GEOFFREY JONES).

610   Legal aid

See LEGAL AID.

611   Loitering with intent to steal—intent necessary for offence

The defendants were charged with loitering with intent to commit theft, contrary to the Vagrancy Act 1824, s. 4. They contended that the prosecution had failed to establish the necessary intent, that of intent to commit an offence of stealing specific property. *Held*, in the light of the decision of the Court of Appeal in *Attorney-General's References (Nos. 1 and 2 of 1979)* [1979] 3 All ER 143, para. 584, it was clear that it was not necessary to prove an intent to steal a specific object.

MILES v CLOVIS (NOTE) [1979] 3 WLR 591 (Queen's Bench Division: ROSKILL LJ, BRISTOW and MICHAEL DAVIES JJ).

612   Manslaughter—husband's failure to get medical assistance for wife—whether reckless disregard of his duty

Due to her past medical history, a woman would have nothing to do with doctors or medical treatment. She became pregnant and concealed the fact from everyone, including her husband, until a few days before the birth, when she told her husband that the baby was not due for over a month. The husband had to deliver the child, which was still-born. The body was secreted by both of them in a cupboard. The woman fell ill and refused a doctor. The husband eventually called a doctor when she became very ill, but did not disclose the full circumstances of the illness, so that the urgency was not apparent to the doctor and he did not arrive until after the woman had died. Medical evidence showed that she could have been saved had the doctor been called earlier. The husband was charged with (1) manslaughter of his wife and (2) concealment of the birth. On the second count he maintained that he and his wife had no intention of concealing the birth permanently, but would have revealed it when they felt up to it. The judge directed the jury that this amounted to a defence. On the first count he directed them that the prosecution had to prove the husband's delay in getting a doctor was in reckless disregard of his duty to care for his wife's health. "Reckless disregard" meant that, fully appreciating the risk to her health, the husband did not get help because he was indifferent or because he deliberately ran a wholly unjustifiable and unreasonable risk. Evidence showed he was not indifferent. There was also evidence that his wife was opposed to calling a doctor. Thus the jury had to balance her right to have her wishes respected against her ability at the time to make a rational decision. The jury convicted the husband of concealment of birth, but were unable to agree on a verdict of manslaughter and were discharged.

R v SMITH [1979] Crim LR 251 (Crown Court at Birmingham: GRIFFITHS J).

613   —— manslaughter "by flight"—alternative verdict on charge of murder

See *DPP v Daley*, para. 723.

614   Mens rea—burglary—burglary with intent to steal—need to prove intent

See *Attorney-General's References (Nos. 1 and 2 of 1979)*, para. 584.

615   —— intent to steal—whether intent to steal specific property necessary

See *Attorney-General's References (Nos. 1 and 2 of 1979)*, para. 584; *R v Walkington*, para. 585; *Scudder v Barrett*, para. 641; *Miles v Clovis*, para. 611.

616   —— recklessness—criminal damage

See *R v Stephenson*, para. 589.

617   —— —— reckless driving

See *R v Clancy*, para. 2312; *R v Davis*, para. 2313.

618   Murder—alternative verdict—evidence of manslaughter—propriety of leaving issue to jury

See *DPP v Daley*, para. 723.

619   —— defence—automatism—medical evidence

At the defendant's trial for murder, he raised the defence of automatism, contending that he had stabbed his victim whilst asleep. The prosecution obtained leave to call doctors to give expert evidence on automatism. The defendant was convicted. He applied for leave to appeal alleging that expert medical evidence was admissible only when insanity or diminished responsibility was in issue and the issue of automatism was a matter for the jury to decide without expert evidence as to the defendant's state of mind. *Held*, the jury were entitled to expert medical or scientific evidence in order to assist them to distinguish between genuine and fraudulent automatism. The application would be dismissed.

R v SMITH [1979] 3 All ER 605 (Court of Appeal: GEOFFREY LANE LJ, SWANWICK and WATERHOUSE JJ). Dicta of Devlin J in *Hill v Baxter* [1958] 1 All ER 193 at 197 applied.

620   —— —— diminished responsibility—medical evidence

The defendant was charged with murder after he killed an eleven year old girl by stabbing her. He sought, inter alia, to raise the defence of diminished responsibility, based on the fact that before the girl's death he was receiving medical treatment for two conditions, the combined effect of which would have had psychological side effects producing an abnormality of the mind, impairing his moral responsibility for his acts. A psychiatrist, who had not been able to question the defendant about his state of mind at the time of the killing, put forward a theoretical reconstruction of the events which supported the defence of diminished responsibility. The jury rejected this and the defendant was convicted. On an application for leave to appeal, the defendant contended that the jury's verdict was unsafe as it had rejected the medical evidence which had not been contradicted by the prosecution. *Held*, on an issue of diminished responsibility, the jury were bound to consider, not only the medical evidence, but also the evidence on the whole facts and circumstances. The jury's verdict was a reasonable one and the application would be refused.

R v Kiszko (1979) 68 Cr App R 62 (Court of Appeal: BRIDGE LJ, WIEN and EASTHAM JJ).

621   Necessity—escape from prison—availability of defence

See *R v Dawson*, para. 603.

622   Obscene publications—articles seized by police—when articles to be brought before magistrate

Acting under a warrant issued under the Obscene Publications Act 1959, s. 3 (1), the police entered certain premises and seized a large quantity of magazines, including a number of identical copies of a magazine published by the plaintiffs. Three weeks later the plaintiffs issued a writ against the police claiming, inter alia, a declaration that they were entitled to the return of the copies of their publication, on the grounds that the police had failed to bring the magazines before a magistrate as required by s. 3 (3) within a reasonable time. They also applied for an interim injunction requiring the return of the articles in question, on the grounds that their retention by the police was an abuse of the powers given by s. 3. The police gave evidence that considerable time was needed for the sorting of the articles and that the magazine in question could not be put before the magistrates separately. The application was refused and the publications were placed before the magistrates prior to the hearing of the plaintiff's appeal. *Held*, the definition of a reasonable time in the context of s. 3 (3) was a question of fact and degree, having regard to the particular circumstances of each individual case. In the present case the conduct of the police could not be questioned, and it would be wrong for the court, at that stage, to interfere with the administration of criminal justice by ordering the return of the magazines.

LORD DENNING MR pointed out that the appropriate remedy for an alleged abuse of powers under s. 3 (1), (2) or (3) was by application for an order of mandamus.

ROANDALE LTD v METROPOLITAN POLICE COMR [1979] LS Gaz R 157 (Court of Appeal: LORD DENNING MR, ROSKILL and CUMMING-BRUCE LJJ).

623   —— enforcement of law relating to pornography—application for mandamus against Metropolitan Police Commissioner

See *R v Metropolitan Police Commissioner, ex parte Blackburn*, para. 2084.

624   Obtaining a pecuniary advantage by deception—evading a debt—whether deception must operate on creditor

In March 1976 a constable took possession of the defendant's car excise licence, which was valid for six months, and replaced it with an undated police memorandum. In October 1977 another constable saw the memorandum on the windscreen of the defendant's car, and was led to believe it was in substitution for a current licence. On a charge of obtaining a pecuniary advantage by deception under the Theft Act 1968, s. 16 (2) (a) the defendant made a successful submission of no case to answer, on the grounds that the person deceived was not the creditor. The prosecutor appealed by case stated. *Held*, there was no requirement that it should be the creditor who was deceived: a causal connection between the deception and the evasion of liability, as had been shown in this case, was sufficient. The case would be remitted to the justices with a direction to that effect.

SMITH v KOUMOUROU [1979] Crim LR 116 (Queen's Bench Division: LORD WIDGERY CJ, GRIFFITHS and GIBSON JJ). Dicta of Lord Reid in *DPP v Turner* [1974] AC 357, 365 applied.

Theft Act 1968 s. 16 (2) (a) is now replaced by Theft Act 1978, see 1978 Halsbury's Abridgment para. 667.

625   **Obtaining property by deception—property subsequently sold— whether accused properly chargeable with obtaining by deception and theft**

The accused signed an hire-purchase agreement in a false name and took delivery of a car. He never made any payments under the agreement and later sold the car. He was charged and found guilty of both obtaining the car by deception and theft. He appealed on the ground that he could not be convicted on both counts. *Held*, the obtaining of possession of the car and the subsequent selling were two separate transactions and the offences were not mutually exclusive. The convictions would be upheld.

R v HIRCOCK [1979] Crim LR 184 (Court of Appeal: LAWTON LJ, MARS-JONES and MAIS JJ).

626   —— **whether deception a question for jury**

A minicab driver who represented himself as an airport taxi driver to a foreigner whom he drove from Heathrow Airport was charged under Theft Act 1968, s. 15 with obtaining property by deception. The jury were directed that they had to be satisfied as to both deception and dishonesty, and that the relevant consideration was whether his claim that he was an airport taxi driver and that he was charging the correct fare led the passenger to believe that his cab was officially regulated. He appealed on the ground that there was no such thing either in fact or law as an airport taxi or correct fare. *Held*, the judge had been correct in leaving the question of deception to the jury and accordingly there was no reason to quash the conviction.

R v BANASTER (1978) 68 Cr App Rep 272 (Court of Appeal: LORD WIDGERY CJ, CUMMING-BRUCE LJ and DRAKE J).

627   **Offensive weapon—possession—article acquired immediately before use as offensive weapon**

On an appeal against a conviction for being in possession of an offensive weapon, contrary to the Prevention of Crime Act 1953, s. 1 (1), the appellant contended that the nature of the offence under s. 1 (1) was the carrying and not the use of a weapon and since he had only borrowed the article for a few moments from another man, despite his intention to use it as an offensive weapon, he had not committed an offence under s. 1 (1). *Held*, the real purpose of the Act was to prevent the carrying of offensive weapons. A person who acquired an article immediately before using it as an offensive weapon, rather than having been previously in possession of it, was not guilty of an offence under s. 1 (1). The appeal would be allowed.

BATES v BULMAN [1979] 3 All ER 170 (Queen's Bench Division: LORD WIDGERY CJ, CROOM-JOHNSON and STOCKER JJ).

628   **Prevention of terrorism—detention of persons liable to examination**

The Prevention of Terrorism (Supplemental Temporary Provisions) (Amendment) Order 1979, S.I. 1979 No. 169 (in force on 18th April 1979), amends art. 10 of the Prevention of Terrorism (Supplemental Temporary Provisions) Order 1976, 1976 Halsbury's Abridgment para. 664. The Order reduces the maximum period for which a person, liable to examination under art. 5 of the 1976 Order, may be detained by an examining officer to a period of 48 hours. The period may however be extended by the Secretary of State by a further period not exceeding 5 days.

629   The Prevention of Terrorism (Supplemental Temporary Provisions) (Northern Ireland) (Amendment) Order 1979, S.I. 1979 No. 168 (in force on 18th April 1979), amends the 1976 Order, 1976 Halsbury's Abridgment para. 665, so as to reduce the maximum period for which a person who may be examined under the 1976 Order may be detained under the authority of an examining officer, to a period of forty-eight hours. That period may be extended, in a particular case, by the Secretary of State, for a further period not exceeding five days.

630   **—— temporary provisions—continuance**

The Prevention of Terrorism (Temporary Provisions) Act 1976 (Continuance) Order 1979, S.I. 1979 No. 352 (in force on 25th March 1979), continues in force the temporary provisions of the Act for a period of twelve months from 25th March 1979.

631   **—— —— proscribed organisations**

The Prevention of Terrorism (Temporary Provisions) Act 1976 (Amendment) Order 1979, S.I. 1979 No.745 (in force on 3rd July 1979), adds the Irish National Liberation Army to Sch. 1 of the 1976 Act, which specifies the organisations which are proscribed for the purposes of the Act.

632   **Prostitution—living on earnings of prostitution—effect of landlord charging prostitute exorbitant rent**

In an appeal against conviction for knowingly living wholly or in part on the earnings of a prostitute, *held*, a landlord who knew his tenant was a prostitute and took advantage of her difficulty in getting accommodation by letting the property at an exorbitant rent far above the normal rent, could be guilty of the offence because he was not then acting merely as a landlord but making his tenant engage in a joint venture, bringing him a part of her immoral earnings over and above the normal rent.

R v CALDERHEAD; R v BIDNEY (1978) 68 Cr App Rep 37 (Court of Appeal; SHAW LJ, LAWSON and SMITH JJ). Dictum of Lord Reid in *Shaw v DPP* [1962] AC 220 at 271 applied.

633   **—— meaning**

An escort agency was set up and run for the purpose of introducing prostitutes to clients. The agency's premises were frequented by several prostitutes and mini-cab drivers and prospective clients would telephone the agency, which was widely advertised, to request an escort. A mini-cab driver would then drive a prostitute to the assignment as arranged on the telephone, and collect from the customer the agency's fee, which he paid to the agency, and the cab fare, which he kept for himself. The prostitutes retained any payment they received. The operator of the agency, his assistant and two mini-cab drivers were convicted under the Sexual Offences Act 1956, s. 30 (1) of living on the earnings of prostitution and sentenced to terms of imprisonment of five years, thirty months and two years each respectively. They appealed against conviction and sentence. *Held*, providing that the evidence established that the money received was earned by prostitutes, in the sense of being the rewards of prostitution, it was not necessary to show that it was actually handed over by the prostitutes. In the present case, where all the appellants knew what the prostitutes intended to do on arriving at their assignments, the money they received as a result of introducing the girls to clients constituted the earnings of prostitution. The convictions would therefore be upheld.

However, in the absence of any evidence of coercion by the appellants on the girls, the sentences imposed were excessive and would be reduced to two years, fifteen months, twelve months and six months respectively.

R v FARRUGIA (1979) (Court of Appeal: LAWTON LJ, THOMPSON and HODGSON JJ (judgment delivered 11th April)). Dicta of Viscount Simonds in *Shaw v DPP* [1962] AC 220 at 237 followed.

634   Public officer—misconduct in public office—elements of offence

A police constable was nearby when a man was ejected from a night club and was killed in the fight which ensued. The police constable did not intervene and when the fight ended he drove away. As a result, he was charged with misconduct in a public office, in that he deliberately failed to carry out his duty as a police constable by wilfully omitting to intervene in the situation. He contended that the indictment disclosed no offence known to the law. The trial judge ruled against the objection and a verdict of guilty was returned. The police constable appealed, contending that not every failure to discharge a duty which devolved on a person as the holder of a public office gave rise to the offence. He argued that non-feasance was not enough; there had to be a malfeasance or misfeasance involving an element of corruption. *Held*, it was true that in most of the cases concerning misconduct in a public office corruption was involved, but this was not a necessary element of the offence. The neglect of duty had to be wilful and not merely inadvertent, and had to be culpable in the sense that it was without reasonable excuse or justification. In this case, the allegation was not of mere non-feasance but of deliberate failure and wilful neglect. This involved an element of culpability which was not restricted to corruption or dishonesty but which had to be of such a degree that the misconduct impugned was calculated to injure the public interest so as to call for condemnation and punishment. Whether such a situation was revealed by the evidence was a question for the jury. The judge's ruling was correct and the appeal would be dismissed.

R v DYTHAM [1979] 3 WLR 467 (Court of Appeal: LORD WIDGERY CJ, SHAW LJ and McNEILL J).

635   Road traffic offences

See ROAD TRAFFIC.

636   Robbery—whether force used "at the time of stealing"

The defendant and his accomplice had entered a house wearing stocking masks. The accomplice went upstairs and took the owner's jewellery box. They then tied and gagged the owner, threatening her, as they left, that they would harm her son if she should phone the police within five minutes of their leaving. The defendant was convicted of robbery. He appealed, contending that the theft was complete at the time of the taking of the jewellery box and the force then used, by way of the threat, was not "immediately before or at the time of stealing" as required by the Theft Act 1968, s. 8 (1). *Held*, the act of appropriation was a continuing one and it was for the jury to decide when it was over. The theft was not over at the time when the owner was tied and gagged. The appeal would be dismissed.

R v HALE (1978) 68 Cr App Rep 415 (Court of Appeal: WALLER and EVELEIGH LJJ and TUDOR EVANS J).

637   Sentencing

See SENTENCING.

638   Sexual offences—indecency with young boys—matters to be considered in passing extended sentence

See *R v Gooden*, para. 2478.

639   Territorial jurisdiction—Law Commission's report

The Law Commission has published a report on the territorial and extra-territorial extent of the criminal law. It recommends, inter alia, that the territorial jurisdiction of the courts in relation to indictable offences should extend to all offences occurring within the outward limits of adjacent territorial waters (i.e. territorial waters as determined by reference to the baseline and internal waters lying behind the baseline.) Also, that the territorial jurisdiction of magistrates' courts should be extended to cover any summary offence occurring beyond the baseline but within the outward limits of territorial waters. This jurisdictional area might, it suggests, be referred to in future legislation as "the ordinary limits of criminal jurisdiction". The Law Commission also recommends that new provisions are required to deal with offences committed on board ship and on shore abroad but it does not recommend changes in relation to British-controlled aircraft or hovercraft outside the United Kingdom. In relation to provisions of the law which are not applied on a territorial basis it makes recommendations only in respect of offences by Crown servants abroad, piracy and the hijacking of ships. A draft Criminal Jurisdiction Bill is appended to the report. See Law Com 91 (HC 75).

640   Theft—appropriation—requirements of appropriation

The defendant was a cashier in a supermarket. She took nearly four pounds from a customer for a purchase but did not ring it up on the till, although she did put the money in there intending to remove it later. She was arrested before she did this and was convicted of theft. She appealed on the ground that although she had formed a dishonest intention to steal, there had been no appropriation as she had put the money in the till. *Held*, the money had been put in the till, without ringing it up, in order that it should accrue for her own benefit and not that of her employers. Accordingly there had been a dishonest appropriation and the appeal would be dismissed.

R v Monaghan [1979] Crim LR 673 (Court of Appeal: Roskill LJ, Mars-Jones and Drake JJ).

641   —— attempted theft—intent necessary for offence

The defendant, who was caught with his hand in another person's bag, was charged with attempted theft. He contended that the prosecution had failed to establish the necessary intention, that he intended to steal specific articles contained in the bag. *Held*, in the light of the decision of the Court of Appeal in *Attorney-General's References (Nos. 1 and 2 of 1979)* [1979] 3 All ER 143, para. 584, it was clear that it was not necessary to prove a specific intention to steal the objects in the bag.

Scudder v Barrett (note) [1979] 3 WLR 591 (Queen's Bench Division: Roskill LJ, Bristow and Michael Davies JJ).

642   —— property—intangible property—confidential information

An information was preferred against a university student who had acquired the proof of an examination paper, alleging that he had stolen certain intangible property, namely, confidential information being the property of the Senate of the university. It was agreed that the student had not intended permanently to deprive the university of the proof itself. The justices dismissed the charge on the grounds that confidential information was not intangible property within the Theft Act 1968, s. 4. The prosecutor appealed by way of case stated. *Held*, there was no property in the confidential information capable of being the subject of a charge of theft. The appeal would be dismissed.

Oxford v Moss (1978) 68 Cr App Rep 183 (Queen's Bench Division: Lord Widgery CJ, Wien and Smith JJ).

643   —— —— property abandoned where owner not liable to discover it—whether intention of permanently depriving owner

Scotland

The defendant was convicted of two separate charges of theft of a motor car. In each case the evidence was that the defendant and co-accused removed the vehicle from where it had been parked, drove it around and subsequently abandoned it. The defendant was the passenger on both occasions but knew that co-accused had had no authority to remove the cars. The defendant appealed, contending that in order to establish the crime of theft it had to be shown that there had been an intention permanently to deprive the owner of his property. *Held*, the fact that on each occasion, the defendant had taken possession of the car without authority and had left it in a place where the owner, by reason of his own investigations, was not liable to find it was sufficient to establish the crime of theft. The appeal would be dismissed.

KIVLIN V MILNE 1979 SLT 2 (High Court of Justiciary).

CRIMINAL PROCEDURE

Halsbury's Laws of England (4th edn.), Vol. 11, paras. 89–480, 611–810

644   **Articles**

The Accused's Spouse as Defence Witness, T. M. S. Tosswill (spouse as compellable witness for spouse-defendant): [1979] Crim LR 696

Arrest by any Other Name, David N. Clarke and David Feldman (nature of arrest and detention in the light of recent cases): [1979] Crim LR 702.

The Authentication of Statements to the Police, Glanville Williams (arguments for introducing the electronic recording of police interrogations): [1979] Crim LR 6.

Bail for the Child in Care: 143 JP Jo 662.

Confessions and the Doctrine of Oppression, John D. Jackson (the extent to which the courts have developed the common law to give more safeguards to the suspect by excluding unfairly obtained evidence): 129 NLJ 264.

Confessions: Wider Aspects of Voluntariness, Dr. A. J. Ashworth (general rule relating to admissibility of confessions, particularly confessions made by mentally handicapped persons): 142 J P Jo 716.

Evidence of Agent Provocateur, F. G. (discretion of court to exclude his evidence): 123 Sol Jo 833.

Homosexuality and Similar Fact Evidence, Frank Bates (in the light of *R v Inder* (1978) 67 Cr App Rep 143, CA, para. 698): 123 Sol Jo 634.

Operation of the Bail Act in London Magistrates' Courts, Michael Zander: 129 NLJ 108.

Pleading Guilty under Mistake of Law, (changing a plea of guilty to not guilty where there has been a mistake of law): 122 Sol Jo 820.

Police Interrogation and the Right to See a Solicitor, John Baldwin and Michael McConville: [1979] Crim LR 145.

Psychiatric Reports: What They Really Mean, Dr. Ian Pullen (relationship between criminal behaviour and mental disorder): 123 Sol Jo 41.

Psychology and the Law, Professor H. J. Eysenck (problems of criminality and the psychologist): 123 Sol Jo 3.

The Relationship of Absconding to Contempt, M. J. Richardson (on how the Crown Court deals with an accused who fails to answer bail): 123 Sol Jo 680.

The Relevance of Psychological Investigation to Legal Issues in Testimony and Identification, Brian R. Clifford: [1979] Crim LR 153.

Self-Defence, Alec Samuels (difficulties arising from the defence of self-defence): 143 JP Jo 74.

645   **Appeal—appeal against sentence—application for bail pending appeal—test to be applied**

See *R v Watton*, para. 659

646   —— —— **concurrent sentences to borstal training**

See *R v Long*, para. 2481.

647　　**—— conviction following plea of guilty on counsel's advice—right of convicted man to appeal**

A man was caught by police officers throwing a pipe over a wall. He denied that it was his, but admitted that he knew it had been used for smoking cannabis, probably at a party the night before. He pleaded guilty to being in possession of cannabis resin under the Misuse of Drugs Act 1971, s. 5 (1) and (2), after having been advised by his counsel that his case fell squarely within the principles of *Bocking v Roberts* [1974] QB 307. However *Bocking v Roberts* was subsequently distinguished in *R v Carver*, where the appellant was acquitted because the quantity of cannabis resin found on him was too small to be used in the manner prohibited by the 1971 Act. The accused's trial was held one day before the decision in *R v Carver*. In the light of that decision he appealed against his conviction. *Held*, by virtue of the Criminal Law Act 1977, s. 44, appeals against conviction where the accused had pleaded guilty were possible. Such appeals could only be allowed at the discretion of the court and in exceptional circumstances. Since the accused might have been acquitted had his trial fallen on a later date, the circumstances could properly be considered exceptional and accordingly the appeal would be allowed.

R v LIDIARD (1978) 122 Sol Jo 743 (Court of Appeal: LAWTON LJ, CAULFIELD AND KENNETH JONES JJ). *R v Carver* [1978] QB 472, 1978 Halsbury's Abridgment para. 615 applied.

648　　**—— irregularity at trial—direction to jury—fitness of accused to plead**

In a case where a doctor gave evidence that the accused was suffering from a condition of paranoid schizophrenia, the question of the fitness of the accused to plead was to be determined by the jury. The trial judge failed to direct the jury that they should base their findings on the ability of the accused to challenge jurors, to instruct counsel, to understand the evidence and to give evidence himself. On appeal *held*, such a failure resulted in a non-direction and the finding of disability would be quashed.

R v BERRY (1977) 66 Cr App Rep 156 (Court of Appeal: GEOFFREY LANE LJ, THESIGER and MICHAEL DAVIES JJ). *R v Pritchard* (1836) 7 C & P 303 and *R v Robertson* [1968] 3 All ER 557, CA, applied.

649　　**—— —— discharge of juror not in open court**

The defendant was tried on a charge of theft. The judge had not completed directing the jury when the court adjourned overnight. In the morning before the court resumed, the judge agreed by telephone to discharge a juror because her husband had died during the night. The judge assumed that the juror's discharge was known and did not mention it in court. The jurors retired and returned a verdict of guilty. Counsel were unaware that only eleven jurors were present. The defendant was sentenced. He appealed against conviction on the ground of a material irregularity in the course of the trial, contending that the judge's decision to discharge the juror could only properly have been taken in open court. *Held*, neither statute nor common law required the discharge of a juror to take place in open court. The only question was whether the juror had been properly discharged, and there was no doubt that she had. The Juries Act 1974, s. 16 (1) clearly contemplated that, given an effective discharge of a juror, the jury could continue; the transfer of jurisdiction from one jury to another did not have to be considered. The appeal would be dismissed.

R v RICHARDSON [1979] 3 All ER 247 (Court of Appeal: LORD WIDGERY CJ, SHAW LJ and McNEILL J).

650　　**—— —— judge's discretion to discharge jury**

The appellant was convicted of wounding with intent and aggravated burglary. At his trial prosecuting counsel produced a witness statement in which it was alleged that the appellant had confessed to the offences. However no deposition was produced nor was the witness available to give evidence. The judge refused to discharge the jury. On an appeal against conviction, *held*, the jury had been put in possession of potentially prejudicial and damaging material with no reasonable prospect of it being supported by evidence. A new jury should have accordingly be empanelled and the appeal would be allowed.

R v BINING [1978] LS Gaz R 1171 (Court of Appeal: LORD WIDGERY CJ, BRIDGE LJ and WIEN J).

651   —— notice of abandonment—application to withdraw notice

A person convicted of burglary, damaging property and actual bodily harm submitted an application for leave to appeal against sentence, but later signed a notice of abandonment of all proceedings. Upon his application for leave to withdraw his notice, *held*, the notice had to be shown to be a nullity and as no evidence was adduced in support, the application would be refused.

R v WILLIAMS [1978] LS Gaz R 1091 (Court of Appeal: WALLER LJ, BRISTOW and STOCKER JJ).

652   —— order for new trial—effect of order—whether order in interests of justice

Jamaica
At the trial of a defendant charged with murder the prosecution case rested wholly on the identification of the defendant by a single eye-witness. The defendant was convicted but the conviction was quashed on appeal on the ground that the identification evidence was insufficient to support the verdict. However, the Court of Appeal, in exercise of its power under the Judicature (Appellate Jurisdiction) Act s. 14 (2), ordered a new trial. The defendant appealed against the order. *Held*, the verdict had been set aside on the grounds that at trial the prosecution had failed to adduce sufficient evidence to justify a conviction, and the effect of the order therefore was to give the prosecution an opportunity of curing the evidential deficiency, which was clearly contrary to the interests of justice. The Court of Appeal had thus erred in principle in exercising its statutory power and the appeal would be allowed.

REID v R [1979] 2 WLR 221 (Privy Council: LORD DIPLOCK, LORD HAILSHAM OF ST MARYLEBONE, LORD SALMON, LORD EDMUND-DAVIES and LORD KEITH OF KINKEL).

653   —— —— grounds for order

Hong Kong
The Court of Appeal of Hong Kong in exercising its unqualified discretionary power to order a retrial had only to act in the "interests of justice" according to the Criminal Procedure Ordinance of Hong Kong. The probability of a conviction was neither a condition precedent to nor a factor of paramount importance in deciding whether to order a new trial.

AU PUI-KUEN v A-G OF HONG KONG [1979] 1 All ER 769 (Privy Council: LORD DIPLOCK, LORD SIMON OF GLAISDALE, LORD SALMON, LORD EDMUND-DAVIES and LORD KEITH OF KINKEL).

654   —— proviso for dismissal of appeal—misdirection to jury on standard of proof

Hong Kong
On arrival at an airport two men were given possession of documents enabling them to collect a parcel of jadestones, which was found also to contain morphine. They were tried on charges of trafficking in dangerous drugs, their defence being that they knew nothing about the morphine. There was a presumption under Hong Kong legislation that possession of a document of title was possession of the drug, unless the defendant's lack of knowledge was proved. It was not established during the trial that the documents in question were documents of title, yet despite this the judge directed the jury that it was to be presumed that the defendants knew the morphine was in the package unless it was proved otherwise. They were convicted and the

Court of Appeal of Hong Kong upheld the conviction, applying a proviso similar to that contained in the Criminal Appeal Act 1968, s. 2 (1). The court held that despite the trial judge's misdirection to the jury, there had been no miscarriage of justice. The defendants appealed. *Held*, allowing the appeal, the only contested issue in the case was the defendants' knowledge. According to the judge's direction the jury were bound to convict if the defendants' knowledge was proved on the balance of probabilities, whereas they should have been acquitted unless their knowledge was proved beyond reasonable doubt. The verdict was therefore unsafe and unsatisfactory and the convictions would be quashed, the case being remitted to the Court of Appeal to consider whether a new trial should be ordered.

KWAN PING BONG AND KONG CHING v THE QUEEN [1979] 2 WLR 433 (Privy Council: LORD DIPLOCK, LORD EDMUND-DAVIES and LORD KEITH OF KINKEL).

655   —— right of appeal—criminal cause or matter

The applicant, who was awaiting trial, brought a private prosecution against an intended witness, the summonses charging the witness with blackmail, obtaining money by deception and swearing a false statement tendered in evidence. The private prosecution was however, taken over by the Director of Public Prosecutions under the Prosecution of Offences Act 1979, s. 4. The justices discharged the witness, as no evidence was offered. The applicant's criminal trial was adjourned when he obtained leave to apply ex parte for an order of mandamus compelling the Director to continue the private prosecution. The application was refused. On the applicant's appeal, it was contended for the Director that the appeal involved a criminal cause or matter and the Court of Appeal had no jurisdiction, by virtue of the Supreme Court of Judicature (Consolidation) Act 1925, s. 31 (1), to hear the appeal without the leave of the House of Lords. *Held*, the present application to the Court of Appeal was a step which would put the witness in the jeopardy of a criminal charge being prosecuted against him and his being convicted; and that step by which the applicant wanted the witness to continue to be prosecuted and possibly convicted was a step in a criminal cause or matter. The Court of Appeal had no jurisdiction, therefore, and the applications would be refused.

R v DIRECTOR OF PUBLIC PROSECUTIONS, EX PARTE RAYMOND (1979) 123 Sol Jo 786 (Court of Appeal: LORD DENNING MR, LAWTON and DONALDSON LJJ). Dictum of Lord Porter in *Amand v Home Secretary and Minister of Defence of Royal Netherlands Government* [1943] AC 147, HL at 164 applied.

656   —— verdict unsafe or unsatisfactory—inadmissible statements made after the trial—whether grounds for appeal

The police saw the appellants put something into the boot of a car and drive away. When the car was stopped, a quantity of explosives was discovered in the boot. The appellants denied all knowledge of the explosives and maintained that they had been planted in the boot. They were convicted of possessing explosive substances. After the trial, a number of statements were obtained, in which two men confessed to having planted the explosives. The Court of Appeal was given power, by the Criminal Appeal Act 1968, s. 7, to allow an appeal against conviction by reason of evidence received or available to be received by them under s. 23 of the 1968 Act. The confession statements were, however, inadmissible as evidence under s. 23, and therefore the appellants appealed on the ground that the jury's verdict was unsafe or unsatisfactory under s. 2 (1), basing their appeal on the confession statements. *Held*, the appellants, who were relying on inadmissible evidence, could not be placed in a stronger position than those relying on s. 23 by basing their appeal on s. 2 (1) rather than on s. 23. It would be unjust to quash a conviction on the basis of information wholly inadmissible in evidence. The appeal would be dismissed.

R v WALLACE (1978) 67 Cr App Rep 291 (Court of Appeal: ROSKILL LJ, CHAPMAN and LAWSON JJ). *Stafford v Director of Public Prosecutions, Luvaglio v Director of Public Prosecutions* [1973] 3 All ER 762, applied.

657   —— —— **test to be applied**

Grenada

A man was convicted of murder. He appealed and the Court of Appeal of Grenada found that there had been a misdirection as to intent by the trial judge. However, the court dismissed the appeal after applying the proviso contained in the West Indies Associated States Supreme Court (Grenada) Act 1971, s. 41 (1), which is substantially the same as the proviso in the Criminal Appeal Act 1968, s. 2 (1). The criterion the Court used in deciding whether to apply the proviso was whether there was evidence on which a reasonable jury could convict. There was a further appeal. *Held*, the Court of Appeal had used the wrong criterion, although the appeal would nevertheless be dismissed. The correct test to be applied was whether the jury's verdict was unsafe or unsatisfactory. Considering all the circumstances, the verdict was safe and satisfactory and no miscarriage of justice had occurred.

FERGUSON V R [1979] 1 All ER 877 (Privy Council: VISCOUNT DILHORNE, LORD EDMUND-DAVIES, LORD FRASER OF TULLYBELTON, LORD SCARMAN and SIR ROBIN COOKE).

658   **Arrest—validity of arrest—conduct likely to cause a breach of the peace**

Police were called to a house where a woman and her daughter appeared to be distressed by the violent behaviour of the woman's husband, from whom she was separated and whom the police believed was subject to a court order excluding him from the house. When the husband refused to comply with his wife's request that he leave, the police purported to arrest him for conduct likely to cause a breach of the peace. In resisting the arrest he injured one of the police officers and was charged with assault occasioning actual bodily harm. He claimed that there was no case to answer because the arrest had been unlawful. *Held*, the police power to arrest was necessarily confined to cases where there was a continuing breach of the peace or a threatened renewal of a previous breach, because otherwise there was no evidence of conduct likely to cause a breach. Accordingly, the husband's arrest had been unlawful and he had been entitled to use such force as was necessary to secure his liberty. There was therefore no case for him to answer.

R V PODGER [1979] Crim LR 524 (Crown Court at Bristol: Mr Recorder JERVIS).

659   **Bail—application for bail pending appeal against sentence—test to be applied**

In November 1978 the applicant, having been granted leave to appeal to the Court of Appeal against sentence, applied for bail pending the appeal, which was likely to be heard in January. The application was refused and he applied to the Court of Appeal on the grounds that since his status had changed from applicant to appellant the principles applicable to pre-trial bail applied and, further, the effect of the Courts Act 1971, s. 13 (4), as amended by the Bail Act 1976, was to widen the powers of the court to grant bail and to remove the test of exceptional circumstances. Alternatively, he submitted that certain personal factors, together with the intervention of the Christmas vacation before the hearing of the appeal, constituted exceptional circumstances. *Held*, the law had not been altered in respect of the granting of bail to offenders appealing against sentence, and the test remained whether exceptional circumstances existed such as to lead the court to the conclusion that justice could only be done by granting bail. Leave to appeal against sentence was merely a factor to be considered, and the application would be refused since the applicant had advanced no exceptional circumstances.

R V WATTON (1978) 68 Cr App Rep 293 (Court of Appeal: GEOFFREY LANE LJ and ACKNER and WATKINS JJ).

660   —— **bail during trial—absconding**

See *R v Tyson*, para. 2490.

661 ——— recognisance—order for forfeiture—correctness of order

See *R v Tottenham Magistrates' Court, ex parte Riccardi*, para. 1793.

662 **Binding over order—restriction on right to return to England or Wales—validity of order under Community law**

See *Case 175/78: R v Saunders*, para. 1220.

663 **Caution—cautioning of person before police officer has made any inquiries as to facts**

See *Dilks v Tilley*, para. 690.

664 **Committal for sentence—offences triable either way—when proceedings commenced**

See *R v Brentwood Justices, ex parte Jones*, para. 1775.

665 **Committal proceedings—papers given to magistrates before hearing—whether formal tendering of evidence**

See *R v Colchester Stipendiary Magistrates, ex parte Beck*, para. 1777.

666 **Community service order—power of Crown Court to revoke order**

See *R v Adair*, para. 561.

667 **Costs—taxation of costs—Crown Court proceedings**

Notes for the guidance of taxing officers in the Crown Court have been published which replace the notes issued in 1972. The notes are divided into four parts. Part I (introductory) sets out, inter alia, the "relevant factors" which the taxing officer should take into account. These include, inter alia, the importance of the case and the importance of it to the defendant, the complexity of the matter, the skill, specialised knowledge and responsibility involved, the documents prepared, the time expended and regional variations in the expense to solicitors of conducting proceedings. Part II deals with counsel's fees. The taxing officer must consider how much work has reasonably been undertaken by counsel having regard to the weight, seriousness, importance and complexity of the case and other relevant factors. Part III deals with solicitors' costs and the general approach includes assessing how much work was done, by whom and if it was reasonably necessary, assessing expense at appropriate hourly rates, and adding the cost of necessary letters, telephone calls and a sum for care and conduct, reasonable disbursements and for attending the hearing. Part IV describes the procedure on taxations.

For the text of the notes, see LS Gaz, 23rd May 1979, pp. 530–535.

668 ——— ——— method of calculation of fees for court attendance

A Chelmsford firm of solicitors appealed against a taxing master's review of an assessment by a taxing officer of their fees, incurred in criminal proceedings, for court attendance. They had calculated their fees according to the system outlined in a Law Society publication "The Expense of Time". On appeal, two questions were certified for the court; (i) whether the taxing officer ought to have accepted, as sufficient evidence of the broad average direct cost of work done in the Chelmsford area, the expense rates shown in the tables prepared by a group of solicitors practising in the Chelmsford Crown Court, on the basis of the method suggested in "The Expense of Time"; and (ii) whether solicitors should be allowed, for attendance at court at the trial, an amount ascertained by multiplying the time actually and reasonably engaged in any one day by the relevant expense rate of the appropriate fee-earner and adding to that a further sum for care and conduct calculated as a percentage of the time charge. Following a detailed examination of the method of calculating the hourly expense rate as outlined in the book, *held* (i), although "The

Expense of Time" was laudable in many ways, it did not, in its present form, provide a reliable basis for the taxation of costs. Thus, while taxation officers were not to disregard altogether calculations of expenses submitted on the basis of the book, they should treat them as no more than one matter to be taken into account. The first question would therefore be answered in the negative. (ii) The present practice of allowing a solicitor a daily fee for court attendance without any mark up for care and conduct was derived from the Legal Aid in Criminal Proceedings (Fees and Expenses) Regulations 1968. To ameliorate the position created by the retention of the solicitors' fees specified in the Sch. an amendment to the 1968 Regulations, in 1977, provided for a taxing master to increase the fees payable under the 1968 Regulations in exceptional circumstances if it appeared that they would not provide fair remuneration. Whilst the court felt that these fixed scales were unfair in an age of inflation, it was not appropriate for it to introduce such a fundamental change. The second question would therefore also be answered in the negative. However, it was suggested that the scope of the regulations be widened to embrace the whole question of solicitors' remuneration for court attendances and in particular the question whether such remuneration should no longer be made on the basis of a fee, but rather on the basis of an hourly expense rate plus a mark up for care and conduct.

R v WILKINSON [1980] 1 All ER 597 (Queen's Bench Division: ROBERT GOFF J sitting with assessors).

669   —— —— **VAT**

See para. 2125.

670   **Criminal Evidence Act 1979**

The Criminal Evidence Act 1979 amends the Criminal Evidence Act 1898, s. 1 (f) (iii); it allows defendants to be asked questions tending to show, inter alia, that they have committed an offence where they have given evidence against another person charged in the same proceedings. Previously, the prosecution or trial judge could only ask such questions where the other person stood charged with the same offence. The provision is not retrospective. The Act received the royal assent on 22nd March 1979 and came into force on 22nd April 1979.

671   **Criminal proceedings—concurrent civil action—power of High Court to stay action pending conclusion of criminal proceedings**

See *Jefferson Ltd v Bhetcha*, para. 2137.

672   **Evidence—admissibility—statement by defendant—self serving statements**

A man was arrested by the police and, in the presence of his solicitor, made a statement. He was then interviewed by the police. The next day he made a second statement. At the trial the judge excluded both statements and part of the interview, on the grounds that they were self serving. On appeal, *held*, three principles governed the admissibility of statements made by a defendant; (i) A statement is never evidence of the facts in the statement unless it contains an admission. An admission is always admissible as a declaration against interest; (ii) (a) A statement that is not an admission is admissible to show the attitude of the accused at the time when he made it. It need not necessarily be a statement made on the first encounter with the police, but the longer the time that has elapsed after the first encounter the less the weight which will be attached to the denial; (ii) (b) It is also admissible if it is made in the same context as an admission, as it would be unfair to admit only statements against interest while excluding other parts of the same interview or series of interviews. The prosecution was under a duty to present the case fairly to the jury; (ii) (c) The prosecution can draw attention to inconsistent denials, although a denial does not become an admission merely because it is inconsistent with another denial. (iii) Although most self serving statements are given in evidence, on the rare occasions when an accused produces a carefully prepared written statement with a view to its being made part of the prosecution evidence, it should be excluded. The principles stated in (ii) (a) and (b) applied in the instant case. The appellant's first statement was relevant to show his attitude at the beginning of the interview. Furthermore as part of the interview had been admitted, the statement should have been admitted in order to put the interview into context. The same principle applied to the rest of the interview and the second statement. The appeal would be allowed and the conviction quashed.

R v PEARCE (1979) 69 Cr App Rep 365 (Court of Appeal: LORD WIDGERY CJ, WALLER LJ and LLOYD J). The principles stated in *R v Donaldson* (1976) 64 Cr App Rep 59 applied; for a summary of this case, see 1976 Halsbury's Abridgment para. 588.

673 —— **analysis of urine sample—dangerous drugs—discretion of court to admit analysis**

Following a raid on his flat in a search for drugs, the accused was required to provide a urine sample. He was not given any caution or warning relating to the use to which the specimen would be put nor offered part of the specimen for his own use. On analysis, the sample was found to contain amphetamines and was used in evidence against him at his trial. Upon his conviction of possession of controlled drugs, the recorder certified that the case was fit for appeal on the ground that the request for a urine sample might have involved the accused in providing evidence against himself. *Held*, it was a matter of discretion as to whether or not the sample would be admitted in evidence. Further, no analogy could be drawn from road traffic cases, where the test was not whether there was any alcohol in the blood at all, but what proportion of alcohol was in the blood. On the facts of this particular case the evidence was fairly admitted and the appeal would be dismissed.

R v BEET (1978) 66 Cr App Rep 188 (Court of Appeal: ORMROD LJ, CUSACK and CROOM-JOHNSON JJ).

674 —— **burden of proof—uttering forged documents—evidence as to falsity of document**

A supervisor at the main contracting company passed certain tax forms to his head office knowing that they had been completed, not by the sub-contractors as required, but by his own foremen. He was subsequently charged and convicted of uttering forged documents and of furnishing false information. On application for leave to appeal against conviction he contended that it was necessary for the prosecution to prove that the documents were false, and this had not been established as the prosecution had adduced no evidence that the completion of the forms had not been authorised by the sub-contractors. *Held*, it was required only for the prosecution to show that the documents had been completed by others and not by the sub-contractors. The burden of proof that the completion had been authorised by the sub-contractors lay on the supervisor. The application would accordingly be refused.

R v HISCOX (1978) 68 Cr App Rep 411 (Court of Appeal: WALLER LJ, BRISTOW and STOCKER JJ). *R v Vincent* (1972) 56 Cr App Rep 281, CA distinguished.

675 —— **character—character of accused**

The accused was convicted on a charge of arson. At his trial the chief prosecution witness, a detective, gave evidence of his confession at an interview. The accused denied this and the recorder then allowed the prosecution to cross-examine him on his character and previous convictions on the basis that the accused had imputed the good character of the witness. On appeal against conviction, *held*, cross examination of the accused as to his character was only permissible when both imputations on the character of the prosecution witness were cast to show his unreliability as a witness independent of the evidence given by him, and when the casting of such imputations was necessary to enable the accused to establish his defence. The attempt to demonstrate the detective's unreliability as to the disputed confession had not been based upon any matter independent of his evidence, nor had the accused's denial been directed at casting imputations to establish a defence but rather it had been a denial

of the charge. Accordingly the accused's criminal record had been incorrectly put
to him.
    R v NELSON (1978) 68 Cr App Rep 16 (Court of Appeal: SHAW LJ, LAWSON and
SMITH JJ).

676   —— —— —— **imputation on witnesses' character**

It was alleged that three people T, TF, and MF went into a jewellers and whilst MF
and T distracted the attention of the shopkeeper, TF stole items from the window
display. During the trial, the defence launched an attack on the character of the
police and consequently TF was asked about his previous convictions of theft from
a jeweller's shop and theft from a shop by distracting attention. Cross-examination
of MF elicited that she too had been jointly convicted with TF of theft from a
jeweller's shop. The Crown did not seek to establish that the evidence fell within
the similar facts rule. TF and MF appealed against conviction on the ground that the
evidence was wrongly admitted. *Held*, the proviso contained in the Criminal
Evidence Act 1898, s. 1 (f) (ii) providing for cross-examination of the defendant as
to character where the defence had made allegations about the character of the
prosecution witnesses, should not have been applied in this case. The cross-
examination had elicited too much detail about the previous offences and should
only have gone so far as to help the jury assess the defendant's credibility. The trial
judge should not have exercised his discretion under the similar facts rule to admit
the evidence either, as it was prejudicial rather than probative. Thus, although even
without this evidence the prosecution case was a strong one, it could not be said that
the evidence might not have influenced the jury, and the appeal would be allowed.
    R v FRANCE AND FRANCE [1979] Crim LR 48 (Court of Appeal: SHAW LJ,
SWANWICK and GRIFFITHS JJ).

677   —— **child aged between ten and fourteen—presumption of
incapacity—admissibility of evidence to rebut presumption**

A boy aged thirteen was tried for blackmail. In the absence of a jury, the
prosecution sought leave to adduce evidence of previous findings of guilt against
the boy in order to rebut the presumption that the boy, as a child aged between
ten and fourteen years, was incapable of forming a criminal intention. The trial
judge ruled that such evidence was admissible. The boy was convicted, and
appealed on the ground that evidence of former findings of guilt against him could
not be adduced to rebut the presumption. *Held*, the prosecution could call relevant
evidence to rebut the presumption of incapacity of forming a criminal intention.
The evidence had to be relevant, and the trial judge could refuse to admit any
evidence which was not relevant to the issue of the boy's capacity to know right
from wrong. The appeal would be dismissed.
    R v B, R v A [1979] 3 All ER 460 (Court of Appeal: LORD WIDGERY CJ, SHAW
LJ and McNEIL J). *B v R* (1958) 44 Cr App Rep 1 applied.

678   —— **confession—confession induced by police officer disguising
himself as fellow prisoner**

Canada
After being arrested for being in possession of narcotics, a man was cautioned and
refused to give a statement. A police officer, disguised as a fellow prisoner, was
placed in a cell with the man, to whom the man then made several admissions. The
trial judge excluded the statements from being presented as evidence, and the man
was acquitted. The Crown appealed. *Held*, allowing the appeal, the statements
should have been admitted at the trial. There had been no oppressive behaviour
and, furthermore, the police officer had not been a person in authority at the time,
because the man had not realised he was anyone in authority when making the
statements. The fact that the statements had been obtained by a trick did not render
them inadmissible.
    The minority opinion of the court was that the officer, by tricking the man, had
subverted the caution and deprived the man of his right to remain silent. In such

circumstances the trial judge had a discretion to refuse admission of the evidence and he had properly exercised that discretion.

R v ROTHMAN (1979) 42 CCC (2d) 377 (Court of Appeal of Ontario).

679 —— —— **confession obtained as result of hypnosis—admissibility**

Canada

A seventeen-year-old youth was charged with the murder of his mother. A statement was obtained from him after intensive interrogation, but did not incriminate him. He was subsequently interviewed by a skilled interrogator who, through the hypnotic quality of his voice, induced the youth to confess in a tape-recorded monologue delivered after the interviewer had left the room. After the hypnosis had worn off, the youth made a second statement confessing his guilt to the interrogator and a third in the presence of the latter and the first interrogators, who recorded what he said. The question arose whether the second and third statements, delivered after the youth emerged from his hypnotic state, were admissible as evidence. *Held*, by a four to three majority, the statements were inadmissible. Two judges considered that the statements should be excluded because the youth had suffered complete emotional disintegration by the end of his interrogation, which precluded anything he said from being considered voluntary; the hypnosis factor was not the crucial issue in determining the admissibility of the statements. Two more judges considered the statements involuntary and therefore inadmissible because they were tainted by the preceding hypnosis. The skilled interrogator's appeal to the youth to speak was irresistible and he could not have refused even had he wanted to.

The minority of the court considered the statements admissible as they had not been obtained by fear of prejudice or hope of advantage held out by a person in authority. The youth had had a strong desire to unburden himself and his statements could only be excluded if the persons in authority had acted improperly or unjustifiably.

HORVATH v R (1979) 93 DLR (3d) 1 (Supreme Court of Canada).

680 —— —— **defendant mentally subnormal—Home Office procedure not followed**

A mentally subnormal woman was indicted on two counts of arson. The only evidence connecting her with the alleged damage was verbal and written confessions obtained during interviews with the police, when no parent or other person responsible for her had been present. This was contrary to the instructions laid down in Home Office Circular 109/1976. The defence submitted that the alleged confessions were inadmissible as evidence. *Held*, the whole case would be withdrawn and the jury directed to find the woman not guilty, because the safeguard designed to protect the mentally subnormal had not been observed.

R v WILLIAMS [1979] Crim LR 47 (Crown Court at Swansea: WATKINS J).

681 —— —— **determination of admissibility on voir dire—admissibility of evidence on voir dire at main trial**

Hong Kong

The appellant was charged with murdering one man and maliciously wounding two others. The only evidence connecting him with the incident was a confession signed by him and given to the police. At the start of his trial the appellant challenged the admissibility of the statement on the grounds that it had not been made voluntarily. The trial judge dealt with the issue in the absence of the jury on the voir dire and on the appellant's evidence ruled that statement inadmissible. However, during the voir dire the appellant admitted under cross-examination that he had been present at and involved in the attack. During the main trial the prosecution sought to establish these facts by calling the reporters of the voir dire to testify as to the appellant's evidence under cross-examination. The trial judge allowed both the reporters' testimony and cross-examination of the appellant as to discrepancies between his evidence on the voir dire and during the main trial. The appellant's appeal against conviction on both counts was dismissed and he appealed to the Privy Council. *Held*, (i), (LORD HAILSHAM dissenting), the sole object of the voir dire was to determine the voluntary nature of the confession for the purpose of ruling as to its admissibility, and the prosecution was therefore not entitled to cross-examine as to its truth; (ii), the distinction between the issue of voluntariness, which was alone relevant to the voir dire, and the issue of guilt, which was to be decided by the jury, should be maintained by excluding from the main trial any evidence regarding the voir dire, regardless of whether the challenged statement was admitted or excluded; and (iii), where a defendant gave evidence in the main trial he could be cross-examined as to his evidence on the voir dire only where the challenged statement had been admitted and where such cross-examination was directed to testing the credibility of the defendant. Accordingly, in this case evidence had been wrongly placed before the jury and the appeal would be allowed.

As to (i), LORD HAILSHAM denied the existence of any limitation on questions which could be tendered on the voir dire other than that of relevance to the issue being determined, which would allow for cross-examination as to the truth of the challenged statement.

WONG KAM-MING v R [1979] 1 All ER 939 (Privy Council: LORD DIPLOCK, LORD HAILSHAM OF ST MARYLEBONE, LORD SALMON, LORD EDMUND-DAVIES and LORD KEITH OF KINKEL). *R v Hammond* [1941] 3 All ER 318, CA, overruled with respect to Hong Kong.

682   —— —— **test of admissibility**

A fifteen-year-old girl was assaulted and thrown from a fast-moving train. She was too ill to give an account of the assault and the police evolved a theory of how the crime was committed. This received wide publicity and the police were notified several weeks later by a group of train passengers who thought that the defendant fitted the publicised description of the assailant. The police arrested the defendant for the attempted murder of the girl. The defendant was aged thirty and single. Evidence given by a psychiatrist, and accepted by the trial judge, showed him to be sub-normal with a mental age of eleven. At his trial the defendant's alleged confessions to the police were challenged by the defence on the ground that the prosecution had failed to prove beyond reasonable doubt that they were made voluntarily without fear of prejudice or by oppression or inducement and that there were a large number of breaches of the Judges' Rules and Administrative Directions. On the question of admissibility, *held*, in determining the admissibility of the alleged confessions the trial judge had to exclude from consideration the weight of the evidence of the confessions, the discrepancies in them, whether there was evidence outside them and the intention of the police during interrogations. If the confessions were obtained by inducements or oppression they had to be excluded. If there was any breach of the Judges' Rules or the Administrative Directions the judge had a discretion to exclude any answers or statements obtained. In this case there had been several breaches of the Rules and Directions in that, inter alia, the defendant had not been informed orally of his rights nor had he been cautioned. The cross-examining had also been of an oppressive nature and included many suggested answers to the defendant. The defendant had been kept for three days before being allowed to see anyone save the police. Thus, taking into account also the mental incapacity of the defendant, the prosecution had failed to prove beyond reasonable doubt the lack of oppression necessary to render the confessions admissible.

R v WESTLAKE [1979] Crim LR 652 (Central Criminal Court: Judge HODGSON).

683   —— —— **whether confession obtained by oppression**

Scotland

A man confessed to having drowned a boy in a burn, whilst cleaning out the burn during the course of his employment. He appealed against his conviction for murder, claiming that his confession should not have been admitted as evidence because it had been obtained under cross-examination. The defence maintained that the man had become demoralised after having been in custody for twelve hours and having been cautioned and questioned in respect of a murder and these circumstances, combined with his youth, had led to his breakdown. Secondly it was argued that even if the confession was admissible, there had been no corroborating evidence. Other evidence consisted of statements by a boy that he had seen a struggle between the victim and an older boy, although the description of the older boy's clothing did not conform to that worn by the convicted man. Furthermore the man had not been instructed to do any work in the water, and his foreman gave evidence that the convicted man never did any work he was not instructed to do. Despite this his clothes had been soiled, indicating that he had entered the water. *Held*, the confession had been rightly admitted. There had been no cross-examination of the man, in the sense of interrogating him in an effort to break down, weaken or prejudice his evidence, or to elicit damaging statements from him. The police had merely questioned the suspect, who had given a confession of his own volition. Although the other two pieces of evidence were scanty, in the circumstances of the case very little corroboration was required. Taken individually, each piece of evidence would not have been enough, but together they were sufficient to corroborate his confession. The appeal would be dismissed.

HARTLEY v H.M. ADVOCATE 1979 SLT 26 (High Court of Justiciary).

684   —— corroboration—confession—whether other evidence sufficient to corroborate confession

See *Hartley v H. M. Advocate*, para. 683.

685   —— —— evidence regarded as corroborative

The appellant was convicted of handling stolen goods. At his trial the thief gave evidence against him. The judge directed the jury to the effect that, as the thief was an accomplice, his evidence had to be corroborated. He did not however give an indication of what evidence would be capable of amounting to corroboration. On appeal, *held*, in failing to identify such evidence the judge's direction was defective. The appeal would be allowed.

R v REEVES (1978) 68 Cr App Rep 331 (Court of Appeal: LORD WIDGERY CJ, BRIDGE LJ and WIEN J).

686   —— cross-examination—cross-examination as to propensity to violence

See *R v Bracewell*, para. 697.

687   —— documents pertaining to committal proceedings—perusal by magistrate in advance of proceedings—whether passing of documents amounted to tendering evidence—validity of proceedings

See *R v Colchester Stipendiary Magistrates, ex parte Beck*, para. 1777.

688   —— driving or being in charge with blood alcohol concentration above prescribed limit—validity of arrest—admissibility of evidence of events subsequent to arrest

See *Morris v Beardmore*, para. 2274.

689   —— evidence irregularly obtained—official instigation of crime—discretion to exclude evidence

The accused, who was indicted on a charge of conspiring with others to utter forged currency, claimed that the crime had only been committed as the result of the activities of an agent provocateur. He contended that the judge had a discretion to exclude prosecution evidence which had been obtained in this way. Such exclusion would inevitably have led to his acquittal. The Court of Appeal upheld the judge's ruling that he had no such discretion. On further appeal, *held*, although a judge always had a discretion to exclude prejudicial evidence of doubtful probative value, that discretion did not apply to relevant admissible evidence which had been obtained by improper or unfair means. It was possible that use of an agent provocateur would give rise to civil or disciplinary action against the police or to criminal proceedings against the police and agent as principal offenders, and might also be a factor in mitigating the accused's sentence, but there was no discretion to exclude evidence obtained in this way, because to do so would be to reintroduce the defence of entrapment. Accordingly, the appeal would be dismissed.

R v SANG [1979] 2 All ER 1222 (House of Lords: LORD DIPLOCK, VISCOUNT DILHORNE, LORD SALMON, LORD FRASER OF TULLYBELTON and LORD SCARMAN). Decision of Court of Appeal [1979] 2 All ER 46, affirmed. *R v McEvilly, R v Lee* (1973) 60 Cr App Rep 150 and *R v Mealey, R v Sheridan* (1974) 60 Cr App Rep 59 applied. *R v Faulkner, Foulkes and Johns* [1973] Crim LR 45, *R v Burnett and Lee* [1973] Crim LR 748 and *R v Ameer, R v Lucas* [1977] Crim LR 104 overruled.

690   —— **evidence of defendant's reply to police questioning—no caution given before questioning—when caution should be given**

The defendant was involved in a motor accident. A police officer arriving on the scene asked the defendant what had happened without first cautioning him. After the defendant told him, he charged the defendant with driving a vehicle without due care and attention. The justices exercised their discretion and excluded evidence of the defendant's reply and held there was no case to answer. They maintained that after the officer had established which vehicle the defendant had been driving, he should have cautioned the defendant before questioning him further. On appeal, *held*, a caution was only required once an officer had evidence which would afford reasonable grounds for his suspicion. The officer had needed to question the defendant in order to get some information about the accident. Therefore before starting to question the defendant he could not have had sufficient evidence to warrant a caution and thus a caution had not been required at that stage. The appeal would be allowed and the case remitted for rehearing by a panel of justices.

DILKS v TILLEY [1979] LS Gaz R 386 (Queen's Bench Division: MICHAEL DAVIES and NEILL JJ).

691   —— **evidence raising possibility of alternative verdict—propriety of leaving issue to jury**

See *DPP v Daley*, para. 723.

692   —— **evidence relating to previous acquittal**

Australia

Two men were charged with abduction and rape. It was alleged that they forcibly took a woman from a railway station and raped her in a nearby park. They were acquitted of abduction, but the jury were unable to agree on the counts of rape. The men were tried again for rape and the trial judge allowed the Crown to lead evidence that the woman had been forcibly taken from the railway station. The men were found guilty and appealed. On appeal it was found that the doctrine of issue estoppel applied in the criminal law, and thus the Crown was precluded from leading evidence in the second trial which was inconsistent with the acquittal, even though such evidence was directed to the question of the woman's consent to intercourse. The convictions were set aside and the Crown appealed to the High Court. *Held*, dismissing the appeal, such evidence was not admissible where it challenged the previous acquittal or denied the accused the full benefit of the acquittal. Where the evidence would be relevant and its inclusion would not be unjust to the accused, it should be led, particularly if its exclusion might lead to artificiality and dangerous speculation. However a clear warning must be made to the jury that the acquittal must not be challenged and that the evidence must be seen in this light; the trial judge's directions to the jury had not been sufficiently clear. The Court was unable to agree as to whether issue estoppel was a doctrine of the criminal law. Those who felt it was held that it would only be applicable where an element of the offence had been determined by the acquittal. As abduction involved several elements, it could not be said that any one element had been so determined.

R v STOREY (1978) 22 ALR 47 (High Court of Australia).

693 —— expert evidence—road traffic offence—opinion of police officer

The appellant's car collided with another vehicle, killing the driver. He had no recollection of the circumstances and there were no effective witnesses. The prosecution called an experienced police officer to give expert evidence and the appellant was convicted. He appealed on the ground that part of the officer's evidence, concerning his opinions on the causation of accidents, was wrongly admitted. *Held*, the police officer was not prevented from giving evidence as an expert if the subject was one in which he had expert knowledge and it was relevant to the case. The officer had kept within his expertise and the appeal would be dismissed.

R v OAKLEY [1979] RTR 417 (Court of Appeal: LORD WIDGERY CJ, WALLER LJ and LLOYD J).

694 —— identification—proper approach for the court

The appellant was charged with dangerous driving and driving with excess alcohol in his blood. His car had been exceeding the speed limit when it was overtaken by a police car and two police officers identified him as the driver but at his trial he gave evidence that his wife had been driving the car. He was convicted and appealed on the ground that the jury had not been properly directed as to the issue of identification, since the judge had failed to give a warning as prescribed by *R v Turnbull* [1976] 3 All ER 549, CA, 1976 Halsbury's Abridgment para. 601. *Held*, *R v Turnbull* was not automatically applicable to every case in which there was evidence of identification. In the present case, where the officers had been in close proximity with the appellant's car and the appellant's evidence had clearly made no impression on the jury, the judge's summing up had been adequate. The appeal would be dismissed.

R v SKILLIN [1978] LS Gaz R 1265 (Court of Appeal: ORMROD and SHAW LJJ and MAIS J).

695 —— Judges' Rules—statement made under caution—statement consisting of questions and answers—whether breach of Judges' Rules

The applicant stabbed a youth at a club, causing his death. He was later taken to a police station and after being cautioned was asked if he wished to make a statement. He agreed but found it difficult to articulate. The officer then asked him a number of questions, both the questions and his replies being taken down verbatim. Upon conviction, he applied for leave to appeal on the grounds that the statement should not have been admitted in evidence. He contended that it was in breach of the Judges' Rules, r. 4 (d), by which all statements had to be made by the person making the statement and no questions were to be asked other than those needed to make the statement coherent. *Held*, provided the police did not put leading questions to the suspect, there was no reason why he should not have the assistance of the police if he experienced difficulty in choosing the correct words. It was arguable whether there had been a breach of rule 4 (d), but there had not been a material irregularity in the trial nor did it affect the satisfactory character of the verdict. Leave to appeal would be refused.

R v WILLIAMS (1977) 67 Cr App Rep 10 (Court of Appeal: WIDGERY CJ, BRIDGE and MAY JJ).

696 —— murder—defences of automatism and diminished responsibility—medical evidence

See *R v Kiszko*, para. 620; *R v Smith*, para. 619.

697 ——— **proof—distinction between legal proof and scientific proof**

Two men were accused of murdering an old man found dead in his house with face and head injuries. At the trial medical evidence was given that the cause of death was heart failure due to manual strangulation, which supported the story of the first accused, that he found the co-accused in a room with the dead man, but during cross-examination the pathologist admitted that the possibility of partial strangulation with a supervening heart attack could not be excluded. The first accused was convicted of manslaughter and the co-accused appealed against his conviction for murder on the grounds, first, that the judge had misdirected the jury in saying that they could be sure that strangulation was the cause of death, and second, that cross-examination of a witness as to the propensity for violence of the first accused should have been allowed. *Held*, there was a distinction between scientific proof and legal proof which had been rightly drawn by the judge and the jury had been correctly directed. Further, evidence of a propensity for violence could only be relevant if true and the judge had been right to exclude it. However, although the grounds of appeal were thus dismissed the verdict, based only on medical evidence and that of the first accused, was unsafe and a conviction for manslaughter would be substituted.

R v BRACEWELL (1979) 68 Cr App Rep 44 (Court of Appeal: ORMROD and WALLER LJJ and CHAPMAN J).

698 ——— **similar facts—sexual offences**

The appellant was convicted of buggery and on four counts of indecent assault on small boys. The trial judge admitted evidence of previous convictions, after the appellant had made imputations of the bad character of a prosecution witness. The judge also admitted the evidence of each boy in relation to the offences involving the others. The questions on appeal were (i) whether reference could properly be made to the appellant's previous record; (ii) how far the evidence of the individual boys could be treated as corroborating the evidence of the other boys. *Held*, (i) the trial judge had not erred in admitting the appellant's previous record but had failed to appreciate the very serious effect which such evidence would have had on the minds of the jury, and had failed sufficiently to remind them that the information was not to be treated as similar fact evidence; (ii) evidence as to other similar offences was admissible as similar fact evidence if it went beyond showing a tendency to commit crimes of that kind and was positively probative with regard to the offence charged. The similarities of fact in this case were those which would be found in all offences of that nature and were not unique. Thus the evidence of one boy was not to be treated as being corroborative of the others' evidence. The trial judge should have directed the jury that the similarities were insufficient to satisfy the test of similar fact evidence. Accordingly the appeal would be allowed and the conviction quashed.

R v INDER (1977) 67 Cr App Rep 143 (Court of Appeal: LORD WIDGERY CJ, BRIDGE LJ and MAY J). *Boardman v DPP* [1974] 3 All ER 887, HL, 1974 Halsbury's Abridgment para. 642 and *R v Scarrot* [1978] 1 All ER 672, CA, 1977 Halsbury's Abridgment para. 661, applied.

699 ——— ——— **shoplifting**

The appellant was convicted of the theft of bacon from a supermarket. At his trial he pleaded mistake, but the trial judge admitted evidence of two previous occasions the year before when the store detective had seen the accused buying bacon. On one occasion the detective had reason to believe he had left the store without paying for the bacon, but no action had been taken. On the second occasion the appellant, noticing that he was being watched, had returned the bacon to the provisions cabinet in the store. On appeal against conviction on the ground that the evidence was wrongly admitted, *held* the evidence had been properly adduced to negative the defence of mistake. The appeal would be dismissed.

R v SEAMAN (1978) 67 Cr App Rep 234 (Court of Appeal: LORD WIDGERY CJ, SHAW LJ and LLOYD J). *Makin v A-G for New South Wales* [1894] AC 57, applied.

700   —— unsworn statement—statement from dock as to good character—whether rebutting evidence admissible

At his trial on a charge of fraudulent trading, the accused made an unsworn statement from the dock representing himself to be an honest businessman. The prosecution successfully applied to call rebutting evidence to show the bad character of the accused. On appeal against conviction on the grounds that the accused's statement from the dock did not allow the prosecution to call rebutting evidence, *held*, the Crown could call evidence in rebuttal of an assertion made in a statement from the dock where, had such a statement been made during the course of sworn evidence, rebutting evidence would have been properly admissible. However the evidence led by the Crown was not evidence of bad character, was wrongly admitted and there was a material irregularity in the trial.

R v CAMPBELL (1979) 69 Cr App Rep 221 (Court of Appeal: BRIDGE LJ, CHAPMAN and KENNETH JONES JJ).

701   —— witness—competence—defendant's spouse

Canada

A husband was charged with arson after setting fire to the motel unit in which his estranged wife was living. The trial judge ruled that the wife was not competent to testify against her husband because the charge did not allege that there had been a threat to her person, life or liberty. On appeal, *held*, a wife could only testify against her husband both where the charge itself involved a threat to her and where such a threat was revealed in the circumstances surrounding the charge. There was no evidence of a threat to the wife in this case, and accordingly the appeal would be dismissed.

R v SILLARS [1979] 1 WWR 743 (Court of Appeal of British Columbia). *R v Yeo* [1951] 1 All ER 864 not followed.

702   —— —— use of notes to refresh memory—contemporaneity of notes

The Court of Appeal has replied in the affirmative to a question put to it by the Attorney-General. The question was whether a police officer, who had taken brief jottings in the course of interviewing an accused person, and within a short time thereafter made a full note in his notebook incorporating and expanding the jottings, would be permitted to refresh his memory from that notebook at the subsequent trial; whether he was bound to retain the original jottings and disclose their existence to the court; and whether it was the duty of the prosecution in such circumstances to make available to the court and the defence copies of the officer's original brief jottings.

ATTORNEY-GENERAL'S REFERENCE (No. 3 OF 1979) (1979) 69 Cr App Rep 441 (Court of Appeal: LORD WIDGERY CJ, FORBES and LLOYD JJ).

703   Indictment—alternative offences—possession of cannabis and intent to supply cannabis

The appellant was convicted on indictment with possessing cannabis with intent to supply. He pleaded guilty to the bare possession of cannabis and the trial judge sentenced him to imprisonment on both counts. On appeal *held*, where there were two counts in the indictment which were in fact alternative, and the appellant was convicted on the more serious charge and pleaded guilty to the lesser offence, the court should not sentence him for the lesser offence, as this would result in duplication. The plea of guilty should remain recorded however. The sentence would be amended to that effect.

R v BEBBINGTON (1978) 66 Cr App Rep 285 (Court of Appeal: ROSKILL LJ, CHAPMAN and LAWSON JJ).

704   —— **amendment of indictment—power of circuit judge to amend voluntary indictment**

Four men were involved in a scheme of hiring self-drive cars and selling them with forged log-books. On an indictment preferred with the consent of a High Court judge in accordance with the Administration of Justice (Miscellaneous Provisions) Act 1933, s. 2 (2) (b), they were charged, inter alia, with conspiring to steal contrary to the Criminal Law Act 1977, s. 1 (1). At the trial the circuit judge, exercising his powers under the Indictments Act 1915, s. 5 (1), amended the indictment to charge the men with conspiracy to defraud at common law, as preserved by s. 5 (2) of the 1977 Act. On conviction they appealed on the grounds, inter alia, that the conspiracy, if any, had to be charged under s. 1 (1) and not under s. 5 (2) of the 1977 Act, and that the circuit judge had no power under s. 5 (1) of the 1915 Act to amend an indictment which owed its authority to a High Court judge under s. 2 (2) (b) of the 1933 Act. *Held*, a conspiracy to steal was properly to be regarded as covered by conspiracy to defraud and accordingly an indictment was not rendered invalid merely because it charged conspiracy to defraud. Further, once an indictment was in existence the power to amend was contained in s. 5 (1) of the 1915 Act and there was no distinction to be made between a voluntary indictment made under s. 2 (2) (b) of the 1933 Act and the usual indictment on committal for trial under s. 2 (2) (a). The appeal would therefore be dismissed.

R v Walters [1979] RTR 220 (Court of Appeal: Lord Widgery CJ, Cumming-Bruce LJ and Neill J). *R v Quinn* [1978] Crim LR 750, 1978 Halsbury's Abridgment para. 600, approved.

This decision was considered by the Court of Appeal in *R v Duncalf*, para. 587.

705   —— **duplicity—alleged possession of cannabis or cannabis resin**

cmThe Court of Appeal has stated that an indictment containing a count of unlawful possession of a controlled drug, being either cannabis resin or cannabis, was not bad for duplicity. Cannabis resin and cannabis were linked in the list of Class B drugs, possession of which was proscribed by the Misuse of Drugs Act 1971 and, as the allegation was a single act of possession of an identified substance, there could be no complaint either at common law or under the Indictment Rules 1971.

R v Best [1979] Crim LR 787 (Court of Appeal: Lord Widgery CJ, Eveleigh LJ and Swanwick J).

706   —— —— **being in control of pecuniary resources or property**

A Hong Kong Ordinance provided that it was an offence for a Crown servant to be "in control of pecuniary resources or property disproportionate to his official emoluments" without satisfactory explanation, the penalty being a sum not exceeding the amount of the pecuniary resources or the value of the property. The accused was charged and convicted of being in control of assets consisting of pecuniary resources and property and ordered to pay a sum equal to the value of the assets. On appeal the Hong Kong Court of Appeal varied the order for payment to one of an amount equivalent to the value of the pecuniary resources alone. On appeal against conviction and cross-appeal by the Attorney-General against the variation, *held*, the word "or" was to be read conjunctively in both cases. Thus, the charge was not bad for duplicity as the section created only one offence which could be committed in one or other or both of two ways. Further the court could, in imposing sentence, match the order to the aggregate of those unexplained assets and it was wrong therefore in principle to reflect only the pecuniary resources. The appeal would be dismissed.

Cheung Chee-Kwong v R; Attorney-General v Cheung Chee-Kwong [1979] 1 WLR 1454 (Privy Council: Lord Edmund-Davies, Lord Russell of Killowen and Lord Keith of Kinkel).

707   —— **joinder of counts**

A man was charged, with others, of causing an affray and with assault, outside a discotheque. Whilst on bail he attempted to coerce the discotheque manager and was subsequently also charged with attempting to pervert the course of justice. He was convicted on all counts, and on appeal contended that the judge should have severed the last charge from the indictment as it was not founded on the same facts, as required by the Indictment Rules 1971, r.9. *Held*, the facts did not have to be identical in substance or virtually contemporaneous for an offence to be joined in the same indictment. The test was whether the charges had a common factual origin. If the subsidiary charge could not have been alleged but for the facts which gave rise to the primary charge, those charges could be legitimately joined together for the purposes of r.9. On that basis, the appeal would be dismissed.

R v BARRELL AND WILSON (1979) 69 Cr App Rep 250 (Court of Appeal: SHAW LJ, BOREHAM and PURCHAS JJ).

708   Information—defect in information—power of Crown Court to amend—whether material defect

The defendant was charged with failing without reasonable excuse to provide a specimen for a laboratory test, contrary to the Road Traffic Act 1972, s. 9 (3). However, the information laid wrongly recited that the requirement to provide a specimen was imposed by s. 8 of the Act, rather than s. 9. He was convicted, and appealed to the Crown Court. The Crown Court quashed his conviction on the ground that the information was defective and that it was too late, at that stage in the proceedings, to amend it under the Magistrates' Courts Act 1952, s. 100 (1). On appeal, *held*, where an information was alleged to be so defective that it could not validly support the conviction without amendment, the question was whether the defect either misled the defendant or was such that injustice might result if the conviction was upheld. The defect in the information was wholly immaterial and amendment could be made under the Magistrates' Courts Act despite the stage in the proceedings. The appeal would be allowed.

LEE v WILTSHIRE CHIEF CONSTABLE [1979] RTR 349 (Queen's Bench Division: BRIDGE LJ and CAULFIELD J). *Garfield v Maddocks* [1974] QB 7 applied. *Meek v Powell* [1952] 1 KB 164 distinguished.

709   Judgment—variation of sentence or other order made by Crown Court—forfeiture order

See *R v Menocal*, para. 593.

710   Legal aid

See LEGAL AID.

711   Magistrates' courts

See MAGISTRATES.

712   Plea—plea of autrefois convict—when plea available

A lorry driver and owner appealed against conviction for the offence of using a goods vehicle when it exceeded the permitted maximum gross weight and two offences of exceeding the permitted maximum axle weight. They contended that only one act of using the lorry with too great a load had been committed, that it was therefore oppressive for more than one penalty to be applied and that the analogous principle of autrefois convict should have been applied. *Held*, if there were three separate offences committed, the fact that they were committed simultaneously was immaterial. The test, of whether there was one offence or three, was whether the facts which constituted the second and third offences would have been sufficient to procure a conviction for the first offence charged. On the facts, the offences concerning the axle weight could not be proved by proving the offence concerning the gross weight and accordingly the three separate offences had been correctly charged. The appeal would therefore be dismissed.

J. THEOBALD (HOUNSLOW) LTD v STACY [1979] RTR 411 (Queen's Bench Division: LORD WIDGERY CJ and LLOYD J). Dictum of Lord Morris in *Connelly v DPP* [1964] AC 1254, HL at 1305 applied.

713   **Police—power to intercept telephone calls**

See *Malone v Metropolitan Police Commissioner*, para. 2093.

714   **Prosecution—plea of not guilty—Crown proposing to offer no evidence—judge's power to direct prosecution to proceed**

A woman pleaded guilty to the theft of four horses. Her lover travelled with her in the horse box and was present when the horses were delivered and the woman was paid. He admitted that he had been suspicious, but pleaded not guilty to assisting in the disposal of stolen property. Counsel for the Crown informed the court that it was not proposed to proceed against the man. However the trial judge held that he should stand trial and he was duly tried and convicted. He applied for leave to appeal on the grounds that the trial judge was wrong in law in directing the prosecution to proceed. *Held*, refusing leave to appeal, the judge had been invited by the prosecution to consent to no evidence being offered; such an invitation was not merely a formality, but entitled him to exercise a discretion in the matter. He had rightly decided to proceed with the prosecution, as injustice would otherwise have been caused in that a man the jury found to be guilty would have escaped conviction.

R v BROAD (1978) 68 Cr App Rep 281 (Court of Appeal: ROSKILL LJ, ACKNER and STOCKER JJ).

715   **Prosecution of offences—duty to enforce the law—Metropolitan Police Commissioner**

See *R v Metropolitan Police Commissioner, ex parte Blackburn*, para. 2084.

716   **Prosecution of Offences Act 1979**

The Prosecution of Offences Act 1979 consolidates certain enactments relating to the prosecution of offences in England and Wales and repeals certain obsolete enactments. The Act received the royal assent on 4th April 1979 and came into force on 4th May 1979.

Destination and derivation tables appear on pages 188 and 189.

DESTINATION TABLE

This table shows in column (1) the enactments repealed by the Prosecution of Offences Act 1979 and in column (2) the provisions of that Act corresponding thereto.

In certain cases the enactment in column (1), though having a corresponding provision in column (2), is not, or is not wholly, repealed, as it is still required or partly required, for the purposes of other legislation.

(1)	(2)	(1)	(2)
Prosecution of Offences Act 1879 (c. 22)	Prosecution of Offences Act 1979 (c. 31)	Prosecution Offences Act 1908 (c. 3)	Prosecution of Offences Act 1979 (c. 31)
s. 1	——	s. 3 (1)	Rep., S.L.R. Act 1927
2	s. 2 (1)	(2)	——
2A	3	Schedule	Rep., S.L.R. Act 1927
ss. 3, 4	Rep., 1884 c. 58, s. 5	Criminal Justice Act 1925 (c. 86)	
s. 5	s. 5		
6	Rep., 1908 c. 3, s. 3 (1), Schedule	s. 34	ss. 7. 10
7	——		
8	s. 9 (1)	Administration of Justice Act 1965 (c. 2)	
9	——		
10	Rep., S.L.R. Act 1894		
		s. 27	s. 9
Prosecution of Offences Act 1884 (c. 58)		Criminal Justice Act 1967 (c. 80)	
s. 1	——	Sch. 6, para. 2	s. 2 (1)
2	Rep., 1908 c. 3, s. 3 (1), Schedule	Criminal Appeal Act 1968 (c. 19)	
3	s. 8		
4	Rep., 1964 c. 48, s. 64 (3), Sch. 10.	Sch. 5, Part I★	ss. 2 (1), 3.
5	Rep., S.L.R. Act 1898		
Prosecution of Offences Act 1908 (c. 3)		Courts Act 1971 (c. 23)	
		Sch. 8, para. 2†	3 (1), 5
s. 1 (1)	s. 1 (1), (2)	13	s. 2 (1)
(2)	(3)		
(3)	——	Criminal Jurisdiction Act 1975 (c. 59)	
(4)	1 (1), (2)		
(5)	(4)		
2 (1)	2 (2)	s. 12 (1), (2)	s. 6 (1), (2)
(2)	Rep., S.L.R. Act 1927	(3)	ss. 6 (3), 10
(3)	s. 4	14 (2) (a)★	——
(4)	——		
(5)	Rep., S.L.R. Act 1927		

★ Repealed in part   † Not repealed

TABLE OF DERIVATIONS

This table shows in the right hand column the legislative source from which the sections of the Prosecution of Offences Act 1979 in the left hand column have been derived. In the table the following abbreviations are used:

1879 = Prosecution of Offences Act 1879 (c. 22)
1884 = Prosecution of Offences Act 1884 (c. 58)
1908 = Prosecution of Offences Act 1908 (c. 3)
1925 = Criminal Justice Act 1925 (c. 86)
1968 = Criminal Appeal Act 1968 (c. 19)
1971 = Courts Act 1971 (c. 23)
1975 = Criminal Jurisdiction Act (c. 59)

Section of Act	Derivation
1 (1)	1908 s. 1 (1), (4).
(2)	1908 s. 1 (1), (4); The Minister for the Civil Service Order 1968 (S.I. 1968/1656) art. 3 (2).
(3)	1908 s. 1 (2); The Minister for the Civil Service Order 1968 (S.I. 1968/1656) art. 3 (2).
(4)	1908 s. 1 (5).
2 (1)	1879 s. 2; Criminal Justice Act 1967 (c. 80) Sch. 6 para. 2; 1968 Part I of Sch. 5; 1971 Sch. 8 para. 13.
(2)	1908 s. 2 (1).
3	1879 s. 2A; 1968 Part I of Sch. 5; 1971 Sch. 8 para. 2.
4	1908 s. 2 (3).
5	1879 s. 5; Sch. 8 para. 2; Criminal Law Act 1977 (c. 45) Sch. 13.
6	1975 s. 12.
7	1925 s. 34; Post Office (Amendment) Act 1935 (c. 15) Sch. 2; Mental Health Act 1959 (c. 72) Sch. 8.
8	1884 s. 3.
9	1879 s. 8; Statutory Instruments Act 1946 (c. 36) s. 1 (2); Administration of Justice Act 1965 (c. 2) s. 27 and Sch. 3.
10	1975 s. 12 (3); 1925 s. 34.

717   **Seizure of property—powers of police—seizure of jewellery of person in custody**

A police constable asked a woman in custody to remove her jewellery for her own protection and that of others. The woman refused and resisted the forcible removal of the jewellery. During the struggle the constable was injured and the woman was charged with assault occasioning actual bodily harm. She contended that the forcible removal of her jewellery had been unlawful. *Held*, the power of the police to seize the property of persons in custody was limited to objects suspected to have been connected with the offence and objects capable of causing injury or effecting an escape. There was no evidence to suggest that the jewellery fell into either category and therefore its seizure had been unlawful and the woman had been entitled to resist the constable.

R v Naylor [1979] Crim LR 532 (Crown Court at Leicester: Judge H. A. Skinner QC).

718   **Summary proceedings—prosecution evidence unsworn—whether justices under duty to rehear charge**

See *R v Uxbridge Justices, ex parte Conlon*, para. 1797.

719   **Transcripts of trial—shorthand transcript—procedure where inaccuracies alleged**

In a Practice Note ((1978) 67 Cr App Rep 50) Lawton LJ noted that where inaccuracies were alleged in the shorthand transcripts of criminal trials, the registrar should be informed. He would then take up the matter with the shorthand writers, and if necessary, with the trial judge. It was unfair to the trial judge for the Court to proceed on an assumption of fact which was not in accordance with the transcript of evidence.

720   **Trial—evidence raising possibility of alternative verdict—right of prosecution to raise issue in closing speech**

See *DPP v Daley*, para. 723.

721   **—— irregularity—plea bargaining—hostile attitude of judge**

A motorist pleaded not guilty to charges of driving while unfit through drink or drugs and failing to provide a laboratory specimen. During the trial the judge saw counsel privately and in the course of proceedings asked more questions than defending counsel. The motorist was convicted on the second count. He appealed on grounds that the judge had made an offer of plea bargaining and that the judge's hostile questioning had prevented him presenting a proper defence. *Held*, there was insufficient evidence of an offer of plea bargaining, although if it had been proved it would have been a very serious matter, and it was possible that a judge who permitted it should not sit on the criminal bench. However, the judge's hostility meant that justice had not been seen to be done, and the conviction would be quashed on the ground of a material irregularity in the trial.

R v Wise [1978] LS Gaz R 1295 (Court of Appeal: Lord Widgery CJ, Cumming-Bruce LJ and Drake J).

722   **—— jury—accused mute of malice—whether right of challenge open to accused**

On charges of assault, the accused refused to plead and a jury was empanelled to determine whether he was mute of malice. The accused was not offered the right of challenge to that jury, which found him mute of malice. The trial proceeded and he was duly convicted. On appeal he contended that the trial was a nullity as no right of challenge had been accorded to him. *Held*, the right of challenge, as contained in the Juries Act 1974, s. 12, assumed that the trial had begun and the accused had already pleaded. No right of challenge lay under s. 12 in the above circumstances. The appeal would be dismissed.

R v PALING (1978) 66 Cr App Rep 299 (Court of Appeal: ROSKILL LJ, CHAPMAN and LAWTON JJ).

723   —— summing up—possibility of alternative verdict—duty of judge to leave issue to jury

Jamaica

In the course of a quarrel between the two defendants and the deceased the defendants threw stones at the deceased who, while trying to escape, fell and was found to be dead. The defendants were charged with murder and at the trial the prosecution opened the case on the basis that the victim had been stoned to death. The evidence which was then given, however, was such as to raise the possibility that the victim had met his death as a result of trying to escape, and in making his closing speech counsel for the prosecution suggested that the jury could return an alternative verdict of manslaughter. The judge left it open to the jury to return the alternative verdict and directed them as to "manslaughter by flight" accordingly. Both defendants were convicted of manslaughter, but their convictions were quashed on appeal on the grounds that the jury were not entitled to return the alternative verdict. The prosecutor appealed. *Held*, where during the trial on an indictment charging murder the evidence adduced left room for a verdict of manslaughter the judge was under a duty to leave it to the jury to decide whether such an alternative verdict was appropriate and to direct them accordingly. Since it was proper for counsel for the prosecution to address the jury on all issues arising from the evidence, he was clearly entitled to address the jury on the possibility of an alternative verdict, and it was within the discretion of the trial judge then to invite counsel for the defence to address him on the issue. In the instant case the jury had therefore been entitled to return the alternative verdict and had been correctly directed as to "manslaughter by flight" in accordance with the principles laid down by the Court of Appeal in *R v Mackie* (1973) 57 Cr App Rep 453. The appeal would be allowed.

DIRECTOR OF PUBLIC PROSECUTIONS v DALEY [1979] 2 WLR 239 (Privy Council: LORD DIPLOCK, LORD HAILSHAM OF ST MARYLEBONE, LORD SALMON, LORD EDMUND-DAVIES and LORD KEITH OF KINKEL). *Kwaku Mensah v The King* [1946] AC 83, PC applied.

724   —— trial by jury—jury vetting—Attorney-General's statement

See para. 1652.

725   Variation of sentence—Crown Court—variation pursuant to breach of undertaking—power to substitute sentence of materially different nature

The accused was charged with having had illegal sexual intercourse with a fifteen-year-old girl. He intended to plead not guilty, but was induced to plead guilty in order to spare the girl, who had since attempted suicide, the ordeal of giving evidence. The recorder had indicated that he would not impose a prison sentence if he pleaded guilty provided that he undertook not to see the girl again. A few days later the accused broke the undertaking, was arrested and committed to the same court for contempt of court. The recorder altered the original suspended sentence to immediate imprisonment relying on the Courts Act 1971, s. 11 (2) which gave Crown Courts the power to vary a sentence within twenty-eight days of it being made. On appeal *held*, s. 11 (2) was not to be used for a fundamental change of mind, converting a sentence which was not immediate into one which was. Nor should it be done because of some event which had taken place after the original sentence had been passed. The appeal would be allowed and the suspended sentence restored.

R v GRICE (1977) 66 Cr App Rep 167 (Court of Appeal: ROSKILL and WALLER LJJ and ACKNER J).

CROWN PROCEEDINGS

Halsbury's Laws of England (4th edn.), Vol. 11, paras. 1401–1580

726   Proceedings against the Crown—Government departments

A revised list of government departments authorised for the purposes of the Crown Proceedings Act 1947, s. 17, and the solicitors on whom documents in proceedings against them may be served has been issued by the Civil Service Department (1st June 1979, H.M. Stationery Office).

AUTHORISED GOVERNMENT DEPARTMENTS	SOLICITORS AND ADDRESSES FOR SERVICES
Administrator of Bulgarian Property	
Administrator of German Enemy Property	
Administrator of Hungarian Property	
Administrator of Italian Property	
Administrator of Japanese Property	
Administrator of Roumanian Property	
Advisory, Conciliation and Arbitration Service	
Board of Trade	
Civil Service Department	
Crown Estate Commissioners	
Custodian of Enemy Property for England	
Ministry of Defence	
Department of Education and Science	
Department of Employment	
Employment Service Agency	
Department of Energy	The Treasury Solicitor
Department of the Environment (see note (3))	3 Central Buildings Matthew Parker Street
Exports Credits Guarantee Department	Westminster
Director General of Fair Trading	London SW1H 9NN
Registry of Friendly Societies	(see notes (1) and (2))
Health and Safety Commission	
Health and Safety Executive	
Department of Health and Social Security (see note (4))	
Home Office	
Department of Industry	
Manpower Services Commission	
Department for National Savings	
Northern Ireland Office	
Public Works Loan Board	
Office of Population Censuses and Surveys (see note (5))	
HM Stationery Office	
Department of Trade	
Training Services Agency	
Department of Transport	
HM Treasury	
Welsh Office (see note (6))	

Ministry of Agriculture, Fisheries and Food (see note (6)) Forestry Commissioners Intervention Board for Agricultural Produce	The Solicitor to the Ministry of Agriculture, Fisheries and Food 55 Whitehall London SW1A 2EY
Commissioners of Customs and Excise	The Solicitor for the Customs and Excise King's Beam House Mark Lane London EC3R 7HE
Commissioners of Inland Revenue	The Solicitor of Inland Revenue Somerset House London WC2R 1LB

NOTES

(1) Sets out the text of the Crown Proceedings Act 1947, ss. 17 (3), 18.

(2) Applies to Scotland.

(3) By s. 1 (3) of the Land Commission (Dissolution) Act 1971, the functions of the Land Commission and all property, rights and liabilities to which it was entitled or subject were transferred to the Secretary of State. The matters transferred are administered by the Department of the Environment and the solicitor to the Department of the Environment continues to conduct litigation in this field. Accordingly, the solicitor and address for service for the purpose of or in connection with any civil proceedings brought by or against the Crown which relate to matters transferred from the Land Commission is the solicitor to the Department of the Environment, 1 Marsham Street, London SW1P 3EB.

(4) The solicitor and address for service for the purpose of or in connection with any civil proceedings brought by or against the Crown which relate to matters described hereunder is the solicitor to the Department of Health and Social Security, State House, High Holborn, London WC1R 4TB:

(i) adjudications under legislation governing war pensions and social security (including child benefit, family income supplement and supplementary benefit) by the Secretary of State, a tribunal or other adjudicating authority;

(ii) recovery of monies under and matters arising from non-receipt of benefit under the legislation mentioned in sub-paragraph (i) and cases stated under s. 87 of the Magistrates' Courts Act 1952 in connection with prosecutions under such legislation;

(iii) determinations by the Occupational Pensions Board.

The Treasury Solicitor is the solicitor acting for the Department of Health and Social Security in all other civil proceedings affecting that department.

(5) The Office of Population Censuses and Surveys (OPCS) was established in 1970 by a fusion of the General Register Office and the Government Social Survey Department; the Registrar General and the General Register Office remain as legal entities within OPCS and are included within that description.

(6) Under the Secretary of State for Wales and Minister of Land and Natural Resources Order 1965 (S.I. 1965 No. 319) and the Transfer of Functions (Miscellaneous) Order 1967 (S.I. 1967 No. 486), and the Transfer of Functions (Wales) Order 1969 (S.I. 1969 No. 388), and the Transfer of Functions (Wales) (No. 1) Order 1978 (S.I. 1978 No. 272), certain functions of the Minister of Agriculture, Fisheries and Food, the former Minister of Housing and Local Government, and the Secretary of State for Social Services, were transferred to the Secretary of State for Wales. The solicitor and address for service for the purpose of or in connection with any civil proceedings by or against the Welsh Office in respect of matters transferred to the Secretary of State for Wales as aforesaid from the Minister of Agriculture, Fisheries and Food is the Solicitor for the Ministry of Agriculture, Fisheries and Food. The Treasury Solicitor is the solicitor acting for the Welsh Office in all other proceedings affecting that office.

The above list is reproduced by permission of the Controller of HMSO.

CUSTOMS AND EXCISE

Halsbury's Laws of England (4th edn.), Vol. 12, paras. 501–1066

727   Alcoholic Liquor Duties Act 1979

The Alcoholic Liquor Duties Act 1979 received the royal assent on 22nd February 1979, and came into force on 1st April 1979. The Act consolidates the enactments relating to the excise duties on spirits, beer, wine, made-wine and cider together with certain other enactments relating to excise.

Derivation and destination tables for this and related consolidating enactments appear on pp. 203–235.

728   —— amendment of enactments

The Alcoholic Liquors (Amendment of Enactments Relating to Strength and to Units of Measurement) Order 1979, S.I. 1979 No. 241 (in force on 1st January 1980), amends the Alcoholic Liquor Duties Act 1979, para. 727, and other enactments so as to replace the proof system of ascertaining the alcoholic strength of spirits and other liquids by the OIML (Organisation Internationale de Metrologie Legale) system of measurement by reference to percentages of alcohol by volume. The Order also replaces any temperatures expressed in degrees Fahrenheit by temperatures expressed in degrees Celsius and any units of measurement expressed in Imperial terms by metric units, expresses existing rates of duty in metric terms and allows for a specified conversion factor to be used for any conversion of gallons at proof to litres of alcohol as may be required by the Commissioners of Customs and Excise.

729   Anti-dumping and countervailing duties

The Customs Duties (ECSC) Definitive Anti-Dumping Order 1979, S.I. 1979 No. 566 (in force on 24th May 1979), imposes a definitive anti-dumping duty on imports of certain angles, shapes and sections of iron or steel into the United Kingdom, originating in Spain and consigned from another country. The order replaces the Customs Duties (ECSC) Provisional Anti-Dumping Order 1979, see para. 732, as regards goods originating in Spain and consigned from other countries, and the Anti-Dumping and Countervailing Duties Order 1978, 1978 Halsbury's Abridgment para. 770. No duty is payable if an application is made to the Commissioners of Customs and Excise, on deliveries intended for European Communities shipbuilding yards.

730   The Customs Duties (ECSC) Definitive Anti-Dumping (No. 2) Order 1979, S.I. 1979 No. 567 (in force on 24th May 1979), imposes a definitive anti-dumping duty on imports into the United Kingdom of certain haematite pig iron and cast iron goods, originating in Brazil and consigned from another country. The order replaces the Customs Duties (ECSC) Provisional Anti-Dumping (No. 2) Order 1979, see para. 733, as regards goods originating in Brazil and consigned from other countries, and the Anti-Dumping and Countervailing Duties Order 1978, S.I. 1978 No. 1147, 1978 Halsbury's Abridgment para. 770.

731   The Customs Duties (ECSC) Definitive Anti-Dumping (No. 3) Order 1979, S.I. 1979 No. 627 (in force on 8th June 1979), imposes a definitive anti-dumping duty on imports into the United Kingdom of certain sheets and plates of iron or steel originating in Spain and consigned to the United Kingdom from other countries. The order replaces the Customs Duties (ECSC) Provisional Anti-Dumping (No. 3) Order, see para. 734, in respect of goods originating in Spain and consigned from other countries, and the Anti-Dumping and Countervailing Duties Order 1978, Halsbury's Abridgment, para. 770. No duty is payable if an application is made by the importer to the Commissioners of Customs and Excise on deliveries intended for European Communities shipbuilding yards.

732   The Customs Duties (ECSC) Provisional Anti-Dumping Order 1979, S.I. 1979 No. 181 (in force on 23rd February 1979), imposed a provisional anti-dumping duty on certain angles, shapes and sections of iron and steel originating in Spain. The duty was imposed in consequence of ECSC Commission Recommendation 267/79, with effect from 13th February 1979.

This order has been revoked; see para. 741.

733   The Customs Duties (ECSC) Provisional Anti-Dumping (No. 2) Order 1979, S.I. 1979 No. 191 (in force on 27th February 1979), imposed a provisional anti-dumping duty from 16th February 1979 on imports of certain haematite pig iron and cast iron, originating in Brazil. The specified rate of the duty might be reduced if the Secretary of State was satisfied that the iron was of inferior quality.

This order has been revoked; see para. 740.

734   The Customs Duties (ECSC) Provisional Anti-Dumping (No. 3) Order 1979, S.I. 1979 No. 231 (in force on 7th March 1979), imposed a provisional anti-dumping duty from 3rd March 1979 on imports into the United Kingdom of certain sheets and plates of iron or steel, originating in Spain. The specified rate of the duty might be reduced if the Secretary of State was satisfied that the goods were of inferior quality.

This order has been revoked; see para. 741.

735   The Customs Duties (ECSC) Provisional Anti-Dumping (No. 4) Order 1979, S.I. 1979 No. 314 (in force on 16th March 1979), imposed a provisional anti-dumping duty from 15th March 1979 on imports into the United Kingdom of certain iron or steel coils for re-rolling, originating in Greece. The specified rate of the duty might be reduced if the Secretary of State was satisfied that the goods were of inferior quality.

This order has been revoked; see para. 742.

736   **—— revocation and suspension of duties**

The Anti-Dumping Duty (Temporary Suspension) Order 1979, S.I. 1979 No. 842 (in force on 18th July 1979), suspends for a period of three months the anti-dumping duty imposed by the Anti-Dumping Duty (No. 2) Order 1977, 1977 Halsbury's Abridgment, para. 748, on certain stainless steel products covered by the ECSC Treaty, originating in Spain.

737   The Anti-Dumping Duty (Temporary Suspension) (No. 2) Order 1979, S.I. 1979 No. 1182 (in force on 18th October 1979), suspends for a further period of three months the anti-dumping duty imposed by the Anti-Dumping Duty (No. 2) Order 1977, 1977 Halsbury's Abridgment, para. 748, on certain stainless steel in so far as it consists of products covered by the ECSC Treaty, originating in Spain.

738   The Anti-Dumping Duty (Revocation) Order 1979, S.I. 1979 No. 104 (in force on 27th February 1979), removes the anti-dumping duty on imports of certain angles, shapes and sections of non-alloy iron and steel originating in Japan. The Anti-Dumping Duty (No. 3) Order 1977, 1977 Halsbury's Abridgment para. 752 is revoked.

739   The Customs Duties (ECSC) Anti-Dumping (Amendment) Order 1979, S.I. 1979 No. 155 (in force on 17th February 1979), lifts payments of duty on Bulgarian iron and steel products previously imposed by Customs Duties (ECSC) Anti-Dumping (Nos. 15, 16) Orders 1978, see 1978 Halsbury's Abridgment paras. 785, 786 respectively. These duties are suspended in consequence of ECSC Commission Recommendation 165/79.

740   The Customs Duties (ECSC) Provisional Anti-Dumping (Revocation) (No. 1)
Order 1979, S.I. 1979 No. 492 (in force on 24th April 1979) revokes the Customs
Duties (ECSC) Provisional Anti-Dumping (No. 2) Order 1979, see para. 733, with
respect to imports into the United Kingdom of certain haematite pig iron and cast
iron originating in and consigned from Brazil. The revocation is in consequence of
Commission Recommendation (ECSC) 720/79.

741   The Customs Duties (ECSC) Provisional Anti-Dumping (Revocation) (No. 2) Order
1979, S.I. 1979 No. 510 (in force on 3rd May 1979), revokes the Customs Duties
(ECSC) Provisional Anti-Dumping Order 1979 and the Customs Duties (ECSC)
Provisional Anti-Dumping (No. 3) Order 1979, see paras. 732 and 734. No duty
is now payable on certain iron and steel products imported into the United Kingdom
originating in and consigned from Spain. Such products originating in Spain, but
consigned from other countries are still subject to duty.

742   The Customs Duties (ECSC) Provisional Anti-Dumping (Revocation) (No. 3) Order
1979, S.I. 1979 No. 1148 (in force on 15th September 1979), removes the anti-
dumping duty on imports of certain iron or steel coils for re-rolling originating in
Greece, imposed by Customs Duties (ECSC) Provisional Anti-Dumping (No. 4)
Order 1979, para. 735 which is revoked.

743   **Bonded goods—customs warehousing**
The Customs Warehousing Regulations 1979, S.I. 1979 No. 207 (in force on 1st
April 1979), prescribe the conditions under which goods may be put into, stored in
and removed from a customs warehouse. The Regulations reproduce many of the
provisions of the Warehousing Regulations 1975, 1975 Halsbury's Abridgment
para. 920 with regard to Customs warehousing, but differ from those provisions by
the inclusion of the requirements of Council Directive (EEC) 69/74.

744   **—— excise warehousing**
The Excise Warehousing Regulations 1979, S.I. 1979 No. 208 (in force on 1st April
1979), prescribe the conditions under which goods may be put into, stored in and
removed from an excise warehouse. The Regulations reproduce many of the
provisions of the Warehousing Regulations 1975, 1975 Halsbury's Abridgment
para. 920 with regard to excise warehousing.

745   **Customs and Excise Duties (General Reliefs) Act 1979**
The Customs and Excise Duties (General Reliefs) Act 1979 received the royal assent
on 22nd February 1979 and came into force on 1st April 1979. The Act consolidates
certain enactments relating to reliefs and exemptions from customs and excise duties,
the Finance Act 1968, s. 7 and related enactments.
    Derivation and destination tables for this and related consolidating enactments
appear on pp. 203–235.

746   **Customs and Excise Management Act 1979**
The Customs and Excise Management Act 1979 received the royal assent on 22nd
February 1979 and came into force on 1st April 1979. The Act consolidates the
enactments relating to the collection and management of the revenues of customs
and excise and in some cases to other matters in relation to which the Commissioners
of Customs and Excise for the time being perform functions, with amendments to
give effect to Law Commission and Scottish Law Commission recommendations.
    Derivation and destination tables for this and related consolidating enactments
appear on pp. 203–235.

747   **Customs duties—Greece**
The Customs Duties (Greece) Order 1979, S.I. 1979 No. 1649 (in force on 1st

January 1980), further amends the Customs Duties (Greece) (No. 3) Order 1977, 1977 Halsbury's Abridgment para. 768, by amalgamating the entries in the Schedule relating to certain fruit originating in Greece and including in the entry certain vegetables originating in Greece which now benefit from the special rates of customs duty. Metric measures are substituted for wine, beer and spirits falling within the common customs tariff, following similar alterations which are being made in respect of such goods in the common customs tariff of the European Economic Community.

748   —— reliefs

The Customs Duties (Standard Exchange Relief) Regulations 1979, S.I. 1979 No. 554 (in force on 11th June 1979) provide for relief, known as standard exchange relief, from customs duty on goods imported into the United Kingdom as replacements for goods exported from the United Kingdom outside the European Community for repair. The regulations implement certain provisions of Council Directives (EEC) 76/119 and 78/1018.

749   The Outward Processing Relief Regulations 1979, S.I. 1979 No. 555 (in force on 11th June 1979), which revoke and replace the Import Duties (Outward Processing Relief) Regulations 1976, 1976 Halsbury's Abridgment, para. 743 and the Agricultural Levies (Outward Processing Relief) Order 1976, 1976 Halsbury's Abridgment para. 33, provide for relief from customs duty and agricultural levy on compensating products and intermediate products imported into the United Kingdom which have been produced or manufactured overseas by outward processing of goods temporarily exported from the United Kingdom or any other member state of the European Community.

750   —— —— personal reliefs

The Customs Duty (Personal Reliefs) (No. 1) Order 1975 (Amendment) Order 1979, S.I. 1979 No. 655 (in force on 18th June 1979), increases the aggregate amount payable by way of duty and tax on personal effects imported by passengers.

751   The Customs Duty (Personal Reliefs) (No. 1) Order 1968 (Amendment) Order 1979, S.I. 1979 No. 1551 (in force on 1st January 1980) converts the existing references to the Sykes proof system in the 1968 Order to the OIML System (Organisation Internationale de Metrologie Legale).

752   —— —— quota relief

The Customs Duties (Quota Relief) Order 1979, S.I. 1979 No. 737 (in force on 1st July 1979), provides for the administration of the United Kingdom's share of the tariff quota opened for the period 1st July 1979 to 29th February 1980 by the EEC, providing exemption from customs duty on import into the United Kingdom for home use of rum, arrack and tafia originating in various African, Caribbean and Pacific States. The Order also provides that application for relief under the Customs Duties (Quota Relief) (Administration) Order 1976, 1976 Halsbury's Abridgment para. 753, must be accompanied by the necessary origin document. Relief is restricted to goods imported for home use.

753   The Customs Duties (Quota Relief) (Paper, Paperboard and Printed Products) Order 1979, S.I. 1979 No. 1717 (in force on 1st January 1980) provides for the opening, during 1980, of duty-free tariff quotas for paper, paperboard and printed products originating in Austria, Iceland, Sweden, Switzerland, Norway and Finland established in accordance with the Agreements between the EEC and those countries.

754   The Customs Duties (Quota Relief) (Paper, Paperboard and Printed Products) (Amendment) Order 1979, S.I. 1979 No. 1718 (in force on 21st December 1979) amends the 1978 Order, 1978 Halsbury's Abridgment para. 809, by increasing the duty-free tariff quota between the EEC and Finland for coated mechanical printing paper weighing not more than a specified weight.

755   The Customs Duties (ECSC) (Quota and Other Reliefs) (Amendment) Order 1979, S.I. 1979 No. 153 (in force on 19th February 1979), amends the Customs Duties (ECSC) (Quota and Other Reliefs) Order 1978, 1978 Halsbury's Abridgment para. 806 by increasing the amounts of the duty-free tariff quotas and the maximum amounts within the quotas which are listed in the 1978 Order, Schedule 1, Part II, columns 2 and 3. The increases are in accordance with the requirements of the European Communities.

756   The Customs Duties (ECSC) (Quota and Other Reliefs) (Revocation) Order 1979, S.I. 1979 No. 1142 (in force on 13th September 1979), revokes the Customs Duties (ECSC) (Quota and Other Reliefs) Order 1978, art. 2, 1978 Halsbury's Abridgment, para. 806, which provides for exemption from customs duty for certain iron and steel products, in relation to certain blooms, billets, slabs and sheet bars of iron and steel, originating in Brazil.

757   The Customs Duties (ECSC) (Quota and Other Reliefs) Order 1979, S.I. 1979 No. 1747 (in force on 1st January 1980), provides for reliefs from customs duty on certain iron and steel products originating in the developing countries named in Sch. 2, in accordance with the decision of the ECSC members of 10th December 1979. The reliefs are provided under the ECSC's Generalised Tariff Preference Scheme for Developing Countries.

758   **Excise Duties (Surcharges or Rebates) Act 1979**

The Excise Duties (Surcharges or Rebates) Act 1979 received the royal assent on 22nd February 1979 and came into force on 1st April 1979. The Act consolidates the Finance Act 1961, s. 9 and Schs. 3, 4 as amended.

Derivation and destination tables for this and related consolidating enactments appear on pp. 203–235.

759   **Excise duty—alcoholic liquors—amendment of units and methods of measurement**

The Alcoholic Liquors (Amendment of Units and Methods of Measurement) Regulations 1979, S.I. 1979 No. 1146 (in force on 1st January 1980) revoke the Strength of Spirits (Ascertainment) Regulations 1954 and amend the Spirits Regulations 1952, the Stills Regulations 1952, the Methylated Spirits Regulations 1952, the Wine and Made-wine Regulations 1975, 1975 Halsbury's Abridgment para. 933, the Cider and Perry Regulations 1976, 1976 Halsbury's Abridgment para. 724, the Beer Regulations 1978, 1978 Halsbury's Abridgment para. 1672 and the Excise Duty (Relief on Alcoholic Ingredients) Regulations 1978, 1978 Halsbury's Abridgment para. 811. The purpose of the amendments is to replace the references to the proof system with references to the OIML (Organisation Internationale de Metrologie Legale) system of measurement. The Fahrenheit scale of temperature measurement is replaced by the Celsius scale and units of measurement are now expressed in metric terms.

760   **——— cider and perry**

The Cider and Perry (Exemption from Registration) Order 1976 (Amendment) Order 1979, S.I. 1979 No. 1218 (in force on 1st January 1980), amends the 1976 Order, 1976 Halsbury's Abridgment para. 725, by replacing the units of measurement expressed in Imperial terms by metric units of measurement.

761   —— tobacco

The Tobacco Products Regulations 1979, S.I. 1979, No. 904 (in force on 1st September 1979) provide the machinery for the administration of the excise duty on tobacco products imposed under Tobacco Products Duty Act 1979, s. 2. They replace, with some amendments, the Tobacco Products Regulations 1977, 1977 Halsbury's Abridgment para. 780.

762   —— wine and made-wine

The Wine and Made-wine Regulations 1979, S.I. 1979 No. 1240 (in force on 1st November 1979) revoke and replace with some amendments the Wine and Made-wine Regulations 1975, 1975 Halsbury's Abridgment para. 933.

763   Exemption from duty—agreement with Greece

Agreement has been reached with Greece whereby, subject to compliance with the relevant Customs regulations, goods and passenger vehicles from one country which are temporarily imported into the territory of the other are exempted from the taxes and charges (other than tolls for the use of bridges, etc.) levied on the circulation and possession of vehicles and from taxes or charges levied on transport operations. No date has been announced upon which the agreement will come into operation. See Agreement between the Government of the United Kingdom and the Government of the Hellenic Republic in respect of the Regulation of Taxation of Road Vehicles in International Traffic (Cmnd. 7409).

764   Export of goods—control

The Export of Goods (Control) (Amendment) Order 1979, S.I. 1979 No. 136 (in force on 12th February 1979), further amends the Export of Goods (Control) Order 1978, 1978 Halsbury's Abridgment paras. 813, by including among the goods of which the export is controlled parts, components and sub-assemblies for the frequency changers specified in the 1978 Order, Sch. 1, Part II, Group 3C.

765   The Export of Goods (Control) (Amendment No. 2) Order 1979, S.I. 1979 No. 164 (in force on 19th March 1979), further amends the Export of Goods (Control) Order 1978, 1978 Halsbury's Abridgment para. 813 by bringing into control the export of goods manufactured or produced more than fifty years before the date of exportation, with certain exceptions.

766   The Export of Goods (Control) (Amendment No. 3) Order 1979, S.I. 1979 No. 276 (in force on 12th March 1979, except for the purposes of Article 2 (b), for which the Order comes into force on 1st April 1979), further amends the Export of Goods (Control) Order 1978, 1978 Halsbury's Abridgment para. 813. It includes among the list of export-controlled goods equipment specially designed for the manufacture or assembly of goods included in the entry relating to centrifuges in Sch. 1, Part II, Group 2.

767   The Export of Goods (Control) (Amendment No. 4) Order 1979, S.I. 1979 No. 1437 (in force on 19th November 1979 except for certain matters coming into operation on 10th December 1979), further amends the Export of Goods (Control) Order 1978. It removes diamonds from the goods subject to export control under Sch. 1, Part I, Group A and abolishes the minimum value criterion for excluding certain goods from the descriptions of iron and steel products included in Group A. With effect from 10th December 1979, there are included among the goods which are subject to export control in Sch. 1, Part II, Group 2 certain mass spectrometer and spectrometer sources and certain pressure gauges, plant for the purification of uranium hexafluoride and equipment, parts and components for plant for the production or purification of that substance. Also with effect from 10th December 1979, there is an extension of the existing control on certain spin-forming and flow-forming machines to exports to all destinations.

768   The Export of Goods (Control) (Amendment No. 5) Order 1979, S.I. 1979 No. 1671 (in force on 13th December 1979), revokes the provisions of the Export of Goods (Control) Order 1978, 1978 Halsbury's Abridgment para. 812 which prohibited the export of goods to any destination in Southern Rhodesia. In future the export of goods to Southern Rhodesia will be governed by the same rules as apply to any other country included in the 1978 Order, Sch. 2, to which Southern Rhodesia has been added.

769   **Finance (No. 2) Act 1979**
See para. 2247.

770   **Hydrocarbon oil duties—composite goods**
The Composite Goods Order 1968 (Revocation) Order 1979, S.I. 1979 No. 1393 (in force on 5th December 1979), abolishes the ad valorem rates of hydrocarbon oil duty on imported composite goods containing hydrocarbon oil. This means that such goods are now charged with duty under the Customs and Excise Management Act 1979, s. 126 on the quantity of oil appearing to have been used in their manufacture, unless, for the protection of the revenue, they are charged with duty as if they consisted of wholly hydrocarbon oil.

771   **Hydrocarbon Oil Duties Act 1979**
The Hydrocarbon Oil Duties Act 1979 received the royal assent on 22nd February 1979 and came into force on 1st April 1979. The Act consolidates the enactments relating to the excise duties on hydrocarbon oil, petrol substitutes, power methylated spirits and road fuel gas.
Derivation and destination tables for this and related consolidating enactments appear on pp. 203–235.

772   **Import of goods—goods manufactured under patent or imported under trade mark—valuation**
Commission Regulation (EEC) 477/79 (in force on 1st July 1979), revokes and replaces Commission Regulation (EEC) 1788/69. The Regulation determines certain exceptions within the meaning of Council Regulation (EEC) 803/68, art. 3 (2), on the valuation of goods manufactured under patent or imported under trade mark, for customs purposes.

773   **Isle of Man—transfer of functions**
An agreement has been concluded (Cmnd. 7747) between the governments of the United Kingdom and the Isle of Man on customs and excise and related matters. This agreement supersedes the agreement between governments dated 30th October 1957 but does not affect the existing arrangements for the sharing of equal duties or of any other revenues. The new agreement provides for the transfer of the revenue and associated control functions of the Customs and Excise Commissioners in the Isle of Man to the Isle of man customs and excise service and makes arrangements for the assumption by the Isle of Man government of agency functions which were formerly carried out by the commissioners in the island. Except as otherwise provided or agreed, the Isle of Man government undertakes to keep the law relating to the management of the customs and excise revenues and associated control functions correspondent with that of the United Kingdom.
This agreement has now been given effect in the Isle of Man Act 1979, para. 774.

774   **Isle of Man Act 1979**
The Isle of Man Act 1979 provides for the repeal and replacement of the Isle of Man Act 1958 which made provision for the Commissioners of Customs and Excise to pay to the Island its share of the customs and excise duties and taxes collected by them in the Island and the United Kingdom. The functions of the Commissioners in the

Island are to be transferred to an Isle of Man customs and excise service from 1st April 1980. The Act received the royal assent on 20th December 1979 and ss. 6, 7, 10 and 11 came into force on that date. The remainder of the Act comes into force on 1st April 1980.

Common duties are defined in s. 1 and the provisions for sharing the duties collected are replaced by new provisions appropriate to the changed circumstances from 1st April 1980: s. 2. Sections 3, 4 and 5 provide for the recovery in the United Kingdom of common duties in the Island, for the enforcement of Isle of Man judgments for common duties and for serving summonses and executing warrants in connection with offences relating to common duties, importation and exportation. The two countries will continue to be treated as a single area for value added tax and car tax: ss 6 and 7. Other provisions deal with the transfer of functions to the Isle of Man service and certain evidential, interpretative and other consequential matters.

775　　Matches and Mechanical Lighters Duties Act 1979

The Matches and Mechanical Lighters Duties Act 1979 received the royal assent on 22nd February 1979 and came into force on 1st April 1979. The Act consolidates the enactments relating to the excise duties on matches and mechanical lighters.

Derivation and destination tables for this and related consolidating enactments appear on pp. 203–235.

776　　Offence—importation of goods—forfeiture of goods—whether gold coins "goods"

The plaintiffs, sellers of gold and silver coins, were fraudulently induced to part with possession of 1,500 Krugerrand by three men who were subsequently convicted of being knowingly concerned in the fraudulent evasion of the prohibition on the importation of gold coins contrary to the Customs and Excise Act 1952, s. 304 (b). The Customs and Excise Commissioners claimed the right to forfeit the coins in accordance with the 1952 Act, s. 44 (f) which provided that any imported goods concealed in a manner intended to deceive customs would be liable to forfeiture. At first instance the court upheld the Commissioner's right to forfeit the coins.

Meanwhile, the three men prosecuted under s. 304 (b) took their case to the European Court, contending that s. 304 (b) was in conflict with the EEC Treaty, art. 30 relating to the free movement of goods between member states. It was held that the Krugerrand were not goods but capital within the meaning of art. 67.

The plaintiffs appealed to the Court of Appeal contending (i) that therefore the Krugerrand were not goods for the purposes of s. 44 (f) and (ii) that the coins belonged to them as innocent owners and the forfeiture was a violation of the European Convention on Human Rights, art. 1 relating to the right of peaceful enjoyment of possessions except where deprivation was in the public interest. *Held,* (i) the court would reject the argument that the Exchange Control Act 1947 put control of gold, silver, bullion and coins into the control of the Treasury. The importation of all those goods were in the hands of the Customs and Excise and were clearly goods within the meaning of s. 44 (f). (ii) There was nothing invalid under art. 1 in a state, under its customs law, forfeiting property brought to that country in breach of those laws. The Krugerrand were forfeitable to the Crown and it was a matter of discretion for the customs authorities as to whether they would return them to the plaintiffs. The appeal would therefore be dismissed.

ALLGEMEINE GOLD-UND-SILBERSCHEIDEANSTALT v CUSTOMS AND EXCISE COMRS (1979) 124 Sol Jo 30, (Court of Appeal: LORD DENNING MR, BRIDGE LJ and SIR DAVID CAIRNS). Decision of Donaldson J [1978] 2 CMLR 292, 1978 Halsbury's Abridgment para. 1189 affirmed.

For the convictions under s. 304 (b) and the appeal, see 1977 Halsbury's Abridgment paras. 1190, 1193. For the decision of the European Court see 1978 Halsbury's Abridgment para. 1219.

Customs and Excise Act 1952, ss. 44 (f), 304 now consolidated in Customs and Excise Management Act 1979, ss. 49 (f), 170.

777 Shipping—reports to customs authorities—commercial vessels

The Ship's Report Regulations 1979, S.I. 1979 No. 565 (in force on 1st July 1979), prescribe revised procedures for the making of a report for a commercial vessel. Such report is to be made in two stages, the first when the vessel is boarded by a Customs Officer or, if not boarded, within three hours of the vessel reaching the place of loading or unloading, and the second within twenty-four hours of the vessel's arrival within the limits of the port.

The Ship's Report, Importation and Exportation by Sea Regulations 1965, Part 1, are revoked.

778 —————— pleasure craft

The Pleasure Craft (Arrival and Report) Regulations 1979, S.I. 1979 No. 564 (in force on 1st July 1979), prescribe procedures for the making of a report for a pleasure craft. Until such a report has been made the craft may not be moved after arrival, nor may any goods be unloaded from it. The Regulations do not apply to craft which are sheltering or waiting for favourable winds or tides.

The Small Craft Regulations 1953 are revoked.

779 Tobacco products—amendment of units of measurement

The Tobacco Products (Amendment of Units of Measurement) Order 1979, S.I. 1979 No. 1489 (in force on 1st January 1980) provides for the rates of excise duty on cigars, hand-rolling tobacco and other smoking and chewing tobacco to be expressed in metric instead of imperial rates. The Order does not materially affect the levels of duty.

780 Tobacco Products Duty Act 1979

The Tobacco Products Duty Act 1979 received the royal assent on 22nd February 1979 and came into force on 1st April 1979. The Act consolidates the enactments relating to the excise duty on tobacco products.

Derivation and destination tables for this and related consolidating enactments appear on pp. 203–235.

781 Value added tax

See VALUE ADDED TAX.

DESTINATION TABLES

Alcoholic Liquor Duties Act 1979

This table shows in column (1) the enactments repealed by the Alcoholic Liquor Duties Act 1979, and in column (2) the provisions of that Act corresponding to the repealed provisions.

In certain cases the enactment in column (1), though having a corresponding provision in column (2), is not, or is not wholly, repealed, as it is still required or partly required, for the purposes of other legislation.

(1)	(2)	(1)	(2)
Customs and Inland Revenue Act 1890 (c. 8)	Alcoholic Liquor Duties Act 1979 (c. 4)	Customs and Excise Act 1952 (c. 44)	Alcoholic Liquor Duties Act 1979 (c. 4)
s. 31 (2)	——	s. 115 (2)	s. 35 (1), (2)
		(3)	(3)
Customs and Excise Act 1952 (c. 44)		116	75
		117 (1)	76 (1), (2)
——		(2)–(4)	(3)–(5)
s. 93 (1)	s. 12 (1), (2)	118	77
(2)	(3)	119 (1)	78 (1), (2)
(3), (4)	(4), (5)	(2), (3)	(3), (4)
(5)	(6)–(8)	120	79
(6)	(9)	121	80
94 (1), (2)	13 (1), (2)	122	9
(3)	(3), (4)	ss. 123, 124	Rep., 1971 c. 12, s. 24
(4)	(5)		(2), Sch. 7
95 (1)–(4)	14 (1)–(4)	s. 125 (1)	s. 47 (1), (2)
(5)	(5), (6)	(2)	(3), (4)
(6)	(7)	(3)–(5)	(5)–(7)
96 (1)	15 (1), (2)	126 (1)	48 (1), (2)
(2)–(5)	(3)–(6)	(2), (3)	(3), (4)
(6)	(7), (8)	127	49
(7)	(9)	128	50
97 (1), (2)	16 (1), (2)	129	51
(3)	(3), (4)	130 (1)	52 (1)
98	17	(2)	(2), (3)
99 (1), (2)	18 (1), (2)	(3)	(4)
(3)	(3), (4)	131	53
(4), (5)	(5), (6)	132	37
100 (1)	19 (1)	133 (1)–(5)	38 (1)–(5)
(2)	(2), (3)	(6)	(6), (7)
101	20	(7)	(8)
102	21	(8)	(9), (10) (b)
103 (1)–(4)	22 (1)–(4)	134	39
(5)	(5)–(7)	135	40
103 (6)–(8)	22 (8)–(10)	136★	Rep., 1959 c. 58, ss.
104	23		1 (6), 37 (5), Sch. 8,
105 (1)	24 (1)		Part I
(1A)	(2)	137 (1)	s. 42 (1), (2)
(2), (3)	(3), (4)	(2)–(4)	(3)–(5)
106	25	138	43 (1)–(3)
107	26 (1)–(4)	139	Rep., 1975 c. 45, s.
108	Rep., 1967 c. 54, s. 6		75 (5), Sch. 14,
	(4) (a), 45 (8), Sch.		Part I
	16, Part II	140	s. 56
109	s. 31	141	Rep., 1975 c. 45, s. 75
110	32		(5), Sch. 14, Part I
111	10	142 (1)	s. 57
112	8	(2)	Rep., 1975 c. 45, s. 75
113 (1)	33 (1), (2)		(5), Sch. 14, Part I
(2)	(3), (4)	143	Rep., 1975 c. 45, s. 75
(3), (4)	(5), (6)		(5), Sch. 14, Part I
114	34	144 (1)	s. 58
115 (1)	Rep., 1958 c. 56, s.		
	40 (5), Sch. 9, Part		
	I		

★ Repealed by the Customs and Excise Management Act 1979, s. 177 (3), Sch. 6, Part I.

(1)	(2)	(1)	(2)
Customs and Excise Act 1952 (c. 44)	Alcoholic Liquor Duties Act 1979 (c. 4)	Customs and Excise Act 1952 (c. 44)	Alcoholic Liquor Duties Act 1979 (c. 4)
s. 144 (2)	Rep., 1975 c. 45, s. 75 (5), Sch. 14, Part I	s. 226 (2)–(5)	s. 81 (3)–(6)
145 (1), (2)	Rep., 1975 c. 45, s. 75 (5), Sch. 14, Part I	227	82
(3)–(5)	s. 59	228	83
146 (1)	65 (1), (2)	237	86 (1), (2)
(2)	Rep., 1959 c. 58, s. 37 (5), Sch. 8, Part I	241 (1)	Rep., 1967 c. 54, ss. 6 (4), 45 (8), Sch. 16, Part II
(3)	s. 65 (4)		s. 28
(4)–(6)	(6)–(8)	(1A), (2)	
147 (1)	65 (5)	(3), (4)	Rep., 1967 c. 54, ss. 6 (4), 45 (8), Sch. 16, Part II
(2)	Rep., 1967 c. 54, ss. 6 (4), 45 (8), Sch. 16, Part II	242	s. 29
148 (1)–(3)	Rep., 1967 c. 54, ss. 5 (1) (a), 45 (8), Sch. 16, Part I	243	30
		263 (3)	46 (1)
(4)	s. 4 (4)	(4), (5)	ss. 46 (2), (3), 61, 64
ss. 149–155*	Rep., 1967 c. 54, ss. 5 (1) (a), 45 (8), Sch. 16, Part I	283 (2)*	8 (2), 10 (2), 13 (3), (5), 15 (4), (5), (7), 16 (2), (3) (b), 17 (2) (a), 18 (6), 19 (2), 20 (1), (2), 21 (3), 22 (9), 24 (4), 25 (1), (2), 28 (2), 29, 31 (3), 33 (1), (5), 34 (2), 35 (3), 40 (2), 44 (2), 46 (3), 47 (7), 48 (4), 49 (2), 50 (2), 51 (2), 52 (1)–(3), 53 (3), 54 (5), 55 (6), 56 (2), 59 (2), 61 (2), 62 (4), (6), 64 (2), 65 (7), 67 (2), 68, 69 (3), (4), 70 (1)–(4), 71 (4), 72 (1)–(3), 73 (4), 75 (5), 77 (3), (4), 78 (4), 80 (1), 81 (5), 82 (2), 84 (3)
s. 156	Rep., 1959 c. 58, ss. 4 (10), 37 (5), Sch. 8, Part I		
157 (1)	s. 66		
(2)	Rep., 1967 c. 54, ss. 5 (1) (a), 45 (8), Sch. 16, Part I		
158	s. 67		
159	68		
160	69		
161	70		
162 (1)	71 (1)		
(2)	(2), (3)		
(3), (4)	(4), (5)		
163 (1)	72 (1), (2)		
(2)	(3), (4)		
164 (1)	73 (1)		
(2), (3)	(3), (4)	306*	s. 90
165	74	306A*	91
166	89	307 (1)†	ss. 1 (1)–(6), 4 (1), 47 (2), 87 (1)
167	84	315 (c), (d)	
168	85	Sch. 10, para. 15	Applied to Scotland
169 (1)	Rep., 1967 c. 54, ss. 5 (1) (a), 45 (8), Sch. 16, Part I	**Finance Act 1953 (c. 34)**	
(2)	s. 87 (1), (2)	s. 2 (1)	s. 38 (1) (a)
(3)	(3)	(2)	(11)
(4)	(5)	**Medical Act 1956 (c. 76)**	
(5)	(6), (7)	s. 52 (1)‡	84 (1) (a)
(6)	Rep., 1959 c. 58, s. 37 (5), Sch. 8, Part I	**Finance Act 1958 (c. 56)**	
170 (1)	s. 88 (1)–(3)	s. 6 (1)	1 (8)
(2)	(4), (5)	(2)	35 (1)
(4)	(6)	(3)	
171 (1), (2)	3 (1), (2)		
(3)	(3)–(5)		
172 (1)–(4)	2 (1)–(4)		
(5)	(5), (6)		
(6)	(7)		
226 (1)	81 (1), (2)		

* Repealed by the Customs and Excise Management Act 1979, s. 177 (3), Sch. 6, Part I.
† Repealed in part.   ‡ Not repealed.

(1)	(2)	(1)	(2)
Finance Act 1959 (c. 58)	Alcoholic Liquor Duties Act 1979 (c. 4)	Finance Act 1967 (c. 54)	Alcoholic Liquor Duties Act 1979 (c. 4)
s. 2 (1)	s. 65 (3)	s. 4 (1)	ss. 12 (3), 48 (3)
(5)	——	(2)	s. 85 (1)
3 (2)	84 (1)	(3)	——
(3)	ss. 85 (1), 86 (1), (3)	(4)	12 (8)
(4)	s. 87 (4), (7), (8)	(5) (a)†	——
(5)		(b)	25 (1) (d)
Finance Act 1960 (c. 44)		(6)	Rep., 1973 c. 36, s. 41 (1), Sch. 6
s. 3 (1)	27 (1), (2)	6 (1)	
(2)	ss. 4 (1), 27 (5)	(2), (3)	s. 27 (3), (4)
(3)	Rep., 1967 c. 54, ss. 6 (4) (b), 45 (8), Sch. 16, Part II	(4)	See against 1967 c. 54, Sch. 9 below
(4)	——	(5)	ss. 4 (1), 27 (5)
(5)	See against 1960 c. 44, Sch. 1, below	(6)	
(6)	——	Sch. 5, para. 2	s. 42 (2)
Sch. 1, para. 1	s. 28 (1), (3)	3	46 (1)
2	29 (1)	4 (1), (2)	44
3	30 (1)	(3)	47 (5)
		Sch. 6, para. 1	76 (4) (b)
Finance Act 1963 (c. 25)		3	70 (1)
s. 6 (1)	41	4	71 (5)
(2)	47 (2), (4)	paras. 7–9	4 (1)
(3)	See against 1963 c. 25, Sch. 2, below	para. 10	87 (4), (7), (8)
(4)	——	11	27 (2) (a)
Sch. 2, para. 1 (1)		Sch. 9, para. 1	21 (2) (a)
(2)	47 (1), (2)	2	65 (4)
(3), (4)	(4), (5)	3	28 (1), (3)
(5)	(7)	paras. 4, 5	29
2	53	para. 6	30 (1)
3	39 (1)		
4	ss. 4 (1), 47 (2)	Finance Act 1968 (c. 44)	
5	——	s. 1 (3)	31 (1) (h)
Weights and Measures Act 1963 (c. 31)		Theatres Act 1968 (c. 54)	
s. 59 (a)	ss. 4 (4), 65 (8)	Sch. 2†	71 (5) (c)
(b)	s. 4 (1)	Decimal Currency Act 1969 (c. 19)	
Sch. 10, para. 1 (d)	——	s. 10 (1)‡	ss. 12 (3), 18 (4), 47 (4), 48 (3), 75 (4), 76 (3), 81 (3)
Finance Act 1964 (c. 49)		Finance Act 1969 (c. 32)	
s. 1 (5)	s. 11	s. 1 (5) (b)	——
2 (5)	ss. 1 (3), 4 (1), 73 (2)	Sch. 7, para. 2	s. 57
(6)	——		
Finance Act 1966 (c. 18)		Finance Act 1970 (c. 24)	
s. 10 (2)‡	s. 26 (5)	s. 6 (1)	ss. 1 (7), 6
Sch. 2, paras. 1†, 2	26 (5)	(2) (a)	s. 1 (7)
s. 1 (5)	See against 1967 c. 54, Sch. 5, below	7 (1)–(4), (6), (7)	——

‡ Not repealed. † Repealed·in part.

(1)	(2)	(1)	(2)
Finance Act 1972 (c. 41)	Alcoholic Liquor Duties Act 1979 (c. 4)	Finance Act 1976 (c. 40)	Alcoholic Liquor Duties Act 1979 (c. 4)
s. 57 (3)	s. 7	s. 2 (1)–(6)	s. 62
(a)	8 (1)	(7)	———
(b)	22 (7)	(8)	1 (6)
(c)	33 (1) (b)	3 (1)	24 (2)
(4)	———	(2), (3)	69 (2), (3)
Finance Act 1974 (c. 30)		Sch. 3, para. 1	2 (7)
		5	64 (1)
s. 4	31 (1)	7 (a)	1 (6)
Finance (No. 2) Act 1975 (c. 45)		(b)	(5)
		9 (a)	55 (5) (b)
s. 9	5	(b)	1 (5)
10 (1)	36		
(2)	ss. 42 (6), 43 (4)	**Finance Act 1977 (c. 36)**	
14 (1)–(4)	s. 54		
(5)	1 (4)	s. 1 (1)	5
15 (1)–(5)	55	(2)	36
(6)	ss. 1 (1), (5), 4 (4), 22	(3)	Sch. 1
	(1), 24 (1), 57, 65	(4)	2
	(1), (6), (8), 66 (1)	(5)	s. 62 (1)
	(d), 67 (1), 76 (4)	(8), (9)	———
	(b)	Sch. 1	Sch. 1
Sch. 3, para. 1 (2)	13 (1), 32 (2), 41,	2	2
	44 (1), 49 (1) (f),	**Criminal Law Act 1977 (c. 45)**	
	51 (1)		
3	s. 22 (5)	s. 27 (1)‡	s. 17 (2)
4	31 (1) (a)	28 (2)‡	17 (2)
5	ss. 9, 10 (1)	(7)‡	4 (1)
6	s. 8 (1)	31 (6)‡	ss. 35 (3), 53 (4), 72 (3)
7	33 (1) (a)	32 (1)‡	17 (2)
9	46 (1)		
15	6	**Finance Act 1978 (c. 42)**	
24	7		
25	24 (1)	s. 2 (1)	45, 60 (1), 63
26	42 (2)	(2)	60 (2)
27	56	Sch. 12, para. 1 (1)	———
28	———	(2)	s. 4 (1)
29	57	(3)(a)	35 (1)
30	———	(b)	42 (4)
31	58 (1)	(c)	58 (1)
32	59	(d)	70 (4)
33	65 (4)	(e)	ss. 71 (1), 73 (1)
34	85 (1)	(f)	s. 74 (b)
35	87 (1)	(4)	ss. 22 (1), (4), 42 (2),
36	88 (1)		43 (2)
37	2 (7)	(5)	s. 56 (2)
42	ss. 46 (2), 61 (1), 64 (1)	(6)	ss. 2 (1), (4), 3 (1), (3)
44 (a)	———	2	s. 11
(b)	s. 1 (4)	3	1 (4)
(d)	ss. 1 (5), 4 (1)	4	1 (5)
45	Applied to Scotland	5	62 (6)
46	Sch. 3, paras. 4, 7	18★	91
47	para. 5 (1), (3)		
	(b)		
Schs. 4, 5			
Sch. 6, para. 5	s. 20 (3)		
6	21 (5)		
7	23 (3)		
8	31 (1) (j)		

‡ Not repealed.

★ Repealed by the Customs and Excise Management Act 1979, s. 177 (3), Sch. 6, Part I.

Customs and Excise Duties (General Reliefs) Act 1979

This table shows in column (1) the enactments repealed and the regulations revoked by the Customs and Excise Duties (General Reliefs) Act 1979, and in column (2) the provisions of that Act corresponding to the repealed and revoked provisions.

In certain cases the enactment in column (1), though having a corresponding provision in column (2), is not repealed as it is still required for the purposes of other legislation.

(1)	(2)	(1)	(2)
Customs and Excise Act 1952 (c. 44)	Customs and Excise Duties (General Reliefs) Act 1979 (c. 3)	Import Duties Act 1958 (c. 6)	Customs and Excise Duties (General Reliefs) Act 1979 (c. 3)
s. 35 (1)	s. 10 (1)	s. 16	——
(2)	Rep., S.I. 1977 No. 1785	Sch. 3, para. 4	s. 1 (4), (5)
(3), (4)	s. 10 (2), (3)	5	(6)
(5)	Rep., S.I. 1977 No. 1785	8 (1)	(3)
(6), (7)	s. 10 (4), (5)	(2)	(2)
36	11	4, para. 2	3 (2)
37 (1), (2)	5 (1), (2)	**Finance Act 1960 (c. 44)**	
(3)	——	s. 10 (1)	s. 3 (5)
41	7	**Defence (Transfer of Functions) Act 1964 (c. 15)**	——
42	8	s. 1*	s. 12 (1), (4), (5)
43	9	**Finance Act 1966 (c. 18)**	——
272 (1)	12 (1), (6)	s. 10 (1)*	s. 18 (3)
(2)–(5)	(2)–(5)	(9)*	(2)
283 (2)*	Sch. 1, para. 3	**Finance Act 1967 (c. 54)**	——
306*	s. 17 (1), (2)	s. 2 (1)	s. 14 (2)
306A*	5 (3)	(2)	(3), (4)
309 (1)	6 (1)	(3)	17 (3)
(3), (4)	(2), (3)	(4)	——
310	Sch. 1	**National Loans Act 1968 (c. 13)**	——
Import Duties Act 1958 (c. 6)		s. 1 (8)*	ss. 4 (3), 10 (2), (3), 11 (1)
s. 4	s. 16, Sch. 2, para. 5	**Finance Act 1968 (c. 44)**	——
5 (1)	1 (1)	s. 7 (1)–(3)	s. 13 (1)–(3)
(1A)	ss. 1, 3 (1)	(4)	17 (1)
(2), (3)	Rep., 1972 c. 68, s. 4, Sch. 3, Part I	(5)	(3), (4), (6)
(4)	s. 4 (1), (2)	(6), (7)	13 (4), (5)
(5)–(7)	Rep., 1972 c. 68, s. 4, Sch. 3, Part I, Sch. 4, para. 1 (1) (a)	**Finance Act 1969 (c. 32)**	——
(8)	s. 4 (3)	s. 54 (1)	——
6 (1)	3 (1), (2)	(2)	s. 3 (1), (3)–(5), (7)
(2)–(6)	(3)–(7)	(3), (4)	——
10 (1)	15		
12 (4)	14 (1)		
13 (1)	Sch. 2, para. 5		
(2)	s. 17 (1), Sch. 12, para. 5		
(3)	s. 17 (3), Sch. 12, para. 5		
(4)	s. 17 (4), (5), Sch. 2, para. 5		
(5)	Sch. 2, para. 5		
(6)	Rep., 1969 c. 16, s. 18 (1)		
15 (1)	ss. 1 (5), 14 (1), 18 (2)		
(2), (3)	——		

* Repealed by the Customs and Excise Management Act 1979, s. 177 (3), Sch. 6, Part I.

(1)	(2)	(1)	(2)
Finance Act 1972 (c. 41)	Customs and Excise Duties (General Reliefs) Act 1979 (c. 3)	Criminal Law Act 1977 (c. 45)	Customs and Excise Duties (General Reliefs) Act 1979 (c. 3)
s. 55 (2)	s. 13 (1), (2)	s. 28 (2)★, (7)★	s. 15 (2) (a), (3) (a)
(3)	(4)	32 (1)★	15 (2) (b)
European Communities Act 1972 (c. 68)		Inward Processing Relief Regulations 1977, S.I. 1977 No. 910	
s. 5 (3)†	ss. 1, 2 (1), 3 (1), 14 (2), 16, 17 (3), (4), 19 (3) (a), Sch. 2, para. 5	reg. 7 (1)	s. 15 (1)
	—	Customs and Excise (Relief for Returned Goods) Regulations 1977, S.I. 1977 No. 1785	
(5)			
(6)	s. 2		
(6A)	ss. 2 (1), 19 (3) (b)	reg. 1	
Sch. 2, para. 2†	s. 17 (1), (2)	2	ss. 10 (1)–(3), 11
4, para. 1 (1)	ss. 1 (1), 3 (1), (3)–(5), (7), 4 (1), 16, 17 (1)		
(2)	s. 4 (1), (2)	Finance Act 1978 (c. 42)	
(3)	3 (1)	s. 6 (8) Sch. 12,	ss. 2 (1), 19 (3) (b)
(4)	—	para. 9	s. 5 (1)
(5)	17 (5), Sch. 2, para. 5	10	9
(6)	—	15	12 (1), (6)
		18★	5 (3)
Finance (No. 2) Act 1975 (c. 45)		19 (7) (a)★	Sch. 1, para. 1 (a)
Sch. 3, para. 1 (1)★	ss. 6 (3), 7, 13 (1), (2) (4), Sch. 1, paras. 1, 2	19 (7) (d)	s. 3 (5)
10	s. 6 (3)	(8)★	Sch. 1, para. 1 (b)
11	Sch. 1, para. 1	20	—
13	—		
Customs Duties (ECSC) Relief Regulations 1976, S.I. 1976 No. 2130		Finance Act 1978 (c. 42)	
reg. 1	—	Sch. 12, para. 24 (1)★, (3)★	s. 15 (2), (3)
2	s. 1 (2), (3)	25	ss. 1, 3 (1)
Finance Act 1977 (c. 36)		26	s. 17 (4), Sch. 2, para. 5
s. 12	—	Customs Duties (Inward and Outward Processing Relief) Regulations 1978, S.I. 1978 No. 1148	
		reg. 2	—

★ Repealed by the Customs and Excise Management Act 1979, s. 177 (3), Sch. 6, Part I.
† Not repealed.

Customs and Excise Management Act 1979

This table shows in column (1) the enactments repealed by the Customs and Excise Management Act 1979, and in column (2) the provisions of that Act corresponding to the repealed provisions.

In certain cases, the enactment in column (1), though having a corresponding provision in column (2), is not, or is not wholly, repealed as it is still required, or partly required, for the purposes of other legislation.

(1)	(2)	(1)	(2)
Customs and Excise Act 1952 (c. 44)	Customs and Excise Management Act 1979 (c. 2)	Customs and Excise Act 1952 (c. 44)	Customs and Excise Management Act 1979 (c. 2)
s. 1 (1), (2)	s. 6 (1), (2)	ss. 38–40	ss. 46–48
(3)	(3), (4)	s. 44	s. 49
2 (1)	175 (2)	45 (1)	50 (1)–(4)
(2), (3)	7	(2), (3)	(6), (7)
3 (1)	6 (5)	46	51
(2), (3)	Rep., 1971 c. 80, s. 4	47 (1)	53 (1), (3)
	(5), Sch. 2, Pt. I	(2)	Rep., 1966 ss. 11, 69
4 (1)	s. 8 (1)		(2), Sch. 1, para. 10,
(2)	(2), (3)		Sch. 14, Pt. VII
ss. 5–9	ss. 11–15	(3)	s. 53 (4), (5)
s. 10 (1)	s. 16 (1), (2)	(4)	(8)
(2)	(3)	(5)	52
11 (1), (2)	17 (1), (2)	48 (1)	60 (1), (3)
(3)	(3), (4)	(2)	(5)
(4), (5)	(5), (6)	(3)	(6), (7)
12	18	49 (1)	57 (1), (3)
13 (1) (a)	19 (1)	(2)	(9)
(b)	(2)	(3)	(10)
(c)	————	(4)	(7)
(2)	(3)	(5)	(5)
14 (1)	20 (1)	50 (1)	61 (1)
(2), (3)	————	(2)	(2), (3)
(4), (5)	(2), (3)	(3), (4)	(5), (6)
15 (1)	21 (1), (2)	(5)	(7), (8)
(2)	(3)	51 (1), (2)	63 (1), (2)
(3)	(4), (5)	(3)	(3), (4)
(4), (5)	(6), (7)	(4)	(5), (6)
(6)	4	52 (1)–(6)	64 (1)–(6)
16	22	(7)	(7), (8)
ss. 17–20	ss. 25–28	ss. 53, 54	ss. 65, 66
s. 21 (1)	s. 29 (1), (2)	s. 55 (1)	s. 67 (1)
(2)	(3)	(2)	(2), (3)
22 (1)	30 (1), (2)	(3), (4)	(4), (5)
(2), (3)	(3), (4)	56 (1)	68 (1)
ss. 23, 24	ss. 32, 33	(2)	(2)–(4)
s. 25 (1)	s. 34 (1)	(3), (4)	(5), (6)
(2)	(2), (3)	ss. 57–59	ss. 69–71
26 (1)–(6)	35 (1)–(6)	s. 60 (1)	s. 72 (1), (2)
(7)	(7), (8)	(2)	(3)
27 (1)	36 (1), (2)	61	73
(2), (3)	(3), (4)	62 (1), (2)	74 (1), (2)
28 (1)	37 (1), (2)	(3)	(3), (4)
(2)	(3), (5)	63	75
(3)	(6), (7)	64 (1)	76 (1)
29 (1)	38 (1)–(3)	(2)	————
(2)	(4)	(3)	(2)
30	39	65 (1)	77 (1), (2)
31 (1)–(3)	40 (1)–(3)	(2)	(3)
(4)	(4), (5)	(3)	(4), (5)
ss. 32, 33	ss. 41, 42	66	Rep., 1968 c. 44, ss. 6
s. 34 (1), (2)	s. 43 (1), (2)		(4), 61 (10), Sch. 20,
(3)	(3), (4)		Pt. I
(4)	(5)	67	s. 79

(1)	(2)	(1)	(2)
Customs and Excise Act 1952 (c. 44)	Customs and Excise Management Act 1979 (c. 2)	Customs and Excise Act 1952 (c. 44)	Customs and Excise Management Act 1979 (c. 2)
s. 68 (1)	s. 81 (2), (3)	s. 255A	s. 121
(2)–(5)	(4)–(7)	ss. 256, 257	ss. 123, 124
69	82	s. 258 (1)	s. 125 (1), (2), Sch.
70	Rep., 1978 c. 42, ss. 5		7, para. 1
	(3), 80 (5), Sch. 13,	(3), (4)	s. 125 (3), (4)
	Pt. I	259 (1)	126 (1), (2), (4)
71 (1)	s. 84 (1)–(3)	(2)	Rep., 1962 c. 44, s. 34
(2), (3)	(4), (5)		(7), Sch. 11, Pt. II
ss. 72–78	ss. 85–91	(3)	s. 126 (5)
s. 79 (1)	s. 5 (1)	ss. 260, 261	ss. 127, 128
(2)	(2), (3)	s. 262 (1)	s. 129 (1), (2)
(3)	(4), (5)	(2)	(3), (4)
(4)	(8)	263 (1), (2)	130
80 (1)	92 (1)	264	131
(1A)–(1C)	(2)–(4)	265	Rep., 1968 c. 2, s. 6
(2)–(5)	(5)–(8)		(2), Schedule
81	Rep., 1975 c. 45, ss.	266	s. 132
	16 (1), 75 (5), Sch.	267 (1)	133 (1)
	14, Pt. I	(2)	(2)–(5)
82 (1), (2)	Rep., 1975 c. 45, ss.	(3)	(6)
	16 (1), 75 (5), Sch.	268 (1)	134 (1)
	14, Pt. I	(2)	(2), (3)
(3)	s. 97	269	Rep., 1968 c. 2, s. 6
ss. 83, 84	Rep., 1975 c. 45, ss.		(2), Schedule
	16 (1), 75 (5), Sch.	270	s. 135
	14, Pt. I	271 (1)	136 (1), (2)
85 (1)	s. 94 (1)–(3), (5)	(2)	(3)
(2)	(4)	(3)†	(4), (5)
(3)	95	273 (1)	137 (1)
86–89	Rep., 1975 c. 45, ss.	(2)	(2), (3)
	16 (1), 75 (5), Sch.	(3)	(4)
	14, Pt. I	274	138
90, 91	ss. 98, 99	275 (1), (2)	139 (1), (2)
s. 92 (1)	s. 100 (1)	(3)	(3), (4)
(2)	(2)–(4)	(4)–(7)	(5)–(8)
233	101	ss. 276, 277	ss. 140, 141
234 (1)	102 (1)	s. 278 (1), (2)	s. 142 (1), (2)
(2)	(2), (3)	(3)	(4)
235	103	279	143
236 (1)	104 (1)	280 (1)	144 (1)
(2)	(2), (3)	(2)	(2), (3)
(3)	(4)	(3)	(4)
238	105	281 (1)	145 (1)
239 (1)	106 (1)	(2)	(2)–(4)
(2)	(2), (3)	(3), (4)	(5), (6)
240	107	282	146
ss. 244–247	ss. 108–111	283 (1)	147 (1)
s. 248 (1)	s. 112 (1), (2)	(2)	156 (3) and
(2)	(3), (4)		passim
(3)	(5)	(3), (4)	147 (3), (4)
249 (1)	113 (1), (2)	(5)	Applied to Scotland
(2)–(5)	(3)–(6)	284	s. 148
ss. 250, 251	ss. 114, 115	285 (1)	Rep., 1977 c. 45, s. 65
s. 252 (1)	s. 116 (1)		(5), Sch. 13
(2)	(2), (3)	(2)	s. 149 (1)
253 (1)	117 (1), (2), (8)	(3)	(3)
(2)	(3), (4)	286 (1)–(3)	150
(3)	(5), (6)	(4)	
(4)	(7)	ss. 287, 288	ss. 151, 152
254	118	s. 289 (1)	s. 153 (1)
255 (1), (2)	119 (1), (2)	(2)	(2), (3)
(3)	(3)–(6)		

† Repealed in part.

(1)	(2)	(1)	(2)
Customs and Excise Act 1952 (c. 44)	Customs and Excise Management Act 1979 (c. 2)	Customs and Excise Act 1952 (c. 44)	Customs and Excise Management Act 1979 (c. 2)
ss. 290, 291	ss. 154, 155	s. 318 (1)	Sch. 4, para. 1
s. 292 (1), (2)	s. 157	(2)	———
(3)	Rep., 1974 c. 22, s. 1, Schedule, Pt. I	ss. 319, 320	Rep., 1974 c. 22, s. 1, Sch., Pt. XI
293 (1)	s. 158 (1), (2)	s. 321	———
(2), (3)	(3), (4)	Sch. 7	Sch. 3
294 (1)–(4)	159 (1)–(4)	10, Part I	4, para. 1
(5)	(5)–(7)	II†	12
(6)	(8)	s. 33 (1)	s. 156 (2) and passim
295	160	35 (2)	
296 (1)	161 (1), (2)		
(2)	(3), (4)	**Finance Act 1957 (c. 49)**	
(3), (4)	(5), (6)	s. 5	s. 126 (3)
297	163	42 (2) (a)	———
298 (1)	164 (1)–(3)	Sch. 2, para. 1 (1)	Sch. 2, paras. 1 (1)–(4), 9
(2)	(4)	(2)	para. 1 (5)
ss. 299, 300	ss. 165, 166	(3)	Rep., 1978 c. 42, ss. 79, 80 (5), Sch. 12, para. 13 (c), Sch. 13, Pt. I
s. 301 (1)	s. 167 (1)		
(2)	(4)	(4), (5)	Sch. 2, paras. 2, 3
(3), (4)	(2), (3)	2	Rep., 1978 c. 42, ss. 79, 80 (5), Sch. 12, para. 13 (c), Sch. 13, Pt. I
ss. 302–304	ss. 168–170		
s. 305 (1)	s. 171 (1)		
(2)–(4)	(3)–(5)	3	Sch. 2, para. 4
306	172	4 (1)	5 (1)
306A	173	(2) (a)	(2)
307 (1)†	1 (1)	(b)	Rep., 1978 c. 42, s. 79, Sch. 12, para. 13 (c)
(2)	(6)		
(3)	———	5	Sch. 2, para. 6
308 (1), (2)	Rep., 1978 c. 42, s. 80 (5), Sch. 13, Pt. I	6 (1)	———
(3)	Sch. 7, para. 3	(2), (3)	Sch. 2, paras. 7, 8
309 (1)‡	s. 174 (1), (3)		
(2)	(2)	**Isle of Man Act 1958 (c. 11)**	
(5)	(4)	s. 2 (1)†	s. 17 (3)
311	Rep., 1978 c. 42, s. 80 (5), Sch. 13, Pt. I		
312		**Finance Act 1958 (c. 56)**	
313 (1), (2)	s. 176 (1)	s. 40 (2) (b)	———
(3)	(2)		
(4) (a)	(3)	**Finance Act 1959 (c. 58)**	
(b)	———		———
314 (1)	Rep., S.I. 1973 No. 2163	s. 37 (2) (a)	———
(2)	Rep., 1962 c. 30, s. 30, Sch. 4, Pt. IV		
(3)	Rep., 1977 c. 18, s. 1 (1), Sch. 1, Pt. X	**Finance Act 1960 (c. 44)**	
(4)	———	s. 79 (2), (3) (a)	———
(5)	Rep., 1973 c. 36, s. 41 (1), Sch. 6, Pt. I	(6)†	———
(6)			
(7)	Rep., 1973 c. 36, s. 41 (1), Sch. 6, Pt. I		
315	Applied to Scotland		
316 (1), (2)			
(3), (4)	Sch. 7, paras. 11, 12		
(5)			
(6)	Rep., 1963 c. 30, s. 1, Schedule		
317	Rep., 1963 c. 9, s. 41 (1), Sch. 4		

† Repealed in part.
‡ Repealed by the Customs and Excise Duties (General Reliefs) Act 1979, s. 19 (2), Sch. 3, Part I.

(1)	(2)	(1)	(2)
Finance Act 1961 (c. 36)	Customs and Excise Management Act 1979 (c. 2)	Finance Act 1967 (c.54)	Customs and Excise Management Act 1979 (c. 2)
s. 11 (1)	s. 176 (4), (6)	s. 3 (2)	s. 10 (2), (3)
(2)	(5)	(3)	(4), (5)
37 (2)	——	4 (5)†	——
		5 (11) (a), (b), (2)	
Finance Act 1962 (c. 44)		Sch. 6, para. 5	112 (5)
		6	
		12	
s. 34 (2)†	——	Sch. 9, para. 7	117 (6)
Pipe-lines Act 1962 (c. 58)		Criminal Justice Act 1967 (c. 80)	
s. 56 (1)	s. 162	s. 93 (4)	149 (2)
(2)	——	106 (2) (b)†	Applied to Scotland
70 (2)*	162	Finance Act 1968 (c. 44)	
Finance Act 1963 (c. 25)			
s. 7 (1), (2)	s. 1 (5)	s. 6	s. 78
(3)		61 (3)	
(4)	112 (5)	Hovercraft Act 1968 (c. 59)	
(5)	——		
73 (3)	——	Schedule, para. 4 (c)	1 (1)
(4)†	——		
Finance Act 1964 (c. 49)		Family Law Reform Act 1969 (c. 46)	
s. 10 (1)	s. 1 (4)		
26 (2), (3)	——	Sch. 1†	108 (2) (a)
Finance Act 1966 (c. 18)		Finance Act 1970 (c. 24)	
s. 10 (1)	2 (1), (3)		
(2)	——	s. 5 (a)	Rep., 1977 c. 36, s. 59 (5), Sch. 9, Pt. II
(3)	23 (1), (3)		
(4) (a)	2 (1)	(b)	——
(b)	164 (4) (e)	7 (5), (8)	——
(c)	23 (2)	36 (3)	——
(5), (6)	2 (4), (5)	Sch. 2, para. 5 (1)	s. 44
(7)	60 (2)–(4)	(2)	43 (4)
(8)	——	(3), (4)	58
(9)	1 (1)		
11 (1)	24 (1), (2)		
(2)	ss. 1 (1), 3 (2), 37 (4)	Hydrocarbon Oil (Customs & Excise) Act 1971 (c. 23)	
(3)	5 (6), (7)		
(4)	s. 3 (1), (3)		
(5)	57 (6)		
(6)	24 (3), (4)	s. 22	ss. 112 (6), 113 (7)
(7)	(5), (6)	Sch. 6, para. 1 (a)	s. 61 (2)
(8), (9)	ss. 96, 97	(b)	——
(10)	1 (1), 24 (2)		
(11)	1 (1), 24 (7)	Courts Act 1971 (c. 23)	
Sch. 2, para. 1†	60 (2), 61 (4), 81 (1), 141 (3), 142 (3), 143 (2)		
		Sch. 9†	s. 147 (3), Sch. 3, para. 11 (1)
Finance Act 1967 (c. 54)			
s. 3 (1)	s. 10 (1)		

* Not repealed. † Repealed in part.

(1)	(2)	(1)	(2)
Misuse of Drugs Act 1971 (c. 38)	Customs and Excise Management Act 1979 (c. 2)	European Communities Act 1972 (c. 68)	Customs and Excise Management Act 1979 (c. 2)
s. 26 (1)	ss. 50 (5), 68 (4), 170 (4)	Sch. 4, para. 2 (1)	
(2), (3)	Sch. 1, paras. 1, 2	(2)	Rep., 1976 c. 40, s. 132 (5), Sch. 15, Pt. I
(4)	Rep., 1977 c. 45, s. 65	(3)	s. 79 (2)
(5), (6)	(5), Sch. 13	(4)	Rep., 1978 c. 42, s. 80 (5), Sch. 13, Pt. I
	——	(5)	Rep., S.I. 1978 No. 1603
Finance Act 1971 (c. 68)		(6)	Rep., 1975 c. 45, s. 75 (5), Sch. 14, Pt. I
		(7)	s. 121
s. 11	——	(8)	125 (1), Sch. 7, para. 1
69 (3)	——		
Sch. 1, para. 1 (1)–(6)	s. 54 (1)–(5)	**Finance Act 1973 (c. 51)**	
(7)	52 (f)		
2	53 (2)	s. 2 (1)–(3)	120
3	55 (1)	(4)	172 (3)
4	56 (1), (2)	59 (3) (a)	——
5	57		
6	59 (1), (2)	**Finance Act 1974 (c. 30)**	
paras. 7, 8	62 (1), (2)		
para. 9	66	s. 1 (7), (8)	
10	——	57 (3) (a)†	——
11 (1),			
(2)		**Finance Act 1975 (c. 7)**	
(3)	54 (7), (8)		
	ss. 53 (6), 54 (9), 57 (12)	s. 4	Sch. 4, para. 12
(4)	s. 56 (4)		
(5)	ss. 53 (7), 54 (10), 57 (11), 59 (6), 62 (4)	**Finance (No. 2) Act 1975 (c. 45)**	
12	s. 59 (3)		
13	ss. 53 (3), 54 (6), 55 (2), 56 (3), 57 (8), 59 (5), 62 (3)	s. 1 (7), (8)	——
		8 (1)–(3)	——
14	s. 59 (4)	(4)	Sch. 7, para. 7
15	ss. 53 (2), 59 (7), 62 (2)	(5)	——
		16 (1)	——
Betting and Gaming Duties Act 1972 (c. 25)		(2)	s. 93 (1), (2)
		(3)–(5)	(3)–(5)
Sch. 2, para. 7	s. 102 (3) (a)	(6)	Rep., 1976 c. 40, s. 15 (3), 132 (5), Sch. 15, Pt. I
4, para. 10	102 (3) (a)		
		(7), (8)	s. 93 (6), (7)
Finance Act 1972 (c. 41)		(9)	——
s. 17 (5)	Sch. 4, para. 12	75 (2)†, (3) (a)	Passim
55 (4)	s. 78 (1)	Sch. 3, para. 1	Sch. 4, para. 12
134 (3) (a)	——	14	11
		23	——
European Communities Act 1972 (c. 68)		paras. 39–41	——
		para. 43	——
s. 5 (4)	s. 1 (7), Sch. 7, para. 5	44 (c)	s. 43 (2) (b)
		Sch. 6, para. 1	46
(7)	9	2	s. 92 (1)
(8)	80	Sch. 6, para. 3	100 (2) (b)
(9)	——	4	——
		14, Part I, para. 2★	Sch. 7, para. 6

★ Not repealed.   † Repealed in part.

(1)	(2)	(1)	(2)
Finance Act 1976 (c. 40)	Customs and Excise Management Act 1979 (c. 2)	Criminal Law Act 1977 (c. 45)	Customs and Excise Management Act 1979 (c. 2)
s. 15 (1), (2)	s. 45	s. 32 (1)*	ss. 13 (b), 16 (2) (b), 24 (5), (6), 50 (4), 53 (5), 63 (6), 64 (8), 68 (3), 100 (4), 129 (4), 159 (7), 167 (2), 168 (2), 170 (3)
(3)	———		
132 (3) (a)	———		
Sch. 3, para. 2	112 (3)		
3	113 (6)		
4	117 (6)		
6	160 (2)		
		Sch. 5, para. 1 (1) (a), (2) (c)	Sch. 1, para. 2
Finance Act 1977 (c. 36)			
		Finance Act 1978 (c. 42)	
s. 8 (1), (2)	122		
(3)	121	s. 3	s. 93 (2) (e)
9 (1)–(3)	124	4	31
(4)	———	5 (1), (2)	83
Sch. 6, para. 21	Sch. 4, para. 9	(3)	———
		79	———
Criminal Law Act 1977 (c. 45)		Sch. 12, para. 7 (1)	ss. 1 (5), 112 (5)
		11	s. 92 (1) (c)
		12	94 (5)
		13	126 (1), (2)
s. 27*	ss. 24 (5), (6), 50 (4), 53 (5), 63 (6), 64 (8), 68 (3), 84 (2), 100 (4), 129 (4), 159 (7), 167 (2), 168 (2), 170 (3), Sch. 1, para. 1	(a)	(3)
		(b)	Sch. 2, paras. 1 (1), 4, 5 (1)
			———
		(c)	s. 130 (1)
		14	149 (1) (b)
		16	151
		17	173
28 (2)*	13 (a), 16 (2) (a), 24 (5), (6), 50 (4), 53 (5), 63 (6), 64 (8), 68 (3), 100 (4), 129 (4), 159 (7), 167 (2), 168 (2), 170 (3), Sch. 1, para. 1	18	1 (1)
		19 (1)	Passim
		(2)	ss. 108 (1), 109 (2), 110, 111 (1), 112 (1)
		(3)	
		(4)	s. 43 (1), (5)
		(5)	ss. 5 (1), 86
		(6)	Passim
(7)*	s. 171 (2)	(7)	
		(a)	ss. 1 (1), 24 (2), 25 (1), 30 (2)
31 (6)*	ss. 12 (3), 27 (2) (b), 30 (4), 41, 60 (6), 61 (5), 64 (4), 70 (5), 71 (4), 72 (3), 85 (1), 91 (1), 101 (4), 107 (2), (3), 139 (7)	(b)	s. 34 (1) (b)
		(c)	159 (5)
		(8)	Passim
		paras. 21, 22 23, 24	Sch. 4, para. 12
			———

* Not repealed.

Excise Duties (Surcharges or Rebates) Act 1979

This table shows in column (1) the enactments repealed by the Excise Duties (Surcharges or Rebates) Act 1979, and in column (2) the provisions of that Act corresponding to the repealed provisions.

In certain cases the enactment in column (1), though having a corresponding provision in column (2), is not, or is not wholly, repealed as it is still required, or partly required, for the purposes of other legislation.

(1)	(2)	(1)	(2)
Finance Act 1961 (c. 36)	Excise Duties (Surcharges or Rebates) Act 1979 (c. 8)	Finance Act 1968 (c. 44)	Excise Duties (Surcharges or Rebates) Act 1979 (c. 8)
s. 9 (1)	s. 1 (2)	s. 10 (2)	s. 1 (1)
(2)	(2)–(4)		
(3)	(1)	Hydrocarbon Oil (Customs & Excise) Act 1971 (c. 12)	
(4) (a)	Rep., 1972 c. 41, s. 134 (7), Sch. 28, Part I		
(b)	———	Sch. 6, para. 2	1 (7)
(c)	s. 1 (2), (5)	s. 3 (5)	1 (1) (b)
(5)	(5)		
(6)	———	Northern Ireland Constitution Act 1973 (c. 36)	
(7), (8)	3 (1), (2)		
(9)	1 (1)		
(10)	3 (3)	s. 40 (2)★	1 (1)
37 (3)★	4 (1)		
Sch. 3, para. 1	———	Finance (No. 2) Act 1975 (c. 45)	
2	2 (6), (7)		
3	(5)	s. 8 (4)★	1 (1)
4, para. 1	———	Sch. 3, para. 1★	1 (1)
2	1 (3)		
3	———	Finance Act 1976 (c. 40)	
4	1 (6)		
5 (1)	———	s. 2 (7)★	1 (1)
(2)	Rep., 1962 c. 44, s. 34 (7), Sch. 11, Part I	6 (6)	1 (1)
6	Rep., 1964 c. 49, s. 26 (7), Sch. 9	Sch. 3, para. 8	1 (1)
7	1 (7)	Finance Act 1978 (c. 42)	
Finance Act 1964 (c. 49)			
		s. 6 (4)†	———
s. 8 (1)	Rep., 1965 c. 25, s. 97 (5), Sch. 22, Part I	10	2 (2)
(2)	s. 1 (1)		
(3)	ss. 1 (2), 2 (3)		
(4)	———		
(5)	s. 2 (3)–(5)		
(6)	(8), (9)		
(7)	———		
26 (3)	4 (1)		

★ Not repealed.   † Repealed in part.

Hydrocarbon Oil Duties Act 1979

This table shows in column (1) the enactments repealed by the Hydrocarbon Oil Duties Act 1979, and in column (2) the provisions of that Act corresponding to the repealed provisions.

In certain cases the enactment in column (1), though having a corresponding provision in column (2), is not, or is not wholly repealed as it is still required, or partly required, for the purposes of other legislation.

(1) Customs and Excise Act 1952 (c. 44)	(2) Hydrocarbon Oil Duties Act 1979† (c. 5)
s. 283 (2)‡	ss. 10 (3), (4), (7), 13 (1), (2), (5), 14 (4), (5), (8), 18 (5), 21 (3), 22 (1), 23 (1), 24 (4)
306‡	s. 25
306A‡	26
Hydrocarbon Oil (Customs & Excise) Act 1971 (c. 12)	
s. 1	1
2	2
3	4
4 (1)	Rep., 1975 c. 45, s. 75 (5), Sch. 14, Part I
(2)	s. 6 (2)
5	3
6	7
7 (1)–(3)	9 (1)–(3)
(4)	(5) (b)
(5)	(4)
8 (1)–(4)	10 (1)–(4)
(5)	(5)–(7)
(6), (7)	(8), (9)
9	11
10 (1)	12 (1)
(2)	27 (1)
(3), (4)	12 (2), (3)
11 (1), (2)	13 (1), (2)
(3)	(3)–(5)
(4), (5)	(6), (7)
12 (1)–(5)	14 (1)–(5)
(6)	(6)–(8)
(7), (8)	(9), (10)
13 (1)	15 (1)
(2)	(2), (3)
(3)	(4)
(4)	
(5)	(5)
14	16
15	17
16	18
17	19
18	20
19 (1)	21 (1) (a), (2)
(2), (3)	(2), (3)
20 (1)	21 (1) (b)
(2) (a)	(3)
(b)	22 (1)
(3)	(2)

(1) Hydrocarbon Oil (Customs & Excise) Act 1971 (c. 12)	(2) Hydrocarbon Oil Duties Act 1979 (c. 5)
s. 21	s. 24
23 (1)	27 (2)
(2)	(1)
ss. 24, 25	
Schs. 1, 2	Schs. 1, 2
Sch. 3	Sch. 3, Parts I, II
4	4
5	5
6, para. 3	6, para. 2
Finance Act 1971 (c. 68)	
s. 3 (1)–(4)	s. 8 (1)–(4)
(6)	21 (1) (c), Sch. 3, Part III
(7) (a)	s. 21 (3)
(b)	23 (1)
(8)	ss. 5, 8, 23 (1), 27 (1), Sch. 3, Part III
(9) (a)	s. 8 (6)
(b)	23 (2)
(10)	8 (7)
(11)	(5)
(12)	
6 (2)	
Sch. 4, Group 7*	
Finance (No. 2) Act 1975 (c. 45)	
s. 11	6 (1)
Sch. 3, para. 2	
16	2 (2)
17	7
18	10 (3)
19	17 (1)
20	18 (1), (2)
21	19 (3)
22	Sch. 3, paras. 8–11
Finance Act 1976 (c. 40)	
s. 9	s. 6 (1)
10	Sch. 1
Finance Act 1977 (c. 36)	
s. 4 (1) (a)	s. 6 (1)
(b)	7, 8 (3), (4) (c), Sch. 6, para. 6

* Not repealed.   † Repealed in part.
‡ Repealed by the Customs and Excise Management Act 1979, s. 177 (3), Sch. 6, Part I.

(1)	(2)	(1)	(2)
Finance Act 1977 (c. 36)	Hydrocarbon Oil Duties Act 1979 (c. 5)	Finance Act 1978 (c. 42)	Hydrocarbon Oil Duties Act 1979 (c. 5)
s. 4 (1) (c)	Sch. 6, para. 1	Sch. 12, paras. 8, 18‡	ss. 1, 2 (4), 4, 24 (3),
(2), (3)	s. 11		Sch. 5, para. 2
(4)	14 (1)		(1), s. 26
(5), (6)	——		
Criminal Law Act 1977 (c. 45)			
s. 27†	s. 10 (7), 13 (5), 14 (8)		
28 (2)†	10 (7), 13 (5), 14 (8)		
32 (1)‡	10 (7), 13 (5), 14 (8)		

† Not repealed.
‡ Repealed by the Customs and Excise Management Act 1979, s. 177 (3), Sch. 6, Part I.
* Repealed in part.

Matches and Mechanical Lighters Duties Act 1979

This table shows in column (1) the enactments repealed by the Matches and Mechanical Lighters Duties Act 1979, and in column (2) the provisions of that Act corresponding to the repealed provisions.

In certain cases the enactment in column (1), though having a corresponding provision in column (2), is not, or is not wholly, repealed as it is still required, or partly required, for the purposes of other legislation.

(1)	(2)	(1)	(2)
Customs and Excise Act 1952 (c. 44)	Matches and Mechanical Lighters Duties Act 1979 (c. 6)	Finance Act 1960 (c. 44)	Matches and Mechanical Lighters Duties Act 1979 (c. 6)
s. 219 (1)	s. 2 (1), (2)	s. 7 (1)†	s. 4 (1)
(2)	(3)	(3)	7 (2), (3)
(3)	(4)	(4)	(1)
220 (1)	3 (1), (2)		
(2)	(3)	Finance Act 1963 (c. 25)	
(3)	1 (2)		
221 (1)	7 (1)	s. 4 (2)	s. 3 (1), (2)
(2)	6 (4)		
(3) (a)	Rep., 1960 c. 44, s. 79 (6), Sch. 8, Part III	Finance (No. 2) Act 1975 (c. 45)	
(b)	6 (5)		
(c)	7 (4)	s. 12	s. 1 (1)
(4)	4 (1)	13	6 (1)–(3)
222 (1)	4 (2)	Sch. 3, para. 1 (2)*	3 (1) (b)
(2)	5 (2)	8	4 (2)
(3)	Rep., 1978, ss. 79, 80 (5), Sch. 12, para. 6 (3), Sch. 13, Part I	12	5 (1)
		38	7 (1) (e)
(4)	——		
(5)–(7)	(3)–(5)	Finance Act 1978 (c. 42)	
283 (2)*	ss. 2 (4), 3 (3), 6 (5), 7 (4)		
306*	3 (4), 7 (5)	Sch. 12, para. 6 (1)	ss. 1 (2), 3 (1) (c)
		(2) (a)	4 (1), 6 (4), 7 (1)
Finance Act 1953 (c. 34)		(b)	
		(3)	——
s. 3 (3)	s. 5 (1)		
(5)			

* Repealed by the Customs and Excise Management Act 1979, s. 177 (3), Sch. 6, Part I.
† Repealed in part.

Tobacco Products Duty Act 1979

This table shows in column (1) the enactments repealed by the Tobacco Products Duty Act 1979, and in column (2) the provisions of that Act corresponding to the repealed provisions.

(1)	(2)	(1)	(2)
Customs and Excise Act 1952 (c. 44)	Tobacco Products Duty Act 1979 (c. 7)	Finance Act 1977 (c. 36)	Tobacco Products Duty Act 1979 (c. 7)
s. 271 (3) (i)	—	s. 2 (2)	ss. 4, 6 (5)
283 (2)*	s. 7 (2)	(4)	s. 1 (3), (6)
306*	9	(5)	(3)
		(6)	(4)
Finance Act 1976 (c. 40)		(7)	(5)
		(8)	—
—		3 (1)	Sch. 1
s. 4 (1), (2)	s. 2	(5)	s. 7 (1)
(3), (4)	7		
(5)	1 (2)	Finance Act 1978 (c. 42)	
(6)	(1), (6)		
5	5	—	
6 (1), (2)	6 (1), (2)	s. 1 (1), (2)	s. 3
(3)	(1)	(3)	ss. 4, 6 (5)
(4), (5)	(3), (4)	(4)	—
7 (1)	8 (1), (2)	Sch. 12, para. 7 (2)	s. 6 (3)
(2)	(3)		

* Repealed by the Customs and Excise Management Act 1979, s. 177 (3), Sch. 4, Part I.

TABLES OF DERIVATIONS

Alcoholic Liquor Duties Act 1979

This table shows in the right hand column the legislative source from which the sections of the Alcoholic Liquor Duties Act 1979 in the left hand column have been derived. In the table the following abbreviations are used:

1952   = The Customs and Excise Act 1952 (c. 44)
1953   = The Finance Act 1953 (and so on as respects subsequent years)
1963 c. 31   = The Weights and Measures Act 1963 (c. 31)
1969 c. 19   = The Decimal Currency Act 1969 (c. 19)
1975 c. 21   = The Criminal Procedure (Scotland) Act 1975 (c. 21)
1975 (No. 2)   = The Finance (No. 2) Act 1975 (c. 45)
1977 CLA   = The Criminal Law Act 1977 (c. 45)
S.I. 1978/1603 = The Customs and Excise (Warehouses) Regulations 1978 (S.I. 1978 No. 1603)
1959 (N.I.)   = The Finance Act (Northern Ireland) 1959 (and so on as respects subsequent years)

Note: In this Table the references to provisions of the Criminal Law Act 1977 are references to those provisions as extended to Northern Ireland by paragraph 24 of Schedule 12 to the Finance Act 1978.

Section of Act	Derivation
1 (1)	1952 s. 307 (1); 1975 (No. 2) s. 15 (6) (part).
(2)	1952 s. 307 (1).
(3)	1952 s. 307 (1); 1964 s. 2 (5).
(4)	1975 (No. 2) s. 14 (5) and Sch. 3 para. 44 (*b*); 1978 Sch. 12 para. 3.
(5)	1975 s. 15 (6) and Sch. 3 para. 44 (*d*); 1976 Sch. 3 paras. 7 (*b*) and 9 (*b*); 1978 Sch. 12 para. 4.
(6)	1976 s. 2 (8), Sch. 3 para. 7 (*a*).
(7)	1970 s. 6 (1) (part), s. 6 (2) (*a*).
(8)	1958 s. 6 (1).
2	1952 s. 172; 1975 (No. 2) Sch. 3 para. 37; 1976 Sch. 3 para. 1; 1978 Sch. 12 para. 1 (6).
3	1952 s. 171; 1978 Sch. 12 para. 1 (6).
4 (1)	1952 s. 307 (1); 1960 s. 3 (2); 1963 s. 6 (3), Sch. 2 para. 4; 1963 (N.I.) s. 19 (3), Sch. 2 para. 3; 1963 c. 31 s. 59 (*b*); 1964 s. 2 (5); 1966 s. 10 (9); 1967 s. 6 (5), Sch. 6 paras. 7, 8 and 9; Hovercraft Act 1968 c. 59, Sch. para. 4; 1975 c. 21 s. 289B (6); 1975 (No. 2) Sch. 3 para. 44 (*d*) (ii); 1977 CLA s. 28 (7); 1978 Sch. 12, paras. 1 (2) and 4.
(2)	—
(3)	—
(4)	1952 s. 148 (4); 1963 c. 31 s. 59 (*a*); 1975 (No. 2) s. 15 (6).
5	1975 (No. 2) s. 9; 1977 s. 1 (1).
6	1970 s. 6 (1); 1975 (No. 2) Sch. 3 para. 15.
7	1972 s. 57 (3) (part); 1975 (No. 2) Sch. 3 para. 24.
8	1952 ss. 112 and 283 (2) and (5); 1972 s. 57 (3) (*a*); 1975 (No. 2) Sch. 3 para. 6.
9	1952 s. 122; 1975 (No. 2) Sch. 3 para. 5.
10	1952 ss. 111 and 283 (2) and (5); 1975 (No. 2) Sch. 3 para. 5.

Section of Act	Derivation
11	1964 s. 1 (5); 1978 Sch. 12 para. 2.
12	1952 s. 93; 1967 s. 4 (1) and (4); 1969 c. 19 s. 10 (1).
13	1952 ss. 94 and 283 (2) and (5); 1975 (No. 2) Sch. 3 para. 1 (2).
14	1952 s. 95.
15	1952 ss. 96 and 283 (2) and (5); S.I. 1978/1603.
16	1952 ss. 97 and 283 (2) and (5).
17	1952 ss. 98 and 283 (2) and (5); 1975 c. 21 ss. 193A and 289B (1); 1977 CLA ss. 27 (1), 28 (2) and 32 (1).
18	1952 ss. 99 and 283 (2) and (5); 1969 c. 19 s. 10 (1).
19	1952 ss. 100 and 283 (2) and (5).
20	1952 ss. 101 and 283 (2) and (5); 1975 (No. 2) Sch. 6 para. 5.
21	1952 ss. 102 and 283 (2) and (5); 1967 Sch. 9 para. 1; 1975 (No. 2) Sch. 6 para. 6.
22	1952 ss. 103 and 283 (2) and (5); 1972 s. 57 (3) (b); 1975 (No. 2) s. 15 (6), Sch. 3 para. 3; 1978 Sch. 12 para. 1 (4); S.I. 1978/1603.
23	1952 s. 104; Decimal Currency (Revenue Duties) Order 1970 (S.I. 1970 No. 1718), Art. 7; 1975 (No. 2) Sch. 6 para. 7.
24	1952 ss. 105 and 283 (2) and (5); 1975 (No. 2) s. 15 (6), Sch. 3 para. 25; 1976 s. 3 (1).
25	1952 ss. 106 and 283 (2) and (5); 1967 s. 4 (5) (b); 1967 (N.I.) s. 17 (1) (part).
26	1952 s. 107; 1966 s. 10 (2) and (9), Sch. 2 paras. 1 and 2.
27 (1), (2), (5) (3), (4), (5)	1960 s. 3 (1) and (2); 1967 Sch. 6 para. 11. 1967 s. 6 (2), (3) and (5).
28	1952 ss. 241 (1A) and (2), 283 (2) and (5); 1960 Sch. 1 para. 1; 1967 Sch. 9 para. 3.
29	1952 ss. 242 and 283 (2) and (5); 1960 Sch. 1 para. 2; 1967 Sch. 9 paras. 4 and 5.
30	1952 s. 243; 1960 Sch. 1 para. 3; 1967 Sch. 9 para. 6.
31	1952 ss. 109 and 283 (2) and (5); 1968 s. 1 (3); 1974 s. 4; 1975 (No. 2) Sch. 3 para. 4, Sch. 6 para. 8.
32	1952 s. 110; 1975 (No. 2) Sch. 3 para. 1 (2).
33	1952 ss. 113 and 283 (2) and (5); 1972 s. 57 (3) (c); 1975 (No. 2) Sch. 3 para. 7.
34	1952 ss. 114 and 283 (2) and (5).
35	1952 ss. 115 (2) and (3), 283 (2) and (5); 1958 s. 6 (2); 1975 c. 21 s. 289C (5); 1977 CLA s. 31 (6); 1978 Sch. 12 para. 1 (3) (a).
36	1975 (No. 2) s. 10 (1); 1977 s. 1 (2).
37	1952 s. 132.
38 (1)–(9) (10), (11)	1952 s. 133 (1)–(8). 1952 s. 133 (8) proviso; 1953 s. 2.
39	1952 s. 134; 1963 Sch. 2 para. 3.
40	1952 ss. 135 and 283 (2) and (5).
41	1963 s. 6 (1) (part); 1975 (No. 2) Sch. 3 para. 1 (2).

Section of Act	Derivation
42	1952 s. 137; 1967 Sch. 5 para. 2; 1975 (No. 2) s. 10 (2), Sch. 3 para. 26; 1978 Sch. 12 para. 1 (3) (*b*) and (4); S.I. 1978/1603.
43	1952 s. 138; 1975 (No. 2) s. 10 (2); 1978 Sch. 12 para. 1 (4); S.I. 1978/1603.
44	1967 Sch. 5 para. 4 (1) and (2); 1952 s. 283 (2) and (5); 1975 (No. 2) Sch. 3 para. 1 (2).
45	1978 s. 2 (1) (part).
46 (1)	1952 s. 263 (3); 1967 Sch. 5 para. 3; 1975 (No. 2) Sch. 3 para. 9.
(2), (3)	1952 ss. 263 (4) (part) and (5), 283 (2) and (5); 1975 (No. 2) Sch. 3 para. 42.
47 (1)	1952 s. 125 (1); 1963 Sch. 2 para. 1 (2); 1963 (N.I.) Sch. 2 para. 1 (2).
(2)	1952 ss. 125 (1), 307 (1); 1963 s. 6 (2), Sch. 2 para. 1 (2) and 4; 1963 (N.I.) s. 19 (2) and Sch. 2 para. 1 (2).
(3)	1952 s. 125 (2).
(4)	1952 s. 125 (2); 1963 s. 6 (2), Sch. 2 para. 1 (3); 1963 (N.I.) s. 19 (2), Sch. 2 para. 1 (3); 1969 c. 19 s. 10 (1).
(5)	1952 s. 125 (3); 1963 Sch. 2 para. 1 (4); 1963 (N.I.) s. 19 (1), Sch. 2 para. 1 (4); 1967 Sch. 5 para. 4 (3).
(6)	1952 s. 125 (4).
(7)	1952 ss. 125 (5) and 283 (2) and (5); 1963 Sch. 2 para. 1 (5); 1963 (N.I.) Sch. 2 para. 1 (5).
48	1952 ss. 126 and 283 (2) and (5); 1967 s. 4 (1); 1969 c. 19 s. 10 (1); S.I. 1978/1603.
49	1952 ss. 127 and 283 (2) and (5); 1975 (No. 2) Sch. 3 para. 1 (2).
50	1952 ss. 128 and 283 (2) and (5).
51	1952 ss. 129 and 283 (2) and (5); 1975 (No. 2) Sch. 3 para. 1 (2).
52	1952 ss. 130 and 283 (2) and (5).
53	1952 ss. 131 and 283 (2) and (5); 1963 Sch. 2 para. 2; 1963 (N.I.) s. 19 (3), Sch. 2 para. 2; 1975 c. 21 s. 289C (5); 1977 CLA s. 31 (6).
54	1975 (No. 2) s. 14 (1)–(4); 1952 s. 283 (2) and (5).
55	1975 (No. 2) s. 15 (1)–(5); 1976 Sch. 3 para. 9 (*a*); 1952 s. 283 (2) and (5).
56	1952 ss. 140 and 283 (2) and (5); 1975 (No. 2) Sch. 3 para. 27; 1978 Sch. 12 para. 1 (5).
57	1952 s. 142 (1); 1969 Sch. 7 para. 2; 1975 (No. 2) s. 15 (6), Sch. 3 para. 29 (*a*); S.I. 1978/1603.
58	1952 s. 144 (1); 1975 (No. 2) Sch. 3 para. 31 (*a*); 1978 Sch. 12 para. 1 (3) (*c*); S.I. 1978/1603.
59	1952 ss. 145 (3)–(5) and 283 (2) and (5); 1975 (No. 2) Sch. 3 para. 32.
60	1978 s. 2 (part).
61	1952 ss. 263 (4) (part) and (5), 283 (2) and (5); 1975 (No. 2) Sch. 3 para. 42.
62	1976 s. 2 (1)–(6); 1977 s. 1 (5); 1978 Sch. 12 para. 5; 1952 s. 283 (2) and (5).
63	1978 s. 2 (1) (part).
64	1952 ss. 263 (4) (part) and (5), 283 (2) and (5); 1975 (No. 2) Sch. 3 para. 42; 1976 Sch. 3 para. 5.
65 (1), (2)	1952 s. 146 (1); 1975 (No. 2) s. 15 (6).
(3)	1959 s. 2 (1); 1959 (N.I.) s. 12 (1).
(4)	1952 s. 146 (3); 1967 Sch. 9 para. 2; 1975 (No. 2) Sch. 3 para. 33.
(5)	1952 s. 147 (1).
(6)	1952 s. 146 (4); 1975 (No. 2) s. 15 (6).

Section of Act	Derivation
65 (7)	1952 ss. 146 (5) and 283 (2) and (5).
(8)	1952 s. 146 (6); 1963 c. 31 s. 59 (a); 1975 (No. 2) s. 15 (6).
66	1952 s. 157 (1); 1975 (No. 2) s. 15 (6).
67	1952 ss. 158 and 283 (2) and (5); 1975 (No. 2) s. 15 (6).
68	1952 ss. 159 and 283 (2) and (5).
69	1952 ss. 160 and 283 (2) and (5); 1976 s. 3 (2) and (3).
70	1952 ss. 161 and 283 (2) and (5); 1967 Sch. 6 para. 3; 1978 Sch. 12 para. 1 (3) (d).
71	1952 ss. 162 and 283 (2) and (5); 1967 s. 5 (1), Sch. 6 para. 4; Theatres Act 1968 s. 19 (1), Sch. 2; 1978 Sch. 12 para. 1 (3) (e).
72	1952 ss. 163 and 283 (2) and (5); 1975 c. 21 s. 289C (5); 1977 CLA s. 31 (6).
73	1952 ss. 164 and 283 (2) and (5); 1964 s. 2 (5) (b); 1978 Sch. 12 para. 1 (3) (e).
74	1952 s. 165; 1978 Sch. 12 para. 1 (3) (f).
75	1952 ss. 116 and 283 (2) and (5); 1969 c. 19 s. 10 (1).
76	1952 s. 117; 1967 Sch. 6 para. 1; 1967 (N.I.) s. 15 (6); 1969 c. 19 s. 10 (1); 1975 (No. 2) s. 15 (6).
77	1952 ss. 118 and 283 (2) and (5).
78	1952 ss. 119 and 283 (2) and (5).
79	1952 s. 120.
80	1952 ss. 121 and 283 (2) and (5).
81	1952 ss. 226 and 283 (2) and (5); 1969 c. 19 s. 10 (1).
82	1952 ss. 227 and 283 (2) and (5).
83	1952 s. 228.
84	1952 ss. 167 and 283 (2) and (5); Medical Act 1956 s. 52 (1); 1959 s. 3 (2); 1959 (N.I.) s. 13 (2).
85	1952 s. 168; 1959 s. 3 (3); 1959 (N.I.) s. 13 (3); 1967 s. 4 (2); 1975 (No. 2) Sch. 3 para. 34.
86	1952 s. 237; 1959 s. 3 (3); 1959 (N.I.) s. 13 (3).
87 (1)	1952 ss. 169 (2), 307 (1); 1975 (No. 2) Sch. 3 para. 35.
(2)	1952 s. 169 (2).
(3)	1952 s. 169 (3).
(4)	1959 s. 3 (4); 1959 (N.I.) s. 13 (4); 1967 s. 5 (1), Sch. 6 para. 10.
(5)	1952 s. 169 (4).
(6), (7)	1952 s. 169 (5); 1967 Sch. 6 para. 10.
(8)	1959 s. 3 (4); 1959 (N.I.) s. 13 (4); 1967 Sch. 6 para. 10.
88	1952 ss. 170 and 315 (e); 1975 (No. 2) Sch. 3 para. 36.
89	1952 s. 166.
90	1952 s. 306.
91	1952 s. 306A.
92	—
93	—

Section of Act	Derivation
Sch. 1	1977 s. 1 (3), Sch. 1.
Sch. 2	1977 s. 1 (4), Sch. 2.
Sch. 3	—
Sch. 4	—

Customs and Excise Duties (General Reliefs) Act 1979

This table shows in the right hand column the legislative source from which the sections of the Customs and Excise Duties (General Reliefs) Act 1979 in the left hand column have been derived. In the table the following abbreviations are used:

1952	=	The Customs and Excise Act 1952 (c. 44)
1958 IDA	=	The Import Duties Act 1958 (c. 6)
1960	=	The Finance Act 1960 (and so on as respects subsequent years)
1972 ECA	=	The European Communities Act 1972 (c. 68)
1975 c. 21	=	The Criminal Procedure (Scotland) Act 1975 (c. 21)
1975 (No. 2)	=	The Finance (No. 2) Act 1975 (c. 45)
1977 CLA	=	The Criminal Law Act 1977 (c. 45)

Section of Act	Derivation
1 (1)	1958 IDA ss. 5 (1) and (1A); 1972 ECA ss. 4 and 5 (3), Sch. 4 para. 1 (1); 1978 Sch. 12 para. 25.
(2), (3)	1958 IDA Sch. 3 para. 8; Customs Duties (ECSC) Relief Regulations 1976 (No. 2130).
(4)–(6)	1958 IDA ss. 5 (1) and 15 (1), Sch. 3 paras. 4 and 5.
2	1972 ECA s. 5 (3), (6) and (6A); 1978 s. 6 (8).
3 (1)	1958 IDA ss. 5 (1A) and 6 (1); 1969 s. 54; 1972 ECA ss. 4 and 5 (3), Sch. 4, para. 1 (1), (3); 1978 Sch. 12 para. 25.
(2)	1958 IDA s. 6 (1), Sch. 4 para. 2.
(3), (4)	1958 IDA s. 6 (2), (3); 1969 s. 54; 1972 ECA s. 4, Sch. 4 para. 1 (1).
(5)	1958 IDA s. 6 (4); 1960 s. 10 (1); 1969 s. 54; 1972 ECA s. 4, Sch. 4 para. 1 (1); 1978 Sch. 12 para. 19 (7) (d).
(6), (7)	1958 IDA s. 6 (5), (6); 1969 s. 54 (2) (a); 1972 ECA s. 4, Sch. 4 para. 1 (1).
4 (1), (2)	1958 IDA s. 5 (4); 1972 ECA s. 4, Sch. 4 para. 1 (1), (2).
(3)	1958 IDA s. 5 (8); National Loans Act 1968 (c. 13) s. 1 (8).
5	1952 ss. 37, 306A, 307 (1); 1978 Sch. 12 paras. 9 and 18.
6	1952 s. 309 (1), (3), (4); 1975 (No. 2) Sch. 3 paras. 1 and 10.
7	1952 s. 41; 1975 (No. 2) Sch. 3 para. 1 (1).
8	1952 s. 42.
9	1952 s. 43; 1978 Sch. 12 para. 10.
10	1952 s. 35 (1), (3), (4), (6), (7); National Loans Act 1968 (c. 13) s. 1 (8); Customs and Excise (Relief for Returned Goods) Regulations 1977 (No. 1785).
11	1952 s. 36; National Loans Act 1968 (c. 13) s. 1 (8); S.I. 1977 No. 1785.
12	1952 s. 272; Defence (Transfer of Functions) Act 1964 (c. 15) s. 1; 1978 Sch. 12 para. 15.
13	1968 s. 7; 1972 s. 55 (2), (3); 1975 (No. 2) Sch. 3 para. 1 (1).
14 (1)	1958 IDA ss. 12 (4) and 15 (1).
(2)	1967 s. 2 (1); 1972 ECA s. 5 (3).
(3), (4)	1967 s. 2 (2); Secretary of State for Trade and Industry Order 1970 (No. 1537) Art. 2 (1).

Section of Act	Derivation
15	1958 IDA s. 10 (1); Inward Processing Relief Regulations 1977 (No. 910) reg. 7 (1); 1975 c. 21 ss. 193A and 289B (1), (6); 1977 CLA ss. 28 (2), (7), 32 (1); 1978 Sch. 12 para. 24.
16	1958 IDA s. 4; 1972 ECA ss. 4 and 5 (3), Sch. 4 para. 1 (1).
17 (1)	1952 s. 306; 1958 IDA s. 13 (2); 1968 s. 7 (4); 1972 ECA ss. 2 and 4, Sch. 2 para. 2 (1), Sch. 4 para. 1 (1).
(2)	1952 s. 306; 1972 ECA s. 2 (4), Sch. 2 para. 2 (2).
(3)	1958 IDA s. 13 (3); 1967 s. 2 (3); 1968 s. 7 (5); 1972 ECA s. 5 (3).
(4)	1958 IDA s. 13 (4); 1968 s. 7 (5); 1972 ECA s. 5 (3); 1978 Sch. 12 para. 26.
(5)	1958 IDA s. 13 (4); 1972 ECA s. 4, Sch. 4 para. 1 (5).
(6)	1968 s. 7 (5).
18	1958 IDA s. 15 (1); 1966 s. 10 (1) and (9).
19 (1), (2)	—
(3)	1978 s. 6 (8).
20	—
Sch. 1	1952 ss. 310, 283 (2) and (5); 1975 (No. 2) Sch. 3 para. 1 (1) and 11; 1978 Sch. 12 para. 19 (7) (a), (8).
Sch. 2	
para. 1	—
2	—
3	—
4	—
5	1958 IDA ss. 4 and 13; 1972 ECA ss. 4 and 5 (3), Sch. 4 para. 1 (5); 1978 Sch. 12 para. 26.
6	—

Customs and Excise Management Act 1979

This table shows in the right hand column the legislative source from which the sections of the Customs and Excise Management Act 1979 in the left hand column have been derived. In the table the following abbreviations are used:

1952	= The Customs and Excise Act 1952 (c. 44)
1953	= The Finance Act 1953 (and so on as respects subsequent years)
1962 c. 58	= The Pipe-lines Act 1962 (c. 58)
1971 c. 38	= The Misuse of Drugs Act 1971 (c. 38)
1972 ECA	= The European Communities Act 1972 (c. 68)
1975 c. 21	= The Criminal Procedure (Scotland) Act 1975 (c. 21)
1975 (No. 2)	= The Finance (No. 2) Act 1975 (c. 45)
1977 CLA	= The Criminal Law Act 1977 (c. 45)
S.I. 1978/1602	= The Customs and Excise (Community Transit Goods) Regulations 1978
S.I. 1978/1603	= The Customs and Excise (Warehouses) Regulations 1978

"R" followed by a number refers to the recommendation of the Law Commission and the Scottish Law Commission of that number contained in their Report (Cmnd. 7418) on this Bill.

Note: In this Table the references to provisions of the Criminal Law Act 1977 are references to those provisions as extended to Northern Ireland by paragraph 24 of Schedule 12 to the Finance Act 1978.

Section of Act	Derivation
1 (1)	1952 s. 307 (1); 1966 ss. 10 (9), 11 (2) and (10); Hovercraft Act 1968 c. 59 Sch. para. 4; Northern Ireland Constitution Act 1973 c. 36 Sch. 5 para. 1; Amendment of Units of Measurement (Nautical Mile) Order 1977 (S.I. 1977, No. 1936); 1978 Sch. 12 para. 19 (1); S.I. 1978/1602; S.I. 1978/1603.

Section of Act	Derivation
1 (2)	—
(3)	—
(4)	1964 s. 10 (1).
(5)	1963 s. 7 (1), (2); 1978 Sch. 12 para. 7 (1).
(6)	1952 s. 307 (2).
(7)	1972 ECA s. 5 (4).
2	1966 s. 10 (1), (4) (*a*), (5) and (6).
3	1966 s. 11 (2) (part) and (4).
4	1952 s. 15 (6).
5 (1)–(5), (8)	1952 s. 79; 1978 Sch. 12 para. 19 (5) and (8).
(6), (7)	1966 s. 11 (3).
6	1952 ss. 1 and 3 (1); Minister for the Civil Service Order 1968 (S.I. 1968 No. 1656).
7	1952 s. 2 (2) and (3).
8	1952 s. 4.
9	1972 ECA s. 5 (7).
10	1967 s. 3; Minister of Technology Order 1969 (S.I. 1969 No. 1498).
11	1952 s. 5.
12	1952 ss. 6 and 283 (2) and (5); 1975 c. 21 s. 289C (5); 1977 CLA s. 31 (6).
13	1952 s. 7; 1975 c. 21 ss. 193A and 289B (1); 1977 CLA ss. 28 (2) and 32 (1).
14	1952 s. 8 and 283 (2) and (5).
15	1952 ss. 9 and 283 (2) and (5).
16	1952 s. 10; 1975 c. 21 ss. 193A and 289B (1); 1977 CLA ss. 28 (2) and 32 (1).
17	1952 s. 11.
18	1952 s. 12.
19	1952 s. 13.
20	1952 ss. 14 and 283 (2) and (5).
21	1952 ss. 15 (1) to (5) and 283 (2) and (5); Air Navigation Order 1976 (S.I. 1976 No. 1783); 1978 Sch. 12 para. 19 (2) and (8).
22	1952 s. 16 and 283 (2) and (5); 1978 Sch. 12 para. 19 (8).
23	1952 s. 283 (2) and (5); 1966 s. 10 (3) and (4) (*c*); 1978 Sch. 12 para. 19 (8).
24 (1)	1966 s. 11 (1).
(2)	1966 s. 11 (1) and (10); 1978 Sch. 12 para. 19 (7) (*a*).
(3), (4)	1966 s. 11 (6).
(5), (6)	1966 s. 11 (7); 1975 c. 21 ss. 193A and 289B (1); 1977 CLA ss. 27, 28 (2) and 32 (1); 1952 s. 283 (2) and (5).
(7)	1966 s. 11 (11).
25	1952 ss. 17 and 283 (2) and (5); 1978 Sch. 12 para. 19 (7) (*a*).
26	1952 ss. 18 and 283 (2) and (5); 1978 Sch. 12 para. 19 (8).
27	1952 ss. 19 and 283 (2) and (5); 1975 c. 21 s. 289C (5); 1977 CLA s. 31 (6); 1978 Sch. 12 para. 19 (8).
28	1952 s. 20; 1978 Sch. 12 para. 19 (8).
29	1952 s. 21.

Section of Act	Derivation
30	1952 ss. 22 and 283 (2) and (5); 1975 c. 21 s. 289C (5); 1977 CLA s. 31 (6); 1978 Sch. 12 para. 19 (7) (*a*) and (8).
31	1978 s. 4; 1952 s. 283 (2) and (5).
32	1952 ss. 23 and 283 (2) and (5).
33	1952 ss. 24 and 283 (2) and (5).
34	1952 ss. 25 and 283 (2) and (5); 1978 Sch. 12 para. 19 (7) (*b*) (8).
35	1952 ss. 26 and 283 (2) and (5); 1978 Sch. 12 para. 19 (8).
36	1952 ss. 27 and 283 (2) and (5).
37	1952 s. 28; 1966 s. 11 (2) (part); Customs and Excise (Entry for Inward Processing) Regulations 1977 (S.I. 1977, No. 1091); S.I. 1978/1602.
38	1952 s. 29.
39	1952 s. 30.
40	1952 s. 31.
41	1952 ss. 32 and 283 (2) and (5); 1975 c. 21 s. 289C (5); 1977 CLA s. 31 (6).
42	1952 s. 33; 1978 Sch. 12 para. 19 (8).
43 (1)	1952 s. 34 (1); 1978 Sch. 12 para. 19 (4).
(2)	1952 s. 34 (2); 1975 (No. 2) Sch. 6 para. 1.
(3)	1952 s. 34 (3).
(4)	1970 Sch. 2 para. 5 (2) (*a*).
(5)	1952 s. 34 (4); 1978 Sch. 12 para. 19 (4).
44	1970 Sch. 2 para. 5 (1).
45	1976 s. 15 (1) and (2).
46	1952 s. 38; 1975 (No. 2) Sch. 6 para. 2.
47	1952 s. 39.
48	1952 s. 40.
49	1952 s. 44; 1975 (No. 2) Sch. 3 para. 1 (1).
50	1952 ss. 45 and 283 (2) and (5); 1971 c. 38 s. 26 (1)–(3); 1975 c. 21 ss. 193A and 289B (1); 1977 CLA ss. 27, 28 (2) and 32 (1); 1978 Sch. 12 para. 19 (8).
51	1952 s. 46; 1975 (No. 2) Sch. 3 para. 1 (1); 1978 Sch. 12 para. 19 (2).
52	1952 s. 47 (5); 1971 Sch. 1 para. 1 (7); S.I. 1978/1603.
53 (1)	1952 s. 47 (1); 1978 Sch. 12 para. 19 (8); S.I. 1978/1602.
(2)	1971 Sch. 1 paras. 2 and 15.
(3)	1952 s. 47 (1) proviso; 1971 Sch. 1 para. 13.
(4), (5)	1952 ss. 47 (3) and 283 (2) and (5); 1975 c. 21 ss. 193A and 289B (1) 1977 CLA ss. 27, 28 (2) and 32 (1).
(6)	1971 Sch. 1 para. 11 (3); 1952 s. 283 (2) and (5).
(7)	1971 Sch. 1 para. 11 (5); 1952 s. 283 (2) and (5).
(8)	1952 s. 47 (4).
54 (1)–(5)	1971 Sch. 1 para. 1 (2)–(6).
(6)	1971 Sch. 1 para. 13.
(7)–(10)	1971 Sch. 1 para. 11 (1)–(3) and (5); 1952 s. 283 (2) and (5).
55 (1)	1971 Sch. 1 para. 3.
(2)	1971 Sch. 1 para. 13.
56 (1), (2)	1971 Sch. 1 para. 4.
(3)	1971 Sch. 1 para. 13.
(4)	1952 s. 283 (2) and (5); 1971 Sch. 1 para. 11 (4).

Section of Act	Derivation
57 (1)–(3)	1952 s. 49 (1); 1971 Sch. 1 para. 5 (1) and (4) (*a*); S.I. 1978/1602.
(4)	1971 Sch. 1 para. 5 (2).
(5)	1952 s. 49 (5).
(6)	1966 s. 11 (5); 1971 Sch. 1 para. 5 (5).
(7)	1952 s. 49 (4).
57 (8)	1971 Sch. 1 paras. 5 (3) and 13.
(9), (10)	1952 ss. 49 (2) and (3), 283 (2) and (5); 1971 Sch. 1 para. 5 (4) (*b*) and (*c*).
(11), (12)	1971 Sch. 1 para. 11 (3) and (5); 1952 s. 283 (2) and (5).
58	1970 Sch. 2 para. 5 (3) and (4).
59 (1), (2)	1971 Sch. 1 para. 6.
(3)	1971 Sch. 1 para. 12 (1).
(4)	1971 Sch. 1 para. 14 (2).
(5)	1971 Sch. 1 para. 13.
(6)	1971 Sch. 1 para. 11 (5); 1952 s. 283 (2) and (5).
(7)	1971 Sch. 1 para. 15.
60 (1)	1952 s. 48 (1).
(2)	1966 s. 10 (7) and Sch. 2 para. 1.
(3)	1952 s. 48 (1); 1966 s. 10 (7) (*b*).
(4)	1966 s. 10 (7) (*a*); 1952 s. 283 (2) and (5).
(5)–(7)	1952 ss. 48 (2) and (3) and 283 (2) and (5); 1975 c. 21 s. 289C (5); 1977 CLA s. 31 (6); 1978 Sch. 12 para. 19 (8).
61 (1)–(3)	1952 s. 50 (1) and (2); 1978 Sch. 12 para. 19 (2).
(4)	1966 Sch. 2 para. 1.
(5)–(8)	1952 ss. 50 (3)–(5) and 283 (2) and (5); 1975 c. 21 s. 289C (5); 1977 CLA s. 31 (6); 1978 Sch. 12 para. 19 (8).
62 (1)	1971 Sch. 1 para. 7.
(2)	1971 Sch. 1 paras. 8 and 15.
(3)	1971 Sch. 1 para. 13.
(4)	1971 Sch. 1 para. 11 (5); 1952 s. 283 (2) and (5).
63	1952 ss. 51 and 283 (2) and (5); 1975 c. 21 ss. 193A and 289B (1); 1977 CLA ss. 27, 28 (2) and 32 (1).
64	1952 ss. 52 and 283 (2) and (5); 1975 c. 21 ss. 193A, 289B (1) and 289C (5); 1977 CLA ss. 27, 28 (2), 31 (6) and 32 (1); 1978 Sch. 12 para. 19 (8).
65	1952 ss. 53 and 283 (2) and (5); 1978 Sch. 12 para. 19 (8).
66	1952 ss. 54 and 283 (2) and (5); 1971 Sch. 1 para. 9.
67	1952 ss. 55 and 283 (2) and (5); 1978 Sch. 12 para. 19 (8); S.I. 1978/1603.
68	1952 ss. 56 and 283 (2) and (5); 1971 c. 38 s. 26 (1)–(3); 1975 c. 21 ss. 193A and 289B (1); 1977 CLA ss. 27, 28 (2) and 32 (1).
69	1952 s. 57.
70	1952 ss. 58 and 283 (2) and (5); 1975 c. 21 s. 289C (5); 1977 CLA s. 31 (6).
71	1952 ss. 59 and 283 (2) and (5); 1975 c. 21 s. 289C (5); 1977 CLA s. 31 (6).
72	1952 ss. 60 and 283 (2) and (5); 1975 c. 21 s. 289C (5); 1977 CLA s. 31 (6).
73	1952 ss. 61 and 283 (2) and (5).
74	1952 ss. 62 and 283 (2) and (5).
75	1952 ss. 63 and 283 (2) and (5).
76	1952 ss. 64 and 283 (2) and (5).
77	1952 ss. 65 and 283 (2) and (5).
78 (1)	1968 s. 6 (1); 1972 s. 55 (4).
(2)–(4)	1968 s. 6 (2) and (3); 1952 s. 283 (2) and (5).

Section of Act	Derivation
79 (1)	1952 s. 67; 1968 s. 6 (4).
(2)	1972 ECA Sch. 4 para. 2 (3); 1975 (No. 2) Sch. 3 para. 1 (1).
80	1972 ECA s. 5 (8); 1952 s. 283 (2) and (5).
81	1952 s. 68; 1966 Sch. 2 para. 1; R 1.
82	1952 s. 69.
83	1978 s. 5; 1952 s. 283 (2) and (5).
84	1952 ss. 71 and 283 (2) and (5); 1977 CLA s. 27.
85	1952 ss. 72 and 283 (2) and (5); Criminal Law Act 1967 (c. 58) s. 12 (5) (a); 1975 c. 21 s. 289C (5); 1977 CLA s. 31 (6).
86	1952 s. 73; 1978 Sch. 12 para. 19 (5).
87	1952 ss. 74 and 283 (2) and (5).
88	1952 s. 75.
89	1952 s. 76.
90	1952 s. 77.
91	1952 ss. 78 and 283 (2) and (5); 1975 c. 21 s. 289C (5); 1977 CLA s. 31 (6).
92 (1)–(4)	1952 s. 80 (1); 1975 (No. 2) Sch. 3 para. 1 (1) and Sch. 6 para. 3; 1978 Sch. 12 paras. 11 and 19 (2); S.I. 1978/1603.
(5)–(8)	1952 ss. 80 (2)–(5) and 283 (2) and (5); S.I. 1978/1603.
93	1975 (No. 2) s. 16 (1)–(5), (7) and (8); 1978 s. 3 and Sch. 12 para. 19 (2); S.I. 1978/1603; 1952 s. 283 (2) and (5).
94	1952 ss. 85 (1) and (2) and 283 (2) and (5); 1978 Sch. 12 para. 12; S.I. 1978/1603.
95	1952 s. 85 (3).
96	1966 s. 11 (8); 1952 s. 283 (2) and (5).
97	1952 s. 82 (3); 1966 s. 11 (9).
98	1952 s. 90; S.I. 1978/1603.
99	1952 s. 91.
100	1952 ss. 92 and 283 (2) and (5); 1975 (No. 2) Sch. 6 para. 4; 1975 c. 21 ss. 193A and 289B (1); 1977 CLA ss. 27, 28 (2) and 32 (1).
101	1952 ss. 233 and 283 (2) and (5); 1975 c. 21 s. 289C (5); 1977 CLA s. 31 (6); 1978 Sch. 12 para. 19 (6).
102	1952 ss. 234 and 283 (2) and (5); Recorded Delivery Service Act 1962 (c. 27) s. 1; Betting and Gaming Duties Act 1972 (c. 25) Sch. 2 para. 7, Sch. 4 para. 10.
103	1952 s. 235.
104	1952 s. 236; 1978 Sch. 12 para. 19 (6).
105	1952 s. 238.
106	1952 ss. 239 and 283 (2) and (5).
107	1952 ss. 240 and 283 (2) and (5); 1978 Sch. 12 para. 19 (6).
108	1952 ss. 244 and 283 (2) and (5); Family Law Reform Act 1969 (c. 46) s. 1 (3) Sch. 1 Pt. I; Age of Majority (Scotland) Act 1969 (c. 39) s. 1 (3) Sch. 1 Pt. I; Age of Majority Act (Northern Ireland) 1969 (c. 28) s. 1 (3) Sch. 1 Pt. I; 1978 Sch. 12 para. 19 (3).
109	1952 s. 245; 1978 Sch. 12 para. 19 (3).

Section of Act	Derivation
110	1952 s. 246; 1978 Sch. 12 para. 19 (3).
111	1952 ss. 247 and 283 (2) and (5); 1978 Sch. 12 para. 19 (3).
112 (1)	1952 s. 248 (1); 1978 Sch. 12 paras. 19 (3) and (6).
(2)	1952 s. 248 (1).
(3)	1952 s. 248 (2); 1976 Sch. 3 para. 2.
(4)	1952 s. 248 (2).
(5)	1963 s. 7 (4); 1967 Sch. 6 para. 5; 1978 Sch. 12 para. 7 (1).
(6)	Hydrocarbon Oil (Customs & Excise) Act 1971 (c. 12) s. 22; 1978 Sch. 12 para. 19 (6).
113	1952 s. 249; Hydrocarbon Oil (Customs & Excise) Act 1971 (c. 12) s. 22; 1976 Sch. 3 para. 3; 1978 Sch. 12 para. 19 (6).
114	1952 ss. 250 and 283 (2) and (5); 1975 (No. 2) Sch. 3 para. 1 (2).
115	1952 ss. 251 and 283 (2) and (5); 1978 Sch. 12 para. 19 (6).
116	1952 s. 252; 1978 Sch. 12 para. 19 (6).
117 (1), (2)	1952 s. 253 (1); 1978 Sch. 12 para. 19 (2) and (6).
(3), (4)	1952 s. 253 (2).
(5)	1952 s. 253 (3); 1975 (No. 2) Sch. 3 para. 1 (2); 1978 Sch. 12 para. 19 (6).
(6)	1952 s. 253 (3); 1967 Sch. 9 para. 7; 1976 Sch. 3, para. 4.
(7)	1952 s. 253 (4).
(8)	1952 s. 253 (1); 1975 (No. 2) Sch. 3 para. 1 (2); R 2.
(9)	1952 s. 315 (e).
118	1952 s. 254; Family Law Reform Act 1969 (c. 46) s. 1; Age of Majority (Scotland) Act 1969 (c. 39) s. 1; Age of Majority Act (Northern Ireland) 1969 (c. 28) s. 1.
119	1952 s. 255; 1975 (No. 2) Sch. 3 para. 1 (1).
120	1973 s. 2; 1975 (No. 2) Sch. 3 para. 1 (1)
121	1972 ECA Sch. 4 para. 2 (7); 1975 (No. 2) Sch. 3 para. 1 (1); 1977 s. 8 (3).
122	1977 s. 8 (1) and (2).
123	1952 s. 256; 1975 (No. 2) Sch. 3 para. 1 (1).
124	1952 s. 257; 1977 s. 9; 1978 Sch. 12 para. 23.
125 (1), (2)	1972 ECA Sch. 4 para. 2 (8).
(3), (4)	1952 ss. 258 (3) and (4), 283 (2) and (5).
126 (1), (2)	1952 s. 259 (1); 1978 Sch. 12 para. 13.
(3)	1957 s. 5; 1978 Sch. 12 para. 13 (a).
(4)	1952 s. 259 (1); 1975 (No. 2) Sch. 3 para. 1 (1).
(5)	1952 s. 259 (3).
127	1952 s. 260; 1975 (No. 2) Sch. 3 para. 1 (1); R 3.
128	1952 s. 261; 1978 Sch. 12 para. 19 (2).
129	1952 ss. 262 and 283 (2) and (5); 1975 c. 21 ss. 193A and 289B (1); 1977 CLA ss. 27, 28 (1) and 32 (1).
130	1952 s. 263 (1) and (2); 1978 Sch. 12 para. 14.
131	1952 s. 264.
132	1952 s. 266.
133	1952 ss. 267 and 283 (2) and (5).
134	1952 s. 268.
135	1952 s. 270.

Section of Act	Derivation
136	1952 ss. 271 and 283 (2) and (5).
137	1952 s. 273; 1970 s. 7 (5); 1978 Sch. 12 para. 19 (2).
138	1952 s. 274; 1978 Sch. 12 para. 19 (2).
139	1952 ss. 275 and 283 (2) and (5); 1975 c. 21 s. 289C (5); 1977 CLA s. 31 (6); 1978 Sch. 12 para. 19 (2).
140	1952 s. 276; 1978 Sch. 12 para. 19 (6).
141	1952 ss. 277 and 283 (2) and (5); 1966 Sch. 2 para. 1; 1978 Sch. 12 para. 19 (2).
142	1952 s. 278; 1966 Sch. 2 para. 1.
143	1952 s. 279; 1966 Sch. 2 para. 1; 1978 Sch. 12 para. 19 (2).
144	1952 s. 280; 1978 Sch. 12 para. 19 (2).
145	1952 s. 281; 1978 Sch. 12 para. 19 (2).
146	1952 s. 282; 1978 Sch. 12 para. 19 (2).
147	1952 s. 283 (1) and (3)–(5); County Courts Act (Northern Ireland) 1959 (c. 25) s. 152 (3) (*a*); Courts Act 1971 (c. 23) Sch. 9; 1978 Sch. 12 para. 19 (2).
148	1952 s. 284; 1978 Sch. 12 para. 19 (2).
149 (1)	1952 s. 285 (2); 1978 Sch. 12 paras. 16 and 19 (2).
(2)	1952 s. 285 (1); Criminal Justice Act 1967 (c. 80) s. 93 (4); 1978 Sch. 12 para. 19 (2).
(3)	1952 s. 285 (3); 1978 Sch. 12 para. 19 (2).
150	1952 s. 286; 1978 Sch. 12 para. 19 (2).
151	1952 s. 287; 1978 Sch. 12 para. 17.
152	1952 s. 288; 1978 Sch. 12 para. 19 (2).
153	1952 s. 289.
154	1952 s. 290; 1978 Sch. 12 para. 19 (2).
155	1952 s. 291.
156 (1)	—
(2)	1953 s. 33 (1).
(3)	1952 s. 283 (2).
(4)	1952 s. 283 (5).
157	1952 s. 292; Family Law Reform Act 1969 (c. 46) s. 1; Age of Majority (Scotland) Act 1969 (c. 39) s. 1; Age of Majority Act (Northern Ireland) 1969 (c. 28) s. 1; 1978 Sch. 12 para. 19 (2).
158	1952 ss. 293 and 283 (2) and (5); 1978 Sch. 12 para. 19 (6).
159	1952 ss. 294 and 283 (2) and (5); 1975 c. 21 s. 193A and 289B (1); 1977 CLA ss. 27, 28 (2) and 32 (1); 1978 Sch. 12 para. 19 (7) (*c*).
160	1952 s. 295; 1976 Sch. 3 para. 6; 1978 Sch. 12 para. 19 (6).
161	1952 s. 296; 1978 Sch. 12 para. 19 (2).
162	1962 c. 58 ss. 56 (1) and 70 (2).
163	1952 ss. 297 and 283 (2) and (5); 1978 Sch. 12 para. 19 (2).
164	1952 s. 298; 1966 s. 10 (4) (*b*); 1978 Sch. 12 para. 19 (8).
165	1952 s. 299.
166	1952 s. 300.
167	1952 ss. 301 and 283 (2) and (5); 1975 c. 21 s. 193A and 289B (1); 1977 CLA ss. 27, 28 (2) and 32 (1).

Section of Act	Derivation
168	1952 ss. 302 and 283 (2) and (5); 1975 c. 21 s. 193A and 289B (1); 1977 CLA ss. 27, 28 (2) and 32 (1).
169	1952 ss. 303 and 283 (2) and (5); 1978 Sch. 12 para. 19 (2).
170	1952 ss. 304 and 283 (2) and (5); 1971 c. 38 s. 26 (1)–(3); 1975 c. 21 ss. 193A and 289B (1); 1977 CLA ss. 27, 28 (2) and 32 (1).
171 (1), (3)–(5)	1952 s. 305; 1978 Sch. 12 para. 19 (2).
(2)	1975 c. 21 s. 289B (6); 1977 CLA s. 28 (7); 1978 Sch. 12 para. 19 (2).
172	1952 s. 306; 1973 s. 2 (4).
173	1978 Sch. 12 para. 18.
174	1952 s. 309 (1), (2) and (5); Copyright Act 1956 (c. 74) Sch. 7 para. 44 (a); 1978 Sch. 12 para. 19 (2).
175 (1)	1952 s. 315 (a), (b), (f) and (g).
(2)	1952 s. 2 (1).
176 (1)–(3), (6)	1952 s. 313.
(4), (5), (6)	1961 s. 11; 1978 Sch. 12 para. 19 (2).
177	—
178	—
Sch. 1	1952 s. 283 (5) proviso; 1971 c. 38 s. 26 (1)–(3); 1975 c. 21 s. 289B (1); 1977 CLA ss. 27 and 28 (2) and Sch. 5 para. 1 (1) (a), (2) (c) and (3); 1978 Sch. 12 para. 24.
Sch. 2	1957 Sch. 2; 1978 Sch. 12 para. 13 (b).
Sch. 3	1952 Sch. 7; County Courts Act (Northern Ireland) 1959 (c. 25) s. 152 (3) (a); Courts Act 1971 (c. 23) Sch. 9.
Sch. 4	
para. 1	1952 s. 318 (1) and Sch. 10 Pt. I.
2	—
3	1975 (No. 2) Sch. 3 para. 1 (1).
4	1975 (No. 2) Sch. 3 para. 1 (1).
5	1975 (No. 2) Sch. 3 para. 1 (2).
6	1975 (No. 2) Sch. 3 para. 1 (1).
7	1975 (No. 2) Sch. 3 para. 1 (1).
8	—
9	1977 Sch. 6 para. 21.
10	—
11	1975 (No. 2) Sch. 3 para. 23.
12	1952 Sch. 10 Pt. II; 1975 s. 4; 1975 (No. 2) Sch. 3 para. 1; 1978 Sch. 12 paras. 19 (2), (6) and (8), 21 and 22; R 4.
Sch. 5	—
Sch. 6	—
Sch. 7	
para. 1	1972 ECA Sch. 4 para. 2 (8).
2	—
3	1952 s. 308 (3).
4	1975 (No. 2) Sch. 3 para. 1 (1).
5	1972 ECA s. 5 (4).
6	1975 (No. 2) Sch. 14 Pt. I para. 2.
7	1975 (No. 2) s. 8 (4).
8	1975 (No. 2) Sch. 3 para. 1 (1).
9	1978 Sch. 12 para. 19 (2), (6) and (8).
10	—
11	—
12	

Excise Duties (Surcharges or Rebates) Act 1979

This table shows in the right hand column the legislative source from which the sections of the Excise Duties (Surcharges or Rebates) Act 1979 in the left hand column have been derived. In the table the following abbreviations are used:

1961	=	The Finance Act 1961 (c. 36)
1964	=	The Finance Act 1964 (c. 49)
1968	=	The Finance Act 1968 (c. 44)
1971 (HO)	=	The Hydrocarbon Oil (Customs & Excise) Act 1971 (c. 12)
1971	=	The Finance Act 1971 (c. 68)
1972 ECA	=	The European Communities Act 1972 (c. 68)
1973 (NI)	=	The Northern Ireland Constitution Act 1973 (c. 36)
1975 (No. 2)	=	The Finance (No. 2) Act 1975 (c. 45)
1976	=	The Finance Act 1976 (c. 40)
1977	=	The Finance Act 1977 (c. 36)
1978	=	The Finance Act 1978 (c. 42)

Section of Act	Derivation
(1 1)	1961 s. 9 (3) (9); 1964 s. 8 (2); 1968 s. 10 (2); 1971 s. 3 (5); 1972 ECA s. 5 (3); 1973 (NI) s. 40 (2); 1975 (No. 2) ss. 8 (4), 14 (5), 15 (6), Sch. 3 para. 1; 1976 ss. 2 (7), 6 (6), Sch. 3 paras. 8 and 9; 1977 s. 10 (4); 1978 s. 6 (4).
(2)	1961 s. 9 (1), (2), (4) (*c*); 1964 s. 8 (3) (4).
(3)	1961 s. 9 (2), Sch. 4 para. 2.
(4)	1961 s. 9 (2).
(5)	1961 s. 9 (4) (*c*), (5).
(6)	1961 Sch. 4 para. 4.
(7)	1961 Sch. 4 para. 7; 1971 (HO) Sch. 6 para. 2.
2 (1)	—
(2)	1978 s. 10.
(3)	1964 s. 8 (3) (5).
(4)	1964 s. 8 (5).
(5)	1961 Sch. 3 para. 3; 1964 s. 8 (5).
(6)	1961 Sch. 3 para. 2 (1).
(7)	1961 Sch. 3 para. 2 (2).
(8), (9)	1964 s. 8 (6).
3 (1)	1961 s. 9 (7).
(2)	1961 s. 9 (8).
(3)	1961 s. 9 (10).
4 (1)	1961 s. 37 (3); 1964 s. 26 (3).
(2)–(4)	—
5	—
Sch. 1	—
Sch. 2	—

Hydrocarbon Oil Duties Act 1979

This table shows in the right hand column the legislative source from which the sections of the Hydrocarbon Oil Duties Act 1979 in the left hand column have been derived. In the table the following abbreviations are used:

1952	=	The Customs and Excise Act 1952 (c. 44)
1971	=	The Hydrocarbon Oil (Customs & Excise) Act 1971 (c. 12)
1971 c. 68	=	The Finance Act 1971 (c. 68)
S.I. 1972/567	=	The Excise Duties (Gas as Road Fuel) Order 1972 (S.I. 1972 No. 567)
1975 c. 21	=	The Criminal Procedure (Scotland) Act 1975 (c. 21)
1975 (No. 2)	=	The Finance (No. 2) Act 1975 (c. 45)
1976	=	The Finance Act 1976 (c. 40)
1977	=	The Finance Act 1977 (c. 36)
1977 CLA	=	The Criminal Law Act 1977 (c. 45)
S.I. 1977/1866	=	The Amendment of Units of Measurement (Hydrocarbon Oil, etc.) Order 1977 (S.I. 1977 No. 1866)
1978	=	The Finance Act 1978 (c. 42)

S.I. 1978/1603 = The Customs and Excise (Warehouses) Regulations 1978 (S.I. 1978 No. 1603)

Note: In this Table the references to provisions of the Criminal Law Act 1977 are references to those provisions as extended to Northern Ireland by paragraph 24 of Schedule 12 to the Finance Act 1978.

Section of Act	Derivation
1	1971 s. 1; S.I. 1977/1866 Art. 2 (*a*); 1978 Sch. 12 para. 8.
2	1971 s. 2; S.I. 1977/1866 Art. 2 (*b*); 1978 Sch. 12 para. 8.
3	1971 s. 5.
4	1971 s. 3; S.I. 1977/1866 Art. 2 (*c*); 1978 Sch. 12 para. 8.
5	1971 c. 68 s. 3 (8); S.I. 1977/1866 Art. 3.
6 (1)	1975 (No. 2) s. 11; 1976 s. 9; 1977 s. 4 (1) (*a*); S.I. 1977/1866 Art. 4.
(2)	1971 s. 4 (2); 1975 (No. 2) Sch. 3 para. 16.
7	1971 s. 6; 1975 (No. 2) Sch. 3 para. 17; 1977 s. 4 (1) (*b*).
8	1971 c. 68 s. 3 (1)–(4), (8), (9) (*a*), (10) and (11); S.I. 1972/567; 1977 s. 4 (1) (*b*).
9 (1)–(4)	1971 s. 7 (1)–(3), (5).
(5)	1971 ss. 7 (4), 21 (1), Sch. 4 para. 1.
10	1971 s. 8; 1975 c. 21 ss. 193A and 289 B (1); 1975 (No. 2) Sch. 3 para. 18; 1977 CLA ss. 27, 28 (2) and 32 (1); 1952 s. 283 (2) and (5).
11	1971 s. 9; 1977 s. 4 (2) and (3), S.I. 1977/1866 Art. 2 (*d*).
12	1971 s. 10.
13	1971 s. 11; 1975 c. 21 ss. 193A and 289B (1); 1977 CLA ss. 27, 28 (2) and 32 (1); 1952 s. 283 (2) and (5).
14 (1)	1971 ss. 12 (1), 21 (1), Sch. 4 para. 1; 1977 s. 4 (4), S.I. 1977/1866 Art. 2 (*e*).
(2)–(10)	1971 s. 12 (2)–(8); 1975 c. 21 ss. 193A and 289B (1); 1977 CLA ss. 27, 28 (2) and 32 (1); 1952 s. 283 (2) and (5).
15	1971 s. 13; S.I. 1978/1603.
16	1971 s. 14; S.I. 1978/1603.
17	1971 s. 15; 1975 (No. 2) Sch. 3 para. 19.
18	1971 s. 16; 1975 (No. 2) Sch. 3 para. 20; 1952 s. 283 (2) and (5).
19	1971 s. 17; 1975 (No. 2) Sch. 3 para. 21.
20	1971 s. 18.
21	1971 ss. 19 and 20 (1) and (2) (*a*); 1971 c. 68 s. 3 (6) and (7) (*a*); 1952 s. 283 (2) and (5).
22	1971 s. 20 (2) (*b*) and (3); S.I. 1977/1866 Art. 2 (*f*); 1952 s. 283 (2) and (5).
23	1971 c. 68 s. 3 (7) (*b*), (8) and (9) (*b*); 1952 s. 283 (2) and (5).
24	1971 s. 21; 1978 Sch. 12 para. 8; 1952 s. 283 (2) and (5).
25	1952 s. 306.
26	1978 Sch. 12 para. 18.
27 (1)	1971 ss. 10 (2) and 23; 1971 c. 68 s. 3 (8).
(2)	1971 s. 23 (1).
28	—
29	—

Section of Act	Derivation
Schedules:	
1	1971 Sch. 1; 1976 s. 10.
2	1971 Sch. 2.
3	1971 Sch. 3; 1971 c. 68 s. 3 (6) and (8); 1975 (No. 2) Sch. 3 para. 22.
4	1971 Sch. 4.
5	1971 Sch. 5; 1978 Sch. 12 para. 8.
6	1971 Sch. 6 para. 3; 1977 s. 4 (1) (b) and (c).
7	—

Matches and Mechanical Lighters Duties Act 1979

This table shows in the right hand column the legislative source from which the sections of the Matches and Mechanical Lighters Duties Act 1979 in the left hand column have been derived. In the table the following abbreviations are used:

1952	= The Customs and Excise Act 1952 (c. 44)
1953	= The Finance Act 1953 (c. 34)
1960	= The Finance Act 1960 (c. 44)
1963	= The Finance Act 1963 (c. 25)
1975 (No. 2)	= The Finance (No. 2) Act 1975 (c. 45)
1978	= The Finance Act 1978 (c. 42)

Section of Act	Derivation
1 (1)	1975 (No. 2) s. 12.
(2)	1952 s. 220 (3); 1978 Sch. 12 para. 6 (1).
2	1952 ss. 219 and 283 (2) (5).
3 (1), (2)	1952 s. 220 (1); 1963 s. 4 (2); 1975 (No. 2) Sch. 3 para. 1 (2); 1978 Sch. 12 para. 6 (1).
(3)	1952 ss. 220 (2) and 283 (2) and (5).
(4)	1952 s. 306.
4 (1)	1952 s. 221 (4); 1960 s. 7 (1); 1978 Sch. 12 para. 6 (2) (a).
(2)	1952 s. 222 (1); 1975 (No. 2) Sch. 3 para. 8.
5 (1)	1953 s. 3 (3); 1975 (No. 2) Sch. 3 para. 12.
(2) to (5)	1952 s. 222 (2) and (5) to (7).
6 (1) to (3)	1975 (No. 2) s. 13.
(4)	1952 s. 221 (2); 1978 Sch. 12 para. 6 (2) (a).
(5)	1952 ss. 221 (3) (b) and 283 (2) and (5).
7 (1)	1952 s. 221 (1); 1960 s. 7 (4); 1975 (No. 2) Sch. 3 para. 38; 1978 Sch. 12 para. 6 (2) (a).
(2), (3)	1960 s. 7 (3).
(4)	1952 ss. 221 (3) (c) and 283 (2) and (5).
(5)	1952 s. 306.
8	—
9	—
10	—
Schedule	—

Tobacco Products Duty Act 1979

This table shows in the right hand column the legislative source from which the sections of the Tobacco Products Duty Act 1979 in the left hand column have been derived. In the table the following abbreviations are used:

1952 = The Customs and Excise Act 1952 (c. 44)
1976 = The Finance Act 1976 (c. 40)
1977 = The Finance Act 1977 (c. 36)
1978 = The Finance Act 1978 (c. 42)

Section of Act	Derivation
1 (1)	1976 s. 4 (6).
(2)	1976 s. 4 (5).
(3)–(5)	1977 s. 2 (4)–(7).
(6)	1976 s. 4 (6); 1977 s. 2 (4).
2 (1)	1976 s. 4 (1).
(2)	1976 s. 4 (2).
3	1978 s. 1 (1) and (2).
4	1977 s. 2 (2) (part); 1978 s. 1 (3) (part).
5	1976 s. 5.
6 (1)–(4)	1976 s. 6 (1)–(5); 1978 Sch. 12 para. 7 (2).
(5)	1977 s. 2 (2) (part); 1978 s. 1 (3) (part).
7 (1)	1976 s. 4 (3); 1977 s. 3 (5).
(2)	1976 s. 4 (4); 1952 s. 283 (2) and (5).
8	1976 s. 7.
9	1952 s. 306.
10	—
11	—
12	—
Sch. 1	1977 s. 3 (1).
Sch. 2	—

DAMAGES AND COMPENSATION

Halsbury's Laws of England (4th edn.), Vol. 12, paras. 1101–1213

782　　Articles

Compensation Orders and Civil Liability, P. S. Atiyah (on whether, under s. 35 of the Powers of Criminal Courts Act 1973, a court is empowered to order the payment of compensation where no civil liability exists): [1979] Crim LR 504.

Damages for Lost Years, Alec Samuels (whether damages are recoverable in respect of shortening of victim's life expectancy): 129 NLJ 8.

Damages for "Lost Years" and Judicial Reform, A. M. Tettenborn (*Pickett v British Rail Engineering* [1979] 1 All ER 774, HL, 1978 Halsbury's Abridgment para. 861: why the change in law it effected was misconceived, and why the House of Lords was not the agency to make it): 123 Sol Jo 591.

Foreign Exchange Losses—The Passing of Risk?, Alex Maitland Hudson (with particular reference to *Miliangos v George Frank (Textiles) Ltd* [1976] 3 All ER 599, 1976 Halsbury's Abridgment para. 770): [1979] LCMLQ 288.

Inflation and the Duty to Mitigate, David Fieldman and D. F. Libling (whether the plaintiff's duty to mitigate extends to inflationary increases in damages): [1979] 95 LQR 270.

Personal Injuries: Interim Payment and Assessment of Damages, Emlyn Williams (procedure to be adopted in order to secure an interlocutory judgment and interim payment order for damages): 129 NLJ 626.

Personal Injury Damages—A Review of the Last Twelve Months, C. Harmer: Law Notes Vol. 98, No. 6, p. 165.

"Responsibility" Under the Civil Liability (Contribution) Act 1978, Tom Hervey (discussion of the ambiguities which have arisen out of the older legislation and the complications posed by the present Act): 129 NLJ 509.

State Benefits in Actions for Personal Injury, Howard E. Roberts (examination of the rules which may be applied when statutory benefits are to be deducted from an award for damages): 129 NLJ 875.

783　　Breach of contract—failure to return shares held on loan—whether damages appropriate remedy—mitigation

Canada

Shares in company A were lent to its president by company B in 1958 under an agreement which required their return no later than the end of the following year. The date for return was later extended to 31st December 1960. In that year B brought an action against the president for specific performance and A brought an action against B for rescission of the agreement due to failure of consideration. In 1966 B brought a third action repeating the claims of the first, which had been commenced too early. The court dismissed the first two actions but awarded B damages for breach of contract. On the question whether damages were the appropriate remedy *held*, as the value of A's shares was easily ascertainable because they were listed on the public exchanges damages were appropriate, but B should have mitigated its loss by buying back the shares in 1967 and therefore the award would be reduced.

ASAMERA OIL CORPN LTD v SEA OIL AND GENERAL CORPN; BAUD CORPN NV v BROOK [1978] 6 WWR 310 (Supreme Court of Canada).

784　　—— whether damages for loss of reputation may be joined with claim of damages for wrongful dismissal

See *McMinn v Town of Oakville*, para. 1049.

785　　Exemplary damages—award of unspecified sum—need to quantify award

See *Attorney-General of St Christopher, Nevis and Anguilla v Reynolds*, para. 324.

786   —— **insufficient notice to terminate tenancy—harassment of tenant by landlord**

See *Tefft v Kooiman*, para. 1697.

787   —— **provocation by plaintiff**

A man was arrested, with others, for being drunk and disorderly. He was put in a cell and thereupon continued to shout and kick the door from 2.30 am until 6.00 am. He obstructed the door and sustained minor injuries, including a cut lip and bruising of the right cheek, when a police sergeant attempted to open the door. Further minor injuries were caused during an attempt to remove his shoes and jacket to prevent him injuring himself. The man brought an action for damages for assault against the police sergeant and the chief officer of police. The judge found that the sergeant had struck one or possibly two blows not justified by the attempts to restrain the man. He also found that the sergeant had been severely provoked by the man. He awarded damages of £125, but no aggravated or exemplary damages. The man appealed, claiming that no police officer was entitled to plead provocation, as the law deemed the police unprovokable. *Held*, dismissing the appeal, the plaintiff's proposition that exemplary damages had to be awarded where a police officer had allowed himself to be provoked was unacceptable. In deciding whether exemplary or aggravated damages were to be awarded, all the circumstances had to be taken into account, including the behaviour of the plaintiff and whether the defendant had been provoked. In this case no exemplary or aggravated damages should be awarded.

O'Connor v Hewitson [1979] Crim LR 46 (Court of Appeal: Megaw and Cumming-Bruce LJJ and Sir Basil Nield).

788   **Industrial disease—pneumoconiosis—compensation**

See Pneumoconiosis (Workers' Compensation) Act 1979, para. 2650.

789   **Measure of damages—breach of contract—contract for sale of goods—liability of seller—date of default**

See *Bunge Corporation v Usines de Stordeur SA*, para. 507.

790   —— —— **contract for sale of land—right of vendor to interest on purchase price**

See *Talley v Wolsey-Neech*, para. 2352.

791   —— —— —— **rule in Bain v Fothergill**

Canada

The vendors agreed to sell certain property to the purchasers, mistakenly believing themselves to be no longer bound by an earlier contract to sell the property to a third party. The third party obtained a decree of specific performance of the earlier contract. The purchasers then brought an action claiming damages for breach of contract. The damages awarded were limited to the purchasers' costs, under the rule in *Bain v Fothergill*; the purchasers could not recover damages for the loss of their bargain as the vendors had acted in good faith, and the rule applied even where the vendors had acted carelessly or recklessly. On appeal, *held*, the rule in *Bain v Fothergill* did not apply where a vendor, having title, had either voluntarily disabled himself from being able to convey or had risked and lost his ability to do so by what were in effect concurrent dealings with two different purchasers. Accordingly, the appeal would be allowed and full damages would be awarded.

AVG Management Science Ltd v Barwell Developments Ltd (1979) 92 DLR (3d) 289 (Supreme Court of Canada). *Bain v Fothergill* (1874) LR 7 HL 158, not applied.

792   —— —— solicitor—failure to give sound advice to vendor of house

See *Inder Lynch Devoy and Co v Subritzky*, para. 2691.

793   —— damage to property—date of assessment

The plaintiffs' garage premises were damaged during the construction of an adjoining multi-storey car park by the defendants in 1968. In an action for damages, the plaintiffs contended that the damages, which were the costs of the repairs, should be assessed as at the date of the hearing in 1978. The judge, however, assessed the damages as at the date on which it was reasonable for the plaintiffs to have begun repairs, 1970. The plaintiffs appealed. *Held*, the general rule was that damages fell to be assessed as at the date when the cause of action arose, but that rule was subject to exceptions. The instant case was such an exception as on the facts the cause of action arose at least two years before the time when the plaintiffs, acting with all reasonable speed, could first have been able to begin the repairs. The true rule was that where there was a material difference between the cost of repair when the repairs could first be reasonably undertaken, the cost of repairs at that time should be taken in assessing the damages. The question of when it was reasonable to do repairs had to be looked at from the point of view of both parties and a balance struck. Further, there was a prima facie presumption that, in a case where the plaintiff had not effected reinstatement by the time of the hearing, the costs then prevailing should be adopted in ascertaining the cost of reinstatement. That presumption could be rebutted if it appeared on the evidence that the plaintiff, acting reasonably, should have undertaken the reinstatement at an earlier date. In the instant case, the plaintiffs were financially able to carry out reinstatement in 1970, but they were commercially prudent in waiting until after the hearing, particularly as the defendants were denying liability and there was a dispute as to what works could and should be done by way of reinstatement. The damages should accordingly be assessed by reference to the cost of repairs in 1978. The appeal would be allowed.

DODD PROPERTIES (KENT) LTD V CANTERBURY CITY COUNCIL [1980] 1 All ER 928 (Court of Appeal: MEGAW, BROWNE and DONALDSON LJJ). Decision of Cantley J [1979] 2 All ER 118, 1978 Halsbury's Abridgment para. 850 reversed.

794   —— death—damages for loss of son's services to family company

Canada

The deceased, aged twenty-four, was killed in a car accident for which the defendants admitted liability. The deceased had been employed for his whole working life by a private company owned by his parents. In an action by his father for damages, the defendants contended that he had not shown that he had suffered a loss as the result of his son's death, because the company, which may have suffered a real loss, was a separate legal entity. *Held*, in the case of family companies it could be concluded on the evidence that the shareholders had suffered a direct and personal loss. Judgment would be given for the plaintiff, the damages to be divided equally between the plaintiff and his wife.

MENSINK V DUECK [1979] 3 WWR 263 (Supreme Court of British Columbia). *Ashcroft v Curtin* [1971] 3 All ER 1208, CA, *Lea v Sheard* [1955] 3 All ER 777, CA applied.

795   —— irrevocable letter of credit—bank's delay in paying under the credit

See *Ozalid Group (Export) Ltd v African Continental Bank Ltd*, para. 197.

796   —— loss of parents—criteria for assessment—whether income from estate to be deducted from award

Canada

Total damages of $35,000 were divided between three children after the death of their parents in an accident. The award was calculated on the bases of lost parental guidance and the probable value of the estate which would have come to them under normal circumstances. Any parental earnings from which the children would ordinarily have benefited were balanced against the annual income from the estates and were found to be exceeded by it, and therefore the former were excluded from the assessment. On appeal against the size of the award, *held*, the correct method for assessing the damages payable was to calculate a capital sum giving the children the equivalent of what would have been spent on them had the parents lived, then to deduct a sum for the benefit accruing from the children's early inheritance of their estates, and thirdly to add a sum representing the extra savings the parents might have accumulated in their lifetime. $70,000 would be a reasonable figure under the first head; the deduction in the second would be offset by the gain under the third head. A further sum to compensate for loss of parental guidance should be added, and thus a total award of $90,000 would adequately reflect their loss.

    CLEMENT V LESLIES STORAGE LTD [1979] 2 WWR 577 (Court of Appeal of Manitoba).

797   —— trespass to land

See *Swordheath Properties Ltd v Tabet*, para. 900.

798   Mitigation—contract for sale of goods—failure to mitigate loss by buyers' representatives

See *Toepfer v Warinco AG*, para. 2332.

799   —— loan of shares—appropriate time to claim return

See *Asamera Oil Corpn Ltd v Sea Oil & General Corpn; Baud Corpn v Brook*, para. 783.

800   Personal injury—deduction in respect of unemployment benefit

A workman was injured in the course of his employment. The employers were found to have been negligent and damages were awarded for personal injury. In calculating damages for loss of earnings, the trial judge took into account the amount of unemployment benefit received by the workman under the Social Security Act 1975 and reduced the amount awarded accordingly. The workman appealed against the decision. *Held*, damages were compensation for net loss. If a victim was in receipt of a benefit, which he would not have received had the injury not occurred, that benefit would reduce his loss. It was argued that unemployment benefit was produced partly by the employee's contributions and hence was similar to insurance and not an alternative to or a continuation of wages. Although the proceeds of insurance were generally disregarded at common law, the insurance element in unemployment benefit was essentially notional and the benefit was in reality a substitute for wages. Accordingly, the appeal would be dismissed.

    NABI V BRITISH LEYLAND (UK) LTD [1980] 1 All ER 667 (Court of Appeal: MEGAW, BROWNE and BRIGHTMAN LJJ). *Parsons v BNM Laboratories Ltd* [1963] 2 All ER 658, CA applied.

801   Personal injury or death—calculation of award—loss of future earnings—interest

Australia

The plaintiff was injured in a motor accident for which the defendant admitted liability. In an action for damages, the plaintiff's award included a sum for future effects of loss of earning capacity. The court also awarded her a lump sum in lieu of interest on the whole amount. The defendant appealed against the award of damages and the plaintiff cross-appealed against the assessment of interest. On the cross-appeal, it was ordered that interest should be paid on the damages awarded for future loss of earning capacity. The defendant appealed. *Held*, in claims for personal injury, interest should not be awarded on damages for any loss to be suffered by the plaintiff after the date of judgment. The plaintiff was not, therefore, entitled to interest on that part of the damages awarded for future effects of loss of earning capacity. The appeal would be allowed.

THOMPSON V FARAONIO [1979] 1 WLR 1157 (Privy Council: LORD DIPLOCK, LORD MORRIS OF BORTH-Y-GEST, LORD HAILSHAM OF ST MARYLEBONE, LORD EDMUND-DAVIES and LORD FRASER OF TULLEYBELTON). *Cookson v Knowles* [1978] 2 All ER 604, HL, 1978 Halsbury's Abridgment para. 863 applied.

802   —— injury to worker—statutory increase in lump sum compensation payable—whether personal representative of deceased worker entitled to payment at higher rate

Australia

A worker, who was entitled to a lump sum payment of compensation for the loss of an eye, died before an award was made. The lump sum was paid to the executrix who appealed against the assessment on the ground that the award ought to have been calculated at the higher rate, as increased by supervening legislation between the date of the injury and the date of the hearing. *Held*, by reference to general law, if a worker died before the statutory amendment was made and before a claim for compensation was heard, his personal representative was entitled to be paid compensation at the higher rate, for the benefit of the worker's estate.

SCHLENERT V H. G. WATSON CONTRACTING CO PTY LTD [1979] 1 NSWLR 140 (Supreme Court of New South Wales).

803   —— interest on damages—exemption from income tax

See para. 1517.

804   —— non-pecuniary loss—effect of inflation

An appeal was brought against an award of damages in respect of pain, suffering and loss of amenity, on the basis that it was too high in comparison with such awards made in similar cases. The defence contended that although occasionally amounts should be increased to take account of the fall in the value of the pound, the courts should not attempt to keep pace with inflation by a continual adjustment in awards. It was in the interests of public policy to restrict such awards in order to help contain inflation. *Held*, although higher than previous awards, the award was appropriate. Damages for non-pecuniary loss should be assessed in the light of inflation, although the application of a rigid multiplier to accord arithmetically with the changing value of money was not desirable. It was certainly not public policy that a plaintiff should suffer a reduction in damages in order to contain inflation. The appeal would be dismissed.

WALKER V JOHN MCLEAN AND SONS LTD [1979] 2 All ER 965 (Court of Appeal: ORR, BRIDGE AND CUMMING-BRUCE LJJ).

805   —— plaintiff unconscious or insensible—whether award should include sum for loss of future earnings

In 1973 a psychiatrist aged thirty-six underwent a minor operation. As a result of the hospital's negligence she suffered brain damage which left her only intermittently, and then barely, sentient and totally dependent on others. She had been a senior psychiatric registrar with good career prospects. Her expectation of life was not substantially reduced. She was awarded damages against the area health authority for, inter alia, pain, suffering and loss of amenities, cost of care and loss of earnings. The defendants' appeal against the quantum of the award was dismissed by a majority of the Court of Appeal. They appealed further, contending inter alia that there should have been no award for loss of future earnings and that in calculating future loss no account should be taken of prospective inflation. *Held*, the defendants' contention that no award should be made for loss of future earnings since in catastrophic cases it did not reflect a real loss was contrary to an established line of authority. Their other contention on this point was that an award of damages for loss of future earnings duplicated the sum awarded for cost of care. There was a risk of duplication in such circumstances and hence certain deductions should be made so that the plaintiff would recover in respect of her future loss a capital sum which would represent her loss of earnings, net after allowing for working expenses, and her cost of care, net after deducting the domestic element or living expenses. A capital sum so assessed would compensate for a genuine loss and for a genuine item of additional expenditure arising from the injury, without any element of duplication.

As to the effect of future inflation, it was settled law that only in exceptional cases, where justice could be shown to require it, would the risk of future inflation be brought into account in the assessment of damages for future loss. Thus damages should first be assessed without regard to the risk of future inflation. Some increase would be permissible only if the assessment would not result in a fair compensation in that particular case. No allowance should have been made for inflation in this case; however, on the facts, the award was correct. The appeal would be dismissed and the award upheld subject to minor variations.

Lim Poh Choo v Camden and Islington Area Health Authority [1979] 2 All ER 910 (House of Lords: Lord Diplock, Viscount Dilhorne, Lord Simon of Glaisdale and Lord Scarman). *Pickett v British Rail Engineering Ltd* [1979] 1 All ER 774, HL, 1978 Halsbury's Abridgment para. 861, *Shearman v Folland* [1950] 2 KB 43, CA, *Taylor v O'Connor* [1971] AC 115, HL and *Young v Percival* [1974] 3 All ER 677, CA, 1974 Halsbury's Abridgment para. 2335 applied. Decision of the Court of Appeal [1979] 1 All ER 332, 1978 Halsbury's Abridgment para. 862 varied.

806   —— quantum of damages

Examples of awards of damages in personal injury or fatal accident cases are arranged in the following order. Cases involving more than one injury are classified according to the major injury suffered.

Death	Internal injuries	Neck and shoulders
Brain damage and paralysis	Burns	Back and trunk
	Skin diseases	Arms and hands
Multiple injuries	Head	Legs and feet

DEATH

807   *Death*

General damages: £15,360. Widow, 62, brought action for damages in respect of husband, 59, Chief Technical Officer, who was killed in a motor accident. Claim under Law Reform Act withdrawn. *Thompson v Brindley*, 8th May 1979 (Queen's Bench Division: Judge Honig).

808   General damages: £8,406. Labourer, single, was standing in front of a parked lorry when a car ran into the back of it. His father, 55, was a scrap merchant who had been seriously ill and his son helped him with the business which enabled the father to earn an extra £12 a week. The above sum was awarded as to £1,750 for loss of expectation of life and £6,656 for loss of future earnings (multiplier of 16 at £8 p.w.). *Gammell v Wilson* 27th July 1979 (Queen's Bench Division: B. A. Hytner QC).

809   Total damages: £65,000 (agreed). Sales representative, 49, died due to injuries after his car was in a collision with a lorry. His widow, 50, received £55,000 and her daughter, aged 10, £10,000. *Pearce v Darling*, 9th November 1979 (Queen's Bench Division: Tudor Evans J).

810   Damages: £35,562. Concrete mixer, 40, married, was killed when he fell off a mobile scaffold. His widow, 46, sued for damages in respect of herself and daughter, 14. Widow awarded £30,562 and daughter £5,000. *Farragher v Campbell Hooper & Austin Wright*, 12th October 1979 (Queen's Bench Division: Michael Davies J).

811   General damages: £26,250. Salesman, single, 23, was killed in a motor accident. He was engaged to be married. Above sum includes £25,000 for future loss of earnings. *Willshire v Gardner*, 6th December 1979 (Queen's Bench Division: Griffiths J).

812   Total damages: £27,066 (Fatal Accidents Acts 1846 and 1959), £1,250 (Law Reform (Miscellaneous Provisions) Act 1934). Company director, 56, married, killed in a motor car accident. His widow, 46, sued for damages and out of the above sum, the daughter, 16, was awarded £4,000. *Gavenca v H. Gavenca Ltd.* 20th December 1979 (Queen's Bench Division: Griffiths J).

BRAIN DAMAGE AND PARALYSIS

813   *Brain*
General damages: £47,500. Labourer, 48, was working on the road when he was knocked down by a motor car. Comminuted depressed fracture of right parietal region of the skull, dura tora and fragmented, brain lacerated. Epilepsy and weakness of left arm and leg, fracture of right tibia and fibula, right leg shortened. Personality change, aggressive, suffers from delusions, poor vision. Above sum includes £25,000 for loss of future earnings. *Philbin v Brady*, 28th June 1979 (Queen's Bench Division: Michael Turner QC).

814   General damages: £136,730. Female school teacher, single, 30, suffered brain damage in a motor accident. Depressed left parietal penetrating injury with extrusion of underlying brain. Operation of acrylic cranioplasty undertaken to simulate a bone graft and reconstitute the brain membranes over severely damaged left temporal lobe. Large sunken scar on left side of head and scar on throat. Facial expression asymmetrical through damage to face nerves. Limited sensory perception of right-hand side of body and limited function of limbs. Can only walk short distances with stick. Intellectual attainment reduced to that of a 7-year old, but aware of her condition. Can only use simple three word sentences. She can never work again or live alone as she requires assistance for all two-handed tasks. Post traumatic epilepsy, depression and reduction of life expectancy, no marriage prospects. Above sum includes £51,690 for future loss of earnings, £53,040 for future care and assistance and £2,000 for loss of pension rights as a teacher. *Summers v Martin*, 6th July 1979 (Queen's Bench Division: Dunn J).

815   Total damages: £22,500 (agreed). Male, 19, single, knocked off pedal cycle by a motor car. Fractured base of skull causing brain damage which partially paralysed his right arm and leg. Has ataxia of gait and grandmal epilepsy, permanent clumsiness of lower limbs, nystagmus and dysarthria. Cannot enjoy sports or social activities for fear of an epileptic attack. Seldom leaves the house. *Hamilton v Bandy*, 5th November 1979 (Queen's Bench Division: Stephen Brown J).

816   General damages: £29,000. Postal executive, 48 married, was knocked down by a car. Fractured skull to left parietal region with 12 inch head wound resulting in brain damage. Deterioration of physical and mental capacities, double vision, weak right arm, loss of accuracy with hands, co-ordination of limbs difficult, impairment of memory and concentration, total absence of libido, 25 per cent of risk of epilepsy. Cannot maintain car or do house repairs, and cannot enjoy walking or bicycling. Breakdown of above award: £17,000 pain and suffering and loss of amenities, £6,000 future loss of earnings, £4,000 loss of pension, £2,000 lump sum he would have received on retirement. *Hewitt v Smith*, 29th November 1979, (Queen's Bench Division: Sheen J).

817   *Brain and knee*
General damages: £24,000. Pattern maker, married, 46, knocked down by motor car. Severe head injury including brain damage, 5 weeks post traumatic amnesia,

numbness on left side of body and face and muscular weakness of left arm. Personality change: now irritable and aggressive, loss of concentration, slow in carrying out jobs, lack of confidence. Fracture of tibial plateau, fibula and left knee and ligamentous damage to right knee joint with detachment of bone on medial side of joint and in intra condylar region. About 10–15 per cent instability in his knees and he cannot kneel, squat or run. He will suffer from osteoarthritis in his knees in later life. Above sum includes £8,000 for future loss of earnings. *Hunter v Maslin*, 11th December 1979 (Queen's Bench Division: Judge William Stabb QC).

818 *Paraplegia*
General damages: £49,000. Spring maker, 29, single, riding on motor cycle when hit by car. Fractured 3 vertebrae damaging spine and causing a transverse spinal chord syndrome. Complete loss of sensation below T 4 segment and of control over both bladder and bowel function. Severe impairment of sexual function. Paralysis of motor function of the middle and lower intercostal muscles, abdominal and lower limbs. *Angus v Jones*, 15th March 1979 (Queen's Bench Division: Stocker J).

819 *Quadriplegia*
General damages: £135,500. Student, single, 22, was a passenger in a car that hit a lamp post. He fractured the 5th cervical vertebra resulting in complete loss of power and sensation below the hips and in the right shoulder and elbow. Permanently paralyzed in both arms and legs, no control over bladder and bowels, total loss of sexual function. He will spend rest of his life in a wheelchair. He used to play golf, rugby and other sports. The award was made up as follows: pain and loss of amenity £40,000, future loss of earnings £58,000, future nursing £35,000 and for his father's future loss of overtime earnings as a fireman £2,500. *Casey v Heaney*, 18th June 1979 (Queen's Bench Division: Smith J).

820 *Tetraplegia*
Total damages: £169,710 (reduced by 50 per cent for contributory negligence). Security guard, married, 42, fractured his 4th and 5th cervical vertebrae in a motorcar accident. No sensation below the elbows or in the hands, requires constant nursing night and day and will never work again. He used to play club cricket and his hobbies included weight-lifting, dancing, home decorating and maintenance. Now confined to a wheel chair. Award includes damages to cover the cost of two nurses for nine years (life expectation). *Wilkinson v Matchett*, 18th June 1979 (Queen's Bench Division: Griffiths J).

MULTIPLE INJURIES

821 *Multiple injuries*
General damages: £3,500. Female machinist, 21, riding a moped fractured right femur, wrist and patella in a collision with a motor car. Deep vein thrombosis. *Floyd v Whitbread*, 16th February 1979, (Queen's Bench Division: Chapman J).

822 Total damages: £17,500 (agreed). Single scaffolder, 38, fell from scaffold when it collapsed. Fracture of right temporal bone radiating down into the posterior cranial fossa, brain contusion affecting his memory. Bleeding from the skull into middle ear and the lateral rectus muscles in the eyes causing facial palsy and slurring speech. Suffered a personality change, now aggressive and unco-operative. Also fractured his pelvis and foot and walks with a limp. *Mullins v Hines Ltd*, 19th February 1979 (Queen's Bench Division: Mars-Jones J).

823 General damages: £400 (husband), £3,000 (wife), £1,000 (eldest daughter), £1,250 (younger daughter). The family were injured in a motor car accident. Husband, 36, roofer, bruised his left shoulder and left leg. Wife, 33, fractured right radius and ulna, lower jaw in three places, left thumb and tore left ear. Permanent bowing of right forearm, limitation in right shoulder and facial scars. She is right-handed and now has difficulty in gardening and doing domestic chores. Eldest daughter, 15, fractured right lower jaw, left forearm and femur. Younger daughter, 13, sustained closed fracture of mid-shaft of the right femur. *Ellis v Spratt*, 24th April 1979 (Queen's Bench Division: Judge Lipfriend).

824   General damages: £3,500. Girl, 20, single, pillion passenger on motor cycle which was in collision with a car. Fractured pelvis, the hips are misaligned which may affect child-bearing, a caesarean section might be required; severe whiplash injury to her neck, fractured right ankle and severe scarring from lacerations to right shin, left knee, both feet and elbows. *Culverwell v Personal Representatives of Barry Davies decd,* 18th October 1979 (Queen's Bench Division: Judge Edgar Fay QC).

825   General damages: £9,000. Roofing contractor, 47, married, fell through an asbestos roof and fractured his pelvis, right acetabulum and pubic rami on left side, neck of right femur, right humerus into avulsion. Right leg shortened by ¾ inch, right wrist stiff. Registered as disabled and gravely at risk in labour market. Above sum includes £1,500 for future loss of earnings. *Walls v Newbold*, 1st November 1979, (Queen's Bench Division: Kenneth Jones J).

826   General damages £15,000. Widow, 66, knocked down on pedestrain crossing and sustained a head injury, multiple fractures of her ribs, left tibia and fibula, right fibula, right lateral malleolus and left clavicle. *Wiszlicki v Caruso*, 30th November 1979 (Queen's Bench Division: Chapman J).

827   General damages: £10,000. Factory production manager, married, 41, injured in motor accident. Fractured nose, jaw, both thighs, left patella and medial femoral condyle, comminuted fracture of left talus, right os calcis, left collarbone, and 3 ribs on left side. Permanent disabilities include stiffness in both knees, limitation of neck movement, scars on chest and legs. There is a high risk of osteoarthritis affecting left knee and ankle. He cannot run, squat or hop and has to climb or descend stairs one step at a time. *Wrenn v Kenton*, 30th November 1979 (Queen's Bench Division; Wien J).

828   General damages: £10,000. Farmer, 54, married, was injured in a motor car accident. Fracture of radius of left forearm, 8/9th ribs on right side, neck and shafts of both femurs and fracture of both patellas, fibula and tibia of both legs and 4/5th metatarsal bones of right foot. Permanent disabilities include stiffness in left arm and weakness in grip, limited movement of the knees, bow deformity of left leg, the legs are different lengths resulting in an awkward gait. Will suffer from osteoarthritis in all injured joints. *Davies v Masterton*, 12th December 1979 (Queen's Bench Division: Balcombe J).

INTERNAL INJURIES

829   *Spleen*

General damages: £8,000. Invoice typist, 21, married, was pillion rider in a road accident. Her spleen was ruptured and subsequently removed leaving 8½ inch para-median scar which is keloid and ugly. Recurrent sublaxation of right patella with patello-femoral chondromalacia. Right knee gives way and locks, limited movement. Anxiety when travelling in motor cars. *Quigley v Hanson*, 30th March 1979 (Queen's Bench Division: Dennis Barker QC).

830   *Loss of sense of smell*

General damages: £1,500. Taxidriver, was in a motor accident as a result of which he suffered a 50 per cent loss of his sense of smell, 15 per cent loss of his hearing and pains in his neck and chest. The accident was a contributory cause of two heart attacks. *Wrobel v Parnell*, 6th December 1979 (Queen's Bench Division: Reeve J).

831   *Mesothelioma*
            General damages £41,300. Marine fitter, 51 married, contracted mesothelioma, a
            respiratory disease, as a result of inhalation of asbestos dust. Persistent pain in left
            side of chest, 50 per cent chance of lung cancer. He had a left pleurectomy and
            decortication. His hobbies of swimming, gardening and long walks restricted.
            Disability assessed at 20 per cent, slow deterioration likely. Above sum includes
            £25,300 for future loss of earnings. *Lord v British Railways Board*, 21st December
            1979 (Queen's Bench Division: Willis J).

BURNS

832   *Burns*
            General damages: £7,000 (agreed). Labourer, 39, was digging with pneumatic
            drill, hit power cable which exploded. Extensive burns of arms, shoulders, hands,
            chest, face, neck and back. About 42 per cent burn area. Developed bacteraemia
            and collapsed lobe of the lung. Skin graft to left hand, scarring, grip impaired,
            permanently deaf in left ear, slightly deaf in both ears before the accident. *Quinn v
            Connaught (Dick Clayden) Ltd*, 3rd May 1979 (Queen's Bench Division: Judge
            Lipfriend).

833   General damages: £8,238. Laundryman, 64, married, sustained severe burns to
            neck, chest, right, shoulder, thighs, ankle and foot, right forearm and hand, when
            boiling water erupted from washing machine. Extensive skin grafts, permanent
            scarring, residual stiffness in right hand, webbing of fingers and impaired grip,
            embarrassment from scars, cannot garden and unable to have sexual intercourse since
            the accident. Above sum includes £1,238 for future loss of earnings. *Barnes v
            Roseacre Laundry Ltd*, 10th May 1979 (Queen's Bench Division: Judge Honig).

834   Total damages: £10,000 (agreed). Production operator, 32, suffered severe
            chemical burns to both eyes, face, chest and left arm when a reactor exploded, gross
            oedema of the eyelids, medium degree of deafness from the blast. Tracheostomy
            performed. *Linbourne v Akzo Chemie UK Ltd*, 16th July 1979 (Queen's Bench
            Division: Michael Davies J).

SKIN DISEASES

835   *Dermatitis*
            General damages: £29,000. Married ship's cook, 49, contracted chronic eczematous
            dermatitis all over both hands after contact with chemical substances i.e. detergents
            or after application of friction, e.g. driving. No longer able to be a ship's cook.
            Above sum includes £21,000 for future loss of earnings. *Torrens v Geest Industries
            Ltd*, 20th February 1979, (Queen's Bench Division: Mars-Jones J).

HEAD

836   General damages: £5,000. Married woman, 84, knocked down by a car. Hairline
            fracture of the skull resulting in permanent gross impairment of memory. She will
            be unable to look after herself when her husband, also aged 84, dies. *Jones v Jones*,
            17th December 1979 (Queen's Bench Division: Griffiths J).

837   General damages: £9,350. Fitter's mate, 61, married, was riding motor cycle when
            it collided with a car. Severe head injury with some brain damage, large contused
            area in the left parietal region. Linear fracture of posterior parietal region extending
            down into base of the skull. Blood clot in both nostrils and peri-orbital
            haematoma. Permanent deterioration in memory and concentration, requires help
            with simple chores, physical movements are unsteady, clumsy handling of objects,
            weakness in right arm. *Hegarty v Muhammad*, 21st December 1979 (Queen's Bench
            Division: Judge William Stabb QC).

838   *Skull*
General damages: £3,000. Work study officer, 40, riding on back of refuse vehicle was flung off when it took a sharp turn. Fractured skull at right occipital bone. Headaches, vomiting and photophobia were slow to improve. *Watson v Chichester District Council*, 3rd July 1979 (Queen's Bench Division: Judge Edgar Fay QC).

839   *Head and wrist*
General damages: £4,500. Married cement technician, 60, was riding his moped when it was hit by a car. Head lacerations and a broken left wrist. Unable to have sexual intercourse, loss of confidence, cannot undertake home decorating. *Coles v Stevens*, 11th December 1978 (Queen's Bench Division: Drake J).

840   *Eye*
Total damages £4,500 (agreed). Boy, 11, injured right eye when another child threw a piece of wood at his face. Corneal abrasion, haemorrhage in anterior chamber, torn iris, bruising of retina and haemorrhage in choroid, subsequent secondary glaucoma. *Stephenson v Inner London Education Authority*, 7th April 1979 (Queen's Bench Division: Barry Chedlow QC).

841   Total damages: £8,000 (agreed). Engine driver, 59, bumped his head on a projection in the engine compartment causing retinal detachment in left eye and loss of sight in that eye. *Shaw v British Railways Board*, 8th October 1979 (Queen's Bench Division: Michael Davies J).

842   General damages: £6,000. Apprentice fitter welder, married, 22, was struck in the right eye by a metal electrode. Permanent loss of most of vision in right eye. Above sum includes £1,875 for future loss of earnings. *Gingell v Croydon Borough Council*, 14th May 1979 (Queen's Bench Division: Judge Lewis Hawser QC).

843   General damages: £10,000. Girl, 8, struck in right eye with a hacksaw blade. Loss of eye, gross disfigurement. Had numerous operations, eye has shrunk and may have to be removed later and artificial eye inserted. Award includes future loss of earning capacity and some diminution in marriage prospects. *Vandome v John*, 25th May 1979 (Queen's Bench Division: Judge Lipfriend).
For substantive proceedings in this case see para. 1961.

844   *Eye and shoulder*
General damages: £8,500. Youth, 19 (13 at time of accident) received lead shot wounds in right eye, face and left shoulder when he was operating a low clay pigeon trap. Complete loss of vision in right eye which has shrunk and he has a divergent squint. Risk of sympathetic involvement of left eye, 7 pellets remain in left shoulder and 5 in the face at the base of the skull and in the maxilla and lower left orbital margin. *Green v Simmons*, 7th December 1979 (Queen's Bench Division: Ackner J).

845   *Face*
General damages £6,700. Hospital receptionist, 44, married, injured in a motor car accident. She fractured her right maxillary antrum and cheek bone and upper part of sternum resulting in a slight broadening of the nose, continued numbness of right side of face and above upper lip. She has a tendency to dribble as right side of mouth is lax. She is nervous of driving and only does so out of necessity. Can only work part-time since the accident. Above sum includes £2,450 future loss of earnings. *Ward v Oudart*, 7th April 1979 (Queen's Bench Division: Judge Lymbery QC).

846   General damages: £1,000. Bank official, 30, married, sustained severe facial lacerations in a motor car accident. Lacerations to nose (1¾ inch scar), eyelids, right cheek and fragments of glass in his eyes. *Moore v Paine*, 14th December 1979, (Queen's Bench Division: Griffiths J).

NECK AND SHOULDERS

847 *Neck*

General damages: £2,500. Married woman supervisor in book company, 56, passenger in a motor car accident. Her neck was strained, symptomless cervical spondylosis already present. She sustained a hiatus hernia, contusion of left side of her chest and suffers from occipal headaches, indigestion, irritability and depression. She cannot do needlework or knitting. *Field v Sycamore*, 2nd February 1979 (Queen's Bench Division: Wien J).

848 General damages: £3000. Carpenter, 55, was a passenger in a van when it stopped suddenly and he sustained a whiplash injury resulting in limitation in flexion and extension and in side to side movement of neck. *McLean v George Brewster & Co Ltd*, 20th July 1979 (Queen's Bench Division: Michael Davies J).

849 General damages: £1,500. Married woman, 24, passenger in motor car accident, sustained a ligamentous strain of lower neck. Some intermittent pain continuing. *Grimwood v Hobbs*, 14th December 1979 (Queen's Bench Division: Judge Lewis Hawser QC).

850 *Neck and shoulder*

General damages: £300. Female grocery shelver, married, 44, strained her neck and shoulder lifting box of baked beans. Had to wear a surgical collar, difficulty in doing domestic chores and carrying shopping. *Youle v Cavenham Ltd*, 8th June 1979 (Queen's Bench Division: Judge Oddie).

851 *Neck and spine*

General damages: £1,000. Surveyor, 65, fell 18ft from ladder when inspecting roof space. Concussional injury and lacerations to scalp and haematoma, and whiplash type of injury to cervical spine. *Oakes v R. J. Cossick Ltd*, 11th October 1979 (Queen's Bench Division: Pain J).

852 *Shoulder*

General damages: £1,250. Labourer, 53, single, knocked off his pedal cycle. Fractured right scapula, reduced grip in right hand. *Kurylo v Dawsonfreight Ltd*, 12th March 1979 (Queen's Bench Division: Barry Chedlow QC).

853 General damages: £2,000. Male, 58, was thrown to the ground when he was struck by a car door. Severely bruised right shoulder resulting in osteoarthritis and palpable grating during rotation, and restricted movement in the shoulder and arm. *Irving v Lefley*, 7th November 1979 (Queen's Bench Division: Michael Davies J).

BACK AND TRUNK

854 *Back*

General damages: £9,000. Female computer operator, single, 23, was impaled in her back by a metal tube when the car she was travelling in hit a fence. She sustained fractures of the transverse processes of L3/4/5 with superficial fractures of the pedicles of L4 and L5. Area of muscle loss 5 inches by 4 inches on left side of lower back, causing a hernia. Disfiguring raised scar of 16 inches across back. Permanent back weakness owing to muscle loss. Disability in labour market. Permanent back ache; cannot lift heavy weights; difficulty in doing domestic chores. Leisure pursuits curtailed. Above sum includes £4,000 for loss of earning capacity. *Simmonds v Hollingsbee*, 22nd January 1979 (Queen's Bench Division: Judge Edgar Fay QC).

855   General damages: £23,000. Glazier, 38, married, twisted his back manoeuvring a large sheet of glass. Decompression by hemi-laminectomy over 4th and 5th segments. Fit for light work only. Depression. Handicapped in labour market. Above sum includes £18,000 for future loss of earnings. *Lawrence v Greater London Council*, 29th March 1979 (Queen's Bench Division: Michael Kempster QC).

856   General damages: £5,000. Married woman, 30, passenger in motor car accident. Fractures of transverse processes on 1st, 2nd, 3rd and 4th lumbar vertebrae on left side, severe lumbo-sacral strain, severe bruising. Disc lesion involved damaged cartilage, tissue devoid of blood therefore no hope of healing. Painful if driving or being driven. She has to wear a steel corset while doing domestic chores. Sporting activities almost wholly curtailed. She will have considerable pain for the rest of her life. *Scadeng v Scadeng*, 30th March 1979 (Queen's Bench Division: Richard Rougier QC).

857   General damages: £3,500. Lorry driver, 29, married, sustained an acute sprain of the lumbar sacral region when he was shifting a heavy crate. Above sum includes £500 for future loss of earnings. *Sharp v Myson Fans Ltd*, 12th October 1979 (Queen's Bench Division: Swanwick J).

858   General damages: £3,750. Female operative, married, 53, was manhandling tray of car pump bodies which jarred and caused a lumbar intervertebral disc lesion. Back has weakened and she is unfit for work involving heavy lifting or bending. *Johnson v Hobourn-Eaton Manufacturing Co Ltd*, 4th June 1979 (Queen's Bench Division: Judge Hawker QC).

859   General damages: £4,500. Married docker, 47, was slinging cases into hatch when one fell and pinned him to the ground. Strained lumbar spine, nervous breakdown and severe mental illness and depression. Unfit to continue dockwork. *Weller v British Leyland Ltd*, 8th November 1979 (Queen's Bench Division: Stephen Brown J).

860   General damages: £1,125. Bank clerk, 32, was hit in the back by a heavy metal box. Bruising of lower back, pain in thighs and groin, weakness of both legs, acute lumbar lesion, prolapsed intervertebral disc. Injury interferes with sexual intercourse, cannot garden, play badminton or tennis. *Perris v Lloyds Bank International Ltd*, 25th April 1979 (Queen's Bench Division: Kenneth Jones J).

861   General damages: £3,000. Female clerk, 53, married, slipped on wet floor and sustained prolapsed intervertebral disc. Was operated on for laminectomy of vertebrae and bilateral partial facetectomy. Permanent limitation of ability to travel and carry out domestic chores. *Adam v Lufthansa German Airlines Ltd*, 17th July 1979 (Queen's Bench Division: Judge Lipfriend).

862   General damages: £7,000. Steriliser, 34, married, had two accidents when pulling a hand truck. In the first accident he slipped on a greasy floor and sustained a wedge compression fracture of the 12th dorsal vertebra and in the second accident the wheels of the truck jammed and the jarring aggravated the previous injury. Slight deformity of the spine which interferes with his hobbies of deep sea fishing, snooker, gardening and dancing. Above award includes £4,000 for future loss of earnings *Hunter v Travenol Laboratories Ltd*, 5th November 1979 (Queen's Bench Division: Neill J).

863   General damages: £2,000. Printing engineer, 45, married, twisted his back unloading equipment. Extensive ligamentous damage in cervical and dorsal regions of the spine with avulsion of small fragment of bone at lower margin of the 5th cervical vertabra. *Bartlett v Arnold Cook Ltd*, 21st December 1979 (Queen's Bench Division: Willis J).

864   *Back and foot*

General damages: £750. Veneer preparer, 55, slipped on oily patch and aggravated pre-existing disc lesion. Flexion and extension of lumbar spine reduced, wasting of right calf and weakness in upward movement of right foot. *Curtis v Uniflex Furniture Ltd*, 10th May 1979 (Queen's Bench Division: Judge Lipfriend).

865   *Back and knee*

General damages: £4,500. Single woman, 70, fell through the floor of the lavatory which her landlord had been ordered by the council to repair. She fell into the cellar and suffered a fracture of the right tibial plateau and the first lumbar vertebra resulting in osteoarthritic changes in the right knee. She will permanently have some pain in the lower lumbar spine and in her knee together with limitation of movement. *Thompson v Nott*, 23rd July 1979 (Queen's Bench Division: T. P. Russell QC).

866   *Spine*

General damages: £8,640. Demolition burner, 42, married, fell off a roof and sustained an unstable fracture—dislocation of the spine between 12th thoracic and 1st lumbar segments. Operation for spinal fusion. He also dislocated left shoulder joint. Only fit for light work. Above sum includes £4,140 for loss of future earnings. *Davies v Hughes & Salvidge (Portsmouth) Ltd*, 15th May 1979 (Queen's Bench Division: McNeill J).

867   *Chest and legs*

General damages: £3,500. Boy, 9, passenger in mini-bus which hit railings. Severe chest injury on left side, paradoxical movement of the left anterior chest wall with inspiratory recession in area of 5th and 6th ribs, crack transverse fractures and greenstick fracture of left tiberia. Haematoma of lower and upper lobe of left lung. Genu valgum deformity of both legs requiring further operation for osteotomy, some paralysis of lateral popliteal nerve. Limitation of movement in left ankle. *Humble v Hobcraft*, 14th December 1978 (Queen's Bench Division: Mais J).

868   *Pelvis and hip*

General damages: £5,500. Girl, copy typist, 19, single, was a passenger in a car accident and sustained a fractured sternum, pelvis, right femur and a fracture of her superior and inferior pubic rami on the right side. Her hip was pinned and painful after sitting or walking for ½ hour. May require further hip surgery to remove the pins. *Ainsworth v West*, 6th June 1979 (Queen's Bench Division: Judge White).

869   *Hip*

General damages: £39,000. Press worker, 45, married, was pushing a trolley when he slipped and injured his right hip: cyst in right acetabulum which was exposed and drilled by operation, bursitis, limitation of flexion, abduction and adduction. *Belardo v London Brick Co Ltd*, 4th April 1979 (Queen's Bench Division: Leonard Caplan QC).

870   General damages: £2,750. Dental student, 23, single, tripped in a depression on a central island and fell in front of a car. Fractured left femur resulting in shortening of left leg, loss of flexion and restrictions in walking. Lacerations to arms, legs and face with permanent scarring to his forehead. *Mullally v London Borough of Bromley*, 18th June 1979, (Queen's Bench Division: Judge Oddie).

General damages: £7,500. Woman factory worker, 41, married, fell on slippery washroom floor. Transcervical fracture of the neck of right femur with a wound at hip after the insertion of a pin. Residual disability: permanent limp. *Page v Goswell Plating Works Ltd*, 5th December 1979, (Queen's Bench Division: Kilner Brown J).

872　　*Hip and knee*
General damages: £2,500. Marketing officer, 23, was riding his motor cycle when he had a collision with a car. Fractured left femur and upper part of left patella and fractures of head of second right metacarpal and proximal phalanx of right index finger. *Job v Merritt*, 11th May 1979 (Queen's Bench Division: Judge Edgar Fay QC).

ARMS AND HANDS

873　　*Arm*
General damages: £1,600. Girl, 18, tripped on uneven surface and fell through a cracked window. Laceration of lower part of left forearm to wrist requiring 15 stitches, leaving a scar and weakness in left hand. She was right-handed. *Lynch v London Borough of Barking*, 28th February 1979 (Queen's Bench Division: Oliver Popplewell QC).

874　　General damages: £2,750. Female filing clerk, married, 57, fell on a doorstep at workplace, severely fractured lower end of right radius and ulna bones. Restricted range of movement of forearm, permanent loss of grip. Difficulty in carrying out domestic chores and lifting heavy files. Restricted movement affects hobbies of dancing and knitting. Some handicap in employment market. *Neale v British Leyland (UK) Ltd*, 11th May 1979 (Queen's Bench Division: Judge Lipfriend).

875　　General damages: £1,000. Fork lift truck driver, 49, married, was struck by the knob of the steering wheel and sustained a fracture of shaft of left ulna. *Wren v Bowater-Scott Corp Ltd*, 22nd November 1979 (Queen's Bench Division: Judge Hawser QC).

876　　Total damages: £25,000 (agreed). Trainee butcher, 19, was riding motor cycle when he collided with stationary dustcart. Multiple superficial abrasions with a severe superficial friction abrasion across left side of neck and shoulder, and left side of brachial plexus palsy leaving him with a useless left arm. Can no longer train as a butcher as he now has the use of only one arm. *Cullip v Horsham District Council*, 19th November 1979 (Queen's Bench Division: Judge Hawser QC).

877　　*Arm and hand*
Total damages: £550. Laundress, 61, was knocked down by a van and sustained a fracture of the left ulna near the wrist affecting the left thumb and triggering off pre-existing symptoms of osteoarthritis of carpo metacarpal joint of thumb. Slight flexion deformity at the proximal interphalangeal joint of the little finger. *Armitage v Nash*, 3rd October 1979 (Queen's Bench Division: Judge William Stabb QC).

878　　*Wrist*
General damages: £2,500. Married woman cleaner, 54, fell on uneven concrete path and sustained a colles's fracture, injury to the triangular cartilage between radius and ulna resulting in some permanent weakness in left wrist. *Dunstan v Board of Governors of Guy's Hospital*, 2nd March 1979 (Queen's Bench Division: Oliver Popplewell QC).

879　　General damages: £3,000. Female kitchen assistant, 52, slipped on jelly spilt on the floor and sustained a left colles's fracture which developed into Sudek's atrophy. Wrist movement limited. Risk of early development of degenerative arthritis. She is at a disadvantage in the open labour market. *Watts v Kent County Council*, 20th June 1979 (Queen's Bench Division: Smith J).

880　　*Hand*
General damages: £10,750. Married physics technician, 48, caught right hand in circular saw. Amputation of ring and little fingers and part of thumb, severed

flexor tendons of index finger and sensory nerves of other fingers. He was right-handed and had to use left hand in which he developed osteoarthritic stiffening of left index finger. Above sum includes £3,750 for loss of future earning capacity. *Mallick v Allied Schools Agency Ltd*, 18th December 1978 (Queen's Bench Division: Lawson J).

881   General damages: £1,750. Battery plant attendant, 48, was struck on left hand by fork lift steering knob. Severe fracture of proximal interphalangeal joint of left middle finger. Permanently stiff and slightly bent which makes it difficult to carry out small precision work. *Jones v British Leyland (U.K.) Ltd*, 8th November 1979 (Queen's Bench Division: Stephen Brown J).

882   General damages: £6,000. Skipper's mate, 41, was guiding tug when his left hand was caught between the davit and its support. Crush injury, amputation of distal phalanx to left index finger, middle phalanx to little finger, proximal inter phalangeal joint shortened to below first joint of middle and ring fingers. *Langton v M. Tugs Ltd*, 2nd November 1979 (Queen's Bench Division: Judge Edgar Fay QC).

883   General damages: £3,000. Senior machine operator, married, 55, caught his left hand between rollers of conveyor belt. Severe crush injury involving fractures of 1st and 2nd metacarpals, avulsion of skin of back of hand, lacerations around inner part of wrist extending to palm and at base of little and ring fingers. Loss of grip and clumsy when handling small objects. Cannot play golf or cricket. Hand is numb and unsightly and the ulnar nerves damaged. Above sum includes £200 for future loss of earnings. *Watson v Mitcham Cardboards Ltd*, 7th December 1979 (Queen's Bench Division: Kilner Brown J).

884   *Fingers*
General damages: £700. Apprentice toolmaker sustained an injury to his right middle finger while setting up a die set. Crush injury to top of finger and compound fracture of the bone and avulsion of nail. Some weakening of grip. He was right-handed. *Cataldo v Cutler Hammer Europa Ltd*, 30th January 1979 (Queen's Bench Division: Forbes J).

885   Total damages: £1,100 (agreed). Wood machinist, married, 57, caught fingers in circular saw. Severe lacerations of left index, middle and ring fingers, unsightly deformity in pulp of middle finger and of nail of ring finger, loss of pincer grip of index finger. Can no longer operate a machine. Handicapped in hobby of gardening. *Sadler v A. Arenson (Holdings) Ltd*, 11th December 1979 (Queen's Bench Division: Judge William Stabb QC).

LEGS AND FEET

886   *Knee*
General damages: £1,000. Warehouseman, 66, tripped over an obstruction and sustained a traumatic fracture of the left patella with some injury to the medial meniscus and considerable retro-patella grating and limitation of movement. Osteo-arthritis partly caused by the injury. Can no longer dance or play tennis. *Clack v Cadbury Schweppes Foods Ltd*, 29th October 1979 (Queen's Bench Division: Neill J).

887   General damages: £6,000. Technical officer, married, 60, fell over an anchor ring in the ground. Severely sprained right knee, meniscectomy performed, hitherto symptomless patella-femoral osteoarthritis exacerbated. Wasting of right thigh and swelling of right knee and calf. Has to use a stick permanently, can only drive and walk short distances, mild deep vein thrombosis in right calf. Previous hobbies of car maintenance, walking and house decorating are all restricted. *Deegan v Post Office*, 23rd May 1979 (Queen's Bench Division: McNeill J).

888   General damages: £1,600. Milkman, 56, knocked down by car in garage forecourt. Knee severely bruised resulting in restriction of movement and exacerbation of previous asymptomatic osteoarthritic changes in his knee. Improvement unlikely. *Porter v Coldham*, 23rd November 1979 (Queen's Bench Division: Judge Edgar Fay QC).

889   *Leg*
General damages: £1,200. Girl, 15, passenger in motor car accident. Transverse fracture of right femur, ¼ inch shortening and some thickening of the leg. *Crowley v Crowley*, 28th March 1979 (Queen's Bench Division: Michael Kempster QC).

890   General damages: £46,110. Police constable, 22, was riding his motor cycle when it collided with a motor car. Fractured upper end of left tibia and fibula with a ligament injury to the inside of his left knee. Some loss of flexion, permanent disability with a risk of osteoarthritis. Unfit to continue career in the police force. Now works as radio telephone operator. Above sum includes £36,110 for future loss of earnings. *Poole v Charvill*, 3rd December 1979 (Queen's Bench Division: Kilner Brown J).

891   *Leg, hand and wrist*
General damages: £4,500. Schoolboy, 18, knocked off his motor cycle. Fracture of left wrist, fracture of head and neck of right radius, lower third of right tibia and bones in right hand; 10° inward angulation of right leg with slight loss of movement, strength and agility. Severe permanent deformity of little and ring fingers with swelling at base of thumb. Post traumatic arthritis in proximal interphalangeal joint of ring finger and thumb. Concussion with retrograde and post traumatic amnesia. Difficulty in concentrating on studies. *Pigrim v Pipe*, 5th October 1979 (Queen's Bench Division: Judge Martin QC).

892   *Ankle*
General damages: £5,250. Married woman, American, 49, knocked down by motor cyclist. Compound fracture, dislocation of right ankle joint, ankle stiff and swollen. She limps and can only walk a limited distance. Marked crepitus under and behind right medial malleolus. Osteoarthritic changes may require future operation to fuse the ankle. The ankle is scarred. Above sum includes £250 for future loss of earnings. *Sumpter v Tonge*, 5th October 1970 (Queen's Bench Division: Patrick Bennett QC).

893   General damages: £1,800. Toolmaker, 48, married, was injured when a bench in a fishing boat fell over. Severe fracture of lateral malleolus of the right ankle with injury to ligament. Permanent 10 per cent restriction of movement, definite risk of osteoarthritis. *Gray v Wood (Sea Enterprises) Ltd*, 27th April 1979 (Queen's Bench Division: Sheen J).

894   General damages: £3,000. Widow, 58, struck on the ankle by a mechanical truck on railway platform. Pott's fracture of right ankle, screw inserted. Ankle thickened by ½ inch with 3 inch linear scar on inside of ankle, permanently swollen limiting movement. Ankle may deteriorate. *Francis v British Railways Board*, 9th November 1979 (Queen's Bench Division: Kenneth Jones J).

895   General damages: £6,500. Scaffolder, 42, fell off a scaffold. Bimalleolar fracture of right ankle requiring insertion of two pins. Walking ability restricted, slight limp, cannot run. Osteoarthritic changes apparent. Unfit for previous employment, could be trained as a welder. Above award includes £2,500 for future loss of earnings. *Hyland v Ralston*, 21st December 1979 (Queen's Bench Division: Sheen J).

896   *Ankle and hand*
General damages: £1,250.   Married packer, 50, was knocked down by a car on a pedestrian crossing.   Fracture of medial malleolus of left ankle and of first metacarpal triquetrum and base of 5th metacarpal of right hand.   *Jackson v Tenorio*, 23rd March 1979 (Queen's Bench Division: Barry Chedlow QC).

897   *Foot*
General damages: £9,798.   Female film maker, single, 31, knocked down by a bus.   Severe crush injury of left foot with fractures of 3 toes, tibia and fibula.   Big toe became gangrenous and was amputated.   Appreciable disfigurement and disability.   Scope and capacity impaired in open labour market and she is liable to loss of earnings.   Above sum includes £2,798 for future loss of earnings.   *Fowke v Reed*, 3rd October 1979 (Queen's Bench Division: Judge Martin QC).

898   —— —— **housewife**
See *The Dragon*, para. 297.

899   **Specific performance—damages at common law on discharge of order**
See *Johnson v Agnew*, para. 2708.

900   **Trespass to land—proof of loss—measure of damages**
A tenant left his flat before the expiry of his fixed term and therefore never became a statutory tenant.   The landlords then claimed possession of the flat and damages for trespass from the two defendants, who had been living there as the tenant's licensees with the landlords' permission.   The court granted possession but refused to award damages because the landlords had not adduced evidence that they could have relet the premises and therefore had not proved actual loss.   On appeal by the landlords, *held*, once a landlord had established that a defendant had remained on residential property as a trespasser he was entitled to damages without proof that he could have re-let the property.   The measure of damages would be the value of the property, which in most cases of this kind would be the ordinary letting value.
SWORDHEATH PROPERTIES LTD v TABET [1979] 1 All ER 240 (Court of Appeal: MEGAW, BROWNE and WALLER LJJ).

901   **Vaccine damage—compensation payments**
See Vaccine Damage Payments Act 1979, para. 1947.

DEEDS

Halsbury's Laws of England (4th edn.), Vol. 12, paras. 1301–1566

902   **Contract—mistake as to contents—influence of son over elderly parents—plea of non est factum**
The defendants, an elderly couple, bought a house, the arrangements being made by their son, a chartered accountant.   In addition to a building society mortgage, the son obtained a loan from the plaintiffs, licensed moneylenders, as part of the purchase price on his agreeing to procure that the defendants would execute a second charge on the house to the plaintiffs.   The defendants executed a second charge to the plaintiffs when the son took them to the plaintiffs' solicitors and told them that there were further documents to be signed in connection with the mortgage to the building society.   The son subsequently disappeared, leaving the loan and interest owing.   The plaintiffs unsuccessfully claimed those sums and possession of the house against the defendants, the judge holding that the defendants had established non est

factum although the plaintiffs and their solicitors had acted honourably. The plaintiffs appealed. *Held*, the defendants could not succeed on non est factum, as they had not exercised the appropriate reasonable care. However, the defendants had left the arrangements to the son and three considerations gave rise to an equity which made the transaction voidable: the plaintiffs appointed the son to procure the transaction; the relationship of the son and his elderly parents; the absence of independent advice. The appeal would be dismissed.

Lord Denning MR dismissed the appeal on the grounds that the son had brought undue pressure on the defendants for the benefit of himself and the plaintiffs and that there was inequality of bargaining power.

AVON FINANCE CO LTD V BRIDGER (1979) 123 Sol Jo 705 (Court of Appeal: LORD DENNING MR, BRANDON and BRIGHTMAN LJJ). *Chaplin & Co Ltd v Brammall* [1908] 1 KB 233 applied.

903   Conveyance—all estate clause—purported mortgage of freehold by one joint tenant

The defendants were joint beneficial owners of their former matrimonial home, which was registered in their joint names. Following their divorce, the first defendant and a woman posing as the second defendant executed a legal charge by way of mortgage on the house in favour of the plaintiffs. The deception having been discovered, the plaintiffs unsuccessfully brought proceedings for a declaration that, by executing the legal charge, the first defendant had charged all his beneficial interest under the statutory trusts for sale to them, and for an order for the sale of the house. The plaintiffs appealed, relying upon the Law of Property Act 1925, s. 63, which provides that every conveyance is effective to pass all interest the conveying parties respectively have in the property conveyed. A mortgage or charge is a conveyance for the purposes of the Act. They contended that, under s. 63, the first defendant's interest in the proceeds of the sale of the house under the statutory trusts for sale constituted an interest in the property conveyed by the legal charge. They further relied on the principle that where a vendor contracts to grant a particular interest in property which is greater than the interest which he is competent to grant, the purchaser can elect to affirm the contract and compel the vendor to grant such less interest as he is competent to grant. *Held*, a beneficial interest in the proceeds of sale of land held upon the statutory trusts for sale was not an interest in that land within the meaning of s. 63. Accordingly, the legal charge was not effective to charge the first defendant's beneficial interest in the proceeds of sale of the house. Further, the plaintiffs, who had contracted for a mortgage of the freehold estate, could not elect to take a charge on the first defendant's interest in the proceeds of sale, as that was an entirely different subject matter from that for which they had contracted.

CEDAR HOLDINGS LTD V GREEN [1979] 3 All ER 117 (Court of Appeal: BUCKLEY, GOFF and SHAW LJJ).

904   Rectification—common intention of parties legitimate avoidance of tax—whether a bar to relief

See *Re Slocock's Will Trusts*, para. 1981.

DEVELOPMENT LAND TAX

Halsbury's Laws of England (4th edn.), Vol. 5, Supp. paras. 300 A–D

905   Article

Development Land Tax—Recent Changes, K. R. Tingley: Taxation 22nd September 1979, p. 445.

906   Finance (No. 2) Act 1979

See para. 2247.

907   Liability to tax—discussions with Development Land Tax Office

The Inland Revenue have issued a Press Release dated 6th February 1979 in which they state that they have modified the practice under which the Development Land Tax Office does not enter into discussions of liability until an assessment has been made. Full details are given in Statement of Practice SP 2/79. District Valuers may now disclose and discuss valuations before an assessment is made, but after the chargeable event, in certain circumstances. These include all cases where a notice has been given under the Development Land Tax Act 1976, Sch. 8, paras. 36 or 37, and other specified cases.

DISCOVERY, INSPECTION AND INTERROGATORIES

Halsbury's Laws of England (4th edn.), Vol. 13, paras. 1–142

908   Articles

Disclosure of Medical Records, R. G. Lee (the inconsistency of judicial opinion concerning disclosure of confidential medical records): 129 NLJ 702.

Need for New Approach to Litigation, Justinian (legal privilege in the light of *Waugh v British Railways Board* [1979] 2 All ER 1169, para. 916): Financial Times, 30th July 1979.

Racial Discrimination: Discovery, Ian MacDonald (decision in *Jalota v Imperial Metal Industry (Kynoch) Ltd* [1979] 1 IRLR 313, para. 912): 129 NLJ 1173.

909   Production of documents—industrial drawings—whether copy-right infringed—use of confidential information

See *Centri-Spray Corpn v CERA International Ltd*, para. 536.

910   —— medical records and letters of complaint—confidence—jurisdiction of court to restrict inspection

A religious sect sued the Department of Health and Social Security and two of its officials for libel in respect of information released to the press and furnished to health authorities abroad. The department objected to discovery of medical records and letters from former members of the sect. An order was made preventing discovery of the medical records except to a medical practitioner nominated by the sect, provided that he undertook not to disclose the contents; the letters were to be disclosed only to the sect's solicitors and then only if they undertook not to reveal the contents to anyone other than counsel and if the sect undertook not to use the information for any collateral purpose. The sect appealed, contending that the court had no jurisdiction to make such an order and that even if it had there had been no grounds for making such an order. *Held*, the court had to ensure that discovery was limited to what was needed for the fair disposal of the action in cases where there was a risk of the right of inspection being used for a collateral purpose. To achieve this, the court was fully entitled to withhold an order unless a suitable undertaking was given. In this case there was a real risk that wide discovery could lead to harassment by members of the sect of those who had written the letters in issue and some restriction on inspection was required. However, the original order was too restrictive and would be replaced by an order in terms agreed by the parties.

CHURCH OF SCIENTOLOGY OF CALIFORNIA v DEPARTMENT OF HEALTH AND SOCIAL SECURITY [1979] 3 All ER 97 (Court of Appeal: STEPHENSON, BRANDON and TEMPLEMAN LJJ). *Warner-Lambert Co v Glaxo Laboratories Ltd* [1975] RPC 354,

CA, 1975 Halsbury's Abridgment para. 2471, *Alterskye v Scott* [1948] 1 All ER 469 and *Riddick v Thames Board Mills Ltd* [1977] 3 All ER 677, CA, 1977 Halsbury's Abridgment para. 918 applied.

911 —— **order by industrial tribunal—complaint of race or sex discrimination—confidential reports**

In an application for discovery of certain documents relating to the assessment, performance, progress and promotional prospects of the claimant and another employee in a case alleging racial discrimination, *held*, the judge or chairman had first to look at the documents in question to see whether discovery was essential in the interests of justice. Before examination however, the judge or chairman had to satisfy himself that the documents were prima facie relevant to the case. Applying these principles, the documents relating to the claimant would be examined to ascertain whether discovery was necessary. However no prima facie case of the relevance of the other employee's file had been made out.

BRITISH RAILWAYS BOARD V NATARAJAN [1979] 2 All ER 794 (Employment Appeal Tribunal: ARNOLD J presiding). *Science Research Council v Nasse; Leyland Cars Ltd v Vyas* [1978] 3 All ER 1196, CA, 1978 Halsbury's Abridgment para. 946 applied.

912 An employee claimed that he had been unlawfully discriminated against on the ground of his race when his application for transfer to a new position was refused. He applied for discovery of various documents or for further particulars in order to establish that it was his employers' policy not to employ coloured people. An industrial tribunal refused his application except in one particular case. The employee appealed, requesting, inter alia, details of the total number of coloured people working for the employers and details of the education and ethnic origin of the successful candidates for the internal vacancies for which he had applied since the beginning of his employment. *Held*, the number of coloured employees was not relevant to whether or not the employers were racially discriminating against the employee when his application for the new position was refused. The only issue that both requests for details could go to was one as to the credit of the employers, namely, that a discreditable racial policy existed. Discovery which related solely to credit was not allowed. Further, it would be undesirable either to require the employers to categorise the colour of their employees or to find out the ethnic origin of the successful candidates for the positions for which the employee had previously applied. It would also be wrong to require the employers to break their confidence with the successful candidates as they would have to do in order to supply the details requested by the employee. Accordingly, the appeal would be dismissed.

JALOTA V IMPERIAL METAL INDUSTRY (KYNOCH) LTD [1979] IRLR 313 (Employment Appeal Tribunal: TALBOT J presiding). *George Ballantine & Son Ltd v F. E. R. Dixon & Son Ltd* [1974] 2 All ER 503, 1974 Halsbury's Abridgment para. 1042 applied.

913 On the hearing of interlocutory appeals against the discharge of orders for discovery of confidential reports made on complaints of racial and sexual discrimination, the House of Lords considered the factors to which an industrial tribunal should have regard when exercising its discretion whether to grant discovery. Discovery of confidential documents relating to both the appellants themselves and to the applicants for the positions for which they had unsuccessfully applied was sought. *Held*, there was no principle of public interest privilege protecting confidential documents such as those with which the appeals were concerned. The documents were not protected from discovery by reason of confidentiality alone, although a tribunal could have regard to the fact that the documents were confidential in the exercise of its discretion to order discovery. Particularly, a tribunal might have regard to the sensitivity of particular types of confidential information, to the extent to which the interests of third parties might be affected by disclosure, to the interest which both employers and employees might have in preserving the confidentiality of personal reports and to any wider interest which might be seen to exist in preserving the confidentiality of systems of personal assessments. Further, the relevance of the documents did not alone provide a sufficient test for ordering discovery. The ultimate test was whether discovery was necessary for disposing fairly of the proceedings, in which case discovery had to be ordered notwithstanding the confidentiality of the documents. However, in order to decide whether disclosure of confidential documents was necessary for that reason the tribunal should first inspect the documents and consider whether justice could be done by special measures such as "covering up", substituting anonymous references for specific names, or, in rare cases, hearing in camera. In the instant case, it followed that the Court of Appeal had rightly held that discovery should not have been ordered in either of the two cases without the respective tribunals first inspecting the documents. Accordingly, the appeals would be dismissed and the cases remitted to the tribunals for examination of the documents and decision on the question of disclosure in the light of their Lordships' observations.

SCIENCE RESEARCH COUNCIL v NASSE; BL CARS LTD (FORMERLY LEYLAND CARS) v VYAS [1979] 3 All ER 673 (House of Lords: LORD WILBERFORCE, LORD SALMON, LORD EDMUND-DAVIES, LORD FRASER OF TULLEYBELTON and LORD SCARMAN). Decision of Court of Appeal [1978] 3 All ER 1196, 1978 Halsbury's Abridgment para. 946 affirmed. Dictum of Arnold J in *British Railways Board v Natarajan* [1979] 2 All ER 794 at 799, para. 911 approved.

914   ———— complaint of unfair dismissal—confidential reports

See *Crown Agents for Overseas Governments and Administration v Lawal*, para. 2880.

915   ———— privilege—Crown privilege—non-disclosure on ground of public interest

A major oil company fell into acute financial difficulties and the Bank of England, acting on Government instructions, came to its aid. An agreement was drawn up whereby certain stock owned by the company was to be sold to the Bank; the Government, however, refused to allow any profit-sharing on resale of the stock. The company was forced to accept the agreement. Subsequently the market price of the stock increased substantially and the company sought to have the agreement set aside on the grounds that the sale was unconscionable, inequitable, unreasonable and at an under-value. The company sought production of certain documents which would disclose the part played by the Government in the negotiations. The Bank objected on the ground that the documents belonged to classes of documents the production of which would be injurious to the public interest. Production was refused both at first instance and by the Court of Appeal. The company appealed. *Held*, the protection given to documents which the Crown claimed were of a high level of public importance was not absolute. If it was likely, reasonably probable or a strong positive case was made out, that the documents contained matter relevant to the case and if on consideration of the ministerial certificate claiming immunity there was a doubt whether the balance of public interest lay against disclosure, the courts had a discretion to review the Crown's claim that the withholding of documents was necessary for the proper functioning of the public service. In reviewing the Crown's claim to privilege the court had to balance the competing interests of preventing harm to the state or public service by disclosure and preventing frustration of the administration of justice by withholding disclosure, and could inspect the documents concerned privately in order to determine where the balance of the public interest lay. Prima facie it was likely that the documents in the instant case would have contained information regarding the Bank's attitude to the terms of the sale; and as this was information necessary for disposing fairly of the case and since disclosure would not be prejudicial to state policy, the court had inspected the documents, but on inspection had concluded that the documents did not contain the relevant information. The appeal would be dismissed.

BURMAH OIL CO LTD v BANK OF ENGLAND [1979] 3 All ER 700 (House of Lords: LORD WILBERFORCE, LORD SALMON, LORD EDMUND-DAVIES, LORD KEITH OF KINKEL and LORD SCARMAN). Decision of the Court of Appeal [1979] 2 All ER 461 affirmed on the other grounds.

916   —— —— legal professional privilege—purpose of document

A train driver was killed in a railway accident. His wife brought an action against the British Railways Board under the Fatal Accidents Acts and sought discovery of a report compiled on the accident by the Board. It was clear from an affidavit produced on behalf of the Board that the report was prepared for a dual purpose; for railway operation and safety purposes and for the purpose of obtaining legal advice in anticipation of litigation, both purposes being described as being of equal rank or weight. Discovery was resisted on the ground of legal professional privilege and the application was refused. On appeal by the widow, *held*, it was established that the public interest in disclosure of a report could be overridden in order that a defendant might properly prepare his case. The question was how close the connection had to be between the preparation of the document and the anticipation of litigation. To qualify for legal professional privilege, the purpose of preparing for litigation had to be the dominant purpose for which the document was prepared. In this case, it was not the dominant purpose and the appeal would be allowed.

WAUGH V BRITISH RAILWAYS BOARD [1979] 2 All ER 1169 (House of Lords: LORD WILBERFORCE, LORD SIMON OF GLAISDALE, LORD EDMUND-DAVIES, LORD RUSSELL OF KILLOWEN and LORD KEITH OF KINKEL). *Birmingham and Midland Motor Omnibus Co Ltd v London and North Western Railway Co* [1913] 3 KB 850, CA, *Ankin v London and North Eastern Railway Co* [1929] All ER Rep 65, CA and *Ogden v London Electric Railway Co* [1933] All ER Rep 896, CA overruled. Decision of the Court of Appeal (1978) 122 Sol Jo 730, 1978 Halsbury's Abridgment para. 952 reversed.

917   —— —— privilege against self-incrimination—claim for privilege on basis of EEC Treaty

An action for infringement of copyright was defended on the grounds, inter alia, that the relief claimed constituted an abuse of the dominant market position held by the plaintiffs in the European Communities, contrary to EEC Treaty, art. 86. On the defendant company's application discovery was granted in respect of documents in the plaintiffs' possession relating to their exercise of any claim to the copyright in question in the Community. The plaintiffs duly served a list of the documents, but claimed privilege in respect of them on the ground that to give discovery would be self-incriminatory to the extent that they established a breach of the EEC Treaty which could give rise to a criminal offence. The defendants then applied for the proceedings to be stayed pending an investigation by the EC Commission as to whether the plaintiffs had abused their dominant market position contrary to art. 86. *Held*, if the plaintiffs' claim to privilege was good the court would be unable to determine the issue of the alleged infringement of copyright, since the necessary documents would be unavailable. However Council Regulation (EEC) No. 17 gave the Commission wide powers of investigation in relation to alleged breaches of art. 86, which would include the power to examine the documents in question. Further, it was clear from the European Communities Act 1972 that a decision of the Commission or, were that decision appealed against, a decision of the European Court, that the plaintiffs had contravened art. 86 would constitute a good defence to the plaintiffs' action. Accordingly, the justice of the case required that the question of the alleged breach of art. 86 should be investigated by the Commission. The proceedings would therefore be stayed pending the final outcome of that investigation.

BRITISH LEYLAND MOTOR CORPN LTD V WYATT INTERPART CO LTD [1979] 3 CMLR 79 (Chancery Division: GRAHAM J).

For proceedings relating to discovery see, para. 919.

918   —— relevance of documents—patents—relevance to validity of patents

See *Halcon International Inc v The Shell Transport and Trading Co Ltd* (*Discovery No. 2*), para. 2022.

919 —— relevance of documents to questions raised in an action— action for infringement of copyright

An action for infringement of copyright was brought following the sale by the defendants in the United Kingdom of spare parts which they had imported from Italy and which were manufactured in Italy by the plaintiffs' subsidiary. The defendants alleged that any consent to the sales of these spare parts in Italy extended to other EEC member-States, including the United Kingdom. They further alleged that the relief sought by the plaintiffs would constitute an abuse of the plaintiffs' dominant position in the EEC, contrary to the EEC Treaty, art. 86. To advance their case, the defendants applied for discovery of documents containing details of prices, terms and conditions relating to the sale and supply by the plaintiffs of spare parts in the United Kingdom and details of conditions imposed on dealers touching the manner, terms and conditions of sale. *Held*, discovery as wide as that sought by the defendants would be oppressive. Discovery should be limited to disclosure of documents relating to the way in which the plaintiffs had exercised any claim to the copyright in question within the EEC.

BRITISH LEYLAND MOTOR CORPN V WYATT INTERPART CO LTD [1979] FSR 39 (Chancery Division: WHITFORD J).

For subsequent proceedings see para. 917.

920 —— undertaking of confidentiality—application for use of documents in foreign proceedings

The plaintiffs applied for certain patents in the Netherlands. The defendants opposed their application in the Netherlands Patents Office. Meanwhile the plaintiffs sought an injunction restraining the defendants from infringing those letters patent granted to the plaintiffs in the United Kingdom. In the English action the defendants made disclosure of a large number of documents to the plaintiffs' legal advisers only, subject to an undertaking of confidentiality. A selection of these documents, the "red file", was made available to the plaintiffs themselves in the English proceedings. The plaintiffs then sought to make the contents of the "red file" available in the Dutch proceedings. The Dutch court in question had no power to order discovery but once produced, any such documents would become available to the public without restraint if the application was successful. *Held*, the "red file" itself did not justify a claim for confidentiality. There was however real evidence that if the file was put forward in the Dutch proceedings, the defendants would be faced with either not putting forward further confidential documents which were material in explaining the "red file" or putting forward the documents and risking them being made public if the plaintiffs' application succeeded. The court would not give permission for the "red file" to be used by the plaintiffs in the Dutch proceedings.

HALCON INTERNATIONAL INC V SHELL TRANSPORT AND TRADING CO [1979] RPC 97 (Court of Appeal: MEGAW, SHAW and WALLER LJJ).

DISTRESS

Halsbury's Laws of England (4th edn.), Vol. 13, paras. 201–500

921 **Distress for rates**

The Distress for Rates Order 1979, S.I. 1979 No. 1038 (in force on 1st September 1979), supersedes the Distress for Rates Order 1972. It prescribes revised fees, charges and expenses in respect of, and incidental to, the levying of distress for rates.

922 —— appeal—jurisdiction of Crown Court

The applicant was arrested for failure to pay rates and taken before a magistrates' court. There was no investigation as to whether the failure to pay was due to wilful refusal or culpable neglect, and warrants of commitment were issued. Distress warrants had been issued twice in the previous year, but the applicant had not received any summons. He appealed to the Crown Court under the General Rate Act 1967, s. 99 (5), as "a person aggrieved by a distress". The Crown Court held that it had no jurisdiction because no distress had been levied. The applicant appealed, and also sought orders of certiorari to quash the distress warrants on the ground that as he had not received any summons, there had been a breach of natural justice, and to quash the warrants of commitment on the grounds that there had been no sufficient inquiry into whether the failure to pay was due to wilful refusal or culpable neglect. *Held*, the warrants of distress would not be quashed; although the applicant had not received notice of the applications for the warrants, where a rating authority had followed the statutory formula and the prescribed procedure with regard to written notice, it could not be said that there was a breach of natural justice. The Crown Court had jurisdiction under s. 99 (5) to hear the appeal because although there was no sufficient distress available, the applicant was prejudiced by the fact that the bailiffs had gone in which had put him at risk of imprisonment on a warrant of commitment. The warrants of commitment would be quashed since the magistrates had failed to make sufficient inquiry into means.

R v LIVERPOOL JJ, EX PARTE GREAVES [1979] RA 119 (Queen's Bench Division: LORD WIDGERY CJ, BRIDGE LJ and CAULFIELD J).

923   —— **application for warrant of commitment—inquiry into conduct or means**

See *R v Liverpool JJ, ex parte Greaves*, para. 922.

924   —— **no summons received—breach of natural justice**

See *R v Liverpool JJ, ex parte Greaves*, para. 922.

925   **Distress for rent—rules**

The Distress for Rent (Amendment) Rules 1979, S.I. 1979 No. 711 (in force on 16th July 1979), amend the provisions of the Distress for Rent Rules 1953 as to the requirement of security for a certificate to act as a bailiff, and prescribe revised fees, charges and expenses recoverable in respect of the levying of distress for rent under these Rules.

DIVORCE

Halsbury's Laws of England (4th edn.), Vol. 13, paras. 501–1352

926   **Articles**

Changes of Name After Family Breakdown, M. D. A. Freeman (some recent cases): 143 JP Jo 331.

Divorce Within the First Three Years of Marriage, Terence Ingman (discussion on Matrimonial Causes Act 1973, s. 3): 9 Fam Law 165.

Family Home On Breakdown: Property Adjustment Order: The Present Situation, Alec Samuels: 9 Fam Law 209.

Foreign Divorces and Financial Provision, J. G. Miller: 123 Sol Jo 4.

Matrimonial Orders for the Payment of Money—What the Books do not Tell You, G. H. Gypps: Law Notes Vol. 98, No. 3, p. 79.

Matrimonial Statistics 1977, Susan Maidment (discussion of *Judicial Statistics* for 1977 (Cmnd 7254, 1977–78)): 129 NLJ 199.

The Parental Obligation to Maintain, J. M. Thomson (the nature of such an obligation and the way in which it can be enforced): 9 Fam Law 71.

Protection For Spouses Resident Abroad, J. G. Miller (consideration, in relation to divorce proceedings in England, of the position of a spouse resident outside the jurisdiction): 123 Sol Jo 224.

Some Principles of Financial and Property Adjustment on Divorce, J. M. Eekelaar (the inadequacies of Matrimonial Causes Act 1973, s. 25(1)): (1979) 95 LQR 253.

927   Access to child—expert report on mother's condition

See *Noble v Robert Thompson (a firm)*, para. 1255.

928   Consent applications—periodical payments direct to child—procedure

See para. 2131.

929   Custody—access—factors to be considered

The parties separated in 1974. The wife was English, the husband Pakistani. The wife obtained an order for custody of their two young children. The husband had access to the children. In June 1976, the husband took the children, who were staying with him for a weekend, to Pakistan without informing the wife. He brought them back in July 1976, when they were found to be in poor health. The wife subsequently refused to allow the husband to see the children. The wife obtained a decree nisi in December 1976. The judge refused the husband's application for access on the grounds that it was doubtful whether access would benefit the children, and that there would be difficulties in supervising access for several years. The husband appealed. *Held*, the paramount consideration when deciding whether to grant access was the benefit of the children. In all the circumstances, the judge had reached the right conclusion in refusing all access to the husband. The appeal would be dismissed.

RASHID v RASHID (1979) 9 Fam Law 118 (Court of Appeal: STAMP and ORR LJJ).

930   —— advice of welfare officer

See *J v J*, para. 1867.

931   —— joint custody—matters to be considered

See *Baker v Baker*, para. 1868.

932   —— postponement for further evidence

The children of marriage, a boy and a girl, were living in Australia with their mother who was having an affair with her young cousin. The children were very distressed and unhappy. A judge, relying on the evidence of a welfare officer's report from Australia, awarded custody of the children to the father. The mother appealed, contending that the decision as to custody should be postponed for evidence from a further welfare officer's report, as the children had had time to settle in their new home and new school since the first report had been made. The mother submitted affidavits from members of her family which contradicted the welfare officer's report, and which had not been available to the judge at first instance. *Held*, on the facts and the additional evidence, the situation of the children was such that it ought not to be allowed to continue. There were proceedings pending in Australia and if further evidence before the Australian court established that the children were no longer unhappy, effective action could be taken by that court. The appeal would be dismissed.

CORBET v CORBET (1979) 9 Fam Law 19 (Court of Appeal: STAMP, ORMROD and CUMMING-BRUCE LJJ).

933   —— taking child out of jurisdiction—application for leave—conditions

A mother applied for leave to take the only child of the marriage to America. She had married an officer in the United States Air Force after her divorce. Leave was granted, but the judge attached conditions to the leave to be supported "by a bond to be agreed in the sum of £10,000". Both parents were wealthy, and the mother had assets of the order of £50,000. No bond was agreed. The mother appealed, proposing an amendment to the order. She proposed that, in place of the bond, the order should require her to deposit a sum of £1,000 which would be forfeit should the court be satisfied that she was or had been in breach of the order. *Held*, as the parties had reached no agreement, a bond in these circumstances was of remarkably little value. The whole concept of the bond in this case was inappropriate and ineffective and also undesirable. If some form of security for the performance of the conditions of the order was desirable, the proposed amendment was a reasonable one. The appeal would be allowed, and an order in the terms proposed by the notice of appeal would be substituted for that part of the order requiring the bond.

BOYD (formerly BICKERDIKE) v BICKERDIKE (1979) 9 Fam Law 122 (Court of Appeal: ORMROD and BROWNE LJJ and SIR DAVID CAIRNS).

934   **Decree absolute—declaration of satisfaction with arrangements for children—issue as to custody**

A wife filed a petition for divorce which was undefended. A decree nisi was pronounced and an appointment made for consideration of arrangements made for the children of the marriage. The husband had not objected to the wife's claim for custody but at the appointment he said that he was applying for legal aid to claim custody. The wife applied for a declaration under the Matrimonial Causes Act 1973, s. 41, which provides that the court must not make absolute a decree of divorce unless it has made a declaration as to arrangements for the welfare of the children. The question of the declaration and custody was adjourned and the wife appealed. *Held*, the question of custody was rightly stood over to give the husband time to make an application for custody. However, the making of the decree absolute should not be deferred, so a declaration would be granted under s. 41 (1) (b) (i) that the wife's arrangements were the best that could be devised in the circumstances. An order would be made in the wife's favour for the interim custody of the children and the husband would be ordered to file an application for custody.

A v A (CHILDREN: ARRANGEMENTS) [1979] 2 All ER 493 (Court of Appeal: ORR, ORMROD and GEOFFREY LANE LJJ).

935   **Domestic courts—constitution**

See paras. 1779, 1780.

936   **Domestic Proceedings and Magistrates' Courts Act 1978—commencement**

The Domestic Proceedings and Magistrates' Courts Act 1978 (Commencement No. 3) Order 1979, S.I. 1979 No. 731 specifies 17th September 1979 as the date of commencement for Domestic Proceedings and Magistrates' Courts Act 1978, s. 40, 1978 Halsbury's Abridgment para. 1509. The date of commencement for ss. 16–18, 28, 29 (1), (2), (5), 30, 75–85, 88 (1)–(4) and certain provisions of Schs. 2 and 3 is 1st November 1979. Schedule 2 of the Order contains transitional provisions adapting certain provisions of the Act under s. 89 (4) in consequence of the partial operation of the Act.

937   **Financial provision—agreement to waive future claims to maintenance—House of Lords decision—whether binding on Judicial Committee of the Privy Council**

See *De Lasala v De Lasala*, para. 1643.

938   **—— lump sum payment—enforcement—appointment of receiver**

A husband was ordered to pay his former wife a lump sum of £2,000, but failed to do so. His only asset was an interest under a trust for sale as a tenant in common with his brother of a house, the former matrimonial home. The brother would not agree to a sale. The wife applied for the appointment of a receiver by way of equitable execution over the husband's interest in the property. *Held*, the court had jurisdiction to appoint a receiver, who would be authorised to take any necessary proceedings in the husband's name to enforce a sale of the property.

LEVERMORE v LEVERMORE [1979] 1 WLR 1277 (Family Division: BALCOMBE J).

939   —— —— **long period of separation before application**

The parties married in 1935 and there were three children of the family. In 1956, the wife left the matrimonial home to live with another man, by whom she had a son in 1957. She continued to live with the other man, making no financial claim on the husband. In 1976, the other man entered a home in order to receive permanent medical care. The wife was living in a flat with her son, who intended to buy the flat with a mortgage. The husband was living in the former matrimonial home, a house and yard valued at £26,500. The wife was granted a decree nisi of divorce in 1978. The wife sought a lump sum payment and an order for the sale of the matrimonial home, the proceeds of sale to be divided, under the Married Women's Property Act 1882, s. 17. *Held*, the wife was in no danger of losing occupation of her present home and was not in need. After a long lapse of time, a party to a marriage should be entitled to take the view that there would be no revival or initiation of financial claims against him; the longer the lapse of time, the less should any claim be encouraged or entertained. Further, even if it could be assumed that the wife was entitled to a lump sum payment, it was unreasonable to expect the husband to raise that amount by the sale of the house and yard or to raise a loan on the equity existing in the premises. Accordingly, the summons would be dismissed.

CHAMBERS v CHAMBERS (1979) 123 Sol Jo 689 (Family Division: WOOD J).

940   —— —— **matters to be considered**

The parties had been married since 1945 and had one married daughter. The wife was granted a decree nisi on the ground that the marriage had irretrievably broken down due to her husband's adultery. She was unemployed, without capital, whilst the husband was a senior civil servant earning £7,152 and due to retire in three years' time, receiving a £9,000 lump sum payment when he did so. The proceeds from the sale of the matrimonial home, a sum of £22,500, were deposited in the parties' joint names, but the husband had further investments in various saving schemes, one of which amounted to £4,400. If the marriage had continued, and the wife survived her husband, she would have received a pension of £1,000. A lump sum of £7,750 was awarded to her which did not take into account the investment savings of £4,400, the lump sum gratuity of the husband or her own pension rights. The wife appealed. *Held*, despite the earlier conclusion that the savings investment was of a different character from that of the remainder of the husband's assets, it was nevertheless evident that had the marriage continued the wife would have benefited from all capital earned or saved by the husband, including pension rights and investments. She was thus entitled to a certain share in all assets. However, her share should not be greater than one third, thereby increasing the payment to £12,000.

RICHARDSON v RICHARDSON (1978) 9 Fam Law 86 (Court of Appeal: STAMP, ORR and BRIDGE LJJ).

941   —— —— —— **matrimonial home**

After cohabiting for a number of years, the parties married. Shortly after the marriage the parties separated and it was dissolved. The husband remained in the matrimonial home, having divided it into flats, for one of which he received rent. The wife applied for a lump sum to be paid to her as her interest in the home. She obtained a surveyor's report on the value of the property but, believing it to be too low, failed to reveal the report to both the husband and the registrar. She put the value at £10,000 whilst the husband put it at between £5,000 and £7,500. The registrar accepted a valuation of £8,000 and ordered the husband to pay a lump sum of £2,300. The husband appealed. *Held*, it was the duty of all concerned to disclose all information relevant to a fair assessment of the value of property where payments of such large amounts were involved; the registrar should have rejected the valuations of both husband and wife as being unreliable. The husband would have been unable to find the sum ordered without selling the house, and therefore part of his means of livelihood, whilst the wife was already securely housed. This should have been taken into consideration as it emphasised the need to obtain an accurate valuation. The appeal would only proceed when a new survey had been carried out.

CHAND v CHAND (1978) 9 Fam Law 84 (Court of Appeal: ORMROD, WALLER and BRANDON LJJ).

942 —— matters to be considered—cohabitation of parties before marriage

The parties had lived together since 1947 and a son was born in 1950. The woman, who had been working part-time in the man's engineering business, took on full-time employment there in 1955. They lived together in a house bought by the man and there was another family home in the country. Both properties were held on trust on behalf of the son. The parties married in 1971 and in 1972 a second matrimonial home was purchased in the son's name. The marriage only lasted four months, however, as the husband refused to continue cohabitation. In 1977, the wife and son, who had joined the family business, bought out the husband's shares with the proceeds from the sale of the second house. A decree nisi was also granted to the wife in that year. She lived in the country house while the husband occupied the former matrimonial home. The wife's application for a lump sum order of £8,000 to enable her to purchase a flat near the business was opposed by the husband on the grounds of inter alia the shortness of the marriage. She also applied for an order for periodical payments. *Held*, a fair and just resolution to the problems had to be reached with the aid of the Matrimonial Causes Act 1973, s. 25. It was important not to limit the court's discretion by a narrow construction of the guidelines. The section required consideration of the "conduct" of the parties and "all the circumstances of the case" and there was nothing in recent authorities to suggest that a broad and general approach to those words was wrong or undesirable. In the present case the wife had given the best years of her life to the husband. She had helped to build up the family business and had managed the home and brought up the son. The wife's behaviour before the marriage had to be taken into account and the sum of £8,000 was not an unreasonable figure to be awarded. It could not be said that the judgment would encourage relationships outside marriage as there would be very few occasions upon which a court would be likely to hold that justice required such recognition of behaviour. Accordingly, the order would be made but the claim for periodical payments would be dismissed.

K v K (1979) Times, 4th December (Family Division: WOOD J).

943 —— —— conduct of parties

The parties married in 1957 and had three children. The husband was a civil engineer working on overseas projects and so the family lived abroad until the breakdown of the marriage in 1972. The wife did not work. Their relationship was turbulent and the wife had attacked and wounded her husband, resulting, on one occasion, in his hospitalisation. She bitterly resented the time her husband spent on his career and maintained that the family had suffered as a result of his ambition. She had however maintained their various homes and cared for the children. A decree nisi was granted to the husband on the basis of five years' separation. On an application by the husband for the decree to be made absolute, the wife sought financial provision for herself. The husband maintained that his wife's conduct was responsible for the breakdown of the marriage and that it had seriously damaged his career, and that he was therefore discharged from his liability to provide for her. *Held*, the wife's behaviour had contributed towards the breakdown both by her violence and her attitude towards her husband and his career, and was a relevant factor to be taken into account when considering her application. She had however made a valuable contribution by looking after the home and the children. Taking into account the husband's own shortcomings, it would be unfair to deprive her of all financial provision, but this would be reduced in view of her behaviour. The matrimonial home would be held on trust for sale, sale to be postponed until the wife died, remarried or ceased to reside, whichever was the earliest. The proceeds of the sale would be divided into 25 per cent for the wife and 75 per cent for the children. The husband would be required to pay a lump sum of £3,000 towards urgent repairs necessary to be made to the house. He would also pay her £1,000 per annum, which should not be reduced if she obtained a job. In view of the fact that the children would benefit from the proper maintenance of the house, she would also receive £800 per annum to cover mortgage repayments and house maintenance. Upon such financial provisions being made, the decree nisi would be made absolute.

BATEMAN v BATEMAN [1979] 2 WLR 377 (Family Division: PURCHAS J).

944   —— —— **conduct of wife—financial needs**

In 1971 a widower aged sixty-one married a woman of fifty-one who was then obliged to surrender her council flat. In 1972 the husband obtained an order on the ground of her cruelty that he need not live with her and that she be excluded from the matrimonial home. After their divorce the wife, who was in receipt of supplementary benefit and living in rented accommodation, claimed financial provision. The husband contended that her conduct and the duration of the marriage entitled him to refuse to make provision. *Held*, the wife's conduct had been deplorable, but in view of her deteriorating health and the surrender of her council flat she should receive £1,000 in full and final settlement of her financial claim.

WARDER v WARDER [1978] LS Gaz R 1060 (Family Division: PURCHAS J).

945   —— **periodical payments—agreement to waive future claims to maintenance—rule of court**

The parties separated in October 1971. They subsequently agreed, in February 1972, that on the granting of a decree of divorce the wife should apply for consent orders for annual maintenance of a certain sum, to be increased during any period when the husband should be a Member of Parliament, during their joint lives or until the wife's remarriage. The wife agreed to consent to her claims for lump sum or secured provision being dismissed and that she would not make any future claims for financial provision whatsoever. The agreement was to be conditional on the approval of the court. On an originating application, the judge was of the opinion that the agreement was fair and reasonable. Minutes of order were drawn up and approved by both parties. On the making of a decree nisi in December 1973, it was ordered that those minutes of order should be made a rule of court. In February 1978, the wife applied for variation of the periodical payments. The husband applied to have his wife's application struck out on the ground of lack of jurisdiction by reason of the order of December 1973. The registrar refused. The husband successfully appealed against the registrar's decision. On appeal by the wife, *held*, on the very face of the order, there was a continuing provision for periodical payments to go on indefinitely "until further order". The order was not a genuinely final order. Further, it was contrary to public policy that a maintenance agreement should be made unalterably binding on a wife. The Matrimonial Causes Act 1973, s. 31 (1) applied and the court had power to vary or discharge the order or to suspend any provision of it for periodical payments. The court therefore had jurisdiction to entertain the wife's application. The appeal would be allowed.

JESSEL v JESSEL [1979] 1 WLR 1148 (Court of Appeal: LORD DENNING MR, BROWNE and GEOFFREY LANE LJJ). *Hyman v Hyman* [1929] AC 601, HL applied. *Minton v Minton* [1979] 1 All ER 79, HL, 1978 Halsbury's Abridgment para. 970 distinguished.

946   —— **provision for children—husband's contribution**

The President of the Family Division, in assessing the amount of maintenance that a husband should be ordered to pay, stated that it was generally accepted that there should be no order under £5 per week, notwithstanding the amount of supplementary benefit paid for a dependent child.

RE L (1979) 9 Fam Law 152 (Family Division: SIR GEORGE BAKER P).

947   —— —— **child of the family**

The husband and wife were married in 1971 when the wife was pregnant by another

man. Another child was born in 1973 of which the husband was not the father.
In 1976 the wife presented a divorce petition, alleging that there were two children
of the family of whom the husband was not the father, but whom he had accepted
and supported as children of the family. The husband signed an acknowledgment
of service and replied "no" to the question whether he wished to apply for custody
of the children. A decree nisi was granted and custody was awarded to the wife
under the Matrimonial Causes Act 1973, s. 42, which confers jurisdiction to make
a custody order only in relation to children of the family. An order was made for
periodical payments in favour of the children. On appeal by the husband against the
order, the judge made a finding of fact that the husband had never accepted the
children as members of the family, but dismissed the appeal on the ground that
notwithstanding that finding of fact, he was bound to hold that the children were
children of the family because the husband was estopped from denying it. On
further appeal by the husband, *held*, there was authority for the proposition that a
custody order involved by necessary implication a decision on the issue whether the
child was a child of the spouses, now replaced by the modern concept of a child of
the family, and thus an estoppel arose on the basis of res judicata. However, the
doctrine of estoppel was in retreat in matrimonial matters and the case relied upon
to support that proposition was wrongly decided. It should be overruled and the
appeal allowed.

ROWE V ROWE [1979] 2 All ER 1123 (Court of Appeal: ORR and CUMMING-
BRUCE LJJ and SIR STANLEY REES). *Lindsay v Lindsay* [1934] P 162, [1934] All ER
Rep 149 overruled.

948   —— —— **maintenance of standard of living of children**

See *Lilford v Glynn*, para. 949.

949   —— **settlement of property—court's jurisdiction to order settlements in favour of children over eighteen**

Following the parties' divorce in 1969, the husband, who was a millionaire, provided
a trust fund of £30,000 for the education of the two children. The wife later
successfully applied for additional periodical payments for the children's benefit.
Subsequently, she sought a variation of the order for periodical payments and an
order for a settlement for the children on the grounds that the current payments
were not sufficient to maintain them at the standard of living they would have
enjoyed if the marriage had continued. The trustees of the fund also claimed that the
income of the trust fund was insufficient to pay the children's school fees. The court
then ordered the husband to make increased secured periodical payments to each
child until the age of 18, to pay their school fees and to make a settlement of £25,000
on each child. The husband appealed against that part of the order requiring him to
pay the school fees and provide the settlement. *Held*, (i) since the husband had
created a trust fund to provide for the education of the children, it would be unjust
to place on him the primary liability for the school fees. Accordingly, the order to
pay the fee would be revoked but the husband would have to undertake to pay any
balance of the fees unpaid by the trustees. (ii) While the court was empowered
under Matrimonial Causes Act 1973, s. 24 (1) (b) to order a settlement, it did not
follow that on divorce, a father whose means permitted it ought to be ordered to
make settlements in favour of his children. As there were restrictions on making
other forms of financial provision in favour of children who had already reached the
age of 18, it was wrong to order settlements which provided for the payment of
income to children during the whole of their life. Furthermore, although under s.
25 (2) of the Act, the court was required to exercise the power to order a settlement
so as to place the children in the financial position they would have been if the
marriage had continued and each party had discharged his financial obligations and
responsibilities towards the children, even the richest father was not to be regarded
as under a financial obligation to provide such settlements where the children were
under no disability and their maintenance and education were secured. Moreover,
in the present case there was no certainty that if the marriage had continued the

father would have made settlements in favour of the children. It followed that the court had been wrong to order the settlements and the appeal would be allowed.

LILFORD v GLYNN [1979] 1 All ER 441 (Court of Appeal: STAMP, ORR and GEOFFREY LANE LJJ). Dicta of Scarman LJ in *Chamberlain v Chamberlain* [1974] 1 All ER 33 at 38 applied.

950 ——— transfer of property—matrimonial home—application for order for sale

See *Chambers v Chambers*, para. 939.

951 ——— ——— charge in husband's favour

The parties married in 1953, when the husband was twenty-eight, and the wife thirty-five, years old. They had a son of eighteen years who had suffered from illness in childhood requiring special care from the wife. The wife lived in the matrimonial home with the son, who contributed towards household expenses. The husband was living in an alcoholics' hospital in deplorable conditions. The wife obtained a decree nisi in 1975. The registrar ordered that the matrimonial home, worth £11,000 with an equity of £10,000, be transferred to the wife. There were difficulties in assessing the husband's contributions to the expenses of the marriage, but the transfer was made subject to a charge of £3,500 in the husband's favour, the charge to be enforceable after five years or the wife's earlier death. On appeal by the wife, the judge ordered that the house be transferred to the wife free of any charge. The husband appealed. *Held*, it would be wrong and unjust to deprive the husband of any interest in the house, despite his alcoholism. However, the order made by the registrar providing for sale of the house to take place after the lapse of five years was a wrong order to make in the circumstances; the wife would be sixty-five years old on the expiry of the five year period and, having no other capital, would be obliged to sell to satisfy the charge. The husband should have an interest of £3,500, but that interest should only become effective on the death of the wife. The appeal would be allowed, and an order made to that effect.

KURYLOWICZ v KURYLOWICZ (1979) 9 Fam Law 119 (Court of Appeal: STAMP, ORR and BRIDGE LJJ).

952 ——— ——— effect of husband's unemployment

The parties, now aged 50, married in 1952. They had two children, one aged 23 and the other aged 18. In April 1978 the wife obtained a decree nisi, custody of the younger child and an order, inter alia, requiring the husband to transfer the whole of the equity in the matrimonial home to the wife. In appealing against the order, the husband contended that the court had not taken note of the fact that he was now unemployed. He had been a chartered secretary and accountant earning over £7,000 per annum and had been in his last employment for nineteen years. *Held*, the husband was looking for new employment at substantially the same remuneration as he had previously enjoyed. This was reasonable if he was to continue providing for the wife and child. The judge had paid too little regard to the difficulties of the husband. The wife would be able to obtain a suitable home for herself out of two-thirds of the proceeds of sale of the matrimonial home. The order would be substituted by an order for sale of the home, two-thirds of the net proceeds of sale after discharging the mortgage debt, to be paid to the wife.

BENNETT v BENNETT (1978) 9 Fam Law 19 (Court of Appeal: STAMP, ORR and BRIDGE LJJ).

953 ——— ——— respective shares—matters to be taken into consideration—availability of alternative accommodation

The wife was granted a divorce and remained in the matrimonial home with her twelve-year-old daughter. The husband lived in a bed-sitting room. The home was bought on mortgage through the proceeds of compensation received by the husband for an industrial injury. The husband was in secure employment and received a disability payment. His wife worked part-time and had paying guests in the summer. The judge ordered, inter alia, that the house be transferred to the husband and wife jointly in equal shares, the wife to live there until her child reached the age of seventeen, or ceased full-time education. On appeal by the wife, *held*, it would be unjust to deprive the husband of all his interests in the matrimonial home. However, the sum realised by the wife upon the sale of the house would probably not be enough for her to obtain secure accommodation for herself. The order would be varied so that the house vested two-thirds in the wife and one-third in the husband.

CAWKWELL v CAWKWELL (1978) 9 Fam Law 25 (Court of Appeal: STAMP and ORR LJJ).

954   Foreign decree—recognition

See CONFLICT OF LAWS.

955   Grounds for divorce—matrimonial relief—suggested reforms

The Family Law Sub-committee of the Contentious Business Committee of the Law Society's Council has prepared a discussion paper on family law reform. The paper considers the deficiencies in the law relating to marital breakdown and puts forward certain suggestions for its reform. Its main recommendations are that the Matrimonial Causes Act 1973, s. 1 should be amended so that the only ground for divorce is the irretrievable breakdown of marriage as shown by the spouses having lived apart for one or more years prior to the presentation of the petition. This would remove all remaining traces of the matrimonial offence and the competitive nature of divorce proceedings so that full attention can be directed to issues such as children's welfare and family finance. Further, a single system of family law should apply to all family matters and the courts' powers to grant matrimonial relief should be extended so as to enable them to make maintenance and custody orders regardless of whether there has been a petition for divorce. An informal family court should be set up with exclusive jurisdiction in all family matters. Attached to the court should be a welfare and counselling service staffed by people qualified to advise on matters such as social security entitlements and the forms of relief obtainable through the court: [1979] LS Gaz 253.

956   Maintenance orders—magistrates' court order—application for remission of arrears—jurisdiction of magistrates

A wife, who brought a summons for arrears of maintenance payments due under a magistrates' order for maintenance, was represented at the hearing by her solicitors. Her husband obtained partial remittance of the arrears under Magistrates' Courts Act 1952, s. 76 because she had hindered his access to their children. She applied for an order of certiorari to quash the order, on the ground that she had not been given a reasonable opportunity to make representations to the court and that hindering access was not a good reason for remitting arrears. *Held*, the wife could not claim she had not had an opportunity to make representations because her solicitors were present in court. Although it was not clear what would constitute a ground for remission, in this case the remission amounted to a punishment for hindering access and should not have been allowed. The order of certiorari would be granted.

R v HALIFAX JJ, EX PARTE WOOLVERTON (1979) 123 Sol Jo 80 (Queen's Bench Division: LORD WIDGERY CJ, BRIDGE LJ and CAULFIELD J).

957   —— reciprocal enforcement

See CONFLICT OF LAWS.

958   Maintenance proceedings—address for service—servicemen

See para. 2135.

959   Matrimonial causes—appeal from registrar—lodgment of notes of evidence and judgment—duty of solicitor—practice

See para. 2130.

960   —— costs

The Matrimonial Causes (Costs) Rules 1979, S.I. 1979 No. 399 (in force on 24th April 1979), replace the Matrimonial Causes (Costs) Rules 1977, 1977 Halsbury's Abridgment para. 956, as amended. They introduce a new composite scale ("the matrimonial scale") for the taxation of costs of matrimonial proceedings in the High Court, in a divorce county court, or in both. So far as proceedings in the High Court are concerned, the new scale follows the scale in RSC Ord. 62, Appendix 2 reasonably closely. So far as proceedings in a divorce county court are concerned, the new scale replaces the divorce scale with a simpler set of provisions, modelled on the scale in Ord. 62, Appendix 2. In addition, the Rules re-enact, with slight modifications, the other provisions in the 1977 Rules affecting costs in connection with matrimonial proceedings in a divorce county court.

961   —— —— taxation—procedure

See para. 2133.

962   —— fees—amendment

The Matrimonial Causes Fees (Amendment) Order 1979, S.I. 1979 No. 966 (in force on 3rd September 1979), amends the Matrimonial Causes Fees Order 1975, 1975 Halsbury's Abridgment para. 1139 by increasing the fee payable on presenting a petition to £25.

963   —— rules

The Matrimonial Causes (Amendment) Rules 1979, S.I. 1979 No. 400 (in force on 24th April 1979) amend the Matrimonial Causes Rules 1977, S.I. 1977 No. 345, 1977 Halsbury's Abridgment para. 956. Rule 64 (1) of the 1977 Rules, as amended now provides for the same procedure for the rescission of decrees of judicial separation by consent, following a reconciliation, as is already provided for the rescission of decrees nisi of divorce or nullity. Appendix 2, para. 5 (c) is amended to allow the petitioner who is proceeding in person to give as the address for service the name or firm and address of a solicitor from whom the petitioner is receiving advice, if the solicitor agrees, or any other address in England and Wales to which documents for the petitioner may be sent.

964   —— —— service of documents—reasonableness of costs

The parties separated in March 1976. On July 7th, the wife petitioned for divorce and issued notice of application for an injunction against molestation. The documents were personally served on the husband on July 13th. He was not legally represented at this time. The husband later broke an undertaking not to molest the wife and, on an ex parte application to commit made by the wife on August 23rd, an order was made directing that the husband be brought before the court. On August 25th, the husband, now legally represented, gave a second undertaking; the order containing this undertaking was also served on him personally. When the second undertaking was broken, the wife made another ex parte application to commit on November 4th, but the husband's solicitors refused to accept service as they no longer had contact with him. Attempts to serve notice of the wife's application were finally abandoned. On taxation, the registrar disallowed the wife's costs of service of notice of application to commit dated July 7th, service of the order made on August 25th and service of notice of application dated November 4th on the ground that those costs were not reasonably incurred within the Matrimonial Causes Rules 1973, r. 119. Rule 119 governs the service of documents where no special mode of service is prescribed. The wife appealed. *Held*, (i) with regard to service of the documents on July 13th, r. 119 (a) did not apply, as the husband was not legally represented then, and the petition had not been served. Applying r. 119 (b), the application for costs was reasonable, as the husband's whereabouts were not known and so the wife's solicitors had no effective option but to serve notice personally or to apply to the registrar for an order dispensing with service. (ii) In relation to service of the order of August 25th, the rules did not specifically mention the service of a notice of an undertaking and so it was open to question whether personal service of the order containing the husband's second undertaking was strictly necessary. Under r. 60, the wife's solicitors had the option of serving the order personally or delivering it to his solicitors. However, the registrar should have considered all the circumstances of the case when deciding whether it had been reasonable to serve the order on the husband personally. (iii) Under the County Court Rules 1936, Ord. 25, r. 68, personal service of notice of the application to commit on November 4th was mandatory, as neither of the prescribed options would have been reasonable. The costs of that personal service had therefore been reasonably incurred. The appeal would be allowed in respect of the costs for service of the orders of July 13th and November 4th. The question of whether costs for the service of the order of August 25th were reasonable would be referred to the registrar for consideration.

. The court repeated the principle that rules of practice should not be allowed to interfere with the care which the judge had to take when considering applications for injunctions in matrimonial cases. Taxation of the costs of service in such cases should be considered in relation to the merits of the individual case and the difficulties facing the petitioner's solicitors.

JACOB v JACOB (1979) 9 Fam Law 57 (Court of Appeal: ORMROD, WALKER and BRANDON LJJ).

1973 Rules, as amended, now consolidated in Matrimonial Causes Rules 1977, 1977 Halsbury's Abridgment para. 955.

965　　　Matrimonial home—transfer of ownership on divorce

See *Bennett v Bennett*, para. 952; *Kurylowicz v Kurylowicz*, para. 951.

966　　　——　——matters to be considered—availabilty of alternative accommodation

See *Cawkwell v Cawkwell*, para. 953.

967　　　Nullity of marriage—approbation of marriage—whether grant of decree statute-barred

The parties married in 1966 but the marriage was never consummated owing to the wife's refusal to have a physical impediment to sexual intercourse cured. The husband knew he could have the marriage avoided but in 1975 the parties adopted two children. In 1976 the husband left the wife and prayed for a decree of nullity. The question arose whether the husband's approbation of the marriage and the effect of the Matrimonial Causes Act 1973, s. 13 (1) precluded the grant of a decree. Section 13 (1) provides that a decree cannot be granted where a petitioner, knowing the marriage to be voidable, has led the respondent reasonably to believe he would not seek annullment and where it would be unjust to the respondent to grant a decree. *Held*, approbation of marriage was not a bar to the grant of a decree of nullity. The husband had led the wife to believe he would not have the marriage avoided but as there would be no injustice to the wife in granting the decree, s. 13 (1) did not create a statutory bar to the grant of one. Accordingly, the decree would be granted.

D v D (NULLITY) [1979] 3 All ER 337 (Family Division: DUNN J).

968　　　—— foreign decree—recognition

See *Perrini v Perrini*, para. 430.

969 Petition—dismissal on grounds of petitioner's responsibility for breakdown—second petition based on respondent's subsequent behaviour—whether petitioner entitled to decree

In 1974, a wife petitioned for divorce alleging that the marriage had broken down irretrievably and that her husband's behaviour was such that she could not reasonably be expected to live with him. The husband defended the petition and in 1976 it was dismissed on the ground that it was the wife's, not the husband's, behaviour that was the cause of the breakdown. The parties however continued to live in the matrimonial home but the husband made life unpleasant for the wife in an attempt to make her leave the home. The wife then presented a second petition on the same grounds as the first. On the question whether the wife could obtain a decree in the second suit, *held*, what had to be considered was whether the marriage had remained 'irretrievably broken down" and whether the husband's behaviour since 1976 was such that his wife could not reasonably be expected to live with him. Although the wife's behaviour was the cause of the breakdown of the marriage, she had established both those facts and accordingly the decree would be granted.

STEVENS V STEVENS [1979] 1 WLR 885 (Family Division: SHELDON J).

970 —— petitioner acting in person—address for service—practice

See para. 2135.

971 —— summons to strike out petition—diplomatic immunity—loss of immunity before summons heard

See *Shaw v Shaw*, para. 1341.

972 Practice—leave to appeal—application for leave to appeal out of time—criterion for grant

See *Williams v Williams*, para. 2104.

973 Preparation for trial—costs—taxation

See *Bwanaoga v Bwanaoga*, para. 2123.

974 Special procedure—application for leave to file an answer out of time—jurisdiction of judge to grant leave

The parties married in 1952. In 1977, the wife filed a divorce petition, which was served on the husband. He gave notice of intention to defend, but did not file an answer. The wife then applied to the registrar for directions for trial under the Matrimonial Causes Rules 1977, r. 33. The registrar gave the appropriate directions and entered the cause for trial in the special procedure list. He granted a certificate that the wife had proved the contents of her petition and fixed a date for pronouncement of the decree by the judge. The husband attended on the appointed day and applied for leave to file an answer out of time. The judge gave leave and took the case out of the special procedure list. The wife appealed. *Held*, the two questions to be decided were (i) whether the judge should have adjudicated on the husband's application at that stage and (ii) what principles should be applied in deciding whether to grant or refuse it. (i) Under the special procedure the process of adjudication was transferred from the judge to the registrar, who under the Matrimonial Causes Rules 1977, r. 48, certified that the petitioner had proved the contents of his petition and was entitled to a decree. The pronouncement of the decree by the judge was merely a formality. Thus the judge should not have entertained the husband's application. (ii) The registrar's certificate in the special procedure was tantamount to a decree nisi under the former procedure and an application by a respondent should therefore be dealt with on the same lines as an application for a re-hearing after a decree nisi; that is, it should be refused unless there were substantial grounds for the belief that the decree would have been obtained contrary to the justice of the case. However, certain handicaps of the respondent under the special procedure that did not exist under the ordinary procedure should be borne in mind in considering whether justice required that his application be granted. On the facts of the present case, the husband had had ample opportunity to file an answer before directions were given and the justice of the case did not require a re-hearing or that he should be permitted to defend. The appeal would be allowed.

DAY v DAY [1979] 2 All ER 187 (Court of Appeal: ORR, ORMROD and TEMPLEMAN LJJ). *Owen v Owen* [1964] 2 All ER 58, DC applied. See further 129 NLJ 11.

975   In a case in which a decree nisi had been granted under the special procedure notwithstanding the husband's attempts to obtain leave to file an answer, ORMROD LJ said that the granting of the decree nisi and the dismissal of the husband's application for leave to file an answer was based on a misunderstanding of the decision in *Day v Day*. It was thought that the effect of that decision was that the judge had no jurisdiction to hear the application, which had to be made to the registrar. In fact the application was not properly made in that case, and nothing was said to the effect that the judge could not hear a properly constituted application.

He added that difficulties might be avoided if the Matrimonial Causes Rules were amended to give more significance, so far as the special procedure was concerned, to the filing of a notice of intention to defend; for example, if the respondent were to be given notice that the registrar was about to give directions for trial under r. 33 (1) or to proceed to consider giving a certificate under r. 48 (1).

SIMS v SIMS (1979) 15th May (unreported) (Court of Appeal: ORR and ORMROD LJJ and SIR DAVID CAIRNS). *Day v Day* [1979] 2 All ER 187, CA, para. 974 explained.

976   **Undefended cause—agreement between parties—agreement made rule of court—enforcement**

See *Herbert v Herbert*, para. 2115.

977   **Unreasonable behaviour—dismissal of petition—second petition based on respondent's subsequent behaviour—whether petitioner entitled to decree**

See *Stevens v Stevens*, para. 969.

978   —— **proof of irretrievable breakdown—appeal—parties continuing to live together after divorce**

The parties married in 1940. The wife petitioned for divorce, alleging that her husband's behaviour was such that it was not reasonable to expect her to live with him. The judge granted her petition, refusing to accept the husband's evidence where it differed from that given by the wife and her witnesses. The husband, who was not in good health and was still being looked after by his wife, appealed. *Held*, the court had to accept the judge's findings of fact, as there was evidence to support those findings. Although the parties were still living together under the same roof, it was reasonably clear that the wife had been looking after her husband for a long time as an act of kindness; it would be wrong to treat the parties as though they were living together in an ordinary married situation. Accordingly, the appeal would be dismissed.

JUDGE v JUDGE (1979) 9 Fam Law 154 (Court of Appeal: ORMROD, WALLER and BRANDON LJJ).

EASEMENTS

Halsbury's Laws of England (4th edn.), Vol. 14, paras. 1–300

979   **Article**

Ancient Lights to a Greenhouse, F. G. (the point of law raised by *Allen v Greenwood* [1979] 2 WLR 187, CA, 1978 Halsbury's Abridgment para. 987, where the question was whether the quantity of light and heat required for a greenhouse could be acquired by prescription by uninterrupted enjoyment of the same for twenty years): 123 Sol Jo 616.

980   **Drainage—connection to private drain from neighbouring property—connection without permission**

See *Cook v Minion*, para. 2496.

981   **Right of way—express grant—means of access**

See *Nickerson v Barraclough*, para. 984.

982   —— —— **reservation of right to claim compensation—assessment of compensation**

The claimants agreed to buy a parcel of land bordering their own from the British Railways Board in April 1973. In May, the Board executed a deed granting a third party an easement to lay and maintain gas mains on the land and undertook not to build within a certain distance of the mains. The right as grantor (an expression which included its successor in title) to claim compensation from the third party was reserved, if the covenant was to affect the grant of any planning permission. The measure of compensation was stated to be the amount which would have been payable in respect of a compulsory acquisition of the easement by the third party. Land was conveyed to the claimants in June, and in November planning permission was granted for the erection of a warehouse and offices on both parcels of land. As the erection of part of these buildings was prevented by the covenant, the claimants, as the Board's successor in title, claimed compensation under the deed. *Held*, (i), the deed of grant related only to the servient land and could not be construed as conferring upon the claimants a right to compensation for injurious affection of the neighbouring land owned by them; (ii), Viscount Dilhorne dissenting, in valuing the servient land in accordance with the Lands Compensation Act 1961, s. 5, its value to the claimants as owners of the neighbouring land could be taken into account even though they were the only purchasers able to realise the full potential of the land by a joint development, as there was evidence of a market apart from the special needs of the claimants. The appeal would be allowed.

Blandrent Investment Developments Ltd v British Gas Corpn (1979) 252 Estates Gazette 267 (House of Lords: Lord Wilberforce, Viscount Dilhorne, Lord Salmon, Lord Keith of Kinkel and Lord Scarman). Decision of Court of Appeal (1978) Estates Gazette 131, 1978 Halsbury's Abridgment para. 989 reversed.

983   —— **prescription—lost modern grant—adverse user**

The plaintiffs claimed in prescription a right of way over a strip of land between the edge of a lane and an adjacent hedge. In order to allow vehicles and caravans to pass freely down the lane, the plaintiffs trimmed back the hedge. It was shown that, before the hedge had been trimmed, there were only two places where vehicles could pass by means of one of the vehicles pulling off the lane on to the verge. On appeal against the decision that no right of way had been established, *held*, the evidence showed that there had been no continuous passage of vehicles over the strip of land between the lane and the hedge. Two passing places were insufficient to create a right of way stretching along the verge at the side of the lane. The user had not been a user asserting a right, but a user relying upon the neighbourly good nature of the owner of the verge to tolerate that use. The claim in prescription therefore failed.

IRONSIDE v COOK (1978) 19th December (unreported) (Court of Appeal: BUCKLEY, GOFF and EVELEIGH LJJ).

984   —— way of necessity—public policy

A plot of building land was conveyed in 1906. The plan on the conveyance included a proposed new road along the route of an unmade lane which ran into a public highway. The lane adjoined the plot, but was separated from it by a dyke. The conveyance expressly provided that the vendor did not undertake either to build the new road or to give any right of way over the lane until such a road was built. The plot was, therefore, apparently land-locked. From 1908, a bridge over the dyke gave access from the lane onto the plot and from 1921 there was user of right of way over the lane. In 1922, the plot was enlarged when a strip of adjoining land was conveyed to the owner of the plot. The entire plot became vested in the plaintiff. The lane and dyke became vested in the defendants. From 1973, the defendants attempted to prevent the plaintiff from exercising a right of way over the lane to the highway. The plaintiff sought (i) a declaration that she was entitled to use a right of way of necessity over the lane; (ii) alternatively, a declaration that, by virtue of the 1922 conveyance and the Law of Property Act 1925, s. 62 (1) (a), a right of way was created from the lane onto the strip that could be used as a means of access from the strip to the rest of the plot. *Held*, (i) there was a rule of public policy that a transaction was not, without good reason, to be treated as effectively depriving land of a suitable means of access because it was in the public interest that land should not be made unusable. The express proviso in the 1906 conveyance was to be construed, in the light of the rule of public policy and the doctrine against derogation of grant, merely as freeing the vendor from any obligation to make up the proposed new road. If such a construction of the proviso was not permissible, public policy required that it should not have the effect of negativing an implied grant of a way of necessity over the lane; (ii) Although the general rule was that the grant of a right of way to reach a plot could not be used as a means of access to a second plot which was beyond the first, this rule would not apply if, at the time of the grant, the first plot formed a means of access to the second. The same rule would apply if the first plot was not used as an actual means of access to the second, but it was the intention of the parties that the first plot should be used in this way. The exception to the general rule applied not only where there was an express grant of the right of way, but also where the grant was implied by 1925 Act s. 62 (1) (a). The declarations would be made accordingly.

NICKERSON v BARRACLOUGH [1979] 3 All ER 312 (Chancery Division: MEGARRY V-C). *Harris v Flower* (1904) 74 LJ Ch 127 distinguished.

985   —— whether right of way capable of being occupied

See *Land Reclamation Co Ltd v Basildon District Council*, para. 1680.

ECCLESIASTICAL LAW

Halsbury's Laws of England (4th edn.), Vol. 14, paras. 301–1435

986   Churches—demolition—public inquiry procedure

The Department of the Environment has issued a Press Notice dated 14th February 1979 concerning a new public inquiry procedure for historic churches. A scheme enabling the Secretary of State for the Environment to hold non-statutory public inquiries into applications by the Church of England to demolish listed, and in some cases unlisted, Churches has now come into operation. The scheme will operate when the Church Commissioners notify the Secretary of State that they are minded to consent to the demolition of a listed church, or an unlisted church in a conservation area, as a result of a pastoral or redundancy scheme made under the Pastoral Measure 1968, and the demolition is opposed by either the Advisory Board for Redundant Churches or the local planning authority, or other circumstances make the Church Commissioners consider that the Secretary of State should be notified. The Secretary of State will then seek the advice of the Historic Buildings Council on whether a local inquiry should be held into the proposed demolition because of the architectural or historic interest of the church.

987   Faculty—painting—ownership of painting—whether gift or loan

By a petition a faculty was sought for the removal of a painting from a church where it had hung since about 1950. The petitioner claimed that the painting had come from his family home and had been introduced into the church by his mother merely on loan. An objection was lodged by the incumbent of the church, asserting that the painting had come to the church as a gift and that title was therefore vested in the churchwardens. *Held*, property in the painting could have passed to the churchwardens in one of two ways: either by the making of a gift of the painting to the church; or by the delivery of the painting into the custody of the churchwardens with the intention of dedicating it to God's service, albeit in the absence of a specific intention to make a gift of it. On the evidence in the case, which showed no indication by the petitioner or his family to any of the various incumbents or churchwardens who had held office since the introduction of the painting into the church that the painting was merely on loan, it was clear that the petitioner's mother, in delivering the painting into the custody of the churchwardens, had intended both to make a gift of it to the church and that it should be dedicated to God's service. Title to the painting had thus passed to the churchwardens in two ways and the petition would therefore be dismissed.

The court pointed out that even had the petitioner successfully established title to the painting in a temporal court, he would still have required a faculty (which would no doubt have been granted) in order to remove the painting from the custody of the church.

RE ESCOT CHURCH [1979] 3 WLR 339 (Exeter Consistory Court: CALCUTT CH).

988   Parochial fees

The Parochial Fees Order 1979, S.I. 1979 No. 194 (in force on 1st July 1979), amends the 1976 Order, 1976 Halsbury's Abridgment para. 925, by establishing a new table of fees payable for certain matters in connection with baptisms, marriages and burials, for the erection of monuments in churchyards and for miscellaneous other matters.

989   Redundant church—disposal of chattels

A church in one parish was declared redundant and, without a faculty, the rector disposed of the two bells to a committee of bellringers in another parish for £20, in the mistaken belief that they only had scrap value. It was then discovered that they were medieval, and the committee sought to dispose of one of them to a third parish for £250. The incumbent of the second parish petitioned for custody of the bells, and his petition was opposed by the first parish. The third parish also brought a petition for the introduction of one bell into its church. *Held*, following a declaration of redundancy, during the waiting period before the confirmation of the scheme, the contents of a redundant church had to be dealt with on proper advice and their disposal authorised. Since the disposal of the bells was not authorised, title to them remained vested in the churchwardens of the first parish. By agreement, one bell would be put at the disposal of the third parish, and the other returned to the first parish, on payment to the bellringers' committee in each case of £100. Accordingly, the first petition would be dismissed and the second granted.

RE WEST CAMEL CHURCH; RE YATTON CHURCH [1979] 2 All ER 652 (Bath and Wells Consistory Court: NEWSOM CH).

990   Redundant Churches Fund

The Grants to Redundant Churches Fund Order 1979, S.I. 1979 No. 478 (in force on 18th April 1979), enables the Secretary of State for the Environment, with the approval of the Treasury, to make grants to the Redundant Churches Fund, during the period 1st April 1979 to 31st March 1984 and payable at such times and on such conditions as he may specify; such grants not exceeding a maximum amount of £1,450,000.

991   —— payments

The Payments to Redundant Churches Fund Order 1979, S.I. 1979 No. 195 (in force on 1st April 1979), prescribes £1,450,000 as the maximum amount which the Church Commissioners must pay to the Redundant Churches Funds during the five year period from 1st April 1979 to 31st March 1984. The maximum amount of payments which may be made to the fund out of the net proceeds of sale and premiums is fixed at £483,000.

EDUCATION

Halsbury's Laws of England (4th edn.), Vol. 15, paras. 1–400

992   Awards

The Local Education Authority Awards Regulations 1979, S.I. 1979 No. 889 (in force on 1st September 1979), consolidate, with amendments, the Local Education Authority Awards Regulations 1978, 1978 Halsbury's Abridgment para. 1000. The principal amendments increase awards and relax the means tests applicable to the maintenance element of awards. The Regulations also take account of Council Regulation (EEC) 1612/68 which directs that children of nationals of member states who are or have been employed in another member state shall be admitted to that state's general educational courses, if such children are residing in its territory.

993   College of education—closure—compensation payable to staff

The applicant was a lecturer at a teachers' training college which was being run down at the direction of the Secretary of State. She accepted a full-time post under a one year contract from September 1976 to August 1977, after which her services would no longer have been required. She was offered and accepted part-time employment from September 1977 to August 1978 but left her post in January 1978. Her claims for both resettlement compensation and long-term compensation under the College of Education (Compensation) Regulations 1975 were rejected by an industrial tribunal. On appeal, *held*, the compensation claimed was for loss of employment and not loss of career. Employment meant the particular set of duties carried out by an employee for an employer. Notwithstanding that she accepted a part-time post, she had lost her employment in August 1977, as at that time her full-time duties came to an end. Her letter of appointment made it clear that her loss of employment was attributable to the Secretary of State's directions, and the fact that she knew her contract would finish at the end of the year was irrelevant. The applicant would be entitled to both resettlement compensation for loss of the particular employment and long-term compensation for loss of employment or diminution of emoluments.

PEARSON v KENT COUNTY COUNCIL (1979) 77 LGR 604 (Queen's Bench Division: FORBES J).

994   —— —— dismissal—whether by reason of redundancy

See *Nottingham County Council v Lee*, para. 1107.

995   Direct grant schools

The Direct Grant Grammar Schools (Cessation of Grant) (Amendment) Regulations 1979, S.I. 1979 No. 1552 (in force on 1st January 1980), amend the Direct Grant Grammar Schools (Cessation of Grant) Regulations 1975, 1975 Halsbury's Abridgment para. 1181. Regulation 3 (2) of the 1975 Regulations is modified in its application to pupils admitted in 1980 so as to permit the payment of a grant where the intention of the proprietors that the school should become a maintained one had become conditional on statutory provisions not being made for a scheme for assisted places at independent schools.

996   Discretionary awards

The Scholarships and Other Benefits (Amendment) Regulations 1979, S.I. 1979 No. 260 (in force on 6th April, 1979), amend the Scholarships and Other Benefits Regulations 1977, Halsbury's Abridgment 1977 para. 976, so as to permit local education authorities to defray clothing expenses of children attending county, voluntary and special schools, even though the clothing could be provided directly by the authority under the Education (Miscellaneous Provisions) Act 1948, s. 5.

997

The Scholarships and Other Benefits (Amendment) (No. 2) Regulations 1979, S.I. 1979 No. 542 (in force on 14th June 1979), revoke the Scholarships and Other Benefits Regulations 1977, 1977 Halsbury's Abridgment para. 976, reg. 5. Accordingly, a local education authority will no longer be required to obtain the approval of the Secretary of State before paying fees etc. in respect of children attending non-maintained schools.

998   Education Act 1979

The Education Act 1979 repeals the Education Act 1976, ss. 1–3. The Act received the royal assent on 26th July 1979 and came into force on that date.

The duty to give effect to the comprehensive principle in education is abolished by s. 1 (1). Subsections 1 (2)–(4) contain transitional provisions allowing the revocation of already approved proposals for adopting the comprehensive principle (s. 1 (3)), and allowing education authorities or school governing bodies to elect to have proposals not yet approved treated as if they had been submitted to the Secretary of State (s. 1 (4)). Any such election must be made in writing before 1st October 1979. Section 2 deals with citation, construction and extent.

999   Education authority—statutory duty to provide education—industrial action resulting in closed schools—injunction to compel authority to open schools

See *Meade v Haringey London Borough Council*, para. 1586.

1000   Grants of land for educational purposes—grants under School Sites Acts—provisions for reverter

Land was conveyed without consideration, pursuant to the School Sites Act 1841. Upon the land ceasing to be used for the purposes of the Act, the question arose as to whether the reverter provisions, contained in s. 2, were to be interpreted as meaning that the legal estate was to revert to those persons entitled under the provisions, or was to remain vested in the successors in title of those persons to whom the conveyance was originally made. *Held*, as soon as a reverter occurred under s. 2, an equitable interest arose in favour of the estate interest out of which the original conveyance was carved. The legal estate would remain with the successors in title of those persons to whom the conveyance was made, who would hold the property in trust for persons entitled under s. 2. When the persons so entitled were ascertained, they would be entitled to a conveyance of the legal estate, pursuant to the Law of Property Act 1925, s. 3 (3).

RE CLAYTON'S DEED POLL [1979] 2 All ER 1133 (Chancery Division: WHITFORD J).

1001   School meals

The Provision of Milk and Meals (Amendment) Regulations 1979, S.I. 1979 No. 695 (in force on 1st August 1979), increase the charge for school dinners in nursery, county and voluntary schools from 25p to 30p, raise the levels of net weekly income below which a parent qualifies for remission of the charge and increase the deduction to be made in calculating net weekly income in respect of a special diet prescribed by a medical practitioner.   The new levels of net weekly income relevant are given in the press notice issued by the Department of Education and Science, on 27th June 1979.

1002   The Provision of Milk and Meals (Amendment) (No. 2) Regulations 1979, S.I. 1979 No. 1686 (in force on 4th February 1980), further amend the Provision of Milk and Meals Regulations 1969 by increasing the charge for school meals at nursery, county and voluntary schools.

1003   State bursaries for adult education—residents of Wales

The State Awards (State Bursaries for Adult Education) (Wales) Regulations 1979, S.I. 1979 No. 333 (in force on 17th April 1979), consolidate with amendments the existing legislation relating to awards in respect of persons ordinarily resident in Wales in so far as they relate to state scholarships for mature students and state bursaries for adult education.

1004   Students' dependants—allowances

The Students' Dependants Allowances Regulations 1979, S.I. 1979 No. 900 (in force on 1st September 1979), consolidate the Students' Dependants Allowances Regulations 1978, 1978 Halsbury's Abridgment para. 1016, with amendments. They are drafted by reference to the Local Education Authority Awards Regulations 1979, para. 992, which increase the amounts prescribed as a student's requirements. An allowance under the present Regulations is payable at a rate determined in part by reference to the principal Regulations and accordingly is payable at an increased rate.   There is power to withhold, or pay at a reduced rate, an allowance where the student concerned maintains a dependant outside the United Kingdom.   The means test for an allowance is relaxed so far as concerns the student's scholarship and similar income and the earned income of his spouse or a person living with him as his spouse.

1005   Teachers—remuneration

The Remuneration of Teachers (Primary and Secondary Schools) (Amendment) Order 1979, S.I. 1979 No. 428 (in force on 4th April 1979) gave effect to the recommendations agreed on by the committee for the consideration of the remuneration of teachers in primary and secondary schools by increasing the amounts of the London Area payments to teachers.
     This order has been revoked, see para. 1007.

1006   The Remuneration of Teachers (Primary and Secondary Schools Burnham Committee) (Variation) Order 1979, S.I. 1979 No. 339 (in force on 23rd April 1979), ends the representation of the Incorporated Association of Head Mistresses, the Incorporated Association of Assistant Mistresses and the Incorporated Association of Assistant Masters on the Burnham Committee concerned with the remuneration of teachers in primary and secondary schools maintained by local education authorities, and of certain other teachers employed by such authorities.

1007   The Remuneration of Teachers (Primary and Secondary Schools) Order 1979, S.I. 1979 No. 1193 (in force on 25th September 1979), brings into operation the scales and other provisions relating to the remuneration of teachers in primary and secondary schools maintained by local education authorities as set out in a document published by Her Majesty's Stationery Office on 21st September 1979.   The Order, which has retrospective effect from 1st April 1979, revokes the Remuneration of

Teachers (Primary and Secondary Schools) (No. 2) Order 1978, 1978 Halsbury's Abridgment para. 1022 and the Remuneration of Teachers (Primary and Secondary Schools) (Amendment) Order 1979, para. 1005.

1008 —— **superannuation**

See PENSIONS.

1009   Transfer of teacher—alleged infringement of human rights— failure to apply for statutory review

See *Harrikissoon v A-G of Trinidad and Tobago*, para. 339.

1010   University—visitor—jurisdiction

A student at a university incorporated by royal charter failed his examinations and was required to withdraw from the university. His request to re-enter was refused and he brought an action against the university for declarations that it had arbitrarily, unreasonably and unlawfully refused him re-admission and lawful access, for an injunction and for exemplary damages. The university contended that the courts had no jurisdiction to hear the case as exclusive jurisdiction was in the visitor of the university. Under the university's charter the Crown had the right to appoint a visitor, but no such appointment had been made. The judge held that, subject to any appointment by the Crown, the Crown was the visitor, the Lord Chancellor exercising visitatorial powers on its behalf. The court had no jurisdiction in the matter, as it fell within the exclusive jurisdiction of the visitor, which extended to all disputes as to membership of the university. On appeal by the student, *held*, the judge was correct in holding that the court had no jurisdiction in the matter. The university's constitution provided for the appointment of a visitor and the subject matter of the dispute fell within the visitor's jurisdiction. The appeal would be dismissed.

PATEL v UNIVERSITY OF BRADFORD SENATE [1979] 2 All ER 582 (Court of Appeal: ORR, ORMROD and GEOFFREY LANE LJJ). Decision of Megarry V-C [1978] 3 All ER 841, 1978 Halsbury's Abridgment para. 1026 affirmed.

1011   Voluntary aided school—dismissal of teacher—absence of rules of management—whether consent of county council required

The head teacher of a Roman Catholic voluntary aided primary school was suspended from his duties by the school managers after his divorce and remarriage in a register office. The Roman Catholic bishop was informed and asked to appoint a tribunal. The tribunal concluded that the teacher should be dismissed and, consequently, the managers summarily dismissed him and the county council stopped paying his salary. The teacher unsuccessfully sought an injunction restraining the managers from purporting to dismiss him without the consent of the county council given after a hearing in accordance with the council's conditions of tenure for teaching staff in primary schools. The teacher appealed. *Held*, the managers had erred when they had referred the matter to the bishop and accepted his tribunal's report; the managers were the parties to the contract and the proper people to exercise power of dismissal. The county council were agents for the managers and the conditions of tenure had been sent by the chief education officer to the teacher on his appointment. The conditions stated that the county council's consent was required to a dismissal and any ordinary person reading them would have believed that they applied to him. Further, no rules of management containing provisions as to dismissal had been made as required by the Education Act 1944, ss. 17 (3), 24 (2) (9). In the absence of rules of management, the court should assume that they would have contained such provisions favourable to the teacher. In accordance with the principle that a person who made a representation which he intended another person to act upon was not allowed to go back on it where the representation had been acted upon and was intended to be binding, an injunction would be granted. The appeal would be allowed.

Jones v Lee [1979] LS Gaz R 1160 (Court of Appeal: Lord Denning MR, Roskill and Cumming-Bruce LJJ). *Crisp v Holden* (1910) 54 SJ 784 and *Smith v Macnally* [1912] 1 Ch 816 applied.

ELECTIONS

Halsbury's Laws of England (4th edn.), Vol. 15, paras. 401–981

1012   Article

Statutory Controls on Election Expenses, J. B. Stewart and F. McMahon: 129 NLJ 160.

1013   Boundary commission—revision of electoral arrangements— equality between voters

See *London Borough of Enfield v Local Government Boundary Commission for England*, para. 1763.

1014   Election campaign—television coverage—whether candidates' consent required

The BBC informed a candidate at a parliamentary election of their intention to film all four candidates in the constituency during the course of the election campaign. The candidate said that he would not willingly take part in any such programme. He was later filmed by the BBC whilst campaigning in spite of his protests to the camera crew. The candidate was granted an injunction restraining the BBC from broadcasting without his consent any item in which both he and the National Front candidate took part. The BBC appealed on the ground that under the Representation of the People Act 1969, s. 9 (1), the candidate had no veto of this kind. Section 9 (1) prohibits the broadcasting of any item if any candidate takes part in the item and the broadcast is not made with his consent. The BBC argued that the words "takes part in the item" contained in the subsection meant "actively participating in the item" and not merely "shown in the item". *Held*, the words "takes part in" applied only when the candidate actively participated in the item. The subsection was designed to protect a candidate who actively participated in a programme by giving him a veto. Further, if the candidate's claim were correct, it would mean that the BBC would no longer be impartial, and this would be contrary to general policy. Accordingly, the appeal would be allowed.

Marshall v British Broadcasting Corpn [1979] 3 All ER 80 (Court of Appeal: Lord Denning MR, Waller and Cumming-Bruce LJJ).

1015   Election petitions—security for costs—recognisance by author- ised person

The Election Petition (Amendment) Rules 1979, S.I. 1979 No. 543 (in force on 15th June 1979), amend the Election Petition Rules 1960, r. 6 (2) which provides that recognisance as security of costs must be acknowledged before a person authorised to take affidavits under the Commissioners for Oaths Acts 1889 to 1891. The amendment makes it clear that persons before whom recognisances may be acknowledged include solicitors to whom the Solicitors Act 1974, s. 81 (1) applies.

1016   Electoral register—requirements

The Representation of the People (Amendment) Regulations 1979, S.I. 1979 No. 1679 (in force on 27th December 1979), amend the Representation of the People Regulations 1974, 1974 Halsbury's Abridgment, para. 1152. The Regulations remove the requirement that the name of any elector who is a service elector be marked with an 'S' and that of a merchant seaman with an 'M' (reg. 3). Regulation 5 adds a provision to the 1974 Regulations whereby the electoral registration officer is required to supply, without fee, to a parish or community council, one copy of so much of the register as relates to that parish or community. The fee payable for copies of the register of electors is increased (reg. 6).

1017   European Assembly elections
See EUROPEAN COMMUNITIES.

1018   Representation of the People Act 1979
The Representation of the People Act 1979 enabled polling in the 1979 general election to be combined with polling for district council elections in England and Wales where they were scheduled to take place on the same day. It also postponed parish or community elections due to have been held on the same date as district council elections for three weeks. The Act received the royal assent on 4th April 1979 and came into force on that date.

1019   Returning officers—expenses
The Returning Officers' Expenses (England and Wales) Regulations 1979, S.I. 1979 No. 429 (in force on 11th April 1979), revoke and replace the Returning Officers' Expenses (England and Wales) Regulations 1974, 1974 Halsbury's Abridgment para. 1155 as amended. They prescribe a revised scale increasing the maximum charges in respect of services rendered and the maximum charges in respect of expenses incurred by a returning officer for the purposes of or in connection with a parliamentary election. Separate charges are prescribed in respect of the preparation of poll cards by manual and by non-manual means. Special provision is also made to cover the case of a parliamentary constituency in which a district council election takes place on the same day as the parliamentary election.

1020   Welsh forms
The Elections (Welsh Forms) Regulations 1979, S.I. 1979 No. 434 (in force on 18th April 1979), amend the Elections (Welsh Forms) Regulations 1975, 1975 Halsbury's Abridgment para. 1220 by prescribing a new form of proxy paper to be used in connection with elections in Wales. They also amend the Welsh versions of certain other forms prescribed by 1975 Regulations, Sch. 2, Part II.

EMERGENCY CONTROLS

1021   Counter-inflation—prices and charges—basic profits—safeguards
The Prices and Charges (Safeguard for Basic Profits) Regulations 1979, S.I. 1979 No. 229 (in force on 28th March 1979), provide safeguards for the profits of enterprises which are subject to restriction under Price Commission Act 1977, s. 13, 1977 Halsbury's Abridgment para. 2842 following a report on an examination carried out by the Price Commission under a direction by the Secretary of State.

The Prices and Charges (Safeguard for Basic Profits) Regulations 1977, 1977 Halsbury's Abridgment para. 1002, are revoked.

1022   —— —— increases
The Prices and Charges (Notification of Increases) (Amendment) Order 1979, S.I. 1979 No. 60 (in force on 25th January 1979) provided that an intended increase in the price of specified animal feeding stuff, principally for cattle, pigs and poultry, need not be notified to the Price Commission. However, particulars relating to

such an increase had to be furnished to the Commission not later than fourteen days after it is implemented.

This Order has been revoked; see para. 1023.

1023   The Prices and Charges (Notification of Increases) (Amendment No. 2) Order 1979, S.I. 1979 No. 178 (in force on 26th March 1979), amended the Prices and Charges (Notification of Increases) Order 1978, 1978 Halsbury's Abridgment para. 1037, by omitting the provisions inserted by S.I. 1979 No. 60, para. 1022 which it revoked.

This Order has been revoked; see para. 1024.

1024   The Prices and Charges (Notification of Increases) (Revocation) Order 1979, S.I. 1979 No. 568 (in force on 24th May 1979), revokes the Prices and Charges (Notification of Increases) Order 1978, 1978 Halsbury's Abridgment, para 1037 and the Prices and Charges (Notification of Increases) (Amendment No. 2) Order 1979, para. 1023. It removes the obligation to give notice of intended increases in prices or charges to the Price Commission.

1025 ———— **newspaper**

The Daily Telegraph Limited (Prices) Order 1979, S.I. 1979 No. 278 (in force on 4th April 1979), prohibited increases in the cover price of the Daily Telegraph and in the rates of advertising charges of the Daily Telegraph during the period ending on 15th October 1979. This Order implements a recommendation of the Price Commission that there should be no such increases.

1026 —— **Price Commission**

The Price Commission (Number of Members) Order 1979, S.I. 1979 No. 795 (in force on 31st July 1979), reduces the minimum number of members of the Price Commission from five to three.

EMPLOYMENT

Halsbury's Laws of England (4th edn.), Vol. 16, paras. 501–1200

1027   **Articles**

Calculating the Quantum of Damages for Wrongful Dismissal, Philip Lehain: 129 NLJ 887.

Constructive Dismissal, J. B. Capstick (in the light of *Western Excavating (ECC) Ltd v Sharp* [1978] 1 All ER 713, CA, 1977 Halsbury's Abridgment para. 2960 and *British Aircraft Corporation v Austin* [1978] IRLR 332, 1978 Halsbury's Abridgment para. 2953): 129 NLJ 499.

Contractual Benefits and Statutory Rights, Bridgit Dimond (dilemmas created by the possibility of choice between applying statutory rights or contractual rights with reference to: *Bovey v Board of Governors of the Hospital for Sick Children* [1977] IRLR 417, 1978 Halsbury's Abridgment para. 1105, and *Inner London Education Authority v Nash* (1978) 122 Sol Jo 860, 1978, Halsbury's Abridgment para. 1107): 123 Sol Jo 446.

Dismissal for Theft, Michael Whincup (a summary of industrial tribunal law and practice in this area): 129 NLJ 591.

Employing an Ex-employee, Norman Selwyn (establishing continuity of employment): 129 NLJ 384.

Fixed Term Contracts: The Continuing Problems, A. E. Morris: 129 NLJ 1195.

Industrial Relations Legislation—1, Henry E. Markson (discussion of proposed changes in law on picketing, the closed shop and providing financial aid for postal ballots for trade unions): 123 Sol Jo 743.

Industrial Tribunals: Orders for Discovery, T. S. Hale and N. J. Fagan (in the light of recent cases based on allegations of discrimination): 123 Sol Jo 174.

Judicial Control of ACAS, R. C. Simpson (analysis of the extent to which the intended role of ACAS is circumscribed and controlled by the courts): 8 ILJ 69.

Recognising a Contract of Employment, Richard Townshend-Smith (examination of recent developments in the area of what constitutes a contract of employment): 129 NLJ 993.

Reform of Labour Law: Prodecural Aspects, Alan C. Neal (an examination of two issues raised by the Government's proposals to amend industrial relations law: "Codes of Practice", and the role of existing bodies for adjudicating employment disputes): 129 NLJ 863.

Statutory Exemptions for Collective Agreements, Colin Bourn (examination of the failure to make use of opportunities for exemption in respect of unfair dismissal and redundancy as compared with guarantee payments): 8 ILJ 85.

Termination of Employment: Some Tax Considerations, A. J. Shipwright (an examination of the tax law applicable to compensation payments and some of the ways in which the tax burden can be mitigated): 123 Sol Jo 191.

Transnational Employment and Employment Protection, M. Forde (handling of disputes involving persons who work wholly or partly outside Great Britain): 7 ILJ 228.

Wrongful Dismissal and Injured Reputation, Henry E. Markson (the case of *McMinn v Town of Oakville* (1978) 85 DLR (3d) 131, High Court of Ontario, para. 1049, as it throws light upon the subject of damages arising from contractual breach): 129 NLJ 653.

1028   Baking industry—Christmas and New Year

The Baking and Sausage Making (Christmas and New Year) Regulations 1979, S.I. 1979 No. 1298 (in force on 16th November 1979), enable women who have reached the age of eighteen to be employed on specific Saturday afternoons and Sundays in December 1979 and January 1980 in the manufacture of meat pies, sausages or cooked meats, or in the pre-packing of bacon, and in the manufacture of bread or flour confectionery (including fruit pies but not biscuits), or in work incidental and ancillary to such work.

1029   Breach of confidence—application for dismissal of action—need for reasonable evidence in support of breach

See *Reinforced Plastics Applications (Swansea) Ltd v Swansea Plastics & Engineering Co Ltd*, para. 2128.

1030   Central Arbitration Committee—jurisdiction—award as to recognised terms and conditions of employment

A trade union made a claim to the Advisory Conciliation and Arbitration Service under the Employment Protection Act 1975, Schedule 11, para. 1, maintaining that the terms and conditions under which the regional health authority employed its ambulancemen were less favourable than the recognised terms and conditions. The claim was referred to the Central Arbitration Committee. The health authority submitted that the Committee had no jurisdiction to hear the claim because under para. 3 no claim could be dealt with by this procedure where the terms and conditions of the employment in question were fixed in pursuance of an enactment. The Committee held para. 3 was only applicable where the terms and conditions were directly affected by a statute. In this case they were fixed by a negotation procedure laid down by regulations made under a statute, but the statute itself did not specify the terms and conditions. The health authority applied for an order of certiorari to quash the award and an order of prohibition to prevent the Committee from hearing and determining the claim. *Held*, granting the application, a negotiation procedure determined by regulations made under a statute amounted to terms and conditions fixed in pursuance of an enactment. The exclusion in para. 3 therefore applied and the Committee had no jurisdiction to make the award.

R v Central Arbitration Committee, ex parte North Western Regional Health Authority [1978] ICR 1228 (Queen's Bench Division: Lord Widgery CJ, Talbot and Ackner JJ).

1031   Confidential information—duty not to disclose—restrictive covenant—reasonableness

See *Greer v Sketchley*, para. 2806.

1032   Constructive dismissal—employee's application to industrial tribunal—employee continuing to report for duty

Disciplinary action was taken against an employee whilst he was off sick and he was demoted and transferred to another depot. The employee claimed that he had been constructively dismissed. When able to work however he continued to report for duty at the depot at which he was previously employed before his transfer. An industrial tribunal dismissed his claim and on appeal, *held*, the employee's behaviour was inconsistent with his contention that he had treated his contract as at an end by reason of his employer's conduct. The appeal would be dismissed.

HUNT V BRITISH RAILWAYS BOARD [1979] IRLR 379 (Employment Appeal Tribunal: BRISTOW J presiding).

1033   Continuity of employment—calculation of length of service—weekly hours—effect of change in legislation

A part time waitress who had worked sixteen hours a week since her engagement in 1974 was dismissed without notice in June 1977 and claimed compensation for unfair dismissal. An industrial tribunal upheld her claim on the ground that she had not received three weeks' notice as required under Contracts of Employment Act 1972, as amended by Employment Protection Act 1975, Schedule 16, Part II. That amendment reduced from twenty-one hours to sixteen the number of hours which an employee had to work in any week which was to be counted in computing a period of employment, and came into force on 1st February 1977. Her employer appealed on the ground that she had worked less than twenty-one hours in all the weeks up to February and therefore those weeks could not be counted. *Held*, when the amendment took effect a person was entitled to have that week counted as a qualifying week, and accordingly all previous weeks in which he had worked sixteen hours or more could also be counted. The waitress therefore had the right to have her whole period of employment counted in the computation of her notice entitlement.

ACTIVE ELDERLY HOUSING ASSOCIATION V SPARROW (1978) 13 ITR 395 (Employment Appeal Tribunal: SLYNN J presiding).

1972 Act, as amended, now Employment Protection (Consolidation) Act 1978.

1034   —— change of employers—associated employers—meaning of companies controlled by third party

An industrial tribunal found that the Merseyside Probation and After Care Service and the Southwood Hostel Management Committee were associated employers and that the claimant was therefore entitled to take his consecutive periods of service with them into account in calculating redundancy payments due to him when he was made redundant by the Southwood Committee. Two employers could be treated as associated employers if they were companies controlled by a third party within the Contracts of Employment Act 1972, Sch. 1, para. 10 (2). On appeal, *held*, the tribunal had erred in its findings. "Companies" meant bodies corporate and therefore did not include these two employers. Further, "control" meant some kind of direction of the operation and not simply funding of the operation as supplied by the Home Office. The appeal would therefore be allowed.

SOUTHWOOD HOSTEL MANAGEMENT COMMITTEE V TAYLOR [1979] ICR 813 (Employment Appeal Tribunal: BRISTOW J presiding).

Contracts of Employment Act 1972, s. 10 (2) now Employment Protection (Consolidation) Act 1978, s. 153 (4) and Sch. 13, para. 8.

1035   —— —— meaning of "associated employers"

A health visitor transferred from one area health authority to another, both of which were controlled by the same regional authority. She was dismissed after ten weeks' employment with the second authority and claimed compensation for unfair dismissal. The authority raised the preliminary point that she had been employed for less than twenty-six weeks. An industrial tribunal ruled that her employment with the first authority counted towards a continuous period of employment within Contracts of Employment Act 1972, s. 10. On appeal, *held*, the 1972 Act contained both a general definition of associated employers in s. 10 (1) and an enlarged definition, to be applied where the employers concerned were companies, in s. 10 (2), which did not limit the general definition. The two health authorities fell within the general definition and therefore the industrial tribunal had been correct in its conclusion.

HILLINGDON AREA HEALTH AUTHORITY V KAUDERS [1979] ICR 472 (Employment Appeal Tribunal: TALBOT J presiding).

1972 Act, s. 10 (1), (2) now Employment Protection (Consolidation) Act 1978, s. 7 (1) and Sch. 13, para. 8.

1036 ———— **time of transfer**

A company was in financial difficulties and the transferee company offered to buy the company. Verbal agreement was reached on Friday, 17th October and the staff were informed that afternoon that their employment had been terminated, and that they would be re-engaged by the transferee company. The final agreement was signed in the evening of the same day. The employee, a worker with the transferor company was dismissed by the transferee company on Monday, 20th October. The transferee company contended that the employee had not the continuity of employment to bring a complaint of unfair dismissal. *Held*, as the employee's normal working hours were over the requisite twenty-one hours per week, by virtue of the Contracts of Employment Act 1972, Sch. 1, paras. 3 and 4, his employment for the week commencing 13th October was deemed to continue until Saturday, 18th October. Therefore at the time the transfer was finally effected, in the evening of the 17th October, the employee was employed by the transferor company and the continuity had not been broken by virtue of Sch. 1, para. 9 (2).

TEESSIDE TIMES LTD V DRURY (1979), Times, 19th December (Court of Appeal: STEPHENSON, GOFF and EVELEIGH LJJ). Decision of Employment Appeal Tribunal [1978] ICR 822, 1978 Halsbury's Abridgment para. 1051 affirmed.

1972 Act, Sch 1, paras 3, 4, 9 now Employment Protection (Consolidation) Act 1978, Sch. 13, paras, 3, 4, 17.

1037 ———— **employee taking another job—whether repudiation of contract**

Scotland

Following a disagreement with her employers, an employee was absent from her work due to sickness. She then began a new job with a different company, without informing her employers or terminating her contract of employment. Three months later she returned to her original job on the same pay and conditions as she had previously enjoyed, having been told by the managing director that her old contract still held good. She was later made redundant and had to show continuity of employment in order to sustain a claim for payment. The employee based her arguments on two premises (i) that she had never resigned from her employment and that until her employers had accepted repudiation of it, the contract was in force and the weeks of absence counted despite the fact that she was in breach of contract herself; (ii) that by virtue of her re-engagement by her employers, she could have been rightly regarded as being absent by arrangement and in such circumstances entitled to count those missing weeks, under the Contracts of Employment Act 1972, Sch. 1, para. 5 (1) (c). *Held,* (i) the abandonment of service with her employers and the taking up of a new job was a clear termination of her contract and no acceptance of such repudiation was necessary; (ii) an arrangement could not be made retrospectively. It had to have been in the contemplation of the parties at the time of the commencement of absence for it to be effective and this was not so in this case. Accordingly the employee could not show continuity of employment and her claim failed.

MURPHY V A. BIRRELL & SONS LTD [1978] IRLR 458 (Employment Appeal Tribunal: LORD MCDONALD MC presiding).

1972 Act, Sch. 1 has been consolidated in the Employment Protection (Consolidation) Act 1978, Sch.13.

1038   —— temporary cessation of work—break in employment following resignation—employment by associated company

A coach driver, who was employed by an East Anglian company, requested a transfer to an associated company in Bristol. Following the company's refusal he resigned and moved to Bristol where, after five and a half weeks, he succeeded in obtaining employment with another company which was associated with the East Anglian company within Contracts of Employment Act 1972. He was dismissed seven weeks later and claimed compensation for unfair dismissal. An industrial tribunal considered that he had been continuously employed for the requisite period, since the five and a half week period of unemployment was an absence from work on account of a temporary cessation of work. The company appealed. *Held*, as there was no evidence of an agreement between the companies that he should transfer there had been no temporary cessation of work. His period of unemployment had arisen from his resignation, and accordingly he could not claim that he had been continuously employed for the requisite period.

WESSEX NATIONAL LTD V LONG (1978) 13 ITR 413 (Employment Appeal Tribunal: PHILLIPS J presiding).

1972 Act, as amended, now Employment Protection (Consolidation) Act 1978.

1039   —— transfer of employers' business—change in partnership

A solicitor was employed in a partnership of two solicitors, one of whom owned 70 per cent of the equity, the other the remaining 30 per cent. On the retirement of the partner with the larger holding, the remaining partner acquired the whole of the equity and carried on the business under the same name. Upon dismissal, the solicitor brought a complaint of unfair dismissal. An industrial tribunal found that the change in the ownership of the firm did not break the solicitor's continuity of service for the purpose of completing the period of employment. On appeal, *held*, where the entire equity of a firm of solicitors was transferred to one of the two former partners there was a transfer of business within the meaning of the Employment Protection (Consolidation) Act 1978, Sch. 13, para. 17 (2). The appeal would accordingly be dismissed.

ALLEN AND SON V COVENTRY [1979] IRLR 399 (Employment Appeal Tribunal: LORD MCDONALD MC presiding).

1040   Contract of employment—construction—whether contract of service or contract for services

A woman worked for a television company as a programme researcher, under contracts for fixed terms and for specific programmes. She was taxed as being self-employed, but under the terms of her contracts the company had virtually exclusive use of her services, the copyright in her work was vested in the company and her work was under the direction of a producer. She was promoted to reporter, under a contract with the same terms. A manager later decided he did not like her voice and, following negotiations with the appropriate union, she was made alternative offers: a return to the rank of researcher with voice training or non-renewal of her contract on its expiry with an ex gratia payment. She accepted the latter. She claimed she had been unfairly dismissed and an industrial tribunal held, on preliminary points, that she was an employee and had been dismissed in law. On appeal against those findings, *held*, in deciding whether the woman was an employee or self-employed it was necessary to look at the contract from the point of view of an ordinary person. To all intents and purposes the company had the exclusive use of her services and her work was entirely under the direction of a producer. Thus the tribunal had correctly found that she was an employee. Furthermore it was found as fact that the contract would have terminated even before she had agreed to its termination and the acceptance of the payment. Thus her acceptance did not alter the fact that she had been dismissed. The appeal would be dismissed.

THAMES TELEVISION LTD v WALLIS [1979] IRLR 136 (Employment Appeal Tribunal: TALBOT J presiding).

1041 —— contract with minor—right of adult party to enforce

See *Toronto Marlboro Major Junior "A" Hockey Club v Tonelli*, para. 1870.

1042 —— existence of contract—church reader—right to claim compensation for unfair dismissal

On an application by a licensed reader in the Church of England for compensation for unfair dismissal, it was held that it did not follow that the holder of an ecclesiastical office could not be employed under a contract of service and hence be an employee for the purposes of the Trade Union and Labour Relations Act 1974. The question was whether the office was one the appointment to which was made by, or was coexistent with, a contract of service; if it was, the reader was entitled to protection under the 1974 Act.

BARTHORPE v EXETER DIOCESAN BOARD OF FINANCE [1979] ICR 900 (Employment Appeal Tribunal: SLYNN J presiding).

1974 Act largely consolidated in Employment Protection (Consolidation) Act 1978.

1043 —— illegality—failure of employee to disclose benefits received to Inland Revenue

A farm worker was held to have been unfairly dismissed and was awarded compensation. His former employer appealed after it was disclosed that the employee did not inform the Inland Revenue of income derived from the sale of cattle given to him by the employer. He contended that though the omission might not render the contract of employment illegal an industrial tribunal should be given an opportunity to consider the matter. *Held*, if an employee without the knowledge of his employer failed to disclose to the Inland Revenue any benefits he received, this did not automatically render the whole contract of employment illegal. Since there was no evidence of the arrangement being a fraud on the Revenue, there were no circumstances which justified remission to a tribunal. The appeal would be dismissed.

McCONNELL v BOLIK [1979] IRLR 422 (Employment Appeal Tribunal: LORD McDONALD MC presiding).

1044 —— —— unenforceability

The manageress of a dry cleaning business was dismissed on its closure. She sought a redundancy payment and compensation for unfair dismissal. Her application was dismissed by an industrial tribunal on the basis that her contract of employment had been illegal, since she drew her wages from the till without making deductions for tax or National Insurance. On appeal against this decision, *held*, as the tribunal had not ascertained whether the employee was aware of the illegality of her contract but had assumed that the knowledge of the employer implied a similar position for the employee, the appeal would be allowed. The case would be remitted to the tribunal for an investigation of the employee's evidence with respect to her understanding of the contract.

DAVIDSON v. PILLAY [1979] IRLR 275 (Employment Appeal Tribunal: SLYNN J presiding).

1045 —— negligence inducing breach—right of action

See *McLaren v British Columbia Institute of Technology*, para. 1977.

1046   —— oral terms—new written contract—whether oral term still effective

An employee was asked to sign a contract of employment form stating that he would be liable to travel thoughout the country. He was unable to do so because of his wife's illness, but was assured by a company manager that if he signed the form he would be able to remain within his home area. During his employment he was never required to travel elsewhere. Three years later the contract was renewed and the employee signed a similar form. Later he was requested to stay at home on basic pay as a stand-by. He telephoned the employers and it emerged that he should have been in Scotland where he refused to go and was subsequently sent a letter stating that he had thereby terminated his employment. The employee was found by an industrial tribunal to have been unfairly dismissed. The employers appealed. *Held*, the employee had been dismissed when the employer insisted that he travelled outside the area, despite an oral promise amounting to a contractual term. There had been no variation in this term by the signing of the second contract and the appeal would be dismissed.

HAWKER SIDDELEY POWER ENGINEERING LTD v RUMP [1979] IRLR 425 (Employment Appeal Tribunal: TALBOT J presiding).

1047   —— repudiation—whether repudiation by employer amounted to fundamental breach

See *Stokes v Hampstead Wine Co Ltd*, para. 2894.

1048   —— whether employee or independent contractor

The employee was principal oboeist with an orchestra registered under the Companies Acts. Every member had one share in the company, the remaining shares being held by the managing director. The employee had no written contract but the offer and acceptance of his engagement was contained in two letters of 1968 and he was informed of the existence of a memorandum from the managing director stating that relations between the orchestra and management were based on a well known formula of unwritten rules. The employee paid national insurance contributions at the self-employed rate and was registered as a supplier for value added tax purposes. In 1978 the board gave the employee three months' notice of the termination of his engagement. On application for compensation for unfair dismissal the company contended that the employee was not an employee within the Trade Union and Labour Relations Act 1974, s. 30 and the industrial tribunal had therefore no jurisdiction to hear the application. The tribunal dismissed the application because the applicant was not engaged under a contract of service. On appeal, *held*, on all the evidence given the applicant was not an employee within the meaning of s. 30.

WINFIELD v LONDON PHILHARMONIC ORCHESTRA LTD [1979] ICR 726 (Employment Appeal Tribunal: BRISTOW J presiding).

Trade Union and Labour Relations Act 1974, s. 30 is now consolidated in the Employment Protection (Consolidation) Act 1978, s. 153.

1049   Dismissal—damages in action for breach of contract—whether joint claim for damages for loss of reputation and wrongful dismissal permissible

Canada

The plaintiff was employed by the defendants as chief planner, his employment being terminable by reasonable notice. On the termination of his employment fifteen months later, the plaintiff brought proceedings for breach of contract claiming damages for wrongful dismissal as well as for loss of reputation. The latter claim was made on the ground that the termination of his employment was publicised in certain newspapers, even though there was no suggestion that the defendants were responsible for the dismissal's being so publicised. On the question whether the law allowed a claim of damages for loss of reputation to be joined with a claim for damages for wrongful dismissal in the same action, *held*, the rule in *Addis v Gramophone Co Ltd* provided that, subject to certain exceptions, compensation for injured feelings could not be included in damages for breach of an employment contract. There was also a separate category of cases applicable only to contracts of employment involving artists, where the contract was for services as well as for the promotion of the artist's reputation. In those cases, damages for loss of opportunity to enhance the artist's reputation could flow from the contractual breach, but such claims were distinct from those arising from ordinary contracts of employment. While the *Addis* principle had allowed claims for damages for physical injuries and mental distress to be included in a breach of contract action, it could not be extended to permit the inclusion of damages for loss of reputation in such an action.

McMINN v TOWN OF OAKVILLE (1978) 85 DLR (3d) 131 (High Court of Ontario). *Addis v Gramophone Co Ltd* [1909] AC 488, HL followed.

1050 —— **resignation of employee after take-over of employer's company—agreement by company to waive notice period—whether employee dismissed**

An employee who knew that his employer's company was about to be taken over and that his job would end began looking for alternative employment. By the time the take-over was effected he had found a new job and the new management accepted his resignation and agreed to waive the period of notice required under his contract. An industrial tribunal found that he had been constructively dismissed because the new management had made it clear that they did not consider themselves bound to employ him. On appeal, *held*, there was a difference between the true case of constructive dismissal where the employee was entitled to terminate his employment by reason of his employer's conduct and the case where the employment had been terminated by mutual agreement. On the evidence this case fell into the latter category and therefore the appeal would be allowed.

L. LIPTON LTD v MARLBOROUGH [1979] IRLR 179 (Employment Appeal Tribunal: BRISTOW J presiding).

1051 —— **resignation of employee after threat of dismissal—resignation not caused by threats—whether employee dismissed**

A company director was threatened with dismissal if he did not resign. Subsequently an agreement was drawn up setting out the terms on which he was prepared to resign, which he duly signed. An industrial tribunal found that he had not been dismissed. On appeal, *held*, normally when an employee resigned upon being threatened with dismissal the case would be treated as being one of dismissal, because the resignation had been by the threat of dismissal. However, in this case the resignation had occurred as a result of the employee being offered terms which were satisfactory to him, and he had not therefore been dismissed.

SHEFFIELD v OXFORD CONTROLS CO LTD [1979] IRLR 133 (Employment Appeal Tribunal: ARNOLD J presiding).

1052 —— **statement of reasons for dismissal—adequacy of statement**

An employee, a part-time town clerk, was dismissed. The council gave reasons for his dismissal in the letter terminating his employment. The employee requested a written statement giving the particulars of the reasons for his dismissal pursuant to the Employment Protection Act 1975, s. 70. The council referred him to the original letter. The employee contended that the council had unreasonably refused to give a written statement. *Held*, a reply to a request made under s. 70 should in itself state the reasons for the dismissal. The council's original letter contained adequate particulars of the reasons for dismissal and the council, in referring back to that letter could not be said to have unreasonably refused to provide the information requested under s. 70.

MARCHANT v EARLEY TOWN COUNCIL [1979] ICR 891 (Employment Appeal Tribunal: SLYNN J presiding). *Horsley Smith & Sherry Ltd v Dutton* [1977] ICR 594, 1977 Halsbury's Abridgment, para. 3012 followed.

Employment Protection Act 1975, s. 70 is now Employment Protection (Consolidation) Act 1978, s. 53.

1053   —— termination of contract with promise of re-engagement— whether employee dismissed

In 1976 the employee was engaged as an engineer officer for six months' voyage with three months' leave. His contract of employment included the terms of a scheme which differentiated between service contract seafarers entitled to regular employment under written contracts and registered seafarers who were engaged by the company when they were required from a pool. A national agreement provided full pay between voyages except in special circumstances. The employee joined the ship but whilst on leave signed a crew agreement for another ship. He then returned home due to his father's ill health, the company offering him re-employment whenever he wished. In 1978 he was informed there was no available work and he claimed compensation for unfair dimissal. The tribunal found he was not dismissed but had terminated his employment by entering into the new agreement. On appeal, *held*, it could not be construed from any document that the employee had had a right to continuous employment. Since the employment was terminated by mutual consent under the terms of the new crew agreement he had not been dismissed.

STEWART v GRAIG SHIPPING CO LTD [1979] ICR 713 (Employment Appeal Tribunal: SLYNN J presiding).

1054   —— unauthorised absenteeism—repudiation of contract of employment by employee—whether employee dismissed

An employee, a fitter, complained of feeling unwell and went home without the necessary permission to do so. He visited a doctor and although he was unable to get a medical certificate, telephoned his employers stating he had a certificate for four weeks. The employee failed to send in a certificate as requested and the employers subsequently discovered he was on holiday. Under the company's rules failure to produce a certificate within three days denoted that the employee had dismissed himself. A letter was sent to the employee stating that he was taken to have terminated his employment. The employee subsequently produced a medical certificate. An industrial tribunal considering whether the dismissal was unfair found that in the circumstances the employee had dismissed himself. The employee appealed. *Held*, the employee, by his failure to comply with company rules and other conduct, had repudiated his contract of employment which justified the employer in treating him as having terminated his contract. The appeal would be dismissed.

SMITH v AVANA BAKERIES LTD [1979] IRLR 423 (Employment Appeal Tribunal: TALBOT J presiding).

1055   Employee—duty of employee—use of confidential information by ex-employee—inspection of drawings

See *Centri-Spray Corpn v CERA International Ltd*, para. 536.

1056   Employer—insurance policy—accident—indemnity if employee acting in course of employment

See *Paterson v Costain and Press (Overseas) Ltd*, para. 1615.

1057   Employment Appeal Tribunal—appeal procedure

See para. 2129.

1058   —— evidence—admissibility of new evidence

On the question whether evidence which had not been presented before an industrial tribunal was admissible in the Employment Appeal Tribunal, *held*, the Employment Appeal Tribunal had been given all the powers of an industrial tribunal, including the right to hear new evidence, by the Employment Protection (Consolidation) Act 1978, Sch. 11, para. 19. It was probable that new evidence would only be admitted if it was credible and might affect the decision, and only if the party concerned could justify its omission from the industrial tribunal hearing.

INTERNATIONAL AVIATION SERVICES (UK) LTD, TRADING AS IAS CARGO AIRLINES v JONES [1979] IRLR 155 (Employment Appeal Tribunal: ARNOLD J presiding).

1059 The appellant, a car park attendant, was bound under his contract of employment to work in any car park to which his employers sent him. He was dismissed for refusing to work in a car park of a type which had not existed when he was first employed. He claimed that, as the new job would involve different duties, the employers had acted unreasonably in expecting him to move. An industrial tribunal rejected his claim for unfair dismissal. The employee then contended that it was an implied term of his employment that he would be required to work only in car parks similar to the one in which he already worked. *Held*, an argument not presented before the industrial tribunal could be argued in appeal only in limited circumstances. In the present case the admission of the new argument would involve further findings of fact by the tribunal. In the circumstances this would not be justified, and the tribunal's decision would be upheld.

KUMCHYK v DERBY COUNTY COUNCIL [1978] ICR 1116 (Employment Appeal Tribunal: ARNOLD J presiding).

1060 **Employment Protection (Consolidation) Act 1978—variation of limits**

The Employment Protection (Variation of Limits) Order 1979, S.I. 1979 No. 1722 (in force on 1st February 1980), varies certain of the limits which are required to be reviewed annually by the Secretary of State under the Employment Protection (Consolidation) Act 1978, s. 148. The amount of guarantee pay payable under s. 15 (1) in respect of any day is increased from £7·25 to £8·00. The amount payable under s. 122 in respect of a debt due to an employee whose employer becomes insolvent is increased from £110 to £120. The amount of a "week's pay" for the purposes of calculating redundancy payments and basic and additional awards of compensation for unfair dismissal under Schedule 14, paras. 8 (1) (a)–(c), is likewise increased from £110 to £120.

1061 **Employment Subsidies Act 1978—renewal of powers**

The Employment Subsidies Act 1978 (Renewal) (Great Britain) Order 1979, S.I. 1979 No. 1579 (in force on 1st January 1980), renews, until 30th June 1981, the powers under the Employment Subsidies Act 1978, s. 1, 1978 Halsbury's Abridgment para. 1079, which would otherwise not be exercisable after the end of 1979. The section authorises the Secretary of State to make payments to employers to enable them to retain employees who would otherwise become unemployed, to take on new employees and generally to maintain or enlarge their labour force.

1062 **Guarantee payments—exemption**

The Guarantee Payments (Exemption) (No. 19) Order 1979, S.I. 1979 No. 1403 (in force on 14th December 1979), excludes the employees of the Motor Vehicle Retail Repair Industry from the operation of the Employment Protection (Consolidation) Act 1978, s. 12, which relates to guarantee payments.

1063 **Health and safety at work**

See HEALTH AND SAFETY AT WORK.

1064 **Industrial diseases—pneumoconiosis—workers' compensation**

See Pneumoconiosis etc. (Workers' Compensation) Act 1979, para. 2650.

1065   Industrial training—industrial training boards—transfer of activities

The Industrial Training (Tranfer of the Activities of Establishment) Order 1979, S.I. 1979 No. 793 (in force on 3rd August 1979), transfers the activities of the establishments specified in Sch. column 1 from the industry of the industrial training board established by the industrial training order specified in Sch, column 2 to the industry of the industrial training board established by the industrial training order specified in Sch, column 3.

1066   —— Rubber and Plastics Processing Board

The Industrial Training (Rubber and Plastics Processing Board) Order 1967 (Amendment) Order 1979, S.I. 1979 No. 1595 (in force on 18th January 1980) amends the Industrial Training (Rubber and Plastics Processing Board) Order 1967, Sch. 1 by including in the industry any establishment engaged in the dealing or fitting of tyres for motor vehicles.

1067   Industrial training levy

Levies have been imposed on employers in the following industries:

	Relevant Statutory Instruments (1979)
Air Transport and Travel	386
Carpet	1548
Ceramics, Glass and Mineral Products	902
Chemical and Allied Products	623
Clothing and Allied Products	544
Construction Board	1207
Cotton and Allied Textiles	1049
Distributive Board	545
Engineering	778
Food, Drink and Tobacco	387
Footwear, Leather and Fur Skin	11
Footwear, Leather and Fur Skin (No. 2)	1271
Furniture and Timber	903
Hotel and Catering	845
Iron and Steel	313
Knitting, Lace and Net	184
Paper and Paper Products	558
Petroleum	185
Printing and Publishing	1492
Road Transport	1024
Shipbuilding	546
Wool, Jute and Flax	251

A right to appeal to an industrial tribunal against an assessment is provided for.

1068   Industrial tribunal—application for case to be struck out for want of prosecution

Industrial tribunal decision:

RAHI v LAND REGISTRY [1979] ICR 93 (complaint of unfair dismissal presented to tribunal in March 1976; applicant then left the country to visit his sick father, returning in May 1977; decided to act for himself and informed tribunal in November; became ill and was hospitalised until May 1978; case finally set down for hearing in September 1978; employers presented application for case to be struck out for want of prosecution; delay of two years not excessive compared with proceedings in other courts; delay excusable; employers not prejudiced by it; application dismissed).

1069 —— application to tribunal—procedure

In a case involving the validity of applications to industrial tribunals, Bristow J held that an originating application sent to the Central Office of the Industrial Tribunals which failed to give the applicant's address, but gave his telephone number, thus enabling him to be identified, was a valid application. Further, there was no objection to two applicants making their applications to the industrial tribunal on one document.

Gosport Working Men's and Trade Union Club Ltd v Taylor (1978) 13 ITR 321 (Employment Appeal Tribunal: Bristow J presiding).

1070 —— decision—application for review—notice of proceedings

An application for a review of a tribunal's decision to grant a protective award against a company on the ground that the company had not received notice of the proceedings was refused by a tribunal. On appeal, *held*, Slynn J dissenting, there was a presumption that all correctly addressed letters sent through the post were deemed to have been received unless the contrary was proved. Accordingly the appeal would be dismissed.

Slynn J said that the question to be considered was whether those persons expecting to have received such mail had established that they did not see the relevant letter.

Migwain Ltd (in liquidation) v Transport and General Workers' Union [1979] ICR 597 (Employment Appeal Tribunal: Slynn J presiding).

1071 —— —— whether gives rise to issue estoppel

See *Green v Hampshire County Council*, para. 1145.

1072 —— evidence—application for further particulars

Employers dismissed an employee for submitting fraudulent expenses claims. The employee claimed that he had been unfairly dismissed, alleging that the employers condoned similar activities in other employees. An industrial tribunal refused to grant the employers' application for further and better particulars. On appeal, *held*, further and better particulars would not normally be required for cases before industrial tribunals, but in this case the application would be granted in order to enable the employers to prepare their case.

International Computers Ltd v Whitley (1978) 13 ITR 399 (Employment Appeal Tribunal: Slynn J presiding).

1073 —— jurisdiction—jurisdiction over non-resident company

Industrial tribunal decision:

Knulty v Eloc Electro-Optiek and Communicatie BV [1979] ICR 827 (proceedings against Dutch company not registered in United Kingdom; employee claiming compensation for unfair dismissal and redundancy payments; whether valid service of originating application to company address in Holland and whether tribunal had jurisdiction to hear complaints; Industrial Tribunals (Labour Relations) Regulations 1974, Sch., r. 14 (1) (e) and (f) allowed service outside United Kingdom where sent to company's registered office; reg. 3 gave tribunal jurisdiction to hear complaint against non-resident company carrying on business in United Kingdom).

1074 —— —— power to accept settlement between parties in lieu of tribunal's decision—reference to Employment Appeal Tribunal

Following a decision of an industrial tribunal, both parties to the action agreed that the decision was in error and agreed upon a proposed settlement. A document was submitted to the registrar, but he maintained that only the Employment Appeal Tribunal had the power to accept the terms of the settlement. *Held*, where both parties to an action wished to reverse a decision of an industrial tribunal, the matter had to be referred to the Employment Appeal Tribunal for ratification. The most advisable course to adopt would be to draw up a formal order which could be incorporated in the appeal tribunal's order, if it was ratified.

COMET RADIOVISION SERVICES LTD V DELAHUNTY [1979] ICR 182 (Employment Appeal Tribunal: KILNER BROWN J presiding).

1075 —— —— power to adjourn hearing—matters to be considered

A company dismissed an employee for breach of contract and serious misconduct, in respect of which they also instituted an action in the High Court. The employee made a complaint of unfair dismissal and the company made a successful application to an industrial tribunal that the hearing of the complaint be postponed until after the decision of the High Court. The Employment Appeal Tribunal allowed an appeal against the tribunal's decision on the ground that the general principle was that complaints should go forward regardless of the existence of other proceedings, unless there were special reasons or unusual circumstances. On appeal, *held*, a tribunal had a complete and wide discretion to postpone proceedings or not as the interests of justice required it. The Employment Appeal Tribunal had no jurisdiction to reverse its decision unless it was wrong in law, perverse or a decision to which no reasonable tribunal could have come. Therefore the appeal would be allowed and the decision of the industrial tribunal restored.

CARTER V CREDIT CHANGE LTD [1980] 1 All ER 252 (Court of Appeal: STEPHENSON, BRIDGE and CUMMING-BRUCE LJJ). Dictum of Arnold J in *Bastick v James Lane (Turf Accountants) Ltd*, para. 1076, approved.

1076

The employee, a manager of a bookmaker's shop, was dismissed for dishonest conduct concerning the improper payment of bets. He complained he was unfairly dismissed but was subsequently charged with theft. The employee applied under the Industrial Tribunal (Labour Relations) Regulations 1974, Sch., r. 11 (2) (b) to the chairman of the industrial tribunal for the hearing to be adjourned until after the criminal trial, stating that the evidence given might be prejudicial to the trial and if he was convicted of theft he would discontinue the tribunal hearing so costs could be saved. The chairman acceded to the employer's submission that the issues were different and that an adjournment would have led to an unacceptable delay in proceedings. On appeal, *held*, before the appeal tribunal would interfere with the exercise of the chairman's discretion to refuse to adjourn proceedings, it was necessary to show that he had improperly taken into account some matter or had failed to take into account some relevant matter. It was clear the chairman had considered all the relevant material and there was no ground for interfering with his decision.

BASTICK V JAMES LANE (TURF ACCOUNTANTS) LTD [1979] ICR 778 (Employment Appeal Tribunal: ARNOLD J presiding).

1077 —— —— power to admit hearsay evidence

The employees, the manager and senior cashier of a squash club, were dismissed for allegedly serving alcohol outside licensing hours. In dismissing the employees, the employers relied upon information given to them by a temporary manager who had received a number of complaints from customers and staff about the way the club was managed. At the hearing of a complaint of unfair dismissal, the tribunal refused to admit the evidence of the temporary manager on the grounds that it was hearsay and that the strict rules of evidence had to be applied where it was alleged that the employees had committed a criminal offence. At the end of the employers' evidence the tribunal found that they had failed to prove that they had acted reasonably in dismissing the employees and held the dismissals to be unfair without hearing the employees' evidence. On appeal by the employers, *held*, in order to make a decision the tribunal had to know what information had been before the employers when they dismissed the employees. They ought therefore to have exercised their discretion not to enforce the strict rules of evidence and to admit the temporary manager as a witness. Although it was within the power of a tribunal to stop the case at the end of the employers' evidence, the case would be remitted to a different tribunal for hearing because the temporary manager's evidence ought to have been presented, which might have resulted in a different decision.

CORAL SQUASH CLUBS LTD V MATTHEWS [1979] ICR 607 (Employment Appeal Tribunal: SLYNN J presiding).

1078 —— —— **power to amend applications**

An employee complained that he had been unlawfully discriminated against on the ground of his race. When the complaint came before an industrial tribunal, the employee applied for leave to amend the originating application in order to include a complaint of unfair dismissal. The tribunal granted the application, holding that it should not be regarded as a new application (which would have been out of time), but as an amendment to an application which had been made in time. The hearing was adjourned to enable the employer to prepare evidence to rebut the new allegation. The employer appealed on the grounds that the amendment raised a new cause of action, that the grounds on which it was based were not adequately stated in the originating application, and that it was prejudicial to the employer. *Held*, although unfair dismissal was not mentioned in the originating application, the facts set out in it would support an arguable case of unfair dismissal as well as an arguable case of unlawful discrimination. Further, in the circumstances, the amendment to include unfair dismissal would neither prejudice nor cause any injustice to the employer. The appeal would be dismissed.

HOME OFFICE V BOSE [1979] ICR 481 (Employment Appeal Tribunal: TALBOT J presiding).

1079 —— —— **power to order adjournment—power to order hearing in private**

An employee was dismissed for allegedly copying and distributing confidential documents relating to his employer's business transactions. The employer brought an action against him, initially in the county court and then in the High Court, for breach of confidence. He was also charged with theft and committed for trial. The employee complained that he had been unfairly dismissed. On application by the employer, the industrial tribunal adjourned his complaint until after the determination of the pending civil and criminal proceedings. The tribunal further ordered that the adjourned complaint be heard in private in view of the confidential nature of the documents. The employee was subsequently acquitted on the criminal charge. The employee appealed on the grounds that the order for adjournment deprived him of a speedy resolution of his complaint and that the order that the complaint be heard in private was ultra vires. *Held*, (i) since the questions whether the documents were confidential and whether the employee could justify his conduct were to be decided by both the High Court and the industrial tribunal, it was clearly right in the interests of justice that the High Court proceedings should be heard first; (ii) since the question of whether the facts should be debated in public would be considered during the High Court proceedings, the tribunal's order that the hearing should be in private would be discharged and the matter of publicity left for the industrial tribunal to reconsider at the adjourned hearing in the light of the views expressed by the High Court. Accordingly, the appeal would be dismissed in relation to the order for adjournment, but allowed in part.

CAHM V WARD AND GOLDSTONE LTD [1979] ICR 574 (Employment Appeal Tribunal: BRISTOW J presiding).

1080 —— —— **power to order discovery and inspection of documents**

See *Science Research Council v Nasse; BL Cars Ltd (formerly Leyland Cars) v Vyas*, para. 913.

1081 —— —— **power to refer case to another tribunal**

Three employees were dismissed by their employers when they refused to be transferred to work on a different machine. They applied to an industrial tribunal for compensation for unfair dismissal and/or a redundancy payment. One member of the tribunal thought that all the claims should be dismissed, the second member thought the claims for redundancy payments should succeed but the claim for unfair dismissal should fail, and the third member thought the employees should be compensated for unfair dismissal but not for redundancy. In the absence of agreement the tribunal decided to refer the case to a different tribunal for a rehearing. The employers applied for an order of prohibition to prevent the rehearing, contending that the tribunal had in fact reached a decision in their favour. *Held*, the employees were potentially entitled to redundancy payments under the Redundancy Payments Act 1965 and to compensation for unfair dismissal under the Trade Union and Labour Relations Act 1974. Where an equal number of justices could not agree they had power to refer the case to another court, and the industrial tribunal had the same inherent jurisdiction. If the tribunal had applied the employers' argument the result would have been unfair as two members of the tribunal believed that the employees deserved some form of compensation although under different heads of legislation.

R v INDUSTRIAL TRIBUNAL, EX PARTE COTSWOLD COLLOTYPE [1979] ICR 174 (Queen's Bench Division: LORD WIDGERY CJ, GRIFFITHS and GIBSON JJ).

1965 Act wholly consolidated and 1974 Act partly consolidated in Employment Protection (Consolidation) Act 1978.

1082   An application was made under the Industrial Tribunal (Labour Relations) Regulations 1974, Sch. r. 12 (2), relating to directions, for a redundancy claim to be heard by a differently constituted tribunal. The original tribunal had adjourned the proceedings after the employers' first witness had given evidence and before the employee had put his case, because they considered there was no basis for a redundancy claim. *Held*, the power to give directions under r. 12 (2) was sufficiently wide to include a direction that a case be heard by a different tribunal. However there was nothing to suggest that the tribunal had reached a conclusion when they adjourned in this particular case and the power would not be exercised.

CHARMAN v PALMERS SCAFFOLDING LTD [1979] ICR 335 (Employment Appeal Tribunal: TALBOT J presiding).

1083   An industrial tribunal heard an employee's complaint of unfair dismissal. The employee applied for the matter to be heard by a different tribunal because he had no confidence in its fairness, alleging it was biased. The tribunal, although considering the allegation of bias as groundless, ordered that the complaint be heard by a differently constituted tribunal on the basis that it could not proceed when one party lacked confidence in it. On appeal by the employers, *held*, the industrial tribunal misdirected itself in law in deciding that it was obliged to discontinue the hearing where the employee lacked confidence in it. This in itself was insufficient grounds for ordering a rehearing and accordingly the case would be remitted to the tribunal to continue the hearing.

AUTOMOBILE PROPRIETARY LTD v HEALY [1979] ICR 809 (Employnent Appeal Tribunal: TALBOT J presiding).

1084   —— —— **requirement of residence**

The employers were a foreign oil corporation operating in Scotland but with a registered office in London. An employee was dismissed and claimed compensation for unfair dismissal, making an originating application to the central office of industrial tribunals in London. It was duly registered because it was considered that the employers came within the residence requirements laid down in the Industrial Tribunals (Labour Relations) Regulations 1974, reg. 3, in that their registered office was in London. The employers asked for the case to be transferred to Scotland but it was found by the regional chairman of tribunals that there was no machinery for such a transferral and the employee had made a valid application. The employer appealed. *Held*, the fact that the employers were a company registered in London was sufficient to satisfy the requirements of residence in reg. 3. The chairman had correctly held that the complaint was properly brought before an English industrial tribunal. The appeal would be dismissed.

ODECO (UK) INC v PEACHAM [1979] ICR 823 (Employment Appeal Tribunal: BRISTOW J presiding).

1085   —— **procedure**

See para. 2142.

1086   —— **review of proceedings—respondent not given notice of proceedings**

An employee obtained an award of compensation for unfair dismissal in the absence of his employers. It later transpired that they had never received notice of the proceedings and they applied for a review under Industrial Tribunals (Labour Relations) Regulations 1974, 1974 Halsbury's Abridgment para. 1834. A tribunal set aside the award in the absence of the employee, who appealed. *Held*, the proceedings on review had been defective because the employee had had no notice of them. Such applications, which involved questions of substance, could not be finally disposed of in the absence of one of the parties, and therefore the review should be re-heard by a differently constituted tribunal.

ALI v NILGUN FASHIONS (1978) 13 ITR 443 (Employment Appeal Tribunal: PHILLIPS J presiding).

1087   **Job Release Act 1977—continuation**

The Job Release Act 1977 (Continuation) Order 1979, S.I. 1979 No. 957 (in force on 30th September 1979), continues in force until 29th September 1980 the Job Release Act 1977, s. 1, 1977 Halsbury's Abridgment para. 1072, which makes financial provision for job release schemes.

1088   **Maternity pay—continuity of employment—calculation of length of service—employer's entitlement to rebate from maternity fund**

The employee had worked as a clerk for the appellant bank on a "one week on, one week off" basis since June 1972. Her contract of employment provided that she could not be made to work during her week off. In 1977 the employee became pregnant and was paid maternity pay by the appellants. The appellants' claim for a rebate from the maternity fund was refused on the basis that the employee had not fulfilled the statutory qualification for maternity pay because she had failed to complete two years' continuous service. The appellants contended that the employee's situation fell within the meaning of the Contracts of Employment Act 1972, Sch. 1, para. 5 (1) (c) which provides that any week during which the employee is absent from work in circumstances such that he is regarded as continuing in the service of the employer shall count as a period of employment. *Held*, to achieve continuity of employment an employee had to work at least sixteen hours each week or be covered by one of the situations specified in para. 5. The present case fell within para. 5 as the employee was absent from work by arrangement with her employers and her contract of employment was regarded as continuing. As all the weeks counted towards the computation of continuous employment she met the two years' service qualification for maternity pay and the appellants were entitled to reclaim that amount from the maternity fund.

LLOYDS BANK LTD v SECRETARY OF STATE FOR EMPLOYMENT [1979] IRLR 41 (Employment Appeal Tribunal: TALBOT J presiding).

1972 Act, Sch. 1, para. 5 now Employment Protection (Consolidation) Act 1978, Sch. 13, para. 9.

1089   **Migrant workers—European Convention**

The Council of Europe has issued the text of the European Convention on the Legal Status of Migrant Workers together with an explanatory report. The convention was opened for signature on 24th November 1977. The convention applies to migrant workers other than frontier workers, artists, other entertainers and sportsmen engaged for a short period and members of a liberal profession, seamen, persons undergoing training, seasonal workers, and workers, who are nationals of a contracting party, carrying out specific work in the territory of another contracting party on behalf of an undertaking having its registered office outside the territory of that contracting party. The convention deals, inter alia, with the migrants' right of exit from and admission to countries, travel facilities, work permits, residence permits, obligations to maintain families, admission of dependants to countries, housing, education, conditions of work, social security, medical assistance, occupational safety and health provisions, taxation, access to the courts and return home. The convention does not derogate from other bilateral or multi-lateral treaties and implementation does not depend on reciprocity. The convention comes into force on the first day of the third month following the deposit of the fifth instrument of ratification, acceptance or approval.

1090   Racial discrimination

See RACE RELATIONS.

1091   Redundancy

For cases concerning unfair dismissal by reason of redundancy, see UNFAIR DISMISSAL.

1092   —— amount of payment—calculation of weekly wage—whether attendance allowance included

An employee who was dismissed for redundancy had his redundancy payment calculated on his basic weekly wage only. The employee claimed an increased payment, contending that it should have taken account of a weekly attendance allowance which he also received. An industrial tribunal upheld his claim for an increased payment on the basis that the attendance award was part of his "week's pay" within the meaning of the Employment Protection Act 1975, Sch. 4, Part III, para. 3 (2). On the employers' appeal, held, the employee was contractually entitled to the attendance award so long as he worked regular hours and the award should therefore be included in his weekly wage. There was no basis for the employers' contention that only payments limited to work done were within the meaning of para. 3 (2).

LONDON BRICK CO LTD v BISHOP [1979] LS Gaz R 102 (Employment Appeal Tribunal: SLYNN J presiding).

1975 Act, Sch. 4, para. 3(2) now consolidated in Employment Protection (Consolidation) Act 1978, Sch. 13.

1093   —— —— effect of supervening misconduct

An employee, who was given five months notice of redundancy, was convicted of stealing from his employers during the intervening period. But for this he would have been entitled to a redundancy payment and he exercised his right to apply to an industrial tribunal to determine whether he should receive a part of that payment. The tribunal awarded him sixty per cent and the company appealed. Held, the tribunal exercised their discretion correctly having regard to all the relevant facts and circumstances. Although the payment was larger than the Appeal Tribunal would have awarded it was not so excessive as to justify interference.

LIGNACITE PRODUCTS LTD v KROLLMAN [1979] IRLR 22 (Employment Appeal Tribunal: PHILLIPS J presiding).

1094   —— —— normal working hours

The employee and two other men worked shifts as fan workers at the defendants' colliery to ensure that the ventilation system was properly functioning and permanently attended. His contract of employment provided for a normal working week of 40 hours but the employee had regularly worked a 56 hour week. The employee was made redundant and his redundancy payment was calculated on the basis of a 40 hour week. On the employee's appeal on the ground that the payment should take account of the overtime worked, an industrial tribunal held that, in the absence of any agreement about his hours of work, the redundancy payment had been properly calculated on the basis of the contract of employment. On appeal, *held*, it was important that the ventilation system should be permanently manned and therefore, although the overtime was not included in the terms of the contract of employment, it could be regarded as compulsory. The industrial tribunal had not made it clear whether it had considered the possibility of an informal agreement regarding overtime. The case would be remitted for reconsideration.

BARRETT v NATIONAL COAL BOARD [1978] ICR 1101 (Employment Appeal Tribunal: PHILLIPS J presiding).

1095　　——cessation or diminution of business—effect of statutory definition

Employers expanded their workforce in expectation of increased production. However, sales did not increase as anticipated, and some employees were dismissed for redundancy. The employees claimed that they had been unfairly dismissed as there was no redundancy situation or, alternatively, that they had been unfairly selected. The tribunal found that the dismissals were fair and were on the ground of redundancy. On appeal by the employees, *held*, where there was overmanning because of over-optimistic expectation of successful trade, the employer might cut out some jobs; a true redundancy situation. If he merely reduced his workforce, as in the instant case, the question was whether or not there was a diminution or cessation of the work on which the dismissed employee was engaged, within the meaning of the Employment Protection (Consolidation) Act 1978, s. 81 (2) (b). The tribunal had failed to analyse the effect of the statutory definition of redundancy on the facts of the case. However, the tribunal had come to the right answer on the merits of the case and the appeals would be dismissed.

KILNER BROWN J considered that as the Department of the Environment was obliged to make a refund to an employer of part of a redundancy payment, the public had a right to insist that the entitlement to a payment was properly and strictly challenged by an employer. There ought to be an examination of the statutory definition of redundancy in the light of the facts of the instant case; the wider aspects should more properly be dealt with by the Court of Appeal.

O'HARE v ROTAPRINT LTD [1979] LS Gaz R 1253 (Employment Appeal Tribunal: KILNER BROWN J presiding).

See also Times, 22nd November 1979.

1096　　—— claim for payment—whether dismissal or resignation

The respondents were sent letters informing them that reductions were being made in staff numbers but that their jobs would last for at least seven months. They gave their notice three months later, left the company and made applications for redundancy payments. The employers contended that the letters were not notices of dismissal and even if the employees had been dismissed with notice, their cross-notices, terminated their employment at an earlier date, were not given within the obligatory period required by the Redundancy Payments Act 1965, s. 4. *Held*, a notice of dismissal had at least to specify an ascertainable date. These letters were merely warnings that employment might terminate in seven months but was not certain to do so, nor were the respondent's cross-notices served within the prescribed time-limit. The respondents had resigned and were not entitled to redundancy payments.

PRITCHARD-RHODES LTD v BOON AND MILLER [1979] IRLR 19 (Employment Appeal Tribunal: SLYNN J presiding).

1965 Act, s. 4 now Employment Protection (Consolidation) Act 1978, s. 85.

1097　　Early in February 1977, the employers told their employee, a motor mechanic, that they were thinking of closing the repair section of their garage business. After discussion, the employee informed the employers that they would have to sack him and make him redundant. The employers did not wish to do this and, after further discussion, drafted an agreement under which the employee was to be self-employed from 28th February 1977, paying the employers a certain weekly sum for the use of their facilities. The agreement was duly signed by both parties on 18th February. The employee started working as a self-employed person at the garage, but was then given notice to terminate his occupation of the premises. The employee applied for a redundancy payment. An industrial tribunal found that the employee had not resigned, that there was no consensual agreement freely entered into by him to terminate his employment, and that he had been dismissed within the meaning of the Redundancy Payments Act 1965, s. 3 (2). The employers appealed. *Held*, as the employee, on the evidence, was clearly aware that his employment would shortly cease, the agreement under which he was to become self-employed was not freely entered into and did not amount to a consensual termination of his employment. The employers themselves fixed the date of termination of his employment at 28th February 1977 in that agreement. A dismissal within the meaning of s. 3 (2) had, therefore, taken place. The appeal would be dismissed.

GLENCROSS v DYMOKE [1979] ICR 536 (Employment Appeal Tribunal: TALBOT J presiding).

1965 Act, s. 3 now Employment Protection (Consolidation) Act 1978, s. 83.

1098 —— **continuity of employment—employer's right to recover rebate**

An employee was made redundant five years after transferring from one company to another in which the first company held shares. At the time of his transfer, his new employers assured him that he would retain the benefits he had acquired as a result of his previous employment. An industrial tribunal found that, by reason of the assurance, the employers were estopped from denying the continuity of his employment and awarded him a redundancy payment reflecting his total period of employment with both companies. The employers successfully appealed against the refusal of the Secretary of State to award a rebate on the full amount under the Redundancy Payments Act 1965, s. 30 (1) (a). The Secretary of State appealed on the ground that the only payment for which the employers were "liable under the Act" within s. 30 (1) (a) was that in respect of the employee's five years' service with them. *Held*, continuity, under s. 1 of the 1965 Act, meant continuity with one employer, and the tribunal was acting outside its jurisdiction under the Act in taking into account the employee's previous service with the first company. The employee retained the benefit of his previous employment by virtue of a contract made with the employers; no question of estoppel arose. Even if anything in the nature of an estoppel did arise, it could only give rise to a contractual obligation and could not make the agreed redundancy payment a payment which the employer was "liable under the Act" to pay, within s. 30 (1) (a). No right to a rebate from the Secretary of State was therefore created.

SECRETARY OF STATE FOR EMPLOYMENT v GLOBE ELASTIC THREAD CO LTD [1979] 2 All ER 1077 (House of Lords: LORD WILBERFORCE, LORD ELWYN-JONES, LORD EDMUND-DAVIES, LORD RUSSELL OF KILLOWEN and LORD KEITH OF KINKEL). Decision of Court of Appeal [1978] 3 All ER 954, 1978 Halsbury's Abridgment para. 1116 reversed. *Evenden v Guildford City Association Football Club Ltd* [1975] QB 917, CA, 1975 Halsbury's Abridgment para. 1290 doubted.

1965 Act, s. 30 now Employment Protection (Consolidation) Act 1978, s. 104.

See further "Continuing redundancy and ambiguity", Justinian, Financial Times, 13th August 1979.

1099 —— **employer's duty to consult trade union—failure to provide written details of redundancies**

Teachers working under fixed term contracts did not have their contracts renewed. Their union applied for a declaration that the employers had failed to provide written details of the redundancies as required by the Employment Protection Act, s. 99 (5). The tribunal refused the application firstly because by s. 119 (7) of the Act employment under a contract for a term of twelve weeks or less is excluded from the provisions of s. 99, unless the employee has been continuously employed for a period of more than twelve weeks. The tribunal held that the definition of continuous employment included the requirement to work a minimum of sixteen hours a week by the Contracts of Employment Act 1972, Sch. 1, para. 4, and as the teachers worked less than sixteen hours a week they were not continuously employed within the meaning of the section. Secondly, the teachers had not been made redundant. Under the Trade Union and Labour Relations Act 1974, Schedule 1, para. 6 (2) the reasons justifying dismissal included redundancy and, under para. 6 (1) (b), "some other substantial reason of a kind such as to justify the dismissal". The tribunal maintained that the reason for non-renewal of the contracts was for some other substantial reason justifying dismissal and was not therefore redundancy. The union appealed. *Held*, allowing the appeal, where the contract of employment was for a fixed term of more than twelve weeks, as it was in this case, irrespective of the number of hours worked in a week, it did not fall within the s. 119 (7) exclusion. The fact that the reason for non-renewal was a substantial reason did not exclude it from also being redundancy. All the reasons listed in para. 6 (2) were substantial, the proviso in para. 6 (1) (b) for "some other substantial reason" merely being a sweeping up category for any substantial reasons not listed in para. 6 (2). The case would not however be remitted back to the tribunal to consider whether the reason was redundancy, as the appeal was merely hypothetical, in that the union was not appealing against the tribunal's refusal to make a protective award.

NATIONAL ASSOCIATION OF TEACHERS IN FURTHER AND HIGHER EDUCATION v MANCHESTER CITY COUNCIL [1978] ICR 1190 (Employment Appeal Tribunal: PHILLIPS J presiding).

1974 Act, Sch. 1, para. 6 (1), (2), now Employment Protection (Consolidation) Act 1978, s. 57.

1100   —— —— **special circumstances preventing compliance—whether pending application for government financial aid a special circumstance**

A company, which was already in severe financial difficulties, applied for a second government loan which was refused, although it was suggested that the Scottish economic planning department might help. They would not do so and the company laid off its entire workforce. A receiver was appointed who dismissed the workforce on the ground of redundancy. The union claimed it had not been consulted about the redundancies in accordance with the Employment Protection Act 1975, s. 99. On a question of whether there were special circumstances rendering it impracticable to comply and whether all reasonable steps had been taken towards compliance, *held*, it was not permissible for a tribunal to assess the prospects of a loan being granted. Insolvency alone was not itself a special circumstance but an application for a loan by a company already in financial difficulties, rendered it impracticable to discuss redundancy generally until the outcome of the application was known. However a substantial measure of confidential consultation could have occurred before the redundancies were declared, but before the outcome of the application was known, in view of the consequences of the refusal of the loan. Therefore, the company had not taken all reasonable steps to comply with s. 99.

ARMOUR (RECEIVER FOR BARRY STAINES LTD) v ASSOCIATION OF SCIENTIFIC, TECHNICAL AND MANAGERIAL STAFFS [1979] IRLR 24 (Employment Appeal Tribunal: LORD McDONALD MC presiding).

1101   —— **entitlement to payment—employee laid off without pay**

Two bricklayers were laid off due to a shortage of work, the employers indicating that they hoped there would be work available in the future. Three months later the bricklayers gave notice of a claim for redundancy payments. One of them was informed orally that work had become available but he turned down the offer on behalf of himself and the other bricklayer, and requested the return of their tax documents and their holiday pay. A formal letter of re-engagement was later sent to them. An industrial tribunal found that they were entitled to redundancy payments. On appeal, *held*, the bricklayers had complied with the statutory requirements of writing notices of their intention to claim redundancy payments and, by orally refusing the employers' offer and requesting the return of their documents, had given notice of their intention to terminate their contracts of employment. The formal offer of re-engagement was not a counter-notice that the employers intended to contest their liability to make redundancy payments. Thus the industrial tribunal had not erred in finding that they were entitled to the payments and the appeal would be dismissed.

FABAR CONSTRUCTION LTD v RACE AND SUTHERLAND [1979] IRLR 232 (Employment Appeal Tribunal: TALBOT J presiding).

1102   —— offer of alternative employment—trial periods—matters to be considered

Employees whose work was about to cease started to work in alternative jobs which the employers had offered, but stated that they were not accepting new contracts. They all left more than four weeks after starting the new jobs and claimed redundancy payments. An industrial tribunal upheld the employers' contention that the employees had accepted the new jobs and were only entitled to a statutory four week trial period, but failed to note that the employees had expressed reservations. The employees appealed. *Held*, in such cases there were three possible situations which an industrial tribunal might have to deal with, each requiring different treatment. An employee might have been told that his work was going to end and that if he did not accept an alternative job he would be dismissed, in which case he would have a period in which to decide whether or not to accept the offer. The length of that period would depend on the facts of the case and the contract would not end until the period expired. He might accept a new job on trial, in which case he would have a similar period in which to make up his mind whether finally to accept the job. Only if he committed himself to the new job by words or conduct so that a new contract came into existence would the statutory four week trial period operate. The tribunal in this case had failed to consider the questions sufficiently and so the appeal would be allowed and the case remitted to a differently constituted tribunal.

TURVEY v C. W. CHEYNEY & SON LTD [1979] IRLR 105 (Employment Appeal Tribunal: KILNER BROWN J presiding).

1103   —— —— whether refusal reasonable

A company ran into financial difficulties and issued redundancy notices to their staff. They then obtained a temporary employment subsidy from the Government. They wrote to their employees, including the respondent, informing them that the redundancies would not be effected and that further employment would be offered them on the same terms and conditions as they had previously enjoyed. The letters noted, however, that trading conditions for the company were still difficult and expressed the hope that there would be greater job security in the future. The respondent refused to accept the offer as he had been offered employment with another firm. On a question of whether his refusal was unreasonable so that he was not entitled to a redundancy payment, *held*, special circumstances affecting the respondent could be taken into account in deciding whether the refusal was reasonable. The fact that the respondent was aged sixty-one, was uncertain as to the future of his employment with the company and had found another job which avoided the possibility of his being unemployed in the future was sufficient to make his refusal reasonable.

PATON CALVERT & CO LTD v WESTERSIDE [1979] IRLR 108 (Employment Appeal Tribunal: SLYNN J presiding).

1104   —— —— —— suitability of employment

An employee was made redundant and offered alternative employment at a nearby factory at a reduced salary. He agreed to work for a trial period, despite the lower salary, but left after a few days. He gave written notice to his employer, stating that the smell of paint and the heat in the new factory made him ill, and that the terms and conditions of the new job meant that it was not suitable alternative employment within the meaning of the Redundancy Payments Act 1965, s. 2 (4). He applied to an industrial tribunal for a redundancy payment. The tribunal held that, since the employee had made it clear the he would have accepted the lower salary had he liked the new job, the difference in pay did not make the job unsuitable. The employee's refusal to accept the offer of alternative employment was therefore unreasonable. The employee appealed. *Held*, the correct test of suitable employment under s. 2 (4) was whether the employment offered was substantially equivalent to the employee's former job; prima facie, a lower salary would make a new job unsuitable, although an unconditional acceptance of a change in pay by an employee would render alternative employment suitable. In the instant case, the employee's willingness to accept the offer of alternative employment was conditional upon his liking the new job. As he clearly did not, the tribunal had erred in law in failing to take this into consideration when deciding whether the new employment was suitable. The appeal would be allowed.

HINDES v SUPERSINE LTD [1979] ICR 517 (Employment Appeal Tribunal: TALBOT J presiding).

1965 Act, s. 2 now Employment Protection (Consolidation) Act 1978, s. 82.

1105   —— **procedure for handling redundancies—statutory time periods**

The Employment Protection (Handling of Redundancies) Variation Order 1979, S.I. 1979 No. 958 (in force on 1st October 1979), varies the provisions of the Employment Protection Act 1975, ss. 99 (3), 101 (1) by reducing to thirty days the period which must elapse between the commencement of consultation with trade union representatives and notification to the Secretary of State and the first of the dismissals, in cases where the employer is proposing to dismiss as redundant ten to ninety-nine employees at one establishment within a period of thirty days or less. The order also varies the protected period specified in s. 101 (5) (b) of the Act by reducing it to thirty days.

1106   —— **protective award—when payable—matters to be considered**

The employers announced the closure of certain of their bakeries without prior consultation with the recognised trade union. The bakeries were sold as going concerns to other companies and nearly all the employees continued to be employed by the new owners without a break in their employment. The trade union claimed a protective award not only in respect of employees dismissed as redundant, but also in respect of employees at the bakeries transferred to new ownership. An industrial tribunal found as a preliminary point that it had the jurisdiction to make the award. On appeal, *held*, an award was available even where the employees had suffered no loss by the lack of consultation. The object of the award was to compensate for failure to consult and in deciding whether to make an award, a tribunal had to consider the loss of days of consultation rather than the loss or potential loss of actual remuneration during the relevant period. Thus even assuming that the transferred employees had suffered no financial loss, the tribunal had jurisdiction to inquire into the merits of making a protective award. The case would be remitted to the tribunal for their decision.

SPILLERS-FRENCH (HOLDINGS) LTD v UNION OF SHOP, DISTRIBUTIVE AND ALLIED WORKERS [1980] 1 All ER 231 (Employment Appeal Tribunal: SLYNN J presiding).

1107   —— **running-down of teachers' training college—whether by reason of redundancy—dismissal**

A teacher had been employed by the local council at a secondary school for fourteen years. He was then seconded to university, where he decided he wished to lecture at a teachers' training college. A post was offered to him at the local college as a temporary lecturer for one year, which was extended for another year, after which he was dismissed as the college was running-down its staff. His claim for unfair dismissal was rejected but his claim for a redundancy payment was upheld by an industrial tribunal. On appeal by the council, *held*, the mere fact that there was a reduction in the amount of work available did not necessarily entitle a person to a redundancy payment. The teacher had accepted the post on a temporary basis in the knowledge that there was a limited and diminishing amount of work available. He was not entitled to a redundancy payment and the appeal would be allowed.

NOTTINGHAM COUNTY COUNCIL v LEE [1979] ICR 818 (Employment Appeal Tribunal: SLYNN J presiding).

1108   Redundancy payments scheme—shipbuilding

The Shipbuilding (Redundancy Payments Scheme) (Great Britain) (Amendment) Order 1979, S.I. 1979 No. 898 (in force on 24th July 1979), amends the scheme established by the Shipbuilding (Redundancy Payments Scheme) (Great Britain) Order 1978, 1978 Halsbury's Abridgment para. 1142, for the payment of benefits to employees of British shipbuilders who are made redundant or transferred to less well paid employment. The order extends the period during which such redundancies or transfers must take place to four years beginning on 1st July 1977. It also makes changes in relation to previous earnings, the class of persons eligible, conditions of eligibility and company schemes.

1109   Sex discrimination

See SEX DISCRIMINATION.

1110   Time off—time off for union duties and activities—entitlement to pay for working hours—whether customary overtime working hours

Industrial tribunal decision:

DAVIES v HEAD WRIGHTSON TEESDALE LTD [1979] IRLR 170 (trade union official who took time off to attend a conference claimed pay for four hours customary overtime as well as pay at basic rate; Employment Protection (Consolidation) Act 1978, s. 27 gave right to pay for "employee's working hours"; working hours were those during which he was contractually bound to be at work; overtime not required by contract so official's claim failed).

1111   —— —— sick pay negotiations—entitlement to pay

Industrial tribunal decision:

DUNCAN v WEIR PACIFIC VALVES LTD [1978] IRLR 523 (shop steward claimed pay for attending meeting with shop stewards of other companies in his employer company's group to discuss sick pay policy; alleged this was a trade union duty within Employment Protection Act 1975, s. 57; employer contended it was an activity for which he was not entitled to pay; as the meeting was designed to improve industrial relations and time off with pay had previously been allowed for discussions about pensions the employer's refusal had been unreasonable).

1975 Act, s. 57 now Employment Protection (Consolidation) Act 1978, s. 27.

1112   —— —— test for determining limit of activities

In two cases concerning time off work for trade union activities, as provided for under the Employment Protection Act 1975, s. 57 it was held that the test for determining the limit of activities, including training courses, which fell within s. 57 was whether the time off required was to enable the trade union official to carry out his duties relevant to the industrial relations between the employer and employees. This did not mean however that he was allowed paid time off in order simply to make himself a better union representative, although the provisions in s. 57 were not to be construed too narrowly.

SOOD v GEC ELLIOTT PROCESS AUTOMATION LTD [1979] IRLR 416; YOUNG v CARR FASTENERS LTD [1979] ICR 844 (Employment Appeal Tribunal: SLYNN J presiding).

Employment Protection Act 1975, s. 57 now Employment Protection (Consolidation) Act 1978, s. 27.

1113   Trade unions
See TRADE UNIONS.

1114   Unfair dismissal
See UNFAIR DISMISSAL.

1115   Vicarious liability—statutory offence—construction—whether a company "uses" a vehicle driven by employee
Scotland
A vehicle driven by an employee was found to have a defective braking system in contravention of motor vehicle regulations. His company was charged with "using" the vehicle in contravention of the Road Traffic Act 1972, s. 40 (5). The company contended that it could not be convicted of "use", only of "causing and permitting" the use of the vehicle. *Held*, the offence created by "use" of the vehicle was one of absolute liability and could be committed both by the actual driver of the vehicle and the company on behalf of whom the vehicle was being driven.

SWAN v MACNAB 1977 SC 57 (High Court of Justiciary). *James and Son Ltd v Smee* [1955] 1 QB 380, DC followed.

1116   Wages—itemised pay statement—failure to provide employee with pay statement
An employee had not agreed her remuneration with her employer when she started work for him. She asked for a gross weekly wage of £40 and he offered her £30 per week net of deductions. She worked for twelve weeks and during that time was paid £30 per week net, but received no pay statement detailing the deductions made from her pay. An industrial tribunal upheld her claim that her employer had failed to comply with the Employment Protection Act 1975, s. 81 by not giving her an itemised pay statement. The tribunal made an award under s. 84 (5), the sum awarded representing the difference between the net pay she would have received calculated on a gross pay of £40 per week, and the pay she actually received. She appealed claiming that the tribunal should have awarded her a sum equal to the total amount of the unnotified deductions, as it had a discretion to do under s. 84 (5). The employer cross-appealed, arguing that no award should have been made. *Held*, upholding the tribunal's decision, although the discretion conferred by s. 84 (5) contained a penal element the tribunal had rightly considered the employer had been penalised by the inconvenience and cost caused to him in having to appear before a tribunal. Nevertheless some award should be made to compensate the employee, as the employer had failed to comply with s. 81. He could not argue that as no gross remuneration had ever been agreed there was no sum from which deductions could be made and therefore no unnotified deductions. It was clear from the evidence that the sum of £30 was arrived at by a process of deductions having been made from a larger sum and that these deductions had not been notified.

SCOTT v CREAGER [1979] IRLR 162 (Employment Appeal Tribunal: ARNOLD J presiding).

1975 Act, ss. 81, 84(5) now Employment Protection (Consolidation) Act 1978, ss. 8, 11(8).

1117   —— payments by health authorities—reimbursement of wages of doctor's staff—employment of doctor's wife or dependant
See *Glanvill v Secretary of State for Social Services*, para. 1945.

1118   —— road haulage workers
The Transport and General Workers' Union made a complaint to the Advisory Conciliation and Arbitration Service on behalf of the road haulage workers employed by the appellant company in respect of the rate of week-day overtime payments, which it maintained should be increased to time and a half. The matter

was referred to the Central Arbitration Committee (CAC) for settlement. The Road Haulage Wages Act 1938, s. 4(3) gives guidance as to how the CAC is to determine the problem, and sub-section (d) provides that remuneration is not unfair if it is equivalent to that payable to similar workers, engaged in the same industry in the same district, in pursuance of any decision of a joint industrial council. By s. 5(3) the CAC has to have regard not only to s. 4(3) but also to the general level of remuneration paid to workers in similar industries. The company argued that although its overtime rates were less favourable than that of others employed in the industry, incentive payments boosted the average hourly rate and that it was more appropriate to compare the overall payment scheme rather than one item, namely overtime. The CAC found that there was in existence an agreement between the company and the union, published by the Joint Industrial Council for the Food Manufacturers' Industry. This agreement provided for overtime at time and a half, and so the existing remuneration was deemed unfair and an award for the new rate was made accordingly. The company applied for orders of certiorari and mandamus on the ground that the CAC had concerned themselves strictly with overtime payments and had not considered the company's argument that the overall payments were high. *Held*, the company's contention would be upheld as the CAC had misdirected itself in law in its approach. The award would be quashed and the matter referred back to the CAC for reconsideration.

R v CENTRAL ARBITRATION COMMITTEE, EX PARTE RHM FOODS LTD [1979] ICR 657(Queen's Bench Division: MOCATTA J).

1119   —— teachers—compensation payable upon closure of college of education

See *Pearson v Kent County Council*, para. 993.

1120   Wages Councils—dressmaking

The Dressmaking and Women's Light Clothing Wages Council (England and Wales) (Variation) Order 1979, S.I. 1979 No. 864 (in force on 1st September 1979), varies the field of operation of the Dressmaking and Women's Light Clothing Wages Council (England and Wales) by the exclusion therefrom of workers employed in the altering, repairing, renovating or remaking of any article of apparel the making of which is included in the dressmaking and women's light clothing trade, where such work is carried on in or about a shop or other place for retail sale, for the purpose of or in connection with such sale.

1121   —— retail trades—food

The Retail Trades Wages Councils (Food and Allied Trades) (Abolition and Establishment) Order 1979, S.I. 1979 No. 862 (in force on 1st September 1979), abolishes with respect to England and Wales the Retail Bread and Flour Confectionery Trade Wages Council, the Retail Food Trades Wages Council and the Retail Newsagency, Tobacco and Confectionery Trades Wages Council and establishes in their place the Retail Food and Allied Trades Wages Council (Great Britain).

1122   ———— non-food

The Retail Trades Wages Council (Non-Food) (Abolition and Establishment) Order 1979, S.I. 1979 No. 863 (in force on 1st September 1979), abolishes the Retail Bookselling and Stationery Trades Wages Council (Great Britain), the Retail Drapery, Outfitting and Footwear Trades Wages Council (Great Britain) and the Retail Furnishing and Allied Trades Wages Council (Great Britain) and establishes in their place the Retail Trades (Non-Food) Wages Council (Great Britain).

1123   Wages Councils Act 1979

The Wages Councils Act 1979 received the royal assent on 22nd March 1979 and came into force on 22nd April 1979. The Act consolidates enactments relating to wages councils and statutory joint industrial councils.

Tables showing the destination of enactments consolidated and the derivation of the new Act are set out at pages 307–309 following.

DESTINATION TABLE

This table shows in column (1) the enactments repealed by the Wages Councils Act 1979 and in column (2) the provisions of that Act corresponding thereto.

In certain cases the enactment in column (1), though having a corresponding provision in column (2) is not, or is not wholly, repealed, as it is still required, or partly required, for the purposes of other legislation.

(1)	(2)
Wages Councils Act 1959 (c. 69)	Wages Councils Act 1979 (c. 12)
s. 1	s. 1
2	2
3	3
4 (1), (2)	4 (1), (2)
(2A), (2B)	(3), (4)
(3)–(6)	(5)–(8)
5	5
6 (1)–(3)	6
(4)	Rep., 1971 c. 72, s. 169, Schs. 8, 9
7	s. 25
8	8
9 (1)	8 Rep., 1975 c. 71, s. 125 (3), Sch. 18
(2)–(5)	s. 7
10	9
11 (1), (2)	14 (1), (2)
(2A)	(3)
(3)	(4)
(3A)	(5)
(4)	(7)
(4A)	(8)
(5)–(8)	(9)–(12)
12 (1)	15 (1)
(1A)	(2)
(2), (3)	(3), (4)
(3A)	(5)
(4), (5)	(6), (7)
13	16
14	17
15	18
16	19
17	20
18	21
19	22
20	23
21	Rep., 1968 c. 73, s 165, Sch. 18, Part IV
22	s. 29
23	30
24	28
25	Rep., 1975 c. 24, s. 10 (2), Sch. 3, and 1975 c. 25, s. 5 (2), Sch. 3, Part I
26	——
27 (1), (2)	——
(3)	s. 32 (3)
Sch. 1, paras. 1, 2	Sch. 1, paras. 1, 2
paras. 2A	para. 3
paras. 3–8	paras. 4–9
s. 2	2
3	3
4	Rep., 1975 c. 71, s. 125 (3), Sch. 18

(1)	(2)
Wages Councils Act 1959 (c. 69)	Wages Councils Act 1979 (c. 12)
Sch. 5, paras. 1–4	——
para. 5	Sch. 5, para. 3
paras. 6–8	——
para. 9	Sch. 5, para. 1
paras. 10–12	——
6	Rep., S.L.(R.) Act 1974
Civil Evidence Act 1968 (c. 64)	
Schedule†	s. 22 (3)
Transport Act 1968 (c. 73)	
Sch. 11†	s. 22 (3) (b)
European Communities Act 1972 (c. 68)	
Sch. 4, para. 9 (4)†	22 (3) (b)
Social Security Act 1973 (c. 38)	
Sch. 27, para. 21	17 (1) (a)
Trade Union and Labour Relations Act 1974 (c. 52)	
Sch. 3.	
para. 9 (1), (2)	
(3)	
(4)–(6)	5
(7)	
(8)	28
	Sch. 1, para. 3
Employment Protection Act 1975 (c. 71)	
s. 89 (1)	ss. 1 (2) (b), (c), 2 (2) (a), (3), (4), 3 (1), (2), (4), (5), 6, 7, 25 (2), (3), 29 (3), 30, Sch. 1, paras. 1, 6, 7
(2), (3)	See against 1975 c. 71, Sch. 7, below
90	s. 10
91	ss. 10 (1), 14, 16, 19 (1)
92	s. 11
93	12

(1)	(2)	(1)	(2)
Employment Protection Act 1975 (c. 71)	Wages Councils Act 1979 (c. 12)	Employment Protection Act 1975 (c. 71)	Wages Councils Act 1979 (c. 12)
s. 94 (1)	13 (1)	para., 5	s. 17 (2)
(2)	13 (2), Sch. 1, para.1	6	ss. 19 (2), 20 (3), 22 (6) 23
95 (1)	24 (1)	7	s. 20 (2)
(2), (3)	(2)	8	22 (3)
(4), (5)	(3), (4)	9	28
96	26	10	Sch. 1, para. 5
117*	s. 24 (6), (7)	Sch. 8	Sch. 4
127 (1) (a), (f)*, (g)	27 (1)	17, para. 11 (1)	
(2)*	(2) (a), (b), (5)	(2)	
(3) (a)*–(f)*	(3)	(3)	Sch. 5, para. 2
(4)*	(4)	12†	
129 (6)*	32 (3)	Road Traffic (Drivers' Ages and Hours of Work) Act 1976 (c. 3)	
Sch. 7, Part I	14 (1)–(5), (7)–		
II	(12)	s. 2 (3)†	s. 22 (3) (b)
III	15	Employment (Continental Shelf) Act 1978 (c. 46)	
IV	Sch. 2		
para., 1	ss. 16 (1), 19 (1), 20 (1), (2)		
2	s. 4 (3), (4)	s. 1 (1)*	27 (2) (c)
3	25 (1)–(3), (5) (a)	2*	(5)
4	16		

†Repealed in part
*Not repealed

TABLE OF DERIVATIONS

This table shows in the right hand column the legislative source from which the section of the Wages Councils Acts 1979 in the left hand column have been derived. In the table the following abbreviations are used:

1959 = The Wages Councils Act 1959
   (7 & 8 Eliz. 2. c. 69)
1971 = The Industrial Relations Act 1971
   (1971 c. 72)
1974 = The Trade Union and Labour Relations Act 1974
   (1974 c. 52)
1975 = The Employment Protection Act 1975
   (1975 c. 71)

This Table does not acknowledge the following Transfer of Functions Orders:—
   The Minister of Labour Order 1959
    (S.I. 1959/1769)
   The Secretary of State for Employment and Productivity Order 1968
    (S.I. 1968/729)

Section of Act	Derivation
1	1959 s. 1; 1975 s. 89 (1)
2	1959 s. 2; 1975 s. 89 (1)
3	1959 s. 3; 1975 s. 89 (1).
4	1959 s. 4; 1975 Sch. 7 Part IV para. 2.
5	1959 s. 5; 1971 Sch. 8; 1974 Sch. 3 para. 9 (3).
6	1959 s. 6; 1975 s. 89 (1).
7	1959 s. 9 (2) to (5); 1975 s. 89 (1).
8	1959 s. 8.
9	1959 s. 10.
10	1975 s. 90, 91.
11	1975 s. 92.
12	1975 s. 93.
13	1975 s. 94.
14 (1) to (5)	1959 s. 11 (1) to (3A); 1975 Sch. 7 Part I.
(6)	Equal Pay Act 1970 (c. 41) s. 4 (1A); 1975 Sch. 16 Part IV para. 13 (8).
(7) to (12)	1959 s. 11 (4) to (8); 1975 Sch. 7 Part I.
15	1959 s. 12; 1975 s. 91, Sch. 7 Part II.
16	1959 s. 13; 1975 Sch. 7 Part IV paras. 1, 4.
17	1959 s. 14; Social Security Act 1973 (c. 38) Sch. 27 para. 21; 1975 Sch. 7 Part IV para. 5.
18	1959 s. 15.
19	1959 s. 16; 1975 Sch. 7 Part IV paras. 1, 6.
20	1959 s. 17; 1975 Sch. 7 Part IV paras. 6, 7.
21	1959 s. 18.
22	1959 s. 19; Minister for the Civil Service Order 1968 (S.I. 1968/1659); Civil Evidence Act 1969 (c. 64) Sch.; Transport Act 1968 (c. 73) Sch. 11; European Communities Act 1972 (c. 68) Sch. 4 para. 9 (4); 1975 Sch. 7 Part IV paras. 6, 8; Road Traffic (Drivers' Ages and Hours of Work) Act 1976 (c. 3) s. 2 (3).
23	1959 s. 20; 1975 Sch. 7 Part IV para. 6.
24	1975 ss. 95, 117.
25	1959 s. 7; 1975 s. 89 (1), Sch. 7 Part IV para. 3.
26	1975 s. 96.
27 (1)	1975 s. 127 (1)(a), (f), (g).
(2)	1975 s. 127 (2); Employment (Continental Shelf) Act 1978 (c. 46) s. 1 (1).
(3), (4)	1975 s. 127 (3), (4).
(5)	Employment (Continental Shelf) Act 1978 (c. 46) s. 2.
28	1959 s. 24; 1975 Sch. 7 Part IV para. 9.
29	1959 s. 22; 1975 s. 89 (1).
30	1959 s. 23; 1975 s. 89 (1).
31	—
32 (1), (2)	1959 s. 27 (3); 1975 s. 129 (6).
(3)	
Sch. 1	
para. 1	1959 Sch. 1 para. 1; 1975 ss. 89 (1), 94(2).
2	1959 Sch. 1 para. 2.
3	1959 Sch. 1 para. 2A; 1974 Sch. 3 para. 9 (8).
4	1959 Sch. 1 para. 3.
5	1959 Sch. 1 para. 4; 1975 s. 89 (1), Sch. 7 Part IV para. 10.
6 to 9	1959 Sch. 1 paras. 5 to 8; 1975 s. 89 (1).
Sch. 2	1959 Sch. 2 as subst. by 1975 s. 89 (2), Sch. 7 Part III.
Sch. 3	1959 Sch. 3; Minister for the Civil Service Order 1968 (S.I. 1868/1659).
Sch. 4	1975 Sch. 8.
Sch. 5	—
Sch. 6	—
Sch. 7	—

ENVIRONMENT

1124   Gypsy encampments—grants

The Department of the Environment has stated in a circular that it is in the national interest that gypsies should be satisfactorily accommodated and that the total amount of grant towards providing the capital cost of gypsy caravan sites is to be found from central government voted expenditure. An appendix to the circular classifies the sites eligible for grant aid, specifies the rate of grant and method of payment and also specifies the qualifying date. The capital costs of providing sites which are eligible for grant are listed in Annex A to the circular (but these need not be followed exactly). The procedure for the approval of schemes and the application for payment of grant is described in Annex B. See Department of Environment circular 11/79.

1125   Waste disposal—disposal licence—prerequisite of planning permission

See *R v Derbyshire County Council, ex parte North East Derbyshire DC*, para. 2776.

EQUITY

Halsbury's Laws of England (4th edn.), Vol 16, paras. 1201–1500

1126   Articles

Covenant "Impeding Some Reasonable User", H. W. Wilkinson (the relevant questions to be considered under the Law of Property Act 1925, s. 84 (1) (aa)): 129 NLJ 523.

Equitable Set-Off, K. P. E. Lasok (a synopsis of *Federal Commerce Ltd v Molena Alpha Inc* (*The Lorfri, Nanfri and Benfri*), [1978] 3 All ER 1066, CA. 1978 Halsbury's Abridgment para. 2609, and other case law): 123 Sol Jo 379.

Extinguishment of Restrictive Covenants, F. Graham Glover (the extinguishment of restrictive covenants where the fee simple of the benefited and burdened land is vested in one person): 129 NLJ 236.

Reservation of Title—The Lessons of *Bond Worth*, Michael Burke: 129 NLJ 651.

Romalpa Clauses: Recent Cases, Hilary E. Pearson (in the light of *Borden (UK) Ltd v Scottish Timber Products Ltd* (1978) 122 Sol Jo 825, 1978 Halsbury's Abridgment para. 512 and *Re Bond Worth* [1979] 3 WLR 629, para. 1137): 123 Sol Jo 207.

1127   Acquiescence—expenditure on property of another—appropriate remedy

The plaintiff told his mistress on several occasions that the house which he had bought for them to live in belonged to her, along with its contents. He encouraged her to spend a substantial part of her capital on repairs, improvements and redecoration, which she continued after he left her to live with another woman. He later claimed possession of the house, but the court upheld her counterclaim that he had made her an absolute gift of the contents of the house and that she had acquired the beneficial interest in the property under a constructive trust. On appeal, *held*, the court had been correct in its finding as to the house contents, but it was not true to say that a constructive trust had come into being because there had been no intention that the house should be hers when it was bought. However, she had spent large sums of money on the house with the plaintiff's acquiescence and therefore she was entitled to equitable relief, either in the form of a licence or of a transfer of title. As equity would not be satisfied unless she was given security of tenure and quiet enjoyment of the property the court would order a transfer of title, since a licence was not registrable as a land charge and could be defeated by a purchaser for value without notice.

PASCOE v TURNER [1979] 2 All ER 945 (Court of Appeal: ORR, LAWTON and CUMMING-BRUCE LJJ).

1128 Conveyance of interest in land for less than full value—whether bargain unconscionable

Canada

Two brothers each had a one-half interest in a farm. One of the brothers, B, had operated the farm and paid the expenses of operation, whilst the other, W, had lived away from the farm for many years. B fell ill and wished to sell the farm. He engaged a solicitor to negotiate with W and the solicitor advised W to get independent legal advice, but W refused to do so. The solicitor persuaded W to convey his interest in the property for $4,500. W's stepson was present in an adjacent room when this bargain was struck, and he gave evidence that he had heard the solicitor browbeating W and claimed that W had broken down and wept after the solicitor had left. The solicitor had used the fact of B's serious illness and the need for an urgent settlement to persuade W to agree, and he also threatened that if W did not agree the resulting litigation would erode much of the proceeds of any sale of the farm. The farm was eventually sold for $35,000. In an action brought by W to get the contract set aside, the defence argued that the transaction was fair, just and reasonable because B had borne the burden of running the farm, thus W was not entitled to the full value of his one-half interest. *Held*, the bargain was unconscionable. The evidence demonstrated that considerable pressure had been put on W by the solicitor, who had the advantage of being a professional man dealing with a sixty-nine year old layman. Furthermore the defence had not discharged the onus of showing that the transaction was fair. W had allowed B to live on the farm rent-free and although B had paid the expenses of running the farm he had also retained all the profits. The contract would therefore be set aside and W would be awarded one-half of the value of the farm.

JUNKIN V JUNKIN (1978) 20 OR (2d) 118 (High Court of Ontario).

1129 Equitable assignment—assignment of after-acquired property— previous charge on property—effect

See *Siebe Gorman & Co Ltd v Barclays Bank Ltd*, para. 245.

1130 Equitable defence—equitable set-off

See *British Anzani (Felixstowe) Ltd v International Marine Management (U.K.) Ltd.*, para. 1704.

1131 Equitable exoneration—mortgage of joint matrimonial home to secure husband's debts—whether wife entitled to be indemnified

See *Re Berry (A Bankrupt)*, para. 219.

1132 Equitable rights—sale of goods to company—retention of equitable title until payment made—whether amounted to equitable floating charge

See *Re Bond Worth*, para. 1137.

1133 Fraud—caveat emptor—amateur building works—liability of vendor in negligence

See *Hone v Benson*, para. 1959.

1134 Restrictive covenant—modification

Lands Tribunal decision:

RE NEW IDEAL HOMES LTD'S APPLICATION (1978) 36 P & CR 476: V. G. Wellings QC (covenant in conveyance of land to use land only for a restricted number of private dwelling-houses; planning permission for larger number of houses granted; application for modification of covenant under Law of Property Act 1925, s. 84 (1) (aa) relating to impeding reasonable user of land; benefit of restriction attached to adjoining land owned by borough council; council objected on grounds that modification of covenant would deprive them of option of selling their land to private developers at a high price for low-density development; objection invalid as any reasonably-minded purchaser would expect to be permitted to develop land at high-density; restriction would be modified).

1135   Subrogation—subrogation rights of guarantor—extinction of rights

See *Brown Shipley and Co Ltd v Amalgamated Investment (Europe) BV*, para. 1400.

1136   Tracing—mistake of fact—money paid under mistake of fact—right to trace and recover

The plaintiff, a New York bank, was instructed to pay a large sum of money to another New York bank for the account of the defendant, a company carrying on business in England. The payment was duly made. Later on the same day, due to a clerical error, the plaintiff made a further payment of the same amount to the same recipient for the account of the defendant. The defendant presented a petition in the English High Court to be wound up compulsorily. A winding up order was made. The defendant was insolvent and the plaintiff could not hope to recover the second sum paid in error, if it proved as a creditor in the winding up. The plaintiff brought an action in England against the defendant claiming a declaration that the defendant was a trustee for the plaintiff's sum paid in error. The defendant contended that the plaintiff was not entitled in equity to trace and recover the mistaken payment because (i) the equitable right of a person to trace and claim money paid by mistake was not part of the substantive law of New York; (ii) under English law the equitable right of tracing depended on the existence of an initial fiduciary relationship arising from a consensual arrangement lacking here; (iii) irrespective of any rights the plaintiff had before the commencement of winding up proceedings, all the defendant's property since that date had been held on a statutory trust requiring its application in discharge of the defendant's liabilities in accordance with the provisions of the Companies Acts, so the plaintiff's only surviving right was to prove as a creditor in the winding up. *Held*, the plaintiff was entitled in equity to trace the mistaken payment because (i) under English law it had the right to do so, since a person who paid money to another in mistake of fact retained an equitable property in it; (ii) on the evidence, it had a similar right under the law of the State of New York; (iii) as a result, under whichever of the two legal systems the plaintiff's title was founded, the assets in the defendant's hands properly representing the plaintiff's money at the commencement of the winding up did not belong to the defendant beneficially and had never formed part of its property subject to the statutory trust under the Companies Acts. A declaration would be granted accordingly and an inquiry ordered into what had become of the sum paid by mistake.

CHASE MANHATTAN BANK NA v ISRAEL-BRITISH BANK (LONDON) LTD [1979] 3 All ER 1025 (Chancery Division: GOULDING J). Dictum of Lord Haldane LC in *Sinclair v Brougham* [1914–15] All ER Rep 622 at 632 applied.

1137   —— vendor of goods—goods incorporated into another product

A company supplied raw fibre to a manufacturer of carpets under a contractual term whereby the supplier transferred the legal property in the fibre but retained the equitable and beneficial ownership of the fibre, any products made from it and the proceeds of sale thereof, until full payment for the fibre had been made. The manufacturer went into liquidation and the supplier contended that, by virtue of the retention of title clause, he held the ownership of the fibre supplied and not paid for, and he accordingly sought beneficial entitlement to the fibre or proceeds of sale (where it had been sold). *Held*, under the contract, the property in the fibre passed to the manufacturer on delivery. If the retention of title clause had operated to confer any equitable rights on the supplier, such rights could only have been by way of an equitable floating charge created by the manufacturer to ensure payment of the purchase price. The *Romalpa* and *Borden* cases were distinguishable on the ground that in those cases neither the legal property nor any equitable ownership in the goods passed until payment had been made. This had made the suppliers bailees of the goods until payment was made and thus a fiduciary relationship had been implied. No such relationship existed in this case and hence the supplier's application to trace, would be dismissed. The floating charge was registrable under the Companies Act 1948, s. 95. It had not been registered and was therefore void against the other creditors.

RE BOND WORTH LTD [1979] 3 WLR 629 (Chancery Division: SLADE J). *Aluminium Industrie Vaassen BV v Romalpa Aluminium Ltd* [1976] 2 All ER 577, 1977 Halsbury's Abridgment, para. 1077 and *Borden (UK) Ltd v Scottish Timber Products Ltd* [1979] 2 Lloyd's Rep 168, 1978 Halsbury's Abridgment para. 512 distinguished. See further 129 NLJ 220.

1138 Resin was supplied to chipboard manufacturers under a contract which provided that property in the goods supplied passed to the manufacturers on full payment of all sums due to the supplier. The supplier was aware that the resin was used in manufacture within two days of delivery, thereafter becoming an inseparable part of the chipboard. The manufacturers became insolvent and a winding up order was made. The supplier claimed against the receivers that under the reservation of title clause any chipboard containing their resin was charged to the same extent with payments due for resin supplied. *Held*, (i) once the manufacturers had used the resin for the manufacture of the chipboard nothing remained for the supplier to trace. The effect of the reservation of title clause was merely to reserve the supplier's propery in the resin as long as it remained unused. Once it had been incorporated into the chipboard it ceased to exist, as did the supplier's title. (ii) In any event there was no special fiduciary relationship between supplier and manufacturers enabling the supplier to trace the resin supplied into the chipboard, because it was supplied under a contract of sale by which the manufacturers received for themselves as purchasers and not in any fiduciary capacity as agents or bailees. (iii) Had the supplier acquired an interest in the chipboard it would have been by way of unregistered floating charge attached to the chipboard or proceeds of sale and as such would have been void under the Companies Act 1948, s. 95, as against the liquidator and other creditors, for want of registration.

BORDEN (UK) LTD v SCOTTISH TIMBER PRODUCTS LTD [1979] 3 WLR 672 (Court of Appeal: BUCKLEY, BRIDGE and TEMPLEMAN LJJ). Decision of Judge Rubin sitting as a deputy High Court judge [1979] 2 Lloyd's Rep 168, 1978 Halsbury's Abridgment para. 512 reversed. Dicta of Jessel MR in *Re Hallett's Estate, Knatchbull v Hallett* [1874–80] All ER Rep at 796–797 applied; *Aluminium Industrie Vaassen BV v Romalpa Aluminium Ltd* [1976] 2 All ER 552, 1976 Halsbury's Abridgment para. 1077 distinguished.

For discussion of this case see "Unsecured creditors given a raw deal", Justinian, Financial Times, 19th November 1979.

ESTOPPEL

Halsbury's Laws of England (4th edn.), Vol 16, paras. 1501–1641

1139 **Article**

Proprietary Estoppel: A Principled Remedy, R. D. Oughton (discussion on *Griffiths v Williams* [1977] LS Gaz R 1130, CA, 1977 Halsbury's Abridgment para. 1146 and *Pascoe v Turner* [1979] 2 All ER 945, CA, para. 1127): 129 NLJ 1193.

1140 **Acquiescence—expenditure on property of another—appropriate remedy**

See *Pascoe v Turner*, para. 1127.

1141   **Business tenancy—application for new tenancy—defective request—whether landlords estopped from denying validity of request**

See *Bristol Cars Ltd v RKH Hotels Ltd* para. 1670.

1142   **Election—ignorance of true facts—whether party barred by election**

See *The Scaplake, Pyxis Special Shipping Co Ltd v Dritsas & Kaglis Bros Ltd*, para. 2526.

1143   **Estoppel by conduct—charter based on fixed hire—secret agreement for repayment of hire by owner—whether charterer estopped from relying on secret agreement as against new owner**

See *The Odenfeld, Gator Shipping Corpn v Trans-Asiatic Oil Ltd SA and Occidental Shipping Establishment*, para. 2532.

1144   **Estoppel by representation—member of international federation—representation that association a member of federation—whether federation estopped from denying association's membership**

See *Reel v Holder*, para. 310.

1145   **Issue estoppel—decision by industrial tribunal—subsequent action in High Court**

In 1972 the plaintiffs, a husband and wife, employed as superintendent and matron of a council-run young persons' home, were dismissed for alleged misconduct. Their complaints of unfair dismissal were dismissed but on appeal the National Industrial Relations Court ordered the case to be reheard by a freshly constituted tribunal. The industrial tribunal dismissed the plaintiffs' complaints and leave to appeal from the High Court was refused. In 1977 the plaintiffs sought a declaration that their dismissals were illegal, ultra vires and void and that the procedure adopted by the council was contrary to the rules of natural justice. *Held*, the decision of the freshly constituted tribunal, which was fully reasoned, was a judicial decision by a judicial tribunal for the purposes of the doctrine of res judicata. The decision gave rise to an issue estoppel binding on the parties. The plaintiffs had been fairly dismissed and accordingly the action would be dismissed.

GREEN v HAMPSHIRE COUNTY COUNCIL [1979] ICR 861 (Chancery Division: FOX J). *Thoday v Thoday* [1964] P 181, CA applied.

1146   **Promissory estoppel—lease—invalid option to renew lease—expenditure incurred on assumption of validity—whether landlords estopped from asserting their strict rights**

Company A were the tenants of no. 22 and company B the tenants of nos. 20 and 21. All three premises were owned by the same landlords, who had purchased nos. 21 and 22 from company B in 1948, subject to a lease of no. 21 being granted back to company B. No. 22 was leased to company A in 1948. The lease contained an option of renewal, subject to company A installing a lift. The 1948 lease to company B contained a provision that if company A did not exercise their option of renewal, the landlords would have the option of terminating the lease of no. 21 fourteen years before it determined. The option to renew in the lease of no. 22 was not registered. In 1960, in *Beesly v Hallwood Estates Ltd*, it was held that an option to renew under a lease was void if not registered. None of the parties were aware of this decision and all believed the option in the lease of no. 22 to be valid. In 1963, company B took a lease of no. 20. The lease contained an option of renewal provided that company A's option in respect of no. 22 had been exercised. In 1975, the landlords became aware that the option might be void for want of registration. In 1976, having installed a lift, company A served notice on the landlords purporting to exercise their option of renewal in the lease of no. 22. When the landlords refused, company A claimed specific performance of that option. Company B also claimed specific performance of the option contained in the 1963 lease and an appropriate declaration in respect of the break clause in the 1948 lease. The questions for consideration were (i) whether company A's option was void against the landlords for want of registration; (ii) if so, whether the landlord was estopped from relying on this ground of invalidity, having regard to the expenditure incurred by company A on the lift with the landlords' concurrence, and (iii) whether, in respect of the two leases to company B, the landlord was estopped from relying on the invalidity of an option which in their own grants they had asserted to be subsisting. *Held*, (i) the option to renew was void in the light of *Beesly v Hallwood Estates Ltd* and subsequent decisions; (ii) In order for the landlords to be estopped from denying the validity of the option, it was necessary to show that it was unconscionable for the landlords to seek to take advantage of the mistake which, at the material time, all the parties shared. The landlords could not have been under a duty to inform company A of the invalidity of the option as they themselves were unaware of the fact at the time. Further, it could not be shown conclusively that company A would have decided not to install the lift if they had known of the invalidity of the option. Their claim for specific performance would fail; (iii) The landlords had obtained the freehold of no. 21 from company B at a price calculated on the basis that the lease would, in all probability, run for the full term. Further, in 1963, company B had been encouraged by the landlords to expend a large sum on the property and to take a lease of no. 20 in the expectation that they would be entitled to renew it when company A exercised their option. It would have been inequitable to have allowed the landlords to frustrate expectations which they themselves had created. Company B's applications would, therefore, succeed.

TAYLOR FASHIONS LTD V LIVERPOOL VICTORIA FRIENDLY SOCIETY (1979) 251 Estates Gazette 159 (Chancery Division: OLIVER J). *Beesly v Hallwood Estates Ltd* [1960] 1 WLR 549, *Greene v Church Commissioners for England* [1974] 3 All ER 609, CA, 1974 Halsbury's Abridgment para. 1907 and *Kitney v MEPC Ltd* [1977] 1 WLR 981, 1977 Halsbury's Abridgment para. 1529 followed.

1147   —— payment for goods on non-contractual document—right of buyer to damages

See *ETS Soule v International Trade Development Co*, para. 483.

1148   —— planning application—whether applicant estopped from re-neging on undertaking

See *Augier v Secretary of State for the Environment*, para. 2775.

1149   Res judicata—custody order—extent of estoppel

See *Rowe v Rowe*, para. 947.

EUROPEAN COMMUNITIES

Halsbury's Laws of England (3rd edn.), Supp. Vol. 39A

1150   Articles

The Community Concept of Force Majeure, Heather Cornwell-Kelly (the defence of force majeure in Community law): 129 NLJ 245.

Constitutional Review and Section 2 (4) of the European Communities Act 1972, Joseph Jaconelli (an examination of the juridical nature of section 2 (4) in the light of the adequacy of existing remedies of administrative law): 28 ICLQ 65.

Consumer Credit—Proposals from the EEC, R. G. Lawson (a review of the draft Council Directive on consumer credit): 129 NLJ 905.

De Minimis Application in Common Market Competition Law, J. Kodwo Bentil: 123 Sol Jo 744.

The Direct Effect of Community Law, Richard D. Hacker: 129 NLJ 43.

European Parliament: Direct Elections and Consequences, Nicholas Bourne: 123 Sol Jo 312.

The Effect of Community Agreements in the United Kingdom under the European Communities Act 1972, Marc Maresceau: 28 ICLQ 241.

The Future of the Legal Profession in the EEC Context, David Edward: [1979] LS Gaz 752.

Judicial Review of EEC Anti-Trust Decisions, J. Kodwo Bentil: 123 Sol Jo 777.

Price, Quantitative Output and Field of Use Restraints in Patent Licences, N. Byrne (situations where prohibition, price and quantitative output restrictions may be necessary): 129 NLJ 45.

Publication and Notification of EEC Legislation, Peter Oliver (the meaning and effect of EEC Treaty, Art 191 with respect to EEC legislation): 129 NLJ 243.

Reference to the EC Court regarding Interlocutory Proceedings, J. Kodwo Bentil (whether reference is to be made to the EC Court in respect of matters or questions arising out of interlocutory proceedings): 123 Sol Jo 42.

Some Problems of EEC Legal Translations, Christopher Dwyer: [1979] LS Gaz 244.

1151 Accession of new member states—transitional measures—interpretation

See Case 231/78: *Re Import of Potatoes*, para. 72.

1152 Accession to the Communities—Greece

A treaty of accession by which Greece will become a full member of the European Communities was signed in Athens on 28th May 1979. This provides for her admission as the tenth member state with effect from 1st January 1981. The treaty permits, in broad terms, a five-year transition period after entry in which Greece will align herself with EEC requirements, but Greek nationals will not be able to take full advantage of the EEC provisions to offer their services on the Community labour market for a further two years. Greece is also expected to join the European Monetary System after the five-year transitional period. See the Guardian, 29th May 1979.

For the implementation of the treaty in the United Kingdom see para. 1192.

1153 Common agricultural policy

See AGRICULTURE.

1154 Common commercial policy — anti-dumping measures — undertakings given by exporters—validity of subsequent definitive measure

Early in 1977 the Commission instituted the procedure provided for under Regulation 459/68, art. 10 in order to determine whether anti-dumping measures were required in consequence of the introduction into Community Markets of large quantities of ball bearings and tapered roller bearings originating in Japan. In accordance with art. 15 of that regulation a provisional anti-dumping duty was then imposed in respect of those products. Subsequently the Commission accepted voluntary undertakings given by the four major Japanese producers to revise their prices so as to eliminate the margin of dumping. However, the Council then adopted, pursuant to art. 17 of the basic regulation, Regulation 1778/78, which introduced a definitive anti-dumping duty in respect of the products in question, to be suspended in the case of the four Japanese producers for only so long as they complied with their undertakings. The regulation also provided for the recovery from the four named Japanese producers of the provisional duty earlier imposed. In proceedings brought under EEC Treaty, art. 173 the four Japanese producers sought the annulment of Regulation 1778/77. *Held*, on the question of the admissibility of the application, although the measure in question was in the form of a regulation it was clear that the suspension of the definitive duty in respect of the applicants, subject to their compliance with the undertakings, and the requirement of payment by them of the provisional duty constituted measures of direct and individual concern. The action was therefore admissible. With regard to the substance of the application, it was unlawful for one and the same anti-dumping procedure to be terminated by the Commission accepting an undertaking under art. 14 of the basic regulation, which provided that such an undertaking led to a termination of the procedure under art. 10, simultaneously with the imposition of a definitive duty under art. 17, the provisions of which could be applied only on completion of that procedure. This principle was equally applicable to the collection of the provisional duty provided for by the regulation in issue: the definitive collection of such duty could only be authorised by a measure adopted under art. 17, the application of which was subject to the above mentioned condition. Regulation 1778/77 would therefore be annulled.

In Case 119/79 the applicants claimed compensation from the Community in respect of (i) payments of provisional duty under Regulation 1778/77, and (ii) loss of profit as a result of an allegedly unlawful obligation contained in their undertaking. The claim was dismissed on the grounds (i) that the annulment of Regulation 1778/77 removed the obligation to pay the provisional duty, and (ii) since the applicants had succeeded in their action for annulment on the basis of their undertaking they were not entitled to rely on the alleged unlawfulness of that undertaking in order to call into question the liability of the Community.

Case 113/77: NTN TOYO BEARING CO LTD v EC COUNCIL; Case 118/77: IMPORT STANDARD OFFICE v EC COUNCIL; Case 119/77: NIPPON SEIKO KK v EC COUNCIL and EC COMMISSION; Case 120/77: KOYO SEIKO CO LTD v EC COUNCIL and EC COMMISSION; Case 121/77: NACHI FUJIKOSHI CORPN v EC COUNCIL [1979] 2 CMLR 257 (European Court of Justice).

1155   —— **imports from non-member states**

Council Regulation (EEC) 926/79 (OJ No. L131, 29.5.79) (in force on 1st June 1979) consolidates existing common rules for imports from non-member states. Annex I sets out the common liberalisation list of products which must not be subject to any quantitative restriction when imported from the third countries listed in Annex II; provision is made for the extension of either list by decision of the Council. The regulation also provides for simplified consultation procedures and surveillance measures in respect of imports which may from time to time require protective measures. Council Regulation 1439/74, as amended, is repealed.

1156   —— **imports from state-trading countries**

Council Regulation (EEC) 925/79 (OJ No. L131, 29.5.79) (in force on 1st June 1979) consolidates existing common rules for imports from state-trading countries. Products which may be imported into the Community without quantitative restriction from certain third countries are listed in the Annex and the regulation provides for simplified consultative procedures and surveillance measures in respect of imports which may from time to time require protective measures. Council Regulation (EEC) 109/70, as amended, is repealed.

1157   —— **trade agreements with non-member states—powers of Community**

In 1978 negotiations were opened under the auspices of UNCTAD, the United Nations agency responsible for the promotion of international trade, for the conclusion of an international agreement on natural rubber. The purpose of the proposed agreement was to achieve a balanced growth between the supply and demand for natural rubber, with a view to stabilising its price, by means of building up a buffer stock. Following a divergence of view between the Council and Commission as to whether the agreement fell within the Community's common commercial policy and the competence of the Community to negotiate and participate in the agreement, the Commission sought the opinion of the European Court pursuant to EEC Treaty, art. 228. *Held*, the subjects covered by the common commercial policy, as enumerated by art. 113, related to traditional measures designed to liberalise, rather than regulate, external trade. However, that list of subjects was not exhaustive, but merely provided examples of the "uniform principles" upon which the policy was expressly based. Accordingly, the concept of the common commercial policy was susceptible to a broad interpretation so as to include any system designed to regulate external trade. Thus, although the proposed agreement in question, in so far as it sought to regulate the world market in natural rubber, fell outside the express definitions contained in art. 113, it fell within the concept of the common commercial policy as envisaged by that provision. It did not, however, automatically follow that the Commission had exclusive competence to negotiate and participate in the agreement on behalf of the member states. Such power would arise only if the burden of financing the buffer stock fell upon the Community budget; if the charges were to be borne directly by the individual member states, their individual participation in the agreement together with the Community would be necessary.

Opinion 1/78 (EEC): RE THE DRAFT INTERNATIONAL AGREEMENT ON NATURAL RUBBER [1979] 3 CMLR 639 (European Court of Justice).

1158   Common transport policy—road transport—licensing of passenger transport operators—grounds for refusing licence

The Danish road passenger transport authority refused to renew a man's licence because of his criminal record. Under the Danish penal code any occupation or position, which could only be held by a person approved by the appropriate public authority, could be denied to someone whose criminal conduct provided grounds for considering that there was imminent danger of misuse by him of such a position. Such a danger was considered to be present by the authority in this case. Council Directive (EEC) 74/562, art. 2 stated that anybody wishing to be a road passenger transport operator should be of good repute, and that each member-state should determine for itself the provisions relating to good repute. An existing operator, under art. 4, who had been authorised before 1st January 1978, was not required to furnish proof that he was of good repute. Consequent upon a claim against the decision of the authority, a number of questions were referred to the European Court concerning the interpretation of the directive. *Held*, the member state did not exceed the margin of discretion given to it by the directive, by deciding good repute on the basis of previous criminal convictions which indicated the danger of a misuse of the position. The provision exempting existing operators from having to provide proof of good repute was of direct effect. However, it did not prevent the authority from refusing to renew a licence where it had found that the operator no longer enjoyed good repute.

Case 21/78: DELKVIST V PUBLIC PROSECUTOR (DENMARK) [1979] 1 CMLR 372 (European Court of Justice).

1159   —— —— tachographs—failure of member state to make installation and use of tachographs compulsory

Under Council Regulation (EEC) 1463/70 the installation and use of automatic recording equipment, the tachograph, was made compulsory for road transport vehicles registered in a member state. Such installation and use was made compulsory by art. 4 in respect of all vehicles used for the carriage of dangerous goods and all other vehicles registered on or after 1st January 1975. Article 23 required member states to adopt all measures necessary for the implementation of the regulation. In the case of new member states the Act of Accession, Annexe VII provided that art. 4 applied with effect from 1st January 1976. However, under United Kingdom legislation the installation and use of tachographs was introduced on an optional basis, while the obligation to keep individual control books, which the regulation had abolished, remained. The Commission, in accordance with EEC Treaty, art. 169, applied to the European Court for a declaration that the United Kingdom had failed to fulfil an obligation under the Treaty. The United Kingdom maintained that national implementation of the regulation was best achieved on an optional basis since the introduction of compulsory measures would meet with active resistance in the sectors concerned. It claimed that the present system complied with the objectives of the regulation and therefore the alleged failure of the United Kingdom to implement its provisions was of a purely technical nature. The United Kingdom also pointed out that since the regulation had been implemented in the other member states its observance was already effectively guaranteed in respect of intra-community transport. *Held*, EEC Treaty, art. 189 provided that regulations were binding in their entirety in member states, and accordingly states were not entitled to apply the provisions of a regulation in an incomplete or selective manner, thereby rendering abortive certain aspects of Community legislation, on the ground of being contrary to the national interest: practical difficulties of implementation could not justify unilateral non-observance of provisions of Community law. Further, the Treaty, while allowing member states to profit from the advantages of the Community, also imposed on them the obligation to respect its rules. Thus, the failure of a state to respect such a rule undermined the duty of solidarity accepted by it by the fact of its adherence to the Community and called into question the equality of member states before Community law. Therefore, by failing to adopt within good time measures necessary for the implementation of Regulation 1463/70 the United Kingdom had failed to fulfil an obligation under the Treaty.

Case 128/78: Re Tachographs: EC Commission v United Kingdom [1979] 2 CMLR 45 (European Court of Justice).

For the subsequent implementation of Regulation 1463/70 see para. 2285.

1160 —— **state aid to transport undertakings—application of general rules on state aid**

See Case 156/77: *EC Commission v Belgium*, para. 1163.

1161 **Community legislation—breach—national legislation concerning equal pay—application for reference to European Court of Justice**

See *Worringham and Humphreys v Lloyds Bank Ltd*, para. 2500.

1162 —— **decision—decision impleaded under European Convention on Human Rights—liability of Communities**

See *Confédération Française Démocratique du Travail v European Communities*, para. 1446.

1163 —— —— **procedure for contesting legality of decision—admissibility of issue of legality in separate proceedings**

Since 1971 the Belgian Government had granted aid to the Belgian national railway company intended to compensate for charges applied to coal and steel in consequence of the establishment under the ECSC Treaty of through international railway tariffs. The European Commission, finding that the aid in question was within EEC Treaty, arts. 92 and 93 and as such could not be justified under either art. 92 or Regulation 1107/70, art. 3 (2), on the granting of aid for transport by rail, road and inland waterway, adopted a decision pursuant to art. 93(2), declaring that the aid was incompatible with the common market to the extent that it should be granted under Regulation 1107/70, art. 4. Belgium failed to comply with that decision and the Commission therefore referred the matter to the European Court in accordance with art. 93 (2). The Belgian Government claimed that the compensation referred to in Regulation 1107/70, arts. 3 (2) and 4 constituted aid within EEC Treaty, art. 77 relating to aid to transport and was thus outside the scope of art. 92. It therefore contested the validity of the Commission's application on the basis of the illegality of the decision. *Held*, the application of arts. 92 and 93, which established a general system for aid granted by member states, could not be excluded by art. 77 in relation to aid for transport. Moreover, Regulation 1107/70, art. 2 specified that arts. 92 to 94 were applicable to aid granted for transport by road, rail and inland waterway. Further, the procedure to be followed by a member state which sought to dispute the legality of a decision addressed to it was laid down by art. 173 which, in order to safeguard the principle of legal certainty, provided for a limitation period of two months. That time having expired in the instant case, the Belgian Government was not entitled to contest the legality of the decision in question in the present proceedings: the purpose of the procedure established by art. 93 (2) was only to enable the Commission to apply to the court for a declaration that a member state had failed to comply with a decision made under that article. To allow a member state to contest the legality of a decision in those proceedings would be irreconcilable with the system of legal remedies established by the Treaty and would jeopardise the principle of legal certainty.

Case 156/77: EC COMMISSION v BELGIUM [1978] ECR 1881 (European Court of Justice).

1164 —— **directive—failure of member state to implement directive**

In 1974 the EC Council issued an outline directive on the approximation of laws of member-states in respect of certain types of tractors which introduced a system of "EEC type-approval". Four further directives were issued covering specific aspects of the system which, together with the outline directive, were to be put into effect by member states within eighteen months of their notification. Italy failed to make the necessary amendments to its national rules within the prescribed period and the EC Commission, after following the procedure under EEC Treaty, art. 169, brought the matter before the European Court. Before the action was heard, however, the Italian government had brought into effect the outline directive, together with enabling provisions for the implementation of the special directives. *Held*, although the substance of Italy's default had been eliminated by the implementation of the outline directive and the adoption of enabling provisions for the implementation of the special directives, the fact remained that the prescribed time limit in respect of the outline directive had been exceeded and the four special directives were still not in force. Accordingly Italy had failed to fulfil its obligations under the Treaty.

Case 69/77: RE TRACTOR TYPE-APPROVAL DIRECTIVE 1974: EC COMMISSION v ITALY [1979] 1 CMLR 206 (European Court of Justice).

1165 —— —— —— **failure due to national difficulties**

Council Directive (EEC) 75/324, on the approximation of laws relating to aerosol dispensers, required member states to adopt the necessary national legislation within eighteen months of its notification. Italy failed to comply and in proceedings brought before the European Court by the Commission pursuant to EEC Treaty, art. 169, explained that the failure, which it did not contest, was due to internal difficulties. *Held*, a member state was not entitled to plead provisions, practices or circumstances existing in its internal legal system in order to justify a failure to comply with the obligations and time-limits imposed by community directives. Accordingly, Italy had failed to fulfil an obligation under the Treaty.

Case 163/78: RE AEROSOL DISPENSERS: EC COMMISSION v ITALY [1979] 2 CMLR 394 (European Court of Justice).

1166 —— **liability of Communities in damages**

See Case 119/77: *Nippon Seiko KK v EC Council and EC Commission*, para. 1154.

1167 —— **national law—compatibility with Community agricultural provisions**

See Case 83/78: *Pigs Marketing Board v Redmond*, para. 62.

1168   —— regulation—action for annulment—requirement of direct and individual concern

See Case 113/77: *NTN Toyo Bearing Co Ltd v EC Council*, para. 1154.

1169   —— —— date of publication—retroactivity

In two cases, questions were raised concerning Commission Regulations (EEC) 649/73 and 741/73 relating to monetary compensatory amounts in the wine sector, in the context of proceedings between German undertakings and the competent customs authority for the repayment of monetary compensatory amounts charged when wine was imported on dates between 9th and 30th March 1973. The questions referred to the European Court of Justice were (i) on what date a regulation was to be regarded as published within the meaning of the EEC Treaty, art. 191, and (ii) from what dates the relevant regulations were to be applied. *Held*, (i) a regulation was to be regarded as published throughout the Community on the date borne by the issue of the Official Journal containing the text of the regulation. However, if there was evidence that the date on which an issue was in fact available at the Office for Official Publications of the European Communities did not correspond to the date appearing on the issue, regard should be had to the date of actual publication; (ii) Regulation 649/73 provided that it was to enter into force on the day of its publication in the Official Journal. The issue of the Official Journal in which it was published bore the date 9th March 1973, but was not in fact available at the Office for Official Publications of the European Communities until 12th March 1973, upon which date it should be deemed to come into force. However, it also provided that the amounts resulting from its application were to apply from 26th February 1973. Generally a Community measure could not take effect from a date before its publication, but exceptionally could do so where the purpose to be achieved so demanded and where the legitimate expectations of those concerned were duly respected. This was such an exceptional case, and hence Regulation 649/73 could validly attribute retroactive effect to itself. Similar considerations applied to Regulation 741/73, which altered the monetary compensatory amounts resulting from Regulation 649/73. Regulation 741/73 was published in the Official Journal on 19th March 1973, on which date it entered into force, but it provided that it applied from 5th March 1973. Such a provision was valid notwithstanding the fact that on that date Regulation 649/73 had not yet been published in the Official Journal. Hence Regulations 649/73 and 741/73 were applicable from 26th February 1973 and 5th March 1973 respectively.

Case 98/78: Firma A. Racke v Hauptzollamt Mainz [1979] ECR 69; Case 99/78: Weingut Gustav Decker KG v Hauptzollamt Landau [1979] ECR 101 (European Court of Justice).

1170   —— —— effect of finding of invalidity

A Dutch importer of feeding stuffs applied to the competent national authority for a protein certificate in respect of certain vegetable feeding stuffs. The application was refused on the ground that the importer had not provided the appropriate security as required by Council Regulation (EEC) 563/76. On the importer's appeal against that decision the Dutch court referred the question of the validity of the regulation to the European Court, which ruled that the regulation was invalid. On the resumption of the national proceedings the importer additionally claimed compensation from the national authorities for damage allegedly suffered as a result of the initial refusal to grant the certificate. The court again stayed the proceedings and referred to the European Court questions on the effect of the invalidity of the regulation and the liability of the Community or the national authority for the alleged damage. *Held*, (i) it was clear, both from EEC Treaty, arts. 173, 174 and 184, under which the European Court had exclusive jurisdiction to review the legality of regulations, and from art. 177, which empowered the Court to give final rulings on the validity of regulations, that all regulations brought into force in accordance with the Treaty were to be presumed valid so long as the Court had not made a finding of invalidity. Accordingly, so long as Regulation 563/76 had not been declared invalid the relevant national authority was obliged to comply with its provisions;

(ii) As stated in an earlier decision of the Court, a finding that the regulation in question was null and void was insufficient by itself to render the Community liable under art. 215 to make good the alleged damage. Further it was not open to the court to determine questions on the application of art. 215 in proceedings under art. 177; (iii) The question of the liability of the national authority was to be determined by the national court in accordance with domestic law; art. 215 related only to the liability of the Community, a matter solely within the jurisdiction of the European Court by virtue of art. 178.

Case 101/78: GRANARIA BV v HOOFDPRODUKTSCHAP VOOR AKKERBOUWPROD-UCKTEN [1979] 3 CMLR 124 (European Court of Justice). Joined Cases 83 and 94/76, 4, 15 and 40/77: Finl v EC Council and Commission [1978] ECR 1209, 1978 Halsbury's Abridgment para. 1193 referred to.

For earlier proceedings in this case see [1977] ECR 1247, 1977 Halsbury's Abridgment para. 77.

1171   —— —— nature—whether regulation in form of a decision

The common organisation of the market in sugar is governed by Council Regulation (EEC) 3330/74, while Council Regulation (EEC) 3331/74 concerns the allocation and alteration of the basic quotas for sugar, and provides for derogations from Regulation 3330/74. Regulation 3331/74 was amended by Council Regulation (EEC) 298/78, which derogated from the provisions of Regulation 3330/74 by providing that France might reduce the basic quota for each undertaking in its overseas departments. The applicants, sugar producers in France's overseas departments, requested the annulment of Regulation 298/78 under the EEC Treaty, art. 173, on the ground that it adversely affected their established rights. *Held*, art. 173 provided that a person might institute proceedings in respect of a decision addressed to him, which, although in the form of a regulation, was of direct and individual concern to him. The nature of Regulation 3331/74 was purely that of a regulation; the derogations provided for by it were not general or special exceptions to the rules governing the basic quotas but an integral part of them. Therefore it could not be considered to constitute a decision. The amendment to it made by Regulation 298/78 was in the same way in the nature of a regulation and could not be considered as a decision. Nor was the regulation itself of direct or individual concern to the applicants; only the measures adopted by the member state concerned pursuant to it could be of direct or individual concern to them. The applications would be dismissed.

Joined Cases 103 to 109/78: SOCIÉTÉ DES USINES DE BEAUPORT v EC COUNCIL [1979] ECR 17 (European Court of Justice).

1172   —— —— regulation imposing penalty—validity

Commission Regulation (EEC) 193/75 lays down rules for the application of the system of import and export licences. It provides that the issue of such licences is conditional upon the giving of a security. It was amended by Commission Regulation (EEC) 499/76, art. 3 of which required evidence of completion of an importation covered by an import licence within six months of expiry of the licence and imposed as a penalty for late submission of the evidence the forfeiture of the security. In an action before the national court, an importer contended that Regulation 499/76, art. 3 was invalid on the ground that the penalty was disproportionate to the end sought. The national court requested the European Court of Justice to give a preliminary ruling on the validity and interpretation of art. 3. *Held*, the penalty for delay in submission of proof of importation was the same as that prescribed for total failure to import. The former infringement was considerably less serious than the latter and hence the penalty prescribed by art. 3 was excessively severe. It was therefore invalid.

Case 122/78: BUITONI SA v FONDS D'ORIENTATION ET DE RÉGULARISATION DES MARCHÉS AGRICOLES [1979] 2 CMLR 665 (European Court of Justice).

1173 ———— regulation requiring national implementation—failure of member states to adopt necessary measures

See Case 128/78: *Re Tachographs*, para. 1159.

1174 ———— validity of additional national conditions

See Case 31/78: *Bussone v Italian Ministry for Agriculture*, para. 63.

1175 ———— regulation subsequently declared invalid—liability of Community

See Case 101/78: *Granaria BV v Hoofdproduktschap voor Akkerbouwprodukten*, para. 1170.

1176 Community proceedings—right to be heard

See Case 85/76: *Hoffmann-La Roche & Co AG v EC Commission*, para. 1177.

1177 Competition policy—abuse of dominant market position

By a decision pursuant to EEC Treaty, art. 86 the Commission found that a Swiss manufacturer and preserver of bulk vitamins had abused the dominant position it held in the Common Market in respect of seven of the eight groups of vitamins it manufactured by the conclusion of certain contracts of sale with twenty-two large purchasers. Under those contracts the purchasers agreed to obtain all or most of their requirements of vitamins from the producer in return for a discount classified as a fidelity rebate. The decision ordered the termination of the consequent infringement of art. 86 and imposed a fine of 300,000 units of account.

In an action for the annulment of that decision the producer claimed (i) that documents which had formed the basis of the Commission's calculations of the relevant market shares had not been disclosed to the producer; (ii) that the Commission had incorrectly interpreted the concept of a dominant position; (iii) that in any event the contracts in question did not constitute an abuse of a dominant position so as to affect intra-community trade; and (iv) that in so far as the producer might have infringed art. 86 it had not done so intentionally or negligently and the fine had therefore been wrongly imposed. *Held*, (i) observance of the right to be heard in all proceedings, including administrative proceedings, in which sanctions or penalties might be imposed was a fundamental principle of Community law. Accordingly, the Commission was not entitled to take into account, to the detriment of an undertaking involved in proceeding under arts. 85 or 86, documents obtained from other undertakings the contents of which it had guaranteed not to disclose pursuant to Council Regulation (EEC) 17, art. 20, on the grounds of professional secrecy. However, since the irregularity in the present case had been corrected during the written procedure before the Court it did not constitute a ground for the annulment of the decision in question. (ii) In deciding whether the applicant held a dominant market position it was necessary first to delimit the relevant markets. The concept of a relevant market implied the possibility of effective competition between the products forming the market on the basis of a sufficient degree of interchangeability between those products as regards their specific uses. In the present case the Commission was correct in finding that a separate market existed in respect of each of the seven groups of vitamins, since each group had a separate function and was therefore not interchangeable either with the other groups or with other products. Further, a consideration of the factors relevant to the establishment of a dominant position in respect of those markets, namely, the relationship between the undertaking concerned and its competitors, the technological lead of the undertaking, the existence of a highly developed sales network and the absence of potential competition showed that the applicant held a dominant position in six of those markets. (iii) The conclusion by the applicant of the contracts of sale in issue constituted an abuse of its dominant position in the relevant markets: obligations such as those imposed by the contracts, whether or not in consideration of the grant of a fidelity rebate, were incompatible with the Treaty objective of undistorted competition in the common market in that they were designed to eliminate or restrict the purchaser's possible choices of sources of supply and to deny either producers access to the markets. Further, the effect of the fidelity rebates was to apply dissimilar conditions to equivalent transactions, thus constituting an abuse as specified by art. 86 (c). (iv) On the question of the imposition and amount of the fine, the circumstances surrounding the negotiation and conclusion of the contracts showed that the applicant had intentionally pursued a commercial policy designed to bar the access to the market of new competitors. The Commission was therefore justified under Regulation 17, art. 15 (2) in imposing the fine, although the amount would be reduced to take account of certain errors in the Commission's calculations of the relevant market shares and the fact that the applicant, in co-operation with the Commission, had amended the contracts during the administrative proceedings. The remainder of the action would be dismissed.

Case 85/76: HOFFMANN-LA ROCHE & CO AG v EC COMMISSION [1979] 3 CMLR 211 (European Court of Justice).

1178   —— —— relevant market—supply of spare parts

A company manufactured cash registers and its subsidiary based in the United Kingdom was a distributor and supplier of spare parts throughout the Community. By a decision of the Commission the company was found to have infringed the provisions of the EEC Treaty, art. 86 because of its failure to supply any spare parts to an English company and by prohibiting their subsidiaries and distributors within the Community from selling such parts outside the distribution network. The Commission contended that the company had abused its dominant position in the relevant market thereby affecting trade between member states. The company applied to the European Court for the annulment of the decision contending that their actions had no affect on inter-state trade. *Held*, for the purposes of art. 86, where a product required specialised parts to be fitted by trained technicians the relevant market was the market for the particular parts for the specialised product. In relation to the effects of conduct by an undertaking on trade between member states, Community law covered any practice likely to threaten free trade between member states, but where the conduct was solely within the territory of one state it would fall under national law. Although the applicant company held a dominant position in the relevant market of spare parts their conduct had no potential effect on inter-state trade since the servicing agreements in question were necessarily local in operation. The court would therefore annul the Commission's decision.

Case 22/79: HUGIN KASSAREGISTER AB AND HUGIN CASH REGISTERS LTD v EC COMMISSION [1979] 3 CMLR 345 (European Court of Justice).

1179   —— —— discovery of documents to show abuse—relevance of documents to question of abuse

See *British Leyland Motor Corpn v Wyatt Interpart Co Ltd*, para. 919.

1180   —— —— investigation of alledged abuse by Commission—stay of English proceedings pending Commission decision

See *British Leyland Motor Corpn Ltd v Wyatt Interpart Co Ltd*, para. 917.

1181   European Assembly—direct elections—conduct of elections

The European Assembly Elections Regulations 1979, S.I. 1979 No. 338 (in force on 3rd April 1979), provide for the conduct of the election of representatives to the Assembly of the European Communities in England, Scotland and Wales. Existing elections legislation, in particular the Representation of the People Acts and subordinate legislation made thereunder, which is to apply to European Assembly elections, is specified, together with appropriate modifications. The modifications take account in particular of the greater size of European Assembly constituencies compared to parliamentary constituencies. Certain forms in the Representation of the People Regulations 1974 and 1975 are amended to enable them to be used in both European Assembly and parliamentary elections. There are transitional provisions with respect to absent voting facilities.

1182   —— —— day of election

The European Assembly Elections (Day of Election) Order 1979, S.I. 1979 No. 219 (in force on 31st March 1979), appoints 7th June 1979 as the day on which the first general election of representatives to the European Assembly would be held.

1183   —— —— election petitions—rules

The European Assembly Election Petition Rules 1979, S.I. 1979 No. 521 (in force on 7th June 1979) regulate the presentation and hearing of an election petition to the High Court which questions the declared result of any election to the European Assembly. They are similar, in form and content, to those made in respect of parliamentary elections by the Election Petition Rules 1960, S.I. 1960 No. 543.

1184   —— —— imposition of particular electoral system in national region—compatibility with European Convention on Human Rights

See *Lindsay v United Kingdom*, para. 1457.

1185   —— —— returning officers

The European Assembly Elections (Returning Officers) (England and Wales) Order 1979, S.I. 1979 No. 220 (in force on 28th March 1979), designates the parliamentary constituencies of which the returning officers at parliamentary elections are to be returning officers at European Assembly elections.

1186 The European Assembly Elections (Returning Officers' Expenses) Regulations 1979, S.I. 1979 No. 588 (in force on 28th May 1979) prescribe for England, Scotland and Wales the maximum charges in respect of services rendered and expenses incurred by the returning officers in connection with the European Assembly Elections. They also provide for a special fee for the counting of ballot papers which took place on 10th June 1979.

1187 The European Assembly Elections (Returning Officers' Expenses) (Northern Ireland) Regulations 1979, S.I. 1979 No. 589 (in force on 28th May 1979) prescribe for Northern Ireland the maximum charges in respect of expenses incurred by the Chief Electoral Officer for Northern Ireland for the European Assembly Elections.

1188   —— —— right to vote

See *Re an Expatriate United Kingdom Citizen; Alliance des Belges de la Communauté Européene v Belguim*, para. 1458.

1189   —— —— Wales

The European Assembly Elections (Welsh Forms) Order 1979, S.I. 1979 No. 368 (in force on the 1st May 1979), prescribes in Welsh and English, the form of the official poll card of an elector and proxy, and certain other forms to be used, for European Assembly elections in Wales.

1190   —— rules of procedure

By a Resolution adopted by the European Parliament on 12th March 1979, OJ No. C 93, 9.4.1979, the following Rules of Procedure entered into force at the first sitting at which the European Parliament met without requiring to be convened (see art. 10 (3) of the Act of 20th September 1976, as annexed to Council Decision 76/787, OJ No. L278, 8.10.1976, p. 1). These Rules are now available from HMSO and are divided into fourteen chapters: I. Session of parliament; II. Verification of credentials; III. Bureau of Parliament; IV. Presidency; V. Agenda of sittings; VI. Official languages; VII. Publicity of proceedings; VIII. Conduct of sittings; IX. Voting; X. Groups and committees; XI. Questions; XII. Petitions; XIII. Secretariat of Parliament: Accounting; and XIV. Miscellaneous provisions. In addition, there are two annexes (implementing procedures for examination of the general budget of the European Communities and supplementary budgets; and guidelines for the conduct of question time) and an index.

1191 European Assembly (Pay and Pensions) Act 1979

The European Assembly (Pay and Pensions) Act 1979 provides for salaries, pensions, allowances and facilities for representatives to the Assembly of the European Communities. The Act received the royal assent on 26th July 1979 and came into force on that date.

Representatives who are not Members of Parliament in the United Kingdom receive the same salary as a member; those who are already members receive a salary of one third of their member's salary: s. 1. By s. 2 the Secretary of State may, with the concurrence of the Treasury, make allowances and facilities available to representatives. Representatives not re-elected to the Assembly receive a grant of three months' salary at the appropriate rate: s. 3. Sections 4–6 deal with pensions, s. 7 provides that salaries, grants and pensions are to be paid from the Consolidated Fund, s. 8 deals with interpretation and s. 9 with short title and extent.

1192 European Communities (Greek Accession) Act 1979

The European Communities (Greek Accession) Act 1979 received the royal assent on 20th December 1979 and came into force on that date. The Act amends the European Communities Act 1972 by providing that the two treaties relating to the accession of Greece to the European Communities, see para. 1152, are included in the definition of "Community Treaties" under s. 1 (2) of that Act. The provisions of those treaties are thus given legal effect in the United Kingdom.

1193 European Court of Auditors—1977 Report

The European Court of Auditors has published its first Annual Report for the financial year 1977 (OJ Vol. 21 No. C313, 30th December 1978).

The Court was set up by a Treaty of 1975 which entered into force on 1st June 1977, and replaces the Audit Board and the office of the ECSC Auditor. The responsibility of the Court under the Treaty is to examine the accounts of all revenue and expenditure of the Communities and institutions, and to this end it is given certain specified powers. For the full text of the Treaty, see OJ Vol. 20 No. L359, 31st December 1977.

1194 European Court of Justice—case law

In reply to a written question from the European Parliament the EC Council issued the following statistics on the case law of the Court of Justice: in 1977 158 cases were referred to the Court and it gave 100 judgments. Direct proceedings took between nine and twelve months, while preliminary rulings took, on average, six months. Of the cases where a member state was in dispute with the EC Commission the Court gave one ruling in favour of the government of a member state (OJ No. C28, 31st December 1978, p. 25).

1195 —— jurisdiction—action by individual—decision in form of regulation

See Cases 103–109/78: *Société des Usines de Beauport v EC Council*, para. 1171.

1196 —— —— jurisdiction to determine liability of Community

See Case 101/78: *Granaria BV v Hoofdproduktschap voor Akkerbouwprodukten*, para. 1170.

1197   —— —— preliminary   ruling—application   in   subsequent proceedings

There was a dispute concerning the legality of contributions to the relevant national board and the case was referred to the European Court of Justice on the interpretation of certain Community provisions, including Council Regulation (EEC) 3330/74 on the common organisation of the market in sugar, in the light of earlier decisions. *Held*, where questions referred to the European Court related to a situation on which a ruling had already been given and no new issues had been raised, the court would refer to and repeat its previous ruling. It was incumbent on the national court to decide whether the previous ruling of the European Court applied to the facts in the case before it.

Case 222/78: I.C.A.P. Distribution Srl v Walter Beneventi [1979] 3 CMLR 475 (European Court of Justice). Case 77/76: *Ditta Fratelli Cucchi v Avez SpA* [1977] ECR 987, ECJ, referred to.

1198   —— —— —— determination of legality of accession of new member states

By an agreement the plaintiff in the main action before a German court undertook to produce, for a financial consideration, market studies in respect of certain products in Spain and Portugal for the defendant company. The agreement, concluded for a period of five years, provided for its earlier termination should the accession of Spain and Portugal to the European Communities in law or in fact prove to be impracticable, the impracticability in law of such accession to be decided by the European Court. In the event of such justified termination the plaintiff was to lose his right to repayment of his expenses. Relying on these provisions the defendant company terminated the agreement and the plaintiff sued to recover his expenses. The German court stayed the proceedings and referred to the European Court questions on the interpretation of EEC Treaty, art. 237, designed to determine the possibility of the accession of Spain and Portugal. *Held*, the division of powers between the European Court and the national courts provided for by art. 177 was mandatory and the exercise of such powers was not to be impeded by, for example, agreement between private persons. Further, the precise procedure laid down by art. 237 for the accession of new member states precluded any prior judicial determination of the legal conditions for such accession, and accordingly the Court had no jurisdiction to answer the questions referred.

Case 93/78: Mattheus v Doego Fruchtimport und Tiefkuhlkost EG [1979] 1 CMLR 551 (European Court of Justice).

1199   —— —— reference by national court—question of compatibility of rules of community and national law

See Case 154/77: *Procureur du Roi v Dechmann*, para. 67.

1200   —— —— review of acts of the Commission

The applicant had supplied the Commission with temporary staff, on a contractual basis, since July 1970. In November 1976 the Commission decided not to renew the contract and issued an invitation to tender for temporary staff under the Finance Regulations 1973, art. 59 (2), which provided that in reaching a decision the Commission could freely choose the tender it thought most attractive taking into account the cost of performance and running costs involved, financial guarantees and guarantees of professional competence. The tenders, including that of the applicant, were submitted for the consideration of the Purchase and Contracts Advisory Committee, which recommended the acceptance of a particular tender, not being that of the applicant. The Commission adopted the recommendation and informed the applicant of its decision. The applicant sought an annulment of that decision under EEC Treaty, art. 173 on the grounds, inter alia, (i) that the failure of the Commission to state the reasons for its decision constituted an infringement of an essential procedural requirement, and (ii) that in rejecting the applicant's tender the Commission had infringed the provision of the Finance

Regulation as to the choice of tender in that, according to the criteria laid down by the provision, the applicant's tender was the most attractive submitted. *Held*, (i) the rejection of the applicant's tender was the necessary and inevitable consequence of the decision to accept another tender and it was therefore unnecessary to give separate reasons, and (ii) in exercising its jurisdiction under art. 173 to review acts of departments of the Commission, the Court had to respect any discretion given to the relevant authorities. In the present case, in providing that the administration might freely choose the offer considered to be the most attractive, the Finance Regulation conferred a discretion on the Commission, whose judgment was, in accordance with the procedure laid down by the Regulation, subject to review by the Purchase and Contracts Advisory Committee. Therefore, provided that the Commission had assessed the tenders fairly, on the same basis and according to the same criteria, as the evidence showed it to have done in this case, the choice of methods employed for the comparison could not be questioned. The application would therefore be dismissed.

Case 56/77: AGENCE EUROPEENNE D'INTERIMS SA v EC COMMISSION [1979] 2 CMLR 57 (European Court of Justice).

1201   —— procedure—oral hearings

The Court of Justice of the European Communities has issued notes for the guidance of counsel at oral hearings before the court. Counsel are asked to provide to the registrar an estimate, in writing, of the time which they require to address the court. They are also asked to restrict their address to the minimum length, bearing in mind that members of the court will have read the papers, the essentials of the arguments will have been summarised and that the object of an oral hearing is, in part, to enable counsel to comment on matters which they were unable to treat in their written pleadings or observations. Attention is drawn to the need to read the report for the hearing before the hearing; amendments may be submitted. Counsel are asked to speak slowly and into the microphone; some members of the court may have to avail themselves of the simultaneous translation service. If a written address has been prepared, a copy should be given in advance to the interpreters. In citing cases, the names of the parties, the case number and the ECR reference should be given. All documents relied on must be annexed to a pleading. Documents will not normally be admitted after the close of the pleadings and this applies to documents submitted at the hearing. For the text of the notes for guidance, see the Law Society's Gazette, 31st October 1979, p. 1068.

1202   —— reference for preliminary ruling—prohibition on quantitative restriction on imports—exception on grounds of public policy or public morality—validity of English legislation

The defendants were convicted under the Customs Consolidation Act 1876, s. 42 of being knowingly concerned in the fraudulent evasion of the prohibition on the importation of indecent or obscene material. On appeal against conviction to the House of Lords, the House stayed the proceedings and referred to the European Court of Justice questions on the interpretation of EEC Treaty, arts. 30 and 36, designed to determine whether: (i) the law of a member state prohibiting the importation of pornographic articles was a quantitative restriction on imports within the meaning of art. 30; (ii) if so, it fell within the exception provided by art. 36 as being justified on the grounds of public policy or public morality; (iii) a member state was entitled to maintain such a prohibition in order to prevent or reduce the possibility of a breach of domestic law; (iv) even if justifiable on the grounds of public policy or public morality, it could amount to a means of arbitrary discrimination or disguised restriction contrary to art. 30.

CASE 34/79; R v HENN; R v DARBY [1979] 2 CMLR 495 (House of Lords: LORD WILBERFORCE, LORD DIPLOCK, LORD SALMON, LORD FRASER OF TULLYBELTON and LORD SCARMAN).

Decision of the European Court reported at [1980] 1 CMLR 246.

1203   European Monetary System

The heads of state and government of the member states of the European Community have passed a resolution to establish a European Monetary System (EMS) based upon a European Currency Unit (ECU). Although the United Kingdom is not participating in the exchange rate mechanism, sterling will be included with other Community currencies in the ECU and the resolution provides for consultation about exchange rate policy decisions between countries inside and outside the exchange rate mechanism. The resolution also describes a system of loans at subsidised interest rates which would be made available to less prosperous member states of the Community participating fully in the EMS exchange rate mechanism. Until the United Kingdom participates in the exchange rate mechanism it will not qualify for such loans nor contribute to the interest subsidies provided for other member states. See "The European Monetary System" (Cmnd. 7419).

Following French reservations the commencing date for the EMS (originally 1st January 1979) was postponed until 13th March 1979. At that date the Italian lira and the Irish pound had fluctuating margins of 6 per cent around the central rates and the currencies of the other participating states had margins of $2\frac{1}{4}$ per cent. See the *Financial Times*, 13th March 1979.

1204   —— introduction into common agricultural policy

See para. 64.

1205   Free movement—rights guaranteed by treaty—national provisions prejudicing exercise of rights—conditions for issue of domestic driving licences

A French national resident in Germany was convicted of driving without a driving licence, his French licence being invalid under German law. On his appeal the court stayed the proceedings and referred to the European Court questions on the mutual recognition of driving licences in relation to nationals of one member state resident in a second state by virtue of EEC Treaty, art. 48. *Held*, since there were no specific provisions of Community law relating to driving licences member states were individually responsible for determining, in relation to national road safety requirements, the necessary conditions for the issue and recognition of licences within their national territory. In view of the wide differences between the laws of member states in this field, national conditions for the recognition of foreign licences held by nationals of another member state who were permanently established in the member state concerned, or for the issue of a domestic licence to such persons, could not be regarded as incompatible with Community law. However, conditions for the issue of a domestic licence to a national of another member state in possession of a licence issued by the authorities of his state of origin, not being conditions in due proportion to the requirements of road safety, could be incompatible with Community law if they were such as to hinder the exercise of rights guaranteed by the Treaty, namely, freedom of movement for workers (art. 48), the freedom of establishment (art. 52) and the freedom to provide services (art. 59).

Case 16/78: CHOQUET [1979] 1 CMLR 535 (European Court of Justice).

1206   Free movement of goods—common customs tariff—transitional period—unilateral adoption of protective measures—validity

In July 1968 an Italian undertaking imported a quantity of Japanese tape recorders into Italy. In February 1971 the Italian customs authorities ordered the importers to pay customs duties on the consignment pursuant to a circular issued in June 1968 by the Ministry of Finance, which had excluded such goods from free circulation treatment. The circular had been issued in application of EEC Treaty, art. 15 (2) which empowered member states, during the transitional period, to take unilateral protective measures in cases of emergency. In the course of national proceedings to recover the charges the importers claimed, first, that the effect of Council Decision (EEC) 66/532 was to bring forward the date of expiry of the transitional period to 1st July 1968, thus precluding the subsequent application of art. 15 (2), and second, that even if the protective measures had been validly adopted, the failure of the ministry to notify the Commission of them as required by art. 15 (2) made them unlawful. The Italian court referred questions of interpretation to the European Court. *Held*, the decision in question referred only to specific actions which were to be taken before 1st July and therefore did not bring forward the date of expiry of the transitional period within the meaning of EEC Treaty, art. 8. Further, although failure to notify under art. 15 (2) involved a breach of the Treaty, such notification was not a condition precedent to the entry into force of measures thus adopted.

Case 27/78: AMMINISTRAZIONE DELLE FINANZE DELLO STATO v RÁSHAM [1979] 1 CMLR 1 (European Court of Justice).

1207 —— common organisation of markets—imports from non-member states—customs duties—charges of equivalent effect—animal health inspection charges

Two consignments of beef and veal imported from Uruguay into Italy were subjected to health inspections in accordance with Italian law. The importer sought to recover charges made in respect of the inspections on the grounds that they constituted charges having an effect equivalent to customs duties and as such were prohibited in relation to imports of beef and veal from third countries under Council Regulation (EEC) 805/68. The Italian court hearing the action referred certain questions for the determination of the European Court concerning the validity and interpretation of that Regulation, which provides for derogation from the prohibition, and related European legislation. *Held*, the established case law of the European Court made it clear that pecuniary charges imposed in respect of health inspectors of meat imported from third countries were charges having an effect equivalent to customs duties within Regulation 805/68, art. 20 (2). However, while in accordance with the principle of free movement of goods the prohibition on the levying of such charges was absolute, the same considerations did not apply to trade with non-member states and, accordingly, Council regulations in that field providing for subsequent derogations were validly made, subject to the requirement of uniform application in member states. Nevertheless, although Council Directive (EEC) 72/462 exempted health inspection charges such as the one in question from the prohibition, the exemption could take effect only when the necessary national implementing measures had been adopted, which excluded its application in the present case.

For the assistance of the Italian court however, the European Court referred to Council Directive (EEC) 64/433 relating to intra-Community trade in fresh meat, which derogates from the prohibition on such charges to the extent necessary to ensure non-discriminatory treatment of traders within the common market and importers from the third countries.

Case 70/77: SIMMENTHAL SpA v AMMINISTRAZIONE DELLE FINANZE DELLO STATO [1978] ECR 1453 (European Court of Justice). Case 84/71: *SpA Marimex v Il Ministero dello Finance* [1972] ECR 89 referred to.

1208 —— —— —— —— —— exemption

See Case 137/77: *City of Frankfurt v Firma Max Neumann*, para. 65.

1209 —— customs duties between member states—charges of equivalent effect—fees for veterinary and public health inspections—imports from non-member states

See Case 70/77: *Simmenthal SpA v Amministrazione delle Finanze dello Stato*, para. 1207.

1210 —— —— —— levy on consumption of precious metals

Under Danish law the production of articles of precious metal was subject to national supervision, the costs of which were covered, inter alia, by contributions paid by manufacturers on the basis of the consumption of precious metal of each undertaking. For the purposes of assessment articles bearing the registered mark of the undertaking or intended for export were included. In the course of national proceedings in respect of non-payment of the levy the Danish court referred certain questions as to the nature of the charges to the European Court of Justice. *Held*, since the levies were charged in respect of products both marketed on national territory and intended for export they were not charges having an effect equivalent to customs duties within EEC Treaty, art. 16, the characteristics of which were that they were imposed specifically and exclusively on exported products. However, the imposition of such charges did constitute a system of internal taxation within art. 95, which was to be construed in the light of the Treaty as referring to the discriminatory application of systems of internal taxation to goods both imported and exported within the Community. In this case, however, where the system was applied to products irrespective of their origin or destination there was no discrimination as prohibited by art. 95. Further, it was irrelevant that exported goods included in the assessment were subjected to an additional charge in the member state of destination, since there were no rules of community law intended to prohibit the effects of double taxation.

Case 142/77: STATENS KONTROL MED ÆDLE METALLER v PREBEN LARSON [1978] ECR 1543 (European Court of Justice).

1211   —— evidence of importation—penalty for late submission of evidence—validity

See Case 122/78: *Buitoni SA v Fonds d'Orientation et de Régularisation des Marchés Agricoles*, para. 1172.

1212   —— gold and silver coins—validity of English customs legislation—whether goods or means of payment

See *Allgemeine Gold-und-Silberscheideanstalt v Customs and Excise Commissioners*, para. 774.

1213   —— quantitative restrictions between member states—measures of equivalent effect—national conditions for quality designations applied to domestic products

Under German law home-produced spirits from wine were entitled to certain quality designations only if at least 85 per cent of the alcoholic content was derived from home-produced wine-distillate and such distillate was stored in the German factory where distillation had taken place. In the course of national proceedings following the refusal of the German authorities to allow the use of the designations in respect of spirits produced from imported French wine distillate the German court referred to the European Court certain questions on the compatibility of the national rules with EEC Treaty, art. 30 (prohibition of quantitative restrictions and measures having equivalent effect on imports). *Held*, although member states were empowered to apply quality standards and designations to domestic products, it was incompatible with the common market for such standards to be linked to a requirement that the whole or part of the production process should take place on national territory: conditions for the granting of such designations should depend solely on the existence of intrinsic objective characteristics of the product in question. Thus a national measure whereby the right to use quality designations for domestic products was subject to the condition that the semi-finished product from which they were manufactured was either produced or treated on national territory, with the effect that the designations were refused where the semi-finished product was imported from another member state, constituted a measure of equivalent effect to a quantitative restriction within art. 30 and was not justified under art. 36.

Case 13/78: FIRMA JOH EGGERS SOHN & CO v FREIE HANSESTADT BREMEN [1979] 1 CMLR 562 (European Court of Justice).

1214   —— —— —— national restrictions on alcohol level in liqueur

A German company wished to import a consignment of French liqueur for sale in

Germany. The relevant national body concerned refused to allow the importation to proceed because the liqueur had insufficient alcoholic strength to be marketed within Germany. The alcoholic content required for such a liqueur was higher than for other alcoholic beverages. The company contended that such a high minimum alcohol level prevented many such products from other member states being sold in Germany. The provision was thus a restriction on the free movement of goods between member states and therefore a measure having an effect equivalent to a quantitative restriction on imports contrary to EEC Treaty, art. 30. The national court stayed the proceedings and referred certain questions on the interpretation of art. 30 to the European Court. *Held*, it was for the member state to regulate matters concerning the marketing of alcoholic beverages and disparity between national laws resulting in the obstruction of free movement of goods had to be accepted in so far as the provision concerned satisfied the protective requirements of the consumer. To impose a minimum alcohol content rule, however, was equivalent to a quantitative restriction on imports under art. 30 and such beverages from other member states could not be refused entry on that ground.

Case 120/78: REWE-ZENTRAL AG v BUNDESMONOPOLVERWALTUNG FÜR BRANNTWEIN [1979] 3 CMLR 494 (European Court of Justice).

1215   —— —— **restrictions on imports into new member states—validity**

See Case 231/78: *Re Import of Potatoes*, para. 72.

1216   —— —— **trade marks—right to contest unauthorised use of mark—protection of industrial property**

An American corporation was the registered proprietor in the Netherlands, Belgium and Luxembourg of the trade mark 'Seresta' and in the United Kingdom of the mark 'Serenid D' for the same pharmaceutical product. The plaintiff Dutch company purchased a quantity of the 'Serenid D' product and marketed it in the Netherlands under the 'Seresta' mark. Under Dutch law the holder of a mark was entitled to contest the unauthorised use of the mark and in proceedings before a Dutch court as to the lawfulness of the company's activities the court referred certain questions on the interpretation of EEC Treaty, art. 36 to the European Court. *Held*, it was clear from the terms of art. 36 that in providing an exception to one of the fundamental principles of the Communities, namely the free movement of goods, in respect of the protection of industrial and commercial property, such an exception could be admitted only to the extent to which it was justified for the purpose of safeguarding rights constituting the specific subject-matter of the property in question. The specific subject-matter of a trade mark consisted in the guarantee to the holder of the mark of the exclusive right to use the mark for the purpose of initially distributing a product. The extent of this exclusive right was to be determined in relation to the essential function of a trade mark, which was to guarantee the identity of origin of a marked product to the ultimate consumer. Therefore, national legislation prohibiting the unauthorised use of marks, in order to maintain the validity of the guarantee, was in accordance with the essential function of a trade mark, and the exclusive right of a proprietor to affix a mark was within the specific subject matter of the property covered by art. 36. Accordingly, a proprietor of a mark protected in one member state was entitled under art. 36 to prevent any unauthorised use of the mark in that member state.

The court pointed out, however, that in cases where the proprietor of the mark in question also marketed identical products under different marks in different member states, it was necessary for the national court to decide whether such activities amounted to a system of marketing designed to partition markets artificially, whereby the exercise of the right to prevent unauthorised use of a mark constituted a disguised restriction on trade between member states under art. 36, and could not therefore be allowed.

Case 3/38: CENTRAFARM BV v AMERICAN HOME PRODUCTS CORPN [1979] 1 CMLR 326 (European Court of Justice).

1217   **Free movement of persons—employment and equality of treatment—housing—enjoyment of rights accorded to national workers**

See *De Falco v Crawley Borough Council; Silvestri v Crawley Borough Council*, para. 1433.

1218   —— **right of establishment—implementation of Community policy by directives—application of directives**

A Dutch national resident in Belgium had worked as a plumbing contractor in Belgium since 1970. In 1976 he applied to the competent Dutch authorities for the necessary authorisation to carry on the same trade in the Netherlands. This application was refused on the grounds that he did not possess the necessary qualifications to carry on the trade in the Netherlands and, as a Dutch national, he was not entitled to benefit from the provisions of Council Directive (EEC) 64/427. That directive provides that where the pursuit of certain economic activities in a member state is subject to the possession of certain qualifications that member state must recognise the actual practice of the activity in question in another member state as proof of those qualifications. The Dutch court hearing the applicant's appeal against the refusal stayed the proceedings and referred to the European Court the question whether the term "beneficiary" referred to in the directive included nationals of the member state in which it was desired to pursue the activity. *Held*, the persons to whom the directive applied were defined by reference to the General Programmes of 1961 for the abolition of restrictions on the freedom to provide services and the right of establishment which, in designating as beneficiaries nationals of member states established within the Community, made no distinction as regards nationality or residence. The provisions of the directive could therefore be relied upon by nationals of all the member states who came within the situations governed by the directive, including nationals of the member state where it was desired to pursue the activity in question.

Case 115/78: KNOORS v SECRETARY OF STATE FOR ECONOMIC AFFAIRS [1979] 2 CMLR 357 (European Court of Justice).

1219   —— —— **mutual recognition of qualifications—application of Treaty provisions**

In French criminal proceedings the defendant was convicted of unlawfully practising as a veterinary surgeon in France. The defendant, originally of Austrian nationality, possessed an Italian degree in veterinary medicine and a certificate entitling him to practice as a veterinary surgeon in Italy. He subsequently took up residence in France and, on acquiring French nationality by naturalisation applied to the competent French authorities for the necessary authorisation to practice in France, on the basis that his Italian degree constituted an equivalent to the necessary French qualifications as provided for under French law. The authorities did not recognise the equivalence, however, and refused his application, but the defendant nevertheless practised as a veterinary surgeon in France, leading to prosecution and conviction. On his appeal against conviction the court stayed the proceedings and referred to the European Court questions on the application of EEC Treaty, arts. 52 and 57 on freedom of establishment in relation to the mutual recognition of qualifications. *Held*, the treaty provided for the achievement of freedom of establishment in two stages. First, art. 52 provided for the abolition of all restrictions on the freedom of nationals of member states to establish themselves in another member state, with a view to ensuring that by the end of the transitional period any national conditions attaching to the right of establishment were applied without discrimination to all Community nationals. Second, since the effect of art. 52 was merely to remove such obstacles to freedom of establishment as resulted from different nationalities, art. 57 provided for the adoption of directives governing the mutual recognition of qualifications in respect of particular activities and professions. Therefore, to the extent that such a directive had not been adopted in respect of the profession of veterinary surgery at the time the situation in question arose, it was not open to nationals of a member state to rely on art. 52 with a view to practising that profession under any conditions other than those laid down by the national legislation of the member state in which it was sought to practice.

The court pointed out, however, that its decision in no way prejudged the effect of Council Directives (EEC) 78/1026 and 78/1027 concerning the mutual recognition of qualifications in veterinary medicine.

Case 136/78: MINISTÈRE PUBLIC v AUER [1979] 2 CMLR 373 (European Court of Justice).

1220   —— workers—national restriction on movement within national territory—validity of restriction

In 1977 a United Kingdom citizen pleaded guilty in the Crown Court to a charge of theft and was ordered to be bound over in her own recognisance of £50 on condition that she immediately proceeded to Northern Ireland and did not return to England or Wales for a period of three years. In breach of that condition in 1978 she returned to Wales and was brought back before the Crown Court for judgment. Before giving judgment, however, the court referred to the European Court questions designed to determine the validity of the 1977 order in the light of EEC Treaty, art. 48, which lays down the principle of freedom of movement for workers, on the basis that the defendant was a worker within the meaning of the Treaty. *Held*, the scope of art. 48 was to be determined in relation to the general principle of non-discrimination with respect to nationality contained in art. 7. Article 48, in application of that principle, aimed to abolish any provision of national legislation under which a national of another member state was discriminated against as regards employment, remuneration and other conditions of work, but did not seek to restrict the power of member states to lay down restrictions within their own territory on the freedom of movement of persons subject to their jurisdiction in implementation of domestic criminal law. Therefore, in the context of a wholly domestic situation such as the one in question, having no connection with any situation envisaged by Community law, provisions of the Treaty on freedom of movement for workers had no application.

Case 175/78: R v SAUNDERS [1979] 2 All ER 207 (European Court of Justice).

1221   Free movement of services—application of community provisions—principle of non-discrimination

A German national resident in France instructed a French bank to carry out on his behalf stock exchange time-bargains on the Paris stock exchange. The resulting gains and losses were respectively credited and debited to his current account with the bank in conjunction with a credit opened by the bank in his favour. He subsequently returned to Germany and the bank brought an action against him in Germany to recover the amount of his overdraft resulting from losses incurred on the transaction. The German court, which had jurisdiction by reason of the debtor's residence, rejected the claim on the ground that the overdraft should be treated in the same way as debts arising out of wagering contracts and as such was not actionable under German law. However, the court referred certain questions to the European Court on the interpretation and application of EEC Treaty, arts. 59 and 60 on the freedom to provide services. *Held*, in carrying out the instructions in question the bank had engaged in activities of a commercial character within art. 60. Further, since the person in receipt of the services took up residence in another member state while the services were still being provided, the requirement of art. 59 was satisfied. However, although arts. 59 and 60 thus applied to the present case, the principle of non-discrimination underlying those provisions had not been infringed by the German limitation on actionability since it applied equally to persons established in Germany and providing services there.

Case 15/78: SOCIETE GENERALE ALSACIENNE DE BANQUE SA v KOESTLER [1979] 1 CMLR 89 (European Court of Justice).

1222   —— **right to provide services—imposition of national licensing requirement—validity**

Under Belgian law, the operation of fee-charging employment agencies for entertainers was subject to the grant of a licence by the competent national authority, and similar agencies operated outside Belgium were allowed to place entertainers in employment in Belgium only through a Belgian agency so licensed. In Belgian criminal proceedings, a Belgian national was charged with having employed the services of a French agency not holding a Belgian licence for the purpose of engaging entertainers for employment in Belgium. The French agency was charged with having placed persons in employment in Belgium without acting through a licensed Belgian agency. The Belgian criminal court stayed the proceedings and referred to the European Court certain questions on the interpretation and application of EEC Treaty, arts. 59 and 63 in order to determine the validity of the national law. *Held*, in providing for the progressive abolition during the transitional period of restrictions on freedom to provide services, art. 59 imposed an obligation to attain a precise result by the end of that period; although art. 63 provided for the implementation of that obligation by means of individual directions issued in respect of particular spheres of activities during the transitional period, it was clear that on the expiry of that period art. 59 became directly and unconditionally applicable. Consequently, in the context of the service of placing entertainers in employment, the imposition of special requirements in order to ensure the application of professional rules, justified by the need to protect the general public or the entertainer, were not incompatible with the treaty, whether imposed on persons established in the member state in question or in another member state which did not impose a similar requirement. A national requirement of this nature in respect of agencies for the employment of entertainers was not objectively justified where the person providing such services was subject to and satisfied comparable conditions imposed by the state in which he was established.

Joined Cases 110/78 and 111/78: MINISTÈRE PUBLIC AND A.S.B.L. v VAN WESEMAEL [1979] ECR 35 (European Court of Justice).

1223   **Harmonisation of laws—food prices—indication of selling price and unit price**

Council Directive (EEC) 79/581 (OJ No. L158, 26.6.79) provides that, in order to increase market transparency and ensure greater protection for consumers, foodstuffs supplied to the final consumer, whether in bulk or pre-packaged, are to bear clear indications of both the selling price and the price per unit of measurement. This requirement also extends to any advertisement which mentions the selling price of foodstuffs. The unit price is to be expressed as the price per litre and the price per kilogram for foodstuffs sold by volume and weight respectively. Member states are required to comply with the provisions of the directive within two years of the date of notification.

1224   —— **household appliances—energy consumption—indication by labelling**

Council Directive (EEC) 79/530 (OJ No. L145, 13.6.79) provides for the harmonisation of national regulations on the publication, particularly by means of labelling, of information on energy consumption of certain household appliances. The relevant information is to be drawn up in accordance with directives adopted in respect of individual types of appliances and, while member states are authorised but not obliged to require all such appliances marketed in their territory to carry the appropriate label, they must ensure that any label in fact attached to an appliance complies with the provisions of this and the relevant implementing directive. The directive is to be complied with within two years of the notification of the first implementing directive (see para. 1225).

1225   —— —— —— —— electric ovens

Council Directive (EEC) 79/531 (OJ No. L145, 13.6.79) applies the provisions of Directive 79/530, para. 1224 to radiant electric ovens and lays down the standards to be observed in providing information on the energy consumption of electric ovens. Member states are required to adopt the necessary national implementing measures within two years of the date of notification of the directive.

1226   Human rights—European Convention on Human Rights—liability of Communities

See *Confédération Française Democratique du Travail v European Communities*, para. 1446.

1227   Jurisdiction of national courts—convention jurisdiction—action against branch or agency—jurisdiction of courts in place where branch established

A German company brought proceedings against a French company with an office in Germany to recover expenses incurred in protecting its property from the possible effect of demolition work carried out in Germany by the French company. The German court hearing the action stayed the proceedings and referred to the European Court questions on jurisdiction under the Convention on Jurisdiction and the Enforcement of Judgments 1968, art. 5 (5). Article 5 (5) provides that a person domiciled in a contracting state may, in another contracting state, be sued in relation to a dispute arising out of the operations of a branch, agency or other establishment, in the courts of the place of the establishment. *Held*, the Convention, concluded pursuant to EEC Treaty, art. 220, was to be interpreted with regard to its principles and objectives and its relationship with the Treaty. Consequently, the need to ensure legal certainty and equality of rights and obligations of the parties required that the concepts referred to in art. 5 (5), which constituted an exception to the general rule on jurisdiction contained in art. 2, be given an independent meaning common to all contracting states. Thus the concept of branch, agency or other establishment implied a permanent place of business with a management and the facilities to negotiate business with third parties independently of the parent body. The concept of operations comprised actions relating to rights and obligations, both contractual and non-contractual, of the management itself, and actions relating to undertakings entered into by the branch in the name of the parent body, to be performed in the contracting state in which the branch was situated. In each case the existence of such a branch and such operations was a question of fact for the national court whose jurisdiction was disputed.

Case 33/78: ETABLISSEMENTS SOMAFER SA v SAAR-FERNGAS AG [1979] 1 CMLR 490 (European Court of Justice).

1228   —— —— application in Germany for enforcement of French order—whether order made in context of bankruptcy or analogous proceedings

Following the winding up of an insolvent French company the liquidator for the creditors applied to the French court, under a provision of the French Act governing bankruptcy and insolvency, for an order that those debts of the company not covered by its assets should be borne by the company's manager. The order was granted and the liquidator then sought to enforce it in Germany pursuant to the Convention on Jurisdiction and Enforcement of Judgments art. 31. The German courts refused the application on the grounds that the order formed part of the winding up proceedings and as such was outside the scope of the Convention, art. 1 of which excludes, inter alia, proceedings relating to bankruptcy and insolvency. On further appeal by the liquidator the German court stayed the proceedings and referred to the European Court questions on the interpretation of art. 1. *Held*, since art. 1 served to indicate the scope of the Convention it was necessary, in order to ensure the uniformity and equality of the rights deriving from it, that the concepts it referred to be interpreted by reference to both the objectives of the Convention and the general principles which stemmed from the legal systems of the contracting states. Thus the exclusion in respect of bankruptcy and winding up proceedings applied only to decisions which derived directly from the bankruptcy or winding up and which were closely connected with those proceedings. It was therefore necessary to consider the legal foundation of the decision in question which, in the case of the present order, was clearly the French Act governing the law of insolvency, since an application for such an order could only be made by the liquidator for the creditors to the court which had originally made the winding up order. Accordingly, the order in question had been granted in the context of proceedings relating to the winding up of an insolvent company and was therefore outside the scope of the Convention.

Case 133/78: GOURDAIN V NADLER [1979] 3 CMLR 180 (European Court of Justice).

1229 —— —— **contract conferring jurisdiction on more than one contracting state**

A contract for the supply of glass by a French company to a German company provided that each party could be sued only in the courts of its respective state. On the default of the German company the French company brought proceedings in the German courts to recover sums due under the contract. The German company raised a defence of set-off and the court hearing the action stayed the proceedings and referred to the European Court questions on the interpretation of the Convention on Jurisdiction and the Enforcement of Judgments 1968, art. 17, in relation to its jurisdiction to take account of the set-off. Article 17 provides, inter alia, that where parties agree that the courts of a contracting state are to have jurisdiction, such jurisdiction is exclusive. *Held*, art. 17 was based on a recognition of the independent will of the parties to a contract in deciding which courts were to have jurisdiction over disputes within the scope of the Convention and, accordingly, although it referred to a single choice, it could not be interpreted as prohibiting an agreement conferring jurisdiction on the courts of more than one contracting state. Further, in accordance with the basis of art. 17 and the need to avoid superfluous procedure, which formed the basis of the Convention as a whole, art. 17 was not to be interpreted as precluding a court hearing proceedings by virtue of an agreement pursuant to that article from taking into account a set-off connected with the legal relationship in dispute.

Case 23/78: MEETH V GLACETAL SARL [1979] 1 CMLR 520 (European Court of Justice).

1230 —— —— **scope of convention—application to disputes arising in divorce proceedings**

In the course of divorce proceedings instituted in France the French court on the application of the husband, authorised, as a provisional protective measure, the putting under seal of certain effects in a German flat owned by the parties and the freezing of the wife's assets and accounts at a German bank. In reliance on the Convention on Jurisdiction and Enforcement of Judgments 1968, art. 31 the husband then applied to a German court for an order enforcing the French order. This application was refused on the ground that the measures authorised by the French court formed part of divorce proceedings and were therefore excluded from the scope of the convention under art. 1. Article 1 provides that the Convention does not apply to, inter alia, the status or legal capacity of natural persons or rights in property arising out of a matrimonial relationship. On the husband's appeal the court stayed the proceedings and referred to the European Court questions on the interpretation of art. 1. *Held*, the term "rights in property arising out of a matrimonial relationship" included both property arrangements specifically and exclusively envisaged by certain national legal systems in the case of marriage and any proprietary relationships resulting from the matrimonial relation or its dissolution. Thus, disputes arising in the course of divorce proceedings relating to the assets of spouses might concern or be closely connected with either questions relating to the status of persons or proprietary relationships between spouses resulting directly from the matrimonial relationship or its dissolution, both of which were excluded from the scope of the Convention. Further, there were no grounds for distinguishing between provisional and definitive measures: their inclusion in the scope of the Convention was to be determined by the nature of the rights they served to protect rather than by their own nature.

Case 143/78: DE CAVEL V DE CAVEL [1979] 2 CMLR 547 (European Court of Justice).

1231   Social policy—principle of equal pay—interpretation

See *Macarthys Ltd v Smith*, para. 2501.

1232   Social security—industrial injury benefit—entitlement where accident occurs on oil rig—reference to European Court of Justice

See *Re The Key Gibraltar Oil Drilling Rig*, para. 2637.

1233   —— iron and steel employees—re-adaptation benefits

The European Communities (Iron and Steel Employees Re-adaptation Benefits Scheme) Regulations 1979, S.I. 1979 No. 954 (in force on 5th August 1979), consolidate with amendments the European Communities (Iron and Steel Employees Re-adaptation Benefits Scheme) Regulations 1974 and amending regulations. The Scheme provides for the payment of benefits to certain steel workers who are made redundant or transferred to new work at lower rates of pay as a result of events which fall within the terms of the ECSC Treaty, art. 56 (2).

1234   —— mineworker's pension—employment in different member states—criterion of nationality—date at which criterion to be satisfied

An Algerian mineworker employed in Germany, who had lost his French nationality on the independence of Algeria in 1962, applied for a German mineworker's pension on the basis of insurance periods completed both in Germany and in France, where he had worked until 1960. His application was rejected on the grounds that, since he was no longer a national of a member state, the provisions of Regulation 1408/71 on social security for migrant workers did not apply and his right to a pension was therefore to be determined solely on the basis of German law. The court hearing his appeal against that decision stayed the proceedings and referred to the European Court questions on the interpretation of Regulation 1408/71, art. 2 (1), which defines persons covered, and the application of its provisions in respect of insurance periods completed before its entry into force. *Held*, in accordance with the principle of legal certainty, which required that any factual situation should normally be examined in the light of the legal rules existing at the time that situation obtained, it was clear that the criterion of nationality of a member state contained in art. 2 (1) was to be examined in relation to the time when the insurance periods were completed. Further, art. 94 (2) provided that insurance periods and periods of employment completed before the regulation came into force were to be taken into account in determining entitlement to benefits under its provisions. Thus the combined effect of art. 2 (1) and art. 94 (2) was that all insurance periods and periods of employment completed under the legislation of a member state prior to the entry into force of the regulation were relevant for the purposes of its provisions, subject to the condition that the worker in question was a national of a member state at the time the relevant periods were completed.

Case 10/78: BELBOUAB V BUNDESKNAPPSCHAFT [1978] ECR 1915 (European Court of Justice).

1235   —— **reimbursement of medical expenses incurred in another member state—delay in issuing documentation—investigation of Parliamentary Commissioner**

A stateless person, who fell ill whilst working in Germany, experienced delay in obtaining form E111 from the Department of Health and Social Security, which was required to meet the expense of urgent medical treatment. The delay was caused by a misunderstanding over whether the applicant was a stateless person or a Chilean national, and was further exacerbated by the fact that his travel document was out of date. The Department apologised for the delay and informed the Commissioner that its procedures were being revised. The Commissioner pointed out that the delay could have been reduced if the applicant had had a valid travel document or if he had applied for E111 before he had left for Germany.

Case 5/67/78: RE MEDICAL TREATMENT IN GERMANY [1979] 1 CMLR 369.

1236   —— **sickness benefit—whether worker in member state entitled to claim benefit based on contributions made in another member state**

National Insurance Commissioner's decision:

RE SICKNESS BENEFIT FOR AN ELDERLY IRISHWOMAN (CS 26/77) [1979] 3 CMLR 442 (Commission referred certain questions to European Court relating to right of fully-insured national of member state to claim sickness benefit in respect of employment in another member state; claimant, Irishwoman fully insured in Ireland, took up work in United Kingdom and paid national insurance contributions into United Kingdom scheme, despite fact that she was aged 60 (upper limit for entry into United Kingdom scheme); fell ill, claimed sickness benefit (which is pension related); disallowed on ground that as she did not satisfy contribution conditions no retirement pension would have been payable and therefore not entitled to sickness benefit; on appeal commissioner put forward questions for European Court; (i) whether she was entitled to pay contributions in United Kingdom while of pensionable age, by virtue of Council Regulations (EEC) 1612/68 at 7 or Council Regulation (EEC) 1408/71, art. 3 both relating to equality of treatment for EEC workers employed in member state other than their own, (ii) whether she was deemed to be fully insured in United Kingdom by an aggregation of insurance under 1408/71 art. 18; (iii) whether art. 18 applied to the acquisition, retention or recovery of the right to sickness benefit where the calculation of sickness benefit was dependent upon the calculation of a notional retirement pension rate).

1237   —— **unemployment benefit—entitlement—conditions to be satisfied**

National Insurance Commissioner's decision:

RE UNEMPLOYMENT BENEFITS (CU 6/79) [1979] 3 CMLR 449 (claimant ended his employment in Netherlands; two and half months later moved to England and registered as unemployed; intervening period spent in Netherlands with occasional weekend visits to England to supervise house removal; claim for unemployment benefit in United Kingdom disallowed as he was absent from Great Britain as provided by Social Security Act 1975, s. 82 (5) (a); further, claimant only allowed to transfer entitlement to benefit from one member state to another if obtained certificate specified in Council Regulation (EEC) 1408/71, art. 69; mere failure to comply with art. 69 not enough to deny worker his entitlement to benefit; however, claimant had also failed to observe legislative rules of member state (United Kingdom) in which benefit was claimed, by failing to register for employment as required by that member state; claim for unemployment benefit dismissed).

Case 27/75: *Bonaffini v Istituto Nazionale Della Previdenza Sociale* [1975] ECR 971, 1976 Halsbury's Abridgment para. 1160 applied.

1238 ———— **retention of rights to benefit in respect of time spent in another member state**

An Italian worker domiciled in Germany brought proceedings in Germany to recover unemployment benefit in respect of five months spent in Italy, initially looking for work but subsequently due to illness. Council Regulation (EEC) 1408/71, art. 69 provides for the retention of rights to unemployment benefit in one member state for a period up to three months spent in another member state looking for work; the period may be extended by the competent national authorities in exceptional circumstances. The court hearing the claim stayed the proceedings and referred to the European Court questions on the interpretation of art. 69. *Held*, while an extension of the three month period was permissible even where the request for the extension was made after the expiry of that period, the decision whether to grant an extension was entirely a matter for the competent national authorities, who were free to take into consideration all factors which were relevant and inherent both in the individual situation of the worker in question and in the exercise of effective control.

Case 139/78: COCCIOLI v BUNDESANSTALT FÜR ARBEIT [1979] 3 CMLR 144 (European Court of Justice).

1239 **Shipping—designation order**

The European Communities (Designation) Order 1979, S.I. 1979 No. 1704 (in force on 28th January 1980), designates the Secretary of State to exercise powers conferred by the European Communities Act 1972, s. 2 (2) to make regulations in relation to sea-going tankers entering or leaving UK ports.

1240 **Taxation—system of internal taxation—application to exports— prohibition on discrimination**

See Case 142/77: *Statens Kontrol Med Ædle Metaller v Preben Larsen*, para. 1210.

1241 ———— **prohibition on discrimination—application**

A German company marketed in Germany spirits imported from Guadaloupe and certain non-member states. The German tax administration assessed tax on the imported products at the ordinary rate, rejecting the company's claim that a lower rate of tax applicable under German law to certain home-produced spirits applied. In the course of national proceedings certain questions were referred to the European Court on the interpretation and scope of the EEC Treaty, art. 95, which prohibits the discriminatory application of internal systems of taxation. *Held*, although Community law did not prohibit member states from granting advantages in respect of certain types of spirits, the effect of art. 95 was that any such preferential system was to be extended without discrimination to spirits coming from other member states, where the criteria underlying art. 95 were satisfied. As to the application of the article, while art. 227 (2) made special provision for the French overseas departments, those areas formed an integral part of the French Republic and, accordingly, after the expiry of the transitional period provided for by art. 227 (2) the Treaty applied automatically to them, by virtue of art. 227 (1). However, there was no provision under the Treaty which prohibited the discriminatory application of systems of internal taxation to goods imported from non-member states.

Case 148/77: HANSEN AND BALLE GMBH & CO v HAUPTZOLLAMT FLENSBURG [1978] ECR 1787 (European Court of Justice).

1242 **Treaties**

The European Communities (Definition of Treaties) (ECSC Decision on Supplementary Revenues) Order 1979, S.I. 1979 No. 292 (in force on 15th March 1979), declares the Decision of the Representatives of the Governments of the Member States of the European Coal and Steel Community, allocating to that Community supplementary revenues for 1978, to be a Community treaty as defined in the European Communities Act 1972, s. 1 (2).

1243   The European Communities (Definition of Treaties) (ECSC Decision of 9th April 1979 on Supplementary Revenues) Order 1979, S.I. 1979 No. 932 (coming into operation on a date to be notified) declares the Decision of the Representatives of the Governments of the Member States of the European Coal and Steel Community, meeting within the Council, of 9th April 1979 to be a Community Treaty as defined in the European Community Act 1972, s. 1 (2). The Decision allocates to the Community supplementary revenues totalling 28 million European Units of Account for the financial year 1979.

1244   The European Communities (Definition of Treaties) (International Wheat Agreement) Order 1979, S.I. 1979 No. 1446 (in force on the day in which the treaty enters into force for the United Kingdom), declares the 1979 Protocols for the Fifth Extension of the Wheat Trade Convention and the Food Aid Convention constituting the International Wheat Agreement 1971 (OJ No. L152) to be Community Treaties as defined in the European Communities Act 1972, s. 1 (2).

EVIDENCE

Halsbury's Laws of England (4th edn.), Vol. 17, paras. 1–400

1245   **Article**

Evidence (competence of witnesses and admissible methods of giving evidence in proceedings in magistrates' courts): Court (Journal of Legal Proceedings in Magistrates' Courts) Autumn 1978.

1246   **Action for breach of confidence—evidence—whether speculative assertion sufficient to found action**

See *Reinforced Plastics Applications (Swansea) v Swansea Plastics & Engineering Co Ltd*, para. 2128.

1247   **Admissibility—evidence given abroad—admissibility in bankruptcy proceedings**

See *Re a Debtor (No. 2283 of 1976)*, para. 214.

1248   —— **letters written "without prejudice"**

See *Finnery Lock Seeds Ltd v George Mitchell (Chester Hall) Ltd*, para. 147.

1249   —— **similar facts—personal injuries action—application for retrial on grounds of fresh evidence**

In 1970 the plaintiff had an operation to restore the hearing of her right ear. As a result, she suffered facial paralysis which she claimed was due to the negligence of the surgeon who performed the operation. Her claim for damages in negligence failed. Subsequently, evidence emerged of an individual who had suffered similar symptoms after undergoing the same operation, performed by the same surgeon. The plaintiff applied for leave to adduce fresh evidence which she claimed was relevant to her case. *Held*, although several features were common to both operations the causes of paralysis had been found to be different. Before "similar fact" evidence could be admitted, there had to be a close degree of similarity between each of the situations. It was a question of degree; varying factors would have varying weight in different cases where "similar fact" evidence was admitted. The fresh evidence which the plaintiff here sought to adduce was not logically probative of the negligence allegedly occurring in the plaintiff's operation. Accordingly, if the evidence had been available at the trial, it would not substantially have affected that decision. There were therefore no grounds for ordering a retrial and the appeal would be dismissed.

REED v VASANT HANSRAJ OSWAL (1979) 22nd November (unreported) (Court of Appeal: MEGAW, SHAW and WALLER LJJ). *Ladd v Marshall* [1954] 3 All ER 745 applied.

1250   Bankruptcy proceedings—debtor abroad—admissibility of evidence—application to hear evidence abroad

See *Re A Debtor (No. 2283 of 1976)*, para. 214.

1251   Criminal cases

See CRIMINAL PROCEDURE.

1252   Cross-examination—application for compulsory purchase order—whether cross-examination on affidavit permissible

See *George v Secretary of State for the Environment*, para. 417.

1253   Documentary evidence—official reports of parliamentary proceedings

The Committee of Privileges has stated that the practice of the House of Commons which prevented reference to the official report of debates in court proceedings except after leave given in reponse to a petition appears to have developed out of a resolution of 26th May 1818 which in terms merely required the leave of the House to be granted for the attendance of its servants to give evidence in respect of the House's proceedings. The resolution continues to provide an essential protection for the House in the matters to which it strictly relates, but the committee consider that no purpose would be served by its extension to the requirement for leave merely for reference to be made to the official report. The committee believe that art. 9 of the Bill of Rights, reinforced by the care taken by the courts and tribunals to exclude evidence which might amount to infringement of parliamentary privilege, amply protects the House's privilege of free speech. Accordingly, the committee have recommended that the practice of presenting petitions for leave to make reference to the official report in court proceedings should not be followed in the future and that such reference should not be regarded as a breach of the privileges of the House. See First Report from the Committee of Privileges (Session 1978–79): Reference to Official Report of Debates in Court Proceedings (HC 102).

1254   Expert evidence—experts' reports—order for exchange of reports—requirements for compliance with order

At the conclusion of his judgment in a personal injuries action, ACKNER J made two observations with regard to orders made under RSC Ord. 38, r. 38 (1) for the disclosure and exchange of experts' reports. Firstly, he pointed out that an order that the substance of the report be exchanged required that not only the factual description of the circumstances of the accident be disclosed but also the opinion of the expert witness in relation to the accident. Secondly, while the court should always be satisfied that it was desirable for experts' reports to be exchanged, such an order would normally be made. The tendency to make orders only in relation to medical reports should be avoided: the whole purpose of Ord. 38, in relation to expert evidence, was to save expense by dispensing with the calling of experts when there was in reality no real dispute and, where there was a dispute, by avoiding the parties being taken by surprise and thereby being obliged to seek adjournments.

OLLETT v BRISTOL AEROJET LTD [1979] 3 All ER 544 (Queen's Bench Division: ACKNER J).

1255   —— **expert witness—terms of reference—whether expert entitled to include relevant observations**

Solicitors asked a consultant psychiatrist to prepare a report on a divorced mother in connection with proceedings for access. He was asked to report on "her present condition and whether in [his] opinion her recovery would be assisted by resuming access to her children". When they received the report the solicitors asked the psychiatrist to omit a passage in it which they regarded as prejudicial in which he stated that access "should not be enforced against the wishes of the children themselves who are in a position to express their views". The psychiatrist refused. *Held*, the psychiatrist had properly refused the request. The terms of reference allowed him to express the views that he did and a report prepared for the purpose of access proceedings was properly concerned with the relationship between the parent and her children.

NOBLE V ROBERT THOMPSON (A FIRM) [1979] LS Gaz R 260 (County court).

1256   —— —— **witness previously consulted by other party—whether a compellable witness**

A handwriting expert was consulted by the plaintiffs in a dispute over a charterparty. When giving his opinion, he said that it was not his practice to accept instructions from one side once he had been instructed by the other side. His opinion was of no assistance to the plaintiffs and he did not hear from them again. Subsequently he was asked by the defendants to give his opinion on the same document and did so before he realised that he had already been consulted on the matter. On realising this, he refused to go further, but received a subpoena ad testificandum from the defendants. The question at issue was whether he was a compellable witness, having already been consulted by the other party. *Held*, it was clearly established that there was no property in the evidence of a witness of fact. An expert witness was in the same position; the court was entitled to have the facts observed by him adduced before it and to have his independent opinion on those facts, subject to any claim for legal professional privilege. Therefore in principle the expert could be subpoenaed. The plaintiffs had contended that the expert was prevented by a contract with them from giving evidence for the defendants. There was no such contract in existence, but at most a statement of practice by the expert that he would not assist the other side. Even if there were such a contract, it would be contrary to public policy and would not be enforced. Hence the expert was a compellable witness.

HARMONY SHIPPING CO SA V DAVIS AND SAUDI EUROPE LINE LTD [1979] 3 All ER 177 (Court of Appeal: LORD DENNING MR, WALLER and CUMMING-BRUCE LJJ).

1257   —— **patent specification—scope of expert evidence in construing specification**

See *American Cyanamid Co v Ethicon Ltd*, para. 2035.

1258   —— **personal injuries action—admissibility**

The plaintiff brought an action for personal injuries following an accident in which his moped collided with one of the defendants' buses. He disclosed a copy of a report on causation, which he had obtained from a firm of consulting engineers, to the defendants' solicitors and then sought to adduce the report in evidence. On the question of whether the report should be admitted at the trial, *held*, in such cases expert evidence was not necessary, since counsel could advance the same arguments with equal force and the case could be argued on a common sense basis.

HINDS V LONDON TRANSPORT EXECUTIVE [1979] RTR 103 (Court of Appeal: LORD DENNING MR, ORR and BRANDON LJJ).

1259   —— —— **agreed experts' reports—procedure**

See para. 2150.

1260   Proceedings in other jurisdictions—Isle of Man

The Evidence (Proceedings in Other Jurisdictions) (Isle of Man) Order 1979, S.I. 1979 No. 1711 (in force on 1st February 1980), extends to the Isle of Man certain provisions of the Evidence (Proceedings in Other Jurisdictions) Act 1975, 1975 Halsbury's Abridgment para. 1460, subject to the modifications made by this Order. The 1975 Act, as so extended, makes fresh provision to enable the High Court of Justice of the Isle of Man to assist in obtaining evidence required for the purposes of proceedings in other jurisdictions.

The Order also extends the Evidence (European Court) Order 1976, 1976 Halsbury's Abridgment para. 1176 to the Isle of Man. Thus, evidence for proceedings before the European Court of Justice may be taken at the request of that Court by the High Court of Justice of the Isle of Man.

1261   Right to remain silent—power of Treasury to require information relating to breach of exchange control restrictions—whether subject to right to remain silent

See *A v H.M. Treasury, B v H.M. Treasury*, para. 1918.

1262   Witness—examination out of court—witness living outside jurisdiction—examination out of jurisdiction—material evidence

Australia

In a patent infringement action the defendants contended, inter alia, that the patent was invalid on the ground of obviousness. They wished to have an independent witness, F, examined on the issue, as he was the technician who, in Sweden, had developed a process analogous to the process in question. However he refused to travel to Australia. The court was therefore asked to exercise its discretion to make an order for the examination of the witness abroad. The defendants argued that F's evidence as to the steps he took in developing his process was material evidence by which the court could be assisted in determining whether the process in question was obvious. Furthermore, it did not matter where in the world the development took place, as long as it was viewed in the light of what was known and used in Australia. *Held*, it had not been established that knowledge and usage in Sweden was the same, or less, than that in Australia at the relevant times, and there were difficulties in comparing F's knowledge with that available to a hypothetical Australian technician. Thus it had not been established on the balance of probabilities that F would be able to give relevant and admissible evidence on the issue of obviousness and the court would not exercise its discretion.

LUCAS INDUSTRIES LTD V CHLORIDE BATTERIES AUSTRALIA LTD [1979] FSR 322 (Federal Court of Australia).

EXECUTION

Halsbury's Laws of England (4th edn.). Vol. 17, paras. 401–586

1263   Charging Orders Act 1979

The Charging Orders Act 1979 makes provision for the imposition of charges to secure payment of money due or to become due under judgments or court orders. It also restrains and prohibits dealings with certain securities and the making of payments in respect of them. The Act, which is based on the recommendations contained in the Law Commission's Report on Charging Orders (1976, Law Com. No. 74, 1976 Halsbury's Abridgment para. 1584), received the royal assent on 6th December 1979 and comes into force on a day to be appointed.

Section 1 provides that the court may, for the purpose of enforcing a judgment or order, make an order imposing a charge on a debtor's property so as to secure payment of money due or to become due under the judgment or court order. Subject to certain exceptions, such an order may be granted by the High Court in respect of a High Court judgment debt of over £2,000 and by the county court in other cases.

Section 2 defines the type of property in respect of which a charging order may be made. A charge may be imposed on a debtor's beneficial interest in a specified asset or under any trust, or, on any interest held by a person as trustee of a trust in certain circumstances. A list of chargeable assets is provided in s. 2 (2).

Section 3 contains supplementary provisions relating to the making of a charging order, its effect, discharge or variation and the manner in which it may be protected. The Lord Chancellor is empowered to extend or reduce, by statutory instrument, the list of chargeable assets in s. 2 (2).

Section 4 provides that the imposition of a charging order constitutes complete execution for the purposes of the insolvency provisions of the Bankcruptcy Act 1914 and the Companies Act 1948.

Definitions as to stop orders and notices are contained in s. 5 which also enlarges the powers of the Rules Committees to make rules of court to prevent dealings, without notice to the creditor, in securities which are subject to a charging order.

Interpretations are contained in s. 6. Section 7 repeals the Administration of Justice Act 1956, s. 35 and the County Courts Act 1959, s. 141 (which relate to the powers of courts to make charging orders). It also makes other consequential amendments and transitional provisions and section 8 deals with citation, commencement and extent.

1264   Equitable execution—appointment of receiver—tenant in common of proceeds of sale of land

See *Levermore v Levermore*, para. 938.

EXECUTORS AND ADMINISTRATORS

Halsbury's Laws of England (4th edn.), Vol. 17, paras. 701–1591

1265   Articles

Family Provision: Relevant Factor, F. Graham Glover (discussion of *Re Coventry* [1979] 3 All ER 815, CA, para. 1266): 9 Fam Law 202.

Intestacy—Rights of Surviving Spouse to Matrimonial Home. Some Problems, L. Jones (problems of surviving spouse in getting legal estate in dwelling-house vested in him or herself): 98 Law Notes, April 1979, p. 109.

1266   Family provision—application by child—child not dependent—meaning of "maintenance"

The deceased and his wife were married in 1927. They acquired a house in which the wife was entitled to a one-third interest. The only child of the marriage, a son, returned to live at home in 1957, when aged twenty-six years. The wife left home shortly afterwards and subsequently received no financial support from the deceased. From 1957–61, the son lived in the house rent-free, but did the domestic work and contributed towards household expenses. In 1961, the son married and he and his wife lived rent-free in the house until the marriage broke up in 1975. The deceased died intestate in 1976. The wife, who was entitled to the whole of the estate under the intestacy, was then aged seventy-four and living on a pension in a council flat. The son was aged forty-six and earning about £52 per week after tax, out of which he was required to pay £12 per week maintenance. He was living in the house and would have to find alternative accommodation if required to move out. The son unsuccessfully applied for provision out of the estate under the Inheritance (Provision for Family and Dependants) Act 1975, s. 1. He appealed, contending that, under s. 3 (5) of the Act, the court should have had regard to events subsequent to the hearing, namely that his financial position had worsened. *Held*, in considering an application for relief out of a deceased's estate, the court should decide whether the provisions governing the disposal of the estate failed to make reasonable financial provision for the applicant. That was a question of fact to be determined by the judge making a value judgment, or a qualitative decision, the question for determination being whether in all the circumstances, looked at objectively, it was unreasonable that the provisions governing the estate did not provide for the applicant, and not whether the deceased had acted unreasonably in so leaving his estate. The judge had properly directed himself and had not erred in principle and his value judgment ought not to be disturbed. Further, the court was not entitled to have regard to events subsequent to the hearing, for under s. 3 (5) it could have regard only to facts "known to the court", and therefore could have regard only to facts which had been properly proved to the court. Accordingly, the appeal would be dismissed.

RE COVENTRY (DECEASED) [1979] 3 All ER 815 (Court of Appeal: BUCKLEY, GEOFFREY LANE and GOFF LJJ). Decision of Oliver J (1978) Times, 14th November, 1978 Halsbury's Abridgment para. 1294 affirmed.

1267   —— —— **reasonable financial provision—matters to be considered**

By her will made in 1963 the deceased left her half share in a house in London to her daughter and a house in Essex owned solely by herself to her son, her residuary estate to be divided equally between them. In 1971 she executed a deed of gift transferring her interest in the London house to her daughter. In 1976 she sold the house in Essex and purchased a smaller property, but died before altering her will so as to entitle her son to the new property, as she had intended. Consequently, the gift of the Essex house could not take effect and the value of the new house was included in her residuary estate. The son applied for an order under the Inheritance (Provision for Family and Dependants) Act 1975, s. 2 for reasonable financial provision to be made for him out of the estate. *Held*, in considering under s. 1 (2) (b) whether the effect of a will was to make such financial provision as in the circumstances would be reasonable for the applicant to receive for his maintenance, the word "maintenance" did not imply that for an applicant to qualify he should be in a state of destitution or financial difficulty. Rather, it referred simply to his way of life and well being, his health and financial security and allied matters. The facts of the present case showed that, while any money received by either the son or the daughter respectively would be of great use to them, it was at all times up to her death the deceased's intention that her daughter should have her interest in the London property and her son her interest in the other. The former part of that intention had been put into effect in 1971 and accordingly it was fair and just that an order should be made for the transfer of the new property to the son.

RE CHRISTIE; CHRISTIE V KEEBLE [1979] 1 All ER 546 (Chancery Division: VIVIAN PRICE QC, sitting as a deputy High Court judge).

1268   —— **person maintained by the deceased otherwise than for full valuable consideration**

The deceased had one legitimate son by his marriage. His will was made in favour of his son, on trust. He had been divorced and lived with the son in the matrimonial home. He advertised for a housekeeper and employed the applicant, an eighteen-year-old girl with an illegitimate child of her own. She became the deceased's mistress and relied on him for her maintenance etc. She had her own child adopted, and a planned child was later born to her and the deceased. The deceased took preliminary steps to have his will changed but died suddenly, leaving his mistress and their child to live on social security. She applied for reasonable financial provision for herself and her son from the deceased's estate, valued at £20,000–£35,000, under the Inheritance (Provision for Family and Dependants) Act 1975 s. 1 (1) (e). *Held*, to be entitled under s. 1 (1) (e) the applicant had to prove that she was being maintained wholly or partly by the deceased otherwise than for full valuable consideration. A submission by the legitimate son that she was in the house under contract as a housekeeper was dismissed. The relationship had been stable and the applicant had been a de facto wife. It was incumbent upon the deceased to provide for her and the child. The son would take equally with the legitimate son of the testator and she would receive £5,000 to cover her needs and resources in the immediate future.

RE McC (1978) 9 Fam Law 26 (Family Division: SIR GEORGE BAKER P).

1269   —— —— couple living as man and wife

The plaintiff and the deceased, a widow, cohabited for thirty-six years in the deceased's bungalow. The plaintiff paid the deceased a fixed weekly amount for accommodation and a regular but variable amount as a contribution to the weekly shopping bill. In addition he drove the deceased around in his car and did the odd gardening and redecorating jobs for which he was paid by the deceased. The deceased did all the housework making it known that the bungalow belonged to her, paying the outgoings and keeping accounts. Although the deceased made a nomination of a number of savings certificates in the plaintiff's favour she made no provision for him in her will. The plaintiff claimed to fall within the provisions of the Inheritance (Provision for Family and Dependants) Act 1975, s. 1 (1) (e) as a person who immediately before the death of the deceased was being maintained wholly or partly by her and applied for an award of financial provision out of the deceased's estate. The executors of the will contended that the application be struck out as disclosing no reasonable cause of action. *Held*, it was not enough for an applicant under s. 1 (1) (e) to show that he was wholly or partly maintained by the deceased unless he also satisfied the provisions of s. 1 (3) as to "substantial contribution" towards his reasonable needs by the deceased. The words in s. 1 (1) (e) "immediately before the death of the deceased" required the court to consider the general arrangement for maintenance of the plaintiff and in the light of s. 3 (4) he also had to establish that the deceased assumed responsibility for his maintenance. Since the plaintiff had failed to establish such an assumption and on the evidence he and the deceased had merely shared their lives together the application should be struck out.

RE BEAUMONT; MARTIN v MIDLAND BANK TRUST CO LTD [1979] 3 WLR 818 (Chancery Division: MEGARRY V-C).

1270   —— —— mistress

The deceased was a successful businessman separated from his wife but making regular voluntary payments to her. After his separation from his wife he had a series of mistresses, one of whom moved into his house with her son and was until his death treated as a wife. In 1965 the deceased met the plaintiff, a young telephonist, and persuaded her to give up working and travel abroad with him. From then on the deceased paid the plaintiff's living expenses, gave her a job in one of his companies, shares and a car and bought flats in Malta and England in their joint names. The deceased made it clear that if he were free to marry the plaintiff he would do so and that in any event her future was secure though there would be no provision for her in his will. However, he drew her attention to the provisions of the Inheritance (Provision for Family and Dependants) Act 1975. On his death in 1977 the deceased made no provision for the plaintiff. Since his death the plaintiff worked on a low salary caring for the elderly and it was doubtful whether she was capable of earning more. The plaintiff applied to the court for reasonable financial provision under the 1975 Act. *Held*, the deceased assumed full responsibility for the plaintiff's maintenance for twelve years during his life on the basis that he would not leave her unprovided for after his death. Accordingly in the absence of reasonable financial provision the court would make an order under s. 2 for a lump sum payment having regard also to the deceased's obligations to the beneficiaries of the will.

MALONE v HARRISON [1979] 1 WLR 1353 (Family Division at Birmingham: HOLLINGS J).

1271   Intestacy—appropriation by personal representatives—matrimonial home—surviving spouse's interest in estate less than value of house

A husband died intestate. The value of the matrimonial home was greater than his widow's absolute interest in the estate. She was prepared to pay the difference in value if the house was transferred to her. By the Intestates' Estates Act 1952, Sch. 2, para. 1 (1), where the intestate's residuary estate comprises an interest in a dwelling house in which the surviving spouse was resident at time of death, the surviving spouse can "require" the personal representatives to exercise their power of appropriation conferred by the Administration of Estates Act 1925, s. 41, "in or towards satisfaction of any absolute interest". At first instance it was held that the widow could not so require the personal representatives to act because para. 1 (1) did not extend to cases where the "satisfaction" would be greater in value than the "interest". On appeal, *held*, the appeal would be allowed. Paragraph 1 (1) should be read in conjunction with para. 5 (2), which extended the meaning of "power of appropriation" in s. 41 of the 1925 Act to include a transaction which was partly appropriation and partly sale. Hence the widow could require appropriation of the house partly in satisfaction of her interest and partly in return for money.

RE PHELPS (DECEASED), WELLS V PHELPS [1979] 3 All ER 373 (Court of Appeal: BUCKLEY, BRIDGE and TEMPLEMAN LJJ). Decision of Foster J [1978] 3 All ER 395 reversed.

1272   **Personal representatives—power of appropriation—extent of power**

See *Re Phelps (deceased), Wells v Phelps*, para. 1271.

1273   **Practice—non-contentious probate—testamentary documents— use of photographic facsimiles**

See para. 2136.

1274   **Probate—grant—procedure—contents of pleadings**

The deceased died in 1977, leaving a will dated 1976 under which the plaintiff, the proprietress of a nursing home in which the deceased had been resident, was sole residuary beneficiary. The plaintiff sought to propound that will. The defendant, by counterclaim, asked the court to reject that will and to pronounce for a will dated 1972, under which he was sole residuary beneficiary, alleging want of knowledge and approval and lack of testamentary capacity. There was no plea of undue influence or fraud. The plaintiff issued a summons asking the court to strike out certain matters alleged by the defendant in support of his plea, as being in contravention of RSC Ord. 76, r. 9 (3), which debars a party who pleads want of knowledge and approval from alleging in support matters which would be relevant in support of pleas of, inter alia, undue influence or fraud, unless that other plea is also included. *Held*, on a literal reading there was force in the plaintiff's contention that facts supporting a plea of want of knowledge and approval could not be pleaded if the allegations would support a plea of undue influence, where that was not expressly pleaded. However, the rule had to have been intended to apply merely to a case where, under cover of a plea of want of knowledge and approval, a pleader was in substance affirmatively alleging undue influence or fraud without specifically introducing it as an alternative plea. An allegation should not be treated as relevant for the purposes of the rule unless, if established, it would, either alone or in conjunction with other facts also pleaded, affirmatively prove the relevant alternative plea. The allegations concerned would not be struck out.

RE STOTT, DECEASED; KLOUDA V LLOYDS BANK LTD [1980] 1 All ER 259 (Chancery Division: SLADE J). *Wintle v Nye* [1959] 1 All ER 552 applied.

1275   **Royal Commission on Legal Services—recommendations—grants to trust corporations**

See para. 1720.

EXPLOSIVES

Halsbury's Laws of England (4th edn.), Vol. 18, paras. 1–200

1276   Explosive substance—whether substance having pyrotechnic effect explosive

A defendant appealed against his conviction on a charge of possessing an explosive substance in contravention of the Explosive Substances Act 1883, s. 4 (1) on the ground that the judge was wrong to apply the definition of explosive in Explosives Act 1875, s. 3, thus including substances which produced a pyrotechnic effect rather than an explosive effect. *Held*, the judge had been entitled to apply the definition in the 1875 Act and therefore the appeal would be dismissed.

R v WHEATLEY [1979] 1 All ER 954 (Court of Appeal: Lord WIDGERY CJ, BRIDGE and WIEN JJ).

EXTRADITION AND FUGITIVE OFFENDERS

Halsbury's Laws of England (4th edn.), Vol. 18, paras. 201–295

1277   Article

Go Back Fugitives, A. N. Khan (some recent developments in the law relating to extradition and deportation): 143 JP Jo 448.

1278   Fugitive offender—application for habeas corpus—double criminality—conditions to be satisfied

The applicants applied for writs of habeas corpus on the ground that the committal warrants upon which they were held pending their extradition to the United States were unlawful. They were to face burglary charges in the United States following the unlawful entry, as trespassers, by members of the Church of Scientology, of several government offices, where they took photocopies of confidential files relating to the affairs of the Church. The burglars had been caught and had revealed that they had been acting on the written instructions of the applicants. The applicants contended that (i) as, by the relevant American law, entry as a trespasser was not an essential element of the crime of burglary as it was in England under the Theft Act 1968, s. 9, the extradition would offend against the principle of double criminality under which a criminal was only to be extradited for the commission of a crime punishable by the laws of both countries; (ii) the offences were of a political character in that the applicants had been engaged in an attempt to change the policy of the United States government towards the Church of Scientology. Further, that the United States government was attempting by indirect means to punish the applicants, not for burglary but for stealing confidential government information. *Held*, (i) it was not necessary that the crime defined in the foreign law satisfied all the essential ingredients of the English crime. It was enough if the crime for which extradition was demanded would be recognised as substantially similar in both countries and there was a prima facie case that the conduct of the accused amounted to the commission of the crime according to English law; (ii) organising burglary for the reasons stated did not amount to offences of a political character, in that they did not challenge the political control or government of the United States. Further, when the offence had not been shown to be of a political character, the English courts would not entertain allegations of bad faith on the part of the requesting country. The applications for habeas corpus would therefore be refused.

R v PENTONVILLE PRISON GOVERNOR, EX PARTE BUDLONG, [1980] 1 All ER 701 (Queen's Bench Division: LORD WIDGERY CJ and GRIFFTHS J).

1279   —— —— Irish warrant—whether offence of political character

Following information received from the Irish police the applicant was arrested in England under the Prevention of Terrorism (Temporary Provisions) Act 1976, s. 12 for a terrorist offence. A warrant was later received from Dublin endorsed for execution in the United Kingdom specifying offences in accordance with the earlier information, and the applicant was re-arrested under the Backing of Warrants (Republic of Ireland) Act 1965. He applied for a writ of habeas corpus on the grounds that the offences specified in the warrant were of a political character within s. 2 (2) of the Act of 1965 and he was therefore exempt from extradition proceedings. *Held*, the applicant had failed to discharge the onus of proving that the offences were of a political character. On being first arrested he had been told that he was being detained for a terrorist offence, which did not justify the conclusion that the offences were therefore political in character. The application would be refused.

R v DURHAM PRISON GOVERNOR, EX PARTE CARLISLE [1979] LS Gaz R 101 (Queen's Bench Division: LORD WIDGERY CJ, KILNER BROWN and ROBERT GOFF JJ).

1280   —— —— second application

A business man who was to have been extradited to Singapore after his application for habeas corpus had been refused, was granted leave to make a second application for habeas corpus. The new application relied on the Fugitive Offenders Act 1967 s. 8 (3) (b), that by reason of the passage of time since the applicant had committed the offences it would be unjust or oppressive to return him. The applicant also contended that under the Administration of Justice Act 1960, s. 14 (2), fresh evidence had arisen to support his case. *Held*, to constitute fresh evidence, the evidence had to be not merely additional to or different from that adduced on the first application, but evidence which the applicant could not have or could not reasonably have put forward. There was no such evidence in this application. The total passage of time was no more than that reasonably caused by the investigation and prosecution of charges which arise upon complicated documents and transactions and did not make it unfair for him to be required to return to Singapore. The application would be refused.

EX PARTE TARLING [1979] 1 All ER 981 (Queen's Bench Division: LORD WIDGERY CJ, GRIFFITHS and GIBSON JJ). *Johnson v Johnson* [1900] P 19, *R v Medical Appeal Tribunal (North Midland Region) ex parte Hubble* [1959] 3 All ER 40, CA, *Yat Tung Investment Co Ltd v Dao Heng Bank Ltd* [1975] AC 581, PC, 1975 Halsbury's Abridgment para. 1349, applied.

For previous proceedings, see *R v Governor of Pentonville Prison, ex parte Tarling* (1977) Times, 30th July, 1977 Halsbury's Abridgment para. 1271, *Tarling v Government of the Republic of Singapore* (1978) Times, 20th April, HL and *Ex parte Tarling* (1978) Times, 6th June, 1978 Halsbury's Abridgment paras. 1310, 1308 respectively.

1281   —— designated Commonwealth countries

The Fugitive Offenders (Designated Commonwealth Countries) Order 1979, S.I. 1979 No. 460 (in force on 30th May 1979) designates Saint Lucia for the purposes of section 1 of the Fugitive Offenders Act 1967.

1282   The Fugitive Offenders (Designated Commonwealth Countries) (No. 2) Order 1979, S.I. 1979 No. 1712 (in force on 24th January 1980), designates Kiribati and Saint Vincent and the Grenadines as independent Commonwealth countries for the purposes of the Fugitive Offenders Act 1967, s. 1 (1).

1283   —— extradition—Denmark

The Denmark (Extradition) (Amendment) Order, 1979, S.I. 1979 No. 1311 (in force on 19th November 1979), applies the Extradition Acts 1870 to 1935 in the case of Denmark in accordance with the Treaty between the United Kingdom and Denmark for the mutual surrender of criminals, signed at Copenhagen on 31st

March 1873, as amended by the supplementary Convention signed on 15th October 1935, and as further amended by the Notes exchanged at Copenhagen on 24th August 1979.

1284 —— —— Norway

The Norway (Extradition) (Amendment) Order 1979, S.I. 1979 No. 913 (in force on 24th August 1979), amends the Extradition Acts 1870 to 1895 in the case of Norway so as to reserve the right of the requested government not to extradite its nationals in accordance with the Treaty between the United Kingdom and Norway for the mutual surrender of fugitive criminals.

1285 Internationally protected persons—specified states

The Extradition (Internationally Protected Persons) Order 1979, S.I. 1979 No. 453 (in force on 24th May 1979), applies the Extradition Acts 1870 to 1895 so as to make extraditable those offences against internationally protected persons mentioned in the Internationally Protected Persons Act 1978, 1978 Halsbury's Abridgment para. 1411, and attempts to commit such offences, in the case of states which are parties to the Convention on the Prevention and Punishment of Crimes against Internationally Protected Persons, including Diplomatic Agents, signed at New York on 14th December 1973.

1286 Suppression of Terrorism Act 1978—convention countries

The Suppression of Terrorism Act 1978 (Designation of Countries) Order 1979, S.I. 1979 No. 497 (in force on 27th May 1979), designates the Republic of Cyprus as a party to the European Convention on the Suppression of Terrorism so that it becomes a convention country within the meaning of the Suppression of Terrorism Act 1978, 1978 Halsbury's Abridgment para. 1321.

FAMILY ARRANGEMENTS, UNDUE INFLU-ENCE AND VOIDABLE CONVEYANCES

Halsbury's Laws of England (4th edn.), Vol. 18, paras. 301–400

1287 Article

Varying a Will after Death, Alan Tunkel (the execution of a deed of family arrangement): 123 Sol Jo 153.

1288 Transfer of property—transfer of interest in land for less than full value—whether transaction fair, just and reasonable

See *Junkin v Junkin*, para. 1128.

1289 Undue influence—when presumption arises—evidence of no improper conduct

Northern Ireland
An elderly and lonely widow, since deceased, was brought home to Ireland from the United States at her own request, by her niece, the applicant. She took up residence in the applicant's home, under her care. Having made known her intention of revoking her will and giving everything to the applicant in an expression of her gratitude for the applicant's kindness, the deceased opened a joint account in a savings bank for the applicant and herself into which she transferred all her funds. The personal representative of the deceased claimed that the money in the account was a part of the estate since there was a presumption that the applicant had been exercising undue influence over the deceased at the time when the account was opened. It was held that the onus was on the applicant to rebut the presumption. Since she had

failed to do so, the money belonged to the estate. She now applied for an order of certiorari to quash the decision on the ground that it bore an error of law on its face in view of the lack of evidence. *Held*, the applicant was under no obligation to rebut a presumption of undue influence. A presumption arose only when the facts were not sufficiently known, and in this instance there was evidence, submitted by witnesses at the bank, that the applicant had taken no part in the arrangements for the opening of the joint account. Furthermore the deputy at the earlier hearing had formed the view that the applicant was a "truthful and reliable witness" and she had stated that her only interest in aiding her aunt was of a purely altruistic nature. Having accepted that the applicant's evidence was truthful there could be no presumption to rebut. An order of certiorari to quash the decision would accordingly be made.

R v HUTTON (No. 2) [1978] NI 139 (Northern Ireland Queen's Bench Division).

FIREARMS

Halsbury's Laws of England (4th edn.), Vol. 11, paras. 875–898

1290   Article

Firearms (a series of articles covering the law relating to possession, use, manufacture, conversion and sale of firearms): Court (Journal of Legal Practice in Magistrates' Courts) Summer 1979.

1291   Fees

The Firearms (Variation of Fees) Order 1979 (Revocation) Order 1979, S.I. 1979 No. 459 (made on 11th April 1979), revokes the Firearms (Variation of Fees) Order 1979, S.I. 1979 No. 86, which prescribed increased fees in respect of firearms certificates and shot gun certificates and in respect of the registration of firearms dealers and the new registration certificates issued to firearms dealers annually. In consequence of the revocation the fees prescribed by the Firearms (Variation of Fees) Order 1978, 1978 Halsbury's Abridgment para. 1329 continue to have effect.

1292   Movement of firearms—control of trafficking

The Council of Europe has published the text of the European Convention on the Control of the Acquisition and Possession of Firearms by Individuals, concluded at Strasbourg on 28th June 1978. The convention is aimed at the suppression of the illegal traffic in firearms and in the tracing and location of firearms transferred from one state to another. The convention does not apply to transactions in which all the principals are states. Inter alia, each contracting state is required to take measures to ensure that any person who sells, transfers or otherwise disposes of a firearm within its territory furnishes particulars to the competent authorities. If firearms are sold, transferred or otherwise disposed of (or if they are permanently transferred without a change of possession) to a person in another state, the authorities of that state and any state through which the firearms pass in transit must be informed. The convention will enter into force at the beginning of the month following a period of three months after the third instrument of ratification, acceptance or approval has been deposited. The text of the convention is published as no. 101 in the European Treaty Series and is available from H.M. Stationery Office.

This convention now published as Cmnd. 7683.

1293   Possession of firearms—parallel offences under two statutes—Malaysia

See *Teh Cheng Poh v The Public Prosecutor, Malaysia*, para. 2716.

1294   —— **possession without a certificate—exemption in respect of antiques—direction to jury**

The appellant was charged with, inter alia, possessing firearms without a certificate contrary to the Firearms Act 1968, s. 1. He contended that they were antiques, thus providing a defence under s. 58 (2) of the 1968 Act. The firearms were not on display and one of them was capable of being fired. The trial judge directed the jury that they must convict on the evidence they had heard, and they duly convicted. On appeal, the appellant contended that the direction was wrong. *Held*, there was a burden on the appellant to show that he had bought the firearms as antiques. He had not discharged this as there was no evidence that he had acquired them as a curiosity or ornament. Nevertheless the jury had not been directed that the question as to whether the firearms were antiques was a question of fact for them decide. The appeal would therefore be allowed and the conviction quashed.

R v BURKE (1978) 67 Cr App Rep 220 (Court of Appeal: SHAW LJ, MAIS and PETER PAIN JJ).

1295   —— **restriction on possession—power of justices to attach prohibition on possession to binding over—common law and statutory powers**

After an incident in which a man fired a shotgun, he was bound over under the Justices of the Peace Act 1361 on condition that he did not possess, carry or use a firearm. Arms and ammunition seized on his premises were ordered to be forfeited under the Firearms Act 1968, s. 52, which provides for such forfeiture following a binding over, where a condition has been attached that the individual shall not possess, use or carry a firearm. The defendant appealed on the grounds that the justices were not entitled to impose a condition on the binding over. *Held*, allowing the appeal, conditions could not be attached to a binding over under the 1361 Act, whereas they could be under the common law power to bind over. The 1968 Act did not create powers which did not exist before, therefore it was only applicable to a binding over under the common law.

GOODLAD v CHIEF CONSTABLE OF SOUTH YORKSHIRE [1979] Crim LR 51 (Crown Court at Sheffield: JUDGE LAURISTON QC sitting with two justices).

FIRE SERVICES

Halsbury's Laws of England (4th edn.), Vol. 18, paras. 401–600

1296   **Pensions**

See PENSIONS.

FISHERIES

Halsbury's Laws of England (4th edn.), Vol. 18, paras. 601–942

1297   **Article**

Fishing, Phillip Stephens (a discussion of the possible legal meanings of "fishing"): 143 JP Jo 376.

1298   **Cod and whiting—licensing**

The Cod and Whiting (Licensing) Order 1979, S.I. 1979 No. 268 (in force on 26th March 1979), prohibits fishing by British fishing boats registered in the United Kingdom for cod and whiting in the North Sea and in specified areas off the West

Coast of Scotland and around Rockall except under licence, but exempts from this prohibition fishing by British fishing boats of registered length less than forty feet. Enforcement powers are conferred on British sea fishery officers.

1299   Common organisation of fisheries—third country fishing

The Third Country Fishing (Enforcement) Regulations 1979, S.I. 1979 No. 1205 (in force on 6th October 1979), make breaches of certain Community regulations relating to third country fishing offences under United Kingdom law where they occur within British fishery limits.

1300   Fishery limits—fishing boats—designated countries

The Fishing Boats (Faroe Islands) Designation Order 1979, S.I. 1979 No. 256 (in force on 10th March 1979), designated the Faroe Islands as a country whose registered fishing boats may fish in the areas specified in the Order for certain sea fish indicated in relation to those areas. The Order expired on 31st March 1979.

1301   The Fishing Boats (Specified Countries) Designation Order 1979, S.I. 1979 No. 504 (in force on 30th April 1979), revoked the Fishing Boats (Specified Countries) Designation (No. 3) Order 1977, 1977 Halsbury's Abridgment para. 1295, as amended, and superseded both it and the Fishing Boats (Faroe Islands) Designation Order 1979, para. 1300, which expired on 31st March 1979. It designated the Faroe Islands, Norway, Spain and Sweden as countries whose registered fishing boats may fish for certain species of sea fish in certain areas of British fishery limits outside the area within twelve miles from the baselines from which the breadth of the territorial sea is measured. The Order, which expired on 31st December 1979, did not affect the rights of fishing boats registered in Norway under the Fishing Boats (Norway) Designation Order 1964.

1302   Fishing boats registry—penalties

The Merchant Shipping (Fishing Boats Registry) (Amendment) Order 1979, S.I. 1979 No. 1455 (in force on 1st January 1980), amends the Merchant Shipping (Fishing Boats Registry) Order 1927 by increasing the specified penalties. The Merchant Shipping Act 1979 enabled the maximum penalty prescribed under that Order to be increased to £50.

1303   Fishing vessels—grants

The Fishing Vessels (Acquisition and Improvement) (Grants) (Variation) Scheme 1979, S.I. 1979 No. 1692 (in force on 15th December 1979), varies the Fishing Vessels (Acquisition and Improvement) (Grants) Scheme 1976, 1976 Halsbury's Abridgment para. 1222, by substituting 1st January 1981 as the date by which applications must be approved for the payment of grants under the 1976 scheme.

1304   Haddock—licensing

The Haddock (West of Scotland and Rockall) Licensing Order 1979, S.I. 1979 No. 71 (in force on 12th February 1979), prohibits fishing by British fishing boats registered in the United Kingdom for haddock in specified sea areas off the West Coast of Scotland and around Rockall, except under licence; but exempts from this prohibition fishing by British fishing boats of registered length less than forty feet. Powers are also conferred on British sea fishery officers for the purposes of enforcement of this Order.

1305   Herring—prohibition

The Herring By-Catch (Restrictions on Landing) (No. 2) (Variation) Order 1979, S.I. 1979 No. 398 (in force on 23rd April 1979), amends the definition of a herring by-catch in the Herring By-Catch (Restrictions on Landing) (No. 2) Order 1976,

1976 Halsbury's Abridgment para. 1231 to any quantity of herring in a catch of which more than 50 per cent consists of other species of sea fish.

1306 The Irish Sea Herring (Prohibition of Fishing) Order 1979, S.I. 1979 No. 1176 (in force on 22nd September 1979, except art. 2 (2), in force on 17th November 1979), prohibits fishing for herring in certain areas and applies the powers of British sea-fishery officers for its enforcement. The order applies to all fishing boats, including foreign vessels.

1307 **Nets—north-east Atlantic**

The Fishing Nets (North-East Atlantic) (Variation) Order 1979, S.I. 1979 No. 744 (in force on 1st July 1979), amends the Fishing Nets (North-East Atlantic Order 1977, 1977 Halsbury's Abridgment para. 1313, by redefining the limits of the Irish Sea, modifying the mesh sizes of nets used to catch certain types of fish and amending the provisions concerning attachments to nets. The Order also adds sea bass to the fish listed in 1977 Order, Sch. 3, which concerns by-catches.

1308 **Sea fish—landing and sale—restrictions**

The Immature Nephrops Order 1979, S.I. 1979 No. 742 (in force on 1st July 1979), prescribes a minimum size for nephrops of twenty-five millimetres. The landing, sale, exposure or offer for sale and possession for the purpose of sale undersized nephrops is prohibited, as is the carriage of undersized nephrops by British fishing boats or foreign fishing boats within British fishery limits.

1309 The Immature Sea Fish Order 1979, S.I. 1979 No. 741 (in force on 1st July 1979), re-enacts the provisions of the Immature Sea Fish Order 1968, S.I. 1968 No. 1618, setting minimum sizes for specified sea fish landed or sold in Great Britain, with an increase in the minimum size for whiting from twenty-five to twenty-seven centimetres. It also extends the statutory provisions against the carriage of undersized fish to foreign fishing boats within British fishery limits.

1310 The Nephrops Tails (Restrictions on Landing) Order 1979, S.I. 1979 No. 743 (in force on 1st July 1979), prohibits the landing of nephrops tails in the United Kingdom, except where the landing consists of a quantity of not more than 290 tails per kilogram of the landed weight.

1311 **Sea fishing—fishing limits—net closed awaiting haulage aboard vessel—whether "fishing" inside limits**

On two separate occasions a fishing vessel was within the three-mile limits off the Cornish coast where fishing with the use of a purse seine net was prohibited by local byelaws. On both occasions the vessel's purse seine net had been "pursed" so that no more fish could be caught and the catch was being pumped on deck. The captain of the vessel was charged on two counts of offences contrary to the local byelaws. He maintained that, on the first occasion the fish had been caught outside the limit and the vessel had drifted inside the limit while the fish were being pumped aboard, and on the second occasion, that although he had been fishing inside the limit, the net had been accidentally "pursed". The justices found the captain guilty on both counts. On appeal, *held*, as further labour was necessary to reduce the fish to useful possession, the "fishing" continued whilst the catch was being hauled aboard in relation to the first incident. On the second occasion as the searching for fish inside the limits had been conceded, the captain had been properly convicted. It was not necessary therefore to decide whether the offence was absolute in relation to the accidental "pursing" of the net. The appeal would accordingly be dismissed.

ALEXANDER v TONKIN [1979] 2 All ER 1009 (Queen's Bench Division: BRIDGE LJ and CAULFIELD J).

1312   —— industry—loans and grants—time limits

The Sea Fish Industry Act 1970 (Relaxation of Time Limits) Order 1979, S.I. 1979 No. 1691 (in force on 15th December 1979), extends the time limits contained in certain provisions of the Sea Fish Industry Act 1970 to the end of 1980.

1313   —— licensing

The Poole Fishery (Variation) Order 1979, S.I. 1979 No. 38 (in force on 13th February 1979), varies the Poole Fishery Order 1915 by the deletion of art. 5(2), which provided for the issue of licences by the grantees of the Order to any person applying for them and paying the prescribed tolls.

1314   The Sea Fishing (Specified Foreign Boats) Licensing Order 1979, S.I. 1979 No. 503 (in force on 30th April 1979), prohibits fishing for certain species of sea fish by fishing boats registered in the Faroe Islands, Spain and Sweden in certain areas within British fishery limits. The prohibition extends for a period expiring on 31st December 1979, but may be avoided by a licence granted by the European Economic Community.

The Sea Fishing (Specified Foreign Boats) Licensing (No. 3) Order 1977, 1977 Halsbury's Abridgment para. 1322, as amended is revoked.

1315   —— prohibition of fishing methods

The Sea Fishing (North-West Scottish Coast Waters) (Prohibition of Fishing Methods) Order 1979, S.I. 1979 No. 1422 (in force on 12th November 1979), prohibits fishing by trawls, ring nets and purse seine nets in specified areas adjacent to the north-west Scottish coast, lying within British fishery limits, from 12th November 1979 to 31st March 1980, inclusive.

1316   White fish subsidy scheme

The White Fish Subsidy (Deep Sea Vessels) (Specified Ports) Scheme 1979, S.I. 1979 No. 421 (in force on 4th April 1979), provides for the payment of grant to the owners or charterers of fishing vessels to which the scheme applies in respect of dock dues levied at Fleetwood, Grimsby or Hull, in relation to voyages made during 1978 for the purpose of catching white fish. Vessels to which the scheme applies are those eighty feet or over in length.

FOOD, DAIRIES AND SLAUGHTERHOUSES

Halsbury's Laws of England (4th edn.), Vol. 18, paras. 1001–1351

1317   Bread—prices

The Bread Prices (No. 2) Order 1976 (Revocation) Order 1979, S.I. 1979 No. 384 (in force on 2nd April 1979), revokes the Bread Prices (No. 2) Order 1976, 1976 Halsbury's Abridgment para. 1242, as amended, which regulated the maximum retail price of most bread loaves of 800 g or less.

1318   Butter—prices

The Butter Prices (Amendment) Order 1979, S.I. 1979 No. 34 (in force on 5th February 1979), further varies the Butter Prices Order 1978, 1978 Halsbury's Abridgment para. 1371, by increasing the maximum retail prices of butter. The Butter Prices (Amendment) Order 1978, 1978 Halsbury's Abridgment para. 1372, is revoked.

1319   Food—labelling of food

The Labelling of Food (Amendment) Regulations 1979, S.I. 1979 No. 1570 (in force on 1st January 1980) further amend the 1970 Regulations. The Regulations inter alia now permit, in declarations of the alcoholic strength of intoxicating liquor pre-packed for sale by retail, certain symbols to be used and revoke the requirement that declarations of alcoholic strength shall appear within a surrounding line. The Regulations also refer to "alcoholic strength by volume" and "alcoholic strength by mass" which are defined in the Alcoholic Tables Regulations 1979, para. 3069.

1320   Hygiene—imported food

The Imported Food (Amendment) Regulations 1979, S.I. 1979 No. 1426 (in force on 1st January 1980) further amend the 1968 Regulations, to give effect to certain EEC Directives.

1321   —— ships

The Food Hygiene (Ships) Regulations 1979, S.I. 1979 No. 27 (in force on 19th February 1979), apply certain provisions concerning food hygiene to the carrying on of a catering business or other retail food business in boats or craft which are moored or which are plying exclusively in inland waters or engaged exclusively in coastal excursions. The provisions correspond to the Food and Drugs (Control of Food Premises) Act 1976, ss. 1–6, which empower a magistrates' court to prohibit the carrying on of a food business at insanitary premises or stalls or in circumstances which would be dangerous to health.

1322   Imported food—unlawful importation of meat—whether importer has possession of meat—availability of statutory defence

The defendants were charged with two offences under the Imported Food Regulations 1968: first, of importing meat without an official certificate and secondly, of unlawfully landing meat in England. They were acquitted of both offences on the basis of the defence contained in the Food and Drugs Act 1955, s. 115. The plaintiff council appealed by way of case stated on the question whether the statutory defence applied to the offences concerned. *Held*, where an offence consisted of "having possession for the purpose of sale", the 1955 Act, s. 115 provided a defence if a person proved that he purchased food as being suitable for lawful sale and had a written warranty to that effect. Therefore, s. 115 only applied to the first offence if an importer "had possession" of meat for sale. The word "possession" should be given its commonsense meaning so that an importer of meat was also in possession of it. Moreover, the 1968 Regulations referred to the statutory defence under s. 155 and clearly intended it to apply to prosecutions under the Regulations. The defendants were entitled to rely on a certificate warranting that the meat had an official certificate as a written warrant for the purposes of s. 115 since they had investigated its accuracy and acted reasonably in relying on it. Accordingly the statutory defence applied to the first offence. It did not apply to the second offence of landing meat in England since that was not an offence covered by s. 115. The appeal would be dismissed in relation to the first offence but allowed in relation to the second.

DOVER DISTRICT COUNCIL v C. R. BARRON LTD (1979) 27th July (unreported) (Queen's Bench Division: LORD WIDGERY CJ, EVELEIGH LJ and WOOLF J). Dicta of Lord Goddard CJ in *Challand v Bartlett* [1953] 2 All ER 832 at 835 applied.

1323   Lead in food

The Lead in Food Regulations 1979, S.I. 1979 No. 1254 (in force on 12th April 1980), replace the Lead in Food Regulations 1961, as amended, which restrict the amount of lead which may be present in food (including drink) intended for sale for human consumption. The Regulations delete and amend certain definitions in the 1961 Regulations and introduce several new definitions. The general limit for lead in food is reduced from 2·0 milligrams per kilogram to 1·0 milligram per kilogram. A number of changes are made to the list of specified foods and the limits for lead which apply to them. The special provision for compound foods in which lead is present in a proportion exceeding the general limit and one of the ingredients is a specified food for which a higher limit is prescribed is amended. The reduced limits will apply after a transitional period of two years in the case of certain specified foods. The Regulations do not apply to food intended for exportation outside the United Kingdom.

1324 Milk—price control

The Milk (Extension of Period of Control of Maximum Prices) Order 1979, S.I. 1979 No. 1602 (in force on 31st December 1979) continues for a further five years from the end of 1979 the power of the Ministry of Agriculture, Fisheries and Food or the Secretary of State under the Emergency Laws (Re-enactments and Repeals) Act 1964, s. 6 to control by order the maximum prices to be charged for liquid milk.

1325 —— prices

The Milk (Great Britain) (Amendment) Order 1979, S.I. 1979 No. 604 (in force on 1st June 1979), further amends the Milk (Great Britain) Order 1977, 1977 Halsbury's Abridgment para. 1339 by increasing the maximum retail prices of milk by 1½p per pint with effect from 3rd June 1979 in England and Wales and from 15th July 1979 in Scotland. The Order also decreases by varying amounts the maximum prices for the sale in Great Britain of raw milk for heat treatment with effect from 1st June 1979. The Milk (Great Britain) (Amendment) (No. 3) Order 1978, 1978 Halsbury's Abridgment para. 1384 is revoked.

1326

The Milk (Great Britain) (Amendment) (No. 2) Order 1979, S.I. 1979 No. 700 (in force on 24th June 1979), further amends the Milk (Great Britain) Order 1977, 1977 Halsbury's Abridgment para. 1339. The Order brings forward from 15th July 1979 to 24th June 1979 increases of 1½p per pint in the maximum retail prices of milk on sales in Scotland.

1327

The Milk (Great Britain) (Amendment) (No. 3) Order 1979, S.I. 1979 No. 1290 (in force on 1st November 1979), further amends the Milk (Great Britain) Order 1977, 1977 Halsbury's Abridgment para. 1339 by revoking and replacing the Milk (Great Britain) (Amendment) Order 1979, para. 1325. The maximum prices for sale in Great Britain of raw milk for heat treatment are thus increased by 1.1 pence per litre from 1st November 1979.

1328

The Milk (Northern Ireland) (Amendment) Order 1979, S.I. 1979 No. 600 (in force on 1st June 1979), further amends the Milk (Northern Ireland) Order 1977, 1977 Halsbury's Abridgment para. 1340. The Order decreases by 2·486p per litre the maximum prices for the sale of raw milk for heat treatment in Northern Ireland with effect from 1st June 1979 and increases by 1½p per pint the maximum retail prices of milk on sale there from 3rd June 1979.

1329 Milk and dairies

The Milk and Dairies (General) (Amendment) Regulations 1979, S.I. 1979 No. 1567 (in force on 1st January 1979), amend the 1959 Regulations by converting (with minor adjustments in two instances) the references to temperatures in reg. 17 from degrees Fahrenheit to degrees Centigrade.

1330 Poultry meat

The Poultry Meat (Hygiene) (Amendment) Regulations 1979, S.I. 1979 No. 693 (in force on 18th July 1979), amend the Poultry Meat (Hygiene) Regulations 1976, 1976 Halsbury's Abridgment para. 1267, so as to implement the provisions of Council Directive (EEC) 78/50 on the universion chilling process and to implement the provisions of Council Directive (EEC) 77/27 on the health marking of large packages of fresh poultry meat. A limited number of other amendments include the clarification of the status of official veterinary surgeons and the requirement of twenty-four hours' notice of intended entry by an authorised officer to premises used solely as a private dwelling house.

1331   Preservatives in food

The Preservatives in Food Regulations 1979, S.I. 1979 No. 752 (in force on 31st July 1979), re-enact, with certain amendments, the Preservatives in Food Regulations 1975, 1975 Halsbury's Abridgment para. 1555.

1332   Price marking—food and drink on premises

See para. 1637.

1333   Prices—EEC requirements

See para. 1223.

1334   —— prohibition of repricing

The Food (Prohibition of Repricing) Order 1979, S.I. 1979 No. 660 (in force on 18th June 1979), amends the 1978 Order, 1978 Halsbury's Abridgment para. 1388. The new Order excludes from the provisions of the 1978 Order any increase in price which is solely attributable to a change in the value added tax chargeable.

1335   Sale—goods not of nature, substance or quality demanded—statutory defence

The purchaser of a can of strawberries which contained a black beetle complained to the food and drug authority. The authority charged the manufacturers with selling to the prejudice of the purchaser a can of strawberries which was not of the substance demanded, contrary to the Food and Drugs Act 1955, s. 2 (1). The manufacturers successfully contended that the presence of the beetle was an unavoidable consequence of the process of collection or preparation and established a defence under s. 3 (3) of the Act. The authority appealed. *Held*, the questions for consideration were whether the presence of the beetle had been a consequence of the process of preparation and collection and, if so, whether it had been unavoidable. The presence of the beetle could not, in its ordinary meaning, be said to be a consequence of that process. The appeal would be allowed.

GREATER MANCHESTER COUNCIL v LOCKWOOD FOODS LTD [1979] Crim LR 593 (Queen's Bench Division: LORD WIDGERY CJ, SHAW LJ and LLOYD J). *Smedleys Ltd v Breed* [1974] AC 839, HL, 1974 Halsbury's Abridgment para. 1434 followed.

1336   Slaughterhouses—conduct—European convention

The member states of the Council of Europe have concluded a Convention for the Protection of Animals for Slaughter (Strasbourg, 10th May 1979; published as European Treaty Series No. 102). The convention applies to domestic solipeds, ruminants, pigs, rabbits and poultry. Express provision is made in Chapter II (arts. 3 to 11) concerning the delivery of animals to slaughterhouses and their lairaging until slaughtered and, in Chapter III (arts. 12 to 19), in respect of their slaughtering. The contracting states are required to take the steps necessary to implement the convention (art. 2). The convention is open to signature by member states of the Council of Europe and of the European Economic Community. It will enter into force six months after the deposit of the fourth instrument of ratification, acceptance or approval by a member state of the Council of Europe (art. 20). An explanatory report on the convention has been published by the Council of Europe.

FOREIGN RELATIONS LAW

Halsbury's Laws of England (4th edn.), Vol. 18, paras. 1401–1908

1337   Article

Draft UK/US Civil Judgments Convention: A US View, Sheila Marshall (Convention on the recognition of foreign judgments on awards of damages arising from products liability claims): 128 NLJ 1199.

1338   Council of Europe—resolution relating to equality of spouses

The Committee of Ministers of the Council of Europe has adopted resolution (78) 37 on the Equality of Spouses in Civil Law. The resolution calls upon governments of member states to take all necessary steps to ensure that the civil law does not contain provisions putting one spouse in a more advantageous position than the other. In relation to personal matters the resolution refers, inter alia, to freedom of movement, pursuit of avocations and studies, and the choice of family residence and family name. In relation to property and financial matters the resolution refers, inter alia, to household expenses, maintenance, occupation of the family home, contracts of marriage, presumptions based upon sex relating to property, rights to property, dowry, and the provision of information to each spouse. In relation to spouses and their children the resolution refers, inter alia, to the family name of the children, equal rights and obligations as to the children, and the provision of rights and obligations in relation to children (on separation or the dissolution of marriage) without discrimination based on the sex of the parents. The resolution (dated 27th September 1978) is published by the Council of Europe together with an explanatory memorandum.

1339   Exchange control—contract contrary to Peruvian exchange regulations—enforceability

See *The American Accord, United City Merchants (Investments) Ltd v Royal Bank of Canada*, para. 1904.

1340   Human rights

See HUMAN RIGHTS.

1341   Immunities and privileges—immunity from civil jurisdiction—divorce petition—loss of immunity before summons heard

The parties were married in the United States of America and later became habitually resident in England. The husband, a diplomatic agent, issued a summons to strike out his wife's petition for divorce on the ground that he was immune from suit under the Diplomatic Privileges Act 1964. He subsequently ceased to be a diplomatic agent and returned to the USA, thereby losing his diplomatic immunity, before the summons was heard. *Held*, the petition was valid at the time of its issue, but could not be entertained whilst the husband relied on his diplomatic immunity. However, since, at the time of the hearing, the husband was no longer so immune, the procedural bar had been removed. The summons would be dismissed.

SHAW v SHAW [1979] 3 All ER 1 (Family Division: BALCOMBE J). *Empson v Smith* [1966] 1 QB 426, CA applied.

1342   —— International Oil Pollution Compensation Fund

A draft agreement has been negotiated by the government with the International Oil Pollution Compensation Fund setting out the immunities, privileges and facilities to be accorded to the fund by the United Kingdom, which is to host the fund. In particular, the fund is given legal personality and, subject to exceptions, is immune from jurisdiction and execution. Its archives are to be inviolable. Within the scope of its official activities, the fund is exempt from direct taxation and goods imported or exported by the fund in exercise of its official activities are exempt from customs and excise duties and other charges and from prohibitions and restrictions on imports and exports. Personal immunity is provided for representatives of the fund whilst exercising their official duties. The director of the fund (unless a citizen of the United Kingdom or a permanent resident) will be accorded the status of a diplomatic agent. Certain immunities are prescribed for staff of the fund. See the Draft Headquarters Agreement between the Government of the United Kingdom and the International Oil Pollution Compensation Fund (Cmnd. 7585).

1343 —— **international organisations**

The INMARSAT (Immunities and Privileges) Order 1979, S.I. 1979 No. 454 (in force on a date to be notified), confers the legal capacities of a body corporate and certain fiscal privileges on the International Maritime Satellite Organisation (INMARSAT).

1344 The INTELSAT (Immunities and Privileges) Order 1979, S.I. 1979 No. 911 (in force on a date to be notified) confers privileges and immunities on the International Telecommunications Satellite Organisation (INTELSAT), on representatives of its members, signatories of its Operating Agreement, its officers and on certain persons participating in arbitration proceedings. The Order revokes the INTELSAT (Immunities and Privileges) Order 1972.

1345 The International Oil Pollution Compensation Fund (Immunities and Privileges) Order 1979, S.I. 1979 No. 912 (in force on a date to be notified), confers privileges and immunities on the International Oil Pollution Compensation Fund, on representatives of its members, its officers and experts. The International Oil Pollution Compensation Fund (Immunities and Privileges) Order 1975, 1975 Halsbury's Abridgment para. 1571 is revoked.

1346 The Oslo and Paris Commissions (Immunities and Privileges) Order 1979, S.I. 1979 No. 914 (in force on a date to be notified) confers privileges and immunities upon the Oslo and Paris Commissions and their officers.

1347 By an exchange of notes between the United Kingdom government and the World Health Organisation, officials of the organisation (who are not citizens of the United Kingdom and colonies and not permanently resident in the United Kingdom) are, from a date on which the relevant United Kingdom legislation comes into operation, to enjoy exemptions whereby services rendered for the organisation will be deemed to be excepted from any employment in respect of which contributions or premiums are payable under United Kingdom social security legislation. See Cmnd. 7591.

Similarly, such exemptions are to be extended to staff members of the International Lead and Zinc Study Group when the group has established its own social security scheme or has joined that of another international organisation (subject to the staff members not being citizens of the United Kingdom and colonies and not being permanently resident in the United Kingdom). See Cmnd. 7592.

1348 **International Court of Justice—jurisdiction**

There is no rule of international law to preclude a joint communiqué issued by heads of government to the press following a conference from constituting an agreement to submit a dispute to arbitration or judicial settlement. Further, a continuing state of negotiations between the parties concerned does not impede the exercise of jurisdiction over the subject matter of the negotiations by the International Court of Justice. But in *Aegean Sea Continental Shelf Case (Greece v Turkey)* ICJ Reports 1978, p. 3, the Court of International Justice, having regard to the terms of a joint communiqué issued by the Prime Ministers of Greece and Turkey on 31st May 1975 and the context in which it was agreed and issued, ruled that it did not constitute an immediate commitment by the parties to accept unconditionally the unilateral submission of their dispute to the court.

1349   International Monetary Fund—consolidation of enactments

See International Monetary Fund Act 1979, para. 1921.

1350   Internationally Protected Persons Act 1978—commencement

The Internationally Protected Persons Act 1978 (Commencement) Order 1979, S.I. 1979 No. 455, brings the whole of the Internationally Protected Persons Act 1978, 1978 Halsbury's Abridgment para. 1411 into force on 24th May 1979.

1351   —— Guernsey

The Internationally Protected Persons Act 1978 (Guernsey) Order 1979, S.I. 1979 No. 573 (in force on 24th May 1979) extends the Internationally Protected Persons Act 1978, 1978 Halsbury's Abridgment para. 1411, to the Bailiwick of Guernsey with exceptions, adaptations and modifications.

1352   —— Isle of Man

The Internationally Protected Persons Act 1978 (Isle of Man) Order 1979, S.I. 1979 No. 574 (in force on 24th May 1979) extends the Internationally Protected Persons Act 1978, 1978 Halsbury's Abridgment para. 1411, to the Isle of Man with exceptions, adaptations and modifications.

1353   —— Jersey

The Internationally Protected Persons Act 1978 (Jersey) Order 1979, S.I. 1979 No. 575 (in force on 24th May 1979) extends the Internationally Protected Persons Act 1978, 1978 Halsbury's Abridgment para. 1411, to the Bailiwick of Jersey with exceptions, adaptations and modifications.

1354   —— overseas territories

The Internationally Protected Persons Act 1978 (Overseas Territories) Order 1979, S.I. 1979 No. 456 (in force on 24th May 1979), extends the 1978 Act, ss. 1, 2, 3, subject to exceptions, adaptations and modifications, to specified territories.

1355   Northwest Atlantic Fisheries Organisation

The parties to the Convention on Future Multilateral Cooperation in the Northwest Atlantic fisheries (concluded at Ottawa, 24th October to 31st December 1978; see Cmnd. 7569) have agreed to establish a Northwest Atlantic Fisheries Organisation. The object of the organisation is to contribute through consultation and co-operation to the optimum utilisation, rational management and conservation of the fishery resources in the defined conservation area. The organisation will comprise a general council, a scientific council, a fisheries commission and a secretariat. The convention entered into force on 1st January 1979.

1356   Sovereign immunity—act of state—doctrine of immunity

In *The I Congresso Del Partido* [1977] 1 Lloyd's Rep 536, 1977 Halsbury's Abridgment para. 1357, Goff J held that the owners of a ship (the Cuban Government) were immune from suit, by reason of sovereign immunity, in an action in rem by a company for damages for non-delivery of Chile-bound cargoes. In an appeal to the Court of Appeal from that decision three judges heard the case but on 10th October 1979 only two judgments were given and leave was therefore given to appeal to the House of Lords.

LORD DENNING MR allowed the appeal. The action by the Cuban Government in diverting the cargoes was a repudiative breach of contract and not an act of foreign policy. The purpose of the repudiation was irrelevant and the motive for the act could not alter its nature.

WALLER LJ upheld the decision of Goff J on the grounds that there was no contractual relationship between the Chilean company and the Cuban Government, and that the act of the latter was purely political, it not being in the commercial interest of Cuba to cease trading with Chile. The act was a foreign policy decision and was covered by the doctrine of sovereign immunity.

Sovereign immunity from suit is now restricted by the State Immunity Act 1978, 1978 Halsbury's Abridgment para. 1421.

1357   ——— ——— ——— **extent—state trading activities**

The Nigerian Ministry of Defence ordered a large quantity of cement from the plaintiffs. Payment was to be by irrevocable letter of credit and accordingly, a letter of credit was issued by an English bank on the advice of the Central Bank of Nigeria in April 1975. The English bank was put in considerable funds to meet the letter of credit, but the Central Bank failed to honour its obligation. In an action by the plaintiffs for damages the judge found in favour of the Central Bank, but an injunction was granted restraining the Central Bank from removing the funds out of the jurisdiction pending an appeal. On appeal by the plaintiffs, the defendants contended that this was not a case for an injunction in the light of the State Immunity Act 1978 and the United States Foreign Sovereign Immunities Act 1976, which provided that the property of a foreign central bank ought not to be taken in execution and that an injunction ought not to be issued so as to impair the dealings of a central bank; these statutes had altered the international law as stated in the *Trendtex* case (which was identical in all material respects to the instant case), that the Central Bank was not a mere organ of the State of Nigeria and that there was no sovereign immunity in regard to a commercial transaction of this nature. *Held,* (i) the 1978 Act did not apply retrospectively and did not, therefore, apply to the transaction in the instant case which took place before it came into force in November 1978; (ii) the 1976 Act did not apply at all because it could be argued that the funds were not being held by the Central Bank "for its own account" as required by that Act, but for the activities of government departments in Nigeria; (iii) the 1976 and 1978 Acts were not sufficient to alter the international law as stated in the *Trendtex* case, and that case was not decided per incuriam; (iv) in accordance with the decision in the *Trendtex* case, there was no sovereign immunity and the injunction should be continued pending an ultimate decision. The appeal would be allowed.

HISPANO AMERICANA MERCANTIL SA v CENTRAL BANK OF NIGERIA [1979] 2 Lloyd's Rep 277 (Court of Appeal: LORD DENNING MR, WALLER and CUMMING-BRUCE LJJ). *Trendtex Trading Corporation v Central Bank of Nigeria* [1977] 1 Lloyd's Rep 581, CA, 1977 Halsbury's Abridgment para. 1356 applied.

1358   —— **action in personam—doctrine of precedent—conflict of authorities**

An English company sought an indemnity in respect of a sum paid by it as guarantor of a Ugandan company subsequently acquired by the Ugandan Government. The latter pleaded sovereign immunity as a defence to the action. *Held,* there were conflicting decisions of the Court of Appeal on the question of sovereign immunity. It was therefore incumbent on the court to anticipate how the Court of Appeal would resolve the conflict. In *Trendtex Trading Corporation v Central Bank of Nigeria* [1977] 1 QB 527, 1977 Halsbury's Abridgment para. 1356, that court had modified the previous doctrine of absolute immunity and had restricted the doctrine of stare decisis. This conflicted with the previously established doctrine of precedent. The earlier doctrine had to be accorded more weight than the modified one, and accordingly the Ugandan Government would be given immunity from suit.

UGANDA CO (HOLDING) LTD v GOVERNMENT OF UGANDA [1979] 1 Lloyd's Rep 481 (Queen's Bench Division: DONALDSON J). *Thai-Europe Tapioca Services Ltd v Government of Pakistan* [1975] 3 All ER 961, CA, 1975 Halsbury's Abridgment para. 1577 applied.

Sovereign immunity from suit is now restricted to acts of a governmental nature by the State Immunity Act 1978, 1978 Halsbury's Abridgment para. 1421, which came into force on 22nd November 1978.

1359   State immunity—Austria

The State Immunity (Federal States) Order 1979, S.I. 1979 No. 457 (in force on 2nd May 1979) applies the provisions of Part I of the State Immunity Act 1978 to the constituent territories of the Republic of Austria, in accordance with paragraph 2 of Article 28 of the European Convention on State Immunity (Cmnd. 5081).

1360   —— dependent overseas territories

The State Immunity (Overseas Territories) Order 1979, S.I. 1979 No. 458 (in force on 2nd May 1979), extends the provisions of the State Immunity Act 1978, 1978 Halsbury's Abridgment para. 1421, with certain minor adaptations, to specified dependent territories.   This will enable effect to be given to the provisions of the European Convention on State Immunity (Cmnd. 5081), the International Convention for the Unification of Certain Rules concerning the Immunity of State-owned Ships (Cmnd. 5672) and the Supplementary Protocol thereto (Cmnd. 5673).

FORESTRY

Halsbury's Laws of England (4th edn.), Vol. 19, paras. 1–100

1361   Felling—exemption from restriction

The Forestry (Exceptions from Restriction of Felling) Regulations 1979, S.I. 1979 No. 792 (in force on 9th August 1979), revoke and re-enact the Forestry (Exceptions from Restriction of Felling) Regulations 1951, 1972 and 1974, as amended.   They omit the provision contained in the 1951 Regulations relating to the ascertainment of the cubic content of trees which is no longer required following the repeal of the relevant part of the Forestry Act 1967, s. 9 (6), by the Forestry Act 1979, para. 1363.   The Regulations provide for further exceptions from the application of the 1967 Act, s. 9 (1), relating to felling licences.

1362   —— procedure

The Forestry (Felling of Trees) Regulations 1979, S.I. 1979 No. 791 (in force on 9th August 1979), make provision for various procedural matters under the Forestry Act 1967.   They revoke and re-enact the Forestry (Felling of Trees) Regulations 1951, with one modification of substance; the provisions which relate to applications for a felling licence specify the information to be submitted on a form to be provided by the Forestry Commission on request.

1363   Forestry Act 1979

The Forestry Act 1979 restates the power of the Forestry Commissioners to make grants and loans, and provides for the metrication of enactments relating to forestry and forest lands.   The Act received the royal assent on 29th March 1979 and came into force on 29th May 1979: s. 3.

Section 1 empowers the Forestry Commissioners, with the approval of the Treasury, to make grants and loans out of the Forestry Fund to owners and lessees of land for forestry purposes.   Section 2 and Sch. 1 substitute metric units of measurement for imperial units in the Forestry Act 1967 and empower the Commissioners by regulations to amend other forestry enactments substituting metric units.   Section 3 relates to citation, commencement and extent.   Schedule 2 lists the repeals to the 1967 Act.

FRIENDLY SOCIETIES

Halsbury's Laws of England (4th edn.), Vol. 19, paras. 101–400

1364   **Fees**

The Friendly Societies (Fees) Regulations 1979, S.I. 1979 No. 1555 (in force on 1st January 1980), increase the fees to be paid for matters to be transacted, and for the inspection of documents, under the Friendly Societies Act 1974.

1365   —— **superannuation and other trust funds**

See TRUSTS.

FUEL AND ENERGY

Halsbury's Laws of England (4th edn.), Vol. 16, paras. 1–490 and
Vol. 19, paras. 401–600

1366   **Coal industry—limit on grants**

The Coal Industry (Limit on Grants) Order 1979, S.I. 1979 No. 1011 (in force on 7th August 1979), increases the limit on the aggregate amount of the grants which may be made to the National Coal Board and other producers of coal and coke to £175 million, the maximum permitted by the Coal Industry Act 1977, s. 5 (3).

1367   **Fuel and electricity—control**

The Fuel and Electricity (Control) Act 1973 (Continuation) (Jersey and Isle of Man) Order 1979, S.I. 1979 No. 1313 (in force on 20th October 1979), continues the Fuel and Electricity (Control) Act 1973 in force in Jersey and the Isle of Man for one year from 30th November 1979.

1368   **Gas—meters**

The Measuring Instruments (EEC Requirements) (Gas Volume Meters) (Amendment) Regulations 1979, S.I. 1979, No. 1224 (in force on 25th October 1979) amend the 1975 Regulations, 1975 Halsbury's Abridgment para. 1612 in consequence of the amendment to Council Directive (EEC) 71/318 by Commission Directive (EEC) 78/365.

1369   The Measuring Instruments (EEC Requirements) (Gas Volume Meters) (Fees) (Amendment) Regulations 1979, S.I. 1979 No. 1257 (in force on 30th October 1979) amend the 1975 Regulations, 1975 Halsbury's Abridgment para. 1613 also in consequence of the amendment to Council Directive (EEC) 71/318 by Commission Directive (EEC) 78/365.

1370   —— **rateable values**

The Gas Hereditaments (Rateable Values) (Amendment) Order 1979, S.I. 1979 No. 1516 (in force on 24th November 1979), amends the Gas Hereditaments (Rateable Values) Order 1976, 1976 Halsbury's Abridgment para. 1304. The 1979 Order substitutes a new formula for apportioning the total rateable value of all gas hereditaments occupied by the British Gas Corporation in all rating areas among the hereditaments in each rating area.

1371   **Hydrocarbon oils—excise duty**

See Hydrocarbon Oil Duties Act 1979, para. 771.

1372   Oil—oil refinery—liability of owners in nuisance—defence of statutory authority

A villager brought an action contending that the odours, vibration, noise and flames caused by a particular oil refinery nearby constituted a nuisance or that the refining company was guilty of negligence in the method of construction and operation of the refinery. The company resisted the claim by a plea of statutory authority under the Gulf Oil Refining Act 1965. The preliminary point of law for the court to decide was whether the company could rely on the Act as having authorised the construction and use of the particular refinery. *Held*, the defence of statutory authority to a claim for nuisance developed in the railway age and a series of cases had established that where the use of the railway was authorised by statute, no action for nuisance would lie. The question of whether the company had been authorised to use the refinery depended therefore upon statutory interpretation. The 1965 Act merely authorised a grant of power to acquire land for the purposes of constructing an unspecified oil refinery, but preserved the planning authority's powers in respect of the proposed change of use of the land acquired from agricultural to industrial. A statute which granted powers to acquire land did not confer statutory authority to construct and use anything built on the land. Accordingly there was no statutory authority to use this particular refinery. The company had merely been granted liberty to build on the land such refinery as they wished, subject only to planning permission and was not entitled to rely on the defence of statutory authority in respect of any nuisance or negligence on their part.

ALLEN v GULF OIL REFINING LTD [1979] 3 WLR 523 (Court of Appeal: LORD DENNING MR and CUMMING-BRUCE LJ). *R v Pease* (1832) 4 B & Ad 30, Jones v Festiniog Railway Co (1868) LR 3 QB 733 and *Hammersmith and City Railway Co v Brand* (1869) LR 4 HL 171, HL applied.

1373   Paraffin—maximum retail prices

The Paraffin (Maximum Retail Prices) (Third Amendment) Order 1979, S.I. 1979 No. 193 (in force on 27th February 1979), further amended the Paraffin (Maximum Retail Prices) Order 1976, 1976 Halsbury's Abridgment para. 1314, by increasing the maximum retail prices for the supply of paraffin intended for use in portable domestic oil burners.

This Order was subsequently revoked: see now para. 1374.

**1374   **The Paraffin (Maximum Retail Prices) (Revocation) Order 1979, S.I. 1979 No. 797 (in force on 12th July 1979), revokes the Paraffin (Maximum Retail Prices) Order 1976, 1976 Halsbury's Abridgment para. 1314 as amended, which imposed maximum retail prices in respect of the supply of paraffin intended for use in portable domestic oil burners.

This Order was subsequently revoked: see now para. 1375.

**1375   **The Paraffin (Maximum Retail Prices) (Revocation) (No. 2) Order 1979, S.I. 1979 No. 1375 (in force on 31st October 1979), effects the revocation of the Paraffin (Maximum Retail Prices) (Revocation) Order 1979, para. 1374. The latter order revoked the Paraffin (Maximum Retail Prices) Order 1976, 1976 Halsbury's Abridgment para. 1314 and subsequent amending orders.

**1376   **The Paraffin (Maximum Retail Prices) (Revocation) (No. 3) Order 1979, S.I. 1979 No. 1383 (in force on 31st October 1979), revokes the Paraffin (Maximum Retail Prices) Order 1976, 1976 Halsbury's Abridgment para. 1314, which imposed maximum retail prices in respect of the supply of paraffin intended for use in portable domestic oil burners, and subsequent amending orders. These orders were revoked earlier by the Paraffin (Maximum Retail Prices) Revocation Order 1979, para. 1374, which has itself been revoked by the Paraffin (Maximum Retail Prices) (Revocation) (No. 2) Order 1979, para. 1375.

1377   **Petrol—lead content**

The Motor Fuel (Lead Content of Petrol) (Amendment) Regulations 1979, S.I. 1979 No. 1 (in force on 1st February 1979), amend the Motor Fuel (Lead Content of Petrol) Regulations 1976, 1976 Halsbury's Abridgment para. 1316. The Regulations (which apply to England, Wales, Scotland and Northern Ireland), specify a new method of testing petrol and reduce the maximum permitted amount of lead per litre of petrol (in accordance with Council Directive (EEC) 78/611, 1978 Halsbury's Abridgment para. 1197).

GIFT AND ESTATE TAXATION

Halsbury's Laws of England (4th edn.), Vol. 19, paras. 601–926

1378   **Articles**

Capital Transfer Tax and Stamp Duty, P. Nellist (stamp duty implications of the more common capital transfer tax transfers): 123 Sol Jo 135.

Exercises in Capital Transfer Tax, H.S.A. Macnair: ACCOUNTANT, 8th March 1979, p. 294.

Loans by Trustees, Barry McCutcheon (on the capital transfer tax effect of loans from a discretionary trust being made at an interest rate lower than the commercial one, or of use made of property at less than commercial rent). [1979] BTR 246.

Payment of CTT by Instalments, B. D. McCutcheon (a discussion of the legislation governing the payment of tax by instalments which attempts to clarify the conditions): Taxation, 15th September 1978, p. 414.

1379   **Capital transfer tax—double taxation relief—arrangements— South Africa**

The Double Taxation Relief (Taxes on Estates of Deceased Persons and on Gifts) (Republic of South Africa) Order 1979, S.I. 1979 No. 576 (made on 23rd May 1979 and to take effect in respect of taxable transfers in the United Kingdom and taxable donations in South Africa arising on or after 1st January 1978), makes provision for taxation of a transferor by the country in which he is domiciled and specifies the type of property which may be taxed by the other country.

1380   —— —— —— **United States of America**

A convention for the avoidance of double taxation and the prevention of fiscal evasion with respect to taxes on estates of deceased persons and gifts between the United Kingdom and the United States of America was signed in London on 19th October 1978. When it comes into operation it will replace the convention signed in Washington in 1945. In the United Kingdom it applies to capital transfer tax and in the United States to Federal gift tax and the Federal estate tax, including the tax on generation-skipping transfers. The convention makes transitional provision for relief in the case of deaths before 27th March 1981. Instruments of ratification have not yet been exchanged.

For the text of the convention, see Cmnd. 7442.

1381   —— —— **Convention—United States of America**

The Double Taxation Relief (Taxes on Estates of Deceased Persons and on Gifts) (United States of America) Order 1979, S.I. 1979 No. 1454 (made on 14th November 1979 and to take effect in respect of capital transfer tax in the United Kingdom and estate and gift taxes in the United States with effect from 10th November 1979), makes provision for taxation of a transferor by the country in which he is domiciled and specifies the type of property which may be taxed by the other country.

1382   —— settled property—interest in possession—exempt securities—whether securities excluded property

A fund consisting of exempt Treasury stock was held on discretionary trust by non-resident trustees for beneficiaries resident and domiciled outside the United Kingdom and certain United Kingdom charities.   The trustees exercised their power of appointment by paying the income of the fund to the non-resident beneficiaries, who immediately became entitled to an interest in possession in the stock.   The Inland Revenue Commissioners claimed that capital transfer tax was payable as there had been a capital distribution under the Finance Act 1975, Sch. 5, para. 6 (2). However, Sch. 5, para. 11 (11) provides that the charge to tax does not apply to excluded property.   The trustees contended that the stock was excluded property within the meaning of the 1975 Act, Sch. 7, para. 3 (1) (b) or 3 (2).   Under Sch. 7, para. 3 (1) (b) excluded property includes securities issued by the Treasury which are exempt from tax as long as they are beneficially owned by a person neither domiciled nor ordinarily resident in the United Kingdom, if such securities are settled property and the person is beneficially entitled to an interest in possession in them.   Under Sch. 7, para 3 (2) if securities are settled and no interest in possession subsists in them, the condition in para. 3 (1) (b) is treated as satisfied if all known persons who might benefit from the settled property are neither domiciled nor ordinarily resident in the United Kingdom. *Held,* (i) the stock was not excluded property under Sch. 7, para. 3 (i) (b) since at the relevant time immediately before appointment there was no interest in possession in the stock.   (ii) However, the stock was excluded property under Sch. 7, para. 3 (2) since at the relevant time it was subject to a discretionary trust whose only individual beneficiaries were not domiciled or resident in the United Kingdom.   Had those trusts failed, the stock would have been held for certain United Kingdom based charities.   However, as the trustees of those charities could not become beneficially entitled they were not known persons who might benefit from the settled property within Sch. 7, para. 3 (2) so the fact that they were based in the United Kingdom did not affect the status of the stock.   Accordingly, as the stock was excluded property there was no charge to tax.

VON ERNST & CIE SA v INLAND REVENUE COMRS [1980] STC 111 (Court of Appeal: BUCKLEY, BRIDGE and TEMPLEMAN LJJ).   Decision of Browne-Wilkinson J [1979] 1 WLR 1325 reversed.

1383   —— —— meaning

The Inland Revenue have issued a Statement of Practice SP10/79 dated 15th August 1979 setting out the view currently taken by the Board of Inland Revenue of the effect for capital transfer tax purposes of the existence and exercise of a power for trustees to allow a beneficiary to occupy a house.   The existence of such a power is not regarded as excluding any interest in possession in the property.   Where there is no interest in possession the exercise of the power will not be regarded as creating one if the effect is to allow non-exclusive occupation or to create a contractual tenancy for full consideration.   Nor will an interest in possession arise on the creation of a lease for a term or a periodic tenancy for less than full consideration, although this will normally give rise to a charge for tax under the Finance Act 1975, Sch. 5, para. 6 (3).   However, if the power is wide enough to cover the creation of an exclusive or joint right of residence, albeit revocable, for a definite or indefinite period, and is exercised with the intention of providing a particular beneficiary with a permanent home, the exercise of the power will normally be regarded as creating an interest in possession.   If in exercise of a power a lease for life for less than full consideration is granted, this will also be regarded as creating an interest in possession.

1384   —— —— whether affected by power of accumulation

Under the terms of a settlement, trustees held the capital and income of the trust fund for such of the settlor's daughters as attained twenty-one or married under that age, subject to a power of accumulation vested in the trustees.   All had attained twenty-one by February 1974 and in 1976 the trustees made an appointment to one of the daughters.   The Revenue claimed that the trustees were liable to capital transfer tax under the Finance Act 1975, Sch. 5, para. 6 (2) since the daughter was not entitled to an interest in possession before the appointment was made. The trustees contended that her interest became an interest in possession in February 1974. *Held*, an interest in possession meant a right of present enjoyment of trust property. The daughter had a vested interest before 1976 and was entitled to enjoyment of the trust income despite the trustees' power of accumulation. Therefore, as she already had an interest in possession, the 1976 appointment was not subject to capital transfer tax.

PEARSON v INLAND REVENUE COMRS [1979] 3 All ER 7 (Court of Appeal: BUCKLEY, BRIDGE and TEMPLEMAN LJJ). Decision of Fox J [1979] 1 All ER 273, 1978 Halsbury's Abridgment para. 1442, affirmed.

1385　　　—— interest on unpaid tax

The Capital Transfer Tax (Interest on Unpaid Tax) Order 1979, S.I. 1979 No. 1688 (in force on 1st January 1980), increases from the 1st January the annual rates of interest on unpaid capital transfer tax from 6 per cent to 9 per cent where interest is payable under the Finance Act 1975, Sch. 4 para. 19 and from 9 per cent to 12 per cent in other cases.

1386　　　—— transfer of value—life assurance premiums

Where a person pays a life assurance premium for the benefit of someone else, this may constitute a transfer of value for capital transfer tax purposes. From 6th April 1979 there is in many cases a right for the payer to make a deduction from the premium in accordance with the system of relief introduced by the Finance Act 1976, s. 34. The Inland Revenue consider that where the payment of such a premium is a transfer of value, the amount of the transfer is the net amount of the premium after any deduction made under the authority of the 1976 Act, Sch. 4 para. 5, or the gross premium where it is paid without deduction: Inland Revenue Press Release dated 17th January 1979.

1387　　　Estate duty—exemption—member of armed forces—whether death caused by war wound—effect of recent decision

In *Barty-King v Ministry of Defence* [1979] 2 All ER 80, 1978 Halsbury's para. 1443, it was held that there did not have to be a direct pathological or physiological connection between a war wound and the cause of death to entitle exemption to be claimed from estate duty (and now capital transfer tax). In refusing a certificate in that case the Defence Council had applied too strict a criterion. In a written reply to a Parliamentary question the Defence Secretary has stated that, following the decision in that case, he had authorised a review of previous unsuccessful applications for certificates. Each case in respect of which papers are still held would be reconsidered and, in appropriate cases, certificates would now be issued. In cases where papers have not been retained (particularly cases where the original applications were made more than ten years previously) it will be necessary to make fresh application with the necessary supporting evidence to the Ministry of Defence (Legal Secretariat). If, following this review, a certificate is issued in any case any estate duty or capital transfer tax paid in respect of the deceased's estate (including any settled fund in which he had a life interest) will be repaid with interest. See Times, 27th November 1979.

1388　　　—— interest on unpaid duty

The Estate Duty (Interest on Unpaid Duty) Order 1979, S.I. 1979 No. 1690 (in force on 1st January 1980), provides that from the 1st January 1980 interest on unpaid estate duty is now payable at 9 per cent, under the various provisions which impose a fixed rate of interest. The limit on the discretionary rate of interest which may be charged where payment of estate duty is postponed on grounds of hardship is correspondingly altered by substituting 9 per cent for 6 per cent (the previous rate).

1389   —— **property deemed to pass—assets of company—amount of benefits accruing to deceased from company**

The deceased, a shareholder in a company, died in 1959 and the Crown claimed that under the Finance Act 1940, s. 46 (1), estate duty was payable on a proportion of the assets of the company. The duty was to be calculated by taking the aggregate amount of benefits accruing to the deceased, dividing it by the net income of the company and applying the fraction to the company's assets. The company conceded this but contended that the "benefits accruing to the deceased" consisted only of dividends actually paid to him. The Crown contended that the benefits should be deemed to include the increase in the value of the shares held by the deceased resulting from the non-distribution by the company of its income. At first instance the court found for the Crown. On appeal, *held*, dismissing the appeal, by s. 47 (1) "benefits accruing to the deceased" included any income of the company which the deceased was entitled to receive or could have become entitled to receive. By s. 58 (3) (e) if the receipt by the company of income mentioned in s. 47 (1) operated to increase the value of property in which the deceased was beneficially interested, then the deceased was deemed to have received income to the amount of that increase. By s. 47 (1) the increase was a benefit accruing to the deceased, and included in the aggregate under s. 46 (1).

INLAND REVENUE COMRS V STANDARD INDUSTRIAL TRUST LTD [1979] STC 372 (Court of Appeal: ORR, ORMROD and TEMPLEMAN LJJ). Decision of Megarry V-C [1977] STC 330, 1977 Halsbury's Abridgment para. 1381 affirmed.

1390   —— **property passing on death—settled property—discretionary power to accumulate trust income**

Scotland

A settlor directed trustees to apply, during the trust period which covered the lives of his children and the survivor of them, the whole of the income of the trust fund in such a manner as they might think fit for the benefit of the beneficiaries. The trustees were also given a discretionary power to accumulate any part or the whole of the income. The settlor died before the trust period expired. The trustees had accumulated the whole of the income accruing to the trust fund from the time of its creation until the settlor's death. The Inland Revenue Commissioners claimed that the power to accumulate was void beyond the life of the settlor by virtue of the restrictions on the accumulation of income corresponding to the Law of Property Act 1925, s. 164. This rendered estate duty payable on the whole of the trust fund on the death of the settlor under the Finance Act 1894, s. 2 (1) (b). On appeal, the trustees contended that the restrictions on accumulation did not render unlawful any discretionary power to accumulate beyond the permitted period if that power was one that the trustees were not obliged to exercise. *Held*, the restrictions were designed to prevent the accumulation of income for longer than the permitted period and it did not matter that, in this case, there was only a power, and not a duty, to accumulate. Accordingly, on the death of the settlor there had been a determination of the power to accumulate causing estate duty to be payable on the whole of the trust fund. The appeal would be dismissed.

BAIRD V LORD ADVOCATE [1979] 2 All ER 28 (House of Lords: LORD DIPLOCK, LORD EDMUND-DAVIES, LORD FRASER OF TULLYBELTON, LORD RUSSELL OF KILLOWEN and LORD KEITH OF KINKEL). Decision of Inner House [1978] STC 282, 1978 Halsbury's Abridgment para. 1444 affirmed in part. See further 129 NLJ 247.

1391   **Finance (No. 2) Act 1979**

See para. 2247.

1392   **Legitimate avoidance of tax—transfer of property by deed—common intention of parties to avoid tax—whether bar to rectification of deed**

See *Re Slocock's Will Trusts*, para. 1891.

GIFTS

Halsbury's Laws of England (4th edn.), Vol. 20, paras. 1–100

1393   Article

Mental Capacity to Make a Gift by Deed, P. K. Virdi (discussion on *Re Beaney* [1978] 2 All ER 595, 1977 Halsbury's Abridgment para. 1387): 9 Fam Law 174.

1394   Gift to unincorporated association—validity

See *Re Grant's Will Trusts*, para. 3096.

GUARANTEE AND INDEMNITY

Halsbury's Laws of England (4th edn.), Vol. 20, paras. 101–400

1395   Guarantee—construction—effect of debtors' repudiation of contract

The plaintiffs made a shipbuilding contract with the buyers. The contract was guaranteed by the defendants who undertook to pay any sums due under the contract in the event of the buyers' default. The buyers defaulted in payment and the plaintiffs rescinded the contract and claimed under the guarantee. *Held*, on its true construction, the guarantee imposed a liability on the defendants to pay the amount due if the buyers defaulted. The defendants were not freed from their obligation to pay past unpaid instalments and their liability remained unaffected by the plaintiffs' rescission. The plaintiffs' claim would be upheld.

HYUNDAI HEAVY INDUSTRIES CO V PAPADOPOULOS [1979] 1 Lloyd's Rep 130 (Court of Appeal: ROSKILL, GEOFFREY LANE and BRIDGE LJJ). *Hyundai Shipbuilding and Heavy Industries Co Ltd v Pournaras* [1978] 2 Lloyd's Rep 502, CA, para. 1396 applied.

1396   —— —— —— extent of guarantors' right of set-off

The terms of four shipbuilding contracts provided for payment by the buyers in five instalments. The payments were secured by letters of guarantee in which the guarantors undertook to pay any sums due under the contract in the event of the buyers' default. When the buyers failed to pay the full amount due under the first two instalments the yard owners chose to treat the contracts as ended and brought a claim for payment under the letters of guarantee. *Held*, on its true construction the guarantee imposed a liability on the guarantors to pay the amounts due if the buyers defaulted. That liability was not reduced either because the yard owners had accepted the buyers' wrongful repudiation or because the guarantors had little hope of reclaiming the money from the buyers. Nor did the guarantors have a right of set-off in respect of any sum which the yard owners might obtain from the buyers in an action for damages for breach of contract. The yard owners' claim would be upheld.

HYUNDAI SHIPBUILDING AND HEAVY INDUSTRIES CO LTD V POURNARAS [1978] 2 Lloyd's Rep 502 (Court of Appeal: STEPHENSON and ROSKILL LJJ).

1397   —— —— survival of guarantor's liability after that of principal debtor

The plaintiff, a British company, deposited money with the defendant bank's branch in East Pakistan as a guarantee for loans made by the bank to an East Pakistani company. When East Pakistan became Bangladesh, the government took over all abandoned property including that of the company, and following the nationalisation of the banks the national bank acquired the defendant bank's right to repayment of the loan. The plaintiff claimed that, as the bank was no longer entitled to repayment of the loan, it was entitled to the return of the deposit. The bank contended that the letter of lien which set up the guarantee gave them a right of set-off against the deposit in the absence of repayment by the East Pakistani company. *Held*, a guarantor normally ceased to be liable after the corresponding obligation of the principal debtor had been extinguished, but on true construction of the letter of lien in this case the plaintiff had become the principal debtor when the East Pakistani company's liability had ceased. Accordingly the bank was entitled to maintain its right of set-off and the plaintiff could not claim return of the deposit.

GENERAL PRODUCE CO v UNITED BANK LTD [1979] 2 Lloyd's Rep 255 (Queen's Bench Division: LLOYD J).

1398   —— enforceability—condition precedent

Canada

The appellant guaranteed a bank loan made to a third party for the purchase of convertible bonds, on the understanding that the bonds would be deposited with the bank as security. The bonds were never deposited, but the bank continued to deal with the third party. The third party defaulted and the bank claimed under the guarantee. The appellant unsuccessfully contended that the deposit of the bonds was a condition precedent to the guarantee being used by the bank. On appeal, *held*, the deposit of the bonds with the bank was a term of the loan agreement, and the bank, by waiving the deposit of the bonds and entering into further transactions with the third party, had altered the original agreement without the appellant's knowledge and consent. The appeal would be allowed.

ROYAL BANK OF CANADA v GIRGULIS [1979] 3 WWR 451 (Court of Appeal of Saskatchewan).

1399   —— mutual guarantee—mutuality of obligation—lack of mutuality—effect

In 1964 a parent company and its subsidiary gave a mutual guarantee to a bank whereby each company undertook to guarantee the indebtedness of the other. In 1967, with the object of extending the guarantee to a further three subsidiaries, a memorandum was executed on behalf of all five companies and indorsed on the original guarantee, thus creating an effective and binding mutual guarantee between those companies. A sixth company later joined the group and, again with the object of including it in the existing guarantee, its name was added to the 1967 memorandum, which was executed on its behalf, although no fresh signatures were obtained from the first five companies. The sixth company subsequently contended that the guarantee, being conditional on mutuality, did not create liability in respect of the indebtedness of the other companies of the group, since the latter had not bound themselves to guarantee the indebtedness of the sixth company. This contention was upheld by the trial judge, but a majority of the Court of Appeal reversed that decision and the company appealed. *Held*, the 1967 memorandum did not, as a matter of construction, create the necessary mutual liability in respect of the first five companies and the sixth. Further, although the group of companies was treated financially as one entity by virtue of the activities of the financial director of the parent company who was also financial advisor to the group, it was clear that in circumstances such as the present involving creditors, the separate legal existence of the constituent companies had to be respected. Thus, in the absence of the necessary contractual act or document as required by the Statute of Frauds 1677, s. 4, the sixth company was not bound by the mutual guarantee. The appeal would be allowed.

FORD AND CARTER LTD v MIDLAND BANK LTD (1979) 23rd May (unreported) (House of Lords: LORD WILBERFORCE, LORD SALMON, LORD EDMUND-DAVIES, LORD FRASER OF TULLYBELTON and LORD KEITH OF KINKEL).

1400   —— **payment under guarantee—reimbursement under counter-guarantee—effect on guarantor's subrogation rights against debtor**

A loan made by a Dutch bank to a Dutch subsidiary of an English company was guaranteed by the plaintiffs, English merchant bankers, who took a counter-guarantee from the English parent company. On the default of the Dutch company the plaintiffs paid the Dutch bank under their guarantee and called upon the English company to pay under the counter-guarantee. The English company was unable to meet the demand, however, and the plaintiffs therefore made a loan of the requisite amount, repayable six months later with interest, to enable payment to be made. Subsequently, the plaintiffs sued the Dutch company for the amount paid under the guarantee, on the ground that, having paid the Dutch bank, they were subrogated to all the latter's rights against the company. *Held*, although the plaintiffs had obtained subrogation rights against the defendants, those rights had been transferred to the English company by operation of law when that company met its liabilities under the counter-guarantee, albeit with the aid of a loan by the plaintiffs. Accordingly, the plaintiffs' claim failed.

BROWN SHIPLEY AND CO LTD v AMALGAMATED INVESTMENT (EUROPE) BV [1979] 1 Lloyd's Rep 488 (Queen's Bench Division: DONALDSON J).

1401   **Guarantor—liability of guarantor—arbitration clause in charter-party—whether guarantor bound by award**

The plaintiffs made an agreement with the defendant for the sale and lease back, by means of a time charter, of the plaintiffs' vessel. The agreement was contained in a contract, bill of sale and an addendum containing an arbitration clause which provided that the defendant was to insure the vessel for not less than the market value and the proceeds of insurance which exceeded the minimum amount was to be shared equally by the parties. In the event the defendant insured the vessel for more than the market value. On completion of the agreement the defendant gave the plaintiffs a general personal guarantee. During the course of a voyage the vessel was wrecked and the defendant claimed the full insurance sum paid. He was not paid the total amount because the plaintiffs claimed a share in the proceeds of insurance but received no satisfaction. The matter was referred to arbitration and the plaintiffs were awarded the sum requested. The plaintiffs never received the sum and issued a writ for payment of the award. The plaintiffs claimed (i) it was an implied term of the contract contained in the addendum that a party would pay any sum awarded by an arbitration tribunal established pursuant to the agreement and the defendant had guaranteed that he would honour the award (ii) the defendant had insured the vessel for more than the market value and therefore in accordance with the agreement had to pay the plaintiffs half the balance. *Held*, (i) general words in a guarantee guaranteeing the due performance of all the obligations of the debtor did not of themselves have the effect that the surety was bound by the arbitration award even where that award arose out of a clause in the agreement containing the obligations guaranteed. (ii) The addendum conferred on the plaintiffs a right to an equal share in any excess of the market price of the vessel over the minimum in the event of a sale. The intention was therefore that the plaintiffs should receive a comparable amount in the event of a sharing of the proceeds of insurance upon a total loss. The plaintiffs would be awarded the requested sum.

THE VASSO, BRUNS v COLOCOTRONIS [1979] 2 Lloyd's Rep 412 (Queen's Bench Division; ROBERT GOFF J). *Re Kitchin* (1881) 17 Ch D 688 applied.

1402   —— **mortgage of husband's and wife's property to secure husband's debt—whether husband and wife co-debtors**

See *Re Berry (A Bankrupt)*, para. 219.

HEALTH AND SAFETY AT WORK

Halsbury's Laws of England (4th edn.), Vol. 20, paras. 401–801

1403   Control of working environment—air pollution, noise and vibration

Convention No. 148 (concerning the protection of workers against occupational hazards in the working environment due to air pollution, noise and vibration) of the International Labour Conference (63rd session, 1977) sets out, inter alia, principles for the protection of workers against these occupational hazards and requires national authorities to establish criteria for determining the dangers of exposure and, where appropriate, the stipulation of exposure limits. The working environment is to be kept as free as possible from such hazards by technical measures applicable to new and existing plants or processes. Where the hazards are not brought within acceptable limits, personal protective equipment must be provided and maintained. The health of workers exposed to such hazards must be supervised. Recommendation No. 156 (dealing with the same subject-matter) supplements the measures referred to in the convention. The government has announced that it proposes to ratify Convention No. 148 and accept Recommendation No. 156 so far as they relate to air pollution on the basis of existing legislation; but it does not intend to extend its acceptance of the provisions relating to noise and vibration until the Health and Safety Commission is satisfied that the requirements in relation to these hazards are fully met. See International Labour Conference: Proposals by Her Majesty's Government in the United Kingdom on two Conventions and two Recommendations adopted at the 63rd Session (1977) of the International Labour Conference (Cmnd 7420).

1404   Dangerous machinery—machinery on loan—duty of bailor

See *Pivovaroff v Chernabaeff*, para. 1957.

1405   Dangerous substances—asbestos

The Health and Safety Commission has published a report (Asbestos: Report of the Advisory Committee, HMSO) recommending stricter standards to be applied to processes involving the use of asbestos on the grounds of health. The recommendations include an obligation on industries using asbestos to seek alternative material; a requirement to reduce exposure to asbestos dust to the practical minimum; a reduction in the limit on the amount of asbestos in the air in factories; a ban on all new uses of blue asbestos; and a requirement that imported raw asbestos be carried only in enclosed, air-tight containers. See the Financial Times, 25th October 1979.

1406   Employer—duty of care—duty to fence machinery—whether machinery being cleaned is being "worked"

Scotland
An employee engaged in building operations was injured when he came into contact with a dangerous part of machinery. At the time the machinery was being cleaned, but the process necessitated it being kept in motion. On a charge of failing securely to fence the dangerous part of the machinery under the Construction (General Provisions) Regulations 1961, the employers contended that the machinery was being cleaned at the relevant time and not being "used" or "worked" for the purpose of the regulations. *Held*, cleaning the machine was an integral part of its normal daily working. The word "works" meant set in motion and included any operation necessary for the activation of the machine.

SMITH v W. AND J. R. WATSON LTD 1977 SC 52 (High Court of Justiciary).

1407 —— —— **whether safe system employed—whether contributory negligence by employee**

The plaintiff, who was employed as a boatswain on the defendant's vessel, was injured when he fell off a ladder to the floor in the hold of the ship. He had been holding the ladder steady whilst another employee mounted the ladder to clean a platform. The other employee had been drinking and the plaintiff, fearing for his safety, also mounted the ladder to try and prevent him falling. The ladder swayed and the plaintiff fell from it. In a claim for damages for personal injuries, *held*, a reasonable employer would have provided a secure method of lashing the ladder and would have provided safety harnesses. The plaintiff was not guilty of contributory negligence as the system was common practice and was not objected to by the officers. The danger to the other employee far outweighed the small risk the plaintiff took in helping him. Damages would therefore be awarded.

O'KEEFE v JOHN STEWART & CO SHIPPING LTD [1979] 1 Lloyd's Rep 182 (Queen's Bench Division: KENNETH JONES J). See further 123 Sol Jo 383.

1408   Explosives Act 1875—exemptions

The Explosives Act 1875 (Exemptions) Regulations 1979, S.I. 1979 No. 1378 (in force on 31st December 1979), provide for the Health and Safety Executive to grant exemptions from any requirement or prohibition imposed by the Explosives Act 1875, Parts I (except ss. 30–32) and II or by any regulation or order made under those provisions or under s. 83 of the Act. Conditions may be attached by the Health and Safety Executive to any such exemption which is only granted if the Executive is satisfied that the health and safety of persons likely to be affected by the exemption and the security of the explosives will not be prejudiced in consequence of it.

1409   Fees for medical examinations

The Health and Safety (Fees for Medical Examinations) Regulations 1979, S.I. 1979 No. 1553 (in force on 7th January 1980), fix the fees payable by employers to the Health and Safety Executive for work done by employment medical advisers appointed under the Health and Safety at Work etc. Act 1974, s. 56 (1) for conducting various medical examinations of employees under or by virtue of the Factories Act 1961.

1410   Industrial diseases—pneumoconiosis—workers' compensation

See Pneumoconiosis etc. (Workers' Compensation) Act 1979, para. 2650.

1411   Petroleum—licensing authority

The Petroleum (Consolidation) Act 1928 (Enforcement) Regulations 1979, S.I. 1979 No. 427 (in force on 1st July 1979), provide that a petroleum-spirit licensing authority, other than the Health and Safety Executive, will be the enforcing authority in its area for the Petroleum (Consolidation) Act 1928 and for instruments made under that Act, except for bye-laws to the extent that they contain provision for their own enforcement.

1412   Safety—provision of signs

Commission Directive (EEC) 79/640 (OJ No. L183, 19.7.79) amends the Annexes to Council Directive (EEC) 77/576, 1977 Halsbury's Abridgment para. 1396, on the provision of safety signs at places of work by prescribing a formula for the determination of the dimensions of safety signs and providing for a new sign warning of the presence of laser beams. Member states are required to adopt the necessary national implementing legislation by 1st January 1981.

HIGHWAYS, STREETS AND BRIDGES

Halsbury's Laws of England (3rd edn.), Vol. 19, paras. 1–822

1413   Diversion order—diversion of footpath—powers of local authority and Secretary of State

A developer obtained planning permission for a housing development on land through which a public footpath ran. Under the Town and Country Planning Act 1971, s. 209, the Secretary of State is empowered to authorise diversions of highways where he is satisfied that a diversion is necessary to enable development to be carried out in accordance with planning permission granted under the Act. Section 210 empowers local authorities to divert footpaths subject to the conditions of s. 209. In 1976, before a diversion order had been made, the developer diverted the path and began building. He was convicted of obstruction and fined. Later that year, the local authority made a diversion order which was confirmed by the Secretary of State. An application by two members of the Ramblers Association to have the order quashed was dismissed and they appealed. The appellants contended that the words "to be carried out" in s. 209 related to the future and could not apply where development had begun or had been completed. *Held*, the question to be considered was whether s. 209 empowered the Secretary of State to make a retrospective order when authorising a diversion order in respect of a new route for a footpath. There was nothing in s. 209 to prevent him from authorising an existing obstruction caused by development already begun. In the present case, the development was still being carried on which necessitated the authorisation of a diversion order at the time. What remained to be done on the houses could not be carried out so long as what had already been done remained unlawful and liable to be removed. Accordingly, the appeal would be dismissed.

ASHBY v SECRETARY OF STATE FOR THE ENVIRONMENT [1980] 1 All ER 508 (Court of Appeal: STEPHENSON, GOFF and EVELEIGH LJJ). Decision of Sir Douglas Frank QC sitting as a deputy High Court judge (1978) 122 Sol Jo 524, 1978 Halsbury's Abridgment para. 1465 affirmed.

1414   Highway—duty to maintain—failure to observe source of danger by inspection—accident—whether authority liable

The first defendant, a motorist, drove at an excessive speed into a pool of water on his side of the road and, as a result, lost control of his car, colliding with the plaintiff's van which was coming in the opposite direction. The plaintiff sued the first defendant in negligence and the highway authority in negligence and for breach of statutory duty, claiming damages for personal injuries and loss. There was evidence that on wet days a pool of water collected at that particular point on the road. *Held*, the water was a potential danger to traffic. The highway authority could reasonably have known about it and should have taken steps to drain it. Failure to do so amounted to a failure to maintain the highway properly. The motorist had failed in his duty to drive in such a way that he could have avoided reasonably foreseeable obstructions. Floods on roads in wet weather were reasonably foreseeable. Liability would therefore be apportioned equally between the first and second defendants.

TARRANT v ROWLANDS [1979] RTR 144 (Queen's Bench Division: CANTLEY J). *Burnside v Emerson* [1968] 3 All ER 741, CA applied.

1415   Highway authority—duty of care—road works—obliteration of traffic sign

A motor accident resulting in injury occurred at the intersection of a priority road with an unclassified country lane. The motorist proceeding along the lane accepted responsibility for the accident, but claimed a contribution from the highway authority as the intersection was "blind" and there was no traffic sign to warn of the priority road. The sign, in the form of white road markings, had been obliterated by the authority during roadsurfacing and no temporary sign had been erected. The trial judge held the authority one-third responsible. The authority appealed on the ground that their removal of the sign gave rise to no duty of care. It was further argued that they were under no duty to guard the motorist against his own negligence or to anticipate it. *Held*, it was clearly foreseeable that there was a risk of drivers misunderstanding their priorities. The authority were under a duty to take reasonable care that the traffic system they had imposed did not deteriorate so as to create a hazard. The authority were in breach of this duty as the placing of a temporary sign was the reasonable precaution to be taken in the circumstances; the authority's failure to place such a sign was therefore negligent. The breach of duty was causative; the absence of the sign contributed to the accident as it caused the motorist to proceed as if he had right of way. Accordingly, the appeal would be dismissed.

BIRD v PEARCE [1979] LS Gaz R 680 (Court of Appeal: MEGAW, EVELEIGH, and BRANDON LJJ). Decision of Wood J [1978] RTR 290, 1978 Halsbury's Abridgment para. 1467 affirmed.

1416   Motorway—public inquiry—procedure

A public inquiry was held regarding the construction of a new motorway, which was approved in principle. At a second inquiry concerning a particular interchange an applicant, who believed that the inspectors would not consider whether the motorway was necessary, took part in a disruptive protest and was excluded from the proceedings. She appealed against the dismissal of her motion to quash the scheme, contending that there had been a breach of natural justice. *Held*, there was an established procedure to be followed in examining objections to proposed schemes, under which inspectors had the right to examine the question of public need for a motorway. As this had been done at the first inquiry it was not necessary to repeat it at the second. Nor could the applicant complain that there had been a breach of natural justice, because her actions had made justice impossible.

LOVELOCK v SECRETARY OF STATE FOR TRANSPORT (1979) 123 Sol Jo 80 (Court of Appeal: LORD DENNING MR, ROSKILL and CUMMING-BRUCE LJJ).

1417   Right of way—private road—obstruction—liability of landlord to tenant

See *Hilton v James Smith and Sons (Norwood) Ltd.*, para. 1690.

1418   —— vehicular and pedestrian rights—conclusiveness of definitive map

When the definitive map of Suffolk was settled under the National Parks and Access to the Countryside Act 1949, a particular right of way was shown as a footpath only. There was no objection to this classification at the time but subsequent research showed that prior to the use as a footpath, the right of way had been used as a cartway for hundreds of years. The defendants, who were the proprietors of an adjacent holiday camp, wished to establish the right of way as a public carriageway and the council asked for a declaration that the definitive map was conclusive evidence that the right of way was a footpath only. The Court of Appeal held that under s. 32 (4) (a) of the Act the definitive map was conclusive evidence that the right of way was a footpath only. With respect to bridleways and roads, s. 32 (4) (b) provided a qualification to the effect that the definitive map was conclusive only of the rights of way shown and not whether the public had any other rights of way. No such qualification was contained in s. 32 (4) (a), however, in relation to footpaths. On appeal *held*, LORD HAILSHAM OF ST MARYLEBONE and LORD FRASER OF TULLYBELTON dissenting, the decision of the Court of Appeal would be upheld. It was the policy and intention of Parliament that any unknown or undiscovered right of way, which had it existed, might have destroyed the status of a footpath, should be regarded as non-existent until an opportunity for revision arose. Under the review provisions of the Act, erroneous entries could be corrected after five years, but until then the definitive map was conclusive evidence that the right of way was a footpath only.

SUFFOLK COUNTY COUNCIL V MASON [1979] 2 All ER 369 (House of Lords: LORD DIPLOCK, LORD MORRIS OF BORTH-Y-GEST, LORD EDMUND-DAVIES, LORD HAILSHAM OF ST MARYLEBONE and LORD FRASER OF TULLYBELTON). Decision of Court of Appeal [1978] 2 All ER 618, 1978 Halsbury's Abridgment para. 1471 affirmed.

1419 Road—meaning of "road"—vehicles on unadopted named road in unfinished housing estate

The defendant was charged with using a motor vehicle on a road in contravention of certain provisions of the Road Traffic Act 1972. The road on which the offences were committed was a named road on a partially built housing estate, was concreted with no kerbs or footpath, had not been adopted by the local authority and, although used by tradesmen, was not used by the general public. The justices found that no prima facie case had been established that the road was a "road" within the meaning of the 1972 Act and they dismissed the case. On appeal by the prosecution, the stated case set out only the evidence. *Held,* even on the assumption that the evidence amounted to findings of fact and whether or not the justices' attention was drawn to the definition of "road" in the 1972 Act, s. 196 (1), it was impossible to say that the justices should have concluded that the road was a "road to which the public has access" within the meaning of s. 196 (1). It was therefore impossible to say that the justices had erred in law and the appeal would be dismissed.

LOCK V LEATHERDALE [1979] RTR 201 (Queen's Bench Division: LORD WIDGERY CJ, WIEN and SMITH JJ).

HIRE PURCHASE AND CONSUMER CREDIT

Halsbury's Laws of England (4th edn.), Vol. 22, paras. 1–400

1420 Article

The Application of the Consumer Credit Act 1974 to Consumer Hire Agreements, Norman Palmer and David Yates (an examination of the disparity in the statutory treatment of such contracts): [1979] CLJ 180.

1421 Consumer Credit Act 1974—commencement

The Consumer Credit Act 1974 (Commencement No. 5) Order 1979, S.I. 1979 No. 1685 (in force on 27th January 1980) brings certain repeals of provisions relating to moneylenders specified in Sch. 5 of the 1974 Act into operation. Transactions made with moneylenders before the appointed day will not be affected by the Order.

1422 Consumer credit—exempt agreements

The Consumer Credit (Exempt Agreements) (Amendment) Order 1979, S.I. 1979 No. 1099 (in force on 1st October 1979), varies the Consumer Credit (Exempt Agreements) Order 1977, 1977 Halsbury's Abridgment para. 1415 which provides that certain consumer credit agreements secured on land are exempt agreements if the creditor is a body specified in the Schedule to that Order. The 1979 Order specifies further bodies to be included in the Schedule.

1423 —— variation of agreements—notice

The Consumer Credit (Notice of Variation of Agreements) (Amendment) Regulations 1979, S.I. 1979 No. 661 (in force on 18th June 1979), amend the 1977 Regulations, 1977 Halsbury's Abridgment para. 1418 (which prescribe the manner in which notice is to be given to the hirer of a variation of a consumer hire agreement under a power contained in the agreement before such variation can take effect). The new Regulations make special provision where the variation relates solely to certain charges in value added tax.

The Consumer Credit (Notice of Variation of Agreements) (Amendment No. 2) Regulations 1979, S.I. 1979 No. 667 (in force on 18th June 1979), correct an error in the above Regulations.

1424 Consumer credit business—licence

The Consumer Credit (Period of Standard Licence) (Amendment) Regulations 1979, S.I. 1979 No. 796 (in force on 1st August 1979), vary the Consumer Credit (Period of Standard Licence) Regulations 1975, 1975 Halsbury's Abridgment para. 1688 by extending the period during which a statutory standard licence is to have effect from three years to ten years.

1425 Contract of hire—implied terms—Law Commission recommendations

The Law Commission has recommended that a contract of hire should include implied terms that the bailor has the right to hire the goods throughout the period of hire and that the bailee is entitled to quiet possession for the same period. Further, it has recommended that the obligation of the supplier of goods under a contract of hire to supply goods corresponding to their description and sample and which are merchantable and fit should be put into statutory form and modelled on the statutory obligations of a seller. See *Law of Contract: Implied Terms in Contracts for the Supply of Goods* (Law Com. No. 95; HC 142).

1426 Control of agreements—agreements to which restrictions apply

The Hire-Purchase and Credit Sale Agreements (Control) (Amendment) Order 1979, S.I. 1979 No. 1223 (in force on 29th October 1979), amends the Hire-Purchase and Credit Sale Agreements (Control) Order 1976, 1976 Halsbury's Abridgment para. 1370 in relation to agreements excluded from control. Restrictions under the 1976 Order no longer apply to certain credit sale agreements for specified goods or to such agreements for motor cars where the cash price under the agreement does not exceed £1,000. The Hire-Purchase and Credit Sale Agreements (Control) (Amendment) Order 1978, 1978 Halsbury's Abridgment para. 1477 is revoked.

1427 Licensing—group licences

It has been announced that group licences effective from 3rd August 1979 were issued by the Director-General of Fair Trading to the Institute of Chartered Accountants in England and Wales, the Scottish and Irish Institutes and the Association of Certified Accountants. The licences relate only to activities arising in the course of practice as a chartered or certified accountant and cover consumer credit, credit brokerage, debt adjusting and debt counselling. See 123 Sol Jo 272.

HOUSING

Halsbury's Laws of England (4th edn.), Vol. 22, paras. 401–900

1428 Articles

Construing the Housing (Homeless Persons) Act 1977, W. T. West (the Act, 1977 Halsbury's Abridgment para. 1427, in the light of *R v Beverley Borough Council, ex parte McPhee* (1978) Times, 27th October, 1978 Halsbury's Abridgment para. 1486): 123 Sol Jo 343.

Government Aid for First Time House Buyers, W. A. Greene: 123 Sol Jo 39.

1429   Assistance for house purchase and improvement—eligibility for subsidy—transitional provisions

The Assistance for House Purchase and Improvement (Transitional Provisions) Regulations 1979, S.I. 1979 No. 1515 (in force on 1st January 1980), make transitional provisions consequential on amendments made to the Housing Subsidies Act 1967, Part II by the Housing Act 1974. The Regulations provide that certain existing option mortgages only continue to be eligible for a subsidy if on 6th April 1980: (i) the balance of the outstanding mortgage loan does not, in general, exceed £25,000, (ii) the property is occupied by the borrower as his only or main residence or is so occupied by his qualifying relative and (iii) the borrower's spouse has no loan in connection with another property which is the spouse's only or main residence and which benefits from option mortgage subsidy or tax relief.

1430   —— variation of subsidy

The Assistance for House Purchase and Improvement (Variation of Subsidy) Order 1979, S.I. 1979 No. 894 (in force on 1st September 1979), provides new scales of percentages in relation to option mortgage subsidy payable under Part II of the Housing Subsidies Act 1967 in respect of interest payable under option mortgages for any period beginning on or after 1st September 1979 where the rate of interest for the time being exceeds 6·67 per cent per annum. An existing Order dealing with previous rates of subsidy is revoked, but its operation is saved in relation to any period ending before 1st September 1979.

1431   Fitness for human habitation—prohibition of back-to-back houses—construction

A company was developing a large estate with various types of housing which included two blocks of four one-bedroomed houses. Each house in the block had two outside walls with windows and two interior party walls, so that the houses were back-to-back as well as side by side. The houses were inexpensive and had been purchased by people from varied occupations. The local housing authority brought an action against the company alleging that the houses were "back-to-back houses intended to be used for the working classes" and therefore prohibited by the Housing Act 1957, s. 5 (1). *Held*, the expression "back-to-back houses" was used in a popular and general sense to mean terraced houses which had three inside walls and only one outside wall. The question was one of fact, and since the houses did not fall within the popular and general meaning, they were not "back-to-back houses" as prohibited by s. 5. Further, even if the houses were "back-to-back houses", the company did not have the necessary intention to erect them for use by "the working classes" to be in breach of s. 5. The action would be dismissed.

CHORLEY BOROUGH COUNCIL v BARRATT DEVELOPMENTS (NORTH WEST) LTD [1979] 3 All ER 634 (Chancery Division at Manchester: BLACKETT-ORD V-C, VICE-CHANCELLOR OF THE COUNTY PALATINE OF LANCASTER). Dicta of Lord Dundas in *Murrayfield Real Estate Co v Edinburgh Magistrates* 1912 SC 217 at 222 and *White v St Marylebone Borough Council* [1915] 3 KB 249 applied.

1432   Homeless persons—statutory duty of local authority to provide accommodation—breach of duty—whether action for damages available

The plaintiff, a homeless person, brought an action in damages in the county court against his local authority for breach of their statutory duty to provide him with accommodation under the Housing (Homeless Persons) Act 1977, s. 3 (4). The judge dismissed the action as disclosing no reasonable cause of action, on the grounds that breach of a statutory duty gave rise only to a right to judicial review by way of mandamus. On appeal, the plaintiff contended that where a statute imposed a duty on a local authority for the benefit of a specified class of persons, but prescribed no special remedy for a breach of that duty, a civil action for damages would lie. *Held*, the local authority owed a duty to an ascertainable class of persons, the homeless.

There was no provision for the enforcement of that duty and an aggrieved person could bring an action in damages for breach of that duty. This would be treated as an action in tort, within the county court's jurisdiction and the plaintiff would have to prove not only breach but resultant damage. The appeal would be allowed and the case remitted to the county court for trial.

THORNTON V KIRKLEES METROPOLITAN BOROUGH COUNCIL [1979] 2 All ER 349 (Court of Appeal: MEGAW and ROSKILL LJJ). *Guardians of the Poor of Gateshead Union v Durham County Council* [1918] 1 Ch 146 and *Cutler v Wandsworth Stadium* [1949] AC 398, HL applied.

For the 1977 Act see 1977 Halsbury's Abridgment para. 1427.

1433   —— —— EEC nationals—whether intentionally homeless

Two Italian nationals working in England applied to a local authority for accommodation for themselves and their families under the Housing (Homeless Persons) Act 1977. One had been unemployed in Italy and had brought his wife and son to England. They stayed with relatives and both husband and wife obtained work, but were subsequently asked to leave. The other, who was married with two children, had decided to return to England with his family when his job in Italy came to an end. They came to England knowing that a flat which they had been promised was no longer available. They also lived with a relative but were later told to leave. Both families were housed in guest houses whilst the local authority made appropriate inquiries to decide whether the applicants were intentionally homeless within the meaning of s. 3 (1), (2) (b) of the 1977 Act. The authority notified the applicants six weeks later of its opinion that they had become homeless intentionally because they came to this country without having ensured that they had permanent accommodation to come to. The applicants applied for mandatory interlocutory injunctions ordering the authority to provide accommodation. They argued that, under Council Regulation (EEC) 1612/68, art. 9.1, a national of a member state employed in the territory of another member state should enjoy all the rights and benefits accorded to national workers in matters of housing and that the authority had not observed the Code of Guidance, para. 2.18 which provided that it would be relevant to consider the most immediate cause of the homelessness rather than events that may have taken place previously. *Held*, no injunction should be granted against a local authority unless a prima facie case was made out that the finding of "intentional homelessness" was invalid. The authority had to have regard to the Code of Guidance under s. 12 of the Act, but having done so, the authority could depart from it. The authority was entitled to find that the applicants had become intentionally homeless, and the injunctions would be refused.

LORD DENNING MR considered the remedies available to an applicant under the 1977 Act if a local authority failed to provide accommodation as required by s. 3 (4). Such an applicant could proceed by action in the High Court or by action for damages in the county court, or by application for judicial review under RSC Ord. 53.

DE FALCO V CRAWLEY BOROUGH COUNCIL; SILVESTRI V CRAWLEY BOROUGH COUNCIL [1980] 1 All ER 913 (Court of Appeal: LORD DENNING MR, BRIDGE LJ and SIR DAVID CAIRNS).

1434   —— —— whether duty complied with by giving advice and assistance

A woman left her matrimonial home in Eire due to her husband's violence and was sent to a women's aid hostel in Bristol with her children. Although she had no local connection with Bristol, the council accepted her as a homeless person with a priority need. However, a community welfare officer for the woman's home town assured the council that accommodation would be provided there if she returned to Eire. The council therefore decided that it could properly fulfil its duty under the Housing (Homeless Persons) Act 1977 by advising the woman to return to Eire, paying her fares and contacting the appropriate authorities there. The woman refused to return to her home town on the ground that she had suffered violence there and applied for an order of mandamus compelling the Bristol council to house her. *Held*, (i) the woman had only suffered violence in the matrimonial home itself and the welfare officer, with full knowledge of her circumstances, had guaranteed her accommodation elsewhere; (ii) under the 1977 Act, s. 6 (1) (c) the council could comply with its duty to provide accommodation by giving the woman any advice and assistance necessary for obtaining accommodation from another person. As the welfare officer was a person who could provide accommodation without risk of violence to the woman or her children, the council had properly fulfilled its statutory duty. The application would be refused.

R v BRISTOL CITY COUNCIL, EX PARTE BROWNE [1979] 3 All ER 344 (Queen's Bench Division: LORD WIDGERY CJ and LLOYD J).

1435   Homes insulation scheme

The Department of the Environment has published a circular (No. 78/60, Welsh Office circular No. 78/108) containing the Homes Insulation Scheme 1978, made by the Secretary of State under the Homes Insulation Act 1978, s. 1. The circular specifies the standard of insulation required in the loft for grant purposes, the persons eligible for a grant and the dwellings in respect of which an application can be made. It also contains an application form and directions as to the establishing of a waiting list for applications.

1436   Housing Act 1974—commencement

The Housing Act 1974 (Commencement No. 6) Order 1979, S.I. 1979 No. 1214, brought into force on 9th October 1979 certain minor and consequential amendments and repeals made by 1974 Act, s. 130 (4), 1974 Halsbury's Abridgment para. 1608.

1437   Housing association grants—administration allowances

The Secretary of State for the Environment has issued a circular (Dept. of Environment circular 16/79) setting out revised administration allowances for housing association grants under the Housing Act 1974, s. 29 (6). The revised allowances apply to housing projects completed for grant purposes after 1st May 1979 where final grant has not been paid; they will remain in force until 31st December 1979.

1438   Housing Corporation—borrowing

The Housing Corporation Advances (Increase of Limit) Order 1979, S.I. 1979 No. 1586 (in force on 3rd December 1979) increases the limit of advances to be made by the Housing Corporation to £750 million in pursuant to the provisions laid down in the Housing Act 1974, s. 7 (5).

1439   Housing finance—rent allowance subsidy

The Housing Finance (Rent Allowance Subsidy) Order 1979, S.I. 1979 No. 234 (in force on 31st March 1979), fixes the amount of rent allowance subsidy payable to a local authority for 1979–80 at 100 per cent of the authority's standard amount of rent allowance for the year.

1440   Rent rebates and allowance schemes

The Rent Rebates and Rent Allowances (Students) (England and Wales) Regulations 1979, S.I. 1979 No. 1014 (in force on 1st September 1979), raise to £8·75 the amount prescribed as the deduction to be made in calculating the rent which is eligible to be met by a rent rebate or a rent allowance under Part II of the Housing Finance Act 1972, as amended, in the case of tenants who are students in receipt of certain awards or grants from public funds for the purpose of their further full-time education.

1441   The Rent Rebate and Rent Allowance Schemes and Services (Amendment) (England and Wales) Regulations 1979, S.I. 1979 No. 1319 (in force on 12th November 1979) vary further the Housing Finance Act 1972, Sch. 3. The variations take effect in respect of any week in a rebate or allowance period beginning on or after 12th November 1979. They provide that a person undergoing full-time education will not cease to be within the definition of "dependent child" in Sch. 3, para. 2 solely by reason of his absence from the tenant's household during term-time. The needs allowance used in calculating the amount of rebate or allowance is increased and the additional allowances available to handicapped persons registered under the National Assistance Act 1948, s. 29 (1) are extended to similarly handicapped persons not so registered. For the purpose of calculating the amount of rebate or allowance, any maintenance payment made to a dependent child under the age of sixteen of either a tenant or his spouse is to be added to the income of the tenant. It is further provided that, in ascertaining income, £5 of the earnings of the tenant and his spouse and also maintenance payments made by the tenant or by his spouse be disregarded. The need to take into account liquid cash resources of the tenant or his spouse is removed. Deductions for non-dependants used in calculating the amount of rebate or allowance are increased. Provision is also made for certain other consequential amendments.

1442   ### Thermal insulation—homes insulation scheme

The Parliamentary Secretary to the Secretary of State for the Environment has stated that the scope of the homes insulation scheme is to be extended to all householders (previously the grant was restricted to private home owners). The eligibility of council tenants to grants under the revised scheme will not affect the moneys already available to local authorities for home insulation. See the Financial Times, 31st October 1979.

1443   ### Unfit house—demolition order—whether capable of being rendered fit at reasonable expense

A local authority made a demolition order in respect of a property under the Housing Act 1957, ss. 16 (1), 17 (1), on the ground that it was unfit for human habitation and was not capable at reasonable expense of being rendered so fit. The order was quashed on the ground that the house could be rendered fit for human habitation at reasonable expense, having regard to the estimated cost of the works necessary to render it so fit and the value which it was estimated that the house would have when the works were completed, as required by the 1957 Act, s. 39 (1). The authority appealed, contending that the judge had failed sufficiently to take into account the provisions of s. 39 (1) in that he had failed to compare the cost of repairs with the difference between the value of the house unrepaired and its value after the repairs had been done. *Held*, it was clear from the judgment that although the judge did not give any figures, he was in fact carrying out such an exercise. It was not necessary for the judge to set out specific figures if it was apparent that he had taken into account the factors required by s. 39 (1). Thus it could not be said that the judge was wrong in law and the appeal would be dismissed.

DUDLOW ESTATES LTD V SEFTON METROPOLITAN BOROUGH COUNCIL (1978) 249 Estates Gazette 1271 (Court of Appeal: MEGAW, BROWNE and WALLER LJJ).

HUMAN RIGHTS

Halsbury's Laws of England (4th edn.), Vol. 18, paras. 1625–1722

1444–
1445   ### Articles

Contempt of Court and Human Rights, M. Jefferson and P. Thornberry (discussion of art. 10 of the European Convention for the Protection of Human

Rights and Fundamental Freedoms 1950 in the light of the Sunday Times case [1973] 3 All ER 54, HL): 123 Sol Jo 416.

Report of the Committee of Data Protection, K. Gottschalk (sociological and constitutional aspects of computer information systems): 129 NLJ 1065.

The Marckx Case, Susan Maidment (implications on English law of illegitimacy of *Re Marckx*, Council of Europe Press Release, para. 1448) 9 Fam Law 230.

1446   Complaint against European Communities—liability of Communities—liability of member states—jurisdiction

The European Commission of Human Rights does not have jurisdiction to examine allegations of violation of the European Convention on Human Rights made against the European Communities.

In proceedings before the European Commission of Human Rights the French applicant organisation alleged violation of the European Convention on Human Rights, arts. 11, 13 and 14 by either the European Communities as such, or the member states of the Communities collectively or individually. The proceedings arose in consequence of a decision of the Council of the European Communities, adopted in accordance with proposals of the governments of member states, designating the representative workers' organisations required to submit lists of candidates for the ECSC Consultative Committee. The applicant organisation was excluded from the proposal of the French government and thus from the decision. Actions then brought by the applicant in the European Court of Justice and the French Conseil d'Etat were both declared inadmissible. The applicant therefore claimed that the decision in question involved liability in the context of the Convention, since it had been denied any judicial remedy. *Held*, the Commission had no jurisdiction ratione personae to examine complaints against the European Communities as such, which were not a Contracting Party to the Convention, and, since the claim against the member states of the Communities collectively was in reality a claim against the Council of the Communities, the Commission lacked jurisdiction on that basis also. Further, with respect to the claim against the member states individually, there was no jurisdiction either as regards France, which had not recognised the right of individual petition under art. 25, or as regards the other member states which, by their participation in a decision of the Council, had not exercised their "jurisdiction" within the meaning of art. 1. The complaint was therefore inadmissible.

CONFEDERATION FRANÇAISE DEMOCRATIQUE DU TRAVAIL v EUROPEAN COMMUNITIES (Case 8030/77) [1979] 2 CMLR 229 (European Commission of Human Rights).

1447   Freedom of information and privacy—Council of Europe

The Parliamentary Assembly of the Council of Europe has recommended that the Committee of Ministers should invite member states which have not yet done so to introduce a system of freedom of information. This is defined as access to government files, comprising the right to seek and receive information from government agencies and departments, the right to inspect and correct personal files, the right to privacy, and the right to rapid action before the courts in these matters. It also has recommended that the Committee of Ministers should implement its decision (taken in 1976) to insert a provision on the right to seek information in the European Convention on Human Rights. See Recommendation 854 (1979).

1448   Respect for family life—right to dispose of property—discrimination against illegitimate child

The Belgian Civil Code required an unmarried mother to recognise her child in order to establish affiliation. However, pursuant to the Code, the effect of recognition was to severely restrict the mother's capacity to give or bequeath property to her child. An unmarried Belgian mother sought a declaration in respect of herself and her child from the European Court of Human Rights that the relevant provisions of the Code constituted, inter alia, a breach of the European Convention, art. 8, respect for private and family life, and art. 14 relating to discrimination. *Held*, art 8 applied to the family life of an illegitimate family as equally as to a legitimate family. The dilemma facing a mother of having to choose whether to recognise her child, and thus lose certain rights to make dispositions she would otherwise have been able to make to him, was not consonant with respect for family life and in breach of art. 8. Further, whilst there was no guaranteed right to acquire possession by intestacy or voluntary disposition, the distinction between the rights of legitimate and illegitimate children lacked objective and reasonable justification and was in breach of art. 14.

RE MARCKX (European Court of Human Rights). See Council of Europe Press Release, Human Rights News C(79) 17, dated 5th June 1979.

1449   Right to bring action for infringement of a right—alternative remedy—whether appropriate

Trinidad and Tobago
A schoolmaster was transferred from one school to another without notice. Instead of seeking a review of the transfer under regulations specifically dealing with the matter, he sought a declaration that the transfer contravened his right to the enjoyment of property enshrined in the Constitution of Trinidad and Tobago, s. 6. Alternatively, he complained it was a breach of his right to equality before the law and to the protection of the law. The claims were founded on the contention that the transfer was a punitive measure taken after he had alleged the existence of improprieties at the first school. *Held*, the schoolmaster's claims were manifestly untenable as no contravention of the rights raised had been disclosed. If he was aggrieved by the transfer he should have sought a review of it under the relevant regulations; the invocation of the constitution to provide a remedy in such a case was an abuse of the process of the court and debased the value of the protection the constitution offered in more serious matters.

HARRIKISSOON V A-G OF TRINIDAD AND TOBAGO [1979] 3 WLR 62 (Privy Council: LORD DIPLOCK, VISCOUNT DILHORNE, LORD EDMUND-DAVIES, LORD RUSSELL OF KILLOWEN and LORD SCARMAN).

1450   —— taxation—whether imposition of levy unconstitutional

Trinidad and Tobago
The Unemployment Levy Act 1970 provided for the imposition of a levy of five per cent on company profits and on individual income over a certain limit. The plaintiff challenged the constitutionality of the levy under the Constitution of Trinidad and Tobago. *Held*, the Act imposed a tax. It was not open to the plaintiff to allege that the scheme of expenditure under the Act conflicted with the provision in the Constitution prohibiting the withdrawal of moneys from public funds unless authorised by Parliament. In any event, there was no necessity for a separate Appropriation Act, nor did the Act infringe the provision in the Constitution guaranteeing protection against the taking of property without due process of law.

MOOTOO V A-G OF TRINIDAD AND TOBAGO (1979) 123 Sol Jo 337 (Privy Council: LORD WILBERFORCE, LORD SALMON, LORD FRASER OF TULLYBELTON, LORD RUSSELL OF KILLOWEN AND SIR WILLIAM DOUGLAS).

1451   Right to fair and public hearing—costs of obtaining judicial separation in Republic of Ireland—whether constitutes bar to right of access to courts

In the Republic of Ireland spouses may be relieved of the duty of living together only by a deed of separation or by a decree of judicial separation granted by the High Court. The complainant wished to obtain a decree but was unable to pay the cost of the proceedings; no legal aid is available in Ireland for such proceedings. She complained, inter alia, that her right of access to a court for the purpose of petitioning for judicial separation was effectively denied due to prohibitive legal costs; this constituted an infringement of art. 6 (1) of the European Convention on Human Rights. On 9th October 1979, the European Court of Human Rights upheld her complaint. The court ruled that, barring access to legal representation, the right of a litigant to conduct his case in person did not constitute an effective right of access to the courts, having regard to the complexity of the procedure and the points of law involved (art. 6 (1)); but in other circumstances it might perhaps have done so. A government could not be heard to say in such instances that the effective reason for the lack of access was the personal circumstances of the complainant; in appropriate situations art. 6 (1) required positive state action; but such action did not necessarily involve free legal aid for every dispute concerning a civil right. The court also stated that the fact that a particular interpretation of a provision of the convention might involve overlapping into social and economic matters did not preclude the acceptance of that interpretation as the true interpretation by the court.

AIREY'S CASE (1979), Council of Europe Press Release dated 9th October 1979.

1452   —— right to hearing within reasonable time

A medical practitioner in Germany had his authorisation to run a clinic withdrawn in 1967 and his authorisation to practise withdrawn in 1971. In those years he commenced proceedings to challenge the withdrawals and he asserted before the European Court of Human Rights that the length of time taken over those proceedings constituted an infringement of his right (guaranteed by art. 6 (1) of the European Convention on Human Rights) to have his civil rights determined within a reasonable time. The court *held*, whether a right was a "civil right" for this purpose had to be determined by reference to the substantive content and effects of the right (not its legal classification) under the relevant domestic law. The rights affected by the withdrawals were private rights and as such within the scope of art. 6 (1). The court ruled that the reasonableness of the duration of proceedings must be assessed according to the circumstances of each case. In the present case, the duration was excessive.

KÖNIG v FEDERAL REPUBLIC OF GERMANY (1978) 2 EHRR 170 (European Court of Human Rights).

1453   Right to family life and home—access to children upon breakdown of marriage—matters to be considered

In principle, a parent always has a right of access to his or her child under art. 8 (1) of the European Convention on Human Rights. However, when deciding questions of access to children on the breaking-up of a marriage, domestic courts may properly take into account, under art. 8 (2), a child's mental stability and physical well-being. Where a national court has before it evidence upon which it could properly conclude that to grant a father a right of access to his children might seriously endanger their health and morals this constitutes, in the view of the European Commission of Human Rights, a justification under art. 8 (2) of the measures taken.

X v SWEDEN (Case 7911/77) Decisions and Reports 12, p. 192.

1454   —— conflict between natural and foster parents—principle to be applied

Reported decisions of the European Commission of Human Rights show that when the question of custody arises in cases of divorce or separation the Commission usually pays special attention to the interests of the child concerned, in particular his physical and mental well-being (see, e.g. *Application 911/60*, Yearbook HR 4, p. 199; *Application 2306/64*, Collection HR 21, p. 23; *Application 2648/65*, Collection HR 26, p. 26). The Commission has ruled that the same principle applies where there is a conflict regarding custody between foster parents and natural parents. Accordingly, where the municipal courts had investigated the position and future prospects of a child and given his interests predominant attention an application for a ruling that the court order for custody infringed the foster parent's right to respect for her private and family life was adjudged to be ill-founded.

X v SWITZERLAND (Case 8257/78) Decisions and Reports 13, p. 248.

1455   —— **right of married prisoner to meet spouse alone**

The refusal of prison authorities to permit married prisoners to meet their spouses in prison without supervision in order to maintain their conjugal life does not constitute an infringement of the right to respect family life guaranteed by the European Convention on Human Rights art. 8 (1). Further, the European Commission of Human Rights has *held*, that this remains valid even if the two spouses are detained in the same prison; such interference with family life is justifiable under art. 8 (2) and as such cannot constitute an infringement of the right to found a family guaranteed by art. 12.

X and Y v SWITZERLAND (Case 8166/78). Decisions and Reports 13, p. 241.

1456   —— **right to found a family—whether includes right to adopt a child**

The right to found a family guaranteed by art. 12 of the European Convention on Human Rights is a right to procreate children. Article 12 does not guarantee a right to adopt or otherwise integrate a child who is not the natural child of the couple concerned into their family. In the view of the European Commission on Human Rights, this is a matter for the national law.

X AND Y v UNITED KINGDOM (Case 7229/75) Decisions and Reports 12, p. 32.

1457   **Right to free elections—elections to European Assembly—imposition of particular electoral system in national region—compatibility with convention**

The officers of the British Ulster Dominion Party brought a complaint against the United Kingdom before the European Commission of Human Rights alleging that the European Assembly Elections Act 1978, by imposing a particular system of voting in Northern Ireland, namely proportional representation, had violated certain provisions of the European Convention on Human Rights. The applicants claimed that this system had been imposed on the region with the intention of depriving a section of its inhabitants of representation which they would otherwise have achieved and thereby violated arts. 3 and 14 of the Convention and art. 3 of the first Protocol. Articles 3 and 14 prohibit inhuman or degrading treatment and discrimination respectively; art. 3 of the Protocol provides for the holding of free elections. *Held*, although art. 3 of the Protocol clearly contemplated elections to national legislatures there was no reason why it should not apply to elections to new representative organs, partly assuming the functions of new legislatures. However, the requirement under that provision that elections should be held under conditions which ensured the free expression of the opinion of the people did not have the effect of imposing a particular kind of electoral system, but included the systems both of simple majority and proportional representation. Further since the latter system was more favourable to minority groups, it clearly fulfilled the requirement of the provision. Similarly, since the system had been adopted in respect of Northern Ireland specifically for the purpose of protecting the rights of the minority, it could not be said to amount to discrimination under art. 14. With regard to art. 3, there was nothing in the adoption of a particular electoral system which could amount to degrading treatment. The application was therefore manifestly ill-founded within the meaning of art. 27 (2) and would be dismissed accordingly.

LINDSAY v UNITED KINGDOM (Case 8364/78) [1979] 3 CMLR 166 (European Commission of Human Rights).

1458   —— —— **national legislation imposing condition of residence on right to vote—compatibility with convention**

A United Kingdom citizen resident in Belgium and a Belgian national resident in France at the time of the direct elections to the European Assembly brought complaints before the European Commission of Human Rights against the United Kingdom and the Kingdom of Belgium respectively, on the grounds that national legislation governing those elections deprived nationals resident in another member state of their right to vote. *Held*, the EC Direct Elections Act of 1976 clearly provided that pending the entry into force of a uniform electoral system the national systems to be adopted for the elections to the European Parliament fell within the competence of each member state. Further, as the Commission had previously held, the requirement of residence for the exercise of the right to vote in Parliamentary elections was not contrary to art. 3 of the Protocol to the European Convention on Human rights dealing with the right to free elections. Accordingly, although the present lack of a uniform electoral procedure applicable to the elections in question was regrettable, it was clear that national legislation governing the procedure on this occasion was not incompatible with art. 3 of the Protocol, on the assumption that provision applied to elections other than those in respect of national legislatures. The applications were therefore manifestly ill-founded within the meaning of art. 27 (2) and would be dismissed.

RE AN EXPATRIATE UNITED KINGDOM CITIZEN (Case 8611/79); ALLIANCE DES BELGES DE LA COMMUNAUTE EUROPEENE V BELGIUM (Case 8612/79) [1979] 3 CMLR 172, 175 (European Commission of Human Rights).

1459   Right to freedom of expression—injunction to restrict

The European Court of Human Rights has ruled that an injunction restraining The Sunday Times from publishing an article tracing the history of the testing, manufacture and marketing of the drug thalidomide was a violation of the European Convention on Human Rights, art. 10. For the purposes of deciding whether there had been a violation of art. 10, the court had to ascertain whether the interference with applicant's freedom of expression was prescribed by law, whether that law had an aim which was legitimate and whether its use in this particular case was necessary. The court rejected the applicant's contention that in view of the uncertainty of the law of contempt and the novelty of the principles enunciated in the House of Lords, the restraint imposed could not be regarded as "prescribed by law". To be prescribed by law a restraint had to satisfy two requirements, (i) that the citizen had to be able to have an adequate indication of the legal rules applicable to a given case, and (ii) he had to be able to foresee, so far as reasonable, the consequences, which a particular action might entail. Those two requirements were satisfied in this case. Further, both the aim of the law of contempt in general and the injunction granted against The Times Newspapers Ltd were legitimate aims for the purposes of art. 10 (2), namely the maintenance of the authority of the judiciary. However, on a question of necessity, the court found, by a majority of eleven to nine, that the injunction did not correspond to a social need sufficiently pressing to outweight the public interest in freedom of expression; the injunction therefore did not have sufficient basis under art. 10 (2), was not proportionate to the legitimate aim pursued and, accordingly, was not necessary in a democratic society for maintaining the authority of the judiciary.

THE SUNDAY TIMES V UNITED KINGDOM [1979] 2 EHRR 245.

See also, Contempt—A European Obligation to Reform: 129 NLJ 508.

1460   Right to liberty and security of person—deprivation of liberty—detention of deportee

The European Commission of Human Rights has ruled that although the term "necessity" is not used in art. 5 (1) (f) of the European Convention on Human Rights it is implicit in the character of art. 5 (1) (f), as an exception clause, that it must be construed strictly and that no criteria other than those mentioned in the exception clause itself may be the basis of any restriction on the right to liberty and security of person. Also, it follows from art. 18 of the convention that the detention of a proposed deportee can be justified under art. 5 (1) (f) only if it is related to the deportation proceedings. Nevertheless, a finding that an application under art. 5 (1) was manifestly ill-founded did not preclude the commission from examining whether art. 5 (4) had been infringed. The complaint under art. 5(4) was declared inadmissible and returned for consideration on its merits.

CAPRINO V UNITED KINGDOM (Case 6871/75). Decisions and Reports 12, p. 14.

1461 ——— **meaning of "security"**

The European Commission for Human Rights has *held*, in the context of the European Convention on Human Rights art. 5, and the "travaux préparatoires" to the Convention, that the word "security" in the phrase "liberty and security of the person" in art. 5 is concerned with an individual's protection against arbitrary interference by a public authority with his personal liberty. Thus any decision taken within the sphere of art. 5 must, in order to safeguard the individual's right to "security of person", conform to the procedural, as well as to the substantive, requirements of law.

EASTERN AFRICAN ASIANS (CITIZENS OF THE UNITED KINGDOM AND COLONIES) v UNITED KINGDOM (Case 4626/70); THREE EAST AFRICAN ASIANS (BRITISH PROTECTED PERSONS) v UNITED KINGDOM (Cases 4715/70, 4783/71, 4827/71) Decisions and Reports 13, p. 17.

1462 **Right to life—appeal against death sentence—delay in consideration of appeal**

Trinidad and Tobago

The applicant was convicted of murder and sentenced to death. His appeal to the Court of Appeal was dismissed and the Judicial Committee of the Privy Council advised dismissal of his appeal in 1976. The applicant then petitioned the Governor-General for mercy. Under the provisions of the Criminal Procedure Ordinance the sentence was postponed pending the Governor-General's decision. Shortly afterwards the republican Constitution came into force and the Governor-General became President, but there was no change in the law regarding pardon by the head of state. The new constitution provided for an advisory committee on the exercise of the power of pardon which was required to report to the designated minister in all cases where the death sentence had been imposed. Only after four months did the government constitute the advisory committee and look at the applicant's petition. In February 1977 the President rejected the petition and ordered execution of the sentence. In March the applicant applied to the High Court by an originating motion for redress under the Constitution, s. 14 alleging that because of the delay in the execution of the death sentence in accordance with the President's warrant it was now contrary to human rights as guaranteed by the Constitution, s. 4 (a). Both the High Court and the Court of Appeal dismissed the motion. On appeal to the Judicial Committee, *held*, although there might be cases where the delay between the passing of the death sentence and the notice of execution was so long as to raise a reasonable belief in the prisoner that his sentence has been commuted to life imprisonment, this was not so here. The executive had been correct to wait until after the election before constituting the advisory committee. The applicant had not established that the period between the setting up of the committee and the rejection of his petition by the president was unreasonable and thus not contrary to the Constitution, s. 4.

ABBOTT v A-G OF TRINIDAD AND TOBAGO [1979] 1 WLR 1342 (Privy Council: LORD DIPLOCK, LORD MORRIS OF BORTH-Y-GEST, LORD EDMUND-DAVIES and LORD FRASER OF TULLYBELTON).

1463 **Right to know accusation—proceedings in language not understood by accused—right to interpreter**

The right of an accused to be informed promptly, in a language which he understands, of the nature and cause of the accusation against him (which is guaranteed by art. 6 (3) (*a*) of the European Convention on Human Rights) entitles him to the free use of an interpreter if he does not understand the language in which the proceedings are conducted. Any attempt to make him pay for the costs of the interpreter would constitute an infringement of art. 6 (3) (*a*).

LUEDICKE, BECKACEM AND KOG v FEDERAL REPUBLIC OF GERMANY (1978) 2 EHRR 149 (European Court of Human Rights).

1464   Right to peaceful enjoyment of property—forfeiture of smuggled goods—deprivation in public interest

See *Allgemeine Gold-und-Silberscheideanstalt* v *Customs and Excise Commissioners*, para. 774.

1465   —— —— whether so excessive as to constitute infringement of right

The applicant was convicted of smuggling goods into Austria. He was required to pay 155,000 schillings in customs duties on the goods (which were valued at 500,000 schillings). In addition, he was fined 100,000 schillings for the offence of smuggling and the smuggled goods were forfeited. He complained to the European Commission of Human Rights that the penalties imposed were disproportionate to the offence and constituted an infringement of his right under the European Convention on Human Rights, Protocol, art. 1 to peaceful enjoyment of his possessions. *Held*, the Commission noted that the sanction of forfeiture of smuggled goods was applied in at least four other member states (including the United Kingdom) and that the level of penalties provided by Austrian legislation in the case of smuggling was below those in some other member states. The fine imposed was in fact below the maximum provided by the legislation. The Commission therefore ruled that, although the sanctions were severe, they were not excessive having regard to the Protocol, art 1, para. 2 to the Convention and ruled that part of the application to be ill-founded.

X v AUSTRIA (Case 7287/75). Decisions and Reports 13, p. 27.

1466   —— meaning of "possessions"

The European Commission of Human Rights, in ruling an application ill-founded, *held*, that the term "possessions" in, the European Convention on Human Rights, Protocol, art. 1 was not restricted in its meaning to movable property but embraced both movables and immovable property. This was clear from the French text which in art. 1 uses the term "biens".

WIGGINS v UNITED KINGDOM (Case 7456/76) Decisions and Reports 13, p. 40.

1467   Right to privacy—legality of telephone tapping by the police

See *Malone v Metropolitan Police Commissioner*, para. 2093.

HUSBAND AND WIFE

Halsbury's Laws of England (4th edn.), Vol. 22, paras. 901–1178

1468   Articles

Abortion—Whose Decision?, Christina M. Lyon and Geoffrey J. Bennett (*Paton v Trustees of British Pregnancy Advisory Service* [1978] 2 All ER 987, 1978 Halsbury's Abridgment para. 1507, with reference to the American position and the difficulties of abortion litigation in both countries): 9 Fam Law 35.

An Equitable Affair?, S. D. Migdal (property rights of a mistress): 9 Fam Law 195.

The Battered Mistress and the Violent Paramour, H. A. Finlay (discussion of the Domestic Violence and Matrimonial Proceedings Act 1976, s. 1): 52 ALJ 613.

Chaos out of Order or Order out of Chaos?, C. J. Allen (problems raised by the wife's interest in the matrimonial home): 123 Sol Jo 411.

The Deserting Spouse's Equity, Peter Smith: 123 Sol Jo 193.

The Domestic Proceedings and Magistrates' Courts Act 1978—Some Points and Problems for Practitioners, Godfrey Gypps: 143 JP Jo 316.

Domestic Violence—A Practitioner's Viewpoint, David C. Robinson (whether the Domestic Violence and Matrimonial Proceedings Act 1976 fulfils its function of providing immediate relief to the battered wife or cohabitee): 129 NLJ 251.

Domestic Violence: No Ansah, David C. Robinson (the function of an ex parte injunction in the light of *Ansah v Ansah* [1977] 2 WLR 760, 1976 Halsbury's Abridgment para. 1476): 129 NLJ 896.

"... For She Has no Right or Power to Refuse Her Consent", Charlotte L. Mitra (a review of the attitude of the law towards rape within marriage): [1979] Crim LR 558.

The Legal Implications of a Relationship Outside Marriage, David Pearl (review of recent developments in the legal position of a cohabiting, but unmarried, couple): [1978] CLJ 252.

The Mistress's Limited Rights of Occupancy, Judith M. Masson (property and occupation rights of unmarried cohabitees in the light of *Davis v Johnson* [1978] 1 All ER 841, CA, 1978 Halsbury's Abridgment para. 1522 and *Chandler v Kerley* [1978] 1 WLR 693, CA, 1978 Halsbury's Abridgment para. 1728): [1979] Conv 184.

Non-Molestation Injunctions, Graham Ritchie: 129 NLJ 1079.

Polygamous Marriages: Wives' Rights, W. T. West: 123 Sol Jo 562.

Polygamy and Capacity to Marry, R. D. James (analysis of the reasoning behind the provisions of Matrimonial Causes Act 1973, s. 11 (d) with suggestions for reform): 42 MLR 533.

Wives "In Actual Occupation", H. W. Wilkinson (issues raised by the wife's interest in property to the purchase of which she has contributed): 129 NLJ 700.

1469   Divorce

See DIVORCE.

1470   Domestic Proceedings and Magistrates' Courts Act 1978—commencement

The Domestic Proceedings and Magistrates' Courts Act 1978 (Commencement No. 3) Order 1979, S.I. 1979 No. 731 specifies 17th September 1979 as the date of commencement for Domestic Proceedings and Magistrates' Courts Act 1978, s. 40, 1978 Halsbury's Abridgment para. 1509. The date of commencement for ss. 16–18, 28, 29 (1), (2), (5), 30, 75–85, 88 (1)–(4) and those provisions of Schs. 2 and 3 as were not brought into force on 20th November 1978, S.I. 1978 No. 1489 is 1st November 1979. Schedule 2 of the Order contains transitional provisions adapting certain provisions of the Act under s. 89 (4) in consequence of the partial operation of the Act.

1471   Maintenance orders—magistrates' court order—application for remission of arrears—jurisdiction of magistrates

See *R v Halifax JJ, ex parte Woolverton*, para. 956.

1472   —— reciprocal enforcement

See CONFLICT OF LAWS.

1473   Marriage—declaration of validity—petitioner's domicile—court's discretion to refuse decree

A German national with a German domicile of origin entered Britain on another person's passport and adopted that person's identity whilst living in England, in an attempt to avoid criminal proceedings being brought against her in Germany. She married an English national, using the name in the passport and giving false particulars about herself in the notice of marriage. The certificate of marriage contained the same false particulars. Although the marriage was consummated the parties never lived together. After the discovery of her true identity, extradition proceedings were commenced against her. She contended that she was a British subject by virtue of the marriage and filed a petition pursuant to the Matrimonial Causes Act 1973, s 45 (1), which provides that any person whose right to be deemed a British subject depends on the validity of a marriage may, if he is domiciled in England, apply for a declaration that the marriage was valid. *Held*, the petition should be dismissed. The marriage was valid under the Marriage Act 1949, s. 49, despite the assumption of a false name and description even though it was the name and identity of a living and indentifiable person. However the petitioner had not obtained a domicile in England for the purposes of s. 45 of the 1973 Act, since her entry into England had been illegal and she had stayed there in order to avoid trial in Germany, rather than with the intention of setting up a permanent home in England. Furthermore the court had a discretion under s. 45 (5) to make such decree as it thought fit in the circumstances; thus even if the petitioner had established that she was domiciled in England the court would not have granted the decree sought in view of her fraud and criminal acts.

PUTTICK v ATTORNEY-GENERAL AND PUTTICK [1979] 3 All ER 463 (Family Division: SIR GEORGE BAKER P).

1474   —— invalidity—one party already married—deceit

See *Beaulne v Ricketts*, para. 1885.

1475   Matrimonial home—domestic violence—exclusion of one party—injunction with power of arrest

A wife was granted injunctions restraining her husband from molesting her and the three children of the family, and from entering the matrimonial home. While in the witness box, the husband made threats against the wife and the judge attached a power of arrest to the injunctions, although there was no evidence of violence by the husband. The husband appealed, contending that the judge had no authority to add the power of arrest to the injunctions. *Held*, a power of arrest could only be attached to one or other of the three types of injunction prescribed by the Domestic Violence and Matrimonial Proceedings Act 1976, s. 2. Further, the judge's jurisdiction to attach such an order only arose if the judge was satisfied that the other party had caused actual bodily harm to the applicant or to the children concerned and it was considered that he was likely to do so again. The only evidence of causing actual bodily harm to the applicant in the instant case was irrelevant because it related to 1976 and there had been virtually no contact between the parties for two years. There was no evidence of violence to any of the children and absolutely no evidence that he was likely to be violent towards them in the future. The judge had, therefore, acted in excess of his jurisdiction. The appeal would accordingly be allowed to the extent of deleting the power of arrest.

MCLAREN v MCLAREN (1979) 9 Fam Law 153 (Court of Appeal: ORMROD, BROWN and BRIDGE LJJ).

1476   An injunction restraining the wife from molestation, with a power of arrest attached, was granted to the husband on an ex parte application. The injunction as made was continued at the inter partes hearing "until further order". During the course of the appeal it was pointed out that under the Domestic Violence and Matrimonial Proceedings Act 1976, s. 2, 1976 Halsbury's Abridgment para. 1392, a power of arrest should only be attached to an injunction if the evidence against the party who had caused bodily harm was particularly strong, and if it was very likely that that party would continue to attempt the same in the future. Even if that should be the case, it was not right to make the order to continue "until further order".

MORGAN v MORGAN (1978) 9 Fam Law 87 (Court of Appeal: STAMP, ORR and BRIDGE LJJ).

1477   —— —— injunction restraining husband from molesting wife—power of arrest

See *McLaren v McLaren*, para. 1456.

1478   —— —— meaning of "man and woman who are living together"

In a case concerning an injunction under the Domestic Violence and Matrimonial Proceedings Act 1976, the Court of Appeal has ruled that the power to make an injunction applied equally to a man and woman who were living together with each other in the same household under s. 1 (2) of the Act. It was not necessary to show that the man and woman were living together at the time of the application. The applicability of the Act depended on the existence of a relationship of a man and woman, living together as husband and wife, and it was a question of fact when the relationship ended.

McLean v Nugent (1979) 123 Sol Jo 521 (Court of Appeal: Ormrod and Eveleigh LJJ).

1479   —— exclusion of spouse—criterion for making order

The parties married in 1974 and had two infant children. The wife petitioned for divorce on the grounds of unreasonable behaviour, alleging, inter alia, excessive drinking and one incident of violence. She left the matrimonial home with her children and went to live with her mother. Her husband refused to leave the matrimonial home and she obtained an order requiring him to do so. On appeal by the husband, *held*, the question of who was to vacate the matrimonial home was usually determined by who kept the children. However, the initial question was whether it was necessary for anyone to leave the matrimonial home. In the circumstances of the case, given that the allegations of unreasonable behaviour were not of a serious nature, there being no evidence to support them, there was no prima facie reason why the wife should not go back. Accordingly the appeal would be allowed and the order would be quashed.

Elsworth v Elsworth (1978) 9 Fam Law 21 (Court of Appeal: Stamp and Orr LJJ and Sir David Cairns).

1480   —— —— jurisdiction to grant injunction in wardship proceedings

See *Re V (A Minor)*, para. 1882.

1481   —— home in joint names—right of indemnity where wife's equity charged for husband's benefit

See *Re Berry (A Bankrupt)*, para. 219.

1482   —— tenancy in husband's name—wife in sole occupation—wife's defence to action for possession by landlord

See *Grange Lane South Flats Ltd v Cook*, para. 2103.

1483   —— wife's unregistered interest—position of mortgagee

See *Williams and Glyn's Bank Ltd v Boland*; *Williams and Glyn's Bank Ltd v Brown*, para. 1934.

1484   Nullity of marriage—approbation—whether grant of decree statute-barred

See *D v D (Nullity: Statutory Bar)*, para. 967.

1485   Publication of secrets of marriage—interlocutory injunction

See *Lennon v News Group Newspapers and Twist*, para. 1749.

IMMIGRATION

Halsbury's Laws of England (4th edn.), Vol. 4, paras. 974–1033

1486   Article

Bail or Temporary Release, David Burgess (the detention of immigrants): 129 NLJ 235.

1487   Appeal—application to Divisional Court against decisions—procedure

See para. 2146.

1488   Deportation order—application for release pending order—jurisdiction of Crown Court

The applicant pleaded guilty to the offence of staying in this country beyond the period of his leave, contrary to the Immigration Act 1971, s. 24 (1) (b). He appealed against the magistrates' recommendation for deportation. This appeal was dismissed and the Crown Court refused to hear an application for his release pending the making of a deportation order on the grounds of lack of jurisdiction. The applicant moved for an order of mandamus requiring the Crown Court to hear and determine the application. *Held*, the magistrates had the power under Sch. 3, para. 2 (1) of the 1971 Act to order the applicant to be detained or released pending deportation. The Courts Act 1971, s. 9 (2) (c) empowered the Crown Court on appeal to make any order which the magistrates could make. The Crown Court had the jurisdiction and an order of mandamus would be granted.

R v INNER LONDON CROWN COURT, EX PARTE OBAJUWANA (1979) 123 Sol Jo 143 (Queen's Bench Division: LORD WIDGERY CJ, EVELEIGH LJ and STEPHEN BROWN J).

1489   Detention order—validity

An immigrant applied for a writ of habeas corpus to secure his release from prison on the ground that the detention order was invalidated by an error in it. A majority of the Divisional Court refused the application and the applicant appealed on the ground that the Divisional Court was wrong in holding that the detention order was valid. An affidavit was put in exhibiting a correct written authority for the continued detention of the applicant, bearing the date of the Divisional Court hearing, which superseded the earlier order. The applicant conceded that he could not in the circumstances argue his appeal, which was dismissed.

RE SHAHID IQBAL (NOTE) [1979] 1 WLR 425 (Court of Appeal: MEGAW, ROSKILL and BROWNE LJJ). Decision of Divisional Court of the Queen's Bench Division [1978] 3 WLR 884, 1978 Halsbury's Abridgment para. 1538 affirmed.

1490   Entry—control of entry through Republic of Ireland

The Immigration (Control of Entry through Republic of Ireland) (Amendment) Order 1979, S.I. 1979 No. 730 (in force on 1st August) amends the Immigration (Control of Entry through Republic of Ireland) Order 1972. Persons entering the Republic from the United Kingdom are now exempt from control under Immigration Act 1971 s. 1 (3).

1491   —— legality of entry into Britain—failure to disclose material consideration upon entry—father settled in Britain

An applicant for a writ of habeas corpus was being detained as an illegal immigrant. She had initially been refused admission to Britain by the British embassy in Karachi, and her passport had been stamped to that effect. She applied for a second passport under a different name and was granted permission to enter Britain. On arrival in this country she did not disclose to immigration officials the existence of the first passport and she told them that her father was in Pakistan, whereas in fact he had settled in Britain, a material consideration in deciding whether someone is a bona fide visitor or in fact intends to settle in Britain. The applicant obtained extensions of stay, the final one expiring in October 1977. In September 1977 she married a man who had settled in Britain and applied for restrictions on her stay to be removed. This was refused on the grounds that the marriage was one of convenience, and upon discovery of her first passport and the whereabouts of her father, she was detained as an illegal immigrant. *Held*, had the immigration officials been aware of the true facts, the applicant would not have been granted entry into Britain. Her deceit about the whereabouts of her father was an additional indication that she had intended to remain permanently in Britain. As she had never been entitled to enter the country, her marriage was not relevant and the application would be refused.

R v SECRETARY OF STATE FOR HOME AFFAIRS, EX PARTE SHAH [1979] LS Gaz R 386 (Queen's Bench Division: LORD WIDGERY CJ, MICHAEL DAVIES and NEILL JJ).

1492   —— —— relevant date for determining applicant's eligibility for entry

A man detained as an illegal immigrant applied for a writ of habeas corpus, claiming he had entered the country legally with a valid entry certificate. An application for an entry certificate had been made on his behalf in 1973, when he was fifteen years old, but due to delay it was not granted until November 1975 when he was eighteen years old. He married early in 1976 and in March of that year he entered the United Kingdom without disclosing his marriage, and was given indefinite leave to enter. Under the Statement of Immigration Rules for Control on Entry 1973, para. 39, the children of settlers in the United Kingdom who are eighteen years or over have to qualify for admission in their own right; however, indefinite leave to enter can be granted to a son who is between eighteen and twenty-one years, unmarried and fully dependent on a parent settled in the United Kingdom. Under para. 10 leave to enter can be refused if there has been "a material change in circumstances" since the date of the grant. When the applicant later applied for his wife to join him he was detained as an illegal immigrant. *Held*, the relevant date for determining the applicant's eligibility to enter was the date of granting the certificate, not the date of application for the certificate. On the date of the grant the applicant had no longer been eligible for entry under para. 39, as he was eighteen and not a fully dependent son. Furthermore the applicant's marriage was a "material change in circumstances" within para. 10 which he should have disclosed at the time of entry. The application for habeas corpus would be refused.

R v SECRETARY OF STATE FOR THE HOME DEPARTMENT, EX PARTE ZAMIR [1979] 2 All ER 849 (Queen's Bench Division: LORD WIDGERY CJ, CUMMING-BRUCE LJ and NEILL J).

1493   Ports of entry

The Immigration (Ports of Entry) (Amendment) Order 1979, S.I. 1979 No. 1635 (in force on 1st January 1980), further amends the Immigration (Ports of Entry) Order 1972, adding Portsmouth to the list of seaports and hoverports specified as ports of entry for the purposes of the Immigration Act 1971. Certain seaports are deleted and Cardiff (Wales) replaces Glamorgan (Rhoose) in the list of airports.

1494   Registration with police—fees

The Immigration (Registration with Police) (Amendment) Regulations 1979, S.I. 1979 No. 196 (in force on 1st April 1979), increase the fees payable where aliens, other than EEC nationals, are required to register with police.

1495   Work permits—proposed restrictions on issue

In a written answer to a parliamentary question the Under-Secretary of State for Employment has stated that, with effect from 1st January 1980, work permits will be restricted to persons holding recognised professional qualifications and persons with a high degree of skill or experience. For most occupations the minimum age at which permits will be issued will be increased from 18 to 23 years. A statement would be made later concerning special arrangements under which a limited number of resident domestic servants and other semi-skilled or unskilled workers would be allowed to enter from certain specified countries. Young people will continue to be allowed to enter for on-the-job training or work experience but will not be allowed to remain in normal employment. See Times, 15th November 1979.

INCOME TAXATION

Halsbury's Laws of England (4th edn.), Vol. 23

1496   Articles

Frost over the Bahamas: Newstead v Frost Examined, Neil Thomas (tax avoidance and the case of *Newstead v Frost* [1979] 2 All ER 129, CA, 1978 Halsbury's Abridgment para. 1557): 129 NLJ 487.

Leasing and Capital Allowances, Robert P. Burrow and A. J. Shipwright (some of the tax implications of leasing machinery or plant): 123 Sol Jo 644.

Migration of Companies: Tax and the Criminal Law, Robert P. Burrow and A. J. Shipwright (consideration of Income and Corporation Taxes Act 1970, s. 482): 123 Sol Jo 171.

The Problems of Arrangements, S. C. Reisbach (the scope and purpose of the Finance Act 1973, ss. 28, 29): [1979] LS Gaz 226.

Remittances, Ian R. Coles (a critical exposition of the current state of the law): [1979] BTR 238.

Remunerative Shares, P. F. Smith (the problem of liability to income tax of benefits conceded by employers to employees): 129 NLJ 897.

Separate Taxation of Wife's Earnings, Simon Owen: TAXATION, 21st July 1979, p. 271.

Stock Relief Updated, K. R. Tingley (a series of articles examining the present availability of stock relief, together with the permanent write-off of unrecovered relief): Taxation 29th September 1979, p. 474.

Tax Aspects of Plant Leasing, Nigel Eastaway: 129 NLJ 275.

Trade, Profession, Employment and Vocation?, A. J. Shipwright (suggestions for the resolution of the question of differences in the tax treatment of people in different lines of employment): 123 Sol Jo 679.

Traders' Golden Handshakes, P. F. Smith (judicial attitude towards the payment of income tax on golden handshakes): 129 NLJ 32.

Voluntary Payments and Trade Receipts, David R. Davies (on the nature of a trade receipt for income tax purposes): [1979] BTR 212.

1497   Appeal—appeal by way of case stated—application to adjourn hearing of appeal to enable determination of whether proceedings before General Commissioners a nullity

A taxpayer appealed by way of case stated against the General Commissioners' determinations of his assessments to income tax. In the meantime, the taxpayer was assessed to surtax in respect of periods during which his total income included the sums in question before the General Commissioners. At the hearing of his appeal before the Special Commissioners against the surtax assessments, the taxpayer applied for an adjournment alleging that the proceedings before the General Commissioners had been improperly conducted and were a nullity. He claimed therefore that the figures forming the basis of the surtax could not stand. The Special Commissioners adjourned the proceedings sine die which meant that they would not be resumed unless one or both parties applied for further hearing. At the appeal by way of case stated, the taxpayer applied for an adjournment of the hearing to enable the Inland Revenue Commissioners to take steps to determine whether the proceedings before the General Commissioners were a nullity having regard to the evidence put before the Special Commissioners. *Held*, the Inland Revenue Commissioners had indicated that they had no intention of taking any of the steps suggested by the taxpayer as they wished to get on with the appeal by way of case stated. Accordingly, the application would be dismissed. However, as the allegations made against the General Commissioners were serious and it would not be right to suppress them by procedural technicalities, an application for adjournment would be considered if the taxpayer wished to apply for judicial review of the proceedings before the General Commissioners under RSC Ord 53.

The court then agreed to stand over the hearing of the appeal until such an application for judicial review was disposed of on the taxpayer's undertaking that it would be made within fourteen days.

DUTTA v DOIG (INSPECTOR OF TAXES) [1979] STC 724 (Chancery Division: GOULDING J).

1498   —— —— **irregularity in proceedings before commissioners—jurisdiction of court**

A freelance draftsman who worked at home was assessed for tax in respect of his fees and interest on a bank deposit account. He appealed against the assessments and claimed that he was entitled to deduct twenty-five per cent for running his home. The commissioners reduced the assessment slightly but permitted only a small deduction for expenses. On appeal by way of case stated, the draftsman claimed that the proceedings before the commissioners had been improperly conducted. *Held*, on an appeal by way of case stated the court could only consider questions of law arising on the case. When a complaint was made as to the conduct of proceedings, it should be dealt with by means of a prerogative order in the Divisional Court of the Queen's Bench Division. Nor was there any ground on which the court could interfere with the assessment and accordingly the appeal would be dismissed.

THOMAS v INGRAM (INSPECTOR OF TAXES) [1979] STC 1 (Chancery Division: FOX J).

1499   —— **appeal to Special Commissioners—procedure**

The Special Commissioners have produced a pamphlet entitled "Notes for parties to appeals or other proceedings before the Special Commissioners". It contains an outline of procedure and draws attention to a number of important points under the following main headings:

Introduction
Preparing for a hearing
The hearing
The decision
Appeal from a decision of the Special Commissioners
Special Commissioners' Office.

Copies may be obtained free of charge by writing to the Clerk to the Special Commissioners, Turnstile House, 94–99 High Holborn, London WC1V 6LQ or by calling at or writing to the Public Enquiry Room, Inland Revenue, New Wing, Somerset House, London WC2R 1LB: Inland Revenue Press Release dated 30th May 1979.

1500   **Assessment—assessment determined by Commissioners—taxpayer's allegations that proceedings before Commissioners a nullity**

See *Dutta v Doig (Inspector of Taxes)*, para. 1497.

1501   —— —— **taxpayer's right to dispute liability to pay tax under assessment**

The Inland Revenue issued a summons under RSC Ord. 14 claiming from the taxpayer tax due under assessments determined by the General Commissioners. The taxpayer's application for leave to defend the action, on the grounds (i) that the assessments were incorrect and (ii) that, as a case had been stated for the opinion of the High Court, final judgment on the summons could not be entered until that case had been heard, was refused, and the Revenue were given leave to sign final judgment against the taxpayer. The taxpayer appealed. *Held*, the statutory machinery for an appeal from a notice of assessment was exclusive and therefore the taxpayer was not entitled, in proceedings to enforce assessments determined by the Commissioners, to dispute his liability in respect of those assessments. Further, the Taxes Management Act 1970, s. 56 (9) expressly provided that the fact that a case had been stated for the opinion of the High Court did not operate as a stay of the taxpayer's liability in respect of assessments which had been the subject of appeals to the General Commissioners. Accordingly, the appeal would be dismissed.

INLAND REVENUE COMRS v SOUL (1976) 51 TC 86 (Court of Appeal: CAIRNS, STEPHENSON and BRIDGE LJJ). *IRC v Pearlberg* [1953] 1 All ER 388 followed.

1502   —— partnership—date of formation of partnership

See *Saywell v Pope (Inspector of Taxes)*, para. 2010.

1503   —— remission of tax—jurisdiction of General Commissioners

See *Slater (Inspector of Taxes) v Richardson and Bottoms Ltd*, para. 1557.

1504   Avoidance—artificial transaction in land—opportunity of realising gain provided by taxpayer

The taxpayer, a United Kingdom resident, settled shares in his company on trust for his family. The trustees, who were resident in Guernsey, set up companies to acquire land from a subsidiary of the taxpayer's company. Planning permission was granted for the land which was then purchased by the taxpayer's company at a greatly increased price. The taxpayer was assessed for the amount of the increase under the Income and Corporation Taxes Act 1970, s. 488, which provides that where land is acquired with the sole or main object of realising a gain from its disposal a person who enables a gain to be realised is to be taxed as if it were his income. He argued that because all the transactions had been for market value, s. 488 did not apply. *Held*, the fact that the land was acquired by the companies realising the gain at market value did not prevent s. 488 from applying, so long as there was an element of tax avoidance. The transactions in this case were clearly entered into for the ulterior motive of tax avoidance. The question was then whether the gain which accrued to the Guernsey companies in respect of the land derived from an opportunity to realise a gain which had been provided directly or indirectly by the taxpayer. The opportunity was not provided directly by him personally, for he was in no position to do so. However, although he lacked the legal capacity to transfer the opportunity by his own act, if he were in a position to procure the trustees to transfer the opportunity to the companies, he could be said to provide the companies with that opportunity indirectly. The Commissioners had not made sufficient findings of fact to determine whether this was so, and the matter would be sent back to them to make further findings.

A further question arose as to the amount of the gain realised. On the sale of the land, the companies only became entitled to a proportion of the purchase price, the balance being payable in instalments upon specified contingencies. Assuming that s. 488 applied to the taxpayer, he would be liable to tax on the proportion of the price payable immediately, subject to deduction of expenses. He would not be taxable on the entire purchase price, since the postponed rights of enjoying the gain could not be regarded as money's worth received by the companies in the tax year in question. The appeal would be allowed and the matter remitted to the General Commissioners for reconsideration.

YUILL v WILSON (INSPECTOR OF TAXES) [1979] 2 All ER 1205 (Court of Appeal: BUCKLEY, GOFF and EVELEIGH LJJ). Decision of Templeman J [1977] 3 All ER 903, 1977 Halsbury's Abridgment para. 1502 reversed.

1505   —— fund administered abroad—whether discretionary beneficiary having powers to enjoy income—statutory provisions

The taxpayers, who resided in the United Kingdom, were beneficiaries under a discretionary trust of overseas property which had been transferred to non-resident trustees. Under the powers contained in the settlement appointments from capital were made to the beneficiaries. The Crown assessed the taxpayers to tax for the previous six years on the basis, under the Income Tax Act 1952, s. 412 (now Income and Corporation Taxes Act 1970, s. 478), that each beneficiary, being an individual ordinarily resident in the United Kingdom, had avoided tax as a result of a transfer of assets abroad resulting in a transfer of income to a person abroad and was thus liable to tax under either s. 412 (1), as having rights by which he had power to enjoy the trustees' income, or s. 412 (2), as having received a capital sum the payment of which was connected with such transfer of assets. Under s. 412 the income of the non-resident trustees of the settlement was deemed to be the income of each beneficiary for the purposes of the Income Tax Acts. To prevent hardship however, the Crown assessed each taxpayer on a proportion of the total income of the trustees. Despite this, one beneficiary who had received a single capital payment of £100,000 was assessed on a total of £274,121. The Chancery Division judge in two separate decisions allowed the taxpayers' appeals, by way of case stated, against the assessments to tax under s. 412 (1) or (2). The Crown appealed direct to the House of Lords. *Held*, in enacting s. 412, Parliament intended the section to have the limited effect of penalising only those persons who transferred assets abroad to avoid tax and did not intend it to refer to beneficiaries under a discretionary trust resulting from such a transfer. An "individual" liable to tax under s. 412 (1), (2) referred only to an individual ordinarily resident in the United Kingdom who sought to avoid his own liability to tax by the transfer of assets abroad while continuing to reside in the United Kingdom.

LORD WILBERFORCE, LORD SALMON and LORD KEITH OF KINKEL held that, in any event, the Revenue's levying of tax on, and apportioning the liability among, the beneficiaries who had received payments from the funds, by the exercise of a self-asserted administrative discretion was unconstitutional as it offended the principle that a citizen could not be taxed unless he was designated in clear terms by a taxing Act as a taxpayer and the amount of his liability was clearly defined. The assessments failed therefore in the case of discretionary beneficiaries.

VESTEY v INLAND REVENUE COMRS (NOS. 1 AND 2) [1979] 3 All ER 976 (House of Lords: LORD WILBERFORCE, VISCOUNT DILHORNE, LORD SALMON, LORD EDMUND-DAVIES and LORD KEITH OF KINKEL). Decisions of Walton J [1977] 3 All ER 1073, 1977 Halsbury's Abridgment para. 1505, [1979] 2 All ER 225, 1978 Halsbury's Abridgment para. 1558 affirmed on other grounds. *Congreve v Inland Revenue Comrs* [1948] 1 All ER 948, HL overruled.

1506 ——**power of commissioners to require information—notice requiring information about unidentified transactions—validity of notice**

The Commissioners of Inland Revenue served a notice on the taxpayer pursuant to the Income and Corporation Taxes Act 1970, s. 490, which is intended to prevent the avoidance of tax by persons concerned with land or the development of land. The taxpayer sought a declaration that the notice was void and of no effect on the grounds that (i) the notice could only be issued under s. 490 (2) (c), because it required particulars of unidentified transactions or arrangements; (ii) the notice was too obscure and covered such a wide variety of matters that it was inordinately burdensome and oppressive that the taxpayer should be required to answer it. *Held*, the commissioners' power to issue such a notice derived from s. 490 (1), which was wide enough to cover unidentified transactions. The commissioners had a discretion to decide what information was necessary and a notice under s. 490 could only be declared invalid if they had acted in bad faith, had failed to take account of relevant matters, had taken into account irrelevant matters or had reached a decision so unreasonable that no reasonable body would have reached it. Oppression did not of itself render a notice void and therefore the taxpayer's claim would fail.

ESSEX v INLAND REVENUE COMRS [1979] STC 525 (Chancery Division: SLADE J). *Royal Bank of Canada v IRC* [1972] Ch 655, *Clinch v IRC* [1974] QB 76, *Associated Provincial Picture House Ltd v Wednesbury Corpn* [1948] 1 KB 223 followed.

1507   —— sale of shares—tax advantage—whether sale a transaction whereby a person received abnormally high dividend

Taxpayers were sole shareholders in five property companies which had profits to be distributed as dividends. In order to reduce their liability to income tax and surtax they devised a complicated series of transactions. This involved a sale of the companies' shares to E, another company over which the taxpayers had control, and it was subsequently agreed that payment for the shares was to be made to company G. The Revenue contended that the taxpayers had acquired an unfair tax advantage. The Special Commissioners rejected the Revenue's contention that the sale of the shares was a transaction whereby E had received an abnormal amount by way of dividend within Income and Corporation Taxes Act 1970, s. 461, para. C. The Revenue appealed and sought to rely on s. 461, para. D, on the ground that the consideration for the shares was connected with the distribution of profits because the transactions were part of one scheme, and the paragraph applied to all five companies on the date when the tax advantage was received because they were all controlled by less than five persons. *Held*, (i) the word "whereby" in para. C meant "by which" not "by means of which" and the sale of the shares was not a transaction by which E had received abnormally high dividend (ii) the relevant date for the purposes of para. D was that of the distribution of profits not that on which the tax advantage had been received. It was not clear whether on that date para. D applied to the companies, since the Revenue had not discharged the burden of proving that they were controlled by less than five persons. Accordingly the appeal would be dismissed.

INLAND REVENUE COMRS V GARVIN [1979] STC 98 (Chancery Division: SLADE J).

This decision has been affirmed by the Court of Appeal; see Times, 29th February 1980.

1508   Benefits—benefits in kind—beneficial loans

The Inland Revenue have issued a Press Release dated 11th April 1979 stating that interest-free loans, or loans at rates of interest less than a rate prescribed for the purpose, which are made to directors and higher paid employees by reason of their employment, may give rise to liability to tax as benefits in kind under the Finance Act 1976, s. 66. In certain circumstances, however, the Inland Revenue will not regard advances made by employers to employees in respect of business expenses as loans giving rise to liability under s. 66. The conditions for the concesssion are that the maximum amount advanced at any one time does not exceed £1,000, the advances are spent within six months, and the employee accounts to his employer at regular intervals for the expenditure of the sum advanced. See Inland Revenue Statement of Practice SP 7/79.

1509   Capital allowance—allowance in respect of industrial building in which "goods" subject to a process—whether notes and coins constitute "goods"

The taxpayer company leased a building to a security company. Part of that building, known as the security area, was used for the storage and sorting out of money for use in wage packets. The security company handled about 10,000 wage packets a week, each containing a breakdown of notes and coins as specified by various employers. The taxpayer company successfully appealed against an assessment to corporation tax on the grounds that it was entitled to an initial allowance in respect of expenditure incurred on the construction of the security area. The General Commissioners reduced the assessment to nil holding that the security area was an "industrial building or structure" within the definition of the Capital Allowances Act 1968, s. 7, thereby entitling the taxpayer company to an allowance by virtue of s. 1 (1) of the Act. The Crown appealed. *Held*, allowance against tax under s. 1 (1) could only be claimed in respect of capital expenditure incurred on the construction of an industrial building or structure. Section 7 (1) (e) defined an "industrial building" as a building in which "goods" were subjected "to any process". While the breaking down of cash into specified quantities of notes and coins for wage packets could be said to be subjecting money to a "process", money itself, in the form of notes and coins did not constitute "goods". Certain money, such as antique coins, could be classified as "goods", but used as a currency money was not within the meaning of that word. The Commissioners were wrong in their decision as the security area was not an "industrial building" for the purposes of the Act. The appeal would be allowed.

BUCKINGHAM (INSPECTOR OF TAXES) v SECURITAS PROPERTIES LTD [1980] STC 166 (Chancery Division: SLADE J).

1510   —— machinery or plant—film production

The Inland Revenue have issued a Statement of Practice SP9/79 dated 10th August 1979 concerning tax treatment of expenditure on producing films and certain similar assets. In future, film production expenditure will qualify for capital allowances as capital expenditure, the asset resulting from the expenditure (the master-print of the film) being regarded as "plant". Similarly, capital allowance claims for expenditure incurred in producing the master copy of records and tapes will be allowed. This change of practice takes effect from 1st June 1979.

1511   —— —— restaurant ship

The taxpayer company purchased a vessel and spent a large sum converting it and fitting it out as a restaurant. It was permanently moored and used as a restaurant. The company claimed capital allowances in respect of the expenditure under the Capital Allowances Act 1968, s. 18, and the Finance Act 1971, s. 41 (1). The question was whether the vessel was "plant", in which case the cost of conversion would be capital expenditure that qualified for the allowance. *Held*, a structure might fall within the definition of "plant" if it was something by means of which the company's business activities were carried on. It would not do so, however, if it played no part in the carrying on of such activities but was merely the place within which they were carried on. Although the vessel was a chattel, and used in connection with the taxpayer company's business, it was not part of the apparatus employed in the commercial activities of the business but was the structure within which the business was carried on. Accordingly, the vessel was not "plant".

BENSON (INSPECTOR OF TAXES) v YARD ARM CLUB LTD [1979] 2 All ER 336 (Court of Appeal: BUCKLEY, SHAW and TEMPLEMAN LJJ). *Yarmouth v France* (1887) 19 QBD 647, DC and *Inland Revenue Commissioners v Barclay, Curle & Co Ltd* [1969] 1 WLR 675, HL applied. Decision of Goulding J [1978] 2 All ER 958, 1978 Halsbury's Abridgment para. 1563 affirmed.

1512   Case stated—hearing of case pending—effect on taxpayer's liability to pay tax under assessment

See *IRC v Soul*, para. 1501.

1513   Child allowance—entitlement—custody of child

Child benefit was claimed for the year 1975/76 in respect of a girl born in 1955, who was the sister of the claimant. Their father died in 1973 when the family was living in India. They came to England in 1974 and the claimant fully supported them, his sister regarding him as being in loco parentis. Child benefit was claimed under the Income and Corporation Taxes Act 1970, s. 10 (1) (b), (2) (b), on the ground that for the year of assessment the claimant had the custody of, and maintained at his own expense, a child other than a child of his who was over sixteen but was receiving full-time instruction at an educational establishment. It was not disputed that the claimant maintained his sister at his own expense or that she was over sixteen but receiving full-time instruction at an educational establishment. The only question was whether for the year of assessment he had custody of the child. *Held*, the claimant could not sensibly be described as having the custody of his sister, who was at the time an adult and an entirely free agent. Thus child allowance was not deductible in respect of her.

ASPEN (INSPECTOR OF TAXES) v BAXI [1979] STC 566 (Chancery Division: BRIGHTMAN J). *Nwagbo v Rising (Inspector of Taxes)* [1978] STC 558, 1978 Halsbury's Abridgment para. 1568 applied.

1514   Close company—undistributed income—apportionment of income—jurisdiction of Special Commissioners to review decision

The taxpayer was a non-trading close company. The Board of Inland Revenue made apportionments of the taxpayer's income for surtax purposes among its participators for the year 1970–71. The Board made the apportionments under the Income and Corporation Taxes Act 1970, s. 296 (5) by reference to the participators' interests in the event of a winding up, instead of the normal apportionment by reference to their interests in income. The taxpayer appealed, contending that the Board's decision to invoke s. 296 (5) was not justified, and that under s. 296 (10) the Special Commissioners had power to review the merits of the Board's decision and to substitute whatever decision they thought proper. The Special Commissioners upheld the apportionment. The taxpayer further appealed. *Held*, on an appeal against apportionment of income of a close company among its participators made under s. 296 (5), the Special Commissioners under s. 296 (10) had a right and a duty to form their own view of the whole matter and, if necessary, to substitute their decision for that of the Board if persuaded that the decision of the Board was wrong. However, on the facts and having regard to the unfettered quality of the power under s. 296 (5), it could not be said that the Board had acted outside that power. Accordingly, the Special Commissioners had not erred in law in affirming the Board's decision. The appeal would be dismissed.

LOTHBURY INVESTMENT CORPN LTD v INLAND REVENUE COMRS [1979] STC 772 (Chancery Division: GOULDING J).

In relation to accounting periods ending after 5th April 1973, 1970 Act, s. 296 (5), (10) was replaced by the Finance Act 1972, Sch. 16, paras. 4 (2), 16 (3).

1515   Compulsory purchase—compensation—deduction for corporation tax

A city council sold back parts of premises compulsorily purchased to enable the original owners of the premises to re-establish their business. It was agreed that compensation would be payable to the owners for loss of profits while the business was being re-established. The question arose as to whether the compensation should be reduced to take account of the corporation tax for which the owners would have been liable in the ordinary course of business if the compulsory purchase order had not been made. The Lands Tribunal held that no such reduction should be made by the council. The council then appealed. *Held*, the decision turned upon the true construction of Finance Act 1969, Sch. 19, para. 11 which provided that where land was compulsorily acquired, the compensation for the acquisition should be apportioned into capital and income elements. The effect of the provision was thus to free compensation for temporary loss of profits of its capital nature and enable it to be treated as a trading receipt. The council should therefore pay the full sum to the owners who in turn could account to the Inland Revenue for their liabilities. The appeal would accordingly be dismissed.

STOKE ON TRENT CITY COUNCIL v WOOD MITCHELL & CO LTD [1979] 2 All ER 65 (Court of Appeal: STEPHENSON, ROSKILL and GEOFFREY LANE LJJ). Decision of Lands Tribunal (1977) 33 P & CR 516, 1977 Halsbury's Abridgment para. 1515 affirmed.

1516   The Inland Revenue have issued a Press Release dated 18th June 1979 stating that as a result of the decision of the Court of Appeal in *City of Stoke on Trent v Wood Mitchell & Co Ltd*, para. 1515, they have changed their practice in relation to compensation for temporary loss of profits and expenses connected with compulsory acquisition of property. Full details are shown in Statement of Practice SP 8/79. In future, any element of compensation received for temporary loss of profits will fall to be included as a receipt taxable under Case I or II of Schedule D. Compensation for losses on trading stock and to reimburse revenue expenditure, such as removal expenses and interest, will be treated in the same way for tax purposes.

1517   Damages for personal injuries—interest—exemption

The Income and Corporation Taxes Act 1970, s. 375A, exempts from income tax interest on damages awarded by a court in the United Kingdom for personal injuries or the death of any person. The Inland Revenue have decided to extend this exemption by extra-statutory concession to interest on damages awarded in corresponding circumstances by a foreign court provided the interest is exempt from tax in the country in which the award is made: Inland Revenue Press Release dated 13th June 1979.

1518   Double taxation relief

The Inland Revenue have issued a Press Release dated 5th June 1979 stating that the leaflet IR6 "Double Taxation Relief" has been revised to take account of the changes in the rules relating to double taxation relief including the introduction of the imputation system of taxation and the renegotiation of a number of the United Kingdom's double taxation agreements since the previous version of the booklet was published in 1969. Copies of the revised booklet are obtainable, free of charge, from the offices of HM Inspectors of Taxes and from PAYE Enquiry Offices.

1519   —— arrangements—Austria

The Double Taxation Relief (Taxes on Income) (Austria) Order 1979, S.I. 1979 No. 117 (made on 6th February 1979 and taking effect in relation to dividends paid on or after 6th April 1973), amends the Convention set out in the Schedule to the Double Taxation Relief (Taxes on Income) (Austria) Order 1970, mainly in relation to the tax treatment of dividends paid by United Kingdom companies to overseas shareholders.

1520   —— —— Canada

A new double taxation convention has been concluded with Canada to replace the existing agreement (dated 12th December 1966). The new convention relates (in the United Kingdom) to income tax, corporation tax, capital gains tax, petroleum revenue tax, and development land tax. The agreement also contains provisions relating to the exchange of information between the appropriate authorities in the two countries for, inter alia, the prevention of fraud. The convention has not yet come into force; but when it is operative it will relate back, in respect of certain dividends to 6th April 1973; it will relate back to 6th April 1976 in respect of income tax and capital gains tax; to 1st April 1976 in respect of corporation tax; to 1st January 1976 in respect of petroleum revenue tax; and to 1st August 1976 in respect of development land tax. See Convention between the Government of the United Kingdom and the Government of Canada for the avoidance of Double Taxation and the Prevention of Fiscal Evasion with respect to Taxes on Income and Capital Gains (Cmnd. 7413).

1521   —— —— Jordan

The Double Taxation Relief (Shipping and Air Transport Profits) (Jordan) Order 1979, S.I. 1979 No. 300 (in force on 14th March 1979), sets out the arrangements made with Jordan under which the profits, income and capital gains arising on or after 1st April 1977 which are derived from shipping and air transport operations by an undertaking of one of the countries are to be exempt from tax in the other country.

1522   —— —— Malawi

The Double Taxation Relief (Taxes on Income) (Malawi) Order 1979, S.I. 1979 No. 302 (in force on 14th March 1979), amends the agreement set out in the Schedule to the Double Taxation Relief (Taxes on Income) (Federation of Rhodesia and Nyasaland) Order 1956, mainly in relation to the tax treatment of dividends paid by United Kingdom companies to overseas shareholders.

1523 —— —— Norway

The Double Taxation Relief (Taxes on Income) (Norway) Order 1979, S.I. 1979 No. 118 (made on 6th February 1969 and to take effect in general from 1st April 1977, except as regards provisions relating to remuneration from employment which take effect from 6th April 1978), amends the Convention with Norway signed on 22nd January 1969, by providing rules for the avoidance of double taxation in respect of income and profits from activities connected with offshore oil and gas exploitation on United Kingdom and Norwegian Continental Shelves.

1524

The Double Taxation Relief (Taxes on Income) (Norway) (No. 2) Order 1979, S.I. 1979 No. 303 (in force on 14th March 1979), amends the Convention set out in the Schedule to the Double Taxation Relief (Taxes on Income) (Norway) Order 1970, mainly in relation to the tax treatment of dividends paid by United Kingdom companies to overseas shareholders.

1525 —— —— Switzerland

A new convention relating to the avoidance of double taxation with respect to taxes on income was concluded with Switzerland on 8th December 1977. The convention has been ratified and it entered into force on 7th October 1978. It relates in Switzerland to any taxable year beginning on or after 1st January 1978 and in the United Kingdom (i) in respect of income tax and capital gains, to any year of assessment beginning on or after 6th April 1978; (ii) in respect of corporation tax, to any financial year beginning on or after 1st April 1978; (iii) in respect of development land tax, to any realised development value accruing on or after 1st April 1978; and (iv) in respect of petroleum revenue tax, to any chargeable period beginning on or after 1st January 1978 (art. 28). The text of the convention has been published as Cmnd 7400.

1526 —— —— United States of America

The Inland Revenue have issued two Press Releases dated 15th March 1979 announcing that on that date a Third Protocol was signed in London further amending the Double Taxation Convention between the United States of America and the United Kingdom signed in London on 31st December 1975 (see 1975 Halsbury's Abridgment para. 1790). The Convention as amended by two earlier Protocols and now by the Third Protocol is not yet in force and cannot be ratified and brought into force unless the Third Protocol is approved by the United States Senate and the House of Commons. The text of the signed Protocol will be published in due course as a Schedule to a draft Order in Council. In view, however, of the widespread interest that there is in the new Convention, arrangements have been made for a limited number of copies of this Protocol to be made available immediately at Somerset House.

1527 —— —— Venezuela

The Double Taxation Relief (Shipping and Air Transport Profits) (Venezuela) Order 1979, S.I. 1979 No. 301 (in force on 14th March 1979), sets out the arrangements made with Venezuela under which the profits, income and capital gains arising on or after 1st April 1977 which are derived from shipping and air transport operations by an undertaking of one of the countries are to be exempt from tax in the other country, provided that at the date of signature of the agreement the undertaking regularly serves an airport or port in the territory of that other country. An undertaking which commences regular services after the date of signature may by mutual agreement be included at a later date.

1528 —— termination—Tanzania

Tanzania has given notice terminating the Double Taxation Arrangement with the United Kingdom. The existing Arrangement will accordingly cease to have effect in the United Kingdom from 6th April 1980 in respect of income tax and 1st April 1980 in respect of corporation tax: Inland Revenue Press Release dated 8th May 1979.

1529 Expenses—expenses of overseas employment—foreign emoluments

The Inland Revenue have issued a Press Release dated 6th August 1979 stating that they have revised the wording of Extra-Statutory Concession A.25 which exempts from tax the reimbursement of certain travelling expenses to and from the United Kingdom to persons working in the United Kingdom in receipt of foreign emoluments. The concession originally applied to United Kingdom employees working abroad as well as to persons in receipt of foreign emoluments but following the enactment of the Finance Act 1977, s. 32, the part relating to United Kingdom employees working abroad became otiose. To avoid misunderstanding, the concession has been revised to make it clear that the recipient of foreign emoluments working in this country is treated in the same way for tax purposes as the United Kingdom resident employee working abroad.

1530 Extra-statutory concession—free coal—whether tax payable on cash benefit given in lieu

A former colliery manager received free coal on his retirement in 1960. When he moved, some years later, to a house heated by gas the National Coal Board paid him a cash allowance in lieu of his free coal, but deducted tax from the cash allowance. His tax office referred him to extra-statutory concession A7 and informed him that "miners" in this provision were understood to be all manual workers at or about a colliery whether on the surface or below ground including men employed on screening and washing plant, haulage etc.; the term included under-officials (overmen, deputies and shotfirers) and weekly-paid industrial staff, and was extended to such persons who had retired on pension and to their widows. The tax office explained that the complainant being a manager at the time of his retirement did not come within the definition and hence was liable to be taxed on the cash allowance. He brought the matter to the attention of the Parliamentary Commissioner. The Revenue explained to the commissioner that where a free delivery of coal to a miner did not qualify for exemption under the concession it did not seek to tax the benefit in kind by reference to the usual rule for benefits in kind (i.e. secondhand value) since its secondhand value was conjectural; but that different considerations applied where a cash allowance was paid in lieu of the benefit in kind. The commissioner found that the rule at the nub of the dispute, the definition of "miner" for the purposes of the concession, had been agreed between the Revenue and the National Coal Board and that accordingly it was not unreasonable for the Revenue to adhere strictly to it. See Case No. 1A/161/78, Parliamentary Commissioner for Administration: Investigations completed—May to July 1978 (HC 664).

1531 Finance Act 1979

The Finance Act 1979 received the royal assent on 4th April 1979 and came into force on that date. The Act continued income and corporation tax at the existing rates, increased the main personal reliefs from income tax, withdrew child tax allowances and continued the limit on relief for interest imposed by the Finance Act 1974, Sch. 1, para. 5. The main financial provisions for 1979/1980 were made in the Finance (No. 2) Act 1979, see para. 2247.

1532 Fraud—power to seize documents—exercise of power—whether warrant should specify offence

The Inland Revenue, suspecting that a tax fraud had been committed, applied to a circuit judge for a search warrant. The warrant was issued under the Taxes Management Act 1970, s. 20c (1) which empowers a judge to issue a search warrant if satisfied by a Revenue officer's sworn information that there is reasonable ground for suspecting that a tax offence has been committed and that evidence of the offence is to be found on specified premises. The Revenue's warrant referred to an officer's sworn information that there was reasonable ground for suspecting a tax offence but did not state that the judge was satisfied by such information of the matters specified in s. 20c (1). Moreover, the warrant did not specify that any particular offence was suspected. Revenue officers searched the taxpayers' homes and business premises, removing many documents in pursuance of the 1970 Act, s. 20c (3). Under s. 20c (3), officers with a search warrant are authorised to seize any documents which they reasonably believe might be required as evidence in proceedings involving a tax fraud. On an application for judicial review of the Revenue's action, the taxpayers were granted (i) an order of certiorari quashing the warrant as being invalid under s. 20c (1) because it did not specify the offence suspected and (ii) a declaration that the seizure was unlawful due to the absence of grounds for "reasonable belief" under s. 20c (3). On appeal by the Revenue, held, LORD SALMON dissenting, (i) the warrant was valid although it did not specify the offence suspected. It was issued under s. 20c (1) which only required disclosure of the premises to be searched and the officers authorised to search. Moreover, its validity was not affected because it did not state that the judge was satisfied of the matters specifed in s. 20c (1). The warrant complied with s. 20c (1) and was therefore valid. (ii) In their application for judicial review, the taxpayers had failed to establish that seizure of the documents under s. 20c (3) was unlawful. Although large quantities of documents were removed, many officers were involved and it would not have taken them long to form a reasonable belief that documents might be required as evidence in proceedings. The fact that some documents might have been taken by mistake did not mean that all other papers were taken without proper examination. Accordingly, as the warrant was valid and the seizure lawful, the appeal would be allowed.

LORD SALMON dissented on the ground that the warrant was invalid because it did not state that the judge was satisfied of the matters specified in s. 20c (1).

INLAND REVENUE COMRS v ROSSMINSTER LTD [1980] STC 42 (House of Lords: LORD WILBERFORCE, VISCOUNT DILHORNE, LORD DIPLOCK, LORD SALMON and LORD SCARMAN). Decision of the Court of Appeal sub nom. *R v Inland Revenue Comrs, ex parte Rossminster Ltd* [1979] 3 All ER 385 reversed.

1533 Group income—election

The Council of the constituent members of the Consultative Committee of Accountancy Bodies after consultation with the Inland Revenue has issued a guidance notice in relation to elections to pay dividends as group income and annual payments and interest without deduction of tax. The Inland Revenue will not take a hard line where there is an accidental failure to make an election due to some genuine reason, provided that acceptance of a late election will not have the effect of disturbing settled claims or assessments that have become final or conclusive. Where only two companies are involved, a single election is acceptable to the Revenue provided that it is signed by a person duly authorised to act on behalf of each company. The Revenue will also accept one election in respect of three or more companies in a group provided that all the necessary facts are shown, that the election is signed on behalf of each company concerned, and that the application of the election between any two companies is clearly shown. The Revenue will accept that any company that is a member of a group may, by resolution of its board, appoint a named person as authorised to make a joint election on behalf of that company for the purposes of the Income and Corporation Taxes Act 1970, s. 256; all the companies in the group may appoint the same person. The guidance note concludes with a draft form of election which is acceptable to the Revenue. See *Accountancy*, July 1979, p.120.

1534 Information—failure to furnish—justification

The taxpayer was sent a notice pursuant to the Taxes Management Act 1970, s. 51, requiring him to make available to the Inspector of Taxes various documents and accounts within ninety days of the date of the notice. The taxpayer did not comply within the time limit and a penalty of £50 was awarded against him. He appealed, claiming he was justified in not sending the documents because, firstly, he had had to send the same documents to the Inspector of Taxes a year earlier, and, secondly, he had written to the Inspector of Taxes and was awaiting a response before sending the documents. *Held*, neither explanation justified not sending the documents. The taxpayer should have written as soon as he received the notice, pointing out that the information had already been made available, whereas his letter was sent only shortly before the time limit expired, and a reply could not have been expected before expiry. The appeal would be dismissed.

GALLERI v WIRRAL GENERAL COMRS [1979] STC 216 (Chancery Division: WALTON J).

1535   Interest—interest on unpaid tax

The Inland Revenue are only prepared to remit or reduce an interest charge which is legally due in very rare and special circumstances: for example, when errors on their part would make an interest charge altogether unconscionable, as might happen if a taxpayer had been positively misled about a due and payable date. An exceptionally long delay by valuation offices before an inspector received valuation figures on which to base capital gains tax assessment and which resulted in the interest provisions of the Finance (No. 2) Act 1975 applying to the case did not in the view of the Revenue constitute such very rare and special circumstances. When the case was taken up by the Parliamentary Commissioner he confirmed that, in his opinion, the consequence of the delay did not justify a remission of the interest charge. See Case No. 1B/766/77, Parliamentary Commissioner for Administration: Investigations completed—May to July 1978 (HC 664).

1536

The Income Tax (Interest on Unpaid Tax and Repayment Supplement) Order 1979, S.I. 1979 No. 1687 (arts. 1, 2 in force on 1st January, art. 3 on 6th January 1980), increases from 9 per cent per annum (but, in the case of development land tax, from 6 per cent per annum) to 12 per cent per annum the rate of increase chargeable on unpaid income tax, surtax, capital gains tax, corporation tax (including advance corporate tax) development land tax, petroleum revenue tax, profits tax, excess profits tax, excess profits levy, and on overpaid land tax. The Order also provides that, for periods beginning on 6th January 1980 Supplement on repayments of income tax, surtax, capital gains tax and corporation tax (including advance corporation tax) will be at the rate of 12 per cent per annum.

1537   —— purchase of cum-dividend securities—liability to tax on proportion of interest attributable to period prior to date of purchase

The taxpayer purchased securities on which the interest was paid half-yearly. The purchase was a purchase cum-dividend; that is the taxpayer paid an additional amount representing interest which had accrued from the last previous dividend date and which entitled him to the full half-year's instalment of interest. The taxpayer was assessed to income tax on this instalment, but he contended that he should be assessed to tax only on the interest which had accrued since the date of purchase. The money with which he had purchased the securities had, prior to the purchase, attracted interest whilst invested with a bank, on which he had paid tax. He contended that to make him liable for tax on both the interest on the purchase money and the interest on the securities arising in the period prior to purchase would amount to double taxation. *Held*, it was clear from *Wigmore v Thomas Summerson and Sons Ltd* that the seller of securities was not liable to tax on any sum received in respect of the purchase of the right to a full instalment of interest, but that it was the purchaser who was so liable. The taxpayer was thus liable to tax on the whole of the instalment in question.

SCHAFFER v CATTERMOLE (INSPECTOR OF TAXES) [1979] STC 670 (Chancery Division: GOULDING J). *Wigmore v Thomas Summerson and Sons Ltd* [1926] 1 KB 131 applied.

1538   —— relief—overdraft secured by deposit of title deeds on house

A taxpayer sought relief from tax on the interest which he had paid on his overdrawn current account. He contended that as he had been granted facilities by the bank to overdraw on his account up to a sum of £3,000, and as he had deposited title deeds to property owned by him as security, the loan was a mortgage and was not an overdraft, the word "overdraft" meaning sums drawn in excess of the amount of the facility permitted by the banker. *Held*, the taxpayer's bank account was a standard current account on which the taxpayer was overdrawn and consequently he was not eligible for relief from tax.

WALCOT-BATHER v GOLDING (INSPECTOR OF TAXES) [1979] STC 707 (Chancery Division: OLIVER J).

1539   Life assurance—relief on premiums

The Inland Revenue have issued a Press Release dated 30th March 1979 reminding taxpayers that a new system for giving relief in respect of life assurance premiums began on 6th April 1979. From that date the arrangements set out in the Finance Act 1976 apply and relief is no longer allowed through an individual's tax coding. Under the new arrangements, in the case of an ordinary branch policy the policy holder will normally deduct and retain 17½ per cent of the premiums when paying them to the life insurance company. The Inland Revenue will then reimburse the company for the amounts deducted. Where, in the case of a policy with an Industrial Office or branch or collecting Friendly Society, the premiums do not exceed £4 per four weeks the individual will normally pay the same premium as now but will receive increased benefits under the policy. If the premiums on such a policy do exceed £4 per four weeks the policy holder will generally have a choice either to go on paying the same premium for an increased benefit, or to pay a premium reduced by 17½ per cent leaving the policy benefits unaltered. The new system applies normally only to residents of the United Kingdom, and relief will be available only when premiums are paid to a United Kingdom company or Friendly Society, or to a United Kingdom branch of an overseas company.

1540   The Income Tax (Life Assurance Premium Relief) Regulations 1979, S.I. 1979 No. 346 (in force on 6th April 1979), amend the Income Tax (Life Assurance Premium Relief) Regulations 1978, 1978 Halsbury's Abridgment para. 1605. Regulation 3 (5) (a) of the 1978 Regulations requires a life office to obtain (unless it already possesses) certain information from the person paying premiums before it can accept payment of premiums under deduction. This regulation is amended to enable the Board to dispense with this requirement in cases where it is unnecessary.

1541   —— —— children's policies

The Inland Revenue have issued a Press Release dated 28th February 1979 stating that they have considered the question of premium relief as it relates to policies effected on the lives of children in the light of the new scheme for premium relief by deduction which commenced on 6th April 1979. Under this scheme, relief may be allowed even if the individual paying the premium is not liable to tax. In order to prevent the selling of ordinary life assurance policies to young children to gain tax advantages resulting in a child's obtaining relief by deduction even though he has no income liable to tax, the Inland Revenue have decided that no relief is due in respect of premiums on a policy taken out by a child of "tender years", since he could not reasonably be regarded as having "made" the contract, having insufficient knowledge and understanding. For this purpose "tender years" indicates a child of less than twelve years old. Details of the practical application of the decision are shown in Inland Revenue Statement of Practice SP 4/79.

1542   The Inland Revenue have issued a Statement of Practice SP 11/79 concerning life assurance premium relief on children's policies. No relief is in strictness due on premiums on a policy taken out by a child under the age of twelve, but the Inland Revenue will not contest life assurance premium relief on premiums on all industrial branch juvenile policies and similar policies issued by registered friendly societies as part of their tax exempt business, subject in each case to the limit in the Finance Act 1976, Sch. 4, para. 11 (3). Where an ordinary branch policy, other than a friendly society policy referred to above, is taken out on the life of a child and is assigned to him or he possesses or acquires the whole interest in the policy, relief on the premiums paid by the child may be allowed (provided that the other conditions are satisfied): (i) where the policy was taken out after the child had attained the age of twelve; (ii) where the policy was taken out prior to 1st March 1979 and before the child attained the age of twelve; (iii) where the policy was taken out on or after 1st March 1979 before the child attained the age of twelve and he has attained that age.

1543   —— —— **premiums on which commission payable to the policyholder**

The Inland Revenue have issued a Press Release dated 19th February 1979 stating that they have considered the position of persons who are entitled as agent of an insurance company to commission on premiums on policies effected on their own account in the light of the provisions for the premium relief by deduction scheme which commenced on 6th April 1979. Formerly Inland Revenue practice was to regard such a person as not liable to tax on such commissions as income in his hands, except that where the premiums were allowable deductions in computing profits or gains for tax purposes or were otherwise allowable under the Taxes Acts, only the net premiums (after deducting the commissions) were allowable. In the light of the new provisions, the position is now that the amount of relief depends on the amount of money which passes between the individual and the life office at the time the premium is paid. Thus relief is only available on the net amount of the premium less the commission: Inland Revenue Statement of Practice SP 3/79.

1544   **Malaysian taxation—acquisition and disposal of property— whether transaction representing trade or business**

A company, the objects of which were dealing in and developing land and investing in shares and securities, bought a parcel of land and entered into contracts for the building of a hotel. It later transferred both the building and land to another company, in consideration for which it received a number of shares. The Revenue contended that this acquisition and disposal represented a trade or business and assessed the resulting profit to tax. The company argued that the profit arose from an isolated transaction which did not amount to a trade or business, or alternatively that it was an investment which was not taxable. *Held*, the transaction had represented a trade or business and therefore the assessment would be upheld.

INTERNATIONAL INVESTMENT LTD v COMPTROLLER-GENERAL OF INLAND REVENUE [1978] TR 247 (Privy Council: LORD DIPLOCK, VISCOUNT DILHORNE, LORD FRASER OF TULLYBELTON, LORD KEITH OF KINKEL and SIR ROBIN COOKE). Dictum of Lord Diplock in *American Leaf Blending Co Sdn Bhd v Director General of Inland Revenue* [1978] TR 243, 1978 Halsbury's Abridgment para. 1623 applied.

1545   —— **exemption from tax for income taxed in Singapore—position where trading losses sustained in Singapore**

Under a Malaysian statute, income of a Malaysian company, wherever it was derived from, was subject to income tax. The statute provided that, when calculating the income for the purpose of tax, trading losses sustained by a company were deductible. A statutory instrument incorporating an agreement between Malaysia and Singapore provided that profits of a Malaysian company which had been taxed in Singapore were exempt from tax in Malaysia. It also provided that the laws of Malaysia were to continue to govern matters of taxation except where there were express provisions to the contrary in the agreement. There were no express provisions regarding trading losses. A company made a profit in Malaysia, but had suffered a loss on its operations in Singapore. The question arose as to whether the company's loss was deductible when calculating tax. *Held*, by the provisions of the statutory instrument the loss could be offset when calculating the tax. There were no express provisions in the agreement regarding losses, therefore Malaysian law must apply. Under that law such losses were deductible when calculating tax.

HOCK HENG CO SDN BERHAD V DIRECTOR-GENERAL OF INLAND REVENUE [1979] STC 291 (Privy Council: LORD DIPLOCK, VISCOUNT DILHORNE, LORD EDMUND-DAVIES, LORD RUSSELL OF KILLOWEN AND LORD HAILSHAM OF ST MARYLEBONE).

1546   Occupational pension schemes—Inland Revenue booklet

A revised edition of the booklet IR12 has been published giving guidance in general terms as to the manner in which the Board of Inland Revenue exercise their discretion under the Finance Act 1970, s. 20, to approve occupational pension schemes for tax relief purposes. It replaces the 1974 edition and takes account of changes in legislation and in the Board's discretionary practice up to the end of March 1979; Inland Revenue Press Release dated 31st August 1979.

1547   Pay As You Earn—coding—husband and wife

A husband and wife are entitled to only one basic rate band on their joint earnings; thus where their joint earnings attract liability to tax at a higher rate, to ensure that they receive only one basic rate it has been the practice in the past to adjust the wife's PAYE coding, increasing her tax liability. In future the adjustment will be made to the husband's coding, unless the wife's earnings are expected to be greater than her husband's or the couple notify the tax office that they would prefer the adjustment to be made to the wife's coding. This has no application to those cases where a wife's earnings election or an election for separate assessment has been made.

The Revenue are changing their practice on correspondence with married women. In future tax offices will always where possible write direct to a married woman about her own tax affairs: Inland Revenue Press Release dated 4th December 1979.

1548   —— payment of emoluments

The Income Tax (Employments) (No. 9) Regulations 1979, S.I. 1979 No. 747 (in force on 6th October 1979), amend the Income Tax (Employments) Regulations 1973, by raising the limit of weekly or monthly pay above which an employer has to operate the PAYE scheme for every employee, to take into account the increased tax allowances proposed for 1979/80.

1549   Payments on termination of employment—tax treatment

The Inland Revenue have issued a Press Release dated 1st August 1979 stating that they have prepared a consultative paper on the tax treatment of payments made on termination of employment. The proposals contained in the paper are that the present distinction between payments for compensation for loss of office and other terminal payments should be ended, and that the top-slicing relief at present used in calculating the tax payable on termination payments should be discontinued, and instead only half the excess of such payments over the prescribed threshold should be taxed. Copies of the paper are available on application in writing or in person to the Public Enquiry Room, New Wing, Somerset House, London WC2R 1LB.

1550   Personal taxation—leaflets

The Inland Revenue have announced in a Press Release dated 8th February 1979 the completion of a new range of explanatory leaflets about personal income tax. The leaflets are:—

IR4   Income Tax and Pensioners
IR4A   Income Tax—Age Allowance
IR13   Income Tax—Wife's Earnings Election
IR22   Income Tax—Personal Allowances
IR23   Income Tax and Widows
IR29   Income Tax and One-Parent Families

IR30   Income Tax—Separation and Divorce
IR31   Income Tax and Married Couples
IR32   Income Tax—Separate Assessment
IR34   Income Tax—PAYE
The leaflets are obtainable from local Tax Offices and Enquiry Offices.

1551   Profit sharing schemes—tax relief—publications

The Inland Revenue has issued a Press Release dated 24th May 1979 stating that two
new publications are now available concerning the provisions of the Finance Act
1978 relating to the tax treatment of profit sharing schemes. They are IR 35
"Income Tax—Profit Sharing", a brief explanatory leaflet designed primarily for
employees, and IR 36 "Approved Profit Sharing Schemes", a booklet giving more
detailed guidance and intended for companies and professional advisers. Copies
may be obtained free of charge from the offices of HM Inspectors of Taxes and from
PAYE Enquiry Offices.

1552   Profits—allowable deductions—annuity payments to charity—whether bona fide commercial transaction

As part of a tax saving scheme, the taxpayer agreed to make five annual payments of
£500 to a registered charity in consideration of payment to him of £2,480. The
taxpayer used that sum to purchase promissory notes payable over the five years
which were lodged with the charity by way of guarantee. The promissory notes
were repaid to the taxpayer the day after he made each payment, and overdraft
facilities were made available to him. He was assessed to surtax for the relevant
years, but successfully contended that the yearly payments were annual payments
within the Income and Corporation Taxes Act 1970, s. 52 (1), and were deductible
from his total income. The Crown appealed, contending that (i) the payments
represented nothing but a repayment to the charity of its own capital; (ii) the payer
of an annual sum was only entitled to make a deduction under s. 52 (1) (c) if such
payments were made wholly out of profits brought in to charge to income tax (and
not by way of promissory notes); (iii) under 1970 Act s. 434 (1), such payments had
to be made for valuable and sufficient consideration; (iv) the scheme was a settlement,
the income of which was to be treated as the income of the settlor under s. 457.
Held, (i) LORD DILHORNE dissenting, having regard to the legal structure of the whole
transaction, the purchase of the annuity was the purchase of an income; the £2,480
when paid became the property of the taxpayer and remained his property even
though he invested it in the promissory notes; (ii) as a general rule, the actual source
out of which money was paid was not significant; it was not disputed that the
taxpayer had, in each relevant year, sufficient taxed income to cover the payments
made, and he could therefore claim the benefit of s. 52 (1) (c); (iii) the price paid was
a full and sufficient consideration for the annuity within s. 434 (1). (iv) LORD
DILHORNE and LORD DIPLOCK dissenting, the expression "settlement" connoted a
transaction containing an element of bounty; s. 457 (1) did not, accordingly, apply
to bona fide commercial transactions such as the one in question, and the annual
payments were therefore deductible in computing the taxpayer's income for surtax
purposes. The appeal would be dismissed.

INLAND REVENUE COMRS v PLUMMER [1979] 3 WLR 689 (House of Lords: LORD
WILBERFORCE, VISCOUNT DILHORNE, LORD DIPLOCK, LORD FRASER OF TULLYBELTON
and LORD KEITH OF KINKEL). Decision of the Court of Appeal [1978] STC 517,
1978 Halsbury's Abridgment para. 1599 affirmed. *Southern-Smith v Clancy* [1941]
1 KB 276, CA, *Chancery Lane Safe Deposit and Offices Co Ltd v Inland Revenue Comrs*
[1966] AC 85, HL, *Bulmer v Inland Revenue Comrs* [1967] Ch 145 and *Inland
Revenue Comrs v Leiner* (1964) 41 TC 589 applied.

Since March 1977, the Finance Act 1977, s. 48, has operated to make such schemes
ineffective.

For a discussion of this case, see Conclusive win for tax avoidance industry,
Justinian: Financial Times, 5th November 1979.

1553 —— —— **capital or income receipts—exchange profits**

Australia

The taxpayer, an Australian company, paid for goods imported from Japan through an agreement with the Bank of New South Wales. The bank's agent in Japan paid for the goods and was then reimbursed in sterling by the bank's London branch. The taxpayer then had ninety days from that date to pay the bank. On one occasion the devaluation of sterling resulted in the taxpayer having to spend fewer Australian dollars to purchase the sterling than it would otherwise have done prior to the devaluation. This exchange gain was included in the taxpayer's assessable income. The taxpayer appealed. *Held,* dismissing the appeal, it was unreal to consider the acquisition of the goods and the financing of that acquisition as two distinct transactions, as the taxpayer's arrangements with the bank had as its purpose the purchasing of the goods. The exchange gains were therefore income and assessable to tax as such.

THIESS TOYOTA PTY LTD v FEDERAL COMMISSIONER OF TAXATION (1978) 23 ALR 89 (Supreme Court of New South Wales)

1554 —— —— **capital or revenue expenditure—payment for improvement to lease**

The lease of a motorway service area provided that the rent payable consisted of two elements, a fixed sum and a variable sum. The tenant paid the landlord a sum in order to reduce the variable element of the rent. The question arose whether that sum was deductible in computing profits for corporation tax purposes; that is, whether it was a payment of a revenue nature, and deductible, or of a capital nature, and not deductible. *Held,* LORD SALMON dissenting, money spent on the acquisition of an identifiable asset of a capital nature should be regarded as capital expenditure, as should money spent on eliminating a disadvantageous asset or making an asset more advantageous. This case was one of once and for all expenditure on a capital asset, namely the lease, designed to make it more advantageous. It was impossible to divorce the payment from the lease and to regard it as simply a payment intended to increase the tenant's share of the profits. Hence the payment should be regarded as being of a capital nature and was therefore not deductible.

TUCKER (INSPECTOR OF TAXES) v GRANADA MOTORWAY SERVICES LTD [1979] STC 393 (House of Lords: LORD WILBERFORCE, LORD SALMON, LORD EDMUND-DAVIES, LORD FRASER OF TULLYBELTON and LORD KEITH OF KINKEL). Decision of Court of Appeal [1979] 1 All ER 23, 1978 Halsbury's Abridgment para. 1603 affirmed.

1555 —— —— —— **payment under guarantee—contract of indemnity**

H, a senior partner in a firm of accountants, entered into a contract with a bank, guaranteeing a loan by the bank to one of the firm's clients. The guarantee was given in H's name to meet the requirements of the bank, although liability under the guarantee was to be treated as that of the partners for the time being. In 1965, D became a partner and it was agreed that any loss that should arise under the guarantee would be borne by H alone. In 1967, H died. D carried on the practice alone until April 1968 when he took R into partnership. In February 1968, the firm made a payment to the bank in settlement of H's liability under the guarantee. The General Commissioners held that the payment was an allowable deduction in computing the firm's taxable profits, and not a capital withdrawal from the partnership. The Revenue appealed, contending that the payment was not deductible because, since the firm was entitled to indemnity against the payment made, it did not suffer any loss as a result of having made the payment. *Held,* one of the assets which D had brought into the partnership with R was the right to have any loss attributable to the guarantee paid out of H's estate under a contract of indemnity. Accordingly, the payment did not fall to be deducted in computing the taxable profits of the firm, under the Income and Corporation Taxes Act 1970, s.130 (k). The appeal would be allowed.

BOLTON (INSPECTOR OF TAXES) v HALPERN AND WOOLF (A FIRM) [1979] STC 761 (Chancery Division: OLIVER J).

1556 ———— ———— trade expenses—payments into trust set up for benefit of employees

A company claimed that payments made into a trust fund it had set up for the benefit of its employees were made wholly and exclusively for the purpose of its trade, were of a revenue nature and thus were deductible in computing its taxable profits. Under the terms of the trust the employees received the dividends on securities purchased by the trust fund, the fund itself being ultimately repayable to the company. The Crown contended that the payments were thus loans or payments of a capital nature and therefore not deductible. *Held*, as in the case of loans, the sums in question could be recalled at will, repayment could be enforced by judicial process and each payment to the trustees gave rise to a corresponding asset of a durable nature, namely the trustees' obligation to repay. Hence the payments were not deductible in computing taxable profits.

RUTTER (INSPECTOR OF TAXES) v CHARLES SHARPS AND CO LTD [1979] STC 711 (Chancery Division: GOULDING J). *Heather (Inspector of Taxes) v P-E Consulting Group Ltd* [1973] 1 All ER 8 distinguished.

1557 Remission of tax—jurisdiction of General Commissioners

In the year 1973–74 the taxpayer company omitted to make declarations, required by the Finance Act 1971, s. 29, in respect of payments made for construction work done by two individual sub-contractors. The sub-contractors had produced exemption certificates under s. 30 of the Act when first taken on, but these had expired before the payments were made. The collector of taxes refused to exercise his discretion to make a direction under the Income Tax (Payments to Sub-contractors in the Construction Industry) Regulations 1971, reg. 6 (3) exonerating the taxpayer from liability. The taxpayer was assessed to tax on this basis and, on appeal against the assessment, the General Commissioners discharged the assessment on the ground that the taxpayer had taken reasonable care to comply with the provisions and had failed to do so because of an error made in good faith. On appeal, *held*, allowing the appeal, the discretion to remit the tax was conferred only on the collector of taxes, and not on the General Commissioners. Thus the General Commissioners had no power to discharge the assessment.

SLATER (INSPECTOR OF TAXES) v RICHARDSON AND BOTTOMS LTD [1979] STC 630 (Chancery Division: OLIVER J).

1558 ———— official error—alteration in financial limits

The Inland Revenue waives arrears of tax either wholly or in part where the arrears arose because of a departmental error which involved the failure to make proper or timely use of information supplied by the taxpayer so he could reasonably believe that his affairs were in order. Since the degree of hardship imposed by the arrears would vary according to the financial resources of the taxpayer the tax is waived by reference to the amount of the taxpayer's income. The income limits governing the practice are to be raised and extra steps introduced into the graduation. The income limits and proportions of arrears waived are as follows:

Income	Proportion of arrears waived
Under £4000	All of arrears waived
£4000–£5,999	Three quarters
£6000–£7,999	One half
£8000–£9,999	One quarter
£10,000 or more	None of arrears waived

A further element of relaxation in the practice is the disappearance of an overriding test related to the level of investment income. Special consideration will continue to be given to the exceptional case of a taxpayer with large family responsibilities whose income is just above the normal limits for full or partial remission. Cases to which the official error remission practice was applied before the date of the commencement of the latest revision cannot be reopened so as to be given the benefit of the new limits: Inland Revenue Press Release dated 7th November 1979.

1559   Rent and receipts from land—rent—payments covered by rent

The taxpayer company demised land for an annual rent, the lease expressly providing
that the tenant was not authorised to take sand, gravel, ballast or other minerals from
the land. By a separate agreement under seal the company authorised the tenant to
remove sand, gravel, ballast and other minerals from the land, the tenant agreeing to
pay royalties. The question to be decided was whether the royalties were part of the
rent for the purposes of taxation under the Income Tax Act 1952, s. 175, for the year
1957–58. The judge at first instance held that they were not. The Inland Revenue
appealed, contending that the lease and the agreement together formed one lease.
The taxpayer conceded this point, but argued that payments under a lease were not
rent unless arrears could be recovered by distress; in this case the taxpayer had no
right of re-entry onto the land when royalties fell into arrears. *Held*, the power of
distress was not dependent upon an express right of re-entry; but even if a landlord
did contract not to exercise the remedy of distress, this would not prevent sums
payable from being rent for the purposes of s. 175, as there was nothing to suggest
that the section was to apply to rents recoverable by distress only. The appeal would
be allowed.

T AND E HOMES LTD v ROBINSON (INSPECTOR OF TAXES) [1979] 1 WLR 452
(Court of Appeal: ORR, ORMROD and TEMPLEMAN LJJ). *Tollemache Settled Estates
Trustees v Coughtrie (Inspector of Taxes)* [1961] 1 All ER 593 followed. Decision of
Goulding J [1976] 3 All ER 497, 1976 Halsbury's Abridgment para. 1447 reversed.

For Income Tax Act 1952, s. 175, see now Income and Corporation Taxes Act
1970, s. 156.

**1560   Restrictive covenant—consideration—undertaking in connection
with employment—whether effect of undertaking to restrict
conduct or activities**

On appeal against an assessment for tax for the year 1972–73, a barrister contended
that the sum of £40,000 paid to him under a deed by a company as an inducement
to him to cease practice at the Bar and enter into a service agreement with the
company, was not an undertaking the effect of which was to restrict him as to his
conduct or activities within the meaning of the Income and Corporation Taxes Act
1970, s. 34. *Held*, for the purposes of s. 34, an undertaking given in connection with
the holding of an office or employment did not include the undertaking of duties
which were inherent and inseparable from that office or employment. The
undertaking by the barrister to cease practice was a statement of a necessary and
inevitable consequence of accepting employment with the company. Accordingly
the payment was not made in respect of a relevant undertaking within s. 34 and did
not fall to be taxed under that section. The appeal would be allowed.

VAUGHAN NEIL v INLAND REVENUE COMRS [1979] STC 644 (Chancery Division:
OLIVER J).

**1561   Retirement annuity contracts—relief on premiums—antedating
premiums—offers in settlement where incorrect returns
submitted**

The Inland Revenue have issued a Statement of Practice SP 12/79. Under the
Income and Corporation Taxes Act 1970, s. 227 (3), if the taxpayer so elects, a
qualifying premium or contribution may be related back to years earlier than the
year in which it is paid, for the purposes of obtaining relief from tax. The conditions
to be fulfilled are that a relevant assessment to tax becomes final and conclusive at a
time after 5th October in the year of assessment to which it relates, that a qualifying
premium is paid after that year of assessment and within six months of the assessment
becoming final and conclusive, and that the election is made by the taxpayer within
that same period of six months. Where incorrect returns and accounts are found to
have been submitted offers in settlement of liability to tax, interest and penalties are
often accepted by the Board of Inland Revenue without assessment of all the tax. In
the absence of relevant assessments the conditions for relief would not be satisfied,
and there would be no entitlement to relief.

Subject to the following conditions, in considering whether an offer in settlement is acceptable the Board will have regard to the reduction in the tax included in the offer but not charged in assessment, and to the consequent reduction in interest and penalties, which would have resulted if assessments to recover this tax has been raised and become final and conclusive, and an election for relief in respect of premiums paid late had been made.

The conditions will be that:—

1. Qualifying premiums or contributions have been paid before the date of the offer and within six months from the agreement of the relevant earnings for the years to which the premium or contribution is to be related.

2. The offeror specifies in writing the premium or contribution paid and the years to which he wishes it to be related and undertakes as part of the offer in settlement that no relief from tax will subsequently be claimed on the premium or contribution.

This practice will be followed in considering all offers made after 30th November 1979.

1562   Returns—failure to deliver income tax returns—failure to furnish information—penalties

The taxpayer was requested to deliver to the inspector of taxes income tax returns for seven years of assessment. He did not comply with the notices and a penalty of £1 in respect of each of the seven notices was awarded. The taxpayer submitted the returns purporting to have fulfilled his duty under the Taxes Management Act 1970, s. 8 to deliver a return of his income specifying each separate source of income and the amount from each source. Against the entries concerning his source of income and amount he wrote "to be ascertained" which the inspector of taxes considered to be insufficient. An application under s. 100 (7) was made for the issue of summonses. The commissioners found that the returns did not comply with the requirements of s. 8 (1) and issued summonses requiring the taxpayer to appear before them. He was further requested for more information regarding his income and given the opportunity to obtain professional assistance before the hearing. The taxpayer amended his returns by enclosing a letter regarding sources of income from five listed companies and said that it was impossible at present to give any indication as to his net amounts of income. The taxpayer was not present at the hearing, a request for an adjournment whilst he sought professional representation being refused, where it was found that the returns were insufficient and a penalty of £560 imposed in each case. The taxpayer appealed, contending that the returns submitted in their amended form were sufficient for s. 8 (1), the information given in them enabling the Revenue authorities to obtain the necessary information. He also contended that there had been a breach of natural justice as he had not been given the opportunity of making representations and the penalties were unreasonable. *Held,* the fact that the Revenue authorities could obtain the information required through other channels was insufficient for compliance with s. 8 (1). There had been no breach of natural justice since the taxpayer had no right to appear when the application was made for the issue of a summons and when the penalties were awarded against him he had been given every opportunity to appear. There were no grounds for interfering with the penalties. The appeal would be dismissed.

Moschi v General Comrs for Kensington [1980] STC 1 (Chancery Division: Goulding J). *R v West London JJ, ex parte Klahn* [1979] 2 All ER 221, para. 1794 applied.

1563   Savings bank interest—exemption—withdrawal

From 21st November 1979 there will no longer be exemption from income tax for interest on ordinary savings accounts with Trustee Savings Banks. At present, the first £70 of total interest is exempt. The effect of this change will not be felt by taxpayers until the tax year beginning in April 1981: Inland Revenue Press Release dated 8th October 1979.

1564   Schedule D—furnished lettings—computation of income—allowable deductions

The taxpayer, who let furnished rooms, appealed against an assessment to income tax under Sch. D, Case VI. In determining the correct assessment, the General Commissioners determined the amount of expenses properly allowable against rents received for the purpose of computing profits or gains arising to the taxpayer. The taxpayer required the Commissioners to state a case for the opinion of the High Court. *Held*, the determination of allowances was purely a question of fact for the Commissioners to determine. No question of law was raised by the case stated and the appeal would be dismissed.

ABIDOYE v HENNESSEY (INSPECTOR OF TAXES) (NOTE) [1979] STC 212 (Chancery Division: WALTON J).

1565   —— profits or gains arising or accruing from any property in the United Kingdom

The taxpayer, who lived in Canada, was the wife of a man who had been convicted and sentenced for robbery, had escaped from prison and been recaptured. After his recapture, the taxpayer made an agreement with an English newspaper to co-operate in the writing of articles about her life and experiences with her husband. In return, she was to receive a sum of money, to be paid in London. The agreement was to be construed in accordance with English law. She was assessed to tax on the sum under Sch. D, Case VI, the Commissioners contending that the money was "annual profits or gains arising or accruing from any property whatever in the United Kingdom", within the Income and Corporation Taxes Act 1970, s. 108, Sch. D, para. 1 (a) (iii). The Special Commissioners upheld the assessment and the taxpayer appealed. *Held*, the Commissioners had found as a fact that the money was received as income and not as capital. There was authority for the proposition that money paid as consideration for the provision of information as a service was properly treated as income. Thus the Commissioners were justified in their finding and the money was received as income.

The other question was whether the money amounted to annual profits or gains "from any property whatever in the United Kingdom". It was accepted by the taxpayer that her rights under the agreement were property. She contended, however, that the payment did not arise from the agreement but from the services rendered by her under it. The services alone did not vest in the taxpayer any right to remuneration; that right stemmed entirely from the agreement. Therefore the money paid to the taxpayer in London was a profit or gain arising or accruing from property in the United Kingdom, and the appeal would be dismissed.

ALLOWAY v PHILLIPS (INSPECTOR OF TAXES) [1979] 1 WLR 564 (Chancery Division: BRIGHTMAN J).

1566   —— voluntary payments

In a test case, the special commissioners have ruled that a literary award is not subject to income tax under Case II of Schedule D. The Inland Revenue had assessed Mr. Andrew Boyle, an author, to tax on a £1,000 Whitbread literary prize awarded to him in 1974 for a biography of Brendan Bracken. The Revenue claimed that the publishers had been left to exploit the book in the most beneficial way and in submitting it for the award had acted as the author's agent. The commissioners, however, ruled that the prize was a voluntary and unsolicited payment and did not represent the proceeds of exploitation of the book either by the author personally or by the publishers in an agency capacity. Further, the award had none of the attributes of a voluntary payment liable to tax as a profit or gain of a trade or profession. *IRC v Boyle*, see the Daily Telegraph, 31st January 1979.

1567   Schedule E—emoluments from office or employment—payment of wages in sovereigns

The taxpayer, who earned about £60 a week, arranged with his employers that his wages would be paid in gold sovereigns. He subsequently received between one and four sovereigns a week which he sold for their open market value. The question at issue was whether his liability to tax was to be assessed on the basis that the sovereigns were to be treated as having their nominal value only, namely £1 each, or on the basis that each sovereign was to be treated as having its actual open market value, which was substantially in excess of its nominal value. *Held*, the Income and Corporation Taxes Act 1970, s. 183 (1), provided that tax under Sch. E was chargeable on the full amount of the emoluments, which were defined as including "all salaries, fees, wages, perquisites and profits whatsoever". The perquisites and profits the taxpayer received were not fully represented by the nominal value of each sovereign. The full amount of his emoluments was the amount for which he was able to realise the sovereigns he received. Therefore the full value of the sovereigns was the proper amount taxable.

JENKINS v HORN (INSPECTOR OF TAXES) [1979] STC 446 (Chancery Division: BROWNE-WILKINSON J).

1568 —— expenses—cost of upkeep of tools or special clothing

An employee who has to bear the cost of upkeep of tools or special clothing necessary for his work is entitled under the Income and Corporation Taxes Act 1970, s. 189 to an allowance for the expenditure incurred. Flat-rate allowances for such expenditure are agreed for most classes of trade between the Inland Revenue and the trade unions concerned, and are given without inquiry as to expenditure actually incurred in the individual case; the individual employee being free to claim as a deduction the actual expenses he has incurred. Revised flat rates are being negotiated and the Inland Revenue have issued a Statement of Practice SP 13/79, which contains a list of those industries where revised allowances have been agreed, and these will be put into effect from 6th April 1980.

1569 —— payments on removal from office

The taxpayer was assessed to Schedule E income tax on £7,450, which comprised a sum awarded to him by an industrial tribunal as compensation for unfair dismissal and payment in lieu of notice. The tribunal found that the taxpayer had spent £500 in seeking other employment and £1,300 for legal representation, and the taxpayer claimed that these sums should be deducted from the assessment, as only the net amount of payments received by him was taxable under the Income and Corporation Taxes Act 1970, s. 187. The general commissioners upheld the taxpayer's claim. On appeal by the Crown, *held*, allowing the appeal, s. 187 (1) brought into charge to tax any payments made to a person in connection with the termination of his holding of an office or employment, with an exemption for the first £5,000 under s. 188 (3). Section 187 (1) was applicable to the whole of the payment and could not be construed otherwise, however unjust the result. Thus the sums of £500 and £1,300 were to be included in the assessment, the total sum of £7,450, minus £5,000 in respect of the s. 188 (3) exception, to be chargeable to tax.

WARNETT (INSPECTOR OF TAXES) v JONES [1980] STC 131 (Chancery Division: SLADE J).

1570 —— payments on retirement from office or employment

The taxpayer retired at the age of sixty-two years and six months. He became entitled to a "temporary pension" payable until he reached sixty-five, under the rules of his employer's pension scheme. The scheme was being considered for approval by the Revenue under the Finance Act 1970, Sch. 5, Part II. Payments in respect of the "temporary pension" were made to the taxpayer by the trustees of the pension fund after deduction of tax. The taxpayer claimed that the payments were either gratuitous or, alternatively, commutations of his rights to a pension and therefore capital. The General Commissioners held that the payments in question had the character of pension payments and were therefore assessable to tax under Schedule E. The taxpayer appealed by way of case stated. *Held*, the sums paid to the taxpayer were income payments and payments of pension. Since the sums were paid under a scheme which was being considered for approval, they were, by Sch. 5, para. 1 (1) of the 1970 Act, mandatorily subject to tax under Schedule E.   Accordingly, the appeal would be dismissed.

ESSLEMONT V ESTILL (INSPECTOR OF TAXES) [1979] STC 624 (Chancery Division: OLIVER J).

1571   Statements of Practice

Following the announcement on 18th July 1978 of the publication of a new comprehensive series of Statements of Practice, the Inland Revenue have issued a Press Release dated 18th June 1979 announcing that a review has been undertaken of statements relating to administrative practice issued before 18th July 1978 which remain valid.   An Index has been published listing the titles of the statements in chronological order together with a brief summary of the point at issue and a reference to publication in the British Tax Review and Taxation where applicable. Where no reference is quoted, the full text of the Statement of Practice is given in an Appendix.   The statements in chronological order are grouped into sections under general subject headings, namely (a) statements applicable to individuals (income tax and interest on tax); (b) statements applicable to individuals and companies (income tax and corporation tax); (c) statements applicable to companies etc. (corporation tax and income tax); (d) statements relating to tax on capital gains (individuals and companies); (e) capital transfer tax; (f) miscellaneous.   Copies of the Index or of individual Statements of Practice may be obtained by calling at or writing to the Public Enquiry Room, New Wing, Somerset House, Strand, London WC2R 1LB.

1572   Tax advantage—transaction in securities—circumstances in which advantage counteracted

A scheme consisting of a number of complex transactions was designed with the purpose of avoiding the substantial tax for which the taxpayers would otherwise become liable on the sale of freehold land owned by their company K Ltd.   It was hoped this would be achieved by converting the profit made from the disposal of the land into the form of loans made to the taxpayers by a company specially set up for the purpose and over which the taxpayers gained control after the loans had been made.   The loans were for all practical purposes interest free and not repayable. The taxpayers were assessed to tax pursuant to the Income and Corporation Taxes Act 1970, s. 460, due to having received a tax advantage in such circumstances as mentioned in s. 461, para. D, in respect of those transactions carried out during the second stage of the scheme, before the taxpayers had received the loans.   This assessment was upheld at first instance.   The taxpayers appealed, but the taxpayers were also technically liable under other provisions of the Act, and the Revenue intended, should they lose the appeal, to assess the taxpayers to tax under these other provisions.   On appeal the taxpayers contended that: (i) the second stage transactions fell within para. E and as the taxpayers had received no repayment of their shares they were entitled to a deferment of tax as provided by para. E(2); (ii) those transactions carried out during the third stage of the scheme, i.e. those transactions relating to the payment of the loans, were not taxable because (a) the taxpayers had received no tax advantage in that a loan could not be a tax advantage and in any event the taxpayers were liable to tax under other provisions of the Act, (b) the loan transactions did not fall within any of the circumstances mentioned in s. 461, (c) the loan transactions were not "transactions in securities" under s. 460 (2).   *Held*, the transactions carried out during the second stage of the scheme fell within both paras. D and E.   But as para. E was the more specific enactment it took precedence over D, and the taxpayers were entitled to a deferment of the tax, but only until the following year, for the transactions carried out during the third stage were liable to tax.   The taxpayers had received a tax advantage by means of the loans, considering the nature of the loans and the circumstances in which they were granted. Furthermore it could not be argued that the taxpayers received no tax advantage merely because they remained technically liable under another provision of the Act.   The circumstances in para. C of s. 461 were applicable to the loan transactions and these transactions were "transactions relating to securities", an expression which was to be given its widest meaning. The appeal would be allowed.

WILLIAMS v INLAND REVENUE COMRS [1979] STC 598 (Court of Appeal: ORR, BRIDGE and CUMMING-BRUCE LJJ). Decision of Browne-Wilkinson J [1978] STC 379, 1978 Halsbury's Abridgment para. 1556 varied. Dictum of Lord Wilberforce in *Inland Revenue Comrs v Joiner* [1975] 3 All ER 1050, HL at 1055, 1975 Halsbury's Abridgment para. 1819 applied.

1573   Trade—adventure in nature of trade—speculation in stocks and shares

The taxpayer, an "operational research consultant", used his expertise in the application of computers to the forecasting of share movements by engaging personally in speculation in the stock market. He made some 200 purchases and sales of stocks and shares over several years. The transactions were not profitable and, in the year ending 31st March 1973, he made a loss. The taxpayer's claim that the transactions constituted an adventure in the nature of a trade and that he was accordingly entitled to relief in respect of the loss under the Income and Corporation Taxes Act 1970, s. 168 (1) was refused. On his appeal, it was found as a fact that the transactions entered into during the year in question did not constitute a trade. The taxpayer further appealed, contending that the commissioners had applied to the admitted facts an erroneous proposition of law, namely that stocks and shares were not a subject matter which could be dealt with by way of trade if the dealing was carried on by an individual on his own account. *Held*, there was a prima facie presumption that an individual engaged in speculative dealings in securities was not carrying on a trade, and it was for the fact finding tribunal to say whether the circumstances took the case out of the norm. In the instant case, the commissioners' conclusion that the taxpayer was not trading was one which, on the facts, was clearly open to them. It followed, therefore, that the taxpayer was not entitled to the relief claimed. The appeal would be dismissed.

SALT v CHAMBERLAIN (INSPECTOR OF TAXES) [1979] STC 750 (Chancery Division: OLIVER J).

1574   Trade receipts—agriculture—premium paid to dairy farmers for undertaking to change to beef production

The taxpayers, a firm of dairy farmers, undertook to change from dairying to beef production for a period of four years, and as a result they became entitled to a grant, known as a premium, pursuant to Council Regulation (EEC) 1353/73. After the first instalment had been paid, they were assessed for income tax on that payment on the basis that it formed part of their trading profit. The taxpayers appealed, contending that the instalment was a capital sum in consideration of their ceasing to engage in dairy farming and was thus not taxable as profit. The General Commissioners found for the taxpayers and the Crown appealed. *Held*, the premium was paid to make good the loss of income resulting from the cessation of dairy farming. The lost income would have been taxable, therefore the premium was taxable. Furthermore the taxpayers did not only undertake to cease dairy farming, but also to conduct their trade in a particular way. This pointed to the premium being income from trade and therefore taxable. The appeal would be allowed.

WHITE (INSPECTOR OF TAXES) v G AND M DAVIES [1979] STC 415 (Chancery Division: BROWNE-WILKINSON J).

1575   —— sale of properties—whether surplus proceeds taxable as trading receipts

Before 1955, the appellant, a quantity surveyor, purchased a number of properties as investments. He then formed a small group of companies for the purpose of acquiring various sites for development. The developments took place and the buildings were sold at a profit. The companies then went into liquidation. The Special Commissioners held that the proceeds of sale in respect of four of the companies were to be treated as giving rise to trading receipts and were taxable accordingly. The Commissioners found that the composite intention of the group was to aim at building up a suitable portfolio of investments, but to allow the final decision, whether to retain a property, to await events. On this basis the decision to liquidate was not inconsistent with the original aim which had been to create investments for retention if possible, or, where it was impossible, for turning to account by way of trade. The liquidator's appeal was allowed at first instance and the Commissioners appealed. *Held*, until a decision was taken to treat a property as an investment, it necessarily followed that the surplus realised on its sale was assessable as a trading profit. By reason of financial pressures and rising costs there could have been no basis for a firm intention to retain the buildings as investments. The appeal would be allowed.

SIMMONS (AS LIQUIDATOR OF LIONEL SIMMONS PROPERTIES LTD) V INLAND REVENUE COMRS [1979] STC 471 (Court of Appeal: ORR, BRIDGE and CUMMING-BRUCE LJJ). Decision of Goulding J [1978] STC 344, 1978 Halsbury's Abridgment para. 1600 reversed.

INDUSTRIAL AND PROVIDENT SOCIETIES

Halsbury's Laws of England (4th edn.), Vol. 24, paras. 1–200

1576   Credit unions—authorised investments

The Credit Unions (Authorised Investments) Order 1979, S.I. 1979 No. 866 (in force on 20th August 1979), prescribes the manner in which credit unions may invest funds not immediately required for their purposes.

1577   —— fees

The Industrial and Provident Societies (Credit Unions) (Amendment of Fees) Regulations 1979, S.I. 1979 No. 1556 (in force on 1st January 1980), increase the fees payable in connection with matters to be transacted and for the inspection of documents under the Industrial and Provident Societies Act 1965 and 1967 and the Credit Unions Act 1979. These regulations apply only in relation to societies registered as credit unions under the Industrial and Provident Societies Act 1965.

1578   —— registration—applications and procedure

The Industrial and Provident Societies (Credit Unions) Regulations 1979, S.I. 1979 No. 937 (in force on 20th August 1979), prescribe the forms of application for and acknowledgement of registration of societies which qualify for registration as credit unions under the Industrial and Provident Societies Act 1965 by virtue of the Credit Unions Act 1979, s. 1, see para. 1579. They also prescribe the forms to be used and the procedure to be followed and make provision for the keeping of documents by the Central Office of the Registry of Friendly Societies and for inspection of documents by the public. They further specify the fees payable in connection with the 1965 Act, the Industrial and Provident Societies Act 1967 and the 1979 Act.

1579   Credit Unions Act 1979

The Credit Unions Act 1979 establishes a legal framework for credit unions in Great Britain. The Act received the royal assent on 4th April 1979 and ss. 32, 33 came into force on that date. The remaining provisions came into force on 20th August 1979, S.I. 1979 No. 936, except for ss. 3 (2), (3), 15 which have not yet been brought into operation.

A society may register as a credit union under the Industrial and Provident Societies Act 1965 if its only objects are those of a credit union and provided that its membership is restricted to persons all of whom fulfil a specific qualification which is stated in the rules, is appropriate to a credit union and which provides a common bond between members: s. 1. Section 2 makes supplementary and transitional provisions relating to registration. Section 3 restricts the use of the term "credit union". Sections 4–6, Sch. 1 deal with rules, membership and voting rights and the minimum and maximum number of members of a credit union. Section 7 provides that all shares in a credit union must be of £1 denomination and that they are not transferable. Subscriptions for shares are generally the only deposits a credit union may take (s. 8) but deposits may be received from persons too young to be members, up to a limit of £250: s. 9.

Section 10 allows credit unions to borrow sums up to half the total of their paid-up share capital, and conversely they may make loans on security to members for provident or productive purposes: s. 11. Section 12 empowers unions to hold, purchase or lease land for the purpose of carrying on business; s. 13 restricts the power to invest surplus funds to investments authorised by the chief registrar. Section 14 deals with the computation and application of profits, s. 15 with unions' obligation to insure against fraud or other dishonesty and s. 16 with the establishment of guarantee funds.

Section 17 extends the powers of registrars to require information under the Industrial and Provident Societies Act 1965, s. 48 (1) to credit unions; s. 18 gives the chief registrar power to appoint an inspector to call a meeting to examine the conduct of a credit union, or to do both. He may further suspend the operation of any credit union if he considers it expedient having regard to the interests of all the members: s. 19, Sch. 2. Section 20 deals with cancellation or suspension of registration and petitions for winding up a credit union. Section 21 applies the 1965 Act. ss. 50, 51 (amalgamations and transfers of engagements between registered societies) to credit unions, s. 23 extends s. 53 of the 1965 Act (conversion of a company with a registered society) to credit unions, but s. 22 expressly does not extend s. 52 (conversion of a company into a society) to them. Sections 24–33 and Sch. 3 contain general, miscellaneous and supplemental provisions.

1580   **Fees**

The Industrial and Provident Societies (Amendment of Fees) Regulations 1979, S.I. 1979 No. 1558 (in force on 1st January 1980), increase the fees to be paid for matters to be transacted and for the inspection of documents under the Industrial and Provident Societies Act 1965 and 1967.

INDUSTRIAL ASSURANCE

Halsbury's Laws of England (4th edn.), Vol. 24, paras. 201–400.

1581   **Fees**

The Industrial Assurance (Fees) Regulations 1979, S.I. 1979 No. 1549 (in force on 1st January 1980), supersede the Industrial Assurance (Fees) Regulations 1976, 1976 Halsbury's Abridgment para. 1463 and increase the fees payable in connection with the exercise by the Industrial Assurance Commissioner of his functions under the Industrial Assurance Act 1923. The fees payable in relation to disputes remain unchanged.

INJUNCTIONS

Halsbury's Laws of England (4th edn.), Vol. 24, paras. 901–1200

1582   **Article**

Injunctions and the Criminal Law, David Feldman: (1979) 42 MLR 369.

1583   Application for leave to appeal against Anton Piller order—no application for discharge of order—order already executed

See *Bestworth Ltd v Wearwell Ltd*, para. 2107.

1584   Breach of negative covenant—injunction to restrain—discretion of court to grant

New Zealand

The appellant company had contracted with the respondent company to buy and freeze meat which the respondent company then exported. The contract ran for twenty years from 1968 and contained provision for either party to request amendments and to submit such requests to arbitration, on certain conditions, at three yearly intervals. Following a takeover and merger of the appellant company, that company, instead of waiting for the contractual interval to lapse, purported to determine or repudiate the contract by giving three days' notice in writing. The contract contained a restrictive covenant that the appellant company would only handle meat for the respondent company. The respondent company sought and obtained an injunction restraining the appellant company from acting in breach of the restrictive covenant. On appeal, *held*, it was within the court's discretion to grant an injunction restraining a breach of a negative covenant in a contract for the sale of goods, even though this might amount, in a roundabout way, to ordering specific performance of the negative covenant for a long period of time. There was nothing in the facts of the present case to suggest that the discretion had been improperly exercised. The appeal would be dismissed.

Thomas Borthwick & Sons (Australasia) Ltd v South Otago Freezing Co Ltd [1978] 1 NZLR 538 (Court of Appeal of New Zealand). *Donnell v Bennett* (1883) 22 Ch D 835, *Esso Petroleum Co Ltd v Harper's Garage (Stourport) Ltd* [1967] 1 All ER 699, and *Wolverhampton & Walsall Railway Co v London and North-Western Railway Co* (1873) LR 16 Eq 433 applied.

1585   Interference with trade—injunction to prevent unlawful act—infringement of copyright

See *Re M's Application*, para. 521; *Rolls-Royce Ltd v Zanelli*, para. 525.

1586   Interlocutory injunction—application to compel local authority to open schools closed as a result of industrial action

The caretakers at a local authority's schools went on strike, as a result of which the schools closed and the children were sent home. The local authority had some sympathy with the industrial action and felt that any action on their part to keep the schools open would escalate the strike and antagonise employees whose co-operation was important. The Secretary of State refused to order an opening of the schools by means of her powers under the Education Act 1944, s. 99. The plaintiff, both as an individual parent and on behalf of the Haringey Schools Trust, brought an action contending that the local authority had failed to discharge its duty to provide full-time education under the Education Act 1944, s. 8 and was in breach of that duty. He sought an interim mandatory injunction compelling the local authority to open the schools. It was refused at first instance and before the appeal was heard the schools reopened. On appeal, *held*, Lord Denning MR dissenting, the injunction would not have been granted. It would have been difficult for the local authority to have known precisely what they had to do in order to open the schools when faced with industrial conflict. Further, it was only in extreme circumstances that the court would interfere by way of mandatory injunction in industrial disputes and negotiations. The appeal would be dismissed.

Meade v Haringey London Borough Council [1979] 2 All ER 1016 (Court of Appeal: Lord Denning MR, Eveleigh LJ and Sir Stanley Rees).

1587 ——— application to prevent breach of confidence—locus standi of plaintiffs

Australia

An interlocutory injunction was sought by members of an Aboriginal council to restrain a distinguished anthropologist and writer from publishing a book containing matters of deep religious and cultural significance to their people, which had been revealed to him in confidence many years earlier. The matters concerned religious secrets known only to adult men, and the members of the council felt that if the book was published these secrets would become known to the women and children, thereby jeopardising the fast disappearing social and religious structure of their people. The members also claimed that they had the right to bring the action on their own behalf, rather than pursuing it by a relator action in the name of the Attorney-General. *Held*, what had been revealed to the author imposed an obligation of confidence on him, for which an injunction could be granted to prevent him breaching that confidence. The feeling that the book was a threat was genuine, and as damages would not compensate the people for any damage caused, an interlocutory injunction was the only appropriate protection until the matter could be heard in full. There was no need to pursue the case by relator action as the members of the council were not only suing as representatives of their people but also on their own behalf as individuals. They were each threatened as individuals by the proposed publication and thus they had sufficient interest to pursue the relief sought. The injunction would be granted.

FOSTER v MOUNTFORD AND RIGBY LTD [1978] FSR 582 (Supreme Court of the Northern Territory).

1588 ——— infringement of copyright

See *Rolls-Royce Ltd v Zanelli*, para. 525; *Re M's Application*, para. 521.

1589 ——— injunction to restrain action in furtherance of a trade dispute

See TRADE UNIONS.

1590 ——— injunction to restrain allegations of breach of copyright

See *Polydor Ltd v Harlequin Record Shops Ltd*, para. 529.

1591 ——— passing off—conversion of second-hand cars

See *Rolls-Royce Ltd v Zanelli*, para. 525.

1592 ——— ——— likelihood of confusion

See *Alfred Dunhill Ltd v Sunoptic SA*, para. 2818.

1593 ——— ——— ——— balance of convenience

The plaintiff company, which owned an established chain of shops all bearing the name Mothercare, sought an interlocutory injunction to restrain a publisher from marketing a book with the title Mother Care. The company had itself published a book entitled the Reader's Digest Mothercare Book, and considered that this might be confusing for the general public. *Held*, in an application for an interlocutory injunction in a passing off action, if a plaintiff satisfied the court that he had a real prospect of succeeding in his claim for a permanent injunction at the trial, the court had to go on to consider the balance of convenience to the parties. In this case the two books were different both in appearance and content, but the relevant question was whether there was any likelihood of damage to the company's goodwill, and it seemed that there was some hope of success at the trial. The balance of convenience between the parties depended on the adequacy of damages as a remedy; on the facts, the publishers were more likely to be adequately compensated by an award of damages in respect of the interlocutory injunction if they succeeded at the trial. Accordingly the injunction would be granted.

MOTHERCARE LTD v ROBSON BOOKS LTD [1979] FSR 466 (Chancery Division: MEGARRY V-C). *American Cyanamid Co v Ethicon Ltd* [1975] AC 396, HL, 1975 Halsbury's Abridgment para. 1864 followed, *John Walker & Son Ltd v Rothmans International Ltd* [1978] FSR 357, 1978 Halsbury's Abridgment para. 2859 and dictum of Browne LJ in *Smith v Inner London Education Authority* [1978] 1 All ER 411 at 419, 1977 Halsbury's Abridgment para. 975 not followed.

1594 —— **restraint on disposition of assets within jurisdiction—circumstances in which injunction may be granted**

Three shipowners each chartered a vessel to the defendants, a company incorporated in Panama. Each charter allowed for arbitration in London and in each case a dispute arose giving the shipowner a claim against the defendants. Each applied to the Commercial Court for a Mareva injunction, which enables a creditor in a proper case to stop his debtor from parting with his assets pending trial. The injunctions were granted. The defendants unsuccessfully applied to discharge them on the ground that they had good defences and would honour any award made against them. On appeal further evidence was adduced, in particular a letter from the defendants' bankers saying that the London account was sometimes in overdraft. The letter said nothing of the defendants' assets and the defendants gave no other evidence of any assets anywhere. No director or officer of the defendants gave any evidence.

LORD DENNING MR set out guidelines governing cases in which a Mareva injunction was sought. The plaintiff should make full and frank disclosure of all matters in his knowledge which are material for the judge to know. He should give particulars of his claim and fairly state the points made against it by the defendant. The plaintiff should have some grounds for believing that the defendant has assets in England; the existence of a bank account is enough whether or not it is in overdraft. He should have some grounds for believing that there is a risk of the assets being removed before the judgment is satisfied. He must give an undertaking in damages, supported by security in suitable cases. In the present case, the defendants, while asserting their own solidity, did not support this by the evidence of any director or by any tangible evidence of financial security. The application to discharge the injunctions would be refused.

THIRD CHANDRIS SHIPPING CORPN, WESTERN SEALANE CORPN, AGGELIKAI PTERA COMPANIA MARITIMA SA v UNIMARINE SA [1979] 2 All ER 972 (Court of Appeal: LORD DENNING MR, LAWTON and CUMMING-BRUCE LJJ.)

1595 A contract for the sale of a ship provided that the vessel was to be delivered in substantially the same condition and with the same class as when it was inspected at Rosario. The buyers were unable to inspect the bottom of the ship at Rosario but they later discovered that it had been damaged. Although two Lloyd's surveys concluded that the ship still retained her class, the buyers claimed damages for breach of contract from the sellers. To secure their claim, the buyers obtained a Mareva injunction immediately before completion, thereby preventing the sellers from dealing with their assets within the court's jurisdiction, including the deposit for the ship and the balance of the purchase price. The sellers completed the sale, unaware of the injunction. When the bank refused to release the proceeds of sale, they successfully applied for the injunction to be discharged. On appeal by the buyers, *held*, (i) a Mareva injunction should be granted only in proper circumstances and its use should not be extended so as to endanger the proper conduct of business. (ii) If the judge had known that the sellers would complete the sale unaware of the injunction, he would not have granted it. (iii) The sellers had given an undertaking not to remove the buyers' deposit from the bank without notice and that was sufficient security for the buyers' claim for damages. Accordingly the appeal would be dismissed.

THE ASSIOS, NEGOCIOS DEL MAR SA v DORIC SHIPPING CORPN SA [1979] 1 Lloyd's Rep 331 (Court of Appeal: LORD DENNING MR, STEPHENSON and SHAW LJJ).

1596 —— —— —— **whether injunction an appropriate remedy**

See *Montecchi v Shimco (UK) Ltd; Navone v Shimco (UK) Ltd*, para. 1598.

1597 —— —— **defendant resident within jurisdiction**

In an action arising out of a charterparty, the plaintiffs applied for a Mareva injunction. The main question for consideration was whether a Mareva injunction could be obtained against a defendant resident within the jurisdiction. The plaintiffs contended that under the Judicature Act 1925, s. 45, the court had a complete discretion in all cases in which it appeared just or convenient to grant an injunction. *Held*, there was a settled practice which prevented the granting of Mareva injunctions against a defendant resident within the jurisdiction. Although it was said in *Rasu Maritima SA v Pertamina* that the court's discretion was unlimited and a Mareva injunction was available against a defendant within or without the jurisdiction, this was an indication of what the law ought to be rather than what it was. Further, the Court of Appeal in that case had intended to draw a distinction between English and foreign based defendants. There was no authority for saying that no such distinction existed. Accordingly, the application would be dismissed.

THE AGRABELE, GEBR VAN WEELDE SCHEEPVAART KANTOOR BV v HOMERIC MARINE SERVICES LTD [1979] 2 Lloyd's Rep 117 (Queen's Bench Division: LLOYD J). *Rasu Maritima SA v Pertamina* [1977] 3 WLR 518, CA sub nom *Rasu Maritima SA v Pertambangan Minyak Dan Gas Bumi Negara*, 1977 Halsbury's Abridgment para. 1578 considered.

1598 —— —— **no evidence to indicate judgment debtor would avoid liability—appropriateness of injunction**

The plaintiffs were Italian businessmen who had supplied goods to the defendant English company. Payment was by bills of exchange which were subsequently dishonoured by the defendants. When the plaintiffs brought actions to recover the amount of the bills, the defendants claimed that in each case the goods were defective and counterclaimed for damages. In the first action the plaintiff was given summary judgment and a stay of execution of the judgment was granted pending the hearing of the defendants' counterclaim. On the plaintiff's appeal, the stay was removed. The second plaintiff was also given summary judgment, but, on the defendants' appeal, a stay of execution was granted until the trial of the counterclaim on condition that the defendants paid the judgment sum into court or into a joint account. An injunction was also granted restraining the plaintiff from dealing with or removing the sum from within the court's jurisdiction. The defendants appealed in the first action and the plaintiff appealed in the second action. *Held*, as between the immediate parties to a bill of exchange, which was to be treated as the equivalent of cash, the defendant's counterclaim for unliquidated damages arising out of the same transaction formed no defence to an action on the bill and was no ground on which he should be granted a stay of execution of the judgment. In the present case the defendants had argued that the two plaintiffs were defendants to their counterclaim and held assets in this country as a result of the judgment being enforced. While the court might in appropriate circumstances grant what was known as a "Mareva" injunction restraining the holder of a bill of exchange from dealing with or removing from its jurisdiction moneys recovered in an action on the bill, such an injunction was only granted when there was good reason to believe that the debtor might defeat his creditor's claim by disposing of or removing his assets from the jurisdiction. In the present case there were no grounds for believing that the plaintiffs were prospective debtors who would attempt to avoid their liability for damages on the counterclaim or that they would be unable to satisfy any judgment entered against them. Accordingly there would be no stay of execution in the first action and the injunction in the second action would be discharged.

MONTECCHI v SHIMCO (UK) LTD; NAVONE v SHIMCO (UK) LTD [1979] 1 WLR 1180 (Court of Appeal: ROSKILL, GEOFFREY LANE and BRIDGE LJJ). Dictum of Lord Denning MR in *Siskina (Owners of cargo lately laden on board) v Distos Compania Naviera SA* [1977] 3 All ER 803 at 809 applied.

1599 —— —— **when injunction can operate**

The plaintiff company, incorporated in Lichtenstein, brought an action against the defendant Nigerian bank claiming the sterling equivalent of $4.5 million, being payment due under a letter of credit opened by the bank in favour of the company in respect of shipments of cement to Nigeria. The company also claimed damages for breach of the terms of the credit. By defence and counterclaim the bank alleged that payments had already been made under the credit against documents which were false and/or forged. The company was granted an interim injunction directing the bank to retain the sum of $5 million within the jurisdiction. The bank's application for security for costs was dismissed and the bank appealed. *Held*, while injunctions of the type granted, namely "Mareva" injunctions, had proved to be of great value, they could only operate where the plaintiffs had a good case that the money in question would become due to them. In the present case, where there was strong evidence of the presentation of forged documents and a possibility of a right to equitable set-off, a "Mareva" injunction was not appropriate. The appeal would be allowed and the plaintiff company ordered to give security for costs.

ETABLISSEMENT ESEFKA INTERNATIONAL ANSTALT V CENTRAL BANK OF NIGERIA [1979] LS Gaz R 101 (Court of Appeal: LORD DENNING MR, LAWTON and BRANDON LJJ).

1600 —— **restraint on financial support given by petrol wholesalers to retailers—whether damages adequate remedy**

The plaintiff company carried on a garage business independent of any contractual ties with any petrol supplier and was able to obtain and retail petrol at relatively low prices. The defendant oil companies were well-established petrol wholesalers whose practice it was, in times of price cutting in any particular area, to give financial support to retailers habitually supplied by them, often under restrictive contracts. On the commercial failure of the garage it claimed that its failure was due to the operation of this subsidy system, which it alleged was unlawful under both the Restrictive Trade Practices Act 1976 and EEC Treaty, arts. 85 and 86. The garage sought an interlocutory injunction restraining the wholesalers from continuing to operate the system. *Held*, although there was clearly a serious and substantial case to be tried the injunction would be refused on the grounds that damages would constitute a sufficient remedy for the garage company in the event of its succeeding at final trial: any damage suffered by the garage before final judgment would be of a character which would be properly compensated for by a sum of money, the amount of which would be clearly quantifiable and, further, while the defendant companies were well able to meet eventual damages the garage company could not offer a cross-undertaking. Two additional grounds for refusing the application were, first, that in view of the existing insolvency of the garage, it could not be said that it would derive any substantial advantage from the injunction sought; and second, it was prima facie clear that so to restrain the oil companies could cause important and possibly irreversible effects to their retailers, who were not represented in the present proceedings.

A submission by the plaintiff company that the principles established by *American Cyanamid Co v Ethicon Ltd* were not applicable in this case, where the alleged illegalities arose from a breach of public legislation, failed: the criteria for granting an interlocutory injunction were not subject to an exception on the grounds of public policy.

CHELMKARM MOTORS LTD V ESSO PETROLEUM CO LTD [1979] 1 CMLR 73 (Chancery Division: GOULDING J). *American Cyanamid Co v Ethicon Ltd* [1975] AC 396, HL, 1975 Halsbury's Abridgment para. 1864 applied.

1601 **Mandatory injunction—preservation of property—ex parte application for search of premises—unlawful interference with business**

See *Carlin Music Corpn v Collins*, para. 520.

1602   Matrimonial home—exclusion of one party

See HUSBAND AND WIFE.

1603   Patent—infringement—perpetual injunction withheld—interlocutory injunction continued

See *American Cyanamid Co v Ethicon Ltd*, para. 2035.

1604   Restrictive covenant—breach—injunction to enforce—reasonableness

See *Greer v Sketchley*, para. 2806.

INSURANCE

Halsbury's Laws of England (4th edn.), Vol. 25, paras. 1–1000

1605   Articles

A Fundamental Principle of Insurance Law, Charles Lewis (identification and quantification of loss before an award can be made): [1979] LCMLQ 275.

Insurance Law Reform: The Law Commission's Proposals, A. M Tettenborn (examination and criticism of the proposals contained in the Law Commission's Working Paper, "Insurance Law: Non disclosure and Breach of Warranty"): 129 NLJ 773.

Motor Insurance, John Gaselee: 123 Sol Jo 154.

1606   Contract of insurance—meaning—entitlement to benefit on occurrence of specified event—nature of benefit

A union of dentists and medical practitioners provided certain services for its members, including the conduct of legal proceedings on their behalf and indemnifying them against claims for damages and costs. A member against whom a claim had been made could merely require the union to consider whether to conduct proceedings on his behalf or provide him with some indemnity; he had no right to require the union to assist him. The union sought a declaration that it did not carry on any class of insurance business within the meaning of the Insurance Companies Act 1974. *Held*, specific forms of insurance business were defined in the Act in terms of effecting and carrying out contracts of insurance. There was no definition of contract of insurance, so the question whether the contracts between the union and its members were contracts of insurance fell to be decided according to the general law. A contract of insurance contained three elements; (i) it had to provide that the assured would become entitled to something on the occurrence of some event; (ii) it had to involve some element of uncertainty; and (iii) the assured had to have an insurable interest in the subject-matter of the contract. The only disputed element was the first; a member's right to have his request properly considered was a benefit to which he became entitled, but it was not one consisting of money or money's worth. Although the term "money or money's worth" might be too narrow a phrase to appear in the first element of a contract of insurance, the term "benefit" was too wide. Therefore the right to have an application properly considered could not suffice for a contract of insurance, and thus the union did not carry on an insurance business and was entitled to the declaration sought.

MEDICAL DEFENCE UNION LTD v DEPARTMENT OF TRADE [1979] 2 All ER 421 (Chancery Division: MEGARRY V-C). *Prudential Insurance Co v IRC* [1904] 2 KB 658 and *Gould v Curtis* [1913] 3 KB 84, CA applied. See further 129 NLJ 13.

1607   Fire insurance—amount recoverable—basis of valuation

The owner of a cottage attempted to sell it for £12,500 but was eventually obliged to reduce his asking price to £4,250. The cottage was insured against fire and other risks for a total of £14,000 under an indemnity policy which stated that the sum was not less than the full value, defined as "the amount which it would cost to replace the cottage in its existing form should it be totally destroyed". The cottage was destroyed by fire before the owner could sell it. The insurers accepted liability but contested the owner's claim for either the full value of the property as defined in the policy or the cost of reinstatement. They contended he was entitled only to the market value of the cottage at the time of the fire, which it was agreed was £3,000. *Held*, under an indemnity policy an insured could not recover more than his actual loss, and the definition in the policy of the full value of the cottage merely laid down the maximum amount recoverable. On the facts of the case the amount which the owner could recover was the agreed sum of £3,000.

LEPPARD v EXCESS INSURANCE CO LTD [1979] 2 All ER 668 (Court of Appeal: MEGAW, GEOFFREY LANE LJJ and DUNN J). *Castellain v Preston* (1883) 11 QBD 380 applied.

1608   The plaintiffs' premises were extensively damaged by fire. Under an insurance policy, the defendant insurers were required to pay for the amount of damage. A professional fees clause provided cover for fees necessarily incurred in reinstating the property; a public authority requirements clause covered certain additional reinstatement costs but imposed a time limit for completion of the work. Both parties negotiated the amount of damage on the basis of the cost of reinstatement although the defendants knew that the plaintiffs were not going to rebuild the property. A figure was settled but the defendants later withheld certain sums on the ground that claims could only be made under the professional fees clause and the public authority requirements clause for reinstatement costs actually incurred. The defendants subsequently contended that the amount of damage was the difference in the market value of the property immediately before and after the fire and not the reinstatement cost. *Held*, (i) the defendants were not prevented from putting forward a new basis for assessing damage as there was no agreement between the parties. However, the primary measure of damage under the policy was the cost of reinstatement and there were no special facts which justified adopting any other measure. (ii) It was clear from the terms of the public authority requirements clause that a claim could only be made if the property was rebuilt: estimated reinstatement costs were not included. Accordingly the plaintiffs' claim relating to the deduction under that clause failed. (iii) However, the professional fees clause, which applied to fees necessarily incurred in reinstatement, contained no time limit for completion of the work. Fees for reinstatement were included whether rebuilding took place or not. Moreover, the words "necessarily incurred" merely described a type of cost and did not mean that the plaintiffs could only recover expenditure actually incurred. Therefore the plaintiffs were entitled to recover an appropriate sum under that clause.

PLEASURAMA LTD v SUN ALLIANCE AND LONDON INSURANCE LTD [1979] 1 Lloyd's Rep 389 (Queen's Bench Division: PARKER J).

1609   **House insurance—insurer's liability to indemnify insured "as occupier"—exclusion of liability where house contents insured under different policy—effect of exclusion**

Australia

A house insurance policy indemnified the insured, as owner and occupier, against claims for compensation resulting from bodily injury arising from an accident on the premises. It further provided that no indemnity was payable where the claim arose out of the insured's occupation of the building if the contents were insured under a different policy, which they were. Following an accident on the premises, the insured obtained a declaration that the insurers were or could be liable to indemnify him. The insurers sought to have the declaration quashed, contending that the exclusion clause absolved them of liability to indemnify the insured. It was agreed that the insured's liability, and consequently his right to an indemnity, was based on his duty as occupier rather than owner of the premises. *Held*, the insured had been sued as occupier of the premises. The words "as occupier" in the insurance document showed that occupation was an essential ingredient of the insured's liability; they were not merely descriptive of the identity or status of the person to whom the liability attached. Consequently, as the contents were insured elsewhere, the exclusion clause operated and the declaration would be quashed.

Tannous v Mercantile Mutual Insurance Co Ltd [1978] 2 NSWLR 331 (Court of Appeal of New South Wales). *Sturge v Hackett* [1962] 3 All ER 166 followed.

1610   Indemnity—double insurance—exclusion clause—contribution

The plaintiffs insured a firm of solicitors against any claim for damages made against them during the period of the insurance in the conduct of the business. The policy provided that written notice should be given of any occurrence which might subsequently give rise to a claim against them; such notice having been given, any subsequent claim should be deemed to have been made during the subsistence of the policy. The policy also contained a clause excluding the plaintiffs' liability to indemnify the solicitors if they were already entitled to indemnity under any other policy. On 24th March, the day that the policy expired, the solicitors gave written notice of an occurrence which might give rise to a claim against them in the future. On 30th April, the defendant issued a certificate referring to a policy (the master policy) by which the solicitors were insured against all loss arising from any claims made against them from midnight on 24th March. The master policy provided that the solicitors should not be indemnified in respect of any loss arising out of an occurrence which had already been notified under any other prior insurance. The plaintiffs claimed that this was a case of double insurance and that they were entitled to a contribution from the defendant. *Held*, there was no sensible distinction between the two exclusion clauses. On the natural construction of the first policy, the time when the claim was actually made had to be looked at in order to determine whether a claim was covered by another policy, and not the time when it was deemed to have been made. The equitable principle of contribution applied and there was no reason why an insurer should bear the whole of the burden of cost; the exclusion clauses were to be treated as cancelling each other out. The plaintiffs were, therefore, entitled to a contribution from the defendant.

National Employers Mutual General Insurance Association Ltd v Hayden [1979] 2 Lloyd's Rep 235 (Queen's Bench Division: Lloyd J). *Weddell v Road Transport and General Insurance Co Ltd* (1931) 41 Ll L Rep 69 and *Austin v Zurich General Accident & Liability Insurance Co Ltd* (1944) 77 Ll L Rep 409 applied.

1611   Insurance brokers—accounts and business requirements

The Insurance Brokers Registration Council (Accounts and Business Requirements) Rules Approval Order 1979, S.I. 1979 No. 489 (in force on 1st July 1979), approves the rules made by the Registration Council in relation to the carrying on of business by practising insurance brokers and enrolled bodies corporate. The rules are set out in the schedule to the Order.

1612   —— indemnity insurance and grants scheme

The Insurance Brokers Registration Council (Indemnity Insurance and Grants Scheme) Rules Approval Order 1979, S.I. 1979 No. 408 (in force on 1st July 1979), approves rules made by the Insurance Brokers Registration Council in exercise of their powers under the Insurance Brokers (Registration) Act 1977, s. 12. The rules require practising insurance brokers and enrolled bodies corporate to take out professional indemnity insurance and also provide for the making of grants to persons who have suffered loss as a result of the negligence or fraud or other dishonesty of insurance broking firms or their employees. Part II of the rules contains the detailed provisions requiring professional indemnity insurance, while Part III deals with the grants scheme. Payment of grants may be financed by a levy on all practising insurance brokers and enrolled bodies corporate. Part IV contains miscellaneous additional provisions.

1613   —— registration and enrolment

The Insurance Brokers Registration Council (Registration and Enrolment) (Amendment) Rules Approval Order 1979, S.I. 1979 No. 490 (in force on 1st July 1979), amends the Insurance Brokers Registration Council (Registration and Enrolment) Rules 1978, 1978 Halsbury's Abridgment para. 1649, by revoking r. 3. The effect of this revocation is to end the exclusion from the 1978 Rules of certain persons, namely practising brokers and bodies corporate (other than Lloyd's brokers) for whom the conditions for the carrying on of business have been specified by rules made under s. 11 of the Act.

1614   Liability insurance—clause requiring notification of third party claim against insured—effect of failure to notify

In 1969 a vessel, insured by its owners with the defendant insurance association, was chartered to the plaintiffs for a single voyage. Due to the subsequent breakdown and immobilisation of the vessel the voyage became commercially frustrated and the plaintiffs were required to charter a second vessel to discharge and re-load their cargo and continue on the original voyage. In 1970, the plaintiffs notified the owners of a preliminary claim in respect of the substantial expenses thereby incurred. The owners did not bring the matter to the attention of the defendant, until 1975, when the plaintiffs petitioned in England for a winding up order against the owners to enable them to claim directly against the defendants under the Third Parties (Rights Against Insurers) Act 1930. By that time the plaintiffs had obtained an American judgment in default against the owners for a substantial sum and an award of the same amount had been made in arbitration proceedings. A winding up order was made against the owners and the plaintiffs then issued a writ against the defendants claiming the same amount as they had been awarded in the earlier proceedings. The action was defended on the grounds, inter alia, first, that r. 13 of the association's rules empowered the defendants to reduce or reject any claim made against them by a member in respect of which they had not received notice by the member within twelve months of the member himself receiving notice of the claim, and second, that r. 8 gave the defendants a discretion to make a deduction from any claim made against them by a member whom the association considered had not acted as a prudent uninsured shipowner would have acted. The defendants maintained that since they were thus entitled to reject any claim which might have been made against them by the owners, they were not liable to the plaintiffs, now subrogated to the owners' rights. *Held*, on the facts of the case r. 13 clearly empowered the defendants to reject any claim made against them by either the owners or the plaintiffs. The questions to be decided were therefore, first, whether the lack of the required notice giving rise to the discretion to reject had caused the defendants some prejudice and, second, whether that discretion had been exercised in accordance with the established principles applicable to a contractual discretion. In relation to the first question, where an insurer sought to escape liability for a claim on the grounds of lack of notice as required by the policy, relatively little prejudice to the insurer had to be shown. In the present case it was clear that had the defendants received timely notice of the claim they would have been able to limit their liability to a considerably smaller sum and thus the test of prejudice had been satisfied. In relation to the second question, the discretion had to be exercised fairly and in good faith, requirements clearly satisfied by the defendants, since they had held several meetings and sought further information before deciding to reject the claim. Accordingly, the defendants were justified in rejecting the claim under r. 13, on the basis of the owners' lack of notice.

However, the defendants were equally entitled to reject the claim under r. 8: the reference to a deduction included, where justified by exceptional circumstances such as the present a deduction of 100 per cent. The defendants were thus entitled to reject any claim made by the owners and therefore by the plaintiffs and accordingly the action failed.

THE VAINQUEUR JOSÉ, CVG SIDERURGICIA DEL ORINOCO SA v LONDON STEAMSHIP OWNERS' MUTUAL INSURANCE ASSOCIATION LTD [1979] 1 Lloyd's Rep 557 (Queen's Bench Division: MOCATTA J). *Farrell v Federated Employers' Insurance Association Ltd* [1970] 3 All ER 632, CA applied.

1615   —— employers' liability policy—application for indemnity from insurers—whether employee acting in the course of his employment

In determining a claim under an insurance policy indemnifying the employers, it fell to be determined whether or not a particular employee was acting in the course of his employment at the time of the accident. The employee was employed on a building site at Bid Boland in Iran. His employers owned a guest house in Abadan for the housing of personnel and the arranging of their travel to and from the site to Abadan. All employees were transported between the two places in the employers' vehicles. When the particular employee arrived at Abadan airport, at the end of his vacation, he was met by the manager of the guest house, who mistakenly informed him that he was required at the site urgently. The employee travelled in the employers' vehicle and was injured in an accident, en route, caused by the negligence of the employers' driver. *Held*, the employee resumed his relationship with the employers on his return to Abadan. In returning to the site in obedience to an order he thought he had received he was, in all the circumstances of the case, in the course of his employment.

PATERSON V COSTAIN AND PRESS (OVERSEAS) LTD [1979] 2 Lloyd's Rep 204 (Court of Appeal: LORD DENNING MR, ORMROD and BROWNE LJJ).

1616   —— insurer's liability to indemnify insured for injury to third party—exclusion clause—validity

See *Tannous v Mercantile Mutual Insurance Co Ltd*, para. 1609.

1617   —— third party's subrogated rights against insurer—enforceability of policy by insured—validity of third party claim

See *The Vainqueur José, CVG Siderurgicia del Orinoco SA v London Steamship Owners' Mutual Insurance Association Ltd*, para. 1614.

1618   Life insurance—accidental death benefit—death caused by deceased's own criminal act

Canada

A driver was killed when she lost control of her car, having an excessive level of alcohol in her bloodstream. She had a personal accident insurance policy which covered "accidental bodily injuries" and her executors sued the underwriters when they refused to meet the claim. On an interpretation of the word "accidental", *held*, the word was to be given its ordinary meaning of "caused by an untoward event". An injury might be accidental even though caused by grossly negligent or dangerous conduct. The death occurred from accidental bodily injuries within the meaning of the policy.

MUTUAL OF OMAHA INSURANCE CO V STATS (1978) 87 DLR (3d) 169 (Supreme Court of Canada).

1619   —— —— exclusion of benefit where death resulting from operation of aircraft—death subsequent to accident

Canada

Under the terms of a pilot's life insurance policy, accidental death benefit was not payable if death resulted from the operation of aircraft. The pilot's aircraft crashed and although not injured in the impact he subsequently fell into a pool and drowned while attempting to walk to safety. On his executor's claim for the accidental death benefit, *held*, the drowning was not even indirectly causally linked to the operation of aircraft and the benefit was therefore payable.

ROYAL TRUST CO V GREAT-WEST LIFE ASSURANCE CO (1978) 94 DLR (3d) 538 (Supreme Court of British Columbia).

1620   Lloyd's—general business—solvency and powers of Secretary of State

The Lloyd's (General Business) Regulations 1979, S.I. 1979 No. 956 (in force on 1st August 1979), implement provisions relating to Lloyd's that are contained in Council Directive (EEC) 73/239 on the taking up and pursuit of the business of direct insurance other than life insurance.

1621   Marine insurance—claim for loss by barratry—allegation that owner consented to sinking—degree of proof required

A ship which had suffered engine failure during the course of a voyage ran into heavy weather and her master was obliged to signal for help. Various attempts were made to attach tow-lines but the only line successfully attached was released without orders for no apparent reason. The crew finally abandoned ship and she sank. The owners made a claim for loss by barratry since it had been established that the officer of the watch had deliberately sunk the ship. The insurers denied liability on the ground that the ship had been sunk with the owners' consent. At first instance the court decided in the owners' favour on the grounds that they had shown on the balance of probabilities that they had had no knowledge of the sinking. Further, the court found that for the owners deliberately to have sunk the vessel was incompatible with their efforts to build up a reputable business, and that in view of the officer's previous involvement in a scuttling it was likely he had acted on his own initiative in sinking the ship. On the insurers' appeal, *held*, it was impossible to say that the owners had presented their claim fraudulently and the insurers had failed to discharge the onus of proving that they had. In the circumstances there were no grounds for interfering with the lower court's decision and the appeal would be dismissed.

THE MICHAEL, PIERMAY SHIPPING CO SA v CHESTER [1979] 2 Lloyd's Rep 1 (Court of Appeal: ROSKILL and BRANDON LJJ and SIR DAVID CAIRNS). Decision of Kerr J [1979] 1 Lloyd's Rep 55 affirmed.

For earlier proceedings between these parties in the Court of Appeal, see [1978] 1 All ER 1233, 1978 Halsbury's Abridgment para. 1276.

1622   —— subrogation—loss of vessel and cargo—right of insurers to bring action against shipowners

Following the loss of a vessel at sea, the cargo-owners received compensation from the cargo's insurers. The insurance premium had been paid by the shipowners as a condition of carrying the cargo in a vessel more than fifteen years old. A preliminary question arose as to whether the insurers could exercise their subrogated rights against the shipowners in the name of the cargo-owners, alleging that the vessel had been unseaworthy at the beginning of the voyage. The questions for the court were whether the cargo-owners had any right to claim against the shipowners for the account of the subrogated underwriters, and if so, whether more than nominal damages would be payable. The shipowners contended (i) that as the cargo-owners had suffered no loss in the light of the insurance pay-out, the insurers could not be placed in a better position; (ii) that if that were not so, the shipowners and cargo-owners were co-assured and the insurers could not exercise a right of subrogation in the name of one assured against a co-assured; (iii) that it was an implied term of the contract, required to give it business efficacy, that the insurers would not exercise rights of subrogation against the shipowners. *Held*, (i) it was well established that the proceeds of insurance were to be disregarded when assessing damages and there was no distinction to be made where the premium was paid by one party on behalf of another; (ii) the shipowners had never intended to insure any interest on their own behalf and consequently could not be considered as co-assured; (iii) there was no basis for implying a term of the nature suggested into the policy; as far as the insurers were concerned it did not matter from whom the premium had been received. Accordingly there was nothing to prevent the insurers from exercising their normal rights of subrogation.

THE YASIN [1979] 2 Lloyd's Rep 45 (Queen's Bench Division: LLOYD J). *Bradburn v Great Western Railway Co* (1874) LR 10 Ex 1, and *Parry v Cleaver* [1970] AC 1, HL applied.

1623   —— third party liability clause—subrogated rights of third party against insurer—enforceability of policy by insured

See *The Vainqueur José, CVG Siderurgicia del Orinoco SA v London Steamship Owners' Mutual Insurance Association Ltd*, para. 1614.

1624   Motor insurance—hire or reward

Since July 1975, the insurance business had regarded contributions to petrol costs alone as not falling within the scope of the "hire or reward" exclusion in motor vehicles insurance.   As a result of consultations, the motor insurers have agreed to widen the previous interpretation and have issued an undertaking in these terms: "The receipt of contributions as part of a car-sharing arrangement for social or other similar purposes in respect of the carriage of passengers on a journey in a vehicle insured under a private car policy will not be regarded as constituting the carriage of passengers for hire or reward (or the use of the vehicle for hiring) provided that: (a) the vehicle is not constructed or adapted to carry more than seven passengers (excluding the driver); (b) the passengers are not being carried in the course of a business of carrying passengers; (c) the total contributions received for the journey concerned do not involve an element of profit."   Policyholders are advised to make inquiries of their insurers if they have any doubt whether a particular car-sharing arrangement is covered by the terms of their policy.   See Department of Transport circular 9/78 (Welsh Office circular 105/78), Annex 4.

1625   —— indemnity—accident resulting in personal injury—disclaimer of liability to indemnify

The plaintiff's car was insured by the defendants.   The policy provided that if the defendants should disclaim their liability to indemnify the plaintiff, legal proceedings had to be instituted within twelve months of the disclaimer or the claim would be deemed to have been abandoned.   In August 1970, the plaintiff was driving when his car was involved in a collision in which one of the plaintiff's passengers was severely injured.   When the passenger claimed damages for her injuries, the defendants refused to meet the claim because the plaintiff was in breach of his policy conditions at the time of the accident.   The plaintiff's solicitors wrote to the defendants questioning their decision.   The defendants replied, in March 1971, that they were not prepared to reconsider their decision concerning indemnity.   The passenger subsequently obtained judgment in default of appearance.   In 1975, the plaintiff's solicitors re-opened correspondence with the defendants, having heard that damages in the passenger's action were to be assessed.   In 1976, judgment was entered for a sum of damages for the passenger.   The plaintiff claimed a declaration that he was entitled to be indemnified by the defendants.   *Held*, the defendants, by their letter of March 1971, clearly disclaimed any liability to the plaintiff for any claim to an indemnity under the policy; they did not at any time repudiate the contract.   The plaintiff's claim was made in 1971, as there was no necessity to have an amount claimed before there was a claim.   The defendants were entitled to disclaim liability in certain circumstances under the contract of insurance, and they had disclaimed liability more than twelve months before the plaintiff had instituted legal proceedings.   Accordingly, the plaintiff's application for a declaration would be dismissed.

WALKER V PENNINE INSURANCE CO LTD [1979] 2 Lloyd's Rep 139 (Queen's Bench Division: SHEEN J).

1626   —— personal injury—limitation of insurer's liability

The plaintiff was the executor of the estate of his son who had suffered grave injuries in a motor accident in British Honduras.   An action in that country had ended with a consent judgment for $175,000 with interest and costs, but the driver responsible was unable to pay any part of the judgment.   The driver had a certificate of insurance, but the insurance company refused to honour the judgment.   The insurance company successfully contended that, as they were only bound to cover the driver in the sum of $4,000 under an ordinance in British Honduras, their liability was limited to that amount. The plaintiff appealed. *Held*, LORD DENNING MR dissenting, it would be wrong to construe the language of the ordinance by reference to different language in different legislation and the ordinance had to be construed as it stood. There was no reason why in principle the legislation should not have provided for limited exemption of liability above a stated figure. Accordingly, the appeal would be dismissed.

HARKER V CALEDONIAN INSURANCE CO [1979] 2 Lloyd's Rep 193 (Court of Appeal: LORD DENNING MR, ROSKILL and CUMMING-BRUCE LJJ).

This decision has been affirmed by the House of Lords; see Times, 4th March 1980.

1627 —— total loss settlement—disposal of vehicle

Following some confusion between the Driver and Vehicle Licensing Centre and motor insurers over the correct method of notifying the disposal of a vehicle subject to a total loss settlement after an accident, the Department of Transport has agreed a procedure with the Motor Conference (representing the interests of motor insurers generally). The motor insurer concerned should advise the policy-holder to notify disposal on the tear-off portion of the registration document by giving the insurer's name and address and ticking the dealer/insurer box (if there is one on the document). If the policy-holder fails to do this, the motor insurer should do it on his behalf. The motor insurer then takes the rest of the registration document and must pass it to the person who buys the vehicle as salvage. If the new purchaser scraps the vehicle he must himself notify the Driver and Vehicle Licensing Centre; but if he repairs the vehicle and sells it the acquirer of the repaired vehicle (unless he is a motor dealer) must notify acquisition on the registration document. This procedure is described in *Case 3B/806/77* in Parliamentary Commissioner for Administration: Investigations Completed—August to October 1978 (HC 111).

1628 Non-disclosure—material facts—criminal record—imputation to insurers of agents' knowledge

A householder insured his property through brokers without disclosing his serious criminal record at that particular time. When he lodged a claim under the policy, the insurers contended that he had failed to disclose material facts and sought to avoid the policy. He contended that the brokers had had previous knowledge of his past and that that knowledge had to be imputed to the insurers. The latter then issued a third party notice seeking an indemnity from the brokers. At first instance the policy was found to be valid and the brokers were ordered to indemnify the insurers. On appeal by both the insurers and the brokers, *held*, the trial judge had accepted and rejected the evidence of certain witnesses for reasons that were manifestly unsound and there was a real possibility that injustice had been done. Accordingly a new trial would be ordered. As to the liability of the brokers to indemnify the insurers, the judge had been correct in imputing the former's knowledge to the latter. If the facts proved to be as found at the trial, the brokers would have no defence against the insurers' claim for an indemnity. Accordingly, although the brokers were not entitled to judgment, the appeal would be allowed so that a decision could be reached at the new trial.

WOOLCOTT V EXCESS INSURANCE CO LTD [1979] 1 Lloyd's Rep 231 (Court of Appeal: MEGAW, SHAW and WALLER LJJ). Decision of Caulfield J [1978] 1 Lloyd's Rep 633, 1977 Halsbury's Abridgment para. 1606 set aside pending a new trial.

1629

The plaintiff insured his property with the defendants through brokers. After a fire at his property, the plaintiff lodged a claim under the policy against the defendants. The defendants contended that they were not liable to the plaintiff because of his failure to disclose his criminal record in his proposal for insurance. The plaintiff successfully argued that the brokers had known of his criminal record before the fire had destroyed the property, and that that knowledge had to be imputed to the defendants. The trial judge, having found for the plaintiff against the defendants, ordered that the brokers should indemnify the defendants. On appeal, a new trial was ordered on the ground that the reasons for acceptance and rejection of certain evidence had been manifestly unsound. It was held, however, that the trial judge had been correct in imputing the brokers' knowledge to the defendants. The point for decision at the retrial was, therefore, whether the plaintiff's past was known to the defendants or the brokers before the contract of insurance was made or the fire occurred. *Held*, on review of the evidence, the brokers did know that the plaintiff had a serious criminal record but had failed to pass this information on to the defendants. Accordingly, the brokers would be ordered to indemnify the defendants.

WOOLCOTT V EXCESS INSURANCE CO LTD AND MILES SMITH ANDERSON AND GAME LTD (No. 2) [1979] 2 Lloyd's Rep 210 (Queen's Bench Division: CANTLEY J).

For earlier proceedings see [1979] 1 Lloyd's Rep 231, CA, para. 1628.

1630   —— —— **previous driving convictions—imputation to principal of agent's knowledge**

Canada

The plaintiff arranged for motor insurance with the agent for the defendant insurance company by telephone. On being questioned about his previous motoring record he said that he had had one accident and had committed a number of minor driving offences, the dates of which he could not remember. The agent assured the plaintiff that more exact information could be acquired by the company from its motor vehicle branch. On attendance at the company office the plaintiff signed documents drawn up by the agent, without reading them. He received the relevant documents and paid his premium. Shortly afterwards he had a car accident and claimed from the insurers; they contended that they were not liable, on the ground that the plaintiff's policy had been rendered invalid by his failure to reveal all the information concerning previous driving offences. *Held*, the policy was valid inasmuch as the plaintiff had given all the information that was known to him concerning his offences. The agent was at fault in not having ascertained, the details of the offences, as he had assured the plaintiff he would, before obtaining the signature of the plaintiff on binding documents.

MOXNESS V CO-OPERATIVE FIRE AND CASUALTY CO [1979] 2 WWR 436 (Supreme Court of Alberta).

1631   **Validity of policy—offer and acceptance**

The plaintiff signed and completed a single premium property bond policy and sent off the application form, together with a cheque, to the defendants. The bond was primarily an investment in property with the benefit of life insurance added and its value as an investment was subject to fluctuation in the property market. The terms of the policy were complicated and detailed, but the basic terms had been explained to the plaintiff and she did not complain about it until seven months later, when the value of her property units had fallen seriously. She brought an action contending that the policy was void as there had never been a concluded contract between her and the defendants in relation to the subject matter of the policy. The judge dismissed the claim on two grounds: (1) that the plaintiff by submitting the application form signed by her and accompanied by her cheque, made an offer to the defendants to invest her money in a property bond policy and the defendants had accepted that offer by allocating property units to her and (2) alternatively, the defendants, by delivering the policy to the plaintiff made an offer to her, which she had implicitly accepted by not objecting to it for seven months. On appeal, *held*, with regard to the first ground for the decision, in ordinary insurance cases a policy could be a binding contract even though the insured had not seen or assented to all the detailed terms of the policy, provided that such terms were the usual terms. Further, in the alternative, it was the inevitable inference from the conduct of the plaintiff in not acting for seven months that she accepted the policy as a valid contract. The judge's decision would be upheld and the appeal would be dismissed.

RUST V ABBEY LIFE ASSURANCE CO LTD [1979] 2 Lloyd's Rep 334 (Court of Appeal: ORR, CUMMING-BRUCE and BRANDON LJJ).

INTOXICATING LIQUOR

Halsbury's Laws of England (4th edn.), Vol. 26, paras. 1–500

1632   Alcohol tables—EEC requirements

See para. 3069.

1633   Alcoholic liquor duties—consolidation

See Alcoholic Liquor Duties Act 1979, para. 727.

1634   Licensing hours—exemptions—special order of exemption—special occasion

A licensee applied for special orders of exemption under the Licensing Act 1964, s. 74 (4), for dates in December and January in respect of his Christmas trade. The justices deleted two dates from the application as not being special occasions, but upheld the remainder. On appeal by the licensee, *held*, the question whether or not it was a special occasion was primarily a question for the justices, using their discretion, as they possessed relevant local knowledge. An application for such an order should be refused if the so-called occasion was too frequent. The special occasion had to be special in the local or national sense. The justices should look first to see whether the occasion was capable of being special and, if it was, decide whether it was special in the instant case. However, the appeal would be dismissed, as the relevant dates had passed.

MARTIN v SPALDING [1979] 2 All ER 1193 (Queen's Bench Division: LORD WIDGERY CJ, GEOFFREY LANE LJ and ACKNER J). *Devine v Keeling* (1886) 50 JP 551 applied.

1635   A licensed sporting club applied for special exemptions from permitted licensing hours, under the Licensing Act 1964, s. 74 (4) (b), in respect of various functions on the club premises including the prize-giving of the club's major annual golf competition, on the ground that they were special occasions within the meaning of s. 74. The justices refused the application on the ground that to be a special occasion it had to be a local or national event external to the club's own activities or a function organised by an outside body. On appeal, *held*, the question whether a function was a special occasion depended on the circumstances. There was no reason why a special sporting occasion organised by a sporting club on its own premises could not be a special occasion and the justices had taken a restricted view of s. 74. The application for a special exemption would be granted.

KNOLE PARK GOLF CLUB v CHIEF SUPERINTENDENT, KENT COUNTY CONSTABU-LARY [1979] 3 All ER 829 (Queen's Bench Division: EVELEIGH LJ and WOOLF J). Dictum of Widgery J in *Lemon v Sargent* [1971] 3 All ER 936 at 937 applied.

1636   Liqueur chocolates

The Licensing Act 1964 (Amendment) Regulations 1979, S.I. 1979 No. 1476 (in force on 1st January 1979), amend the Licensing Act 1964, s. 167 (1) by providing that the reference to the proportion of intoxicating liquor in liqueur chocolates, now computed as at proof spirit, is now to be expressed with a reference to the quantity of ethyl alcohol amounting to 57 per cent of the volume of the liquor inclusive of the alcohol contained in it as at 20 degrees Centigrade.

1637   Price marking—drink on premises

The Price Marking (Food and Drink on Premises) Order 1979, S.I. 1979 No. 361 (in force on 30th July 1979), requires prices to be displayed on any premises where an indication is given that food or drink is or may be for sale for consumption there. The display of prices is not required in bona fide clubs, staff canteens or canteens in educational establishments, nor for food prepared by special request or for which a price has been agreed in advance.   The Price Marking (Drinks on Premises) Order 1975, 1975 Halsbury's Abridgment para. 1908, is revoked.

1638   Sale of intoxicating liquor outside permitted hours—liability of absent licensee

A licensee was convicted of having sold, by his servants, intoxicating liquor outside the permitted hours contrary to the Licensing Act 1964, s. 59 (1) (a).   The magistrates found as fact that the licensee was unconnected with the company which operated a restaurant on the premises covered by the licence and was not present at the time the offences were committed, but they convicted on the grounds that a licensee was responsible for all breaches of the terms of the licence.   On appeal by case stated, *held*, the magistrates had been wrong in holding that a conviction could be founded on mere possession of the licence: for the licensee to be guilty it had to be shown that the liquor had been sold by him or his servants.   The conviction would be quashed.

TAYLOR v SPEED [1979] Crim LR 114 (Queen's Bench Division: LORD WIDGERY CJ, GRIFFITHS and GIBSON JJ).

1639   —— sale under occasional licence

The defendant was granted an occasional licence to sell intoxicating liquor on certain premises during the normal licensing hours applicable in that area.   Alcohol was sold outside the permitted hours.   The defendant was convicted of selling intoxicating liquor when he did not have a licence authorising him to do so, contrary to the Licensing Act 1964, s. 160.   The justices held that the occasional licence ended after the hours specified in it.   On the defendant's appeal, *held*, s. 59, which created the offence of selling liquor outside permitted hours, did not apply when the sale was under an occasional licence.   Section 160 also covered the offence of selling liquor without a licence, and for selling liquor in a place not authorised for such sale by the licence.   The section did not cover the sale of alcohol outside permitted hours.   The justices had erred in holding that s. 160 applied to the present case and the appeal would be allowed.

SOUTHALL v HAIME [1979] LS Gaz R 158 (Queen's Bench Division: LORD WIDGERY CJ, BRIDGE LJ and CAULFIELD J).

JUDGMENTS AND ORDERS

Halsbury's Laws of England (4th edn.), Vol. 26, paras. 501–600

1640   Article

.Enforcement of Judgments: Charging Orders and Receivers, R. N. Hill (an examination of the two methods of enforcement): Law Notes Vol. 98, No. 10, p. 274.

1641   Agreement between parties—agreement made rule of court—whether enforceable as order or judgment of the court

See *Herbert v Herbert*, para. 2115.

1642   Charging Orders Act 1979

See para. 1263.

1643   Judgment—House of Lords decision—whether binding on Judicial Committee of the Privy Council

Hong Kong
The parties to a divorce agreed that the husband would not defend the wife's petition

and that he would make certain financial provisions for her. In return she promised to consent to the dismissal of her claim for financial provision in the petition. At all material times the Hong Kong legislation relating to financial provision was in the same terms as English legislation. The wife was granted a decree nisi and a consent order approving the parties' financial arrangements was made. The wife's subsequent application for variation of the consent was refused, but that decision was reversed by the Hong Kong appeal court. The husband appealed to the Judicial Committee of the Privy Council contending that, according to a judgment of the House of Lords delivered prior to the hearing before the Board, the Hong Kong court had been acting out of its jurisdiction. The House of Lords had decided that, under Matrimonial Causes Act 1973, s. 23 (1) (b), there was no jurisdiction to make a maintenance order in favour of a wife after the refusal of her original application for financial relief. The wife contended that the Privy Council was not bound by the House of Lords decision when hearing the appeal from the Hong Kong court. *Held*, in considering whether a decision of the House of Lords was binding on a colonial court, there was a distinction to be drawn between common law and statute. A decision in relation to the common law was of only persuasive authority, although the common membership of the Board and the Judicial Committee meant that the Board was unlikely to diverge from a decision made by its members in its alternative capacity. A decision in relation to statutory interpretation was binding because there was no question of divergent development of the law. Both the Hong Kong appeal court and the Board were accordingly bound to follow the House of Lords decision and the husband's appeal would be allowed.

DE LASALA v DE LASALA [1979] 2 All ER 1146 (Privy Council: LORD DIPLOCK, LORD FRASER OF TULLYBELTON and LORD RUSSELL OF KILLOWEN). *Minton v Minton* [1979] 1 All ER 79, 1978 Halsbury's Abridgment para. 970 applied.

1644   Judgment debt—interest—rate of interest

The Judgment Debts (Rate of Interest) Order 1979, S.I. 1979 No. 1382 (in force on 3rd December 1979), increased to $12\frac{1}{2}$ per cent per annum the rate of interest on judgment debts under the Judgment Act 1838, s. 17.

1645   Judgment on admissions of fact—negligence—action for damages—negligence admitted—whether sufficient for judgment

The plaintiff lorry driver brought an action for damages against the defendants, his employers, after he slipped on a pool of glucose in the defendants' filling shed. The defendants admitted negligence, and the plaintiff obtained an order under RSC Ord. 27, r. 3, which provides that where admissions of fact are made by one party, the other party can apply to the court for a judgment or order upon those admissions, without waiting for a determination of any other questions between the parties. The plaintiff believed that all that remained to be settled was the quantum of damages and applied for judgment. The defendants appealed against the order on the ground that, although they had admitted negligence, they had not admitted that the plaintiff suffered damage or injury as a result of the incident, and that accordingly, an order under Ord. 27, r. 3 ought not to have been made. *Held*, in any action for negligence the cause of action had two elements, breach of duty to the plaintiff and damage suffered by the plaintiff. The plaintiff did not establish a right to judgment without proof or admission of both of these. The defendants had not admitted that the plaintiff sustained any injury in the manner alleged. Accordingly the order ought not to have been made and the appeal would be allowed.

RANKINE v GARTON SONS & CO LTD [1979] 2 All ER 1185 (Court of Appeal: STEPHENSON and GEOFFREY LANE LJJ and DUNN J). *Blundell v Rimmer* [1971] 1 All ER 1072 followed.

1646   Setting aside judgment—judgment where applicant did not appear at trial—applicant in contempt—court's jurisdiction to set aside judgment

A father granted his son an option to purchase a farm but, before the son could exercise it, the father conveyed the farm to his wife for substantially less than its market value. The son sought specific performance of the option or alternatively damages for conspiracy. The statement of claim alleged that the father and his wife had conspired to defraud him by means of the conveyance. The parties all died and the action was carried on by the son's executors against the wife's executor and the father's executrix, the applicant in the present proceedings. The applicant failed to comply with an order for discovery and her defence was struck out. Judgment in default of defence was entered against her for damages for conspiracy and an inquiry as to damages was ordered. The applicant had failed to plead plene administravit praeter and sought to amend her defence in order to do so. The application was refused. She then applied under RSC Ord. 35, r. 2 (1), to set aside the judgment on the ground that the facts pleaded in the statement of claim could not support a judgment for damages for conspiracy, since a husband and wife were in law incapable of conspiring together. She did not offer to purge her contempt in failing to comply with the order for discovery. *Held*, the court could exercise its discretion under Ord. 35, r. 2 (1), to set aside a judgment which the court had not had jurisdiction to enter because it was insupportable in law, notwithstanding that the applicant was in serious contempt. Therefore if the applicant succeeded in establishing that the judgment entered against her was insupportable in law, the court would set it aside on terms that the order for discovery was complied with. However, although a husband and wife could not be indicted for the crime of conspiracy, this did not apply to the tort of conspiracy, since public policy did not require it. Thus the facts pleaded in the statement of claim supported the son's claim and the court had jurisdiction to enter judgment against the applicant. The motion would be dismissed.

MIDLAND BANK TRUST CO LTD v GREEN (No. 3) [1979] 2 All ER 193 (Chancery Division: OLIVER J). *Gordon v Gordon* [1904–7] All ER Rep 702 and dictum of Salmon J in *Marrinan v Vibart* [1962] 1 All ER 869 at 871 applied.

For previous proceedings, see *Midland Bank Trust Co Ltd v Green* [1978] 3 All ER 555, 1977 Halsbury's Abridgment para. 1636 (reversed on appeal; see para. 1657) and *Midland Bank Trust Co Ltd v Green (No. 2)* [1979] 1 All ER 726, 1978 Halsbury's Abridgment para. 1290.

1647   Summary judgment—leave to defend—counterclaim—whether leave should be granted

A company contracted with builders for the construction of a warehouse and car park. The company refused to pay outstanding sums of £52,000 for the warehouse and £17,000 for the car park, contending that the floor of the former and the composition of the latter did not meet the specifications prescribed. The counterclaims amounted to £67,000 in respect of the warehouse, based on the report of consultant engineers, coupled with loss of rents on the warehouse, and a similar figure in respect of the car park. On the builders' application for summary judgment the company were given leave to defend as to £20,000 in respect of the warehouse and £17,000 in respect of the car park. On the company's appeal, *held*, (i) although the counterclaim relating to the warehouse seemed exaggerated it was at least arguable that the drastic remedial work suggested by the engineers would have to be undertaken. Accordingly, the builders could not be given leave to sign judgment for more than the difference between the sum outstanding on the contract and the counterclaim. (ii) The claim relating to the car park was also doubtful. There was no identifiable sum in respect of which judgment could be given and the company therefore had to be allowed to defend in respect of the whole sum outstanding on the contract. The company's additional contention that the counterclaim relating to the car park should be treated as an equitable set-off against the sum due on the warehouse would not be upheld; the lower court had reasonably exercised its discretion in refusing to allow it and that decision would stand.

SABLE CONTRACTORS LTD v BLUETT SHIPPING LTD [1979] 2 Lloyd's Rep 33 (Court of Appeal: LORD DIPLOCK and LORD RUSSELL OF KILLOWEN).

1648   —— stay of execution pending counterclaim—Mareva injunction

See *Montecchi v Shimco (UK) Ltd; Navone v Shimco (UK) Ltd*, para. 1598.

JURIES

Halsbury's Laws of England (4th edn.), Vol. 26, paras. 601–700

1649   **Articles**

An American Experience, Judge Peter Mason (jury vetting in the United States): 129 NLJ 1192.

Jury-Vetting: A Challenging Task, Jeremy Smith (a criticism of the prosecution's guidelines on the practice of jury-vetting): 129 NLJ 484.

The Representativeness of Juries, John Baldwin and Michael McConville: 129 NLJ 284.

1650   **County court—action for false imprisonment—right to trial by jury**

See *Harmsworth v London Transport Executive*, para. 553.

1651   **Juror—discharge of juror—discharge not in open court—whether a material irregularity**

See *R v Richardson*, para. 649.

1652   **Jury vetting—Attorney-General's statement**

The Attorney-General has stated in the House of Commons that there will be no vetting of jurors in criminal trials in future except where he has given his direct approval.   See Times, 11th December 1979.

LAND CHARGES

Halsbury's Laws of England (4th edn.), Vol. 26, paras. 701–900

1653   **Article**

Land Charges and the Dead Man's Handle. A. M. Prichard (on whether a land charge can effectively be registered against the name of a deceased person): [1979] Conv 249.

1654   **Estate contract—right of pre-emption—whether interest in land**

In 1944, vendors, a husband and wife, sold a hotel to a purchaser, but retained adjoining land.   The vendors covenanted that neither they nor their survivor would sell the retained land without first giving the purchaser an option to purchase the retained land during his lifetime, at a certain sum, the fixtures to be at a valuation. The covenant was registered under the Land Charges Act 1925.   In 1954, the hotel was sold to the first and second defendants.   In 1959, the vendors granted the plaintiff a lease of the retained land containing an option to purchase the land after the death of the survivor of the vendors.   In 1964, a second lease was granted to the plaintiff which repeated the option.   That option was also registered under the 1925 Act.   After the wife's death, the husband's health deteriorated and in 1971 his nephew, the third defendant, was appointed as his receiver under the Mental Health Act 1959.   The third defendant agreed to sell the retained land to the first and second defendants subject to certain conditions.   The husband died before completion. The plaintiff then purported to exercise his option, and issued a writ seeking specific performance and an order setting aside the conveyance to the first and second defendants as being a conspiracy to defeat his rights. His application was refused. On appeal by the plaintiff, *held*, the grant of the right of pre-emption in 1944 created a mere spes which the vendors, as grantors, might either frustrate by choosing not to fulfill the necessary conditions or might convert into an option to purchase and thus an equitable interest by fulfilling the conditions. The plaintiff's option, being an interest in land, took priority over the prior registered right of pre-emption. It was further held (GOFF LJ dissenting) that the grant of a right of pre-emption could bind a grantor's successor in title. The appeal would be allowed.

PRITCHARD v BRIGGS [1979] 3 WLR 868 (Court of Appeal: STEPHENSON, GOFF and TEMPLEMAN LJJ). Decision of Walton J (1977) 122 Sol Jo 96, 1977 Halsbury's Abridgment para. 1633 reversed.

1655   Local land charges—fees for registration—increase

The Local Land Charges (Amendment) Rules 1979, S.I. 1979 No. 1404 (in force on 3rd December 1979), amend the Local Land Charges Rules 1977, 1977 Halsbury's Abridgment para. 1635 by increasing the fees payable in connection with the registration of local land charges.

1656   Option to renew lease—failure to register—whether landlords estopped from asserting strict rights

See *Taylor Fashions Ltd v Liverpool Victoria Friendly Society*, para. 1146.

1657   Registration—failure to register—estate contract—position of purchaser—purchaser for money or money's worth

In 1961 a father in consideration of £1 granted his son an option to purchase a farm belonging to him, which was worth at least £40,000. The option was not registered under the Land Charges Act 1925. In 1967 the father conveyed the farm to his wife for £500. The son purported to exercise the option by issuing a formal notice which was not complied with and he brought an action to enforce the option. It was held that the option was void for non-registration under the Land Charges Act 1925, s. 13 (2), the wife being a purchaser for money or money's worth. On appeal by the son, *held*, SIR STANLEY REES dissenting, "money or money's worth" meant a fair and reasonable value in money or money's worth, not an undervalue, particularly a gross undervalue or mere token, as here. Hence the wife was not a purchaser for money or money's worth. Accordingly, she took the estate subject to the option and the purported exercise of the option by the son was valid. The appeal would be allowed.

LORD DENNING MR considered that the appeal should also be allowed because the provisions protecting a purchaser were of no avail when the sale was made in fraud of the holder of the estate contract; and fraud in this context covered any dishonest dealing done so as to deprive innocent parties of their rightful dues. The conveyance was executed deliberately to deprive the son of the benefit of the option, and this amounted to a fraud on him.

SIR STANLEY REES, dissenting, considered that the evidence did not support a finding of fraud against the father and his wife and that "money or money's worth" should not be construed to mean a fair and reasonable value.

MIDLAND BANK TRUST CO LTD v GREEN [1979] 3 All ER 28 (Court of Appeal; LORD DENNING MR, EVELEIGH LJ and SIR STANLEY REES). Decision of Oliver J [1978] 3 All ER 555, 1977 Halsbury's Abridgment para. 1636 reversed.

Land Charges Act 1925, s. 13 (2), now Land Charges Act 1972, s. 4 (6).

1658   Vacation of register—illegal advance by building society on second mortgage

See *Nash v Halifax Building Society*, para. 263.

LAND REGISTRATION

Halsbury's Laws of England (4th edn.), Vol. 26, paras. 901–1490

1659   Chief Land Registrar—annual report

The Chief Land Registrar's report for 1978–79 has been published and is available from HMSO. The number of registered titles now exceeds 6 million and it is thought that this represents approximately 50 per cent of the number of titles which will be registered in England and Wales when all titles have been registered. The Registrar reports that, with few exceptions, certificates of search have been issued on the date of receipt of applications when the applications related to the whole of the land in a registered title. When the applications related to part of the land in a title, the certificates have been issued on the day following receipt. Indemnity was paid in respect of 109 claims during the year (ninety-eight claims in the previous year). The report also covers the Land Charges Department where most certificates of search were despatched within twenty-four hours of receipt and the remainder within forty-eight hours. During the year more than 11 per cent of all full searches were made by the telephone search service. The index of names of registered proprietors in the Registration of Title Department is expected to be fully computerised by 1983 and the manual part of the index will be closed.

1660   District registries—areas served

The Land Registration (District Registries) Order 1979, S.I. 1979 No. 1019 (in force on 19th November 1979), replaces the Land Registration (District Registries) Order 1978, 1978 Halsbury's Abridgment para. 1697. A new district land registry is constituted at Weymouth and responsibility for the registration of titles in the countries of Hampshire and Isle of Wight is transferred from the Gloucester District Land Registry to Weymouth. The areas of the remaining district registries remain unchanged.

1661   Estate contract—right of pre-emption—prior registration— whether interest in land

See *Pritchard v Briggs*, para. 1654.

1662   Priority—registration of deeds—deed of settlement registered before earlier conveyance—Trinidad and Tobago

The beneficiary under a settlement of a parcel of land, which was registered after the owner sold the land to her lessee but before the sale was registered, claimed after the owner's death that his prior registration entitled him to the fee simple under the Registration of Deeds Ordinance. *Held*, on the true construction of the Ordinance an unregistered deed did not affect the title of a subsequent purchaser of land who took the conveyance without notice of the deed. The conveyance had to be registered in order that the validity of the first deed could be challenged and, therefore, the lessee was entitled to the fee simple.

MAHABIR v PAYNE [1979] 1 WLR 507 (Privy Council: LORD DIPLOCK, LORD RUSSELL OF KILLOWEN and LORD SCARMAN).

1663   Registration of title—private caveat—application for removal of caveat—balance of convenience

Malaysia

The vendors were the registered proprietors of land in Malaysia. They contracted to sell the land to the purchaser. On the purchaser's default, the vendors served notice on him terminating the contract for breach. The purchaser commenced an action for specific performance of the contract and entered a private caveat on the register to the extent of the whole share. The Malaysian system of private caveats is substituted for the equitable doctrine of notice. The vendors applied for removal of the caveat, supporting their application by an affidavit exhibiting the written contract of sale. The purchaser also filed an affidavit which contained assertions which conflicted with that of the vendors. The judge rejected the purchaser's affidavit as false, inadmissible and unlikely and ordered the removal of the caveat. On appeal by the purchaser, the order was set aside on the ground that once the purchaser had asserted that the contract of sale had not been lawfully terminated and had begun an action for specific performance, the judge was bound to leave the caveat on the register until that action had been disposed of. The vendors appealed. *Held*, when an application for the removal of a caveat was made by the registered proprietor of the land, the purchaser, as caveator, was in a position analogous to that of a plaintiff in an action for specific performance seeking an interlocutory injunction to restrain the vendor from disposing of the land pending the trial of the action; the caveator had to satisfy the court that there was a serious issue to be tried and, having done so, to show that on the balance of convenience the status quo should be maintained until trial. On the evidence, the judge had decided that the purchaser had not shown that there was a serious issue to be tried, and that decision should not be interfered with on appeal. The appeal would be allowed.

ENG MEE YONG V LETCHUMANAN S/O VELAYUTHAM [1979] 3 WLR 373 (Privy Council: LORD DIPLOCK, LORD MORRIS OF BORTH-Y-GEST, LORD HAILSHAM OF ST MARYLEBONE, LORD EDMUND-DAVIES and LORD FRASER OF TULLYBELTON). *American Cyanamid Co v Ethicon Ltd* [1975] 1 All ER, HL, 1975 Halsbury's Abridgment para. 1864 applied.

1664   **Unregistered interest in property—position of mortgagee claiming possession**

See *Williams and Glyn's Bank v Boland*; *Williams and Glyn's Bank Ltd v Brown*, para. 1851.

LANDLORD AND TENANT

Halsbury's Laws of England (3rd edn.), Vol. 23, paras. 985–1746

1665   **Articles**

A Tale of Unlawful Eviction, Stephen D. Migdal (the legal steps to be taken should a tenant be evicted and barred from access to the property and his belongings): 129 NLJ 937.

Alteration of Terms in New Lease of Business Property, C. Baxter (general propositions guiding the court in deciding the validity of such terms): 129 NLJ 434.

Business Lease: Break Clause, Henry E. Markson (in the light of *Adams v Green* (1978) 247 EG 49, CA, 1978 Halsbury's Abridgment para. 1704): 123 Sol Jo 396.

Determining Fair Rents, Peter Robson and Paul Watchman (progress in the determination of fair rents under the Rent Acts): 128 NLJ 1209.

Eviction, Harassment and Exemplary Damages, Stephen D. Migdal (a review of some cases involving actions for unlawful eviction and the awarding of exemplary damages): 129 NLJ 849.

Harassment and Unlawful Eviction, Henry E. Markson (a survey of some statutory provisions and certain recent developments concerning the subject): 123 Sol Jo 629.

Landlord's Liability for Repairs, Charles Bennett (the exceptions to the general rule regarding the liability of landlords of dwelling-houses and the effect of the law of misrepresentation): 129 NLJ 727.

Leasehold Covenants for Title, M. J. Russell (basic problems concerning the landlord's covenant for quiet enjoyment): [1978] Conv. 418.

Limited Owners and Inflation-Proof Rents, Martin Dockray (on the breadth of statutory powers of disposition enjoyed by a tenant for life, and the possible introduction of rent review clauses): [1979] Conv 258.

The Lessons of *Ravenseft*, H. W. Wilkinson (the problem of the tenant's liability to repair inherent defects in the light of *Ravenseft Properties Ltd v Davstone (Holdings) Ltd* [1979] 1 All ER 929, para. 1689): 129 NLJ 839.

Mesne Profits and Married Quarters, S. D. Hall-Jones (the problems of initiating proceedings against non-occupying servicemen; discussion of cases): 129 NLJ 260.

Mortgagee's Right to Possession, Jonathan S. Fisher (decision in *Quennell v Maltby* [1979] 1 All ER 568, 1978 Halsbury's Abridgment para. 1736): 123 Sol Jo 775.

The Penalty of Improvements, P. F. Smith (business tenancies to which Pt II of the Landlord and Tenant Act 1954 applies): [1979] Conv 215

Public Sector Tenancies, Henry E. Markson (summary of recent consultation papers on public sector tenancies): 129 NLJ 210.

Refusal of Consent to Sub-let, H. W. Wilkinson (on the question raised by the decision in *West Layton Ltd v Ford* [1979] 2 All ER 657, CA, para. 1686): 129 NLJ 955.

Renewal on Different Terms, Trevor M. Aldridge (review of terms, other than terms and rent, of business tenancy): 123 Sol Jo 811.

Rent Review—Valuing the Incomparable, Ronald Bernstein (notional lettings for which no comparable transactions can be found, because the terms of the notional letting are unusual): [1979] LS Gaz 674.

Rent Revision and Tenant's Improvements, Paul Robertshaw: 129 NLJ 615.

Repairing Covenants and Inherent Defects, I. G. C. Stratton (the tenant's liability for inherent defects in a building in the light of *Ravenseft Properties Ltd v Davstone (Holdings) Ltd* [1979] 2 WLR 897, para. 1689): 123 Sol Jo 510.

Revocation of Licences, J. Warburton (the question of whether an equitable licence, once established, can be revoked by the subsequent misconduct of the licensee, as raised by *Williams v Staite* [1978] 2 All ER 928, CA, 1978 Halsbury's Abridgment para. 1725): 123 Sol Jo 463.

The Saga of Campden Hill Towers, D. J. Hughes (*Campden Hill Towers v Gardner* [1977] 1 All ER 739, 1976 Halsbury's Abridgment para. 1579 and its effect upon the repairing obligations between landlords and the tenants of dwelling-houses): 129 NLJ 691.

Some Aspects of Rent Review: An Alternative Slant, P. F. Smith (judicial interpretation of rent review clauses): [1979] Conv. 10.

Some Recent Cases on the Rent Act 1977, Catherine Hand (some cases which illustrate the difficulty of interpreting the word "family" as used in Sch. 1, Part 1 of the Rent Act 1977): 129 NLJ 629.

Standard Rent Review, Trevor M. Aldridge (rent review clauses for leases of commercial property): 123 Sol Jo 759.

Succession Rights: Rent Acts and Secure Tenancies, Henry E. Markson (a short comparative reference between succession rights of tenants under the Rent Acts and secure tenancies): 129 NLJ 536.

Transfer of a Tenancy: The Landlord's Position, Tony Radevsky (position of landlord where tenancy involved contains a covenant against assignment): 129 NLJ 1069.

Transfer of Tenancy and the Matrimonial Homes Act 1967, N. E. Hickman (power of a divorce court to order a transfer of a protected or statutory tenancy under the Matrimonial Homes Act 1973, s. 24): 129 NLJ 52.

Who is the Tenant? James Goudie (whether person not entered as tenant on a lease may claim right to statutory tenancy): 128 NLJ 1239.

1666   Agreement to provide accommodation—whether agreement a licence or a lease—principles for determining nature of agreement

Upon an application by the plaintiffs for a possession order, the defendant contended that he and his former co-occupant were joint tenants, that the agreement they entered into with the plaintiffs gave rise to a joint tenancy and not separate licences. *Held*, the occupants had signed separate but identical agreements which upon construction, created non-exclusive licences. The fact that the agreements were used to avoid the operation of the Rent Acts did not mean that the court could refuse to give effect to those agreements.

ALDRINGTON GARAGES v FIELDER (1978) 247 Estates Gazette 557 (Court of Appeal: STEPHENSON, ROSKILL and LAWTON LJJ).

1667   The plaintiffs shared a flat under separate agreements purporting to be licences by which each paid rent separately to the landlord. They applied for a declaration that they held a protected tenancy under the Rent Acts. *Held*, the fact that rent was payable one month in advance, despite the owner's purported contractual right to terminate the agreement on one week's notice, was not consistent with the existence of a licence. Nor was there any provision which could be said to preclude exclusive possession of the flat by the two sharing tenants. The agreements did not reflect the real arrangement and there could be a joint tenancy, despite the fact that each joint tenant would be personally liable only for his share of the total rent.

    DEMUREN v SEAL ESTATES LTD (1979) 249 Estates Gazette 440 (Court of Appeal: MEGAW, ROSKILL and BROWNE LJJ). *Somma v Hazlehurst* [1978] 2 All ER 1011, CA, 1978 Halsbury's Abridgment para. 1726 and *Aldrington Garages v Fielder* (1978) 247 Estates Gazette 557, CA, para. 1666 distinguished.

1668   Upon an application by the plaintiff for a possession order, the defendant contended that he was a tenant and that the agreement he had entered into with the plaintiff gave rise to a tenancy and not a licence. The application was refused. On appeal, *held*, on its true construction, the written agreement between the parties against the background of the evidence created a tenancy and not a licence. It was found as fact that a previous oral agreement had been firmly concluded in the terms of a tenancy and not in the terms of a licence. The written agreement was not a genuine attempt to record the verbally agreed terms, but a sham devised to avoid the provisions of the Rent Act 1974. Accordingly, the appeal would be dismissed.

    O'MALLEY v SEYMOUR (1978) 250 Estates Gazette 1083 (Court of Appeal: STEPHENSON, LAWTON and GEOFFREY LANE LJJ). *Somma v Hazlehurst* [1978] 2 All ER 1011, CA, 1978 Halsbury's Abridgment para. 1726 and *Aldrington Garages v Fielder* (1978) 247 Estates Gazette 557, CA, para. 1666 distinguished.

1669   **Agricultural tenancies**

    See AGRICULTURE.

1670   **Business tenancy—application for new tenancy—defective request—whether defect waived—estoppel**

    A lease of business premises was due to expire on 31st October 1976. By a request dated 4th February 1976 and made under Landlord and Tenant Act 1954, s. 26, the tenants requested a new tenancy commencing on 16th February 1976. Section 26 (2) provides that the commencement date must be not more than 12 nor less than 6 months after the making of the request and must not be earlier than the date on which the current tenancy would come to an end. The landlords' receiver acknowledged receipt on 10th February 1976 and the period of two months for notifying opposition passed without any notice being given. Application to the court was duly made on 13th May 1976 and by virtue of s. 64 of the Act any defect as regards the date for commencement of the new term became academic. Subsequently the premises were sold. Negotiations continued but no agreement resulted. Proceedings were adjourned but the action was later restored. The landlords applied for determination of interim rent, the foundation for such an application being the application for a new tenancy.

    In April 1977 the landlords said that the original request for a new tenancy was defective as it did not comply with the requirements of s. 26 (2) and themselves sent a notice under s. 25 terminating the tenancy. They stated for the first time that they would oppose a new tenancy on the ground that they intended to demolish or reconstruct the premises. They applied to strike out the tenants' application on the ground of its invalidity because of the defect in the request. The county court held that the landlords had waived the defect. On appeal, *held*, the defect was capable of being waived, the requirements of s. 26 being procedural. By asking the court to grant an interim rent the landlords had waived any defect. A majority of the court also based their decision on the alternative ground of estoppel. The tenants had been led to believe that the grant of a new tenancy would not be opposed. Their position had so altered that it would be unfair to allow the validity of the request to be contested and the new tenancy opposed. In the circumstances the landlords were estopped from denying the validity of the request when they had, innocently, led the tenants to believe that a new tenancy would not be opposed.

BRISTOL CARS LTD v R K H HOTELS LTD (1979) 38 P & C R 411 (Court of Appeal: MEGAW, BRIDGE and TEMPLEMAN LJJ). *Kammins Ballrooms Co Ltd v Zenith Investments (Torquay) Ltd* [1971] AC 850, HL applied.

1671 —— —— **interim rent and new rent—factors to be taken into consideration when determining rent—state of disrepair of premises**

Upon the expiry of a lease of business premises the tenant applied for a new tenancy under the Landlord and Tenant Act 1954, Part II. The landlord objected to the terms of the new tenancy proposed by the tenant and applied for a determination by the county court of the rent it would be reasonable for the tenant to pay whilst the tenancy continued by virtue of s. 24 of the Act. The premises were in a considerable state of disrepair, and the county court judge, in determining both the interim rent under s. 24A and the rent for the new tenancy under s. 34, refused to take into account the state of disrepair. He maintained that the court had no power either under s. 24A or s. 34 to award a differential rent, i.e. a rent which would vary according to the situation with regard to the state of repair of the premises. Furthermore the landlord was subject to a full repairing covenant and the tenant's proper remedy was in damages for breach of the covenant. The tenant appealed against the rents determined. *Held*, under s. 34 the rent the court had to determine was that at which, having regard to the terms of the new tenancy, the holding might reasonably be expected to be let in the open market by a willing lessor. Such a market rent might well be affected by the state of repair of the premises. If the premises were in a poor state of repair, and under the terms of the tenancy the landlord was under an obligation to carry out repairs, taking both factors into account, the resulting rent would be a differential one, varying over the period of time it took the landlord to carry out the repairs. The same considerations applied to the determination of rent under s. 24A, where the court had to determine the rent at which the holding might reasonably be let from year to year, having regard to the terms of the existing tenancy. The appeal would therefore be allowed.

FAWKE v VISCOUNT CHELSEA [1979] 3 All ER 568 (Court of Appeal: STEPHENSON, GOFF and BRANDON LJJ).

1672 —— —— **opposition—landlord's intention to occupy holding**

The owner of a property subject to a business tenancy died and her interest vested in the two executors, who were also entitled under the will to equal shares in the residue, which included the property in question. The tenants' application for a new tenancy was opposed by the beneficiaries under the Landlord and Tenant Act 1954, s. 30 (1) (g), which provides that a new lease is not to be granted if the landlord proves that on the termination of the current tenancy he intended to occupy the holding for the purposes of a business to be carried on by him. One of the beneficiaries intended to purchase the other's interest and use the property for the purposes of a business. The 1954 Act, s. 41 (2), provides that where the landlord's interest is held on trust, references to the landlord are to be construed as including references to the beneficiaries under the trust. The beneficiary intending to use the property contended that as a beneficiary entitled to a half share in the residue he was a beneficiary under a trust and was entitled by virtue of s. 41 (2) to call himself the landlord for the purposes of s. 30 (1) (g). *Held*, the words "beneficiaries under the trust" in s. 41 (2) should be limited to persons occupying by virtue of their interests as beneficiaries. In this case, the beneficiary was not entitled to be let into occupation of the property as beneficiary, as he only had a half share of the residue. This was demonstrated by the necessity to purchase the other beneficiary's interest. Accordingly, the beneficiary could not be regarded as the landlord for the purposes of s. 30 (1) (g) and the tenants' application would be granted.

CARSHALTON BEECHES BOWLING CLUB LTD v CAMERON (1978) 249 Estates Gazette 1279 (Court of Appeal: STEPHENSON, BRIDGE and SHAW LJJ). *Frish Ltd v Barclays Bank Ltd* [1955] 2 QB 541, CA applied.

1673   A landlord served a notice opposing the grant of a new business tenancy upon the ground specified in the Landlord and Tenant Act 1954, s. 30 (1) (g), that he intended to occupy the premises for the purpose of a business carried on there by him. In fact, the premises were to be used by the company in which the defendant had a controlling interest. The plaintiff tenants contended that the notice was accordingly defective. *Held*, s. 30 (3) of the 1954 Act had been amended to provide that opposition to a new tenancy could be established not only by the landlord intending to carry on a business personally, but also through the medium of a limited company in which he had a controlling interest. The validity of a notice under s. 30 (1) (g) could be satisfied by the proving of an interest such as that in s. 30 (3). The notice was therefore valid.

     HARVEY TEXTILES LTD v HILLEL (1979) 249 Estates Gazette 1063 (Chancery Division: WHITFORD J).

1674   —— —— **option to purchase freehold in original tenancy—inclusion of term in new tenancy**

In May 1977 the landlords gave notice to terminate the lease in November 1977. In September 1977 the tenants made an application under the Landlord and Tenant Act 1954, Part II, for a new five-year tenancy. The original lease had contained an option to purchase the freehold on three months' notice prior to the termination of the term. The landlords did not oppose the grant of a new lease but objected to the option to purchase being included. The county court judge included the option in the new lease. On appeal, the landlords contended that neither s. 32(3) nor s. 35 of the 1954 Act gave the court jurisdiction to do this. Section 32(3) provided that rights enjoyed under the original lease could be included in a new tenancy and s. 35 gave the court power to determine the terms of the tenancy in default of agreement between the tenant and landlord. *Held*, the original tenancy did not include the right to exercise an option, such a right having lapsed three months before the term expired, therefore s. 32(3) was inapplicable. The object of Part II of the Act was to give security of tenure to business tenants, not to grant them a saleable asset. The court's discretion under s. 35 was not wide enough to create a new option to purchase where none had previously existed. The appeal would be allowed and the option deleted from the new lease.

     KIRKWOOD v JOHNSON (1979) 38 P & CR 392 (Court of Appeal: ORR, ORMROD and GEOFFREY LANE LJJ). *G. Orlik (Meat Products) Ltd v Hastings and Thanet Building Society* [1974] 29 P & C R 126, CA 1974 Halsbury's Abridgment para. 1922 and dictum of DENNING LJ in *Gold v Brighton Corpn* [1956] 3 All ER 442, CA, applied.

1675   —— —— **right to apply to court—previous request by tenant**

A lease of business premises expired on 15th July 1979. On 11th August 1978 the tenant made a request for a new tenancy commencing on 16th July 1979. The landlord served a counternotice stating the grounds on which he proposed to oppose any application to the court for a new tenancy. However, the tenant did not apply to the court for a new tenancy within the time prescribed by the Landlord and Tenant Act 1954, s. 29 (3). On 12th January 1979, the tenant purported to make a further request for a new tenancy commencing on 16th July 1979. The landlord contended that the second request was invalid and reiterated his grounds of opposition. The tenant then applied to the court for a new tenancy based on his request of 12th January 1979. *Held*, it was only possible for a tenant to make one request for a new tenancy, and the tenant's application was invalid as being out of time following his original request. It was irrelevant that the two requests specified the same date for the commencement of the new tenancy. The application would be dismissed.

     POLYVIOU v SEELEY [1979] 3 All ER 853 (Court of Appeal: MEGAW and BROWNE LJJ). *Stile Hall Properties Ltd v Gooch* [1979] 3 All ER 848, para. 1676 applied.

1676   A tenant of business premises under a lease expiring on 6th January 1967 served on his landlords a valid request, under the Landlord and Tenant Act 1954, s. 26, for a new tenancy, specifying 29th September 1967 as the commencement date for the new tenancy. The effect of the request was to continue the current tenancy until 28th September 1967, by virtue of s. 26 (5) of the Act. The tenant did not, however, apply to the court for a new tenancy within the time prescribed by s. 29 (3). Two days before the current tenancy would have determined, the tenant served a second request for a new tenancy, specifying a new commencement date, and purported to withdraw the first request. The landlords successfully claimed possession of the premises on the ground that the tenancy had determined on 28th September 1967 by virtue of the first request. The tenant appealed. *Held*, the effect of a request by a tenant for a new tenancy was to fix the date for the termination of the current tenancy by reference to the date on which the new tenancy was to commence. If a tenant failed to apply to the court within the prescribed period, he lost the right to a new tenancy under the 1954 Act, because it would frustrate the scheme of the Act if a tenant could serve successive requests for a new tenancy which prolonged the current tenancy. Since the tenant had failed to apply to the court within the prescribed period, the current tenancy had determined on 28th September 1967, and the landlords were accordingly entitled to possession. The appeal would be dismissed.

STILE HALL PROPERTIES LTD V GOOCH (1968) [1979] 3 All ER 848 (Court of Appeal: DANCKWERTS, DAVIES and EDMUND-DAVIES LJJ).

1677   ———— variation of terms of tenancy

On an application by the tenants for a new tenancy under the Landlord and Tenant Act 1954, Part II, the landlords wished to vary the terms of the tenancy to the effect that the tenants would be liable for comprehensive variable contributions to the cost of repairs etc. of the property. This was to replace the fixed service charge they had paid under the old tenancy. In considering such an application for variation by the landlords, the court had to take into account the terms of the current tenancy and all the relevant circumstances. *Held*, the landlord's proposals had to satisfy four tests (i) whether they had given good reasons for the variation (ii) whether the tenants would be compensated by an adjustment in rent; (iii) whether the tenants could continue their business or profession; (iv) whether the variation was fair and reasonable between the parties on the facts of this case. (i) A variable contribution to the cost of repairs made the reversion a more valuable and marketable asset to a person who did not want to suffer the effect of price fluctuation in the cost of repairs etc.; (ii) the parties had agreed a reduction in the rent which fairly compensated the tenants; (iii) the tenants were a well-established firm of solicitors who would not be adversely affected by the change in the terms; (iv) the variation was fair and reasonable in all the circumstances. The landlords' proposed variation satisfied all the tests and the new tenancy would be granted on their terms.

O'MAY V CITY OF LONDON REAL PROPERTY CO LTD (1979) 249 Estates Gazette 1065 (Chancery Division: GOULDING J).

1678   ——— interim rent—commencement date for payment of rent

In May 1975, lessors of premises served a notice to the lessees which purported to determine their tenancy as from November 1975. Negotiations then began between the parties for a new tenancy under Landlord and Tenant Act 1954, Part II. These negotiations subsequently broke down and in June 1977 the lessors made an application to determine the interim rent payable under s. 24A of the Act in respect of the premises. The amount of the rent and the date to which it was payable had been agreed upon by both parties. The question arose as to whether the date of commencement of the rent was June 1977, the date of the application or November 1975, the date of the expiry of the notice. *Held*, on the true construction of s. 24A (2) of the 1954 Act, interim rent could only take effect from the date of application for the rent. Thus, a landlord who knew of his rights could put in his notice under s. 24A in time to avoid any substantial hardship. The date of commencement of the interim rent was therefore June 1977.

VICTOR BLAKE (MENSWEAR) LTD V WESTMINSTER CITY COUNCIL (1978) 38 P &

C R 448 (Chancery Division: MICHAEL WHEELER QC sitting as a deputy High Court judge). *Stream Properties Ltd v Davies* [1972] 2 All ER 746 applied. *Secretary of State for Social Services v Rosetti Lodge Investment Co Ltd* (1975) 119 Sol Jo 339, CA, 1975 Halsbury's Abridgment para. 2750 distinguished.

1679   —— occupation for business purposes—meaning of "activity"

In 1973 the defendants took an assignment of a lease, which expired in 1978, of certain shop premises, intending to use those premises to store material from two other shops at which alterations were to be made. Delays occurred to the alterations and the defendants allowed licensees to occupy the premises. In late 1977 the building work started and the premises were used as a dumping ground for the waste materials from the two shops. In 1978, upon being served with a notice terminating the tenancy, the defendants served a counter-notice and applied for a new tenancy. The plaintiffs, who owned the reversionary interest, brought an action claiming possession and a declaration that the Landlord and Tenant Act 1954, s. 23 did not apply to the premises because they had not been occupied by the defendants for the purpose of a business carried on by them. The judge held that s. 23 did not apply and that the plaintiffs were entitled to possession. The defendants appealed. *Held*, the great bulk of the material dumped at the premises was rubbish and the premises were not used for the purpose of a business carried on by the defendants but for the purpose of affording facilities to the builders to make alterations at the other two shops. Assuming that the activities of the builders were those of the defendants, the dumping of rubbish was not an "activity" within the meaning of s. 23 (2). The word "activity" connoted some general use and not some casual operation. Though an activity was not strictly a trade, profession or employment, it had to be something analogous and was a question of fact and degree. The appeal would accordingly be dismissed.

HILLIL PROPERTY AND INVESTMENT CO LTD v NARAINE PHARMACY LTD (1979) 123 Sol Jo 437 (Court of Appeal: MEGAW, SHAW and CUMMING-BRUCE LJJ).

1680   —— —— whether right of way capable of being occupied

A local authority granted to a company a right of way over a private road for a term of seven years. The road gave access to land used for the company's waste disposal business and the use of the road by the company was restricted to certain times and was not exclusive. On the expiry of the tenancy the company applied for the grant of a new tenancy under the Landlord and Tenant Act 1954, Pt. II. *Held*, an incorporeal right such as a right of way was not capable of being occupied for business purposes within the 1954 Act. As the road was not part of the property comprised in the tenancy the question whether the road was occupied was irrelevant, but in any event the enjoyment of the right of way did not amount to occupation of the road for the purpose of the Act as it was intermittent and non-exclusive.

LAND RECLAMATION CO LTD v BASILDON DISTRICT COUNCIL [1979] 2 All ER 549 (Court of Appeal: BUCKLEY, SHAW and BRANDON LJJ). Decision of Brightman J [1978] 2 All ER 1162, 1978 Halsbury's Abridgment para. 1712 affirmed.

1681   —— option to renew lease—failure to register—estoppel

See *Taylor Fashions Ltd v Liverpool Victoria Friendly Society*, para. 1146.

1682   —— public house—action for possession—whether non-alcoholic transactions a substantial proportion of the business

The defendant was lessee and licensee of a public house the freehold of which was vested in the plaintiffs. On the expiry of the defendant's lease, the plaintiffs sought to obtain possession of the public house. The defendant unsuccessfully claimed that she was entitled to security of tenure under the Landlord and Tenant Act 1954, Part II. As protection under the Act does not extend to premises licensed for the sale of intoxicating liquor for consumption on the premises, the defendant relied on the exception provided in s. 43 (1) (d) (i) of the Act. The section provides an exception to exclusion from Part II where business includes the reception of guests to sleep on the premises or the carrying on of a restaurant, or both, and where a substantial proportion of the business consists of transactions other than the sale of intoxicating liquor. The defendant appealed, contending that non-alcoholic sales accounted for between 17 per cent and 18 per cent of her business. *Held*, it was impossible to lay down any precise figure as a test of substantiality. The question was whether, on the facts of the case, with regard to the nature of the business as a whole which was primarily that of a public house, it could be said that the transactions relating to non-alcoholic sales represented a substantial proportion of the total. Even after assuming every possible fact in favour of the defendant, it could not be said that the proportion of business attributable to transactions relating to non-alcoholic sales was a substantial one. The appeal would therefore be dismissed.

GRANT v GRESHAM (1979) 252 Estates Gazette 55 (Court of Appeal: ROSKILL and ORMROD LJJ and SIR DAVID CAIRNS).

1683   Covenant—contribution by tenants to maintenance costs— waiver by landlord—effect on original tenant and assignees

The leases of flats in a block each contained a covenant that the tenants would contribute towards excess expenses incurred by the landlord. The roof required urgent attention and the landlord orally undertook to repair it at his own expense, but later he tried to enforce the covenant in respect of expenses incurred in the repair against both an original tenant, who had received an assurance before she signed her lease, and against two assignees. *Held*, the assurance to the original tenant had constituted an oral collateral contract and to allow the landlord to enforce the covenant in these circumstances would be inequitable. The assignees could not rely on a collateral contract, but the assurances made to their assignors had constituted a waiver which subsisted over the subsequent assignments, so they had taken the leases free from any obligation to contribute towards the cost of the roof repairs.

BRIKOM INVESTMENTS LTD v CARR [1979] 2 WLR 737 (Court of Appeal: LORD DENNING MR, ROSKILL and CUMMING-BRUCE LJJ).

1684   —— covenant against carrying on offensive trade—meaning of offensive

Canada

The lease of restaurant premises provided that they should not be used for an offensive trade or business. The lessee began to provide entertainment in the form of topless waitresses and nude dancing. The lessee appealed against the finding of the trial judge that the covenant in the lease had been breached and that the lease had been properly terminated. *Held*, the word "offensive" did not have a definite legal meaning and it should be read in the context of the lease. Read in relation to other provisions contained in the lease, it was correct to conclude that "offensive" encompassed nude dancing and topless waitresses in this instance. The appeal would be dismissed.

RE KOUMOUDOUROS AND MARATHON REALTY CO LTD (1978) 89 DLR (3d) 551 (High Court of Ontario).

1685   —— covenant against underletting, assigning or parting with possession—breach—acquiescence by landlords

A lease of a flat contained a covenant that the tenant would not assign, underlet or part with possession of the flat. The tenant granted a sub-tenancy, the sub-tenant believing that the tenant was the owner of the flat and being unaware of the covenant. After three years, when the landlords became aware of the situation, they brought an action for possession. An order for possession was granted and the sub-tenant appealed. *Held*, the porters who serviced the block of flats had known of the sub-tenancy and had not challenged the sub-tenant. Their knowledge and acquiescence were deemed to be the landlords' knowledge and acquiescence. The landlords had thus waived the breach of covenant and the sub-tenancy was lawful under the Rent Act 1977, s. 137. The appeal would be allowed.

METROPOLITAN PROPERTIES CO LTD v CORDERY (1979) 251 Estates Gazette 567 (Court of Appeal: MEGAW, BRIDGE and TEMPLEMAN LJJ).

1686 ——— ——— **consent—reasons for withholding consent**

A lease, granted in 1971, of a butcher's shop with living accommodation above, contained a covenant restricting sub-letting to a letting or fully-furnished tenancy for which the landlord's consent was required, such consent not to be unreasonably withheld. The landlord refused to allow the sub-letting of the living accommodation to two respectable and responsible persons. The tenant obtained a county court order declaring that the landlord's consent had been unreasonably withheld. On appeal, *held*, the lease was granted before the Rent Act 1974 which extended protection to furnished tenancies. The effect of the tenant's request was to invite the landlord to alter the nature of the demised property from commercial property, a butcher's shop with residential accommodation above, to a property let on a multiple tenancy, the separate sub-tenancy upstairs attracting protection from the 1974 Act. Further, the only entrances to the residential accommodation were through the shop itself and this would have resulted in a general loss of control over the premises. The consent therefore had not been unreasonably withheld and the appeal would be allowed.

WEST LAYTON LTD v FORD [1979] 2 All ER 657 (Court of Appeal: MEGAW, ROSKILL and LAWTON LJJ). *Bickel v Duke of Westminster* [1976] 3 All ER 801, 1976 Halsbury's Abridgment para. 1542 applied.

1687 ——— ——— ——— **unreasonable withholding of consent**

A lease of premises contained a clause prohibiting assignment without the previous consent in writing of the landlords, such consent not to be unreasonably withheld. It contained a proviso that if the tenants wished to assign, they first had to offer to surrender the lease to the landlords. In an action by the landlords for possession, the tenants sought a declaration that the above proviso was void by virtue of the Landlord and Tenant Act 1927, s. 19 (1), which provides that in all leases containing a provision against assignment without consent, that provision is, notwithstanding any express provision to the contrary, to be deemed to be subject to a proviso that such consent is not to be unreasonably withheld. *Held*, as a result of s. 19 (1), the parties could not abrogate the court's power to decide by an objective standard whether or not a withholding of consent was reasonable. Thus if the parties purported to specify the circumstances in which the landlord could withhold his consent, such a term would be invalid. Hence it had been held that a term was invalid if it provided that a refusal of consent should not be deemed to be unreasonable if, when the landlord refused, he offered to accept a surrender of the tenancy. However, it had also been decided that a stipulation, by a proviso, that before the tenant applied for consent to assign, he should offer to surrender the lease was valid, as it avoided the inclusion of a provision deeming anything not to be unreasonable. The difference between the two formulae was semantic and the practical result the same. However, on balance, the latter formula should be regarded as valid as the weight of authority was on its side, it had been widely used in leases and there was no good policy reason for interfering further with freedom of contract in such a context. Thus the clause in question was valid and the declaration would be refused.

BOCARDO SA v S and M HOTELS LTD [1979] 3 All ER 737 (Court of Appeal: MEGAW, LAWTON and BROWNE LJJ). *Adler v Upper Grosvenor Street Investment Ltd* [1957] 1 All ER 229 applied.

1688 —— covenant to repair—application by tenants' association—jurisdiction of court to amend application

See *Hermitage Court Owners' Association v Clyftville Properties Ltd*, para. 552.

1689 —— —— inherent defects in premises—liability of tenant

The lease of a block of flats contained covenants by the tenants to repair the premises. Remedial works, including the insertion of expansion joints, were rendered necessary by the stone cladding on the concrete frame of the flats becoming loose and dangerous. The tenants refused to pay for the repairs, contending that where wants of reparation arose which were caused by some inherent defect in the premises demised, the results of the inherent defect could never fall within the ambit of a covenant to repair. The landlords brought an action to recover the cost of the repairs. *Held*, the tenants' contention was incorrect; the true test was that it was always a question of degree whether that which the tenant was being asked to do could properly be described as repair, or whether it would involve giving back to the landlord a wholly different thing from that which he demised. In this case, the expansion joints formed only a trivial part of the whole building and did not amount to such a change in the character of the building as to take them out of the ambit of the covenant to repair. Thus the landlords were entitled to recover the cost of the repairs.

RAVENSEFT PROPERTIES LTD v DAVSTONE (HOLDINGS) LTD [1979] 1 All ER 929 (Queen's Bench Division: FORBES J). Dictum of Lord Esher in *Lister v Lane and Nesham* [1891–4] All ER Rep at 390, *Lurcott v Wakely and Wheeler* [1911–13] All ER Rep 41, *Pembery v Lamdin* [1940] 2 All ER 434, *Sotheby v Grundy* [1947] 2 All ER 761 and *Brew Brothers Ltd v Snax (Ross) Ltd* [1970] 1 All ER 587 applied.

1690 Disturbance—obstruction of tenant's access and parking—liability of landlord

Landlords owned a terrace of shops at the back of which was a private cul-de-sac providing rear access and parking for the tenants. The tenant of one shop was continually prevented from parking or obtaining access to the back of his premises and brought an action for damages and an injunction against the landlords for breach of their covenant of quiet enjoyment, for derogation from grant or, alternatively, in nuisance. The county court awarded maximum damages and granted an injunction restraining the landlords from causing, permitting or suffering any obstruction of access or parking. On the landlord's appeal, *held*, applying the principles laid down in *Sedleigh-Denfield v O'Callaghan* it was clear that the landlords had no answer to the tenant's claims, upon whichever basis they were made. They had been aware of the problem and had had the power to solve it but had failed to do so. The appeal would therefore be dismissed. The injunction would, however, be limited to restraining obstruction of the tenant's access; the parking problem was one that the tenant was quite capable, as occupier of the land, of solving by actions in trespass if not by other more practical means.

HILTON v JAMES SMITH AND SONS (NORWOOD) LTD (1979) 251 Estates Gazette 1063 (Court of Appeal: LORD SCARMAN, ORMROD and EVELEIGH LJJ). *Sedleigh-Denfield v O'Callaghan* [1940] AC 880, HL applied.

1691 Forfeiture—breach of covenant not to assign—service of notice on assignor or assignee

A landlord granted a lease of business premises, the lessee covenanting not to assign the lease without the consent of the landlord. The lessee assigned the lease in breach of the covenant and the landlord served a notice of forfeiture on the lessee under the Law of Property Act 1925, s. 146 (1). The question arose as to whether the notice should have been served on the lessee or the assignee. *Held*, the assignment, though a breach of covenant, was an effective assignment and any notice under s. 146 should be served on or addressed to the assignee, who was the person concerned to avoid forfeiture.

OLD GROVEBURY MANOR FARM LTD v W. SEYMOUR PLANT SALES AND HIRE LTD (No. 2) [1979] 3 All ER 504 (Court of Appeal: LORD RUSSELL OF KILLOWEN and BROWNE LJ).

1692 **—— relief—breach of covenant against subletting—relief for sub-tenant**

Premises consisting of a shop and flat above were let for 21 years in 1959. The lease contained a covenant against assignment or subletting, subject to a proviso permitting letting of the flat on the basis of a furnished tenancy only. Furnished tenancies were unprotected until 1974. In breach of the covenant the flat was let unfurnished in 1976. The lessee died and the rent was no longer paid. The subtenant claimed relief against forfeiture under Law of Property Act 1925, s. 146 (4). This was refused. On appeal, the subtenant contended that the landlord could not have complained if the tenancy had been furnished and that as since 1974 both furnished and unfurnished tenancies were protected, the landlord was no worse off. *Held*, the granting of relief would result in the landlords being unable to deal with the premises properly as one whole. The appeal would be dismissed.

CLIFFORD v PERSONAL REPRESENTATIVES OF JOHNSON (1979) 251 Estates Gazette 571 (Court of Appeal: LORD DENNING MR, LAWTON and GEOFFREY LANE LJJ).

1693 **Harassment of tenant by landlord—insufficient notice to terminate tenancy—award of exemplary damages**

See *Tefft v Kooiman*, para. 1697.

1694 **Lease—term of lease—term protecting other tenants from nuisance—extent of lessee's obligation**

Landlords brought an action for possession against one of their tenants on the grounds that she had been in breach of a term in the lease, by permitting certain acts on the premises which were a nuisance to other tenants. The tenant was receiving unwanted attention from a male admirer, and the other tenants were disturbed by his persistent attempts to get in touch with her. The landlords appealed against a finding of the county court that she was not in breach of the lease. *Held*, the tenant could only be said to have permitted the nuisance in question if the landlords could show that the tenant had failed to take reasonable steps to prevent the nuisance. On the evidence the tenant had done all she reasonably could to abate the nuisance. The appeal would be dismissed.

COMMERCIAL GENERAL ADMINISTRATION LTD v THOMSETT (1979) 250 Estates Gazette 547 (Court of Appeal: ORR, ORMROD and GEOFFREY LANE LJJ).

1695 **—— term of years running from date prior to date of execution—obligations arising upon commencement of term—liability of tenant to fulfil obligations**

The Landlord and Tenant Act 1954, Part II applied to a tenancy, which would otherwise have expired on 24th March 1974. On 11th January 1977 a consent order was made in the county court granting a new lease for a term of ten years from 25th March 1974 at a rent of £1750 per annum, with a provision for reviews of the rent during the term. The new lease, executed on 10th March 1978, stated that the property was to be let from 25th March 1974 for ten years, the tenant paying a rent for the first four and three quarters years at £1750 per annum, the rent for the remainder of the term to be determined in accordance with provisions in the lease. The tenant covenanted in the lease to pay during the term the reserved rents at the times and in the manner specified. During the period 25th March 1974 to 10th March 1978 the tenant had paid a rent of £312 per annum, and he refused to pay any additional sums for this period on the ground that his obligations to pay £1750 per annum had not arisen until the execution of the new lease. *Held*, a lease might create a term of years which was expressed to run from a date prior to its execution, yet the term created would not commence until the date of execution, in which case normally no act or omission prior to the execution date would constitute a breach of the terms of the lease. But there was nothing to prevent the parties from making contractual provisions or creating obligations under the lease which took effect from a date prior to execution. On the construction of the consent order and the new lease the rent of £1750 per annum was to be paid from 25th March 1974.

BRADSHAW v PAWLEY [1979] 3 All ER 273 (Chancery Division: MEGARRY V-C).

1696   Leasehold enfranchisement or extension

See LEASEHOLD ENFRANCHISEMENT.

1697   Notice to quit—insufficient notice—harassment of tenant by landlord—award of exemplary damages

Canada

The landlord gave the tenant insufficient written notice to terminate the monthly tenancy. Subsequently the water to the tenant's house was turned off without an adequate explanation from the landlord. As a result of the landlord's conduct, the tenant vacated the house earlier than he would have been required to do by law. The tenant was subjected to considerable harassment as a result of the landlord's conduct, not least in the many visits he had to make to the landlord's agent and to his own legal advisers. *Held*, the facts clearly established a claim for damages in tort as well as for breach of contract. Special and general damages would be awarded, together with an award of punitive or exemplary damages as an indication to the landlord that the rights of the tenant under the tenancy agreement should have been respected.

TEFFT V KOOIMAN (1978) 87 DLR (3d) 740 (Court of Queen's Bench of Manitoba).

Drane v Evangelou [1978] 2 All ER 437, CA, 1977 Halsbury's Abridgment para. 1678, was not considered by the court.

1698   —— validity—clerical error in notice

Landlords purported to issue a notice to quit to a tenant under the Landlord and Tenant Act 1954, s. 25, but the wrong date was put on the tenant's copy. The notice was sent with a covering letter which referred to the correct date. The court granted the landlords a declaration that the notice was good. On appeal, *held*, the correct test was whether the notice would be clear to a reasonable tenant. The covering letter ensured that no reasonable tenant would be misled and therefore the notice was valid.

GERMAX SECURITIES LTD V SPIEGAL (1979) 123 Sol Jo 164 (Court of Appeal: BUCKLEY, ROSKILL and GOFF LJJ). *Carradine Properties Ltd v Aslam* [1976] 1 WLR 442, 1976 Halsbury's Abridgment para. 1562 applied.

1699   Protected tenancy—rooms sub-let to students—whether tenancy a protected tenancy—contemplated use of premises

A house was let to a university college which then sub-let it to five students. Each student had his own room and gave a separate cheque for his share of the total rent. The college unsuccessfully applied for a declaration that the house was the subject of a protected tenancy under the Rent Act 1977, s. 1. Section 1 provides that a tenancy under which a dwelling-house is let as a separate dwelling is a protected tenancy for the purposes of the Act. On appeal by the college the question was therefore whether the house had been let as a separate dwelling within the meaning of s. 1. *Held*, in deciding whether premises were a separate dwelling for the purposes of the Act, the contemplated use of the premises had to be determined. On its true construction, the lease granted the college a tenancy of a building which contained a number of units of habitation; the premises were therefore not let as a separate dwelling within the meaning of s. 1.

ST CATHERINE'S COLLEGE V DORLING [1979] 3 All ER 250 (Court of Appeal: MEGAW, EVELEIGH and BRANDON LJJ).

1700   Recovery of possession—dwelling-house let on a regulated tenancy—required as residence by only one joint owner-occupier

Two joint owners of a house, which had been occupied by one of them, let it on a regulated tenancy. They subsequently brought proceedings for possession under the Rent Act 1968, Sch. 3, Part II, Case 10, on the grounds that one of them had occupied the house as her residence, had let it on a regulated tenancy and as owner-occupier required it as a residence. The application was refused on the ground that for Case 10 to apply, the house had to be required as a residence for both owners. The joint owner who had occupied the house appealed. *Held*, LORD FRASER OF TULLYBELTON dissenting, the conditions stated in Case 10 were satisfied notwithstanding that only one of the joint owners required it as a residence. She had occupied the house as her residence, had let it on a regulated tenancy, even though for the letting to be effective the other joint owner had to join in, and required it as a residence for herself. The appeal would be allowed.

TILLING V WHITEMAN [1979] 1 All ER 737 (House of Lords: LORD WILBERFORCE, LORD DIPLOCK, LORD SALMON, LORD FRASER OF TULLYBELTON and LORD SCARMAN). Decision of the Court of Appeal [1978] 3 All ER 1103, 1978 Halsbury's Abridgment para. 1733 reversed. For a discussion of the case, see Justinian, Financial Times, 19th March 1979.

The Rent Act 1968 has been consolidated by the Rent Act 1977.

1701   —— expiry of fixed term—continuing acceptance of payments of rent—whether new tenancy created

A tenant, an antique dealer, occupied certain premises under an underlease, using them for both residential and business purposes. A month before the underlease determined, the landlords informed the tenant that they would require possession on the expiry of the term. The tenant replied that he wished to exercise his rights of security of tenure in respect of the residential portion of the premises. The landlords continued to accept rent paid by the tenant whilst they tried to persuade him to leave. Having written numerous letters to the tenant, the landlords eventually applied for an order for possession of the premises. The tenant sought a declaration that he was a protected tenant. The trial judge, refusing both applications, held that a new contractual periodic tenancy had been created by the payment and acceptance of rent after the determination of the underlease. Both parties appealed. *Held*, in the circumstances, a contractual tenancy had not been impliedly agreed after the expiry of the underlease; it was clear from the parties' correspondence that the tenant had remained in occupation because he had declined to leave, not because the landlords had agreed that he could stay. Accordingly, the tenant's appeal would be dismissed and an order for possession would be made in favour of the landlords.

LONGRIGG, BURROUGH & TROUNSON V SMITH (1979) 251 Estates Gazette 847 (Court of Appeal: LORD SCARMAN, ORMROD and TEMPLEMAN LJJ).

1702   —— premises let to company being wound up—jurisdiction of Companies Court to make order

See *Re Blue Jeans Sales Ltd*, para. 354.

1703   Rent—restriction on underletting—effect on valuation

The lease of an office block contained a restriction on underletting to the effect that the tenants could not allow the premises to be used other than for the business of consulting engineers. The landlords applied for a rent review based on the full market value of the property. The tenants contended that the rent should be reduced to take account of the restriction, but the landlords argued against this on the ground that it was always open to them to waive the restriction. The arbitrator and the court made an assessment in favour of the tenants. On appeal by the landlords *held*, it had not been possible for the arbitrator to assess the rent on the basis that the landlord would relax or waive the restrictions wholly gratuitously. It was impossible to assess the sum the landord would require as consideration for such a relaxation or waiver and the arbitrator was accordingly entitled to find that the restriction had such a depressing effect that the rent ought to be reduced. The tenant's claim would therefore be upheld

PLINTH PROPERTY INVESTMENTS LTD V MOTT, HAY AND ANDERSON (1979) 38 P & C R 361 (Court of Appeal: LORD DENNING MR, SHAW AND BRANDON LJJ).

1704   —— recovery—breach of agreement by landlord—tenant's equitable right of set-off

The plaintiffs developed reclaimed land by building and leasing warehouses. They agreed to construct two warehouses and lease them to the defendants. The lease contained no covenant to repair but the agreement provided for the remedying of defects. When defects appeared and caused the warehouses to be evacuated the defendants refused to pay any further rent. The plaintiffs claimed possession, unpaid rent and mesne profits. The court had to decide whether the defendants were entitled to deduct or set off against their admitted liability the damages claimed for breach of the agreement. *Held*, the principle of equitable set-off applied where the sum sought to be set-off was an unliquidated sum such as that of an unspecified amount of damages; further it was available against a claim for rent if the tenant's cross-claim arose from the lease itself or the relationship of landlord and tenant. Whilst the agreement and the lease were separate entities there was a close connection between them and it would be manifestly unjust to allow the plaintiffs to recover their rent without taking into account the damages which the defendants had suffered through the plaintiffs' failure to perform their part of the agreement. The defendants were therefore entitled to defend the plaintiffs' action by raising as set-off damages for the plaintiffs' breach of the agreement.

BRITISH ANZANI (FELIXSTOWE) LTD v INTERNATIONAL MARINE MANAGEMENT (U.K.) LTD [1979] 2 All ER 1063 (Queen's Bench Division: FORBES J). *Banks v Jarvis* [1903] 1 KB 549, DC, *Waters v Weigall* (1795) 2 Anst 575, *Beasley v D'Arcy* (1800) 2 Sch & Lef 402 and dicta of Morris LJ in *Hanak v Green* [1958] 2 All ER at 150 applied. *Hart v Rogers* [1916] 1 KB 646 doubted.

1705   —— review clause—construction of clause

The developers of a newly constructed commercial block of property ran out of resources before the building was finally completed. The tenants of the third floor carried out all the building works required to make the floor fit for use, in recognition of which they paid only a peppercorn rent for the first six months of their tenancy. The lease provided for a rent review after seven years, clause 6 providing that the value attributable to the tenants' initial improvements was to be disregarded in re-assessing the rent. The landlord and the tenants adopted wholly different valuation methods in regard to the above clause and the court was asked by the arbitrator to decide the bases upon which the valuation should be made. *Held*, having regard to all the facts and taking into account that any valuation had to reflect properly the intention of the parties, in view of the possibility of inflation, the rent had to be reviewed at the 7th and 14th years in order to do justice between the landlord and the tenants. In view of the tenants' expenditure, they were to be credited with the rental equivalent of their initial expenditure (which itself might be subject to inflation). The improvements themselves would enure for the benefit of the landlord and should, therefore, be regarded as far as the tenants were concerned, as a wasting asset. The valuers were to bear in mind that with the passage of time the improvements would no longer be new.

GREA REAL PROPERTY INVESTMENTS LTD v ROY GRAINGER WILLIAMS (RECEIVER ON BEHALF OF CREDIT LYONNAIS) (1979) 250 Estates Gazette 651 (Queen's Bench Division: FORBES J).

1706   Tenants occupied four properties, the ground floors of which were shops, under a lease for a term of fifty-three years. The tenants covenanted not to use the upper floors of the premises otherwise than as offices, but improvements were required in order to permit their use as such. The lease prescribed a rent which was initially to be reviewed after five years, and then at successive periods of five years. At the first review, the parties could not agree on the rent and an arbitrator was appointed under the terms of the rent review clause. The arbitrator valued the ground and upper floors separately, arriving at the rental value of the upper floors by deducting the calculated average annual cost of improvements from the rental value that the upper floors would have had, had improvements been carried out. The landlord was dissatisfied with his award and applied to have it set aside, arguing that the arbitrator had misconstrued the terms of the lease. *Held*, the intention of the parties had to be observed in relation to the parties' realisation that in an inflationary period the rent at the beginning of the lease would not represent a fair rent at the end. The parties would also have realised that the tenants were paying for improvements which would eventually inure to the benefit of the landlord and would have intended that the landlord should not, therefore, have the benefit of those improvements in terms of rent. The arbitrator's method of calculating the rental value of the upper floors was probably not in accordance with the parties' intention; the cost of the improvements, calculated to take account of inflation, was not necessarily the same as the value of the improvements in an inflationary period in terms of rent; further, the cost of the improvements would not be incurred by the tenants at each successive review date. There was an error on the face of the award and accordingly it would be remitted to the arbitrator for reconsideration.

ESTATES PROJECTS LTD v GREENWICH LONDON BOROUGH (1979) 251 Estates Gazette 851 (Queen's Bench Division: FORBES J). *GREA Real Property Investments Ltd v Roy Grainger Williams (Receiver on Behalf of Credit Lyonnais)* (1979) 250 Estates Gazette 651, para. 1705 applied.

1707 Repair—notice to tenants of obligation to repair—validity of notice—whether defects in notice capable of waiver

Landlords were the owners of a block of flats which was the subject of a dangerous structure notice. They served notice on the tenants requiring them to carry out the repairs to the premises, which stated that if the tenants wished to claim the benefit of the Leasehold Property (Repairs) Act 1938, they should serve a counternotice on the landlords within twenty-eight days. The tenants' solicitors sent a letter which purported to claim the benefit of the Act, but the tenants later claimed that the landlords' notice had been invalid because it did not comply with the requirements of s. 1 of the Act. The landlords alleged that the tenants' solicitors' letter had waived the invalidity. *Held*, while it was not necessary that the wording of s. 1 be followed precisely, the landlord was not entitled to issue a notice which did not give the tenant a clear idea of what protection was afforded by the Act. The notice in this case was not sufficient to comply with that requirement and was accordingly invalid. Although the invalidity was capable of waiver it had not been waived. The letter from the tenants' solicitors had been written on the basis that the notice was valid, but did not indicate that they would not rely on any invalidity which was subsequently alleged.

BL HOLDINGS LTD v MARCOLT INVESTMENTS LTD (1979) 249 Estates Gazette 849 (Court of Appeal: STEPHENSON and BRANDON LJJ and SIR DAVID CAIRNS).

1708 —— matrimonial home—tenancy in husband's name—wife in sole occupation—wife's defence to action for possession by landlord

See *Grange Lane South Flats Ltd v Cook*, para. 2103.

1709 Statutory tenancy—right of succession—member of tenant's family—friend treated as nephew

In 1957, the defendant, a young man, became friendly with an elderly widow and moved into the flat of which she was a tenant. The relationship was purely platonic. They regarded each other as aunt and nephew, but were not in fact related. The widow paid the rent, but all other expenses were shared. They resided together in the flat until the widow's death in 1976. During that period, the widow's contractual tenancy expired and she became a statutory tenant. After her death, the landlords sought possession. The defendant claimed that he was a member of the original tenant's family for the purposes of the Rent Act 1968, Sch. 1, para. 3, and accordingly had become the statutory tenant by succession on her death. *Held*, the word "family" in para. 3 was to be given its ordinary, natural meaning and did not have the same meaning as the word "household". Two adults who lived together in a platonic relationship could not establish a familial nexus by acting as members of each other's family even if they addressed and regarded each other as such.

CAREGA PROPERTIES SA (formerly JORAM DEVELOPMENTS LTD) v SHARRATT [1979] 2 All ER 1084 (House of Lords: LORD DIPLOCK, VISCOUNT DILHORNE, LORD ELWYN-JONES, LORD FRASER OF TULLYBELTON and LORD RUSSELL OF KILLOWEN). Decision of Court of Appeal sub nom *Joram Developments v Sharratt* [1978] 2 All ER 948, 1978 Halsbury's Abridgment para. 1753 affirmed.

Rent Act 1968, Sch. 1 now Rent Act 1977, Sch. 1, paras. 1–11.

1710   —— termination of protected tenancy—occupation by tenant's ex-wife—right to assert tenancy through ex-husband

In an appeal against an order for possession, a divorcee asserted a statutory tenancy against the landlord through her ex-husband, who had been the tenant of the matrimonial home. The husband had not occupied the premises for several years prior to their divorce and she had remained in the house and paid the rent. *Held*, a tenant who no longer occupied the premises, and who did not wish to return or reside, had abandoned possession and the protection of the Rent Acts and could not therefore extend such protection to his ex-wife who, after the divorce, was a stranger to him and not in occupation as his representative. The appeal would therefore be dismissed.

HEATH ESTATES LTD v BURCHELL (1979) 251 Estates Gazette 1173 (Court of Appeal: ORMROD, GEOFFREY LANE and EVELEIGH LJJ). *Robson v Headland* (1948) 64 TLR 596, CA, followed.

LAW REFORM

1711   Article

The Profession of the Future, Sir Henry Benson (personal view of the legal professions): 53 ALJ 497.

1712   Contract—implied terms—Law Commission recommendations

See para. 488.

1713   Criminal law—territorial jurisdiction—Law Commission's report

See para. 639.

1714   Hire purchase—contract of hire—implied terms—Law Commission recommendations

See para. 1425.

1715   Marital breakdown—suggested reforms

See para. 955.

1716   Method of taxation of costs—court attendance—calculation of fees

See para. 668.

1717   Parliamentary reports—qualified privilege—extension of rule

See para. 1751.

1718   Personal injuries actions—procedure

The Report of the Personal Injuries Litigation Procedure Working Party (Cmnd. 7476) under the chairmanship of Cantley J has been presented to Parliament. Amongst the recommendations of the working party is a recommendation to implement the suggestion made in para. 352 of the Report of the Committee on Personal Injuries Litigation (1968, Cmnd. 3691) (under the chairmanship of Winn LJ) that the summons for directions be abandoned and replaced by automatic directions without summons and without order. A draft rule for automatic directions is set out as App. H to Cmnd. 7476. The working party also recommends that if, within 18 months after the issue of the writ in a personal injuries case, the action has not been set down for trial, the plaintiff's solicitor should be required to report to the court the stage which the proceedings have reached; thereafter the court may issue a court summons for directions in the action. The working party further recommends a change in relation to striking out for want of prosecution; the court should not normally grant such an order unless the defendant has previously obtained an "unless" order from the court and the plaintiff has failed to comply with it; the working party has proposed a draft rule to this effect (see App. J to Cmnd. 7476). The working party's other recommendations include a panel of twelve suitably experienced deputy High Court judges to be available, an extension of the powers of district registrars under RSC Ord. 34, r. 5(3), to include the issue of a court summons after an action has been set down but before it is listed for trial, reducing the period for service of a writ under RSC Ord. 6, r. 8, to six months, encouraging judges to examine pleadings to see whether undue expense has been incurred by defective pleadings, increasing the time for service of the defence to 28 days, permitting interim payments (even where contributory negligence is alleged) where the plaintiff is likely to recover substantial damages, further consideration being given to the advantages of a split trial where the uncertainty of medical evidence would cause delay in the trial of the issue of liability, and permitting a defendant to make a formal offer on liability after a separate trial of that issue has been ordered.

1719   Restrictive practices—stock exchange—proposed legislation

See para. 2723.

1720   Royal Commission on Legal Services—recommendations

The Royal Commission on Legal Services was appointed in July 1976 to inquire into the law and practice relating to the provision of legal services in England, Wales and Northern Ireland, to consider what changes were desirable in the public interest, in the structure, organisation, training, regulation of and entry to the legal profession, including the arrangements for determining remuneration, and in the rules which prevent laymen from undertaking conveyancing and other legal business on behalf of others. The Commission, which made its report in October 1979, read 3,000 submissions of written evidence, and heard 153 witnesses.

Legal Services
The Commission found that the legal profession generally had an unsatisfactory image. Although many criticisms were unfairly directed at practising lawyers (Chapter 3, para. 29 (3.29)) the Commission recommended that all possible steps be taken to remove the causes of this indifferent image (3.3).

The Commission recorded that the demand for legal services was growing (3.1) and that there was an especial need for lawyers skilled in social welfare law (3.38). It was also suggested that a scheme for interest-free loans, to encourage private practitioners to areas of need, be introduced (12.16, 26, 29).

With regard to the provision of legal services the Commission felt that a competent, accessible, independent national network of basic generalistic advice was needed (7.1–3). It was agreed that the Citizens Advice Bureaux (CABx) should continue to provide such advice with the aid of local law societies, which should ensure that every CAB is properly serviced by solicitors to whom CABx could refer their clients (7.9, 10), and that a rota system of barristers and solicitors should be established where necessary (7.16). The Commission considered that CABx should continue to be financed out of public funds (7.20).

After commissioning surveys into the work undertaken by law centres and legal aid centres (Section 3) the Commission found that there was now a need to consolidate the centres under proper administrative and financial control. The establishment of Citizen Law Centres (CLCs) to provide legal advice, assistance and representation to those in its locality with special emphasis on social welfare law, was therefore suggested (8.17–21). A small government-controlled agency should manage the CLCs which would all be financed out of public funds (8.27). The Senate and the Law Society would retain responsibility for professional standards of lawyers employed in such centres (8.35, 36).

Legal aid

The Commission recommended the transfer of responsibility for legal aid in criminal cases from the Home Secretary to the Lord Chancellor (11.22), thus making the latter responsible for all forms of legal aid, although it was accepted that the separate system of aid for civil and criminal cases be retained (11.24).

The separate methods of assessing income contributions based on the "green form scheme" (legal advice and assistance) and on the civil aid scheme, the Commission felt, led to anomalies and that they ought to be assimilated (12.34). The present fee limits of disposable capital and disposable income ought to be increased (12.40, 43) and the contributions from income and capital, above the present free limit, reduced (12.48, 52). The method of calculating disposable capital was recommended to be revised (12.58), the scope of civil legal aid extended (13.70, 72) and the forms and procedure governing the administration, reviewed (13.13, 38, 68).

The Commission proposed that legal aid in criminal cases should be available to all defendants except for offences triable by magistrates (14.9) and set out the criteria for refusing legal aid in such cases (14.10). Contributions in respect of legal aid as to costs in magistrates courts should no longer be required (14.30, 31).

In a chapter entitled "Alternatives to Legal Aid" the Commission rejected the system of remunerating lawyers by contingency fees and felt that a Contingency Legal Aid Fund ought not to be established (16.6, 12).

Barristers

Many recommendations are made in Chapter 33 in relation to barristers' practising arrangements. It was agreed that the Senate should maintain an up-to-date register of vacancies in chambers (33.47) and develop strong policies to increase the amount of accommodation available to barristers (33.53), and ought, in proper cases, to waive the rules against practice from a barrister's residence (33.32). Further, it was proposed that no arbitrary upper limit ought to be placed on the number of barristers working in a set of chambers.

The earnings of young barristers were discovered to be low (36.2) and financial support for all beginners at the Bar was recommended to enable persons of all classes of society to set up practice (36.25, 26). It was agreed that barristers should ensure that an efficient system of fee-rendering and collection operated in their chambers (37.119). In order to maintain earnings at a time of inflation and economic difficulties, the Commission recommended the establishment of a Fees Advisory Committee (37.91). The Commission also recommended that a barrister maintain records of time spent on preparatory work and paper work for which a fee other than a standard fee was payable (37.87). The Commission reached the view that in lengthy matters a barrister (and a solicitor) should receive regular payments on account in respect of work done (37.124, 125).

The conclusion was reached that an employed barrister ought to be able to deal with conveyancing (20.27–31) and to instruct counsel to advise in non-contentious matters (20.35).

A report of the special committee on Partnership (Section 13) led to the conclusion that there was no reason to abolish the rule against partnerships (33.66).

It was recommended that a barrister should not be compelled to have a clerk (34.7) and that all chambers staff should have training in accountancy and administration (34.30, 31).

The Commission recorded that no change ought to be made in the present law relating to a barrister's immunity from suit (24.6). All practising barristers should, however, be required to have professional indemnity insurance cover against claims for negligence (24.12).

It was remarked that the problems identified by the Peace Commission had not yet been solved (32.28, 56.61). The Commission recommended that the organisation and functions of the circuits ought to be reviewed (32.54).

The Commission considered that the structure of the Senate be changed (32.67) and the majority of its members elected (32.70, 74) and that they retire from active administration on reaching the age of seventy (32.78 (l)). Further, that a compulsory subscription to the Senate should be paid by all barristers and an annual meeting held (32.78 (h), (k)). The Commission recorded that the Senate should continue to have vested in them the properties of the Inns (37.76), and that the collegiate functions of the Inns be preserved (32.62).

It was proposed that the Senate should include in their chambers guidelines, information on the obligation to maintain equal opportunity for women and members of ethnic minorities (35.21, 40), and that the governing bodies should have the power to reserve seats for those people if necessary (35.29, 43). It was also proposed that courses be established for women returning to practice (35.27) and that the possibility of establishing a crèche in or near the Inns explored (35.26).

Solicitors
The Commission expressed concern that the profession was not sufficiently responsive to lay opinion and the needs of the public (29.18). It also reached the view that the Law Society was entitled to a greater measure of support than was provided by local societies and solicitors (29.23), and suggested that a district organisation be formed, by re-grouping or re-organising local societies, which would be responsible for implementing the policies of the Law Society throughout the country (29.43–47).

With regard to private practice, the Commission found that the present system of holding the client's money was sound and well administered (23.7, 22) and in the event of misuse, the compensation arrangements were satisfactory (23.5). However the Commission suggested that the Solicitor's Practice Rules should be amended (25.8) and that the powers of the Professional Purpose Committee and the Solicitors Disciplinary Tribunal be extended (25.46, 50).

The Law Society's pamphlet on the complaints procedure was recommended to be regularly updated and the Commission placed upon the Law Society a responsibility to analyse and publish details of complaints received (25.24, 29, 35), and to ensure that independent legal advice was available for those who alleged negligence.

The Commission found that the remuneration of salaried solicitors was low in comparison with earnings in other forms of salaried employment (36.63). It was agreed that partnership between solicitors and members of other professions ought not to be permitted (30.15), similarly the incorporation of a solicitor's business with limited liability (30.18).

It was considered that employed solicitors should be able to deal with conveyances on behalf of, and give free legal advice to, fellow employees (20.16). All solicitors should be required to take out indemnity insurance (20.17, 27).

The Commission proposed that the Law Society issue guidance to solicitors on their obligation to maintain equal opportunities for women (35.21) and should set up bodies to monitor all matters relating to equality of opportunity for women (35.22) and ethnic minorities (35.60).

Legal Education and training
The Commission agreed that the legal profession should continue to be organised into two branches (17.45, 45). It recommended that a law degree should be the normal, but not exclusive, mode of entry into the profession (39.11).

The Commission recognised the need for all lawyers to be given a grounding in EEC law, and acknowledged the profession's contribution to the development of Community law (28.8, 10). It was also proposed that social welfare law and company law should be taught at either the academic, vocation stage or both (39.48). With regard to students at the Bar, the collegiate life in the Inns was recommended to be retained (39.54), although it was felt that the dining arrangements ought to be reviewed (39.55). A record of training in prescribed form during pupillage was suggested (39.64). At the end of the first 6 months this, together with a pupil master report, should be lodged with the appropriate authority, call to the Bar being deferred until satisfactory completion of the initial period of pupillage (39.69).

The Commission approved the recommendations of the Law Society's Working Party on Articles (Annex 39.1) and recommended their implementation. It further proposed that the Law Society ought to ensure that all solicitors who accepted articled clerks were able to give them adequate training (39.77). The Commission recorded that adequate minimum salaries for articled clerks ought to be fixed (39.101).

Grants, the Commission felt, should be mandatory for the vocation stage (39.98) and should extend to the first 6 months of pupillage in the case of barristers (39.108). It was agreed that law ought also to be taught in schools (4.26).

The Layman
The Commission felt that laymen, other than litigants in person, should not have rights of audience in the superior courts (18.12), but that guidelines should be laid down for the exercise of judicial discretion in county courts to allow laymen rights of audience in certain cases (18.20). It was felt however that the layman's right of audience in tribunals ought not to be further restricted (18.21).

The Commission recognised the need for information to be made available to the public, but also noted the need to restrict advertising and touting by the profession in order to protect the public and maintain high standards of integrity and performance by the profession (Chapter 27).

The Commission noted that the Law Society was willing to allow laymen onto its committees and the Commission recommended that they sit on committees concerned with remuneration, education, public relations, discipline (29.40, 41) and the assessment of fees (37.14). The Senate's committees too should include co-opted laymen (32.77).

The Commission upheld the present constriction on conveyancing by non-lawyers (21.32) but agreed that a person buying or selling a house should continue to be entitled to act for himself (21.28).

See also 129 NLJ 1116.

1721 Social security—benefits—proposed reform

See para. 2601.

1722 Work permits—proposed restrictions on issue

See para. 1495.

LEASEHOLD ENFRANCHISEMENT OR EXTENSION

Halsbury's Laws of England (3rd edn.), Vol. 23, Supp. paras. 1747–1845

1723 Article

Leasehold Reform Act 1979, Trevor M. Aldridge (a look at the object of the Act): 123 Sol Jo 311.

1724 Acquisition of freehold—rateable value—whether consecutive tenancies to be treated as single tenancy

The applicant's mother was granted a long tenancy at a low rent in 1961. In 1964, the mother died and the lease vested in the applicant. In 1973, the applicant surrendered the 1961 lease and a new long tenancy was simultaneously granted to her at the same rent. In 1975, she applied under the Leasehold Reform Act 1967 for an order that she was entitled to acquire the freehold of the house. In 1973, the rateable value of the house was £1,272. Under the 1967 Act, s. 1 (6), a tenant is entitled to acquire the freehold of a house where the rateable value is not more than £1,500, provided that the tenancy was created on or before 18th February 1966 (subject to certain other conditions that the applicant's tenancy fulfilled). For tenancies created after that date, the highest qualifying rateable value is set at £1,000, which would have excluded the applicant's tenancy. The applicant contended that the effect of s. 3 (3) of the Act was that the tenancies of 1961 and 1973 were to be treated as a single tenancy created in 1961, and that s. 1 (6) could therefore be applied. Section 3 (3) provides that, in the case of a tenant holding consecutive long tenancies of the same property, the Act is to apply as if a single tenancy had been granted for a term beginning at the same time as the term under the earlier tenancy. The freeholders successfully argued that the words "as if" in s. 3 (3) imposed only an assumption as to the continuance of the term, in contrast to assumptions as to its date of commencement in s. 3 (2), in which the word "deemed" was used; the word used in s. 1 (6) (c) was "created", as opposed to "granted" in s. 3 (3), and s. 3 (3) did not therefore apply so as to affect the date of the creation of the tenancy under s. 1 (6) (c). The applicant appealed. *Held*, in its clear and unambiguous meaning, s. 3 (3) provided that the tenancies of 1961 and 1973 were to be treated as a single tenancy for the purposes of Part I of the Act. Where a tenancy had been validly granted, a tenancy had necessarily to have been created; the effect of s. 3 (3) in relation to s. 1 (6) (c) was that the tenancy was to be treated as having been created in 1961; the conditions of s. 1 (6) were therefore satisfied and the appeal would be allowed.

BATES v PIERREPOINT (1978) 37 P & CR 420 (Court of Appeal: MEGAW and CUMMING-BRUCE LJJ and SIR BASIL NIELD).

1725   Leasehold Reform Act 1979

The Leasehold Reform Act 1979 gives a tenant in possession claiming to acquire the freehold under the Leasehold Reform Act 1967 further protection against artificial inflation of the price he has to pay. The Act received the royal assent on 4th April 1979 and came into force on that date.

Section 1 (1) provides that as against a tenant in possession claiming under the 1967 Act, s. 8, the price payable on a conveyance for giving effect to that section cannot be made less favourable by reference to a transaction since 15th February 1979 involving the creation or transfer of an interest superior to, whether or not preceding, his own, or an alteration since that date of the terms on which such an interest is held. This applies to any claim made on or after 4th April 1979 and additionally to any claim made before that date if the price had not by then been determined by agreement or otherwise: s. 1 (3). Section 2 deals with citation and extent.

This Act abrogates the decision of the House of Lords in *Jones v Wentworth Securities Ltd* [1979] 1 All ER 286, 1978 Halsbury's Abridgment para. 1764.

LEGAL AID AND ADVICE

Halsbury's Laws of England (4th edn.), Vol. 11, paras. 751–779; (3rd edn.), Vol. 30, paras. 901–1036

1726   Articles

British and American Legal Aid: A Comparison, David Tiplady: 129 NLJ 724.
Legal Aid Acts 1974 and 1979, R. L. Waters (the amendments made by the 1979 Act to the 1974 Act): 123 Sol Jo 327.

The New Magistrates' Court Legal Aid Scheme: A Criticism and Counter Proposal, Edward Irving, Brian Langstaff, Clive Million and Richard Tyson: [1979] Guardian Gazette 651.

Setting Up a Legal Aid Practice, Peter Soar (a series of articles concerning the setting up and running of a practice): 129 NLJ 911.

1727   Criminal proceedings—assessment of resources

The Legal Aid in Criminal Proceedings (Assessment of Resources) (Amendment) Regulations 1979, S.I. 1979 No. 61 (in force on 1st March 1979), amend the Legal Aid in Criminal Proceedings (Assessment of Resources) Regulations 1978, 1978 Halsbury's Abridgment para. 1774. They increase the figures contained in the 1978 Regulations for determining whether a person should be granted legal aid, and whether a person to whom legal aid is ordered should be required to make a contribution in respect of his legal aid costs.

1728   —— fees and expenses

The Legal Aid in Criminal Proceedings (Fees and Expenses) (Amendment) Regulations 1979, S.I. 1979 No. 360 (in force on 1st May 1979), amend the Legal Aid in Criminal Proceedings (Fees and Expenses) Regulations 1968, S.I. 1968 No. 1230. They facilitate the operation of the Law Society as taxing authority in the magistrates' courts where counsel is instructed although the legal aid order does not provide for the services of counsel. They also give the taxing authority a discretion as to the award of fees to a solicitor or counsel assigned in respect of persons whose cases are to be heard jointly, and empower the Secretary of State to intervene in a review by a taxing master and, if necessary, to appeal to the High Court from any decision of the taxing master in that review.

1729   —— magistrates' courts—counsel not assigned by the court

The agreement between the Law Society and the Bar Council concluded in 1963 relating to the payment of counsel's fees where counsel had been instructed in criminal cases in magistrates' courts but not assigned by the court ceased to have effect on 1st May 1979 when it was superseded by the Legal Aid in Magistrates' Courts (Criminal Proceedings) (Amendment) Scheme 1979. Under the scheme, where counsel is instructed but not assigned he should, at the end of the case, complete a case memorandum and fee note form and return it with the brief to the instructing solicitor. Where more than one counsel has appeared, the memorandum and form should be submitted on behalf of all counsel by the clerk to the counsel whose name appears first on the brief. The solicitor should send the legal aid order, his report on the case (in revised form, LA/REP/3B, containing instructions and a summary of the procedure to be followed), counsel's brief, the case memorandum and the fee note form to the area committee. The committee first assesses the fee which would have been payable had the solicitor done all the work himself ("the maximum fee") and then assesses fair remuneration for the work actually and reasonably done by counsel and the solicitor; such amounts (not exceeding the maximum fee) will be paid direct to counsel and the solicitor (apportioning the maximum fee, if need be). If more than one counsel has appeared, the fee is paid direct to counsel whose name appears on the brief, the case memorandum and fee note. Counsel and solicitors have the right of appeal to the council of the Law Society under the scheme. (Where counsel has been assigned by the court, no change in procedure has been made.) See the Law Guardian, 25th April 1979, p. 110.

1730   —— order made by Crown Court—whether order of retrospective effect

An order for legal aid made by the Crown Court does not cover expenses incurred in respect of work done by solicitors prior to the date of the order.

Following his committal for trial the accused applied to the Crown Court for legal aid and was told that an order would be made only upon payment of a £50 deposit on account of any subsequent contribution order which might be made. The deposit was paid a month later and an order was made assigning the appellants as the accused's solicitors. At the end of the trial the solicitors submitted their bill of costs for taxation including a claim for work undertaken and disbursements incurred between the date of committal and the date of the issue of the legal aid order. The claim was rejected by the taxing authority and the solicitors appealed. *Held*, on a true construction of the relevant provisions of the Legal Aid Act 1974, Pt. II, namely, ss. 28 (12), 30 (1) and 37 (1), (2), payment under a legal aid order could be made only in respect of the costs of representation by a solicitor assigned by the court, and accordingly no payment could be made in respect of work undertaken by a solicitor prior to the making of the order. The appeal would be dismissed, but leave would be granted to appeal to the High Court.

R v ROGERS [1979] 1 All ER 693 (Sup. Ct. Taxing Office: MASTER MATTHEWS). *R v Tullett* [1976] 2 All ER 1032, 1976 Halsbury's Abridgment para. 1602 not followed.

1731   —— recommendations of Royal Commission on Legal Services

See para. 1720.

1732   Legal advice and assistance—financial conditions

The Legal Advice and Assistance (Financial Conditions) Regulations 1979, S.I. 1979 No. 166 (in force on 6th April 1979), increase from £25 to £35 a week the disposable income above which a person receiving legal advice and assistance under the Legal Aid Act 1974, 1974 Halsbury's Abridgment para. 1985, is required to pay a contribution. They also make consequential amendments to the scale of contributions.

1733

The Legal Advice and Assistance (Financial Conditions) (No. 2) Regulations 1979, S.I. 1979 No. 350 (in force on 6th April 1979), increase the disposable income limit for the availability of legal advice and assistance under the Legal Aid Act 1974 from £52 to £75 a week and increase the disposable capital limit from £365 to £600.

1734

The Legal Advice and Assistance (Financial Conditions) (No. 3) Regulations 1979, S.I. 1979 No. 1395 (in force on 12th November 1979), increase the disposable income limit for eligibility for legal advice and assistance under the Legal Aid Act 1974 from £75 to £85 a week.

1735

The Legal Advice and Assistance (Financial Conditions) (No. 4) Regulations 1979, S.I. 1979 No. 1164 (in force on 12th November 1979) increase from £35 to £40 a week the disposable income above which a person receiving legal advice and assistance under the Legal Aid Act 1974, 1974 Halsbury's Abridgment para. 1985 is required to pay a contribution. The scale of contributions is amended accordingly.

1736   —— resources—assessment—allowance   for   spouse   and dependants

The Legal Advice and Assistance (Amendment) Regulations 1979, S.I. 1979 No. 281 (in force on 6th April 1979), further amend the Legal Advice and Assistance Regulations 1973 by increasing the allowances for a spouse, dependent child or dependent relative when assessing disposable income.

1737   Legal Aid Act 1979

The Legal Aid Act 1979 amends the Legal Aid Act, 1974 Halsbury's Abridgment para. 1985, and the corresponding Scottish provisions. The Act received the royal assent on 4th April 1979. Sections 4, 13 (1) (for the purposes of Sch. 1, para. 13 only), 13 (2) (in respect of 1974 Act, s. 9 (2) only) came into force on 20th July 1979,

S.I. 1979 No. 756. Remaining provisions come into force on days to be appointed: s. 14.

Section 1 extends the scope of advice and assistance to allow representation in circumstances to be specified in regulations. Section 2 (3), (4) of the 1974 Act are repealed. Legal aid committees have power to deny legal aid where assistance by way of representation would be more appropriate: s. 1 (3). Section 1 (4) extends 1974 Act, ss. 3, 14, relating to the power to award costs out of the legal aid fund to successful unassisted parties, to assistance by way of representation.

Sections 2–5 contain further amendments to the 1974 Act, relating respectively to the financial limits on the prospective cost of advice and assistance, contributions from recipients of advice or assistance, contributions from recipients of legal aid and the charge on property recovered for persons receiving legal aid.

Part II, ss. 6–10 make similar provision with respect to Scotland. Section 11 deals with financial provision, s. 12 with interpretation, s. 13 and Schs. 1, 2 with minor amendments and repeals and s. 14 with citation, commencement and extent.

1738   Legal aid—certificate—costs—charging order on matrimonial home

In January 1972 the wife was granted a full legal aid certificate to enable her, inter alia, to pursue a suit for divorce. The husband and wife were subsequently divorced and applications were made for ancillary relief. An order was made requiring the matrimonial home to be sold and the proceeds divided equally. The wife appealed against the order and the house was transferred to her absolutely. Costs amounted to £8,000 and a charge on the house was registered by the Law Society. The wife had difficulty maintaining the house in good repair and wished to sell it. She was informed that the Law Society had no power to register a charge on a replacement house. The value of the equity was £10,000. She sought a declaration in the Queen's Bench Division that she had not recovered or preserved any property within the Legal Aid Act 1974, s. 9 (6) by virtue of the proceedings for ancillary relief brought by her against her husband. The matter was transferred to the Family Division. *Held*, the wife's legal aid certificate extended to all matters under dispute between the parties and the proceedings were not to be compartmentalised according to different aspects of the litigation. The wife recovered the whole house as a result of proceedings and the Law Society were entitled to a charge upon it in respect of all the costs incurred on her behalf.

HANLON v THE LAW SOCIETY (1979) 123 Sol Jo 437 (Family Division: REEVE J). This decision has been affirmed by the Court of Appeal; see [1980] 1 All ER 764.

For ancillary proceedings see *Hanlon v Hanlon* [1978] 1 WLR 592, 1977 Halsbury's Abridgment para. 947.

1739   Legal aid—financial conditions

The Legal Aid (Financial Conditions) Regulations 1979, S.I. 1979 No. 351 (in force on 6th April 1979), increase the financial limits of eligibility for legal aid laid down in the Legal Aid Act 1974. The income limits are increased to make legal aid available to those with disposable incomes of not more than £3,600 a year (instead of £2,600) and available without payment of a contribution to those with disposable incomes of less than £1,500 a year (instead of £815). The capital limits are increased to make the upper limit of disposable capital, above which legal aid may be refused if it appears that the applicant could afford to proceed without legal aid, £2,500 (instead of £1,700) and the lower limit of disposable capital, below which no contribution in respect of capital may be required, £1,200 (instead of £365).

1740   The Legal Aid (Financial Conditions) (No. 2) Regulations 1979, S.I. 1979 No. 1394 (in force on 12th November 1979), increase the disposable income limit for eligibility for legal aid under the Legal Aid Act 1974, Part I from £3,600 to £4,075 a year. The disposable income limit for eligibility for legal aid without payment of a contribution is increased from £1,500 to £1,700 a year.

1741   —— general amendments

The Legal Aid (General) (Amendment) Regulations 1979, S.I. 1979 No. 263 (in force on 6th April 1979), further amend the Legal Aid (General) Regulations 1971 so as to empower local and area secretaries to approve applications for legal aid in all cases; to provide that a certificate shall not extend to representation by an EEC lawyer unless it expressly provides for it; and to make further provisions for the merging, discharge and revocation of emergency certificates.

1742   —— recommendations of Royal Commission on Legal Services

See para. 1720.

1743   —— resources—assessment

The Legal Aid (Assessment of Resources) (Amendment) Regulations 1979, S.I. 1979 No. 280 (in force on 6th April 1979), further amend the Legal Aid (Assessment of Resources) Regulations 1960 by removing the need to disregard £104 of income; specifying the employment expenses which may be deducted from income; increasing the deductions from income for dependants; and removing the deductions from capital for dependants and low income.

1744   Magistrates' courts—counsel's fees—Legal Aid Scheme

See para. 1728.

1745   Royal Commission on Legal Services—recommendations

See para. 1720.

LIBEL AND SLANDER

Halsbury's Laws of England (4th edn.), Vol. 28, paras. 1–300

1746   Cause of action—parties to action—whether trade union can sue in libel

See *Electrical, Electronic, Telecommunication and Plumbing Union v Times Newspapers Ltd*, para. 2836.

1747   Criminal libel—committal proceedings—evidence—admissibility

At committal proceedings in a case of criminal libel, the defendants, authors and publishers of the book in which the libel was alleged to be contained, sought to adduce evidence of the general bad reputation of the person instituting the proceedings. The evidence was excluded by the magistrate on the ground that it impinged on the merits of the case which the defence had conceded were not relevant at that stage of the proceedings and that it was not relevant to the question to be determined, namely whether there was a prima facie case for trial. The defendants applied for orders of certiorari setting aside the committal orders on the ground that the evidence had been wrongly excluded. The Divisional Court refused the application and the defendants appealed to the House of Lords. *Held*, the magistrate had to decide whether evidence of bad character was relevant to the question whether there was sufficient evidence that there had been publication of a criminal libel. The defendants had contended that there was no prima facie case unless the public interest was involved to such an extent as to require a prosecution, and that the bad character of the person alleged to be libelled meant that there was no such public interest requiring a prosecution. When a case came before examining justices, the prosecution was already instituted and it was not their task to decide whether the public interest was involved to such an extent as to require a prosecution before deciding whether or not to commit for trial. It was not right to say that a libel to be criminal must involve the public interest or must be likely to provoke a breach of the peace. A criminal libel had to be a serious libel; a libel could be serious even if the person libelled had the bad character alleged and therefore proof of bad character was irrelevant. In addition, it would be extraordinary if evidence of bad character could be given at committal proceedings when evidence of justification was prohibited by the Libel Act 1843. The appeal would be dismissed.

It was suggested that it would be an improvement in the law if no prosecution for criminal libel could be instituted without leave of the Attorney General or the Director of Public Prosecutions.

GLEAVES v DEAKIN [1979] 2 All ER 497 (House of Lords: LORD DIPLOCK, VISCOUNT DILHORNE, LORD EDMUND-DAVIES, LORD KEITH OF KINKEL and LORD SCARMAN. *R v Sir Robert Carden* (1879) 5 QBD 1 applied. Decision of the Divisional Court of the Queen's Bench Division sub nom. *R v Wells Street Stipendiary Magistrate, ex parte Deakin* [1978] 3 All ER 252, 1978 Halsbury's Abridgment para. 1784 affirmed.

1748   Defences—fair comment—when defence available

Canada

In a case where the defendant newspaper claimed that the defence of fair comment was available to a libel action brought in respect of a letter written to the newspaper and which the newspaper believed reflected the writers' honest beliefs, *held*, as the writers were not called as witnesses there was no evidence as to their honest beliefs and neither did the defendants agree with the opinions in the letter. The defence of fair comment would therefore not be put to the jury.

CHERNESKY v ARMADALE PUBLISHERS LTD AND KING [1978] 6 WWR 618 (Supreme Court of Canada).

1749   —— justification—interlocutory injunction

A well-known pop star sought an interlocutory injunction to restrain his ex-wife from publishing an article in a newspaper containing details of their former married life, claiming that details already published were libellous. The defence maintained that the matters revealed in the article were true. The plaintiff further contended that, even if the article was true, because it concerned the private details of his married life, publication should be restrained, following *Argyll v Argyll*. The injunction was refused and the plaintiff appealed. *Held*, an injunction would not be granted on the basis that the article was libellous, because a defence of justification had been raised. Neither could an injunction be granted on the basis of *Argyll*, because both parties had permitted previous articles to be published in the press concerning their married life, and the relationship had thus ceased to be their own private affair. The appeal would be dismissed.

LENNON v NEWS GROUP NEWSPAPERS LTD AND TWIST [1978] FSR 573 (Court of Appeal: LORD DENNING MR and BROWNE LJ). *Argyll v Argyll* [1967] Ch 302 distinguished.

1750   —— privilege—absolute and qualified privilege—statement by minister to reporters outside Parliament

Canada

A Minister of a Government department read a defamatory statement in Parliament, which was protected by the principle of absolute privilege accorded to all parliamentary proceedings. In response to reporters' questions outside the House of Commons, he repeated his remarks. On the question of whether privilege extended to the comments made outside the House, *held*, the Minister was not protected by the defence of absolute privilege, despite the statement being the same in substance as that made inside the House, nor was the defence of qualified privilege available to him. The latter defence was dependent upon the duty of the speaker to communicate and the listener to hear it. The Minister had no duty to speak, his remarks having been recorded in Parliament by Hansard, nor had the reporter any duty to receive the statements. The defence of privilege was not therefore available.

STOPFORTH v GOYER (1978) 20 OR (2d) 262 (High Court of Ontario).

1751 —— —— qualified privilege—parliamentary reports

The Committee of Privileges has recommended that the qualified privilege accorded by the Parliamentary Papers Act 1840, s. 3, to extracts from or abstracts of parliamentary reports and papers (published on the authority of either House of Parliament) where the defendant can show that he had published them bona fide and without malice should be extended to all fair and accurate reports of parliamentary proceedings. The purpose of the proposed change in the law is to ensure that those who, bona fide and without ulterior motive, report parliamentary proceedings (the publication of which has been authorised by Parliament) should be protected against any civil or criminal consequences which might otherwise flow from such publication. The qualified privilege under s. 3 has been extended to broadcasting by the Defamation Act 1952. The committee emphasises the obligation that this change would impose upon Members of Parliament to have regard, in any decision to make statements in the House (which if made outside might be defamatory or even criminal), to the widespread effect of such statements when reported in the press and broadcast and to the prejudice and possibly undeserved injury which might result to individuals who would have neither remedy nor right of reply. See Second Report from the Committee of Privileges (Session 1978–79), HC 222, paras. 1–10.

LIBRARIES

Halsbury's Laws of England (4th edn.), Vol. 28, paras. 301–324

1752 Article

The Significance of the Public Lending Right Act 1979, Gavin McFarlane (the background to and provisions of the Act, see para. 1754): 123 Sol Jo 395.

1753 Arts and libraries—transfer of functions

See para. 454.

1754 Public Lending Right Act 1979

The Public Lending Right Act 1979 provides for a right, to be known as public lending right, to be conferred on authors, by virtue of which payments will be made to them in respect of loans of their works from public libraries. The Act received the royal assent on 22nd March 1979 and came into force on 1st March 1980: S.I. 1980 No. 83.

Section 1 confers on authors a right, known as public lending right, to receive from time to time out of a Central Fund payments in respect of their books which are lent out to the public by local library authorities, in accordance with a scheme to be prepared by the Secretary of State: s. 1 (1). The classes, descriptions and categories of books in respect of which the right subsists and the scales of payments to be made are to be determined by or in accordance with the scheme: s. 1 (2). A Registrar of Public Lending Right is to be appointed by the Secretary of State: s. 1 (3); his terms and conditions of office are set out in the Schedule. The Registrar must maintain a register of books in respect of which public lending right subsists and the persons entitled to the right, and determine any sums due by way of public lending right: s. 1 (4), (5). Provision is made for the duration, registration, transmission and renunciation of public lending right: s. 1 (6), (7).

Section 2 provides for the constitution of a Central Fund by the Secretary of State under the control and management of the Registrar. Out of the Fund there are to be paid the sums due to authors under the scheme and the expenses of administering the scheme. The Fund is to be financed out of money provided by Parliament, which is not to exceed £2 million in any year. The Secretary of State is empowered with Treasury consent to increase this limit by order, subject to affirmative resolution of the House of Commons.

Section 3 requires the Secretary of State to make, subject to the affirmative resolution of each House of Parliament, a scheme for the purposes of the Act by means of an order in a statutory instrument. The scheme must make entitlement to public lending right dependent on the number of occasions on which books are lent out from particular libraries. It may be varied from time to time by the Secretary of State.

Section 4 provides for the keeping of a register of books and authors, containing prescribed particulars. It must indicate the person for the time being entitled to public lending right in respect of any particular book. It is an offence in connection with any entry on the register to make a statement known to be false in a material particular, or to do so recklessly; the offence is punishable on summary conviction by a fine of not more than £1,000. Section 5 provides for citation, commencement and extent.

LIEN

Halsbury's Laws of England (4th edn.), Vol. 28, paras. 501–600

1755   Article

The Problem of Bona Fide Liens, A. M. Tettenborn (consent to the creation of lien): 129 NLJ 1045.

1756   General lien—lien contained in contract with third party—whether necessary to defendants' business

The defendant warehousemen had regularly done business with a container shipping line under the terms of the General Conditions of contract of the National Association of Warehousekeepers. The terms purported to give the warehouse-keeper a "lien on all goods for all money due to him" and "a general lien on all goods for any money due to him from the customer or the owners of such goods upon any account whatsoever". The plaintiff owners of goods sent them to the shipping lines who then sent them to the defendants for packing in containers. The shipping line then went into liquidation. The defendants purported to exercise their general lien over the goods. The plaintiffs paid the sum necessary for their release, but then brought an action to recover that sum on the ground that the lien was invalid. *Held*, on construction of the General Conditions the defendants had the right to refuse to deliver the goods up to the plaintiffs until they had been paid by the shipping line. However the general lien was not necessary for the defendant's business. Nor could the court imply that the plaintiff had agreed that the shipping line should sub-contract the containerisation to the defendants. The plaintiff's claim would accordingly be allowed.

CHELLARAM AND SONS (LONDON) LTD v BUTLERS WAREHOUSING AND DISTRIBUTION LTD [1978] 2 Lloyd's Rep 412 (Court of Appeal: MEGAW, ORMROD and BRIDGE LJJ). Decision of Mocatta J [1977] 2 Lloyd's Rep 192, 1977 Halsbury's Abridgment para. 1722 reversed.

1757   Possessory lien—solicitor—right to lien over client's documents for unpaid bills

See *Gamlen Chemicals Co (UK) Ltd v Roche Ltd*, para. 2696.

LIMITATION OF ACTIONS

Halsbury's Laws of England (4th edn.), Vol. 28, paras. 601–1000

1758   **Article**

The Renewal of Writs, R. B. L. Prior (relaxation in courts' attitudes towards the renewal of writs): 122 Sol Jo 835.

1759   **Limitation period—extension—action for personal injury on behalf of minor—whether minor entitled to commence fresh action within extended time limit.**

See *Tolley v Morris*, para. 2169.

1760   **Personal injury—date of commencement of limitation period— plaintiff's knowledge**

Scotland

The employers owned and managed a pottery where the employee worked for thirty years. When he left his employment he was suffering from pneumoconiosis. Fourteen years later he instituted proceedings against the employers claiming damages for personal injuries. The claim was prima facie barred by the three-year limitation period under the Scottish equivalent of the English Limitation Act 1963 (now repealed). The employee relied on a provision that the defence was not available to the employers since material facts of a decisive character were not known to him until a date not earlier than three years before the action was brought, in that he did not know that he had a good cause of action against the employers. *Held,* the aim of the legislation was to remedy the injustice that arose where a man suffering from an industrial disease might not know of its seriousness or connect it with his place of work for many years. The limitation period ran therefore from when he knew all the material facts. To grant an extension of time when a victim knew all the facts would introduce a dimension of wide and dangerous implications. The employee, on the evidence, knew all the material facts regarding his illness and its causation on the termination of his employment. His ignorance of the fact that on this basis he could have raised an action against the employers was not a material fact. The employers could therefore rely on the three-year period of limitation.

McINTYRE v ARMITAGE SHANKS LTD (1979) 130 NLJ 91 (House of Lords: LORD HAILSHAM OF ST. MARYLEBONE LC, LORD WILBERFORCE, LORD FRASER OF TULLYBELTON, LORD RUSSELL OF KILLOWEN and LORD KEITH OF KINKEL).

Different provisions are now in force in England; see Limitation Act 1975, s. 1.

1761   **—— expiry of limitation period—court's power to override time limits—circumstances to be considered**

The plaintiff was employed by the defendant company from 1961 to 1977 during which time he contracted an industrial disease. In October 1971 his solicitors issued a writ against the defendants claiming damages for personal injury. The plaintiff's solicitors informed the plaintiff that he did not have a good claim and no statement of claim was delivered. In 1972 the plaintiff instructed another firm of solicitors who wrote to the defendants' solicitors asserting the defendants' liability. They replied that if the action was proceeded with, they would apply to have it dismissed for want of prosecution. No further steps were taken although the action was not discontinued. In 1974 the plaintiff consulted a third firm of solicitors who, upon expiry of the limitation period under the Limitation Act 1939, s. 2A, as added by the Limitation Act 1975, issued another writ against the defendants asserting the same cause of action. A master granted the defendant's application for dismissal of the second action on the grounds that it was frivolous, vexatious and an abuse of the process of the court, as it was brought in respect of the same matter as the first action. On appeal the masters' order was set aside on the plaintiff's undertaking to discontinue the first action. However, no direction was given by the court under s. 2D as to whether it would be just and equitable to allow the second action to proceed outside the limitation period. The Court of Appeal upheld that decision and decided that, as there was insufficient evidence presented to decide whether an application to proceed under s. 2D would be granted, the plaintiff would be given the opportunity to adduce further evidence. On appeal by the defendant, *held*, where a plaintiff started an action within the primary limitation period prescribed by s. 2A he could only in the most exceptional circumstances invoke s. 2D in respect of a second action brought after the expiry of the primary limitation period, to enforce the same course of action. Having brought the first action within the limitation period, he could not claim that s. 2A had "prejudiced" him under s. 2D (1) (*a*). Nor did the fact that the first action was no longer in existence constitute prejudice as this had been caused by the plaintiff's or his legal adviser's own dilatoriness. The plaintiff could not therefore rely on s. 2D. However, even if he had been entitled to apply under s. 2D for an order allowing the second action to proceed, the court was entitled, on the evidence before it on the summons, to strike out the second action. The appeal would be allowed and the masters' order that the second action be struck out would be restored.

WALKLEY V PRECISION FORGINGS LTD [1979] 2 All ER 548 (House of Lords: LORD WILBERFORCE, VISCOUNT DILHORNE, LORD DIPLOCK, LORD EDMUND-DAVIES and LORD KEITH OF KINKEL). Decision of the Court of Appeal [1979] 1 All ER 102, 1978 Halsbury's Abridgment para. 1798 reversed.

LOCAL GOVERNMENT

Halsbury's Laws of England (4th edn.), Vol. 28, paras. 1001–1403

1762 Articles

Challenging the Validity of a By-law, Jonathan S. Fisher: 143 JP Jo 636.

Injunctions and Tree Preservation Orders, Colin Manchester (questions on the subject raised by *Kent County Council v Batchelor (No. 2)* [1978] 3 All ER 980, 1978 Halsbury's Abridgment para. 1811): 129 NLJ 579.

1763 Boundary commission—revision of electoral arrangements— criteria for revision—priority of electoral equality

A Local Government Boundary Commission recommended that in the interests of effective and convenient local government a borough should have sixty-six councillors and thirty-three wards. The borough council contended it should have seventy councillors and thirty-five wards. The council scheme provided as nearly as possible that each elector's vote would have the same weight throughout the borough, as required by the Local Government Act 1972, Sch. 11, para. 3 (2) (a). The council applied for a declaration that the commission's proposals were invalid as they failed to comply with the rule in Sch. 11, para. 3 (2) (a) relating to electoral equality. *Held*, para. 3 (2) made it clear that electoral equality was to take priority in fixing boundaries and in relation to local ties, but there was no corresponding provision giving it priority in fixing the number of councillors. Under s. 47 of the Act the only proposals which the commission was authorised to make were proposals for changes which appeared desirable in the interests of effective and convenient local government. It was the duty of the commission having decided on the required number of councillors for effective and convenient local government to give effect so far as was reasonably practicable to the requirements of para. 3 (2) and then as nearly as possible secure electoral equality.

LONDON BOROUGH OF ENFIELD V LOCAL GOVERNMENT BOUNDARY COMMISSION FOR ENGLAND [1979] 3 All ER 747 (House of Lords: LORD DIPLOCK, VISCOUNT DILHORNE, LORD SALMON, LORD FRASER OF TULLYBELTON and LORD SCARMAN). Decision of the Court of Appeal [1978] 2 All ER 1073, 1978 Halsbury's Abridgment para. 1801 affirmed.

1764 Elections—effect of general election—simultaneous polling

See Representation of the People Act 1979, para. 1018.

1765 Local authorities — breach of statutory duty — remedies of aggrieved person

See *Thornton v Kirklees Metropolitan Borough Council*, para. 1432.

1766 —— functions—Isles of Scilly

The Isles of Scilly (Functions) Order 1979, S.I. 1979 No. 72 (in force on 1st March 1979), makes provision, under the Local Government Act 1972, s. 265, for the exercise and performance in the Isles of Scilly of functions which are for the time being conferred or imposed on local authorities. The Order replaces the provision for the exercise and performance of functions contained in existing orders made under the Local Government Act 1933, which are consequently revoked. It also provides for the exercise and performance by the Council of the Isles of Scilly of the functions conferred or imposed on district councils by the Local Land Charges Act 1975.

1767 —— miscellaneous provisions

The Local Authorities (Miscellaneous Provision) Order 1979, S.I. 1979 No. 1123 (in force on 5th October 1979), makes further provisions under the Local Government Act 1972 relating to the amendment of certain Acts, the variation of orders for grouping parishes and committees, the transfer of property between specified authorities and various other matters.

1768 Officers—allowances

The Local Government (Allowances) (Amendment) Regulations 1979, S.I. 1970 No. 1565 (in force on 29th December 1979) further amend the Local Government (Allowances) Regulations 1974, 1974 Halsbury's Abridgment para. 2030, by increasing the maximum rate of attendance allowance payable to members of a local authority for the performance of an approved duty.

The Local Government (Allowances) (Amendment) Regulations 1978, 1978 Halsbury's Abridgment para. 1815 are revoked.

1769 —— fees for inquiries

The Fees for Inquiries (Variation) (Amendment) Order 1979, S.I. 1979 No. 569 (in force on 21st July 1979), increases to £70 the maximum daily fee payable under the Local Government Act 1972, s. 250 (4) for the services of an officer engaged in an inquiry held under that section.

1770 Rate support grants

The Rate Support Grant Regulations 1979, S.I. 1979 No. 1514 (in force on 1st April 1980), provide for carrying into effect the statutory provisions concerning the payment of rate support grants to local authorities for the year 1980–81.

1771 —— needs element

The Rate Support Grants (Adjustment of Needs Element) (Amendment) Regulations 1979, S.I. 1979 No. 337 (in force on 1st April 1979), amend the Rate Support Grants (Adjustment of Needs Element) Regulations 1976, 1976 Halsbury's Abridgment para. 1640 and, in respect of each establishment of further education (including polytechnics), increase the amounts of capital expenditure from revenue in a financial year to which those regulations apply.

1772   Travelling and subsistence allowances—rates

The Secretary of State for the Environment and the Secretary of State for Wales have specified revised rates for travelling and subsistence allowances which are the maximum rates which may be paid to members of local authorities and other bodies within the Local Government Act 1972, Pt. VIII. The rates are effective from 4th December 1979 and are set out in the Appendix to Department of the Environment Circular 30/79 (Welsh Office Circular 66/79). The rate for travel by public transport may not exceed the ordinary fare or any available cheap fare unless the authority determines that first class fares may be paid. Where more than one class of fare is available the rate shall be determined by reference to first class fares in the case of travel by ship, and by reference to second class fares in any other case unless the authority determines that first class fares shall be substituted (Appendix, Pt. I, para. 1 (1)). Special rates are payable for travel by a member's own solo motor cycle (not exceeding 500 cc) (see Appendix, Pt. I, para. 2 (1)). The rate for the use of a member's own private motor vehicle (other than such motor cycle) is 6·8p per mile (Appendix, Pt. I, para. 2 (2)) unless he can show that such travel (a) results in a substantial saving of his time, or (b) is in the interests of the authority, or (c) is otherwise reasonable, when a higher rate may be paid. The higher rate may not exceed: (i) for the use of a solo motor cycle exceeding 500 cc, a motor cycle with side-car, or a tri-car not exceeding 500 cc, 7·8p per mile; (ii) for the use of a motor car not exceeding 500 cc, 12·9p per mile; and (iii) for the use of a motor car or a tri-car (a) between 500 cc and 999 cc, 12·9p per mile, (b) between 999 cc and 1199 cc, 14·1p per mile, and (c) exceeding 1199 cc, 15·6p per mile (Appendix, Pt. I, para. 2 (2)). Additional amounts may be paid in respect of certain passengers, fees for tolls, ferries or parking and garaging (in respect of overnight absences (see Appendix, Pt. I, para. 2 (3)). Travel by taxi may be reimbursed by the rate for travel by appropriate public transport, except in cases of urgency or where no public transport is reasonably available when the actual fare and any reasonable gratuity may be reimbursed (Appendix, Pt. I, para. 3). The rate for the use of other hired vehicles may not exceed the rate applicable had the vehicle belonged to the member; the authority may, however, approve a payment not exceeding the actual cost (Appendix, Pt. I, para. 4). Provision is also made for payments in respect of travel by air (see Appendix, Pt. I, para. 5). Subsistence allowances are at the rate of (i) for between four and eight hours, £3·66, (ii) for between eight and twelve hours, £6·43, (iii) for between twelve and sixteen hours, £9·10, (iv) for more than sixteen hours, £10·88, in the case of absences not involving an absence overnight, and (v) for overnight absence, £27·06 plus (in certain circumstances) a supplementary allowance not exceeding £3·44 (Appendix, Pt. 2, para. 1 (1)).

LONDON GOVERNMENT

Halsbury's Laws of England (4th edn.), Vol. 29, paras. 1–200

1773   Housing—staff transfer

The Greater London Council Housing (Staff Transfer and Protection) Order 1979, S.I. 1979 No. 1737 (in force on 2nd January 1980), makes general provision for the transfer of certain persons employed by the Greater London Council to those authorities to whom, after 31st March 1979, land or housing accommodation is transferred by an order under the London Government Act 1963, s. 23 (3), and for the protection of those persons.

MAGISTRATES

Halsbury's Laws of England (4th edn.), Vol. 29, paras. 201–600

1774 Articles

Adults and Juveniles Appearing Before Court, John Richman: 143 JP Jo 130.

Changes in the Role of the Magistrates' Clerk, Nicholas Crampton: 129 NLJ 208.

The Court at Work (organisation of magistrates' courts and role of various officers in the court proceedings): Court (Journal of Legal Proceedings in Magistrates' Courts) Winter 1978.

Magistrates' Assessments of Compensation for Injury, Julie Vennard (reasons for the infrequency with which magistrates award compensation for injury, and attempts to overcome the problem): [1979] Crim LR 510.

Prosecution Costs in the Magistrates' Courts, Alec Samuels: 129 NLJ 133.

1775 Committal for sentence—offences triable either way—when proceedings commenced

In May 1978 a driver was arrested, charged with driving while disqualified and bailed to appear before magistrates on 2nd August. On 17th July 1978 the Criminal Law Act 1977, Sch. 12 came into force in respect of "proceedings commenced" after that date, as provided by Sch. 14, para. 1, making it possible for justices to commit for sentence to the Crown Court under the Magistrates' Courts Act 1952, s. 29 defendants found guilty of offences triable either way, such as the one in question. On 2nd August the driver pleaded guilty and was committed to the Crown Court for sentence, which decided that it lacked jurisdiction as the proceedings had commenced before the schedule came into force. An application was made for an order of mandamus directing the justices to proceed to sentence. *Held*, the proceedings had commenced when the defendant was charged, not at the date of the hearing and the application would be granted. The court pointed out, however, that such an interpretation was contrary to the view expressed in a Home Office circular on the subject.

R v BRENTWOOD JJ, EX PARTE JONES [1979] Crim LR 115 (Queen's Bench Division: LORD WIDGERY CJ, GRIFFITHS and GIBSON JJ).

1776 —— young offender—validity of committal—date of conviction

The defendant was found guilty at a juvenile court of handling stolen goods and was remanded for sentence. He was committed to the Crown Court for sentence. The defendant attained the age of fifteen after the date that he had been found guilty but before the date of his committal for sentence. The Magistrates' Courts Act 1952, s. 28 provides that a person who is not less than fifteen but under twenty-one may, on conviction by a magistrates' court of an offence punishable on summary conviction with imprisonment, be committed to the Crown Court for sentence. The question of whether the committal was defective in view of s. 28, as the defendant was only fourteen when found guilty, depended on whether the date of conviction was the date of a finding of guilt or the date of committal to the Crown Court. *Held*, the fact that both the words "conviction" and "commit" were used in s. 28 indicated that those words had different meanings. On its proper construction, s. 28 meant that the date of conviction was the date of the finding of guilt. The committal was, therefore, defective. The case would be remitted to the juvenile court.

R v T (A JUVENILE) [1979] Crim LR 588 (Crown Court at Snaresbrook: JUDGE FINESTEIN QC).

1777 Committal for trial—magistrate reading papers before proceedings—validity of proceedings

A stipendiary magistrate read some papers pertaining to committal proceedings in advance of the hearing itself. During the hearing it was submitted that the magistrate should discharge himself, but he refused to do so. Later the defendants were committed for trial. They applied for a judicial review and an order of certiorari to quash the committal, on the ground that, by reading the papers before the hearing, the magistrate was in breach of the Magistrates' Courts Act 1952, the Magistrates' Courts Rules 1968 and the rules of natural justice. *Held*, the Act of 1952 and the Rules of 1968 referred to the formal tendering of evidence in court, and since the handing of the documents to the magistrate prior to the trial did not amount to tendering evidence, there was no breach of the legislation. Furthermore, it was part of a magistrate's duty to separate in his mind admissible from inadmissible evidence; thus there was no possibility of bias resulting from his reading the documents before the hearing.

R v COLCHESTER STIPENDIARY MAGISTRATES, EX PARTE BECK [1979] 2 WLR 637 (Queen's Bench Division: LORD WIDGERY CJ, KILNER BROWN and ROBERT GOFF JJ). *Metropolitan Properties Co (FGC) Ltd v Lannon* [1969] 1 QB 577, CA applied.

1778   Domestic courts—adoption proceedings

See para. 1856.

1779   —— constitution

The Domestic Courts (Constitution) Rules 1979, S.I. 1979 No. 757 (in force on 27th July 1979), contain provisions for setting up domestic court panels for the purpose of the Domestic Proceedings and Magistrates' Courts Act 1978, s. 80 (in force on 1st November 1979). Section 80 inserts in the Magistrates' Courts Act 1952, a new s. 56A containing provisions relating to domestic courts and, in particular, requiring members of a domestic court to be drawn from a panel of justices specially appointed to deal with domestic proceedings. These rules relate to domestic court panels in areas outside the inner London borough and the City of London and provide for the composition and appointment of chairmen of these courts.

1780   The Domestic Courts (Constitution) (Inner London) Rules 1979, S.I. 1979 No. 758 (in force on 27th July 1979), contain provisions for setting up domestic court panels for the purpose of Domestic Proceedings and Magistrates' Courts Act 1978, s. 80 in the inner London borough and the City of London and for the composition and appointment of chairmen of these courts.

1781   Guardianship—access to minors by grandparents

see para. P1528a.

1782   Information—conflict between details in information and evidence—justices' power to amend information

An omnibus had defects in its rear off-side tyre, in contravention of the Motor Vehicles (Construction and Use) Regulations 1973, reg. 91(1). Informations in respect of each defect were preferred against the owners of the vehicle, describing the tyre as having been on the rear near-side of the vehicle. After hearing a constable's evidence, the justices amended each information to read "rear off-side tyre", under the powers conferred on them by the Magistrates Courts Act 1952, s. 100. The owners applied for an order prohibiting the justices from hearing the case, claiming the amended informations created a new offence and prosecuting it would be unjust and contrary to s. 104 of the 1952 Act. *Held*, the offence in question was having a defective tyre and the owners knew which tyre it was as they had brought it to court and exhibited it there. It was only the location of the tyre that had been misdescribed in the information, and as no injustice had been caused the owners' application would be refused.

R v SANDWELL JJ, EX PARTE WEST MIDLANDS PASSENGER TRANSPORT BOARD [1979] Crim LR 56 (Queen's Bench Division: LORD WIDGERY CJ, MELFORD STEVENSON and CANTLEY JJ).

1783   Jurisdiction—summary offence committed within Stannaries—election to be tried by county court

The defendant was charged with the summary offence of using an unlicensed motor vehicle on a public road within the area of Cornwall known as the Stannaries. He contended that as a privileged tinner, he was entitled to be tried by the court now exercising the Stannaries Court jurisdiction, which by the Stannaries Court (Abolition) Act 1896, s. 1 (1), was the county court. The justices held that they had no jurisdiction to hear the matter as he had elected to be tried by the county court. The prosecutor applied for a judicial review of the decision. *Held*, under the Magistrates' Court Act 1952, s. 2 (1), the justices had jurisdiction to hear all summary offences committed within their area. Thus they had power to hear and determine the case. Alternatively, even if there was any surviving criminal jurisdiction in the Stannaries Court in 1896, the 1896 Act, s. 1 (1), only transferred the court's civil jurisdiction to the county court and thus the defendant could not claim that he was entitled to be tried by the county court for a summary offence. Orders of certiorari and mandamus would be granted.

R v EAST POWDER JJ, EX PARTE LAMPSHIRE [1979] 2 All ER 329 (Queen's Bench Division: LORD WIDGERY CJ, KILNER BROWN and ROBERT GOFF JJ).

1784   Justices' clerks' assistants—qualifications

The Justices' Clerks (Qualifications of Assistants) Rules 1979, S.I. 1979 No. 570 (in force on 1st July 1979 for the purposes of r. 4 (2) and on 1st October 1980 for all other purposes) make provision for the qualifications required, subject to certain exceptions, for a person to be employed to assist a justices' clerk as a clerk in a magistrates' court.

1785   Justices of the Peace Act 1979

The Justices of the Peace Act 1979 consolidates certain enactments relating to justices of the peace (including stipendiary magistrates), justices' clerks and the administrative and financial arrangements for magistrates' courts, and to connected matters, with amendments to give effect to recommendations of the Law Commission (Cmnd. 7583). The Act received the royal assent on 6th December 1979 and comes into force on 6th March 1980.

Tables showing the derivation of the Act and the destination of enactments consolidated are set out on pages 478–488.

DESTINATION TABLE

This table shows in column (1) the enactments repealed by the Justices of the Peace Act 1979, and in column (2) the provisions of that Act corresponding to the repealed provisions.

In certain cases the enactments in column (1), though having a corresponding provision in column (2), is not, or is not wholly, repealed as it is still required, or partly required, for the purposes of other legislation.

(1)	(2)	(1)	(2)
Justices Jurisdiction Act 1742 (c. 18)	Justices of the Peace Act 1979 (c. 55)	Justices' Clerks Act 1877 (c. 43)	Justices of the Peace Act 1979 (c. 55)
s. 1	s. 65	s. 1	
2	Rep., S.L.R. Act 1867	ss. 2–4	Rep., 1949 c. 101, s. 46 (2), Sch. 7, Part III
3	Rep., 1971 c. 23, s. 56 (4), Sch. 11, Part IV		
		s. 5	Not re-enacted; see Law Com. No. 94, para. 3
Justices Protection Act 1848 (c. 44)		ss. 6, 7	Rep., 1949 c. 101, s. 46 (2), Sch. 7, Part III
ss. 1–3	ss. 44–46		
s. 4	47, 49 (1)	s. 8	Rep., 1914 c. 58, s. 44, Sch. 4
ss. 5, 6	s. 48		
s. 7	50	9	Rep., 1949 c. 101, s. 46 (2), Sch. 7, Part III
ss. 8, 9	Rep., S.L.R. Act 1894		
s. 10	s. 51		
ss. 11, 12	Rep., 1893 c. 61, s. 2, Sch.	10	Rep., S.L. (R.)A. 1978, s. 1, Sch. 1, Part I
s. 13	s. 52		
14	Rep., 1893 c. 61, s. 2, Sch.	Local Government Act 1888 (c. 41)	
15	s. 72 (3)		
ss. 16, 17	Rep., S.L.R. Act 1875	s. 42 (12)	s. 66 (2)
s. 18	Rep., S.L.R. Act 1950		
19	Rep., S.L.R. Act 1875	Metropolitan Police Courts Act 1897 (c. 26)	
Stipendiary Magistrates Act 1858 (c. 73)		ss. 1, 8	58 (3)
ss. 1–3	s. 16 (3)–(5)	Administration of Justice Miscellaneous Provisions) Act 1938 (c. 63)	
s. 4	Rep., 1964 c. 42, s. 41 (8), Sch. 5		
5	Rep., 1952 c. 55, s. 132, Sch. 6	Sch. 2†	48 (1)
6	Rep., 1964, c. 42, s. 41 (8), Sch. 5		
8	Rep., S.L.R. Act 1875	Justices of the Peace Act 1949 (c. 101)	
ss. 9–12	Rep., 1971 c. 23, s. 56 (4), Sch. 11, Part IV	s. 1 (1)–(3)	7 (1)–(3)
s. 13	Rep., 1869 c. 34, s. 1	(4)	Rep., 1968 c. 69, s. 8 (2), Sch. 5, Part II
14	Rep., 1949 c. 101, s. 46 (2), Sch. 7, Part III	(5)	s. 68 (1)
		3 (1)–(4)	s. 64 (1)–(4)

† Repealed in part

(1)	(2)	(1)	(2)
Justices of the Peace Act 1949 (c. 101)	Justices of the Peace Act 1979 (c. 55)	Justices of the Peace Act 1949 (c. 101)	Justices of the Peace Act 1979 (c. 55)
s. 3 (5)	Rep., 1975 c. 20, s. 24 (2), Sch. 2	s. 25 (5), (6)	Rep., 1968 c. 69, s. 8 (2), Sch. 5
5	ss. 7 (4), 64 (5)	26 (1), (2)	s. 56 (1), (2)
13 (1)	s. 18 (1)	(3)	(2)–(4)
(2)–(4)	17	27 (1)	61 (1)
(5), (5A)	18 (2), (3)	proviso	(2), (3)
(6)	(5)	(2)	59 (1), (2)
15 (5)†	18 (4)	(3)	(3)
16 (1)	19 (1)	(4)	———
(2)	(2), (3)	(5), (6)	59 (4), (5)
(3)	Rep., 1972 c. 70, ss. 217 (7) (a), 272 (1), Sch. 27, para. 5 (3), Sch. 30	(7)	61 (2)
		(8)	Rep., 1972 c. 70, ss. 217 (7) (a), 272 (1), Sch. 27, para. 10 (3), Sch. 30
(4)	———	(9)	s. 61 (4)
(5)	s. 69	(10) (a)	Rep., 1972 c. 71, ss. 61 (3), 64 (2), Sch. 6, Part II
(6)	Rep., 1972 c. 70, s. 272 (1), Sch. 30	(b), (c)	s. 61 (7)
17	s. 63 (1)	(d)	59 (6)
18 (1)–(3)	23 (1)–(3)	(e)	Rep., 1968 c. 69, s. 8 (2), Sch. 5, Part II
(4)	(5)	(11)	Rep., 1972 c. 71, ss. 61 (3), 64 (2), Sch. 6, Part II
(5)–(7)	24 (1)–(3)	(12)	s. 61 (5)
(8)	23 (4)	42	See Sch. 1, para. 13 (1)
(9)	24 (6)	43 (1)★	s. 59 (1)
(10)	(5)	44 (1)	ss. 4 (4), 18 (1), 70
(11)	(4)	(2)–(4)	
19 (1)	25 (1)	s. 44 (5)	Cf. s. 71 (4)
(2)–(6)	27 (1)–(5)	Sch. 4, para. 1 (1)	s. 20 (1)
(7)	(6), (7)	(2)	(3)
(8), (9)	25 (2), (3)	(2A)	(2)
(10)	Rep., 1972, c. 70, ss. 217 (7) (a), 272 (1), Sch. 27, para. 7 (2), Sch. 30	(3)	Rep., 1971 c. 23, ss. 53 (1), 56 (4), Sch. 7, para. 2 (2), Sch. 11, Part IV
(11)	s. 25 (4)	(4)–	
(12)	Rep., 1952 c. 55, s. 132, Sch. 6	(6)	s. 20 (4)–(6)
(13)	Rep., 1953 c. 46, s. 168, Sch. 10	(7)	21 (1), (3)
20 (1), (2)	s. 26 (1), (2)	(8)	(2)
(4)	(3), (4)	(9)	(4)
(5)	(5)	2	19 (3)
(7)	———	3	Rep., 1972 c. 70, ss. 217 (7) (a), 272 (1), Sch. 27, para. 14 (9), Sch. 30
21 (1)	s. 29 (1), (2)		
(2), (3)	Rep., 1952 c. 55, s. 132, Sch. 6	4	Rep., 1971 c. 23, ss. 53 (1), 56 (5), Sch. 7, para. 2 (2), Sch. 11, Part IV
(4)	See Sch. 1, para. 14		
(5)	———	5	s. 22 (3)
(6)	Rep., 1952 c. 55, s. 132, Sch. 6	6	19 (4)
(7)	Rep., 1968 c. 69, s. 8 (2), Sch. 5, Part II	7	22 (7)
(8)	———	8	(6)
23 (1)		9	(1), (2)
(2)	See Sch. 1, para. 10	10	(4)
(3)–(6)	———	11	(5)
(7)	See Sch. 1, para. 11		
(8)–(10)	Rep., 1953 c. 25, s. 23 (1), Sch. 3, para. 8		
(11)	See Sch. 1, para. 11 (3)		
(12)	———		
25 (1)–(4)	s. 55		

† Repealed in part   ★ Not repealed

(1)	(2)
Magistrates' Courts Act 1952 (c. 55)	**Justices of the Peace Act 1979 (c. 55)**
s. 116 (1)	s. 66 (1)
118 (3)	30 (1), (2)
118 (4)†	(1)
121 (1)	16 (1)
Sch. 5★	61 (1)
Metropolitan Magistrates' Courts Act 1959 (c. 45)	
s. 2 (1), (2)	34 (1), (2)
(3)	67 (4)
(4)	34 (3)
Administration of Justice Act 1964 (c. 42)	
s. 2 (1), (2)	2 (1)
(3)	ss. 2 (2), 4 (2), 19 (1)–(3), 20 (1), (3), 21 (2), 22 (2), 23 (1), (2), (4), 24 (5), 57 (1), 66 (1)
(3A)	Rep., 1968 c. 22, ss. 86 (2), 89 (2), Sch. 3
(4)	Rep., 1973 c. 15, s. 19 (1), Sch. 5, Part II
3	s. 3
9	33
10 (1)–(5)	31 (1)–(5)
(6)–(8)	32
13 (1)	ss. 19 (1)–(3), 20 (1), 21 (2), 22 (2), 23 (1), (4), 35 (1)
(2)–(5)	s. 35 (2)–(5)
(6)	38 (2)
(7)	35 (6)
14	36
15 (1), (2)	37 (1), (2)
(3)	38 (3)
(4)–(6)	37 (3)–(5)
(7)	(6), (7)
(8)	ss. 25 (5), 27 (9)
16 (1)	s. 38 (1)
(2)	63 (2)
(3)	38 (4)
17 (1), (2)	58 (1), (2)
(3), (4)	(4), (5)
(5)	See ss. 55, 56
ss. 27, 28	ss. 53, 54
s. 30 (1), (2)	s. 67 (1), (2)
(3), (4)	Rep., 1968 c. 69, s. 8 (2), Sch. 5, Part II
s. 30 (5)	s. 67 (5)
32	See Sch. 1, para. 13 (1)
36 (1)	ss. 36 (1), 37 (6), (7), 53 (4)
(2)	
37 (4)	s. 60, Sch. 2, para. 26
38 (1)★	70

(1)	(2)
Administration of Justice Act 1964 (c. 42)	**Justices of the Peace Act 1979 (c. 55)**
Sch. 3, para. 2	s. 26 (4)
12 (1)	66 (2)
20 (6)	57 (1), (2)
(7)	59 (6)
Justices of the Peace Act 1965 (c. 28)	
s. 1 (1)	26 (3) (a)
(2)	(4) (b)
2	
General Rate Act 1967 (c. 9)	
s. 2 (5)★	49 (2)
116 (1)★	49 (1)
Superannuation (Miscellaneous Provisions) Act 1967 (c. 28)	
s. 15 (8)(j),★ (9)★	58 (2)
Justices of the Peace Act 1968 (c. 69)	
s. 1 (2)	s. 39 (1)
(3)	67 (3)
3	18 (3)
5 (1)	28 (1), (2)
(2)	27 (8)
(3)	28 (3), (4)
Sch. 2, para. 1	39 (2)
2	40 (1), (4)
paras. 3, 4	40 (2), (3)
3, para. (1) (a)★	39 (4)
(b)★	ss. 41 (1), 57 (3), 59 (6)
2 (1)	s. 39 (3)
(2)	Rep., 1971 c. 23, s. 56 (4), Sch. 11, Part IV
3	ss. 4 (2), 19 (2), 20 (1), 21 (2), 22 (2), 41 (1), 57 (3), 59 (6), 66 (1)
4 (4)	19 (3), 42
8★	s. 30 (1)
15	See Sch. 1, para. 12
16	See Sch. 1, para. 13 (2)
Courts Act 1971 (c. 23)	
s. 3†	s. 5 (2)
53 (1)†	
Sch. 7, para. 1	
2 (1)	20 (1), (2)
(2)	
3	22 (3)
Sch. 8, para. 2★	ss. 61 (5), 64 (1)

† Repealed in part   ★ Not repealed

(1)	(2)
Courts Act 1971 (c. 23)	Justices of the Peace Act 1979 (c. 55)
Sch. 8, para. 43 (1)	s. 35 (5)
(3),	54 (1), (2)
(4)	
Superannuation Act 1972 (c. 11)	
Sch. 7, para. 5	59 (2)
Local Government Act 1972 (c. 70)	
s. 216 (2)†	69
217 (1), (2)	See Sch. 1, paras. 3 (1), (2), 4 (2)
(3)	ss. 4 (1), 19 (2)
(5)	s. 55 (1), (2)
Sch. 27, para. 1	68 (1)
paras. 2–4	Rep. 1973 c. 15, s. 19 (1), Sch. 5, Part II
para. 5(1)	19 (1)
(2)	(2), (3)
(3)	———
(4)	69
6 (1), (2)	23 (1), (2)
(3)	24 (1), (2)
(4)	23 (4)
(5)	24 (6)
(6)	(4)
7 (1)	25 (2), (3)
(2)	———
8	———
9	55 (1), (2)
10 (1)–	———
(3)	———
(4)	59 (6)
11	Rep., 1973 c. 15, s. 19 (1), Sch. 5, Part II
12	———
13	s. 4 (2)
14 (1)	20 (1)
(2)	(2), (3)
(3)–	
(5)	(4)–(6)
(6)	21 (1), (3)
(7)	(2)
(8)	19 (3)
(9)	———
(10)	22 (2)
15	See s. 16 (3)
17 (1)	
(2)	ss. 57 (1), 59 (6)
19 (1)	4 (2), 19 (2), 20 (1), 21 (2), 22 (2), 41 (1), 57 (3), 59 (6)
(2)	s. 19 (3)
29, para. 1 (2)*	64 (1)
Criminal Justice Act 1972 (c. 71)	
s. 61 (1)	61 (6)
(2)	59 (1)–(3)
(3)	———

(1)	(2)
Criminal Justice Act 1972 (c. 71)	Justices of the Peace Act 1979 (c. 55)
s. 62 (1)	s. 63 (5)
(2)	
(3)	———
(4)	62 (1)
	ss. 62 (2), 63 (6)
Administration of Justice Act 1973 (c. 15)	
s. 1 (1)	ss. 1, 5 (1)
(2)	6, 11 (1); and see Sch. 1, para. 4 (1)
(3)	11 (2), 43
(4) (a)	s. 11 (3)
(b)	8 (1)
(5) (a)	(5)
(b)	10 (3)
(6)	ss. ss. 6 (2), 39 (1) proviso, 43
(7), (8)	68, 69
2 (1)	s. 13 (1), (2)
(2)	(3)
s. 2 (3)	s. 16 (2)
(5)	14 (1) proviso
(6)	ss. 13 (4), (5), 31 (1), (7)
(7)	s. 15
3	63 (3), (4)
20 (3), (4), (5).†	See Sch. 1, paras. 2 (1).
(6)†	(2), 3 (1), (3), 4 (1), 5 (1), 7–9
Sch. 1, para. 1	ss. 14, 31 (6)
3★	31 (6)
4 (1)	8 (2), (3); and see Sch. 1, para. 5 (2)
(2)–	
(4)	(4)–(6)
(5)	68 (2)
(6)	8 (7)
Sch. 6, paras. 5, 6	ss. 9, 10
para. 8 (1)–	
(3)	s. 12 (1)–(3)
(3A)	(4)
(4)–	
(6)	(5)–(7)
9 (1)	ss. 7 (1)–(3), 71 (3); and see Sch. 1, para. 6
12	s. 59 (1) (b)
Social Security Act 1973 (c. 38)	
Sch. 27, para. 98★	12 (1)
Powers of Criminal Courts Act 1973 (c. 62)	
Sch. 5, para. 14★	Sch. 2, para. 26

† Repealed in part   ★ Not repealed

(1)	(1)	(1)	(2)
Social Security Pensions Act 1975 (c. 60)	Justices of the Peace Act 1979 (c. 55)	Domestic Procceedings and Magistrates' Courts Act 1978 (c. 22)	Justices of the Peace Act 1979 (c. 55)
Sch. 4, para. 5	s. 58 (2) (b)	s. 86 (1)	ss. 2 (2), 4 (2), 19 (1)– (3), 20 (1), 21 (2), 22 (2), 23 (1), (2), (4), 57 (1)
Administration of Justice Act 1977 (c. 38)			
s. 21 (1)	17 (2)		
(2)	18 (2) (c)		
Sch. 2, para. 5 (a)	12 (4)	(2)	s. 17 (3)
(b)	(6) (a)	Sch. 2, para. 10★	

★ Not repealed

TABLE OF DERIVATIONS

This table shows in the right hand column the legislative source from which the sections of the Justices of the Peace Act 1979 in the left hand column have been derived. In the table the following abbreviations are used:

1742	=	The Justices Jurisdiction Act 1742 (16 Geo. 2. c. 18).
1848	=	The Justices Protection Act 1848 (11 & 12 Vict. c. 44)
1858	=	The Stipendiary Magistrates Act 1858 (21 & 22 Vict. c. 73)
1888	=	The Local Government Act 1888 (51 & 52 Vict. c. 41)
1897	=	The Metropolitan Police Courts Act 1897 (60 & 61 Vict. c. 26)
1938	=	The Administration of Justice (Miscellaneous Provisions) Act 1938 (1 & 2 Geo. c. 63)
1949	=	The Justices of the Peace Act 1949 (12, 13 & 14 Geo. 6, c. 101)
1952 (c. 55)	=	The Magistrates' Courts Act 1952)15 & 16 Geo. 6 & 1 Eliz. 2. c. 55)
1953	=	The Licensing Act 1953 (1 & 2 Eliz. 2. c. 46)
1959	=	The Metropolitan Magistrates' Courts Act 1959 (7 & 8 Eliz. 2. c. 45)
1964 (c. 26)	=	The Licensing Act 1964
1964 (c. 42)	=	The Administration of Justice Act 1964
1965	=	The Justices of the Peace Act 1965 (c. 28)
1967 (c. 9)	=	The General Rate Act 1967
1967 (c. 28)	=	The Superannuation (Miscellaneous Provisions) Act 1967
1968	=	The Justices of the Peace Act 1968 (c. 69)
1968	=	The Decimal Currency Act 1969 (c. 19)
1971	=	The Courts Act 1971 (c. 23)
1972 (c. 11)	=	The Superannuation Act 1972
1972 (c. 70)	=	The Local Government Act 1972
1972 (c. 71)	=	The Criminal Justice Act 1972
1973 (c. 15)	=	The Administration of Justice Act 1973
1973 (c. 38)	=	The Social Security Act 1973
1973 (c. 62)	=	The Powers of Criminal Courts Act 1973
1975	=	The Social Security Pensions Act 1975 (c. 60)
1977	=	The Administration of Justice Act 1977 (c. 38)
1978	=	The Domestic Proceedings and Magistrates' Courts Act 1978 (c. 22)
R (followed by a number))	=	The recommendations set out in the paragraph of that number in the Appendix to the Report of the Law Commission (Cmnd. 7583).

Section of Act	Derivation
1	1973 (c. 15) s. 1 (1)
2 (1)	1964 (c. 42) s. 2 (1)
(2)	1964 (c. 42) s. 2 (3); 1978 s. 86
(3)	R10.
3	1964 (c. 42) s. 3; R11.
4 (1)	1072 (c. 70) s. 217 (3).
(2)	1949 s. 44 (1); 1964 (c. 42) s. 2 (3); 1968 Sch. 3 para. 3; 1972 (c. 70) Sch. 27, paras. 13, 19 (1); 1978 s. 86.
5 (1)	1973 (c. 15) s. 1 (1).
(2)	1971 s. 3.
6 (1)	1973 (c. 15) s. 1 (2).
(2)	1973 (c. 15 s. 1 (2), (6).
7 (1)–(3)	1949 s. 1 (1)–(3); 1973 (c. 15) Sch. 1 para. 9 (1) (a).
(4)	1949 s. 5.

Section of Act	Derivation
8 (1)	1973 (c. 15) s. 1 (4).
(2)–(7)	1973 (c. 15 s. 5, Sch. 1, para. 4 (1)–(4), (6).
9	1973 (c. 15) Sch. 1 para. 5.
10	1973 (c. 15) Sch. 1 para. 6.
11	1973 (c. 15) s. 1 (2)–(4).
12 (1)	1973 (c. 15) Sch. 1 para. 8 (1); 1973 (c. 38) Sch. 27 para. 98.
(2), (3)	1973 (c. 15) Sch. 1 para. 8 (2), (3)
(4)	1973 (c. 15) Sch. 1 para. 8 (3A) (inserted by 1977 Sch. 2 para. 5).
(5)	1973 (c. 15) Sch. 1 para. 8 (4).
(6)	1973 (c. 15) Sch. 1 para. 8 (5); 1977 Sch. 2 para. 5.
(7)	1973 (c. 15) Sch. 1 para. 8 (6).
13 (1), (2)	1973 (c. 15) s. 2 (1).
(3)	1973 (c. 15) s. 2 (2).
(4), (5)	1973 (c. 15) s. 2 (6).
14 (1)	1973 (c. 15) s. 2 (5), Sch. 1 para. 1 (1).
(2)	1973 (c. 15) Sch. 1 para. 1 (2).
15	1973 (c. 15) s. 2 (7); R15.
16 (1)	1952 (c. 55) s. 121 (1).
(2)	1973 (c. 15) s. 2 (3).
(3)	1858 s. 1.
(4)	1858 s. 2.
(5)	1858 s. 3.
17 (1)	1949 s. 13 (2).
(2)	1949 s. 13 (3) (substituted by 1977 s. 21 (1)).
(3)	1949 s. 13 (4); 1978 Sch. 2 para. 10.
18 (1)	1949 ss. 13 (1), 44 (1) ("county justice"); R5.
(2)	1949 s. 13 (5); 1977 s. 21 (2).
(3)	1949 s. 13 (5A) (inserted by 1968 s. 3).
(4)	1949 s. 15 (5).
(5)	1949 s. 13 (6).
(6)	1949 s. 44 (1).
19 (1)	1949 s. 16 (1); 1964 (c. 42) ss. 2 (3), 13 (1); 1972 (c. 70) Sch. 27 para. 5 (1); 1978 s. 86.
(2)	1949 s. 16 (2); 1964 (c. 42) ss. 2 (3), 13 (1); 1968 Sch. 3 para. 3; 1972 (c. 70) Sch. 27 paras. 5 (2), 19 (1); 1978 s. 86; R14.
(3)	1949 s. 16 (2), Sch. 4 para. 2; 1964 (c. 42) ss. 2 (3), 13 (1); 1968 Sch. 3 para. 4 (4); 1972 (c. 70) Sch. 27 paras. 5 (2), 14 (8), 19 (1); 1978 s. 86; R14.
(4)	1949 Sch. 4 para. 6.
20 (1)	1949 Sch. 4 para. 1 (1); 1964 (c. 42) ss. 2 (3), 13 (1); 1968 Sch. 3 para. 3; 1972 (c. 70) Sch. 27 para. 14 (1); 1978 s. 86.
(2)	1949 Sch. 4 para. 1 (2A) (inserted as para. 1 (2) by 1971 Sch. 7 para. 2 (1) and re-numbered para. 1 (2A) by 1972 (c. 70) Sch. 27 para. 14 (2)).
(3)	1949 Sch. 4 para. 1 (2); 1964 (c. 42) s. 2 (3); 1972 (c. 70) Sch. 27 para. 14 (2).
(4)–(6)	1949 Sch. 4 para. 1 (4)–(6); 1972 (c. 70) Sch. 27 para. 14 (3)–(5).
21 (1)	1949 Sch. 4, para. 1 (7); 1972 (c. 70) Sch. 27 para. 14 (6).
(2)	1949 Sch. 4 para. 1 (8); 1964 (c. 42) s. 2 (3); 1968 Sch. 3 para. 3; 1972 (c. 70) Sch. 27 para. 14 (7); 1978 s. 86.
(3)	1949 Sch. 4 para. 1 (7); 1972 (c. 70) Sch. 27 para. 14 (6).
(4)	1949 Sch. 4 para. 1 (9).

Section of Act	Derivation
22 (1)	1949 Sch. 4 para. 9 (1).
(2)	1949 Sch. 4 para. 9 (2); 1972 (c. 70) Sch. 27 para. 14 (10).
(3)	1949 Sch. 4 para. 5 (substituted by 1971 Sch. 7 para. 3); R8.
(4)	1949 Sch. 4 para. 10.
(5)	1949 Sch. 4 para. 11.
(6)	1949 Sch. 4 para. 8.
(7)	1949 Sch. 4 para. 7.
23 (1)	1949 s. 18 (1); 1964 (c. 42) ss. 2 (3), 13 (1); 1972 (c. 70) Sch. 27 para. 6 (1); 1978 s. 86.
(2)	1949 s. 18 (2); 1964 (c. 42) s. 2 (3); 1972 (c. 70) Sch. 27 para. 6 (2); 1978 s. 86.
(3)	1949 s. 18 (3).
(4)	1949 s. 18 (8); 1964 (c. 42) ss. 2 (3), 13 (1); 1972 (c. 70) Sch. 27 para. 6 (4); 1978 s. 86.
(5)	1949 s. 18 (4).
24 (1)	1949 s. 18 (5); 1972 (c. 70) Sch. 27 para. 6 (3).
(2)	1949 s. 18 (6); 1972 (c. 70) Sch. 27 para. 6 (3).
(3)	1949 s. 18 (7).
(4)	1972 (c. 70) Sch. 27 para. 6 (6).
(5)	1949 s. 18 (10); 1964 (c. 42) s. 2 (3).
(6)	1949 s. 18 (9); 1972 (c. 70) Sch. 27 para. 6 (5).
25 (1)	1949 s. 19 (1).
(2)	1949 s. 19 (8); 1972 (c. 70) Sch. 27 para. 7 (1).
(3)	1949 s. 19 (9); 1972 (c. 70) Sch. 27 para. 7 (1).
(4)	1949 s. 19 (11).
(5)	1964 (c. 42) s. 15 (8).
26 (1)	1949 s. 20 (1).
(2)	1949 s. 20 (2).
(3)–(5)	1949 s. 20 (4); 1964 (c. 42) Sch. 3 para. 2; 1965 s. 1; 1968 s. 8 (2), Sch. 5 Pt. II; Justices of the Peace Act 1968 (Commencement No. 1) Order 1968 (1968/2035).
27 (1)	1949 s. 19 (2); 1953 Pt II, s. 168 (1), (5), Sch. 10 (as read with 1964 (c. 26) Pt. VII, Sch. 14, para. 1).
(2)–(7)	1949 s. 19 (3)–(7).
(8)	1968 s. 5 (2).
(9)	1964 (c. 42) s. 15 (8).
28 (1), (2)	1968 s. 5 (1).
(3), (4)	1968 s. 5 (3); R12.
29 (1), (2)	1949 s. 21 (1); R5.
(3)	—
30 (1), (2)	1952 (c. 55) s. 118 (3), (4); 1968 Sch. 3 para. 8; R9.
(3)	R9.
31 (1)	1964 (c. 42) s. 10 (1); 1973 (c. 15) s. 2 (6) (a).
(2)–(5)	1964 (c. 42) s. 10 (2)–(5).
31 (6)	1973 (c. 15) Sch. 1 paras. 1, 3.
(7)	1973 (c. 15) s. 2 (6).
32	1964 (c. 42) s. 10 (6)–(8).
33	1964 (c. 42) s. 9.
34 (1), (2)	1959 s. 2 (1), (2).
(3)	1959 s. 2 (4); Minister for the Civil Service Order 1971 (1971/2099).

Section of Act	Derivation
35 (1)–(4)	1964 (c. 42) s. 13 (1)–(4).
(5)	1964 (c. 42) s. 13 (5) (substituted by 1971 Sch. 8 para. 43 (1)).
(6)	1964 (c. 42) s. 13 (7).
36	1964 (c. 42) ss. 14, 36.
37 (1), (2)	1964 (c. 42) s. 15 (1), (2).
(3)–(5)	1964 (c. 42) s. 15 (4)–(6).
(6), (7)	1964 (c. 42) ss. 15 (7), 36 (1).
38 (1), (2)	1964 (c. 42) s. 16 (1), (2).
(3)	1964 (c. 42) s. 13 (6).
(4)	1964 (c. 42) s. 15 (3).
(5)	1964 (c. 42) s. 16 (3).
39 (1)	1968 s. 1 (2); 1973 (c. 15) s. 1 (6).
(2)	1968 Sch. 2 para. 1.
(3)	1968 Sch. 3 para. 2.
(4)	
40 (1)	1968 Sch. 2 para. 2 (1).
(2)	1968 Sch. 2 para. 3.
(3)	1968 Sch. 2 para. 4.
(4)	1968 Sch. 2 para. 2 (2).
41 (1)	1968 Sch. 3 paras. 1 (b); (3); 1972 (c. 70) Sch. 27 para. 19 (1); R13.
(2)	R13.
42	1968 Sch. 3 para. 4 (4).
43	1973 (c. 15) s. 1 (3), (6).
44	1848 s. 1.
45	1848 s. 2; R2.
46	1848 s. 3.
47	1848 s. 4.
48 (1)	1848 s. 5 (substituted by 1938 Sch. 2).
(2)	1848 s. 6.
49 (1), (2)	1848 s. 4; 1967 (c. 9) ss 2 (5), 116 (1).
(3)	—
50	1848 s. 7.
51	1848 s. 10.
52	1848 s. 13; 1969 s. 10 (1), Sch. 1.
53 (1)–(3)	1964 (c. 42) s. 27 (1)–(3).
(4)	1964 (c. 42) ss. 27 (4), 36 (1).
(5), (6)	1964 (c. 42) s. 27 (5), (6).
54 (1)	1964 (c. 42) s. 28 (1); 1971 Sch. 8 para. 2.
(2), (3)	1964 (c. 42) s. 28 (2), (3).
55 (1)	1949 s. 25 (1); 1972 (c. 70) s. 217 (5), Sch. 27 para. 9 (1).
(2)	1949 s. 25 (2); 1972 (c. 70) Sch. 27 para. 9 (2); R7.
(3), (4)	1949 s. 25 (3), (4).
56 (1)	1949 s. 26 (1).
(2)	1949 s. 26 (2), (3).
(3), (4)	1949 s. 26 (3).

Section of Act	Derivation
57 (1), (2)	1964 (c. 42) ss. 2 (3), 17 (5), Sch. 3 para. 20 (6); 1972 (c. 70) Sch. 27 para. 17 (2); 1978 s. 86.
(3)	1968 Sch. 3 paras. 1 (*b*), 3; 1972 (c. 70) Sch. 27 para. 19 (1).
58 (1)	1964 (c. 42) s. 17 (1).
(2)	1964 (c. 42) s 17 (1); 1967 (c. 28) s. 15 (8), (9); 1975 Sch. 4 para. 5.
(3)	1897 ss. 1, 8.
(4), (5)	1964 (c. 42) s. 17 (3), (4).
59 (1)–(3)	1949 ss. 27 (2) (as substituted by 1972 (c. 71) s. 61 (2)), 43 (1); 1972 (c. 11) Sch. 7 para. 5; 1973 (c. 15) Sch. 1 para. 12.
(4), (5)	1949 s. 27 (5), (6).
(6)	1949 s. 27 (10) (*d*); 1964 (c. 42) Sch. 3 para. 20 (7); 1968 Sch. 3 paras. 1 (*b*), 3; 1972 (c. 70) Sch. 27 paras. 10 (4), 17 (2).
60	1964 (c. 42) s. 37 (4); 1973 (c. 62) Sch. 5, para. 14.
61 (1)	1949 s. 27)1); 1952 (c. 55) Sch. 5; R5.
(2)	1949 s. 27 (1) proviso)a), (7).
(3)	1949 s. 27 (1) proviso (*b*).
(4)	1949 s. 27 (9).
(5)	1949 s. 27 (12); 1971 Sch. 8 para. 2; R5.
(6)	1972 (c. 71) s. 61 (1).
(7)	1949 ss. 27 (10), 44 (1); R5.
62 (1), (2)	1972 (c. 71) s. 62 (3), (4).
63 (1)	1949 s. 17.
(2)	1964 (c. 42) s. 16 (2).
(3)	1973 (c. 15) s. 3 (1).
(4)	1973 (c. 15) s. 3 (2).
(5)	1972 (c. 71) s. 62 (1).
(6)	1972 (c. 71) s. 62 (4).
64 (1)	1949 s. 3 (1); 1971 Sch. 8 para. 2; 1972 (c. 70) Sch. 29 para. 1 (2); R4, 5.
(2)–(4)	1949 s. 3 (2)–(4); R5.
(5)	1949 s. 5.
65	1742 s. 1; R1.
66 (1)	1952 (c. 55) s. 116 (1); 1964 (c. 42) s. 2 (3); 1968 Sch. 3 para. 3.
(2)	1888 s. 42 (12); 1964 (c. 42) Sch. 3 para. 12 (1).
67 (1), (2)	1964 (c. 42) s. 30 (1), (2).
(3)	1968 s. 1 (3).
(4)	1959 s. 2 (3).
(5)	1964 (c. 42) s. 30 (5).
68 (1)	1949 s. 1 (5); 1972 (c. 70) Sch. 27 para. 1; 1973 (c. 15) s. 1 (7).
(2)	1973 (c. 15) s. 1 (7), Sch. 1 para. 4 (5).
69	1949 s. 16 (5); 1972 (c. 70) s. 216, Sch. 27 para. 5 (4); 1973 (c. 15) s. 1 (8).
70	1949 s. 44 (1) ("justices' clerk", "magistrate", "prescribed"); 1964 (c. 42) s. 38 (1) ("officer", "the Receiver", "stipendiary magistrate"); R6.
71 (1), (2)	—
(3)	1973 (c. 15) Sch. 1 para. 9 (1).
(4)	—
72	—
Sch. 1	
para. 1	—
2	—

Section of Act	Derivation
3	1973 (c. 15) s. 20 (3) (*a*).
4	1973 (c. 15) ss. 1 (2), 20 (3) (*b*).
5	1973 (c. 15) s. 20 (6), Sch. 1 para. 4 (1) proviso.
6	1973 (c. 15) Sch. 1 para. 9 (1).
7	1973 (c. 15) ss. 2, 20 (5).
8	1973 (c. 15) s. 20 (5) proviso (*a*), (*c*).
9	—
10	1949 s. 23 (1), (2); Justices of the Peace Act 1949 (Commencement No. 3) Order 1951 (1951/1941).
11	1949 s. 23 (1), (7).
12	1968 Sch. 3 para. 15; Justices of the Peace Act 1968 (Commencement No. 3) Order 1969 (1969/1373).
13	1949 s. 42; 1964 (c. 42) s. 32; 1968 Sch. 3 para. 16.
14	1949 s. 21 (4); Justices of the Peace Act 1949 (Commencement No. 3) Order 1951 (1951/1941).
15	1949 Sch. 2; 1973 (c. 15) Sch. 5 Pt. I
16	—
17	—
18	—
Sch. 2 paras. 1–25	—
26	1964 (c. 42) s. 37 (4); 1973 (c. 62) Sch. 5, para. 14.
27–31	—
Sch. 3 repeal of Justices' Clerks Act 1877.	R3.
other repeals.	—

1786   **Magistrates' courts—domestic proceedings—justices' reasons**

See *Faulkner v Faulkner*, para. 1871.

1787   —— **forms**

The Magistrates' Courts (Forms) (Amendment) Rules 1979, S.I. 1979 No. 1220 (in force on 1st November 1979), amend the Magistrates' Courts (Forms) Rules 1968 in consequence of the coming into force of certain provisions of the Domestic Proceedings and Magistrates' Courts Act 1978, 1978 Halsbury's Abridgment para. 1509. New forms are prescribed for use in connection with ss. 16 and 18.

1788   —— **rules**

The Magistrates' Courts (Amendment) Rules 1979, S.I. 1979 No. 1221 (in force on 1st November 1979), amend the Magistrates' Courts Rules 1968 in consequence of the coming into force of certain provisions of the Domestic Proceedings and Magistrates' Courts Act 1978, 1978 Halsbury's Abridgment para. 1509. The relevant provisions are ss. 16–18 and 77 which relate to family protection orders and payments to a child.

1789   —— **sentencing practice—Home Office Report**

See para. 2489.

1790   **Maintenance order—application for remission of arrears—jurisdiction of magistrates**

See *R v Halifax JJ, ex parte Woolveron*, para. 956.

1791   **Powers—committal for non-payment of fine—offender already in prison for other offences—whether issue of warrant without notification a breach of natural justice**

Fines payable in weekly instalments were imposed on the offender by magistrates for motoring offences. He was later convicted and sentenced to fifteen months' imprisonment for burglary. He informed the magistrates' court of his sentence and consequential inability to pay the remaining balance of the fine. At the hearing, of which he was not informed, the magistrates, in his absence, ordered him to serve sixty days' imprisonment in default of payment, to run consecutively to his sentence for burglary. He sought an order of certiorari to quash the committal warrant on the grounds that as he was not informed of the hearing, neither he nor his representative could attend, which amounted to a breach of the rules of natural justice. *Held*, ROBERT GOFF J dissenting, the Criminal Justice Act 1967, s. 44 (6) gave the magistrates express power to issue a committal warrant for non-payment of fines without the accused being present as he was serving a term of imprisonment. The magistrates therefore had implied authority to commit him without giving him notice of the hearing and the application would be refused.

R v DUDLEY JJ, EX PARTE PAYNE [1979] 2 All ER 1089 (Queen's Bench Division: LORD WIDGERY CJ, MICHAEL DAVIES and ROBERT GOFF JJ).

1792   —— **power to attach condition to binding over—common law and statutory powers**

See *Goodlad v Chief Constable of South Yorkshire*, para. 1295.

1793   **Recognisance—forfeiture—culpability of surety**

A man who entered into a recognisance to ensure the attendance of his son in court was ordered to forfeit the full amount when he failed to appear. The son had disappeared on the 19th/20th August. The father failed to inform the police until three days later, when he requested release from his suretyship, which was refused.

The justices considered that the father was guilty of culpable neglect in failing immediately to inform the police of his son's disappearance and that no reduction of the full amount could be made. On an application for an order of certiorari to quash the order to forfeit the full amount, *held*, a surety was liable to pay the full amount unless there were mitigating circumstances which would enable the court to reduce the amount payable. The justices had expressed an opinion which it was perfectly open for them to express and which any reasonable bench would have made. The application for certiorari would be refused.

R v TOTTENHAM MAGISTRATES' COURT, EX PARTE RICCARDI (1977) 66 Cr App Rep 150 (Queen's Bench Division: LORD WIDGERY CJ, EVELEIGH and FORBES JJ). *R v Southampton Justices, ex parte Green* [1976] QB 11, CA, 1975 Halsbury's Abridgment para. 636 and *R v Horseferry Road Stipendiary Magistrate, ex parte Pearson* [1976] 2 All ER 264, DC, 1976 Halsbury's Abridgment para. 1673 applied.

1794   Summons—application for issue—right of proposed defendant to be heard

The applicant, a solicitor, acted on behalf of the plaintiffs in civil proceedings in the county court in which judgment was entered against the defendant. The defendant then commenced proceedings in the High Court against the plaintiffs for conspiracy to defraud and injure him by giving false evidence in the county court proceedings. His application to join the applicant as defendant was dismissed. He then applied to a metropolitan magistrate for the issue of a summons against the applicant, alleging that he had committed perjury in an affidavit used in the High Court proceedings. The applicant applied to the magistrate to be heard in relation to the application. The magistrate held that he had no power to hear the applicant and that the applicant had no right to be heard. The applicant sought a writ of mandamus to require the magistrate to hear and determine his objections. *Held*, the duty of a magistrate in considering an application for the issue of a summons was to exercise a judicial discretion; in deciding whether or not to issue it, he should consider the whole of the relevant circumstances. In the majority of cases, the magistrate would not need to consider material beyond that provided by the informant, but he had a residual discretion to hear a proposed defendant if he felt it necessary. However, a proposed defendant had no locus standi and no right at that stage to be heard. Thus the magistrate did have power if he wished to hear the applicant, but the applicant had no right to address him. Hence the magistrate was justified in refusing to hear the applicant and the application would be refused.

R v WEST LONDON JJ, EX PARTE KLAHN [1979] 2 All ER 221 (Queen's Bench Division: LORD WIDGERY CJ, EVELEIGH LJ and STEPHEN BROWN J). Dictum of Lord Goddard CJ in *R v Wilson, ex parte Battersea Borough Council* [1947] 2 All ER at 570 applied.

1795   Travelling and subsistence allowances—rates

New rates of travelling allowance and subsistence allowance for justices of the peace have been announced. The new rates took effect on 31st January 1979. The rates prescribed for the use of a justice's own private vehicle (provided that it is shown that this results in a substantial saving of the justice's time or is otherwise reasonable) are: for the use of a motor cycle (exceeding 500 c.c.), a motor cycle combination, or a tri-car not exceeding 500 c.c., 5·8p per mile; for the use of a four-wheeled vehicle not exceeding 500 c.c., 11·3p per mile; for the use of a motor car or tri-car exceeding 500 c.c. but not exceeding 999 c.c., 11·3p per mile; for the use of a motor car or tri-car exceeding 999 c.c. but not exceeding 1199 c.c., 12·4 per mile; and for the use of a motor car or tri-car exceeding 1199 c.c., 13·7p per mile. Extra rates may be claimed for the carriage of a passenger and for overnight garaging. Separate rates are prescribed for travel by public service, by hired motor car, by own motor cycle not exceeding 500 c.c., and by air. Subsistence rates for absence from the usual place of residence (not involving overnight absence) are: for more than four but not more than eight hours, £3·13; for more than eight but not more than twelve hours, £5·50; for more than twelve but not more than sixteen hours, £7·78; and for absences of more than sixteen hours, £9·30. The subsistence allowance for overnight absence is £22·09 plus (for an absence overnight in Greater London) a supplementary allowance not exceeding £2·12. See Home Office Circular 27/1979.

1796   Trial—applicant charged before seventeenth birthday—remission to juvenile court—validity

A youth was charged with certain offences one month before his seventeenth birthday, but appeared before magistrates some time after it. When the court remitted the case to the juvenile court the youth applied for an order of certiorari to quash the decision. *Held*, since the youth was over seventeen years of age when he appeared before the magistrates, his case could not be remitted to the juvenile court. The case would be returned to the magistrates.

R v BILLERICAY JJ, EX PARTE JOHNSON [1979] Crim LR 315 (Queen's Bench Division: LORD WIDGERY CJ, EVELEIGH LJ and STEPHEN BROWN J).

1797   —— prosecution evidence unsworn—whether justices under duty to rehear charge

A store detective brought a prosecution for shop-lifting, and at the proceedings before the magistrates acted as both advocate and witness. A plea of not guilty to the charge of theft was entered and the detective knowingly gave unsworn evidence from the witness box. The magistrates upheld a submission of no case to answer on the ground that there was no prosecution evidence of the facts alleged, and the detective applied for an order of certiorari to quash the decision and an order of mandamus directing the magistrates to rehear and determine the charge of theft. *Held*, while the magistrates had the power to rehear the case they were not obliged to do so and it was important to remember that they were inhibited from taking any step which would appear to be leaning towards the prosecution. There had been no breach of duty by the court and the applications would be refused.

R v UXBRIDGE JJ, EX PARTE CONLON [1979] LS Gaz R 157 (Queen's Bench Division: LORD WIDGERY CJ, BRIDGE LJ and CAULFIELD J).

MARKETS AND FAIRS

Halsbury's Laws of England (4th edn.), Vol. 29, paras. 601–716

1798   Article

Markets, Planning Law and the Shops Act 1950, Henry E. Markson (recent cases concerning markets which highlight some problems in shop legislation where it relates to planning law): 123 Sol Jo 413.

1799   Sunday trading—degree of permanence of business

The first defendant was an organiser of Sunday markets in and around the plaintiff council's district. The second defendant owned three sites in that district, which were used in rotation as sites for Sunday markets organised by the first defendant. A stallholder was convicted of contravening the Shops Act 1950, s. 47, which provides that shops must be closed on Sundays. The defendants were convicted of aiding and abetting. The plaintiff council obtained an interlocutory injunction restraining the defendants from Sunday trading in contravention of the 1950 Act. On appeal, the question was whether the markets had been "at a place where any retail trade or business is carried on as if that place were a shop" as provided by s. 58 of the 1950 Act. *Held*, whether a business carried on at a place had a sufficient degree of permanence to justify it being within s. 58 was a question of fact and degree. A trader who regularly or frequently rented a stall each Sunday at the markets, on whichever site they were held, showed a sufficient continuity of the trade or business, and the "pitch" on which he had his stall on any particular day was a "place" within

s. 58.   Accordingly s. 47 would apply as if that "place" were a shop, and the trader would be in breach of the Act and liable to prosecution, and the defendants would be liable for aiding and abetting. The use of the sites in this manner would not be permitted and the injunction would stand.

NEWARK DISTRICT COUNCIL v E & A MARKET PROMOTIONS LTD (1979) 77 LGR 6 (Court of Appeal: BUCKLEY and GOFF LJJ).   *Maby v Warwick Corporation* [1972] 2 QB 242 applied.

MEDICINE, PHARMACY, DRUGS AND MEDICINAL PRODUCTS

Halsbury's Laws of England (3rd edn.), Vol. 26, paras. 1–667

1800   Articles

Abortion—A Clarification, T. G. A. Bowles and M. N. M. Bell: 129 NLJ 944.
Some Legal Implications of Embryo Transfer, Douglas J. Cusine: 129 NLJ 627.

1801   Chloroform—prohibition

The Medicines (Chloroform Prohibition) Order 1979, S.I. 1979 No. 382 (in force on 28th March 1980), prohibits the sale or supply of medicinal products which are for human use and which consist of or contain chloroform.   There are certain exemptions from the prohibition, which include certain sales or supplies of medicinal products by medical and dental practitioners and from registered pharmacies and hospitals, the sale or supply of chloroform as an anaesthetic, the sale or supply of medicinal products where the chloroform content does not exceed specified limits, or for use in dental surgery, or solely for external use, the sale or supply of medicinal products for export, the sale or supply of chloroform for use as an ingredient, in specified circumstances, in the preparation of a substance or article.

1802   Contact lens fluids

The Medicines (Committee on Dental and Surgical Materials) Amendment Order 1979, S.I. 1979 No. 1535 (in force on 1st January 1980), amends the Medicines (Committee on Dental and Surgical Materials) Order 1975, 1975 Halsbury's Abridgment para. 2217, under which the Committee was established, by extending its functions to cover certain substances and fluids for use with contact lenses for human use or the blanks from which such lenses are prepared.

1803   The Medicines (Contact Lens Fluids and Other Substances) (Appointed Day) Order 1979, S.I. 1979 No. 1539 (in force on 1st January 1980), brings into force the licensing restrictions on marketing, manufacture and wholesale dealing imposed by the Medicines Act 1968, ss. 7, 8 and the restrictions on clinical trials imposed by s. 31, with regard to certain substances and fluids for use with contact lenses for human use or the blanks from which such lenses are prepared, subject to certain transitional exemptions contained in ss. 16 and 37.

1804   The Medicines (Contact Lens Fluids and Other Substances) (Exemption from Licences) Order 1979, S.I. 1979 No. 1585 (in force on 1st January 1980), gives exemption from the restriction imposed by the Medicines Act 1968, s. 8 (2) on the labelling, except in accordance with a manufacturer's licence, of certain substances and fluids for use with contact lenses or blanks.   The exemption applies to doctors, pharmacists and registered ophthalmic opticians where certain specified conditions are met.

1805   The Medicines (Contact Lens Fluids and Other Substances) (Exemption from Licences) Amendment Order 1979, S.I. 1979 No. 1745 (in force on 1st January 1980), amends the Medicines (Contact Lens Fluids and Other Substances) (Exemption from Licences) Order 1979, art. 1, para. 1804 so as to remove a possible ambiguity in the reference to "contact lens".

1806   The Medicines (Contact Lens Fluids and Other Substances) (Labelling) Regulations 1979, S.I. 1979 No. 1759 (in force on 1st February 1980), lay down special requirements as to the particulars to be furnished with certain substances and fluids for use with contact lenses or blanks which are for sale or supply, either on a label on the container or package or in an accompanying leaflet. The substances and fluids concerned are those described in the Medicines (Specified Articles and Substances) Order 1976 Sch. 2, para. 1, 1976 Halsbury's Abridgment para. 1685. The regulations also make certain transitional provisions.

1807   The Medicines (Contact Lens Fluids and Other Substances) (Advertising and Miscellaneous Amendments) Regulations 1979, S.I. 1979 No. 1760 (in force on 1st February 1980), lay down requirements as to the particulars which must be contained in advertisements in the form of information sheets sent or delivered to pharmacists and ophthalmic and dispensing opticians relating to certain substances and fluids for use with contact lenses or blanks. They amend the Medicines (Data Sheet) Regulations 1972 so that those regulations do not apply to data sheets which relate to such substances and fluids, and prescribe special particulars for such data sheets sent or delivered to doctors. They also contain certain transitional provisions.

1808   ## Dangerous drugs—offences

See CRIMINAL LAW.

1809   ## Dentists—ancillary dental workers

The Ancillary Dental Workers (Amendment) Regulations 1979, S.I. 1979 No. 142 (in force on 1st July 1979), amend the Ancillary Dental Workers Regulations 1968 by providing for the name and title of the class of ancillary dental workers known as dental auxiliaries to be changed to dental therapists. Certificates of fitness to practise as dental auxiliaries will continue to qualify their holders for enrolment in the renamed roll, and no change is made to the training requirements or to the effect of enrolment.

1810   ## —— striking off register—infamous or disgraceful conduct

The Disciplinary Committee of the General Dental Council found a dentist guilty of infamous or disgraceful conduct in a professional respect due to his having permitted unqualified staff to fill cavities in a patient's teeth after he had completed the drilling. The legal assessor had advised the Committee to decide the "appropriate standard each practitioner should adhere to, not a special standard greater than is ordinarily to be expected, but the ordinary standard of the profession". The dentist appealed against the finding and the erasure of his name from the register. *Held*, the assessor's advice was wrong in law, since it implied that merely negligent conduct was enough for a finding of guilt, whereas the conduct should be "deserving of the strongest reprobation and . . . so heinous as to merit . . . the extreme professional penalty of striking off". However the misdirection would not have had sufficient effect on the Committee's decision as the Committee had been referred to decisions in previous cases which correctly stated the law. Although the sentence was severe it would not be overturned as it was not wrong or unjustified.

McENIFF v GENERAL DENTAL COUNCIL [1980] 1 All ER 461 (Privy Council: LORD EDMUND-DAVIES, LORD SCARMAN and LORD LANE). *Felix v GDC* [1960] AC 704 applied.

1811   General Medical Council—constitution

The General Medical Council (Constitution) Order 1979, S.I. 1979 No. 112 (in force on 7th March 1979), provides, under the Medical Act 1978, for the reconstitution of the General Medical Council as from 27th September 1979. It empowers the universities and other bodies, listed in the Schedule, to choose those members of the General Council who are appointed. It also contains provisions as to members' tenure of office.

1812   Medical Act 1978—commencement

The Medical Act 1978 (Commencement No. 2) Order 1979, S.I. 1979 No. 920 brings the following provisions of the 1978 Act into force on 27th September 1979: ss. 1 (13), (14), 3, 5, 15, 16, 31 (1) (part), (2) (part), (3), Sch. 1, Sch. 6, paras. 1–3, 5–12, 14, 19, 37, 48 (a), 49 (part), 56, 59, and Sch. 7 (part). For the Act see 1978 Halsbury's Abridgment para. 1864.

1813   Medical practitioners—defence union—whether carrying on insurance business

See *Medical Defence Union Ltd v Department of Trade*, para. 1606.

1814   —— obstetrician—negligence

See *Whitehouse v Jordan*, para. 1986.

1815   —— overseas qualified practitioners — registration — Review Board

The General Medical Council (Review Board for Overseas Qualified Practitioners Rules) Order of Council 1979, S.I. 1979 No. 29 (in force on 15th February 1979), prescribes the constitution, quorum and procedure of the Review Board established to hear applications by medical practitioners with qualifications obtained overseas for a review of certain decisions made by the General Medical Council under the Medical Act 1978, s. 28, relating to their registration.

1816   —— prescribed experience

See para. 1944.

1817   —— registration—General Medical Council

The General Medical Council (Registration Regulations) Order of Council 1979, S.I. 1979 No. 844 (made on 17th July 1979), approves the Medical Practitioners Registration (No. 2) Regulations 1979, which make provisions concerning the Principal List and the Overseas List of the register of medical practitioners. The General Medical Council (Registration Regulations) Order of Council 1970, as amended by S.I. 1977 No. 1266, 1977 Halsbury's Abridgment para. 1808, is revoked.

1818   —— —— Ireland

The Irish Republic (Termination of 1927 Agreement) Order 1979, S.I. 1979 No. 289 (in force on 30th April 1979), is made under the Medical Act 1978, s. 4, 1978 Halsbury's Abridgment para. 1864. Following the termination of the 1927 Agreement made between the United Kingdom and the Republic of Ireland providing for reciprocal recognition of qualifications, the Order makes consequential repeals or modifications of legislation concerning doctors and dentists. The rights relating to registration as medical practitioners in the United Kingdom of persons who now have, or before 30th April 1985 acquire, the medical qualifications of the Republic of Ireland, are preserved. Irish members of the General Medical Council are to continue in office.

1819   —— **suspension from register—whether contract of employment frustrated**

A registered medical practitioner, employed by a regional health board, was suspended from the register for twelve months after he had been found guilty of infamous conduct. The regional health board informed him that his contract of service had been frustrated and was therefore terminated. In 1974 the board was superseded by the area health authority. The doctor brought an action against the authority for breach of contract. *Held*, dismissing the action, the Medical Act 1956, s. 28 (1) stipulated that no-one could hold an appointment as a medical officer in a hospital unless he was fully registered. Sub-section 33 (1) (b), as amended, provided that a person who was suspended should be treated as not being registered. Thus once the holder of an appointment was suspended he was no longer able to continue holding that appointment, and the contract of employment was consequently frustrated.

Tarnesby v Kensington, Chelsea and Westminster Area Health Authority (Teaching) (1978) 123 Sol Jo 49 (Queen's Bench Division: Neill J).

1820   **Medical profession—General Medical Council—quorum rules**

The General Medical Council (Quorum Rules) Order of Council 1979, S.I. 1979 No. 1358 (in force on 8th November 1979), approves the rules which prescribe the quorum of the Council as reconstituted under the Medical Act 1978.

1821   **Medicines—licences and certificates—exemption**

The Medicines (Exemption from Licences) (Assembly) Order 1979, S.I. 1979 No. 1114 (in force on 2nd October 1979), exempts certain medicinal products for human use from the restrictions imposed by the Medicines Act 1968, s. 8 (2) on the labelling without a manufacturer's licence of any medicinal product. The Order specifies the persons to whom and the conditions upon which exemption is granted, its duration in certain cases and the circumstances in which it may be terminated by the licensing authority.

1822   —— —— **fees**

The Medicines (Fees) Amendment Regulations 1979, S.I. 1979 No. 899 (in force on 1st September 1979), amend certain fees and methods of calculating certain fees laid down in the Medicines (Fees) Regulations 1978, 1978 Halsbury's Abridgment, para. 1878.

1823   —— **sale or supply**

The Medicines (General Sale List) Amendment Order 1979, S.I. 1979 No. 315 (in force on 12th April 1979), amends the Medicines (General Sale List) Order 1977, 1977 Halsbury's Abridgment, para. 1832, by making changes in the List with regard to named products for human use, named products for veterinary use and products sold by automatic machines.

1824   The Medicines (Phenacetin Prohibition) Order 1979, S.I. 1979 No. 1181 (in force on 27th March 1980) prohibits the sale, supply or importation of medicinal products which consist of or contain phenacetin, with certain specified exceptions.

1825   The Medicines (Prescriptions Only) Amendment Order 1979, S.I. 1979 No. 36 (in force on 10th February 1979), amends the Medicines (Prescriptions Only) Order 1977, 1977 Halsbury's Abridgment para. 1831, as amended by S.I. 1978 No. 987, 1978 Halsbury's Abridgment para. 1883. The Order grants temporary exemptions until 11th February 1980 from the restrictions imposed by the Medicines Act 1968, s. 58 (2), which relate to medicinal products for human and animal use, where the selling, supplying or administering of the medicinal product could have been lawfully done before 11th August 1978 otherwise than in accordance with a prescription.

1826   The Medicines (Prescription Only) (Amendment) (No. 2) Order 1979, S.I. 1979 No. 1040 (in force on 7th September 1979), further amends the Medicines (Prescription Only) Order 1977, 1977 Halsbury's Abridgment para. 1831, by excluding from the classes of specified medicinal products those products consisting of or containing Tylosin Phosphate where the product is sold or supplied for incorporation in feed as a growth promoter for figs.

1827   —— —— **veterinary drugs—exemption**

The Medicines (Exemptions from Restrictions on the Retail Sale or Supply of Veterinary Drugs) Order 1979, S.I. 1979 No. 45 (in force on 11th February 1979), consolidates the Medicines (Exemptions from Restrictions on the Retail Sale or Supply of Veterinary Drugs) Orders 1977 and 1978, 1977 Halsbury's Abridgment para. 1835 and 1978 Halsbury's Abridgment para. 1885. It also replaces the schedules to those orders and provides for certain additional exemptions from the restrictions in Medicines Act 1968, s. 52.

1828   The Medicines (Exemptions from Restrictions on the Retail Sale or Supply of Veterinary Drugs) (Amendment) Order 1979, S.I. 1979 No. 1008 (in force on 1st September 1979), amends the 1979 Order, para. 1827, by replacing all the schedules in that order with updated new schedules.

1829   **Nurses—conditions of work**

Convention No. 149 (concerning the employment and conditions of work and life of nursing personnel) of the International Labour Conference (63rd session, 1977) is designed to improve the conditions of employment of those providing nursing care, with a view to promoting and developing effective nursing services and ensuring the highest possible standards of nursing care internationally. Recommendation No. 157 (which deals with the same subject-matter) supplements the provisions of the convention. The government has stated that it does not intend at present to ratify the convention. Although the practices of the health authorities satisfy the terms of the convention, the government does not regulate the working conditions of nurses outside the national health services and is not contemplating the enactment of legislation to do so. Further, the convention's conditions could not be applied in all respects to the armed forces nurses. See the International Labour Conference: Proposed action by Her Majesty's Government in the United Kingdom on two Conventions and two Recommendations adopted at the 63rd Session (1977) of the International Labour Conference (Cmnd 7420).

1830   —— **nurses qualified in Community member states—right to work in United Kingdom**

The Nursing Qualifications (EEC Recognition) Order 1979, S.I. 1979 No. 1604 (in force on 1st January 1980) amends the Nurses Act 1957, Nurses (Scotland) Act 1951 and the Nurses and Midwives Act (Northern Ireland) 1970 so as to apply the provisions of Council Directives (EEC) 77/452, 453, 1977 Halsbury's Abridgment para. 1202 relating to the mutual recognition of qualifications of nursing staff. The Order gives nurses qualified in another member state of the Community the right to be registered and practice in the United Kingdom.

1831   —— **training**

The Nurses and Enrolled Nurses (Amendment) Rules Approval Instrument 1979, S.I. 1979 No. 49 (in force on 22nd February 1979), amend the Nurses Rules 1969, S.I. 1969 No. 1675 and the Enrolled Nurses Rules 1969, S.I. 1969 No. 1674, in particular by providing for a cessation of reduction in training in respect of the holders of certain qualifications and by making new provision as to the retaking of the Final State Written Examination.

1832   Nurses, Midwives and Health Visitors Act 1979

The Nurses, Midwives and Health Visitors Act 1979 establishes a United Kingdom Central Council for Nursing, Midwifery and Health Visiting and four National Boards. It also contains provisions as to the education and training requirements and other conditions for admission to a register to be kept by the Council. The Act received the royal assent on 4th April 1979, and comes into force on a day or days to be appointed except ss. 21 (2) and 24 which came into force on the passing of the Act.

Section 1 establishes the United Kingdom Central Council for Nursing, Midwifery and Health Visiting, the constitution of which is dealt with in Sch. 1. Section 2 lays down the Council's functions with regard to prescribing the standards of education, training and professional conduct of those wishing to be included on the register which is to be kept by the Council. On all matters relating to midwifery the Council is required to consult a Midwifery Committee which is to be set up by order of the Secretary of State: ss. 3, 4.

Section 5 establishes National Boards for Nursing, Midwifery and Health Visiting, one each for England, Scotland, Wales and Northern Ireland and s. 6 lays down the Boards' functions relating to the provision of training for those seeking registration. The constitution of the Boards is dealt with in Sch. 2. The Boards are obliged to consult committees set up by order of the Secretary of State on matters relating to midwifery and finance: s. 7. The Secretary of State is required to make an order for the establishment of a joint committee of the Council and the Boards to be known as the Health Visiting Joint Committee: s. 8, and he is empowered to order the setting up of local training committees of the Boards: s. 9.

The Council is required to set up a professional register of qualified nurses, midwives and health visitors: s. 10, and to make rules relating to conditions of admission to and removal from that register: ss. 11, 12. Further provisions as to proceedings under s. 12 are contained in Sch. 3. Section 13 deals with the right of appeal against decisions of the Council and s. 14 provides offences and penalties for those who falsely claim to be qualified persons.

Sections 15–17 contain miscellaneous provisions relating to midwives and the practice of midwifery. Section 15 empowers the Council to make rules regulating midwifery practice. Section 16 lists the bodies responsible as local supervising authorities for midwives and gives the Council power to prescribe the qualifications of persons who may be appointed to such authorities. Unqualified persons may not generally attend a woman in childbirth: s. 17. Midwives practising in Scotland are exempted from jury service: s. 18.

Financial provisions are set out in ss. 19–20. Section 19 empowers the Council and Boards to charge fees and the Secretary of State to make grants for the establishment and expenses of the Council and Boards and to promote improvements in training. The Council and Boards are required to keep accounts: s. 20, Sch. 4.

Supplementary and transitional provisions, minor and consequential amendments and repeals are contained in ss. 21–24 and Schs. 5–8.

1833   Opticians—General Optical Council—registration and enrolment

The General Optical Council (Registration and Enrolment Rules) (Amendment) Order of Council 1979, S.I. 1979 No. 1638 (made on 10th December 1979), approves the Registration and Enrolment (Amendment) Rules 1979. They require registered opticians and enrolled bodies corporate carrying on business as opticians to show all practice addresses in the registers and lists maintained by the General Optical Council, subject to specific exceptions. They also increase the fees charged in respect of registration, enrolment and retention.

1834   Professions supplementary to medicine—registration

The Professions Supplementary to Medicine (Registration Rules) (Amendment) Order of Council 1979, S.I. 1979 No. 365 (made on 27th March 1979), approves rules made by the Council for Professions Supplementary to Medicine. The rules increase with effect from 1st April 1979 the registration fees and retention fees payable to the Boards established under the Professions Supplementary to Medicine Act 1960.

1835   Transplantation—European convention

The Committee of Ministers of the Council of Europe has adopted Resolution (78)29 concerning the Harmonisation of Legislation of Member States relating to the Removal, Grafting and Transplantation of Human Substances. The rules appended to the resolution apply to the removal, grafting, transplantation and other use of substances of human origin removed or collected for therapeutic or diagnostic purposes for the benefit of persons other than the donor and for research purposes (art. 1.1). But the transfer of embryos, the removal and transplant of testicles and ovaries and the utilisation of ova and sperm are expressly excluded (art. 1.2). The rules require information about possible consequences of the removal to be given in advance to the donor and, except in cases of close personal or family relationships, for the anonymity of donor and recipient to be respected (art. 2). The donor must consent freely (art. 3). Safeguards for persons under a legal disability who act as donors are provided by art. 6. No substance may be offered for profit but a donor may be reimbursed for loss of earnings and expenses (art. 9). Special rules apply to the removal of substance from the bodies of deceased persons, including a safeguard (art. 10) where the deceased has expressed an objection, or may be presumed to have objected. The identity of the donor and recipient must not be disclosed (art. 13).

1836   The Council of Ministers of the Council of Europe in furtherance of Resolution (78) 29, para. 1835, has adopted Recommendation R (79) 5 calling upon member states to take all appropriate measures: (i) to facilitate the international exchange and transportation of specific substances of human origin; (ii) to ensure the safe, speedy and priority transport of such substances; (iii) to ensure the exchange of information on the demand for and availability of the substances, and on matters relating to their preservation, transportation and processing; (iv) to exempt the substances and their containers from all duties and taxes on import and export.

MENTAL HEALTH

Halsbury's Laws of England (3rd edn.), Vol. 29, paras. 790–1125

1837   Articles

The Mental Health Act 1959, Douglas Miller (proposed reforms to the 1959 Act): 129 NLJ 151.

Unimpeded Access to Courts, Larry Gostin (examination of the Mental Health Act 1959, s. 141): 129 NLJ 213

1838   Admission for treatment—application—application for substitution of acting nearest relative—evidence

The respondent, who was her daughter's nearest relative within the Mental Health Act 1959, s. 27 refused to give her consent to an application being made under s. 26 for her daughter's detention in hospital for treatment. Accordingly, the mental welfare officer applied for an order under s. 52 that he be appointed to act as the nearest relative for the purpose of making the s. 26 application, on the ground that the respondent had unreasonably objected to the application. At the hearing of the s. 52 application, two medical reports that had been prepared for the purpose of the s. 26 application were handed to the respondent's solicitor. The hearing was adjourned to give the solicitor an opportunity of considering the reports. The solicitor did not show the reports to the respondent, but told her that two doctors had recommended that her daughter be kept in hospital. The mental welfare officer's application was granted. The respondent appealed, contending that the requirement of the proviso to the County Court Rules, Ord. 46, r. 18 para. 5 that a respondent be told the substance of any part of a report bearing on his fitness or conduct had not been complied with, as she had not seen the medical reports; that the evidence tendered at the hearing did not comply with either s. 26 or other statutory provisions. *Held*, to comply with the proviso to r. 18 it was sufficient if a report was handed to the respondent's legal adviser in circumstances where the legal adviser could give advice and take instructions. The object of an application under s. 52 was to enable the provisions of s. 26 to be brought into operation, and any defects in the form of the medical reports for the purposes of s. 26 were irrelevant for the purposes of the s. 52 application. The judge was concerned with the medical content of the reports and not their statutory form. Since the medical content of the reports made it clear that the daughter did require compulsory detention, there was prima facie evidence on which the judge could hold that the mother's objection had been unreasonable. The appeal would be dismissed.

B v B (MENTAL HEALTH PATIENT) [1979] 3 All ER 494 (Court of Appeal: MEGAW, LAWTON and BROWNE LJJ).

1839   Criminal procedure—interview by police of mentally subnormal person—necessity for presence of independent person during interview

See *R v Williams*, para. 680.

1840   Ill-treatment of patient in mental hospital—what constitutes ill-treatment

A mental nurse was charged with ill-treating a patient contrary to the Mental Health Act 1959, s. 126. The evidence showed that the ill-treatment consisted of one slap to the patient's face. The defence submitted that a single assault could not constitute ill-treatment, as it was necessary to show a course of conduct. *Held*, rejecting the submission, there was no need to show a course of conduct; a single act was sufficient to constitute ill-treatment.

R v HOLMES [1979] Crim LR 52 (Crown Court at Bodmin: JUDGE LAVINGTON).

MINES, MINERALS AND QUARRIES

Halsbury's Laws of England (4th edn.), Vol. 31, paras. 1–1000

1841   Coal industry—redundant workers—concessionary coal

The Redundant Mineworkers and Concessionary Coal (Payments Scheme) (Amendment) Order 1979, S.I. 1979 No. 385 (in force on 31st March 1979), further amends the Redundant Mineworkers Payments Scheme scheduled to the Redundant Mineworkers and Concessionary Coal (Payments Schemes) Order 1973, and the Redundant Mineworkers and Concessionary Coal Payments Scheme scheduled to the Redundant Mineworkers and Concessionary Coal (Payments Schemes) Order 1978, 1978 Halsbury's Abridgment para. 1897. The principal charge made is the addition of a new table of basic weekly benefit for those who become redundant on or after 6th April 1979, the minimum rate for both schemes now being £6·62.

1842   Continental shelf—designated areas

The Continental Shelf (Designation of Additional Areas) Order 1979, S.I. 1979 No. 1447 (made on 14th November 1979), designates further areas of the Continental Shelf in the northern North Sea as areas in which the rights of the United Kingdom with respect to the sea bed and subsoil and their natural resources may be exercised.

1843   Health and safety—coal mines—electric lighting for filming

The Coal and Other Mines (Electric Lighting for Filming) Regulations 1979, S.I. 1979 No. 1203 (in force on 20th October 1979), make provision for electric lighting for filming in mines of coal, stratified ironstone, shale and fireclay. The Regulations stipulate the circumstances in which lighting may be used and place duties on the manager of the mine in relation to the testing of equipment and the testing for the presence of flammable gas. The Regulations also supersede and revoke a number of Regulations which made similar provision for individual mines.

1844 Industrial disease—pneumoconiosis—workers' compensation

See Pneumoconiosis etc. (Workers' Compensation) Act 1979, para. 2650.

1845 Ironstone Restoration Fund

The Ironstone Restoration Fund (Standard Rate) Order 1979, S.I. 1979 No. 211 (in force on 1st April 1979), prescribes a standard rate of £782 per acre as the rate of payments to be made to ironstone operators in respect of the restoration of worked ironstone land in compliance with conditions of a planning permission.

1846 National Coal Board—borrowing powers

The Coal Industry (Borrowing Powers) Order 1979, S.I. 1979 No. 1012 (in force on 7th August 1979) increases the overall limit which the National Coal Board is empowered to borrow, temporarily or otherwise, under the Coal Industry Act 1965, s. 1, as amended, from £1,800 million to £2,200 million.

1847 Offshore installations—life-saving appliances

The Offshore Installations (Life-saving Appliances and Fire-fighting Equipment) (Amendment) Regulations 1979, S.I. 1979 No. 1023 (in force on 1st September 1979), amend the Offshore Installations (Life-saving Appliances) Regulations 1977, 1977 Halsbury's Abridgment para. 1862, by substituting a new table of rates for examination of life-saving appliances, higher than those previously set out. These Regulations revoke the Offshore Installations (Life-saving Appliances) (Amendment) Regulations 1978, 1978 Halsbury's Abridgment para. 1908.

1848 Opencast coal—compensation—rate of interest

The Opencast Coal (Rate of Interest on Compensation) Order 1979, S.I. 1979 No. 942 (in force on 4th September 1979), increases the rate of interest payable in addition to compensation under the Opencast Coal Act 1958, s. 35 from thirteen to fourteen and a half per cent. The Opencast Coal (Rate of Interest on Compensation) (No. 4) Order 1978, 1978 Halsbury's Abridgment para. 1911, is revoked.

1849 Safety in mines—precautions against inrushes

The Mines (Precautions Against Inrushes) Regulations 1979, S.I. 1979 No. 318 (in force on 9th April 1979), replace the existing provisions for controlling inrushes in mines, repeal the Mines and Quarries Act 1954, ss. 75 to 77 and revoke, inter alia, the Coal and Other Mines (Precautions Against Inrushes) Regulations 1956. The new regulations impose on owners and managers of mines duties to take precautions against inrushes of gas, water and material which flows or is likely to flow when wet.

MINORS

Halsbury's Laws of England (4th edn.), Vol. 24, paras. 401–900

1850 Articles

Abandonment of Children, W. T. West (meaning of "abandonment" in the light of *Wheatley v Waltham Forest LBC* [1979] 2 WLR 543, para. 1864): 123 Sol Jo 727.

Adoption; Minor Corrections and Major Innovation, J. F. Josling (provisions relating to adoption contained in the Domestic Proceedings and Magistrates' Courts Act 1978): 123 Sol Jo 74.

Changing A Child's Surname, F. Graham Glover (arguments for and against changing a child's surname on the mother's remarriage): 128 NLJ 1240.

Illegitimacy: Law Commission's Working Paper, Jennifer Levin (examination of the contents of the paper): 129 NLJ 672.

Intermediate Treatment (the legal structure of intermediate treatment: its origins and development, with an examination of some of the problems to which it gives rise in the courts): 143 JP Jo 431.

Judicial Discretion in Child-Snatching Cases, Godfrey Cole: 129 NLJ 64.

"Kidnapping" One's Own Child, D. W. Fox and A. N. Khan (a review of the courts attitude towards the "kidnapper" of his or her own child in the light of *Re C (minors)* [1978] 2 All ER 230, CA, 1977 Halsbury's Abridgment para. 1881): 9 Fam Law 68.

Magistrates' Courts, Children and the 1978 Act, M. D. A. Freeman (consideration of the new law relating to children in matrimonial proceedings contained in the Domestic Proceedings and Magistrates' Courts Act 1978, 1978 Halsbury's Abridgment para. 1509): 143 JP Jo 388.

The Nature of Care Proceedings (with particular reference to *Shropshire County Council v S (A Child)* (1975) (unreported), and *Humberside County Council v R* [1977] 3 All ER 964, 1977 Halsbury's Abridgment para. 1243): 9 Fam Law 60.

Parents Under Disability in the Juvenile Court, William Evans (the inadequacy of the facilities for legal representation of disadvantaged parents in care and similar proceedings): 129 NLJ 558.

Recent Developments in the Law Relating to Children, Martin L. Parry: 123 Sol Jo 526.

Remember *Re M?*, Vaughan Bevan (review of prerogative power of wardship in the light of recent cases): 9 Fam Law 170.

Retaining a Child in Care, M. D. A. Freeman (consideration of the effect of the Court of Appeal's decision in *Johns v Jones* [1978] 3 All ER 1222, 1978 Halsbury's Abridgment para. 1926): 129 NLJ 223.

Wardship of Court and the Chess Game (problem regarding wardship when the child involved is a Polish citizen): 129 NLJ 84.

Wardship and Kidnapping, G. Ritchie (a review of some cases involving the removal of children from the court's jurisdiction by one parent in a dispute over custody): 129 NLJ 873.

Who Cares? Some Comments on the Lewisham Case, M. D. A. Freeman (a questioning of the decision in *London Borough of Lewisham v Justices of Lewisham Juvenile Court* [1979] 1 All ER 297, HL, para. 1863): 129 NLJ 648.

1851 Access—access proceedings—duty of court making order to hear representations from local authority

At the hearing of an application for access to the children of a broken marriage the judge made a care order in favour of the local authority. The authority was not represented at the hearing and had had no opportunity to make representations. On appeal by the children's mother, *held*, the judge had no jurisdiction to make an order without allowing the local authority to make representations in accordance with the Matrimonial Causes Act 1973, s. 43 (2). The court had no alternative but to set the care order aside.

MONK v MONK [1979] LS Gaz 102 (Court of Appeal: ORR and ORMROD LJJ).

1852 —— order that access to be determined by welfare officer—appropriateness of order—court's responsibility in deciding issue

At the hearing of a father's application for access to the child of the family, only the welfare officer gave evidence. The judge adjourned the application and made an interim order that the father should have such supervised access to the child as the welfare officer should determine. The mother appealed against the order. *Held*, while it was quite proper for the welfare officer to have given evidence, it was unfair to leave the ultimate decision as to access to him. It was the court's responsibility to decide the issue of access and the appeal would be allowed on the merits of the case.

MNGUNI v MNGUNI (1979) 123 Sol Jo 859 (Court of Appeal: ORMROD and CUMMING-BRUCE LJJ and SIR DAVID CAIRNS).

1853   Adoption—order—refusal to perfect order—appeal—application for mandamus

See *R v Colchester and Clacton County Court, ex parte ADW and BAW*, para. 544.

1854   —— paramountcy of child's welfare—application by parent and step-parent

After separating from her husband, a wife gave birth to a boy whom the husband saw briefly at the nursing home. The marriage was dissolved two and a half years later and the mother of the child married a man whom she had been associated with since the child was aged six months. They applied to adopt the boy, and obtained the formal consent of the child's natural father. This consent was subsequently withdrawn by him. The application for adoption was turned down in the light of the Children Act 1975, s. 10 (3), 1975 Halsbury's Abridgment para. 1838, which provides that adoption in these circumstances should be permitted only if it advances the welfare of the child to a greater degree than existing arrangements. The mother and her husband appealed against the decision. *Held*, it would be in the best interests of the child to allow the adoption order to be made. Referring to an earlier case, *Re S* [1977] 3 All ER 671, CA, 1977 Halsbury's Abridgment para. 1871, where an application for adoption had been refused under s 10 (3), it was noted that the opinion of the judge had been that "adoption imposes an artificial status" where "custody recognises the reality of the situation". This opinion had been true of the earlier case, but in the present case the relationship of the boy to his stepfather had been the only paternal relationship he had known, and thus could not be seen as "artificial". Therefore in order to legalise the child's relationship with his stepfather and place it on the same footing as a normal family situation, it was acceptable to permit the adoption order to go through. With these aims in view it would be unreasonable of the boy's natural father to withhold his consent.

RE S (1978) 9 Fam Law 88 (Court of Appeal: STAMP, LAWTON and ORMROD LJJ).

1855   —— rules—county court

The Adoption (County Court) (Amendment) Rules 1979, S.I. 1979 No. 978 (in force on 3rd September 1979), amend the Adoption (County Court) Rules 1976, 1976 Halsbury's Abridgment para. 1747 by enabling an adoption application in respect of a child whose parents are divorced to be made to the divorce county court where the divorce was obtained.

1856   —— —— magistrates' court

The Magistrates' Courts (Adoption) (Amendment) Rules 1979, S.I. 1979 No. 1222 (in force on 1st November 1979), amend the Magistrates' Courts (Adoption) Rules 1976, 1976 Halsbury's Abridgment para. 1732 by transferring adoption proceedings from juvenile courts to domestic courts and by requiring adoption proceedings to be heard and determined in camera.

1857   Child—meaning—whether includes illegitimate child—interpretation of Bermuda Constitution

The defendant, a Bermudian, married the mother of four illegitimate children whom he accepted as children of his family on their arrival in Bermuda. In an action to prevent their deportation the defendant sought to establish that they "belonged to Bermuda" as his stepchildren under the Bermuda Constitution, s. 11 (5) (d). The plaintiffs contended however that "child" did not include illegitimate child for the purposes of the Constitution. The Bermuda Court of Appeal upheld the defendant's submission. On appeal, *held*, although the Constitution had been established by an English Act of Parliament, it had been influenced by the European Convention of Human Rights and interpretation had to be guided, therefore, by the principle of giving full recognition and effect to the fundamental rights and freedoms with which the Constitution was concerned. In that context the provision amounted to a clear recognition of the unity of the family as a group and acceptance of the principle that young children ought not to be separated from a group which as a whole "belonged to Bermuda". References to "child" therefore included an illegitimate child and the appeal would be dismissed.

MINISTER OF HOME AFFAIRS v FISHER [1979] 3 All ER 21 (Privy Council: LORD WILBERFORCE, LORD HAILSHAM OF ST MARYLEBONE, LORD SALMON, LORD FRASER OF TULLYBELTON and SIR WILLIAM DOUGLAS).

1858   Child care—assumption of parental rights and duties—local authority resolution

A local authority passed a resolution under the Children Act 1948, s. 2 (1), as substituted by the Children Act 1975, s. 57, vesting in themselves parental rights and duties in respect of three children, on the ground set out in s. 2 (1) (b) (v), i.e. that the parents had so consistently failed without reasonable cause to discharge the obligations of parents as to be unfit to have care of the children. The resolution was confirmed by the juvenile court. On appeal by the parents, *held*, under s. 2 (1) (b) (v) the obligations of a parent included the natural and moral duty of a parent to show affection, care and interest towards his child and also the common law or statutory duty to maintain his child financially. Failure to discharge those obligations had to be culpable to a high degree, e.g. as evidenced by some callous or self-indulgent indifference to the child's welfare, and for a parent to have consistently failed to discharge those obligations it had to be shown that his behaviour over a period had constantly adhered to the pattern of which complaint was made. In determining whether such a failure was without reasonable cause, the court should look to see whether the cause was reasonable or unreasonable according to what a reasonable parent would have done in all the circumstances. In the instant case the evidence supported the juvenile court's conclusion, and the appeal would be dismissed.

M v WIGAN METROPOLITAN BOROUGH COUNCIL [1979] 2 All ER 958 (Family Division: SIR GEORGE BAKER P and SHELDON J). *Re P (Infants)* [1962] 3 All ER 789, *Re C (an infant)* [1964] 3 All ER 483 and *Re D (minors)* [1973] 3 All ER 1001 applied.

1859   —— care and protection—care order

Two children were made wards of court under the supervision of the local authority. The children were later committed to the care of the local authority and the grandparents were granted staying access at weekends and in school holidays. The grandfather's appeal was dismissed by the Court of Appeal and the access arrangements deleted. The House of Lords restored the order and returned the matter to the Family Division for reconsideration of the changed circumstances. The mother and grandfather sought care and control. *Held*, the mother was now a stable person with full-time employment and a home for the children. It would therefore be appropriate to grant care and control to the mother with reasonable access by the grandfather and a supervision order would be made in favour of the local authority.

B v W [1979] LS Gaz R 1131 (Family Division: DUNN J).

For the proceedings relating to wardship see *B v W (wardship: appeal)* [1979] 3 All ER 83, HL, para. 1877.

1860   —— —— —— application by local authority—development of children threatened

The father, a serving soldier, was granted custody of his two children in divorce proceedings. In March 1974 he voluntarily put the children into the care of the county council because he was posted to Hong Kong. The children lived with foster parents until March 1976 when the father, now stationed in Northern Ireland, wished to re-marry and take the children to live with himself and his new wife in Northern Ireland. The council sought a care order in the juvenile court, believing that it was not in the interests of the children to be uprooted. The registrar held that the children's proper development was not being unavoidably prevented or neglected within the meaning of the Children and Young Persons Act 1969, s. 1 (2) (a) and that accordingly a care order could not be granted. On appeal, *held*, that section of the Act was only concerned with presently existing events and not future events, no matter how imminent those events might be. The decision of the registrar would be upheld and the county council's appeal dismissed.

ESSEX COUNTY COUNCIL v TLR AND KBR (1978) 9 Fam Law 15 (Queen's Bench Division: LORD WIDGERY CJ, KILNER BROWN and ROBERT GOFF JJ).

1861   —— —— —— —— parent's right of cross-examination

A local authority applied to take a child into care. It was alleged that the mother had attempted to poison the child by giving him too much salt. At the magistrates' court the child and his parents were separately represented. The mother applied for a preliminary ruling on whether she could cross-examine the local authority's witnesses. The justices ruled that she had no right to cross-examine and she applied for a judicial review on the ground that the court had an inherent jurisdiction to permit the cross-examination in the interests of justice. *Held*, under the Magistrates' Courts (Children and Young Persons) Rules 1970, r. 14B, in care proceedings a parent, although not a party to the proceedings, had the power to defend himself by calling or giving evidence. Although the right of cross-examination was omitted in r. 14B, the justices had the power to allow cross-examination in so far as it was a necessary ancillary to the right of a parent to meet the challenge against him by calling or giving evidence.

R v MILTON KEYNES JJ, EX PARTE R [1979] 1 WLR 1062 (Queen's Bench Division: LORD WIDGERY CJ, MICHAEL DAVIES and NEILL JJ).

1862   —— children in care of local authority—independent welfare report

The mother of seven children by five different fathers had led an unstable life and all the children were taken into care at an early age. The two youngest, now aged eleven and nine years old, were taken into care in 1975 when the mother had a nervous breakdown. They lived in a residential home and visited their mother regularly. The local authority sought to place the children with foster parents and the mother made them wards of court and sought care and control of them. *Held*, the children were intelligent and mature and had expressed views on their future. It was important for the court to have a reliable account of their views, the weight to be placed on them depending on the circumstances of the case. The interests of the children would be best served by an independent welfare report. Such a report having been made, it would be in the children's best interests if the authority's proposal were carried out. They should remain wards of court in the authority's care and the mother should have access to them at the authority's discretion.

RE A (MINORS) (1979) 123 Sol Jo 553 (Family Division: DUNN J).

1863   —— recovery of child in care—notice by parent

On 12th July 1977, a child was taken into care by a local authority with his mother's consent under the Children Act 1948, s. 1 (1). On 18th April 1978, the mother gave written notice to the authority of her desire to resume the care of the child in a month's time. On 25th April 1978, the authority passed a resolution assuming parental rights and duties in respect of the child under the 1948 Act, s. 2 (1), which authorises the passing of such a resolution in relation to a child in the authority's care. Notice of the resolution was served on the mother, who served a counter-notice. The authority complained to the juvenile court, which held that it had no jurisdiction to hear the complaint. The Divisional Court dismissed an application by the authority for an order of mandamus requiring the juvenile court to hear the complaint, and the authority's appeal was dismissed. All the courts held that they were bound to hold that the authority had had no power under s. 2 to pass the resolution because the child had ceased to be in care as soon as the mother's notice of 18th April 1978 was received. On further appeal, *held*, the 1948 Act, s. 1 (3), provided that an authority was not authorised to keep a child taken into care under

s. 1 (1) if its parent or guardian desired to take over the care. Thus where the parent demanded the return of the child, the authority had no legal right to retain the child in care under s. 1, where it had been in care for less than six months. However, the child would continue to be in care until the parent removed him and until then the authority would have the power to pass a resolution under s. 2. Where, as in this case, a child had been in care for six months or more, s. 1 (3A) provided that a parent had to give at least twenty-eight days' notice of his intention to take away the child. A child did not cease automatically to be in the authority's care from the moment when the parent notified the authority of his intention, but remained in care at least until the month expired and probably until the parent came to take the child away. Hence the child was in care under s. 1 at the time when the authority passed the resolution, and the resolution was valid. The appeal would be allowed.

LONDON BOROUGH OF LEWISHAM V LEWISHAM JUVENILE COURT JUSTICES [1979] 2 All ER 297 (House of Lords: LORD WILBERFORCE, VISCOUNT DILHORNE, LORD SALMON, LORD KEITH OF KINKEL and LORD SCARMAN). *Johns v Jones* [1978] 3 All ER 1222, CA, 1978 Halsbury's Abridgment para. 1926 overruled.

1864   On 17th December 1976, a child was taken into care by a local authority under the Children Act 1948, s. 1 (1). On 6th July 1977, the mother gave written notice to the authority of her desire to resume the care of the child in a month's time. On 20th July 1977, the authority passed a resolution assuming parental rights and duties in respect of the child under the 1948 Act, s. 2 (1), which authorises the passing of such a resolution in certain circumstances in relation to a child in the authority's care. Notice of the resolution was served on the mother, who served a counternotice. The authority complained to the juvenile court, which made an order that the resolution should not lapse. On appeal by the mother, *held*, it was contended that the authority had no power to pass the resolution because the child had ceased to be in care as soon as the mother's notice of her desire to resume care was received. The 1948 Act, s. 1 (3A), made it a criminal offence for a parent to take away a child in care before the expiration of twenty-eight days from the date of her notice of her intention to do so, if the child had been in care throughout the preceding six months. Thus a child remained in care after receipt of the notice for at least twenty-eight days subsequently. Accordingly, the child was in care at the time the resolution was made, and the authority had power to make it. However, it had not been proved that the mother had so consistently failed without reasonable cause to discharge the obligations of a parent as to be unfit to have the care of the child, as required by s. 2 (1), and accordingly the appeal would be allowed and the resolution would lapse.

WHEATLEY V LONDON BOROUGH OF WALTHAM FOREST [1979] 2 WLR 543 (Family Division: SIR GEORGE BAKER P and WATERHOUSE J).

1865   ### Children and Young Persons Act 1969—transitional modifications

The Children and Young Persons Act 1969 (Transitional Modifications of Part I) Order 1979, S.I. 1979 No. 125 (in force on 1st March 1979), excludes the application of the Children and Young Persons Act 1969, ss. 23 (2), (3), which provide for the committal of young people to prison, to girls under the age of 17.

1866   ### Custody—order—breach of order—removal from jurisdiction— effect of contempt on party's appeal

A care order was made concerning the parties' five children. Care of the elder three boys was committed to the father, and care of the younger two boys to the mother. The children were made wards of court and it was further ordered that they should not be taken out of the jurisdiction without the authority of the court or the consent of the parents. The father subsequently took all five children to Sicily. There was no indication that he intended to bring them back. The father appealed in respect of the order as to the elder of the two boys whose care was committed to the mother. The father, being in breach of the order and therefore in contempt, recognised that he was not entitled to pursue his appeal, but submitted that the proper course was for the court to stand over the appeal that he might have an opportunity of purging his contempt by bringing the children back. *Held*, there was no useful purpose to be served by standing over the appeal. It was apparent that, if and when the father returned to England with the children, the situation would be quite different from that which the judge at first instance had been confronted with. It was clear that a completely new situation had arisen which was one which ought to be dealt with by a judge of first instance. Further, there was no indication that the father had any intention of bringing the children back to the jurisdiction and, therefore, no indication of any intention to purge the contempt. Accordingly, the appeal would be dismissed.

RE A MINOR (1979) 9 Fam Law 151 (Court of Appeal: LORD SCARMAN, STAMP and ORR LJJ). *Hadkinson v Hadkinson* [1952] 2 All ER 567, CA, considered.

1867   —— paramountcy of child's welfare—advice of welfare officer not followed

The parties were married for a period of five years, during which time they had a child, a boy now five years old. The mother left the home and went to live with another man, and custody of the child was given to the father owing to the uncertainty of her domestic arrangements. The father, unable to cope with the child on his own, went to live with his parents, taking the child with him. He proposed to marry a young woman later. Meanwhile the wife had secured her relationship with her cohabitee, whom she intended marrying as soon as she was free to do so. In view of this she was awarded custody of the child. The husband appealed. *Held*, despite the fact that all four people concerned were evidently anxious to do all that was best for the child, and though the welfare officer advised awarding the father custody of him, it was to be presumed that a child of so few years had greater need of his mother than of his father. Furthermore, the mother's immediate future was of a more stable nature than that offered by the father, and so could give the child greater security. It was also felt that a feeling of bitterness and unfairness existed in the attitude of the father towards the mother which tended to favour the mother. The appeal would therefore be dismissed.

J v J (1978) 9 Fam Law 91 (Court of Appeal: ORMROD and BRIDGE LJJ).

1868   —— —— application for joint custody

Canada

The parties were married in 1964 and their son was born in 1970. Financial difficulties arose shortly afterwards due to the child's ill health. The wife then developed emotional and physical problems and excessive alcohol intake resulted in her being unable to cope with domestic responsibilities. The marriage deteriorated and the husband petitioned for divorce in 1976. The wife cross-petitioned on grounds of cruelty and both parties claimed custody of the child. The wife's cross-petition was granted by the trial judge who held that as both parties appreciated their role in the child's life and were qualified to give him affection and guidance, joint custody would be awarded with the mother having care and control and the father having liberal access. The husband appealed. *Held*, from the facts it did not appear that the parties were willing and able to co-operate as loving parents. The court had to take a realistic and practical approach to joint custody and limit it to exceptional circumstances which were rarely present in cases of disputed custody. It might be encouraged as a voluntary alternative for relatively stable amicable partners behaving maturely but should not be considered when those conditions were not present. The trial judge should have asked which parent would best promote the child's welfare instead of starting from the presumption that both parties were fit parents entitled to joint custody. Further, as the other issues central to the petition had not been adequately dealt with, the case would be remitted for rehearing.

BAKER V BAKER (1979) 95 DLR (3d) 529 (Court of Appeal of Ontario).

1869   —— —— impression made by father

The marriage of the husband and wife failed after four years during which time a child, now four and a half years old, had been born. The mother left the matrimonial home and went to live with her parents, taking the child with her. The father was in the Army but intending to leave it in eighteen months' time. He had difficulty in gaining access to the child while she was in the care of the mother, and partly on account of this and also because he had created a favourable impression of his ability to look after the child, he was awarded custody. The mother appealed. *Held*, since the mother was naturally better equipped to administer to the needs of her child, and further, since the child had spent her whole life with the mother, custody should be awarded to her. The reasons for giving custody to the father, however good and capable a man he was, were insufficient as compared with the needs of the child which were paramount. Difficulties of access could be resolved through orders of court. The appeal would therefore be allowed.

M v M (1978) 9 Fam Law 92 (Court of Appeal: STAMP, ORMROD and BRIDGE LJJ).

1870   Employment—contract—whether beneficial to minor—right of adult party to enforce

Canada

A seventeen-year-old amateur hockey player contracted to play for an amateur hockey club for several years and to pay the club 20 per cent of his earnings in his first three years as a professional. The club also had other rights under the contract, including the right to terminate it at any time. When he reached the age of eighteen, the player repudiated the contract and entered into an agreement with a professional club. The amateur club brought an action for damages but the contract was held to be voidable at the player's option. On appeal, *held*, a contract of service could only be enforced against a minor if it had been made for his benefit; the burden of proving the benefit was on the adult party. The contract in question was clearly not beneficial to the player and accordingly neither he nor his agent were liable in damages to the amateur club.

TORONTO MARLBORO MAJOR JUNIOR "A" HOCKEY CLUB v TONELLI (1979) 23 OR (2d) 193 (Court of Appeal of Ontario).

1871   Guardianship—proceedings—magistrates' court—variation of custody order—justices' reasons

A husband and wife were divorced in 1978. Custody of the two young children of the marriage was granted to the husband, who had remarried, as the wife was in severe financial difficulties. In 1979, the wife successfully applied for variation of the custody order, as her circumstances had improved. The husband appealed. *Held*, the justices, in supplying reasons to justify their decision, had endeavoured to answer criticisms made in the grounds of appeal. That was throughly bad practice. The justices were not required to see the notice of appeal, and if they did see the notice they should not be influenced by its contents in formulating the reasons. By attempting to answer the points raised in the grounds of appeal the justices were entering the arena. However, looking at the evidence as a whole, the justices had not come to a wrong decision, and the appeal would be dismissed.

FAULKNER v FAULKNER (1979) 123 Sol Jo 751 (Family Division: SIR JOHN ARNOLD P and BOOTH J).

1872   Juvenile courts—constitution

The Juvenile Courts (Constitution) (Amendment) Rules 1979, S.I. 1979 No. 952 (in force on 1st October 1979), amend the Juvenile Courts (Constitution) Rules 1954 by providing that members of a juvenile court panel commence their service from 1st January following the date of their appointment.

1873   —— proceedings against minor—attainment of full age during proceedings

See *R v Billericay JJ ex parte Johnson*, para. 1796.

1874   —— —— **intention to commit criminal offence—child aged eleven**

Two boys aged eleven and thirteen visited a car showroom where the elder intended to prove that he could drive. He reversed a car into a sliding door, damaging both the car and the door. The boys were jointly charged with taking a conveyance and with criminal damage, and the elder admitted both charges. The younger was convicted on the ground that he had in no way discouraged his friend or dissociated himself from his action. On appeal, *held*, although the younger child was a party to a joint taking, the prosecution had failed to establish that he took part with the necessary intent. This was particularly important in this case because the boy had only just reached the age of criminal responsibility. The appeal would be allowed.

C v Hume [1979] Crim LR 328 (Queen's Bench Division: Eveleigh LJ and Stephen Brown J).

1875   **Legal proceedings—proceedings on behalf of minor—action by next friend—whether minor entitled to commence fresh action within extended limitation period**

See *Tolley v Morris*, para. 2169.

1876   **Magistrates' courts—guardianship**

The Magistrates' Courts (Guardianship of Minors) (Amendment) Rules 1979, S.I. 1979 No. 953 (in force on 17th September 1979), amend the Magistrates' Courts (Guardianship of Minors) Rules 1974, 1974 Halsbury's Abridgment para. 1737, in consequence of the Domestic Proceedings and Magistrates Courts Act 1978, s. 40, relating to access to minors by grandparents.

1877   **Wardship—access to ward—variation of order—grounds for variation**

Conflict arose between the parents and grandparents of two children concerning their upbringing. The grandfather applied to have the children made wards of court. The application was granted and the children were put in the care of the local authority. It was ordered that they attend a certain school and spend weekends and school holidays with the grandparents. The Court of Appeal varied the order by deleting the provisions granting the grandparents weekend and holiday access. On appeal by the grandfather, *held*, the question was whether the Court of Appeal was entitled to vary the order. It should not have done so unless it was clearly satisfied that the judge was wrong. Unlike the judge, the Court of Appeal had taken a very hostile view of the grandfather and were especially influenced by a letter to the court from a social worker, which criticised the grandfather. The existence and terms of the letter were unknown to the grandfather and his advisers and in relying on it the Court of Appeal acted irregularly and unjustly. It was not possible to say that the judge's access order was wrong. The appeal would be allowed and the original order restored.

B v W (Wardship: Appeal) [1979] 3 All ER 83 (House of Lords: Lord Diplock, Viscount Dilhorne, Lord Edmund-Davies, Lord Keith of Kinkel and Lord Scarman). Dicta of Viscount Simon LC in *Charles Osenton & Co v Johnston* [1941] 2 All ER at 250 and Lord Wright in *Evans v Bartlam* [1937] 2 All ER at 654 applied.

1878   —— **application—existing care order—jurisdiction of High Court**

Two children were made subject to care orders under the Children and Young Persons Act 1969, s. 1. The mother had access to one of the children but the local authority became concerned about the effect on the child of the mother's visits and decided that there should be no further access. With a view to overturning the authority's decision and securing rights of access to the children, the mother issued a wardship summons. The judge refused to exercise the court's prerogative jurisdiction in wardship by way of a review of the merits of the authority's decision taken in exercise of its statutory discretion under the 1969 Act. The court would only interfere if the authority had acted improperly or in excess of its jurisdiction. On appeal, *held*, the judge's decision would be upheld and the appeal dismissed.

RE W (MINORS) (WARDSHIP: JURISDICTION) [1979] 3 All ER 154 (Court of Appeal: ORMROD, BROWNE and BRIDGE LJJ). *Re M (an infant)* [1961] Ch 328, CA and *Re T (AJJ) (an infant)* [1970] Ch 688, CA applied.

1879   The father and mother had a child in January 1975. In 1976 the father left the mother and child and went to live with another woman. In 1978 the mother assaulted the child causing severe bruising, as a result of which the local authority obtained a place of safety order in respect of the child. The local authority then instituted care proceedings and obtained an interim care order from the juvenile court. The father applied to the magistrates' court for, inter alia, an order for custody of the child, which was refused. He then applied by summons to the High Court for an order that the child be made a ward of the court and that care, custody and control be given to him. On a question of whether the High Court could exercise its wardship jurisdiction, *held*, although a juvenile court could not make a custody order in care proceedings, the magistrates' court could have made such an order if it felt it was in the best interests of the child to do so. The High Court would only exercise its wardship jurisdiction where the powers of the lower court were inadequate, or where there had been some irregularity or excess in the powers of the local authority or where there were special circumstances necessitating its intervention. In the present case there was no reason for the High Court to exercise its discretion as the case was straightforward and disclosed no unusual features. The summons would accordingly be dismissed.

M v HUMBERSIDE COUNTY COUNCIL [1979] 2 All ER 744 (Family Division: SIR GEORGE BAKER P). *Re T (AJJ) (an infant)* [1970] 2 All ER 865, CA applied.

1880   ——jurisdiction—existing care order

See *Re W (Minors) (Wardship: Jurisdiction)*, para. 1878 and *M v Humberside CC*, para. 1879.

1881   ——proceedings—address for service—servicemen

See para. 2135.

1882   —— —— court's   jurisdiction   to   grant   non-molestation and exclusion orders

The parties married in February 1976 and a child, who was not the husband's child, was born two months later. In wardship proceedings, the child was made a ward of court and care and custody was granted to the wife. The husband was ordered not to molest the wife, who returned to the matrimonial home with the child. The husband assaulted the wife who then applied in the wardship proceedings for an injunction to restrain him. The husband sought to exclude his wife from the matrimonial home and also sought a non-molestation order. *Held*, under its wardship jurisdiction the court had the power to grant an injunction restraining the husband or father from molesting the mother, if this was in the interests of the child. It did not however have any power to make an order excluding the mother from the matrimonial home; such an application should be made under the Domestic Violence and Matrimonial Proceedings Act 1976 or the Matrimonial Homes Act 1967. The husband had assaulted the mother and it was in the interests of the child that he be excluded from the matrimonial home and such an order would be granted.

RE V (A MINOR) (1979) 123 Sol Jo 201 (Family Division: SIR GEORGE BAKER P).

1883   ——removal of ward from jurisdiction—effect of contempt on party's appeal

See *Re A Minor*, para. 1866.

MISREPRESENTATION AND FRAUD

Halsbury's Laws of England (4th edn.), Vol. 31, paras. 1001–1137

1884   Article

Mis-statement and the Unfair Contract Terms Act 1977, John R. Murdoch (provisions of 1977 Act governing use of exemption clauses and their effect upon the exclusion of liability for misrepresentation): 129 NLJ 4.

1885   Deceit—action for damages—plaintiff entering into invalid marriage as result of fraudulent misrepresentation

Canada

The plaintiff and the defendant went through a form of marriage in 1970. The defendant represented himself to be a bachelor, but was already married. The plaintiff did not discover until 1976 that the previous marriage had not been dissolved. In 1971, the plaintiff had a hysterectomy operation as the result of a miscarriage. She claimed special damages for a sum of money that she had given the defendant whilst believing him to be her husband and general damages for injury to her character and person because of the defendant's deceit and assaults by way of sexual intercourse to which she consented due to his misrepresentation that she was his lawful wife. *Held*, as a result of the deceit of the defendant, the plaintiff's prospects of a proper marriage had been seriously prejudiced, she had suffered a hysterectomy and she had lost a claim to maintenance that she would have had had the marriage been valid. Accordingly, damages would be awarded.

BEAULNE v RICKETTS [1979] 3 WWR 270 (Supreme Court of Alberta).

1886   Fraud—action for damages—plaintiff in breach of exchange control provisions—effect

See *Shelley v Paddock*, para. 1903.

MISTAKE

Halsbury's Laws of England (4th edn.), Vol. 32, paras. 1–101

1887   Article

Over-crediting a Customer's Account and Estoppel, S. Dilwar Hussain (application of estoppel against a bank when it mistakenly over-credits a customer's account): 122 Sol Jo 837.

1888   Mistake of fact—recovery of money paid under mistake of fact—payment of cheque by bank—cheque previously stopped by drawer

A customer of a bank drew a cheque in favour of a building company in payment of a debt. He later instructed the bank to stop the cheque, but due to an oversight by an employee it was paid. The bank brought an action for repayment of the amount as money paid under a mistake of fact. *Held*, where a person paid money to another under a mistake of fact which caused him to make the payment, he was prima facie entitled to recover it as money paid under a mistake of fact; however, his claim would fail if (i) he intended that the payee should have the money at all events; (ii) the payment was made for good consideration, in particular in discharge of a debt; or (iii) the payee had changed his position in good faith or was deemed in law to have done so. Where a bank paid, under a mistake of fact, a cheque drawn on it by a customer, it was prima facie entitled to recover payment from the payee if it had acted without mandate, such as overlooking a notice of countermand, and the payee had not in good faith changed his position or was not deemed in law to have done so. The defendants contended that since the bank had failed to give notice of its claim on the day when the cheque was paid, they had been deprived of giving notice of dishonour on that day and so should be deemed to have changed their position. However, under the Bills of Exchange Act 1882, s. 50 (2) (c), notice of dishonour was dispensed with as regards the drawer where the drawer countermanded payment. Hence in the case of a simple unindorsed cheque, payment of which had been countermanded, notice of dishonour was not required and the defence in question was not available. Therefore since there was no actual or deemed change of position by the defendants, the bank was entitled to succeed.

BARCLAYS BANK LTD v W. J. SIMMS SON & COOKE (SOUTHERN) LTD [1979] 3 All ER 522 (Queen's Bench Division: ROBERT GOFF J). *Kleinwort, Sons & Co v Dunlop Rubber Co* (1907) 97 LT 263, *Kerrison v Glyn, Mills Currie & Co* [1911–13] All ER Rep 417, *RE Jones Ltd v Waring & Gillow Ltd* [1926] All ER Rep 36, *Aiken v Short* [1843–60] All ER Rep 425 and dictum of Parke B in *Kelly v Solari* [1835–42] All ER Rep at 322 applied.

1889   —— —— right to trace and recover

See *Chase Manhattan Bank NA v Israel British Bank (London) Ltd*, para. 1136.

1890   Mistake of law—overpayment to shareholders by liquidator in winding up—whether recoverable

See *Taylor v Wilson's Trustees*, para. 380.

1891   Rectification—common intention of parties—legitimate avoidance of tax—whether a bar to relief

The first plaintiff was entitled as a residuary legatee to the proceeds of the sale of land to a development company. A management company was set up to facilitate the transaction with the development company, and the various beneficiaries of the proceeds of the sale were allotted shares in the management company. The first plaintiff purported to surrender her life interest in the proceeds of the sale to the second and third plaintiffs, in order to avoid the payment of capital transfer tax. But her solicitor erroneously believed that the shares in the management company carried with them the beneficial interest, and he drew up a deed which transferred the shares only, without the beneficial interest. The plaintiffs issued a summons seeking rectification of the deed to give effect to their common intention. *Held*, the court would order rectification of the deed. The common intention of the parties was the legitimate avoidance of tax, and it would be an incorrect exercise of the court's discretion to refuse rectification merely because it would deprive the Crown of tax.

RE SLOCOCK'S WILL TRUSTS [1979] 1 All ER 358 (Chancery Division: GRAHAM J).

1892   Unilateral mistake—mistake of subject matter of contract—incidence of loss

A dispute arose over the contract for sale of copper cable between the defendants, a company carrying on business in the United Arab Emirates, and the plaintiffs, a company in the United Kingdom. The defendants wished to sell electric cable to the plaintiffs. There were two varieties of copper cable and each party believed that they had entered into the contract of sale with the other and the goods shipped conformed with the requirements of the contract. The defendants however believed they were selling one type of cable whilst the plaintiffs believed they were buying another type. The situation arose through misunderstanding on both sides and the purpose of the action was to decide who should bear the resulting loss. Two issues arose: (i) whether there was an ostensible contract for goods of any description; (ii) if there was an ostensible contract, whether it was void on the grounds of unilateral mistake of fact. *Held*, on the evidence of the complex correspondence given there was an ostensible contract between the parties but the contract was subject to such latent ambiguities that it was void for mistake and it was probable that the parties were at cross purposes from the beginning. Where both parties made mistakes it seemed hard that the plaintiffs alone should bear the loss but there was no rule of equity to apportion the loss.

HARIS AL-AFAQ LTD v CAMERON DEMPSEY AND IVY LTD (1979) 15th November (unreported) (Queen's Bench Division: MUSTILL J). *Scriven Brothers & Co v Hindley & Co* [1913] 3 KB 564 distinguished.

MONEY AND MONEYLENDERS

Halsbury's Laws of England (4th edn.), Vol. 32, paras. 101–401

1893   Article

The Floating Pound, Alan Greenwood (effect of devaluation of the pound on recognition given to foreign currencies by the English courts): 129 NLJ 23.

1894   Asian Development Bank—replenishment of Asian Development Fund

The Asian Development Bank (Second Replenishment of the Asian Development Fund) Order 1979, S.I. 1979 No. 1225 (in force on 10th October 1979), provides for the payment to the Asian Development Fund, established in 1973 by Resolution of the Governors of the Asian Development Bank, of a sum of £55,172,379 as a contribution by way of the second replenishment of the Fund and of a sum of £4,158,987 as a supplementary contribution. The Order also provides for the redemption of non-interest-bearing and non-negotiable notes issued by the Minister of Overseas Development in payment of the contribution and supplementary contribution. It is further provided that any sums which may be received by the Government of the United Kingdom in pursuance of the arrangements are to be paid into the Consolidated Fund.

1895   Borrowing control

The Control of Borrowing (Amendment) Order 1979, S.I. 1979 No. 794 (in force on 3rd August 1979), further amends the Control of Borrowing Order 1958, S.I. 1958 No. 1208. Issues of sterling securities by or on behalf of an open ended investment trust company (as defined in the Order), which is resident in the scheduled territories but outside the United Kingdom, are exempted from borrowing control under Part I of the 1958 Order.

1896   Counter-inflation

See EMERGENCY CONTROLS.

1897   Deposits—control of deposit-taking institutions

See Banking Act 1979, para. 192.

1898   European Monetary System

See Cmnd. 7419, para. 1203.

1899   Exchange control—authorised dealers and depositaries

The Exchange Control (Authorised Dealers and Depositaries) (Amendment) Order 1979, S.I. 1979 No. 321 (in force on 2nd April 1979), amends the lists of the banks and other persons authorised under the Exchange Control Act 1947 to deal in gold and foreign currencies, and those who are entitled to act as authorised depositaries for the purpose of the deposit of securities as required by that Act.

1900   The Exchange Control (Authorised Dealers and Depositaries) (Amendment) (No. 2) Order 1979, S.I. 1979 No. 740 (in force on 13th July 1979), amends the lists of those persons authorised under the Exchange Control Act 1947 to deal in gold and foreign currencies and those who are entitled to act as authorised depositaries for the purpose of the deposit of securities as required by that Act.

1901   The Exchange Control (Authorised Dealers and Depositaries) (Amendment) (No. 3) Order 1979, S.I. 1979 No. 1194 (in force on 2nd October 1979) further amends the Exchange Control (Authorised Dealers and Depositaries) Order 1978, 1978 Halsbury's Abridgment para. 1954 in relation to the lists of banks and other persons authorised under the Exchange Control Act 1947 to deal in gold and foreign currencies and those who are entitled to act as authorised depositaries for the purpose of the deposit of securities as required by the Act.

1902   The Exchange Control (Authorised Dealers and Depositaries) (Amendment) (No. 4) Order 1979, S.I. 1979 No. 1338 (in force on 24th October 1979) further amends the Exchange Control (Authorised Dealers and Depositaries) Order 1978, 1978 Halsbury's Abridgment para. 1954. Authorised dealers in gold and foreign currency no longer have special functions under the Exchange Control Act 1947, ss. 1 (1) and 2 (1) and thus cease to be authorised dealers. Authorised depositaries continue to have that status though they no longer have any special functions under ss. 15 and 16 of the Act.

1903   —— **breach—effect on action for damages for fraud**
The plaintiff agreed to buy a house in Spain from the defendants, who represented that they were agents to sell the house for the owner. The plaintiff paid a cash deposit in Spain to the defendants, in contravention of the Exchange Control Act 1947. She subsequently paid the balance of the purchase price into the defendants' own bank account in England, contravening both the 1947 Act and Treasury requirements, of which she was totally unaware. On learning that the defendants could not give her any title to the house, the plaintiff began an action in tort for the recovery of her money as damages for fraud. The trial judge found that as the plaintiff's breaches of the 1947 Act were the result of her ignorance of the Act, public policy did not prevent her from being awarded compensation for the defendants' fraud. The defendants appealed. *Held*, the principle that a plaintiff founding a cause of action on an illegal act could not recover damages in an action for fraud did not apply, as the defendants had swindled the plaintiff from the beginning, she did not participate in the fraud, and the parties were not in pari delicto. Accordingly, the appeal would be dismissed.
      SHELLEY v PADDOCK (1979) 123 Sol Jo 706 (Court of Appeal: LORD DENNING MR, BRANDON and BRIGHTMAN LJJ). Decision of Bristow J [1978] 3 All ER 126, 1978 Halsbury's Abridgment para. 1957 affirmed. *Kiriri Cotton Co Ltd v Dewani* [1960] AC 192 applied, *Helman v Johnson* (1775) 1 Cowp 341 distinguished.
      Exchange control restrictions have now been lifted: see para. 1908.

1904   —— **contract contrary to Peruvian exchange regulations—enforceability**
A Peruvian company contracted to buy a glass fibre forming plant from a British company. On receiving a quotation of the price the Peruvians asked that the estimate be doubled and that they be allowed to pay the surplus in United States dollars to another company with an office in Miami. When the British company attempted to enforce payment the Peruvians claimed that the contract was unenforceable because it involved a breach of the Bretton Woods Agreements as to exchange controls, which were incorporated into the law of both countries and prohibited exchange contracts which were contrary to the regulations of any member country. Peruvian law prohibited the maintaining or establishment of deposits in a foreign currency in banks in Peru or abroad and made it an offence of fraud to overvalue imports and obligations payable in foreign currency. *Held*, the

purpose of the contract had obviously been to get money out of Peru unlawfully, and the fact that the British company had been prepared to double its quotation and to allow payment of the surplus money to the Miami company showed that it was prepared to ignore the true nature of the transaction. The agreement was undoubtedly an exchange contract in disguise and the court could not enforce it because to do so would be to evade the Bretton Woods Agreements.

THE AMERICAN ACCORD, UNITED CITY MERCHANTS (INVESTMENTS) LTD V ROYAL BANK OF CANADA [1979] 1 Lloyds Rep 267 (Queen's Bench Division: MOCATTA J).

1905 —— directions—revocation

The Exchange Control (Revocation) Directions 1979, S.I. 1979 No. 1339 (in force on 24th October 1979) revoke all directions at present in force under the Exchange Control Act 1947, ss. 26, 34 (2), 40 and 41 (2) except the Exchange Control (Branches and Residence) Directions 1951, art. 2 and the Exchange Control (Reserve Bank of Rhodesia) (Residence) Directions 1966.

1906 —— —— —— Southern Rhodesia

The Exchange Control (Revocation) (No. 2) Directions 1979, S.I. 1979 No. 1662 (in force on 13th December 1979) revoke the Exchange Control (Exports to Southern Rhodesia) Directions 1965 and the Exchange Control (Reserve Bank of Rhodesia) (Residence) Directions 1966, thus completing the removal of all exchange control restrictions.

1907 The Control of Gold and Treasury Bills (Southern Rhodesia) (Revocation) Directions 1979, S.I. 1979 No. 1661 (in force on 13th December 1979) revoke the Control of Gold and Treasury Bills (Southern Rhodesia) Directions 1965. Controls on gold and treasury bills to Southern Rhodesia have now been abolished.

1908 —— exemptions

The Exchange Control (General Exemption) Order 1979, S.I. 1979 No. 1660 (in force on 13th December 1979) abolishes all obligations and prohibitions imposed by or under the Exchange Control Act 1947, following the lifting of sanctions imposed in relation to Southern Rhodesia. Earlier orders, which had granted exemptions except in relation to Southern Rhodesia, have been revoked.

1909 —— —— corporate bodies

The Exchange Control (Bodies Corporate) (Exemption) Order 1979, S.I. 1979 No. 1337 (in force on 24th October 1979) has the effect that the Exchange Control Act 1947, s. 30 (2) now only prohibits acts done with intent to secure that a corporate body controlled by residents of the United Kingdom becomes controlled by residents of Southern Rhodesia. Complete exemption is granted from the provisions of s. 30 (3) (permission required for a loan to a resident corporate body controlled by non-residents) and s. 30 (3A) (permission required for a non-resident corporate body to issue or negotiate financial instruments).

The Exchange Control (Non-resident Controlled Banks) (Exemption) Order 1977, 1977 Halsbury's Abridgment para. 1909 is revoked.

This Order has been revoked; see para. 1908.

1910 —— —— gold and foreign currency

The Exchange Control (Gold and Foreign Currency) (Exemption) Order 1979, S.I. 1979 No. 1331 (in force on 24th October 1979) exempts from the provisions of the Exchange Control Act 1947, s. 1 the buying, borrowing, selling and lending of gold and foreign currency other than Southern Rhodesian currency, subject to the condition that such gold or foreign currency is not used in connection with payments to Southern Rhodesian residents. The order also provides that ss. 2 (surrender of gold and foreign currency), 3 (bailees of gold and foreign currency) and 4 (4) (encashment of traveller's cheques) no longer apply except, in the case of s. 3, to gold held on behalf of a Southern Rhodesian resident.

The following orders, which have thus become redundant, are revoked: The Exchange Control (Bailees Exemption) Order 1947; The Exchange Control (Temporary Visitors' Exemption) Order 1947; The Exchange Control (Specified Currency and Prescribed Securities) Order; The Exchange Control (Specified Currency and Prescribed Securities) (Amendment) Order 1968; The Exchange Control (Purchase of Foreign Currency) Order 1970; The Exchange Control (Purchase of Foreign Currency) (Amendment) Order 1977, 1977 Halsbury's Abridgment para. 1910; The Exchange Control (Purchase of Foreign Currency) (Amendment) Order 1978, 1978 Halsbury's Abridgment para. 1958; The Exchange Control (Purchase of Foreign Currency) (Amendment No. 2) Order 1978, 1978 Halsbury's Abridgment para. 1959; and the Exchange Control (Gold Coins Exemption) Order 1979, para. 1916.

This Order has been revoked; see para. 1908.

1911   —— —— imports and exports

The Exchange Control (Import and Export) (Exemption) Order 1979, S.I. 1979 No. 1334 (in force on 24th October 1979) exempts all imports and exports from the prohibitions imposed by The Exchange Control Act 1947, ss. 21 and 22 except in relation to the export of export securities and related documents and gold coin and bullion owned by persons resident in Southern Rhodesia.

The following Orders are revoked: The Exchange Control (Import and Export) Order 1966, The Exchange Control (Import and Export) (Amendment) Order 1975, 1975 Halsbury's Abridgment para. 2294; The Exchange Control (Import and Export) (Amendment) Order 1977, 1977 Halsbury's Abridgment para. 1908 and The Exchange Control (Import and Export) (Amendment) Order 1979, para. 1917.

This Order has been revoked; see para. 1908.

1912   —— —— payments etc.

The Exchange Control (Payments etc.) (Exemption) Order 1979, S.I. 1979 No. 1332 (in force on 24th October 1979) exempts from the provisions of the Exchange Control Act 1947, ss. 5 (payments in the United Kingdom), 6 (payments outside the United Kingdom), 7 (compensation deals) and 24 (collection of certain debts) all payments except payments made in respect of Southern Rhodesia made in respect of Southern Rhodesian residents.

The following orders are revoked: The Exchange Control (Payments) Order 1967, arts. 2, 5 and 6; and the Exchange Control (Payments) (Amendment) Order 1971.

This Order has been revoked; see para. 1908.

1913   —— —— securities etc.

The Exchange Control (Securities etc.) (Exemption) Order 1979, S.I. 1979 No. 1333 (in force on 24th October 1979) exempts from the provisions of the Exchange Control Act 1947, ss. 8–14 and 28, which impose restrictions on the issue, transfer, substitution and registration of securities, all transactions in securities except those involving Southern Rhodesian residents. The Order also abolishes unconditionally (i) the obligation to place certain securities in the custody of an authorised depositary; (ii) the restrictions on authorised depositaries parting with securities already in their custody; and (iii) the restrictions relating to the deposit of certificates of title.

The following Orders are revoked: The Exchange Control (Transfer from Custodian Exemption) Order 1947; the Exchange Control (Declarations and Evidence) Order 1968; and the Exchange Control (Deposit of Securities) (Exemption) Order 1970.

This Order has been revoked; see para. 1908.

1914   —— —— settlements

The Exchange Control (Settlements) (Exemption) Order 1979, S.I. 1979 No. 1336 (in force on 24th October 1979) has the effect that the Exchange Control Act 1947, s. 29 now only applies to settlements conferring an interest in property on a resident in Southern Rhodesia and to the exercise of a power of appointment in favour of such a person.

This Order has been revoked; see para. 1908.

1915   —— exports—Southern Rhodesia

The Exchange Control (Exports) (Southern Rhodesia) Order 1979, S.I. 1979 No. 1335 (in force on 24th October 1979) replaces the Exchange Control (Payments) Order 1967, art. 3. The Exchange Control Act 1947, s. 23 now only applies to exports to destinations in Southern Rhodesia.

The Exchange Control (Payments) Order 1967, arts. 3, 4 and 7 is revoked.

This Order has been revoked; see para. 1908.

1916   —— gold coins

The Exchange Control (Gold Coins Exemption) Order 1979, S.I. 1979 No. 648 (in force on 13th June 1979), revokes the Exchange Control (Gold Coins Exemption) Order 1975, 1975 Halsbury's Abridgment para. 2293 and the Exchange Control (Gold Coins Exemption) (Amendment) Order 1977, 1977 Halsbury's Abridgment para. 1907. The Order allows gold coin (but not gold bullion) to be bought, sold, borrowed and lent without permission under the Exchange Control Act 1947, s. 1 (1) and to be held without permission under s. 2 (1) of the Act. Persons holding gold coins as bailees continue to be exempted from the obligation, imposed by s. 3, to notify the Bank of England.

This Order has been revoked; see para. 1910.

1917   —— import and export

The Exchange Control (Import and Export) (Amendment) Order 1979, S.I. 1979 No. 647 (in force on 13th June 1979), amends the Exchange Control (Import and Export) (Amendment) Order 1977, 1977 Halsbury's Abridgment para. 1908. Travellers abroad may now take out of the United Kingdom up to £1,000 worth of foreign currency notes.

This Order has been revoked; see para. 1911.

1918   —— power of Treasury to require information—extent of power— whether exercisable after person charged and cautioned

For the purpose of investigations of offences against the Exchange Control Act 1947, Customs and Excise officers seized documents belonging to several companies. A and B were directors of some of these companies. B refused to answer a questionnaire served on him. He was later arrested and cautioned and charged with offences under the Act and conspiracy to defraud the public revenue. The Treasury, in exercise of their powers under Sch. 5, Part I, para. 1 (1) of the Act served B with a letter of direction requiring him to answer the questionnaire and produce certain documents, failure to comply being an offence under the Act. It was conceded that B could have incriminated himself in answering the questionnaire. A, who had not been arrested or charged, was served with a similar letter of direction, questionnaire and request for documents, all directed towards obtaining information relevant to the conspiracy charge against B. A and B sought the court's determination as to whether they were bound in law to comply with the letters of direction. *Held*, on the true construction of para. 1 (1) the power to direct a person to provide information could not be invoked once that person had been charged and cautioned, for otherwise the right of such a person to remain silent would be removed. B was accordingly not bound to comply. However A had not been arrested or charged and he was to be treated like any other potential witness from whom information was sought. Accordingly A was bound to comply with the letter of direction served on him.

A v H.M. TREASURY, B v H.M. TREASURY [1979] 2 All ER 586 (Queen's Bench Division: T. P. RUSSELL QC sitting as a deputy High Court judge).

1919   **Exchange Equalisation Account Act 1979**

The Exchange Equalisation Account Act 1979 consolidates the enactments relating to the Exchange Equalisation Account. The Act received the royal assent on 4th April 1979 and came into force on 4th May 1979.

Derivation and destination tables appear on page 518.

DESTINATION TABLE

This table shows in column (1) the enactments repealed by the Exchange Equalisation Account Act 1979 and in column (2) the provisions of that Act corresponding thereto.

In certain cases the enactments in column (1), though having a corresponding provision in column (2) is not wholly repealed as it is still partly required for the purposes of other legislation.

(1)	(2)	(1)	(2)
Finance Act 1932 (c. 25)	Exchange Equalisation Account Act 1979 (c. 30)	Finance Act 1946 (c. 64)	Exchange Equalisation Account Act 1979 (c. 30)
s. 24 (1) (2)	s. 1 (1), (2) Rep., 1968 c. 13, ss. 7 (4), 24 (2), Sch. 6, Part I	s. 63 (1) (2)	s. 1 (3) (b) Rep., S.L.R. Act 1950
(3) (4)	ss. 1 (3) (a), 3 (1) (a) Rep., 1968 c. 13, ss. 7 (1), 24 (2), Sch. 6, Part I	National Loans Act 1968 (c. 13)	
		s. 7 (1)–(3) (4)	s. 2 (1)–(3)
(5), (6)	Rep., 1968 c. 13, s. 24 (2), Sch. 6, Part I		
(7) 25 (7)★	s. 4 s. 3 (3)	International Finance, Trade and Aid Act 1977 (c. 6)	
Bretton Woods Agreements Act 1945 (c. 19)		s. 3 (1) (2) (3)	1 (3) (d) 3 (1) (b), (2) 4
s. 2 (2)†	1 (3) (c)		

★ Repealed in part.

† Repealed in part by the International Monetary Fund Act 1979, s. 6 (1), Schedule, Part I.

TABLE OF DERIVATIONS

This table shows in the right hand column the legislative source from which the sections of the Exchange Equalisation Account Act 1979 in the left hand column have been derived. In the table the following abbreviations are used:

      1932 = The Finance Act 1932
              (22 & 23 Geo. 5 c. 25)
      1945 = The Bretton Woods Agreements Act 1945
              (9 & 10 Geo. 6 c. 19)
      1946 = The Finance Act 1946
              (9 & 10 Geo. 6 c. 64)
      1968 = The National Loans Act 1968
              (1968 c. 13)
      1977 = The International Finance, Trade and Aid Act 1977
              (1977 c. 6)

Section	Derivation
1 (1) (2)	1932 s. 24 (1).
(3) (a)	1932 s. 24 (3).
(b)	1946 s. 63.
(c)	1945 s. 2 (2).
(d)	1977 s. 3 (1).
2	1968 s. 7 (1)–(3).
3 (1) (a)	1932 s. 24 (3).
(b)	1977 s. 3 (2).
(2)	1977 s. 3 (2).
(3)	1932 s. 25 (7).
4	1932 s. 24 (7); 1977 s. 3 (3).
5	Short title, repeals and commencement.
Sch.	[Enactments repealed.]

1920 Interest—claim for interest on sums already paid—power of court to award interest simpliciter

See *Tehno-Impex v Gebr van Weelde Scheepvaartkantoor BV*, para. 145.

1921 International Monetary Fund Act 1979

The International Monetary Fund Act 1979 consolidates the enactments relating to the International Monetary Fund and repeals as obsolete the European Monetary Agreement Act 1959. The Act received the royal assent on 4th April 1979 and came into force on 4th May 1979.

Derivation and destination tables appear below.

DESTINATION TABLE

This table shows in column (1) the enactments repealed by the International Monetary Fund Act 1979, and in column (2) the provisions of that Act corresponding thereto.

In certain cases the enactment in column (1), though having a corresponding provision in column (2), is not, or is not wholly, repealed as it is still required, or partly required for the purposes of other legislation.

(1)	(2)	(1)	(2)
Bretton Woods Agreements Act 1945 (c. 19)	International Monetary Fund Act 1979 (c. 29)	National Loans Act 1968 (c. 13)	International Monetary Fund Act 1979 (c. 29)
Preamble, para. (a)	——	Sch. 2*	ss. 1 (1), 3, 4 (2)
s. 2 (1) (b)–(d)	s. 1 (1) (b)–(d)		
(2)*	(3)	International Monetary Fund Act 1970 (c. 49)	
(4)*	4		
3 (1)*	5 (1)	Preamble, s. 1	Rep., 1977 c. 6, s. 8 (3), Sch. 2
(2)†	(2), (3)	s. 2	s. 2 (4)
(4)*	(1)	3	——
International Bank and Monetary Fund Act 1959 (c. 17)		International Finance, Trade and Aid Act 1977 (c. 6)	
Preamble*	——	s. 1 (1)	1 (1)
International Monetary Fund Act 1962 (c. 20)		(2)	2 (2)
		(3)	ss. 1 (2), 2 (3)
Preamble	2 (5)	2 (1), (2)	——
s. 1 (1)	(1), (4)	(3)	s. 1 (1) (b)
(2)	Rep., 1970 c. 49, s. 2	(4)	(d)
2	——	(5)	4 (1)
		(6)	——

*Repealed in part   †Not repealed.

TABLE OF DERIVATIONS

This table shows in the right hand column the legislative source from which the sections of the International Monetary Fund Act 1979 in the left hand column have been derived. In the table the following abbreviations are used:

1945 = The Bretton Woods Agreements Act 1945
        (9 & 10 Geo. 6, c. 19)

1962 = The International Monetary Fund Act 1962
        (10 & 11 Eliz. 2, c. 20)

1968 = The National Loans Act 1968
        (1968 c. 13)

1970 = The International Monetary Fund Act 1970
        (1970 c. 49)

1977 = The International Finance, Trade and Aid Act 1977
        (1977 c. 6)

1978 = The Interpretation Act 1978
        (1978 c. 30)

Section	Derivation
1 (1)	See 1968 Sch. 2; 1977 s. 1 (1)
(a)	1977 s. 1 (1) (b).
(b)	1945 s. 2 (1) (b); 1977 s. 2 (3).
(c)	1945 s. 2 (1) (c).
(d)	1945 s. 2 (1) (d); 1977 s. 2 (4).
(2)	1977 s. 1 (3).
(3)	1945 s. 2 (2).
2 (1)	1962 preamble and s. 1 (1).
(2), (3)	1977 s. 1 (2), (3).
(4)	1962 s. 1 (1); 1970 s. 2.
(5)	1962 preamble and s. 1 (1).
3	1968 Sch. 2.
4 (1)	1945 s. 2 (4); 1977 s. 2 (5).
(2)	1945 s. 2 (4); 1968 Sch. 2.
5 (1)	1945 s. 3 (1).
(2)	1945 s. 3 (2); 1978 Sch. 1, definition of "colony".
(3)	1945 s. 3 (2).
6	[Repeals and saving].
7	[Short title and commencement].
Sch.	[Enactments repealed].

1922   **National Savings Stock Register—limit on stock which may be purchased in one day—exemption**

The National Savings Stock Register (Amendment) Regulations 1979, S.I. 1979 No. 1677 (in force on 4th January 1980), amend the 1976 Regulations, 1976 Halsbury's Abridgment para. 1784. The Regulations exempt the Accountant-General of the Supreme Court from the £5,000 limit on the amount of stock of any one description which may be purchased by any one person on any one day.

1923   **Overseas aid**

The Caribbean Development Bank (Further Payments) Order 1979, S.I. 1979 No. 1160 (in force on 17th September 1979), provides for payments to be made to the bank to increase its authorised capital stock.

1924   **Savings certificates**

The Savings Certificates (Amendment) Regulations 1979, S.I. 1979 No. 1388 (in force on 2nd December 1979), which amend the Savings Certificates Regulations 1972, consolidate the list of maximum permitted holdings of certificates and distinguish between the two types of certificates listed as being on sale at a price of £10 per unit certificate, namely index-linked certificates of the Retirement Issue and certificates of the 18th Issue.

1925   The Savings Certificates (Amendment) (No. 2) Regulations 1979, S.I. 1979 No. 1533 (in force on 3rd December 1979) further amend the Savings Certificate Regulations 1972 by increasing the maximum permitted holding of the index-linked Retirement Issue of National Savings Certificates from 70 to 120.

1926   **Securities—exchanges and conversions**

The Exchange of Securities (General) Rules 1979, S.I. 1979 No. 1678 (in force on 1st January 1980), consolidate the Exchange of Securities (General) Rules 1963 as amended. They prescribe the general procedure to be followed with respect to exchanges and conversions of government securities except National Savings Certificates. They also make amendments to the definitions of "exchange", "new securities," and "old securities".

1927   **Sterling deposit market—code of conduct**

The Bank of England has issued a code of conduct for the guidance of principals and brokers in the sterling deposit market. Participants are required to adhere to the spirit as well as to the letter of the code which relates explicitly to sterling deposits and certificates of deposit. To the extent that sterling markets deal in other unquoted instruments, the principles enshrined in the code should be applied. The code deals, inter alia, with confidentiality, rules of conduct and standards; it also contains a schedule of accepted market terminology and definitions. A joint standing committee has been established to assist the Bank of England to monitor observance of the code and for the resolution of disputes between principals and brokers concerning the application of the code or market practice.

MORTGAGE

Halsbury's Laws of England (4th edn.), Vol. 32, paras. 401–1052

1928   **Articles**

The Mortgagee's Right to Possession—The Modern Law, R. J. Smith (a review of the working of the Administration of Justice Act 1970, as amended, with reference to its effect on the right of possession): [1979] Conv. 266.

Mortgages, A New Equity, H. W. Wilkinson (mortgaging problems raised by the judgment in *Quennel v Maltby* [1979] 1 All ER 569, CA, 1978 Halsbury's Abridgment para. 1736): 129 NLJ 624.

1929   Building society—illegal advance on second mortgage—rights of building society

See *Nash v Halifax Building Society*, para. 263.

1930   Legal charge executed by one joint tenant—whether effective to charge share in proceeds of sale

See *Cedar Holdings Ltd v Green*, para. 903.

1931   Matrimonial home—mortgage of joint matrimonial home to secure husband's debt

See *Re Berry (A Bankrupt)*, para. 219.

1932   Mortgagee—valuation of mortgaged property—structural survey by mortgagor

See para. 2366.

1933   Remedies of mortgagee—action for possession—application for suspension of possession order—likelihood of mortgagor being able to pay sums due

In return for a loan, the defendant mortgaged his dwelling-house to the plaintiffs. The deed provided that the defendant was to repay the principal sum on a certain date, but in fact he was permitted to defer repayment indefinitely. The deed also provided, inter alia, that should he default on his instalments of interest, the principal would become due immediately. He fell into arrears with his payments of interest and the plaintiffs obtained an order for possession of the house. The defendant applied for an order under the Administration of Justice Act 1970, s. 36 (2) staying or suspending execution of the possession order. The court, before granting an order under s. 36 (2), has to take into account the likelihood of the mortgagor being able, within a reasonable period, to pay any sums due under the mortgage. Under the Administration of Justice Act 1973, s. 8, where the mortgagor can defer payment of the principal, but may also be liable to an earlier payment in the event, of his default, then, for the purposes of s. 36, a court may treat as due only those sums the mortgagor would have been required to pay if there had been no such provision for earlier payment. The defendant claimed his case fell within s. 8, with the result that the only sums due were the interest and costs owing under the mortgage, which there was a reasonable possibility he could pay. But the plaintiffs contended that because, according to the mortgage deed, the principal was to be repaid in a single sum on a specified date and there was no provision for deferment, s. 8 did not apply. Thus the sums due included the principal, which the defendant was unlikely to be able to repay within a reasonable time. *Held*, the court should take into account not merely the legal stipulations contained in the mortgage, but also their practical effect in equity. The mortgage was to be construed as permitting the mortgagor to defer payment of the principal, thus bringing it within s. 8. On the evidence the defendant would, within a reasonable time, probably be able to pay off the costs and the interest outstanding, and the court would therefore, under s. 36 (2), suspend the execution of the order for possession.

CENTRAX TRUSTEES LTD V ROSS [1979] 2 All ER 952 (Chancery Division: GOULDING J).

1934   —— —— effect of unregistered interest of mortgagor's wife

In two actions for possession of land a bank claimed and was granted possession of the matrimonial home, as in both cases the husband had charged the house to the bank as security, without the wife's knowledge.   The wife in both cases had made a substantial contribution to the purchase of the home, but had failed to register any form of caution, restriction or notice, the husband being registered as sole proprietor.   In neither case did the bank make an inquiry as to the interest which might be held by the wife.   On appeal, *held*, the wives were equitable tenants in common under trusts for sale, the legal estates being vested in the husbands as sole trustees.   Although the wives' interests were "minor interests" within the meaning of the Land Registration Act 1925, s. 3 (xv) (a), they were "interests . . . affecting the estate transferred or created" by the charges "subsisting in reference" to the land and so capable of being overriding interests under ss. 20 (1) (b) and 70 (1) of the Act; and as the wives were in "actual occupation of the land" for the purposes of s. 70 (1) (g), they were overriding interests to which the bank's charges were subject.   The court considered that those lending money on the security of matrimonial homes should realise that most wives now have proprietary interests and should therefore make the necessary inquiries.

WILLIAMS AND GLYN'S BANK LTD v BOLAND; WILLIAMS AND GLYN'S BANK LTD v BROWN [1979] 2 WLR 550 (Court of Appeal: LORD DENNING MR, ORMROD AND BROWNE LJJ).   Decision of Templeman J (1978) Times, 29th April, 1978 Halsbury's Abridgment para. 1978 reversed.   *Elias v Mitchell* [1972] Ch 652, *Bull v Bull* [1955] 1 QB 234 and *Cooper v Crutchley* [1955] Ch 431 applied.   *Caunce v Caunce* [1969] 1 WLR 286 and *Bird v Syme Thomson* [1978] 3 All ER 1027, 1978 Halsbury's Abridgment para. 1979 not followed.   See further 129 NLJ 270.

1935   Terms—power of sale subject to consent of mortgagee—whether sale without consent valid

See *100 Main Street v W. B. Sullivan Construction Ltd*, para. 2360.

NATIONAL HEALTH SERVICE

Halsbury's Laws of England (3rd edn.), Vol. 27, paras. 981–1186

1936   Boards of Governors

The National Health Service (Preservation of Boards of Governors) Order 1979, S.I. 1979 No. 51 (in force on 22nd February 1979), preserves from abolition under the National Health Service Reorganisation Act 1973, s. 14, the Boards of Governors of the teaching hospitals specified in the order.   This preservation will extend until 31st March 1982 and applies in relation to the Boards various statutory provisions with or without modification.

1937   Charges

The National Health Service (Charges for Drugs and Appliances) Amendment Regulations 1979, S.I. 1979 No. 681 (in force on 16th July 1979), further amend the National Health Service (Charges for Drugs and Appliances) Regulations 1974, 1974 Halsbury's Abridgment, para. 2216, increasing the charges specified for the supply of drugs and certain appliances, the sums prescribed for the grant of prepayment certificates of exemption from those charges and the allowance for exemption from those charges on grounds of low income.

1938   The National Health Service (Dental and Optical Charges) Amendment Regulations 1979, S.I. 1979 No. 677 (in force on 16th July 1979), amend the National Health Service (Dental and Optical Charges) Regulations 1978, 1978 Halsbury's Abridgment, para. 1984, increasing the charges for the supply of certain dental appliances and the provision of dental treatment.

1939   —— proposed increase

The government has announced, in its public expenditure plans for 1980–81, that on 1st April 1980 prescription charges will be increased from 45p to 70p. It has also stated that the present exemptions will not be altered (see the Financial Times, 2nd November 1979). It was later announced that the cost of prepayment certificates (season tickets) will rise in April 1980 from £8 to £12 for a year; a four-month certificate will also be available for £4.50 (see the Daily Telegraph, 3rd November 1979).

1940   Family Practitioner Committees—membership and procedure

The National Health Service (Family Practitioner Committees: Membership and Procedure; Regulations 1979, S.I. 1979 No. 739 (in force on 27th July 1979), consolidate with amendments the National Health Service (Family Practitioner Committees: Membership and Procedure) Regulations 1973, as amended. They provide for the appointment and term of office of, and the procedure of, Family Practitioner Committees and alter the dates of termination of office of certain members of those committees in England from 31st July to 30th November and adjust appropriately the term of office of the original members.

1941   Health authorities—breach of statutory duty—remedies

A number of orthopaedic patients at a hospital in Birmingham sought declarations against the Secretary of State, the regional health authority and the area health authority that they were in breach of their duty under the National Health Service Act 1977, s. 1 to continue to promote a comprehensive health service designed to improve health and prevent illness and under s. 3 to provide accommodation, facilities and services for those purposes. The patients had waited longer for treatment than was medically advisable, because of a shortage of facilities arising from a decision not to build a new hospital block on the grounds of cost. *Held*, it was not the court's function to direct Parliament what funds to make available to the health service and how to allocate them. The Secretary of State had a discretion as to the disposition of financial resources. The court could only interfere if the Secretary of State acted in such a way as to frustrate the purpose of the Act, no such breach having been shown in this case. As there were specific remedies available under the Act against the area or regional health authorities the court could not grant a declaration against them. Even if a breach of duty was proved, there was no remedy in damages available under the Act. The application would therefore be dismissed.

R v SECRETARY OF STATE FOR SOCIAL SERVICES, EX PARTE HINCKS (1979) 123 Sol Jo 436 (Queen's Bench Division: WIEN J).

1942   —— membership

The National Health Service (Health Authorities: Membership) Regulations 1979, S.I. 1979 No. 738 (in force on 27th July 1979), consolidate with amendments the National Health Service (Health Authorities: Membership) Regulations 1977, 1977 Halsbury's Abridgment para. 1940, as amended. They provide for the appointment and tenure of office of chairmen and members of Regional and Area Health Authorities and alter the dates of termination of office of certain members of Health Authorities in England from 31st July to 30th September and adjust appropriately the tenures of office of the original members.

1943   Hospital charges—vicitims of road accidents—proposed increase in charges

The government has announced in its public expenditure plans for 1980–81 that the hospital charges payable under the Road Traffic Act 1972 for the treatment of victims of road accidents would be increased. See the Financial Times, 2nd November 1979.

1944 **Medical practitioners—prescribed experience**

The National Health Service (Vocational Training) Regulations 1979, S.I. 1979 No. 1644 (in force on 16th February 1980), prescribe the medical experience which under the National Health Service Act 1977, s. 31, a medical practitioner is required to have acquired or be exempt from the need to do so before applying to be included in a medical list to provide general medical services.

1945 **Payments by health authorities—reimbursement of wages of doctors' staff—employment by doctors of wife or dependant—validity of directions by Secretary of State**

A scheme governing the remuneration of general practitioners within the National Health Service prevented a general practitioner from being recompensed out of public funds if he employed his wife or any other dependant of his as ancillary staff in his practice, although reimbursement was available in other cases. A general practitioner was granted a declaration that the directions given by the Secretary of State, which the scheme embodied, were void on the ground that the Secretary of State, in making the exclusions, had exercised his power unreasonably and unlawfully. The Secretary of State appealed and by cross-notice the general practitioner sought a declaration that the judge was wrong to reject his contention that the Secretary of State, in making the exclusions, had exceeded his powers. On the cross-notice, *held*, the directions in question were not ultra vires. The Health Services and Public Health Act 1968, s. 29 (1), (2), under which the Secretary of State was empowered to make the directions, did not restrict his powers and gave him a wide discretion. Hence he was entitled to restrict the class of ancillary staff in respect of whom reimbursement was available.

On the appeal, *held*, a regulation, determination or decision made under powers delegated by statute was invalid if some material factor was taken into account which should not have been taken into account, or some material factor was not taken into account which should have been taken into account. It was also invalid if the regulation, determination or decision was such that no reasonable person could have made it. In this case, the Secretary of State had had all relevant factors brought to his notice, including the effect on doctors' morale and the traditional and important position of doctors' wives in practices. Nor was the provision, which had been agreed with representatives of the profession, so unreasonable that no reasonable minister could have made it. The appeal would be allowed.

GLANVILL v SECRETARY OF STATE FOR SOCIAL SERVICES (1979) Times, 20th November (Court of Appeal: MEGAW, SHAW and WALLER LJJ). *Associated Provincial Picture Houses Ltd v Wednesbury Corpn* [1948] 1 KB 223, CA, applied. Decision of Talbot J (1978) 122 Sol Jo 611, 1978 Halsbury's Abridgment para. 1988 reversed.

1968 Act s. 29 (1), (2) now consolidated in National Health Service Act 1977, s. 99.

1946 **Public Health Laboratory Service Act 1979**

The Public Health Laboratory Service Act 1979 extends the powers conferred on the Secretary of State by the National Health Service Act 1977, s. 5 (2) (c) regarding the provision of a microbiological service, and amends certain provisions of that Act relating to the Public Health Laboratory Service Board. The Act received the royal assent on 29th March 1979 and came into force on that date.

1947 **Vaccine Damage Payments Act 1979**

The Vaccine Damage Payments Act 1979 provides for payments to be made out of public funds in cases where severe disablement occurs as a result of vaccination against certain diseases or of contact with a person who has been vaccinated against any of those diseases. The Act received the royal assent on 22nd March 1979 and came into force on that date. Section 1 specifies the amount of the payment and provides for the Secretary of State to make payment. Subsection (2) lists the diseases for which vaccination has been offered as part of public vaccination policies since

1948; provision is made for additional diseases to be added to the list by order. Subsection (3) ensures that payment may be made to a person who is severely disabled as a result of vaccination given to his mother before he was born and to a person severely disabled as a result of contracting a disease through contact with a vaccinated third person. Subsection (4) provides that for the purposes of the scheme, a person is to be treated as severely disabled if his disablement is eighty per cent or more as assessed for the purposes of social security legislation. Section 2 contains the main conditions for entitlement. Section 3 deals with the determination of claims, which will initially be dealt with by the Secretary of State. If he is not satisfied that the claimant is severely disabled as a result of vaccination he may refer the matter to an independent medical tribunal. Section 4 provides for review of cases by these tribunals. Section 5 enables the Secretary of State to reconsider a determination that a payment should or should not be made. Section 6 provides that payment is to be made direct where the disabled person is over 18 and capable of managing his own affairs; in all other cases payment is to trustees. Section 7 deals with cases where claims have been made prior to royal assent. Section 8 authorises the making of regulations as to the mode of making claims, medical examinations, the disclosure of medical evidence and the functions of tribunals. Section 9 provides for penalties for the making of fraudulent statements in connection with a claim. Sections 10 and 11 amend the Scotland Act 1978 and the Wales Act 1978 respectively so as to provide that the functions of the Secretary of State under this Act be included in devolved matters. Section 12 contains financial provisions and s. 13 contains the short title and specifies that the Act applies to Northern Ireland and the Isle of Man.

1948   —— claims

The Vaccine Damage Payments Regulations 1979, S.I. 1979 No. 432 (in force on 6th April 1979), contain provisions relating to claims for payment made under the Vaccine Damage Payments Act 1979, para. 1947, s. 1 (1), the information to be given when claiming and for treating claims made prior to the passing of the 1979 Act as claims falling within s. 3 (1) of that Act. The Regulations provide that vaccinations given outside the United Kingdom and the Isle of Man to serving members of Her Majesty's forces and members of their families are to be treated as carried out in England. They also make provision for the appointment by the Secretary of State of vaccine damage tribunals, for the procedure of the tribunals and for the reconsideration of the Secretary of State's determination in certain circumstances.

1949   —— disability from disease contracted from vaccinated person

The Vaccine Damage Payments (Amendment) Regulations 1979, S.I. 1979 No. 1441 (in force on 13th December 1979), amend the Vaccine Damage Payments Regulations 1979 by adding a new regulation. The regulation prescribes the circumstances in which the provisions of the Vaccine Damage Payments Act 1979, para. 1947, are to have effect with respect to a person who is severely disabled as a result of contracting a disease through contact with a third person who was vaccinated against it as if the vaccination had been given to him and the disablement resulted from it. The circumstances prescribed are that the person suffering the disablement has been in close physical contact with a person who has been vaccinated against poliomyelitis with orally administered vaccine within a period of sixty days beginning with the fourth day immediately following the vaccination. The disabled person must also have been, within the sixty day period, either looking after the vaccinated person or himself being looked after together with the vaccinated person.

1950   —— tribunals

See para. 23.

NEGLIGENCE

Halsbury's Laws of England (3rd edn.), Vol. 28, paras. 1–120

1951   Articles

A Question of Contributory Negligence, C. P. Walker (on whether the court can make a finding of contributory negligence in the absence of a plea to that effect, in the light of *Fookes v Slaytor* [1979] 1 All ER 137, CA, 1978 Halsbury's Abridgment para. 1997): 129 NLJ 674.

Defective Premises: Negligence Liability of Builders, Nigel P. Gravells (developments in the common law of negligence since the Defective Premises Act 1972) [1979] Conv. 97.

Hospital Admissions—Duty of Care, R. G. Lee (the question of when a duty of care arises in relation to a person presenting himself at a hospital with or without an accident and emergency department): 129 NLJ 567.

Occupiers, Trespassers and the Unfair Contract Terms Act, J. Mesher (restrictions on the exclusion of occupiers' liability): [1979] Conv. 58.

Safe System of Work, Henry E. Markson (extent to which claim in negligence may be met by the defence that there was a safe system of work): 129 NLJ 99.

When a Weak Case Meant a Strong One, P. J. Davies (*Hill v James Crowe (Cases) Ltd* [1978] 1 All ER 812, 1977 Halsbury's Abridgment para. 1959 and the concept of strict tortious liability for defective products): 123 Sol Jo 345.

1952   Contributory negligence—spectator at game

Canada

A spectator at a game of ice-hockey was hit in the eye by a flying hockey-stick, whilst he was standing near the front. He brought an action for damages against the owners of the arena. *Held*, the owners ought reasonably to have foreseen that someone might get hit with a hockey-stick, as similar incidents occurred four or five times a year. Furthermore, reasonable care had not been taken to protect spectators. There was no protective shielding, which was relatively cheap to instal, and no warning of the danger of standing near the front. However there was substantial contributory negligence on the spectator's part in that he ought to have been aware of the dangers of standing too near the front. Thus the owners would be liable for only one-third of the total damages.

KLYNE V BELLEGARDE, BELLEGARDE, LLOYD AND INDIAN HEAD [1978] 6 WWR 743 (Court of Queen's Bench of Saskatchewan).

1953   —— standard of care required—common sense

Australia

A trainee shunter was employed on railway shunting operations when he moved in front of rolling stock, tripped and was run over, sustaining serious injuries. His damages were reduced on the ground of contributory negligence, on the basis that common sense should have indicated the dangerous nature of what he was doing. On appeal by the Commissioner of Railways and cross-appeal by the employee against the finding of contributory negligence, *held*, reliance on a plaintiff's common sense might in the absence of special circumstances justify a finding of contributory negligence. However, common sense was a quality of the reasonable man which could readily be affected by special circumstances, such as those which applied in this case, in that the plaintiff was a trainee and was given very little advice or supervision. It was not established that he knew or ought to have known that his actions were dangerous. The appeal would be dismissed and the cross-appeal allowed.

RAILWAYS COMR V HALLEY (1978) 20 ALR 409 (High Court of Australia).

1954   Duty of care—admission of liability—whether an order for judgment on admissions would lie

See *Rankine v Garton Sons & Co*, para. 1645.

1955   —— architect—duty to advise clients of planning requirements

See *BL Holdings Ltd v Robert J. Wood and Partners*, para. 258.

1956   —— auditor—negligent error in certified accounts—duty to third party

See *Scott Group Ltd v McFarlane*, para. 347.

1957   —— bailee and bailor—dangerous machinery

Australia

The defendants, a bailor and bailee, were farmers and one gratuitously lent the other an onion sorting machine. The machine when new had been supplied with a guard more as a visible warning of danger than as a method of protection for the user. The bailor removed the guard and operated the machine without it. He gave directions to the bailee on how to operate the machine and of its potential dangers particularly where children were concerned. The bailee operated the machine with the assistance of the plaintiff, a thirteen year old boy, and in the course of working the machine the plaintiff's hand was severely injured. The plaintiff in his action for damages contended that the bailee failed to acquaint himself with the methods of operating the machine in a safe manner and that the bailor had supplied the machine without proper information concerning its dangers. The defendants contended that they took all necessary precautions for the plaintiff's safety and alleged contributory negligence on his part asserting he had failed to observe the directions given to him. The trial judge found the bailee had been negligent in his supervision of the machine and was liable to the plaintiff in damages. The bailor was under a duty to warn of the possible dangers of the machine and he had discharged this duty sufficiently. The action against him was therefore dismissed. The plaintiff appealed. *Held*, the bailor might owe a duty of care to children in the vicinity of the machine, but it did not follow that he owed a similar duty of care to children employed by the bailee contrary to the instructions given. The decision of the trial judge would be affirmed.

PIVOVAROFF V CHERNABAEFF (1979) 21 SASR 1 (Supreme Court of South Australia).

1958   —— bank manager—liability of bank for negligent misstatement

A consultant engineer, employed by an undertaking to head a new project, was also allowed to work on his own account. In September 1974 he prepared a quotation for the supply of steel to a company in Canada which he submitted to an intermediary company there. The former company accepted the quotation after the delivery dates had been confirmed. In October, the engineer resigned from his position and assumed control over a group of companies with which he had developed close connections. The group was insolvent and he hoped to rescue it by means of the contract to supply steel which he had previously concluded. He asked the bank to provide the necessary finance, submitting a cash flow forecast for the next six months. The manager agreed, provided the engineer took out a policy issued by the Export Credit Guarantee Department, in which case the consent of head office to the advance would be a mere formality. The bank manager failed to explain the difference between the policy and a Banker's Guarantee (Bills and Notes) issued by the same department. The engineer applied for the latter which he failed to obtain. Meanwhile the Head Office had informed the bank manager that there was not the slightest possibility of such an amount being sanctioned. The company ran into financial difficulties and the engineer brought an action for damages in negligence on the grounds that he had suffered loss by relying on the careless statements made by the bank manager about the availibility of finance. *Held*, although the bank manager was not obliged to predict the outcome of an application for a loan, if did so he was under a duty to take reasonable care since he knew that his prediction would be relied upon. He had failed to exercise the reasonable care to be expected of a competent bank manager as he had given the engineer the impression that the granting of a loan would be a mere formality once the policy had been obtained. Therefore, the bank was liable on the *Hedley Byrne* principle and damages would be awarded accordingly.

Box v MIDLAND BANK LTD [1979] 2 Lloyd's Rep 391 (Queen's Bench Division: Lloyd J). *Hedley Byrne & Co Ltd v Heller & Partners* [1964] AC 465, [1963] 2 All ER 575, HL applied.

1959 —— builder—liability of amateur builder as vendor

Purchasers of a restaurant alleged that the vendors, who had built the premises, had been negligent in the construction of the hot water and central heating system. On the question whether the claim for damages for negligence was properly founded and if so, whether the Law Society's General Conditions of Sale (1970 edn.), condition 4 (2) (a), which states that a purchaser is deemed to buy with full knowledge of the state and condition of the property, afforded the vendors a defence, *held*, there was no reason why a building owner who carried out work himself should not be liable for negligent construction in the same way as a professional builder, and a purchaser from him would be the person to whom he owed a duty of care. This duty was not limited by the principle of caveat emptor which had always applied to sales of land. In order for condition 4 (2) (a) to give the vendors a defence it would have to be construed as an exemption clause and it was not apt in its wording to exempt them from liability in negligence.

HONE v BENSON (1978) 248 Estates Gazette 1013 (Queen's Bench Division: JUDGE EDGAR FAY QC sitting as a deputy High Court judge). Dicta of Lord Denning MR in *Dutton v Bognor Regis UDC* [1972] 1 QB 373, CA, and of Lord Wilberforce in *Anns v Merton London Borough Council* [1977] 2 WLR 1024, HL, 1977 Halsbury's Abridgment para. 2175 applied. *Canada SS Ltd v R* [1952] AC 192, PC followed.

1960 —— carrier—liability for personal injury—validity of exemption clause

See *The Dragon*, para. 297.

1961 —— dangerous tool—parent's duty to prevent child from obtaining possession of tool

The plaintiff, a child, was playing outside her home with her five year old sister and the defendants' two children when an accident occurred causing her to lose the sight of one eye. The accident was caused by the defendants' four year old son who was playing with a sharpened hacksaw blade from his father's tool bag. The plaintiff claimed damages contending that the defendants had failed to take reasonable care to keep the blade out of their son's possession and to supervise him properly. *Held*, a parent had a duty in such cases to take reasonable care to prevent his child obtaining possession of any article which could cause damage to any person with whom he could reasonably foresee the child would come into contact. Here, the matters which had to be considered were the nature of the tool and the risk of injury and the care actually taken to keep the child away from it. It could not be argued that ordinary household articles such as kitchen knives could cause similar injuries. Greater care had to be taken to keep tools out of a child's reach as a child was likely to be more interested in his father's tools than in everyday household articles. As the defendants had failed to exercise the necessary care, the plaintiff's claim would succeed.

VANDOME v JOHNS [1979] LS Gaz R 680 (Queen's Bench Division: JUDGE LIPFRIEND sitting as a deputy High Court judge).

For the quantum of damages awarded in this case, see para. 843.

1962 ── driver—articulated lorry in adverse weather conditions

An articulated lorry nearly fifty feet long attempted to cross a dual carriageway in fog when visibility was less than one hundred yards. The plaintiff's car collided with the side of the lorry half-way along its length and the lorry driver continued on his course. The plaintiff's widow sued for damages but her claim was dismissed at first instance. On appeal, *held*, the manoeuvre of driving across the carriageway was little short of lethal in the circumstances and it had been negligent of the lorry driver to do so. However, no amount of care could have prevented the collision once he had embarked on it so he was not to be blamed for driving on after the impact. The appeal would be allowed and an agreed sum of damages would be payable.

LANCASTER v H B & H TRANSPORT LTD [1979] RTR 380 (Court of Appeal: STEPHENSON, GEOFFREY LANE LJJ and DUNN J).

1963 ── ── duty owed to passenger of hired vehicle

The plaintiff hired a taxi and sat in the front passenger seat. In getting out at her destination in a dimly lit street, she tripped over the seat belt, fell and broke her ankle. In a claim for damages she claimed, inter alia, that no interior light was provided in the car and that the seat belt amounted to an obstruction when not properly fastened on its hook. Her claim was dismissed and on appeal, *held*, the driver had a duty to take reasonable care to provide a safe vehicle for his passengers. This included the passengers' entrance and exit from the car, and preventing the vehicle's equipment from becoming a danger or obstruction. The driver was in breach of that duty by failing to switch on the interior light or warn the plaintiff about the seat belt. The plaintiff, being unfamiliar with the car, had not contributed in any way to her accident and the driver's negligence was the sole cause of the accident. The appeal would therefore be allowed.

McCREADY v MILLER [1979] RTR 186 (Court of Appeal: STEPHENSON and BRANDON LJJ and SIR DAVID CAIRNS).

1964 ── ── duty owed to person lying in driveway of driver's premises

Australia
Before sunrise a driver slowly approached the driveway to his home in poor conditions of visibility and light. He entered the driveway and ran over a man, whom he did not see, lying prostrate. The victim could not explain his presence but had made his way there whilst under the influence of alcohol. He sued the driver for damages for his injuries. *Held*, it was not reasonable, in the circumstances, to expect the driver to have seen the man in the driveway and the victim had not established that the driver owed him a duty of care. If a duty of care had existed however, it had not been established that the driver had failed to exercise the standard of care required of a prudent and reasonable man in the circumstances. The action would be dismissed.

MAZINSKI v BAKKA (1978) 20 SASR 350 (Supreme Court of South Australia).

1965 ── employer

See EMPLOYMENT.

1966 ── highway authority—road works—obliteration of traffic sign

See *Bird v Pearce*, para. 1415.

1967 ── insurance broker—omission to renew policy—contributory negligence of assured

Canada
The defendant was the plaintiff's insurance agent for twenty years issuing him fire insurance policies on his house for three year terms. On the expiry of each policy

the defendant automatically sent a renewal policy and invoice for the premium. Due to the worsening economic climate changes were made in the fire insurance industry leading to policies being issued annually. At the end of a three year term the plaintiff's policy was not renewed and he was not notified. The plaintiff failed to realise he had no fire insurance cover until after his house was destroyed nearly eighteen months later. The plaintiff sought damages from the defendant. *Held*, he could recover 25 per cent of the damages claimed. The standard of reasonable care required the defendant to notify the plaintiff in some way that his policy was not being renewed and his failure to do so amounted to negligence. Equally the plaintiff's failure to keep informed over such a long period regarding his insurance cover amounted to contributory negligence.

MORASH V LOCKHART AND RITCHIE LTD (1978) 95 DLR (3d) 647 (Supreme Court of New Brunswick, Appeal Division).

1968   —— **patent agent—duty owed to client**

See *Andrew Master Hones Ltd v Cruickshank and Fairweather*, para. 2033.

1969   —— **ship owner—seaworthiness of ship**

See *The Hellenic Dolphin*, para. 2518.

1970   —— **solicitors—attestation of will**

See *Ross v Caunters*, para. 2698.

1971   —— **surgeon—artery operation—whether patient informed of risks inherent in operation**

Canada

A neurosurgeon decided to perform an operation on an artery, which involved cutting dangerously into the patient's neck. The neurosurgeon obtained the patient's consent for the operation, but did not inform him of the attendant risks. As a result of the operation the patient suffered a massive stroke which paralysed the right hand side of his body. The patient sued the neurosurgeon in negligence for failing to disclose and advise him of the degree of risk involved in the operation. *Held*, on a majority decision, the manner in which the nature of the degree of risk was explained to a particular patient was to be left to the judgment of the doctor concerned. The neurosurgeon adequately informed the patient of the contrasting risks and effects of undergoing the operation and of not undergoing the operation. The neurosurgeon would not be liable in negligence.

REIBL V HUGHES (1978) 21 OR (2d) 14 (Court of Appeal of Ontario). Decision of High Court of Ontario (1977) 16 OR (2d) 306, 1977 Halsbury's Abridgment para. 1964 reversed.

1972   —— **vendor of dangerous motor car—adequacy of warning**

The plaintiff was severely injured when a car owned and driven by a friend, in which he was a passenger, crashed due to the chassis snapping where it was very seriously corroded. At the date of the accident, third party liability insurance in respect of passengers was not compulsory and the plaintiff's friend was not insured against this risk. The plaintiff therefore brought an action against the previous owner, a garage owner who was not a qualified mechanic. On buying the car, he had looked underneath it and realised that it could not be driven, but bought it to sell for scrap. The car was sold at an auction "as seen and with all its faults and without warranty". The plaintiff's friend failed to buy the car at the auction but bought it immediately afterwards from the purchaser. *Held*, the case turned on a question of fact: the extent of the previous owner's knowledge of the dangerously corroded state of the chassis. If he only knew that the car was dangerous to drive, the duty of care which he owed to those who might be injured as a result of its dangerous character after he had parted with possession of it would be satisfied by the warning that it was being sold "as seen and with all its faults." If, however, he knew the precise nature of the defect, a more specific warning of the danger was needed to satisfy the duty of care. On the evidence, it could only be shown that the previous owner was aware of the potential danger of driving the car without further examination and the doing of any necessary repairs. In that case, the warning that the car was to be sold "as seen and with all its faults" was adequate to satisfy the duty of care owed to the plaintiff, and hence the previous owner had not been negligent.

HURLEY V DYKE (1979) (unreported) (House of Lords: LORD DIPLOCK, VISCOUNT DILHORNE, LORD HAILSHAM OF ST MARYLEBONE, LORD KEITH OF KINKEL and LORD SCARMAN).

For discussion of this case, see Law does not spoon-feed unwary buyers, Justinian, Financial Times, 23rd April 1979.

1973   Fatal accident—damages—loss of parents—criteria for assessing award

See *Clement v Leslies Storage Ltd*, para. 796.

1974   Foreseeability—nervous shock—shock resulting in behavioural disorder in young child—right of child and mother to damages

Canada

A motorist negligently reversed into a parked car containing a baby. The baby suffered shock and his mother, who was not present at the time of the accident, became hysterical when she arrived at the scene and heard him screaming. The baby subsequently developed a serious behavioural disorder, which was exacerbated by his mother's inability to cope. On the mother's and baby's claim for damages for nervous shock, *held*, the accident had carried with it the foreseeability of some injury to the baby through nervous shock. Provided that some shock was foreseeable, it was irrelevant that the precise kind or severity of it could not be foreseen. The baby was therefore entitled to damages against the negligent driver. The mother's shock was not, however, foreseeable as she was not even present at the time of the accident. Had she been there and been able to see that the baby had suffered no physical injury she would have reacted differently.

DUWYN V KAPRIELIAN (1978) 22 OR (2d) 736 (Court of Appeal of Ontario).

1975   Highway—overhanging wires—liability

Canada

Whilst being driven on a road a farmer's cultivator became entangled in guy wires supporting a telephone authority's telephone line. The farmer brought an action for negligence, claiming that the authority's wires must have been sagging; evidence showed that two days earlier the guy wires had been taut and firmly secured. The trial judge found that the authority was not negligent, but instead of dismissing the action he allowed an amendment to the pleadings, setting up nuisance as a fresh cause of action, and found the authority liable in nuisance. The authority appealed. *Held*, such an amendment to the pleadings should not have been allowed after all the evidence had been heard, unless the court was satisfied that all the evidence on the new issue had been heard. In this case the court had not taken sufficient steps to ensure that all the evidence on the issue of nuisance had been submitted, and the authority may well have been prejudiced as a result. The trial judge also erred in finding the authority liable in nuisance. On the evidence the authority had not allowed the guy wires to fall into a state of disrepair; indeed there was evidence that they were in good repair two days earlier. Furthermore the guy wires were installed pursuant to statutory authority and, in the absence of negligence, no liability arose.

ASSIE V SASKATCHEWAN TELECOMMUNICATIONS (1978) 90 DLR (3d) 410 (Court of Appeal of Saskatchewan). Decision of the Court of Queen's Bench of Saskatchewan [1977] 4 WWR 611, 1977 Halsbury's Abridgment para. 1988 reversed in part.

1976　　**Negligence by agent—liability of principal—whether agent acting within authority**

See *Nelson v Raphael*, para. 44.

1977　　**Negligence inducing breach of contract—whether right of action exists—contract of employment**

Canada

A teacher brought an action for wrongful dismissal. He sought to include a claim that his former employer and fellow employees had caused his dismissal, in that their negligent acts had induced the breach of his contract of employment. A number of incidents had taken place whilst the teacher was employed at the college, which he claimed had undermined his standing as a teacher. These included the questioning of his teaching ability in front of the students, the rebelling of students which, he claimed, was encouraged by the other teachers and the making of statements by the teachers which, he alleged, were reckless and negligent. Furthermore the college was negligent in that it had failed to recognise the situation and take steps to prevent it from affecting the teacher's ability to continue teaching. *Held*, there was no right of action for negligence inducing breach of contract and the categories of negligence should not be extended to include such a right. The parties to a contract were free to impose any rights and obligations they wished on each other, but if there existed a right of action in negligence for inducing breach of contract, the parties could impose a limitless variety of duties of care on third parties. The amendments sought would therefore be refused.

McLaren v British Columbia Institute of Technology [1978] 6 WWR 687 (Supreme Court of British Columbia).

1978　　**Negligent misstatement—statement made by bank manager—existence of duty of care—liability of bank**

See *Box v Midland Bank Ltd*, para. 1958.

1979　　**Occupier's liability—duty owed to visitor—degree of care expected of visitor—volenti non fit injuria**

Canada

A surveyor was injured on a construction site when an unfinished wall blew on top of him in a severe gale. It was known to the site owner, a sub-contractor engaged in work on the site and to the surveyor that in abnormal weather the wall might topple but he ignored the risk. On the surveyor's claim for damages for personal injury, *held*, it was clear that the wall's construction and support accorded with normal building practice and so the site owner and sub-contractor could not be held negligent in that respect. If a person with no inkling of the hazards had been injured then the crucial issue would have been whether measures could have been taken to avoid any accident as the weather deteriorated. However, the surveyor was aware of the risks he was running and was consequently the author of his own misfortune. Although the defence of *volenti non fit injuria* could not apply in the absence of an agreement between the surveyor and site owner waiving the former's right of action in the event of injury, neither the latter nor the sub-contractor was in breach of his statutory duty to a visitor as the degree of care expected of a visitor varied according to the circumstances.

Epp v Ridgetop Builders Ltd (1978) 94 DLR (3d) 505 (Supreme Court of Alberta).

1980　　**Public policy—failure of doctor to carry out abortion—right of mother to damages for birth of child**

See *Sciuriaga v Powell*, para. P1318.

1981   Res ipsa loquitur—application of maxim—facts sufficiently known

The plaintiff and his friends were travelling on the top deck of a bus. The plaintiff went to look out of the window and as he leant against it it gave way and he fell out onto the ground. He brought an action against the bus company, and the judge held that the plaintiff had not used undue force. While rejecting the allegation that the windows were of unsafe design, he held that the defendants were negligent on the basis of res ipsa loquitur since they were unable to discharge the burden of proving that they had an adequate system of inspection which would have revealed any defect. On appeal, *held*, the judge was wrong to hold that the doctrine of res ipsa loquitur applied. The doctrine was dependent on the absence of explanation of the occurrence and it was clear that it was the plaintiff's action, whatever its precise nature, which triggered off the collapse of the window. Accordingly the burden of proof remained on the plaintiff, and he had not discharged it. He had failed to show that the accident was caused by an antecedent defect in the window which an inspection would have revealed. The appeal would be allowed.

JOHNSON v LONDON TRANSPORT EXECUTIVE (1979) 25th May (unreported) (Court of Appeal: STEPHENSON, ROSKILL and BROWNE LJJ).

1982   Road accident—driver—duty of care

See *Lancaster v HB & H Transport Ltd*, para. 1962.

1983   —— —— standard of care—defence of impaired judgment

The defendant's car collided head-on with a parked car, damaging the car beyond repair and injuring a woman and her child. The woman's husband brought an action against the defendant for damage to the car, and she claimed damages for injuries suffered by herself and her child. There was no dispute that the circumstances of the collision established a prima facie case of negligence against the defendant entitling the plaintiffs to damages. The defendant however contended that he was not liable to the plaintiffs because twenty minutes before the accident he had unknowingly suffered a stroke, causing his conciousness to be impaired. From then on, through no fault of his own, he was unable to control the car properly or appreciate the fact that he was no longer fit to drive. Evidence showed that shortly before the collision with the plaintiffs' car he had struck a van and knocked a boy off a bicycle when there would have been plenty of room to pass. He stated that before each collision he felt odd but fine afterwards. The question was whether the defendant's physical condition absolved him from liability for negligence. *Held*, the defendant was unable to escape liability for negligence where shortly before the accident his conciousness was impaired unless the facts established that his actions were wholly beyond his control, namely what the law recognised as automatism. The defendant retained some control and his driving judged objectively was below the required standard but remained similar to that of an old or infirm driver. The defendant was alternatively liable to the plaintiffs on the grounds that he continued to drive when unfit to do so and should have been aware of his unfitness particularly following the earlier collision with the parked van. Although due to his mental state he was unable to appreciate that he should have stopped and he was in no way morally to blame that was irrelevant to the question of legal liability since impairment of judgment was not a defence.

ROBERTS v RAMSBOTTOM [1980] 1 All ER 7 (Queen's Bench Division sitting at Manchester: NEILL J). *Hill v Baxter* [1958] 1 All ER 193 and *Whatmore v Jenkins* [1962] 2 All ER 868 applied.

1984   —— expert evidence—admissibility

See *Hinds v London Transport Executive*, para. 1258.

1985 **Standard of care—parental responsibility for children—whether parents negligent**

Canada

The plaintiff, a child, lost the sight of one eye when he was shot by a boy aged thirteen with a pump-action pellet gun. The boy's father, who thought that the gun was far less powerful than it was, had not given his son any instruction in its use. But he had told him that the gun was only to be used in the presence of himself, his wife or an older brother. The gun and ammunition were kept in an unlocked cupboard and drawer in the house. The son disobeyed the instructions, took the gun and ammunition and, following an argument, shot the plaintiff in the eye. The plaintiff brought an action for damages against the son and his parents. *Held*, judgment should be given against the boy and his parents. The negligence of the son was conceded. The parents had been negligent in leaving the gun and ammunition readily available and unattended. This made it easily possible for the son to disregard their instructions. They were also negligent in failing to give the boy proper instruction in the use of what was not a toy but a dangerous weapon.

FLOYD V BOWERS (1978) 21 OR (2d) 204 (High Court of Ontario).

1986 **—— profession of special skill—doctor**

An obstetrician was sued in negligence for the brain damage suffered by a baby he had delivered, which, following a forceps examination, he had delivered by Caesarean section. At first instance he was held liable in negligence and damages were awarded against him. On appeal *held*, DONALDSON LJ dissenting, the judge's finding that the obstetrician had pulled too long and too hard with the forceps and that he was thus guilty of such want of skill and care that it was he who caused the baby's cerebral haemorrhage, would be reversed. There was no evidence of negligence disclosed, other than in a report by two professors which could not stand up against the reports of the other distinguished men. In any event, had the forceps examination been too long and too hard, it would not have been negligent but an error of judgment. In a professional man an error of judgment was not negligent. The appeal would therefore be allowed. Both LORD DENNING MR and LAWTON LJ noted that to allow findings of negligence on flimsy evidence or to regard failure to produce an expected result as strong evidence, would lead to the practice of defensive medicine (that was adopting procedures which were not for the benefit of the patient or refusing to treat patients for fear of being accused of negligence).

WHITEHOUSE V JORDAN [1980] 1 All ER 650 (Court of Appeal: LORD DENNING MR, LAWTON and DONALDSON LJJ).

For a discussion of this case see Justinian, Temptation to stretch the law resisted, Financial Times, 10th December 1979.

1987 **—— —— driving instructor**

The plaintiff, a learner driver, had been receiving driving lessons in a dual control car over a period of several months and had made satisfactory progress. During one lesson her instructor allowed her to drive her husband's car which did not have dual controls. The plaintiff drove satisfactorily for several miles, but when making a left turn she took the corner too widely and then over corrected the steering so that she was driving towards a tree. The instructor pulled on the handbrake, but could not prevent an accident. Neither the instructor nor the plaintiff were wearing seat belts, and were more seriously injured than they would have been if they had been wearing them. The plaintiff brought an action for damages against the instructor and the driving school on the grounds of negligence and breach of contract in allowing her to drive a car without dual controls and for failing to prevent the collision. *Held*, in the limited time available the instructor had done all that a reasonable driving instructor could be expected to do to prevent an accident. The instructor had not been unreasonable in allowing the plaintiff to drive a car without dual controls; it was a natural progression in her driving instruction. The instructor had been negligent in failing to make a proper recommendation for wearing seat belts but that negligence was not a cause of the accident and therefore did not found a claim in the action.

GIBBONS V PRIESTLEY [1979] RTR 4 (Queen's Bench Division: JUDGE LYMBERY QC sitting as a deputy High Court judge).

1988   —— shipping collision—apportionment of liability

See *The Devotion II*, para. 2536.

1989   Strict liability of defendant—damage caused by plaintiff's negligence—defence of circuity of action

See *Post Office v Hampshire County Council*, para. 2731; *Post Office v Mears Construction Ltd*, para. 2732.

NORTHERN IRELAND

Halsbury's Laws of England (4th edn.), Vol. 8, paras. 1637–1647

1990   Emergency provisions

The Northern Ireland (Emergency Provisions) Act 1978 (Amendment) Order 1979, S.I. 1979 No. 746 (in force on 3rd July 1979) adds the Irish National Liberation Army to the list of proscribed organisations contained in the Northern Ireland (Emergency Provisions) Act 1978 Sch. 2, 1978 Halsbury's Abridgment, para. 2034.

1991   House of Commons—number of Irish members

See para. 2005.

1992   Northern Ireland Act 1974—interim period extension

The Northern Ireland Act 1974 (Interim Period Extension) Order 1979, S.I. 1979 No. 816 (in force on 11th July 1979), extends until 16th July 1980 the period specified in the Northern Ireland Act 1974, s. 1 (4), as extended by S.I. 1978 No. 957, 1978 Halsbury's Abridgment para. 2033, for the operation of the temporary provisions for the government of Northern Ireland contained in Sch. 1 to the Act.

1993   Northern Ireland (Emergency Provisions) Act 1978—continuance

The Northern Ireland (Emergency Provisions) Act 1978 (Continuance) Order 1979, S.I. 1979 No. 817 (in force on 25th July 1979), continues in force the temporary provisions of the Northern Ireland (Emergency Provisions) Act 1978 for a period of six months from 25th July 1979.

1994   The Northern Ireland (Emergency Provisions) Act 1978 (Continuance) (No. 2) Order 1979, S.I. 1979 No. 1683 (in force on 25th January 1980), continues in force the temporary provisions of the Northern Ireland (Emergency Provisions) Act 1978 for a period of six months from 25th January 1980.

NUISANCE

Halsbury's Laws of England (3rd edn.), Vol. 28, paras. 152–245

1995   Construction work—damage to adjoining property—date of assessment of damages

See *Dodd Properties (Kent) Ltd v Canterbury City Council*, para. 793.

1996   **Continuance of nuisance—landlord's liability to tenant—obstruction of access**

See *Hilton v James Smith and Sons (Norwood) Ltd*, para. 1690.

1997   **Defence—defence of statutory authority—statutory power to "use" an oil refinery—whether available as a defence—meaning of "use"**

See *Allen v Gulf Oil Refining Ltd.*, para. 1372.

1998   **Escape—no negligence by defendant—blockage in sewer**

Canada

The respondents were landowners and their premises were severely damaged as a result of a blocked sewer constructed and maintained by the appellants, a municipal authority. The respondents sued alleging negligence and claiming also in nuisance. The trial judge found that where a municipality constructed and operated a sewer pursuant to legislation and was not negligent in the construction it was nevertheless liable in nuisance. The municipal authority appealed against the attribution of liability for nuisance and the respondents cross-appealed against the finding absolving the appellants of negligence. *Held*, affirming the decision of the trial judge, the essence of the tort of nuisance was interference with the enjoyment of land not necessarily accompanied by negligence. The test was whether the defendant's use of the land interfered with the use and enjoyment of the plaintiff's land and that the interference was unreasonable.

ROYAL ANNE HOTEL CO LTD v VILLAGE OF ASHCROFT; SAITO v VILLAGE OF ASHCROFT (1979) 35 DLR (3d) 756 (Court of Appeal of British Columbia).

1999   **Neighbouring properties—hazard arising from natural causes—encroachment on neighbouring property—liability of occupier**

The plaintiffs' houses stood at the foot of a hill owned and occupied by the National Trust. Over a number of years, as a result of natural causes, falls of soil and other detritus took place from the hill onto the plaintiffs' land. The plaintiffs complained, but no action was taken. In 1976 a heavy fall occurred onto the plaintiffs' properties. The National Trust denied responsibility and the plaintiffs commenced an action in nuisance. An interlocutory injunction was granted and the National Trust carried out work on the land. At the hearing of the main action, the National Trust was held liable in nuisance. They appealed, contending that neither the owner nor the occupier of land from which, solely as the result of natural causes, natural mineral material encroached on to, or threatened to encroach on to, adjoining land, causing damage, was under any liability to the adjoining land owner. *Held*, the question was whether the decision in *Goldman v Hargrave*, to the effect that there was liability in such a situation, correctly represented the law of England. The Privy Council in that case had held that the effect of the decision of the House of Lords in *Sedleigh-Denfield v O'Callaghan* was to impose a general duty upon occupiers in relation to hazards occurring on their land, whether natural or man-made. The House of Lords' decision in the *Sedleigh-Denfield* case was that an occupier was liable for a nuisance arising from a latent defect, including a defect in the land itself, or from the act of a trespasser it he failed to remedy it when he became, or ought to have become, aware of it.

If this decision was correct, then the adoption of it in *Goldman v Hargrave* was an accurate statement of the law. However, the National Trust argued that the House of Lords was not entitled to reach the decision because in doing so it departed from the principle laid down in *Rylands v Fletcher*. There was nothing in the true ratio decidendi of *Rylands v Fletcher* which rendered the decision in the *Sedleigh-Denfield* case incorrect. The true decision in *Rylands v Fletcher* was that there was strict liability where the defendant erected or brought upon his land something of an unusual nature which was essentially dangerous in itself. It was not authority for the proposition that a person who had not used his land in a non-natural way was in no circumstances liable if something from his land encroached on his neighbour's land. Thus the *Rylands v Fletcher* principle was irrelevant in the *Sedleigh-Denfield* case and the House of Lords was not precluded by it from reaching its decision.

Nor was there any decision subsequent to that in the *Sedleigh-Denfield* case which prevented the court from holding that the law as laid down in the *Sedleigh-Denfield* case was correctly stated in *Goldman v Hargrave*. Finally, as a matter of policy there should be a duty in a case such as the present. Hence the Privy Council's decision in *Goldman v Hargrave* was a correct exposition of the law; there was a duty to do what was reasonable in all the circumstances to prevent or minimise the known or foreseeable risk of damage or injury to one's neighbour or his property. The National Trust was in breach of this duty and the appeal would be dismissed.

LEAKEY v NATIONAL TRUST FOR PLACES OF HISTORIC INTEREST OR NATURAL BEAUTY [1980] 1 All ER 17 (Court of Appeal: MEGAW, SHAW and CUMMING-BRUCE LJJ). *Goldman v Hargrave* [1967] AC 645, PC, *Sedleigh-Denfield v O'Callaghan* [1940] AC 880, HL applied; *Davey v Harrow Corpn* [1958] 1 QB 60, CA approved; *Rylands v Fletcher* (1868) LR 3 HL distinguished; *Giles v Walker* (1890) 24 QBD 656, DC and *Ponterdawe RDC v Moore-Gwyn* [1929] 1 Ch 656 overruled. Decision of O'Connor J [1978] 3 All ER 234, 1978 Halsbury's Abridgment para. 2038 affirmed.

OPEN SPACES AND HISTORIC BUILDINGS

Halsbury's Laws of England (3rd edn.), Vol. 28, paras. 246–441

2000   Ancient Monuments and Archaeological Areas Act 1979

The Ancient Monuments and Archaeological Areas Act 1979 consolidates and amends the law relating to ancient monuments and makes provision for the investigation, preservation and recording of matters of archaeological or historical interest. The Act received the royal assent on 4th April 1979. Sections 48, 49 came into force on 16th July 1979: S.I. 1979 No. 786. Remaining provisions come into force on days to be appointed: s. 65.

Ancient Monuments

Part I deals with the protection of ancient monuments. Section 1 provides for a Schedule of monuments to be compiled and maintained by the Secretary of State, who must also publish a list of the monuments included. Under s. 2, it is an offence to execute, cause or permit the execution of works damaging or otherwise affecting a scheduled monument unless such works are authorised by written consent of the Secretary of State ("scheduled monument consent"). Schedule 1, Part I, deals with applications for such consent. Section 3 deals with the grant of scheduled monument consent by order of the Secretary of State, and s. 4 and Sch. 1, Part II, with its duration, modification and revocation. Section 5 empowers the Secretary of State to carry out any works urgently necessary for the preservation of a scheduled monument. Section 6 provides powers of entry for the inspection of scheduled monuments with a view to ascertaining their condition. Sections 7–9 provide for the payment of compensation for loss or damage following the refusal or conditional grant of scheduled monument consent, or where works cease to be authorised. There is also provision for the recovery of compensation on a subsequent grant or modification of consent.

Section 10 enables the Secretary of State to acquire an ancient monument compulsorily for the purpose of securing its preservation, and s. 11 authorises acquisition by agreement or gift. Sections 12–14 enable the Secretary of State or local authorities to become the guardian of a monument, and deal with the effect and termination of guardianship. Sections 15 and 16 provide for the acquisition and guardianship of land in the vicinity of ancient monuments, and for the acquisition of easements and similar rights over such land. Section 17 enables the Secretary of State and local authorities to make agreements concerning ancient monuments and land in their vicinity providing for maintenance and public access. Section 18 empowers limited owners to enter into guardianship and other agreements. Section 19 provides for a right of public access to monuments under the ownership or guardianship of the Secretary of State or a local authority. Section 20 deals with the provision of facilities and information for the public in connection with ancient monuments. Section 21 provides for the transfer of ancient monuments between local authorities and Secretary of State. Sections 22 and 23 relate to the Ancient Monuments Boards, their membership, functions and annual reports. Section 24 provides for expenditure by the Secretary of State or local authorities on the acquisition and preservation of ancient monuments. Section 25 enables the Secretary of State to advise on ancient monuments and to superintend works. Section 26 confers power to enter on land believed to contain an ancient monument for the purpose of investigating, recording information and excavating. Section 27 contains general provisions as to compensation for depreciation under Part I. Section 28 creates an offence of damaging certain ancient monuments and s. 29 provides for compensation orders for damage to monuments under guardianship. Section 30 empowers the Secretary of State or local authorities to dispose of land acquired by them under Part I. Section 31 authorises receipt of voluntary contributions towards expenditure on monuments. Section 32 deals with interpretation of Part I.

Archaeological areas
Part II deals with areas of archaeological importance. Section 33 authorises the designation of areas of archaeological importance and Sch. 2 deals with the making, variation and revocation of designation orders. Section 34 provides for the appointment of investigating authorities to carry out archaeological investigations in such areas. Section 35 makes it an offence to carry out, or cause or permit to be carried out, operations which disturb the ground or involve flooding or tipping, without first serving an operations notice. A local authority may seek an injunction to prevent operations in contravention of s. 35. Section 36 provides for the issue of certificates to accompany operations notices. Section 37 confers exemptions from an offence under s. 35 and provides defences. Section 38 provides investigating authorities with powers to enter and excavate a site of operations covered by an operations notice and s. 39 confers on them power to investigate in advance of an operations notice any site which may be acquired compulsorily. Section 40 contains a power for persons authorised by the Secretary of State or the Royal Commission on Historical Monuments to enter on a site of operations covered by an operations notice. Section 41 deals with interpretation of Part II.

Miscellaneous
Part III deals with miscellaneous and supplementary matters. Section 42 provides for restrictions on the use of metal detectors on the site of a protected monument or in an area of archaeological importance. Section 43 authorises entry onto land for the purpose of surveying or valuing it in connection with acquisition or compensation. Section 44 contains supplementary provisions relating to powers of entry. Section 45 provides for expenditure on archaeological investigation. Section 46 relates to compensation for damage to land or chattels caused by the exercise of powers conferred by the Act. Section 47 contains general provisions with respect to claims for compensation. Section 48 provides for the recovery of grants for expenditure in conservation areas and on historic buildings. Section 49 makes provision for grants to the Archaeological Heritage Fund. Section 50 relates to Crown land, s. 51 to ecclesiastical property, s. 52 to the Isles of Scilly and s. 53 to monuments in territorial waters. Section 54 enables temporary custody to be taken of finds of archaeological or historical interest. Section 55 provides for appeals to the courts against certain orders and decisions under the Act. Sections 56–61 are supplemental. Sections 62 and 63 make special provision for Scotland and Wales. Section 64 and Schs. 3, 4 and 5 make transitional provisions and provide for consequential amendments and repeals. Section 65 deals with commencement and extent.

2001   Listed building—church—demolition

See para. 986.

PARLIAMENT

Halsbury's Laws of England (3rd edn.), Vol. 28, paras. 442–924

2002   General election—effect on local elections—simultaneous polling

See Representation of the People Act 1979, para. 1018.

2003   House of Commons—Members' Fund

The Resolution of the House of Commons, dated 10th December 1979 (S.I. 1979 No. 1667), passed in pursuance of the House of Commons Members' Fund Act 1948, s. 3, varies from 1st December 1979 the maximum annual amounts of the periodical payments which may be made out of the House of Commons Members' Fund under the House of Commons Members' Fund Act 1939.

2004   —— standing orders

The Standing Orders of the House of Commons, Public Business, 1979 have been published as HC 78 (HM Stationery Office). The publication includes a table showing the dates on which the individual Standing Orders were passed and, where relevant, amended; it also includes a subject index.

2005   House of Commons (Redistribution of Seats) Act 1979

The House of Commons (Redistribution of Seats) Act 1979 increases the number of Northern Irish constituencies to between sixteen and eighteen. In normal conditions the number should be seventeen. The Act received the royal assent on 22nd March 1979 and came into force on that date.

2006   Parliamentary proceedings—sub judice rule

Four members of Parliament in supplementary questions on 20th April 1978 identified "Colonel B" (a witness in criminal proceedings) at a time when the legality of identifying "Colonel B" was the subject of proceedings before the Divisional Court. The Speaker ruled that this was in breach of the sub judice rule on 24th April 1978. The question of the application of the sub judice rule was referred to the Committee of Privileges who, after consideration, decided not to recommend any alteration of the rule. The rule is founded on resolutions of 23rd July 1963 and 28th June 1972: "That subject to the discretion of the chair and the right of the House to legislate on any matter (1) matters awaiting or under adjudication in all courts exercising a criminal jurisdiction . . . should not be referred to . . . (c) in any question to a Minister including a supplementary question". The committee stated that it was possible to contend that in referring to "Colonel B" and in stating his name the members were not referring to matters awaiting or under adjudication in a court since they were merely repeating in the House statements as to identity which, having been made by others outside the House, had become the subject of the proceedings. The committee said that it might therefore be argued that the members were not commenting on the legality of what had been done and were not referring to any matter under adjudication. The committee found, however, that such contention was unduly narrow and technical. Reference in the House to matters which are the factual basis for the issues before a court, or even to facts so closely connected with those matters as to be liable to prejudice the interests of the due administration of justice is, in the committee's view, clearly within the scope of the rule. See Second Report from the Committee of Privileges (Session 1978–79), HC 222, paras. 11–18.

2007   Reports—qualified privilege

See para. 1751.

2008 **Statutes—royal assent**

During 1979 sixty public general Acts received the royal assent. Of these, four related to Scotland. Of the remainder, fifteen were consolidation Acts.

PARTNERSHIP

Halsbury's Laws of England (3rd edn.), Vol. 28, paras. 925–1169

2009 **Existence of partnership—agreement for development of land**

A dispute arose out of an agreement between property developers and builders to build dwelling houses on certain land. The question was whether the agreement constituted a partnership or was merely a building contract. *Held*, the relation between the parties had to be determined from the evidence and from all the admissible surrounding circumstances; the only evidence in the instant case was contained in the agreement. The agreement provided expressly for sharing profits but not for sharing losses, for consultation with regard to the appointment of estate agents, and for the project to be advertised as a joint project. The parties were accordingly carrying on a business in common and the agreement was for a joint development enterprise with a reasonable distribution of financial burden, coupled with a degree of sharing of the overheads. Despite some contrary indications, the agreement constituted a partnership.

WALKER WEST DEVELOPMENTS LTD v F. J. EMMETT LTD (1979) 252 Estates Gazette 1171 (Court of Appeal: BUCKLEY, GOFF and EVELEIGH LJJ). Dicta of North J in *Davis v Davis* [1894] 1 Ch 393 at pages 398, 399 applied.

2010 **—— assessment to income tax**

In 1960 S and P were partners in a firm carrying on the business of dealing in and repairing agricultural machinery. There was no written partnership agreement. In 1972 R and J were employed, undertaking a small amount of work. The accounts showed that salaries had been paid to them. In 1973 the firm obtained a major marketing franchise and R and J enjoyed a more active position with the firm. In 1975 a written partnership agreement was signed by all four parties providing that the partnership should commence from April 1973 and that the profits of the business as shown by the accounts should be divided. R and J were also informed that they would become liable for the firm's debts. No notice as to the change of the partnership was given to the bank, creditors or customers, nor did R and J introduce any capital into the business or have drawing rights from the partnership bank account. The accounts for 1973–74 showed share profits credited to R and J. In assessing the firm to income tax for 1973–74 and 1974–75 the Inspector of Taxes proceeded on the assumption that at no time between April 1973 and 1975 were R and J partners. The General Commissioners upheld the decision of the Inspector and the parties appealed. *Held*, (i) where a written partnership agreement stated that it should take effect from a date prior to its execution it cannot legally operate where the partners in truth had not been partners from that date; (ii) receipt by a person of a share in the business profits was prima facie evidence of a partnership. Although the accounts for the relevant years showed a credit sharing of the net profit to R and J there was no evidence as to when the accounts were drawn up and they were never accompanied by the drawing of shares by R and J. The accounts did not prove a receipt of a share of the profit of the firm by R and J within the Partnership Act 1890 s. 2 (3). In the circumstances R and J were not partners of the firm.

SAYWELL v POPE (INSPECTOR OF TAXES) [1979] STC 824 (Chancery Division: SLADE J). Dicta of Rowlatt J in *Waddington v O'Callaghan (Inspector of Taxes)* (1913) 16 Tax Cas 187 at 197 and North J in *Davis v Davis* [1894] 1 Ch 393 at 399 followed.

2011   **—— registration for VAT—liability of one party for tax**

Value added tax tribunal decision:

PETER V CUSTOMS AND EXCISE COMRS (1979) MAN/76/88 (unreported) (taxpayer agreed to go into business with antique dealer; taxpayer dealt in coins in conjunction with antique business from same premises; taxpayer and antique dealer opened bank account in their joint names; antique dealer notified the commissioners that he had entered into partnership with taxpayer; commissioners registered taxpayer and antique dealer as taxable persons; partnership was later dissolved; partnership assessed for tax; taxpayer appealed on ground that he was never a partner in antique business as coin business was carried on separately; taxpayer had raised no objection when form of notification specified partnership; accounts for both coin and antique businesses kept in one book; taxpayer had held himself out as a partner in his business dealings; a partnership did exist).

PATENTS AND INVENTIONS

Halsbury's Laws of England (3rd edn.), Vol. 29, paras. 1–388

2012   **Application—amendment of claim—exercise of discretion to amend—evidence required before discretion exercised**

Two applications for patents were filed in the United States of America, concerning related subject matters. In an application for a patent in the United Kingdom, the two subject matters were combined in one claim, with the result that the United Kingdom patent would not get priority from its being founded upon either of the earlier applications in the United States of America, but would take priority only from the date of filing in the United Kingdom. The applicants applied under the Patents Act 1949, s. 29 to amend the United Kingdom application by splitting the claim into two claims, each relating to one of the American applications. This was granted by the superintending examiner in the Patent Office and upheld by the Appeal Tribunal. The applicants had produced evidence that their American patent agents were responsible for the form in which the application was made. The opponents appealed on the ground that evidence should also have been produced as to what advice was given and what decisions were made by the firm of British patent agents who filed the application in the United Kingdom. *Held*, allowing the appeal, under s. 29 it was for the applicants to demonstrate that the form in which the claim was made was not the form in which it was intended to be made. As no evidence had been produced as to the role played by the British agents in filing the application, there was not sufficient information concerning the reasons for the mistake and the discretion to amend the application could not be exercised.

SCM CORPORATION'S APPLICATION [1979] RPC 341 (Court of Appeal: BUCKLEY and GOFF LJJ).

2013   **—— anticipation—prior publication without consent of applicant**

An application for a patent was opposed on the grounds, inter alia, that the article had been invented by one of the opponents and that the invention had been anticipated by being published before the priority date of the claim. The applicant sought to rely on the Patents Act 1949, s. 50 (2) which provided that an invention was not anticipated where the information had been obtained from the applicant and published without his consent. The evidence demonstrated that the opponents had published the information before the priority date against the applicant's express wishes. The superintending examiner was unable to decide, on the evidence, who was the inventor and therefore held that, as the applicant had not positively proved the invention was his, he could not therefore establish that the invention had been obtained from him. Furthermore he was unable to demonstrate lack of consent, because he had not given the information to the opponent in confidence. The Patents Appeal Tribunal reversed this decision, finding that the applicant was the true inventor and holding that confidentiality was not pertinent to the question of consent, the applicant's express opposition to publication being sufficient lack of consent. The opponents appealed, contending that the appellate court was not justified in coming to a different conclusion on the facts from that of the superintending examiner. *Held*, dismissing the appeal, the appeal tribunal had not upset any finding of fact of the examiner. The examiner came to no conclusion as to which party was the inventor, and therefore the appellate court had been free to decide that issue. It has also rightly considered the matter of confidentiality irrelevant to the question of consent.

TIEFEBRUN'S APPLICATION [1979] FSR 97 (Court of Appeal: BUCKLEY, GOFF and EVELEIGH LJJ).

2014   —— manner of new manufacture—change in colour of article

A patent application was brought relating to a blue squash ball; the applicant maintaining that the colour blue gave enhanced visual impact during play. The principal examiner refused to allow the application to proceed, on the basis that although it related to a manner of manufacture it was not a manner of new manufacture. The applicants appealed. *Held*, the application would be allowed to proceed. The evidence indicated that the colouring of the ball may have added a desirable characteristic to it; the ball had been commercially successful and competitors had started to manufacture blue balls. The idea of a blue ball was not necessarily obvious, as it had not been thought of before and the visual effect of the ball had come as a surprise when it was first tried out. The case was not one where the application should at that stage be refused.

ITS RUBBER LTD'S APPLICATION [1979] RPC 318 (Chancery Division: WHITFORD J).

2015   —— —— topograms enabling identification of diamonds

An application for a patent was refused by both the examiner and the Patents Appeal Tribunal on the ground that no new manufacture had been disclosed, and the applicants appealed to the Court of Appeal. The application related to a procedure whereby photographic records of the X-ray diffraction patterns of diamonds were made. Records of this type, known as topograms, were known at the date of application, but the procedure in question differed from others in that these particular topograms enabled diamonds to be individually identified. *Held*, it was not simply topograms that were to be manufactured, but topograms made by a procedure which was claimed to be new and which enabled identification of diamonds. The procedure constituted a new manner of manufacture, the novelty lying not in the making of topograms, but making them by a procedure which resulted in them being able to be used for a totally new purpose. The appeal would be allowed.

DE BEERS CONSOLIDATED MINES LTD'S APPLICATION [1979] FSR 72 (Court of Appeal: BUCKLEY, ORR and GOFF LJJ).

2016   —— opposition—prior claiming—substance of claims

A patent application related to claims concerning a developer composition for electrostatic images primarily for use in copying machines. The application was opposed on the basis of prior claiming. The hearing officer decided that although the phraseology of each relevant claim was different, the invention claimed was in substance the same as in the earlier specification. He also decided that amendment was necessary to meet this finding and further directed that a reference under the Patents Act 1949, s. 9 should be inserted into the specification. The applicant appealed against his decision and further contended that a s. 9 reference should be dealt with in separate proceedings. On appeal, *held*, the claims did not involve any question of inventive concept, merely the requirement that the developer materials should have certain properties. The pre-requisite properties were in substance the same in both the earlier and later claim. The appeal would be dismissed.

It was further held that a s. 9 reference should be dealt with as soon as the matter came to the notice of the tribunal, whether raised by the parties or not.

XEROX CORPN (CHATTERJI'S) APPLICATION [1979] RPC 375 (Patents Appeal Tribunal: WHITFORD J).

2017   —— —— **prior user—burden of proof**

An application for a patent concerning a wheel for tubeless tyres was made. The opponents relied on prior user as a ground of objection to the patent being granted. Their evidence was not challenged but the applicants contended that the burden was on the opponents to prove not only the prior user but also that it had been non-secret which they had failed to establish. The opponents contended that the burden of proof as regards the question of secrecy lay with the applicants. *Held*, the burden was on the opponents to prove all the necessary elements of a ground of opposition and in this case it was necessary to establish that prior use was not secret. If however the question of the secrecy of the prior user was not raised as an evidential issue, the opponents were to be taken as having discharged their burden without having to prove non-secrecy. The evidential burden might shift during the course of the proceedings. The opponents' evidence was clearly in the direction of non-secret use and so the evidential burden shifted to the applicants. The opponents' evidence, having been unchallenged, was to be taken at face value and the opposition would therefore be upheld.

DUNLOP HOLDINGS LTD'S APPLICATION [1979] RPC 523 (Court of Appeal: BUCKLEY, BRIDGE and WALLER LJJ).

2018   —— —— **use of confidential documents**

See *Halcon International Inc v Shell Transport and Trading Co*, para. 920.

2019   —— **request for preliminary examination and search—"relevant prescribed period"**

An application was filed on 2nd October 1978 claiming priority under the International Convention over an Italian application filed a year earlier. The applicants did not file the appropriate forms for a preliminary examination and search within the specified time period. The Comptroller of the Patent Office held that he had no power to extend the time limit or to treat the matter as an irregularity in procedure which he could, in his discretion, rectify under the Patents Rules 1978, rr. 100 and 110, and therefore in accordance with the provisions of the Patents Act 1977, s. 15 (5), the application was taken to have been withdrawn. The applicants appealed. *Held*, the "relevant prescribed period" in s. 15 (5) was different for filing the claims and abstract and for requesting a search and r. 25 which prescribed different time limits was hence not ultra vires. The applicants' failure to request a search was an irregularity in the procedure necessary to obtain a patent and had occurred "in proceedings before the Office". It could therefore be rectified in accordance with r. 100. The Comptroller had a discretionary power to rectify the irregularity notwithstanding that the correction would necessarily involve an enlargement of the time specified by r. 25. The appeal would be allowed.

FATER SpA's APPLICATION [1979] FSR 647 (Patents Court: GRAHAM J).

2020   **Comptroller-General of Patents—annual report**

The 96th Report of the Comptroller General of Patents, Designs and Trade Marks (HC 2) draws attention to the Patents Act 1977 which came into operation on 1st June 1978. The substantive law and procedure laid down is so different from that laid down by the old law that practically all comparisons between the statistics of 1978 and those of the preceding years are meaningless. Nevertheless the report notes that 50,324 applications for United Kingdom patents were made in 1978; 925 applications were made under the European Patent Convention and 56 applications under the Patent Co-operation Treaty. In the same year there were 5,147 applications for new registrations of designs; this is the highest figure since 1972 and represents an increase of 15 per cent over the 1977 figure. There was also a sharp rise in the number of applications for trade marks. The figure of 18,150 for 1978 represented an increase of 12 per cent over the 1977 figure.

2021   **Extension—invention of wholly exceptional character—benefit to public**

The petitioners applied for an extension of the term of the patent on segmented skirts for containing the air cushion of hovercraft, claiming that theirs was an exceptional case and merited the maximum entitlement of ten years. *Held*, since this was an invention which could truly be said to have contributed to the public good in an exceptional way (in particular via the export market), and which would increasingly continue to do so, an order for the extension of the patent for a further ten years would be made. The development of the hovercraft had depended largely on the invention of the segmented skirt, and a great deal of money had been spent in abortive research before arriving at the present solution. In order to recoup the losses incurred in research and development it was possible that an extension period would redress the balance in favour of those who had devoted their time and energy to the development of a product as commercially and economically beneficial as the hovercraft.

HOVERCRAFT DEVELOPMENT LIMITED'S PATENT EXTENSION [1979] FSR 481 (Patents Court: WHITFORD J).

2022   **Infringement—action for infringement—discovery of documents**

The defendants intended to import into the United Kingdom material produced by a process in which they used insoluble catalysts. The plaintiffs held two patents for the process, but they had previously used only soluble catalysts. In an action for infringement of the patents, the defendants alleged that the process involving the use of soluble catalysts had been published at the priority date of one of the patents. They contended that the patents were invalid for obviousness, insufficiency and utility. The defendants sought orders for discovery of documents relating to the plaintiffs' research, which they contended were relevant to the validity of the patents and to the question of whether the named inventor had in fact invented insoluble catalysts. *Held*, (i) documents relating to the plaintiffs' research might be of considerable assistance to the court in determining the question of obviousness and ought to be disclosed; (ii) documents recording the plaintiffs' experiments might disclose either that the plaintiffs had failed to use insoluble catalysts, or that they had attempted to use insoluble catalysts, but had been unsuccessful, which might be of relevance to the issues of insufficiency and utility. Accordingly, discovery would be ordered.

HALCON INTERNATIONAL INC v THE SHELL TRANSPORT AND TRADING CO LTD (DISCOVERY NO. 2) [1979] RPC 459 (Chancery Division: WHITFORD J). Dictum of Edmund-Davies LJ in *Woven Plastics Products Ltd v British Ropes Ltd* [1970] FSR 47 applied.

For previous proceedings in this case, see [1979] RPC 97, para. 920.

2023   **—— —— whether carrier or warehouseman an infringer—meaning of "keeps"**

An airline which had possession of an infringing product in its bonded warehouse was made a defendant in the proceedings for patent infringement. The patentee contended that the airline had infringed the patent under the Patent Act 1977, s. 60 (1) (a), by keeping the product in its warehouse. The airline sought relief by way of interpleader to secure its release from the action, an order removing the product from its custody and payment of the costs and charges incurred. *Held*, it was clear under the law in force before the 1977 Act that an innocent carrier or warehouseman of an infringing product did not infringe a patent. One of the purposes of the 1977 Act was to give effect to the Community Patent Convention, which provided that a Community patent conferred the right to prevent others from making, offering, putting on the market or using a product or importing or stocking the product for those purposes. The word "keeps" in s. 60 (1) (a) was therefore to be construed in the same sense as the convention and connoted a keeping in some capacity and for a purpose other than that of a mere custodian. The airline had not therefore done anything which constituted an infringement. Further, it was also entitled to recover its costs and charges from the patent infringers, except in so far as they related to the patentee's unnecessary accusation of patent infringement against the airline.

SMITH KLINE AND FRENCH LABORATORIES v R D HARBOTTLE (MERCANTILE) LTD [1979] FSR 555 (Patents Court: OLIVER J).

2024   —— application for order of inspection—inadequacy of evidence in support of contention

A patent for bin activators, held by the plaintiffs, had as part of its specification a device, named a baffle member, which prevented material from flowing straight down through the discharge outlet by virtue of its conical shape. In the defendants' bin activator the use of a device, resembling the ribs of an umbrella, prompted the plaintiffs to contend that it would perform a job similar to their baffle member, by causing material to form a cone over the ribbed structure. On the grounds that they suspected infringement, the plaintiffs sought an order for inspection so that they might take measurements for the purpose of experiment. The defendants sought to have the action struck out as being frivolous and an abuse of the process of court, but they were willing to allow the plaintiffs access to the apparatus. *Held*, in view of the speculative nature of the assertion and the unlikelihood of the device performing the same functions as that of the plaintiff's baffle member, since material would fall through the "ribs" of the umbrella, an order for inspection would be refused. A viewing of the machine by the plaintiff's solicitors should prove adequately whether the assertion had been correct. However, the action would not be struck out since this would imply that no infringement had taken place, and this had not yet been proved or disproved.

WAHL AND SIMON-SOLITEC LTD v BUHLER-MIAG (ENGLAND) LTD [1979] FSR 183 (Chancery Division: WHITFORD J).

2025   —— declaration of non-infringement—written description of article—whether production of article also required

A company brought an action under the Patents Act 1949, s. 66 for a declaration that a particular process did not infringe three patents held by the patentee. Subsection 66(1) stipulates that the plaintiff must show that he has applied in writing to the patentee for a written acknowledgement to the effect of the declaration claimed and has furnished him with full particulars in writing of the process in question; this the company had done. The patentee sought by notice of motion to establish whether the company should also have furnished the patentee with a specimen of the article produced by this process. *Held*, ss. 66(1) clearly stated that full particulars in writing were all that was required, and there was no obligation on the company to furnish, in addition, a specimen.

PLASTICISERS LTD v PIXDANE LTD [1979] RPC 327 (Chancery Division: D. W. FALCONER QC sitting as a deputy High Court judge).

Patents Act 1949, s. 66 now Patents Act 1977, s. 71.

2026   —— finding of infringement—refusal to grant perpetual injunction

See *American Cyanamid Co v Ethicon Ltd*, para. 2035.

2027   —— foreign action pending—applicable for stay pending determination of foreign action

See *Western Electric Co Inc v Racal-Milgo Ltd*, para. 441.

2028   —— infringement by company—liability of director

Canada

The plaintiffs brought an action for infringement against the defendants, who were a small company engaged in the business of the assembly and selling of retractable pens. The defendant company was controlled and part owned by its managing director who was involved in the day to day running of the company. The defendants were found guilty of the infringement but the action against the managing director personally was dismissed. On appeal, *held*, an incorporated company was a separate legal entity from its officers. The degree of involvement by which a person made the tortious act his own was a question of fact. There were no circumstances in this case from which it was reasonable to calculate that the director was deliberately and wilfully pursuing a course likely to constitute infringement. The appeal would be dismissed.

MENTMORE MANUFACTURING CO LTD V NATIONAL MERCHANDISING MANUFACTURING CO INC (1978) 89 DLR (3d) 195 (Federal Court of Canada).

2029   —— specifications—whether specifications essentially similar

See *Catnic Components Ltd v Hill and Smith Ltd*, para. 532.

2030   —— statement of claim—details required for particulars of infringement

The defendants sold metal-coated diamond grit. The plaintiffs alleged infringement of their patent because metal-coated diamond grit was being embedded in a resin bond by customers of the defendants. The defendants moved to strike out the statement of claim as disclosing no cause of action, and at the same time the plaintiffs sought an order of discovery regarding the defendants' customers and supplier. At first instance the judge refused to strike out the statement of claim and granted the order for discovery. The defendants appealed. *Held*, by RSC Ord. 104, r. 5 (2) the particulars of the infringement should contain at least one instance of each type of infringement alleged. The first two paragraphs of the particulars of the infringement in the plaintiff's statement of claim contained no specific instances of the alleged infringements and thus disclosed no cause of action. Although paragraph three did contain a particular instance of the sale of the grit to a particular customer, selling articles to be used for the purpose of infringing a patent was not in itself an infringement of the patent on the part of the vendor, neither did it amount to procuring others to infringe the patent; thus paragraph three did not disclose a cause of action either. The appeal would be allowed.

BELEGGING-EN EXPLOITATIEMAATSCHAPPIJ LAVENDER BV V WITTEN INDUSTRIAL DIAMONDS LTD [1979] FSR 59 (Court of Appeal: BUCKLEY, GOFF and EVELEIGH LJJ).

2031   —— validity of patent—application for statement of nature of challenge to validity

The plaintiffs in a patent infringement action brought an application requiring the defendants to produce statements regarding certain advertisements which the defendants were claiming amounted to prior publication. The plaintiffs wished to know which features of the machinery, disclosed in the advertisements, corresponded with features of each claim of the patents; and which features disclosed in the advertisements would have been combined, by a man skilled in the art, with which other features, to produce a machine having the integers of each claim of the patents. *Held*, it was possible to make an order requiring such statements, but it would not be made in this case, because both the machinery and the advertisements were clear and uncomplicated, and the plaintiffs should not have any problems in deciding what was disclosed by the advertisements.

POWERSCREEN INTERNATIONAL LTD V J. FINLAY (ENGINEERING) LTD AND SURE EQUIPMENT LTD [1979] FSR 108 (Chancery Division: WHITFORD J).

2032   —— —— evidence—examination of witness outside jurisdiction

See *Lucas Industries Ltd v Chloride Batteries Australia Ltd*, para. 1262.

2033   Patent agent—negligence—duty of care owed to client

The plaintiffs developed a device enabling a marine crankshaft to be machined in situ, and instructed the defendants, a firm of patent agents to obtain a patent for the device as soon as possible. The defendants considered that the patent was invalid and informed the plaintiffs, who did not reply. The defendants failed to put in order the complete specification by the last possible date and the application for letters patent became void. The plaintiffs sued for negligence. The defendants contended that no valid patent would have been obtained and in advising the plaintiffs of that they had done all that was reasonably necessary. If they had been negligent, any monopoly could have been avoided by various modifications. *Held*, the degree of knowledge and care to be expected was that degree possessed by a duly qualified person practising in the profession. Applying that standard, the defendants had been negligent in that they had taken a superficial and incorrect view of the prior art and had failed to ascertain from the plaintiffs the features of the device which distinguished it from prior art. Further, they should not have assumed that the plaintiffs had decided to abandon the application, and had failed to establish that the monopoly would not have been effective against competitors had the device been registered.

ANDREW MASTER HONES LTD v CRUICKSHANK AND FAIRWEATHER [1979] FSR 268 (Chancery Division: GRAHAM J).

2034   Specification—amendment—obviousness

The plaintiffs were patentees of a device for securing containers to transporters. The device was designed to fit into sockets in the containers, but could be retracted so that it would be flush with the carrying surface of the transporter when other loads were being carried. During an infringement action the patentees sought to amend the verbal specification of the device on the ground of obvious mistake, because it was described as lying entirely within the body of the housing when in the retracted position, although in fact it projected below the housing. The claim was allowed by the patent judge and the Court of Appeal. On appeal by the defendants, *held*, there had been no intention to exclude from the patent devices which projected below the housing, and anyone who examined the specification with the drawings would see that such devices were intended to be included. Accordingly the specification would be amended.

HOLTITE LTD v JOST (GREAT BRITAIN) LTD [1979] RPC 81 (House of Lords: LORD DIPLOCK, LORD KILBRANDON, LORD SALMON, LORD EDMUND-DAVIES and LORD SCARMAN).

2035   —— construction—scope of expert evidence

The plaintiffs owned a patent relating to the process of manufacturing a synthetic, absorbable, surgical suture. The patent specification claimed that the suture was made from the homopolymer PHAE, derived from the homopolymerisation of glycolide. The defendant company manufactured a similar suture from a copolymer of glycolide and lactide in the proportions 90 per cent and 10 per cent respectively. The plaintiffs, by an action which was quia timet, sued for infringement of the patent and the defendant company counterclaimed for revocation on the basis of its invalidity. *Held*, in order to decide the issue of infringement it was necessary to determine, as a matter of construction, whether the claim of the patent specification included copolymers of glycolide and lactide. In view of the complexity of modern inventions and the consequent technical nature of patent specifications such as the one in question, the guidance of earlier cases as to the correct scope of expert evidence was inadequate. In cases such as the present, while it remained the function of the judge finally to construe the specification, the court should, in the interest of justice, ascertain the meaning of whole phrases and sentences of the specification as understood by the various experts to whom it was to be regarded as being addressed. Thus, in the light of expert evidence so received, the claim in the specification covered sutures formed from a copolymer of glycolide and lactide in the proportions used by the defendant company since the suture so formed possessed the essential qualities and characteristics of the homopolymer PHAE. Accordingly the patent, which the defendant company had failed to prove to be invalid, had been infringed.

However, a perpetual injunction would not be granted since to do so would deprive the defendant company of protection should it succeed on appeal. The existing interlocutory injunction would therefore be continued, subject to a cross-undertaking in damages given by the plaintiffs, until judgment in the Court of Appeal or further order, on the defendant also giving an undertaking that an appeal would be entered within an appropriate period and prosecuted with due diligence. Leave to appeal against the order would be granted.

AMERICAN CYANAMID CO v ETHICON LTD [1979] RPC 215 (Chancery Division: GRAHAM J). Dicta of Lord Westbury LC in *Hills v Evans* (1862) 31 LJ Ch 457 at 460 and of Lord Russell in *EMI v Lissen Ltd* (1939) 56 RPC 39 at 41 followed.

For interlocutory proceedings see 1975 Halsbury's Abridgment para. 1864.

PENSIONS AND SUPERANNUATION

2036   Articles

Occupational Pensions and the 1975 Inheritance Act, D. S. Rosettenstein (issues raised by the use of the provisions of the Inheritance (Provision for Family and Dependants) Act 1975, 1975 Halsbury's Abridgment para. 1478, to gain access to benefits payable under an occupational pension scheme): 123 Sol Jo 661.

Pensions (a collection of articles on self-administered pension schemes, tax aspects of pension planning, retirement, job changes, key executives, pension consultants and the partnerplan scheme): NLJ Supplement, 15th March 1979.

2037   Appeal tribunals—rules

The Pensions Appeal Tribunals (England and Wales) (Amendment) Rules 1979, S.I. 1979 No. 1744 (in force on 29th January 1980) increase some of the amounts payable by the Pensions Appeal Tribunals by way of allowances and expenses.

2038   British Railways Board—pensions

The British Railways Board (Funding of Pension Schemes) (No. 7) Order 1979, S.I. 1979 No. 1724 (in force on 31st December 1979), varies the British Railways Board (Funding of Pension Schemes) (No. 1) Order 1974, 1974 Halsbury's Abridgment para. 2705 and subsequent orders made under the Railways Act 1974. The present order reduces from approximately £39 million to £21 million the sums which, under the previous orders, the Board is to provide by annual instalments from 1st April 1980 to 1st April 1986 for the purpose of funding the British Railways Superannuation Fund (Amalgamated Sections).

2039   Children's pensions—earnings limit

The Superannuation (Children's Pensions) (Earnings Limit) Order 1979, S.I. 1979 No. 680 (in force on 16th July 1979), revokes the 1965 Order, S.I. 1965 No. 1026. The Administration of Justice (Pensions) Act 1950 permits the payment of a children's pension under that Act to continue after the age of sixteen if the child is undergoing training for a trade, profession or vocation. One of the conditions is that the emoluments received during training, excluding the return of any premiums, do not exceed £104 per year. This is now increased to £598 per year.

This order has been revoked, see para. 2040.

2040   The Superannuation (Children's Pensions) (Earnings Limit) (No. 2) Order 1979, S.I. 1979 No. 1275 (in force on 12th November 1979), revokes the Superannuation (Children's Pensions) (Earnings Limit) Order 1979, para. 2039. The order increases the financial limit on emoluments received during training, excluding premium returns by children over sixteen, from £598 to £694 per year.

2041   Civil service—superannuation

The Superannuation (Lyon King of Arms and Lyon Clerk) Order 1979, S.I. 1979 No. 1540 (in force on 18th January 1980), adds the office of Lord Lyon King of Arms and the office of Lyon Clerk and Keeper of the Records of Court and Office of Lyon King of Arms to the offices listed in the Superannuation Act 1972, Sch. I, thereby bringing persons holding either of these positions within the principal civil service pension scheme made under s. 1 of the Act. The order takes effect from 1st July 1979.

2042   Coal industry—mineworkers' pension scheme—limit on contributions

The Mineworkers' Pension Scheme (Limit on Contributions) Order 1979, S.I. 1979 No. 374 (in force on 28th March 1979), amends the National Coal Board (Finance) Act 1976, s. 2 (3) (b), 1976 Halsbury's Abridgment para. 1716, by substituting the sum of £36·48 million for the sum of £34 million (minimum aggregate of payments by Secretary of State to the National Coal Board to reimburse expenditure incurred towards reducing or eliminating deficiencies in the Mineworkers' Pension Scheme).

2043   Firemen—pensions

The Firemen's Pension Scheme (Amendment) Order 1979, S.I. 1979 No. 407 (in force on 1st May 1979), amends the Firemen's Pension Scheme 1973, by increasing the rate of interest payable by a fire authority on a transfer value in respect of a fireman who has ceased to be a member of that authority's brigade, to take effect from 1st April 1979.

2044   The Firemen's Pension Scheme (Amendment) (No. 2) Order 1979, S.I. 1979 No. 855 (in force on 20th August 1979), amends the Firemen's Pension Scheme 1973 by extending the definition of infirmity caused by a particular injury to include cases where an injury which became apparent only after retirement so aggravated an infirmity as to result in death or disablement. The Order also gives the widows of firemen an option to take a smaller pension and a lump sum instead of the pension provided by the scheme. Provision is also made for the payment of a lump sum to widows of firemen who die in service due to injuries sustained on duty.

2045   The Firemen's Pension Scheme (Amendment) (No. 3) Order 1979, S.I. 1979 No. 1286 (in force on 12th November 1979), amends the Firemen's Pension Scheme 1973 and other previous Schemes in so far as they continue to have effect. Under these schemes, the amounts of certain awards are determined by reference to flat rates which do not qualify for increases under the Pensions (Increase) Act 1971 as amended. The order increases these flat-rates with effect from 12th November 1979. In cases where a widow is entitled to a minimum pension, the order makes a reduction for so much of the increase as is attributable to that minimum pension.

2046   The Firemen's Pension Scheme (War Service) Order 1979, S.I. 1979 No. 1360 (in force on 1st December 1979), supplements the Firemen's Pension Scheme Order 1973 and certain earlier Schemes in the case of firemen who retired before April 1972. The order, which has effect from 1st April 1975, makes special provisions for firemen who have completed a period of war service and who meet other specified requirements.

2047   Judicial pensions

The Superannuation (Judicial Offices) (Amendment) Rules 1979, S.I. 1979 No. 668 (in force on 16th July 1979), revoke and replace with an amendment the Superannuation (Judicial Offices) (Assistant Registrar of the Lancaster Palatine Court) Rules 1972, which applied the provisions of the Superannuation (Judicial Offices) Rules 1970 to any person holding the office of assistant registrar of the Court of Chancery of the county palatine of Lancaster immediately before January 1st 1972. Such a person may now elect that the whole of his service before and after that date be aggregated for the purpose of determining his superannuation benefits.

2048   —— widows' and children's benefits

The Judicial Pensions (Widows' and Children's Benefits) (Amendment) Regulations 1979, S.I. 1979 No. 210 (in force on 1st April 1979), make amendments to the Judicial Pensions (Widows' and Children's Benefits) Regulations 1974, 1974 Halsbury's Abridgment para. 2499.

2049   Local government—superannuation

The Local Government Superannuation (Amendment) Regulations 1979, S.I. 1979 No. 2 (in force on 1st February 1979), amend the Local Government Superannuation Regulations 1974, 1974 Halsbury's Abridgment para. 2502. They provide for employees to make certain payments to avoid any reduction in the prospective retirement allowance or death gratuity. Other regulations are amended to allow for this.

2050

The Local Government Superannuation (Amendment) (No. 2) Regulations 1979, S.I. 1979 No. 592 (in force on 2nd July 1979), further amend the Local Government Superannuation Regulations 1974, 1974 Halsbury's Abridgment para. 2502 by providing that for the purposes of regulation A7 the duty of an acting returning officer includes duties required to be discharged by such an officer at a European Assembly election.

2051

The Local Government Superannuation (Amendment) (No. 3) Regulations 1979, S.I. 1979 No. 1534 (in force on 1st January 1980), further amend the Local Government Superannuation Regulations 1974, 1974 Halsbury's Abridgment para. 2502 in relation to the preservation and transfer of certain pension rights.

2052   —— superannuation payments—interpretation of forfeiture clause

The defendant worked for Birmingham County Borough Council until his suspension in March 1974 (he had been City Architect from 1966). He resigned at the end of that month and in June stood trial and was sentenced to two and a half years' imprisonment for conspiracy to corrupt. In April 1974 the Birmingham County Borough Council was superseded by the Birmingham District Council. The defendant's pension rights were governed by the Local Government Superannuation Acts 1937–53, and his pension was liable to forfeiture by the employing authority in consequence of fraud or misconduct. In March 1972 the 1937–53 Acts were replaced by the Superannuation Act 1972. The rights under the old Acts were preserved by Regulations in 1974. A committee established by the Birmingham District Council resolved that as the defendant had resigned in consequence of gross misconduct in connection with his duties, he should forfeit a proportion of his pension. The Secretary of State however determined that the committee had no jurisdiction to sanction the forfeiture. The plaintiffs, as administering authority of the appropriate superannuation fund, applied for the determination of the court. *Held*, the forfeiture provision under the 1937–57 Acts applied until 1974 (when the new authority came into being) and the defendant's pension remained liable to forfeiture until that date. After that date, it would be unfair if the defendant's pension was not subject to the risk of forfeiture. Further, it was not unfair that the question of forfeiture be decided by a new body which had never been the defendant's employer. The committee could accordingly direct a forfeiture of a pension.

WEST MIDLANDS COUNTY COUNCIL v MAUDSLEY (1979) 16th March (unreported) (Chancery Division: BRIGHTMAN J).

2053   —— —— **pre-entry war service**

The Department of the Environment has stated that broad agreement has been reached on the terms and conditions under which pensionable employees and pensioners may reckon periods of pre-entry war service for the purposes of local government superannuation. The basic requirements are: (a) entry in local government employment on or before 30th June 1950; (b) continuous employment in local government (apart from intervals of less than 12 months) from the date of entry until 1st April 1978 (or until retirement in the case of a pensioner or deferred pensioner on that date); (c) all local government employment must be reckonable for calculating the benefits of local government superannuation. Regulations effective from 1st April 1978 will be made at a future date. If local authorities make increased payments in appropriate cases in anticipation of the regulations and if such payments are challenged on audit the Secretary of State has indicated that, where appropriate, he would be prepared to give his sanction under the Local Government Act 1972, s. 161 (1). See Department of the Environment Circular 24/79.

2504   **Occupational pension schemes—public service**

The Occupational Pension Schemes (Public Service Pension Schemes) (Amendment) Regulations 1979, S.I. 1979 No. 1645 (in force 1st January 1980), amend the Occupational Pension Schemes (Public Service Pension Schemes) Regulations 1978, 1978 Halsbury's Abridgment para. 2107, by adding two further occupational schemes to the Schedule.

2055   **Overseas pensions—increase**

The Increase of Pensions (India, Pakistan and Burma) (Amendment) Regulations 1979, S.I. 1979 No. 1276 (in force on 12th November 1979), amend the Increase of Pensions (India, Pakistan and Burma) Regulations 1972 so as to provide for increases payable in respect of the pensions specified in Schedules 1 and 2 to those regulations, to be calculated by reference to increases payable on a Civil Service pension under the Social Security Pensions Act 1975, s. 59, following the coming into operation of those provisions.

2056   **Overseas service—pensions**

The Overseas Service (Pensions Supplement) (Amendment) Regulations 1979, S.I. 1979 No. 1277 (Part I in force on 12th November 1979 and Part II in force on 1st July 1980 whereupon reg. 6 ceases to have effect), amend the Overseas Service (Pensions Supplement) Regulations 1977, 1977 Halsbury's Abridgment para. 2058. They provide for overseas public service pension supplements to be calculated by reference to increases payable on a Civil Service pension under the Social Security Pensions Act 1975, s. 59; for the alteration of the beginning date for supplements in respect of certain officers' pensions; for the removal of the restriction debarring overseas pensioners from receiving supplements under a current Review order; and for a transitional date for the determination of additions to the sterling value of overseas pensions due to changes in rate of exchange before Part II of the regulations comes into force.

2057 **Parliamentary Commissioner—pensions**

The Pensions Increase (Parliamentary Commissioner) Regulations 1979, S.I. 1979 No. 622 (in force on 4th July 1979), apply prospectively the provisions of the Pensions (Increase) Act 1971 to pensions for Parliamentary Commissioners who exercise the right of election.

2058 **Past Prime Ministers—pensions**

The Pensions Increase (Past Prime Ministers) (Amendment) Regulations 1979, S.I. 1979 No 771 (in force on 30th July 1979), amend the Pensions Increase (Past Prime Ministers) Regulations 1972, S.I. 1972 No. 1654.

2059 **Pension fund—temporary pension—whether payments subject to income tax**

See *Esslemont v Estill* (*Inspector of Taxes*) para. 1570.

2060 **Pensioner's Payments and Social Security Act 1979**

See para. 2648.

2061 **Pensions increase—review**

The Pensions Increase (Review) Order 1979, S.I. 1979 No. 1047 (in force on 12th November 1979), increases the rates of public service pensions. Pensions beginning before 2nd July 1978 are increased by 16 per cent and those beginning after 1st July 1978 are increased by between 11·7 per cent and 1·5 per cent. The Order also increases certain lump sum payments and provides that guaranteed minimum pensions may be reduced.

2062 **Police—pensions**

The Police Pensions (Amendment) Regulations 1979, S.I. 1979 No. 406 (in force on 1st May 1979), amend the Police Pensions Regulations 1973, S.I. 1973 No. 428, by increasing the rate of interest payable by a police authority on a transfer value in respect of a policeman who has retired from the police force maintained by that authority, to take effect from 1st April 1979.

2063 The Police Pensions (Amendment) (No. 2) Regulations 1979, S.I. 1979 No. 1287 (in force on 12th November 1979), amend the Police Pensions Regulations 1973 and, in so far as they continue to have effect, the Police Pensions Regulations 1971. Under those Regulations the amounts of certain widows' pensions and children's allowances are determined by reference to flat rates which do not qualify for increases under the Pensions (Increase) Act 1971, as amended. The present Regulations increase these flat rates with effect from 12th November 1979. In cases where a widow is entitled to a minimum pension corresponding to a guaranteed minimum pension under the Social Security Pensions Act 1975 a reduction is made by reg. 6 for so much of the increase as is attributable to that minimum pension.

2064 The Police Pensions (War Service) Regulations 1979, S.I. 1979 No. 1259 (in force on 6th November 1979), supplement the Police Pensions Regulations 1971 and 1973. The Regulations make special provision for regular policemen who have completed a period of war service and meet certain other qualifications. A qualified policeman may elect to increase his own pension by buying additional years of reckonable service up to half his period of war service, or he may pay more and provide also a corresponding increase in the benefits under the pension scheme for widows and children. Where a qualified policeman dies without electing to increase his widow's pension in this way, she may in certain circumstances exercise the right to elect. The Regulations have retrospective effect from 1st April 1975.

2065   —— —— payments to widows

The Police Pensions (Lump Sum Payments to Widows) Regulations 1979, S.I. 1979 No. 1406 (in force on 3rd December 1979), provide for the payment of a gratuity of £10 in the case of a policeman's widow, in receipt of a discretionary increase in the police widow's pension under the Police Pensions Regulations 1971, during the week beginning the 3rd December 1979 if she is not entitled to a payment by virtue of the Pensioners' Payments and Social Security Act 1979, s. 1 (1).

2066   Police cadets—pensions

The Police Cadets (Pensions) (Amendment) Regulations 1979, S.I. 1979 No. 75 (in force on 1st March 1979), amend the Police Cadets (Pensions) Regulations 1973 so as to attract amendments made by the Police Pensions (Amendment) Regulations 1976, 1976 Halsbury's Abridgment para. 1920 and the Police Pensions (Amendment) (No. 2) Regulations 1978, 1978 Halsbury's Abridgment para. 2114 from the appropriate dates, subject to the exclusion of particular provisions. Retrospective effect is authorised by the Superannuation Act 1972, ss. 12, 15.

2067   Retirement pensions

See SOCIAL SECURITY.

2068   —— surviving spouse

The Social Security (Maximum Additional Component) Amendment Regulations 1979, S.I. 1979 No. 1428 (in force on 9th November 1979), amend the Social Security (Maximum Additional Component) Regulations 1978, 1978 Halsbury's Abridgment para. 2119, by substituting new provisions for reg. 2 of these Regulations. The new provisions relate the calculation of the maximum additional component prescribed for the purposes of the Social Security Pensions Act 1975, s. 9 (3), 1975 Halsbury's Abridgment para. 3191, to the date on which a surviving spouse would (but for the Social Security Act 1975, s. 27 (6)) have become entitled both to a Category A and to a Category B retirement pension, or would have become so entitled if he or she had retired.

2069   Speakers of House of Commons—pensions

The Pensions Increase (Speakers' Pensions) (Amendment) Regulations 1979, S.I. 1979 No. 762 (in force on 30th July 1979) amend the Pensions Increase (Speakers' Pensions) Regulation 1972, S.I. 1972 1653.

2070   Special constables—pensions

The Special Constables (Pensions) (Amendment) Regulations 1979, S.I. 1979 No. 76 (in force on 1st March 1979), amend the Special Constables (Pensions) Regulations 1973 to extend amendments made by the Police Pensions (Amendment) Regulations 1975, 1975 Halsbury's Abridgment para. 2516 and the Police Pensions (Amendment) (No. 2) Regulations 1978, 1978 Halsbury's Abridgment para. 2114 to special constables, from the appropriate dates, subject to the exclusion of particular provisions. Retrospective effect is authorised by the Superannuation Act 1972, ss. 12, 15.

2071   Teachers—superannuation

The Teachers Superannuation (Policy Schemes) Regulations 1979, S.I. 1979 No. 47 (in force on 19th February 1979), apply to teachers who are subject to a superannuation scheme providing benefits secured by means of assurance policies. The regulations provide that, firstly, the policies are to vest in the Secretary of State and that, secondly, the Teachers Superannuation Regulations 1976, 1976 Halsbury's Abridgment para. 944, are to be subject to various modifications.

2072   The Teachers' Superannuation (Amendment) Regulations 1979, S.I. 1979 No. 1206 (in force on 1st November 1979), amend the Teachers' Superannuation Regulations 1976, 1976 Halsbury's Abridgment para. 944 in relation to the keeping of an account of the expenditure and revenue on teachers' superannuation.

2073   ### Transport—National Freight Corporation—pensions

The National Freight Corporation (Funding of Pension Schemes) (No. 3) Order 1979, S.I. 1979 No. 1416 (in force on 1st December 1979), further amends the National Freight Corporation (Funding of Pension Schemes) (No. 1) Order 1978, 1978 Halsbury's Abridgment para. 2126. The order increases the sum to be provided by the Corporation for the funding of certain obligations owed in respect of the NFC (1978) Pension Fund.

2074   ### War—civilians' pensions

The Personal Injuries (Civilians) Amendment Scheme 1979, S.I. 1979 No. 270 (arts. 1, 3, 4, 5 (a), (c) and (d), 6 and 7 in force on 2nd April 1979, arts 2 and 5 (b) on 6th April 1979), amends the Personal Injuries (Civilians) Scheme 1976, 1976 Halsbury's Abridgment para. 1910, which provides for compensation to or in respect of civilians injured or killed in the 1939–45 war. The Scheme amends the principal Scheme relating to unemployability, invalidity and treatment allowances and amends the rates of the invalidity allowance, the personal allowance element of the treatment allowance and allowance payable on the death of a member in respect of the member's children.

2075   The Personal Injuries (Civilians) Amendment (No. 2) Scheme 1979, S.I. 1979 No. 1232 (in force on 12th November 1979), further amends the Personal Injuries (Civilians) Scheme 1976, 1976 Halsbury's Abridgment para. 1910. It provides for rent allowances to widows to be continued for twenty-six weeks from the date upon which any child, for whom the allowance was paid, ceases to be a member of the household. It makes provision for the commencement of payment of awards made following reviews of assessments and successful appeals against the reduction or withholding of an award. The order also increases the rates of retired pay, pensions, gratuities and death and disablement allowances in the Second World War, and raises the maximum amount of annual earnings of a disabled person deemed to be unemployable for unemployability allowance purposes.

2076   ### —— service pensions

The Injuries in War (Shore Employments) Compensation (Amendment) Scheme 1979, S.I. 1979 No. 1506 (in force on 12th November 1979), provides that the maximum weekly allowance payable to ex-members of the Women's Auxiliary Forces who suffered disablement from their services during the 1914–1918 War is to be increased from £31.90 to £38.00 and that other allowances are to be increased proportionately.

2077   The Naval, Military and Air Forces etc. (Disablement and Death) Service Pensions Amendment Order 1979, S.I. 1979 No. 113 (arts. 1, 3, 4 (a), (c), (d), 5, 6 in force on 2nd April 1979; arts 2, 4 (b) in force on 6th April 1979), further amends the Naval, Military and Air Forces etc. (Disablement and Death) Service Pensions Order 1978, 1978 Halsbury's Abridgment para. 2134. It provides for the receipt of an additional component within the meaning of the Social Security Pensions Act 1975, s. 6 (1) (b) or of a graduated retirement benefit under the National Insurance Act 1965 no longer to render a member of the forces ineligible for an award of unemployability allowance under the 1978 Order, art. 18. It also down-rates in respect of a member's children the increase of unemployability allowance and the additional allowance element of treatment allowances; rebands the rates of invalidity allowances and the personal allowance element of treatment allowances; and up-rates allowances payable on the death of a member in respect of the members' children.

2078   The Naval, Military and Air Forces etc. (Disablement and Death) Service Pensions Amendment (No. 2) Order 1979, S.I. 1979 No. 1312 (in force on 12th November 1979), further amends the Naval, Military and Air Forces etc. (Disablement and Death) Service Pensions Order 1978, 1978 Halsbury's Abridgment para. 2134. It provides for rent allowances to widows of servicemen and unmarried dependants who lived as wives to be continued for twenty-six weeks from the date upon which any child, for whom the allowance was paid, ceases to be a member of the household. It makes provision for the commencement of payment of awards made following successful appeals against their reduction or withholding. The order also increases the rates of retired pay, pensions, gratuities and death and disablement allowances due to service during the First World War and after 2nd September 1939, and raises the maximum amount of annual earnings of a disabled person deemed to be unemployable for unemployability allowance purposes.

PERPETUITIES AND ACCUMULATIONS

Halsbury's Laws of England (3rd edn.), Vol. 29, paras. 561–709

2079   Accumulations—discretionary power to accumulate—whether within restrictions

See *Baird v Lord Advocate*, para. 1390.

PLEADING

Halsbury's Laws of England (3rd edn.), Vol. 30, paras. 1–78

2080   Probate action—contents of pleadings

See *Re Stott, deceased; Klouda v Lloyds Bank Ltd*, para. 1274.

2081   Striking out—reasonable cause of action at date of writ—amendment of writ

See *Roban Jig and Tool Co Ltd v Taylor*, para. 522.

POLICE

Halsbury's Laws of England (3rd edn.), Vol. 30, paras. 79–237

2082   Article

Unlawful Searching of Premises by Police Officers, J. Kodwo Bentil: 123 Sol Jo 542.

2083   Cadets

The Police Cadets Regulations 1979, S.I. 1979 No. 1727 (in force on 1st February 1980), consolidate, with minor amendments, the Police Cadet Regulations 1968 as amended, with particular reference to those provisions concerning pay, allowances and general conditions of employment.

2084   Metropolitan Police Commissioner—duty to enforce the law against obscene publications—application for mandamus to compel performance of that duty

A private individual made an application for mandamus directed to the Metropolitan Police Commissioner requiring him, inter alia, to enforce or secure the enforcement of the law against those who illegally published or sold obscene material. The applicant had made two similar applications in 1968 and 1973, both of which had been rejected. When the present proceedings commenced in 1978 the Prosecution of Offences Regulations 1946 were in force. Regulation 1 (c) provided that it was the duty of the Director of Public Prosecutions (DPP) to institute or undertake criminal prosecution in certain cases, which included any case which appeared to him to be of importance or difficulty or for any other reason which required his intervention. Regulation 6 (2) (d) required the chief officer of every police district to report all cases of obscene or indecent libels, exhibitions or publications to the DPP. The DPP and the Commissioner made an arrangement that all proceedings under the Obscene Publications Act 1959 ss. 2, 3, as amended, relating to the publication of obscene articles and the empowering of magistrates to issue search and seizure warrants, would be conducted by the DPP under reg 1 (c) and that he would be consulted before any searches were made. These arrangements were still in force when the applicant first commenced his action. Later in 1978 the system was changed and new regulations replaced the 1946 regulations. Regulation 6 (2) (d) was revoked but the DPP added the offences involving obscene exhibitions or publications to the list of offences required to be reported under reg. 6 (2). The new arrangements provided that proceedings under the 1959 Act ss. 2, 3 were no longer to be normally conducted by the DPP. District police officers would still be required to submit a report to the Obscene Publications Branch at New Scotland Yard before applying for a search warrant but they were not bound to follow any advice as to whether to proceed under s. 2 or s. 3. A report to the DPP was still required where a chief officer contemplated criminal prosecution but not, in general, where he considered proceedings under s. 3 were appropriate. The applicant contended that the "centralisation policy" and "bureaucratic procedures" under the new system made the effective enforcement of the law against pornography impossible. *Held*, the matter would be approached by considering whether, since 1973, there had been any change in the circumstances or in the nature of the relief claimed that would make it right for the court to grant the relief which had been refused in 1968 and 1973 by the Court of Appeal. The new system had removed some of the applicant's original complaints as to the role of the DPP and to s. 3 proceedings. It was impossible to say that the Commissioner was not entitled to use his discretion to give instructions that the police should consult their legal advisers and that the more serious legal proceedings should be conducted by him. Nor was the effect of the Commissioner's instructions to remove from constables the power of arrest in obscenity cases. The motion therefore failed and would be dismissed.

R v METROPOLITAN POLICE COMMISSIONER, EX PARTE BLACKBURN (1979) Times, 1st December (Queen's Bench Division: LORD WIDGERY CJ, BROWNE LJ and WATKINS J).

For previous proceedings see [1968] 1 All ER 763, CA and [1973] 1 All ER 324, CA.

This decision has been affirmed by the Court of Appeal; see Times, 7th March 1980.

2085   Misconduct—failure to carry out duty as a police officer

See *R v Dytham*, para. 634.

2086   Pay and allowances

The Police (Amendment) Regulations 1979, S.I. 1979 No. 694 (in force on 23rd July 1979), amend the Police Regulations 1971 by increasing, with effect from 1st May 1979, rates of pay for police officers in England and Wales and the London Allowance which is payable to all members of the City of London and metropolitan police forces. Retrospective effect is authorised by the Police Act 1964, s. 33 (4).

2087   The Police (Amendment) (No. 2) Regulations 1979, S.I. 1979 No. 1216 (in force on
1st November 1979), amend the Police Regulations 1971 by increasing, with effect
from 1st September 1979, rates of pay for police officers in England and Wales and
the London allowance payable to all members of the City of London and
metropolitan police forces. London weighting and university scholars' supplementary pay are increased with effect from 1st July 1978. Retrospective effect is
authorised by the Police Act 1964, s. 33 (4).

2088   The Police Cadets (Amendment) Regulations 1979, S.I. 1979 No. 1543 (in force on
1st January 1980), amend the Police Cadet Regulations 1968 by increasing the pay
of police cadets and the charges payable by them for board and lodging provided by
police authorities.

2089   Pensions
See PENSIONS.

2090   Police Complaints Board—annual report
During 1978 the Police Complaints Board received a total of 7,329 complaints cases
and the Board received 4,828 reports under s. 2 (4) of the Police Act 1976 giving
information as to the stage reached in dealing with complaints over four months
old. During the year the Board completed action on 7,164 cases, some of which had
been submitted at the end of 1977. The average period from receipt of the papers
by the Board to completion of action on the case was 24 calendar days. See the
Report of the Police Complaints Board 1978 (HC 4).

2091   Police regulations—consolidation
The Police Regulations 1979, S.I. 1979 No. 1470 (in force on 1st January 1980),
consolidate, with minor amendments, the Police Regulations 1971, as amended.

**2092   Powers—arrest—validity of arrest—conduct likely to cause a
breach of the peace**
See *R v Podger*, para. 658.

**2093   —— power to intercept telephone conversations—restrictions on
power**
The plaintiff had been charged with handling stolen goods and the prosecution had
admitted at the trial that there had been interception of the plaintiff's telephone
conversations on the authority of the Secretary of State's warrant. The plaintiff
issued a writ claiming that such an interception was unlawful and sought by motion
an injunction against the Metropolitan Police Commissioner to restrain interception
or monitoring of his telephone conversations. It was agreed to treat the motion as
the trial of the action. The plaintiff then sought declarations that: (i) the interception
of confidential conversations on his lines without his consent was unlawful even if
done pursuant to a warrant of the Home Secretary, and that disclosure of those calls
to third parties, the police or the Home Secretary was similarly unlawful; (ii) that he
had a right of property, privacy and confidentiality in respect of telephone calls and
that any interception was in breach of those rights; (iii) that the interception violated
the Convention for the Protection of Human Rights and Fundamental Freedoms,
art. 8 which entitled everyone to respect for his private and family life, his home and
correspondence; (iv) there was no remedy in respect of breaches of (i) and (ii) or of
violation of (iii). *Held* (i) insofar as telephone tapping meant recording by the Post
Office for use by the police in the prevention or detection of crime, no unlawful
conduct had been established since there was no law against it. Telephone tapping
was not authorised by statute, but by the Post Office Act 1969, s. 80, Parliament had
provided a clear recognition of the warrant of the Home Secretary as having an
effective function in law. (ii) The plaintiff could have no immunity from telephone

tapping based on a right of property because no property (apart from copyright) existed in words transmitted over the telephone. Further there was no right of privacy recognised by English law and an offence under the Wireless Telegraphy Act 1949, s. 5 related only to unauthorised information obtained by wireless telegraphy apparatus ("bugging"). Finally, there was no contractual right of confidentiality between the plaintiff and the Post Office. Even if there was a general duty of confidentiality binding on those who heard a telephone conversation, a breach by the police would be excused where the telephone tapping was done for the purposes of detecting or preventing crime, where no use was made of material obtained except for those purposes and where knowledge of information not relevant for those purposes was confined to the minimum number of people reasonably required to be engaged in the tapping. In the circumstances of the present case if there had been a breach of confidence by the police, there was just cause and excuse for it. (iii) The court's power to make declaratory judgments was confined to matters justiciable in the English courts. The Convention had the status of a treaty and was not justiciable in England. (iv) Declarations could only be made in respect of legal or equitable rights and not moral, social or political matters. Therefore the court did not have the power to make any formal declarations.

In any event the claim for all the declarations would fail for the interception of the telephone conversations was not made by the defendants but by the Post Office.

The court considered that telephone tapping was a complex matter and was a subject for legislation.

MALONE v METROPOLITAN POLICE COMR (No. 2) [1979] 2 All ER 620 (Chancery Division: MEGARRY V-C).

2094   —— power to stop motorist—power to require breath test where no traffic offence committed

See *Shersby v Klippel*, para. 2273.

2095   —— seizure of property from person in custody

See *R v Naylor*, para. 717.

2096   Promotion

The Police (Promotion) Regulations 1979, S.I. 1979 No. 991 (in force on 1st October 1979), consolidate with amendments the Police (Promotion) Regulations 1968 which govern promotion to the rank of sergeant or inspector in a police force in England and Wales. The Police (Promotion) (Amendment) Regulations 1975, 1975 Halsbury's Abridgment, para. 2545 are revoked.

PORTS, HARBOURS AND THE SEASHORE

Halsbury's Laws of England (3rd edn.), Vol. 35, paras. 1247–1311 and Vol. 39, paras. 767–891

2097   Port health authorities

See PUBLIC HEALTH.

POST OFFICE

Halsbury's Laws of England (3rd edn.), Vol. 30, paras. 238–362

2098   Legal effect of communication by post—application by post—time when made

See *North West Traffic Area Licensing Authority v Brady*, para. 2292.

2099   **Telephone—monitoring of conversations—power of police to order**

See *Malone v Metropolitan Police Commissioner*, para. 2093.

POWERS

Halsbury's Laws of England (3rd edn.), Vol. 30, paras. 363–546.

2100   **Power of appointment—investment clause—power of appointment created by order of court—whether donee authorised to alter trustees' powers of investment**

A settlement made in 1931 contained a narrow investment clause which gave no general power to invest in equities. In 1961 a power of appointment was conferred on the plaintiff by an arrangement approved by an order of the court under the Variation of Trusts Act 1958. Clause 5 of the arrangement provided for the trustees, subject to the power of appointment, to hold the trust money on trust for certain persons with such provisions for maintenance, education and advancement and otherwise at the discretion of any person and with such gifts over and generally in such manner for the benefit of those persons or such of them as the plaintiff should by deed appoint. In 1979 the plaintiff exercised her powers of appointment by deed and purported to grant to the trustees much wider powers of investment by providing that the trust money could be employed in the purchase of stocks, funds, shares, securities etc. The deed provided that it should be void unless wholly validated by the court. On a summons for a declaration that the power had been validly exercised, *held*, clause 5 on its true construction, including such phrases as "and otherwise at the discretion of any person" and "generally in such manner" gave the plaintiff a general authority to confer on the trustees any additional administrative powers of investment which she, in the exercise of her discretion, thought would enure for the benefit of the appointees.

RE RANK'S SETTLEMENT TRUSTS; NEWTON v ROLLO [1979] 1 WLR 1242 (Chancery Division: SLADE J).

PRACTICE AND PROCEDURE

Halsbury's Laws of England (3rd edn.), Vol. 30, paras. 547–1036

2101   **Articles**

Anton Piller Discovery, Cedric D. Bell (Chancery judges' attitude towards granting ex parte applications for the entry of premises and inspection of documents): 122 Sol Jo 838.

Anton Piller Orders and the Dishonest Trader, David Lyons (necessary safeguards in the execution of such orders): 129 NLJ 512.

Civil Remedies: Procedural Developments, Henry E. Markson (a short survey of recent procedural developments concerning civil remedies): 123 Sol Jo 480.

Foreign currency judgments, D. G. Powles (power of court to give judgment for sum of money expressed in a foreign currency): [1979] LMCLQ 485.

Precedent Prevalent, Henry E. Markson (recent decisions reaffirming that established principles of precedent are still prevalent): 123 Sol Jo 6.

Prerogative Proceedings, Henry E. Markson (recent changes in procedure): 123 Sol Jo 211.

Prerogative Proceedings 1978, Henry E. Markson (study of Judicial Statistics Annual Report 1978, Cmnd. 7627): 123 Sol Jo 779.

2102   Admiralty actions—commencement of proceedings

The following Practice Direction ([1979] 2 All ER 155) has been issued by the Admiralty Registrar with effect from 2nd April 1979.

(1) The practice of allowing a writ in an action in rem and a writ in an action in personam to be combined in one document and issued as a single writ will no longer be followed.

(2) The appropriate prescribed forms must be used and if it is desired to commence proceedings both in rem and in personam separate writs must be issued.

2103   Appeal—appeal against exercise of judge's discretion—circumstances in which Court of Appeal will interfere

A husband and wife lived in the matrimonial home, a flat on a monthly tenancy in the husband's name. In 1977, they separated and the husband left. In May 1978, the landlords served notice to quit and brought an action for possession against both husband and wife. The wife filed a defence in which she relied on the statutory tenancy of her husband and on the Matrimonial Homes Act 1967, s. 1 (5), which provided that occupation by one spouse had to be treated for the purposes of the Rent Acts as possession by the other. In October 1978, the registrar granted an order for possession against the husband. At that time, the landlords' solicitors were aware of the decision in *Penn v Dunn* [1970] 2 QB 686, which made it clear that if the order for possession stood, the wife would lose her defence under the 1967 Act, as the Act did not confer on a wife any greater right to a statutory tenancy than was afforded by the possession of her husband, and the husband had lost his right to possession. The wife's solicitors did not become aware of the decision until March 1979. In June 1979, the action came on for hearing between the landlords and the wife. The judge ordered that the action be stood over on the undertaking that an application for leave to appeal out of time against the order should be made within fourteen days. The recorder, sitting as a deputy judge, refused the application on the ground that although the registrar was wrong, *Penn v Dunn* had not been brought to his attention, and the case and its implications had been known to the wife's solicitors since March 1979. The wife appealed. *Held*, the recorder had not fully directed his mind to the correct considerations. Although cogent reasons were normally required to justify an appeal out of time, in the instant case the registrar's order was not made against the intending appellant but against a co-defendant and it affected her only by a side wind. There would be no injustice in allowing her appeal out of time so as to enable her defence to be fully argued, and the registrar's order clearly ought not to have been made. Further, the landlords' solicitors had known of the decision in *Penn v Dunn* and it had been their duty to bring it to the attention of the registrar. The court had therefore to interfere with the manner in which the recorder had exercised his discretion, and the appeal would be allowed.

GRANGE LANE SOUTH FLATS LTD v COOK [1979] LS Gaz R 1226 (Court of Appeal: MEGAW, BROWNE and BRIGHTMAN LJJ).

See also Times, 28th November 1979.

2104   —— appeal to Court of Appeal—application for leave to appeal out of time—criterion for grant

The parties were divorced in 1973. The husband, who was serving in the Army, was ordered to pay periodical payments to the wife and their child. In 1977, the husband left the Army and received a gratuity. The wife applied for a lump sum payment in September 1977, but the matter was delayed and did not come before the registrar until May 1978. The registrar reserved judgment and sent his written judgment to the parties by post. The substance of his judgment was communicated to the wife's solicitors on 16th June 1978, and the wife's notice of appeal against the registrar's decision reached the court on 22nd June 1978. The wife was one day out of time on a five day notice. Her application for an extension of time for filing her notice of appeal was refused. The wife appealed. *Held*, the objection that the appeal was out of time was the most naked formality. It was a total denial of justice if the wife was to be precluded from challenging the registrar's decision on an important matter like a lump sum order because she was one day out of time on filing her notice of appeal. Accordingly, the appeal would be allowed.

WILLIAMS V WILLIAMS (1979) 9 Fam Law 154 (Court of Appeal: ORMROD, WALLER and BRANDON LJJ).

2105 ——— application for retrial on basis of fresh evidence

See *Reed v Vasant Hansraj Oswal*, para. 1249.

2106 ——— review of exercise of discretion—wardship proceedings— when variation of order justified

See *B v W (Wardship: Appeal)*, para. 1877.

2107 Application for leave to appeal against Anton Piller order—no application for discharge of order—order already executed

An application for leave to appeal against an Anton Piller order was opposed on the grounds that, firstly, the defendants, against whom the order was made, were given an express right to apply to discharge the order, and had not availed themselves of that right; secondly, that the order had, for all practical purposes, been executed and thus an appeal would be of no practical use. *Held*, a defendant had the right, subject to the necessary leave, to challenge an order in the Court of Appeal on the ground that it should never have been granted in the first place. An Anton Piller order was of such a drastic and far-reaching nature, that a defendant should not be deprived of this right, unless there were strong grounds for doing so. Such grounds had not been disclosed in the instant case, and leave to appeal would be granted.

BESTWORTH LTD V WEARWELL LTD [1979] FSR 320 (Chancery Division: SLADE J).

2108 Barristers

See BARRISTERS.

2109 Chancery Division—Companies Court—applications and orders heard by registrar—exercise of functions by chief clerk

See para. 2113.

2110 ——— proceedings in chambers—transaction of business by post

See para. 2114.

2111 ——— direction for speedy trial—procedure

The following Practice Direction ([1979] 1 All ER 364) has been issued by the direction of the Vice-Chancellor.

1. When a judge, on hearing a motion, directs a speedy trial of the action it is now usual for the judge to treat the summons for directions in the action as before him (subject to the issue of a pro-forma summons) and to give preliminary directions, adjourning the rest of the summons to the master on a fixed date in order that the master may consider the progress of the action and give such further directions as may be necessary to enable the action to be set down for hearing without delay.

2. Solicitors are reminded that the master needs to be supplied with copies of the relevant papers before the date fixed by the judge. The solicitors to the party at whose instance the order for speedy trial was made and who have issued the pro-forma summons (normally the plaintiff's solicitors) must accordingly, not less than two days before the date of the adjourned hearing, lodge with the master's summons clerk: (a) copies of the writ and all subsequent pleadings and notices, (b) a copy of the summons for directions issued pro-forma, (c) a certified or office copy of the judge's order or, if it has not yet been perfected, a copy of the draft order or, if it has not been

drafted, counsel's brief endorsed with the judge's directions and (d) the duplicate appearance and a copy of any civil aid certificate.

3. If the master has not been supplied with these papers in due time before the adjourned hearing and accordingly has to order a further adjournment it is likely to be at the expense of the party in default.

2112 Commercial Court—procedure

The Commercial Court committee has been considering whether any procedural changes could be introduced in order to further the object of achieving an efficient service for the resolution of commercial disputes.

The Court has always adopted a flexible approach to procedure and has tried to adjust procedures so as to enable each case to be disposed of as speedily and economically as possible. The committee therefore agree that it would be a retrograde step to try to lay down any new rules of procedure. The committee nevertheless wish to draw the attention of practitioners to certain matters.

The summons for directions, which is heard by a judge, should be issued as early as possible in the action. Practitioners should then consider how the twin objectives of speed and economy can best be achieved.

In some cases very considerable savings in time and costs can be made by, for example, dispensing with pleadings and discovery or replacing oral evidence with agreed statements of fact or written evidence. In other cases this is not desirable and the greatest saving in time and money will in the end be achieved by full and accurate pleadings and full discovery, not only of documents but even, if necessary, by way of interrogatories. By such means each party will be forced to make a realistic appraisal of the strength or weakness of its case at a comparatively early stage.

Interlocutory applications in the right case and for the above objects are therefore desirable if initial applications by letter are refused. Parties who refuse such applications may expect to have to pay the costs of an application to the court if they are subsequently ordered to give particulars or discovery which they have refused. On the other hand parties who endeavour to use interlocutory applications for the purposes of delay and seek to obtain unnecessary particulars or discovery, may expect to have to pay the costs on the failure of their applications.

The English tradition is for oral hearings, but there is a body of opinion which favours avoiding unnecessary reading aloud in court as involving a waste of valuable time. Thus, it is said, much time could be saved if the judge were given the pleadings, the correspondence and, in appropriate cases, written summaries of the parties' submissions together with a list of authorities and read them in his room either before or in the course of the hearing. Against this it has been said the oral guidance given by counsel will enable the judge to confine his reading to the essential documents and that the preparation of written submissions takes more time than is saved in court. Further suggestions have been that there should be time limits upon the arguments of counsel and that the examination in chief of expert witnesses, whose proofs have been exchanged, should be confined to a few questions designed to enable the witness to confirm his proof and to explain particular points of importance.

Experience has shown that established procedures are generally the most efficient. For example, it has been found in many cases to take more time to remove from the judge's mind an impression mistakenly formed from unguided reading than to present the case in the traditional way. There are however many individual cases when, by agreement between the parties, some parts of the suggested variations are valuable. If requested by both parties to do so the judges frequently read certain documents overnight or before trial in order to save time reading them in court. In suitable cases they will, whenever reasonably possible, continue to cooperate in agreed measures designed to save costs provided that this does not interfere with the need to ensure that justice is administered in public nor involve the infringement of some substantive provision of the law or mandatory rule of procedure.

The judges of the court wish it to be known that they regard it as a very important part of their duty to be available at short notice at any stage in the progress of an action on the initiative of either party. Subject to what has been said above, the costs of attendance at court will be regarded, prima facie, as part of the general costs of the cause. Practice Directions, 7th February 1979: 123 Sol Jo 132.

2113   Companies Court—applications and orders heard by registrar— exercise of functions by chief clerk

The following Practice Direction ([1979] 3 All ER 613) has been issued by the direction of the Vice-Chancellor.

1. It has been decided that the chief clerk of the Companies Court may assist the registrar in the hearing of the following applications and making orders thereon: (i) applications by the Official Receiver to consider reports of first meetings of creditors and contributories, to dispense with the submission of statements of affairs and to extend the time for holding first meetings of creditors and contributories; (ii) applications to extend the time for filing affidavits verifying winding-up petitions; (iii) applications to extend the date of hearing of winding-up petitions; (iv) applications for leave to amend proceedings; and (v) applications for substituted service within the jurisdiction by post only.

2. The evidence (if any) in support of any such application must be lodged in Room 312, Thomas More Building, and will be considered by the chief clerk who will deal provisionally with the application. The registrar will initial the note of any order made before the order takes effect.

3. The chief clerk may also without reference to the registrar (a) give leave to file affidavits notwithstanding any irregularity in their form, and (b) sign certificates of attendances in chambers for the purpose of taxation of costs.

4. Any party may require the application to be heard by the registrar instead of the chief clerk; and when an application has been heard by the chief clerk any party dissatisfied with the chief clerk's decision may thereupon require the matter to be adjourned to the registrar who will consider it afresh.

5. Nothing in this Practice Direction will prevent the registrar from dealing with any of the matters listed above if it is more appropriate or convenient for him to do so.

2114   —— proceedings in chambers—transaction of business by post

The following Practice Direction ([1979] 3 All ER 602) has been issued by the direction of the Vice-Chancellor.

1. These directions apply to proceedings in chambers in the High Court in London under the Companies (Winding-up) Rules 1949 and under RSC Ord. 102. They are made with a view to enabling certain formal business in the chambers of the companies court registrar in London to be transacted by post when this is more expeditious, economical or convenient. They will be reviewed from time to time and, in the light of practical experience, may be varied, extended or withdrawn as seen fit. Parties may nevertheless continue to transact such business by personal attendance if they so wish.

2. In these directions, "Ord. 102" means Ord. 102 of the Rules of the Supreme Court, "the Winding-up Rules" means the Companies (Winding-up) Rules 1949, and "the registrar" means the registrar and the companies court registrar as defined in the Winding-up Rules and Ord. 102 respectively.

3. The classes of business which may be transacted by post subject to the general and specific provisions of this Practice Direction are set out in the schedule hereto.

4. *General directions.*
(1) The use of postal facilities is at the risk of the solicitor or party concerned who should have regard to any material time limits prescribed and should enclose all necessary papers.
(2) Applications for the conduct of business by post must be made by a letter signed by or on behalf of the solicitor for a party or by the party if he is acting in person (a) specifying precisely what the court is being asked to do, (b) enclosing any

requisite documents, and (c) enclosing an adequately stamped envelope of adequate size properly addressed to the sender for the return of any relevant documents to him.

(3) The letter of application together with any requisite documents must be posted in a prepaid envelope properly addressed to—

> The High Court of Justice
> Companies Court
> Registrar's Chambers: Room 312
> Thomas More Building
> Royal Courts of Justice
> Strand
> London WC2A 2LL

If any deficiency is found in or among the necessary documents, a note marked "Please call" will be sent to the solicitors or litigant in person but the deficiency will not be specified. It will not be possible to enter into correspondence concerning deficiencies.

(4) Applications will be treated as having been made at the date and time of the actual receipt of the requisite documents in the registrar's chambers and for this purpose the date and time of despatch will be disregarded.

(5) If an acknowledgement of the receipt of papers is required they must be accompanied by a list setting out the papers in question, sent with a stamped and addressed envelope. The court will not accept responsibility for papers which are alleged to have been sent to it unless an acknowledgement is produced.

(6) The documents required for the conduct of any business by post will include all those documents which would have been required had the business been conducted by personal attendance.

(7) Any application by post which does not comply with the relevant rules or with this direction will be rejected and, in any other case, the court may exercise its power to decline to deal with a postal application. If any application is rejected the party making the application will be notified by post and he should then conduct the business in question by personal attendance in the ordinary way.

(8) It is emphasised that any party applying for the issue of proceedings by post will be responsible for the service of all documents requiring to be served under the rules in the same way as if the proceedings had been issued on personal attendance and that the costs of any adjournment occasioned by non-service of any necessary documents are likely to be awarded against the party responsible.

(9) On making any application by post the proper amount of any court fees payable must be enclosed together with a stamped addressed envelope. Any cheque or other draft should be made payable to HM Paymaster-General.

5. *Particular classes of business*
(1) The presentation of petitions
  (a) *Winding-up petitions under s. 210 of the Companies Act 1948.* A typed copy and at least two additional copies (not carbons) certified by the petitioner or his solicitor to be true copies of the typed copy of the petition should be sent to the court. To facilitate the verification of petitions within the time limit imposed by the Winding-up Rules the court will generally accept and file affidavits sworn within seven days before receipt of the petition at the registrar's chamber and sent with the petition.
  (b) *Petitions to confirm reduction of capital or to sanction schemes of arrangement.* A typed copy of the petition and one other copy (not a carbon) certified by the petitioner's solicitor to be a true copy of the typed copy should be sent to the court together with the appropriate fee and stamped addressed envelope.

(2) The issue of summonses and applications for the restoration or adjournment of summonses
In dealing with any postal application for the issue of a summons not being an originating summons requiring an appearance, the proper officer of the court will allocate an appropriate time and date for the first hearing and will seal and return one copy of the summons for service, if necessary. Any specific requests for a particular date will be considered by the proper officer but there can be no guarantee that they

can be met. Generally speaking, the first available appointment will be allotted, having regard to any time needed for service of the summons, for swearing and filing evidence and for completion of any other necessary formalities. Counsels' appointments at 12 o'clock will not be allotted unless specifically requested.

Applications for the restoration or adjournment of summonses will be dealt with in similar manner.

An originating summons requiring an appearance will be sealed and returned to the sender for service.

(3) The issue of notices of motion

A typed copy and two additional copies of the notice of motion should be sent to the court together with the appropriate fee payable (if any) and a stamped addressed envelope. The typed copy must be signed by the applicant personally or by his solicitors. The proper officer will appoint the date for hearing the motion allowing sufficient time for service if necessary and will seal and return one copy of the notice to the sender.

6. *Drawing up of orders*

In future, subject to the exception mentioned below, all orders, whether made by the judge or registrar, and whether made in court or in chambers, will, unless otherwise directed, be drafted in the chambers of the registrar. It is therefore of the utmost importance that solicitors should ensure that all documents required to enable such orders to be drawn expeditiously (eg briefs, copy charges etc) are lodged in chambers as soon as possible after the matter has been heard, particularly in cases where limitations as to time are involved. In the case of any order other than a winding-up order, a copy of the draft order will be sent to the solicitors for the parties, together with an appointment to settle the same. Should the parties be in agreement with the form of the order as drafted they may return the same marked "approved" and the order will be engrossed in that form and the appointment to settle vacated. If any variation in the form of order is desired by any party he must notify all other parties of the variation desired and thereafter all parties must attend on the appointment to settle and discuss the matter with the appropriate official.

The exceptions referred to above are (i) orders by the registrar on the application of the Official Receiver or for which the Treasury Solicitor is responsible under the existing practice, (ii) orders of the registrar or the judge in relation to reductions of capital, share premium account or capital redemption reserve fund or in relation to schemes of arrangement under ss 206 to 208 of the 1948 Act.

7. This Practice Direction will come into effect on 15th October 1979.

THE SCHEDULE

(1) The presentation of petitions under Ord. 102 and the Winding-up Rules.
(2) The issue of summonses under Ord. 102 and the Winding-up Rules.
(3) The issue of notices of motion under Ord. 102 and the Winding-up Rules.
(4) The issue of third party notices (where leave to issue such notice has been granted) and notices under r. 68 of the Winding-up Rules.
(5) The filing and lodging of affidavits, exhibits and other documents required to be filed or lodged.
(6) Entry of appearances.
(7) The issue of notices of appointments for the hearing of originating summonses to which an appearance is required.
(8) Fixing appointments for the restoration of adjourned summonses.
(9) Drawing up orders.
(10) The issue of certificates of taxation.
(11) The adjournment of summonses by consent.
(12) Notification that proceedings have been disposed of.

2115   Compromise of action—agreement between parties—rule of court—effect of breach

The parties to the wife's undefended divorce suit made an agreement relating to certain contentious matters, after a decree nisi had been granted. The agreement was signed by both parties and the registrar and made a rule of court. Upon an alleged breach of the agreement, the wife sought to commit her husband. At the hearing of the summons, *held*, an agreement which had been made a rule of the court had the same effect as an order or judgment of the court and was enforceable by either party.

HERBERT v HERBERT (1978) 122 Sol Jo 826 (Family Division: A. S. MYERSON QC sitting as a deputy High Court judge).

2116 **Conveyancing—contract races—Law Society direction as to practice**

See para. 2354.

2117 **Costs—costs of arbitration—principles to be applied**

See *The Aghios Nicolaos*, para. 159.

2118 **—— criminal cases**

See CRIMINAL PROCEDURE.

2119 **—— divorce cases**

See DIVORCE.

2120 **—— House of Lords—petition for leave to appeal**

See para. 2138.

2121 **—— interlocutory matters—counsel's fees**

A new list of counsel's fees on interlocutory matters in accident cases has been agreed by the chief taxing master and the Senate. The following fees are regarded as properly allowable on taxation where the item has been dealt with fully; lower fees may, however, be appropriate where an item has not been dealt with comprehensively, was unusually simple or where more than one item was dealt with simultaneously. Any higher fee which has been agreed will have to be justified on taxation. The new scales became effective on 1st December 1979.

	Personal Injury Cases	Running Down Cases
Statement of claim	£25	£18
Defence without counterclaim	£20	£15
Defence plain admission	£8	£8
Particulars, request and answers	£10	£10
Reply with or without defence to counterclaim	£15	£12
Third party notice (not to stand as statement of claim)	£15	£15
Interrogatories and answers	£20	£20
Advice on evidence	£25	£25
Opinion (including opinion on appeal)	£25	£25
Opinion on liability	£25	£25
Opinion on *quantum*	£25	£25
Opinion on liability and *quantum*	£35	£35
Notice of appeal to Court of Appeal and counternotice	£25	£25
Brief on summons before master	£20	£20

Conference fees

Queen's Counsel	£20 for first ½ hour	£15 ⎤	for each
		⎬	succeeding
Junior Counsel	£10 for first ½ hour	£ 8 ⎦	half hour

See (1979) LS Gaz, 1285.

2122 —— security for costs—counterclaim—whether costs arising from counterclaim or action

Plaintiffs in an action for patent infringement sought security for the costs of a counterclaim, because the defendant was a company in liquidation. The question for the court was whether those costs would arise from the counterclaim or from the defence to the action, since the issue to be determined was that of the validity of the patent. *Held*, costs in respect of the issue of validity would arise in the course of the action. Such costs as might arise from a counterclaim would be nominal, and security would only be awarded for a nominal sum.

NORPRINT LTD v SPJ LABELS LTD [1979] FSR 126 (Chancery Division: WHITFORD J).

2123 —— taxation—Family Division—telephone calls

Solicitors sought a review of the taxation of costs in the Family Division, in respect of telephone calls made in preparation for trial. *Held*, time spent on telephone calls made in preparation for trial should be recorded and allowed on taxation at the same rate as that spent in personal interviews. Routine calls should be charged for as a substitute for a letter. The proper rate in this case would be £13 an hour plus fifty per cent for care and attention.

BWANAOGA v BWANAOGA [1979] 2 All ER 105 (Family Division: PAYNE J sitting with assessors).

2124 —— —— procedure

A Practice Direction ([1979] 1 All ER 958) has been issued by the Chief Master of the Supreme Court Taxing Office laying down the procedure to be followed in relation to the taxation of bills of costs under the Rules of the Supreme Court, Ord. 62, App. 2 (as amended by the Rules of the Supreme Court (Amendment) 1979, S.I. 1979 No. 35, para. 2154), and providing guidelines as to the operation of that procedure.

2125 —— —— VAT

The following Practice Direction ([1979] 2 All ER 1008) has been issued by the Chief Taxing Master

1. Attention is drawn to the Practice Direction issued on 9th March 1973 ([1973] 1 All ER 847) as varied by the Practice Direction issued on 28th January 1974 ([1974] 1 All ER 847, 1974 Halsbury's Abridgment para. 2630) and the Practice Direction issued on 12th March 1973 ([1973] 1 All ER 971) as varied by the Practice Direction issued on 28th January 1974 ([1974] 1 All ER 848, 1974 Halsbury's Abridgment para. 2629).

2. The increase in the rate of value added tax (VAT) from 8% to 15% which, subject to para 3 below, will be effective on and after 18th June 1979 will apply to all bills of costs the taxation of which is completed on or after that date.

3. Paragraph 4 of motion no. 2 of the budget statement however provides as follows:

"Where a supply in fact made wholly or partly before the said 18th June, or a supply which, apart from the other provisions of the said section 7, would be treated as so made by subsection (2) or (3) of that section, is treated under those other provisions as made on or after that date, the person making the supply may account for and pay tax on the supply or, as the case may be, on the relevant part of it as if the rate of tax had not been increased by paragraph (1) (*b*) above.'

4. Where all or a part of work was undertaken prior to 18th June 1979 it will be assumed, unless a contrary indication is given in writing, that an election to charge VAT at 8% has been made and VAT will be calculated on that part of the bill at 8%. VAT will be calculated at 15% on all work undertaken on or after that date.

5. In any case in which an election to charge the lower rate is not made such decision must be justified in accordance with the principles of taxation which are applicable to the basis on which the costs are ordered to be taxed.

6. Until a further direction is made all bills of costs, fee notes and disbursements on which VAT is chargeable must be divided into separate parts so as to show the work done on a day-to-day basis before and on and after 18th June 1979. Where however a lump sum charge is made for work any part of which was performed before 18th June 1979, the lump sum must also be apportioned. The totals of profit costs and disbursements in each part must be carried separately to the summary.

7. Where in addition work was undertaken prior to 1st April 1973 the bill must be divided to show work undertaken before that date in accordance with existing practice.

8. With the concurrence of the Senior Registrar of the Family Division and the Admiralty Registrar, this direction is to apply to all costs in the Supreme Court taxed under their respective jurisdictions.

2126   —— **value added tax tribunal**

See *Jocelyn Feilding Fine Art Ltd v Customs and Excise Comrs*, para. 3035.

2127   **Dismissal of action—abuse of process of court—simultaneous proceedings**

See *Mantovani v Carapelli SpA*, para. 136.

2128   —— **application for dismissal of action in respect of breach of confidence—evidence—whether speculative assertion sufficient to found action**

Whilst giving judgment in an action involving an alleged breach of confidence, WHITFORD J observed that in cases where assertions were made concerning the disclosure of confidential information by an employee who had transferred to a rival firm, those assertions should not be of a speculative nature, but reasonable evidence should be demonstrated in support of them. Unless information was actually being used by the defendants, then the action only involved a waste of time and money and disclosed the very information alleged to be confidential.

REINFORCED PLASTICS APPLICATIONS (SWANSEA) LTD v SWANSEA PLASTICS & ENGINEERING CO LTD [1979] FSR 182 (Chancery Division: WHITFORD J).

2129   **Employment Appeal Tribunal—appeal procedure**

The following Practice Direction ([1979] 1 All ER 640) has been issued by the President of the Employment Appeal Tribunal, substituting the following paragraph for paragraph 10A of the Practice Direction dated 3rd March 1978 ([1978] 2 All ER 293) (listing of appeals in England and Wales), which is revoked.

A. *England and Wales*—(a) When the respondent's answer has been received and a copy served on the appellant, the case will be put in the list of cases for hearing. At the beginning of each calendar month a list will be prepared of cases to be heard on specified dates in the next following calendar month. That list will also include a number of cases which are liable to be taken in each specified week of the relevant month. The parties or their representatives will be notified as soon as the list is prepared. When cases in the list with specified dates are settled or withdrawn cases warned for the relevant week will be substituted and the parties notified as soon as possible. (b) A party finding that the date which has been given causes serious difficulties may apply to the listing officer before the 15th of the month in which the case first appears in the list. No change will be made unless the listing officer agrees, but every reasonable effort will be made to accommodate parties in difficulties. Changes after the 15th of the month in which the list first appears will not be made other than on application to the President of the Employment Appeal Tribunal; arrangements for the making of such an application should be made through the listing officer. (c) Other cases may be put in the list by the listing officer with the consent of the parties at shorter notice, eg where other cases have been settled or withdrawn or where it appears that they will take less time than originally estimated. Parties who wish their cases to be taken as soon as possible and at short notice should notify the listing officer. (d) Each week an up-to-date list for the following week will be prepared including any changes which have been made (in particular specifying cases which by then have been given fixed dates). (e) The monthly list and the weekly list will appear in the daily cause list and will also be displayed in room 6 at the Royal Courts of Justice and at 4 St James's Square, London SW1. It is important that parties or their advisers should inspect the weekly list as well as the monthly list. (f) If cases are settled or to be withdrawn notice should be given at once to the listing officer so that other cases may be given fixed dates.

2130   Family Division—appeals from registrar—lodgment of notes of evidence and judgment—practice

The following Practice Direction ([1979] 1 WLR 284) has been issued by the President with the concurrence of the Lord Chancellor.

1. As from March 12th 1979, on entering an appeal to a judge from a judgment, order or decision of a registrar exercising Family Division jurisdiction in the High Court or in the county court the following procedure will apply.

2. Where the appellant is represented by a solicitor, he shall (a) at the time of entering the appeal, certify (if this is the case) that it has been agreed with the solicitor for the respondent that nothing in any oral evidence taken before the registrar is relevant to any issue arising on the appeal, and that no notes of evidence will be lodged, and (b) unless otherwise directed, and subject as aforesaid, lodge prior to the hearing of the appeal a copy of the registrar's notes of evidence and judgment (if any) or a copy of such notes as have been prepared and agreed by the parties' legal advisers and approved by the registrar.

3. Where the appellant is acting in person, he should lodge a copy of any notes of evidence and judgment that are available to him. If none are available the respondent's solicitor (if any) shall, after service of the notice of the appeal, comply with the obligations imposed by paragraph 2 (a) and (b) above as if he were acting for the appellant and inform the appellant of the lodging of such notes and (if so requested) supply to him a copy thereof on payment of the usual copying charges.

4. Where both parties to the appeal are acting in person, the registrar shall, where possible, make a note for the assistance of the judge hearing the appeal and shall, prior to the hearing, furnish each party with a copy of that note or certify that no note can be made.

2131   —— consent applications—periodical payments to child—procedure

The following Practice Direction ([1979] 1 All ER 831) has been issued by the Family Division, and cancels paragraph 2 of Practice Direction [1976] 1 All ER 272, 1976 Halsbury's Abridgment para. 868.

Where a consent summons or notice of application seeks an order which includes agreed terms for periodical payments direct to a child in excess of the amounts qualifying for the time being as "small maintenance payments" under s. 65 of the Income and Corporation Taxes Act 1970, it is no longer necessary for the solicitor to certify whether the child is or is not living with the party who will be making the payments under the proposed terms.

2132   —— maintenance and wardship proceedings—address for service—servicemen

The following Practice Direction ([1979] 2 All ER 1106) has been issued by the

Senior Registrar of the Family Division substituting the following for para. (3) of Practice Direction [1973] 1 All ER 61 and setting out the appropriate addresses to which relevant enquiries should be made.

In cases where the person sought is known to be serving or to have recently served in any branch of HM Forces, the solicitor representing the applicant may obtain the address for service of maintenance or wardship proceedings direct from the appropriate service department. In the case of army servicemen the solicitor can obtain a list of regiments, and of the various manning and record offices from the Officer in Charge, Central Clearing Wing, Higher Barracks, Exeter EX4 4ND.

The solicitor's request should be accompanied by a written undertaking that the address will be used solely for the purpose of service of process in the proceedings and that so far as is possible the solicitor will disclose the address only to the court and not to the applicant or any other person, except in the normal course of the proceedings.

Alternatively if the solicitor wishes to serve process on the person's commanding officer under the provisions contained in s. 101 of the Naval Discipline Act 1957, s. 153 of the Army Act 1955 and s. 153 of the Air Force Act 1955 (each as amended by s. 62 of the Armed Forces Act 1971) he may obtain that officer's address in the same way.

Where the applicant is acting in person the appropriate service department is prepared to disclose the address of the person sought, or that of his commanding officer, to a registrar on receipt of an assurance that the applicant has given an undertaking that the information will be used solely for the purpose of serving process in the proceedings.

In all cases the request should include details of the person's full name, service number, rank or rating, and his ship, arm or trade, corps, regiment or unit or as much of this information as is available. Failure to quote the service number and the rank or rating may result in failure to identify the serviceman or at least in considerable delay.

2133   —— **matrimonial causes—costs—taxation**

A Practice Direction ([1979] 2 All ER 150) has been issued by the Senior Registrar of the Family Division laying down the procedure to be followed in relation to the taxation of bills of costs in matrimonial proceedings following the introduction of a new "Matrimonial Scale" by the Matrimonial Causes (Costs) Rules 1979, para. 960, and providing guidelines as to the operation of that procedure.

2134   The following Practice Direction ([1979] 3 All ER 896) has been issued by the Senior Registrar of the Family Division.

In the Practice Direction [1979] 2 All ER 150, para. 2133, on the new practice on taxation it was laid down that bills must be divided into parts to show, inter alia, the work done in the High Court and the divorce county court.

There appears to be some degree of misunderstanding about the method of setting out the work in the two courts and the object of this note is to clarify this method.

Where work is begun in the county court and transferred to the High Court (or, rarely, vice versa) items 10 (*a*) and 10 (*b*) relating to that work must be set out at the end of that part of the bill. In any subsequent transfer between the High Court and the county court the same procedure will apply.

The Family Division has not been asked to approve any form of bill and will not accept as correct any form of bill that does not conform with the earlier Practice Direction, as explained in the present Practice Direction.

2135   —— **petitions—petitioner acting in person—address for service**

The following Practice Direction ([1979] 2 All ER 45) has been issued by the Family Division with the concurrence of the Lord Chancellor and lays down the procedure to be observed in the light of the Matrimonial Causes (Amendment) Rules 1979, para. 963.

Paragraph 5(*c*) of App 2 to the Matrimonial Causes Rules 1977 is amended by the Matrimonial Causes (Amendment) Rules 1979 with effect from 24 April 1979.

As from that date a petitioner, though acting in person, may give as his address for service the name and address of a solicitor, providing that (a) that solicitor has given him legal advice and assistance and (b) that solicitor agrees. That petitioner, however, will remain on the record as acting in person.

Where a solicitor has agreed to his name and address being used as the address for service of the petitioner but subsequently wishes to withdraw his agreement, he should notify the court to this effect, give the petitioner's last known address and certify that he has notified the petitioner of the withdrawal of his agreement.

2136 —— **probate—testamentary documents—use of photographic facsimilies**

The following Practice Direction ([1979] 3 All ER 859) has been issued by the Senior Registrar of the Family Division.

To assist in the preparation of fiat copies of testamentary documents, it has been decided that, subject to the registrar's discretion, as an alternative to typewritten engrossments, facsimile copies produced by photography may be used in the following circumstances:

1. where a complete page or pages are to be excluded,
2. where words on the same page below the testator's signature can be excluded by masking out, and
3. where the original has been altered but not re-executed or republished and there exists a photocopy of the original executed document.

This extended practice will apply in the district probate registries and sub-registries as well as in the Principal Registry.

2137 **High Court—power to stay action—concurrent criminal proceedings—disclosure of defence**

The plaintiff company issued a writ claiming against the defendant, a former employee, the recovery of a certain sum, on the grounds that the defendant had misappropriated certain cheques drawn by the plaintiff in favour of its suppliers. The statement of claim did not assert fraud or any criminal offence. The defendant was however, committed to stand trial at the Crown Court, the charge being founded on the same matters as the civil action. The plaintiff applied by summons under RSC Ord. 14 for summary judgment for the amount claimed on the basis of an affidavit sworn by the financial controller of the company. At the hearing of the application the judge made an order that the summons would stand adjourned until the conclusion of the criminal proceedings. The plaintiff appealed against the order and the defendant cross-appealed, contending that the appropriate form of relief was not an order adjourning the summons, but an order staying the action until the conclusion of the criminal proceedings. The defendant maintained that if she was required to swear an affidavit in opposition, which she was bound to do if summary judgment was not to be entered against her, she would of necessity be disclosing the whole of her defence and thereby many matters which would be put to the financial controller of the company in cross-examination at the criminal trial. *Held*, there was no principle of law that, if criminal proceedings were pending against a defendant in respect of the same subject matter, he, the defendant, would be entitled to be excused from taking in the civil action any procedural step necessary or desirable for him to take in furtherance of his defence in the civil action if that step would have the result of disclosing his defence to the criminal proceedings. The protection given to one facing a criminal charge, the right of silence, did not extend to give the defendant, as a matter of right, the same protection in contemporaneous civil proceedings: this was a matter for the discretion of the judge if it appeared that justice required it. There was however, in this case, no evidence that it would be just or convenient to stay the civil action. The appeal would be allowed and the Ord. 14 summons restored for re-hearing.

JEFFERSON LTD v BHETCHA [1979] 2 All ER 1108 (Court of Appeal: MEGAW and BRANDON LJJ).

2138 House of Lords—costs—petition for leave to appeal

The following Procedure Direction ([1979] 1 All ER 846) has been issued by the Clerk of the Parliaments.

The Appeal Committee have determined that, where leave to brief counsel before them has been obtained pursuant to Direction 8, agents will be permitted to make a charge for preparing counsel's brief.

Item (xvi) on p. 6 of the Forms of Bills of Costs applicable to Judicial Taxations in the House of Lords (1977) will be amended accordingly.

2139 —— petition for leave to appeal—criminal causes—procedure

The following Procedure Direction ([1979] 2 All ER 359) has been issued by the Clerk of the Parliaments.

Criminal petitions for leave to appeal to the House of Lords in respect of which no certificate has been granted by the court below under section 1 (2) of the Administration of Justice Act 1960 or section 33 (2) of the Criminal Appeal Act 1968 will not be received in the Judicial Office.

This accords with the decision of this House in *Gelberg v Miller* [1961] 1 WLR 459; [1961] 1 All ER 618, which has been held by the Appeal Committee to apply to section 33 (2) of the Criminal Appeal Act 1968 as it applies to section 1 (2) of the Administration of Justice Act 1960.

2140 —— —— petitions out of time

At the conclusion of the hearing of a petition for leave to appeal by Warinco A. G. from a decision of the Court of Appeal [1979] 1 Lloyd's Rep 450, para. 2341, the Chairman of the Appeal Committee, LORD EDMUND-DAVIES, said ([1979] 1 WLR 884):

We have heard this petition for leave to appeal on its merits, and we dismiss it. But I think it is right to point out that it is as a matter of indulgence that we have allowed the merits to be gone into at all, because this is a petition which is six and a half months out of time. A wholly inadequate attempt has been made to explain the delay. The excuses offered, even when taken at their face value, explain some three and a half months only of the delay which has occurred, leaving a substantial period of time wholly unexplained.

Laxity in relation to compliance with Standing Orders is increasing and it must be curbed. Earlier this year, in February, in *Unitramp Ltd. v Carnac Grain Co. Inc.*, the noble and learned Viscount, Lord Dilhorne, said in words that we respectfully adopt:

"The Standing Orders of this House are meant to be complied with. There are very experienced firms of solicitors acting on both sides, and there is a great deal of money involved. The Standing Orders of this House really cannot be treated as if they meant nothing, so that the parties can ignore them. The fact that there is no excuse for it is a matter we shall have to consider . . ."

We have considered the non-compliance in this case very carefully, and we want it to become known that laxity of this kind will not be tolerated. If it is persisted in, the day will dawn when parties seeking leave to appeal will find that they are out of court for that reason alone, regardless of the merits. Disobedience to the clear rules as to time disorganises business in this House and shows disrespect if non-compliance occurs which is wholly or (as in the present case) largely unexplained. We refuse leave to appeal.

Standing Order No. II requires a petition for leave to appeal to be lodged within the Parliament Office within one month from the date of the last order or judgment appealed from.

2141 —— —— procedure

The following Procedure Direction ([1979] 2 All ER 224) has been issued by the Clerk of the Parliaments and supersedes the earlier Procedure Direction [1976] 2 All ER 445, 1976 Halsbury's Abridgment para. 522 on petitions for leave to appeal.

1. As from 1st October 1976 petitions for leave to appeal to the House of Lords will be referred to an appeal committee consisting of three Lords of Appeal, who will consider whether the petition appears to be competent to be received by the House and, if so, whether it should be referred for an oral hearing.

For the purposes of this direction, petitions are incompetent if they fall under one of the following heads: (a) petitions for leave to appeal to the House of Lords against a refusal of the Court of Appeal to grant leave to appeal to that court from a judgment of a lower court; (b) petitions for leave to appeal to the House of Lords barred by s. 108 (2) (b) of the Bankruptcy Act 1914; (c) petitions for leave to appeal to the House of Lords barred by para. 4 of Sch. 4 to the Housing Act 1957; (d) petitions for leave to appeal to the House of Lords brought by a petitioner in respect of whom the High Court has made an order under s. 51 of the Supreme Court of Judicature (Consolidation) Act 1925, as amended by the Supreme Court of Judicature (Amendment) Act 1959, unless leave to present such a petition has been granted by the High Court or a judge thereof pursuant to that section.

2. Petitions for leave to appeal will be referred for an oral hearing if any member of the appeal committee (i) considers that the petition is competent or expresses doubts as to whether it is incompetent; and (ii) considers that it is fit for an oral hearing.

3. Where a petition is not considered fit for an oral hearing, the Clerk of the Parliaments will notify the parties that the petition is dismissed.

2142   Industrial tribunal—procedure

In order to avoid delays at hearings before industrial tribunals and to avoid adjournments, the President of Industrial Tribunals (England and Wales) has requested solicitors acting for parties to prepare a bundle containing all correspondence and other documents on which they intend to rely at the hearing arranged in correct sequence and numbered consecutively. A list of the documents should be sent to the other party and, whenever practicable, there should be an agreed bundle of documents. Three sets of documents should be made available for the use of the tribunal. See notice published in the Law Society Gazette, 17th January 1979, p. 48.

2143   Legal aid

See LEGAL AID.

2144   Parties—joinder—additional defendant to copyright action

The plaintiffs brought an action alleging breach of copyright against the sole United Kingdom importers of conveyor chains manufactured in Germany. The plaintiffs sought to join the German company as a defendant to the action under RSC Ord. 15, r. 6. *Held*, as the German company was so closely connected with the dispute it would be proper to join it as a defendant to the action.

REXNORD INC v ROLLERCHAIN DISTRIBUTORS LTD [1979] FSR 119 (Chancery Division: FOX J).

2145   Preservation of subject-matter of cause of action—ex parte application for discovery—unlawful interference with business

See *Carlin Music Corpn v Collins*, para. 520.

2146   Queen's Bench Division—Divisional Court—applications against immigration decisions—presentation

The following Practice Direction ([1979] 2 All ER 880) has been given by LORD WIDGERY CJ.

In order to simplify the presentation of applications to the Divisional Court against decisions reached under the Immigration Act 1971, three forms have been prepared. Form 1 is for use in connection with applications in respect of a refusal of leave to enter; form 2 is for applications in respect of refusal to vary leave or an appeal against a variation of leave; form 3 is for applications made where the applicant has been detained after entry and where no application to remain or for variation of leave to remain has been made.

Copies of the forms may be obtained from the chief clerk of the Crown Office and should be used in all appropriate cases.

2147   —— **judgment—judgment upon default of defence—indorsement of judgment before entry**

The following Practice Direction ([1979] 2 All ER 1062) has been issued by the Senior Master of the Supreme Court, in consequence of the abolition of the requirement for the indorsement of service on the writ of summons, by the Rules of the Supreme Court (Amendment No. 2) 1979, para. 2145.

Having regard to the abolition of the requirement for the indorsement of service on the writ of summons, and in order to ensure that a judgment in default of the service of his defence by the defendant is not entered prematurely, the following indorsement must first be signed and dated by the solicitor for the plaintiff, or by the plaintiff if he is acting in person, on the back of the court copy of the judgment which he tenders for entry against the defendant for default of service of his defence:

"I/WE, SOLICITORS FOR THE PLAINTIFF CERTIFY THAT THE TIME FOR SERVICE OF THE DEFENCE BY THE DEFENDANT PRESCRIBED BY THE RULES OF COURT OR EXTENDED BY ORDER OF THE COURT OR THE CONSENT OF THE PARTIES HAS EXPIRED AND THAT THE DEFENDANT IS IN DEFAULT IN SERVING HIS DEFENCE WITHIN SUCH TIME

DATED. . . . .
                                        SOLICITORS FOR THE PLAINTIFF"

2148   —— **Masters' summonses—return dates**

The Senior Master of the Supreme Court has issued the following Masters' Practice Direction ([1979] 1 WLR 1038).

1. The arrangements for return dates for the hearing of Summonses before the Queen's Bench Masters in Chambers (Masters' Practice Direction [1977] 3 All ER 943, 1977 Halsbury's Abridgment para. 2144) have been revised and the current practice will continue.

2. Masters' Practice Direction 16A (1) (Return Dates for Masters' Summonses) is therefore amended by deleting the first three paragraphs and substituting therefor the following paragraphs:

"1. The current practice for the hearing of Summonses before the Queen's Bench Masters in Chambers will continue.

2. Two Masters will sit each day to hear Summonses in Chambers and they will sit as at present in Rooms 95 and 96 at 10.30 am.

3. The present 'Supplementary Lists' on Tuesdays and Thursdays will continue but will be listed for hearing before the Master at 2.00 pm and the Master will sit in Room 95 or 96, as necessary. If the business before the Masters makes it necessary or desirable, the Masters may take an occasional 'Additional List'."

In all other respects the Practice Direction referred to above will continue to apply.

2149   —— **orders—time for drawing up orders**

The Senior Master of the Supreme Court has directed that in cases where no time is specified for the drawing up of an order to be indorsed on a summons, notice or other document in the Queen's Bench Division the parties need no longer seek the leave of the Master before drawing up the order. Masters' Practice Direction 19 is amended accordingly by the deletion in para. (1). of the words "or, if no time is specified, 21 days after the making of the order". Nevertheless, the parties are still under an obligation in these cases to draw up the necessary order as soon as is reasonably practicable after it is made. See 129 NLJ 756.

2150   —— personal injury actions—agreed experts' reports

The following Practice Direction ([1979] 1 All ER 818) has been issued by the Senior Master of the Supreme Court.

1. In personal injury actions it would be of great convenience and assistance to the trial judge to have the opportunity before the trial to read the reports of the experts, both medical and other experts, which have been agreed between the parties.

2. Accordingly, in personal injury actions a copy of the reports of the medical and other experts which have been agreed between the parties must be lodged by the plaintiff with the proper officer (as defined in RSC Ord 34, r. 3 (5)) at the place where the action has been set down for trial, within 14 days after such reports have been agreed or as soon after setting down as is practicable.

3. These reports will be placed by the proper officer with the documents required to be lodged with him when setting an action down for trial under RSC Ord 34, r. 3, and they will accompany such documents for the use of the trial judge.

4. Each such report should state on the face of it the name of the party on whose behalf the expert has given that report and the date on which it was given.

2151   —— —— expert reports—order for disclosure

See *Ollett v Bristol Aerojet Ltd*, para. 1254.

2152   Representative action—action in tort—whether representative action should be permitted

A question arose as to whether a minority shareholder of a company could bring a representative action on behalf of the other shareholders against two of the company's directors, seeking a declaration of entitlement to damages for conspiracy. The directors contended that a representative action could not be brought where the cause of action of each member of the class purported to be represented was a separate cause founded in tort and proof of damage was therefore a necessary ingredient. *Held*, such an action could be permitted provided that it would not have the effect of conferring on any member of the class a right he could not have claimed in a separate action or of barring a defence that could have been raised in a separate action; normally therefore only declaratory relief would be granted and not damages. Furthermore the issue to be decided should be one common to all the members of the class. The action in the instant case would be permitted and should the declaration be granted, the issues covered by the declaration would be res judicata between the shareholders and the directors; thus the individual shareholders would still have to bring their own actions to establish damage within the limitation period running from the date of the cause of action.

PRUDENTIAL ASSURANCE CO LTD V NEWMAN INDUSTRIES LTD [1979] 3 All ER 507 (Chancery Division: VINELOTT J).

2153   Rules of court—indorsement of writs—prescribed form—effect of exchange control changes

Until such time as changes are made in the rules of court and the prescribed forms of writ, a plaintiff must continue to indorse the writ to the effect that payment by the defendant should be made into court where the plaintiff, or the person on whose behalf the payment is made, is resident outside the scheduled territories as required by RSC Ord 6, r. 2. The Lord Chancellor's Department drew attention to this in a notice dated 8th November 1979 (see 123 Sol Jo 772). The notice also stated that because of the lifting of exchange controls, certain rules (i.e. RSC Ord 22, r. 9; Ord 45, r. 2; Ord 46, r. 7; Ord 49, r. 7; and CCR Ord 46, r. 12) apply only to cases where the plaintiff is resident in Southern Rhodesia. The notice stated that the Accountant-General has directed that the forms currently used in connection with court funds (in particular Forms 2, 10, 11, 13, PF2 and PF3) should be adapted by inserting "in Southern Rhodesia" for the words "outside the scheduled territories" wherever the latter appear.

2154   **Rules of the Supreme Court**

The Rules of the Supreme Court (Amendment) 1979, S.I. 1979 No. 35 (in force on 5th February 1979, except rr. 4, 5, which came into force on 24th April 1979), amend the Rules so as to (i) prevent the plaintiff from obtaining a judgment in default of a defence if a summons under Ord. 86 has been served; (ii) allow a respondent the same time for appealing against a decision of the court below as he has at present for serving a respondent's notice; (iii) introduce a new scheme for the taxation of costs; (iv) substitute new fixed costs for the basic costs allowable under Ord. 62, Appendix 3 where the sum recovered is either £350 or between £350 and £1,200; and (v) extend Ord. 73, r. 10 so as to cover the enforcement of awards under the Arbitration Act 1975.

2155   The Rules of the Supreme Court (Amendment No. 2) 1979, S.I. 1979 No. 402 (in force on 24th April 1979), amend the Rules of the Supreme Court so as (i) to allow service by post in many situations in which personal service is required under the existing rules; (ii) to change the rules in respect of joinder of parties and the enforcement of a judgment for contribution or indemnity, following the coming into force of the Civil Liability (Contribution) Act 1978; (iii) to make minor changes in Ord. 62, Appendix 2, regarding the taxation of costs; and (iv) to allow two months for the service of an application for a new tenancy under the Landlord and Tenant Act 1954, Part II, instead of one month, as at present.

2156   The Rules of the Supreme Court (Amendment No. 3) 1979, S.I. 1979 No. 522 (in force on 7th June 1979 except rr. 4–9, which come into force on the day appointed for the coming into force of the Arbitration Act 1979), amend the Rules so as (i) to raise the fees payable to examiners of the Court, (ii) to allow a person making an affidavit to give a "work address" in certain circumstances and also to apply for permission to omit the address altogether, (iii) to make provision for proceedings under the Arbitration Act 1979 once the "case stated" procedure 1950 Act has ceased to be available, (iv) to make provision for proceedings affecting the International Oil Pollution Compensation Fund and (v) to amend the rules applicable to summary proceedings for possession of land so as to require Form No. 11A to be used in every case.

2157   The Rules of the Supreme Court (Amendment No. 4) 1979, SI 1979 No. 1542 (in force on 2nd January 1980), amend the Rules so as to (i) widen the scope of provisions for service out of jurisdiction of summonses, notices and orders in arbitration proceedings, (ii) amend provisions concerning the enforcement of exchange controls, (iii) require a registrar to inform the police immediately the court varies or discharges an injunction with a power of arrest attached under the Domestic Violence and Matrimonial Proceedings Act 1976, s. 2 or directs that a magistrates' court order with a power of arrest attached is to cease to have effect under the Domestic Proceedings and Magistrates' Courts Act 1978, s. 28, (iv) extend the appeals procedure under the Matrimonial Proceedings (Magistrates' Courts) Act 1960 to appeals under the Domestic Proceedings and Magistrates' Courts Act 1978 and (v) provide for the registration of the assignment of book debts.

2158   The Rules of the Supreme Court (Amendment No. 5) 1979, S.I. 1979 No. 1725 (in force on 2nd January 1980) amend the rules by removing all provisions concerned with the enforcement of exchange controls.   Previous amendments to those provisions, see para. 2157 are revoked.

2159   —— **writ and appearance**

The Rules of the Supreme Court (Writ and Appearance) 1979, S.I. 1979 No. 1716 (in force on 3rd June 1980) amend the Rules primarily by prescribing new forms of writ of summons and replacing the entry of appearance by acknowledgment of service.   There will be a combined form of writ in place of the various forms now used in the Central Office and district registries and revised forms of writ in Admiralty actions in rem and limitation actions.

2160   Service of process—substituted service—defendant outside the jurisdiction—when substituted service may be granted

The plaintiff, by writ dated 14th April 1977, claimed damages for conspiracy to defraud against the defendant, a solicitor residing and practising in Jersey. Attempts to effect personal service on the defendant, during a short visit by him to England, failed. The plaintiff obtained an order for substituted service on the defendant under RSC Ord. 65, r. 4, which was subsequently set aside. The trial judge rejected the plaintiff's initial appeal against the setting aside of the order. The plaintiff further appealed. *Held*, although RSC Ord 65, r. 4 gave a discretion, it should only be exercised to avoid conflict with other rules. The general rule was that an order for substituted service could not be made where at the time of the issue of the writ there could not be good personal service because the defendant was outside the jurisdiction. In the instant case, the defendant was in Jersey on 14th April 1977. Accordingly, the appeal would be dismissed.

MYERSON V MARTIN [1979] 3 All ER 667 (Court of Appeal: LORD DENNING MR, WALLER and EVELEIGH LJJ).

2161   Setting action down for trial—setting down after expiry of period fixed by court order—procedure

The following Masters' Practice Direction 16A (2) (a) ([1979] 1 WLR 1040) has been issued by the Senior Master of the Supreme Court and revokes Practice Direction [1964] 3 All ER 496.

1. Subject to compliance with RSC Ord 3, r. 6 (requirement of service of notices of intention to proceed after a year's delay), where applicable, the plaintiff need not obtain the leave of the Court or the consent of the defendant or the defendants, if there are more than one, before setting an action down for trial after the expiry of the period fixed by an order made under RSC Ord 34, r. 2 (1).

2. The foregoing change in the practice in no way relieves the plaintiff of his obligation to set the action down for trial within the time fixed by the order of the Court, and his failure to do so may entail the dismissal of the action for want of prosecution under RSC Ord 34, r. 2 (2).

2162   Solicitor—absence from hearing—return after hearing—unreasonableness of Commissioners

See *R and D McKerron Ltd v IRC*, para. 2687.

2163   Stay of proceedings—stay granted pending decision of European Commission

See *British Leyland Motor Corpn Ltd v Wyatt Interpart Co Ltd*, para. 917.

2164   Striking out—appeal against striking out of action—whether reasonable cause of action

Serious constructional defects were discovered in a number of tower blocks in 1971 ten years after they were built by contractors. In 1976, the council, as owner of the properties, claimed damages for breach of contract and negligence from the contractors who contended that such an action was statute barred under the Limitation Act 1939. The council claimed that its right of action had been concealed by the contractors' fraud in hiding the defects and that time did not start to run until discovery of the fraud. The council's statement of claim was struck out on the ground that any defects could and should have been discovered by its own architects and supervisors. On appeal, *held*, the council was not prevented from arguing that its action was concealed by fraud merely because it employed its own architects and supervisors. The question of whether or not the 1939 Act applied should be determined and therefore it was wrong to strike out the claim. The appeal would be allowed.

LEWISHAM LONDON BOROUGH V LESLIE & CO LTD(1978) 250 Estates Gazette 1289 (Court of Appeal: LORD DENNING MR and BRANDON LJ).

2165   Summons—Masters' summons—adjournment, withdrawal or transfer from lists—procedure

The following Masters' Practice Direction 16A (1) (a) ([1979] 1 WLR 1039) has been made by the Senior Master of the Supreme Court.

1. *Summons in the Ordinary List*

A Summons in the ordinary list may be adjourned or withdrawn or transferred to Counsel's List or for a special appointment without reference to a Master:
(a) by consent; or
(b) if the summons has not been served.

In all other cases application must be made to the Master to whom the summons has been assigned.

2. A Summons may be restored to the ordinary list for hearing:
(a) without the leave of a Master if for any reason the summons has not been heard, or, if heard, has not been fully disposed of;
(b) in other cases, by leave of a Master.

3. *Special Appointments before the Masters*

An application for the adjournment of a special appointment given by a Master must be made to the Master who gave the appointment personally.

4. Where the matter involved in a summons for which a Master has given a special appointment has been settled, it is the duty of solicitors for the parties and particularly the solicitor who obtained that appointment to notify that Master immediately.

2166   Supreme Court fees

The Supreme Court Fees (Amendment) Order 1979, S.I. 1979 No. 968 (in force on 3rd September 1979), amends the Supreme Court Fees Order 1975, 1975 Halsbury's Abridgment para. 2638. The fee payable on the issue of a writ for a liquidated sum not exceeding £2,000 is increased to £25 and in any other case the fee is increased to £30.

2167   Supreme Court funds

The Supreme Court Funds (Amendment) Rules 1979, S.I. 1979 No. 106 (in force on 1st March 1979), amend r. 35 (1) of the Supreme Court Funds Rules 1975 by raising the rate of interest allowed on money in a short-term investment account from 10 per cent to 12½ per cent per annum.

2168   The Supreme Court Funds (Amendment No. 2) Rules 1979, S.I. 1979 No. 1620 (in force on 1st January 1980), amend r. 35 (1) of the Supreme Court Funds Rules 1975 by raising the rate of interest allowed on money in a short term investment account from 12½ per cent to 15 per cent per annum.

2169   Want of prosecution—dismissal of action—delay—action brought on behalf of a minor—whether minor entitled to bring fresh action within limitation period

The infant plaintiff suffered personal injury, including brain damage, when she was struck by a car in 1964. In 1967 the father commenced an action for personal injury on her behalf and a writ was served in 1968. No further action was taken until 1977 when the plaintiff's new solicitors gave notice of intention to proceed and issued a statement of claim. The action was dismissed for want of prosecution by the district registrar and an appeal from his decision failed. The Court of Appeal reversed that decision, and allowed the action to proceed, on the ground that under the Limitation Act 1939, s. 22 as amended, where a minor had a right of action for personal injury, the limitation period for bringing such an action was extended until three years after attaining the age of eighteen. On appeal by the defendant, *held*, LORD WILBERFORCE and VISCOUNT DILHORNE dissenting, the decision of the Court of Appeal would be upheld. Although there had been a delay prejudicial to the defendant, dismissal of the action for want of prosecution would not avail the defendant, as the plaintiff had the right to bring a further action within three years of attaining the age of eighteen. Once an action had been commenced a defendant had a remedy under the rules of court for any excessive delay on the part of the plaintiff. The appeal would be dismissed.

TOLLEY v MORRIS [1979] 2 All ER 561 (House of Lords: LORD WILBERFORCE, VISCOUNT DILHORNE, LORD DIPLOCK, LORD EDMUND-DAVIES and LORD KEITH OF KINKEL). Decision of the Court of Appeal [1979] 1 WLR 205, 1978 Halsbury's Abridgment para. 2225 affirmed.

2170   —— —— —— delay jeopardising likelihood of fair trial

The defendants allegedly infringed the plaintiff's patent from 1964 until 1967, and their stocks were not finished until 1973. The plaintiffs issued a writ in 1972, and the patent expired in 1974. Six and a half years elapsed before the plaintiffs restored their summons for directions for hearing. The defendants applied to have the action struck out in view of the delay between the issue of the writ and the summons for directions. *Held*, despite the plaintiffs' avowed difficulty in finding an expert witness it had been incumbent upon them to bring the action as soon as possible after the issue of the writ. As a result of the long delay the witnesses in the case were at a greater disadvantage than earlier with respect to their recollection of the facts. Furthermore, since advances had been made in the industry, the patent in question had been superseded, and different people had replaced the original employees, thereby increasing the defendants' difficulty in collecting the evidence necessary for a fair trial. The action would accordingly be struck out.

THE HORSTMAN GEAR LTD v SMITHS INDUSTRIES LTD [1979] FSR 461 (Patents Court: GRAHAM J). *Birkett v James* [1978] AC 297, 1977 Halsbury's Abridgment para. 2157, applied.

2171   —— —— effect of dismissal of action on new writ issued outside limitation period

See *Walkley v Precision Forgings Ltd*, para. 1761.

2172   Writ of summons—revision

See para. 2159.

PRESS AND PRINTING

Halsbury's Laws of England (3rd edn.), Vol. 30, paras. 1037–1091

2173   Newspaper—agreement with prosecution witness—whether improper

The Press Council has severely censured the Sunday Telegraph over an agreement with Mr Peter Bessell who was a prosecution witness in the trial of Mr Jeremy Thorpe. Under the agreement (signed two months after the defendants had been charged) the newspaper acquired exclusive world rights to publish extracts from a book being prepared by Mr Bessell on "The Thorpe Affair" for immediate publication after the criminal proceedings were completed. Payment was to to be £17,000 on execution of the agreement, £8,000 by April 1979 and a further £25,000 on publication. If, on legal advice, the newspaper was unable to publish the extracts, Mr Bessell would provide alternative articles for publication and be paid £25,000. The first two payments were made but the contract was terminated after Mr Bessell had finished giving evidence but before the trial was completed. Mr Bessell's solicitor had contacted the office of the Director of Public Prosecutions concerning the contract before it was signed. The Press Council ruled that it was improper and a breach of its declaration of principle on such matters for a newspaper to make any contract with a witness once criminal proceedings have begun for his story about the case. It was grossly improper to do so where the contract takes the form (in the judge's phrase) of "double your money" in the event of a conviction. The judge's view that the evidence had previously "crystallised" in Mr Bessell's mind may have saved the newspaper from proceedings for contempt of court but afforded no defence to a complaint of breach of the Press Council's declaration of principle. See the Daily Telegraph, 26th October 1979.

PRISONS

Halsbury's Laws of England (3rd edn.), Vol. 30, paras. 1092–1231

2174   Articles

Prison Discipline and the Courts, Graham Zellick: 129 NLJ 308.
Prisoner's Access, Alan Beaver: 95 LQR 393.

2175   Disciplinary offences—hearing before prison board of visitors— board's powers and duties in conducting hearings

Following prison riots certain prisoners were charged with and found guilty of offences under the Prison Rules 1964, by the prison's board of visitors. They each applied for an order of certiorari to quash the board's findings on the grounds that it had failed to observe the rules of natural justice in refusing to allow the prisoners to call their own witnesses and in admitting and acting upon statements made by the governor based on reports by prison officers who had not given oral evidence. Furthermore that the Prison Rules, r. 49 (2), which states that a prisoner should be given a full opportunity of hearing what is alleged against him and of presenting his own case, had not been observed. *Held*, quashing some of the board's findings, the following principles should be observed when adjudicating under the prison disciplinary procedure. Under r. 49 (2) a prisoner had the right to be heard himself and the right to call evidence which was likely to assist in establishing the vital facts in issue. The discretion conferred upon the board's chairman to refuse to allow a prisoner to call witnesses was a necessary part of the procedure in view of the fact that the board was dealing with prisoners, but it had to be exercised reasonably, in good faith and on proper grounds. Hearsay evidence could be admitted, but the board's right to do so was subject to the overriding obligation to provide the accused with a fair hearing, which might mean the cross-examination of witnesses whose evidence was initially before the board in the form of hearsay evidence. The board should refuse to admit hearsay evidence if the prisoner was disputing it and wished to question the witness, and the witness's attendance at the hearing was for some reason impossible.

R v HULL PRISON BOARD OF VISITORS, EX PARTE ST GERMAIN (No. 2) [1979] 3 All ER 545 (Queen's Bench Division: LORD WIDGERY CJ, GEOFFREY LANE LJ and ACKNER J).

2176   Parole Board—annual report

The Report of the Parole Board for 1978 (HC 105) notes that in 1978 the board considered 5303 fixed-term prisoners for release on parole. The board recommended that 3913 be released (62 per cent of the cases examined); the Home Secretary was unable to accept the recommendation in the case of seven prisoners. In total 4808 prisoners were granted parole during the year, the figure including those released by the Home Secretary on the advice of local review committees. During 1978, 440 fixed-term prisoners were recalled to prison during their parole period and had their licences revoked. An appendix to the report sets out the criteria for selection for parole.

PUBLIC AUTHORITIES AND PUBLIC OFFICERS

2177   British Airports Authority—statutory powers—power to ban minicabs—validity of banning notice

Minicab drivers were not permitted to offer their services whilst at an airport. An unlicensed minicab driver had numerous convictions for touting for passengers at the airport and allegedly regularly overcharged them. The airport authority invoked a byelaw and gave the driver written notice that he was prohibited from entering the airport. The byelaw prevented a person so prohibited from entering the airport except as a bona fide airline passenger. The driver sought declarations that (i) the Airports Authority Act 1975 and the Heathrow Airport–London Byelaws 1972 constituted a code under which the airport, as a public authority, was to be operated and it was not open to the authority to act as an ordinary landowner could; (ii) the authority had no power to ban individuals from the public part of the airport; (iii) the byelaw relied on was void as being unreasonable and too wide; (iv) if the authority had such power, it could only be exercised in accordance with the principles of natural justice and the driver should, therefore, have been given an opportunity to be heard. *Held,* the position of a public authority could not be equated with that of a private landowner, as it would be wholly alien to the purpose for which such an authority was set up that it should have the same power of arbitrary exclusion as a private landowner had. However, the authority had the power to exclude members of the public provided that that power could not be exercised unreasonably; the authority were not, in the circumstances, acting unreasonably in banning the driver from the airport. The byelaw was not too wide; it was not unreasonable to prevent the driver from pursuing his legitimate commercial and leisure activities at the airport, as he had abused the system so often before in order to wait at the airport and tout for trade. In a normal case, the authority would have had to hear any objections from the driver before imposing the prohibition, as it affected his means of earning a living. However, as the driver's only expectation was to continue flouting the byelaws and indulging in criminal activity, the rules of natural justice did not apply. The declarations would be refused.

CINNAMOND V BRITISH AIRPORTS AUTHORITY [1979] RTR 331 (Queen's Bench Division: FORBES J). Dictum of Diplock LJ in *Mixnam's Properties Ltd v Chertsey Urban DC* [1964] 1 QB 214 CA, at 237 applied.

This decision has been affirmed by the Court of Appeal; see Times, 23rd February 1980.

PUBLIC HEALTH

Halsbury's Laws of England (3rd edn.), Vol. 31, paras. 1–638

2178   Aircraft

The Public Health (Aircraft) Regulations 1979, S.I. 1979 No. 1434 (in force on 1st January 1980) consolidate the Public Health (Aircraft) Regulations 1970 and all amending regulations, providing for public health control of aircraft arriving in or leaving England and Wales.

2179   —— Isle of Man

The Public Health (Aircraft) (Isle of Man) Order 1979, S.I. 1979 No. 1315 (in force on 1st December 1979) extends the Public Health (Aircraft) Regulations 1970 to the Isle of Man, subject to specified exceptions, modifications and adaptations.

2180   Building regulations—inner London

The Building (Repeals and Amendments) Regulations 1979, S.I. 1979 No. 601 (in force on 27th June 1979), are made in consequence of the Building (First Amendment) Regulations 1978, 1978 Halsbury's Abridgment para. 2246, which came into force on 1st June 1979 and made provisions for the purpose of furthering the conservation of fuel and power in England and Wales apart from inner London. These provisions make redundant, in relation to factories, regulations made under the Thermal Insulation (Industrial Buildings) Act 1957. Since the Act will still apply in inner London, the present regulations modify the definition of "local authority" in the Act so that the only local authority in England and Wales which will be able to enforce the requirements of the regulations made under the Act will be the Greater London Council in inner London.

2181 —— type relaxation

Type relaxation direction 3 (relating to cavity insulation work) has been made under the Health and Safety at Work etc. Act 1974, s. 66, dispensing with the requirements of regs. A10 and C9 (2), and other regulations of the Building Regulations 1976, 1976 Halsbury's Abridgment para. 2013, (as amended) as applied by reg. A7 subject to conditions. The building matters to which the dispensation is applied are specified. Subject to savings, type relaxation direction 1 dated 16th October 1975 is revoked. See Department of Environment circular 29/79.

2182 Dangerous substances—restrictions on marketing and use

Council Directive (EEC) 79/663 (OJ No. L197 3.8.79) supplements Council Directive (EEC) 76/769, 1976 Halsbury's Abridgment para. 2017, on the approximation of the laws of member states relating to restrictions on the marketing and use of certain dangerous substances by adding to the Annex of that directive certain toxic, harmful and flammable liquids. Member states are required to adopt the necessary national implementing legislation within twelve months of the date of notification of the directive.

2183 Drain—connection to private drain from neighbouring property— connection without permission

See *Cook v Minion*, para. 2496.

2184 Local authority—exercise of powers under Public Health Act— compensation for damage

See *Leonidis v Thames Water Authority*, para. 2497.

2185 Port health authority—Fowey

The Fowey Port Health Authority Order 1979, S.I. 1979 No. 1085 (in force on 1st October 1979), constitutes the Port of Fowey, together with that part of the Port of Falmouth which lies to the east of Port Holland, as a port health district and constitutes a joint board, consisting of representatives of Restormel Borough Council and Caradon District Council, to be port health authority for that district. This Order supersedes similar orders made under the Public Health Acts and confers upon the joint board functions under general Acts relating to public health and food and drugs.

2186 —— Stroud

The Stroud Port Health Authority Order 1979, S.I. 1979 No. 134 (in force on 1st April 1979), constitutes part of the Port of Gloucester as a port health district, and constitutes Stroud district council as port health authority for that district. It lays down the jurisdiction and powers of the council as port health authority. The Order supersedes similar orders made under the Public Health Acts and confers upon the port health authority functions under general Acts relating to public health and food and drugs.

2187   Public Health Laboratory Service Act 1979

See para. 1946.

2188   Ships

The Public Health (Ships) Regulations 1979, S.I. 1979 No. 1435 (in force on 1st January 1980) consolidate the Public Health (Ships) Regulations 1970 and all amending regulations, providing for public health control of ships arriving in or leaving England and Wales.

2189   —— Isle of Man

The Public Health (Ships) (Isle of Man) Order 1979, S.I. 1979 No. 1316 (in force on 1st December 1979) extends the Public Health (Ships) Regulations 1970 to the Isle of Man, subject to specified exceptions, modifications and adaptations.

2190   Sports grounds—safety

The Safety of Sports Grounds (Designation) Order 1979, S.I. 1979 No. 1022 (in force on 1st January 1980), designates certain sports stadia as requiring safety certificates under the Safety of Sports Grounds Act 1975, 1975 Halsbury's Abridgment para. 2670.

RACE RELATIONS

Halsbury's Laws of England (4th edn.), Vol. 4, paras. 1034–1100

2191   Article

The Grounds of Discrimination under the Race Relations Act 1976 (1976 Halsbury's Abridgment para. 259) in the United Kingdom, Lawrence Lustgarten: 28 ICLQ 221.

Indirect Discrimination and the Race Relations Act, Geoffrey Bindman (the extent to which the law deals with indirect discrimination): 129 NLJ 408.

2192   Discrimination—complaint of discrimination in employment— amendment to include unfair dismissal—jurisdiction of industrial tribunal

See *Home Office v Bose*, para. 1078.

2193   —— —— production of documents—when production of confidential reports should be ordered

See *Jalota v Imperial Metal Industry (Kynoch) Ltd*, para. 912; *Science Research Council v Nasse; BL Cars Ltd (formerly Leyland Cars) v Vyas*, para. 913.

2194   —— Report of Commission for Racial Equality

Appendix II of the annual report (1978) of the Commission for Racial Equality includes information on a number of cases supported by the commission, mainly relating to unlawful discrimination in the field of employment and heard by industrial tribunals, where compensation was awarded for injury to feelings. The quantum of awards ranged from £25 to £250, most of the awards falling within the range £50 to £150.

2195   Employment—discrimination on racial grounds—refusal of qualifying body to grant access to training course

Industrial tribunal decision:

GHAFFAR v COUNCIL OF LEGAL EDUCATION (1979) 8147/79/A (unreported) (Pakistani citizen who had been living in England since 1971 had Pakistani law degree and English law doctorate and had been employed as civil servant and teacher in England; applied for certificate of eligibility to complete his training as barrister by taking diploma course over one year period; respondant refused on ground that overseas graduate required to take two year course because might not otherwise have basic knowledge of law and where to find it; condition did not amount to discrimination on ground of national origin; respondent decided test was that student had to have basic knowledge of core subjects before doing one year diploma; studies made by Pakistani in obtaining degrees not sufficient equivalent to core subjects to justify exemption; no provision for any other kind of assessment; tribunal not competent to question standards set for any profession unless standard patently unreasonable).

2196   —— —— —— remedies

Industrial tribunal decision:

BOHON-MITCHELL v COMMON PROFESSIONAL EXAMINATION BOARD; BOHON-MITCHELL v COUNCIL FOR LEGAL EDUCATION [1978] IRLR 525 (United States citizen who had been living in England for five years applied for a certificate of eligibility to complete her training as a barrister by taking a diploma course over a one year period; respondents refused on ground that overseas graduates were required to take a two year course because otherwise they might not have sufficient knowledge of English social and economic environment; condition amounted to discrimination on grounds of national origin which would cause the applicant to suffer financial hardship; award of compensation inappropriate; recommendation that respondents amend their regulations so that overseas graduates who were required to take the two year course be given reasons so they might appeal).

2197   —— —— selection of employees—indirect discrimination

Industrial tribunal decision:

HUSSEIN v SAINTS COMPLETE HOUSE FURNISHERS [1979] IRLR 337 (shop advertised vacancies stipulating that candidates should not live in city centre, on ground that such employees attracted undesirables to the shop; applicant, coloured youth, applied for job; refused on ground he resided in city centre; claimed unlawful discrimination on ground of racial origin; tribunal satisfied no direct discrimination by shop, however, city centre population was fifty per cent coloured whereas in suburbs was only two per cent; condition excluded larger number of coloured people than white; evidence therefore of indirect discrimination; shop advised to cease residential requirements).

2198   —— —— —— whether reason for selection justifiable

A Sikh who applied for a job in a confectionery factory was rejected because he would not comply with a rule which would require him to shave off his beard. His claim that he had been unlawfully discriminated against was rejected by an industrial tribunal because although the rule would apply to more Sikhs than non-Sikhs it was justifiable under Race Relations Act 1976, s. 1 on grounds of hygiene. On appeal, *held*, the tribunal had been correct in equating what was justifiable with what was equitable and reasonable. The factory owners' rule could not be said to be merely convenient, as it was supported by medical advice and had the support of the local food and drugs officer, and was in fact a commercial necessity. The appeal would be dismissed.

SINGH v ROWNTREE MACKINTOSH LTD [1979] IRLR 199 (Employment Appeal Tribunal: LORD McDONALD MC presiding).

2199　Immigration

See IMMIGRATION.

RAILWAYS, INLAND WATERWAYS AND PIPELINES

Halsbury's Laws of England (3rd edn.), Vol. 31, paras. 639–1403

2200　British Railways Board—borrowing powers

The British Railways Board (Borrowing Powers) Order 1979, S.I. 1979 No. 944 (in force on 11th August 1979) raises to £900 million the limit on the borrowing powers of the British Railways Board. The limit (which covers the Board's commencing capital debt and the principal of moneys borrowed by them under the Transport Act 1962, s. 19) at present stands at £600 million but can be increased to £900 m by Order of the Minister, approved in draft by resolution of the House of Commons.

2201　International carriage of goods—dangerous goods

In accordance with an additional protocol dated 7th February 1970, dangerous goods carried under the International Convention Concerning the Carriage of Goods by Rail, Berne 1970 (CIM), or the International Convention Concerning the Carriage of Passengers and Luggage by Rail (CIV), to or from the United Kingdom must comply with the regulations contained in Annex 1 (RID) to the CIM and also with the United Kingdom conditions for the carriage of dangerous goods by rail and sea. This is until a special appendix (which is in the course of preparation) containing special regulations for rail-sea carriage of dangerous goods between the Continent and the United Kingdom enters into force. A new edition of the International Regulations Concerning the Carriage of Dangerous Goods by Rail (RID) incorporating amendments agreed by the committee of experts has been published and replaces the 1977 text. The text of the 1978 edition of RID is available from HMSO.

Amendment No. 1 to the 1978 edition is now also available from HMSO.

RATING

Halsbury's Laws of England (3rd edn.), Vol. 32, paras. 1–272

2202　Article

Conveyancing: Rating of Unoccupied Property, J. Gilchrist Smith: 123 Sol Jo 105.

2203　Assessment—appeal—jurisdiction of local valuation court—increase in assessment

The ratepayers owned oil refineries and manufacturing plants and over a three-year period were conducting negotiations with the valuation officer concerning valuation of the hereditaments for rating purposes. Objections were raised in each case to the ratepayers' proposals prior to agreement being reached on the assessments, which were lower than the figures in the proposals. Hence it was necessary to transmit the proposals to the local valuation court to effect alterations to the valuation list. At the hearing agreed figures were produced by the ratepayers and valuation officer but the rating authority claimed the right to call evidence and question the parties. The local valuation court, having decided that the figures were agreed, stated that the authority had no further right to be heard. The rating authority appealed to the Lands Tribunal. The ratepayers contended that it was contrary to the spirit of present rating legislation that the rating authority which had not taken part in any negotiations should be allowed to go before the local valuation court and seek to prove that the figures should be higher than those agreed where those agreed figures were lower than those in the proposals and that therefore the Lands Tribunal had no jurisdiction to increase the figures found by the local valuation court. The Tribunal held that it had jurisdiction and the ratepayers appealed. *Held*, the provisions of the General Rate Act 1967, Pt. 5 recognised that the valuation officer, ratepayer and rating authority must always have an interest in the compilation and alteration of the valuation list. The provisions defined the function of the local valuation court which was to assess the impact of all contentions of the appellant upon the force of the objections. It was for the court to decide to what extent the objections were refuted by facts proved before them. There was no reason why the rating authority could not appear before the local valuation court since they had no obligation to take part in the earlier negotiations and when a matter was referred to the Lands Tribunal its jurisdiction corresponded to that of the local valuation court. Therefore it could arrive at a figure higher than that determined by the valuation court but it could not entertain a different proposal from that to which the objection was made. Hence the Lands Tribunal could make a higher assessment than that determined by the valuation court so long as it was not greater than that contained in the proposal.

ELLESMERE PORT AND NESTON BC v SHELL UK LTD [1980] 1 All ER 383 (Court of Appeal: MEGAW, SHAW and WALLER LJJ).

2204   British Gas Corporation

The Natural Gas Terminals (Rateable Values) (Amendment) Order 1979, S.I. 1979 No. 1373 (in force on 27th November 1979), amends the Natural Gas Terminals (Rateable Values) Order 1976, 1976 Halsbury's Abridgment para. 2047, by substituting certain new formulae and by adding certain premises to Schedule 1 of that Order.

2205   Distress for rates

See DISTRESS.

2206   Rate rebate scheme

The Rate Rebate (Amendment) Regulations 1979, S.I. 1979 No. 417 (in force on 26th April 1979), amend the statutory rate rebate scheme provided in the Rate Rebate Regulations 1978, 1978 Halsbury's Abridgment para. 2278. They enable the grant of a rebate from the beginning of the period mentioned below, to a residential occupier who is in receipt of supplementary benefit, if he will have received less payment in supplementary benefit than he would otherwise have received in rate rebate and any rent rebate or allowance, during the period from twelve months prior to the date of his application for a rebate or such later date on which he receives supplementary benefit to the date when he ceases to receive supplementary benefit.

2207

The Rate Rebate (Amendment) (No. 2) Regulations 1979, S.I. 1979 No. 1303 (in force on 12th November 1979) amend the statutory rent rebate scheme, provided for in the Rate Rebate Regulations 1978, 1978 Halsbury's Abridgment para. 2278. They provide for increases in the needs allowances and increases in the amounts to be deducted for non-dependants. The Regulations revoke the provision requiring liquid cash resources to be taken into account in calculating a residential occupier's income. They also provide that, in ascertaining income for the purpose of rate rebate, certain earnings of the residential occupier and his spouse and maintenance payments made by either the occupier or the spouse, will be disregarded. Further a person does not now cease to be within the definition of a "dependent child" solely by reason of his absence from the occupier's household during term-time.

2208   Rate support grants

See LOCAL GOVERNMENT.

2209   Rateable occupation—actual and exclusive occupation—extent of actual use and enjoyment required

The respondent purchased a house in May 1973, but he and his wife did not move into the house until November 1975. The respondent did not sleep in the house during the intervening period, but he made visits to decorate and maintain it. Gas and electricity were consumed and the telephone was used. The respondent kept some chattels in the house, although the majority of his furniture was in store. The rating authority preferred a complaint against the respondent when he failed to pay rates for the year commencing 1st April 1974. The magistrates concluded that there was not sufficient enjoyment of the hereditament to constitute rateable occupation. The rating authority appealed by way of case stated on the question of whether the magistrates' conclusion was one which, on the facts found, they could reasonably have reached and whether those facts were facts upon which as a matter of law they could reach the conclusion that they had. *Held*, although there was evidence of exclusive occupation and some enjoyment which would indicate rateable occupation, there was sufficient evidence for the magistrates reasonably to reach the opposite conclusion. Accordingly, the appeal would be dismissed.

WIRRAL BOROUGH COUNCIL v LANE (1979) 251 Estates Gazette 61 (Queen's Bench Division: LORD WIDGERY CJ, CUMMING-BRUCE LJ and NEILL J).

2210   —— occupation by spouse—husband and wife divorced—whether husband in rateable occupation

After the parties' divorce, a house was purchased to provide a home for the two children of the marriage and the ex-wife. The house had never been a matrimonial home. There was a maintenance order in existence for the benefit of the ex-wife and children. The ex-wife was rated as the occupier of the house but justices refused to issue a distress warrant against her for non-payment on the ground that the ex-husband was still under an obligation to provide accommodation for the children even after the divorce. On appeal by the ex-husband, *held*, the warrant should be issued against the ex-wife because she was in permanent beneficial occupation of the house. There was no evidence to support the contention that the ex-husband was providing a home for the children, in which the mother was living as a person having either custody or care and control, and accordingly the ex-husband was not the rateable occupier. The appeal would be allowed.

CHELMSFORD DISTRICT COUNCIL v CARROLL [1979] RA 45 (Queen's Bench Division: LORD WIDGERY CJ, MAY and TUDOR EVANS JJ).

2211   Rateable value—assessment—Lands Tribunal decisions

BRITISH AIRWAYS BOARD v RIDGEON (VALUATION OFFICER) [1979] RA 266: J. H. Emlyn Jones FRICS (ratepayer appealed against assessment of large composite hereditament used for aircraft maintenance consisting of hangars, workshops, offices, car parks and apron areas; contended, inter alia, that incorrect to have regard to rents or assessments of other properties within airport perimeter used for other purposes, because warehouse value provided no true indication of industrial value and value of small properties used, for example, as offices, did not give indication of value of offices forming integral part of large composite hereditament; comparables within airport not to be excluded; unrealistic to assume hypothetical landlord and hypothetical tenant would exclude from their minds the levels of values in the locality for different classes of hereditaments).

2212

CIVIL AVIATION AUTHORITY v LANGFORD (VALUATION OFFICER): CIVIL AVIATION AUTHORITY v CAMDEN LONDON BOROUGH COUNCIL [1979] RA 1: J. H. Emlyn Jones FRICS (ratepayers and rating authority agreed office building to be treated as completed in 1968; before first letting building found to have structural defects;

extensive reconstruction commenced; ratepayers asked to be permitted to pay nominal rates; ratepayers deemed to have carried out all reasonable repairs, but reconstruction was not repair; rates reduced because building could not have been let at date of deemed completion).

2213 COMMERCIAL UNION ASSURANCE CO LTD v BURNE (VALUATION OFFICER) [1978] RA 173: E. C. Strathon FRICS (ratepayers occupied premises used as offices in High Street; applied for reduction in assessment of gross value; no other ground floor offices in High Street so ratepayers claimed assessment should be related to ground floor offices outside High Street, but increased by 25 per cent to reflect additional value of direct access to High Street; but more dependable assessment based on what prospective tenants would consider reasonable rent; prospective tenants comprised such bodies as insurance companies and government departments who required central point for collection of money and therefore interested in High Street location; reasonable rent based on High Street rental values of banks, less 25 per cent for narrower access and poorer internal planning and quality of ratepayers' premises compared to banks).

2214 CORSER (VALUATION OFFICER) v GLOUCESTERSHIRE MARKETING SOCIETY LTD [1979] RA 31: R. C. Walmsley FRICS (auction hall used as fruit and vegetable market by local growers; valuation officer contended the hall was not an agricultural building because the business carried on there was independent of agricultural operations, and therefore it was a rateable property; hall should be regarded as an agricultural building used solely by the growers to sell their produce, which was connected with agricultural operations).

2215 EYSTON v MUNDY (VALUATION OFFICER) [1978] RA 200: J. H. Emlyn Jones FRICS (ratepayer appealed against assessments of gross and rateable values on mansion; property had been restored; condition of restoration grant that mansion should be open to public one day a week in summer; ratepayer claimed condition made property unlettable; assessment reduced slightly, but condition imposed on ratepayer did not affect assessment; condition not restrictive covenant running with land, but personal arrangement between ratepayer and Ministry of Works, therefore imposed no obligation on hypothetical tenant or hypothetical landlord, thus did not make property unlettable, indeed large number of wealthy people who might wish to rent premises).

2216 LEICESTER CITY COUNCIL v NUFFIELD NURSING HOMES TRUST [1979] RA 299: J. H. Emlyn Jones FRICS (hereditament comprised of modern clinic; some bedrooms not occupied by patients; assessment made by reference to comparables; no rental evidence available and profits basis valuation impossible as ratepayers were charity; rating authority appealed against assessment, relying on contractors' basis and applying 6 per cent to costs of buildings; in valuation on contractual basis, 6 per cent was appropriate rate; although cost of construction was met largely by subscription, it was assumed that benefaction was to be made available on annual basis and therefore available to pay rent; percentage was to be applied for surpluses as full use was not being made of bedrooms intended for patients; examination of comparables gave no real indication of where clinic should properly appear on comparative basis and no adjustment should therefore be made to gross value).

2217 MARSHALL v EBDON (VALUATION OFFICER) [1979] RA 238: W. H. Rees FRICS (property listed prior to 1976 as two hereditaments; ratepayer informed valuation officer in December 1975 that property was unoccupied, under reconstruction, and requested that assessment be reduced to nil; no amendment made to list on that basis; valuation officer proposed to delete two entries in favour of one composite one and assessed property on that basis at £380 gross value; ratepayer contended proposal invalid on grounds, inter alia, that no proposal could be made until completion notice served or until property occupied and used, property was subject to two separate assessments and at relevant date no one would have paid rent for it because

of poor condition; property not newly-erected building, completion notice
procedure did not therefore apply; valuation officer could make proposal for
alteration at any time; property constituted single hereditament as was unoccupied,
situated in one rating area and formed one geographical unit; hypothetical landlord
would have carried out repairs and no support for ratepayer's contention that no one
would pay any rent for property; assessment therefore upheld).

2218   NATIONAL CAR PARKS LTD v GUDGION (VALUATION OFFICER): NATIONAL CAR
PARKS LTD v BURROWS (VALUATION OFFICER): WEST (VALUATION OFFICER) v
NATIONAL CAR PARKS LTD [1979] RA 85: J. D. Russell Davies FRICS (re-assessment
of rates of several multi-storey car parks; plaintiffs claimed reduction in first which
was held under licence for consideration; alleged this was similar to a tenancy and
the consideration was a good indication of market value; one-third of parking space
was set aside for local authority and charges and opening hours were prescribed;
valuation reduced on latter grounds, but the tribunal accepted that the licence
represented a management agreement for consideration and could not be used to
assess market value; plaintiffs claimed reduction in valuation for second because
access had been impeded by the introduction of a one-way system after the car park's
construction; tribunal upheld valuation based on rent paid under current lease and
comparables; valuation officer claimed increase in valuation of third by reference to
comparables and alleged that the current rent was too low because it had been
negotiated as part of a larger business transaction; revaluation permitted).

2219   STOKE ON TRENT CITY COUNCIL v MCMILLAN (VALUATION OFFICER) [1979] RA
359: J. H. Emlyn Jones FRICS (appellant local authority owned and occupied multi-
storey car park; appealed against assessment and put forward valuation based on
contractor's test, effective capital value of land as a whole, including land and site
works, deducted fifty per cent for surplusage (car park only completely full on two
days per week) and applied 4½ per cent to give gross value; valuation officer offered
twenty per cent surplusage and 6 per cent to produce gross value; valuation officer's
assessment upheld; twenty per cent surplusage sufficient as unrealistic to expect car
park to be fully occupied throughout all daylight hours; further, proper commercial
rate per cent to be adopted to convert effective capital value into gross value was 6
per cent).

2220   VESTA LAUNDERETTES LTD v SMITH (VALUATION OFFICER) [1979] RA 317: E. C.
Strathon FRICS (ratepayers appealed against assessment to rates in respect of
launderette; assessed on zoning method of valuation; ratepayers contended that
shops were not acceptable comparables and that zoning method was not relevant as
front area of a launderette had higher value than back area; further contended that
valuation should be made by reference solely to other launderettes on basis of price
per machine; launderette was of same mode or category of use as a shop; zoning
method, customarily acceptable for shops, was applicable; valuation on basis of price
per machine rejected).

2221   ——— **proposal for reduction—application of legislation—
jurisdiction**

A ratepayer sought a reduction in her rates. She contended that an extension to her
house built after 1st April 1974 had to be ignored under the Local Government Act
1974, s. 21 (1) in determining the rateable value. *Held*, s. 21 (1) applied only to
proposals under the General Rate Act 1967, s. 69, for an increase in the gross value;
it did not apply where a ratepayer sought a reduction. The 1967 Act, s. 9, dealing
with refunds by rating authorities, similarly was of no assistance to the ratepayers as
refunds were strictly a matter for rating authorities; the courts had no jurisdiction.
Accordingly, the assessment would stand.

WHITE v BROMIDGE (VALUATION OFFICER) (1979) 251 Estates Gazette 469 (Court
of Appeal: MEGAW, EVELEIGH and BRANDON LJJ).

2222   **Surcharge—unused   commercial   buildings—exemption—industrial purposes**

A garage was built in 1932 and used until December 1975 for the preparation for sale and sale of new and used cars, for vehicle repairs and the sale of petrol. At no time were vehicles manufactured on the premises, which had been vacant since 1975. The local rating authority sought a rating surcharge from the owners and a distress warrant was issued against them. On appeal the owners contended that the property was exempt from the surcharge by virtue of the Rating Surcharge (Exemption) Regulations 1974, reg. 3 which provided that no surcharge was payable on hereditaments constructed or adapted as factories or other premises of similar character for use for industrial purposes. *Held*, the premises were registered under the Factories Act 1961 and as 72 per cent of them were used for the repair of vehicles, in which nearly thirty people were employed, they were properly to be regarded as a factory for use wholly or mainly for industrial purposes. At the least, they were premises of a similar character for such purposes. The appeal would therefore be allowed.

POST OFFICE v OXFORD CITY COUNCIL [1979] RA 255 (Queen's Bench Division: MICHAEL DAVIES and NEILL JJ).

2223   **Unoccupied property—service of completion notice—effect of subsequent division of hereditament**

A completion notice was served under the General Rate Act 1967, Sch. 1 in respect of a six-storey building. A subsequent agreement in July 1974 specified November 1974 as the date from which unoccupied property rates were payable. In June 1975 the two floors were leased to the defendants and the local rating authority claimed empty property rates in respect of those two floors. The defendants resisted the claim on the ground, inter alia, that a separate hereditament had come into existence in June 1975. *Held*, there was a valid and properly constituted completion date specified to be November 1974 and the notice had been served with reference to each floor separately. The notice therefore applied to any part of the building which became a separate hereditament at a later date. Unoccupied property rates were payable therefore from June 1975.

BRENT LONDON BOROUGH COUNCIL v LADBROKE RENTALS LTD (1979) 252 Estates Gazette 702 (Queen's Bench Division: KILNER BROWN J). *Camden London Borough Council v Post Office* [1977] 2 All ER 795, CA, 1977 Halsbury's Abridgment para. 2229 applied.

2224   **—— unused commercial property—application of empty property rate to offices—construction of local authority recommendation**

In February 1975 the Finance and Policy Co-ordination Committee of the defendant district council made a recommendation that the provisions of the General Rate Act 1967, s. 17 (1) should henceforth be applied in relation to offices. Section 17 (1) provides that a rating authority may resolve that the provisions of Sch. 1 of the Act apply to the rating of unoccupied property. The plaintiff company owned an unoccupied office block on which it failed to pay the rates. The defendant council were granted a distress warrant in respect of those rates and the plaintiff, on appeal, contended that the recommendation did not refer to the provisions of the Schedule but merely to s. 17 (1), under which the power existed to apply those provisions. *Held*, it would be incorrect to construe the recommendation formally. The resolution had made it sufficiently clear that the plaintiff's unoccupied premises were to be rated. The appeal would be dismissed.

GRAYLAW INVESTMENTS LTD v HARLOW DISTRICT COUNCIL (1979) 251 Estates Gazette 573 (Queen's Bench Division: GEOFFREY LANE LJ and ACKNER J). *Sheffield City Council v Graingers Wines Ltd* [1978] 2 All ER 70, CA, 1977 Halsbury's Abridgment para. 2228 applied.

2225   **—— —— properties not in valuation list—validity of rate demand**

A magistrates' court authorised the issue of a distress warrant against the plaintiffs in respect of non-payment of rates on certain unoccupied warehouses owned by the plaintiffs. The plaintiffs appealed against the decision on the ground, inter alia, that although rates could be recovered in respect of occupied property, notwithstanding that the property was not in the valuation list, this did not extend to unoccupied property (even if a proposal had been made by a valuation officer). *Held*, on the basis of the General Rates Act 1967, s. 6 and the decision of the Court of Appeal in *B Kettle Ltd v Newcastle-under-Lyme Borough Council* it was not necessary for there to be an actual entry in a valuation list before rates could be demanded and a proposal by the valuation officer was a sufficient foundation for the valuation. Further, there was no reason for limiting this principle to occupied property only. Once the rating authority had passed a resolution under s. 17 bringing into force the provisions of the Act relating to the rating of unoccupied property it was entitled to demand the rates notwithstanding that the property was not in the list. The appeal would therefore be dismissed.

BAR HILL DEVELOPMENTS LTD v SOUTH CAMBRIDGESHIRE DISTRICT COUNCIL [1979] RA 379 (Queen's Bench Division: LORD WIDGERY CJ, EVELEIGH LJ and WOOLF J). Decision of Court of Appeal in *B Kettle Ltd v Newcastle-under-Lyme Borough Council* [1979] RA 223, CA, para. 2227, applied.

2226   —— —— **property subject to unoccupied property rates and surcharge—application for relief on grounds of hardship**

A company completed the purchase of property, for development purposes, prior to the rating authority's decision that the provisions of the General Rate Act 1967, Sch. 1 relating to the rating of unoccupied property should apply to their area. Just before completion the Local Government Act 1974, s. 15, gave authorities the power to make a surcharge payable for non-use of a commercial building. The company applied for rates relief on the ground of hardship but the application was refused without reasons. On appeal the company contended that the authority's refusal was so unreasonable that a reasonable authority could not have reached such a decision. *Held*, it was necessary for the rating authority to ask themselves whether, in all the circumstances, the company had satisfied them that the payment would cause it such hardship that, having regard to the purpose of the relief provisions, they should reduce or remit the payment. The question of hardship was a matter of degree; it did not follow that merely because the company had suffered some hardship, such as loss of profits, relief should be granted. In all the circumstances, including the company's refusal to supply the authority with information concerning its finances, the authority's decision had not been unreasonable.

R v LIVERPOOL CITY COUNCIL, EX PARTE WINDSOR SECURITIES LTD [1979] RA 159 (Court of Appeal: MEGAW, LAWTON and CUMMING-BRUCE LJJ).

2227   **Valuation list—alteration—inclusion of new hereditament**

In September 1975, the valuation officer proposed to include a new hereditament in the valuation list. A general resolution for levying rates had been passed by the rating authority for the forthcoming year from April 1975. The ratepayer lodged an objection alleging that the proposed rateable value of the hereditament was too high. Pending the decision of the valuation court concerning the rateable value, the rating authority demanded payment of rates on the proposed value. On the ratepayer's refusal, the rating authority was granted a distress warrant. The ratepayer appealed on the question whether, when a proposal has been made for an addition to the valuation list, the rating authority has the right to distrain and levy the sum before that proposal is put into the valuation list. His appeal was dismissed and he appealed further. *Held*, although the General Rate Act 1967, s. 2 (4) provided that the rate was to be levied in accordance with the valuation list in force, that provision was "subject to the provisions of the Act" and was qualified by later provisions. In particular, s. 6 (2) of the Act provided for amendments when "a proposal . . . has been made by a valuation officer." The authority was therefore able to make the amendment as soon as the proposal was made in September 1975, and was entitled to recover the rate in respect of the premises for the rating year beginning in April 1975. The appeal would be dismissed.

B. KETTLE LTD. v NEWCASTLE UNDER LYME BOROUGH COUNCIL [1979] RA 223 (Court of Appeal: LORD DENNING MR, LAWTON and GEOFFREY LANE LJJ). Decision of Divisional Court of the Queen's Bench Division [1977] RA 181, 1977 Halsbury's Abridgment para. 2230 affirmed.

2228   —— cancellation of revaluation

The government has announced the cancellation of the proposed rating revaluation. A new list was originally due to come into operation in 1978 but this was postponed to 1980 by the General Rate Act 1975, 1975 Halsbury's Abridgment para. 2682. In a written answer to a parliamentary question, the Secretary of State for the Environment has stated that work on the preparation of the new lists due to take effect in 1980 has been cancelled and that the government intends to take the opportunity to consider the longer term future of the rating system. See the Financial Times, 23rd June 1979.

2229   —— compilation—proposal not served on ratepayer—distress warrants for non-payment—power of magistrates to go behind list

A ratepayer sought orders of mandamus directing the justices and the stipendiary magistrate to state cases for the opinion of the High Court. The justices and the stipendiary magistrate had issued two separate distress warrants in respect of non-payment of rates, but in each case had refused to state a case on the grounds that the applications were frivolous. The ratepayer contended that the valuation officer's proposal, upon which the assessment had been made, was not valid because it had not been served on her, and that the entry in the list was therefore of no effect. *Held*, the valuation shown in a valuation list was conclusive as to its correctness and the duty of a magistrate was to give effect to it and issue a distress warrant where it was shown that the ratepayer had been properly summoned to the court. The magistrates had no power to go behind the valuation list and their refusal to state a case was therefore justified. The application for mandamus would accordingly be refused.

R v THAMES MAGISTRATES' COURT, EX PARTE CHRISTIE [1979] RA 231 (Queen's Bench Division: LORD WIDGERY CJ, GEOFFREY LANE LJ and ACKNER J). *County and Nimbus Estates Ltd v Ealing Borough Council* (1978) 76 LGR 624, DC, 1978 Halsbury's Abridgment para. 2285, applied.

2230   —— necessity for property to be in list—rate demand for unoccupied property

See *Bar Hill Developments Ltd v South Cambridgeshire District Council*, para. 2225.

2231   —— validity of proposal—existing entry—caravan site—proposal for new entry—caravan and pitch

Lands Tribunal decision:

HOLDERNESS DC v HINGLEY (VALUATION OFFICER) [1979] RA 347: V. G. Wellings QC (valuation officer made proposal for alteration of valuation list to include a particular caravan on a caravan site; site already on list as one entry; proposal did not seek to amend that entry; local authority contended proposal therefore invalid as related to hereditament already included in list; contention rejected; caravans and pitches were to be treated as separate hereditaments; proposal valid notwithstanding that no amendment to existing entry proposed and that without amendment, double assessment would ensue).

REAL PROPERTY

Halsbury's Laws of England (3rd edn.), Vol. 32, paras. 273–606

2232　Article

Co-Ownership Schemes for Commercial Property Investment, R. G. Finch and R. S. Broadhurst: [1979] LS Gaz 234.

RECEIVERS

Halsbury's Laws of England (3rd edn.), Vol. 32, paras. 607–792

2233　Appointment—appointment by court—appointment by way of equitable execution

See *Levermore v Levermore*, para. 938.

2234　—— appointment under debenture—collection of value added tax—whether money payable to debenture holder

See *Re John Willment (Ashford) Ltd*, para. 357.

2235　—— —— receiver acting as company's agent—duty to account—detail required

See *Smiths Ltd v Middleton*, para. 358.

2236　—— effect upon authority of company's agent

See *Re Peek Winch & Tod Ltd*, para. 385.

2237　Fees and disbursements—fund for payment—whether receivership extends to capital

A husband owned a club and held the premises under a lease with an option to purchase the freehold. In 1973 an order was made appointing a receiver to receive in satisfaction of arrears of maintenance for his wife "the rents, profits and moneys receivable in respect" of the husband's "interest" in the club. By a further order in 1974, the receiver was also ordered to manage the club, of which he had already taken charge. The club made a loss and the wife applied for an order giving the receiver leave to exercise the option and sell it and an order for the husband to pay the costs of the receivership. A charging order nisi was made on the premises in respect of the maintenance arrears, but it was held that the 1973 order created a receivership in respect of income only and did not extend to capital. Hence as the club did not make a profit, there was no fund from which to pay the receiver's fees and disbursements. On appeal by the receiver, *held*, since the 1973 order referred to "moneys receivable in respect" of the husband's "interest" in the club, it created a receivership over corpus. However, the order did not extend to the business and therefore the receiver could not claim fees as a manager, but only receivership fees. However, that defect was cured by the 1974 order. The appeal would be allowed.

SMITH v SMITH (1979) 123 Sol Jo 584 (Court of Appeal: LORD SALMON, STEPHENSON and GOFF LJJ).

REGISTRATION CONCERNING THE INDIVIDUAL

Halsbury's Laws of England (3rd edn.), Vol. 32, paras. 793–887

2238   Births, deaths and marriages—registration—fees

The Registration of Births, Deaths and Marriages (Fees) Order 1979, S.I. 1979 No. 149 (in force on 1st April 1979), increases certain fees payable under the Acts relating to the registration of births, deaths and marriages and associated matters. Different fees are payable for the attendance of a registrar at a marriage at a register office and a marriage which takes place in a building registered for the solemnisation of marriages.

The Registration of Births, Deaths and Marriages (Fees) Order 1977, 1977 Halsbury's Abridgment para. 2237 is revoked.

2239   —— —— New Hebrides

The Registration of Births and Deaths (Consular Officers) (Amendment) Regulations 1979, S.I. 1979 No. 1072 (in force on 24th September 1979), amend the Registration of Births and Deaths (Consular Officers) Regulations 1974, 1974 Halsbury's Abridgment para. 2795 by providing that births and deaths of citizens of the United Kingdom and Colonies in the New Hebrides may be registered by United Kingdom Government officers serving there.

REVENUE

Halsbury's Laws of England (3rd edn.), Vol. 33, paras. 1–622

2240   Articles

Finance (No. 2) Act 1979, Julia Kerr and Brian Harvey (a résumé of the Act, para. 2247): 123 Sol Jo 611.

Residence and Domicile, J. B. Morcom (a discussion of the differences between the two concepts together with the legislation that governs them): 129 NLJ 752.

2241   Appropriation Act 1979

The Appropriation Act 1979 appropriates the supplies granted in the 1978/1979 session of Parliament. The Act received the royal assent on 4th April 1979 and came into force on that date.

2242   Appropriation (No. 2) Act 1979

The Appropriation (No. 2) Act 1979 applies a sum out of the Consolidated Fund to the service of the year ending on 31st March 1980, appropriates the supplies granted by Parliament and repeals the Consolidated Fund, Consolidated Fund (No. 2) and Appropriation Acts 1977, see 1977 Halsbury's Abridgment paras. 2242–2244. The Act received the royal assent on 27th July 1979 and came into force on that date.

2243   Consolidated Fund Act 1979

The Consolidated Fund Act 1979 applies certain sums out of the Consolidated Fund to the service of the years ending 31st March 1979 and 1980. The Act came into force on receiving the royal assent on 22nd March 1979.

2244   Consolidated Fund (No. 2) Act 1979

The Consolidated Fund (No. 2) Act 1979 applies certain sums out of the Consolidated Fund to the service of the years ending on 31st March 1980 and 1981. The Act came into force on receiving the royal assent on 20th December 1979.

2245   Customs and excise

See CUSTOMS AND EXCISE.

2246   Finance Act 1979

See para. 1531.

2247   Finance (No. 2) Act 1979

The Finance (No. 2) Act 1979 grants and alters certain duties, amends the law relating to the National Debt and the Public Revenue and makes further provisions in connection with finance. The Act received the royal assent on 26th July 1979 and came into force on that date except for ss. 2, 3 which came into force on 12th June 1979 and 13th August 1979 respectively.

Part I   Value Added Tax and Excise Duties
Section 1 abolishes the higher rate of value added tax and increases the standard rate to 15 per cent with effect from 18th June 1979. Section 2 increases the excise duty on hydrocarbon oil and reduces the rebates allowed on certain fuels and oils. The duty on cigarettes is altered by s. 3. Section 4 provides that orders under the Excise Duties (Surcharges or Rebates) Act 1979 may be made or may continue in force after the end of August 1980.

Part II   Income Tax, Corporation Tax and Capital Gains Tax
Section 5 charges income tax for the year 1979–80 at the basic rate of 30 per cent. A lower rate of 25 per cent will be chargeable on the first £750 of a person's taxable income and higher rates not exceeding 60 per cent will be chargeable on taxable income over £10,000. The investment income surcharge will be 15 per cent on investment income exceeding £5,000. The rate of advance corporation tax for the financial year 1979 will be 3/7: s. 6. The rate of corporation tax payable by small companies for the financial year 1978 will be 42 per cent on profits not exceeding £60,000 and 52 per cent on profits exceeding £100,000 with marginal relief at 3/20: s. 7. Section 8 deals with personal reliefs. A married man's allowance is increased to £1,815 and a single person's to £1,165; a wife's earned income relief also becomes £1,165. A married man's age allowance is increased to £2,455 and a single person's to £1,540 with a general limit on income for the full allowance of £5,000. Additional relief for widows and others in respect of children under their care is increased to £650. Pensions and allowances payable in respect of war injuries or death due to war service are exempt from income tax: s. 9. Section 10 extends the transitional provisions giving relief for interest payments on certain bank loans. Section 11 and Sch. 1 contain provisions consequential on the withdrawal of child tax allowances by the Finance Act 1979, Key No. P909. Section 12 and Sch. 2 amend various statutes in consequence of the Social Security Pensions Act 1975, 1975 Halsbury's Abridgment, para. 3191. The relief for increase in stock values is extended: s. 13 and Sch. 3. Provisions concerning capital allowances for certain motor vehicles are contained in s. 14. Section 15 reduces to 30 per cent the rate for deductions from payments made to certain sub-contractors in the construction industry. Section 16 enables an arrangement to be made between the United Kingdom and the United States for double taxation relief. Compensation paid by the Department for National Savings for delays in making certain payments due to industrial action is exempt from income tax, corporation tax and capital gains tax: s. 17.

Part III   Petroleum Revenue Tax
Section 18 increases the rate of petroleum revenue tax to 60 per cent. The supplement for allowable expenditure for an oil field is reduced to 35 per cent: s. 19. The allowance for the cost of transporting oil from the field to the United Kingdom is extended: s. 20. Section 21 halves the oil allowance and provides for the metrication of amounts in the Oil Taxation Act 1975, s. 8, 1975 Halsbury's Abridgment para. 2784. Section 22 abolishes the British National Oil Corporation's exemption from tax.

Part IV   Miscellaneous and Supplementary
Section 23 defers the capital transfer tax on discretionary trusts until 1st April 1982. Section 24 and Sch. 4 deal with development land tax. The rate of tax on development value realised on a disposal on or after 12th June 1979 is reduced to 60 per cent; the amount of development value which may be realised without liability to tax is increased to £50,000. Miscellaneous supplementary provisions and repeals are contained in s. 25 and Sch. 5.

2248   Income tax

See INCOME TAXATION.

2249   Stamp duties

See STAMP DUTIES.

2250   Value added tax

See VALUE ADDED TAX.

ROAD TRAFFIC

Halsbury's Laws of England (3rd edn.), Vol. 33, paras. 623–1383

2251   Articles

Cycle Lore, Richard Macrory (problems and uncertainties in the present law relating to cycles): 129 NLJ 602.

Goods Vehicles and the EEC, John Pugh (examination of the complexities contained in EEC Regulations affecting goods vehicles): 143 JP Jo 360.

Ignoring a Policeman's Signal, Jonathan S. Fisher (discussion of Road Traffic Act 1972, s. 22): 129 NLJ 224.

Minibus Law, Alec Samuels (legal provisions relating to minibuses): 129 NLJ 75.

Road Traffic Cases, James Morton (a refresher course): 129 NLJ 729.

To Obey or Not to Obey: That is the Question, A. N. Khan and K. Gillance (the powers of the police over the stopping and regulating of vehicles): 123 Sol Jo 628.

Obstruction of the Highway—A Question of Reasonableness? T. I. McLeod (on the application of the Highways Act 1959, s. 121 (1)): 143 JP Jo 618.

Zebra Crossings: No Longer Black and White, Jonathan S. Fisher (overtaking a stationary vehicle at a pedestrian crossing: *Conner v Patterson* [1977] 3 All ER 516, 1977 Halsbury's Abridgment para. 2342): 129 NLJ 513.

2252   Accident—failure to stop and report accident—necessity to remain at scene of accident

A man who had been drinking collided with the perimeter fence of a depot whilst driving his car. After inspecting the car for damage he left it there and went home on foot, without exchanging details with the depot employee on duty or informing the police. He was charged with failing to stop and failing to report the accident contrary to the Road Traffic Act 1972, s. 25. The justices dismissed the informations, being of the opinion that leaving his car at the scene of the accident, enabling him to be identified, amounted to compliance with s. 25. The prosecutor appealed. *Held*, the obligation to stop under s. 25 (1) meant an obligation to remain near the vehicle for a sufficient period to enable the exchange of details between parties to take place. The defendant had not remained with his vehicle for a sufficient period and, having neither exchanged details with the other party, nor informed the police within a reasonable time, he had not fulfilled his duties under s. 25. He should therefore be convicted.

WARD v RAWSON [1979] Crim LR 58 (Queen's Bench Division: LORD WIDGERY CJ, BOREHAM and DRAKE JJ).

2253   Breath test device—approval

The Home Secretary has approved the Alcolyser device for use by the police in England and Wales for the purpose of carrying out breath tests. The device comprises an indicator tube (marked with the name "Alcolyser"), a mouth piece and a measuring bag. See the Breath Test Device (Approval) (No. 1) Order 1979 (not in the S.I. series).

2254   Carriage by road

See CARRIERS.

2255   Causing death by dangerous driving—period of disqualification

A bus-driver with a year's learner-driving experience and ten weeks' experience of bus-driving failed to take a slight bend whilst driving a bus and collided with a car, killing the car driver instantly. His defence was that he had been momentarily distracted by a bee or wasp flying through the open door of the cab. Nevertheless he was convicted of causing death by dangerous driving, the judge describing his driving as appalling and disqualifying him under the Road Traffic Act 1972, s. 93 (1), from driving for ten years. He appealed against the disqualification, claiming it was excessive in that the trial judge, in describing his driving as appalling, had wrongly confused the consequences of the accident with the cause of it. *Held*, allowing the appeal, it being open to argument whether the accident was caused by a momentary lapse by an inexperienced driver, rather than reprehensible driving, the court would reduce the period of disqualification from ten years to two years, and would make a further order under s. 93 (7) that he be further disqualified until he passed a driving test appropriate to whatever licence he desired to hold.

R v HESLOP [1978] RTR 441 (Court of Appeal: LAWTON LJ, SWANWICK and GIBSON JJ).

2256   Cycle racing

The Cycle Racing on Highways (Special Authorisation) (England and Wales) Regulations 1979, S.I. 1979 No. 233 (in force on 1st April 1979), vary provisions of the Cycle Racing on Highways Regulations 1960 in relation to the number of competitors who may take part in specified races.

2257   Dangerous driving—appeal against conviction—appeal allowed—lesser charge of careless driving preferred—whether Crown Court had jurisdiction

See *Killington v Butcher*, para. 560.

2258   —— causing death by dangerous driving—expert evidence—admissibility

See *R v Oakley*, para. 693.

2259   Disqualification—special reason for not ordering disqualification—emergency

A motorist who pleaded guilty to a charge of driving with a blood-alcohol concentration in excess of the prescribed limit, contended that there were special reasons within Road Traffic Act 1972, s. 93 (1) for not ordering her disqualification. She claimed that she had been obliged to drive her husband home from a party because he was a paraplegic and required a specially fitted lavatory. There was no-one else who could have driven him and she did not have enough money for a taxi. *Held*, the question whether an emergency amounted to a special reason was to be decided by considering whether a defendant had acted responsibly and reasonably. The emergency in this case was the result of the motorist's own irresponsibility in that she had failed to make provision for the possibility that her husband might need lavatory facilities, and therefore she had not established a special reason why she should not be disqualified.

POWELL V GLIHA [1978] LS Gaz R 1296 (Queen's Bench Division: LORD WIDGERY CJ, GRIFFITHS and GIBSON JJ).

2260   A husband and wife went to a party at which there was a disturbance. The husband drove his wife away in a car and on being stopped by the police, was found to have excess alcohol in his blood. He pleaded guilty but contended there were special reasons for not disqualifying him, because his wife, who had suffered a brain haemorrhage and been advised by her doctor to avoid getting excited, might have suffered a second haemorrhage following the disturbance at the party, had she not been driven home immediately. The defendant was not disqualified. The prosecutor appealed. *Held*, the court should not have exercised its discretion not to disqualify until it had heard full details of the special reasons relied on by the defence; the evidence presented to the court had not established that a sudden medical emergency had arisen. The defendant should therefore be disqualified.

PARK V HICKS [1979] Crim LR 57 (Queen's Bench Division: LORD WIDGERY CJ and WIEN J).

2261   **Drivers' hours—exceeding statutory hours—defence of unavoidable delay—delay on outward journey**

A mini-bus driver was charged with having a working day which exceeded sixteen hours, contrary to the Transport Act 1968, s. 93 (3) (c). A puncture had delayed his outward journey for two and a half hours, but on his return journey he had spent several hours in a cafe and leisure centre. The justices allowed the driver a defence under s. 96 (11) (i), that the puncture had caused unavoidable delay. On appeal, *held*, the puncture was not the reason for the journey being completed more than sixteen hours after the driver had set out, as it happened on the outward not the return journey. The driver, therefore, had no defence under s. 96 (11) (i).

GREEN V HARRISON [1979] LS Gaz R 321 (Queen's Bench Division: LORD WIDGERY CJ, CUMMING-BRUCE LJ and NEILL J).

2262   **Driving or being in charge whilst unfit through drink or drugs—additional charge of driving or attempting to drive—whether roadside breath test necessary**

A constable noticed that the defendant was unsteady on his feet and when the latter attempted to start his car, the constable arrested him under the Road Traffic Act 1972, s. 5 (5) for being drunk in charge of a motor vehicle contrary to s. 5 (2). At the police station a breath test proved positive and a laboratory test revealed excess blood-alcohol. He was charged with offences under s. 5 (2) and s. 6 (1), attempting to drive when over the prescribed limit. The magistrates found that there was no case to answer on s. 6 (1) as the breath test had not been carried out at or nearby the scene of the offence as required by s. 8 (1). On appeal by the prosecution, *held*, a motorist could properly be charged under both s. 5 (2) and s. 6 (1). It was irrelevant whether a breath test was taken as prescribed by s. 8 (1) as the s. 6 offence was committed if a laboratory specimen given under s. 9 proved positive. Section 8 (7) provided for a breath test to be given at the police station whether the person was arrested under s. 5 (5), as in this case, or under s. 8 following the taking of a breath test on the spot. Accordingly the case would be remitted to the justices to continue the hearing.

SHARPE V PERRY [1979] RTR 235 (Queen's Bench Division: LORD WIDGERY CJ, GRIFFITHS and GIBSON JJ).

2263   **Driving or being in charge with blood-alcohol concentration above prescribed limit—arrest—admissibility of evidence of events subsequent to arrest**

See *Morris v Beardmore*, para. 2274.

2264   —— —— **validity**

A police constable called at a motorist's home following an accident in which he was involved and required him to take a breathalyser test. The motorist refused and was arrested. He contended that the constable had failed to establish that he had reasonable cause to suspect him of having alcohol in his body, but was convicted. On appeal, *held*, the mere fact that the constable had asked for a breath test was not sufficient to establish that he suspected the motorist of having alcohol in his body and accordingly the arrest had not been valid.

SIDDIQUI V SWAIN [1979] Crim LR 318 (Queen's Bench Division: EVELEIGH LJ and STEPHEN BROWN J).

2265   The Divisional Court of the Queen's Bench Division has ruled that where a motorist is required to take a breathalyser test by one of two police officers acting jointly, but is arrested by the other, the arrest is valid.

KNIGHT V TAYLOR [1979] Crim LR 318 (Queen's Bench Division: EVELEIGH LJ and STEPHEN BROWN J).

2266   —— **blood or urine sample—grounds for requiring sample— evidence**

The defendant, at a hospital as a patient after a road accident, was required by a constable to provide a breath test specimen which he failed to do. However, analysis of a laboratory test specimen provided revealed an excess of alcohol in his bloodstream and he was charged under the Road Traffic Act 1972, s. 6. At his trial no evidence was adduced to establish that the constable had reasonable cause to suspect the defendant of having alcohol in his body before requiring him to provide a laboratory test specimen. On appeal against conviction, *held*, as there was no evidence put before the justices to enable them to conclude that the constable had reasonable cause to suspect the defendant of having alcohol in his body and no inference could be drawn to fill the gap in evidence, the appeal would be allowed and the conviction would be quashed.

GRIFFITHS V WILLETT [1979] RTR 195 (Queen's Bench Division: BRIDGE LJ and CAULFIELD J).

2267   —— **breath test—grounds for requiring—proof of occurrence of accident**

A police van was parked on a slope. A person was seen to approach it and shortly after the van rolled down the slope and crashed. A police officer suspected that the defendant had previously taken the van and driven it away. He required him to take a breath test under the Road Traffic Act 1972, s. 8 (2), as a person whom he had reasonable cause to believe was driving or attempting to drive a vehicle which was involved in an accident. The defendant refused to do so and resisted arrest. He was charged with failing to provide a specimen and resisting a police officer in the execution of his duty. Justices dismissed the information, concluding that there had not been an "accident" and thus proceedings under s. 8 (2) were not appropriate. On appeal by the prosecutor, *held*, the court should not attempt to define "accident" when Parliament had refrained from so doing. On the facts, any ordinary person would conclude that there had been an accident. The appeal would be allowed and the matter remitted to the justices.

CHIEF CONSTABLE OF THE WEST MIDLANDS POLICE V BILLINGHAM [1979] 2 All ER 182 (Queen's Bench Division: BRIDGE LJ and CAULFIELD J).

2268   —— —— —— **reasonable cause for suspicion**

The defendant was obliged to stop abruptly at a junction to allow a vehicle to pass in front of him because his view to the right was obscured. He was approached by two police officers who smelt alcohol on his breath and a breath test subsequently administered proved positive. He was charged with driving with an excess of alcohol in his blood contrary to the Road Traffic Act 1972, s. 6. Before the justices, the prosecutor contended that the constable had reasonable cause to suspect that the defendant had alcohol in his blood as a result of the manner in which he drove at the junction. No submissions were made on the basis of the constable having smelt alcohol on the defendant's breath. The justices found no case to answer, as the defendant's driving at the junction had been normal and could not, therefore, have given rise to a reasonable cause for suspicion. The prosecutor appealed by way of case stated. *Held*, although the initial suspicion was not aroused by circumstances which could amount to reasonable cause, that suspicion had been sustained by subsequent events sufficiently proximate in time to have occurred whilst the defendant was still driving. The constable's request for a specimen of breath was therefore lawful. The appeal would be allowed, and the case remitted to the justices.

MULCASTER V WHEATSTONE [1979] Crim LR 728 (Queen's Bench Division: EVELEIGH LJ and WOOLF J). *Hay v Shepherd* [1974] RTR 64, CA applied.

2269 —— —— mouthpiece of device incorrectly assembled

The defendant carelessly collided with a stationary vehicle and was required to provide a specimen of breath. The constable produced the appropriate device, but as he had failed to attach the mouthpiece to the tube correctly, the bag failed to inflate. He then fully inserted the mouthpiece and returned the device to the defendant who failed to provide a specimen. There was no suggestion of the constable not acting bona fide. The defendant was arrested and, on refusing to provide a laboratory test specimen, was charged accordingly. At first instance the case was dismissed on the ground that as the device had been incorrectly assembled the defendant should have been offered a new device before being required to provide a breath specimen. On appeal, *held*, the device was correctly assembled the second time and there was no risk of prejudice to the defendant after the error had been rectified. The appeal would therefore be allowed and the case would be remitted to the magistrates.

PRICE V DAVIES [1979] RTR 204 (Queen's Bench Division: LORD WIDGERY CJ, GRIFFITHS and GIBSON JJ).

2270 —— —— refusal to provide a specimen—mandatory disqualification—special reasons for not imposing disqualification

A man, after drinking in a public house, drove his car a short distance across a car park, colliding with another vehicle. The accident prevented him from driving the car further that night, so he returned to the public house and consumed more drink whilst waiting for a lift home. The police arrived some time after the accident and they asked him to take a breath test. He refused and after they had arrested him, he again refused to give a specimen of breath, blood or urine. As he had had another drink between the time of the accident and the request for a specimen, the specimen, if taken, could not have been used to convict him. Nevertheless he was guilty of failure to provide a specimen under the Road Traffic Act 1972, s. 9 (3), and it was therefore necessary to consider whether there were special reasons for the court not to impose disqualifications for the mandatory period of twelve months, as required by s. 93 (1) of that Act. At first instance it was held that because the specimen could not have been used to convict him, this was a special reason not to impose the mandatory sentence and he was not disqualified. The prosecutor appealed. *Held*, the justices had misdirected themselves and the fact that the driver could not have been convicted on the evidence provided by the specimen was not a special reason for not imposing on him the mandatory disqualification laid down by s. 93 (1), for his failure to provide a specimen. The appeal would be allowed.

COURTMAN V MASTERSON [1978] RTR 457 (Queen's Bench Division: LORD WIDGERY CJ, CUMMING-BRUCE LJ and PARK J).

2271   —— —— **result of test disputed—admissibility of urine specimen as evidence**

A motorist was required to provide a breath specimen. The police evidence was that it was positive, as was a subsequent test. The motorist disputed that either breath test was positive. He later gave a laboratory test specimen which showed an excess of alcohol in his blood. The trial judge directed the jury that if they were in doubt that there was any material on which it could have appeared to the police that either of the breath tests were positive, they should acquit. The jury asked whether they could conclude from the results of the laboratory test specimen that the breath tests were likely or certain to have been positive. They were further directed that although the specimen result could not be regarded as conclusive, they should look at the evidence as a whole. The motorist was convicted and appealed, submitting that as there were issues as to the legality of two of the necessary steps in the procedure leading to the giving of the specimen of urine, the jury should have been directed to resolve those issues without any regard to the evidence of the specimen analysis. *Held,* if there had been some failure to comply lawfully with the requirements of the antecedent procedure leading to the provision of a specimen, then the evidence of an analysis of that specimen could not provide an admissible foundation for a conviction under s. 6 (1). However, once evidence of the result of such an analysis was properly before the jury, as it had been in this case, then the jury could have regard to all the evidence before them, including the evidence of the analysis of the specimen, if the analysis result was relevant to the issue to be decided. The judge was therefore right to direct the jury that they could consider the whole of the evidence, including the analysis of the appellant's urine. The appeal would be dismissed.

R v CARPENTER (1979) 27th April (unreported) (Court of Appeal: BRIDGE LJ, CHAPMAN and LAWSON JJ).

2272   —— —— **validity of test**

A police constable who smelt alcohol on a motorist's breath ascertained that he had been drinking a short while before and required him to take a breath test on an Alcotest (R) 80 device. The manufacturer's instructions stated that the device was not to be used if the suspect had been drinking within the preceding twenty minutes. The motorist was charged with driving with a blood alcohol concentration above the prescribed limit, but contended that the test had been taken too soon. The jury were directed that the relevant question was not whether the breath test had been taken at the right time, but whether the constable had been acting reasonably and in good faith. The motorist applied for leave to appeal against conviction. *Held,* a police constable should not be put in a position in which he was forced to rely on everything a suspect said and accordingly the direction to the jury had been correct. Leave to appeal would be refused.

R v MOORE [1979] RTR 98 (Court of Appeal: EVELEIGH LJ, O'CONNOR and GRIFFITHS JJ).

2273   —— —— **vehicle stopped before commission of any traffic offence**

A vehicle was stopped by a uniformed constable who had no reason to suspect the commission of a traffic offence. When the driver stepped out of the car, the policeman suspected him of having alcohol in his body and gave him a breathalyser test, which proved positive. The driver was charged with driving with excess alcohol in his bloodstream. The magistrates believing that the constable, not having a reasonable cause to stop the car, was not entitled to require the breath test, dismissed the case. On appeal by the prosecutor *held,* the constable was entitled to initiate the breath test. There would not be a retrial as the magistrates had added a note to the appeal to the effect that they were advised by their clerk that their decision was wrong. The case would be remitted with a direction to convict.

SHERSBY v KLIPPEL [1979] Crim LR 186 (Queen's Bench Division: LORD WIDGERY CJ, GRIFFITHS and GIBSON JJ).

2274   —— **failure to provide specimen—arrest by police on private property without lawful authority—validity of arrest**

Police officers went to the defendant's home following an accident which involved his car. They were invited in by the defendant's son. The defendant refused to see them, informing them through his son that they were trespassers and he wished them to leave. The officers then entered the defendant's bedroom and requested him to take a breath test. He refused and was arrested. At the police station he refused to provide breath, blood or urine samples. He was charged with failure to provide such specimens under the Road Traffic Act 1972, ss. 8 (3), 9 (3). The justices dismissed the informations on the ground that as the officers were trespassers, the request for the breath specimen had not been made by police constables and the defendant's arrest was therefore unlawful, rendering all subsequent evidence inadmissible. On appeal by the prosecutor, the point of law raised was whether a uniformed constable, who had been invited into a private house by someone other than the occupier, and whose permission to remain therein had been subsequently withdrawn by the occupier, continued to be a constable under s. 8 of the 1972 Act who could lawfully arrest a person who had refused to take a breath test. *Held*, the officers did not cease to be constables empowered to require a breath test merely because their invitation to enter the house had been withdrawn and they had become trespassers. As long as they had complied with the conditions precedent to the grant of such a power, they had the right to require a breath test. Therefore, even if they were trespassers at the time of the request, that fact did not affect the validity of the defendant's arrest after he had refused to take the breath test nor did it affect the admissability of evidence of matters subsequent to the arrest. Furthermore, since there had been a lawful arrest, the justices had erred in law in holding that such evidence was inadmissible. If that admissible evidence had in fact been obtained in an oppressive manner, the justices would have had a discretion to exclude it. Accordingly the appeal would be allowed and the case remitted to the justices with a direction to decide whether to exercise their discretion to exclude admissible and relevant evidence which they wrongly thought inadmissible.

MORRIS v BEARDMORE [1979] 2 All ER 290 (Queen's Bench Division: CUMMING-BRUCE LJ and NEILL J). *Spicer v Holt* [1976] 3 All ER 71, HL, 1976 Halsbury's Abridgment para. 2141 applied.

2275   —— —— **defective information—power to amend**

See *Lee v Wiltshire Chief Constable*, para. 708.

2276   —— —— **discretion of police to allow motorist to telephone solicitor**

The defendant motorist was arrested as the result of a positive breath test and taken to the police station. He was required to provide specimens of urine or blood. The defendant asked to be allowed to telephone his solicitor, but after repeatedly failing to contact him, the police withdrew the concession and told him to provide the specimen. The defendant said he did not know what to do and was charged with failing to provide a specimen under the Road Traffic Act 1972, s. 9. On appeal against conviction, *held*, the longer a motorist was able to delay the provision of a specimen the more favourable it was to him and the less likelihood there would be that the blood–alcohol concentration would correctly reflect his state at the time of driving. The police had a discretion to allow a motorist to telephone his solicitor, relative or doctor, but if they felt that the time taken for doing so was too long, they could withdraw the concession and demand that a specimen be provided. Once the concession had been withdrawn, if the motorist still failed to provide a specimen he was guilty of the offence. The appeal would be dismissed.

BROWN v RIDGE [1979] RTR 136 (Queen's Bench Division: LORD WIDGERY CJ, GRIFFITHS and GIBSON JJ). *Pettigrew v Northumbria Police Authority* [1976] RTR 177, DC, 1976 Halsbury's Abridgment para. 2140, *Hockin v Weston* [1972] RTR 136, DC applied.

2277   —— —— **reasonable excuse**

While driving his car one evening the defendant collided with a bridge and fell into a river. He was pulled out by a passing driver who gave him some brandy and drove him home. The defendant then started drinking sherry and continued doing so until the police arrived two hours after the accident. The defendant refused to provide a specimen of breath on the ground that he had taken alcohol in the past twenty minutes. He was then arrested and taken to the police station where he refused to provide breath, blood or urine samples. He was charged with, and convicted of, contravening the Road Traffic Act, s. 9 (3) 1972 in failing, without reasonable excuse, to provide specimens for laboratory tests. On appeal that the meaning of "reasonable excuse" should not be limited to physical and mental matters *held*, an excuse could not be regarded as reasonable unless the person from whom the specimen was required was physically or mentally incapable of providing it. The appeal would be dismissed.

WILLIAMS V CRITCHLEY [1979] RTR 46 (Queen's Bench Division: LORD WIDGERY CJ, MAY and TUDOR EVANS JJ). *R v Lennard* [1973] 2 All ER 831, CA applied.

2278   The defendant, a Libyan with a limited command of English, was stopped when driving and required to take a breath test which proved positive. He was arrested and taken to the police station where he was asked to provide a blood or urine specimen for a laboratory test. Although he was warned that failure to provide a specimen might lead to imprisonment, a fine and disqualification he refused. He was charged under the Road Traffic Act 1972, s. 9 (3) with failing, without reasonable excuse, to provide a specimen. At first instance the court found that as the defendant was unable to understand fully the consequences of refusal, he did have a reasonable excuse. On appeal *held*, the purpose of the warning was to ensure that the defendant could not be guilty of the offence unless he appreciated the consequences of refusal. The court had come to the correct conclusion and the appeal would be dismissed.

BECK V SAGER [1979] LS Gaz R 158 (Queen's Bench Division: BRIDGE LJ and CAULFIELD J).

2279   A motorist, who had failed to inflate a breathalyser bag when asked to take a breath test, maintained that the result of a second test taken at the police station was negative and refused to supply a blood or urine sample. Magistrates found that the test had been positive but that his belief that it was negative constituted a reasonable excuse for not providing a sample. On appeal, *held*, in law a reasonable excuse for not providing a sample had to relate to the capacity of the person concerned to provide it, and therefore the motorist in this case did not have a reasonable excuse.

MALLOWS V HARRIS [1979] Crim LR 320 (Queen's Bench Division: EVELEIGH LJ and STEPHEN BROWN J).

2280   —— —— —— **mental inability to provide sample**

A man was required to provide a blood specimen and although initially willing to do so he felt himself mentally incapable owing to a fear of blood being taken from his body. The justices found that he was not guilty of failure to provide a specimen without reasonable excuse. On appeal, by way of case stated, the question for the court was whether there were grounds upon which the justices could have properly reached their decision. *Held*, no excuse could be adjudged to be a reasonable one unless the person from whom the specimen was required was physically or mentally unable to provide it or unless he suffered from an invincible repugnance of the use of the needle. The man was of good character and had admitted that he was terrified of giving blood and that it made him feel ill. He had fainted on two previous occasions when required to give specimens and was unable to be a blood donor. There was therefore evidence upon which the justices could have decided as they did and the appeal would be dismissed.

ALCOCK V READ [1979] Crim LR 534 (Queen's Bench Division: GEOFFREY LANE LJ and ACKNER J). *R v Lennard* [1973] 2 All ER 831, CA applied.

2281   Goods vehicles—excess weight—offences in respect of gross weight and axle weight—whether duplication

See *J Theobald (Hounslow) Ltd v Stacy*, para. 712.

2282   —— international journeys—fees

The Goods Vehicles (Authorisation of International Journeys) (Fees) (Amendment) Regulations 1979, S.I. 1979 No. 42 (in force on 15th February 1979), amend the Goods Vehicles (Authorisation of International Journeys) (Fees) Regulations 1976, 1976 Halsbury's Abridgment para. 2149, by substituting a new definition of "community authorisation". This takes account of an amendment to Council Regulation (EEC) No. 3164/76 concerning the quota for the carriage of goods by road between member states.

2283   —— operators' licences—fees

The Goods Vehicles (Operators' Licences) (Fees) Regulations 1979, S.I. 1979 No. 1732 (in force on 1st February 1980), consolidate with amendments the Goods Vehicles (Operators' Licences) (Fees) Regulations 1974, 1974 Halsbury's Abridgment para. 2922 and the Goods Vehicles (Operators' Licences) (Fees) (Amendments) Regulations 1976, 1976 Halsbury's Abridgment para. 2161. The fees payable whenever a vehicle is specified in an operator's licence and for an interim direction under the Transport Act 1968, s. 68 (5) on the grant of an operator's licence are increased.

2284   —— —— licensing system

The committee appointed to enquire into the effectiveness of the operators' licensing system of road freight transport introduced by the Transport Act 1968, has reported to the Secretary of State for Transport. The committee has made 44 major recommendations and a further 47 minor recommendations. Amongst the major recommendations the committee has suggested that a permanent independent committee should be set up to review track costs annually and to make and publish recommendations for the appropriate level of vehicle excise duty to be charged on each category of vehicle. The committee also recommends that licensing authorities should be encouraged in future to give more of their attention to offences concerning drivers' behaviour since this is regarded as the most important cause of vehicle accidents; and that licensing authorities should be able to suspend for a substantial period of time the heavy goods vehicle driving licence of a driver driving a vehicle which should, but does not, have an operator's licence. The committee further recommends that there should be a hirer's licence for non-operators who hire out heavy goods vehicles. See *Road Haulage Operators' Licensing: Report of the Independent Committee of Inquiry* (HMSO).

2285   —— tachographs—installation

The Passenger and Goods Vehicles (Recording Equipment) Regulations 1979, S.I. 1979 No. 1746 (in force on 14th January 1980), apply to passenger and goods vehicles to which the Transport Act 1968, Part VI (Drivers' Hours) applies. They amend that part of the Act by substituting new ss. 97 to 97B for the existing s. 97 which relates to the installation and operation of recording equipment in vehicles. The regulations provide for the implementation of Council Regulation (EEC) 1463/70, as amended, and as read with the Community Road Transport Rules (Exemptions) Regulations 1978, 1978 Halsbury's Abridgment para. 2400, on the introduction of recording equipment (tachographs) in road transport. The new s. 97 makes it an offence, punishable on summary conviction by a fine of up to £200, to use vehicles to which the Council Regulation applies without the installation of a tachograph, or to fail to use it where it has been installed. Defences are provided for in certain cases. Requirements relating to the tachographs are imposed upon crew members of vehicles and their employers, and timetables are specified for the coming into force of those requirements. Failure to comply with the requirements is also an offence punishable on summary conviction by a fine up to £200. Provision is made for the use of tachograph record sheets as evidence in proceedings in the 1968 Act. The regulations also make consequential adaptions to various enactments and provide for ministerial approval of tachograph fitters and workshops and for a period of retention of records by crew members.

The Passenger and Goods Vehicles (Recording Equipment) Regulations 1977, 1977 Halsbury's Abridgment para. 2281 are revoked.

2286 **———— whether to be used as evidence of exceeding speed limits**

The Minister for Transport has stated, in a written reply to a parliamentary question, that the implementation of Council Regulation (EEC) 1463/70 to fit tachographs in goods vehicles would not have the effect of making tachograph records admissible as the sole evidence in prosecutions for speeding offences. See the Daily Telegraph, 3rd November 1979.

For the implementation of the EEC Regulation see para. 2285.

2287 **Highways—failure to maintain—accident—liability for accident**

See *Tarrant v Rowlands*, para. 1414.

2288 **Indorsement—notification**

Home Office Circular 54/1978 has been supplemented by Circular 159/1979 which contains amendments to the notes on indorsement of driving licences and preparation of notifications by courts of orders for indorsement which accompanied the earlier Circular. The main purpose of the amendments is to make the "other sentence" details more readily understandable and to incorporate those instructions in the main body of the text (instead of in a separate appendix). Code MS70 has been introduced for driving with uncorrected eyesight (formerly code MS40) and code MS80 has been introduced for refusing to submit to any eyesight test (also formerly code MS40).

2289 **International road haulage permit—forged document**

A man displayed a forged document resembling an international road haulage permit on a vehicle belonging to him. He was convicted of possessing an international road haulage permit with intent to deceive, contrary to the Road Traffic Act 1972, s. 169 (1) (a). He appealed. *Held*, the document was not an international road haulage permit, therefore he could not be convicted of possessing such a permit with intent to deceive. A prosecution under s. 169 (1) (b) for having in his possession a document closely resembling such a permit with intent to deceive, might have succeeded. The conviction would be quashed.

HOLLOWAY V BROWN [1979] Crim LR 58 (Queen's Bench Division: LORD WIDGERY CJ, BOREHAM and DRAKE JJ).

2290 **International road transport**

The United Kingdom has ratified the European Agreement concerning the Work of Crews of Vehicles engaged in International Road Transport (AETR) and the agreement entered into force for the United Kingdom on 18th August 1978. Subject to exceptions, the agreement applies in the territory of each contracting party to all international road transport performed by any vehicle registered in its territory or in the territory of any other contracting parties (art. 2). The agreement prescribes requirements inter alia, as to drivers' ages, daily rest periods, weekly rest periods, periods of driving and of continuous driving, manning and individual control documents (arts. 5–12). Each contracting party is required to apply provisions in its own territory not less strict than those of the agreement (art. 3) and in international road transport the undertaking and crew members are required to observe (in relation to rest periods, driving periods and manning) the rules laid down by the domestic law of the district of the scale in which the crew member normally exercises his occupational activities and by arbitral awards or collective agreements in force in that district (art. 4). On depositing its instrument of ratification the United Kingdom made the reservation that transport operations between Member States of the European Community should be regarded as national transport operations within the meaning of AETR insofar as such operations do not pass through the territory of a third state which is a contracting party to the AETR. Other countries which have ratified or acceded to the AETR are: Austria, Belgium, Czechoslovakia, Denmark, East Germany, France, Greece, Luxembourg, the Netherlands, Norway, Portugal, Spain, Sweden, Switzerland, the USSR, West Germany, and Yugoslavia. The text of AETR has been published as Cmnd. 7401

2291   Licences—driver's licence

The Motor Vehicles (Driving Licences) (Amendment) Regulations 1979, S.I. 1979 No. 1412 (in force on 5th December 1979), amend the Motor Vehicles (Driving Licences) Regulations 1976, 1976 Halsbury's Abridgment para. 2153 by extending to one year the period during which a person who became resident in Great Britain may be treated as a licence holder if he holds a specified permit. Certain conditions which such a person must satisfy are modified.

2292   —— —— heavy goods vehicle—application for grant—when application made

The respondent posted an application for a heavy goods vehicle driver's licence to the appellant licensing authority on 22nd December 1976, having obtained the necessary medical certificate two days earlier. The Road Traffic (Drivers' Ages and Hours of Work) Act 1976, Sch. 2, para. 3 (3) provided that nothing should prevent a licensing authority from granting a full licence if the application was made during 1976 by a person such as the respondent. The licensing authority declined to deal with the application because it was not received until 5th January 1977, the envelope bearing the postmark 4th January 1977. The justices considered that the respondent had made his application in 1976, as it was posted on a date which, in the ordinary course of posting, meant that it would have reached the authority during that year and ordered that he should be granted a licence. The licensing authority appealed on the ground that an application is "made" within the meaning of the Schedule at the time when the application is received by the licensing authority. It was argued on behalf of the respondent that he had done all that he could be expected to do to submit his application in time and that the words "application . . . is made" in their ordinary meaning are directed simply to what it is that the applicant himself has to do. *Held*, MICHAEL DAVIES J dissenting, for an application to be "made", it was necessary not only for it to be sent, but also for it to be received by the person who had to deal with it. The appeal would be allowed.

NORTH WEST TRAFFIC AREA LICENSING AUTHORITY v BRADY [1979] RTR 500 (Queen's Bench Division: LORD WIDGERY CJ, MICHAEL DAVIES and NEILL JJ). *Watts v Vickers Ltd* [1916] 116 LT 172 applied.

2293   —— —— national conditions for issue of domestic licences to Community nationals

See Case 16/78: *Choquet*, para. 1205.

2294   Licensing—public service vehicle—expiry of licence—whether contract carriage

The defendant owned a fifty-two-seater coach. The certificate of fitness of the coach had expired so that the defendant's public service vehicle licence had automatically determined. He used the coach to transport forty children to school for hire or reward under contract to a local authority. He was charged with using the coach as a contract carriage without a public service vehicle licence, contrary to the Road Traffic Act 1960, s. 127 (1). Section 117 (1), (4) of the Act defines a contract carriage as a public service vehicle not carrying passengers at separate fares. The justices found that the coach was not being used as a contract carriage, as there was no evidence of any payment being made for the carrying of the children, as required by s. 118 (3) (a). On appeal by way of case stated, *held*, as the coach was obviously being used to carry the children to school at a contract fare and not at separate fares, all the preconditions of a contract carriage were satisfied. The appeal would be allowed and the case remitted to the justices with a direction to continue the hearing.

MIDDLEMAS v MCALEER [1979] RTR 345 (Queen's Bench Division: LORD WIDGERY CJ, GRIFFITHS and GIBSON JJ).

2295   Metrication—heavy vehicles—weight limit

The Car Tax (Description of Vehicles) Order 1979, S.I. 1979 No. 1647 (in force on 1st January 1980), converts to a convenient metric equivalent the weight limit above which heavy vehicles become not chargeable with tax.

2296   Motor vehicles—approval marks

The Motor Vehicles (Designation of Approval Marks) Regulations 1979, S.I. 1979 No. 1088 (in force on 1st October 1979), replace the Motor Vehicles (Designation of Approval Marks) Regulations 1976, 1976 Halsbury's Abridgment, para. 2166. The 1976 Regulations have been largely re-enacted with the addition of certain marks relating to lighting, prevention of fire risks and head restraints.

2297   —— authorisation of special types

The Motor Vehicles (Authorisation of Special Types) General Order 1979, S.I. 1979 No. 1198 (in force on 1st November 1979), authorises the use on roads of certain vehicles which do not comply with the Motor Vehicles (Construction and Use) Regulations 1978, 1978 Halsbury's Abridgment para. 2364, or the Motor Vehicles (Construction and Use) (Track Laying Vehicles) Regulations 1955. The order consolidates, with minor amendments, the Motor Vehicles (Authorisation of Special Types) General Order 1973, as amended.

2298   —— construction and use—agricultural or forestry tractors

The Motor Vehicles (Construction and Use) (Amendment) (No. 2) Regulations 1979, S.I. 1979 No. 843 (in force on 16th August 1979) further amend the Motor Vehicles (Construction and Use) Regulations 1978, 1978 Halsbury's Abridgment para. 2364 by making new provisions as to agricultural or forestry tractors. The regulations also provide alternative requirements as to the particulars to be shown on the manufacturers' plates with which certain vehicles are required to be equipped.

2299   —— —— brakes

The Motor Vehicles (Construction and Use) (Amendment) Regulations 1979, S.I. 1979 No. 138 (in force on 13th March 1979), amend the Motor Vehicles (Construction and Use) Regulations 1978, 1978 Halsbury's Abridgment para. 2364, by amending the requirements as to the brakes of locomotives and land tractors.

2300   —— —— goods vehicle—maximum weight exceeded—"nearest" weighbridge

The defendant drove a lorry from certain docks to the premises at which he delivered his load. The lorry was weighed at those premises and found to exceed the maximum permitted gross weight. The defendant told a police officer that the weighbridge had been used to record the amount delivered. He was charged with using a goods vehicle on a road which exceeded the maximum permitted gross weight, contrary to the Road Traffic Act 1972, s. 40 (5). The defendant contended that when the lorry was being used on the road it was proceeding to the nearest available weighbridge for the purpose of being weighed and that he therefore had a defence under 1972 Act s. 40 (6) (a). The weighbridge at the delivery premises was the nearest weighbridge to the docks in a straight line on a map, but not the nearest to the docks by road. He was convicted. On appeal, *held*, the 1972 Act was concerned with ensuring that potentially unsafe vehicles were used on the road for the shortest possible distance and "nearest" within s. 40 (6) (a) accordingly meant the nearest weighbridge to which a lorry could go to be weighed. The Act referred to the distance by road. Further, the defence under s. 40 (6) (a) was not available to a driver going to a weighbridge solely to weigh the load in connection with delivering it. The appeal would be dismissed.

LOVETT v PAYNE [1979] Crim LR 729 (Queen's Bench Division: EVELEIGH LJ and WOOLF J). *Hayes v Kingsworth Foundry Co Ltd* [1971] RTR 286 followed.

2301   —— —— **seat belts—goods vehicle**

The defendants' driver attempted to pass the plaintiff, who was driving up a hill in a 1963 van. He failed to pass and caused the plaintiff's van to strike a lamp-post. The plaintiff, who was thrown out and suffered injuries, brought an action for damages. The defendants sought to establish that their driver had not been negligent and if he had, then the plaintiff had also been negligent in failing to have seat belts fitted to his van. The defendants and their driver were held wholly liable for the accident, and appealed. *Held*, the Motor Vehicles (Construction and Use) Regulations 1973, reg. 17 requiring the fitting of seat belts did not apply to goods vehicles registered before 1st January 1966. As the plaintiff was not under a statutory obligation to have seat belts fitted he could not be guilty of contributory negligence.

HOADLEY v DARTFORD DISTRICT COUNCIL [1979] LS Gaz R 158 (Court of Appeal: MEGAW, WALLER and EVELEIGH LJJ).

2302   —— —— **seat belts and anchorage points**

The Motor Vehicles (Construction and Use) (Amendment) (No. 3) Regulations 1979, S.I. 1979 No. 1062 (in force on 20th September 1979), further amend the Motor Vehicles (Construction and Use) Regulations 1978, 1978 Halsbury's Abridgment para. 2364, by consolidating with amendments the provisions which relate to seat belts and anchorage points.

2303   —— **Italjet motor cycle—whether a mechanically propelled vehicle**

A youth was convicted, inter alia, of driving a motor cycle whilst under age and without a crash helmet and of using a motor vehicle without insurance. On appeal he contended that the Italjet motor cycle he was riding at the time of the alleged offences was not a motor vehicle within the meaning of the Road Traffic Act 1972, s. 190 (1). *Held*, Italjet was a two-wheeled vehicle propelled by a 22 cc internal combustion engine with a seat and handle bars. The justices had sufficient grounds therefore for deciding that it fell within s. 190 (1) and the appeal would be dismissed.

O'BRIEN v ANDERTON [1979] RTR 388 (Queen's Bench Division: LORD WIDGERY CJ, BRIDGE LJ and CAULFIELD J). Dictum of Lord Parker CJ in *Burns v Currell* [1963] 2 All ER 297, DC applied.

2304   —— **lighting**

The Road Vehicles (Rear Fog Lamps) (Amendment) Regulations 1979, S.I. 1979 No. 1145 (in force on 1st October 1979), amend the Road Vehicles (Rear Fog Lamps) Regulations 1978, 1978 Halsbury's Abridgment para. 2372, by substituting a new definition for the "approval mark" with which certain rear fog lamps are required to be marked.

2305   —— **tests**

The Motor Vehicles (Tests) (Amendment) Regulations 1979, S.I. 1979 No. 439 (in force on 1st July 1979), amend the Motor Vehicles (Tests) Regulations 1976, Sch. 3, Part IV, 1976 Halsbury's Abridgment para. 2118, by obliging vehicle testing stations to use beam-setting equipment for testing the direction of the head lamp beams of vehicles in Class III, IV or V.

2306   The Motor Vehicles (Tests) (Amendment) (No. 2) Regulations 1979, S.I. 1979 No. 1215 (in force on 1st November 1979), raises certain fees prescribed by the Motor Vehicles (Tests) Regulations 1976, 1976 Halsbury's Abridgment para. 2118. The charge for the supply of forms for use as certificates is now £18.00, the fee for examination of a motor bicycle is now £3.36 and the fee for examination of any other motor vehicle is now £5.60.

2307   —— type approval

The Motor Vehicles (Type Approval) (Amendment) Regulations 1979, S.I. 1979 No. 1089 (in force on 1st October 1979), amend the Motor Vehicles (Type Approval) Regulations 1973, in relation to heating systems, wheel guards, liquid fuel tanks, rear underrun protection, braking devices, external projections, head restraints and recording equipment.

2308   The Motor Vehicles (Type Approval) (Great Britain) Regulations 1979, S.I. 1979 No. 1092 (in force on 1st October 1979), consolidate the Motor Vehicles (Type Approval) (Great Britain) Regulations 1976, 1976 Halsbury's Abridgment para. 2174, as amended. They also add regulations concerning radio interference suppression, exhaust emissions, lights, brakes, interior fittings, external projections and speedometers.

2309   —— vehicle exceeding maximum prescribed length—meaning of indivisible load

A lorry was found to be longer than the permitted overall length for articulated vehicles. An exception to the limitation was provided whereby carriage was permissible if the load carried was exceptionally long and unable to be broken down into smaller loads. On a question of whether an exceptionally long container carrying livestock fell within the exception, *held*, livestock was not an indivisible load. The purpose of the exception was to provide for the carriage of loads which could not, without undue expense or risk of damage, be easily sub-divided and it was not the container but the contents of the container which constituted the load.

PATTERSON v REDPATH BROTHERS LTD [1979] 2 All ER 108 (Queen's Bench Division: LORD WIDGERY CJ, GRIFFITHS and GIBSON JJ).

2310   Parking—off-street parking—appeals procedure

The Control of Off-Street Parking outside Greater London (Appeals Procedure) (England and Wales) Regulations 1979, S.I. 1979 No. 236 (in force on 3rd April 1979), prescribe the procedure for appeals to the Secretary of State in connection with the grant of licences under the provisions of the Control of Off-Street Parking (England and Wales) Order 1978, 1978 Halsbury's Abridgment para. 2392.

2311   Pelican pedestrian crossings

The "Pelican" Pedestrian Crossings (Amendment) Regulations 1979, S.I. 1979 No. 401 (in force on 1st June 1979), amend the "Pelican" Pedestrian Crossings Regulations and General Directions 1969, with regard to the siting of signals and indicators and the alternative phasing of light signals and pedestrian indicators.

2312   Reckless driving—causing death by reckless driving—test of recklessness

A motorist was charged with causing death by reckless driving, contrary to the Road Traffic Act 1972, s. 1 as substituted by the Criminal Law Act 1977, s. 50 (1). The case against him centred on his speed. The jury were initially directed to apply the test of whether they would have considered the motorist's driving to have been reckless had they been at the scene. After submissions by counsel, the jury were further directed that the motorist's driving had been "reckless" if he knew that by the manner of his driving there was a risk of such an accident; that in spite of that knowledge he drove in such a manner that an accident of this sort would possibly occur; that he could have avoided the risk had he chosen to do so. The motorist was convicted. He applied for leave to appeal on the ground that the initial direction to the jury was wrong and had confused them. *Held*, the jury must have approached the case with the further direction on the meaning of "reckless" firmly in mind and there was, therefore, no reason to suppose that the verdict was unsafe or unsatisfactory. The application would be refused.

R v CLANCY [1979] RTR 312 (Court of Appeal: LORD WIDGERY CJ, EVELEIGH LJ and NEILL J).

2313   An accident occurred when the driver of a pantechnicon, having lost control after driving too fast round a bend, hit a vehicle travelling in the opposite direction, killing its occupant. The driver was tried on a charge of causing death by reckless driving, contrary to the Road Traffic Act 1972, s. 1, as substituted by the Criminal Law Act 1977, s. 50 (1). The jury were directed that recklessness involved deliberately doing something which one knew involved a risk, in this case, a risk of getting out of control. One might be guilty of reckless driving without a collision, or if one was merely reckless of one's own safety. The driver was convicted. He applied for leave to appeal on the ground that the jury were misdirected as to the meaning of "reckless" in s. 1. *Held*, on the assumption that a subjective rather than objective test was correct, the jury were not misdirected. Further, on the evidence the jury were entitled to conclude that the facts fulfilled the proper definition of "reckless" given by the judge. Accordingly, the application would be refused.

R v DAVIS [1979] RTR 316 (Court of Appeal: GEOFFREY LANE LJ, ACKNER and WATKINS JJ).

2314   **Road—meaning of "road" for purpose of determining contravention of road traffic regulations**

See *Lock v Leatherdale*, para. 1419.

2315   **Road traffic accident—cost of full police report**

The Home Office have announced that the cost of obtaining a full accident report of a road traffic accident from the police has been increased from £10 to £12. Similarly, the charge for interviews has been increased from £7.20 to £13.50. Both increases took effect from 1st July 1979. See the Law Society's Gazette, 11th July 1979, p. 709.

2316   **Street collections—metropolitan police district**

The Street Collections (Metropolitan Police District) Regulations 1979, S.I. 1979 No. 1230 (in force on 1st January 1980), contain provisions relating to the collection of money and the sale of articles in any street or public place within the metropolitan police district. Regulations dated 2nd July 1926, S.R. & O. 1926 No. 848 are revoked.

2317   **Taking motor vehicle without authority—defence of owner's consent—defendant unaware of owner's possible consent at time of committing offence**

A man, together with four others, was charged with taking a conveyance without the authority of the owner, contrary to the Theft Act 1968, s. 12 (1). He pleaded guilty. The owner of the car gave evidence that the defendants were old friends of his, who would have had his permission to drive the car. The defendant appealed against his conviction, on the ground that his plea of guilty was based on a fundamental mistake of fact in thinking that the owner would not have consented. *Held*, the defendant had no defence because at the material time he did not believe that he had lawful authority to take the car or that the owner would have consented had he known of the defendant's taking the car. The appeal would be dismissed.

R v AMBLER [1979] LS Gaz R 321 (Court of Appeal: LAWTON LJ, THOMPSON and HODGSON JJ).

2318   Taximeters—EEC requirements—implementation

The Taximeters (EEC Requirements) Regulations 1979, S.I. 1979 No. 1379 (in force on 1st December 1979), implement Council Directive (EEC) 77/95, OJ L26, 31.1.1977, relating to taximeters. Provision is made for the Secretary of State, an application being made for that purpose, to approve patterns of taximeters which comply with the Directive (reg. 6). Provision is also made for him to carry out partial verification of such instruments to determine whether they comply with the approved pattern, granted in the United Kingdom or in another member State, and with the requirements of the Directive, and for the affixing to the instrument of the mark of EEC partial verification (reg. 7). The Regulations also provide for offences (regs 9–12, 14–17) and penalties (reg. 12) and include powers of inspection of instruments not incorporated in a vehicle and entry on premises other than private dwelling houses, where such instruments are manufactured or stored, for the enforcement of the Regulations (reg. 15).

2319   Vehicles—lighting

The Road Vehicles Lighting (Amendment) Regulations 1979, S.I. 1979 No. 803 (in force on 9th August 1979), amend the Road Vehicles Lighting Regulations 1971, S.I. 1971 No. 694, by prescribing regulations as to reflectors to be fitted to pedal cycles having four or more wheels, cycles, mechanically-powered bicycles, sidecars and invalid carriages.

2320   Vicarious liability—defective braking system—whether company "uses" a vehicle driven by employee

See *Swan v Macnab*, para. 1115.

ROYAL FORCES

Halsbury's Laws of England (3rd edn.), Vol. 33, paras. 1348–1866

2321   Army, Air Force and Naval Discipline Acts—continuation

The Army, Air Force and Naval Discipline Acts (Continuation) Order 1979, S.I. 1979 No. 906 (made on 26th July 1979), continues in force the Army Act 1955, the Air Force Act 1955 and the Naval Discipline Act 1957 until 31st August 1980.

2322   Imprisonment and detention—army

The Imprisonment and Detention (Army) Rules 1979, S.I. 1979 No. 1456 (in force on 1st January 1980), consolidate the Imprisonment and Detention (Army) Rules 1956, as amended. The Rules are in certain cases applicable to members of the other armed forces serving sentences of detention. Provisions are made for the control, inspection and classification of places where sentences may be served and the duties of the managing staff. Furthermore, provisions regarding remission of sentences, corrective training and parole together with the treatment of soldiers under sentence are made. Education and earning schemes are provided for and punishable offences whilst under detention laid down.

2323   Pensions

See paras. 2077, 2078.

2324   Royal Air Force—terms of service

The Royal Air Force Terms of Service (Amendment) Regulations 1979, S.I. 1979 No. 215 (in force on 5th April 1979), amend the Royal Air Force Terms of Service Regulations 1977, 1977 Halsbury's Abridgment para. 2366 by removing the requirement that a person must have completed four years' service before giving notice to extend his term of service to one exceeding fifteen years. Regulations 9 (2) and 9 (3) of the 1977 Regulations are revoked.

2325   Royal Navy—terms of service

The Royal Navy Terms of Service (Amendment) Regulations 1979, S.I. 1979 No. 192 (in force on 1st May 1979), amend the Royal Navy Terms of Service Regulations 1967, S.I. 1967 No. 1821, by extending the maximum period by which a person entered into naval service may extend his service from five years to ten.

SALE OF GOODS

Halsbury's Laws of England (3rd edn.), Vol. 34, paras. 1–321

2326   Articles

The Passing of Property in Part of a Bulk, Andrew G. L. Nicol (problems arising from Sale of Goods Act 1893, s. 16): 42 MLR 129.

Physical Loss, Economic Loss and Products Liability, Peter F. Cane (rules governing liability for defective products): 95 LQR 117.

Reservation of Title and the Right to Trace, Michael Burke (reservation of title clauses and the equitable doctrine of tracing in the light of recent cases): 129 NLJ 1183.

Section 25 (1) of the Sale of Goods Act 1893: The Reluctance to Create a Mercantile Agency, L. A. Rutherford and I. A. Todd: [1979] CLJ 346.

2327   Bill of lading—cargo discharged after fire damage—notation in bill—whether bill clean

A bill of lading bore a notation that the cargo covered by the bill had been destroyed by fire whilst on board the delivery ship. The buyer, who had purchased the cargo on c and f terms under which the seller would be entitled to be paid the price, whether or not the shipment was lost, upon tender of a clean, on board, bill of lading, rejected the bill. The seller claimed that it was clean for the purposes of claiming the price of the discharged cargo. The arbitrators decided in favour of the buyer in that the bill of lading was not clean by reason of the notation attached to it. The matter was referred to the court by way of special case stated, and the judge found in favour of the seller on the ground that a bill of lading was not clean only if it contained a clause the effect of which was to make it unacceptable or unmerchantable in the ordinary course of trade. On appeal, *held*, the judge's decision would be upheld. The arbitrators had been incorrect in law in construing "clean" in its narrow sense. A clean bill of lading was one in which there was nothing to qualify the admission that the goods were in good order and condition at the time of shipment.

M. GOLODETZ AND CO INC v CZARNIKOW-RIONDA CO INC, THE GALATIA. [1980] 1 All ER 50 (Court of Appeal: MEGAW, SHAW and WALLER LJJ). Decision of Donaldson J [1979] 2 All ER 726 affirmed.

2328   Breach of contract—covenant in restraint of trade—negative covenant—whether injunction to enforce covenant may be granted

See *Thomas Borthwick & Sons (Australasia) Ltd v South Otago Freezing Co Ltd*, para. 1584.

2329   —— force majeure and prohibition clauses—liability of seller

See *Bunge GmbH v Alfred C Toepfer*, para. 500.

2330   —— force majeure clause—construction

See *Sociedad Iberica de Molturacion SA v Tradax Export SA*, para. 494.

2331   —— —— liability of buyer

See *Coloniale Import-Export v Loumidis Sons*, para. 499.

2332   —— goods not in conformity with contract—liability of seller

A contract provided for the sale of fine-ground soya bean meal f.o.b. Hamburg. After the greater part of the meal had been loaded, supervisors appointed by the buyers discovered that it was coarse-ground. Loading was stopped and the remainder of the shipment was fine-ground. The buyers had resold the whole shipment as fine-ground meal to sub-buyers and incurred expense in separating the meal and compensating the sub-buyers. The buyers then claimed damages from the sellers for breach of contract. The Board of Appeal of GAFTA decided that the buyers had waived their right to damages by appointing supervisors to check the meal but stated their award in the form of a special case. *Held*, (i) the contract was for the sale of goods by description and as the term "fine-ground" was part of the description, it was a condition of the contract that the meal was fine-ground; (ii) the supervisors' failure to protest about the meal when loading began was an unequivocal representation to the sellers that they had no objection to the coarse-ground meal. However, the supervisors had no implied authority to vary any term of the contract between the buyers and the sellers and therefore their conduct did not amount to a waiver of the buyers' right to damages; (iii) the supervisors did have implied authority to stop the loading of coarse-ground meal as soon as reasonably possible but had failed to do so. Therefore the buyers, through their representatives' delay, had failed to act reasonably to mitigate their loss and were entitled to nominal damages only. Accordingly the award would be remitted for reconsideration.

TOEPFER v WARINCO AG [1978] 2 Lloyd's Rep 569 (Queen's Bench Division: BRANDON J.).

2333   —— liability of seller—assessment of damages—date of default

See *Bunge Corporation v Usines de Stordeur SA*, para. 507.

2334   —— payment made on non-contractual document—whether buyers estopped from claiming damages for breach

See *Ets Soule v International Trade Development Co*, para. 483.

2335   C and f contract—clause providing for payment based on delivered weight—short cargo delivered to wrong port—construction of clause

Sellers sold buyers 6000 long tons of tapioca pellets c and f Rotterdam under a contract incorporating GAFTA 100, cl. 16, which provided that final settlement was to be made on the basis of gross delivered weight, weighing to be done at the time and place of discharge. The sellers preserved the right to superintend the weighing. The buyers agreed that the shippers could discharge the cargo at Bremen instead of Rotterdam without seeking the sellers' agreement. When the cargo was weighed at Bremen a 280 ton shortfall was discovered. The sellers claimed that, as they had never agreed to make an adjustment on the basis of discharged weights and as there were no Rotterdam weights according to contract, there could be no final settlement and accordingly they refused to pay the buyers' invoice for the shortfall. *Held*, a party whose rights to adjust figures in his favour arose under cl. 16 had to proceed in accordance with that clause, which was intended to be construed so as to cover all commercial situations which might arise between the parties. The injustice which appeared to result from a strict construction of cl. 16 was outweighed by the commercial advantage of knowing that they could make an adjustment within the terms of cl. 16. The sellers' claim would therefore be upheld.

KROHN AND CO V MITSUI AND CO EUROPE GmbH [1978] 2 Lloyd's Rep 419 (Court of Appeal: STEPHENSON and CUMMING-BRUCE LJJ).

2336   C.i.f. contract—absence of evidence of contract of carriage— buyers' right to reject documents

The buyers of a quantity of soya beans rejected allegedly defective shipping documents tendered under the c.i.f. contract of sale on the grounds, inter alia, that they contained no evidence of the contract of carriage to the port of discharge. In an action for damages the sellers contended (i) that there was incorporated into the contract of sale a documents clause under which, in the event of any omissions or errors in any documents, the buyers were still bound to perform the contract if the sellers guaranteed performance in accordance with the contract; (ii) that the alleged defects were not of a nature to entitle the buyers to reject the documents, even in the absence of the documents clause; and (iii) that the documents clause was effective in depriving the buyers of any right they may have had to reject the documents. The sellers failed at first instance and appealed. *Held*, (i) although the buyers failed to sign and return their copy of the documents clause, there was a common understanding between the parties based on previous dealings and general trading practice that any sale by the sellers' organisation would include a documents clause of that nature; (ii) the defects in the documents as to the contractual destination of the soya beans were serious enough to render the documents not reasonably and readily fit to pass in commerce and the buyers had been entitled to reject them; (iii) the documents clause was to be strictly construed and accordingly the letters of guarantee sent to the buyers were not a guarantee of performance but merely a promise to reimburse the buyers for costs and expenses. Thus the buyers were entitled to reject the documents and the appeal would be dismissed.

S.I.A.T. DI DEL FERRO V TRADAX OVERSEAS SA (1979) 25th May (unreported) (Court of Appeal: MEGAW, EVELEIGH and BRANDON LJJ). Decision of Donaldson J [1978] 2 Lloyd's Rep 470, affirmed.

2337   —— notice of shipment tendered out of time—validity of further notice

Sellers sold yellow soya beans to be shipped c.i.f. Rotterdam from certain United States ports in June 1977. The contract incorporated the terms of a standard form contract (FOSFA No. 24), under which the sellers had to give the buyers a notice containing particulars of shipment. Notices had to be passed on with due despatch by intermediate buyers and sellers. On June 10th, the sellers received a notice (from the seller to them) relating to goods shipped under a bill of lading dated June 1st. They were obliged to accept the notice as it had been passed with due despatch. The sellers did not pass on the notice until June 15th; the buyers rejected it as being out of time. On June 23rd, the sellers passed on a new notice relating to different goods. This notice was not out of time. The buyers rejected the new notice, contending that the sellers, having already given a valid declaration of shipment, albeit out of time, could not give a further declaration without withdrawing the first declaration; such a withdrawal could not be made without the buyers' consent. The dispute was referred to arbitration and the Board of Appeal of FOSFA found in favour of the sellers but stated their award in the form of a special case. *Held*, a valid declaration of shipment could not, in any circumstances, be applied by a stale notice. The notice should not be regarded as something distinct from the declaration of shipment; the buyers could not both maintain that the notice was a valid declaration of shipment which could not be withdrawn without their consent and that it was invalid because it was sent to them out of time. The buyers were thus liable in damages to the sellers.

GERTREIDE IMPORT GESELLSCHAFT mbH V ITOH & CO (AMERICA) INC [1979] 1 Lloyd's Rep 592 (Queen's Bench Division: DONALDSON J).

2338   Consumer protection

See CONSUMER PROTECTION.

2339   Contract—default by buyer—effective date of default

See *Toprak Mahsulleri Ofisi v Finagrain Compagnie Commerciale Agricole et Financiere SA*, para. 504.

2340   Defective goods—buyer's right of rejection—effect of delay

Textile wholesalers rejected a quantity of cloth sent to them by an Italian textile manufacturer. The disputed goods were delivered to the wholesalers in March and April 1974 but not rejected until 8th July owing to the wholesalers' difficulty in ascertaining from their own buyers how much cloth was defective. The manufacturer contended that the delay in rejecting the goods was unreasonable. *Held,* the wholesalers were entitled to spend time ascertaining exactly how much of the cloth was defective, especially as the manufacturer was alleging that rejection would be considered a breach of contract. On the facts, the delay was not unreasonable and the wholesalers had not therefore forfeited their right of rejection.

MANIFATTURE TESSILE LANIERA WOOLTEX v J. B. ASHLEY LTD [1979] 2 Lloyd's Rep 28 (Court of Appeal: MEGAW, LAWTON and CUMMING-BRUCE LJJ).

2341   Delivery by instalments—non-acceptance of one instalment— whether repudiation of entire contract

The sellers agreed to sell to the buyers a quantity of crude rapeseed oil, half to be shipped in September and half in October. On receipt of the September shipment, the buyers rejected it on the ground that it was not in accordance with the specification. The sellers replied that they could only supply identical goods for the October quota and that if they were rejected, the sellers would consider the buyers to be in breach of contract. The buyers notified them by telex that they would refuse the shipment if it was not in accordance with the contract. The sellers accepted the refusal to take up and pay for the September quota as a repudiation of the whole contract. When the matter came before the Commercial Court it was held that the sellers ought not to be allowed unilaterally to turn a dispute about one instalment into a dispute about the contract as a whole. On appeal, *held,* the buyers' telex notifying the sellers that the goods would be rejected if not in accordance with the contract amounted to a repudiation of the contract itself. It clearly indicated to the sellers that if goods of an identical nature to those refused in September were supplied in respect of the October shipment, these too would be rejected. The sellers' acceptance of the refusal to pay for the September quota as a repudiation of the contract amounted to clear acceptance of repudiation. The appeal would be allowed.

WARINCO AG v SAMOR SpA [1979] 1 Lloyd's Rep 450 (Court of Appeal: LORD DENNING MR, STEPHENSON and SHAW LJJ). Decision of Donaldson J [1977] 2 Lloyd's Rep 582, 1977 Halsbury's Abridgment para. 2378 reversed.

2342   F.o.b. contract—incorporation of second contract—conflict of terms—extension of time for loading contract goods

The sellers sold soya beans to be shipped f.o.b. from certain Brazilian ports. The contract incorporated the terms of the standard Anec f.o.b. contract, which gave detailed provisions for adequate notice in relation to nomination of vessels. The terms of a Grain and Feed Trade Association (GAFTA) contract were also incorporated where such terms did not conflict with the Anec contract. The sellers rejected the buyers' nomination of ships because one was due to arrive at the port of loading outside the contract time and they elected to treat the contract as null and void. The buyers initially sought to extend the time for loading the vessels under the terms of the GAFTA contract but finally accepted the sellers' repudiation as an anticipatory breach and claimed damages. A special case was referred to the court on the question whether the provisions as to extension of time in the GAFTA contract were incorporated into the sale contract. It was held that the Anec contract clearly excluded the extension provisions of the GAFTA contract and that the sellers had therefore been entitled to treat the contract as null and void. On appeal by the buyers, *held*, the question was one of construction only, and on the true construction of the contract, there was no contradiction between the provisions of the Anec contract and the extension provisions of the GAFTA contract. The buyers were therefore entitled to damages from the sellers for breach of contract. Damages were to be assessed at the date on which the buyers would, on the evidence, have performed the contract. The appeal would be allowed.

BREMER HANDELSGESELLSCHAFT mbH v J. H. RAYNER & CO LTD [1979] 2 Lloyd's Rep 217 (Court of Appeal: MEGAW, BRIDGE and TEMPLEMAN LJJ). Decision of Mocatta J [1978] 2 Lloyd's Rep 73, 1978 Halsbury's Abridgment para. 2415 reversed. *Societe Co-operative Suisse des Cereales et Matieres Fourrageres v La Plata Cereal Co SA* (1947) 80 Ll L Rep 530 applied.

2343   Implied condition—fitness and merchantable quality—effect of warning by seller

A chemical company sold a certain chemical to the buyer, a company manufacturing disinfectants. The presence of the chemical in the disinfectant produced caused the tainting of foodstuffs by airborne infection and the buyer sought damages contending, inter alia, that the chemical was not reasonably fit for the purpose for which it was bought and that it was not of merchantable quality. The buyer was successful at first instance. On appeal by the seller, *held*, the court would accept the evidence of the seller's sales liaison officer that, as a result of articles published in independent technical journals, he had warned the buyer that the chemical could taint certain foodstuffs. A claim under the Sale of Goods Act 1893, s. 14 (3), relating to fitness for purpose, would fail therefore because the circumstances showed that the buyer did not rely on the seller's skill and judgment. Further, the claim under s. 14 (2), relating to merchantable quality, would also fail, as the potential defect in the chemical was clearly brought to the buyer's attention. The appeal would accordingly be allowed.

JEYES GROUP LTD v COALITE AND CHEMICAL PRODUCTS LTD (1979) 15th May (unreported) (Court of Appeal: MEGAW, BRIDGE and TEMPLEMAN LJJ).

2344   Mistake—unilateral mistake as to subject matter of contract—apportionment of loss

See *Haris Al-Afaq Ltd v Cameron Dempsey & Ivy Ltd*, para. 1892.

2345   Non-acceptance—sellers' duty to tender shipping documents—validity of documents

A contract for the sale of goods provided for payment to be made in exchange for certain shipping documents, including an insurance certificate; the sellers were required to insure the goods against certain specified risks whilst they were in transit between warehouses. In February 1974 the contract was varied by agreement which provided for the goods to be delivered from a warehouse during April 1974; the sellers were also required to provide free insurance for a period after presentation of the appropriate documents. On 26th April 1974 the sellers tendered an insurance certificate which did not apply to goods stored in a warehouse or cover the risks specified in the original insurance clause. The buyers rejected the insurance certificate. The sellers then obtained insurance covering the goods in store against all specified risks but the cover note delivered to the buyers on 1st May 1974 was also rejected. The buyers contended that the documents tendered were not in accordance with the contract. The Board of Appeal of GAFTA found in favour of the sellers, but stated their award in the form of a special case. *Held*, (i) although the insurance clause in the original contract did not apply to goods in store, the provisions requiring insurance against specified risks remained in force notwithstanding the variation of the contract. Therefore the sellers' insurance certificate tendered on 29th April was inadequate as those risks were not covered. (ii) The insurance certificate was also inadequate because it covered the goods from warehouse to warehouse only whereas the contract as varied applied to goods stored in a warehouse. Moreover, the sellers were not entitled to rely on the cover note delivered on 1st May since it did not constitute an insurance certificate. (iii) Neither the insurance certificate nor the cover note complied with the contract since no provision was made for free insurance for a period after presentation of the shipping documents. Accordingly the buyers were entitled to reject all the documents tendered.

PROMOS SA v EUROPEAN GRAIN & SHIPPING LTD [1979] 1 Lloyd's Rep 375 (Queen's Bench Division: PARKER J).

2346   Passing of property—goods supplied on credit terms—reservation of title by vendor—vendor's right to trace

See *Borden (UK) Ltd v Scottish Timber Products Ltd*, para. 1138; *Re Bond Worth Ltd*, para. 1137.

2347   Price marking—food and drink on premises

See para. 1637.

2348   Sale of Goods Act 1979

The Sale of Goods Act 1979 consolidates the law relating to the sale of goods. The Act received the royal assent on 6th December 1979 and came into force on 1st January 1980.

Tables showing the derivation of the Act and the destination of enactments consolidated are set out on pages 619–625.

DESTINATION TABLE

This table shows in column (1) the enactments repealed by the Sale of Goods Act 1979, and in column (2) the provisions of that Act corresponding to the repealed provisions.

In certain cases the enactment in column (1), though having a corresponding provision in column (2), is not, or is not wholly, repealed as it is still required, or partly required, for the purposes of other legislation.

(1)	(2)	(1)	(2)
Sale of Goods Act 1893 (c. 71)	Sale of Goods Act 1979 (c. 54)	Sale of Goods Act 1893 (c. 71)	Sale of Goods Act 1979 (c. 54)
s. 1 (1)	s. 2 (1), (2)		3, Part II; but see Sch. 4, para. 3
(2)	(3)	s. 25 (1)	s. 24
(3)	(4), (5)	(2)	25 (1), (2)
(4)	(6)	(3)	26
2	3	27	27
3	4	28	28
4	Rep., 1954 c. 34, s. 2, and 1954 c. 26 (N.I.), s. 2	29 (1)	29 (1), (2)
		(2)–(5)	(3)–(6)
ss. 5–7	ss. 5–7	30 (1)	30 (1)
s. 8 (1)	s. 8 (1)	(2)	(2), (3)
(2)	(2), (3)	(3), (4)	(4), (5)
9	9	ss. 31–34	ss. 31–34
10 (1)	10 (1), (2)	s. 35	s. 35 (1)
(2)	(3)	ss. 36–39	ss. 36–39
11 (1) (a), (b)	11 (2), (3)	s. 40	Applied to Scotland
(c)	11 (4), Sch. 1, para. 2	ss. 41–45	ss. 41–45
(2)	Applied to Scotland	s. 46 (1)	s. 46 (1)–(3)
(3)	s. 11 (6)	(2)	(4)
12 as originally enacted	Sch. 1, para. 3	ss. 47–54	ss. 47–54
12 (1)	s. 12 (1), (2)	s. 55 as originally enacted	Sch. 1, para. 12
(2)	(3)–(5)	s. 55 as substituted[2]	11
13 (1)	13 (1), (2)	s. 55 (1), (2)	s. 55 (1), (2)
(2)	(3)	(3)–(11)	Rep., 1977 c. 50, s. 31 (4), Sch. 4
s. 14 as originally enacted	Sch. 1, para. 6	55A	Rep., 977 c. 50, s. 31 (4), Sch. 4; but see Sch. 1, para. 13
s. 14 as substituted[1]	5	56	s. 59
s. 14 (1), (2)	s. 14 (1), (2)	57	60
(3)	ss. 14 (3), 61 (1)	58	57
(4), (5)	s. 14 (4), (5)	59	Applied to Scotland
(6)	Rep., 1974 c. 39, s. 192 (3), Sch. 5, Part I	60	Rep., S.L.R. Act 1908
15	s. 15 (1), (2)	61 (1)–(4)	s. 62 (1)–(4)
ss. 16–21	ss. 16–21	(5)	Applied to Scotland
s. 22 (1)	s. 22 (1)	(6)	Rep., 1977 c. 50, s. 31 (4), Sch. 4; but see Sch. 1, paras. 11, 13
(2)	Rep., 1967 c. 58, s. 10 (2), Sch. 3, Part III. and 1967 c. 18 (N.I.), s. 14 (1), Sch. 2, Part II; but see Sch. 1, para. 8	62 (1)	s. 61 (1), Sch. 1, paras. 11, 13, 14
		(1A)	ss. 14 (6), 15 (3), Sch. 1, para. 5
(3)	s. 22 (2)	(2)–(4)	s. 61 (3)–(5)
23	23	s. 63	Rep., S.L.R. Act 1908; but see s. 1 (1)
24	Rep., 1968 c. 60, s. 33 (3), Sch. 3, Part III. and 1969 c. 66 (N.I.), s. 31 (2), Sch.	64	—
		Schedule	Rep., S.L.R. Act 1908

[1] As substituted by 1973 c. 13, s. 3, but without the amendments made by 1974 c. 39, s. 192 (3), Sch. 4, para. 3, Sch. 5, Part I.

[2] As substituted by 1973 c. 13, s. 4, but without the amendments made by 1977 c. 50, s. 31 (3), (4), Schs. 3, 4.

(1)	(2)	(1)	(2)
Misrepresentation Act 1967 (c. 7)	Sale of Goods Act 1979 (c. 54)	Supply of Goods (Implied Terms) Act 1973 (c. 13)	Sale of Goods Act 1979 (c. 54)
s. 4 (1)	—	s. 6	Rep., 1977 c. 50, s. 31 (4), Sch. 4; but see Sch. 1, paras. 11, 13
(2)	s. 35 (1)		
5³	See s. 1 (2), Sch. 1, paras. 2, 10	7 (1)	s. 61 (1), Sch., paras. 11, 13, 14
6 (3)⁴	—	(2)	ss. 14 (6), 15 (3), Sch. 1, para. 5
		s. 18 (2)	
Criminal Law Act 1967 (c. 58)		(5)³	See s. 1 (2), Sch. 1, paras. 3, 4, 6, 7, 12, 15
s. 12 (1)³	See s. 1 (2), Sch. 1, para. 8		
		Consumer Credit Act 1974 (c. 39)	
Supply of Goods (Implied Terms) Act 1973 (c. 13)		s. 192 (4)³	See s. 1 (2), Sch. 1, paras. 5, 9
		Sch. 4, para. 3	ss. 14 (3), 61 (1)
s. 1	s. 12	4	s. 25 (2)
2	13 (3)	**Unfair Contract Terms Act 1977 (c. 50)**	
3	14 (1)–(5), Sch. 1, para. 5		
	55, Sch. 1, para. 11		
4	Rep., 1977 c. 50, 31 (4), Sch. 4; but see Sch. 1, para. 13	s. 31 (2)	See s. 1 (2), Sch. 1, paras. 11, 13, 14
5 (1)		Sch. 3⁴	ss. 55 (1), 61 (1)
(2)	Sch. 2, para. 15		

³ Not repealed.
⁴ Repealed in part.

TABLE OF DERIVATIONS
This table shows in the right hand column the legislative source from which the sections of the Sale of Goods Act 1979 in the left hand column have been derived.

The following abbreviations are used in this table:

1889 (c. 45)	=	Factors Act 1889 (52 & 53 Vict. c. 45)
1890 (c. 40)	=	Factors (Scotland) Act 1890 (53 & 54 Vict. c. 40)
1893 (c. 71)	=	Sale of Goods Act 1893 (56 & 57 Vict. c. 71)
1908 (c. 49)	=	Statute Law Revision Act 1908 (8 Edw. 7. c. 49)
1967 (c. 7)	=	Misrepresentation Act 1967
1967 (c. 58)	=	Criminal Law Act 1967
1967 (c. 14 N.I.)	=	Misrepresentation Act (Northern Ireland) 1967
1967 (c. 18 N.I.)	=	Criminal Law Act (Northern Ireland) 1967
1973 (c. 13)	=	Supply of Goods (Implied Terms) Act 1973
1974 (c. 39)	=	Consumer Credit Act 1974
1977 (c. 50)	=	Unfair Contract Terms Act 1977

Section of Act	Derivation
1 (1)	1893 s. 63; 1908 (c. 49) s. 1 proviso
(2)	1967 (c. 7) s. 5; 1967 (c. 58) s. 12 (1); 1973 (c. 13) s. 18 (5); 1974 (c. 39) s. 192 (4); 1977 (c. 50) s. 31 (2)
(3)	—
(4)	—
2 (1)	1893 s. 1 (1)
(2)	1893 s. 1 (1)
(3)	1893 s. 1 (2)
(4)	1893 s. 1 (3)
(5)	1893 s. 1 (3)
(6)	1893 s. 1 (4)
3 (1)	1893 s. 2
(2)	1893 s. 2
(3)	1893 s. 2
4 (1)	1893 s. 3
(2)	1893 s. 3
5 (1)	1893 s. 5 (1)
(2)	1893 s. 5 (2)
(3)	1893 s. 5 (3)
6	1893 s. 6
7	1893 s. 7
8 (1)	1893 s. 8 (1)
(2)	1893 s. 8 (2)
(3)	1893 s. 8 (2)
9 (1)	1893 s. 9 (1)
(2)	1893 s. 9 (2)
10 (1)	1893 s. 10 (1)
(2)	1893 s. 10 (1)
(3)	1893 s. 10 (2)
11 (1)	1893 s. 11 (1), (2)
(2)	1893 s. 11 (1) (a)
(3)	1893 s. 11 (1) (b)
(4)	1893 s. 11 (1) (c)
(5)	1893 s. 11 (2)
(6)	1893 s. 11 (3)
(7)	—

Section of Act	Derivation
12 (1)	1893 s. 12 (1) (*a*) ⎫
(2)	1893 s. 12 (1) (*b*) ⎪
(3)	1893 s. 12 (2) ⎬ substituted by 1973 (c. 13) s. 1.
(4)	1893 s. 12 (2) (*a*) ⎪
(5)	1893 s. 12 (2) (*b*) ⎭
(6)	—
13 (1)	1893 s. 13 (1) (re-numbered by 1973 (c. 13) s. 2)
(2)	1893 s. 13 (1) (re-numbered by 1973 (c. 13) s. 2).
(3)	1893 s. 13 (2) (inserted by 1973 (c. 13) s. 2)
(4)	—
14 (1)	1893 s. 14 (1) (substituted by 1973 (c. 13) s. 3)
(2)	1893 s. 14 (2) (substituted by 1973 (c. 13) s. 3)
(3)	1893 s. 14 (3) (substituted by 1974 (c. 39) Sch. 4 para. 3)
(4)	1893 s. 14 (4) (substituted by 1973 (c. 13) s. 3)
(5)	1893 s. 14 (5) (substituted by 1973 (c. 13) s. 3)
(6)	1893 s. 62 (1A) (inserted by 1973 (c. 13) s. 7 (2))
(7)	—
(8)	
15 (1)	1893 s. 15 (1)
(2)	1893 s. 15 (2)
(3)	1893 s. 62 (1A) (inserted by 1973 (c. 13) s. 7 (2))
(4)	—
16	1893 s. 16
17 (1)	1893 s. 17 (1)
(2)	1893 s. 17 (2)
18	1893 s. 18
19 (1)	1893 s. 19 (1)
(2)	1893 s. 19 (2)
(3)	1893 s. 19 (3)
20 (1)	1893 s. 20
(2)	1893 s. 20, proviso 1
(3)	1893 s. 20, proviso 2
21 (1)	1893 s. 21 (1)
(2)	1893 s. 21 (2)
22 (1)	1893 s. 22 (1)
(2)	1893 s. 22 (3)
(3)	—
23	1893 s. 23
24	1893 s. 25 (1)
25 (1)	1893 s. 25 (2)
(2)	1893 s. 25 (2); 1974 (c. 39) Sch. 4 para. 4
(3)	—
(4)	—
26	1893 s. 25 (3); 1889 (c. 45) s. 1 (1); 1890 (c. 40) s. 1
27	1893 s. 27
28	1893 s. 28
29 (1)	1893 s. 29 (1)
(2)	1893 s. 29 (1)
(3)	1893 s. 29 (2)
(4)	1893 s. 29 (3)
(5)	1893 s. 29 (4)
(6)	1893 s. 29 (5)

Section of Act	Derivation
30 (1)	1893 s. 30 (1)
(2)	1893 s. 30 (2)
(3)	1893 s. 30 (2)
(4)	1893 s. 30 (3)
(5)	1893 s. 30 (4)
31 (1)	1893 s. 31 (1)
(2)	1893 s. 31 (2)
32 (1)	1893 s. 32 (1)
(2)	1893 s. 32 (2)
(3)	1893 s. 32 (3)
33	1893 s. 33
34 (1)	1893 s. 34 (1)
(2)	1893 s. 34 (2)
35 (1)	1893 s. 35; 1967 (c. 7) s. 4 (2)
(2)	—
36	1893 s. 36
37 (1)	1893 s. 37
(2)	1893 s. 37
38 (1)	1893 s. 38 (1)
(2)	1893 s. 38 (2)
39 (1)	1893 s. 39 (1)
(2)	1893 s. 39 (2) and s. 62 (1)
40	1893 s. 40
41 (1)	1893 s. 41 (1)
(2)	1893 s. 41 (2) and s. 62 (1)
42	1893 s. 42
43 (1)	1893 s. 43 (1)
(2)	1893 s. 43 (2)
44	1893 s. 44
45 (1)	1893 s. 45 (1)
(2)	1893 s. 45 (2)
(3)	1893 s. 45 (3)
(4)	1893 s. 45 (4)
(5)	1893 s. 45 (5)
(6)	1893 s. 45 (6)
(7)	1893 s. 45 (7)
46 (1)	1893 s. 46 (1)
(2)	1893 s. 46 (1)
(3)	1893 s. 46 (1)
(4)	1893 s. 46 (2)
47 (1)	1893 s. 47
(2)	1893 s. 47
48 (1)	1893 s. 48 (1)
(2)	1893 s. 48 (2)
(3)	1893 s. 48 (3)
(4)	1893 s. 48 (4)
49 (1)	1893 s. 49 (1)
(2)	1893 s. 49 (2)
(3)	1893 s. 49 (3)

Section of Act	Derivation
50 (1)	1893 s. 50 (1)
(2)	1893 s. 50 (2)
(3)	1893 s. 50 (3)
51 (1)	1893 s. 51 (1)
(2)	1893 s. 51 (2)
(3)	1893 s. 51 (3)
52 (1)	1893 s. 52
(2)	1893 s. 52
(3)	1893 s. 52
(4)	1893 s. 52
53 (1)	1893 s. 53 (1)
(2)	1893 s. 53 (2)
(3)	1893 s. 53 (3)
(4)	1893 s. 53 (4)
(5)	1893 s. 53 (5)
54	1893 s. 54
53 (1)	1893 s. 55 (1) (substituted by 1973 (c. 13) s. 4; amended by 1977 (c. 50) Sch. 3)
(2)	1893 s. 55 (2) (substituted by 1973 (c. 13) s. 4)
(3)	—
56	—
57	1893 s. 58
58	1893 s. 59
59	1893 s. 56
60	1893 s. 57
61 (1)	1893 s. 62 (1); 1973 (c. 13) s. 7 (1) and 1977 (c. 50) Sch. 3 ("business"); 1974 (c. 39) Sch. 4 para. 3 ("credit-broker")
(2)	1893 s. 62 (1)
(3)	1893 s. 62 (2)
(4)	1893 s. 62 (3)
(5)	1893 s. 62 (4)
(6)	—
62 (1)	1893 s. 61 (1)
(2)	1893 s. 61 (2)
(3)	1893 s. 61 (3)
(4)	1893 s. 61 (4)
(5)	1893 s. 61 (5)
63	—
64	—
Schedule 1 para. 1	—
2	1967 (c. 7) s. 5; 1967 (c. 14 N.I.) s. 5
3	1893 s. 12 (as originally enacted); 1973 (c. 13) s. 18 (5)
4	1973 (c. 13) s. 18 (5)
5	1893 ss. 14 and 62 (1A) (as substituted and inserted by 1973 (c. 13) ss. 3 and 7 (2)); 1974 (c. 39) s. 192 (4)
6	1893 s. 14 (as originally enacted); 1973 (c. 13) s. 18 (5)
7	1893 s. 15 (as originally enacted); 1973 (c. 13) s. 18 (5)
8	1967 (c. 58) s. 12 (1); 1967 (c. 18 N.I.) s. 14 (1)
9	1974 (c. 39) s. 192 (4)
10	1967 (c. 7) s. 5; 1967 (c. 14 N.I.) s. 5

Section of Act	Derivation
Schedule 1—*cont.*	
para. 11	1893 s. 55 (substituted by 1973 (c. 13) s. 4); 1893 s. 61 (6) (inserted by 1973 (c. 13) s. 6); 1893 s. 62 (1) (definition of "contract for the international sale of goods" inserted by 1973 (c. 13) s. 7 (1)); 1977 (c. 50) s. 31 (2)
12	1893 s. 55 (as originally enacted); 1973 (c. 13) s. 18 (5)
13 (1), (3)	1893 s. 55A (inserted by 1973 (c. 13) s. 5(1)); 1893 s. 61 (6) (inserted by 1973 (c. 13) s. 6); 1893 s. 62 (1) (definition of "contract for the international sale of goods" inserted by 1973 (c. 13) s. 7 (1)); 1977 (c. 50) s. 31 (2)
13 (2)	1977 (c. 50) Sch. 4
14	1977 (c. 50) s. 31 (2)
15	1973 (c. 13) s. 18 (5)
Schedule 2	—
Schedule 3	—
Schedule 4	—

SALE OF LAND

Halsbury's Laws of England (3rd edn.), Vol. 34, paras. 322–668

2349   Articles

Condominiums and Co-Ownership, Frederick S. Lane (American and English ideas on shared forms of residential and business tenure): [1979] JPL 505.

Contract Subject to Specific Performance, F. Graham Glover (in the light of *Singh v Nazeer* [1978] 3 All ER 817, 1978 Halsbury's Abridgment para. 2434): 129 WLJ 692.

Damage by Subsidence: The Conveyancing Problem, Harry Street: [1979] Conv 241.

Damages in Lieu of Rescission, F. Graham Glover (the question of the circumstances in which damages can be awarded when a contract for the sale of land is rescinded): 129 NLJ 841.

The Estate Agents Bill: Reform at Last, Michael Buck: 129 NLJ 232.

Estate Agents' Commission, C. P. Seepersad (when commission payable): 123 Sol Jo 695.

Gazumping—A Suggested Practical Solution, Ernest H. Scamell: [1979] LS Gaz 959.

House Buyers and the Misrepresentation Act 1967, A. M. Tettenborn (on what measure of damages may be awarded where an innocent misrepresentation leads to a contract, under the Misrepresentation Act 1967, s. 2 (1)): 123 Sol Jo 669.

Options Open in Enforcing Contracts for Sale of Land, A. Tettenborn: 123 Sol Jo 427.

The Sale of Council Houses, I. R. Storey (*Storer v Manchester City Council* [1974] 3 All ER 824, CA, 1974 Halsbury's Abridgment para. 477 and *Gibson v Manchester City Council* [1979] 1 All ER 972, HL, para. 2357: two important cases where the issue was whether a binding contract had been formed): 129 NLJ 663.

Standard Conditions, a New Form, H. W. Wilkinson (a consideration of the new set of standard conditions for conveyancing by E. H. Scamell): 129 NLJ 286.

Still a Matter of Title—the Article 9 Certificate, Brian Rust Howell (procedure to be followed should local authorities fail to have issued an Article 9 certificate in accordance with the provisions of the Local Authorities etc. (England) (Property etc: Further Provision) Order 1974, 1974 Halsbury's Abridgment para. 2054): [1979] LS Gaz 958.

Time of the Essence—Waiver, H. W. Wilkinson (discussion of notices to complete: *Buckland v Farmer & Moody* [1978] 3 All ER 929, CA, 1978 Halsbury's Abridgment para. 2435): 129 NLJ 185.

2350   Completion—date of completion—contractual obligation—liability of vendor

The vendor agreed to complete the sale of his house to the defendant on 12th July 1977, and on the same day the defendant was to complete the sale of his house to the plaintiff. The vendor was unable to complete on the due date, for reasons unconnected with title. The plaintiff had already vacated his home and was forced to rent accommodation until he obtained vacant possession of the defendant's house. In accordance with the Law Society's Conditions of Sale 1973, condition 19, the defendant gave the vendor notice to complete within twenty-eight days and completion took place on 11th August. The defendant's contract with the plaintiff was completed on that day and the plaintiff was let into possession. The plaintiff sued and was awarded damages against the defendant for the expenses incurred due to the delay in completion. The defendant served the vendor with a third party notice claiming indemnity. The questions for the court were whether (i) there had been a breach of contract on 12th July, or within a reasonable time thereafter, which was able to be remedied in damages; (ii) the service of a notice pursuant to condition 19 varied the original date for completion so that if completion took place before the new date, there was no breach of contract. It was accepted by the parties that if the vendor was in breach of contract he was liable to indemnify the plaintiff. *Held*, (i) the vendor committed a breach of contract by failing to complete on 12th July. Although a claim for specific performance of the contract would have been refused on the ground that the stipulation as to time was not of the essence of the contract, that was no ground for relieving the vendor or defendant from liability for failure to complete; (ii) service of the notice presupposed that the sale was not completed on the original date. This did not however discharge any accrued right or cause of action vested in the person who served the notice. Hence the defendant had not been deprived of any cause of action in damages against the vendor which had accrued before service of the notice to complete. The vendor was thus liable to indemnify the defendant for damages paid to the plaintiff.

RAINERI V MILES (WIEJSKI, THIRD PARTY) [1979] 3 All ER 763 (Court of Appeal: BUCKLEY, BRIDGE and TEMPLEMAN LJJ). Dicta of Fry LJ in *Howe v Smith* [1881–5] All ER Rep 201 at 209 and of Lord Parker of Waddington in *Stickney v Keeble* [1914–15] All ER Rep 73 at 81 applied.

2351　　Contract—breach—measure of damages—rule in Bain v Fothergill

See *AVG Management Science Ltd v Barwell Developments Ltd*, para. 791.

2352　　—— —— rescission—damages—right of vendor to interest on purchase price—Law Society's General Conditions of Sale

The sale of a house fell through owing to the purchaser's failure to complete. Apart from agreed damages to cover the vendor's loss in reselling at a lower price and in arranging the sale, he claimed interest at 15 per cent per annum (the rate specified in the contract as payable under the Law Society's General Conditions of Sale, condition 16) on the purchase price for the period from the original completion date to the actual completion date on resale. He further claimed interest on the original purchase price, including the deposit, from the date of proposed completion to the date he rescinded the contract and put the house back on the market. At first instance it was held that condition 16 did not apply where there was a resale, with the result that the vendor was not entitled to interest on the purchase price between the original and actual completion dates. The vendor was, however, awarded interest at a rate determined by the court on the purchase price for the period between original completion and rescission. The purchaser appealed, contending that the agreed damages, which were provided for by condition 19 of the General Conditions, were all that the vendor was entitled to receive. *Held*, condition 19 clearly provided that a vendor could either rescind and sue for restitution or affirm and sue for breach of contract, either reselling or not, or for specific performance. If he elected to rescind he was only entitled to liquidated damages as defined by that condition. Accordingly, the vendor was not entitled to the sums of interest claimed and the appeal would be allowed.

The court considered, however, that the trial judge had been correct in refusing to award interest under condition 16 where there had been a resale.

TALLEY V WOLSEY-NEECH (1978) 38 P & CR 45 (Court of Appeal: STEPHENSON, BROWNE and WALLER LJJ).

2353　　—— deposit—deposit forfeited on failure to complete—court's discretion to order repayment

Under a contract for the sale of property in London the purchasers paid a substantial deposit, being 10 per cent of the purchase price. However, due to a change in exchange control regulations the purchasers were prevented from transferring funds from Nigeria to London to cover the balance of the purchase price, and were unable to complete on the due date or within the following twenty-eight days pursuant to the completion notice served on them by the vendors under the terms of the contract. The vendors rescinded the contract and purported to forfeit the deposit. The purchasers brought an action claiming repayment of the deposit on the grounds that either the contract had been frustrated or the court should exercise its discretion to order repayment of the deposit under the Law of Property Act 1925, s. 49 (2).

The trial judge held that the court had no discretion under s. 49 (2) to order repayment, as the purchasers could not have successfully resisted an action for specific performance. The purchasers appealed. *Held*, although the purchasers had been unable to complete by the completion date, the contract was not incapable of performance and had therefore not been frustrated. Section 49 (2) gave the court an unqualified discretion to order repayment of the deposit, where this was necessary to do justice between the parties. The question as to whether the vendor should repay the deposit should be decided by the trial judge or tried as a separate issue. The appeal would be allowed.

UNIVERSAL CORPN v FIVE WAYS PROPERTIES LTD [1979] 1 All ER 552 (Court of Appeal: BUCKLEY and EVELEIGH LJJ). Decision of Walton J [1978] 3 All ER 1131, 1978 Halsbury's Abridgment para. 2429 revised.

2354   —— exchange of contracts—"contract races"

The Council of the Law Society has re-issued a direction concerning the practice where a vendor of land instructs his solicitor to submit forms of contract to more than one prospective purchaser. Where the solicitor is acting only for the vendor he must at once disclose the decision to submit a form of contract to more than one prospective purchaser direct to the solicitor acting for each prospective purchaser (if no solicitor is acting, disclosure must be made to the prospective purchaser in person). The disclosure must be confirmed at once in writing if originally made orally. Disclosure must be made with the vendor's consent; if he does not consent, the solicitor must cease to act forthwith. The Council of the Law Society warn of the increased dangers of a conflict of interest arising in such cases where the solicitor is entitled to act for both the vendor and for one of the prospective purchasers. If, exceptionally, a solicitor feels that he can so act, he must also disclose this decision direct to both clients and to the solicitor acting for every other prospective purchaser (or, if no solicitor is acting, to each such prospective purchaser in person). This disclosure must also be confirmed at once in writing if originally made orally. Where forms of contract are submitted to more than one prospective purchaser, a solicitor must not accept instructions to act for more than one purchaser. See the Guardian Gazette, 28th November 1979, p. 1177.

2355   —— —— exchange by telephone—authority of solicitors to dispense with actual exchange

In an action by the intending purchaser for specific performance of a contract for the sale of a house, the vendor denied that a binding agreement for sale had been made. An agreement for sale subject to contract had been made and the vendor and purchaser had each signed their part of the contract and sent it to their respective solicitors. The vendor's part, however, was not sent to the purchaser's solicitors, but a telephone conversation took place between the two solicitors in which they agreed that the contracts would be treated as immediately exchanged by telephone at that moment. The purchaser contended that the conversation was effective in law to effect an exchange of contracts and bind the parties. This was rejected in the Chancery Division and on appeal, *held*, a client impliedly and ostensibly authorised his solicitor to effect an exchange of contracts in such manner as his solicitor thought fit. The practice of exchanging contracts by telephone was a common and necessary practice in conveyancing. A solicitor who had ostensible authority to deliver the documents to the other solicitor was entitled to effect constructive delivery by undertaking to hold them on behalf of the other solicitor. Thus, immediately after the telephone conversation an effective exchange of contracts took place, creating a binding contract.

TEMPLEMAN LJ noted that, in order to prevent uncertainty about the terms and effect of a telephone conversation, it was desirable that a formula, which effected an exchange by telephone, be devised and adopted by the profession.

DOMB v ISOZ [1980] 1 All ER 942 (Court of Appeal: BUCKLEY, BRIDGE and TEMPLEMAN LJJ). Decision of Brian Dillon QC sitting as a deputy High Court judge (1978) 122 Sol Jo 573, 1978 Halsbury's Abridgment para. 2430, reversed.

2356   —— **exemption clause—whether effective to exclude liability**

See *Hone v Benson*, para. 1959.

2357   —— **existence of contract—principles for establishing existence— whether decree of specific performance appropriate**

A council tenant who wished to purchase the freehold interest in his house filled in an application form supplied by the council. Following an inspection of the premises the council wrote him a letter which informed the tenant that it might be prepared to sell him the house on terms stated, and invited him to make a formal application on the attached form. He filled in the form and returned it with a letter stating that he wished to continue with the purchase. The council subsequently reversed its policy of selling council houses to tenants, and the tenant applied for a decree of specific performance. The Court of Appeal granted the application on the grounds that the parties' correspondence had evinced an intention on behalf of both that they intended to be contractually bound, and that the tenant had made improvements at his own expense in reliance on that contract. The council appealed. *Held*, the language of the council's letter stating that it might be prepared to sell the house was such that it could not be converted into a firm offer capable of acceptance. Accordingly there was no legally enforceable contract of sale and the appeal would be allowed.

    Gibson v Manchester City Council [1979] 1 All ER 972 (House of Lords: Lord Diplock, Lord Edmund-Davies, Lord Fraser of Tullybelton, Lord Russell of Killowen and Lord Keith of Kinkel. Decision of Court of Appeal [1978] 2 All ER 583, 1978 Halsbury's Abridgment para. 2431 reversed. See further 129 NLJ 268.

2358   —— **frustration—purchaser intending to develop land—development prohibited—whether contract frustrated**

Canada

The appellants purchased land from the respondents, intending to develop it. The respondents were aware of this intention, which was reflected in the purchase price. After the contract had been executed, the land was rendered useless for such development by subsequent legislation. The appellants sought a declaration that the agreement was frustrated and appealed against an order for specific performance granted to the respondents. *Held*, the agreement to sell land was not frustrated by the enactment of legislation prohibiting its development, although both parties were aware that the purchaser intended such development. The effect of the legislation was not such as to alter the fundamental character of the agreement so that it no longer reflected its original basis. The appeal would be dismissed.

    Victoria Wood Development Corpn Inc v Ondrey (1978) 22 OR (2d) 1 (Court of Appeal of Ontario).

2359   —— **order for specific performance—failure to comply—discharge of order—entitlement to damages at common law**

See *Johnson v Agnew*, para. 2780.

2360   —— **sale subject to consent of mortgagee**

Canada

Vendors agreed to sell certain premises to the purchasers. These premises were subject to an agreement with the mortgagees of the property not to sell without their consent. The purchasers refused to disclose confidential financial statements in order that the mortgagees might agree to the sale and repudiated the agreement. The vendors sued for damages for breach of contract. *Held*, the agreement between the vendors and the mortgagees imposed a condition precedent and without its fulfilment there could be no agreement to sell. The request for financial statements was reasonable and the refusal to comply prevented the vendors from fulfilling the agreement; the purchasers had no right to rely upon their own non-compliance to repudiate the agreement and were in breach. In assessing damages, the vendors bore the burden of proving their loss and the purchasers the burden of showing that the loss had not been mitigated. The damages were to be calculated on the difference between the contract price and the market price at the date fixed for completion.

100 MAIN STREET LTD v W. B. SULLIVAN CONSTRUCTION LTD (1978) 20 OR (2d) 401 (Court of Appeal of Ontario).

2361 —— specific performance—sale subject to entries on register

Properties, part freehold, part leasehold, were put up for auction by the defendants. The plaintiff bought one lot of the property which was registered at the Land Registry with either absolute freehold or absolute leasehold title. The contract of sale incorporated the National Conditions of Sale (19th edn.), cl. 6 (iii) whereby if any property sold was subject to a covenant, copies of the relevant documents could be examined at the vendor's solicitors and the purchaser would be deemed to purchase with prior notice. A special condition of sale provided that the property would be sold subject to the entries on the register of title. The plaintiff's solicitor found that the property was subject to certain restrictive covenants contained in a deed of 1883 which had not been available on first registration. The plaintiff issued a vendor and purchaser summons asking, inter alia, for a declaration that good title had not been shown. *Held*, on construction of the contract, the plaintiff was bound to take the property subject to the entries on the register. However, there had been no attempt to state that there was a difficulty in the title or that the property was subject to the contents of a deed which could not be produced. Specific performance of such a contract could not be enforced and the plaintiff was entitled to the return of his deposit, under the Law of Property Act 1925, s. 49 (2).

FARUQI v ENGLISH REAL ESTATES LTD [1979] 1 WLR 963 (Chancery Division: WALTON J).

2362 —— undertaking by solicitor to pay over purchase price to vendor on registration—enforcement of undertaking

See *Damodaran S/O Raman v Choe Kuan Him*, para. 2707.

2363 —— vendor's obligation to show good title—presumption of facts on which title depends

Vendors entered into a contract with purchasers for the sale of business premises subject to a trust for sale. The purchasers took out a vendor and purchaser summons to determine whether the vendors had shown good title as there was evidence of an option to purchase the premises together with a contract of sale made in 1912, which was suspended by deed in 1930, but remained unperformed. On appeal by the vendors against a decision that they had not shown a good title, it was held that the evidence supported a presumption of abandonment of the option and the 1912 contract. The purchasers appealed. *Held*, from 1933 onwards, all the evidence pointed to an abandonment of the 1912 contract and to the impossibility of a claimant obtaining specific performance of it. In particular, an agreement for a twenty-one year lease of the premises granted in 1933 made no reference to the contract and a deed of appointment of new trustees made in 1936 reciting the administration and history of the trust made no reference to the option. Further, the grantee of the option had died in 1942 and no claim had been made on behalf of his estate since. On the facts, it was beyond reasonable doubt that there was an abandonment of the contract of sale before 1936. Accordingly, the appeal would be dismissed.

MEPC LTD v CHRISTIAN-EDWARDS [1979] 3 All ER 752 (House of Lords: LORD WILBERFORCE, VISCOUNT DILHORNE, LORD SALMON, LORD RUSSELL OF KILLOWEN and LORD KEITH OF KINKEL). Decision of the Court of Appeal [1978] 3 All ER 795, 1978 Halsbury's Abridgment para. 2436 affirmed. Dictum of Lord Cozens-Hardy in *Smith v Colbourne* [1914] 2 Ch 533 at 541 and *Johnson v Clarke* [1928] Ch 847 applied.

2364   Conveyancing—preliminary inquiries—local authority fees

The fees payable to local authorities for preliminary inquiries are increased with effect from 1st December 1979. The new fees are:

Part I Inquiries

(a) one parcel of land   £5.75
(b) several parcels of land
          — first parcel   £5.75
          — each addition   £1.40

Part II Inquiries
each printed inquiry   £0.45
each additional inquiry   £1.10

The Local Authorities Association is to remind its members to use first class post in every case. Some time will inevitably elapse before the new fees appear on the printed forms. See the Law Society's Gazette, 7th November 1979, p. 1108.

2365   —— recommendations of Royal Commission on Legal Services

See para. 1720.

2366   Conveyancing practice—valuation for mortgage purposes

Following discussions with the Office of Fair Trading, the Building Societies Association has recommended to its members that they should consider having the valuer for the building society carry out a structural survey for the applicant for a mortgage. Alternatively, a building society should permit a valuation for its purposes to be carried out by a surveyor proposed by the applicant for a mortgage and who is considered suitable by the building society. The building society and the prospective house purchaser would each receive a separate report. The Office of Fair Trading, commenting on the announcement, has advised house buyers to inform the building society if they want a structural survey before the valuation is arranged. The office added that the house buyer should discuss the scope of the survey and the fee direct with the surveyor. See also *Financial Times*, 24th July 1979.

2367   Estate Agents Act 1979

The Estate Agents Act 1979 regulates certain activities of estate agents in relation to the acquisition or disposal of interests in land, with the object of protecting users of their services. The Act received the royal assent on 4th April 1979 and comes into force on days to be appointed.

Section 1 limits the application of the Act to estate agency work, which is defined as the introduction of prospective vendors and purchasers of an interest in land, and activities designed to ensure the disposal or acquisition of that interest. An interest in land is defined as a legal estate in fee simple absolute in possession or a lease which, by reason of the level of the rent, the length of the term or both, has a capital value which may be lawfully realised on the open market: s. 2.

Section 3 empowers the Director General of Fair Trading to make orders prohibiting persons from carrying on estate agency work, either generally or in relation to a particular aspect of it, on the grounds specified in that section and Sch. 1, including convictions of certain criminal and statutory offences and the commission of discrimination in estate agency work. He is also empowered to issue warnings to persons liable to have such an order made in respect of them: s. 4. The procedure for the making of orders and issuing of warnings is laid down in s. 5 and Sch. 2. Under s. 6, on application by the person concerned, the Director General may vary or revoke any order or warning and Sch. 2 prescribes the procedure to be followed. Decisions of the Director General under ss. 3, 4 and 6 are subject to a right of appeal to the Secretary of State, and there is provision for a further appeal to a court on a point of law: s. 7. Section 8 requires the Director General to establish and maintain a register of all measures taken under ss. 3, 4 and 6.

Section 9 authorises the Director General by notice to require any person to supply any information or documents specified in the notice, but s. 10 provides that any information so obtained is to be disclosed only with the consent of the person or persons to whom it relates. Under s. 11 officers of enforcement authorities are empowered to enter business premises and to inspect and seize any books or documents found.

Section 12 defines client money as including any money received by an estate agent in the course of estate agency work being a contract or pre-contract deposit; money received by him is held on trust for the person paying it who is entitled to have it paid back to him or by his direction. If the estate agent receives the money as stakeholder, it is held on trust for the person who may become entitled on occurrence of the event against which the money is held: s. 13. Under s. 14, estate agents must pay any client money received into a separate client account with an institution authorised under regulations made by the Secretary of State; such regulations may also require the keeping of specific accounts and records in relation to clients' money. The Secretary of State may also make regulations requiring estate agents to account for interest earned by clients' money on deposit: s. 15. Section 16 provides that an estate agent may receive client money only if he is covered by authorised arrangements against his possible failure to account for that money. However, the Director General is given a discretion to grant exemptions from the requirement of s. 16: s. 17.

By s. 18 an estate agent must inform the client of all his financial liabilities consequent on the proposed transaction, including the remuneration payable for the estate agent's services, prior to the client entering into an agreement for those services: failure to do so will make the agreement unenforceable at the instance of the agent. Section 19 provides that, in relation to estate agency work carried out in England, Wales or Northern Ireland, regulations may impose an upper limit for pre-contract deposits payable by prospective purchasers of an interest in land; pre-contract deposits are prohibited in relation to estate agency work carried out in Scotland: s. 20. Where an estate agent has any beneficial interest in property which is the subject of a proposed transaction, or the proceeds of sale thereof s. 21 requires him to disclose that interest.

Under s. 22 regulations may be made establishing a minimum standard of competence of persons engaged in estate agency work, and prescribing the means of attaining such a standard; bankrupts are prohibited from engaging in estate agency work except as employees of another: s. 23. Section 24 amends the Tribunal and Inquiries Act 1971 to bring the adjudicating functions of the Director General under the supervision of the Council on Tribunals. Section 25 imposes a general duty on the Director General to oversee the working and enforcement of the Act and to keep its operation under review. In Great Britain the local weights and measures authorities are responsible for enforcement, while in Northern Ireland it is the responsibility of the Department of Commerce: s. 26. The obstruction of authorised officers of enforcement authorities acting in pursuance of the Act is subject to penalties under s. 27. Section 28 makes available to all persons charged with an offence under the Act the general defence of showing that they took all reasonable precautions and exercised due diligence to avoid the commission of the offence. General and supplementary provisions are contained in ss. 29–35. Section 36 deals with short title, commencement and extent.

2368   Latent defect of quality—landslip affecting land subject of sale— duty of vendor

Canada

Purchasers of land contended that the vendors' failure to notify them of landslips affecting the land and dwelling they had acquired amounted to a latent defect rendering the premises uninhabitable. *Held*, in some circumstances a vendor could be liable to a purchaser in respect of premises which were not new if he knew of the defect, but the purchaser had to prove his knowledge or show that he had concealed the circumstances or had shown reckless disregard for the truth of his representations. The vendor's liability would not be founded on *Donoghue v Stevenson* [1932] AC 562, HL and the cases after it, as they were concerned with manufacturer's or product liability. Similarly, a vendor could be liable for a defect rendering premises inherently dangerous, but such liability also could not be founded on *Donoghue v*

Stevenson. In the present case the vendor was not in breach of any duty recognised in the cases. Further, the purchasers had failed to establish all the facts alleged in the pleadings and accordingly their claim would be dismissed.

McGRATH v MacLEAN (1979) 22 OR (2d) 784 (Court of Appeal of Ontario).

2369   Memorandum—sale of land and chattels—chattels not mentioned in written memorandum—whether sufficient note of terms

Fiji

In 1968 the vendors agreed to sell their leasehold interest in two parcels of land together with some chattels to the purchasers for £5,000. The sum was not apportioned between land and chattels. The vendors signed a memorandum stating the sum but referring only to the land. In 1970 the vendors refused to complete the sale. In 1973 the purchasers brought an action against the vendors and obtained an order for specific performance of the contract and damages. The Court of Appeal held the contract and price specified in the memorandum related to both chattels and land and the memorandum was sufficient for the purposes of the Indemnity, Guarantee and Bailment Ordinance, s. 59 (d). The order for specific performance was set aside on the grounds of laches and the case remitted to the trial judge for assessment of damages for breach of contract. The vendors appealed. *Held,* (i) on an action to enforce a contract for the sale of both land and chattels a memorandum referring to land only was sufficient for s. 59 (d). (ii) Since the purchasers had asserted an indivisible contract for an indivisible price, it was not open to the court to treat the terms of the agreement which related to chattels as collateral and apportion the purchase price for the purpose of bringing the memorandum within the section. Accordingly the memorandum was insufficient and the contract unenforceable.

RAM NARAYAN v RISHAD HUSSAIN SHAH [1979] 1 WLR 1349 (Privy Council: LORD DIPLOCK, LORD FRASER OF TULLYBELTON and LORD RUSSELL OF KILLOWEN).

SENTENCING

Halsbury's Laws of England (4th edn.), Vol. 11, paras. 481–573

2370   Articles

The Advisory Council and the Suspended Sentence, A. E. Bottoms (the suspended sentence of imprisonment as reported in "Sentences of Imprisonment" by the Advisory Council on the Penal System, 1978 Halsbury's Abridgment para. 2540): [1979] Crim LR 437.

Community Service Order, Alec Samuels (the role of the court in selecting community service as an appropriate course of action with an offender): 123 Sol Jo 528.

A Last Look at Section 3, P. J. Davies (discussion of Criminal Justice Act 1961, s. 3): 129 NLJ 88.

The Law and Practice on Sentencing the Drug Offender, Alec Samuels: 129 NLJ 899.

The Role of Prosecuting Counsel in Sentencing, Graham Zellick (on whether the prosecuting counsel should play a larger role at the sentencing stage): [1979] Crim LR 493.

2371   Appeal—examples

Examples of sentencing appeals are set out under the following headings:

OFFENCES AGAINST GOVERNMENT AND PUBLIC ORDER (Possessing an offensive weapon; Perjury).

OFFENCES AGAINST THE PERSON (Manslaughter; Manslaughter (diminished responsibility); Causing grievous bodily harm; Wounding with intent; Malicious wounding; Assault occasioning actual bodily harm; Assault with intent to rob;

Possessing a firearm with intent to endanger life; Rape; Attempted rape; Indecent assault; Kidnapping; Neglect of child).

OFFENCES AGAINST PROPERTY (Robbery; Conspiracy to rob; Burglary; Aggravated burglary; Theft; Attempted theft; Handling stolen goods; Receiving stolen goods; Making false statements to defraud the Inland Revenue; Obtaining pecuniary advantage by deception; Obtaining property by deception; Conspiracy to defraud; False accounting; Taking a motor vehicle without authority; Going equipped for taking a motor vehicle without authority; Arson; Arson with intent to endanger life; Criminal damage; Forgery).

OFFENCES AGAINST DECENCY AND MORALITY (Buggery; Bigamy; Importuning for immoral purposes).

OFFENCES RELATING TO DRUGS (Fraudulent evasion of prohibition on importation of controlled drug; Being knowingly concerned in fraudulent evasion of prohibition on importation of controlled drug; Possession of controlled drug with intent to supply (cannabis); Possession of cannabis; Possession of cannabis resin).

DRIVING OFFENCES (Causing death by dangerous driving; Causing death by reckless driving; Driving with excess alcohol in blood).

OFFENCES AGAINST GOVERNMENT AND PUBLIC ORDER

2372   *1. Possessing an offensive weapon.   2. Damaging property*
Sentence: 1. Three months' imprisonment, 2. Three years' imprisonment concurrent. Woman, aged 40, born in Belfast. Marriage broken up and five children (aged 2–12) in care. Previous convictions for assault and manslaughter of a child (put on probation). Appellant lived in block of flats. Police called to the premises, she was found with a 10 inch carving knife in her hand and smashing her front door with a bottle. Police had been called a number of times to her premises when her behaviour was violent. Since her conviction for manslaughter in 1967 she had been in and out of hospital 23 times. Medical opinion was that she should be in a secure hospital but none were prepared to take her because her mental condition was not serious enough for a special hospital under the Mental Health Act 1959. Sentenced as above. On appeal, *held*, it was absolutely wrong for the criminal courts to be put in a position of having to apply the criminal law and sentences of imprisonment simply because there were no proper hospital facilities. Accordingly, the trial judge had no option, there being no suitable hospital for the appellant, but to impose the sentence he did for the protection of the public. *R v Scanlon*, 6th February 1979 (Court of Appeal: Waller LJ, Mais and Jupp JJ).

2373   *Perjury (3)*
Sentence: 15 months' imprisonment concurrent. Man, aged 47. No previous convictions. Various employments, inter alia, as a Government printer in West Africa and latterly as an export director and credit controller. Fell in love with a married woman who was seeking a divorce. In the course of giving evidence in her divorce proceedings he gave perjured evidence which was very material to the court reaching a decision as to the future of the children of the marriage. Pleaded guilty to the three charges and sentenced as above. On an application for leave to appeal *held*, the sentence passed for deliberate perjury was in all the circumstances a proper one. *R v Medley*, 2nd February 1979 (Court of Appeal: Bridge LJ and Caulfield J).

OFFENCES AGAINST THE PERSON

2374   *Manslaughter*
Sentence: 8 years' imprisonment. Man, aged 41, of previous good character. Joined Merchant Navy after attending a nautical school. Worked with shipping companies until 1962 and later was a stock control clerk until he joined an oil company in 1966. Married in 1962. Shortly after marriage his medical condition showed he could not father children. He and his wife adopted two boys. The couple then became friendly with S, the victim. When S's wife left him, the appellant's wife formed a liaison with him. She finally went to live with him and gave birth to his

child. The appellant found out about this after someone had sent him the child's birth certificate. One night, after he had a certain amount to drink while brooding about his wife's relationship with S, he decided to go to the latter's home to find out the true position. He took a sharp pointed kitchen knife with him and used it to break into the house. S came downstairs and a struggle ensued during which he was stabbed eleven times. The appellant was charged with murder but the jury returned a verdict of manslaughter "because they were not sure that intention to kill or do serious bodily harm had been proved". Sentenced as above. There was no history of any psychiatric or emotional disturbance of a serious kind. On appeal *held*, the trial judge had rightly dealt with the case. Although the facts did not in law amount to provocation, the appellant was under mental stress due to marital unhappiness. It was a savage attack on a man in his home which deprived him of his life. The sentence would stand. *R v Saunders*, 13th March 1979 (Court of Appeal: Lawton LJ, Thompson and Hodgson JJ).

2375   Sentence: 6 years' imprisonment. Married man, aged 44, with three children. Lived with mistress and children. Born in Eire and visited the country annually. Regular employment since leaving army in 1957 and yard foreman for the last eight years. A heavy drinker. While on last visit to Eire, his mistress left home with the children and went to live with the victim. She refused to return to the appellant who had found out about the victim. He went to the latter's house and started arguing with him. The victim, who was a larger man and six stones heavier, punched the appellant in the face and threw him into a hedge. The appellant then produced a sheath knife. He claimed that the victim "ran onto the knife" which entered his stomach and went right through his heart. The victim died shortly afterwards. A plea of manslaughter on grounds of provocation was accepted and the appellant was sentenced to 8 years' imprisonment. The judge held that while there was a long history of matrimonial unhappiness, the killing was the result of a savage blow with an unpleasant weapon. On appeal *held*, in all the circumstances, having regard to the provocation involved and the fact that the victim was the aggressor from the beginning of the fight, the court would vary the sentence from eight to six years. *R v Farrell*, 2nd July 1979 (Court of Appeal: Cumming-Bruce LJ, Park and Smith JJ).

2376   Sentence: 4 years' imprisonment. Single man, aged 25, with no previous convictions. After leaving school, worked as a garage apprentice and then as a semi-skilled fitter. Excellent home background and no history of violence. After a heavy drinking session, got into an unnecessary drunken fight with the victim outside a public house. During the fight the victim's head hit the pavement, fracturing his skull. He became unconscious. The appellant, who had received blows to his eyes and mouth, then deliberately sat astride the victim and rained blows onto the latter's face before being dragged away. The victim died in hospital. A post mortem revealed that his death was due to asphyxia caused by swallowing the blood from his facial injuries. The appellant was charged with murder but his plea to manslaughter was accepted and he was sentenced to 6 years' imprisonment. On appeal, *held*, no court doing its duty to stop that sort of drunken behaviour could do other than pass a severe sentence. Nevertheless, taking all the mitigating factors into consideration, the sentence passed was too high and it would be reduced to four years. *R v Hatch*, 19th July 1979 (Court of Appeal: Roskill LJ, Mars-Jones and Drake JJ).

2377   *Manslaughter (diminished responsibility).*
Sentence: 7 years' imprisonment. Man, aged 35, with four children. Married victim in 1962 but marriage was not a happy one. Continuous employment since leaving school at 15 until 1976 when he left his employment with a firm of painters of his own accord. Unemployed on arrest. Spent convictions. Paralysis of left arm since birth. In 1976 and 1977, the appellant spent periods in a mental hospital and during his last stay there in 1977 his wife obtained an injunction preventing him from living in the matrimonial home. In December 1977, he broke into the

matrimonial home, pushed his 14 year old son aside, ran into his wife's bedroom and barricaded himself in. Neighbours heard his wife's screams. The appellant then appeared at the bedroom window and shouted "It's done now. I'm just waiting for her to die then I'm going to slash my wrists". The police were called and forced their way into the bedroom and arrested the appellant. His wife was found bleeding from a number of stab wounds. She died in hospital the next day. A pathologist's report revealed that the wife had put up a struggle and had received seven knife wounds on her arm and two on her leg before the appellant inflicted the fatal 6½ inch deep wound into her abdomen. Medical and psychiatric reports showed that part of the appellant's trouble was due to excessive drinking, he also suffered from mild psychopathy unsusceptible to treatment. The reports revealed that the appellant's control over his emotions had diminished to such an extent as to bring him within the Homicide Act 1957, s. 2. The trial judge accepted a plea of manslaughter and sentenced him to life imprisonment. On appeal *held*, it was doubtful whether on the medical evidence put forward, the plea should have been accepted. These cases of homicide were to be tried by judges and juries not psychiatrists. The trial judge had accepted the plea of diminished responsibility and sentenced the appellant to life imprisonment on the ground that he was a potentially dangerous man, subject to outbursts of violence for no good reason. However, the court found that the degree of diminished responsibility shown in the psychiatrist's report did not come within the sort of mental imbalance which justified a life sentence. Accordingly, a sentence of 7 years' imprisonment would be substituted. *R v Robinson*, 8th March 1979. (Court of Appeal: Lawton LJ, Thompson and Hodgson JJ).

2378   *Causing grievous bodily harm*
Sentence: probation for 3 years on terms that the appellant undergoes medical treatment. Man, aged 47, divorced. Chief river pollution prevention officer until 1974 when he retired after a nervous breakdown. Said to be suffering from a form of manic depressive disorder. During attacks liable to be very irritable and aggressive if provoked or thwarted. Victim was his second wife with whom he had lived for a considerable time before his first wife would divorce him. He had been treating her violently since 1976. In December 1977, the victim obtained an injunction against him but eight days later he went to her house, caused a disturbance and was arrested. He agreed to undergo hospital treatment as an alternative to imprisonment for breach of the injunction. Shortly afterwards he was diagnosed as a hypomaniac by a psychiatrist. He then began to pester the victim with telephone calls for two days and threatened her with a pitchfork. The following day, he broke down her front door and assaulted her. Her neighbours came to her rescue and the police were summoned. Sentenced to 3 years' imprisonment. Since the sentence, medical reports have stated that it is no longer necessary to imprison the appellant for the safety of the public or the victim. With the aid of drugs he is said to be safe when released. On appeal *held*, the court had two courses open to it, to uphold the sentence or vary it under the Powers of Criminal Courts Act 1973, s. 3. Accordingly, the court would vary the sentence as set out above on terms that the appellant underwent medical treatment. *R v Billington*, 30th April 1979 (Court of Appeal: Lord Widgery CJ, Lane LJ and Ackner J).

2379   Sentence: 18 months' imprisonment. Married man, aged 22, with one child. Eight previous convictions mainly for dishonesty, assault and offences connected with cars for which he was fined, sent to attendance and detention centres, put on probation and imprisoned. The appellant and co-accused kicked and punched the victim who was hospitalised for a week with a broken rib, an injured eye, extensive bruising and lacerations. The appellant and co-accused accused each other of inflicting the injuries on the victim. The appellant was sentenced as above. The jury disagreed on the co-accused's guilt. At his re-trial, he pleaded guilty to assault occasioning actual bodily harm and was sentenced to 6 months' imprisonment and ordered to pay the victim £10 compensation. The appellant appealed against disparity of sentence. *Held*, it was impossible to say that the appellant's sentence was excessive for not only was it a very bad assault, but the appellant had a bad record for such offences going back to when he was 14 years' old. He needed to be kept in check by substantial sentences.

The co-accused on the other hand had a much shorter record with only two previous convictions for assault. *R v Priavix*, 2nd July 1979 (Court of Appeal: Lord Widgery CJ, Shaw LJ and McNeill J).

2380   Sentence: 15 months' imprisonment. Married man, aged 33, with children and a good work record. Two previous convictions for violence, both in 1966. The appellant and his two brothers were in a public house on Boxing Day 1977 when a brawl commenced. One of the brothers made an unprovoked and vicious attack on a young man, seizing him by the hair and poking his eyes. The appellant joined in and the man was struck several times while on the floor. They then left the public house but later returned and became involved in another violent attack on the already injured young man. The appellant was sentenced as above and his brother received 30 months' imprisonment. On appeal against severity of sentence on grounds of the appellant's good work record and family background, *held*, as it was a public house fight of an extremely serious nature, the sentence would stand. *R v O'Leary*, 19th July 1979 (Court of Appeal: Roskill LJ, Mars-Jones and Drake JJ).

2381   Sentence: 5 years' imprisonment. Divorced man, aged 34, with 3 children. When arrested employed as a process worker. Separated from wife in 1976. In 1978, when the wife was asleep one night, the appellant let himself into the house and went to her bedroom. He woke her up and hit her over the head with a bottle, causing blood to pour down her face. She staggered downstairs where he again attacked her, stabbing her in the stomach several times. He then dragged her into the living room, hit her with various objects and attempted to strangle her. The wife was taken to hospital by the police who had been summoned by neighbours. In sentencing the appellant to 7 years' imprisonment, the trial judge said it was one of the worst cases of causing grievous bodily harm with intent that he had come across. On appeal, the wife accepting that she was responsible for the breakdown of the marriage and perhaps to blame for driving her husband into a state of desperation, *held*, the sentence was not excessive or out of proportion to the terrible crime committed, nevertheless, as an act of mercy, the court would vary the sentence as set out above. *R v Price*, 29th October 1979 (Court of Appeal: Cumming-Bruce LJ, Phillips and Michael Davies JJ).

2382   *Wounding with intent*
Sentence: 5 years' imprisonment. Single man, aged 27, with no previous convictions. Victim was the woman with whom he had been living for 15 months. There had been problems with the relationship and arguments and previous violence because he had objected to her going out with other men. There was an attempted reconciliation after a parting, but, following a further argument the appellant again suspected that she was involved with another man. While they were driving home, the appellant attacked his girlfriend. He stabbed her three times with a knife that happened to be in the car. She was rushed to the hospital and only care and treatment saved her life. Sentenced as above. Medical and psychiatric reports showed that although not suffering from any state which required treatment, his personality was such that he was liable to behave in a violent manner and the offence took place because of the physical and emotional stress he was under. On appeal, *held*, the sentence passed was not wrong in principle or too long in all the circumstances. *R v Smith*, 23rd October 1979 (Court of Appeal: Eveleigh LJ, Phillips and Michael Davies JJ).

2383   *Wounding with intent; unlawful wounding*

Sentence: 5 years' and 3 years' imprisonment concurrent. Man, aged 21. Unemployed for a year. Number of previous convictions including one of criminal damage for which he was fined and another of being drunk and disorderly. In 1976, sentenced to 3 months at detention centre for wounding with intent and causing grievous bodily harm. Bad start in life. Sent into care at the age of 13 because his parents could not cope with him and he went to an approved school. Difficult father who broke his arm when drunk. The appellant went to a public house with his girl friend early on Christmas Day 1977 to help with the cleaning. The victim was staying there. The appellant thought that he was making a "pass" at his girlfriend and kicked him to the ground. A witness said that while the victim was on the ground unconscious and covered with blood, the appellant had stood over him and kicked and stamped him in the face. The victim suffered severe injuries. When the girlfriend tried to stop the appellant he threw a stool at her hitting her in the face and causing a wound. He then dragged her outside and she had bruises and cuts which needed stitching. She forgave him and has since married him. Sentenced as above. On appeal *held*, it was impossible to say that the sentences imposed for such an offence, even for a young man of 21, were wrong in principle or manifestly excessive. Having regard to his history and the medical evidence before the Court, it appeared that a severe sentence was the best prospect for the appellant to come to his senses in the future as well as for the public's welfare. *R v Dunne*, 5th June 1979 (Court of Appeal: Roskill LJ, Bristow and Michael Davies JJ).

2384   *Malicious wounding*
Sentence: Immediate release (4 months' imprisonment served). Married man, aged 30. Six previous convictions since 1965 of shopbreaking, burglary, motoring offences etc, but none for violence. Probation three times, fined three times for eight offences, one suspended sentence and sentenced to 18 months in all for three burglaries, larceny as a servant, schoolbreaking. The appellant had a New Year party. One O was there who had too much to drink. Party became boisterous. O hit his wife and the appellant's girlfriend and the appellant's father. The appellant then picked up the first thing he saw in the kitchen, a paring knife, and stabbed O with it. One stab went near the heart and the other penetrated O's abdomen and injured his colon. Sentenced to 12 months' imprisonment. On appeal, *held* owing to the exceptional circumstances leading up to the offence, although an immediate prison sentence was called for, it should have been in the order of six months. Accordingly the sentence would be varied to allow the appellant's immediate release. *R v Van Dongen*, 6th February 1979 (Court of Appeal: Waller LJ, Mais and Jupp JJ).

2385   *Assault occasioning actual bodily harm*
Sentence: borstal training. Youth, aged 18, living with parents. Worked as a labourer since leaving school at 15. Three previous convictions for dishonesty for which he had received a supervision order, a fine and six month's detention. Had a girl friend who was seen amongst a group of young people talking to two boys aged 14 and 15. The appellant who took objection to this, threatened one of the boys and as they walked home he and his friends attacked them. The appellant kicked and punched one of the boys. Sentenced as above. On appeal *held*, it was a typical bullying attack by a gang egged on by the appellant for no reason at all on two young boys who were unable to protect themselves or escape. A custodial sentence was clearly called for, and, as a detention sentence was inappropriate, the sentence of borstal training would stand. *R v Rix*, 12th January 1979 (Court of Appeal: Lawton LJ, Cantley and Willis JJ).

2386   Sentence: immediate release (2 months' imprisonment served); compensation order for £250. Pakistani waiter who came to England in 1966. The victim, a woman, was disturbed by young hooligans who rang the doorbell of her place of work and ran off. She pursued the boys who ran up the stairs leading to the restaurant where the appellant worked. He, instead of chiding the boys, pushed the woman down the stairs. Her reaction was to return upstairs and box his ears. Further violence occurred and the victim was given hospital treatment for a black eye, swollen cheek, bruised spine and a deep cut on her nose which required stitches. Sentenced to 9 months' imprisonment and ordered to pay £250 compensation to the victim. On appeal against the term of imprisonment, *held*, as it was not contemplated violence but had occurred on the spur of the moment, and bearing in mind that the appellant had already served 2 months' imprisonment, the sentence would be varied to allow his immediate discharge. *R v Miah*, 13th September 1979 (Court of Appeal: Shaw LJ, Bristow and Watkins JJ).

2387 Sentence: 9 months' imprisonment. Divorced man, aged 30. Six previous convictions including three for assault. Last conviction in 1975 for which he was fined. The appellant lived in the same house as the victim and his wife. After a heated argument with the wife, the appellant slapped her face. When the victim appeared, the appellant struck him on the jaw, fracturing it, and knocking him unconscious. The prosecution conceded that there was some evidence of provocation. Sentenced as above. On appeal, *held*, it was impossible to say that the sentence of imprisonment was excessive. The offence was committed by a man with a previous record of violence and the sentence was fully justified. *R v Wright*, 23rd October 1979 (Court of Appeal: Eveleigh LJ, Phillips and Michael Davies JJ).

2388 Sentence: 12 months' imprisonment. Married man, aged 33, with children. Eight previous convictions (3 spent) for a similar offence, damaging property, threatening behaviour and for being drunk and disorderly for which he received a 3 month suspended sentence, was fined, put on probation and conditionally discharged. The appellant and three other men were engaged in a heated argument in a public house car park. They were shouting and using bad language. A police officer requested them to quieten down and move on. The other men did so but the appellant remained and directed obscenities at the officer. A police car then arrived with two other officers, the appellant assaulted one of them, striking him on the face and breaking his teeth causing bleeding in his mouth. Sentenced as above, the trial judge stating that such assaults on the police could not be tolerated. On appeal, *held*, deliberate drunken assaults on police officers had to be punished with immediate custodial sentences. The present sentence was an appropriate one for such a nasty assault and was imposed to act as a deterrent in an area where such offences were prevalent. *R v Bowater*, 9th November 1979 (Court of Appeal: Roskill and Ormrod LJJ and Bristow J).

2389 *Assault occasioning actual bodily harm; cruelty to persons under sixteen*
Sentence: 15 months' imprisonment concurrent suspended for 2 years (6 months' imprisonment already served), supervision order. Man, aged 23, living with his girlfriend and her three children. Two of the children, one of whom was the appellant's son, aged 15 months, were involved in the offences of assault. The other was a little girl aged 3. The appellant's illtreatment of both children over a period of time resulted in them being taken to hospital where his son was found to have fractured ribs and bruising all over his body. The little girl also had bruises on her body. Sentenced to 2 years' imprisonment concurrent on the two assault charges and to 18 months' imprisonment concurrent on the two cruelty charges (2 years in all). On appeal, *held*, although the court would have normally passed a sentence of imprisonment on such an offender, in the present case, the fact that the children did not shy away from the appellant and had expressed feelings of love for him had persuaded the court to vary the sentence to that set out above. *R v Taylor*, 13th November 1979 (Court of Appeal: Shaw LJ, O'Connor and Comyn JJ).

2390 *Assault with intent to rob; going equipped for theft*
Sentence: 3 years' imprisonment (first offence); 6 months' imprisonment concurrent (second offence). Youth, aged 20. Previous conviction for stealing money from employers, for which he had been dismissed. Appellant, armed with a claw hammer and with a scarf over his face, went to an all night petrol filling station. Threatened the cashier with the hammer, and demanded all the cash from the till. The cashier told the appellant the night's takings were already in the night safe and that the till was empty. Appellant abandoned attempted robbery. Cashier phoned the police. Two evenings later the police picked up appellant, who was riding a bicycle and was

still armed with the hammer. He admitted the attempted robbery; he said he had no intention of committing a similar offence, but if such a situation arose he might be "tempted to try it again". Sentenced as above. On appeal *held*, the sentence was not excessive. Apart from a borstal sentence the only alternative was 6 months' imprisonment which would have been a derisory and wholly inappropriate sentence. The case illustrated the embarrassment caused by the statutory restrictions (Criminal Justice Act 1961, s. 3) on the courts' powers of sentencing young people under 21. Appellant was doing well in prison, and any relief asked for had to be extended to the parole board. Appeal dismissed. *R v Mitchell*, 9th November 1978 (Court of Appeal: Lord Widgery CJ, Bridge LJ and Wien J).

2391   *Assault with intent to rob*
Sentence: 9 months' imprisonment (suspended 2 years); £200 fine. Student, aged 22, in receipt of maximum grant of £1,100 per annum. Previous good character. A female student walking through the city centre was grabbed from behind by the appellant. He pulled at her shoulder bag, she screamed and a car drew up alongside. The appellant ran off and was pursued and arrested. The girl's trousers had been ripped and her gold bracelet broken open. She suffered delayed shock. Sentenced as above. On appeal *held*, the sentence of imprisonment imposed was a lenient one and would stand even though it was an isolated offence. Further, there was no objection in principle to adding a fine to a suspended sentence, even though the intention of the fine was not to relieve an offender of the profits of his crime, as in the instant case. The appeal would be dismissed. *R v Giuffrida*, 2nd March 1979 (Court of Appeal: Lawton LJ, Thompson and Hodgson JJ). *R v Ffoulkes* [1976] Crim LR 758 and *R v Genese* [1976] 2 All ER 600, 1976 Halsbury's Abridgment para. 2335 applied.

2392   *Possessing a firearm with intent to endanger life*
Sentence: 9 months' imprisonment. No previous convictions. The appellant worked at a riding establishment. While the proprietor was away on holiday, the victim was left in charge. One night after the appellant had had a lot to drink, a fight broke out between him and two other employees. The appellant went to the cellar where he knew a gun was kept and returned with a shot gun and some ammunition. He loaded the gun and then threatened to shoot the victim. The latter wrestled with the appellant and the gun went off. The appellant was overpowered and the gun was taken away from him. Sentenced to 2 years' imprisonment. On appeal, *held*, a conviction could be obtained under the Firearms Act 1968, s. 16 without proving an immediate and unconditional intention to endanger life, thus, the gravity of the offence was considerably reduced. Accordingly, the sentence imposed was excessive and would be varied as set out above. *R v Cook*, 30th October 1979 (Lord Widgery CJ, Browne LJ and Watkins J).

2393   *Rape*
Sentence: life imprisonment. Married man, aged 20. Child died July 1975 and mother died December 1975. In March 1976, convicted of indecent exposure and fined. The following year he attacked a married woman who was walking home one evening, threw her on the ground and stripped and raped her. Victim also suffered scratches and bruises. In April 1977, he was convicted of three offences of indecent exposure and put on probation. The second and third cases of rape occurred on the same day in December 1977. At 5.30 p.m. he attacked and raped an 18 year old girl after indecently exposing himself to another woman. An hour later, he attacked, stripped and raped a 20 year old girl three times after subjecting her to various other degrading forms of sexual activity. In both cases he threatened to kill the girls. Sentenced to concurrent terms of life imprisonment. Social enquiry and medical reports showed that the appellant's child died shortly after birth, his mother died of cancer and that his wife was divorcing him. The reports showed that there was nothing psychiatrically wrong with him. On appeal, *held*, the court agreed with the trial judge that the appellant was a menace to unaccompanied girls and women. It was a classic case where life imprisonment was

appropriate (assuming a hospital and restriction order under the Mental Health Act 1959, ss. 60, 65 was inappropriate) as opposed to a long fixed term sentence. *R v Thornett*, 11th January 1979 (Court of Appeal: Browne LJ, Lawson and Phillips JJ).

2394   Sentence: 5 years' imprisonment. Single man, aged 22, born in Bangladesh. No previous convictions. The complainant was a married Mauritian woman who came to England in 1977. She had gone out shopping for some storage containers. The appellant came up to her and engaged her in conversation. He asked her if she was from Mauritius and told her his parents were from there. He then offered to show her where to get the containers and subsequently tricked her into entering a house where, after threatening her with a knife, he violently assaulted and raped her. At his trial he alleged that she had been acting as a prostitute. Sentenced as above. On appeal, *held*, it was a bad case of rape which was made worse by the appellant's defence at his trial. After having raped the victim in private he had then verbally raped her in open court. The sentence imposed was a lenient one and would stand. *R v Aziz*, 27th September 1979 (Court of Appeal: Lawton LJ, Park and Peter Pain JJ).

2395   *Attempted rape*
Sentence: 12 months' imprisonment suspended 2 years (2 months' imprisonment served). Married man, aged 56, of previous good character. Married for 25 years but wife had been periodically mentally unwell. Although the marriage was a happy one, sexual relations between the two had been unsatisfactory or non-existent for some time. Victim was the wife's aunt, also aged 56. She suspected that the appellant was attracted to her and the year before had told him not to go to her house unless accompanied by his wife. He arrived one day on the victim's doorstep stating that his wife was following. In his hands were a pair of tights. As the victim was bringing him tea, he suddenly advanced upon her with the tights stretched between his fists, said "I am sorry I have to do this" and pinned her down with the tights against her throat. He looked strange and smelt of drink. There was a struggle, she kicked him in the groin and told him to leave. He came to his senses, apologised, said he did not know what had come over him and left. The tights had formed a ligature around her neck. The appellant pleaded guilty and was sentenced to 12 months' imprisonment. On appeal *held*, it was an unusual charge and a most unusual case. On the basis that the offence was highly unlikely to be repeated, the sentence would be suspended. *R v Cunnew*, 11th January 1979. (Court of Appeal: Browne LJ, Lawson and Phillips JJ).

2396   *Indecent assault; incest*

Sentence: 5 years' imprisonment on two counts of incest and 5 years' imprisonment concurrent on six counts of indecent assault. Married man, aged 39. Three sons and three daughters. No previous convictions. The offences involving the daughters were committed over a period of 5 years, the children being aged 12, 9 and 8 years old respectively at the initiation of the offences. Sentenced as above. On appeal on ground that he had made a full confession to the police, expressed remorse, was a good supporter of his family and a hard worker, *held*, the sentences imposed fully reflected the mitigating circumstances of the case but for which the sentences imposed might well have been longer. In fact, they were not a day too long. *R v Jones*, 2nd April 1979 (Court of Appeal: Lord Widgery CJ, Melford Stevenson and Michael Davis JJ).

2397   *1. Kidnapping   2. Burglary   3. Taking a conveyance without authority   4. Aggravated burglary (2).   5. Shortening shotgun   6. Trespassing with a firearm   7. False imprisonment*
Sentence: 1, 2 and 7: life imprisonment; 3, 4 and 5: five years in all concurrent. Man aged 38. Very bad criminal record with long history of criminal offences going back before he was 21. In his adult life had been sentenced to between 17 and 18 years' imprisonment. Went to Borstal 3 times. Most of offences for burglary

and similar crimes—last sentence 1973 for robbery with a shotgun—robbed a lady in her home at gunpoint. Sentenced to five years' imprisonment. Released on parole 1976. Present offences committed within 2 days in October 1977. Broke into house of acquaintance and stole a shotgun and cartridges. Then kidnapped B at gunpoint, forced B to drive him in B's car and then forced B out of the car. A massive police hunt ensued. He changed to another car, went to an unoccupied cottage and sawed off a double-barrelled shotgun and stole property worth £480. Then went to house of a nurse and her patient, threatened her with a gun, she telephoned the police—he escaped. He then went to farmhouse and threatened occupier. The occupier's family arrived and he forced the occupiers' grandson, aged 18, at gunpoint to drive him in a Land Rover past a police check point. A police chase ensued and he was eventually overcome. Psychiatrist of opinion that the appellant suffered from severe character neurosis but not serious enough to warrant a s. 60 Mental Health Act 1959 order. No prognosis possible. Sentenced as above as very dangerous man against whom the public had to be protected. Said to have deprived background. On appeal a fixed term of imprisonment was asked for. *Held*, that having regard to the uncertain prognosis it was the classic case for the imposition of a life sentence of imprisonment. It was a merciful sentence, for if the court were to substitute a fixed term of imprisonment it would have undoubtedly been a very, very long sentence indeed. *R v Herpels*, 1st February 1979 (Court of Appeal: Lord Widgery CJ, Bridge LJ and Caulfield J).

2398   *Neglect of child*
Sentence: 18 months' imprisonment. Single woman, aged 27, with 2 children, one born in 1972 and the other born in 1976. In September 1977 appellant left her parents' home and took the two children to live with her lover. From September 1977 to February 1978 the lover persistently ill treated the younger child then aged between 18 and 23 months of age. Appellant saw that child trembled at lover's approach. Final episode occurred one night when child was seen vomiting; child died early the following day. Post mortem examination revealed 86 bruises. Cause of death was a kick by the lover to the child's abdomen, rupturing her internal organs. Lover was convicted of murder and appellant of wilful neglect. She was sentenced as above. Trial judge was of the opinion that appellant did not intefere on the child's behalf because she had wilfully blinded herself to the situation. On appeal, *held*, it was appellant's duty to protect child, but facts showed serious and manifest cruelty and a custodial sentence was rightly imposed. Its length was for the discretion of the trial judge and the sentence imposed was neither too harsh nor too severe. *R v Green*, 19th December 1978 (Court of Appeal: Waller and Cumming-Bruce LJJ and Jupp J).

OFFENCES AGAINST PROPERTY

2399   *Robbery; possession of imitation firearm*
Sentence: 7 years' imprisonment (first offence); 2 years' imprisonment concurrent (second offence). Man, aged 24. Employed as electrician at teaching hospital. One previous conviction of possessing an offensive weapon for which he had been fined £10. Planned a wages robbery on his employers. Put on a mask and armed himself with an imitation ·38 firearm and a container of hydrochloric acid. Hid himself in a cupboard of the wages office on a day when he knew £35,000 was to be delivered to pay hospital staff. Jumped out on a security man, squirting some acid at him. Ordered three other employees to do as he told them, and hid the money and firearm in the motor room. Went back to his work as if nothing had happened. When the money and firearm were discovered appellant pleaded guilty to both offences and was sentenced to 10 years' imprisonment for the robbery and 2 years' imprisonment consecutive for the possession of the imitation firearm. On appeal, *held*, although it was a carefully premeditated offence the sentence imposed was that usually given to professional robbers. The imitation firearm was part of the robbery and a concurrent sentence should have been imposed. The serious aspect of the case was the use of hydrochloric acid. The sentence imposed was excessive and would be varied as set out above. *R v Barker*, 9th November 1978 (Court of Appeal: Lord Widgery CJ, Bridge LJ and Wien J).

2400 *Robbery*

Sentence: 3 years' imprisonment. Man, aged 20, with four previous convictions for dishonesty for which he was fined. An elderly man of 68 had gone to a van after collecting wages from the bank for his employers. When sitting in the driving seat of the van, he was attacked, kicked and punched by the appellant and co-accused. The wages bag was snatched from the victim who suffered shock and was taken to hospital. The police found the appellant hiding in a ditch. He told them where the stolen money was and it was recovered. He made a statement admitting the offence and told them that the information leading to the commission of the offence had been given by a girl who had received a suspended sentence of 12 months' imprisonment. The appellant maintained that he had not kicked the victim but had merely grabbed him by the collar in an attempt to separate him from his wages bag. The appellant and co-accused both got 5 years' imprisonment. On appeal, it was contended that although a prison sentence was inevitable, the sentence imposed was too great for one who had no previous custodial sentence. *Held*, as the co-accused was the older man with the worse record and was in fact more involved in the offence, the appellant's sentence would be varied to 3 years' imprisonment. *R v Owens*, 2nd March 1979 (Court of Appeal: Shaw LJ, Smith and Mustill JJ).

2401 Sentence: $2\frac{1}{2}$ years' imprisonment. Man, aged 31. Number of previous convictions but had not served a prison sentence since 1971. Lived in the same building as the co-accused, a violent man who had a previous conviction for robbery in 1975. A prostitute, known to the co-accused, took a sailor to the co-accused's room. The co-accused and appellant then went to the room and the former threatened the sailor with a knife. They took from him his watch, ring and some money. The appellant played a minor part in the episode. At their trial, the appellant was sentenced to 6 years' imprisonment, the co-accused pleaded not guilty but was subsequently sentenced by a different judge to 4 years' imprisonment. On appeal, *held*, the 6 year sentence was excessive taking into consideration the parts played by both men and the fact that the appellant may have been in some fear of the co-accused. Accordingly, the sentence would be varied to $2\frac{1}{2}$ years' imprisonment. *R v Gillard*, 12th July 1979 (Court of Appeal: Lord Widgery CJ, Shaw LJ and McNeill J).

2402 *1. Robbery. 2. Taking a conveyance without authority*

Sentence: 1. Twelve months' imprisonment. 2. Fifteen months' disqualification from driving. Man of previous good character. Managed a bakery, invited by a friend to rob the bakery company's safe. Took a car for the purpose of robbery. Sentenced to 12 months' imprisonment for robbery and two years disqualification for taking a vehicle without authority. Appeal against disqualification on grounds that he did not drive the car, had not been previously convicted of a similar sort of offence and was not invited to commit the offence because of any driving skill or experience on his part. *Held*, there was nothing wrong in principle with the sentence of disqualification, especially as the term of imprisonment was short. There was evidence however that the appellant might have difficulty finding employment on his release and for that reason the period of disqualification would be reduced. *R v Mulroy* [1979] RTR 214 (Court of Appeal: Browne LJ, Lawson and Phillips JJ).

2403 *Conspiracy to rob*

Sentence: 3 years' imprisonment. Youth, aged 16 at time of offence. Lived with parents. Salesman at time of arrest. Previous good character. Offences took place between autumn 1976 and summer 1977. Appellant and seven other youths aged between 17 and 19 went to a public lavatory, a well known meeting place for homosexuals, with the express intention of assaulting homosexuals. The victims would be robbed not only of money but also of articles such as cheque books or cheque cards. On one occasion a victim had his glasses broken and his shoes removed; another had his hearing aid removed and a third suffered a fractured rib. The gang was arrested when an innocent heterosexual member of the public was assaulted and robbed in the lavatory, and informed the police. Appellant admitted being with the gang, all of whom pleaded guilty, on five occasions of assaulting homosexuals. Sentenced as above. Since being in prison had done extremely well and hoped to move into full time education to obtain RSA and GCE 'O' level qualifications. On appeal, *held*, although a 3 year sentence was a long one for a young boy, his changed attitude since going to prison showed that the judge had passed the right sentence. It would be wrong to substitute a borstal sentence. *R v Oke*, 21st November 1978 (Court of Appeal: Roskill LJ, Lawson and Neill JJ).

2404   *Burglary*

Sentence: 18 months' imprisonment concurrent. Married man, aged 27, with 2 children. No previous convictions. Started business of his own in 1972 and made substantial profits. The burglaries were committed after the business came to an end in 1977. Offences took place between July and October 1977. Broke into store shed and stole a hammer drill worth £150. Two nights later he broke into another store shed and stole central heating equipment of considerable value. He later returned to the same building site and stole further items of hardware. The value of the property stolen in these three burglaries was between £2,250 and £3,000. The ten cases taken into consideration were similar type burglaries involving £3,500 worth of property. Many of the goods stolen were passed on to two co-defendants for money. Social inquiry report suggested a suspended sentence with a compensation order. Sentenced as above. On appeal *held*, a compensation order would be unrealistic. The prison service report was good and suggested that he would not offend again, but the sentence imposed was correct in principle and not excessive. *R v Hill*, 9th November 1978 (Court of Appeal: Orr LJ, Boreham and Stephen Brown JJ).

2405   Sentence: 30 months' imprisonment. Man, aged 45. Long list of convictions dating back to 1950. From 1963, his record included shopbreaking and larceny for which he was made subject to a Mental Health Act 1959, s. 60 order. In 1968, he received 4 years' imprisonment for burglary and stealing silverware. Released in 1971 and in 1972 he was put on probation for two years for burglary and larceny, but six months later for similar offences he received 4 years' imprisonment reduced to 2 years on appeal. From then until 1976 he kept out of trouble until the current offence which consisted of smashing the window of a West End store and stealing a silk carpet worth £2,500. He hid it 40 yards away and was arrested shortly after. Appellant was given an extended sentence of 5 years' imprisonment. On appeal, *held*, taking into account the appellants' offence and his background and criminal history, it was inappropriate to impose an extended sentence even though he was eligible for it. The sentence would be varied as set out above. *R v Cohen*, 23rd January 1979 (Court of Appeal: Browne LJ, Lawson and Phillips JJ).

2406   Sentence: 5 years' imprisonment concurrent. Single man, aged 57, unemployed. Left Merchant Navy in 1970 due to ill health. Said to have been unable to adjust to civilian life after 35 years at sea. Four convictions for dishonesty before 1946, then kept out of trouble until 1972 when sentenced to 2½ years imprisonment for 4 offences of deception. In September 1975, sentenced to 5 years' imprisonment for 8 offences of burglary and escaped from prison in April 1976 when serving that sentence. Current offences consisted of breaking into three separate houses. Two of the owners he knew to be stamp collectors and he stole stamps valued at £5,000 and £8,500 respectively. At the third burglary he was disturbed by the occupier but £2.29 was found stolen. The appellant escaped but a complete burglar's kit was found in nearby gardens. In December 1977, he attempted to sell some of the stamps and was arrested. About £1,500 was recovered. Sixteen cases were taken into consideration consisting of 4 burglaries (two involving theft of stamps), 11 cases of obtaining by deception (all cheque offences) and one attempted deception. Sentenced as above. On appeal against the severity of the sentence on grounds of mercy, *held*, the deliberation, cleverness and persistence in the commission of the offences made it necessary for the public to be protected from a man of such criminality. The sentence would stand. *R v Hardress-Lloyd*, 1st March 1979 (Court of Appeal: Lord Widgery CJ, Cumming-Bruce LJ and Neill J).

2407   Sentence: 2 years' imprisonment. Youth, aged 18. Eight findings of guilt and two previous convictions including several offences of burglary and others of dishonesty, criminal damage and driving offences. For the burglary offences sentenced to borstal training. The appellant was caught emerging from a clubhouse early one morning. The groundsman had heard footsteps and had summoned the police. £16.50 was found to be missing from a fruit machine. This sum was later recovered but a window which the appellant had damaged in forcing his way into the clubhouse cost £18 to repair. Sentenced as above. The offence was committed only 21 days after his release from borstal and a remand centre report stated that borstal training had nothing further to offer him. On appeal, *held*, having regard to his deplorable record, no further leniency was justified and the sentence imposed was correct. *R v Hostettler*, 27th September 1979 (Court of Appeal: Lawton LJ, Park and Peter Pain JJ).

2408   Sentence: supervision order (3 months served in borstal). Youth, aged 15. Fifty previous findings of guilt. Since 1975, constant appearances before juvenile court for serious offences of burglary, theft, arson etc. Had been given numerous conditional discharges, care and attendance centre orders and small fines all of which were ineffective. Five months before the present offences, sentenced to 3 months' detention for burglary. The present offences involved the appellant and other youths breaking into a store and stealing £5,000 worth of goods which were mostly recovered. He asked for 6 similar cases to be taken into consideration. Sentenced to borstal training. On appeal, *held*, in view of his having completed a sentence of detention and the undesirability of following one period of detention by another, the court would vary the sentence to a supervision order under a local probation officer. *R v O'Connor*, 26th October 1979 (Court of Appeal: Eveleigh LJ, Phillips and Michael Davies JJ).

2409   Sentence: orders under Mental Health Act 1959, ss. 60, 65 (detention in hospital without limit of time). Single man, aged 35, of no fixed abode. Five previous findings of guilt and 19 convictions mainly for offences of violence, dishonesty and criminal damage. Has been in and out of prison or borstal since the age of 15 and has a long history of mental illness. The appellant broke into a shop late one night and stole £4 in cash, a bar of chocolate, a bag of nuts and a can of soft drink (total value £5). On the following night he broke into a greengrocer's shop, took an apple and ate it. The police found him hiding in the shop. While it was acknowledged that he needed hospital treatment, no hospital was available at the date of the trial so the appellant was sentenced to concurrent terms of 5 years' imprisonment on the ground that he was a danger to the public. Pending the appeal he was transferred to a mental hospital. On appeal, *held*, the sentence would be varied, the term of imprisonment quashed and in its place ss. 60, and 65 hospital orders would be made. *R v Ledger*, 13th November 1979 (Court of Appeal: Donaldson LJ, Thompson and Bush JJ).

2410   Sentence: 3½ years' imprisonment concurrent. Divorced man, aged 30. Made subject of a Mental Health Act 1959, s. 60 order at the age of 16 when he was said to be suffering from certain abnormalities. At 19, convicted of robbery and housebreaking and again made subject of a s. 60 order and s. 65 restriction order. Went into a mental hospital and was conditionally discharged in 1973. Now considered to be of average intelligence. Living with girlfriend and their child. In 1977, convicted twice of burglary, given a suspended sentence for the first offence but on conviction of the second offence received a total sentence of 21 months' imprisonment. He committed the current offences shortly after his release from prison. The main offence involved burgling a house and stealing property worth £268. The nine offences taken into consideration were also burglaries, committed over a ten day period. The goods stolen were valued at £435 and were all from dwelling houses. Sentenced as above. While waiting to appeal against the sentence, the appellant escaped from prison and committed another burglary for which he received 6 months' imprisonment concurrent to the present sentence. On appeal, *held*, a favourable probation officer's report could not be considered in view of the appellant's activities since conviction and accordingly, the imposed sentence would stand. *R v Sturman*, 29th November 1979 (Court of Appeal: Waller LJ, Thompson and Bush JJ).

2411   *Burglary; theft*

Sentence: 12 months' and 3 months' imprisonment consecutive (15 months' imprisonment in all). Man, aged 32. Long history of dishonesty and previous imprisonments for theft and burglary. He broke into a flat, forced open the electricity meter and stole £10 in cash and a radio cassette recorder and two cassettes valued at £50. He then ran downstairs, was arrested and granted bail. Absconded from bail and was not recaptured until a year later. He met an American sailor who wanted to change a $20 bill, the appellant offered to change it for him but the sailor said they would go together to change the money. The appellant then snatched the note from the sailor and ran off. He spent the money obtained from it on drink. He later met up with the sailor and two others who beat him up. Sentenced to 12 months' imprisonment consecutive for each offence, 2 years in all. On appeal *held*, the sentence imposed for the burglary was lenient and there could be no complaint about it. The theft sentence however was a little excessive and would be varied to 3 months' imprisonment to run consecutively to the burglary sentence (15 months' imprisonment in all). *R v Perry (alias Wearn)*, 5th June 1979 (Court of Appeal: Lawton LJ, Wien and Eastham JJ).

2412   *Aggravated burglary*

Sentence: orders under Mental Health Act 1959, ss. 60, 65. Man, aged 40. Paranoid schizophrenic with long history of mental illness, but no previous history of violence. He wandered around housing estates, stealing ladies' underwear from clothes lines. After seeing two women he was overcome with a feeling of injuring women. He entered a house and saw a girl, aged 12, in bed. He hit her on the head with a bottle, but did not cause serious injury. He was later arrested and sentenced to life imprisonment. Trial judge was originally of the opinion that s. 60 and s. 65 mental health orders were appropriate, but no suitably secure hospital was available. On appeal, *held*, medical reports since the trial suggested that appellant's admission to Broadmoor or a similar hospital was not necessary. As a suitably secure hospital had been found and the risk of his committing a similar offence was sufficiently small to justify his detention in such a hospital ss. 60, 65 orders would be substituted, with no limitation of time. *R v Bromley*, 7th November 1978 (Court of Appeal: Browne LJ, Phillips and Michael Davies JJ).

2413   *Theft*

Sentence: 15 months' imprisonment. Married man, aged 39, with 2 children. No previous convictions. Worked as a delivery driver. Between January 1975 and December 1976 he stole a bath, basin, bidet, toilet set and quantity of gold fittings valued at £1,300 belonging to his employers. He sold those items for £930. The police interviewed him in June 1977 when he first denied the theft but then confessed and asked for four similar cases to be taken into consideration—two pairs of two offences of theft of bathroom equipment, valued at £900 in each case. He had sold that property. Probation officer's report before the court took the view that he was unlikely to offend again. The company's managing director thought the offence was out of character and appellant's employer at time of trial said appellant was a good worker and was in position of trust. Sentenced as above. On appeal submitted that suspended sentence would have been more appropriate, *held*, the offences were deliberate and had involved planning. Sentence imposed was the proper one for such serious offences. *R v Broadrib*, 9th November 1978 (Court of Appeal: Orr LJ, Boreham and Stephen Brown JJ).

2414   Sentence: immediate release (6½ months' imprisonment served). Married man, aged 53. Good record. Employed as a station warden by RAF for 22 years. A storeman at the RAF station disliked banks and kept £3,000 in cash in his locker. The money disappeared and was discovered to have been stolen. Appellant was seen acting suspiciously. Interviewed by police. Appellant denied stealing money but later confessed having shown police where it was hidden in his house. Further investigations revealed that appellant had, at various times, taken articles belonging to RAF and hidden them in his home, but had not used them. As a result of committing offences appellant lost his pension. Medical reports revealed appellant suffered from anxiety and depression over a period of years. Sentenced to 18 months' imprisonment concurrent. On appeal, *held*, as appellant had served period of imprisonment and it was unlikely he would offend again, and with regard to the fact he had lost his pension, sentence would be varied to immediate release. *R v Whelan*, 16th November 1978 (Court of Appeal: Ormrod and Shaw LJJ and Mais J).

2415   Sentence: 3 years' imprisonment. Married man, aged 39 with four teenage sons. An insurance agent of previous good character. In 1977, when treasurer of a football thrift club, he helped himself to £11,900 of the club's money thereby reducing the balance to £1,400. He then took the rest of the balance, left part of it with his family and went to London where he claimed he threw £1,000 into the river and spent the remainder. Said he had spent the money paying bills and on drink and gambling. In sentencing the appellant to four years' imprisonment the judge held that he had deprived the club members of substantial sums of money which they had invested every week for the Christmas draw. On appeal, *held*, while it was a very serious offence committed by a man in breach of trust, in view of the appellant's special family circumstances, his wife had just undergone a serious operation and there were the four boys to look after, the sentence would be varied as set out above. *R v Sumners*, 15th January 1979 (Court of Appeal: Lawton LJ, Cantley and Willis JJ).

2416   Sentence: 6 months' imprisonment concurrent. Married woman, aged 47, living with second husband and two grown-up daughters. Has had psychiatric problems for the last 20 years and had been in a mental home 20 years ago. Since 1973, employed as a cashier at a frozen food centre and appointed to head cashier in 1977. Her duties included controlling and operating three tills and cashing up other tills. In June 1978, large discrepancies were found, appellant admitted to stealing £6,000 but the sum was in fact about £1,800. The appellant was sentenced as above. On appeal that the trial judge should have seen her psychiatric report which also showed that she had been in a mental hospital in 1971, *held*, the short term of imprisonment imposed was not only justified but had been beneficial to the appellant. Even if the trial judge had seen the psychiatric report it would have proved no basis for a probation order on terms that she underwent treatment. The appeal would be dismissed. *R v Woodley*, 16th January 1979 (Court of Appeal: Lawton LJ, Cantley and Willis JJ).

2417   Sentence: 3 months' imprisonment; £100 prosecution costs. Married man, aged 43, with one son. No previous convictions. Employed as a driver for a firm of caterers at London Airport. He and the co-accused went to collect foodstuff from an aircraft which had just landed. The appellant took a basket of fruit from the aircraft and put it in his lorry. The co-accused broke the seals of three barred boxes containing dutiable goods. From one, he took a package of ten miniature bottles of gin and placed it in the fruit basket on the lorry. The appellant was present and watching all the time. Both men were later questioned by customs officers about the broken seals and after denials they made statements. The co-accused confessed and later pleaded guilty but the appellant was convicted. The value of the gin stolen was £5. The appellant was sentenced as above and the co-accused received a suspended 2 year sentence with £50 prosecution costs. On appeal against disparity and on grounds of previous good character, *held*, the appellant was acting in the course of his duty and held a position of trust. The judge had taken all mitigating factors into consideration and the distinction between the two men's sentences was well justified. *R v Hollyman*, 6th August 1979 (Court of Appeal: Roskill LJ, Thompson and Gibson JJ).

2418   Sentence: probation for 3 years. Single girl, aged 18, from respectable family. Obtained work as a petrol pump attendant at a garage. During the following 4 months she stole sums of money amounting to £400 and car accessories worth £217 from the garage. She passed the accessories on to various friends who were convicted of handling stolen goods. Sentenced to borstal training and sent to a remand centre where she was let out on bail. On appeal, *held*, borstal training was not necessarily as effective for girls as it was for boys; as the appellant had no previous convictions the Court would vary the sentence as set out above. In view of the appellant's persistent thefts, a longish period of close supervision under a probation officer would be a better way of dealing with her. *R v Corbett*, 9th October 1979 (Court of Appeal: Lawton LJ, Tudor Evans and McNeill JJ).

2419   *Theft; burglary*
Sentence: immediate release (9 months' imprisonment served). Married man, aged 33, with 4 children. Worked for components firm. Two spent convictions as a juvenile. Three offences of theft consisted of stealing considerable quantities of scrap metal from his employers. Burglary consisted of breaking into a factory and stealing steel worth several thousand pounds. Sentenced to concurrent terms of 18 months' imprisonment. Since sentence letters etc. before the court suggested appellant had good qualities and was led to commit the offences by economic pressures. On appeal, *held*, although the 18 month sentence was fully merited the court would, in mercy, vary it as set out above to give appellant an opportunity of redeeming himself by hard work to support his family. *R v O'Neill*, 21st November 1978 (Court of Appeal: Roskill LJ, Lawson and Neill JJ).

2420   *Theft; criminal damage*
Sentence: 12 months' imprisonment concurrent. Man aged 27. Numerous previous convictions since 1970, most spent. Since 1974, numerous convictions involving drink and being drunk and disorderly. In 1977, received 12 months' imprisonment for criminal damage and breach of a suspended sentence. Described as a thorough nuisance to the public. Appellant burgled an army canteen and stole chewing gum and biscuits to the value of £4·40 which were later recovered. A gaming machine had been damaged. Sentenced as above. On appeal, *held*, the sentence would stand because if it was reduced the appellant would think that his offences were of minor importance and he would have no motive for curbing his drinking habits. *R v Dale*, 6th February 1979 (Court of Appeal: Geoffrey Lane LJ, Lawson and Wien JJ).

2421   *Theft; false accounting*
Sentence: 2 years' imprisonment concurrent. Married man, aged 49, with three children. Born in Portugal. No previous convictions. In catering trade for most of his life. Catering manager of Wembley Stadium from 1974 to 1977. During that time his initial salary of £3,500 rose to £5,000 a year. In March 1975, he found himself in financial difficulties which worsened until he left for other employment in December 1977. The first theft was £300 from the office safe. In May 1975, he stole a further £300 and in August his household and gambling commitments led him to steal £1,200. From then until December 1977 he made periodic raids on the office safe totalling £10,604. The three counts of false accounting related to cheques received by the appellant in middle to late 1977 and banked by him but not recorded in the Stadium cash book. The cheques were for the sums £2,515, £3,216 and £2,308. The appellant made a full confession of the offences to the police. In sentencing him to 3½ years' imprisonment concurrent on each count, the judge said that a position of high personal responsibility had been abused and a number of breaches of trust had been committed over a period of time. On appeal, *held*, although the total amount was large and the appellant was

grossly in breach of trust over a period of time of two years or more, there were strong mitigating factors such as his previous good character and working record. He had also made a full confession and pleaded guilty and had returned to England to stand trial after having taken up an appointment in Algeria. Imprisonment of 3½ years was therefore too much and would be varied as set out above. *R v Ferrinho*, 2nd March 1979 (Court of Appeal: Lawton LJ, Thompson and Hodgson JJ).

2422 *Theft (shoplifting)*

Sentence: 6 months' imprisonment. Married woman, aged 29, with two small children. Separated from husband. A semi-trained nurse with a complicated life-history. Married a policeman who left her on birth of her second child. Since 1969, four convictions for dishonesty and one for posing as a State registered nurse for which she was fined, put on probation and conditionally discharged. Committed two offences of shoplifting in 1978, four months after last offence, she went into a supermarket, loaded a trolley with groceries valued at about £30 and wheeled it out without paying for the goods. When questioned by a security officer, she claimed that she had paid £15 for them but later admitted to stealing the goods. Sentenced as above. On appeal, *held*, the time had come to impress upon the appellant that the consequences of continued shoplifting were very serious. The imposed sentence would stand. *R v Power*, 10th July 1979 (Court of Appeal: Geoffrey Lane LJ, Swanwick and Waterhouse JJ).

2423 Sentence: 2 years' imprisonment. Woman, aged 39, unemployed. Seventeen previous convictions mostly for shoplifting from 1972 onwards. Sent to prison for terms of up to 30 months. Was on probation on condition she undertook psychiatric treatment. The appellant stole 19 records from a record shop and was later seen in a nearby churchyard removing the wrappers and price tags by two plain-clothes police officers. In a written statement, she admitted to having taken the records. Sentenced as above. The trial judge remarked that the leniency shown to her in the past had been misplaced as she needed to realise that stealing was a serious offence which could attract a considerable sentence of imprisonment. She appealed. Psychiatric reports before the court suggested a personality disorder but stated that the appellant's behaviour was not compulsive or due to any psychiatric illness. *Held*, it was impossible to say that 2 years' imprisonment was excessive or wrong in principle as the appellant could voluntarily seek psychiatric treatment if she needed it. *R v Grodinski*, 16th October 1979 (Court of Appeal: Bridge LJ, Forbes and Sheldon JJ).

2424 *Theft; uttering a forged document; demanding money on a forged instrument*

Sentence: immediate release (2 months' imprisonment served). Woman, aged 37. Separated from husband but living with a man and her 10 year old son in a council house. On social security. One previous conviction in 1974 for theft of two pension books and six offences of obtaining by deception (110 other offences taken into consideration). All current offences related to a giro cheque, a social security fraud which was very common and difficult to detect. The giro in question belonged to her husband who reported to the authorities that he had not received it. The appellant cashed the cheque. After initially denying the charge, she admitted to it and to other similar offences on a previous occasion. Sentenced to concurrent terms of 4 months' imprisonment. On appeal, *held*, such social security frauds were hard to detect and had to be punished. However, as the appellant was living with a respectable man who was looking after her child, the sentence would be reduced to allow her immediate release. The court warned that if she continued to offend she would receive a very long sentence. *R v Davies*, 20th July 1979 (Court of Appeal: Roskill LJ, Mars-Jones and Drake JJ).

2425 *Theft; uttering a false document; furnishing false information.*

Sentence: 6 months', 4 years' and 3 years' imprisonment concurrent. (Twenty-nine similar offences taken into account.) Married man aged 55. No previous convictions. Senior partner in firm of solicitors used clients' money to bolster-up his own failing business speculations over a period of three years. Total amount of money involved was £260,000. When discovered he co-operated fully with the police and Law Society. Struck off solicitors' roll and made bankrupt. Sentenced as above. On appeal, contended that as he had pleaded guilty and co-operated with police etc. his personal circumstances should be taken into account. His wife was mentally unstable and there was a real danger of her committing suicide as long as her husband was in prison. *Held*, retributive and deterrent elements very strong in sentencing in a case of this kind. Breach of trust by a solicitor was a very grave offence. Hardship to family was not a matter which the court could take into consideration. Appeal dismissed. R v DAVIES (1978) 67 Cr App Rep 207 (Court of Appeal: Lawton LJ, Mars-Jones and Gibson JJ).

2426 *Attempted theft; breach of suspended sentence*
Sentence: 18 months' imprisonment (first offence); 6 months' imprisonment concurrent (second offence). Youth, aged 18. Long history of convictions for theft and burglary with numerous other offences taken into consideration. In February 1978 he received a suspended sentence of 6 months' imprisonment for burglary and theft from an infant school. Four days later he was convicted of a similar offence and given a deferred sentence. Current offence of attempted theft committed in June 1978 when two police officers saw appellant board a bus and try to remove a purse from a lady's bag. He was arrested after a short chase. Sentenced to 12 months' imprisonment for that offence and the deferred sentence of 6 months' imprisonment was activated to run consecutively (18 months in all). On appeal, *held*, in view of s. 3 of the Criminal Justice Act 1961 the 12 months' sentence could not have added to it an activated sentence of 6 months to provide an 18 months sentence. This was permissible only where a defendant had already served a borstal sentence. Accordingly the court would vary the sentence to one of 18 months' imprisonment and order that the suspended sentence run concurrently, making 18 months' imprisonment in all. *R v Halse* [1971] 3 All ER 1149 applied. *R v McCalla*, 21st November 1978 (Court of Appeal: Roskill LJ, Lawson and Neill JJ).

2427 *Handling stolen goods*
Sentence: 6 months' imprisonment suspended for 2 years. Single woman, aged 33, with one child. Good education and stable upbringing, GPO trained telephonist. No previous convictions. Unemployed for three years prior to arrest. Had been living for several years with a man with a substantial criminal record, who stole property from air terminals, stations and cars. The stolen property was largely luggage but in one case included £3,000 worth of equipment. When the appellant was interviewed by police, about eight stolen suitcases were found in her house. She admitted to having handled them knowing them to have been stolen. Sentenced to 18 months' imprisonment concurrent suspended for 2 years. On appeal, *held*, while it was right to impose a sentence of imprisonment and then suspend it, the imposed sentence should be appropriate to the offence committed. In the present case it would be varied to 6 months and for deterrent effect be suspended for 2 years. *R v Monk*, 8th August 1979 (Court of Appeal: Roskill LJ, Thompson and Gibson JJ).

2428 Sentence: 3 years' imprisonment concurrent. Married man, aged 31. Eleven previous convictions for dishonesty for which he received terms of imprisonment. He had not been in trouble since his marriage in 1975. Owner of a second-hand shop. The appellant told the police that a man was trying to sell him a second hand radio. The police searched the appellant's premises and recovered about 500 items worth approximately £1000. Sentenced to 4 years' imprisonment for "gross dishonesty", the 14 separate offences having been committed between 1977 and 1978. On appeal, *held*, the sentence imposed was too high and would be varied to that set out above. *R v Watts*, 5th November 1979 (Court of Appeal: Lord Widgery CJ, Wien and Watkins JJ).

2429 Sentence: 3 months' imprisonment concurrent. Married man, aged 29, with children. One previous conviction in 1977 for theft of a licence disc for which he was fined. Ran an unsuccessful second-hand business. A house was burgled and the missing items included a cassette recorder valued at £35, a heated hair roller set valued at £22 and a watch valued at £21. The missing items were found in the appellant's shop. He admitted that a schoolboy had brought the articles to his shop on three separate occasions and also admitted that he had had an idea that they were stolen but had bought them because his business was doing badly. He confessed that he did not normally buy anything from young boys, that he had never done so before and would be more careful in the future. Sentenced to 6 months' imprisonment on the first count and to 9 months' imprisonment concurrent on the second and third counts (9 months' imprisonment in all). On appeal, *held*, while an immediate sentence of imprisonment was required to show disapproval of second-hand dealers who acquired goods from juvenile thieves, the sentence imposed was too long and would be varied to 3 months' imprisonment concurrent on each count. *R v Dilworth*, 29th November 1979 (Court of Appeal: Waller LJ, Thompson and Bush JJ).

2430   *Receiving stolen goods*
Sentence: 12 months' imprisonment. Single man, aged 33, living with widowed mother. Various jobs, a publicity agent at time of arrest. Two previous convictions for handling stolen goods for which he was fined. The two co-accused followed a public house manager who was carrying £2,000 in three canvas bags to the bank. One of the men snatched two of the bags containing £1,600 and they then jumped into a getaway car and drove off. Half a mile further on they deposited the bags in a second car driven by the appellant. The appellant was arrested ten minutes after the robbery and the two bags were found in his car. He gave the police sufficient information to arrest one of the co-accused. The appellant then made a full statement about the incident and pleaded guilty. The first co-accused who had pleaded guilty received 3½ years' imprisonment, the second who, after his subsequent arrest, had pleaded not guilty was acquitted. The appellant was sentenced as above. On appeal on grounds of his minimal involvement, his assistance to the police and his plea of guilt, *held*, the trial judge had given sufficient consideration to the mitigating factors, as the appellant had received the proceeds of the robbery and had knowingly helped in the offence, the sentence imposed was a lenient one. *R v Wiggins*, 6th August 1979 (Court of Appeal: Roskill LJ, Thompson and Gibson JJ).

2431   *Making false statements to defraud the Inland Revenue*
Sentence: 3 months' imprisonment concurrent. Divorced man, aged 49, with one son. Two findings of guilt and two convictions, all spent. Worked in building trade for last 20 years. When working as a roofing contractor he succeeded in misleading his accountants and, through them, the Inland Revenue, by paying considerable amounts of his profits into a bank account, the existence of which he kept hidden. From 1962 to 1964 he failed to declare the amount of money on which he should have paid tax. In 1965 the Inland Revenue received a tip-off as a result of which investigating officers interviewed appellant on three occasions. He maintained that he had submitted the correct accounts. It later appeared that the Revenue had been deprived of £1,612 tax. Appellant disappeared and went on the run for 13 years. Formed a friendship with a woman who had some connection with the Inland Revenue, and the investigators then caught up with him. He repaid all he owed before his trial. Sentenced to 9 months' imprisonment concurrent. On appeal, *held*, appellant had been punished enough and his sentence would be reduced as set out above. *R v Francis*, 19th December 1978 (Court of Appeal: Geoffrey Lane LJ, Ackner and Watkins JJ).

2432   *Obtaining pecuniary advantage by deception*
Sentence: immediate release (4½ months imprisonment served). Married man, aged 57, with 4 children. No previous convictions. Petty officer in second World War. A hard worker, and had run a café for 25 years. In 1973, the café was compulsorily purchased. As the appellant received less compensation money than he had expected, he was unable to set up his café again. He was unemployed until

1977 when he went into the road haulage business with the co-accused, a long distance lorry driver. They bought a lorry worth £7,000 with a bank loan and traded as a transport company with the co-accused as the driver. The lorry was insured, but not when it was abroad. It broke down in Italy where it was too expensive to have it repaired. The appellant and co-accused decided to make a false insurance claim stating that the lorry had been stolen in England. The co-accused cut the chain of the yard where the lorry had previously been kept and reported the lorry as stolen to the police. He then made a claim on the insurance company in respect of the supposed theft. Later, he telephoned the insurers and told them the lorry had been found in Italy. The insurers eventually recovered the lorry at the cost of £983. The appellant and co-accused confessed to attempting to obtain the insurance money by deception and were sentenced to 12 months' imprisonment. On appeal that the case was not one for immediate imprisonment under the Powers of Criminal Courts Act 1973, s. 20 (1), *held*, a sentence of immediate imprisonment was clearly right in the circumstances of the case; however, in view of the appellant's previous excellent character, his age and favourable social inquiry reports, the court would vary the appellant's sentence to permit his immediate release. *R v O'Reilly*, 26th March 1979 (Court of Appeal: Browne LJ, Gibson and Drake JJ).

2433   Sentence: £1,000 fine on each of 3 counts; 9 months' imprisonment suspended 2 years. Compensation order quashed. Married man, aged 47 with seven children. Born in Kashmir but has lived in England for 20 years. Since 1974, employed in an iron foundry earning £60 a week. Also earning undisclosed sums from two laundrettes and from a number of houses belonging to him and his wife which were tenanted. Previous convictions, none relevant. In 1975, he applied to the local council for four improvement grants under the Housing Act 1974, s. 74 (1). Each of the four applications was accompanied by a certificate of owner occupation. The appellant received the grants from the local council but he and his family only lived in one of the properties. The applications were made in the names of three of his sons and his own name. The council made grants totalling £5,111.25. Sentenced as above plus a compensation order for the latter mentioned sum. On appeal that the compensation order should not be made, *held*, it was wrong to make a compensation order without an application for it by the local council. Only the latter had the right to reclaim the money, for compensation orders were a summary remedy and were not to be made if there were any complications about the case. The fines would stand. *R v Shan (Ali)*, 2nd April 1979. (Court of Appeal: Browne LJ, Gibson and Drake JJ.)

2434   *Obtaining pecuniary advantage by deception (counts 3 and 14); theft (counts 6, 9, 11, 15, 16); obtaining property by deception (counts 12 and 17); taking a conveyance without authority (count 10)*

Sentence: (1) Six months' imprisonment on counts 3, 6 and 9 consecutive; (2) Six months' imprisonment on counts 10, 11 and 12 concurrent but consecutive to (1); (3) Six months' imprisonment consecutive on count 14 and 6 months' concurrent on counts 15 to 17 but consecutive to the other sentences making 3 years' imprisonment in all. Man aged 61, divorced. When arrested, a self employed photographer. Previous convictions from 1949 to 1967 which included larceny as a bailee (probation order) and four offences of obtaining money by deception (corrective training and up to 7 years' preventive detention). No offences since 1967 until the present offences which took place between 1974 and 1978. They consisted of: acquiring a car under a false name and running up bills totalling £154 (count 3); stealing photographic equipment worth £200 (count 6); stealing a camera worth £15 under a false name (count 9); obtaining £2,650 in loans and bills from his landlady, borrowing her car without permission and stealing £15 worth of tools from it (counts 10 and 11); pledging the said tools for £5 (count 12); obtaining evasion of a debt of £550 by false representation (count 14); stealing cameras and lenses worth £595 and selling part of the equipment for £120 to a secondhand dealer (counts 15 to 17). The appellant was arrested and made a statement.

Sentenced to 6 months' consecutive imprisonment on each count (5 years in all). On appeal that overall sentence excessive, *held*, the sentences were excessive. The offences fell into three groups (1) counts 10, 11, 12, (2) counts 15, 16, 17, (3) counts 3, 6, 9, 14. The sentences would be varied as set out above bearing in mind that the appellant, after a serious record of dishonesty, had not been in prison since 1967. *R v Heritage*, 27th April 1979 (Court of Appeal: Bridge LJ, Chapman and Lawson JJ).

2435   *Obtaining property by deception; bankrupt obtaining credit*

Sentence: 12 months' imprisonment concurrent. Man, aged 36, married with family. Self employed builder with no relevant previous convictions. He told a friend that he would obtain a billiard table for him receiving the friend's table in part exchange. The friend never got the table but paid a further £50 towards its price. The appellant then induced another friend to lend him £400, telling him that if the money could be borrowed for three weeks to buy the table involved in the first deception, he would be given £100 of the profit. The second friend received neither the £400 nor the £100. At the time of the offences the appellant was an undischarged bankrupt. Sentenced to 2 years' imprisonment concurrent on the deception counts and 18 months concurrent on the bankruptcy charges. On appeal, *held*, in view of the appellant's previous good character, the sentence imposed was too long and would be varied as set out above. *R v Maplesdon*, 6th August 1979 (Court of Appeal: Roskill LJ, Thompson and Gibson JJ).

2436   *Obtaining property by deception (9); forgery (8)*

Sentence: 3 years' imprisonment for the first offence and 2 counts of the second offence, 2 years' imprisonment concurrent on remaining counts of the second offence (3 years' in all). Married man, aged 53, of previous good character. Employed as a clerk with a firm of underwriters and insurance brokers in London. His wife inherited a house in Derbyshire and moved there and the appellant subsequently joined her. As a result he had to spend £1,200 a year on rail fares to London, a figure totally disproportionate to his salary. Between 1974 and 1977 he appropriated approximately £6,000 from his employers by fraudulently obtaining signatures for small cheques in respect of supposedly overpaid premiums, by forging benefit claims and supporting documents and paying himself the amounts of the claims and by forging the signatures of authorised signatories. He left the company before his deceptions were discovered. Sentenced to 4 years' imprisonment on the first 9 counts and on 2 of the forgery counts and to concurrent terms of 2 years' imprisonment on the other counts. On appeal, *held*, in view of the appellant's previous good character and unblemished record, the court would vary the sentences as set out as above. *R v Parker*, 13th November 1979 (Court of Appeal: Donaldson LJ, Thompson and Bush JJ).

2437   *Obtaining property by deception; theft*

Sentence: 12 months' imprisonment concurrent. Married man, aged 34, with a son aged 2½ who is a haemophiliac. Joined a bank after leaving school and rose from position of bank clerk to note dealer. On arrest, a sales representative with a business firm. No previous convictions. The theft offences took place when he was working as a foreign note dealer in the bank. Between September 1977 and August 1978 he made about £2000 for himself by entering into deals with the chief cashier of a travel agent firm. The arrangement was to generate a surplus of foreign currency which they stole and divided between themselves. The deception charges involved various transactions in which the appellant exchanged money in his possession at a rate of exchange which enabled him to make a personal profit. To ensure that it worked he used false names on the documentation to show they were deals with bank customers in the normal course of business. On discovery, the appellant admitted guilt and in a statement described his method of operation in each transaction. He was dismissed from the bank. In sentencing him as above, the judge said that the offences were serious and had been committed over a long period of time. The fact that the appellant had pleaded guilty had been taken into account but the only appropriate sentence was imprisonment. On appeal on the ground that the offences were committed for the purpose of acquiring money to make life easier for his haemophiliac son, *held*, the offences were serious ones committed by a trusted bank employee and the sentence imposed showed the maximum amount of mercy. *R v Templeman*, 11th August 1979 (Court of Appeal: Roskill LJ, Thompson and Gibson JJ).

2438   *Conspiracy to defraud*

Sentence: 5 years' imprisonment concurrent to sentences being served. Single man, aged 19, living with parents. No regular employment since leaving school. Twelve previous court appearances mainly for burglary, theft, handling stolen goods and criminal damage for which he was fined, sent to detention centre and conditionally discharged. Between 1976 and 1977, with the three co-accused, the appellant obtained £27,400 from certain London Clearing Banks by presenting stolen cheques backed by stolen guarantee cards. The cheques and cards were stolen and had been purchased for between £5 and £7. The original signature on each cheque card was blanked out with solvents and the intended user substituted a signature in his own handwriting. They worked in pairs, moving from bank to bank. The appellant was arrested and while on bail received 2 years' imprisonment for similar offences committed prior to the instant one, where he had obtained £6,600 on 136 cheques. He also received 6 months' imprisonment for criminal damage. Sentenced to 6 years' imprisonment and all the sentences were ordered to run consecutively making 8½ years' imprisonment in all. None of the stolen money was recovered. In sentencing him the trial judge said that that type of crime threatened to destroy the whole structure of the bank card system and the particular offence was so sophisticated that neither age nor the circumstances could be taken into account. On appeal against severity of sentence, *held*, there was no doubt that the sentences imposed were entirely proper but in total 8½ years was too long for a nineteen-year old. The necessary deterrent sentence would be met by making the overall figure 5 years (the main sentence being reduced to 5 years and the others to take effect concurrently). *R v Hewitt*, 9th October 1979 (Court of Appeal: Bridge LJ, Forbes and Sheldon JJ).

2439   *False accounting; theft; obtaining property by deception*

Sentence: 30 months' imprisonment concurrent; compensation order for £10,287. Married man, aged 47, with 6 children. Employed as a bookkeeper-accountant with a company. Stole £200 from petty cash by making false entries in the cash books. On four occasions he stole company cheques signing his own name as "payee" and induced a company officer to sign cheques without filling in the payee's name. Total amount lost by the company was £10,287. The appellant paid back £4,300 to the company. The offences taken into consideration were of a similar nature. Sentenced to 5 years' imprisonment concurrent plus the above compensation order. On appeal, *held*, it was a mean fraud against his employers. However, for someone like the appellant who had a previous good character and a settled matrimonial background, imprisonment was a very grave penalty indeed. It would be best if he could come out of prison as soon as possible and pay off the balance of the money owed to the company. Accordingly, the sentence would be reduced to 30 months' imprisonment. *R v Karia*, 3rd July 1979 (Court of Appeal: Geoffrey Lane LJ, Swanwick and Waterhouse JJ).

2440   *Taking a motor vehicle without authority*

Sentence: probation for 2 years. Married man, aged 25, with three children. Minor previous offences. A good worker. Children in care from time to time and wife on probation for unspecified offences. He and two others took a car, the appellant started it up with a spare battery and the other two drove it off. The appellant admitted to the offence and was sentenced to 3 years' imprisonment and disqualified for 6 months. On appeal *held*, because of his domestic situation, the court would set aside the sentence of imprisonment and substitute a probation order.　*R v Thomas*, 5th July 1979 (Court of Appeal: Lord Widgery CJ, Shaw LJ and McNeill J).

2441　　*Taking a motor vehicle without authority; attempting to take a motor vehicle without authority; theft*

Sentence: 18 months' imprisonment concurrent in each case.　Two brothers, aged 23 and 25, both with several previous convictions some of which in respect of offences similar to those currently charged.　One night, after the elder brother's car had broken down, they attempted to take a car from outside its owner's house but were unable to start it.　They took a radio cassette player valued at £76, from it. The brothers then managed to drive away another car but were followed by the police.　The car collided with a parked vehicle rendering the latter beyond repair and causing considerable damage to its own right wing.　In sentencing both men to 3 years' imprisonment concurrent, the judge said they had to be kept out of circulation for a long time for the benefit of the public and that the sentences would have been longer if they had been older.　On appeal against severity of sentence on the ground that the three offences were the result of one incident, *held*, although the offence was inexcusable, the case was one where the total sentence should be reduced to 18 months' imprisonment concurrent.　*R v Norris and Norris*, 18th July 1979 (Court of Appeal: Waller LJ, Kilner-Brown and Neill JJ).

2442　　*Taking a motor vehicle without authority; theft*

Sentence: 9 months imprisonment (first offence) and 6 months imprisonment consecutive (second offence) (15 months in all).　Young man, separated from wife and two children.　Previous convictions and in 1977 one for similar offences for which he was sentenced to 3 months' detention.　Took a car from outside a club and eventually "dumped it".　He opened the boot where he found a number of track suits belonging to a football team.　He took nine track suit tops and sold them a month later.　Sentenced as above.　On appeal, *held*, as he had committed two distinct crimes the court would support the trial judge's view that consecutive rather than concurrent sentences were appropriate.　*R v Taylor*, 30th October 1979 (Court of Appeal: Roskill LJ, Bristow and Hollings JJ).

2443　　*Going equipped for taking a motor vehicle without authority; attempting to take a motor vehicle without authority; damaging property*

Sentence: 2 years' imprisonment concurrent (first and second offences); 6 months' imprisonment concurrent (third offence).　Youth, aged 18.　Since leaving school at 16 has had two short periods of employment as a labourer.　Unemployed since May 1978.　Five findings of guilt and seven previous convictions for dishonesty and offences connected with motor vehicles.　Dealt with by conditional discharge, detention centre, borstal and two suspended sentences of which he is in breach. Current offences consisted of breaking into a car using keys given to him by an accomplice (who was not apprehended).　The appellant was caught trying to force open the crook lock on the car's steering wheel with a screwdriver he had taken from the boot using the same keys.　He was given the maximum sentences for the first and second offences under the Theft Act 1968, s. 25 (1) and 6 months' concurrent for the third offence.　The judge took the view that the public needed protection against further offences by him.　On appeal, *held*, as the appellant had already been to borstal, it was possible to pass a sentence of less than 3 years (see Criminal Justice Act 1961, s. 3), and, although his record was very bad, it was not so serious a case of taking a motor vehicle without authority as would warrant the maximum sentence.　Accordingly, the sentences for the first and second offences would be varied as set out above.　*R v Watson*, 5th June 1979 (Court of Appeal: Lord Widgery CJ, Waller LJ and Lloyd J).

2444　　*Arson*

Sentence: 7 years' imprisonment concurrent.　Married man, aged 21.　Had a personality disorder and a drink problem, making him irresponsible and unaware of what he was doing. Disagreements with his wife. Convicted of culpable manslaughter of his brother in Scotland and sentenced there to 3 years' imprisonment. Offences consisted of twice starting fires at a boarding house at which he was staying. No-one was injured but considerable damage caused. Shortly afterwards set fire to a hotel lavatory. Sentenced to life imprisonment. On appeal contending that an indeterminate sentence was not called for, *held*, he had little regard for the safety and interests of other people. It was not the sort of case which warranted or required an indeterminate sentence. Nevertheless, for the safety of the public, a substantial sentence of imprisonment was called for, and it would be varied as set out above. *R v Hutchison*, 27th November 1978 (Court of Appeal: Lord Widgery CJ, Shaw LJ and Drake J).

2445   Sentence: 4 years' imprisonment. Man, aged 25. Museum attendant for five years. He went into an empty room there, poured inflammable spirit on the floor and on the stairs leading to the floor above where a valuable collection of natural history specimens was housed. After igniting the spirit he left the building, telling a colleague he had been attacked by an intruder who had set fire to the museum. The museum was vacated and the fire put out. Damages to the value of £300,000 had been caused. Appellant admitted offence to police. Said he was very depressed and had been receiving treatment from his doctor for some years. Admitted starting two small fires and also perpetrating a bomb hoax. Said his father had been a part-time fireman and he wanted to join the fire service. On searching his flat police found 12 toy fire engines. Sentenced as above. Doctors and psychiatrists who had examined him found no mental illness. One said his release on parole would not be a good thing. On appeal, *held*, it would be wrong to interfere with the sentence which was fully warranted, and necessary even in the interests of the appellant. Appeal would be dismissed. *R v Jones*, 28th November 1978 (Court of Appeal: Lord Widgery CJ, Shaw LJ and Drake J).

2446   Sentence: probation order for 2 years on condition that the appellant undergoes medical treatment. Man, aged 37. Previous convictions. Antipathy to police and tendency to set fire to things. Defect in personality due to a mental condition, however, susceptible to treatment and a hard worker. Addicted to drink. Set fire to a wooden shed in a coal merchant's yard which resulted in £100 worth of damage. Nine months later set fire to a litter bin and was arrested by police. Sentenced to 3 years' and 1 years' imprisonment concurrent. At the time he was under two suspended sentences for (1) assault on police and (2) damaging a railway line. The suspended sentences of 12 months in all were brought into effect and ordered to run consecutively to the 3 years making a total of 4 years' imprisonment. On appeal, on the ground that the appellant had been in custody for about 15 months and had served the activated sentences, *held*, the Court would vary the sentence as set out above to a term of probation on condition that the appellant underwent hospital treatment as an in-patient. *R v Buckby*, 11th April 1979 (Court of Appeal: Roskill LJ, Ormrod LJ and Watkins J).

2447   Sentence: 4 years' imprisonment; compensation order for £2000 to be paid within 6 months or 12 months' imprisonment in default. Married man, aged 47, with seven children. Educated in India until 1949. Two previous convictions, for affray in 1961 (15 months' imprisonment) and for breach of the peace and possession of an offensive weapon (£100 fine) in 1975. Said to have a very good work record in the United Kingdom. In 1975, he bought a house in Leicester which was at the time let to a woman whom he asked to leave. She did not do so and remained in the house with her family. The appellant did not take legal steps to evict her but decided to "smoke her out" engaging the services of three youths and one of his sons to do so. In 1977, during the woman's absence, the house was doused with petrol and set on fire. There was no danger to life involved but the house and its contents were damaged by the fire. It was clear to the police that the fire was deliberately caused and when questioned, the appellant after initially denying it, admitted that he had paid three youths to do it. The elder youth received three years' detention and the two younger ones were sent to borstal. In sentencing the appellant to 7 years' imprisonment and making the above compensation order, the judge said it was a very serious offence. He had attempted to terrorise his tenant into leaving and had got the three youths to do his "dirty work" for him. The sentence had to be such as to deter like-minded people. On appeal, *held*, a sentence as long as 7 years was unnecessary, it would be varied to 4 years' imprisonment and the compensation order would stand. *R v Pargat Singh*, 2nd July 1979 (Court of Appeal: Lord Widgery CJ, Shaw LJ and McNeill J).

2448 Sentence: probation for 2 years (6 months' imprisonment served). Married man, aged 36, in regular employment. Two previous offences in 1973 and 1974 but no previous prison sentence. Offence committed in appellant's own home, a council house, after a series of arguments with his wife. When he returned home after a drinking bout she locked him out of the house. With her in the house were her three children. The appellent got some paraffin and unsuccessfully attempted to set the back door alight. He then managed to set the front door partly on fire by pouring paraffin over it. His son jumped through the window and summoned help. The cost of the damage was £10. The appellant expressed remorse and his plea of simple arson, to a charge of arson with intent to danger life, was accepted. On sentencing him to 4 years' imprisonment the judge said arson was a very serious offence because of the damage it could do. On appeal, *held*, while the judge's views on arson were correct, the offence varied greatly in gravity. The present case was at the lower end of the scale, the appellant having acted in a moment of hysteria and frustration when affected by drink, his object being to gain access to the house rather than to cause serious damage. As he had served 6 months' imprisonment, the court would vary the sentence as set out above. *R v Walls*, 2nd July 1979 (Court of Appeal: Geoffrey Lane LJ, Swanwick and Waterhouse JJ).

2449 Sentence: hospital orders under Mental Health Act 1959, ss. 50, 65 (detention in hospital without limit of time). Single woman, aged 31. Seven previous convictions for offences of dishonesty and damage and subject to a Mental Health Act 1959, s. 50 order for theft in 1969. Lived in a guest house with her boyfriend. When told to leave, the appellant started a fire in the basement of the house above which was an oil tank. The fire was discovered and put out by a resident. Sentenced to life imprisonment, for although she had received treatment in the past for mental illness and had been a patient in various mental institutions, no suitable hospital was available. Since her sentence, a medical report showed that the appellant was suffering from a psychiatric disorder within the meaning of the Mental Health Act. On appeal, *held*, in view of the changed circumstances, the fact that the latest report advised detention in a mental hospital for treatment and that one such hospital had become available, the sentence would be varied as set out above. *R v Beck*, 7th August 1979 (Court of Appeal: Roskill LJ, Thompson and Gibson JJ).

2450 Sentence: probation for 2 years on terms. Single man, aged 30, in spasmodic employment. Seven findings of guilt and 15 previous convictions for offences of theft, arson, assault occasioning bodily harm, burglary, forgery and handling stolen goods. Dealt with by fines, periods of approved school, detention centre, and borstal, conditional discharge and prison sentences from 3 months to 5 years. Current offences committed while released on licence. Set fire to a garden shed in the middle of the night. The fire was quickly discovered and extinguished before the fire brigade arrived, the appellant having assisted in the removal of the shed contents. One night, a month later, he started another fire in an empty block of flats causing £3,000 worth of damage. He admitted the offences to the police. Sentenced to concurrent terms of 4 years' imprisonment. Since the sentence, a report has suggested that the appellant would benefit from psychiatric treatment. On appeal, *held*, the court would vary the sentence to that set out above on the basis that the appellant was under the supervision of a probation officer and underwent psychiatric treatment. *R v Taylor*, 4th December 1979 (Court of Appeal: Lord Widgery CJ, Shaw LJ and Park J).

2451   *Arson; burglary; office breaking and causing criminal damage*

Sentence: care order to remain in force until the appellant reaches the age of 18. Youth, aged 14. Subject of previous care order which placed him in a children's home. On the next day he set fire to the premises causing £100 damage. Two months later, he burgled an Army Careers office stealing £15. Five days later he burgled a hairdressing saloon stealing £15 and ten days later committed a similar offence at the same saloon. Arrested and released. A week later, with a gang of boys, he broke into a solicitor's office and did appalling damage. Admitted to this offence a month later. Sentenced to 3 months' detention by the Juvenile Court and sent to the Crown Court after his release for the criminal damage offence. Returned to detention centre for 6 months. On appeal, *held*, as it was wrong in principle to sentence a youth to what amounted to 9 months at a detention centre, in view of the appellant's age a fresh care order would be made as set out above and the detention sentence set aside. *R v Jones*, 8th August 1979 (Court of Appeal: Roskill LJ, Thompson and Gibson JJ).

2452   *Arson; possession of article with intent to endanger property*

Sentence: probation for 3 years on condition that the appellant undergoes medical treatment. Man, aged 23, joined police force from school. Unhappy youth, mother disappeared and he was put in a home. The mother later returned. Keen and energetic police officer. Disturbances at home caused depression resulting in the current offences which were committed for no apparent reason. All offences occurred late at night after the appellant had been drinking. They consisted of lighting fires in outbuildings and a waiting room at a railway station and setting fire to a church hall which was gutted. He then reported the fires to the police. Damage exceeded £20,000. The offences occurred between March and May 1978. In June he was seen carrying a polythene container filled with paraffin by a station guard. He dropped the container and ran off. Later, when apprehended, he confessed to the offences attributing them to drink and domestic problems. He was sentended to concurrent terms of 3 years' imprisonment. He appealed on the ground that as a policeman if he went to prison he would have to claim protection for his own safety which would mean solitary confinement equivalent to 4 years' imprisonment. Medical opinion was that if the appellant served the full term of imprisonment he would come out a more serious risk to the public than when he went in. *Held*, the sentence would be varied to probation on condition he underwent medical treatment. *R v Cassidy*, 24th April 1979 (Court of Appeal: Lord Widgery CJ, Geoffrey Lane LJ and Ackner J).

2453   *Arson with intent to endanger life*

Sentence; immediate release (almost 8 months' imprisonment served). Married man, aged 45. Apart from a minor offence, of previous good character. History of mental illness going back to 1974. Also suffers from heart disease which has caused some degree of brain damage. Has lived in a council house for 8 years. In a fit of severe depression he set fire to the house one night in an attempt to put an end to his own life and that of his wife because he could no longer stand her nagging. He lit strips of paper and put them under the living-room sofa. His wife woke up around midnight unable to breathe because of the smoke. She raised the alarm and she and the appellant had to be rescued by the fire brigade. Sentenced to 2 years' imprisonment. On appeal *held*, although arson with intent was a serious offence, in view of recent medical reports that the appellant was unlikely to commit a further offence and was no danger to himself or the public provided he continued the medical treatment he was undergoing, the Court would reduce the sentence to allow his immediate release. *R v Allott*, 5th June 1979 (Court of Appeal: Lord Widgery CJ, Waller LJ and Lloyd J).

2454   *Criminal damage*

Sentence: hospital order under Mental Health Act 1959, s. 60. Woman, aged 22. Said to have been a problem child, admitted to children's psychiatric hospital at the age of 4. Behaviour problems resulted in her being placed in a hostel for maladjusted children at 13. She absconded from there frequently and committed offences of larceny. Put on probation and sent to approved school. She was unsettled until the age of 18 when at above psychiatric hospital she showed aggression to the staff and smashed 45 windows in 72 hours. Returned to remand centre and because of self injurious behaviour thought unsuitable for borstal training and sent to Broadmoor. There for 4½ years. Currently charged with breaking a window. Psychiatric report said that the appellant was a very impulsive, immature girl unable to cope with the demands of society when free, yet becoming hostile, aggressive and attention-seeking when in captivity. Said to be of average intelligence and may suffer from epilepsy. At great risk from effects of institutionalisation in a secure environment but difficult to see what the alternative arrangements could be. Judge made orders under Mental Health Act 1959 ss. 60, 65. She appealed on the ground that she had been in Broadmoor since 1975 and had only been convicted of trifling offences before the current one which took place in 1975. *Held*, justice and humanity demanded that a risk should be taken to remove the restriction order under s. 65. *R v Hodge*, 13th March 1979 (Court of Appeal: Shaw LJ, Smith and Mustill JJ).

2455   Sentence: 6 months' imprisonment. Man, aged 20. Unemployed since 1975 when he discharged himself from the Merchant Navy. Seven previous convictions for dishonesty, dealt with by fines, probation and borstal training. He had a 2 year affair with a girl of 17 and had a child by her who died. In 1977, she ended the affair but the appellant continued to pester her refusing to accept that it was over. He was sent to borstal until September 1978 when he tried to contact her again. Eventually, he spoke to her at a discotheque and threatened her with violence. She managed to get away from him and the next day found that her car had been extensively damaged. The appellant was arrested and returned to borstal where he completed his sentence in November 1978. He was remanded in custody and sentenced to 2 years' imprisonment. On appeal, *held*, a custodial sentence was appropriate, but as he had no previous convictions for criminal damage the 2 year sentence was excessive. However, in view of his age, although a 12 month sentence was appropriate, only sentences of 18 months and 6 months were allowed for under the Criminal Justice Act 1961, s. 3. Accordingly, the sentence would be varied as set out above. *R v Shinkwin*, 12th July 1979 (Court of Appeal: Lord Widgery CJ, Shaw LJ and McNeill J).

2456   Sentence: 6 months' imprisonment; previous suspended sentence of 6 months' imprisonment (for 2 assaults occasioning actual bodily harm and criminal damage) activated (12 months in all). Man, aged 66, with criminal record dating back to 1932 and prone to bouts of heavy drinking. Previous convictions mainly for being drunk and disorderly, criminal damage and for offences of deception. Described as a recidivist with no real work record. The day after the imposition of the aforementioned suspended sentence, he went to his nephew's flower shop to ask for money. His request was refused and at midnight he returned and smashed three of the shop windows causing £420 worth of damage. In mitigation, the appellant said that he would be "better off" in prison. Sentenced to 30 months' imprisonment and the suspended sentence activated and ordered to run consecutively (3 years in all). He appealed against severity of sentence, on grounds of age and the fact that he was a recidivist. *Held*, the appellant's record had to be considered in sentencing him, in the present case a sentence of 30 months' imprisonment was too long for the offence committed and would be varied to 6 months' imprisonment with the activated suspended sentence to run consecutively. *R v Jones*, 5th November 1979 (Court of Appeal: Lord Widgery CJ, Wien and Watkins JJ).

2457   *Forgery*
Sentence: immediate release (6½ months' imprisonment served). Married man, aged 36, with 6 children. Served in Royal Marines and discharged with a good character in 1965. He had various employments but unemployed since 1976. Seven previous convictions, three for motoring offences and the others for damage to property,

abstracting electricity, attempted burglary in 1973 and theft in 1977 for which he was fined.   The appellant then acted as a "broker" for the co-accused who had discovered a method of altering Ministry of Transport Test Certificates so that they could be extended for a further 12 months.   The appellant supplied a number of persons with the altered certificates at £7 each, £5 of which went to the co-accused, and together, they ran a thriving business.   Both men, and a large number of other accused, were charged with contravening the Road Traffic Act 1972, s. 169 (1) (b). The co-accused received 21 months' imprisonment and the appellant 15 months' imprisonment.   On appeal, *held*, it was a serious fraud which required to be dealt with severely by way of a custodial sentence, but as the co-accused was far more to blame and had a worse record than the appellant, the court would vary the appellant's sentence to allow him to be released forthwith.   *R v Vidler*, 22nd January 1979 (Court of Appeal: Browne LJ, Lawson and Phillips JJ).

OFFENCES AGAINST DECENCY AND MORALITY

2458   *1. Buggery.   2. Indecent assault.   3. Gross indecency.*

Sentence: 1. Eight years' imprisonment, 2. eight years' imprisonment concurrent, 3. five years' imprisonment concurrent (eight years in all).   Single man, aged 40, unemployed and a paedophile.   In 1974, when a schoolmaster, conditionally discharged for indecent assault.   Over a period of months he committed buggery and acts of gross indecency with a number of boys aged between 14 and 15.   He set up a photographic business and paid the boys to be models for nude photographs. He then took photographs of the boys indulging in sexual activity with himself and with each other and sold the photographs for considerable sums of money.   The activities were finally exposed by a national newspaper.   Sentenced to 10 years' imprisonment for the buggery and indecency offences and 5 years' imprisonment concurrent for the gross indecency offence.   On appeal against severity of sentence, *held*, by a series of sexual offences involving boys the appellant had provided the pornographic trade with material out of which money could be made by others. That trade could only be stopped if the Court made it clear that the public would not tolerate such behaviour and those who indulged in it would have to suffer the consequences.   However, as the appellant had been frank and co-operative with the police since his arrest, the sentence would be varied as set out above.   *R v Saunders*, 11th October 1979 (Court of Appeal: Lawton LJ, Tudor Evans and McNeill JJ).

2459   *Bigamy*

Sentence: immediate release (2½ months' imprisonment served).   Man, aged 40. Originally married in 1957 when he and his wife went to Rhodesia.   They separated in 1960 and she returned to UK.   No contact since.   In 1973 he married a divorcee, but the marriage was never consummated and lasted only a few weeks.   Marriage annulled in 1975 but before that happened appellant went through a form of marriage with another woman.   He told her he was divorced.   They went to Jamaica and she had a child there.   Returned to England in November 1975 when it was discovered that appellant was already married.   When seen by police he said he thought his original marriage had ended in divorce.   Pleaded guilty and sentenced to 18 months' imprisonment, the judge referring to appellant as a compulsive husband.   On appeal, *held*, on the first count the marriage had never been consummated so no injury had been done.   On the second count the woman had not been asked if she would have started living with appellant if she had known he was married.   Sentence of immediate imprisonment was properly imposed for offence of bigamy but 18 months' imprisonment was out of all proportion to the gravity of the offence.   Sentence would be varied as set out above.   *R v Crowhurst*, 18th December 1978 (Court of Appeal: Waller and Cumming-Bruce LJJ and Jupp J).

2460   *Importuning for immoral purposes*

Sentence: 3 months' imprisonment.   Married man, aged 31, wife living in America.   Four previous convictions for importuning dealt with summarily by fines and a conditional discharge. Police officers saw the appellant walking up and down a street in an effeminate manner. He approached four men on four separate occasions. Finally, he approached one of the police officers, spoke to him and asked him back to his flat. He was then arrested. Sentenced as above. On appeal on ground that sentence was excessive in view of the fact that it was his first custodial sentence, *held*, the trial judge had rightly thought that the appellant had to be dealt with differently this time. The sentence imposed was not excessive and would stand. *R v Chan*, 6th August 1979 (Court of Appeal: Roskill LJ, Thompson and Gibson JJ).

OFFENCES RELATING TO DRUGS

2461   *Fraudulent evasion of prohibition on importation of controlled drug*
Sentence: 3 years' imprisonment (first count); one year's imprisonment consecutive (second count). Married man, aged 42, with 2 children. Unemployed since 1962 but said to be supported by family and friends and was not on social security. No previous convictions. Said he tried to set up in business with a general stores, but his health deteriorated—he suffered from bad asthma and chronic bronchitis. In April 1978 arrived at Heathrow from Damascus. His suitcase had a fake bottom which contained 3703 grammes of opium. Appellant confessed that he had brought it from Delhi. Then admitted importing a kilo of cannabis in February 1978, and selling it in London for £150. In mitigation he said he had gone to Bangladesh to recover business debts owed him and there, by chance, had been offered the opium. Sentenced as above on the grounds that he was a carrier of prohibited drugs. On appeal, *held*, the court was dealing with a man who had imported large amounts of prohibited drugs. Such importation had to be severely dealt with and the sentence imposed was comparatively lenient. *R v Quadir*, 9th November 1978 (Court of Appeal: Orr LJ, Boreham and Stephen Brown JJ).

2462   Sentence: 2 years' imprisonment. Jamaican man, aged 22. Telephone technician with excellent character. Belonged to a Jamaican sect known as the Rastafarians who made extensive use of cannabis. The appellant arrived with a woman friend at Heathrow airport. Each had a suitcase with a false bottom in which was compressed 5.15 kilogrammes of cannabis, altogether worth £5,000. The appellant was said to consume a pound or two of cannabis a week. Sentenced to three years' imprisonment, the woman to two years' imprisonment suspended for two years. On appeal on grounds that the case was not one of commercial importation, the appellant having a good job in Jamaica, *held*, he was the active partner in the deliberate smuggling of drugs which were forbidden goods. A sentence of imprisonment was called for but justice would be met by varying the sentence to two years' imprisonment. *R v Williams*, 12th January 1979 (Court of Appeal: Lawton LJ, Cantley and Willis JJ).

2463   Sentence: 3 years' imprisonment. Man, aged 34. Except for a minor offence committed long ago, a person of good character. In regular work as a carpenter. Was apprehended in 1972 for driving while disqualified and with excess alcohol (offences for which he was dealt with in 1978 at the same time as the instant offence and sentenced to 12 months' imprisonment) but absconded while on bail. He was lost sight of until early 1978 when with the co-accused he was stopped coming through customs. A substantial quantity of cannabis was found concealed in the rear seat of the vehicle in which they were travelling. The appellant confessed to the offence, pleaded guilty and was sentenced to 5 years' imprisonment. The co-accused received 18 months' imprisonment. The cannabis was 47 lb in weight and worth £30,000. The appellant's share was £2,000. On appeal, *held*, in view of the appellant's previous good character, his regular work as a carpenter and confession to the offence, the sentence imposed was too long and would be varied to that set out above. *R v McCormack*, 25th April 1979 (Court of Appeal: Bridge LJ, Chapman and Lawson JJ).

2464   Sentence: 5 years' imprisonment concurrent. Pakistani man, aged 43, married with three children. A one time leading Pakistani actor, film distributor and cinema owner. Said to earn about £50,000 per annum in Pakistan. With the three co-accused, he developed a scheme to get large quantities of cannabis resin, worth about £100,000, into the UK from Pakistan by inserting it into spools of film. The consignments of film arrived in the country in October 1976 and May 1977. The scheme involved the formation of a bogus company in the UK. The appellant supplied the money, two bank accounts being opened, one by the co-accused who was a UK resident and the other, an external account, by the appellant himself. At the time of his arrest there was about £25,000 in the external account. The co-accused were sentenced to between 2 and 3 years' imprisonment; the appellant was sentenced to concurrent terms of 5 years' imprisonment and fined £25,000 with 12 months' imprisonment consecutive in default of payment. On appeal against sentence, *held*, the appellant had not only infringed the laws of the UK but also those of Pakistan in two respects, firstly, the export of cannabis was forbidden in that country and secondly, in order to effect the exportation, he had dealt with "black money". As he had made a genuine attempt to pay the fine but had been refused permission to remove his money from Pakistan by the authorities, the fine would be quashed. The sentence of imprisonment would stand however as the Court had always taken a firm line on the illegal importation of drugs. *R v Durrani,* 12th October 1979 (Court of Appeal: Lawton LJ, Tudor Evans and McNeill JJ).

2465   *Being knowingly concerned in fraudulent evasion of prohibition on importation of controlled drug.*
Sentence: 3 years' imprisonment. Man, aged 31, with no previous convictions. Certain African carvings were left at London Airport by a person not allowed to enter the United Kingdom. Customs officials discovered a large quantity of cannabis, said to be worth between £16,000 and £20,000, concealed in the carvings. The officers replaced the carvings. The appellant and co-accused then arrived at the airport and removed them. They were arrested by the police and the co-accused made a full confession stating that he was in touch with people in Africa regarding the importation of cannabis and gave information about the distribution organisation in the United Kingdom. The appellant denied complicity but was convicted. It appeared that he only found out what was happening when he arrived at the airport with the co-accused. Both sentenced as above. The co-accused received his sentence because he had confessed and helped the police but the appellant fought the case throughout. On appeal on grounds of disparity, *held*, knowingly to take part in an international plan to import cannabis into the United Kingdom by the sophisticated hiding of the drug in carvings was a very serious offence and the three years' imprisonment imposed was by no means a severe sentence. *R v McClurkin,* 19th February 1979 (Court of Appeal: Waller LJ, Lawson and Jupp JJ).

2466   *Possession of controlled drug with intent to supply (cannabis)*
Sentence: 15 months' imprisonment. Man, aged 23, squatting with his common law wife and child. Unemployed. Four previous convictions, two for dishonesty, one for attempting to obtain cannabis (£200 fine) and one for possession of cannabis (£50 fine). In September 1977 police officers with a search warrant went to appellant's house. He was there with three adults and a child. The police found a set of brass scales and weights, a wallet containing £56, a tin box containing a blade, cannabis, some herbal mixture, four cigarettes and a packet of cigarette papers, and a piece of silver paper containing more cannabis. Appellant admitted to owning those items. The cannabis resin seized weighed 138 grammes. Appellant admitted being a dealer in cannabis resin. Sentencing appellant to 2 years' imprisonment, the judge said evidence that appellant had sold cannabis to visitors to his home was irresistible. On appeal, *held*, the proper sentence was one of 15 months' imprisonment, bearing in mind that appellant had pleaded guilty and had not been to prison before, although convicted of two offences involving drugs. *R v Delahaye,* 16th November 1978 (Court of Appeal: Roskill LJ, Lawson and Neill JJ).

2467　Sentence: 6 years' imprisonment. Married (now divorced) man, aged 30, with two children. Born in India and came to United Kingdom in 1966. Sentenced to 2 years' imprisonment in 1975 for facilitating illegal immigration. Stopped by the police whilst driving his car along the M1 motorway. In the well of the back seat was found a cardboard box containing 1.221 kilogrammes of cannabis resin. A later examination of the car revealed another 0.5 grammes of the same drug wrapped up on the floor by the front passenger seat. The value of this consignment in the retail market was estimated at £16,000. It was described by the police as "one of the largest hauls in the country of this particular commodity". At the time, the appellant was on social security. The police discovered he had sent substantial sums of money abroad purportedly to help a relative. He had bought a house on mortgage and had a car which in one month alone had done 2,500 miles. Sentenced as above on ground he was a courier of the drug, not an organiser. On appeal, *held* it was clear he was a courier of the drug on a very large scale. *R v Sajnum Singh*, 30th January 1979 (Court of Appeal: Browne LJ, Mais and Phillips JJ).

2468　*Possession of cannabis*

Sentence: 3 months' imprisonment concurrent. Man, aged 28. Previous offences for taking and driving away vehicles and one for possessing a controlled drug. Police found the appellant in possession of two quantities of cannabis weighing 1.83 grammes and 487 milligrammes. Sentenced as above. On appeal, *held*, although the volume of cannabis found on the appellant did not suggest any sort of trafficking or selling, the offences called for an immediate sentence of imprisonment and the above sentence was in no way excessive. *R v Minott*, 25th April 1979 (Court of Appeal: Lord Widgery CJ, Geoffrey Lane and Ackner JJ).

2469　*Possession of cannabis resin*

Sentence: £10 or 1 months' imprisonment in default. The appellant and her co-accused husband were travelling to a pop festival when they were stopped by the police and 2·1 grammes of cannabis resin were found in the car. Sentenced to 4 months' imprisonment suspended for 18 months. On appeal, *held*, it was a simple case in which no sentence of imprisonment, whether immediate or suspended, was appropriate. The matter could have been better dealt with by the imposition of a fine. Accordingly, a fine of £10 would be substituted with 1 months' imprisonment in default. *R v Leaman*, 12th July 1979 (Court of Appeal: Lord Widgery CJ, Shaw LJ and McNeill J).

Driving Offences

2470　*Causing death by dangerous driving*
Sentence: immediate release (twenty-one days already served). Man, of previous good character. Attempted to overtake two cars and a milk float travelling at approximately twenty miles per hour. Failed to notice sign for right hand bend. Collided with lorry coming in opposite direction. Passenger in car killed. Appellant convicted of causing death by dangerous driving and sentenced to twenty-eight days imprisonment and disqualified for three years. Appealed on ground that as he had neither been drinking nor driving too fast there were no aggravating circumstances. *Held*, hazards at accident location were not extraordinary and there were no aggravating circumstances. Sentence of imprisonment would be quashed but disqualification would stand. *R v Bruin* [1979] RTR 95 (Court of Appeal: Lord Widgery CJ, Browne LJ and Stocker J).

2471　Sentence: £300 fine; disqualified for 2 years. Man, aged 38, medical officer in RAF; 2 previous speeding convictions. The appellant was driving at dusk and proceeded from a minor road straight across stop lines, past a "giveway" sign on to a major road into the path of an oncoming car. As a result, the driver and passenger in that car died from their injuries. He was fined £300 and disqualified for five years. He appealed against the length of the period of disqualification. *Held*, it was a serious case of dangerous driving. However it would be impossible for the appellant to enter private practice without the use of a car and the length of disqualification would cause additional hardship when he wanted to have access to his daughter, in the custody of his former wife. The period of disqualification would be reduced to 2 years. *R v Fenwick* [1979] RTR 506 (Court of Appeal: Bridge LJ, Chapman and Lawson JJ).

2472   Sentence: £500 fine; disqualified for 3 years. Man, aged 19. No previous convictions. Held provisional driving licence. One night the appellant was driving under the supervision of a full licence holder and carrying 2 passengers. The speed limit was 30 m.p.h. The supervisor, who knew the road instructed him to slacken speed because of a bend ahead. He ignored the instructions and increased speed as a result of which the car skidded, overturned and collided with a lamp post. One of the passengers later died. His speed was estimated to be 60–65 m.p.h. according to the driver of the car behind. Sentenced as above. On appeal, *held*, since the appellant was the holder of a provisional licence and had ignored the advice given to him by the supervising driver to slacken speed, it was a severe case of causing death by dangerous driving. The fine was proper and the period of disqualification not excessive. *R v O'Connor* [1979] RTR 467 (Court of Appeal: Geoffrey Lane and Bridge LJJ and Lawson J).

2473   *Causing death by dangerous driving: driving with excess alcohol in blood.*
Sentence: 6 months' imprisonment; disqualified for 4 years (first offence); 6 months' imprisonment concurrent; disqualified for 4 years to run concurrently (second offence). Man, aged 29, of previous good character. After a drinking session with several friends appellant's car was involved in an accident. He was not driving at excessive speed but car collided with a traffic sign and overturned, killing one of the passengers. Appellant found to have 157 milligrammes of alcohol in 100 milligrammes of blood. Sentenced to 15 months' imprisonment and disqualified for 7 years for dangerous driving, and sentenced to 6 months' imprisonment and 7 years disqualification for driving with excess alcohol in blood. On appeal *held*, an immediate prison sentence was correct, but the sentence imposed was too severe and would be varied as set out above. An appeal against sentence was appeal against the whole sentence and, although appellant had not sought a reduction in his period of disqualification, it would be reduced to 4 years. *R v Midgley* [1979] RTR 1 (Court of Appeal: Lord Widgery CJ, Cumming-Bruce LJ and Drake J).

2474   *Causing death by reckless driving*
Sentence: 6 months' imprisonment; disqualified for 7 years. Minicab driver who had previous convictions for dangerous driving, collided head-on with another vehicle killing a passenger. He was convicted of causing death by reckless driving and sentenced as above. He appealed against the disqualification contending that every day of the disqualification would mean a day of unemployment. *Held*, while it was understandable that the case called for a lengthy period of preventive disqualification, in the circumstances such a disqualification could be counter-productive and it would be accordingly reduced to five years. *R v Farrugia* [1979] RTR 422 (Court of Appeal: Lord Widgery CJ, Waller LJ and Lloyd J).

2475   *Driving with excess alcohol in blood*
Sentence: £75 fine; £100 prosecution costs; disqualified for 18 months. Man, aged 29, stable work record. One previous conviction. At 1 a.m., the appellant was seen by a police officer driving a van in a haphazard manner until he stopped in an awkward position. The appellant was found to have 222 milligrammes of alcohol in 100 millilitres of his blood. He was fined, sentenced to 7 days' imprisonment, ordered to pay prosecution costs of up to £100 and disqualified for 3 years. On appeal, *held*, the sentence of imprisonment would be quashed as it was not appropriate and the period of disqualification reduced to 18 months. The fine of £75 would remain and he would be ordered to pay the prosecution costs, limited to £100. *R*

v Beardsley [1979] RTR 472 (Court of Appeal: Browne LJ, Phillips and Michael Davies JJ).

2476   Sentence: disqualified for 12 months. Man, aged 24, self-employed dealer, needed to travel to earn living. First road traffic offence. In respect of other matters, was subject to sentences of 5 years' imprisonment. The appellant was found to have 136 milligrammes of alcohol in 100 millilitres of blood. He was disqualified for 3 years. On appeal, *held*, since the appellant was subject to 5 years' imprisonment, the punitive effect of the disqualification would be delayed for a considerable period; since he had no record of a previous offence and needed to drive to earn his living, the period of disqualification would be reduced to 12 months. *R v Cunningham*, [1979] RTR 465 (Court of Appeal: Lord Widgery CJ, Eveleigh LJ and Swanwick J).

2477   Sentence: 3 months' imprisonment and disqualified for 18 months. Man, aged 59, in continuous employment as planning engineer. Unblemished record after a life of driving. Appellant had driven onto hard shoulder of motorway interchange. Car parked at an angle of approximately 45°. A breath test proved positive and he was found to have 267 milligrammes of alcohol in 100 millilitres of his blood. Sentenced to 3 months' imprisonment and disqualified for 3 years. On appeal against sentence, *held*, since the appellant's blood-alcohol concentration was enormously high, the sentence of imprisonment was proper. However, in view of the appellant's age and experience the period of disqualification would be reduced to 18 months. *R v Salters*, [1979] RTR 470 (Court of Appeal: Lawton LJ, Thompson and Hodgson JJ).

2478   —— **extended sentence—matters to be considered**

The defendant was convicted of a number of offences of indecency with young boys. He was sentenced to concurrent terms of eight years' imprisonment for four offences of indecent assault on young boys and to two years of imprisonment concurrent for one offence of indecency with a child. He appealed against the total sentence of eight years' imprisonment. *Held*, such heavy sentences had been passed on the defendant because he had been before the court for similar offences on several previous occasions and the judge had considered that he was a persistent offender from whom the public needed to be protected. However, unless an offender qualified for an extended sentence under the Powers of Criminal Courts Act 1973, s. 28, he should be sentenced only on the basis of the facts proved and not for the purposes of public protection. The gravity of the particular acts committed had to be considered bearing in mind the guidelines provided by *R v Willis*, [1975] 1 All ER 620, 1975 Halsbury's Abridgment para. 884. A persistent course of conduct over a period of time had to be regarded as serious but the degree of seriousness varied with the acts. In the present case the acts were not too serious and there were a number of mitigating circumstances that could be taken into account. Accordingly, the sentence would be reduced to four years.

R v GOODEN [1979] LS Gaz R 1283 (Court of Appeal: LAWTON LJ, CHAPMAN and WOOLF JJ).

See also Times, 5th December 1979.

2479   —— **matters to be considered—bribery of Crown official**

Two defendants were convicted of corruptly giving a gift or consideration to their co-defendant, who was convicted of corruptly accepting, as a Crown official, the gift or consideration. The offences related to the sale of Chieftain tanks to the government of Iran to equip its army. The first defendant received a suspended sentence, the second eighteen months' imprisonment and their co-defendant three years' imprisonment. They all appealed against their convictions and the second defendant and third defendant against sentence. *Held*, there had been no miscarriage of justice and all the appeals against conviction would be dismissed. On a question of sentence, it was important to prevent the spread of corruption in public and commercial life and thus heavy sentences had to be imposed as a deterrent. There was therefore nothing wrong in principle with the sentences, but as an act of mercy the second defendant would be released because of his age and ill health.

R v WELLBURN (1979) 69 Cr App Rep 254 (Court of Appeal: LAWTON LJ, CANTLEY and WILLIS JJ).

2480   Binding over—power to attach conditions—firearms offences

See *Goodlad v Chief Constable of South Yorkshire*, para. 1295.

2481   Borstal training—concurrent sentence—power of court to recommend period of training

The appellant, already serving a sentence of borstal training, pleaded guilty to burglary and taking a conveyance without authority. At his trial he was sentenced to a fresh concurrent period of borstal training. The trial judge refused however to give him an indication that the fresh term would not interfere with his optimum sentence already imposed for his earlier offences. On appeal from that refusal, *held*, the question of the appropriate release date of a borstal trainee was a matter for the jurisdiction and discretion of the borstal authorities. However the court could give an indication that the second sentence should not necessarily result in the appellant serving any longer in custody than he would have served had he been subject only to the first borstal sentence. Nonetheless the appellant was not entitled to have any sense of grievance if the borstal authorities decided on a different release date.

R v LONG [1979] Crim LR 598 (Court of Appeal; LORD WIDGERY CJ, CUMMING-BRUCE LJ and NEILL J).

2482   —— sentence subsequent to sentence of detention imposed for other offences

The appellant, a youth of eighteen, committed offences in October 1976, January 1977, March 1977 and May 1977. In July 1977 he was sentenced to three months in a detention centre in respect of the January and March offences. Following his release from the centre, he was convicted of the October and May offences and sentenced to borstal training. His co-defendants, being over twenty-one, were given custodial prison sentences. On appeal contending that borstal training was inappropriate because he had been given a good detention centre report, *held*, the nature of the October and May offences, assaults on the police, could only be dealt with by an immediate custodial sentence, despite his good report from the detention centre. Further, it would be unfair if he were to go unpunished when his co-defendants were sentenced to imprisonment. The appeal would be dismissed.

R v FRANCIS (1978) 66 Cr App Rep 335 (Court of Appeal: SHAW LJ, O'CONNOR and LAWSON JJ). *R v Gooding* (1955) 39 Cr App Rep 187, CA distinguished.

2483   Community service order—power of Crown Court to revoke order

See *R v Adair*, para. 561.

2484   —— whether may be accompanied by a fine

In an appeal against a sentence of a fine and a period of community service, *held*, notwithstanding the provisions of the Powers of Criminal Courts Act 1973, ss. 14 (1), (8), 30, the intention of Parliament was that, by analogy with a probation order, a community service order, should stand alone. This was to avoid complications when an offender, who failed to comply with a probation order or a community service order, was brought back to court and punished for the original offence.

R v CARNWELL (1979) 68 Cr App Rep 58 (Court of Appeal: LAWTON LJ, KENNETH JONES and SMITH JJ).

2485   Deprivation of property used for crime—variation of order made by Crown Court

See *R v Menocal*, para. 593.

2486 Imprisonment—power of magistrates' court to sentence accused in his absence—accused in prison for other offences—sentence for non-payment of fines

See *R v Dudley Justices, ex parte Payne*, para. 1791.

2487 Practice—robbery with violence

In an appeal against sentence on convictions, inter alia, of robbery and conspiracy to rob, *held*, the purpose of what was said by the Court of Appeal in *R v Turner* was not to fix a ceiling which had to be slavishly followed in all future cases of robberies with violence on banks, but to give guidance to Crown Courts throughout the country, where so many bank robbery cases had to be tried, as to the length of sentence which might be appropriate.

R v WILDE (1978) 66 Cr App Rep 339 (Court of Appeal: ROSKILL and EVELEIGH LJJ and STOCKER J). *R v Turner* (1975) 61 Cr App Rep 67, CA, 1975 Halsbury's Abridgment para. 842 explained.

2488 Prostitution—living on earnings of prostitution—absence of evidence of coercion—effect on sentence

See *R v Farrugia*, para. 633.

2489 Sentencing practice in magistrates' courts—Home Office Report

The Home Office have issued a Press Release, dated 30th November 1979, concerning its research into sentencing practice in magistrates' courts. The research, covering the years between 1971–1975, confirmed that sentencing discrepancies existed between different courts and that they were sometimes quite large. Whilst some variations were explained by a difference in the types of offenders before the courts and by the courts' resources and by local circumstances, it was evident that courts did have different ways of dealing with similar types of offenders, and a number of reforms were suggested. The report, Sentencing Practice in Magistrates' Courts, Home Office Research Study No. 56, is published by HMSO.

See also 129 NLJ 1218.

2490 Suspended sentence—activation of sentence—absconding

In the course of his trial for attempted rape and assault occasioning bodily harm, the appellant absconded to France. The trial continued in his absence, resulting in conviction and sentence. The appellant subsequently returned to England and surrendered to the police. At the Crown Court he admitted absconding contrary to the Bail Act, s. 6. The judge dealt with the matter summarily as if it were a criminal contempt of court. The appellant was sentenced to six months' imprisonment for absconding. A six month suspended sentence previously incurred was activated to run consecutively to the sentence for absconding, both sentences to run consecutively to the sentences imposed for the offences tried on indictment. The appellant objected to the activation of the suspended sentence on the ground that the Powers of Criminal Courts Act 1973, s. 23, the authority under which the judge had acted, did not apply to criminal contempt of court. *Held*, unless it would be unjust to activate the suspended sentence, the terms of s. 23 of the 1973 Act were mandatory. The Bail Act 1976, s. 6, created a new statutory offence of absconding. Since bail was granted much more freely under the 1976 Act, it was important to show that the provisions of s. 6 would be firmly applied to persons who absconded. The judge had acted correctly and the appeal would be dismissed.

R v TYSON (1979) 68 Cr App Rep 314 (Court of Appeal: LAWTON LJ, CANTLEY and WILLIS JJ). *Morris v Crown Office* [1970] 2 QB 114, distinguished.

2491 Young offender—committal for sentence—validity

See *R v T (a juvenile)*, para. 1776.

SET-OFF AND COUNTERCLAIM

Halsbury's Laws of England (3rd edn.), Vol. 34, paras. 669–755

2492   Counterclaim—leave to defend—whether leave should be granted

See *Sable Contractors Ltd v Bluett Shipping Ltd*, para. 1647.

2493   Set-off against freight—availability as between principal and agent

See *James & Co Scheepvaarten Handelmij BV v Chinecrest Ltd*, para. 2547.

2494   Set-off against rent—repairs covenant by landlord—agreement collateral to lease

See *British Anzani (Felixstowe) Ltd v International Marine Management (U.K.) Ltd*, para. 1704.

SETTLEMENTS

Halsbury's Laws of England (3rd edn.), Vol. 34, paras. 756–1141.

2495   Investment clause in settlement—continuation—power of appointment created by order of court—whether power authorised alteration of trustees' powers of investment

See *Re Rank's Settlement Trusts; Rollo v Newton*, para. 2100.

SEWERS AND DRAINS

Halsbury's Laws of England (3rd edn.), Vol. 31, paras. 290–397

2496   Private sewer—connection of drain from neighbouring house with permission—second connection without permission—remedy

The owner of a house number seventeen, who was the plaintiff's predecessor, gave permission to the owner of numbers nineteen and twenty-one to attach the drains of those houses to a pipe which ran from his property into the main sewer, and which had been laid by the local authority. The defendant bought numbers nineteen to twenty-three, and reconstructed the drains so that the sewage from all three houses flowed into the pipe which belonged to number seventeen, then owned by the plaintiff. On the plaintiff's claim that he owned the pipe and that the defendant should disconnect his drains, *held*, although the local authority had laid the pipe, it was not a sewer within the definition in Public Health Act 1936, s. 343, and therefore ownership vested in the plaintiff. The drains from numbers nineteen and twenty-one had been connected to the pipe with the permission of the plaintiff's predecessor, at the defendant's predecessor's expense and a permanent right of drainage had thereby been acquired. However, the connection of the drains from number twenty-three was a trespass, which entitled the plaintiff to an injunction in equity, but as this would be oppressive to the defendant the court would make an award of damages.

COOK v MINION (1979) 37 P & CR 58 (Chancery Division: GOULDING J).

2497 Sewer—damage caused by laying sewer—compensation—loss of profit

The plaintiff, a garage owner, was awarded compensation by an arbitrator under the Public Health Act 1936, s. 278, in respect of business loss suffered by him from road closures ordered by the defendant water authority under statutory powers for the purpose of reconstructing a sewer. The defendant authority refused to pay the amount awarded, contending that (i) liability could not arise when there was no physical interference with access to the plaintiff's premises, and (ii) that compensation was limited to cases of injury to land. *Held*, (i) there was no rule that there had to be direct physical interference with access, nor was it a defence that the authority in exercising its powers did not create an obstruction greater than was reasonably necessary for the proper carrying out of their duties. (ii) There was direct authority that compensation could be awarded for loss of profit. Judgment would be given for the plaintiff.

The court also considered the alternative procedures for enforcing an award. The normal practice was for an applicant first to go to arbitration and then to bring an action on the award rather than to proceed by way of application under the Arbitration Act 1950, s. 26, and RSC Ord. 73, r. 3, for leave to enforce the award. However, there was nothing to prevent a claimant from adopting the latter course if he wished to do so.

LEONIDIS v THAMES WATER AUTHORITY (1979) 251 Estates Gazette 669 (Queen's Bench Division: PARKER J). *Lingke v Christchurch Corpn* [1912] 3 KB 595 applied.

SEX DISCRIMINATION

Halsbury's Laws of England (4th edn.), Vol. 16, paras. 771:2–771:38

2498 Articles

Access to the Courts—Sex Discrimination provides a new model, Jennifer Corcoran (a review of the powers of assistance held by the Equal Opportunities Commission and the Commission for Racial Equality): [1979] LS Gaz 870.

Equality in the Equal Pay Act 1970, A. N. Khan (provisions of and recent judicial developments relating to the Act): 123 Sol Jo 660.

Sex Discrimination Act's blow against chivalry (discussion of the Court of Appeal's decision in *Jeremiah v Ministry of Defence,* see para. 2506): Justinian, Financial Times, 22nd October 1979.

Sex Discrimination in Employment, A. N. Khan and Terrence Ingman (recent judicial decisions on the difficulties raised by such discrimination): 129 NLJ 731.

The Sex Disqualification (Removal) Act—60 Inglorious years, Francis Bennion (the relevance of the 1919 Act today): 129 NLJ 1088.

2499 Discovery of documents—power of industrial tribunal to order

See *Science Research Council v Nasse; BL Cars Ltd (formerly Leyland Cars) v Vyas,* para. 913.

2500 Equal pay—exclusion of requirement for equal treatment—contributory pension scheme—application for appeal to European Court of Justice

n a case concerning a bank-operated pension scheme whereby female employees did In a case concerning a bank-operated pension scheme whereby female employees did not contribute to the fund until over the age of twenty-five whereas male employees did and male employees therefore received 5 per cent more gross pay, the employees conceded that the case fell within the Equal Pay Act 1970, s. 6 (1A) (b), which excluded from its ambit "terms related to death or retirement, or any provision made in relation to death or retirement" consequent upon the decision of the Court of Appeal in *Roberts v Cleveland Area Health Authority, Garland v British Rail Engineering Ltd* and *Turton v MacGregor Wallcoverings Ltd* [1979] 2 All ER 1163. It was argued however that the provisions of the English statute did not comply with the EEC Treaty, art. 119, which provided for equal pay for men and women doing the same work. The Court of Appeal was asked to refer the matter to the European Court of Justice. *Held*, although the applicants were excluded from having their complaints of discrimination in pay considered under the Equal Pay Act 1970, the case would be referred to the European Court of Justice.

WORRINGHAM AND HUMPHREYS v LLOYDS BANK LTD [1980] 1 CMLR 293 (Court of Appeal: LORD DENNING MR, SHAW and TEMPLEMAN LJJ).

2501   —— **like work—employment in succession—application of statutory provisions**

Four months after a man left his position as a stockroom manager a woman was appointed to the position, at a lower wage. The industrial tribunal which heard the woman's claim against her employer for equal pay found that she was employed on like work with her predecessor and that the difference in pay was due exclusively to the difference in sex. The tribunal therefore held that she was entitled to be paid at the higher rate and awarded her extra remuneration. The decision was upheld by the Employment Appeal Tribunal and the employers appealed on the grounds that the Equal Pay Act 1970, s. 1 (2) (a) (i), as substituted by the Sex Discrimination Act 1975, s. 8, applied only to cases where the man and woman were employed at the same time. Section 1 (1) and (2) (a) (i) provided that where a woman is employed on like work with a man in the same employment an equality clause is to be included either expressly or by implication, in the woman's contract of employment. *Held*, LORD DENNING MR dissenting, it was clear from the wording of the statute that that provision was intended to apply only in cases where the man and woman were employed at the same time. However, that interpretation of the provision could be applied only if it was consistent with EEC Treaty, art. 119, the overriding nature and effect of which was established by the European Communities Act 1972, s. 2. While art. 119 clearly placed an obligation on member states to ensure and maintain the application of the principle of equal pay for equal work the ambit of that article was uncertain, and accordingly the proceedings would be stayed pending the opinion of the European Court on the construction and application of art. 119.

LORD DENNING MR considered that s. 1 (2) (a) (i) and art. 119 should be construed together: since, in his opinion, art. 119 clearly applied to cases of both contemporaneous and successive employment, s. 1 (2) (a) (i) was to be interpreted likewise, with the result that there was no conflict between the two provisions and that the United Kingdom had fulfilled its Treaty obligations. He therefore saw no necessity for a reference to the European Court and would have dismissed the appeal. Nevertheless, he acquiesced in the decision to refer.

MACARTHYS LTD v SMITH [1979] 3 All ER 325 (Court of Appeal: LORD DENNING MR, LAWTON and CUMMING-BRUCE LJJ).

On 10th August 1979 a reference for a preliminary ruling under EEC Treaty, art. 177 was lodged at the Registry of the European Court on the question of the construction and application of art. 119 and Council Directive (EEC) 75/117, with particular reference to the situation outlined above. The reference was designated Case 129/79 (OJ No. C.224, 6.9.79).

2502   —— —— **material difference other than sex**

A female machinist who worked twenty-six hours forty minutes a week claimed that she was entitled to the same hourly rate of pay as a man who worked forty hours a week. An industrial tribunal rejected her claim on the ground that the difference in contractual weekly hours was a material difference other than sex which justified the variation in the rate of pay. On appeal, *held*, the industrial tribunal had been correct in its conclusion because the difference in the hourly rate arose out of a difference in the company's productivity. This was clear from the fact that women who worked forty hours also earned more than the claimant. Nor did this conflict with the Treaty of Rome, art. 119, which did not prohibit differences in pay resulting from differences in working time.

HANDLEY v H. MONO LTD [1978] IRLR 534 (Employment Appeal Tribunal: SLYNN J presiding).

2503   A female university lecturer brought a claim under the Equal Pay Act 1970 for modification of her contract of employment after a younger male lecturer was appointed to the same point on the salary scale as herself. The plaintiff believed that the equality between them did not reflect her greater qualifications and that her position had become relatively less favourable. Further, that under the ordinary arrangements in the university, the older a person was, the higher the points he or she got. Her claim was rejected by the industrial tribunal and the Employment Appeal Tribunal. On appeal, *held*, there was no term in her contract less favourable than the equivalent term in the man's contract, nor was her grading less favourable. The "age wage" was not a contractual term but was an internal system for guidance. The grading system of the university depended upon age, qualifications and experience, irrespective of sex and did not infringe the 1970 Act.

POINTON v THE UNIVERSITY OF SUSSEX [1979] IRLR 119 (Court of Appeal: LORD DENNING MR, LAWTON and BRANDON LJJ). Decision of Employment Appeal Tribunal [1977] IRLR 294, 1977 Halsbury's Abridgment para. 2535 affirmed.

2504   A woman employed as a clerk by a company was paid less than a male clerk in the company's press shop. The position of press shop clerk had been successively filled by employees who had become too ill and too old to carry out their usual work; the present press shop clerk had previously been a shop floor worker, but had been transferred to his new position for these reasons. The male clerk had originally been paid at the same rate as the previous press shop clerk, which was slightly less than he had been earning on the shop floor, but he received staff benefits and a staff salary increase that resulted in his earning more than he had been whilst on the shop floor. The woman made a claim under the Equal Pay Act 1970, contending that the male clerk had, in effect, been promoted from the shop floor, and that the company could not therefore claim that his higher wage was due to the fact that his wage was being protected. The tribunal found that the employers had a defence under s. 1 (3) of the 1970 Act, as the material difference between the case of the woman and the case of the male clerk was that of age and illness rather than sex. The woman appealed. *Held*, it was clear from the evidence that the company gave jobs to employees of both sexes who were ill. The tribunal had been entitled, on its finding, to hold that the variation in salary was genuinely due to a material difference between the case of the woman and the case of the male clerk other than the difference of sex. The appeal would be dismissed.

METHVEN v COW INDUSTRIAL POLYMERS LTD [1979] IRLR 276 (Employment Appeal Tribunal: SLYNN J presiding).

2505   **Equal treatment—licensing of premises for wrestling—licence subject to condition prohibiting women from taking part**

A professional female wrestler applied to a promotional company for a wrestling engagement but was refused on the ground that the licence, at the proposed venue, was subject to a condition prohibiting women from taking part. Her complaint, against the licensing authority, of unlawful sexual discrimination was upheld by an industrial tribunal. On appeal, the authority contended that the licence came within the exception provided in the Sex Discrimination Act 1975, s. 51 (1) (b) whereby an instrument made under an Act passed before 1975 was not rendered unlawful after 1975 notwithstanding that it was discriminatory. *Held*, the Local Government Act 1963 provided for the licensing of premises used for wrestling. The licensing authority had been given powers under the 1963 Act to include in the licence such terms as it thought proper. The licence was an instrument granted intra vires the 1963 Act and was therefore exempt under s. 51 (1) (b), notwithstanding that the licence itself had been granted after 1975. The appeal would accordingly be allowed.

GREATER LONDON COUNCIL v FARRAR [1979] LS Gaz R 1253 (Employment Appeal Tribunal: SLYNN J presiding).

2506   —— like work—women not required to work in particular area—whether men under a disadvantage by comparison with women

Work in a particular shop in a munitions factory which produced colour bursting shells involved wearing protective clothing and taking showers after normal working hours. This necessitated overtime working. Male examiners who volunteered for overtime were occasionally required to work in the colour bursting shops whether they wished to do so or not. However, women examiners who volunteered for overtime were never required to work in such shops. A male examiner complained that the practice amounted to unlawful discrimination against male employees on the ground of their sex. Both an industrial tribunal and the Employment Appeal Tribunal upheld his complaint. The employers appealed,. contending inter alia that women employees objected to working in the colour bursting shops, facilities did not exist for them to work there and that the men were compensated financially for the dirty work. *Held*, the case turned on the meaning of the Sex Discrimination Act 1975, ss. 1(1), 2(1), 6(2)(b). The effect of those provisions was that the difference of treatment referred to constituted unlawful discrimination if it put men examiners under a disadvantage by comparison with women examiners or if it subjected them to some detriment by comparison with the latter. From the facts it appeared that the male examiners were treated less favourably than their female counterparts on the ground of their sex. The employers could not buy the right to discriminate by making extra payments to the men. Accordingly, the appeal would be dismissed.

MINISTRY OF DEFENCE v JEREMIAH [1979] 3 All ER 833 (Court of Appeal: LORD DENNING MR, BRANDON and BRIGHTMAN LJJ). Decision of Employment Appeal Tribunal [1978] IRLR 402, 1978 Halsbury's Abridgment para. 2569 affirmed.

2507   Retirement—age of retirement—post-retirement benefit—meaning of "a provision in relation to death or retirement"

The Sex Discrimination Act 1975, s. 6 (4), provides that it is not unlawful to treat women less favourably than men in respect of "a provision in relation to death or retirement". Three cases arose on the interpretation of this section, and were heard together.

The first applicant was employed by a local authority, whose policy was to retire men at sixty-five and women at sixty years of age. She claimed that the different retiring ages amounted to unlawful discrimination. Her complaint was rejected by an industrial tribunal and the Employment Appeal Tribunal on the ground that her complaint fell within the s. 6 (4) exclusion.

The second applicant was employed by a company, which gave both men and women travel concessions for themselves, their spouse and any dependent children. After retirement however, although men enjoyed the same concessions as before, women were only allowed concessions for themselves. An industrial tribunal rejected, and the Employment Appeal Tribunal upheld, her complaint that the concessions were not a provision in relation to retirement but were privileges accorded during employment which continued after retirement.

The third applicant's complaint concerned her employer's policy of giving redundant employees additional payments above the statutory minima. This included an age gratuity given to redundant employees over the age of sixty, which was in fact given to men only as women retired at the age of sixty. Her complaint was upheld by both an industrial tribunal and by the Employment Appeal Tribunal.

On appeal, *held*, the exclusion from the scope of the 1975 Act of "a provision in relation to death or retirement" had to be interpreted widely to mean a provision about death or retirement. On that basis: in the first case the age at which employees were required to retire was within the meaning of s. 6 (4) and her appeal would be dismissed; the fixing of a retiring age was a provision in relation to retirement, and the sole reason why the third applicant did not receive the age gratuity was because of the fixing of that age at sixty. Further, with regard to the second case, a provision whereby a man or a woman was granted, on retirement, certain travel facilities was a provision under s. 6 (4) and the difference between the concessions granted to the man and the woman was not therefore unlawful.

ROBERTS v CLEVELAND AREA HEALTH AUTHORITY; GARLAND v BRITISH RAIL ENGINEERING LTD; TURTON v MACGREGOR WALLCOVERINGS LTD [1979] 2 All ER 1163 (Court of Appeal: LORD DENNING MR, LAWTON and GEOFFREY LANE LJJ). Decisions of Employment Appeal Tribunal in *Roberts v Cleveland Area Health Authority* [1978] ICR 370 affirmed; *Garland v British Rail Engineering Ltd* [1978] 2 All ER 789 reversed; *Turton v MacGregor Wallcoverings Ltd* [1978] ICR 541 reversed. See 1977 Halsbury's Abridgment paras. 2521, 2523, 2549.

2508   Scope of legislation—application to justice of the peace—nature of appointment as justice

After being interviewed, a woman was not recommended for appointment as a justice of the peace. She alleged that during her interview she was asked questions that amounted to unlawful discrimination on the ground of her sex. The tribunal found that it had no jurisdiction to hear the complaint. The applicant appealed. *Held*, dismissing the appeal, the office of justice of the peace did not constitute "employment", as a justice was not paid a salary and was not subject to direction as to the manner in which he fulfilled his obligations. The Sex Discrimination Act 1975, s. 85 (2) (a) conferred the protection of the Act upon those performing service for the purposes of a Minister of the Crown or a government department, other than those holding a statutory office; and a justice of the peace fell within the exception of "those holding a statutory office". Similarly there was no protection under s. 85 (2) (b) because service of a justice of the peace was service for the Crown itself, and not service on behalf of the Crown for the purposes of a person holding a statutory office or purposes of a statutory body. Section 86 (2) imposed a prohibition on the Minister on doing any act which would have been unlawful under s. 6 had the Crown been the employer. Even assuming that justices of the peace were appointed by a Minister of the Crown, the acts prohibited by this section did not constitute acts of unlawful discrimination within Part II (ss. 6–21) of the Act, so as to confer, under s. 63 (1) (a), jurisdiction on an individual tribunal to deal with the matter.

KNIGHT v A-G [1979] ICR 194 (Employment Appeal Tribunal: SLYNN J presiding).

2509   —— services for purposes of person holding statutory office or of statutory body—rent officer

A woman applied for a job as a rent officer but was refused an interview. She complained that she had been unlawfully discriminated against on the ground of her sex. An industrial tribunal found that it had jurisdiction to hear her claim, as a rent officer performed a service on behalf of the Crown for purposes of a person holding a statutory office or statutory body, within the meaning of the Sex Discrimination Act 1975, s. 85 (2) (b). The Department of the Environment appealed. The woman contended that a rent officer performed a service on behalf of the Crown, that a rent officer, as the holder of a statutory office, could be working for the purposes of his own statutory office, and that a rent officer was working for the purposes of a statutory body, the rent assessment committee. The Department argued that a rent officer carried out an independent function given to him by the legislature, and that public service was not necessarily service on behalf of the Crown. *Held*, a rent officer's job was service on behalf of the Crown, as no distinction should be drawn between public service generally and service on behalf of the Crown unless Parliament had made the distinction clear. However, a rent officer, as holder of a statutory office, could not be giving services for his own purposes. Further, a rent officer was not working for the purposes of a statutory body, as a rent officer had his own separate function. Section 85 (2) (b) did not, therefore, apply. The appeal would be allowed.

DEPARTMENT OF THE ENVIRONMENT v FOX [1980] 1 All ER 58 (Employment Appeal Tribunal: SLYNN J presiding).

2510   Selection for appointment—concern of employers that applicant only woman in a team

A woman was refused a place in a painting and decorating team because she would have been the only woman in the team, and problems had arisen in the past where one woman had been alone as part of the team. An industrial tribunal found that the employers had acted fairly and had not discriminated against the woman. She appealed. *Held*, allowing the appeal, even though the employers' intention may have been to act in the best interests of the woman, this did not justify the discrimination in question; neither did the fact that the employers would also have discriminated against a man where the rest of the team consisted of women. *Peake v Automotive Products Ltd* was distinguishable from this case in that it related to people who were already employed, whereas in this case there was a refusal of employment and only the exceptions in the Sex Discrimination Act 1975, s. 7 could justify refusal of employment on the grounds of sex. Furthermore the discrimination in *Peake v Automotive Products Ltd* was *de minimis* and was merely concerned with chivalrous and courteous conduct, which was not so in this case. The refusal of employment in this case was in itself inherently hostile to the interests of the woman.

GRIEG V COMMUNITY INDUSTRY [1979] IRLR 158 (Employment Appeal Tribunal: SLYNN J presiding). *Peake v Automotive Products Ltd* [1978] 1 All ER 106, CA, 1977 Halsbury's Abridgment para. 2550 distinguished.

2511   —— effect of marital status and dependent children

Industrial tribunal decision:

THORNDYKE V BELL FRUIT (NORTH CENTRAL) LTD [1979] IRLR 1 (married woman with three children claimed discrimination on grounds of sex for post as security officer; also on grounds of marital status for post as supervisor; no discrimination proved for first post, five out of the nine security officers employed were female; denied opportunity of competing on equal terms for second post on account of dependent children; no actual loss flowed from discrimination as not proven she would have been appointed; damages limited to compensation for injury to feelings).

2512   —— research fellowship—charitable nature of institution—effect of European legislation

In a case concerning the refusal to grant a research fellowship to a female applicant by a university college, because women were excluded from membership by the college statutes, it was held, (i) the case fell within the provisions of the Sex Discrimination Act 1975 because of the contractual relationship between the college and the research fellow. Although a research fellow was not employed under a contract of service he was engaged in the execution of work and labour within the definition of employment in s. 82 (1) of the Act. (ii) However under s. 43 (2) due to the charitable nature of the college statutes, the exceptions to Part II of the the Act applied so that the discrimination was lawful. (iii) An EEC Directive, on the principle of equality for men and women in vocational training and employment, which was not directly applicable and had not been incorporated into English Law had no effect on the operation of the college statute and did not prevent the provisions of the Act from rendering the discrimination lawful.

HUGH-JONES V ST JOHN'S COLLEGE, CAMBRIDGE [1979] ICR 848 (Employment Appeal Tribunal: SLYNN J presiding).

SHERIFFS AND BAILIFFS

380   Halsbury's Laws of England (3rd edn.), Vol. 34, paras. 1142–1252.

2513   Sheriffs—fees—mileage allowance

The Sheriffs' Fees (Amendment) Order 1979, S.I. 1979 No. 1442 (in force on 17th

December 1979) increases the mileage fee payable to sheriffs on execution of writs of fieri facias, possession or delivery to 16·4 pence per mile.

SHIPPING AND NAVIGATION

Halsbury's Laws of England (3rd edn.), Vol. 35

2514   Articles

The Himalaya Clause, D. G. Powles (the question of its validity as a defence in the light of the decision in *The Eurymedon* [1974] 1 All ER 1015): [1979] LCMLQ 331.
Oil Pollution and the Common Law, John Gibson: [1979] LMCLQ 498.
Some topical considerations in the event of a casualty to an oil tanker, D. W. Abecassis: [1979] LMCLQ 449.
Waybills and Short Form Documents: A Lawyer's View, Richard Williams (examination of the new "short form" and standardised document movement promoted by SITPRO and the General Council of British Shipping): [1979] LCMLQ 297.

2515   Admiralty jurisdiction

See ADMIRALTY.

2516   Berth—safety of berth—requirements

A vessel let under a time charterparty was berthed at a Chilean port where it suffered extensive damage by contact with the pier during bad weather. At the time the vessel was berthed there was no indication of bad weather but during the following night the weather changed and a light was displayed warning of the onset of bad weather. The ship's master immediately summoned a stand-by pilot and tug in order to move the ship from the exposed berth into the bay. However, the presence of two other ships anchored in the bay left no room to manoeuvre and, the operation could not be completed until those ships had first been moved, by which time the damage had occurred. The owners of the vessel claimed damages from the charterers on the ground that, contrary to an express clause in the charterparty, they had ordered the vessel to a port or berth which was unsafe. On a reference to arbitration the umpire found in favour of the owners and his decision was upheld on a case stated. The charterers appealed. *Held*, while it was clear that a port or berth was not necessarily unsafe merely because a vessel might have to leave it due to bad weather, four requirements had to be satisfied in such a case: first, there had to be an adequate weather forecasting system; second, pilots and tugs had to be adequately available; third, there had to be adequate searoom to manoeuvre; and fourth there had to be an adequate system for ensuring that searoom and room for manoeuvre were always available. On the facts of the present case neither the third nor the fourth requirement had been satisfied with the result that the vessel could not leave the berth. Accordingly, the appeal would be dismissed.

THE KHIAN SEA, ISLANDER SHIPPING ENTERPRISES SA v EMPRESA MARITIMA DEL ESTADO SA [1979] 1 Lloyd's Rep 545 (Court of Appeal: LORD DENNING MR, STEPHENSON and SHAW LJJ). *The Stork* [1955] 1 Lloyd's Rep 349, *The Eastern City* [1957] 2 Lloyd's Rep 153 and *The Dagmar* [1968] 2 Lloyd's Rep 563 applied. Decision of Donaldson J [1977] 2 Lloyd's Rep 439, 1977 Halsbury's Abridgment para. 2564 affirmed.

2517   Cargo—damage to cargo—exclusion clause contained in Hague Rules—application

Cement being transported in the hold of the defendants' ship was damaged by water entering through a hatch that was open in heavy weather. In answer to the cement-owners claim for damages, the defendants pleaded the Hague Rules, art. IV, r. 2 (a), (p) which exclude liability for loss or damage arising or resulting from the act, neglect or default of the master, mariner, pilot or the servants of the carrier in the navigation or management of the ship, or arising or resulting from a latent defect not discoverable by due diligence. *Held*, the defendants were in breach of art. III, r. 2, which made the carrier responsible for carefully loading, handling, storing, carrying, keeping, caring for and discharging the cargo. The onus of proving that the cause of the damage fell within art. IV was on the defendants and they had failed to discharge it. The hatch would not have been opened in the course of the navigation or management of the ship and if it had been opened surreptitiously by a crew member the exclusion clause could not apply. Nor had any latent defect been discovered and accordingly the defendants were liable for the damage.

THE BULKNES [1979] 2 Lloyd's Rep 39 (Queen's Bench Division: SHEEN J).

2518   **Carriage of goods by sea—damage to goods—seaworthiness of ship**

The defendant's ship carried asbestos belonging to the plaintiffs on her return voyage from Lourenco Marques to Piraeus. When the ship called at Venice, the defendants found that the asbestos had been damaged by seawater which had leaked through a deep indent in the ship's outer plating. The plaintiffs claimed damages. *Held*, the entry of seawater through an undetected defect in the ship's plating constituted damage by perils of the sea; therefore the defendants were not liable unless the plaintiffs could prove that the ship was unseaworthy when the asbestos was loaded at Lourenco Marques. As no incident had been recorded in the ship's logbook it was impossible to determine whether the indent was made before or after loading. Moreover, in the absence of clear evidence the court would not draw an inference either way. Even if the ship was unseaworthy before loading, the defendants were still not liable unless the unseaworthiness was due to their lack of due diligence. However, the defendants ensured that the ship was fully classed at all material times and that she was thoroughly examined after every complete trip. Routine inspections were also made during each voyage. If the defect existed before the asbestos was loaded, it was a latent defect not discoverable by due diligence and accordingly the defendants were not liable in damages.

THE HELLENIC DOLPHIN [1978] 2 Lloyd's Rep 336 (Queen's Bench Division: LLOYD J).

2519   **—— freight—arbitration clause—time limit—application for extention of time**

See *Sanko Steamship Co v Tradax Export SA*, para. 139.

2520   **—— goods damaged during transhipment—application of Hague Rules**

Canada

Carriers undertook to ship the plaintiff's goods from Madras to Vancouver. The goods were contained in lift vans which the carriers knew to be not waterproof. The plaintiff paid freight for carriage below deck. He was advised that the vans would be transhipped at some point in the voyage, as two vessels would be used. The vans were shipped from Madras to Singapore by the carriers' first vessel. The bill of lading contained a term on its reverse side incorporating the Hague Rules. The plaintiff had worked in the shipping industry and was aware that the bill of lading contained terms on the reverse side, but was at no time shown the carriers' standard form of bill of lading. The carriers' agents made arrangements for storage of the vans at Singapore. The carriers were aware that the vans were stored uncovered for nineteen days. The vans were then shipped to Vancouver by the carriers' second vessel. It was agreed at the time of discharge that the goods had been badly damaged by contact with fresh water during storage. The plaintiff brought an action claiming damages for the breach of contract. The carriers argued that since, by cl. 2 of the bill of lading, the contract incorporated the Hague Rules, the period that the vans were in storage at Singapore was covered by the rules, and by art. IV, r. 5, their liability was limited to $500 per unit. The plaintiff denied that the clause formed part of the contract since no effort had been made to bring it to his attention, and he had not seen the bill of lading until after the damage had occurred. *Held*, the Hague Rules were effectively incorporated into the contract because the bill of lading, as the standard shipping document, had to be taken as evidence of the contract between the parties. However, the part of the contract relating to the storage of the goods at Singapore awaiting loading upon the second vessel was not within the rules because it did not relate to the carriage of goods by water. The carriers' liability was not, therefore, subject to the financial limitation.

CAPTAIN V FAR EASTERN STEAMSHIP CO [1979] 1 Lloyd's Rep 595 (Supreme Court of British Columbia).

2521   Certification of competence—masters, officers and ratings

An international convention was signed in London on 1st July 1978 setting out the requirements as to service, age, medical fitness, training, qualification and examination for certificates for masters, officers and ratings. The convention also prescribes the form of indorsement of certificates issued to masters and officers. The convention applies to seafarers serving on board sea-going ships entitled to fly the flag of any contracting party, other than those serving upon warships, naval ships etc., fishing vessels, pleasure yachts not engaged in trade and wooden ships of primitive build. The United Kingdom has not yet ratified the convention. See International Convention on Standards of Training, Certification and Watchkeeping for Seafarers 1978 (Cmnd. 7543).

2522   Charterparty—arbitration clause—guarantee—whether guarantor bound by award

See *The Vasso*, para. 1401.

2523   —— consecutive voyage charter—calculation of freight

A consecutive voyage charterparty, dated October 1973, provided that the freight rate was to be 250 per cent of the rate stipulated in the Worldscale Schedule as applicable at the date of each loading. The Worldscale Schedule is a schedule of nominal freight rates used by the shipping community as a standard of reference. A revised schedule, based on weighted average bunker prices for the preceding year, is published annually, with effect from 1st January of each year. However, due to a sharp increase in bunker prices in 1973, an additional bunker index was issued each month during 1974. The first, January, index was accompanied by explanatory notes from the publishers stating that the indices were in no way to be construed as an amendment to the basic schedule and that their use was to be subject to the specific agreement of the parties concerned. The charterers paid freight in respect of voyages made in 1974 in accordance with the revised Schedule for 1974 and the owners sought to recover increments resulting from the bunker indices. *Held*, since the publishers of Worldscale expressly stated that the monthly indices did not constitute an amendment to the basic Schedule and it was clear that there had been no express agreement between the parties as to their use, the charterparty was not effective in incorporating the indices into its terms. The owners' claim therefore failed.

THE MARITSA, POLE STAR COMPANIA NAVIERA SA v KOCH MARINE INC [1979] 1 Lloyd's Rep 581 (Queen's Bench Division: MOCATTA J).

2524   —— construction—bunker escalation clause—whether applicable to voyage chartered ship

A contract of affreightment in the form of a charterparty required ship owners to provide vessels nominated by them for the carriage of oil. Under a bunker escalation clause, the charterers had to reimburse the owners for any increase in the cost of bunkers. In 1973 the parties orally agreed to vary the method of preparing increased bunker costs in respect of ships chartered by the owners, as opposed to their own ships nominated under the contract. The charterers settled a number of claims prepared on the agreed basis. They then discovered that the owners had not purchased the bunkers themselves as the ships concerned had been voyage chartered to them. The charterers made a claim for recovery of the payments and the dispute was referred to arbitration. The arbitrator decided against the claim but stated his award in the form of a special case. *Held*, (i) on a true construction of the bunker escalation clause, "reimburse" meant "pay back" and therefore the clause could not apply as the owners did not pay for the bunkers themselves; (ii) the 1973 agreement was not a course of dealing which altered the true construction of the clause; it merely applied to increased bunker costs under charters to which the escalation clause applied, such as time or demise charters; (iii) the charterers had not waived their right to rely on the true construction of the clause. They made the payments under a mistake of law, unaware that the ships had been voyage chartered from another party who was responsible for the cost of bunkers. Moreover, the owners did nothing to inform them of the true position. Accordingly the charterers were entitled to recover the payments and the award would be remitted to the arbitrator.

SARONIC SHIPPING CO LTD v HURON LIBERIAN CO [1979] 1 Lloyd's Rep 341 (Queen's Bench Division: MOCATTA J).

2525　　—— —— despatch money

A dispute involving two charterparties was referred to arbitration and, following the making of awards, the charterers issued motions to set aside or remit the awards for alleged errors of law. The two issues which arose were firstly whether the motions were out of time and secondly whether the arbitrators' decision was correct. Under RSC Ord 73, r. 5 a motion to set aside or remit might be made at any time within six weeks after the award had been made and published to the parties. The question was whether the awards had been made and published on the day of receipt of the notice that the awards were available for collection, in which case the charterers were four days out of time, or on the day the copy of the awards was received. The dispute itself was whether under the terms of the two charterparties the charterers would include Sundays and holidays as laytime saved in the calculation of despatch money; the arbitrators decided that they could not. *Held*, time ran from receipt of the notice that the awards were available and the charterers had thus been out of time, but in view of the circumstances, including the short delay of four days, the court would exercise its discretion to extend the time.

Under the terms of the charterparty the laytime allowed for the loading and discharging of the vessel did not, except in certain circumstances, include Sundays and holidays and it was clear that the excepted days were not to count as working time. Thus Sundays and holidays were not to be included as laytime saved in the calculation of despatch money. The motions would be dismissed.

THE ARCHIPELAGOS AND DELFI, BULK TRANSPORT CORPN v SISSY STEAMSHIP CO LTD, BULK TRANSPORT CORPN v IFLED SHIPPING CORPN [1979] 2 Lloyd's Rep 289 (Queen's Bench Division: PARKER J). *Brooke v Mitchell* (1840) 9 LJ (NS) Ex 269 and *Mawson Shipping Co Ltd v Beyer* [1914] 1 KB 304, applied.

2526　　—— —— different parties named as "charterer" and "actual charterer"—liability under charterparty

The plaintiffs let their ship to a Cypriot company "as charterers" for the carriage of goods. The charter provided for freight and demurrage to be guaranteed by the defendants, a Greek company, as "actual charterers". Before the charter was agreed, the plaintiffs had insisted that if the charterers were not Greek, the charter had to be countersigned by the original charterers registered in Greece. The charter was duly signed by the plaintiffs and the Cypriot company; the defendants also signed in two places. The ship was damaged and in May 1976 the plaintiffs began arbitration proceedings against the Cypriot company. In July 1976 they petitioned for the arrest of a ship as security for their claim against the Cypriot company before discovering that the company did not own the ship or have any substantial means. In April 1977 the plaintiffs dropped their arbitration proceedings against the Cypriot company and instead began proceedings against the defendants. The defendants denied liability, contending that the charterers were the Cypriot company. Alternatively they claimed that the plaintiffs' actions showed that they had elected to hold the Cypriot company liable under the charter and were therefore barred from continuing arbitration proceedings against the defendants. *Held*, (i) since the defendants had signed the charter twice and were described in it as "actual charterers", their liability could not be limited to guaranteeing freight and demurrage; (ii) the defendants had countersigned the charter in accordance with the plaintiffs' original requirement which showed that they accepted liability as charterers and were bound by the arbitration clause; (iii) the plaintiff could only be barred by election if they acted with full knowledge of the facts. However, they did not discover that the defendants had more substantial means than the Cypriot company until sometime after commencing proceedings against the company in July 1976. Moreover, the defendants had not been prejudiced in any way by the plaintiffs' actions. Accordingly, the plaintiffs were not barred from continuing arbitration proceedings against the defendants.

THE SCAPLAKE, PYXIS SPECIAL SHIPPING CO LTD v DRITSAS & KAGLIS BROS LTD [1978] 2 Lloyd's Rep 380 (Queen's Bench Division: MOCATTA J).

2527   —— —— when demurrage incurred— meaning of "used laytime"

See *The Tsukuba Maru*, para. 2529.

2528   —— demurrage—claim for interest on demurrage paid late

See *Tehno-Impex v GEBR Van Weede Scheepvaartkantoor BV*, para. 145.

2529   —— —— expiry of laytime—exception clause

A vessel was chartered under a voyage charterparty which provided for a total period of laytime to cover loading and discharge and specified the rate of demurrage payable on such time used in loading and discharging cargo and other "used laytime" as exceeded the agreed laytime. Under clauses 6 and 7 of the charterparty laytime was not to run until six hours after receipt of the notice of readiness to discharge, and time between anchoring and berthing at the port of discharge and any delay in berthing due to bad weather were not to count as "used laytime". Under clause 8, on the happening of certain events, including the break-down of the vessel or shore equipment, demurrage was either not payable or was to be reduced. The permitted laytime was exceeded at the loading port, making demurrage payable in respect of the excess period. On arrival at the port of destination the master gave notice of readiness, but was unable to berth for several days due to bad weather. The cargo was not finally discharged until nearly a month later, during part of which time the vessel's boiler required repairs and certain shore unloading equipment broke down. The owners claimed demurrage in respect of the whole of the time from arrival at the port, subject to the agreed reductions and exceptions under clause 8. On a case stated by the arbitrators, *held*, the charterers' submission that the phrase "used laytime" was a term of art defining the period in respect of which demurrage was payable could not be supported: from the moment they exceeded the agreed laytime they were in continuous breach of contract and liable to pay demurrage. Since it was clear that such liability could be negatived only by a clearly worded exclusion clause the charterers could not claim exemption under clauses 6 and 7 since they were merely exceptions preventing time from running and contained nothing to indicate that they applied once the vessel was on demurrage, as in this case. Thus the vessel continued to be on demurrage for the whole of the time from its arrival at the port of discharge, subject only to the exemption and reduction under clause 8, which was sufficiently clearly worded as to constitute an exception.

The charterers' further submission on the basis of causation also failed: where laytime was agreed under a charterparty it imposed an absolute obligation on the charterers, for the non-performance of which, in the absence of a clearly worded exception clause they were answerable. The concept of causation in relation to demurrage was largely irrelevant.

THE TSUKUBA MARU, NIPPON YUSEN KAISHA v SOCIÉTÉ ANONYME MAROCAINE DE L'INDUSTRIE DU RAFFINAGE [1979] 1 Lloyd's Rep 459 (Queen's Bench Division: MOCATTA J). *Union of India v Compania Naviera Aeolus SA* [1964] AC 868, HL, and *Dias Compania Naviera SA v Louis Dreyfus Corporation* [1978] 1 All ER 724, HL, 1978 Halsbury's Abridgment para. 2595 applied.

2530   —— freight—freight payable on delivery of cargo—cargo contaminated—whether cargo delivered

A charterparty provided that freight was payable on delivery of the cargo. The cargo shipped was "Bachaquero Crude" oil which had the special quality of being free from paraffin and therefore suitable for processing into high quality lubricating oils. The charterers took delivery of the oil, but alleged that on discharge the oil contained paraffin left over from a previous cargo. In arbitration proceedings, the arbitrators stated their award in the form of a consultative case. The question for the court was whether the shipowners were entitled to payment of freight in full on the assumption that the cargo was delivered in a state which was either unmerchantable as Bachaquero Crude or was not identical commercially with the cargo loaded. *Held*, where goods had been damaged during shipment, the test whether there had been delivery of the cargo so as to entitle the shipowner to freight was whether, on discharge, an honest merchant would be forced to qualify the description applicable to the goods on shipment to such an extent as to destroy it, or whether he would merely qualify the cargo as goods of the description shipped but damaged. The mere fact that on delivery the oil was not identical commercially with the oil loaded, or was not of merchantable quality, did not necessarily deprive the shipowners of the right to freight. The award would be remitted to the arbitrators to make the appropriate further award.

THE CASPIAN SEA [1979] 3 All ER 378 (Queen's Bench Division: DONALDSON J). Dictum of Lord Esher in *Asfar & Co v Blundell* [1896] 1 QB 123 at 127–8 applied.

2531   —— hire—owner's right to withdraw ship failing punctual payment—whether charterer made payment "in cash"

Under a charterparty, hire was payable in cash and the owners could withdraw the ship failing punctual and regular payment. An instalment of hire was due on 22nd January 1976. On that date the charterers' bank sent a telex to the owners' bank transferring the amount due "value 26". This meant that although the money could be paid to the owners immediately, interest on the sum did not begin to run in their favour until 26th January 1976. The owners instructed their bank to refuse the payment and withdrew the ship, contending that hire had not been paid punctually in cash. The charterers claimed damages for wrongful withdrawal and the dispute was referred to arbitration. The arbitrator decided in favour of the charterers but stated his award in the form of a special case. *Held*, in determining whether the telex transfer was a payment in cash under the charter, the sole test to be applied was whether or not the owners were given an unconditional right to immediate use of the money on 22nd January. The words "value 26" in the telex made the transfer conditional on interest not accruing to the owners until 26th January. Therefore, the payment was not in cash as it did not give them an unconditional right to immediate use of the money on the specified date for payment. Accordingly, the owners were entitled to withdraw their ship.

THE CHIKUMA, A/S AWILCO v FULVIA SpA DI NAVIGAZIONE [1979] 1 Lloyd's Rep 367 (Queen's Bench Division: ROBERT GOFF J). Dicta of Brandon J in *Tenax Steamship Co Ltd v Reinante Transoceanica Navegacion SA (The Brimnes)* [1973] 1 All ER 769 at 782, applied.

2532   —— —— secret agreement for repayment of hire by owner—whether charterer entitled to rely on secret agreement as against new owner

The owners of a ship were anxious to borrow money and chartered their ship for ten years at a fixed rate of hire which could be used as security for a loan. The charter also provided for hire to be assessed by an independent panel after two years; if the assessed rate was less than the fixed rate, the defendant charterers had to pay the fixed rate and the difference was to be treated as advance hire. However, the defendants refused to pay more than the assessed market rate and the parties made a separate agreement by letter whereby the owners guaranteed to repay the defendants any difference in rates. The owners subsequently obtained a loan from the plaintiffs and assigned their right to payment of hire as security. The plaintiffs were shown the charter but not the letter. In April 1975 the panel assessed the market rate for hire as being less than the fixed rate specified in the charter. The defendants paid the plaintiffs the fixed rate until December 1975 but the owners only repaid the excess over the assessed rate up to September 1975. The defendants stopped payments altogether in January 1976. The plaintiffs then discovered the existence of the letter containing the owners' guarantee to repay hire and unsuccessfully called in their loan. The ship was laid up in July 1976 at the plaintiffs' expense. In September 1976 title in the ship was transferred to the plaintiffs who claimed that the defendants were liable for the fixed rate of hire under the charter from January to September 1976. The defendants contended that the charter had ended in January 1976. *Held*, (i) even if the owners had repudiated their obligations under the letter, the defendants were not entitled to stop paying hire and determine the charter since the charter and the letter were designed to operate independently of each other. (ii) The plaintiffs had suffered considerable loss as a direct result of the defendants' conduct in their dealings with the owners: the defendants entered the charter knowing that the owners would use it as security for a loan and conceal the separate agreement for repayment of hire. Accordingly the defendants were estopped from denying that the charter was the only material agreement with the owners which affected their duty to pay hire. (iii) By laying up the ship in July 1976 the plaintiffs had terminated the charter and therefore the defendants were liable for the fixed rate under the charter from January to July 1976.

THE ODENFELD, GATOR SHIPPING CORPN v TRANS-ASIATIC OIL LTD SA AND OCCIDENTAL SHIPPING ESTABLISHMENT [1978] 2 Lloyd's Rep 357 (Queen's Bench Division: KERR J).

2533   —— —— **underpayment—acceptance of underpayment—owner's right to withdraw vessel**

Charterers hired a vessel for eight to ten months under a charterparty which provided for withdrawal of the vessel in default of payment of hire. The hire was to be paid monthly in advance without discount except for the final month's hire which was subject to certain deductions. At the beginning of the ninth month, the charterers sent the owners a credit note for the month's hire, showing a deduction from the amount due. The owners informed the charterers that the deductions were not acceptable, but did not instruct their bank to refuse payment. The reduced amount was paid into the owners' account and on the following day the charterers supplied details of the deductions, from which it was apparent that they estimated the ninth month to be the last one of hire. The owners correctly maintained that the charter would extend into another month and that the deductions were not therefore allowable. When requested full details of the deductions were not forthcoming, the owners withdrew the vessel, claiming that the underpayment constituted a default in payment. The charterers successfully contended that the owners were in breach of the charterparty as they had waived their right of withdrawal by accepting the underpayment, by requesting further details of the deductions, and by failing to return the hire in respect of the period after withdrawal. On appeal by the owners, *held*, the owners' acceptance of the hire could not amount to waiver; on the date of payment there was no default that the owners could waive, as the charterers had until the following day to make good the deficiency. Further, the owners were entitled to a reasonable time to ascertain whether the charterers' estimated deductions were correct before deciding to exercise a right of withdrawal, as the right would accrue to them only if the deductions were wrong. The retention by the owners of the excess hire did not make the act of withdrawal any less unequivocal and therefore did not amount to waiver, although the owners would have to give credit for the excess paid on the settling of accounts. Accordingly, the appeal would be allowed.

CHINA NATIONAL FOREIGN TRADE TRANSPORTATION CORPN v EVLOGIA SHIPPING CO SA OF PANAMA, THE MIHALIOS XILAS [1979] 2 All ER 1044 (House of Lords: LORD DIPLOCK, VISCOUNT DILHORNE, LORD SALMON, LORD FRASER OF TULLYBELTON and LORD SCARMAN). Decision of Court of Appeal [1979] 1 All ER 657 reversed.

2534   —— time charter—ship damaged due to act of crew member—
time lost during repairs—claim of right of set-off

A ship was chartered on terms incorporating the Hague Rules. During the voyage
she collided with a quay while docking and the charterers lost the opportunity of a
cargo owing to the time taken for repairs. The charterers alleged that the accident
was due either to the negligence of the crew or a defect in the engine, and claimed
a right of set-off against the hire charge. *Held*, it was clear on the evidence that there
was no defect in the engine and therefore the accident could only have been caused
by a crewmember's act for which the owners could not be held liable under the
Hague Rules. The charterers claim would therefore be dismissed.

THE ALIAKMON PROGRESS, ALIAKMON MARITIME CORPN V TRANSOCEAN
CONTINENTAL SHIPPING LTD [1978] 2 Lloyd's Rep 499 (Court of Appeal: LORD
DENNING MR and GEOFFREY LANE LJ).

2535   —— —— suspension of payments—whether charterers entitled to
give notice of suspension

A group of companies built a plant in Abu Dhabi for liquefying natural gas, which
was then to be shipped to Japan. The plant consisted of two entirely separate units,
each producing half the required output, independently of each other. One unit was
to start production before the other and the second was to start six months later,
production to be built up to the contract average in the second six months. By a
charterparty of March 1973 the owners let their vessels on a time charter until 1995,
delivery of the vessels to coincide with the build up in production. Clause 59 (a) of
the charter provided that if through any cause beyond the reasonable control of the
charterers, production was interrupted or terminated, the charterers could suspend
operation of the charter including the payment for hire for a maximum of six
months in any five-year period. Further by sub-clause (b) in the event of the
charterers exercising their option to suspend the charter they would do so in writing
and then consult with the owners for a maximum period of thirty days in an
endeavour to find alternative employment for the vessel, at the end of which sub-
clause (a) would come into operation.

Production started on the first unit in August 1976, defects occurred and no gas
was produced until January 1977. It was then further delayed, due to the
malfunctioning of an instrument until March. As a result of defects in the first unit,
the second unit was modified and production did not commence until August
1977. In September there was a total failure of both plants and only one unit
resumed production later that month. The vessels came on hire by the end of 1976
but there was no cargo for them to load. The first vessel loaded her first cargo in
April 1977 but an unloading incident in Japan in September had the effect of cutting
back production at the plant. The second vessel loaded her first cargo in August and
the third vessel in September. In March 1977 the charterers, in accordance with cl.
59 gave notice suspending the payment of hire of the second vessel. Owing to the
incident which occurred in September the first vessel was in Singapore for a tank
inspection and as it was unlikely to be required before December, the charterers
advised the owners that its would be withdrawn from service for two or three
months. The third vessel was in Singapore when, in October, the charterers gave
their second notice suspending payment of hire under the first and second vessel
charterparties. In an action for payment disputes arose as to, inter alia, whether the
charters were entitled to give notice of suspension of hire and the meaning in cl. 59 (a)
of the words "production being interrupted". *Held*, although delivery of the
vessels was intended to coincide with the build up in production, it did not follow
that cl. 59 was not intended to operate during the build up period, nor was there any
reason why such a restriction should have been implied. The clause applied as soon
as there was any production capable of being interrupted. By September 1977 the
first unit had been in production for eight months and the second unit a month and
there was therefore sufficient production and it was interrupted due to causes
reasonably beyond the control of the charterers. The charterers were entitled
therefore to exercise their option under cl. 59 in relation to their October notice
suspending payment of hire of the first and second vessels. In March, however, full

production had not started, the second unit not commencing production until August and cl. 59 did not apply.

THE HILLI, KHANNUR AND GIMI, GOLAR GAS TRANSPORT INC v LIQUEFIED GAS SHIPPING CO LTD [1979] 1 Lloyd's Rep 153 (Queen's Bench Division: LLOYD J).

2536   Collision—apportionment of liability—negligence of both parties

Scotland

A fishing vessel sighted the defendants' vessel heading for her. Each ship presumed the other would alter course and each failed to keep a proper lookout. In trying to take avoiding action the ships collided and the defendants' vessel struck the fishing vessel causing her to sink. In an action for negligence the fishing vessel's owners contended, inter alia, that the defendants had failed to keep a proper lookout. Further, that as the defendants' ship was fitted with a whaleback deck which was not a normal fitting and impaired visibility from the wheelhouse, the defendant had a duty to institute a system of work so that a proper lookout was kept. *Held*, the collision was caused by the failure of both parties to keep a lookout and liability would be equally apportioned. Further, the whaleback deck was a common feature on vessels and there was no evidence that such precautions were necessary or desirable. Nor was there any evidence that the slight impairment of vision occasioned by the whaleback deck played any part in the collision.

THE DEVOTION II [1979] 1 Lloyd's Rep 509 (Outer House).

2537   The plaintiffs' ship and the defendants' ship had to navigate a narrow channel in opposite directions. According to usual practice, an outward bound ship such as the plaintiffs' left the lock at the north of the channel shortly before high water; an inward bound ship such as the defendants' arrived at the lock after high water. However, the plaintiffs' ship was delayed until after high water. The pilot of the defendants' ship, which had already left her anchorage outside the channel, reduced speed and subsequently stopped all engines; the ship was blown over to the extreme eastern side of the channel and then proceeded slowly northwards. The pilot eventually saw the plaintiffs' ship travelling down the channel at considerable speed. He began to steer the defendants' ship over to her own starboard side of the channel so as to pass the plaintiffs' ship port to port in accordance with the Collision Regulations, r. 25. A collision occurred. The plaintiffs claimed that the defendants' ship should have stayed out of the way on the eastern side of the channel. The defendants contended that it was clear that their ship would turn to starboard. *Held*, (i) the defendants' pilot was not at fault in leaving anchorage when he did or in allowing his ship to drift over to the eastern side of the channel. However, he was clearly in breach of the Collision Regulations, r. 25 in failing to steer the ship over to her own starboard side of the channel in good time. (ii) The plaintiffs' pilot was at fault in failing to anticipate the clear possibility that the defendants' ship would cross over to her own starboard side. In view of that possibility, the plaintiffs' ship should have been travelling at a slower rate. (iii) The action by the defendants' pilot in turning to starboard was the main cause of the collision and liability would be apportioned 70 per cent to the defendants and 30 per cent to the plaintiffs.

THE CITY OF LEEDS [1978] 2 Lloyd's Rep 346 (Queen's Bench Division: BRANDON J).

2538   —— regulations—distress signals

The Collision Regulations and Distress Signals (Amendment) Order 1979, S.I. 1979 No. 462 (in force on 14th May 1979), further amends the Collision Regulations and Distress Signals Order 1977, 1977 Halsbury's Abridgment para. 2597, by making the necessary amendment in respect of the traffic separation schemes adopted by IMCO. It also adds a further five countries to the list of foreign countries to whose vessels the Regulations apply.

This order has now been revoked, see para. 2539

2539   The Safety (Collision Regulations and Distress Signals) Regulations 1979, S.I. 1979 No. 1659 (in force on 9th January 1980), further amend the Collision Regulations and Distress Signals Order 1977 and revoke art. 2 (2) of the Amendment Order, 1977 Halsbury's Abridgment para. 2597. The order also revokes the Collision Regulations and Distress Signals (Amendment) Orders 1978, 1978 Halsbury's Abridgment paras. 2612, 2613 and para. 2538 supra.

2540   **Colonies—merchant shipping**

The Merchant Shipping (Colonies) (Amendment) Order 1979, S.I. 1979 No. 1449 (in force on 17th December 1979), amends the Merchant Shipping (Colonies) Order 1927 by deleting Bermuda from the Schedule to the Order. The Order is consequent upon the enactment in Bermuda of the Merchant Shipping Act 1979, which, inter alia, replaces the provisions of the Merchant Shipping (International Labour Conventions) Act 1925 so far as they relate to ships registered in Bermuda.

2541   **Continental shelf—protection of installations**

Various Orders have been made specifying as safety zones certain sea areas (being areas within a radius of 500 metres of certain offshore installations). Ships are forbidden to enter those zones except with permission of the Secretary of State, or in specified circumstances. The Orders concerned are: Continental Shelf (Protection of Installations) Order 1979, S.I. 1979 No. 641 (in force on 12th June 1979); Continental Shelf (Protection of Installations) (No. 2) Order 1979, S.I. 1979 No. 1058 (in force on 23rd August 1979); Continental Shelf (Protection of Installations) (No. 3) Order 1979, S.I. 1979 No. 1083 (in force on 30th August 1979); Continental Shelf (Protection of Installations) (No. 4) Order 1979, S.I. 1979 No. 1136 (in force on 11th September 1979).

2542   The Continental Shelf (Protection of Installations) (Variation) Order 1979, S.I. 1979 No. 1273 (in force on 2nd November 1979), varies the Continental Shelf (Protection of Installations) Order 1979 and the Continental Shelf (Protection of Installations) (No. 4) Order 1979, para. 2541, by deleting incorrect designations of the installations from the Schedules to those Orders and inserting the correct designations.

2543   **Contract of affreightment—construction—bunker escalation clause**

See *Saronic Shipping Co Ltd v Huron Liberian Co*, para. 2524.

2544   **Crew accommodation**

The Merchant Shipping (Crew Accommodation) (Amendment) Regulations 1979, S.I. 1979 No. 491 (in force on 1st July 1979), amend the Merchant Shipping (Crew Accommodation) Regulations 1978, 1978 Halsbury's Abridgment para. 2618, in those provisions relating to the minimum floor area to be provided in sleeping rooms for officers and cadets so as to take account of the case where two cadets are accommodated in one sleeping room.

2545   **Fishing vessels**

See FISHERIES.

2546   **Food hygiene—ships**

See para. 1321.

2547   **Freight—collection by agent—agent's right to set off lost profit against freight**

The defendants were appointed the plaintiffs' agents for the purpose of establishing a regular shipping line between the United Kingdom and Nigeria. The defendants were responsible for the collection of freight. They contended that the plaintiffs had contracted to provide one ship a month and that when that frequency was not achieved they were entitled to regard the plaintiffs as having repudiated the contract. The defendants did not, however, pay over the freight they had collected. The plaintiffs sought a declaration and an account and payment of money due on the account under RSC Ord. 14. The defendants counterclaimed for damages for the loss they had suffered in consequence of the plaintiffs' failure to provide one ship a month. The trial judge held that the defendants had no right of set off and ordered them to bring into court a sum representing the whole of the unpaid freight. On the defendants' appeal, *held*, the claim was clearly one for freight notwithstanding the fact that it was brought under the contract of agency. The case could not be distinguished from *The Brede* [1974] QB 233, CA or *The Aries* [1977] 1 All ER 398, HL, 1977 Halsbury's Abridgment para. 2580 and therefore the defendants' claim could only be brought as a cross-action; it could not be pleaded as a defence or set-off. Further, the trial judge had been quite entitled to order the whole sum into court as a condition of staying execution on the judgment.

JAMES & CO SCHEEPVAARTEN HANDELMIJ BV V CHINECREST LTD [1979] 1 Lloyd's Rep 126 (Court of Appeal: STEPHENSON and LAWTON LJJ).

2548   Hovercraft—application of enactments

The Hovercraft (Application of Enactments) (Amendment) Order 1979, S.I. 1979 No. 1309 (in force on 2nd November 1979), amends the Hovercraft (Application of Enactments) Order 1972, Sch. 1 by adding references to the Transport Act 1962, s. 67 (2) and the Transport Act 1968, Sch. 16, para. 4 (5). The power of the British Railways Board to make bylaws relating to ships operated by them or by their subsidiaries is thus extended to hovercraft operated by the Board.

2549   —— civil liability

The Hovercraft (Civil Liability) Order 1979, S.I. 1979 No. 305 (in force on 1st April 1979), revokes and re-enacts the provisions of the Hovercraft (Civil Liability) Order 1971, with modifications with regard to the limit of the carrier's liability for the carriage of cargo, injury or death to passengers, passengers' baggage and damage caused by a hovercraft other than damage to passengers and their baggage.

2550   —— fees

The Hovercraft (Fees) (Amendment) Regulations 1979, S.I. 1979 No. 1280 (in force on 1st December 1979), amend the Hovercraft (Fees) Regulations 1978, 1978 Halsbury's Abridgment para. 2631 by prescribing increased fees payable to the Secretary of State for the issue of operating permits.

2551   Insurance

See INSURANCE (marine).

2552   Maritime lien—nature of lien—ship let on demise charter—whether lien extinguished

Owners of a ship contracted with charterers to surrender all their rights of possession and control during the term of the charter. Following a collision in which the ship was involved, an action in rem was brought against the ship, on the basis of a maritime lien. Her owners sought to set aside the action on the ground that such a lien was a right over property by way of security for personal liability, and that as they had had no control over the ship at the time of the collision they could not be personally liable. *Held*, a maritime lien consisted of a right to arrest a ship, which had originally been necessary when her owners were not easily available. It had previously been held that the right would remain if a ship had been sold to new owners after a collision, and accordingly it would remain where she had been let out on a demise charter. This decision was reinforced by the fact that it corresponded with the maritime law of other countries, and English law was bound to aim for uniformity in such cases.

THE FATHER THAMES [1979] 2 Lloyd's Rep 364 (Queen's Bench Division: SHEEN J).

2553   —— possessory lien—right of consulting engineer to advance payments in respect of personal liability incurred

A consulting engineer carried out an inspection of a ship's engine which was in need of repair, assessed those repairs which would be necessary and engaged sub-contractors to do the work. As the work progressed he experienced difficulty in securing advance payments from the ship's owners so he withheld certain engine parts which he had in his possession and submitted a claim for the balance of the account. The owners alleged in defence that the work had been badly done and that the engineer had not exercised the professional skill which he had held himself out as possessing. They also disputed his claim for advance payments. *Held*, on the evidence the engineer had exercised all reasonable care and skill in performing his duties, and the problems which had arisen during the course of the repairs were due to circumstances beyond his control. Although he had been acting as the owners' agent, in hiring the sub-contractors he had incurred personal liability for which he was entitled to be secured in advance. He had been entitled to retain the engine parts under a possessory lien until he received payment from the owners, and would be awarded the whole of his claim in the form of a money judgment.

THE IJAOLA, FRASER v EQUITORIAL SHIPPING CO LTD [1979] 1 Lloyd's Rep 103 (Queen's Bench Division: LLOYD J).

2554   Merchant shipping—confirmation of legislation—Bermuda

The Merchant Shipping (Confirmation of Legislation) (Bermuda) Order 1979, S.I. 1979 No. 1448 (in force on 17th December 1979), confirms an Act of the legislature of Bermuda which repeals certain provisions of the Merchant Shipping Acts 1894 and 1906 and the Merchant Shipping (Seamen's Allotment) Act 1911, the Merchant Shipping (Certificates) Act 1914, the Merchant Shipping (Amendment) Act 1923 and the Merchant Shipping (Superannuation Contributions) Act 1937 so far as they relate to ships registered in Bermuda.

2555   —— fees

The Merchant Shipping (Fees) Regulations 1979, S.I. 1979 No. 798 (in force on 1st September 1979 for the purpose of reg. 3 (2), Sch. Part XI and 1st August 1979 for all other purposes), revoke and re-enact both Merchant Shipping (Fees) Regulations 1978, 1978 Halsbury's Abridgment para. 2626 and Merchant Shipping (Fees) (Amendment) Regulations 1979, S.I. 1979 No. 631. The fees for marine surveys and other services have been increased, except in respect of the following: fishing vessel surveys and inspections; certificates of service; registration of ships; wreck; submersible craft.

2556   —— foreign deserters

The Merchant Shipping (Foreign Deserters) (Disapplication) Order 1979, S.I. 1979 No. 120 (in force on 7th March 1979), provides that the Merchant Shipping Act 1970, s. 89, which prescribes the United Kingdom procedure for dealing with deserters from ships of certain foreign countries, is to cease to apply to Estonia, Japan, Latvia and Romania.

2557   —— load lines

The Merchant Shipping (Load Line) (Amendment) Rules 1979, S.I. 1979 No. 1267 (in force on 1st January 1980), amend the Merchant Shipping (Load Line) Rules 1968, S.I. 1968 No. 1053, by deleting references to the surveyor's report which formerly formed part of the record of particulars relating to conditions of assignment of freeboards issued to ships complying with the load line requirements.

2558 —— **Manchester pilotage**

The Manchester Pilotage (Amendment) Order 1979, S.I. 1979 No. 712 (in force on 1st September 1979), extends the limits of the Manchester Pilotage District.

2559 —— **marine engineer officers—certification**

The Merchant Shipping (Certification of Marine Engineer Officers) (Amendment) Regulations 1979, S.I. 1979 No. 599 (in force on 1st September 1981), amend the Merchant Shipping (Certification of Marine Engineer Officers) Regulations 1977, 1977 Halsbury's Abridgment para. 2611, in relation to certificates of competency and service.

2560 —— **metrication**

The Merchant Shipping (Metrication) (Hong Kong) Order 1979, S.I. 1979 No. 1706 (in force on 24th January 1980), extends to Hong Kong the Merchant Shipping Act 1970, s. 90 and the Merchant Shipping (Metrication) Regulations 1973, which adapt certain measurement provisions of the Merchant Shipping Acts dealing with the marking on ships' sides to the metric scale.

2561 —— **repatriation**

The Merchant Shipping (Repatriation) Regulations 1979, S.I. 1979 No. 97 (in force on 1st March 1979), re-enact with amendments the Merchant Shipping (Repatriation) Regulations 1972, S.I. 1972 No. 1805, with regard to seamen left behind or shipwrecked. The two major amendments are (i) an employer is obliged to return a seaman who has been unable, for reasons beyond his control, to inform his employer, his employer's agent, a superintendent or other proper officer of his whereabouts, as soon as he receives confirmation that the seaman wishes to return. That obligation ceases when the employer receives written notice from the seaman that he does not wish to be returned. (ii) An employer is obliged to make provision for a seaman's relief and maintenance, including reasonable legal costs in certain criminal proceedings. Other amendments simplify the requirements for seamen's wages and accounts.

2562 —— **returns of births and deaths**

The Merchant Shipping (Returns of Births and Deaths) Regulations 1979, S.I. 1979 No. 1577 (in force on 1st January 1980), revoke and re-enact the provisions of the Merchant Shipping (Returns of Births and Deaths) Regulations 1972 and contain certain additional provisions. Under reg. 7, where a master is unable to perform the duty imposed on him by the Regulations because he has himself died or is incapacitated or missing, and the death in question has been established, the Registrar General of Shipping and Seamen is required to record the specified information about the death. Where an inquest has been held, or there has been a post-mortem examination or a preliminary investigation and the coroner is satisfied that an inquest is unnecessary, and it appears to the coroner that the death occurred in a ship registered in the United Kingdom or in an unregistered British ship or, if outside the United Kingdom, was of a person employed in such a ship, the coroner is required to send specified particulars to the Registrar General of Shipping and Seamen. The Registrar General of Shipping and Seamen must then send a certified copy of that record or return to the appropriate specified Registrar General. The maximum penalty which can be imposed on any master who fails to make any return of birth or death required by the Regulations is increased to £50.

2563 —— **ships' names**

The Merchant Shipping (Ships' Names) Regulations 1979, S.I. 1979 No. 341 (in force on 18th April 1979), replace the Board of Trade Regulations dated 28th August 1907, SR & O 1907 No. 740, as amended by SR & O 1936 No. 390, which dealt with the registration of ships' names.

2564   —— sterling equivalents

The Merchant Shipping (Sterling Equivalents) (Various Enactments) Order 1979, S.I. 1979 No. 790 (in force on 1st August 1979), specifies the sterling amounts which are to be taken as equivalent to the amounts expressed in gold francs in the following enactments: Merchant Shipping (Liability of Shipowners and Others) Act 1958; Carriage of Goods by Sea Act 1971; Merchant Shipping (Oil Pollution) Act 1971, Merchant Shipping Act 1974, 1974 Halsbury's Abridgment para. 3067; Unfair Contract Terms Act 1977, 1977 Halsbury's Abridgment para. 540.

2565   Merchant Shipping Act 1970—commencement

The Merchant Shipping Act 1970 (Commencement No. 6) Order 1979, S.I. 1979 No. 809, brought into force on 1st August 1979, 1970 Act, ss. 15, 19, 95 (2) and the repeals in s. 100 (3), Sch. 5 of Merchant Shipping Act 1895, ss. 157, 158 and of Merchant Shipping (International Labour Conventions) Act 1925, s. 1, Sch. 1, part 1.

2566   Merchant Shipping Act 1974—commencement

The Merchant Shipping Act 1974 (Commencement No. 4) Order 1979, S.I. 1979 No. 808, brought into force on 1st August 1979, 1974 Act ss. 14, 15, Sch. 4, 1974 Halsbury's Abridgment para. 3067. Those provisions empower the Secretary of State to make orders for the protection of shipping and trading interests.

2567   Merchant Shipping Act 1979

The Merchant Shipping Act 1979 amends the law of pilotage, carriage by sea, shipowners' and salvors' liability and pollution from ships. The Act received the royal assent on 4th April 1979. The Merchant Shipping Act 1979 (Commencement No. 1) Order 1979, S.I. 1979 No. 807, brought certain provisions into force as follows.

The date of commencement of the provisions listed in Sch. 1 is 1st August 1979. The provisions are: ss. 1–6, 12, 13 (1) (in relation to the provisions brought into force by Sch. 2 to the Order), (5), 16, 20–22, 26, 32 (1), 33, 34, 35 (1) (in relation to fishing vessels), 36 (1)–(3), 37 (1)–(3), (5), (7), (8), 39–41, 47 (1), (2) (in relation to the provisions listed in Sch. 1 to the Order), (3), 48, 49, 50 (1), (2), (4) (in relation to the repeals in Sch. 7 to the Act brought into force by Sch. 1 to the Order), 51 (1)–(3), 52, Schs. 1, 2 (part) and the repeals in Sch. 7 set out in the appendix to Sch. 1 to the Order.

The date of commencement of the provisions listed in Sch. 2 is 1st October 1979. The provisions are: ss. 27, 28, 46 (excluding part of sub-s. (1)), 47 (in relation to the provisions listed in Sch. 2 to the Order), 50 (4) (in relation to the repeals in Sch. 7 to the Act brought into force by Sch. 2 to the Order) and the provisions of Sch. 7 set out in the appendix to Sch. 2 to the Order.

The date of commencement of the provisions listed in Sch. 3 is 1st January 1980. The provisions are: ss. 13 (1) (in relation to the provisions brought into force by Sch. 2 to the Order), (2)–(4), 29, 30, 42–45, 47 (2) (in relation to s. 45 and the repeals in Sch. 7 to the Act brought into force by Sch. 3 to the Order), 54 (in relation to the repeals in Sch. 7 to the Act brought into force by Sch. 3 to the Order), Schs. 2 (part), 6 and the provisions of Sch. 7 set out in the appendix to Sch. 3 to the Order.

The Merchant Shipping Act 1979 (Commencement No. 2) Order 1979, S.I. 1979 No. 1578, brought into force on 17th December 1979 the following provisions of the 1979 Act which enable Orders to be made to extend certain provisions to countries outside the United Kingdom: ss. 15 (1), (2) (part), 19 (2), (3), 38 (5), 47 (1), (3) and (2) so far as it relates to ss. 48–52 and Sch. 7, Part I.

The remaining provisions will come into force on days to be appointed.

Section 1 establishes a Pilotage Commission of between ten and fifteen persons to be selected by the Secretary of State from specified categories of those having knowledge of pilotage. Schedule 1 makes detailed provision relating to the constitution of the Commission, tenure of office of members, their remuneration, proceedings etc. The Commission may make schemes requiring pilotage authorities to pay sums to it from time to time to cover the cost of the performance of its functions: s. 2. Such schemes must be approved by the Secretary of State, and copies must be given to each pilotage authority affected: ibid. Section 3 limits the borrowing power of the Commission to £200,000, which may be increased to £500,000 by order. The section also makes provisions relating to accounting and the appointment of auditors.

The Commission's functions are outlined in s. 4. Its role is advisory and its scope may be extended by the Secretary of State. Under s. 5 the Commission must produce an annual report on the performance of its functions. Sections 6–13 make other provision relating to pilotage. By s. 6 the Commission must keep under review the organisation of pilotage services and non-compulsory pilotage areas; s. 7 empowers the Secretary of State to make regulations relating to pilotage orders and s. 8 amends the Pilotage Act 1913. s. 11. Section 9 gives pilotage authorities the right to draw up a list of charges for pilotage services in its district. Section 10 deals with the refusal and cancellation of pilotage certificates and s. 11 with the employment of pilots by pilotage authorities. Pilots' pension and compensation schemes may be established and maintained by the Commission: s. 12. Section 13 and Sch. 2 make minor amendments to the Pilotage Act 1913.

Sections 14–16 concern the carriage of passengers and luggage by sea. Section 14 gives effect to the Convention relating to the Carriage of Passengers and their Luggage contained in Sch. 3, Pt. I, and s. 15 makes supplementary provisions. The Convention may be applied to international carriage before s. 14 comes into force and also to domestic carriage, by Order in Council: s. 16.

Section 17 gives effect in the United Kingdom to the Convention on Limitation of Liability for Maritime Claims 1976, as set out in Sch. 4, Pt. I. Section 18 excludes British shipowners from liability both for loss of or damage to property arising from fire on board and for loss or damage to gold, silver, watches, jewels or precious stones lost through theft or any dishonest conduct, where their nature and value was not declared to the ship's master in the bill of lading or otherwise in writing. Supplementary provisions are contained in s. 19 and Sch. 5.

Section 20 enables effect to be given to three international agreements relating to pollution from ships and to any future such agreements. Agreements can be brought into force with respect to the United Kingdom before they come into force internationally.

The Secretary of State is empowered by s. 21 to make regulations for securing the safety of United Kingdom ships, persons on them and any provisions of an international agreement ratified by the United Kingdom so far as it relates to the safety of ships, persons on them and their health. Section 22 makes supplementary provision relating to safety regulations.

Sections 23–25 deal with discipline on board merchant ships. By s. 23, regulations may be made to deal with breaches by seamen of codes of conduct and local industrial agreements. Section 24 extends the regulation-making power in the Merchant Shipping Act 1970, s. 9 so as to enable the amount of deductions from the wages of those employed in fishing vessels to be determined by a body set up or approved under s. 23. Section 25 imposes a maximum fine of £1,000 on summary conviction, or up to two years' imprisonment and a fine on conviction on indictment for offences relating to unauthorised liquor on fishing vessels.

Sections 26–28 relate to the appointment and powers of Department of Trade inspectors. Section 29 amends the Merchant Shipping Act 1970 in respect of inquiries into deaths of crew members and others. Section 30 amends the 1970 Act in relation to returns by masters of deaths in United Kingdom registered ships and deaths outside the United Kingdom of persons employed in such ships.

Sections 31–41 contain miscellaneous provisions relating to dues for space occupied by deck-cargo, shipping casualties, the Commissioners of Northern Lighthouses and Irish Lights, the repeal of spent provisions, minor amendments, the replacement of gold francs by special drawing rights for certain purposes of the Merchant Shipping (Oil Pollution) Act 1971 and the Merchant Shipping Act 1974, attachment of earnings, foreign action affecting shipping and the application of the Merchant Shipping Acts to certain structures.

Sections 42–46 deal with offences. Section 42 alters the time for certain summary prosecutions, s. 43 and Sch. 6 alter certain penalties, s. 44 provides for the punishment of masters and owners of dangerously unsafe ships, s. 45 amends certain offences provisions in the Merchant Shipping Act 1970 and s. 46 relates to offences by the officers of bodies corporate. Sections 47–51 are supplemental, and Sch. 7 contains repeals.

2568 Oil pollution—convention countries

The Prevention of Oil Pollution (Convention Countries) (Additional Countries) Order 1979, S.I. 1979 No. 721 (in force on 25th July 1979), declares that the Republic of Korea, the German Democratic Republic and the Yemen Arab Republic have accepted the International Convention for the Prevention of Pollution of the Sea by Oil 1954.

2569 —— Hong Kong

The Prevention of Oil Pollution Act 1971 (Hong Kong) Order 1979, S.I. 1979 No. 1452 (in force on 17th December 1979), extends to Hong Kong those provisions of the Prevention of Oil Pollution Act 1971 that enable measures to be taken to prevent, mitigate or eliminate grave and imminent damages to the coastline or related interests from pollution or threat of pollution of the sea by oil, following upon a maritime casualty.

2570

The Prevention of Oil Pollution Act 1971 (Hong Kong) (No. 2) Order 1979, S.I. 1979 No. 1453 (in force on 17th December 1979), applies the Prevention of Oil Pollution Act 1971, ss. 12–15, as extended to Hong Kong, to ships not registered in Hong Kong and which are outside the territorial waters of Hong Kong. Section 12 enables the Governor to give directions, or take action, to prevent or reduce oil pollution or risk of oil pollution which threatens Hong Kong on a large scale as a result of a shipping casualty. Section 13 enables persons unreasonably suffering loss or damage as a result of such directions or action to recover compensation from the Governor.

Sections 12–15 only apply under this Order where the Governor is satisfied that there is a grave and imminent danger of oil pollution from which the coast and waters of Hong Kong need to be protected. The power to give directions and the offence of obstruction only relate to individuals who are citizens of the United Kingdom or bodies corporate established under Hong Kong law.

2571 —— international compensation fund

The participating oil companies have announced that the maximum amount payable in compensation for oil pollution at sea from the International Oil Pollution Compensation Fund has been increased from £19 million to £28·5 million. The increased compensation limit is applicable from 20th April 1979. See the Financial Times, 25th April 1979.

2572 —— merchant shipping—compulsory insurance

The Oil Pollution (Compulsory Insurance) (Amendment) Regulations 1979, S.I. 1979 No. 1593 (in force on 2nd January 1980), amend the Oil Pollution (Compulsory Insurance) Regulations 1977, 1977 Halsbury's Abridgment para. 2619 by increasing the fee to be paid on application for a certificate of compulsory insurance from £12 to £19.

2573 —— —— convention countries

The Merchant Shipping (Oil Pollution) (Parties to Conventions) (Amendment) Order 1979, S.I. 1979 No. 1450 (in force on 17th December 1979), amends the Merchant Shipping (Oil Pollution) (Parties to Conventions) Order 1975, 1975 Halsbury's Abridgment para. 3057, by adding the Republic of Chile, the German Democratic Republic, the Republics of Ghana, Indonesia, Italy and Korea and the Yemen Arab Republic to the list of countries to which the International Convention on Civil Liability for Oil Pollution Damage has entered into force. The Merchant

Shipping (Oil Pollution) (Parties to Conventions) (Amendment) (No. 2) Order 1977, 1977 Halsbury's Abridgment para. 2621 is revoked.

2574 Penalties

The Merchant Shipping (Increased Penalties) Regulations 1979, S.I. 1979 No. 1519 (in force on 1st January 1980), pursuant to the Merchant Shipping Act 1979, Sch. 6, Pt. VI, increase the maximum penalties which may be imposed on summary conviction for breach of certain specified regulations, which are accordingly amended.

2575 Protection of wrecks—restricted areas

The Protection of Wrecks (Designation No. 1) Order 1979, S.I. 1979 No. 31 (in force on 9th February 1979), designates an area in Cardigan Bay, round the site of what is believed to be a wreck of historical and archaeological importance, as a restricted area for the purposes of the Protection of Wrecks Act 1973.

2576

The Protection of Wrecks (Designation No. 1 and No. 4 Orders 1978) (Amendment) Order 1979, S.I. 1979 No. 56 (in force on 16th February 1979), amends the Protection of Wrecks (Designation No. 1) Order 1978, 1978 Halsbury's Abridgment para. 2646, and the Protection of Wrecks (Designation No. 4) Order 1978, 1978 Halsbury's Abridgment para. 2649. The centre of the site dealt with in the first has been redefined and the size of the restricted area in both has been increased.

2577

The Protection of Wrecks (Revocation) Order 1979, S.I. 1979 No. 6 (in force on 31st January 1979), revokes the Protection of Wrecks (Designation No. 6) Order 1974, 1974 Halsbury's Abridgment para. 3073, which designated an area in the Sound of Mull round the site of the vessel HMS *Dartmouth* as a restricted area. The wreck is no longer considered to require protection.

2578 Safety convention—Hong Kong

The Merchant Shipping (Safety Convention) (Hong Kong) (Amendment) Order 1979, S.I. 1979 No. 1707 (in force on 25th May 1980), amends the following Orders: Merchant Shipping Safety Convention (Hong Kong) No. 1 Order 1953 and Merchant Shipping (Safety Convention) (Hong Kong) Order 1965. The amendments take into account the entry into force for Hong Kong of the International Convention for the Safety of Life at Sea 1974.

2579 Salvage—award—appeal against award—jurisdiction of arbitrator

A British cargo vessel ran aground and a salvage tug was orally engaged by the shipowners with reference to the Lloyds standard form of salvage agreement. Pursuant to the agreement, Lloyds appointed an arbitrator who found that both the shipowners and the cargo-owners had to pay for the salvage service in proportion to the value of their respective properties salved. All the owners sought to appeal but due to a clerical error the original notice of appeal was made solely on behalf of the shipowners. The appeal arbitrator set aside the original award and awarded a lesser sum. However the total contributions to be paid by the parties amounted to more than the award in so far as the contribution to be paid by the cargo-owners was not reduced due to their lack of notice of appeal. By a notice of motion all the owners applied for an order remitting the award to the appeal arbitrator on the grounds that he had misconducted himself and exceeded his jurisdiction as to the calculation of the award. *Held*, the law of salvage imposed on the owners of the property salved the obligation to pay a salvage award which was assessed with reference, inter alia, to the value of the property salved and the owners were severally liable to pay the whole award. It was important to preserve the principle that each party to the salvage operation should decide for himself whether to appeal against the original award. The arbitrator on appeal had correctly assessed the total remuneration due to the salvors and since the cargo-owners had failed to give due notice of appeal, no injustice had been done to any party. The motion would be dismissed accordingly.

THE GEESTLAND (1979) 130 NLJ 45 (Queen's Bench Division: SHEEN J).

2580   —— **extent of contract—liability for expenses of cargo salvage**

A ship ran aground, and it became necessary to take cargo off the ship and store it on shore. A firm of salvors was engaged by the ship's master as agent for, inter alia, the cargo owners under the Lloyd's standard form of salvage agreement. The voyage was abandoned and, although the cargo-owners agreed to pay for all subsequent storage expenses, they refused to pay those expenses incurred before it was abandoned. In an action brought against them they contended that (i) the shipowners were liable because (a) they were bailees for reward of the cargo until the voyage was abandoned and (b) the cargo was being stored on shore at the shipowners' request; further that (ii) the Lloyd's agreement was limited to the performance of salvage services and did not extend to any services rendered after the cargo arrived on shore. *Held*, as the Lloyd's agreement had been signed on behalf of the cargo owners, it had created a direct contractual relationship between them and the salvors. The contract of bailment between the cargo owners and shipowners had ended when the cargo came into the possession of the salvors, and a new bailment between the salvors and cargo owners was created. There was no express or implied agreement between the salvors and the shipowners that redelivery of the cargo was to be made to the shipowners or that it was to be stored in their name or to their account. The Lloyd's agreement provided that the salvors had implied authority to take responsibility for the cargo whilst on shore, in the absence of express directions from the cargo owners, and to charge reasonable expenses; but even without this provision the salvors would have been entitled to compensation from the cargo owners, as the owners had benefited from their services.

CHINA-PACIFIC SA v FOOD CORPORATION OF INDIA, THE WINSON [1979] 2 All ER 35 (Queen's Bench Division: LLOYD J).

2581   —— **intervention—rights of superseded salvors—nature of remedy**

The master of a ship which had been grounded accepted help from salvors and signed the Lloyd's Standard Form of Salvage Agreement No Cure No Pay, in the mistaken belief that the salvors had been sent by his employers. The salvors made various preparations to tow the ship off, but were dismissed when her master realised his mistake and his employers' salvors completed the salvage. The salvors claimed damages for breach of contract and/or salvage remuneration. The question which arose before the court was whether the salvors were entitled to moneys in addition to salvage for services actually rendered and whether they were entitled to restitution in integrum either as compensation or as damages for breach of contract. *Held*, there was a difference between cases in which salvors were engaged without a written agreement and those in which there was such an agreement. In the former there was no obligation on either party to continue the agreement and therefore a salvor could be superseded. He would then be entitled to remuneration in the nature of salvage as a reward for services rendered and by way of compensation for loss of the opportunity to complete the service. In the latter the salvors were under an obligation to complete the salvage and the ship's master was under a corresponding obligation not to prevent them from doing so. The salvors would have a remedy in damages in such a case, but could not recover payment for services rendered as well.

THE UNIQUE MARINER (No. 2) [1979] 1 Lloyd's Rep 37 (Queen's Bench Division: BRANDON J).

For previous proceedings concerning this salvage see *The Unique Mariner* [1978] 1 Lloyd's Rep 438, 1978 Halsbury's Abridgment para. 2637.

2582 —— salvage award—liability of parties

See *The Geestland*, para. 2579

2583 —— —— interest

The defendants' motor tug ran aground in a gale and was severely damaged. The plaintiffs' trawler, which should have been fishing but was sheltering in a nearby harbour, was asked by the local lifeboat to assist in the rescue of the tug. She set off immediately accompanied by the lifeboat. The rescue took six hours and the plaintiffs claimed a salvage award for services rendered. *Held*, the tug was in a position of grave danger and alternative assistance would have arrived too late. Accordingly, a salvage award would be made, with interest, taking into account the state of the weather, the degree of damage and danger to the tug and the trawler, the time employed and the value of the property.

THE RILLAND [1979] 1 Lloyd's Rep 455 (Queen's Bench Division: SHEEN J). *The Industry* (1835) 3 Hag Adm 203 and *The Aldora* [1975] 2 All ER 69, 1975 Halsbury's Abridgment para. 3090 applied.

2584 Seabed—public right of navigation—extent of right to moor and fix moorings

See *Crown Estate Comrs v Fairlie Yacht Slip Ltd*, para. 3066.

2585 Shipbuilding industries—increase of shipbuilders' borrowing powers

See para. 2788.

2586 Shipbuilding (Redundancy Payments) Act 1978—redundancy payments scheme

See para. 1108.

2587 Tonnage—Monegasque ships

The Monegasque Tonnage Order 1979, S.I. 1979 No. 306 (in force on 12th April 1979), provides that the tonnage shown in the certificates of registry or other national papers of Monegasque ships shall be recognised in the same way as the tonnage shown in the certificate of registry of a British ship.

SOCIAL SECURITY

Halsbury's Laws of England (3rd edn.), Vol. 27, paras. 897–980, 1187–1570

2588 Articles

Giving with One Hand, Audrey Harvey (on the effect of the new right of appeal from a decision of a supplementary benefit appeal tribunal to a national insurance commissioner): 129 NLJ 970.

One-Parent Families, Family Income Supplement and the New Poverty Trap, M. D. A. Freeman (comparison of the advantages and disadvantages between working and claiming FIS and not working and claiming supplementary benefit): 129 NLJ 800.

The Self-Employed and the EEC Social Security Rules, M. Forde (the integration of the self-employed into social security systems): 8 ILJ 1.

2589 Accommodation—provision by local authority—charges

The National Assistance (Charges for Accommodation) Regulations 1979, S.I. 1979 No. 823 (in force on 12th November 1979), increase the minimum weekly amounts which a person is required to pay for accommodation managed by a local authority. They also increase the weekly sum for personal requirements which the local authority will allow in assessing a person's ability to pay for accommodation. The National Assistance (Charges for Accommodation) Regulations 1978, 1978 Halsbury's Abridgment para. 2659, are revoked.

2590   Attendance allowance

The Social Security (Attendance Allowance) Amendment Regulations 1979, S.I. 1979 No. 375 (in force on 2nd April 1979), further amend the Social Security (Attendance Allowance) (No. 2) Regulations 1975, 1975 Halsbury's Abridgment para. 3107, by inserting a new Part IIIA in the 1975 Regulations consisting of regulations 5A, 5B and 5C. Where conditions have been satisfied with respect to an earlier claim, regulation 5A allows a gap of up to 2 years to intervene between the qualifying period and the new period with respect to which the Attendance Allowance Board determine that attendance conditions are, or are likely to be, again satisfied. Regulations 5B and 5C apply to persons suffering from renal failure who are undergoing renal dialysis.

2591   The Social Security (Attendance Allowance) Amendment (No. 2) Regulations 1979, S.I. 1979 No. 1684 (in force on 14th January 1980), amend the Social Security (Attendance Allowance) (No. 2) Regulations 1975, 1975 Halsbury's Abridgment para. 3107. Regulations 2, 3 vary the provisions of the 1975 Regulations concerning non-payability of allowances for persons in accommodation provided at public expense. Regulation 4 removes the obligation of the Attendance Allowance Board to give reasons in writing when making decisions on review favourable to claimants and in cases where claimants forego their rights to be given reasons, but enables them and the Secretary of State subsequently to apply for such reasons. Regulation 5 makes consequential amendments to provisions stating the time limits for appeals to the Commissioner. Regulation 6 updates some references to the enactments specified in the Schedule to the 1975 Regulations. Regulation 7 removes conditions formerly applicable to persons born outside the United Kingdom and to aliens.

2592   —— entitlement—meaning of "night"

National Insurance Commissioner's decision:
    Decision R(A) 1/78 (attendance allowance sought in respect of the care of a child throughout the night; interpretation of the word "night"; night meant the period of inactivity through which each household went in the dark hours once that household had retired; it did not extend to the time between the child's bedtime and the retiring time of the household).

2593   —— —— requirements of natural justice

National Insurance Commissioner's decision:
    Decision R (A) 4/78 (claimant for attendance allowance required renal dialysis at home; had previously been awarded allowance on basis of two sessions a week; further claim disallowed; claimant contended decision contrary to natural justice, as condition was unchanged; no breach of natural justice as different mind had reached different conclusion on claim for subsequent period: could not be said as matter of law that medical requirements for allowance must be found to be satisfied by two sessions a week, or that no reasonable person could hold that requirements were not so met; no allowance payable).

2594   Benefits—availability—potential claimants not informed of availability of benefits—report by Parliamentary Commissioner for Administration

See Annual Report of Parliamentary Commissioner for Administration: H of C Paper (1978–79) No. 302, para. 21.

2595   —— computation of earnings

See para. 2596.

2596   —— overlapping benefits

The Social Security (Overlapping Benefits and Miscellaneous Amendments) Regulations 1979, S.I. 1979 No. 359 (in force on 6th April 1979), further amend the Social Security (Overlapping Benefits) Regulations 1975, 1975 Halsbury's Abridgment para. 3108, and amend the Social Security Benefit (Computation of Earnings) Regulations 1978, 1978 Halsbury's Abridgment para. 2662. For the purposes of the 1975 Regulations, references to additional component include references to increases of additional component and guaranteed minimum pensions increments. Minor adjustments are made in relation to widows over pensionable age, in respect of certain dependency benefits and to ensure equality of treatment of widows and widowers in certain circumstances. A provision relating to priority as between husband and wife in relation to increase of benefit for dependent children is amended. The scope of certain of the 1978 Regulations are extended so that they apply to increases of certain benefits whether or not the dependant resides with the beneficiary. Certain provisions are revoked in consequence of the passing of the Social Security Act 1979, para. 2664.

These regulations have been revoked; see para. 2597.

2597   The Social Security (Overlapping Benefits) Regulations 1979, S.I. 1979 No. 597 (in force on 29th June 1979), revoke and consolidate the Social Security (Overlapping Benefits) Regulations 1975, 1975 Halsbury's Abridgment para. 3108, as amended. They contain provisions relating to adjustment of benefits under the Social Security Act 1975 by reference to other benefits payable for that same period. The principal matters dealt with are adjustment of personal benefit under Chapters I, II and IV of Part II of the Act, earnings-related supplement and dependency benefit. The regulations also contain miscellaneous provisions incidental to those matters.

2598   —— persons abroad

The Social Security Benefit (Persons Abroad) Amendment Regulations 1979, S.I. 1979 No. 463 (in force on 17th April 1979), further amend the Social Security Benefit (Persons Abroad) Regulations 1975, 1975 Halsbury's Abridgment para. 3116, by modifying the restrictions relating to entitlement to industrial injuries benefit under the Social Security Act 1975 in the case of earners in employment relating to the exploitation of natural resources suffering accidents or contracting prescribed diseases in specified areas by reason of their employment in those areas.

2599   The Social Security Benefit (Persons Abroad) Amendment (No. 2) Regulations 1979, S.I. 1979 No. 1432 (in force on 10th November 1979), further amend the Social Security Benefit (Persons Abroad) Regulations 1975, 1975 Halsbury's Abridgment para. 3116. The Regulations modify the conditions relating to entitlement to basic component and additional component of retirement pension, and to the payment of up-rating increases, in relation to persons absent from and not ordinarily resident in Great Britain. They prescribe upper limits by which Category A retirement pensions of persons who are absent from Great Britain may be increased by any Category B pensions to which they become entitled. The Regulations also adapt and apply the provisions of the 1975 Regulations to the up-rating of increments in guaranteed minimum pensions, and to the up-rating of pensions payable to widowers and others on the contributions of their former spouses.

2600   —— repayment of overpaid benefit

The Social Security (General Benefit) Amendment Regulations 1979, S.I. 1979 No. 1067 (in force on 15th October 1979), amend the Social Security (General Benefit) Regulations 1974, reg. 13, 1974 Halsbury's Abridgment para. 3086, so as to bring within its scope decisions requiring repayment of overpaid benefit which are made under the Social Security Act 1975, s. 119 (2A), added by the Social Security Act 1979, para. 2664.

2601   —— report of Department of Health and Social Security—proposed reform

The Department of Health and Social Security issued a Press Release on 29th November 1979 announcing the publication of a Government White Paper "The Reform of the Supplementary Benefits Scheme". The supplementary benefits scheme is to be reformed and simplified. The reconstructed scheme is to be introduced in November 1980 and the main changes proposed are to form part of a new Social Security Act. The Supplementary Benefits Commission is to be abolished and a new body will replace it and the National Insurance Advisory Committee, to advise on the whole range of social security schemes. The proposed changes in supplementary benefit include reducing the existing qualifying periods, reducing the children's scale rates, bringing the main supplementary benefit rates into line with the corresponding National Insurance rates and simplifying the rules relating to the treatment of capital and income in assessing benefit.

2602   ——unemployment, sickness and invalidity

The Social Security (Unemployment, Sickness and Invalidity Benefit) Amendment (No. 3) Regulations 1979, S.I. 1979 No. 1299 (in force on 19th October 1979) further amend the Social Security (Unemployment, Sickness and Invalidity Benefit) Regulations 1975, 1975 Halsbury's Abridgment para. 3117 by inserting a new regulation 3 (3) which provides that a person who is found to be not incapable of work by reason only of the fact that he has done some work may be deemed incapable of work if the work done satisfies certain conditions. Regulation 7 (1) (a) of the 1975 Regulations is revoked.

2603   —— —— seasonal workers

The Social Security (Unemployment, Sickness and Invalidity Benefit) Amendment (No. 2) Regulations 1979, S.I. 1979 No. 940 (in force on 27th July 1979), amend the Social Security (Unemployment, Sickness and Invalidity Benefit) Regulations 1975, 1975 Halsbury's Abridgment para. 3117 by imposing additional conditions regarding the receipt of unemployment benefit by seasonal workers during their off-season.

2604   —— —— students

The Social Security (Unemployment, Sickness and Invalidity Benefit) Amendment Regulations 1979, S.I. 1979 No. 934 (in force on 27th July 1979), amend the Social Security (Unemployment, Sickness and Invalidity Benefit) Regulations 1975, 1975 Halsbury's Abridgment para. 3117 by imposing an additional condition regarding the receipt of unemployment benefit by full-time students.

2605   —— up-rating

The Social Security Benefits Up-rating Order 1979, S.I. 1979 No. 993 (in force on 12th November 1979), increases with effect from specified dates in the week beginning 12th November 1979 the rates and amounts of the benefits and increases of benefit (except age addition) specified in the Social Security Act 1975, Sch. 4, Parts I, III, IV and V. It also increases the rates and amounts of certain benefits under the Social Security Pensions Act 1975, Part II, and the rate of graduated retirement benefit under the National Insurance Act 1965. It increases the rates laid down in the Industrial Injuries and Diseases (Old Cases) Act 1975 for the maximum weekly rate of lesser incapacity allowance supplementing workmen's compensation and the weekly rate of allowance under the Industrial Diseases Benefit Schemes where disablement is not total. Further, the Order increases the amount, specified in the

Social Security Act 1975, s. 30 (1), of weekly earnings which must be exceeded before retirement pension is reduced by reference to earnings. The Social Security Benefits Up-rating Order 1978, 1978 Halsbury's Abridgment para. 2669, is revoked.

2606 The Social Security Benefits Up-rating Regulations 1979, S.I. 1979 No. 1278 (in force on 12th November 1979) and made in consequence of the Social Security Benefits Up-rating Order 1979. The regulations specify the circumstances in which the rate of benefit which is awarded before the date from which the altered rates became payable is not automatically altered by the Social Security Act 1975, Sch. 14, para. 2. They also apply the provisions of the Social Security Benefit (Persons Abroad) Regulations 1975, 1975 Halsbury's Abridgment para. 3116, relating to persons absent from and not ordinarily resident in Great Britain at the time of the increase in the weekly rate of certain benefits, to the increases of benefit provided by the up-rating order. The regulations also further amend the Social Security (Non-Contributory Invalidity Pension) Regulations 1975, 1975 Halsbury's Abridgment para. 3171 and the Social Security (Industrial Injuries) (Benefit) Regulations 1975, 1975 Halsbury's Abridgment para. 3154 so as to raise to £13 a week and £676 a year the earning limits in respect of work a person may do in certain circumstances while in receipt of a benefit under those regulations. The Social Security Benefits Up-Rating Regulations 1978, 1978 Halsbury's Abridgment para. 2670 are revoked.

2607 The Social Security Benefits Up-rating (Amendment) Order 1979, S.I. 1979 No. 1429 (in force on 10th November 1979), substitutes for the Social Security Benefits Up-rating Order 1979, art. 8, para. 2606, which revoked the Social Security Benefits Up-rating Order 1978, 1978 Halsbury's Abridgment para. 2669, a new art. 8. This excludes from the revocation art. 1 and so much of art. 6 as increased to £45 the amount of weekly earnings which must be exceeded before increases of benefit payable with retirement pension, invalidity pension and unemployability supplement in respect of certain wives are reduced by reference to the wives' earnings. £45 thus remains the relevant amount for this purpose.

2608 —— widow's allowance—earnings-related addition

The Social Security (Earnings-Related Addition to Widow's Allowance) (Special Provisions) Regulations 1979, S.I. 1979 No. 1431 (in force on 6th January 1980), modify the Social Security Act 1975, Sch. 6, Part I in cases where the late husband had attained pensionable age and during the whole or part of the relevant year would have had liability for Class 1 contributions but for the Social Security Pensions Act 1975, s. 4 (1). The earnings-related addition will be calculated in these cases by reference to the late husband's earnings and not to an earnings factor which is based on Class 1 contributions.

2609 —— widow's benefit and retirement pensions

See paras. 2683, 2684.

2610 Child benefit—rates

The Child Benefit and Social Security (Fixing and Adjustment of Rates) Amendment Regulations 1979, S.I. 1979 No. 998 (in force on 12th November 1979), further amend the Child Benefit and Social Security (Fixing and Adjustment of Rates) Regulations 1976, 1976 Halsbury's Abridgment para. 2417. They increase the weekly rate of child benefit payable under the Child Benefit Act 1975 in respect of a child living with one parent by £0·50 to £2·50.

2611 Claims and payments

The Social Security (Claims and Payments) Regulations 1979, S.I. 1979 No. 628 (in force on 9th July 1979), consolidate the Social Security (Claims and Payments) Regulations 1975, 1975 Halsbury's Abridgment para. 3125, as amended. They provide for the manner in which claims for and payments of benefits, including industrial injuries benefit, under the Social Security Act 1975, 1975 Halsbury's Abridgment para. 3187 are to be made.

2612   The Social Security (Claims and Payments) Amendment Regulations 1979, S.I. 1979 No. 781 (in force on 5th September 1979), amend the Social Security (Claims and Payments) Regulations 1979, para. 2611, so as to make provision to allow certain claims for unemployment benefit to be made for a period falling partly after the date on which the claim is made. Amendments are made to the special provisions in the principal Regulations relating to claims for unemployment benefit during the periods connected with public holidays. The definition of "medical certificate" is amended in the provisions of the principal Regulations relating to forward allowances and disallowances of incapacity benefits to include a doctor's statement based on a written report from any other doctor.

2613   The Social Security (Claims and Payments) Amendment (No. 2) Regulations 1979, S.I. 1979 No. 1199 (in force on 25th October 1979), amend the Social Security (Claims and Payments) Regulations 1979, para. 2611. They enable the Secretary of State to arrange for weekly payments of guardian's allowance to be made on Mondays instead of Tuesdays.

2614   **Contributions**

The Social Security (Contributions) Amendment Regulations 1979, S.I. 1979 No. 358 (in force on 6th April 1979), further amend the Social Security (Contributions) Regulations 1975, 1975 Halsbury's Abridgment para. 3216 by reducing the percentage rate of secondary Class 1 contributions payable in respect of registered dock workers to whom the provisions of the Employment Protection (Consolidation) Act 1978, s. 81 (redundancy payments) do not apply. They also modify the Social Security Act 1975, s. 134 (destination of contributions) by providing for a corresponding reduction in the employment protection allocation.

These regulations have been revoked; see para. 2615.

2615   The Social Security (Contributions) Regulations 1979, S.I. 1979 No. 591 (in force on 6th July 1979), revoke and consolidate the Social Security (Contributions) Regulations 1975, 1975 Halsbury's Abridgment para. 3126, as amended. They make provision for the assessment and collection of contributions, for exception from, and, in the case of Class 1 and Class 4 contributions, deferment of, liability for contributions and for the appropriation, reallocation and refund of contributions. They also apply with necessary adaptations the provisions of the Stamp Duties Management Act 1891 and the Post Office Act 1953, s. 63, to stamps prepared and issued for the purpose of the Social Security Act 1975, 1975 Halsbury's Abridgment para. 3187. They also make provision for the treatment of late paid and unpaid contributions. Further, they make provision, in relation to contributions, for special classes of earners, namely, airmen, persons employed in connection with the continental shelf, mariners, married women and widows, members of the forces and persons outside Great Britain. In the latter category, provision is made prescribing the conditions of residence or presence in Great Britain for liability or entitlement to pay contributions.

These regulations hve been amended; see para. 2616.

2616   The Social Security (Contributions) (Earnings Limits) Amendment Regulations 1979, S.I. 1979 No. 1483 (in force on 6th April 1980), amend the Social Security (Contributions) Regulations 1979, para. 2615, by substituting new lower and upper earnings limits for Class 1 contributions for the tax year beginning 6th April 1980.

2617   **——— exemptions—Inter-American Development Bank**

By an exchange of notes between the government and the Inter-American Development Bank (Cmnd. 7567) certain bank officials will be exempted, when the agreement comes into force, from United Kingdom social security contributions. The agreement does not relate to those officials of the bank who are citizens of the United Kingdom or permanent residents of the United Kingdom.

2618   —— re-rating

The Social Security (Contributions, Re-rating) Consequential Amendment Regulations 1979, S.I. 1979 No. 9 (in force on 6th April 1979), further amend the Social Security (Contributions) Regulations 1975, 1975 Halsbury's Abridgment para. 3126, by increasing the special rate of Class 2 contributions payable by share fishermen.

2619   The Social Security (Contributions, Re-rating) Order 1979, S.I. 1979 No. 1694 (in force on 6th April 1980), increases the rates of Class 1, 2 and 3 contributions payable under the Social Security Act 1975. It increases the amount of earnings below which an earner may be excepted from liability for Class 2 contributions, and the lower and upper limits of profits or gains between which Class 4 contributions are payable.

2620   The Social Security (Contributions, Re-rating) (No. 2) Order 1979, S.I. 1979 No. 1736 (in force on 6th April 1980), substitutes a lower rate of secondary Class 1 contribution in the Social Security Act 1975, s. 4 (6) (b) and amends s. 134 (4) by reducing the percentage there specified in relation to the appropriate employment protection allocation. The Order comes into operation immediately after the coming into operation of the Social Security (Contributions, Re-rating) Order 1979 on 6th April 1980, see para. 2619, supra.

2621   **Determination of claims and questions**

The Social Security (Determination of Claims and Questions) Amendment Regulations 1979, S.I. 1979 No. 1163 (in force on 5th November 1979), amend the Social Security (Determination of Claims and Questions) Regulations 1975, 1975 Halsbury's Abridgment para. 3133, by substituting new provisions for those of reg. 38. The new provisions continue to enable benefit, if paid under an earlier decision but subsequently by decision on review or appeal found not to be payable, to be treated as properly paid to the extent that, but for such payment, more pension or allowance under the Supplementary Benefits Act 1976 would have been paid instead. The restriction to cases where repayment of benefit would have been required is removed and reg. 38 is extended to cases where there can be no review of a decision but where the facts found for the purposes of a subsequent decision do not support payments made under the earlier one. There are exceptions from these provisions in respect of dependency benefits.

2622   **Earnings factor**

The Social Security (Earnings Factor) Regulations 1979, S.I. 1979 No. 676 (in force on 16th July 1979), consolidate the Social Security (Earnings Factor) Regulations 1975, 1975 Halsbury's Abridgment para. 3134, as amended. They prescribe rules for deriving from contributions paid or credited under the Social Security Act 1975 the earnings factor by reference to which the contribution conditions for contributory benefits are expressed in Sch. 3 to the Act, the rate of earnings-related supplement or addition to certain benefits is calculated under Sch. 6 to the Act, the additional component in the rate of long-term benefits is calculated by virtue of the Social Security Pensions Act 1975, s. 6, and an earner's guaranteed minimum is calculated under the 1975 Act, s. 35.

2623   —— revaluation

The Social Security Revaluation of Earnings Factors Order 1979, S.I. 1979 No. 832 (in force on 16th July 1979), increases the earnings factors relevant to calculating the additional component in the rate of any long term benefit for the 1978–79 tax year by 13·3 per cent. The Order also provides for the adjustment of fractional amounts.

2624   Family income supplement

The Family Income Supplements (General) Amendment Regulations 1979, S.I. 1979 No. 160 (in force on 3rd April 1979), amend the Family Income Supplements (General) Regulations 1971, reg. 5. A single person with at least one dependent child is now to be treated being engaged and normally engaged in remunerative full-time work if he is engaged and normally engaged in remunerative work for not less than twenty-five hours a week.

2625   The Family Income Supplements (General) Amendment (No. 2) Regulations 1979, S.I. 1979 No. 1504 (in force on 31st December 1979), further amend the Family Income Supplements (General) Regulations 1971. Regulation 2 defines "advanced education", "education authority", "educational maintenance allowance" and "recognized educational establishment". Regulation 3, together with the definitions contained in reg. 2, adds mobility allowance and educational maintenance allowance to the list of deductions to be made in the calculation of normal gross income for the purposes of the Family Income Supplements Act 1970. Regulation 3 also provides that certain income of a child derived, directly or indirectly, from a parent or person under a legal obligation to maintain that child is to be included in the normal gross income of the family of which that child is a member. Regulation 4 amends the 1971 Regulations so that if any claim for benefit is made after a regulation under the 1970 Act is made, but before it comes into operation, the transitional provisions (enabling certain persons to claim benefit) will apply provided the claim is made not more than fifty-six days before that regulation comes into operation. Regulation 5, together with the definitions contained in reg. 2, prescribes the circumstances in which a person of or over the age of sixteen is to be treated as a child. Regulation 6, limits the Supplementary Benefits Commission's power to review a decision, in certain circumstances, on the ground that it was made in ignorance of a material fact of which the claimant was, or ought reasonably to have been, aware in respect of any period earlier than twelve months before that material fact was disclosed to the Secretary of State.

2626   —— claims and payments

The Family Income Supplements (Claims and Payments) Amendment Regulations 1979, S.I. 1979 No. 1505 (in force on 31st December 1979), amend the Family Income Supplements (Claims and Payments) Regulations 1971. Regulation 8 of the 1971 Regulations is amended to provide that payment of family income supplement may be suspended by the Secretary of State pending the determination of an appeal.

2627   —— computation

The Family Income Supplements (Computation) Regulations 1979, S.I. 1979 No. 939 (in force on 13th November 1979), raise the prescribed weekly amount of a family's resources below which the supplement is payable to £54 for a family with one child plus £4·50 for each additional child. They also provide that the weekly rate of supplement is not to exceed £12·50 for a family with one child plus £1·00 for each additional child. The Family Income Supplements (Computation) Regulations 1978, 1978 Halsbury's Abridgment para. 2690, are revoked.

These Regulations have been revoked, see para. 2628.

2628   The Family Income Supplements (Computation) (No. 2) Regulations 1979, S.I. 1979 No. 1430 (in force on 13th November 1979), specify the prescribed amount for any family and the weekly rate of benefit under the Family Income Supplements Act 1970 in accordance with the amendments made to the 1970 Act by the Child Benefit Act 1975. These Regulations revoke the Family Income Supplements (Computation) Regulations 1979, para. 2627, immediately after they come into operation.

2629   **Hospital in-patients**

The Social Security (Hospital In-Patients) Amendment Regulations 1979, S.I. 1979 No. 223 (in force on 6th April 1979), amend the Social Security (Hospital In-Patients) Regulations 1975, 1975 Halsbury's Abridgment para. 3146, by substituting for the "standard rate", the "basic component", which means the weekly rate of basic component specified in the Social Security Pensions Act 1975, s. 6 (1) (a).

2630   **Industrial injuries—prescribed diseases**

The Social Security (Industrial Injuries) (Prescribed Diseases) (Amendment) Regulations 1979, S.I. 1979 No. 264 (in force on 6th April 1979), amend the Social Security (Industrial Injuries) (Prescribed Diseases) Regulations 1975, 1975 Halsbury's Abridgment para. 3164, reg. 49 with regard to the right to appeal to a medical appeal tribunal against a decision of a pneumoconiosis medical board on a diagnosis question relating to pneumoconiosis or byssinosis.

2631   The Social Security (Industrial Injuries) (Prescribed Diseases) Amendment (No. 2) Regulations 1979, S.I. 1979 No. 265 (in force on 6th April 1979), amend the Social Security (Industrial Injuries) (Prescribed Diseases) Regulations 1975, 1975 Halsbury's Abridgment para. 3164, reg. 2 so that, for the purpose of deciding whether byssinosis is a prescribed disease in relation to a person, it is no longer necessary that he should have been employed for a specific minimum period in an occupation prescribed in relation to byssinosis.

2632   The Social Security (Industrial Injuries) (Prescribed Diseases) Amendment (No. 3) Regulations 1979, S.I. 1979 No. 632 (in force on 8th August 1979), extend the Social Security (Industrial Injuries) (Prescribed Diseases) Regulations 1975, to include nasal carcinoma in the case of persons employed in buildings where the manufacture or repair of footwear or components of footwear made wholly or partly of leather or fibre board, is carried out.

2633   The Social Security (Industrial Injuries) (Prescribed Diseases) Amendment (No. 4) Regulations 1979, S.I. 1979 No. 992 (in force on 3rd September 1979), amend the Social Security (Industrial Injuries) (Prescribed Diseases) Regulations 1975, 1975 Halsbury's Abridgment para. 3164. They extend the definition of occupational deafness to substantial permanent sensorineural hearing loss of at least 50dB in each ear, being due in the case of at least one ear, to occupational noise, and also add a number of occupations to those prescribed in relation to occupational deafness.

2634   The Social Security (Industrial Injuries) (Prescribed Diseases) Amendment (No. 5) Regulations 1979, S.I. 1979 No. 1569 (in force on 7th January 1980), widen the description of the disease specified in the Social Security (Industrial Injuries) (Prescribed Diseases) Regulations 1975, 1975 Halsbury's Abridgment para. 3164, Sch. 1, Pt. I, para. 21 and enlarge the range of occupations to which it applies. Cover under the industrial injuries provisions of the Social Security Act 1975 is thus extended to infection by leptospira of all kinds in relation to persons employed in occupations involving work in places infested or liable to be infested by rats, field mice or voles; work at dog kennels or the care or handling of dogs; and contact with bovine animals or pigs or the meat products of either. The Regulations also contain transitional provisions relating to persons, not covered by earlier regulations, who are already suffering from the disease on the date on which they come into operation.

2635   —— —— **occupational deafness—computation of period worked in prescribed employment**

National Insurance Commissioner's decision:

R (I) 3/78 (claim for industrial disablement benefit in respect of occupational deafness; claimant worked continuously in prescribed occupation for fourteen years and for part of six remaining years, in vicinity of prescribed plant; insurance officer contended that twenty year prescription test not therefore satisfied; claimant who carried out more than one function in exercise of his skills, was employed in single occupation for purposes of computing period he worked in prescribed occupation; twenty year period made up and occupational deafness therefore prescribed in relation to claimant).

2636   —— —— whether prescribed in relation to claimant

National Insurance Commissioner's decision:

R (I) 2/78 (claim for disablement benefit for prescribed disease of occupational deafness; claimant employed as welder in chemical factory making cast metal linings for vessels; used high-speed grinding tools to dress new cast metal which arrived from suppliers in manufactured or fabricated form; question whether occupation was prescribed in relation to occupational deafness under Social Security (Industrial Injuries) (Prescribed Diseases) Regulations 1975, 1975 Halsbury's Abridgment para. 3164, being use of high-speed grinding tools in dressing of cast metal within Sch. 1, Part I, para. 48 (a); para. 48 (a) not restricted to operations involved in fabrication of cast metal; dressing of already manufactured cast metal fell within paragraph, which was not confined to the metal manufacturing industry; therefore disease was prescribed in relation to claimant).

2637   Industrial injury benefit—entitlement where accident occurs on oil rig in Dutch waters—referral to European Court of Justice

National Insurance Commissioner's decision:

Decision CI 202/1977: RE THE KEY GIBRALTAR OIL DRILLING RIG [1979] I CMLR 362 (worker injured whilst working on oil rig belonging to English company, claimed industrial injury benefit; rig positioned on part of Continental Shelf over which Netherlands exercised sovereign rights; question as to worker's entitlement to U.K. benefit; case referred to European Court of Justice for interpretation of Council Regulation (EEC) 1408/71, arts. 14 and 55; whether under art. 14 (1) (a) oil rig worker to be regarded as having been posted to member state on whose part of Continental Shelf rig stationed; whether under art 14 (1) (c) was pursuing activity in territory of two or more member states; if either of these, whether responsibility for payment of benefit fell on member state to whose legislation worker subject within meaning of art. 14; whether, within meaning art. 55 (1) (a), worker was staying in member state on whose part of Continental Shelf rig stationed; if so whether, under art. 55 (1) (a), member state was responsible for payment of benefit, even though worker was staying in another member state at time of accident).

2638   Invalidity   benefit—entitlement—change   from   sickness   to invalidity benefit—whether time barred

National Insurance Commissioner's decision:

R (S) 3/79 (claimant aware that earnings limit for payment of increase in sickness benefit in respect of wife precluded payment in his case; unaware of different conditions and earnings limit which applied to increase of invalidity benefit; claimed promptly once he knew of entitlement but out of time; claimant had good excuse for failure to claim; had knowledge of limit in relation to sickness benefit and could not be expected to enquire if position different in relation to invalidity benefit; claim therefore allowed).

2639   —— —— review of decision—where obtaining different medical opinion is change of circumstances

National Insurance Commissioner's decision:

Decision R (S) 6/78 (claimant's doctor certified incapacity of claimant to work for a number of weeks; award of invalidity benefit made accordingly; medical officer of Department of Health and Social Security inspected claimant; found him capable of work; insurance officer reviewed decision to award benefit as he considered there had been a relevant change of circumstances under Social Security Act 1975, s. 104 (1) (b); obtaining different medical opinion not in itself a change of circumstances within s. 104 (1) (b), although it might have been evidence of such a change if there was other evidence of it).

2640   —— **non-contributory invalidity pension—entitlement**

National Insurance Commissioner's decisions:

Decision R (S) 4/78 (claimant, a housewife, disabled by paralysis of the left arm; could perform household duties but only very slowly; it took her all day to do housework; not entitled to non-contributory invalidity pension unless she was incapable of performing normal household duties under Social Security Act 1975, s. 36 (2); under Social Security (Non-Contributory Invalidity Pension) Regulations 1975, reg. 13A (2), a woman could be treated as so incapable if she was unable to perform household duties to any substantial extent; she was not incapable of performing normal household duties under s. 36 (2) and was not to be treated as incapable under reg. 13A (2); claimant not entitled to pension).

2641   Decision R(S) 5/78: (claimant for non-contributory invalidity pension; claimant had use of one arm only and deformity in one foot; able to do limited household chores slowly; claimant established that she was incapable of performing normal household duties under Social Security (Non-Contributory Invalidity Pension) Regulations 1975, reg. 13A; test was subjective; amount she could perform was substantially less than capable housewife).

2642   Decision R(S) 7/78 (claimant, a housewife, had extensive coronary thrombosis and consequently developed angina as a result of which ability to perform household duties restricted; entitlement to non-contributory invalidity pension; whether incapable of performing normal household duties; not necessary to establish that there were virtually no household duties she could perform; incapacity depended on establishing that by reason of disablement she was effectively prevented from running household in manner and to standard to be expected of housewife in her circumstances; claimant was so incapable and thus entitled to benefit).

2643   **Maternity allowance—entitlement—earnings-related supplement**

National Insurance Commissioner's decision:

Decision R (G) 1/78 (claimant received maternity allowance for period 12th January 1976 to 22nd May 1976; also earnings-related supplement for period beinning 19th January 1976; rate of supplement calculated by reference to 1973/74 tax year because maternity allowance period linked with period of incapacity for work in October 1975 by virtue of Social Security Act 1975, s. 17 (1); claimant contended linking provisions of s. 17 (1) should not have been applied and thus relevant year for calculation of supplement was 1974/75; although express reference to maternity allowance omitted from s. 17 (1), it should be implied from context; thus linking provisions applied and relevant year was 1973/74).

2644   **Mobility allowance**

The Mobility Allowance Amendment Regulations 1979, S.I. 1979 No. 172 (in force on 21st March 1979), amend the Mobility Allowance Regulations 1975, 1975 Halsbury's Abridgment para. 3175 by prescribing more precisely the circumstances in which a person is to be treated as suffering from physical disablement such that he is virtually unable to walk. They also ensure that mobility allowance may be payable to a person who has the use of a vehicle provided by the Secretary of State under the Health Services and Public Health Act 1968, s. 33, where that vehicle is not a power driven road vehicle controlled by the occupant.

2645 —— entitlement—inability or virtual inability to walk

National Insurance Commissioner's decisions:

Decision R (M) 1/78 (claimant spastic child with unpredictable liability to epileptic seizures; able to walk but doctor advised she should not be allowed to walk unattended; whether satisfied condition for mobility allowance of being unable or virtually unable to walk; condition not satisfied; claimant physically capable of walking a mile or more, thus could not be said to be unable or virtually unable, by reason of physical disablement, to walk).

2646   Decision R (M) 2/78 (claimant mongol boy physically capable of walking but due to mental handicap could not walk unaided; whether satisfied condition for mobility allowance of being unable or virtually unable to walk because of physical disablement; erratic behavour which seriously impaired mobility directly due to condition of mongolism which was a physical disorder, being due to faulty genetic inheritance; since physical factor present thoughout in causation of inability to walk, he was virtually unable to walk because of physical disablement).

2647 —— —— —— test to be applied

National Insurance Commissioner's decision:

R(M) 3/78 (claimant aged 29 suffering from imbalance and subject to disabling fits and tachycardia on exertion; medical appeal tribunal, after examination, satisfied she was not "unable to walk or virtually unable to walk" for purposes of Mobility Allowance Regulations 1975; insufficient evidence to show that exertion required to walk would constitute danger to life or serious deterioration in health; claimant contended test was ability to walk such a distance as would enable person to lead normal life; decision of tribunal upheld; "walk" meant movement by means of legs and feet, and regulations did not require test of environmental circumstances).

2648 Pensioners' Payments and Social Security Act 1979

The Pensioners' Payments and Social Security Act 1979 makes provision for lump sum payments to pensioners and modifies the Social Security Act 1975, s. 125, relating to the review of the amount of earnings of a beneficiary's wife which must be exceeded before a pension is reduced by reference to the excess. The Act received the royal assent on 26th July 1979 and came into force on that date.

Section 1 provides for a lump sum payment of £10 to be made in respect of certain persons who are entitled, or treated as entitled, to payment of specified qualifying benefits in respect of a day in the week beginning 3rd December 1979: s. 1 (1). A further payment of £10 can also be made in respect of the spouses of certain of those persons where both spouses have attained pensionable age: s. 1 (2). The payment is not taxable and will be disregarded when a person's means are assessed under any other legislation: s. 1 (4).

Section 2 relates to interpretation of provisions as to payments. Section 3 deals with the administration of the lump sum payment.

Section 4 requires the Secretary of State in 1980, and in each subsequent year, to lay a draft order before Parliament providing for another payment of £10 or a larger sum if he considers it appropriate, having regard to the economic situation, the standard of living and other such matters.

Section 5 modifies the up-rating provisions in the Social Security Act 1975, s. 125 so as to remove from the Secretary of State the duty of reviewing the amount of the earnings limit for dependent wives in ss. 45 (3) and 66 (4) of the 1975 Act, and of laying a draft order before Parliament relating to such sums.

Sections 6 and 7 contain supplemental provisions and s. 8 provides for citations and repeals.

2649 Pneumoconiosis, Byssinosis and Miscellaneous Diseases—benefit scheme

The Pneumoconiosis, Byssinosis and Miscellaneous Diseases Benefit (Amendment)

Scheme 1979, S.I. 1979 No. 996 (in force on 8th August 1979) amends the 1966 Scheme by adding nasal carcinoma to the list of diseases for which benefit is payable out of the National Insurance Fund.

2650　Pneumoconiosis (Workers' Compensation) Act 1979

The Pneumoconiosis etc. (Workers' Compensation) Act 1979 renders persons disabled by pneumoconiosis, byssinosis or diffuse mesothelioma eligible for lump sum compensation payments if no damages have already been recovered from any employer, no claim has been compromised and there is no relevant employer available to be sued for damages. Dependants of those disabled by the above diseases prior to death are also eligible. The Act received the royal assent on 4th April 1979 and came into force on 4th July 1979.

Section 1 enables compensation to be paid and lists the diseases for which it is payable. Regulations may be made prescribing the level of compensation for different cases, classes of cases and different circumstances. Section 2 lays down the conditions of entitlement. In the case of a person disabled by a relevant disease, he must be in receipt of disablement benefit in respect of it, no relevant employer may still be carrying on business, and he must not have brought any action or compromised any claim for damages in respect of his disablement. In the case of a dependant of a person disabled prior to death, the dependant must be entitled to death benefit by reason of the deceased's disablement, or the deceased must have been receiving disablement benefit while alive. Every relevant employer must have ceased carrying on business, no payment may have been made to the deceased in respect of the disease during his lifetime, and neither the deceased nor his personal representatives nor any relatives may have brought any action or compromised any claim for damages in respect of the disablement or death. Actions dismissed other than on the merits, for example for want of prosecution, do not preclude a disabled person or dependant from making a successful claim.

Dependants are limited to spouses and relatives wholly or mainly dependent on the deceased at the date of his death: s. 3. Section 4 empowers the Secretary of State to appoint a person to hold an inquiry into any question arising on a claim, and extends the Social Security Act 1975, s. 94, allowing appeals on questions of law, to determinations made under this Act. Section 5 allows the Secretary of State to reconsider determinations against applicants for compensation where there has been a material change of circumstances since the determination was made. He may also reconsider cases decided either in the applicant's favour or against him where the decision was made in ignorance of, or was based on a mistake as to some material fact. Any payments to minors or those incapable of managing their affairs must be made to trustees: s. 6. Section 7 deals with the making of regulations under the Act, s. 8 prescribes a maximum fine of £1,000 for anyone making a fraudulent statement or furnishing false documents or information for the purpose of obtaining a payment for himself or any other person. Section 9 contains financial provisions and s. 10 deals with short title, construction, commencement and extent.

2651　—— determination of claims

The Pneumoconiosis etc. (Workers' Compensation) (Determination of Claims) Regulations 1979, S.I. 1979 No. 727 (in force on 4th July 1979), prescribe the manner in which claims for payment must be made for determination by the Secretary of State under the Pneumoconiosis etc. (Workers' Compensation) Act 1979, para. 2650. They also prescribe the manner in which applications for reconsideration of such determinations must be made. Time limits for making such claims and applications are prescribed, although the Secretary of State has power to extend these time limits where appropriate.

2652　—— payment of claims

The Pneumoconiosis etc. (Workers' Compensation) (Payment of Claims) Regulations 1979, S.I. 1979 No. 1726 (in force on 1st January 1980), prescribe the amount or level of payments to be made under the Pneumoconiosis (Workers' Compensation)

Act 1979, para. 2650, to persons disabled by a disease to which the Act applies or to dependants of persons who immediately before they died were disabled by such a disease.

2653   Reciprocal agreements

The Social Security (Reciprocal Agreements) Order 1979, S.I. 1979 No. 290 (in force on 6th April 1979), provides for specified Orders in Council, which give effect to agreements made between the United Kingdom Government and other countries providing for reciprocity in certain social security matters, to have effect subject to modifications to take account of changes in social security law made by the Social Security Pensions Act 1975. The modifications make provision for the treatment in those agreements of the additional component of retirement pension, widow's benefit and invalidity pension introduced by that Act.

2654   —— Finland

A treaty with Finland was signed in London on 12th December 1978 extending and modifying the convention establishing reciprocity between the two countries in the field of social security in 1959. The treaty provides for each country to extend the obligations and advantages under its social security legislation (specified, in the case of England, as the Social Security Act 1975 and the Child Benefit Act 1975) to persons and their dependants from the other country who become residents in the first country. A protocol attached to the convention entitles a national of either country who needs immediate medical treatment during a temporary stay in the territory of the other country to receive, on production of his passport, the necessary medical treatment under the same conditions (including payment of charges) as a person ordinarily resident in that territory. Instruments of ratification have not yet been exchanged. For the text of the convention, see Cmnd. 7498.

2655   —— Portugal

The Social Security (Portugal) Order 1979, S.I. 1979 No. 921 (in force on 1st October 1979), makes provision for modification of the Social Security Act 1975 and that part of the Child Benefit Act 1975 relating to child benefit so as to give effect to the Convention on Social Security between the United Kingdom and Portugal signed in London on 15th November 1978. The text of the Convention is set out in the Schedule, and see also Cmnd. 7721. It relates to reciprocity in contributions, short-term benefits, invalidity benefit, retirement pensions, widow's benefit, industrial injuries benefits, death grant, guardian's allowance and child benefit.

2656   Retirement pension—entitlement—late claim for increase

National Insurance Commissioner's decision:

R (P) 1/79 (claimant retired in 1971, was awarded retirement pension and ascertained he was not entitled to increase for wife because of her earnings; earnings rule subsequently relaxed; claimant entitled to increase from April 1976, but did not claim until March 1977, being unaware of change; whether good cause for delay in claiming; necessary to consider whether ignorance reasonable; failure to make inquiries not necessarily fatal if claimant able to show he could not reasonably have been expected to have been aware of rights or that claimants' mistaken belief reasonably held was responsible for failure to assert rights; claimant entitled to increase from April 1976).

2657   —— increase in rate—entitlement to increase—whether ordinarily resident in Great Britain

National Insurance Commissioner's decision:

Decision R(P) 1/78 (claimant in receipt of retirement pension left Great Britain in 1973 to live in husband's home in Rhodesia; intended to remain there while political situation stable and to return to Great Britain for part of each year; returned to Great

Britain for several months in 1974, 1975 and 1976 and stayed with relations and friends; claimed increases in benefit from 1973 onwards; three of increases became operative on dates on which claimant absent from Great Britain; claimant only entitled to increases if ordinarily resident in Great Britain immediately before relevant dates; she ceased to reside here in 1973 and was not ordinarily resident here while in Rhodesia, since matrimonial home was in Rhodesia and claimant had no settled home here; nor was she ordinarily resident in Great Britain when she stayed here in 1974, 1975 and 1976 as ordinary residence connoted some degree of continuity; claimant not entitled to increases).

2658   **Sickness benefit—entitlement—absence abroad for convalescence**

National Insurance Commissioner's decisions:

Decision CS 175/77: RE CONVALESCENCE IN GERMANY [1978] 1 CMLR 390 (claim by English worker for United Kingdom sickness benefit in respect of time spent in Germany for rest and change of air; benefit of rest and freedom from worry did not constitute treatment under Social Security Benefit (Persons Abroad) Regulations 1975 or Council Regulation (EEC) 1408/71; claimant therefore not within exeption to disqualification under either provision; validity of reciprocal convention with Germany on exemption from disqualification for sickness benefit uncertain in light of EEC Treaty, art. 6 and the Secretary of State had indicated that the discretion to grant that exemption would not be exercised in respect of claims made after the entry into force in the United Kingdom of Regulation 1408/71; claimant disqualified from receiving benefit).

2659   Decision CS 622/78: RE AN ITALIAN WORKER [1979] 2 CMLR 441 (claimant resided in England and was domiciled in Italy; became totally disabled and received English sickness benefit; returned to Italy for six weeks for convalescence and applied for benefit for convalescent period; Council Regulation (EEC) 1408/71 provided for payment of benefit to workers of member states and superseded national legislation; claim disallowed; travel abroad for convalescent purposes was not travel in order to receive treatment within Reg. 1408/71; claimant was not residing in Italy at relevant time, therefore was not covered by exception allowing retention of benefit when authorised to return to member state where he resided).

2660   **—— —— claim by Irish national—effect of United Kingdom disqualification**

An Irish national resident in Great Britain claimed sickness benefit under the National Insurance Act 1965 in respect of a period spent in hospital while serving a term of imprisonment in Ireland. His claim was rejected by the Insurance Officer on the basis that he was disqualified under s. 49 (1) (b) of the Act from receiving a benefit for a period during which he was imprisoned. He appealed to the National Insurance Commissioner, who stayed the proceedings and referred to the European Court questions as to the interpretation and application of Community rules against discrimination. On the resumption of the proceedings, *held*, on the basis that s. 49 (1) (b) applied only to terms of imprisonment served in Great Britain, although the disqualification would thus discriminate against British nationals, such discrimination did not offend any principle of Community law. Further, while Community law did not prohibit the treatment of corresponding facts in one member state as equivalent to such facts occurring in national territory, there was no duty to do so, and since the British authorities had no discretion to allow such an approach the disqualification could not therefore apply to the claimant. Moreover, it was not possible to apply the disqualification to imprisonment outside Great Britain since the exemptions to the disqualification were confined to Great Britain. Nationals of other member states would therefore be unable to claim the benefit of the exemptions and would thus be discriminated against, contrary to the overriding prohibition of discrimination contrary to EEC Treaty, art. 7, which the European

Court had held to be directly applicable within the scope of Council Regulation (EEC) 1408/71. Accordingly, the claimant was entitled to receive benefits in respect of the period in question.

Case CS 539/76: KENNY v INSURANCE OFFICER [1979] 1 CMLR 433 (National Insurance Commissioner).

The ruling of the European Court of Justice is reported at [1978] ECR 1489, 1978 Halsbury's Abridgment para. 1264.

National Insurance Act 1965, s. 49 (1) (b) is now Social Security Act 1975, s. 82 (5) (b).

2661 —— —— —— **reference to European Court**

National Insurance Commissioner's decision:

RE SICKNESS BENEFIT FOR AN ELDERLY IRISHWOMAN (C(S) 26/77) [1979] 3 CMLR 442 (Commissioner referred certain questions to European Court relating to right of fully-insured National of member state to claim sickness benefit in respect of employment in another member state; claimant, Irishwoman fully insured in Ireland, took up work in United Kingdom and paid National Insurance contributions into United Kingdom scheme, despite fact that she was aged 60 (upper limit for entry into United Kingdom scheme); fell ill, claimed sickness benefit (which is pension related); disallowed on ground that as she did not satisfy contribution condition no retirement pension would have been payable and therefore not entitled to sickness benefit; on appeal commissioner put forward questions for European Court; (i) whether she was entitled to pay contributions in United Kingdom while of pensionable age, by virtue of Council Regulations (EEC) 1612/68 art. 7 or Council Regulations (EEC) 1408/71, art. 3 both relating to equality of treatment for EEC workers employed in member state other than their own; (ii) whether she was deemed to be fully insured in United Kingdom by an aggregation of insurance under 1408/71 art 18; (iii) whether art 18 applied to the acquisition, retention or recovery of the right to sickness benefit where the calculation of sickness benefit was dependant upon the calculation of a notional retirement pension rate).

2662 —— —— **incapacity for work**

National Insurance Commissioner's decision:

R (S) 4/79 (during claimant's illness (deep vein thrombosis in leg), his wife ran shop in which they were partners; claimant helped when felt fit; whether claimant incapable of work within Social Security Act 1975, s. 17 (1) (a) (ii); "work" construed as work for which an employer would be willing to pay, or work as a self-employed person in some gainful occupation; claimant's intermittent tinkering in business not work; however, under Social Security (Unemployment, Sickness and Invalidity Benefit) Regulations 1975, reg. 7 (1) (g), day not to be treated as day of incapacity for work if person does any work on that day, other than, inter alia, work which, although not part of medical treatment, claimant has good cause for doing; "work" had different meaning from in s. 17 (1) (a) (ii) and included type of work done by claimant; however, claimant had good cause for doing it for therapeutic reasons; hence claimant incapable of work and entitled to benefit).

2663 —— —— **whether expiry of time limit bar to claim for benefit**

National Insurance Commissioner's decision:

R (S) 5/79 (production worker claimed sickness benefit for two month period; claim received by Department of Health and Social Security after expiry of time limit because had been sent to employer first; responsibility of claimant to ensure claim sent to Department in good time; failure by intermediary to deliver claim in time attributable to claimant as claimant reasonably expected to make inquiry if no payment or acknowledgment of claim received from Department).

2664 **Social Security Act 1979**

The Social Security Act 1979 makes a number of miscellaneous changes in the law relating to social security. The Act received the royal assent on 22nd March 1979 and came into force on that date with the following exceptions: ss. 11, 12, Sch. 1, paras. 2–22, Sch. 3, paras. 5–7, 11, 14–20, 22, 23, 29 (a), (b) came into force on 6th April 1979; s. 3 (3), so far as it relates to women between the ages of sixty and sixty-five on 22nd March 1979, comes into force on days to be appointed.

For women born between 7th June 1918 and 22nd March 1919 inclusive, the operative date is 29th March 1979 in relation to the making and determination of claims for mobility allowance, and 6th June 1979 for all other purposes: S.I. 1979 No. 369.

For women born between 29th November 1914 and 6th June 1918 inclusive, the operative date is 5th September 1979 in relation to mobility allowance and 28th November for all other purposes: S.I. 1979 No. 1031.

Section 1 deals with interpretation. Section 2 amends the Social Security Act 1975, s.35, by giving power to vary the qualifying period for the attendance allowance and providing for regulations to be made to enable those undergoing renal dialysis to qualify for the allowance, except where they are hospital out-patients.

Section 3 amends s. 37A of the 1975 Act relating to increases in mobility allowances. The upper age limit for receipt of the allowance is increased to seventy-five and the application of regulations made under the 1975 Act is extended. Section 4 amends the provisions relating to earnings after retirement age. Section 5 and Sch. 1 amends the 1975 Act as regards entitlement to invalidity allowance and Category D non-contributory pensions, as well as amending retirement pension contribution conditions. Further amendments relate to contribution requirements under the Social Security Pensions Act 1975 and to pensions under Social Security (Miscellaneous Provisions) Act 1977. Defects in both 1975 Acts are additionally remedied.

Sections 6–9 deal with appeals from and to the Supplementary Benefits Appeal Tribunals. Section 6 and Sch. 2 insert s.15A and a new Sch. 4 in the Supplementary Benefits Act 1976 making provision for changes in the appeal system, in particular enabling the introduction of rules to allow for appeals from the tribunals to the National Insurance Commissioner. Sections 7, 8 amend the Social Security Act 1975, concerning incompatible benefits and the repayment of benefits. Under s.9 solicitors may be appointed as National Insurance Commissioners.

Sections 10, 11 amend the Social Security Pensions Act 1975. The former amends the provisions for the review and revaluation of earnings factors, the latter rectifies defects relating to increases in official pensions. Section 12 provides for the uprating of increments in a person's guaranteed minimum pension.

Sections 13–21 make miscellaneous provisions. Section 13 obliges the Secretary of State to review the rates of maternity and death grants annually, s. 14 gives him power to adjust secondary Class 1 contributions where the employees in question do not have a right to redundancy payments. Section 15 provides for the adjustment of benefits where there is an overlap with benefits payable under the legisation of another member state of the EEC. Section 16 re-defines "business" for the purposes of certain criminal proceedings, s. 17 exempts certain proposed regulations from having to be referred to the National Insurance Advisory Committee and s. 18 concerns the treatment of insignificant amounts. Section 19 relates to Northern Ireland, s. 20 makes financial provisions and s. 21 deals with short title, commencement and extent. Schedule 3 makes minor and consequential amendments.

2665   Social Security Pensions Act 1975—commencement

The Social Security Pensions Act 1975 (Commencement No. 13) Order 1979, S.I. 1979 No. 171, brings provisions of the 1975 Act relating to mobility allowance into force for men born between 7th June 1918 and 21st December 1919 inclusive. Sections 22, 65 (1) and Sch. 14 (part) came into force on 7th March 1979 for the purposes of making claims for, and the determination of claims and questions relating to, mobility allowance; for all other purposes they come into force on 6th June 1979.

2666

The Social Security Pensions Act 1975 (Commencement No. 15) Order 1979, S.I. 1979 No. 394, brought into force s. 22, Sch. 4, paras. 47, 49, 51–53 of the 1975 Act in relation to women born on or after 23rd March 1919 but before 21st December 1919. The date of commencement in relation to mobility allowance is 31st March 1979, and for all other purposes is 6th June 1979. The Order also revokes the Social Security Pensions Act 1975 (Commencement No. 14) Order 1979, S.I. 1979 No. 367, which contained an error in drafting.

2667   The Social Security Pensions Act 1975 (Commencement No. 16) Order, S.I. 1979 No. 1030, brought into force ss. 22, 65 (1) (in relation to the paragraphs of Sch. 4 brought into force by the Order), Sch. 4, paras. 47, 49, 51–53 of the 1975 Act in relation to persons born after 28th November 1914 but before 7th June 1918. The date of commencement in relation to mobility allowance is 5th September 1979 and for all other purposes 28th November 1979.

2668   —— **transitional provisions**

The Social Security (Benefit) (Transitional) Regulations 1979, S.I. 1979 No. 345 (in force on 6th April 1979, except for reg. 7, which came into force on 24th March 1979), make provision for transitional matters connected with the coming into force of the Social Security Pensions Act 1975. Modifications are made to the Social Security Act 1975 and the Social Security Pensions Act 1975 and certain regulations made under them in their application to persons who, immediately before 6th April 1979, were contributors under the Social Security Act 1975 or were entitled to, or had a prospective right to, or expectation of, benefit under that Act or the National Insurance Act 1965. The modifications relate to entitlement to Category A and Category B retirement pensions, widowed mother's allowance and widow's pension.

2669   **Supplementary benefit—calculation of benefit—right to reduce allowance—whether reduction validly made**

The applicant, having registered for work, applied for supplementary allowance and unemployment benefit. When his supplementary allowance application came before the Supplementary Benefits Commission, his claim for unemployment benefit had been suspended, pending inquiries into whether he had contributed to his own unemployment. The Commission calculated the amount of supplementary allowance which would normally be payable to him and then deducted 40 per cent, purporting to act under the Supplementary Benefits Act 1976, Sch. 1, para. 9. Under para. 9, an applicant's supplementary allowance could be reduced by 40 per cent if, in the opinion of the Commission, he would, if his claim for unemployment benefit had been determined, be disqualified for that benefit by virtue of the Social Security Act 1975, s. 20 (1) by reason of conduct resulting in unemployment. A tribunal dismissed the applicant's appeal against the deduction on the grounds that the allowance had been correctly calculated and the deduction had been correctly applied. In reply to an inquiry made on behalf of the applicant, the tribunal subsequently stated that it had not been in a position to decide to what extent, if any, the applicant had contributed to his own unemployment. This applicant applied for an order of certiorari to quash the tribunal's decision on the ground that the tribunal could not make a deduction under para. 9 without first forming an opinion as to whether the applicant would have been disqualified from receiving unemployment benefit if his claim to that benefit had been determined. *Held,* a tribunal had to form such an opinion before it could make a deduction under para. 9, despite the difficulties involved. On the evidence, the tribunal had not formed its own opinion as to whether the applicant would have been disqualified from receiving unemployment benefit and had therefore erred in deducting 40 per cent. An order for certiorari would be granted.

R v GREATER BIRMINGHAM SUPPLEMENTARY BENEFIT APPEAL TRIBUNAL, EX PARTE KHAN [1979] 3 All ER 759 (Queen's Bench Division: LORD WIDGERY CJ, SHAW LJ and LLOYD J).

2670   —— **determination of requirements**

The Supplementary Benefits (Determination of Requirements) Regulations 1979,

S.I. 1979 No. 997 (in force on 12th November 1979), vary the provisions of the Supplementary Benefits Act 1976, Sch. 1, Part II, concerning the calculation of requirements in relation to supplementary benefits.

2671 —— entitlement—minor receiving full time education

A minor's application for supplementary benefit was refused by the Supplementary Benefits Commission on the grounds that he was receiving a full time education and was not entitled to claim supplementary benefit by virtue of the Supplementary Benefit Act 1976, s. 7 (1). The appeal tribunal dismissed his appeal holding that there were no exceptional circumstances to justify the discretion given in the section. The minor appealed, contending that the tribunal had failed to consider that he was ill and not undergoing full time education at the time of his application. He also claimed that the tribunal misdirected itself as to the meaning of the words "exceptional circumstances" contained in the Act. *Held*, while the boy had been ill and had spent long periods in hospital and at home, the words "attending a school" in the Act should not be construed as referring to a single moment in time. Further, it was also a question of fact whether there were exceptional circumstances which would justify the granting of supplementary benefit to the applicant in his own right. The tribunal had inquired into all the applicant's circumstances and had not found them exceptional. The appeal would be dismissed.

BLOOMFIELD V SUPPLEMENTARY BENEFITS COMMISSION (1979) 123 Sol Jo 33 (Queen's Bench Division: SHEEN J).

2672 —— —— whether claimant receiving full-time instruction of a kind given in schools

The claimant, who was seventeen years old, attended a technical college. Her father received benefits in respect of her under the Child Benefit Act 1975. Her claim for supplementary benefit during the Easter holidays was rejected by an officer of the Supplementary Benefits Commission, on the ground that she was receiving full-time instruction of a kind given in schools and therefore under the Supplementary Benefits Act 1976, s. 7 (1), she was not entitled to supplementary benefit. Her appeal to the Tribunal was dismissed. She appealed, contending that the Commission, through its officer and the decision of the Tribunal, had misdirected itself in interpreting s. 7 (1). *Held*, for the purpose of the receipt of benefits under the Child Benefit Act, education was divided into "advanced" and "non-advanced" education. Benefit was not available in respect of children receiving "advanced" education. Hence for the purposes of the Child Benefit Act it had already been decided that the claimant was receiving "non-advanced" education. The Commission had adopted a policy of interpreting "instruction of a kind given in schools" in s. 7 (1) as meaning "non-advanced" education according to the opinion of the local education authority. On this interpretation, a child in respect of whom child benefit was payable was not entitled to claim supplementary benefit. It was clear that the officer had regarded himself as being bound absolutely by this interpretation, to the exclusion of any other considerations. He had ascertained that the claimant was receiving "non-advanced" education in the opinion of the local education authority, and had held that this disentitled her to supplementary benefit. The expressions "advanced" and "non-advanced" education might be useful as a yardstick, but there should not be a complete abdication of the responsibility to look at the facts of each case. Hence the officer had misdirected himself in considering himself bound by that interpretation and the Tribunal had insufficiently understood the extent to which he had shackled himself. The appeal would be allowed and the matter remitted to the Tribunal for reconsideration.

SAMPSON V SUPPLEMENTARY BENEFITS COMMISSION (1979) 123 Sol Jo 284 (Queen's Bench Division: WATKINS J).

2673 Unemployment benefit—disqualification—whether claimant directly interested in trade dispute

Scotland

Craftsmen imposed sanctions in one of the employers' two factories in pursuance of a wage claim. This resulted in a number of hourly-paid workers being laid off. The union negotiated a new wage structure affecting all union members in both factories and the craftsmen resumed normal work. One of the hourly-paid workers, a storeman, claimed unemployment benefit for the three months he had been laid off. The National Insurance Commissioners refused his claim on the ground that, under the National Insurance Act 1965, s. 22 (1), the storeman was directly interested in the trade dispute which caused the stoppage of work and was thus disqualified from receiving benefit. The storeman appealed contending the decision was, inter alia, ultra vires. *Held*, to be directly interested in a trade dispute, a person had to have a clearly identifiable interest in the subject matter of the dispute itself so that the outcome virtually automatically affected him. The commissioner had misconstrued the meaning of the words and had therefore acted ultra vires.

WATT v LORD ADVOCATE 1979 SLT 137 (Inner House).

2674   Employees at a building site of a power station demanded free protective clothing, which was refused. This eventually lead to a withdrawal of labour for a period of six months, for which the employees claimed unemployment benefit. The National Insurance Commissioner held that as the stoppage of work was caused by a trade dispute within the meaning of the Social Security Act 1975, s. 19, the employees were therefore disqualified from receiving benefit. On appeal, *held*, the cause of the stoppage was the single disputed question of who was to pay for the protective clothing, which the employers were then willing to provide and it was clearly a trade dispute. The appeal would therefore be dismissed.

R v NATIONAL INSURANCE COMMISSIONER, EX PARTE THOMPSON (1979) Appendix to R (U) 5/77 (Queen's Bench Division: LORD WIDGERY CJ, MICHAEL DAVIES and NEILL JJ). Decision of National Insurance Commissioner R (U) 5/77, 1978 Halsbury's Abridgment para. 2728, affirmed.

2675   ―― entitlement—absence abroad

National Insurance Commissioner's decision:

Decision CU 251/78: RE A FARM MANAGER [1979] 1 CMLR 445 (claim by unemployed British farm manager for unemployment benefit for week spent in France looking for work; claimant had been registered as unemployed in Great Britain for two months; claim refused under Social Security Act 1975, s. 82 (5) (a) on grounds of absence from Britain; disqualification under s. 82 (5) (a) did not extend to days of arrival and departure; Council Regulation (EEC) 1408/71, art. 69 gave worker registered as unemployed in one member state for at least four weeks right to benefit for up to three months spent in another member state looking for work, subject to being registered as unemployed in the new member state within seven days of arrival; where worker left within seven days unnecessary to register; claimant entitled to benefit).

2676   See *Re Unemployment Benefits*, para. 1237.

2677   ―― ―― Crown employees—receipt of special payment— whether payment a bar to benefit

A member of the Armed Forces received a special capital payment on the termination of his employment due to compulsory redundancy. The Chief National Insurance Commissioner held that this precluded him from receiving unemployment benefit for one year since it was a payment in lieu of wages within Social Security (Unemployment, Sickness and Invalidity Benefit) Regulations 1975, reg. 7 (1) (d), 1975 Halsbury's Abridgment para. 3117. The court upheld his appeal on the ground that, although there was an element of payment in lieu of wages, that element could not be precisely ascertained. On appeal by the Commissioner, *held*, a capital payment made to a member of the Armed Forces on redundancy was not intended to be compensation in lieu of future remuneration, since entitlement and quantum depended on past service, not future loss. Such a payment was similar to that made to men returning from active service, which was intended to give them a new start in life, not to provide them with an income during a period of unemployment.

R v NATIONAL INSURANCE COMR, EX PARTE STRATTON [1979] 2 All ER 278 (Court of Appeal: LORD DENNING MR, BRIDGE and TEMPLEMAN LJJ). Decision of Divisional Court of the Queen's Bench Division [1979] 1 All ER 1, 1978 Halsbury's Abridgment para. 2726 affirmed.

2678 —— —— **effect of industrial tribunal's decision on question whether claimant unfairly dismissed**

National Insurance Commissioner's decision:

Decision R (U) 4/78 (maintenance fitter summarily dismissed for threatening violence against works engineer; found by industrial tribunal to have been fairly dismissed; National Insurance tribunal followed their decision and found that claimant had been dismissed for misconduct within Social Security Act 1975 s. 20 (1) (a); on appeal Commissioners upheld their decision; National Insurance tribunal not bound by industrial tribunal decision but bound to take cognisance of any evidence given to an industrial tribunal).

2679 —— —— **satisfaction of contribution conditions**

National Insurance Commissioner's decision:

RE WORK IN GERMANY [1979] 1 CMLR 267 (claim in United Kingdom for unemployment benefit; question whether German contributions paid by claimant working in Germany during relevant contribution period counted for United Kingdom unemployment benefit purposes; commissioner directed question to be determined by Secretary of State under Social Security Act 1975, s. 93 (1) (b); decision of Secretary of State determined question in two alternative ways, on basis of National Insurance Acts and on basis of application of Council Regulation (EEC) 1408/71; commissioner regretted absence of reasoned opinion; applied second alternative on basis of presumed intention of Secretary of State; effect of Regulation 1408/71, art. 71 (1) that United Kingdom contribution conditions satisfied by claimant).

2680 —— **increase for child dependants—entitlement**

National Insurance Commissioner's decision:

Decision R(U) 3/78 (claimant, who received increase of unemployment benefit in respect of wife and children with whom he was living, imprisoned; released on 11th October 1976; fresh claim for benefit from 13th October 1976, but claimant did not return to wife and children and sent no money for maintenance until 27th October 1976; on 6th July 1977 claimant gave written undertaking to contribute to maintenance; whether claimant entitled to increase in respect of children for period 13th to 27th October 1976; claimant not so entitled as had not contributed to their maintenance in respect of that period; could not be deemed to be making contributions by reason of undertaking as undertaking could not be given retrospective effect to extent of more than a week).

2681 **Vaccine damage payments**

See Vaccine Damage Payments Act 1979, para. 1947.

2682 **Welfare food**

The Welfare Food (Amendment) Order 1979, S.I. 1979 No. 1568 (in force on 1st January 1980), further amends the Welfare Food Order 1977, 1977 Halsbury's Abridgment para. 1016, by stopping the entitlement to welfare milk and food of expectant mothers and nursing mothers and the young children, not in a family in special circumstances, when the tokens issued before the coming into operation of this order expire; and by increasing the prices of children's vitamin drops to 14p per bottle and vitamin tablets for expectant and nursing mothers to 30p per container.

2683   Widow's benefit and retirement pensions

The Social Security (Widow's Benefit and Retirement Pensions) Regulations 1979, S.I. 1979 No. 642 (in force on 10th July 1979), consolidate the Social Security (Widow's Benefit and Retirement Pensions) Regulations 1974, 1974 Halsbury's Abridgment para. 3122, as amended. They contain provisions relating to widows' benefits, retirement pensions and age addition under the Social Security Act 1975, 1975 Halsbury's Abridgment para. 3187, and the Social Security Pensions Act 1975, 1975 Halsbury's Abridgment para. 3191.

2684   ⸺ transitional provisions

The Social Security (Widow's Benefit, Retirement Pensions and Other Benefits) (Transitional) Regulations 1979, S.I. 1979 No. 643 (in force on 10th July 1979), consolidate the Widow's Benefit, Retirement Pension and Other Benefits (Transitional) Regulations 1974, 1974 Halsbury's Abridgment para. 3088, as amended. They make provision for transitional matters connected with the coming into force of the Social Security Act 1975 and the Social Security Pensions Act 1975.

2685   Workmen's compensation—scheme

The Workmen's Compensation (Supplementation) (Amendment) Scheme 1979, S.I. 1979 No. 1190 (in force on 14th November 1979), amends the Workmen's Compensation (Supplementation) Scheme 1966 by making adjustments to the intermediate rates of lesser incapacity allowance consequential upon the increase in the maximum rate of that allowance made by the Social Security Benefits Up-rating Order 1979, para. 2605. The Scheme also makes transitional provisions.

SOLICITORS

Halsbury's Laws of England (3rd edn.), Vol. 36, paras. 1–358

2686   Articles

A Canadian Preview of our Royal Commission Report?, Michael Zander (a study of the Canadian legal profession): 129 NLJ 599.

Blueprint for the Future, S. P. Best (position of solicitors in the future): 123 Sol Jo 55.

Confidentiality and Privilege in the EEC Context, David Edward (obligation of confidentiality between lawyer and client in the European context): 128 NLJ 1208.

Do Lawyers Do More Harm than Good? John D. Ayer (discussion on the United States' legal profession): 129 NLJ 1040.

The Report of the Royal Commission on Legal Services, P.A.L., [1979] LS Gaz 953.

Royal Commission: expensive and ineffective, Justinian (a brief, condemnatory view of the report by the Royal Commission on Legal Services): Financial Times 8th October 1979.

Royal Commission on Legal Services: Principal Recommendations: 129 NLJ 964.

The Solicitor and the Silicon Chip, Theodore Ruoff (answers to some of the questions asked concerning the usefulness of the computer in the solicitor's office): 123 Sol Jo 670.

Solicitors and Professional Liabilities: A Step Forwards, K.M. Stanton (a solicitor's liability in negligence): (1979) 42 MLR 207.

2687   Absence from hearing—return after hearing—unreasonableness of Commissioners

Scotland

Where a company solicitor was absent when his appeal against a corporation tax assessment came before the General Commissioners, their decision to refuse to hear the solicitor who arrived after the disposal of the appeal was held to be unreasonable.

R AND D MCKERRON LTD v INLAND REVENUE COMRS [1979] STC 815 (Inner House).

2688   Advertising—form of advertising to be allowed—Law Society statement

The Council of the Law Society has issued a statement of how solicitors may announce themselves and their work within the Solicitors Practice Rules 1936–72, r. 1. The statement covers collective announcements in the press which may be made by local law societies. It refers also to announcements of the opening of a new office in the legal press and in the non-legal press and also to information concerning amalgamations and dissolutions, admissions of new partners, retirements of partners, and changes in firm name, address, office hours, telephone number or telex details. Reference may be made to a telephone for use when the office is shut and to a telephone answering machine. The form of the announcements is laid down and examples are given of announcements regarded as suitable for insertion in the local press. The statement refers also to the inclusion of announcements in directories open to the whole profession, and specifically to announcements in the Yellow Pages and in the Legal Aid Solicitors List. In referring to announcements on office premises the statement draws attention to self-adhesive notices relating to types of work which are available from the Law Society. The statement also deals with announcements inside the office and the despatch of circulars to established clients. For the text of the statement, see the Law Society's Gazette, 11th October 1979, pp. 982, 983.

2689   —— recommendations of Royal Commission on Legal Services

See para. 1720.

2690   Authority—authority to conclude contracts—exchange of contracts by telephone

See *Domb v Isoz*, para. 2355.

2691   Breach of contract—failure to give sound advice to vendor of house—measure of damages

New Zealand

Solicitors acted for both the vendor and purchasers of a house. They also acted for the vendor in the purchase of a building plot. Before the purchasers' cheque had been cleared, they advised the vendor to give up possession of her house. The purchasers moved in but a dispute arose over certain contents of the house and they stopped the cheque, saying that they would waive their claim for the contents they alleged were missing if $400 was deducted from the price. The vendor at first refused to accept the lower price but later asked for payment. The disputed $400 was not paid but the vendor successfully sued for it. Owing to the delay in payment, the cost to the vendor of building on her plot had escalated and eventually she had to settle for a lesser house than originally intended. She sued the solicitors for breach of contract and was awarded damages representing the difference between the original and new building estimates. On the solicitors' appeal as to the measure of damages, *held*, there was a link between their failure to ensure the purchase price was in hand before the vendor gave up possession of her house and the vendor's inability to build on her plot as planned. The damages reasonably payable included sums for interest on the money for the period she was kept out of it, the expense of providing accommodation for that period and the additional expense incurred in the recovery of the purchase price and the final $400. The increase in building costs and the lack of available builders were not, however, matters which followed from breach of the solicitors' obligation to advise on the delivery of possession of the vendor's house and the total damages payable would accordingly be reduced.

INDER LYNCH DEVOY AND CO v SUBRITZKY [1979] 1 NZLR 87 (Court of Appeal of New Zealand).

2692   Breach of trust—liability of solicitor's partner—value of dissipated asset

Between 1940 and 1947 the widow and son of the settlor dissipated the assets of a trust fund in breach of trust, including selling a farm to the trustees of the son's voluntary settlement. H, a partner in a firm of solicitors, who acted for the trustees of the settlement and for the son personally, knew of the breaches and assisted in some of them. The breaches were discovered in 1967 after the deaths of the widow and son. The plaintiffs who had contingent interests under the settlement commenced an action against H, the executors of his partner's estate and the son's executor, claiming replacement of the sums dissipated. The questions for the court were: (i) whether H's partner was liable even though he did not know of the breaches and was not negligent; (ii) at what date the value of the farm was to be assessed for the purpose of replacement; (iii) whether in assessing liability, the fact that certain duties had been waived which would have been payable had the fund not been dissipated, were to be taken into account. *Held*, (i) the solicitor had acted as an agent of express trustees and no liability for breach of trust could be imposed on his partner H; (ii) the farm would have properly been sold in 1949 by the trustees for the voluntary settlement, the defendants were liable only to account for the profit made by the voluntary settlement trustees; (iii) a trustee could not benefit from his own breach of trust by retaining sums which would have been paid in tax had the breach of trust not been committed.

RE BELL'S INDENTURE; BELL v HICKLEY (1979) 123 Sol Jo 322 (Chancery Division: VINELOTT J).

2693   Costs—taxation—fees for court attendance in criminal proceedings

See *R v Wilkinson*, para. 668.

2694   —— —— VAT

See para. 2125.

2695   —— unpaid bill of costs—solicitor's duty to inform client of his rights

The plaintiff, a solicitor, submitted his bill to the defendants in 1976. When the defendants queried the bill of costs he sent them, in June 1976, a copy of the Solicitors' Remuneration Order 1972 referring them to art. 2 relating to matters to be taken into consideration in assessing a solicitor's remuneration. The bill remained unpaid and in May 1977 the plaintiff wrote a letter before action informing the defendants that his earlier letter had complied with the requirements of art. 3 (1), (2), as to informing them of their right to a certificate from the Law Society that the sum was fair and reasonable and of the relevant provisions of the Solicitors Act 1957 relating to taxation. In the action he claimed, and was awarded, interest on the amount on the unpaid bill from June 1976. On appeal it was held that the letter of June 1976 had not complied with the 1972 Order and interest was payable only from May 1977. The plaintiff appealed. *Held*, in the letter of June 1976 the plaintiff should have called to the defendants' attention the whole of the Order, in particular the clients' right to a certificate granted by the Law Society and to have the costs checked by an officer of the court. The appeal would therefore be dismissed.

CLEMENT-DAVIS v INTER GSA (1979) 123 Sol Jo 505 (Court of Appeal: STEPHENSON and BRANDON LJJ).

2696   —— unpaid fees—lien over client's documents—when solicitor has lien

A firm of solicitors informed its clients that it could no longer continue to act for them and they therefore requested payment. The clients refused and the solicitors issued a summons for relief under RSC Ord 67, r. 6 (1) to have themselves removed from the record. The clients consulted new solicitors, gave notice of change and sought to recover their documents and papers from their former solicitors. An order was made directing their former solicitors to deliver the papers to the new solicitors, the latter undertaking, inter alia, to hold them subject to the former solicitors' lien. On appeal, *held*, if a client discharged a solicitor, the solicitor's lien endured and the court had no rights to call for the documents to be handed over. However, if the solicitor discharged himself in the course of an action then the summons sought followed as a matter of course. On inference from the facts, the former solicitors could not claim that they did not discharge themselves and the appeal would be dismissed.

GAMLEN CHEMICAL CO (UK) LTD v ROCHEM LTD (1979) 123 Sol Jo 838 (Court of Appeal: GOFF and TEMPLEMAN LJJ). *Robins v Goldingham* (1872) LR 13 Eq 440 applied.

See also Times, 6th December 1979.

2697 Disciplinary proceedings—recommendations of Royal Commission on Legal Services

See para. 1720.

2698 Duty of care—attestation of will

Solicitors drafted a will for a testator, under which the plaintiff was a beneficiary, and gave instructions as to its execution. After the testator's death, the gift to the plaintiff was found to be void, as her husband had attested the will. The plaintiff alleged that the solicitors had been negligent. The solicitors admitted the allegation, but contended that their obligation to take reasonable care in the making of the will was owed to the testator alone, and that they owed no duty of care to the plaintiff. *Held*, a solicitor might not only be liable to his client in contract, he might be liable both to his client and to others for the tort of negligence. A solicitor who was instructed by his client to carry out a transaction that would confer a benefit on an identified third party owed a duty of care towards that third party in carrying out that transaction, in that the third party was a person within his direct contemplation as someone who was likely to be so closely and directly affected by his acts or omissions that he could reasonably foresee that the third party was likely to be injured by those acts or omissions. The mere fact that the loss caused was purely financial was no bar to a claim against the solicitor. The plaintiff's claim would succeed.

ROSS v CAUNTERS [1979] 3 All ER 580 (Chancery Division: MEGARRY V-C), *Donoghue v Stevenson* [1932] All ER Rep 1, *Ministry of Housing and Local Government v Sharp* [1970] 2 QB 223, CA and *Midland Bank v Hett, Stubbs and Kemp* [1978] 3 All ER 571, 1977 Halsbury's Abridgment para. 1960 applied.

2699 Duty of solicitor—evidence—lodgment of notes of evidence—Family Division—appeal from registrar

See para. 2130.

2700 Investment for clients—whether solicitor acting in professional capacity

Canada

In an action against a solicitor for compensation for pecuniary loss by reason of misappropriation of funds, the question arose in what circumstances a solicitor could be said to be acting in his professional capacity when he invested clients' money. *Held*, as a general rule, funds received by a solicitor for investment in mortgages were received in his capacity as a solicitor. However, moneys left with a solicitor for use in a purely private commercial venture in which the solicitor and client were joint participants were not received in such a capacity. A solicitor who acted as a guarantor of the proposed investment did not receive the moneys in his professional capacity. In determining the question, the following factors had also to be considered: whether the solicitor was acting as the investor's lawyer at all times; the nature of the services to be provided; whether the solicitor was taking any personal financial risk; the reasonableness of the fees payable and whether the moneys were received by the solicitor in trust or were to be transferred to the alleged commercial venture immediately.

RE PATCHETT AND LAW SOCIETY OF BRITISH COLUMBIA (1978) 92 DLR (3d) 12 (Supreme Court of British Columbia).

2701   Lay observer—annual report

The lay observer has itemised what he sees to be the main areas of client dissatisfaction as: inadequate explanations (which may result in complaints about delays, costs, forecast chances of success or quantum of compensation), estimates of time and cost, delays, lien (in respect of which the lay observer states that there appears to be a need for a swift and cheap procedure whereby clients can recover property withheld on lien; also, that the exercise of the right of lien is only acceptable when the business has been completed), the handling of wills and estates (in respect of which the lay observer states that he feels that the question of the competence of solicitors was most in question), petitions and affidavits in divorce (for example, "he would never have said that in the affidavit if the solicitor had not encouraged it"), the need to advise a client before reaching the door of the court about what may be an acceptable compromise, the belief of clients that solicitors are primarily at fault for last-minute changes of counsel, and the failure to introduce unadmitted staff to the client with suitable expressions of confidence. See Fourth Annual Report of the Lay Observer 1978 (HC 16).

In an appendix to the report the lay observer sets out his recommendations to the Royal Commission on Legal Services: 1. The Law Society should take note of the substance of complaints made by clients and inform the individual firm, and the profession generally if appropriate, of those elements where, in the opinion of the society, a better service might have been given. 2. The lay observer should be directed to inform the Law Society where a practice by the profession seems to him to be against the general interests of clients, and make recommendations accordingly.

2702   Liability on undertakings—whether acting as agent for client

Canada

During the course of an action the defendants' solicitor informed the plaintiff that the defendant was prepared to pay a certain sum in settlement. When it became apparent that the defendants could not pay, the plaintiff contended that the solicitor had given a personal undertaking to pay the sum in the event of default. *Held*, the solicitor had clearly been acting as the defendants' agent and so could not be said to have given a personal undertaking to pay.

JOST V McINNES, COOPER AND ROBERTSON (1978) 87 DLR (3d) 756 (Supreme Court of Nova Scotia).

2703   Negligence—advice given to solicitor by specialist counsel—extent of counsel's duty towards solicitor

Canada

An insured person retained a solicitor to assist in bringing a claim under a fire insurance policy. The firm of solicitors was successfully sued by the insured for negligently allowing the limitation period for bringing claims under the policy to expire. An experienced insurance counsel was retained to advise on the preparation of proofs of loss, and his firm was joined as a third party by the solicitors, and had a third of the damages awarded against them. They appealed. *Held*, the insurance expert was taken on merely to advise on the preparation of proofs of loss and there was no evidence that he was to have been responsible for giving advice with respect to the limitation period. The appeal would be allowed.

SMITH V MCINNIS (1979) 91 DLR (3d) 190 (Supreme Court of Canada).

2704 Professional privilege—documents disclosed to the taxing master

Letters written by a solicitor to his client, a legal aid committee and another firm of solicitors, fell into the hands of the plaintiffs, after the letters had been disclosed to an officer of the court for the purposes of taxation. The plaintiffs alleged that the letters were libellous. The solicitor, claiming professional privilege, applied to have the action stayed, for an injunction restraining any further proceedings and for an order for the return of the letters. *Held*, although the letters had not been disclosed in the previous action, they were covered by professional privilege by analogy, in that they had been disclosed for the purposes of taxation and it was in the public interest that the solicitor should be able to disclose all the necessary papers to the taxing master without fear of litigation. The action would therefore be stayed and the injunction and order granted.

HAYWARD V WEGG-PROSSER [1978] LS Gaz R 1202 (Queen's Bench Division: TUDOR EVANS J).

2705 Rights of audience—recommendations of Royal Commission on Legal Services

See para. 1720.

2706 Royal Commission on Legal Services—recommendations

See para. 1720

2707 Undertaking by solicitor—sale of land—undertaking to pay purchase price to vendor—refusal to pay—order for payment into court—appeal

Malaysia

The vendor agreed to sell land, of which he was the registered proprietor, to the purchaser. At all material times there was a lis pendens order on the register of titles in favour of a third party claiming a half share in the land. A solicitor acting for both the vendor and the purchaser received the purchase price and gave the vendor an undertaking to pay over the money to him on registration of the transfer of the land. The transfer of title was registered, but the solicitor refused to pay over the money to the vendor because the vendor's action to have the lis pendens order set aside had been dismissed. In an action by the vendor to enforce the undertaking, the solicitor was ordered to pay the money into court to safeguard the interests of the third party should he succeed in his claim. The order was upheld on appeal, but on the ground that if the third party's claim were to succeed, the purchaser would not have obtained an unencumbered title and he would accordingly have a claim against the vendor and probably also against the solicitor. The vendor further appealed. *Held*, the possibility of claims being made in the future by a stranger to the proceedings, even where those claims arose out of the transaction in relation to which the solicitor's undertaking was given, was not a matter which the court was entitled to take into consideration as a ground for ordering payment into court instead of to the plaintiff vendor. The main purpose of a solicitor's undertaking in transactions for the sale of land was that it was enforceable against the solicitor independently of any claims against each other by the parties to the contract of sale.

Accordingly, the appeal would be allowed and an order made that the solicitor pay the purchase money over to the vendor.

DAMODARAN S/O RAMAN V CHOE KUAN HIM [1979] 3 WLR 383 (Privy Council: LORD DIPLOCK, LORD MORRIS OF BORTH-Y-GEST, LORD EDMUND-DAVIES and LORD FRASER OF TULLYBELTON).

SPECIFIC PERFORMANCE

Halsbury's Laws of England (3rd edn.), Vol. 36, paras. 359–529

2708 **Contract for sale of land—order for specific performance—failure to comply—discharge of order—entitlement to damages at common law**

A contract was entered into for the sale of property which was subject to a mortgage. The purchaser failed to complete and the vendors obtained an order for specific performance. No steps were taken to enforce the order and the mortgagees enforced the mortgage by selling the property. The vendors sought an order that the purchaser should pay the balance of the purchase price and an inquiry as to damages, or a declaration that they were entitled to treat the contract as repudiated and an inquiry as to damages. The Court of Appeal made an order discharging the order for specific performance and an order for an inquiry as to damages in lieu of specific performance under the Chancery Amendment Act 1858 (Lord Cairns' Act). On appeal by the purchaser, *held*, in a contract for the sale of land, if the purchaser failed to complete after time became of the essence, the vendor could either treat the contract as repudiated and seek damages for breach of contract, or seek an order for specific performance with damages for loss arising from delay. If the vendor treated the purchaser as having repudiated, he could not thereafter seek specific performance, since the contract was discharged. If, however, an order for specific performance was made, the contract remained in effect and was not merged in the judgment. If the order for specific performance was not complied with, the vendor could either apply to the court for enforcement of the order or apply to the court to dissolve the order and put an end to the contract. The only remaining question was whether if the vendor took the latter course, as in this case, he was entitled to recover damages for breach of contract. The line of authority for the proposition that damages were not recoverable in such circumstances was unsound and should no longer be regarded as of authority. Deciding the matter on principle, since the effect of acceptance of a repudiation of a contract was not to rescind the contract ab initio but only to discharge the parties from further performance, rights and obligations which had already arisen and causes of action accruing from the breach continued unaffected. The vendors were thus entitled to damages at common law upon discharge of the contract.

In a case where a breach occurred and the innocent party reasonably continued to try to have the contract completed, damages should be assessed not at the date of the original breach but the date which, otherwise than by his default, the contract was lost. In this case that date would be that on which the mortgagees contracted to sell the property. The appeal would be dismissed subject to the above variations in the order.

JOHNSON V AGNEW [1979] 1 All ER 883 (House of Lords: LORD WILBERFORCE, LORD SALMON, LORD FRASER OF TULLEYBELTON, LORD KEITH OF KINKEL and LORD SCARMAN). *Henty v Schröder* (1879) 12 Ch D 666, *Barber v Wolfe* [1945] Ch 187, *Horsler v Zorro* [1975] Ch 302, 1975 Halsbury's Abridgment para. 2993 and *Capital and Suburban Properties Ltd v Swycher* [1976] Ch 319, CA, 1976 Halsbury's Abridgment para. 2481 overruled. Decision of the Court of Appeal [1978] 3 All ER 314, 1977 Halsbury's Abridgment para. 2742 varied. See further 129 NLJ 292.

2709 **—— sale of local authority house—whether agreement for sale concluded**

See *Gibson v Manchester City Council*, para. 2357.

STAMP DUTIES

Halsbury's Laws of England (3rd edn.), Vol. 33, paras. 480–622

2710   Article

The Contingency Principle, G. N. Benson (recent cases on the contingency principle for stamp duty): 123 Sol Jo 311.

2711   Stamping practice—postmaster's service

The facility whereby documents for stamping could be handed in to a main post office for transmission to Bush House or a linked provincial office (known as the "postmaster's service") has been withdrawn as from 1st April 1980. Documents of a kind which have hitherto reached Bush House or a provincial office via this service should thereafter be posted by direct mail. See the Law Society's Gazette, 28th March 1979, p. 314.

STATUTES

Halsbury's Laws of England (3rd edn.), Vol. 36, paras. 530–750

2712   Article

Legislative Technique, Francis Bennion (drafting of statutes): 129 NLJ 1170.

2713   Act amending or repealing common law—proceedings begun under common law before Act came into force

A man was charged with the common law offence of keeping a disorderly house. A few weeks later the Criminal Law Act 1977, s. 53 came into force, which converted the common law offence into a statutory one. Section 53 (3) provided that no-one should be charged under the common law, and the stipendiary magistrate held that the sub-section deprived him of any jurisdiction to hear the case. The prosecution applied for an order of mandamus, to order the magistrate to hear the case. *Held*, s. 53 (3) extended to proceedings begun before but not concluded by the time the Act came into force. The Interpretation Act 1889, s. 38 (2) (now the Interpretation Act 1978, s. 16), which provided that the repeal of an enactment by another Act did not affect matters instigated before the repeal, did not apply to common law offences. The application would be refused.

R v WELLS STREET STIPENDIARY MAGISTRATES, EX PARTE GOLDING [1979] Crim LR 254 (Queen's Bench Division: LORD WIDGERY CJ, BRIDGE LJ and CAULFIELD J).

2714   Construction—deprivation of property—right to compensation

Canada

A company operated a business in Manitoba, whereby it purchased freshwater fish from fishermen, which it then processed and sold to customers in the United States and Canada. With the passing of the Freshwater Fish Marketing Act 1970, which gave the exclusive right to the State to carry on the business of exporting fish from Manitoba and elsewhere in Canada, the company was put out of business. The Act provided for compensation to the owners of plant and equipment that would be rendered redundant by the Act. The Manitoba government refused to pay the company compensation and the Canadian government claimed that the payment of compensation was entirely the responsibility of the Manitoba government. The company commenced an action against the Canadian government claiming compensation for loss of its business, including loss of goodwill. At first instance it was held that the legislation did not amount to a taking of the company's property and that consequently no compensation was payable. This decision was upheld on appeal to the Federal Court of Appeal. The company appealed to the Supreme Court of Canada. *Held*, allowing the appeal, unless the words of a statute clearly stated the opposite, it was not to be construed so as to take away the property of a subject without compensation. There was no intention expressed in the 1970 Act that no compensation was to be payable; furthermore the provisions of the Act did amount to a taking away of the company's property. The term "property" included goodwill and the company, in being deprived of its customers who were now forced to buy from the State, had had its goodwill taken away by the Act. Although the Canadian government had placed responsibility for the payment of compensation on the governments of the provinces, the company was entitled to bring its claim against the Canadian government, as the Act which had put the company out of business was one passed by the Parliament of Canada.

MANITOBA FISHERIES LTD v R [1978] 6 WWR 496 (Supreme Court of Canada).

2715   —— offence committed—subsequent increase in penalty— whether legislation retroactive

The Queen's Bench Division has re-affirmed the principle that, without clear words, new legislation is not retroactive. Thus, magistrates could not impose the new penalty (increased by an Act effective from January 1977) on a group of fishermen who were found guilty in February 1977 of an offence committed in November 1976. The sentences would be quashed and the case remitted to the magistrates.

R v PENRITH JJ, EX PARTE HAY (1979) 123 Sol Jo 621 (Queen's Bench Division: LORD WIDGERY CJ, EVELEIGH LJ and WOOLF J).

2716   —— parallel provisions in two statutes—statutes of general and special application—whether special provisions applicable

Malaysia
A man was charged with the offences of being in possession of a firearm and ammunition after he was found with a revolver and ammunition in Penang. There were two Acts in force in Malaysia which made such possession criminal offences, the Internal Security Act 1960 and the Arms Act 1960, the penalty under the former being death but under the latter, imprisonment. The man was charged under the former as he had been found in a security area. Penang had been declared a security area for the purposes of the Internal Security Act by a proclamation which purported to bring the offences within the Essential (Security Cases) (Amendment) Regulations 1975. The regulations provided inter alia for trial by a single judge rather than trial by jury. The man was convicted and appealed on three grounds; that the Security Cases Regulations were ultra vires, the proclamation making Penang a security area was no longer in force on the date of the alleged offences and the Attorney-General should have brought the prosecution under the Arms Act, rather than the Internal Security Act. *Held*, the Security Cases Regulations were ultra vires, thus the court would set aside the conviction and order a retrial before a jury. As regards the security area proclamation, proclamations remained in force until revocation by the Monarch on the advice of the Cabinet, or annullment by both Houses of Parliament. Failure to revoke in circumstances where a proclamation ought to be revoked, could only be remedied by an order of mandamus against the Cabinet requiring them to advise the Monarch to revoke the proclamation. Whether the security area proclamation should have been revoked or not, no order of mandamus had been sought or made at the time of the alleged offences, thus the proclamation had still been in force. The Attorney-General had been right to bring the prosecution under the Internal Security Act, which related specifically to offences committed within security areas, whereas the Arms Act, which came into force after the Internal Security Act, was of general application. Thus the maxim *generalia specialibus non derogant* applied, whereby the special provisions in a statute took precedent over general provisions contained in a subsequent statute.

TEH CHENG POH v THE PUBLIC PROSECUTOR, MALAYSIA [1979] 2 WLR 623 (Privy Council: LORD DIPLOCK, LORD SIMON OF GLAISDALE, LORD SALMON, LORD EDMUND-DAVIES and LORD KEITH OF KINKEL).

2717   —— **statute giving effect to international convention**

See *Quazi v Quazi*, para. 429.

2718   —— **"use" by statutory authority—whether available as a defence to action in nuisance**

See *Allen v Gulf Oil Refining Ltd*, para. 1372.

2719   **Interpretation—duty imposed by statute to build properly—work begun before commencement—whether statute applied**

The plaintiff brought an action against the defendants claiming damages for breach of the duty imposed by the Defective Premises Act 1972, s. 1 (1). Section 1 (1) of the Act requires a person who takes on work in connection with the provision of a dwelling to ensure that the work is done in a professional manner with proper materials and that the property will be fit for human habitation when completed. The agreement between the parties for the purchase and conversion of a property into flats had been made in 1972 before the Act came into force in 1974, but the work was not completed until after its commencement. A master ordered that a preliminary issue be tried as to whether s. 1 (1) applied to the 1972 agreement and the work done pursuant to it. The trial judge held, dismissing the action, that the relevant date in determining whether the section applied was the date when the agreement was entered into, and not the date when it was completed. The plaintiff appealed, contending that there was a duty to provide a dwelling fit for human habitation on completion which continued until the work was completed and therefore the section applied. *Held*, the duty imposed by s. 1 (1) arose when the contract to do the work was entered into or at latest when the work was commenced. The duty was required to be performed while the work was being carried out. On that construction, and applying the presumption that the Act was not intended to be retrospective in effect, the duty only applied to work started after the commencement of the Act. The appeal would therefore be dismissed.

ALEXANDER V MERCOURIS [1979] 3 All ER 305 (Court of Appeal: BUCKLEY, GOFF and WALLER LJJ). Dictum of Lindley LJ in *Lauri v Renad* [1892] 3 Ch 402 at 421 applied.

2720   **Retrospective operation—pending proceedings—effect**

Malaysia

A police constable in the Malaysian police force was convicted of an offence. He was dismissed on that ground by a chief police officer in 1972. Under the Constitution of Malaysia, a constable could only be dismissed by an authority having the power to appoint constables. The Malaysia Police Force Commission had delegated to chief police officers the power to dismiss constables but not the power to appoint them. The constable successfully claimed that his dismissal contravened the Constitution and was therefore void. In 1976, the Constitution was amended so that a constable could effectively be dismissed by chief police officers in pursuance of the power delegated to them by the Police Force Commission. The amendment was to operate retrospectively from 31st August 1957. The Malaysian government successfully appealed, relying on the amendment. The constable appealed contending that the amendment could not apply as his action had been commenced and judgment given on his claim before the amendment came into force. *Held*, for pending actions to be affected by retrospective legislation, the enactment did not have to state expressly that it applied to such actions but its language had to be such that no other conclusion was possible. On the true construction of the amendment, no actions commenced after 31st August 1957, whether proceeding or not commenced when the amendment was made, could succeed on the ground that the power to dismiss had not been exercised by someone with power to appoint. Accordingly, the appeal would be dismissed.

ZAINAL BIN HASHIM V GOVERNMENT OF MALAYSIA [1979] 3 All ER 241 (Privy Council: LORD WILBERFORCE, VISCOUNT DILHORNE, LORD EDMUND-DAVIES, LORD RUSSELL OF KILLOWEN and LORD KEITH OF KINKEL). Dictum of Evershed MR in *Hutchinson v Jauncey* [1950] 1 All ER 165, at 168, CA applied.

STOCK EXCHANGE

Halsbury's Laws of England (3rd edn.), Vol. 36, paras. 751–970

2721   Article

Unit Trusts (a selection of articles on the condition of the unit trust industry; on the selection and taxation of unit trusts; on investments for non-UK residents; and on share exchange schemes): NLJ Supplement, 11th October 1979.

2722   Securities and unit trusts—licence holders

The Department of Trade has published *Particulars of Dealers in Securities and Unit Trusts 1979* (available from HMSO). Part I lists the holders of principals' licences granted under the Prevention of Fraud (Investments) Act 1958, s. 3. Part 2 states that the Stock Exchange is a recognised stock exchange for the purposes of s. 15 (1). Part 3 lists the associations of dealers in securities authorised under s. 15 (1). The dealers declared to be exempted dealers under s. 16 are listed in Part 4. Part 5 lists the unit trust schemes authorised under s. 17. Where a date is stated to be relevant the date given is 31st January 1979; any changes in the particulars given will be published in *Trade and Industry* on the second Friday in each month.

2723   Stock exchange agreement—restrictive practices

The Secretary of State for Trade announced in the House of Commons that he had rejected a request from the Council of the Stock Exchange to remove the Stock Exchange agreement from the scope of the restrictive practices legislation. It was intended, however, to introduce an amendment to the Competition Bill whereby the effect of orders by the Restrictive Practices Court might be deferred to enable the interested parties to revise their practices in the light of the order. Any such revised agreements would have to be re-submitted to the court for approval. See the Financial Times, 24th October 1979.

2724   Stock Exchange (Completion of Bargains) Act 1976—commencement

The Stock Exchange (Completion of Bargains) Act 1976 (Commencement) Order 1979, S.I. 1979 No. 55 brought the 1976 Act, 1976 Halsbury's Abridgment para. 349, into force on 12th February 1979.

2725   Transfer of securities to or from nominee—prescribed forms

The Stock Transfer (Addition of Forms) Order 1979, S.I. 1979 No. 277 (in force on 4th April 1979), amends the Stock Transfer Act 1963, Sch. 1 by adding forms for use where securities are transferred to or from a nominee. These are to be known as sold transfer and bought transfer forms and may be used as alternatives to the stock transfer form. The Order also amends s. 1 by providing that a form used to transfer securities to a nominee need not specify particulars of consideration or the address of the nominee, and that a form used to transfer securities from a nominee where the transferor is a body corporate need not be executed under hand but will be treated as duly executed if it bears a facsimile of the transferor's corporate seal.

TELECOMMUNICATIONS AND TELEVISION

Halsbury's Laws of England (3rd edn.), Vol. 36, paras. 971–1123

2726   Article

Tapping Telephones in the United States, Clive Morrick (its history, mechanics and a comment on *Malone v Metropolitan Police Commissioner* [1979] 2 WLR 700, para. 2093): 129 NLJ 575.

2727 Broadcasting—BBC licence

The term of the deed of licence and agreement concluded between the Postmaster General and the British Broadcasting Corporation and dated 7th July 1969 was extended by a supplemental licence and agreement (dated 7th April 1976) for a period of three years from 31st July 1976 to 31st July 1979. By a supplemental licence and agreement the principal deed of licence and agreement has been further extended from 31st July 1979 to 31st July 1981. Also the annual renewal fee payable by the BBC to the Secretary of State for each of the years 1979 and 1980 has been increased from £30,000 to £36,000. See Supplemental licence and Agreement dated 8th March 1979 between HM Secretary of State for the Home Department and the BBC, Cmnd. 7508.

2728 —— Channel Islands

The Independent Broadcasting Authority Act 1973 (Channel Islands) Order 1979, S.I. 1979 No. 114 (in force on 6th February 1979), extends the Independent Broadcasting Authority Act 1973, as amended, to the Channel Islands with adaptations and modifications, one of the effects of which is to exclude the provision of local sound broadcasting under the Act in the Channel Islands. The Television Act 1964 (Channel Islands) Order 1964 and the Sound Broadcasting Act 1972 (Channel Islands) Order 1973 are revoked.

2729 —— Independent Broadcasting Authority licence

The period of the licence granted to the Independent Broadcasting Authority and dated 1st August 1973 has been further extended to 31st December 1981 by a supplemental licence dated 18th June 1979. The renewal fee for 1979 and 1980 is £28,000 or such other sum as the Secretary of State for the Home Department may determine; the Secretary of State may determine the amount of the fee for the period 31st July to 31st December 1981. See Cmnd. 7616.

2730 —— Isle of Man

The Independent Broadcasting Authority Act 1978 (Isle of Man) Order 1979, S.I. 1979 No. 461 (in force on 12th April 1979), extends the Independent Broadcasting Act 1978, s. 1, 1978 Halsbury's Abridgment para. 2760, to the Isle of Man. This amends the Independent Broadcasting Act 1973, which has already been extended, so as to extend the duration of the Independent Broadcasting Authority's function until 31st December 1981.

2731 Damage to telegraphic lines—strict liability—negligence of Post Office

The action of a local authority employee damaged a Post Office cable, but he had been acting upon the advice of Post Office officials. The Post Office claimed compensation under the Telegraph Act 1878, s. 8, whereby anybody damaging a telegraphic line is liable to pay compensation for the damage, even though he has not been wilful or negligent in causing the damage. At first instance it was found that the Post Office employee had acted negligently. The trial judge held that, following *Postmaster General v Liverpool Corporation*, liability under s. 8 did not arise where the damage had been caused by the negligence of the Post Office, and no compensation was payable. The Post Office appealed. *Held*, the trial judge was right in finding the Post Office negligent. However, the real ratio of *Postmaster General v Liverpool Corporation* was that liability under s. 8 did not arise where it could be shown that the act occasioning the damage was not that of the third party but of the Post Office itself. As the act occasioning the damage in this case had undoubtedly been that of the local authority employee, the case did not afford a defence, but it was possible for the local authority to sue the Post Office for damages in negligence, for having caused the authority to become liable under s. 8. In order to prevent a situation arising whereby the authority would claim back in damages what they had paid in compensation, they could plead circuity of action instead; that was not merely a counterclaim, but afforded a defence where the plaintiff had been wholly responsible for the damage caused. The appeal would therefore be dismissed.

POST OFFICE v HAMPSHIRE COUNTY COUNCIL [1979] 2 All ER 818 (Court of Appeal: ORR, ORMROD and GEOFFREY LANE LJJ). *Workington Harbour and Dock Board v Towerfield* [1951] AC 112, HL and *Ginty v Belmont Building Supplies Ltd* [1959] 1 All ER 414 applied, *Postmaster General v Liverpool Corporation* [1923] AC 587, HL distinguished.

2732   Contractors carrying out building work relied on a plan on which the Post Office had marked up details of underground cables that were in the construction area. There was a disclaimer attached to the plan to the effect that the Post Office did not guarantee the accuracy of the information. The plan was inaccurate and, due to their reliance on the plan, the contractors caused damage to a Post Office cable. The Post Office claimed compensation under the Telegraph Act 1878, s. 8, whereby anybody damaging a telegraphic line was liable to pay compensation for the damage, even though he had not been wilful or negligent in causing the damage. The contractors admitted liability under s. 8, but counterclaimed in negligence contending that the Post Office, knowing that the plan would be relied upon by the contractors, owed a duty to give accurate information. *Held*, the Post Office's duty was merely to supply a plan which indicated roughly where the cables were to be found and its knowledge of the contractor's reliance on the plan did not impose on it any greater obligation. It was clear from the type of plan it was that the information could not be relied upon in detail. Furthermore the disclaimer absolved the Post Office from any liability for the inaccuracy of the information. The Post Office claim would be allowed and the counterclaim dismissed.

POST OFFICE v MEARS CONSTRUCTION LTD [1979] 2 All ER 813 (Queen's Bench Division: WILLIS J).

2733   **Independent Broadcasting Authority Act 1979**

The Independent Broadcasting Authority Act 1979 empowers the Authority to equip itself to transmit an additional television broadcasting service, but not to provide it. The Act received the royal assent on 4th April 1979 and came into force on that date.

Section 1 empowers the Authority to equip itself to broadcast the new service. This includes granting it powers to establish and install any necessary wireless telegraphy stations, but does not exempt it from obtaining any licences necessary under the Wireless Telegraphy Act 1949. Section 2 makes financial provision and s. 3 deals with short title and extent.

2734   **Licence charges**

The Wireless Telegraphy (Broadcast Licence Charges and Exemption) (Amendment) Regulations 1979, S.I. 1979 No. 841 (in force on 31st July 1979) amend the Wireless Telegraphy (Broadcast Licence Charges and Exemption) Regulations 1970, by substituting a new scale of fees for those licences related to the number of premises connected to the licensee's apparatus, and by amending the definition of the licence, now described as a "broadcast relay apparatus licence".

2735   The Wireless Telegraphy (Broadcast Licence Charges and Exemption) (Amendment) (No. 2) Regulations 1979, S.I. 1979 No. 1490 (in force on 24th November 1979), raise the amount of the basic fee for television licences from £10 to £12 in the case of monochrome and from £25 to £34 in the case of colour.

2736   **Telephone—interception of conversations—powers of police**

See *Malone v Metropolitan Police Commissioner*, para. 2093.

2737   Television—information as to sale and hire

The Wireless Telegrams Act 1967 (Prescribed Forms etc.) Regulations 1979, S.I. 1979 No. 563 (in force on 1st August 1979), makes new provision as to the information to be supplied by television dealers in place of the provisions contained in the Wireless Telegraphy Act 1967 (Prescribed Forms and Addresses) Regulations 1967, S.I. 1967 No. 1692.

2738   Television coverage of election campaign—candidate's consent

See *Marshall v BBC*, para. 1014.

THEATRES AND OTHER PLACES
OF ENTERTAINMENT

Halsbury's Laws of England (3rd edn.), Vol. 37, paras. 1–132

2739   Cinemas—levy—collection

The Cinematograph Films (Collection of Levy) (Amendment No. 7) Regulations 1979, S.I. 1979 No. 1751 (in force on 10th February 1980), further amend the 1968 Regulations by charging the normal rate of levy, increasing the amount by reference to which total or partial exemption from payment of levy is allowed in respect of cinemas at which takings are small and changing the marginal rate of levy.

2740   —— —— distribution

The Cinematograph Films (Distribution of Levy) (Amendment) Regulations 1979, S.I. 1979 No. 1750 (in force on 10th February 1980), amend the 1970 Regulations by setting a limit on the total payments which may be made to the maker from the British Film Fund to £500,000 in the case of a long film and £50,000 in the case of a short film.   The Order also ceases to apply to low-cost long films the multiple of two and a half times their earnings for the purpose of computing the payments to be made to their maker from the British Film Fund.   In the case of short films, other than newsreels, the multiple of two and a half times their earnings is only to be applied until the maker has been paid £30,000 by the British Film Fund.

2741   —— —— limits

The Cinematograph Films (Limits of Levy) Order 1979, S.I. 1979 No. 395 (in force on 1st April 1979), amends the Cinematograph Films Act 1957, s. 2 (3) (b), which provides for the limits on the yield of levy on exhibitors of films, by increasing the maximum limit from £7 million to £12 million.

2742   Films Act 1979

The Films Act 1979 amends the Films Act 1960 which contains provisions to ensure that exhibitors show an appropriate quota of British films in any one year.   The Act received the royal assent on 22nd February 1979 and came into force on that date.

The Act replaces the Films Act 1960 s. 6 (1) and provides that when certain foreign films are shown at a cinema, the exhibitor may be allowed to satisfy the quota requirement for British films over a two year period, on condition that each foreign film is exhibited for such continuous period exceeding eight weeks as is specified by the Secretary of State.

TIME

Halsbury's Laws of England (3rd edn.), Vol. 37, paras. 133–185

2743   **Time when application made—application by post—whether made when posted or when received**

See *North West Traffic Area Licensing Authority v Brady*, para. 2292.

TORT

Halsbury's Laws of England (3rd edn.), Vol. 37, paras. 186–280

2744   **Articles**

The Civil Liability (Contribution) Act 1978, A. M. Dugdale (a review of the Act): 42 MLR 182.

The Commercial Exploitation of Real Names, Peter Russell (on the rights of celebrities over their names and reputations where they are being used commercially): 129 NLJ 791.

The Individual Striker and Tort Liability, P. M. L. Glover (on the protection offered to the individual union member if he is sued as an individual rather than as a union man): [1978] LS Gaz 962.

2745   **Conspiracy—conspiracy between husband and wife—whether gives rise to tortious liability**

See *Midland Bank Trust Co Ltd v Green (No. 3)*, para. 1646.

TOWN AND COUNTRY PLANNING

Halsbury's Laws of England (3rd edn.), Vol. 37, paras. 281–816

2746   **Articles**

Agricultural Compensation: The Way Forward, Malcolm Bell (suggestions for improvements in planning law where compensation for interest in land fails to recognise the full cost of readjusting a working holding): [1979] JPL 577.

Challenging Planning Decisions, Henry E. Markson: 123 Sol Jo 647.

Determining Development Rights: An Unfulfilled Need?, A. J. Ward (the inadequacies of the Town and Country Planning Act 1971, ss. 53, 94 in this area): [1979] JPL 352.

Discontinuance Orders, H. W. Wilkinson (planning authorities' powers to issue discontinuance notices): 129 NLJ 423.

The Good Life: Agricultural Pursuits in Residential Areas, R. T. F. Turrall-Clarke (problems raised by ss. 22 (2) and 22 (2) (e) of the Town and Country Planning Act 1971): [1979] JPL 449.

Injunctions—A Useful Aid to Planning Control, D. B. Kerrigan (on whether local authorities can make greater use of injunction proceedings as a means of planning control): [1979] JPL 597.

Large New Stores: Planning Appeals, Alec Samuels (obtaining planning permission for large new stores): 123 Sol Jo 360.

Law and Fact in the Assessment of Compensation, P. H. Clarke (balance of law and fact in assessment of compensation for compulsory purchase): (1979) JPL 277.

Locus Standi in Planning Law, Henry E. Markson (a few developments in connection with the subject): 123 Sol Jo 531.

Material Considerations in Planning Law, Henry E. Markson (a collation of recent decisions on a subject which gives rise to certain difficulties of interpretation): 123 Sol Jo 575.

Operations or Use? Henry E. Markson (the interpretation and application of the concept of development in town and country planning law): 123 Sol Jo 151.

Planning Appeals: Policies and Principles, Henry E. Markson (discussion of *Seddon Properties Ltd and James Crosbie & Sons Ltd v Secretary of State for Environment* (1978) 248 Estates Gazette 950, para. 2781): 123 Sol Jo 812.

Planning Conditions, Henry E. Markson (recent points concerning conditions in planning law): 123 Sol Jo 329.

Planning Decisions by Estoppel, S. J. Sellers (ability of local government officers to make decisions binding on local planning authorities in the absence of express delegation): 129 NLJ 161.

Planning Inquiry Complaints, Henry E. Markson (some planning inquiry complaints investigated by the Parliamentary Ombudsman, with regard to the practical problems they illustrate): 123 Sol Jo 444.

Planning Permission and the Eccentric Millionaire, John Alder (on whether a planning authority should take the cost of development into account when deciding whether to grant planning permission): 129 NLJ 704.

Planning Permission, Outline and Detail, H. W. Wilkinson (whether the holder of outline planning permission can apply for a second approval of reserved matters once a first approval has been given): 129 NLJ 61.

Planning Permission Problems, Henry E. Markson (examination of some recent cases): 123 Sol Jo 545.

Planning Permissions—Blowing Hot and Cold, John Alder (whether landowner free to ignore an unnecessary planning permission): [1979] JPL 815.

Planning Precedents, Henry E. Markson (on whether granting permission for a particular proposed development might serve as an undesirable precedent for later applications 123 Sol Jo 681.

Public Inquiry Problems, Henry E. Markson (discussion of Parliamentary Commissioner for Administration's First Report for Session 1978–79, HC 111 concerning planning decisions): 123 Sol Jo 697.

Section 52 Agreements: A Case for New Legislation?, Roger W. Suddards (the problems of planning by agreement in the urban area): [1979] JPL 661.

2747   Appeal—inquiry—matters to be included in inspector's report

A developer appealed against refusal of planning permission for residential development on the outskirts of a town. An inquiry was held and the inspector found that there was a need for increased allocation of development land due to an anticipated population increase in the area. His report omitted to include the evidence of a planning officer that land required for housing to meet the anticipated population increase had already been allocated. The Secretary of State allowed the appeal. His decision was subsequently quashed on the ground that although the court would not usually intervene it was permissible to bring evidence to show that a matter of real importance had been wholly ignored or completely misunderstood so that the Secretary of State was given the wrong picture. It was open to the inspector to consider the evidence and reject it but in this case he had failed to consider it at all. On appeal, *held*, the omission was likely to have misled the Secretary of State, and the order quashing his decision would be upheld.

EAST HAMPSHIRE DISTRICT COUNCIL v SECRETARY OF STATE FOR THE ENVIRONMENT (1979) 251 Estates Gazette 763 (Court of Appeal: LORD DENNING MR, EVELEIGH LJ and SIR STANLEY REES). Decision of Slynn J (1977) 248 Estates Gazette 43, 1978 Halsbury's Abridgment para. 2792 affirmed.

2748   —— —— procedure—powers of inspection—evidence

A man inherited a house which had been built twenty years previously by an eminent architect. His application for planning permission to build a second house in the grounds of the existing house, which was too small for his requirements, was refused. On appeal, the inspector granted planning permission on the grounds that refusal would be unreasonable and that any extension to the existing house built as an alternative would spoil a building that deserved preservation. He had visited the house himself and had refused to allow the local authority to bring expert evidence as to the architectural merits of the house. The authority unsuccessfully appealed, contending that the refusal of the application for leave to call an expert witness was a breach of natural justice and that when the inspector visited the house and site he was receiving new evidence of which he should have notified the authority. On the authority's further appeal, *held*, the architectural quality of the house was a matter of aesthetic taste and expert evidence was not, therefore, necessary. The inspector's view of the site constituted real evidence, but not "new evidence" and so the inspector would not have been obliged to give notice of the visit to the authority. Accordingly, the appeal would be dismissed.

WINCHESTER CITY COUNCIL v SECRETARY OF STATE FOR THE ENVIRONMENT (1979) 251 Estates Gazette 259 (Court of Appeal: LORD DENNING MR, WALLER and CUMMING-BRUCE LJJ). Decision of Forbes J (1978) 36 P & C R 455 affirmed.

2749   —— —— reasons for decision—whether decision based on issue not raised at inquiry

An application for planning permission for residential development of land was refused on the ground that the land was in the green belt. On appeal, an inquiry was held, and the inspector dismissed the appeal. The applicant then appealed under the Town and Country Planning Act 1971, s. 245, on the ground that the inspector had decided the matter on the basis that the proposal was premature pending approval of the structure plan for the area, an issue that had not been raised at the inquiry, which amounted to a breach of natural justice. *Held*, on an examination of the inspector's decision letter, it was clear that he had decided the case on the basis of the approved green belt situation then existing, not on the prematurity of the application. In any event, the matter of the structure plan had been mentioned at the inquiry. In the circumstances there had been no breach of natural justice and the appeal would be dismissed.

CHARLES CHURCH LTD v SECRETARY OF STATE FOR THE ENVIRONMENT (1979) 251 Estates Gazette 674 (Queen's Bench Division: SIR DOUGLAS FRANK QC sitting as a deputy High Court judge).

2750   Derelict land—clearance areas

The Derelict Land Clearance Areas Order 1979, S.I. 1979 No. 334 (in force on 17th April 1979), amends the Derelict Land Clearance Areas Order 1978, 1978 Halsbury's Abridgment para. 2779 with regard to those areas now specified as part of the City of Birmingham Special Area.

2751   Development—control—industrial development certificates

The Town and Country Planning (Industrial Development Certificates) Regulations 1979, S.I. 1979 No. 838 (in force on 7th August 1979), revoke the Town and Country Planning (Industrial Development Certificates) Regulations 1972 to 1977. They direct that an industrial development certificate is not required for the erection of any industrial building in any employment office area described in the Schedule or for a change of use as a result of which premises in any such area which are not an industrial building become an industrial building.

These regulations have been amended; see para. 2753.

2752   The Town and Country Planning (Industrial Development Certificates: Exemption) Order 1979, S.I. 1979 No. 839 (in force on 7th August 1979), revokes the Town and Country Planning (Industrial Development Certificates: Exemption) Order 1976, 1976 Halsbury's Abridgment, para. 2533. Under the 1979 Order industrial development requires an industrial development certificate only if the industrial floor space to be created by the development together with the industrial floor space created by any related development exceeds 50,000 square feet. The existing exemption whereby no industrial development certificate is required in respect of any industrial development of land in the development and intermediate areas, is not affected.

2753   The Town and Country Planning (Industrial Development Certificates) (Amendment) Regulations 1979, S.I. 1979 No. 1643 (in force on 1st January 1980), amend the Town and Country Planning (Industrial Development Certificates) Regulations 1979, para. 2751, so as to include the employment office area of Corby.

2754   —— —— **office development**

The Control of Office Development (Cessation) Order 1979, S.I. 1979 No. 908 (in force on 6th August 1979), provides for the cessation of the control of office development in England and Wales, by revoking the relevant provisions of the Town and Country Planning Act 1971.

2755   —— **permitted development—use classes—extension of non-residents' bar in private hotel**

The appellants were granted planning permission to use a small area of the ground floor of their hotel as a non-residents' bar. They later sought to extend the bar to cover a much larger area. After being granted a licence to operate the enlarged bar, an enforcement notice was served upon the appellants requiring them to cease using the enlarged area as a non-residents' bar. The appellants appealed to the Secretary of State under the Town and Country Planning Act 1971, s. 88. The Secretary of State concluded that planning permission was required for the extension, as the facilities it was offering were much the same as those of a public house, with the consequent increase in customers, noise and traffic sufficient to constitute a material change in the use of the premises. The Secretary of State refused planning permission. An appeal was brought under s. 246 of the Act. *Held*, allowing the appeal, use of the premises as a public house would be materially different from use as a private residential hotel, but under the Town and Country Planning (Use Classes) Order 1972, art. 3, where a building was used for a specified class of purpose, the use of the building for any other purpose within that class would not be deemed a development of the land. The use of the premises prior to the extension of the bar fell within Use Class XI specified in the Schedule to the 1972 Order as "use as a boarding or guest house, or an hotel providing sleeping accommodation". The extension of the bar did not change the use of the premises sufficiently to take it outside the ambit of Class XI; hence the extension was not a development of land. The matter would be remitted to the Secretary of State to be dealt with in accordance with the judgment of the court.

EMMA HOTELS LTD v SECRETARY OF STATE FOR THE ENVIRONMENT (1978) 250 Estates Gazette 157 (Queen's Bench Division: LORD WIDGERY CJ, BRIDGE LJ and CAULFIELD J).

2756   —— **structure and local plans**

The Town and Country Planning (Structure and Local Plans) (Amendment) Regulations 1979, S.I. 1979 No. 1738 (in force on 31st January 1980), amend the Town and Country Planning (Structure and Local Plans) Regulations 1974, 1974 Halsbury's Abridgment para. 3224. A reasoned justification of the policy and proposals submitted in the structure plan written statement, as provided for by reg. 9 (3) of the 1974 Regulations, is no longer required. The time limit by which objections to proposed modifications may be made is now exactly six weeks after the date of first publication of the modifications.

2757   —— —— **Buckinghamshire**

The Town and Country Planning Act 1971 (Commencement No. 51) (Buckinghamshire) Order 1979, S.I. 1979 No. 1624, brought into force on 2nd January 1980, s. 20 and Sch. 23, Part I (part) for the county of Buckinghamshire. These provisions relate to structure and local plans.

The above provisions replace the provisions of the 1971 Act relating to development plans which are repealed by the Town and Country Planning (Repeal of Provisions No. 23) (Buckinghamshire) Order 1979, S.I. 1979 No. 1625 (in force on 2nd January 1980).

2758 ———— **Cheshire**

The Town and Country Planning Act 1971 (Commencement No. 46) (Cheshire) Order 1979, S.I. 1979 No. 891, brought into force on 13th August 1979, s. 20 and Sch. 23, Part I (part) for the county of Cheshire. These provisions relate to structure and local plans.

The above provisions replace the provisions of the 1971 Act relating to development plans which are repealed by the Town and Country Planning (Repeal of Provisions No. 18) (Cheshire) Order 1979, S.I. 1979 No. 890 (in force on 13th August 1979).

2759 ———— **Hertfordshire**

The Town and Country Planning Act 1971 (Commencement No. 48) (Hertfordshire) Order 1979, S.I. 1979 No. 1187, brought into force on 15th October 1979, s. 20 and Sch. 23, Part I (part) for the county of Hertfordshire. These provisions relate to structure and local plans.

The above provisions replace the provisions of the 1971 Act relating to development plans which are repealed by the Town and Country Planning (Repeal of Provisions No. 20) (Hertfordshire) Order 1979, S.I. 1979 No. 1189 (in force on 15th October 1979).

2760 ———— **Humberside**

The Town and County Planning Act 1971 (Commencement No. 45) (Humberside) Order 1979, S.I. 1979 No. 329, brought into force on 16th April 1979, s. 20 and Sch. 23, Part I (part) for the county of Humberside. These provisions relate to structure and local plans.

The above provisions replace the provisions of the 1971 Act relating to development plans which are repealed by the Town and Country Planning (Repeal of Provisions No. 17) (Humberside) Order 1979, S.I. 1979 No. 328 (in force on 16th April 1979).

2761 ———— **Isle of Wight**

The Town and Country Planning Act 1971 (Commencement No. 42) (Isle of Wight) Order 1979, S.I. 1979 No. 140, brought into force on 9th March 1979, s. 20 and Sch. 23, Part I (part) for the Isle of Wight. These provisions relate to structure and local plans.

The above provisions replace the provisions of the 1971 Act relating to development plans which are repealed by the Town and Country Planning (Repeal of Provisions No. 14) (Isle of Wight) Order 1979, S.I. 1979 No. 139 (in force on 9th March 1979).

2762 ———— **Norfolk**

The Town and Country Planning Act 1971 (Commencement No. 52) (Norfolk) Order 1979, S.I. 1979 No. 1625, brought into force on 3rd January 1980, s. 20 and Sch. 23, Part I (part) for the county of Norfolk. These provisions relate to structure and local plans.

The above provisions replace the provisions of the 1971 Act relating to development plans which are repealed by the Town and Country Planning (Repeal of Provisions No. 24) (Norfolk) Order 1979, S.I. 1979 No. 1627 (in force on 3rd January 1980).

2763 ———— **North East Lancashire**

The Town and Country Planning Act 1971 (Commencement No. 49) (North East

Lancashire) Order 1979, S.I. 1979 No. 1485, brought into force on 10th December 1979, s. 20 and Sch. 23, Part I (part) for North East Lancashire. These provisions relate to structure and local plans.

The above provisions replace the provisions of the 1971 Act relating to development plans which are repealed by the Town and Country Planning (Repeal of Provisions No. 21) (North East Lancashire) Order 1979, S.I. 1979 No. 1486 (in force on 10th December 1979).

2764   —— —— Oxfordshire

The Town and Country Planning Act 1971 (Commencement No. 44) (Oxfordshire) Order 1979, S.I. 1979 No. 201, brought into force on 2nd April 1979, s. 20 and Sch. 23, Part I (part) for the county of Oxfordshire. These provisions relate to structure and local plans.

The above provisions replace the provisions of the 1971 Act relating to development plans which are repealed by the Town and Country Planning (Repeal of Provisions No. 16) (Oxfordshire) Order 1979, S.I. 1979 No. 203 (in force on 2nd April 1979).

2765   —— —— Peak District National Park

The Town and Country Planning Act 1971 (Commencement No. 50) (Peak District National Park) Order 1979, S.I. 1979 No. 1622, brought into force on 2nd January 1980, s. 20 and Sch. 23, Part I (part) for the Peak District National Park. These provisions relate to structure and local plans.

The above provisions replace the provisions of the 1971 Act relating to development plans which are repealed by the Town and Country Planning (Repeal of Provisions No. 22) (Peak District National Park) Order 1979, S.I. 1979 No. 1623 (in force on 2nd January 1980).

2766   —— —— Rutland

The Town and Country Planning Act 1971 (Commencement No. 53) (Rutland) Order 1979, S.I. 1979 No. 1628, brought into force on 4th January 1980, s. 20 and Sch. 23, Part I (part) for the county of Rutland. These provisions relate to structure and local plans.

The above provisions replace the provisions of the 1971 Act relating to development plans which are repealed by the Town and Country Planning (Repeal of Provisions No. 25) (Rutland) Order 1979, S.I. 1979 No. 1629 (in force on 4th January 1980).

2767   —— —— Suffolk

The Town and Country Planning Act 1971 (Commencement No. 47) (Suffolk) Order 1979, S.I. 1979 No. 1043, brought into force on 10th September 1979, s. 20 and Sch. 23, Part I (part) for the county of Suffolk. These provisions relate to structure and local plans.

The above provisions replace the provisions of the 1971 Act relating to development plans which are repealed by the Town and Country Planning (Repeal of Provisions No. 19) (Suffolk) Order 1979, S.I. 1979 No. 1042 (in force on 10th September 1979).

2768   —— —— West Berkshire

The Town and Country Planning Act 1971 (Commencement No. 43) (West Berkshire) Order 1979, S.I. 1979 No. 200, brought into force on 2nd April 1979, s. 20 and Sch. 23, Part I (part) for certain areas of Berkshire. These provisions relate to structure and local plans.

The above provisions replace the provisions of the 1971 Act relating to development plans which are repealed by the Town and Country Planning (Repeal of Provisions No. 15) (West Berkshire) Order 1979, S.I. 1979 No. 202 (in force on 2nd April 1979).

2769   Development corporations—limit on borrowing

The New Towns (Limit on Borrowing) Order 1979, S.I. 1979 No. 204 (in force on 2nd March 1979), increases the limit for the total of the sums outstanding at any one time in respect of the principal of sums advanced by the Secretary of State to development corporations and the Commission for New Towns, to £3,250 million.

2770   Enforcement notice—contents of notice—material change of use—reversion to earlier lawful use

The owners purchased a site that had previously been used for light industrial purposes as a repair garage. They proceeded to develop it and use it as a bus depot. They were served with an enforcement notice alleging breach of planning control and requiring them to cease using the site for any purpose in connection with the operation of a bus station. The owners appealed against the notice, contending that they were using the site for light industrial purposes and that there had, therefore, been no material change of use. The Secretary of State dismissed their appeal in view of the varied activities carried out on the site in addition to the repair of buses. The owners further appealed, contending that the Secretary of State should have taken the Town and Country Planning Act 1971, s. 23 (9) into account when considering whether to amend the notice. Section 23 (9) gives a landowner permission to go back to any use of the land which could lawfully have been carried out if development had never occurred. *Held*, the Secretary of State had been correct in adopting the whole site as the planning unit for the purpose of deciding that there had been a material change of use. However, he should also have considered whether any use, such as the light industrial use involved in the repair of buses, safeguarded by the provisions of s. 23 (9) had been adequately safeguarded in the enforcement notice. Accordingly the appeal would be allowed and the decision of the Secretary of State would be remitted to him for further consideration.

DAY V SECRETARY OF STATE FOR THE ENVIRONMENT (1979) 251 Estates Gazette 163 (Queen's Bench Division: LORD WIDGERY CJ, CUMMING-BRUCE LJ and NEILL J).

2771   ——— whether sufficiently specified matters constituting breach—validity of stop notice

The plaintiffs, the owners and occupiers of a sports stadium, began to adapt the existing greyhound track for use by motor cycles and for speedway racing. The local authority served an enforcement notice in relation to the alteration of the track and a stop notice requiring them to cease their operations. The plaintiffs contended (i) that the enforcement notice did not specify the matters alleged to have constituted the breach of planning control and, (ii) that the stop notice did not sufficiently describe specific operations to cease. *Held* (i) a general description was enough, provided it was sufficient to identify the activity, thus the notice was not void; (ii) where the stop notice incorporated the terms of the enforcement notice, any deficiency in the particularity of the stop notice would be validated by the language of the enforcement notice. Both notices were accordingly valid.

BRISTOL STADIUM LTD V BROWN (1979) 252 Estates Gazette 803 (Queen's Bench Division: LORD WIDGERY CJ, EVELEIGH LJ and WOOLF J). *Miller-Mead v Minister of Housing and Local Government* [1963] 1 All ER 459, CA followed.

2772   Established use certificate—immunity from enforcement notice—change in character of use of land

An established use certificate was issued in respect of a rural timber yard in a predominantly rural area of woodland and farmland. The ownership of the land changed and the timber yard developed into a bulk storage depot, an industrial timber yard. The authority served an enforcement notice, in respect of the change of use, which was quashed by the Secretary of State on appeal. The authority challenged his decision. *Held*, the purpose of an established use certificate was to obviate investigation as to the nature of the established use at the date of the certificate. The certificate had been issued in respect of a timber yard and had not specified any limits on the scope and intensity of that use. There was no material change of use. Local authorities should draft their certificates with care and expressly limit them to the precise use in question. The Secretary of State's decision would be upheld.

BROXBOURNE BOROUGH COUNCIL v SECRETARY OF STATE FOR THE ENVIRONMENT [1979] 2 All ER 13 (Queen's Bench Division: LORD WIDGERY CJ, KILNER BROWN and ROBERT GOFF JJ)

2773 Footpath—diversion order—powers of local authority and Secretary of State

See *Ashby v Secretary of State for the Environment*, para. 1413.

2774 Highway—motorway—public inquiry—procedure

See *Lovelock v Secretary of State for Transport*, para. 1416.

2775 Planning permission—conditional planning permission—enforcement of condition—right of Secretary of State to rely on applicant's good faith—estoppel

Landowners were refused planning permission to extract sand and gravel from their land on the ground that visibility at the junction of a necessary access road would be poor. The Secretary of State subsequently granted permission subject to visibility splays being provided at the junction. A local preservation society applied to have his decision quashed on the grounds that the permission was in a form that did not ensure that the revised lay-out would be provided, and that there was insufficient evidence on which the Secretary of State could be satisfied that improved sight lines would be provided. *Held*, whether or not the landowners' undertaking to provide visibility splays, which they could only do by acquiring extra land from a third party, was enforceable in law, the Secretary of State had been entitled to rely on their good faith in the matter. In any event, the landowners would be estopped from denying that implementation of the permission was conditional on their complying with the undertaking and from claiming that there was no power to require their compliance with it.

AUGIER v SECRETARY OF STATE FOR THE ENVIRONMENT (1978) 38 P & CR 219 (Queen's Bench Division: SIR DOUGLAS FRANK QC, sitting as a deputy High Court judge). *Associated Provincial Picture Houses Ltd v Wednesbury Corporation* [1948] 1 KB 223, CA, *Hughes v Metropolitan Railway Co* (1877) 2 App Cas 439, HL, *Central London Property Trust Ltd v High Trees House Ltd* [1947] KB 130 and *H. Clark (Doncaster) Ltd v Wilkinson* [1965] Ch 694, CA applied.

2776 —— —— planning permission as prerequisite of disposal licence—whether material change of use

In 1969 a local planning authority granted a third party conditional planning permission. Backfilling of excavated land was required, but twenty-one acres remained unfilled when working ceased in 1978. A company obtained an option to purchase the land, intending to use it as a tip site. Before acquiring the land, the company was assured by the authority that no further planning permission for tipping would be required. The company was granted a waste disposal licence under the Control of Pollution Act 1974 and subsequently purchased the site in August 1978. The District Council applied for an order of certiorari to quash the disposal licence. Section 3 (2) of the 1974 Act states that a disposal licence shall not be issued for a use of land for which planning permission is required, unless such permission is in force. The District Council contended that the use solely for tipping was a totally different use from the mixed use involved in concurrent extraction and backfilling; further planning permission would be required because of the change of use and the issue of the disposal licence was therefore ultra vires the county court. *Held*, a condition of the 1969 permission contemplated and required that the site should be backfilled after the completion of excavations, and that as that condition was still enforceable by law, there was no reason why the company, as present occupiers, should not be entitled to comply with the condition voluntarily. The application would therefore be dismissed.

R v DERBYSHIRE COUNTY COUNCIL EX PARTE NORTH EAST DERBYSHIRE DC (1979) 77 LGR 389 (Queen's Bench Division: LORD WIDGERY CJ, BRIDGE LJ and CAULFIELD J).

2777   —— —— **validity of condition—powers of Secretary of State**

Two building firms appealed against the deemed refusal of a local authority to grant planning permission for the construction of two housing estates. The parties subsequently came to an agreement on the development subject to the builders' providing play areas for children, public open spaces and a social/shopping centre. In the light of this agreement the local authority invited the Secretary of State to allow the appeal. He nevertheless dismissed it on the ground, inter alia, that he could not grant permission subject to conditions which did not relate to the development applied for. Subsequently the High Court held that the conditions could be imposed. On appeal, *held*, the Secretary of State could deal with the applications as if they had been made to him in the first instance, and was not confined to accepting the proposed conditions as they stood or rejecting the applications outright.

ROBERT HITCHINS BUILDERS LTD v SECRETARY OF STATE FOR THE ENVIRONMENT; BRITANNIA (CHELTENHAM) LTD v SECRETARY OF STATE FOR THE ENVIRONMENT (1979) 251 Estates Gazette 467 (Court of Appeal: MEGAW, EVELEIGH and BRANDON LJJ). Decision of Sir Douglas Frank, QC, sitting as a deputy High Court judge, (1978) 247 Estates Gazette 301, 1978 Halsbury's Abridgment para. 2784, affirmed on different grounds.

2778   —— —— —— **reasonableness**

Scotland

The British Airports Authority (BAA) applied to a local planning authority for planning permission to carry out certain developments at an airport to cater for growing air transport traffic. Permission was granted subject to certain conditions. The conditions, designed to control the mischief of aircraft noise, restricted the operational flying hours at the airport and controlled the direction of take off and landing. BAA appealed to the Secretary of State against the imposition of the conditions, and a public local inquiry was held. Following the inquiry, the Secretary of State refused to discharge the conditions and merely varied their terms. BAA further appealed, contending, inter alia, that both conditions were ultra vires in that neither was fairly and reasonably related to the permitted development; that the condition controlling take off and landing was so unreasonable that no reasonable planning authority could have imposed it. *Held*, the Secretary of State was entitled to find that there was a close relationship between the permitted development and future noise levels and that the conditions designed to control the mischief of aircraft noise associated with the use of the runway were fairly and reasonably related to that development. However, as the control of the direction of take off and landing was outside the jurisdiction of BAA, the imposition of the second condition was ultra vires the Secretary of State because there were no steps that BAA could take to achieve the desired result. It was a misuse of power to attempt to use BAA as an intermediary by the device of attaching conditions to the permitted development, in order that a certain result be obtained. Planning permission had to be quashed for it was as a whole ultra vires. The appeal would be remitted to the Secretary of State for reconsideration.

BRITISH AIRPORTS AUTHORITY v SECRETARY OF STATE FOR SCOTLAND 1979 SLT 197 (Court of Session).

2779   —— **exercise of power by Secretary of State—original decision quashed—material considerations arising after original decision**

An application was made for planning permission for residential development of a site. Permission was refused on the grounds of sewage and highway difficulties, although a draft structure plan indicated that the construction of housing was in accordance with the county council's proposals. An inquiry was set up and the subsequent inspector's report recommended that the developer's appeal be allowed subject to the special condition that the houses to be erected on the site should not be occupied in advance of improvement to the highway and to the sewage works. The Secretary of State, however, decided that the inspector's recommendation was not practicable and dismissed the appeal. On the developer's further appeal, the Secretary of State's decision was quashed on the ground that the Secretary of State, reasonably directing himself on the available evidence, could not have come to that conclusion as all the evidence pointed clearly to the practicability of imposing the condition. Following that decision, there was correspondence between the Secretary of State and the developer on the questions of sewage and highway problems and the provisions of the draft structure plan. The Secretary of State having failed to issue a decision on the planning appeal since his original decision was quashed, the developer sought a declaration against the Department of the Environment in order that the Secretary of State should make a decision. The developer contended that the judgment quashing the original decision had removed the sole impediment to the Secretary of State's grant of planning permission and, further, that it was not open to the Secretary of State to take into account any other considerations which arose after the date of the original decision, including his own subsequent modifications to the draft structure plan. *Held*, the judge had not said that such a condition could never be imposed, but that there was no material on which the Secretary of State could have found that it was impracticable to impose such a condition in the instant case. The Secretary of State was therefore entitled to reconsider the matter or to consider other questions on which he could found another decision. Further, when a decision of the Secretary of State was quashed, it had to be treated as not having been made; the Secretary of State had to make another decision in accordance with any view of the law which the court hearing the appeal may have indicated. Under the Town and Country Planning Act 1971, s. 36, the Secretary of State, in coming to a fresh decision, was entitled to take into account any material consideration which had arisen whether before his original decision or after it. Accordingly, the application would be dismissed.

It was suggested that cases asking purely for declaratory relief between a disappointed appellant and the Department of the Environment would be better dealt with in the Divisional Court when such cases were in the nature of mandamus rather than purely declaratory matters.

PRICE BROS (RODE HEATH) LTD v DEPARTMENT OF THE ENVIRONMENT (1979) 252 Estates Gazette 595 (Queen's Bench Division: FORBES J).

2780   —— —— reasons for decision

A local planning authority refused an application by a company for planning permission. The company successfully appealed to the Secretary of State. The authority applied for an order under the Town and Country Planning Act 1971, s. 245, that the Secretary of State's decision be quashed. The authority contended that the Secretary of State had failed to give any reasons for rejecting one of the substantial grounds upon which the authority had relied in refusing planning permission, namely, that the development would be contrary to a draft district plan. *Held*, although the Secretary of State had not expressly mentioned the plan in his decision, it was clear that he had considered the company's appeal against the background of the development history relating to the area in question. That development history had included, especially, the draft district plan. The application would be dismissed.

SHEFFIELD CITY COUNCIL v SECRETARY OF STATE FOR THE ENVIRONMENT (1979) 251 Estates Gazette 165 (Queen's Bench Division: DRAKE J).

2781   —— —— relevant considerations

A local authority refused an application for planning permission to develop a site north of Macclesfield for residential use because it was apparent that the proposed rate of development would interfere with the local structure plan and create an undesirable increase in traffic on local main roads unless a condition was imposed that only a certain number of houses could be built before a relief road was completed. The Secretary of State upheld the decision and stated that it would be futile to impose a time condition because the applicants might find themselves in possession of a permission which had expired due to circumstances beyond their control. On appeal, *held*, the Secretary of State had erred because he had failed to notice the applicants' offer to phase the development to align with the structure plan. His objection to the time condition was unrealistic, since a permission could expire only if he himself placed a time limit on it and it would plainly be an abuse of powers for him to impose a time limit which would make a time condition illusory. Accordingly the appeal would be dismissed on the ground that he had failed to take into account relevant considerations and had taken account of irrelevant considerations.

SEDDON PROPERTIES LTD AND JAMES CROSBIE & SONS LTD V SECRETARY OF STATE FOR THE ENVIRONMENT (1978) 248 Estates Gazette 950 (Queen's Bench Division: FORBES J).

2782   —— material consideration—finance received from development

An inspector was appointed to determine an appeal, by the trustees of a private school, against the local authority's refusal of planning permission for the development of unused playing fields. The inspector allowed the appeal on the basis that the site was not of such visual and physical importance that development should be excluded; further that as the school was a listed building and required considerable finance for its upkeep, the development of the site would provide that finance. The local authority applied to have this decision quashed, claiming that the finance of the upkeep of the school was not a material consideration. *Held*, normally, when considering an application for planning permission, the applicant's intentions regarding any finance to be received from the development of the site in question, were not a consideration that should be taken into account. However, there was an exception where the finance was to be used for planning purposes. Because the school was a listed building, its upkeep was a planning matter and thus was a relevant consideration. The inspector's decision would be upheld.

BRIGHTON BOROUGH COUNCIL V SECRETARY OF STATE FOR THE ENVIRONMENT (1979) 249 Estates Gazette 747 (Queen's Bench Division: SIR DOUGLAS FRANK QC sitting as a deputy High Court judge). *Niarchos (London) Ltd v Secretary of State for the Environment* (1977) 76 LGR 480, 1977 Halsbury's Abridgment para. 2790 applied, *J. Murphy and Sons Ltd v Secretary of State for the Environment* [1973] 2 All ER 26 distinguished.

2783   —— outline planning permission—revocation—compensation—Lands Tribunal decision

LOROMAH ESTATES LTD V HARINGEY LONDON BOROUGH (1978) 248 Estates Gazette 877: V. G. Wellings QC (outline planning permission granted in 1965 subject to certain conditions; application for approval of reserved matters in 1970; revocation order made in 1971 and confirmed by Secretary of State in 1973; compensation sought for depreciation in value of land, for loss of money, being interest on bank overdraft, incurred by the non-payment of compensation and for payment of development land tax on any sum awarded for such depreciation; planning authority based compensation figures on deemed refusal of the 1970 application; authority could not rely on own failure to consider that application, 1970 scheme was good, compensation would be assessed on basis that it had been approved; claim for compensation for the delay in the assessment of compensation inadmissible; claim for compensation for development land tax also dismissed).

2784   —— refusal—appeal against decision of Secretary of State—access to development site

Builders appealed against the Secretary of State's refusal of planning permission for residential development. Permission had been refused on the grounds that access to the site would have had a detrimental effect on existing adjacent housing estates and that a proposed alternative access route could not be approved as the builders only had a licence over it; they did not therefore have "control" for the purposes of the Town and Country Planning Act 1971, s. 30 (1) (*a*). *Held*, on the facts the Secretary of State had been justified in refusing permission on the ground that the builders did not have sufficient control over the proposed access route. However, he was at fault in not having considered the alternative of imposing a negative condition under s. 29 prohibiting access through the existing housing estates. The appeal would accordingly be allowed.

GEORGE WIMPEY & CO LTD v NEW FOREST DISTRICT COUNCIL (1979) 250 Estates Gazette 249 (Queen's Bench Division: SIR DOUGLAS FRANK QC sitting as a deputy High Court judge).

2785   —— unauthorised grant of permission—validity

A district council recommended that permission should be granted to a retail company to build a hypermarket on the outskirts of a town. This recommendation was to have been discussed at a county council meeting before a final decision to grant planning permission was made. The solicitors for the vendors of the site in question wrote a letter to the district council, asserting that the council had, on the day it decided to recommend granting planning permission, actually granted permission and had wrongfully failed to issue the appropriate grant of permission. The solicitors threatened to bring an action for mandamus and damages. The clerk to the district council issued the grant of permission on his own initiative, the grant being back-dated to the date of the recommendation. The vendors produced the grant to the retail company, who promptly completed the purchase of the site. At a later date the district council purported to confirm the action taken by the clerk. The Attorney-General, in a relator action, challenged the validity of the grant. *Held*, a grant of planning permission was to be made only in the public interest and should not be pre-empted by the mistaken issue of a printed form by a clerk. The recommendation of the district council was not a grant of planning permission, thus the clerk had issued the grant without any authority. The fact that the company had purchased the land in good faith, on the strength of the document, could not validate the grant. For although a grant of planning permission ran with the land and no-one could look behind it to discover the true facts, this only applied to grants which had initially been authorised. The grant in the instant case had never been authorised and was thus ultra vires and void. The subsequent purported confirmation of the clerk's action could not ratify the grant, as an act which was ultra vires could not be ratified. Neither could the district council retrospectively validate the permission so as to make it effective from the date of the recommendation. Thus planning permission had never been granted.

A-G v TAFF ELY BOROUGH COUNCIL (1979) 250 Estates Gazette 757 (Court of Appeal: LORD DENNING MR, ORMROD AND BROWNE LJJ). *Slough Estates v Slough Borough Council* [1969] 2 Ch 315, distinguished, *Ashbury Carriage Co v Rich* (1875) LR 7 HL 653 and *Norfolk County Council v Secretary of State for the Environment* [1973] 1 WLR 1400 followed.

2786   Stop notice—restrictions on service—activity beginning more than twelve months earlier

In September 1975, the plaintiffs were granted conditional planning permission to carry on an open-air market. The permission expired on 30th June 1978, but the plaintiffs continued to conduct a market in breach of planning control. The local planning authority sought to serve a stop notice on the plaintiffs under the Town and Country Planning Act 1971, s. 90, as amended. The plaintiffs sought a declaration that they were not entitled to do so on the ground that s. 90 (2) provided that a stop notice could not be served where the activity in question has been carried on for more than twelve months previously, as in this case. The declaration was refused on the ground that s. 90 (2) should be construed as providing that the activity in question must have been carried on in breach of planning control for more than twelve months previously, which was not the case here. On appeal by the plaintiffs, *held*, BRANDON LJ dissenting, the language of the section was unequivocal. There was no justification for saying that "activity" in s. 90 (2) meant an activity carried on in breach of control. Since the plaintiffs had in fact carried on the activity in question for more than twelve months previously, s. 90 (2) prohibited the service of a stop notice. The appeal would be allowed.

SCOTT MARKETS LTD v LONDON BOROUGH OF WALTHAM FOREST (1979) 77 LGR 565 (Court of Appeal: BUCKLEY, SHAW and BRANDON LJJ). Decision of Mars-Jones J [1978] LS Gaz R 1172, reversed.

2787　Town and Country Planning Act 1971—commencement

See paras. 2757–2768.

TRADE AND INDUSTRY

Halsbury's Laws of England (3rd edn.), Vol. 38, paras. 1–600

2788　Aircraft and shipbuilding industries—increase of shipbuilders' borrowing powers

The British Shipbuilders Borrowing Powers (Increase of Limit) Order 1979, S.I. 1979 No. 961 (in force on 28th July 1979), increases to £300 million, the financial limit specified in the Aircraft and Shipbuilding Industries Act 1977, s. 11 (7), see 1977 Halsbury's Abridgment para. 2819. Section 11 (7) limits the aggregate, of the borrowings by British Shipbuilders and its subsidiaries (other than excluded loans) and the public dividend capital received by British Shipbuilders, to £200 million, but makes provision for that limit to be increased to not more than £300 million.

2789　—— loans by Secretary of State

The British Aerospace (Design, Development and Production of Civil Aircraft) (Payments) Order 1979, S.I. 1979 No. 165 (in force on 19th February 1979), deals with the power of the Secretary of State under the Aircraft and Shipbuilding Industries Act 1977, s. 45, 1977 Halsbury's Abridgment para. 2819, to make payments to British Aerospace for promoting the design, development and production of civil aircraft. The aggregate of those payments, less any sums received by the Secretary of State, otherwise than by way of payment of interest on money lent under s. 45, is limited to £50 million.

2790　Assisted areas

The Assisted Areas Order 1979, S.I. 1979 No. 837 (in force on 18th July 1979), upgrades certain areas to intermediate, development and special development areas and downgrades certain other areas. Various Orders are also revoked.

2791

The Assisted Areas (Amendment) Order 1979, S.I. 1979 No. 1642 (in force on 12th December 1979), amends the Assisted Areas Order 1979, para. 2790 by upgrading certain areas.

2792　Census of production

The Census of Production (1980) (Returns and Exempted Persons) Order 1979, S.I. 1979 No. 1484 (in force on 31st December 1979), prescribes the matters about which a person carrying on an undertaking may be required to furnish returns for the Census of Production being taken in 1980 and exempts from such an obligation any person carrying on an undertaking in the exploration for and extraction of petroleum on land and offshore.

2793   Certificate of origin—Arab boycott

The Foreign Office has announced that, following an extensive review of the working of the Arab boycott, the practice of authenticating signatures on "negative" certificates of origin of goods would be maintained. The Foreign Office is, however, issuing separate notices pointing out that the signatures on boycott documents refer only to their authenticity and do not condone their contents. See the Financial Times, 6th November 1979.

2794   Employment Agencies Act 1973—exemption

The Employment Agencies Act 1973 (Exemption) Regulations 1979, S.I. 1979 No. 342 (in force on 1st May 1979), exempt from the licensing and other provisions of the 1973 Act certain professional institutes providing services for their members and registered students.

2795   The Employment Agencies Act 1973 (Exemption) (No. 2) Regulations 1979, S.I. 1979 No. 1741 (in force on 4th February 1980), exempt from the licensing and other provisions of the 1973 Act certain named organisations which provide services for their members and registered students and also the Crown Agents for Overseas Governments and Administrations, which as from 1st January 1980, became a body corporate.

2796   Employment agencies and businesses—licence—fee

The Employment Agencies and Employment Businesses Licence Fee Regulations 1979, S.I. 1979 No. 770 (in force on 1st August 1979), revoke the Employment Agencies and Employment Businesses Licence Fee Regulations 1978, 1978 Halsbury's Abridgment para. 2823, and prescribe the increased fees payable on the grant or renewal of a licence under the Employment Agencies Act 1973 to carry on an employment agency or business.

2797   Export credit—Export Credits Guarantee Department—revision of schemes

The Export Credits Guarantee Department (ECGD) has announced some changes in the cover it provides for large export orders (see the Financial Times, 1st November 1979). For contracts of £5,000,000 or more financed on a buyer-credit basis the exporter will in future be able to make an initial payment of 10 per cent; subsequent payments being related to draw down of the bank loan. Although in practice the ECGD's 100 per cent recourse to the exporter (on a buyer-credit scheme) has been reduced to about 25 per cent this will now be reduced further to a maximum of 10 per cent; a cut-off period will be introduced after which the exporter will be released from his recourse obligation. A conditional guarantee scheme will be introduced as an alternative to the normal buyer-credit scheme; under the conditional scheme the banks will be responsible for the loan conditions and documentation and, as such, will undertake some of the risk. The tender-to-contract scheme will only be available in future if the exporter opts for it shortly after he applies for basic ECGD cover.

2798   Export guarantees—subsidies to exporters—extension of period

The Export Guarantees (Extension of Period) Order 1979, S.I. 1979 No. 180 (in force on 23rd February 1979), extends the period during which arrangements by the Secretary of State for export subsidies may be made for one year from 26th March 1979.

2799   Hosiery and Knitwear Industry—scientific research levies

The Hosiery and Knitwear Industry (Scientific Research Levy) (Amendment) Order 1979, S.I. 1979 No. 1740 (in force on 1st January 1980), amends the Hosiery and Knitwear Industry (Scientific Research Levy) Order 1969. The order provides that such levies under the Industrial Organisation and Development Act 1947 will cease to be payable in the hosiery and knitwear industry in respect of any period after that ending on 30th June 1982, and, from 1st January 1980 extends the exemption from liability to pay the levy to persons carrying on business in the industry with a chargeable turnover of not more than £250,000.

2800   Industrial development—special development area

The Special Development Area (Falmouth) Order 1979, S.I. 1979 No. 269 (in force on 12th March 1979), upgrades the employment office area of Falmouth from a development area to a special development area.

2801   Industry Act 1979

The Industry Act 1979 raises the statutory financial borrowing limits of the Welsh Development Agency and the National Enterprise Board (including their subsidiaries) to £250 million, which may be increased by order to £400 million, and £3,000 million, which may be increased to £4,500 million respectively: s. 1, Schedule. The borrowing limit of the Scottish Development Agency has also been increased. Section 2 deals with short title. The Act received the royal assent on 4th April 1979 and came into force on that date.

2802   Monopolies and Mergers Commission—investigation of alleged monopoly situation—factors to be taken into account

In considering whether a complex monopoly situation existed under s. 6 (1) (c) and (2) of the Fair Trading Act 1973, the Monopolies and Mergers Commission was not required (where there were shown to be alternative ways of competing) to consider the total competitiveness of the suppliers rather than a particular aspect of it. In determining whether conduct was restrictive of competition there was no valid distinction between conduct that was "anti-competitive" and that which was merely "non-competitive". See Electricity Supply Meters: A Report on the Supply and Export of Electricity Supply Meters (Monopolies and Mergers Commission) (Cmnd. 7639, 1979).

2803   Price Commission (Amendment) Act 1979

The Price Commission (Amendment) Act 1979 amends the Price Commission Act 1977, 1977 Halsbury's Abridgment para. 2842. The Act received the royal assent on 12th February 1979 and came into force on that date.

Section 1 excuses the Secretary of State from having to make regulations under 1977 Act, s. 9, relating to the safeguarding of minimum profit levels of enterprises during and after their investigation by the Price Commission. The section also contains consequential amendments, repeals and transitional provisions. By s. 2, the provisions repealed by s. 1 revive after one year, subject to the possibility of the revival's postponement for not more than one year at a time by Order in Council. Section 3 deals with short title.

2804   Prices—footwear

The Distribution of Footwear (Prices) (Amendment) Order 1979, S.I. 1979 No. 129 (in force on 12th February 1979), amends the Distribution of Footwear (Prices) Order 1978, 1978 Halsbury's Abridgment para. 2843, by adding specified distributors to those who are exempt from the 1978 Order, and who are listed in the Schedule to that Order.

2805   Regional development grant—percentages

The Regional Development Grants (Variation of Prescribed Percentages) Order 1979, S.I. 1979 No. 975 (in force on 31st July 1979), varies the rate of regional development grant payable under the Industry Act 1972 on capital expenditure incurred in providing assets on qualifying premises in development areas or for use in those areas. The amount of grant is reduced from twenty per cent to fifteen per cent of the expenditure incurred. Expenditure will remain eligible for regional development grant at the old rate if it is incurred in respect of assets provided before 1st August 1980 or if it was defrayed before 18th July 1979.

2806   Restraint of trade—covenant not to compete—injunction to enforce—reasonableness

On being appointed a director in 1974, the plaintiff signed a covenant declaring that should he resign from the company he would not take up a position in a similar business anywhere in the United Kingdom for a period of twelve months from the date of the termination of his contract. In 1977 the plaintiff left the employ of the defendant company and sought a declaration that the covenant was unenforceable. The defendants entered a counterclaim to restrain the plaintiff from taking up his new employment. The covenant was declared invalid. The defendants appealed, contending additionally that if the covenant were amended to exclude the plaintiff from working for a competing rather than a similar business, it would be enforceable. *Held*, the decision of the trial judge would be upheld, despite the added contention, on the grounds that the covenant laid its restriction over too wide a geographical area, into parts of which the defendants had not expanded. It was unreasonable to curtail completely all chance of going into another job in the one business in which the plaintiff was ever likely to be employed. The only valid reason for imposing such a restriction was for the prevention of the disclosure of confidential information and the plaintiff had already undertaken not to disclose such information as there was. The appeal would therefore be dismissed.

GREER v SKETCHLEY LTD [1979] FSR 197 (Court of Appeal: LORD DENNING MR, SHAW and WALLER LJJ).

2807   Scientific research—industrial levy

The Iron Casting Industry (Scientific Research Levy) (Amendment) Order 1979, S.I. 1979 No. 748 (in force on 1st July 1979), further amends the Iron Casting Industry (Scientific Research Levy) Order 1971 so as to provide that in future the amount of that part of the levy on the iron castings industry to finance scientific research which is determined by the amount of iron castings produced will be determined by reference to a 1975-based index of the wholesale selling prices of iron castings produced in the United Kingdom instead of a 1970-based index.

2808   Shipbuilding Act 1979

The Shipbuilding Act 1979 raises the limits imposed by the Aircraft and Shipbuilding Industries Act 1977, s. 11 in relation to the finances of British Shipbuilders and their wholly owned subsidiaries. The Act also extends the application of the Industry Act 1972, s. 10 to include the alteration of completed and partially constructed ships and mobile offshore installations. The Act received the royal assent on 20th December 1979 and came into force on that date.

Section 1 increases the limit under the Aircraft and Shipbuilding Industries Act 1977, s. 11 (7) on the amount of external finance which British Shipbuilders and its wholly owned subsidiaries may borrow or receive by way of public dividend capital. The original limit was £200m. which was increased to the maximum of £300m. by order. The new limit is £500m. which may be increased by order to £600m.

Section 2 extends the power of the Secretary of State under the Industry Act 1972, s. 10 to guarantee payment of sums borrowed by a person in the United Kingdom, the Channel Islands or the Isle of Man to finance the construction or the completion in the United Kingdom of a ship or mobile offshore installation. The Act provides that guarantees may be given in relation to finance for the alteration of a vessel or partially built vessel as well as for construction or completion.

2809   Shops—Sunday observance—exemption—Jewish traders

The Shops Regulations 1979, S.I. 1979 No. 1294 (in force on 1st December 1979), amend the Shops Regulations 1937, S.I. 1937 No. 271 and the Shops (Procedure for Jewish Tribunals) Regulations 1937, S.I. 1937 No. 1038. The Shops Act 1950, s. 53 (1), (3) provides that a Jewish trader is entitled to be registered by a local authority, under certain conditions, and permitted, so long as the shop is closed on Saturdays, to serve customers on Sundays. In order to obtain registration the trader is required to submit the statutory declaration prescribed in the Shop Regulations 1937, Sch. The 1979 Regulations require that in addition to the above statutory declaration, a person must also make a declaration that he has not been employed or engaged on the Jewish Sabbath in any trade or business and that an application must be supported by a certificate from a panel appointed by the Board of Deputies of British Jews. Notification of the holding of an inquiry into an application must now be sent by registered letter.

TRADE DESCRIPTIONS

2810   False trade description—act or default of some other person

The defendants, who were motor dealers, sold a second-hand car after turning the odometer back to zero. The sale was made with full disclaimers and was therefore lawful. The purchasers sold the car to a dealer, who later resold it with a false trade description because the odometer then recorded 5,000 miles. The defendants were convicted of contravening the Trade Descriptions Act 1968, s. 23, in that by virtue of their turning the odometer to zero a subsequent offence under the Act had been committed. On appeal against conviction, *held*, the commission of the offence by the dealer was not due to the defendants' act or default which was in any case not wrongful. They had ceased to be responsible before the sale took place. The conviction was misconceived and would therefore be quashed.

K. LILL HOLDINGS LTD v WHITE [1979] RTR 120 (Queen's Bench Division: LORD WIDGERY CJ, WIEN and SMITH JJ).

2811   —— coal—weight deficiency due to moisture loss—duty to compensate

A coal merchant loaded his lorry with 1 cwt sacks of coal which had a high moisture content, although he knew that it would lose weight as the moisture evaporated. The load was supposed to weigh 1.5 tons but was subsequently found to be some 140 lbs short. He was charged with applying a false trade description but was acquitted on the ground that he could only have compensated for the moisture loss by gross overweighing and to require this would be unreasonable. On appeal, *held*, there was no requirement to overweigh to compensate for moisture loss, but the coal merchant should have attempted to achieve the correct weight. He had failed to show that he had taken all the necessary precautions and the magistrates would be directed to convict him.

KINCHIN v HAINES [1979] Crim LR 329 (Queen's Bench Division: EVELEIGH LJ and STEPHEN BROWN J).

2812   Textile products—composition

The Textile Products (Determination of Composition) (Amendment) Regulations 1979, S.I. 1979 No. 749 (in force on 30th July 1979), amend the Textile Products (Determination of Composition) Regulations 1976, 1976 Halsbury's Abridgment para. 2611 which specified the best methods to be used to determine the composition of certain textile products, thereby implementing Council Directive (EEC) 79/76.

TRADE MARKS, TRADE NAMES
AND DESIGNS

Halsbury's Laws of England (3rd edn.), Vol. 38, paras. 811–1135

2813   Hallmarking

The Edinburgh Assay Office Order 1979, S.I. 1979 No. 1587 (in force on 5th December 1979) confers powers upon and varies existing statutory provisions relating to the Incorporation of Goldsmiths of the City of Edinburgh including the alteration of its constitution, appointment of officers, acquisition and disposal of land and other investments and provisions of benefits to employees.

The Order repeals certain provisions relating to the Incorporation in ancient enactments.

2814   Passing-off—application for interlocutory injunction—likelihood of confusion

The plaintiffs and defendants were both manufacturers of pharmaceutical products. The plaintiffs had marketed a suppressor for the menstrual cycle in capsule form under the name DANOL since November 1974. Whilst considering the registration of the name they became aware of the defendants' mark, DE-NOL, but proceeded to register the name DANOL. The defendants had marketed a liquid preparation for the treatment of ulcers under various names incorporating the word DE-NOL for many years. The name DE-NOL (alone) had been registered in July 1973. Both products would normally be prescribed by a hospital consultant, but DE-NOL could be bought without a prescription. The defendants wished to market DE-NOL in solid form when a satisfactory formulation could be found, which they estimated would take two to three years. The plaintiffs became aware of their intention and sought an injunction to restrain passing-off, arguing that if DE-NOL were marketed in solid form there would be a substantial likelihood of confusion with their product. The defendants admitted the likelihood of confusion, but claimed that the plaintiffs should be restrained as their mark, DE-NOL, had been registered first, and it was an accepted practice to use the same trade name for a re-formulated product. Both parties had build up considerable goodwill. It was established that the two names had been confused on several occasions, but the mistakes had been corrected by either the prescribing doctor or the dispensing chemist. *Held*, (i) there was no likelihood of confusion in relation to the two products whilst DE-NOL continued to be sold in liquid form, as doctors and pharmacists were trained to take very great care and DANOL was not available to the public without a prescription; a real likelihood of confusion would only arise if the defendants marketed their product in solid form. (ii) The plaintiffs did not enter the market knowing that there was a risk of confusion, and it was not reasonable to hold that they should have anticipated that DE-NOL might be sold in solid form at some future date. The defendants' claim would fail. The plaintiffs were entitled to judgment, but, since there was no immediate market threat, it would be inappropriate to grant an injunction.

STERWIN AG v BROCADES (GREAT BRITAIN) LTD [1979] RPC 481 (Chancery Division: WHITFORD J).

2815   —— business name—likelihood of confusion

The plaintiffs were members of a group of companies operating a parcel delivery service throughout the country via British Rail called the "Red Star" parcel delivery service. The plaintiffs advertised their business under the name "City Link" which appeared on the parcels but was not used by their agents. The defendant, a taxi driver who had been employed by an agent of the plaintiffs, commenced business as a taxi firm under the registered business name "City Link Travel Service", delivering parcels directly by road. The plaintiffs applied for an injunction restraining the use of the name by the defendant. The defendant contended that at the time of commencing business he did not know of the name "City Link". *Held*, the defendant did not adopt the name for any improper motive. The words "City Link" were descriptive although this would not prevent the plaintiffs establishing a second meaning and thereby a reputation. It was difficult to infer from the evidence that the name "City Link" had come to denote a service of the plaintiffs rather than a description used in connection with the Red Star service and by the trial date it was the defendant who had built up a local reputation as a taxi and parcel delivery service under the name. The relief would be refused.

CITY LINK TRAVEL HOLDINGS LTD v LAKIN [1979] FSR 653 (Chancery Division: WHITFORD J).

2816   —— interlocutory injunction—conversion of second-hand cars

See *Rolls-Royce Ltd v Zanelli*, para. 525.

2817   —— —— likelihood of confusion

The plaintiffs, American publishers of a magazine called "Newsweek", sought interlocutory relief restraining the defendants from broadcasting a programme also called "Newsweek". They contended that the magazine and the programme would be linked and that the defendants were liable for passing-off. *Held*, the test was whether there was a misrepresentation likely to lead to confusion and, except amongst a few tourists, there was little likelihood of confusion. The word "Newsweek" was a descriptive title and a shortened form of "news of the week". It would be unfair to allow anyone a monopoly of the word. The application would be refused.

NEWSWEEK INC v BRITISH BROADCASTING CORPN [1978] LS Gaz R 1171 (Court of Appeal: LORD DENNING MR, STEPHENSON and SHAW LJJ).

2818   A Swiss company marketed sunglasses and spectacle frames under the trade mark "CD Christopher Dunhill, London". The mark was used by agreement with a great-grandson of the founder of the plaintiff company, whose business embraced the sale of sunglasses in the United States. The latter sought an interlocutory injunction banning the Swiss company from operating in specified countries, contending that it was deliberately exploiting their name and perpetrating a blatant fraud. They further contended that damages would be an inadequate remedy if the injunction were refused. The relief was refused at first instance on the ground that the plaintiffs would suffer no significant loss if the injunction were not granted. On appeal, *held*, the facts of the case were substantially in dispute and so consideration of the respective merits of the parties could not provide the basis for a decision. Damages would be an inadequate remedy for the plaintiffs and in any case it was unclear whether the Swiss company would be able to pay any damages which might be awarded. By contrast, the loss to the Swiss company if an injunction were granted would be relatively slight. Accordingly, an injunction would be granted banning the sale of the Swiss company's products in the United Kingdom and Switzerland.

ALFRED DUNHILL LTD v SUNOPTIC SA [1979] FSR 337 (Court of Appeal: MEGAW, ROSKILL and BROWNE LJJ). *American Cyanamid v Ethicon* [1975] AC 396, HL, 1975 Halsbury's Abridgment para. 1864 followed.

2819   —— —— —— balance of convenience

See *Mothercare Ltd v Robson Books Ltd*, para. 1593.

2820   —— —— —— distinctiveness of trade name

The plaintiffs were manufacturers in Holland of an alcoholic drink known as "advocaat", the principal ingredients of which were eggs and spirit. It was imported and sold in the United Kingdom, where it acquired substantial reputation and goodwill. The defendants, an English company, began to manufacture and sell in the United Kingdom a drink known as "Keeling's Old English Advocaat", consisting of eggs and Cyprus sherry. Since it attracted the lower rate of excise duty appropriate to fortified wines instead of spirits, the defendants were able to under-sell the plaintiffs and capture a large proportion of the market. In a passing-off action, the plaintiffs were granted an injunction restricting the defendants from selling and distributing their product as advocaat. The defendants' appeal was allowed and the plaintiffs appealed. *Held*, there were five characteristics which had to be present in order to create a valid course of action for passing off: (1) a misrepresentation, (2) made by a trader in the course of trade, (3) to prospective customers of his or ultimate consumers of goods or services supplied by him, (4) which was calculated to injure the business or goodwill of another trader (in the sense that this was a reasonably foreseeable consequence) and (5) which caused actual damage to a business or goodwill of the trader by whom the action was brought or (in a quia timet action) would probably do so. The goodwill which was thus damaged could belong to an identifiable class of people and not just to one individual. If one could define the type of product that had acquired a reputation in the market by reason of its recognisable and distinct qualities, one could identify the members of the class entitled to the goodwill as those who supplied that product in England. It was irrelevant whether the recognisable and distinct qualities of the product were the result of it having been made in a particular locality or of its having been made from particular ingredients. In the present case, the type of product that had gained reputation and goodwill for the name "advocaat" was defined by reference to the nature of its ingredients. The class of traders entitled to that goodwill were those who supplied an egg and spirit drink in broad conformity with an identifiable recipe. The plaintiffs fell into that class. All five characteristics necessary to create a valid cause of action were present and hence the appeal would be allowed and the injunction restored.

ERVEN WARNINK BV v J. TOWNEND & SONS (HULL) LTD [1979] 2 All ER 927 (House of Lords: LORD DIPLOCK, VISCOUNT DILHORNE, LORD SALMON, LORD FRASER OF TULLYBELTON and LORD SCARMAN). Decision of the Court of Appeal (1978) Times, 20th April, 1978 Halsbury's Abridgment para. 2860 reversed. *Bollinger v Costa Brava Wine Co Ltd* [1960] Ch 262 approved.

2821   Registration—application—whether design new or original

The applicants applied for registration of a design in respect of a football shirt. The shirt was of a conventional shape but had red and blue bands running around the collar, from the collar over the shoulder down the arm to the cuff and on the cuffs themselves. The shirt was, in fact, that worn by the England football team. The applicants were refused on the ground that the design did not display the novelty nor the originality required by the Registered Designs Act 1949, s. 1, striping constituting a trade variation only and the colours not importing sufficient novelty where none existed to justify registration. On appeal, *held*, notwithstanding that variations in striping were commonly to be found on football shirts, and that if there had been no limitation on colour in the registration the previous decision would have been correct, the appeal would be allowed. It was not only the significance of the colours used that was important but also their positioning on the shirts. It was the essential combination of the features of stripes and colour for which protection was sought. The application would be allowed to proceed.

RE COOK AND HURST'S DESIGN APPLICATION [1979] RPC 197 (Registered Designs Appeal Tribunal: WHITFORD J).

2822   —— application for rectification of register—non-use by registered proprietor

The applicants acquired the use of a trade mark from the registered proprietors in 1966, but their use of the mark did not comply with the restriction to which the registration was subject. The interveners, who had used the same mark in the United States, later acquired the mark from the applicants, but the applicants sought rectification of the register in their own favour on the ground that the registered proprietor had not been using the mark. The interveners appealed against the registrar's decision that the mark be removed from the register. *Held*, it was clear that the registered proprietors had not used the mark since 1966 and, since the applicants had not complied with the registration restriction, the register would be rectified in the interveners' favour.

McGregor Trade Mark [1979] RPC 36 (Chancery Division: Whitford J).

2823 —— —— —— **use of mark with alterations not substantially affecting its identity**

The respondents, manufacturers of jeans and other casual clothing, decided to adopt the name "Huggers" for their products. They applied to register the mark "Huggers" but, following objection from the registry, they registered the mark "Huggars" instead, but continued to use the mark "Huggers" on their products. In an application to have the mark removed from the register the applicants relied on the Trade Marks Act 1938, s. 68, which defines a trade mark as a mark "used or proposed to be used". They contended that as the respondents had never proposed to use the mark "Huggars", it did not fall within the Act's definition. The respondents sought to rely on s. 30, which provides that where a registered trade mark needs to be proved for any purpose, the use of a trade mark with alterations not substantially affecting its identity is acceptable as an equivalent for the use required to be proved. The respondents claimed that the mark "Huggers" was not substantially different from "Huggars". *Held*, the application would be granted. The word "Huggars" was not "Huggers" with an "alteration not substantially affecting its identity", as the latter suggested the tight-fitting quality of the clothing manufactured by the respondent, which the former did not.

Re Huggars Trade Mark [1979] FSR 310 (Chancery Division: Goulding J).

2824 —— **descriptive word—whether word capable of distinguishing the goods**

Canada

A Canadian company was a wholly owned subsidiary of an American company. The latter was registered as the owner of the trade mark "OFF!" in respect of personal insect repellent, and the Canadian company as a registered user thereof. The Canadian company manufactured and sold in Canada the insect repellent under its own name, using the trade mark. The American company never used the trade mark in Canada. The defendant company marketed in Canada, under the name "BUGG OFF!", an insect repellent towel and the American and Canadian companies sued, inter alia, for infringement. The defendant counter-claimed, inter alia, for expungence of the trade mark on the ground that it was descriptive and not distinctive of the goods of the trade mark owner. *Held*, the message communicated to the Canadian public by the use of the word "OFF!" by the Canadian company was that the goods originated with the Canadian company and not with the American company. Accordingly the trade mark did not serve to distinguish the goods of the owner from the goods of all others (including the Canadian company) and was not therefore distinctive. The permitted use of the trade mark by the Canadian company did not mean that that company could be considered the owner, it merely permitted use without contravening the owner's rights. The counter-claim would be allowed and the trade mark expunged.

Re "OFF!" Trade Mark [1979] FSR 243 (Federal Court of Canada).

2825 —— **opposition—likelihood of confusion**

New Zealand

An Australian company's application for registration in New Zealand of a trade mark was opposed by the American proprietors of a strikingly similar mark. The opponents had made no sales in New Zealand because of import restrictions, but its business and mark were well known there as a result of advertising in overseas publications. They successfully contended that the use of the mark by the Australian company would be likely to deceive or cause confusion because of the existing reputation of their mark. On appeal by the Australian company, *held*, the purpose of the relevant legislation, which was equivalent to the Trade Marks Act 1938, s. 11, was to protect the public rather than the proprietary rights of traders; the likelihood of confusion had to be decided with reference to the awareness in the relevant New Zealand market and not based on the actual use of the mark there. The American mark had been sufficiently brought to public notice by the advertising for it to be concluded that use of the Australian mark would be reasonably likely to cause deception and confusion. Accordingly, the appeal would be dismissed.

PIONEER HI-BRED CORN CO v HY-LINE CHICKS PTY LTD [1979] RPC 410 (Court of Appeal).

2826   An application was made to register the mark FIF for dietetic and non-alcoholic drinks. It was opposed by the registered proprietors of the mark JIF, which included non-alcoholic drinks and fruit juices, and had been extensively used in the marketing of lemon juice. They contended that registration should be refused on the ground of likelihood of confusion and deception, and submitted questionnaires from traders as evidence to support their contention. The applicants, who also adduced questionnaires in evidence, argued that the opponents' questionnaires consisted of leading questions which made subsequent declarations worthless. The registrar decided that the applicants had shown that there was no real, tangible danger of phonetic or visual confusion under the Trade Marks Act 1938, ss. 11 and 12 (1), and allowed the application to proceed. The opponents appealed. *Held*, the evidence adduced by both parties was so inconclusive as to be of practically no assistance. When considering the visual aspect of mono-syllabic trade marks, greater importance should be attached to the initial letter of the mark. Prima facie, the marks were neither visually nor phonetically so close as to be likely to lead to confusion if used upon the same or similar goods. The appeal would be dismissed.

FIF TRADE MARK [1979] RPC 355 (Chancery Division: WHITFORD J).

TRADE UNIONS

Halsbury's Laws of England (3rd edn.), Vol. 38, paras. 601–677

2827   **Articles**

The Golden Formula: Some Recent Developments, Keith Ewing (the development of a restrictive interpretation of the term "in contemplation or furtherance of a trade dispute"): 8 ILJ 133.

Secondary Picketing, Michael Wright (comment on the picketing of premises of an employer not directly involved in a particular dispute): 129 NLJ 111.

What Can a Picket Lawfully Do?, A. T. Goff (legal position of pickets): 123 Sol Jo 103.

2828   **Action in furtherance of trade dispute—interlocutory injunction to restrain action—action in contemplation or furtherance of dispute**

Members of the National Union of Journalists employed by provincial newspapers went on strike over pay. Officers of the NUJ called a strike by union members employed by the Press Association so as to support the main strike by preventing the supply of news to the provincial papers. In addition, union members working for national newspapers were instructed to refuse to handle material issued by the Press Association. Neither the Press Association nor the national newspapers were otherwise involved in the pay dispute. A national newspaper was granted an interlocutory injunction restraining the union's action in inducing the newspaper's employees who were union members to break or not to perform their contracts of employment by refusing to use the Press Association material. The union officers appealed, contending that they had acted in furtherance of a trade dispute. *Held*, the action of the officers was taken by "a person in contemplation or furtherance of a trade dispute" and therefore was protected by the Trade Union and Labour Relations Act 1974, s. 13 (1), as amended. The correct test to be applied in deciding whether an act was in furtherance of a trade dispute was a subjective not objective one as s. 13 (1) clearly referred to the state of mind of the person taking the action. Therefore it was sufficient that the union officers honestly and reasonably believed that their actions might help the existing dispute; the court was not required to decide whether in fact they were reasonably capable of doing so. Accordingly the appeal would be allowed.

LORD WILBERFORCE allowed the appeal but considered that there was an objective element in the test whether the action was reasonably capable of furthering the dispute.

EXPRESS NEWSPAPERS LTD v MACSHANE [1980] 1 All ER 65 (House of Lords: LORD WILBERFORCE, LORD DIPLOCK, LORD SALMON, LORD KEITH OF KINKEL and LORD SCARMAN). Decision of the Court of Appeal [1979] 2 All ER 360 reversed. *Conway v Wade* [1908–10] All ER Rep 344, HL applied; *British Broadcasting Corpn v Hearn* [1978] 1 All ER 111, CA, 1977 Halsbury's Abridgment para. 1031 approved.

2829   The plaintiff company obtained their raw materials from the suppliers but collected the materials in their own lorries driven by their own employees. During a dispute between the Transport and General Workers' Union (TGWU) and member companies of the Road Haulage Association (RHA), a picket line was established outside the suppliers' premises. Although there was no dispute between the plaintiffs, who were not members of the RHA, their drivers or the union, nor between the suppliers and its employees, the plaintiffs' vehicles were not allowed to cross the picket line. An agreement was later reached with the TGWU whereby the plaintiffs would be allowed through. This, however, was restricted by the defendant picket to the collection of one lorry load per day, instead of the usual three. On an application by the plaintiffs for an interlocutory injunction, they contended that the defendant's action in causing a picket line to interfere with the plaintiffs' collection, was unlawful as not being "in contemplation of or furtherance of a trade dispute". *Held*, there was a limitation to be placed upon these words, and three separate bases for determining whether the defendants' action was unlawful. These tests were, whether the action (i) was in furtherance of a dispute or merely a consequence of a dispute; (ii) gave practical, and not simply moral, support to the cause; (iii) was reasonably capable of achieving the directive of the dispute. On the facts of this case the action failed to satisfy any of these tests. Further, the behaviour of the defendant was inconsistent with the union's instructions and there was evidence that the union had given permission for the plaintiffs to cross the picket line.

UNITED BISCUITS (UK) LTD v FALL [1979] IRLR 110 (Queen's Bench Division: ACKNER J).

This case must be read in the light of *Express Newspapers Ltd v MacShane* [1980] 1 All ER 65, HL, para. 2828.

2830   —— —— **balance of convenience**

Officials of the National Graphical Association, a printers' union, ordered their members to black advertisements submitted to the publications on which they worked by sixteen companies. Those companies regularly advertised in the Nottingham Evening Post, even though they had been asked not to by the NGA officials. They claimed to have issued the order because they wanted recognition for the purpose of collective bargaining by the owner of that newspaper who, unlike other newspaper owners, refused to operate a closed shop. The companies affected by the blacking order alleged that it constituted both unlawful interference with their trade and unlawful inducement to breach of contract by NGA members, which was not intended to further a recognition dispute but to remove the managing director of the Post and, possibly, to protect a union monopoly. The officials appealed against the grant of an interlocutory injunction restraining them from continuing the action on the ground that they were acting in furtherance of a trade dispute which was rendered lawful by statute. *Held*, the aim of a court in granting an interlocutory injunction was to set the balance fairly between the parties during the period leading up to the trial. The arguments put forward by the parties were sufficient to show that there was a serious issue to be tried. The officials had failed to establish that the balance of convenience was in favour of refusing the injunction, since they were unlikely to be able to meet a claim for damages of the order envisaged if the companies were successful at the trial of the main action, but any damage caused to themselves if they succeeded would be minimal. The appeal would be dismissed.

ASSOCIATED NEWSPAPERS GROUP LTD v WADE [1979] IRLR 210 (Court of Appeal: LORD DENNING MR, LAWTON and GEOFFREY LANE LJJ).

2831 —— —— **circumstances governing grant of injunction**

The new owners of a vessel formerly registered in Norway registered the vessel in Hong Kong. A Hong Kong crew was engaged at very much lower wages to take the place of the Norwegian crew. The International Federation of Transport Workers (ITF), a federation of seamen's unions, considered that the vessel, as a vessel registered in a country which was not the domicile of its beneficial owner, was using a "flag of convenience" in order to employ cheap labour. When the vessel berthed in the U.K. the ITF, having unsuccessfully sought an agreement from the owners on ITF terms, informed the owners that the vessel would be "blacked" unless ITF conditions of employment were complied with. The owners were granted an injunction restraining the ITF from "blacking" the vessel. The injunction was discharged on appeal on the ground that it was likely that the ITF would succeed in establishing an immunity under Trade Union and Labour Relations Act 1974, s. 13 when the action came to trial, by showing that their "blacking" of the vessel was in contemplation or furtherance of a trade dispute. The owners' appeal against a refusal to grant a second injunction on new evidence was subsequently dismissed on the same ground. The owners appealed against both decisions. *Held*, the ITF qualified as "workers" for the purposes of s. 29 (4) of the 1974 Act and the dispute between the ITF and the owners was clearly, on the evidence, a trade dispute as defined in s. 29 (1). The ITF would almost certainly succeed in showing that the threatened action of "blacking" the vessel would have been in contemplation or furtherance of that dispute. Accordingly, the appeal would be dismissed.

Their Lordships considered the effect of s. 17 (2) of the Act, that the court must, in exercising its discretion whether or not to grant an injunction, have regard to the likelihood of the party succeeding in establishing a statutory defence at the trial of the action. As the balance of convenience as to the grant of an interlocutory injunction was, on the face of it, heavily weighted in favour of the employer in the case of threatened industrial action, the court should, in exercising its discretion, have regard to practical realities in considering the balance of convenience in favour of the defendant; in particular, that the grant of an injunction was tantamount to giving final judgment against the defendant. However, the likelihood of successfully establishing the defence should not be treated as of over-riding or paramount importance.

NWL LTD v NELSON; NWL LTD v WOODS [1979] 3 All ER 614 (House of Lords: LORD DIPLOCK, LORD FRASER OF TULLYBELTON and LORD SCARMAN). Decisions of the Court of Appeal [1979] IRLR 321 affirmed. *The Camilla M* [1979] 1 Lloyd's Rep 26, CA, 1978 Halsbury's Abridgment para. 2871 overruled.

2832 —— —— **legitimate trade object—extraneous motive**

It has been re-stated by the Court of Appeal that if third parties intermeddle by making threats or demands for some extraneous motive and not for any legitimate trade object, they do not act in contemplation or furtherance of a trade dispute.

In a case where the defendants acted unofficially, contrary to the rules of their union, by ordering picketing and the "blacking" of the plaintiff's business, *held*, their motive was one of anger with their National Executive Council for overruling them by reaching a settlement with another union in respect of who was to operate exclusive union membership and negotiate rights for the men employed in the plaintiff's company. Thus they were not acting genuinely with a view to achieving a trade union objective and an injunction would be granted against them.

PBDS (NATIONAL CARRIERS) LTD v FILKINS [1979] IRLR 356 (Court of Appeal: LORD DENNING MR and TEMPLEMAN LJ). Dictum of Lord Denning MR in *The Camilla M, Star Sea Transport Corporation of Monrovia v Slater* [1978] IRLR 507, CA, at 510, 1978 Halsbury's Abridgment para. 2871 applied.

2833 Advisory, Conciliation and Arbitration Service—statutory duties—validity of decision to defer inquiries pending judicial proceedings

An independent trade union, the Engineers' and Managers' Association (EMA) sought recognition on behalf of professional staff at engineering works. EMA started a recruitment campaign in the works but the Trade Union Congress (TUC) Disputes Committee instructed it to cease recruitment and not to seek recognition. EMA then made an application to the Advisory, Conciliation and Arbitration Service for recognition, and also issued a writ against the TUC claiming that its instructions were invalid. Despite hopes for an early trial, the trial was fixed for March 1980. In deference to this trial ACAS decided to postpone its inquiries as the outcome of the trial would be a material factor in the recognition issue. EMA issued a writ against ACAS asking for a declaration that ACAS had failed to carry out its statutory duty under the Employment Protection Act 1975, s. 14 (1) to ascertain the opinions of the workers concerned within a reasonable period of time. At first instance this was refused and on appeal the questions for the court were whether ACAS had a discretion to defer its inquiries and if so, whether it had had reasonable grounds to do so in this case. *Held*, the requirement to ascertain the opinions of the workers was mandatory, not directory. ACAS did have a discretion as to the method of its inquiries but could not use its discretion to avoid its statutory duty. Nor were the reasons for the delay reasonable in view of the date of the trial and the fact that it had been petitioned by the workers requesting that inquiries be made. Accordingly ACAS had erred in law in considering that it was entitled to wait until the difficulties posed by EMA's legal action against the TUC had been resolved before proceeding with its inquiries and the declaration would be granted.

ENGINEERS' AND MANAGERS' ASSOCIATION v ADVISORY, CONCILIATION AND ARBITRATION SERVICE [1979] IRLR 246 (Court of Appeal: LORD DENNING MR, LAWTON and CUMMING-BRUCE LJJ). Decision of Oliver J [1978] ICR 875, 1978 Halsbury's Abridgment para. 2872 reversed.

This decision has been reversed by the House of Lords; see [1980] 1 All ER 896.

2834 Certification officer—fees

The Certification Officer (Amendment of Fees) Regulations 1979, S.I. 1979 No. 1385 (in force on 1st December 1979), increase certain fees payable to the certification officer and revoke the Certification Officer (Amendment of Fees) Regulations 1978, 1978 Halsbury's Abridgment para. 2875.

2835 Collective bargaining—disclosure of information

A union which was recognized for collective bargaining purposes complained to the Central Arbitration Committee (CAC) that the company had not disclosed to union representatives the full text of a national survey of salaries in the data processing industry. The survey was published by a third party who claimed copyright in it and stated that the survey was confidential to subscribers. The survey was taken into account by the company in determining salary structures; and although the company was prepared to disclose specific statistics to the union it refused to disclose the whole text of the survey. The union claimed that this failure constituted a breach by the company of its duty as an employer to disclose, under the Employment Protection Act 1975, s. 17 (1), information relating to the undertaking, the absence of which would impede collective bargaining and the disclosure of which would constitute good industrial practice. The CAC dismissed the complaint on the ground that the survey did not relate to the company's undertaking and hence did not fall within s. 17. The CAC added that, had its decision been otherwise, it would have regarded the survey as falling within the exception to disclosure provided by s. 18 (1) (b) (prohibition on disclosure of information imposed by an enactment) and also that provided by s. 18 (1) (c) (information disclosed in confidence). See Award no. 78/212 (*Joint Credit Card Co Ltd v National Union of Bank Employees*) available from HMSO.

2836 Legal proceedings—capacity—right to sue in own name for defamation

A trade union claimed that it had been libelled in two articles in the defendant newspaper. As a preliminary issue two questions arose for the court to decide; (i) whether a trade union (not being a special register body) could maintain an action in its own name for damages for defamation in relation to its own reputation as a legal entity and (ii) whether it was able to maintain an action on behalf of each individual member of the union without identifying any particular member, in relation to a publication which impugned their several reputations as members of the union. *Held* (i) after the decision in *Taff Vale Railway Co v Amalgamated Society of Railway Servants* [1901] AC 426, HL, it had become apparent that an unincorporated association had the necessary legal personality for it to be sued in its own name and that had been the basis upon which unions, as quasi-corporate bodies, had sued in libel. In 1971 effect was given to the recommendation that trade unions should be bodies corporate and the Industrial Relations Act 1971 was passed. This was repealed by the Trade Union and Labour Relations Act 1974. Section 2 (1) of the 1974 Act stated unequivocably that a trade union was not and could not be treated as a body corporate. The Act had removed from a trade union a status which had been granted to it from 1901 until 1971 and despite the absurdity of the result, a trade union therefore did not possess the necessary personality which it could protect by an action in defamation. (ii) A representative action was not available to a number of individuals where the relief sought was damages. The individual reputations of the members would be different and insofar as any of them could sue, the damages would also be different.

ELECTRICAL, ELECTRONIC, TELECOMMUNICATION AND PLUMBING UNION V TIMES NEWSPAPERS LTD (1979) 124 Sol Jo 31 (Queen's Bench Division: O'CONNOR J).

2837 —— representation of union—whether counsel necessary

See *Engineer's and Managers' Association v Advisory, Conciliation and Arbitration Service (No. 1)*, para. 574.

2838 Recognition—recommendation by Advisory, Conciliation and Arbitration Service—validity of recommendation

The Advisory, Conciliation and Arbitration Service were asked to decide a question of recognition involving a union that wished to represent the professionally qualified engineers working within a company. There were already a number of unions representing the company's employees, and these unions opposed the recognition of the union. ACAS recommended that the union should not be recognised. The union challenged the recommendation in the High Court and the judge found the ACAS report a nullity and of no effect because ACAS had failed to discharge its duties under the Employment Protection Act 1975. ACAS appealed to the Court of Appeal. *Held*, dismissing the appeal, ACAS had not fulfilled its obligations under s. 12 (4) of the Act because it had not set out its findings in the form of an objective assessment of the case, but merely stated the views of the parties. In particular it had not established whether the engineers were an effective group for collective bargaining purposes who needed separate representation. Furthermore ACAS had not fulfilled its obligations under s. 1 (2). This section laid upon ACAS two duties, namely the improvement of industrial relations and the development and, where necessary, the reform of collective bargaining machinery. Where the two duties clashed it was necessary to weigh the two against each other.

LORD DENNING MR considered the special duty to encourage the development of collective bargaining took priority over the general duty to improve industrial relations, under the maxim *generalia specialibus non derogant*. ACAS had not considered the need to reform the collective bargaining machinery, but had instead based its recommendation entirely upon the objections of the other unions and the possible consequences recognition might have for industrial relations.

UNITED KINGDOM ASSOCIATION OF PROFESSIONAL ENGINEERS v ADVISORY, CONCILATION AND ARBITRATION SERVICE [1979] 2 All ER 478 (Court of Appeal: LORD DENNING MR, LAWTON and BRANDON LJJ).

This decision has been reversed by the House of Lords; see [1980] 1 All ER 612.

2839   The Advisory Conciliation and Arbitration Service were asked to decide a question of recognition involving a union that wished to represent a company's head office employees. The union claimed that 105 of the employees were members. A circular suggesting that there should be a staff council, instead of the union, to negotiate with the management met with little success. A second union expressed an interest in the inquiry, but later withdrew. ACAS sent a questionnaire to all the employees with an accompanying letter. Neither the questionnaire nor the letter mentioned any body other than the union. On the basis of the employees' response to the questionnaire, ACAS recommended that the union should be recognised. The company refused and applied for a declaration that ACAS had misdirected itself submitting that it was the duty of ACAS to ascertain the degree of support for other unions as well as the support for the union named in the questionnaire, and that ACAS acted as no reasonable body could have acted in adopting the questionnaire as the means of ascertaining the opinions of the employees. *Held*, ACAS had not misdirected itself, as there was no evidence that the failure to refer expressly to the second union or the staff council had any distorting effect on the answers to the questionnaire. The Employment Protection Act 1975 conferred on ACAS a discretion as to what inquiries it should make and it was reasonable in this case for ACAS to have regarded as irrelevant the degree of support for other unions. When the questionnaire was sent to the employees, a number of experts thought it appropriate; the decision to use the questionnaire was not, therefore, a decision that no reasonable body could have come to. The application would be dismissed.

NATIONAL EMPLOYERS LIFE ASSURANCE CO LTD v ADVISORY, CONCILIATION AND ARBITRATION SERVICE [1979] IRLR 282 (Chancery Division: BROWNE-WILKINSON J). *Powley v Advisory, Conciliation and Arbitration Service* [1977] IRLR 190, 1977 Halsbury's Abridgment para. 2888 distinguished.

2840   Right to trade union membership and activity—appropriate time—remedy for infringement of right

Industrial tribunal decision:

CARTER v WILTSHIRE COUNTY COUNCIL [1978] IRLR 331 (firemen's independent trade union held meeting, without permission, in social club of fire station after hours; members of union subject to disciplinary action as result; applicant contended this contravened right under Employment Protection Act 1975, s. 53 (1), not to have action taken against him for taking part in independent trade union activities at any appropriate time; employer could not claim exemption from s. 53 solely on ground that activities took place on his premises; appropriate time included the time when applicant entitled to be on premises, at social club; no inconvenience or extra expense incurred by employers; declaration that employers took action against applicant contrary to 1975 Act).

1975 Act, s. 53 (1), now Employment Protection (Consolidation) Act 1978, s. 23.

2841   —— compensation for infringement

Industrial tribunal decision:

CHEALL v VAUXHALL MOTORS LTD [1979] IRLR 253 (security officer was member of ACTSS and later joined APEX; wife died while he was on shift work, and consequently he gave it up, but continued receiving shift allowance; dispute arose between two unions over incorrect transfer procedures, resulting in decision to exclude security officer on six weeks' notice; all representations by APEX on behalf of security officer for an extension of shift allowance payment refused by employers as a consequence of decision; shift payments stopped after two months;

employee contended that right of representation had been infringed as penalisation for membership of APEX, and that employers had contravened s. 53 (1) (a) of Employment Protection Act 1975; she also claimed reimbursement for lost shift allowance; contravention of s. 53 (1) (a) confirmed since employee still union member at time of application; compensation for frustration of lack of representation only, as there was no reason to suppose an extension of allowance would have been forthcoming).

1975 Act, s. 53 now Employment Protection (Consolidation) Act 1978, s. 23.

2842   **Rules—construction—"withdrawal from employment"**

The National Executive Council of the National Union of Journalists voted for an all-out strike of its members employed by provincial newspapers and sanctions and disruptive measures to be applied by its other members. When the strike was settled disciplinary action was taken against those members who had not complied with the union's instructions. Rule 20 (b) of the union's rules provided that no withdrawal from employment affecting a majority of union members could be sanctioned without a ballot. No ballot had been taken. The plaintiffs, members against whom action had been taken, sought an interim injunction to restrain the union from taking further disciplinary action and an order that they would be restored to membership pending trial of the action. It was refused at first instance and on appeal, *held*, the National Executive Council had acted unconstitutionally in calling a strike without holding a membership ballot. "Withdrawal from employment" included not only total strike but partial withdrawal, disruptions and sanctions and those "affected" by the withdrawal constituted a majority of union members. The injunction would therefore be allowed.

PORTER v NATIONAL UNION OF JOURNALISTS [1979] IRLR 404 (Court of Appeal: LORD DENNING MR, SHAW and TEMPLEMAN LJJ).

TRANSPORT

Halsbury's Laws of England (3rd edn.), Vol. 31, paras. 639–1403

2843   **Articulated lorries—vehicle exceeding maximum prescribed length—meaning of indivisible load**

See *Patterson v Redpath Brothers Ltd*, para. 2309.

2844   **Carriage by Air and Road Act 1979**

See para. 289.

2845   **International passenger services**

The Road Transport (International Passenger Services) (Amendment) Regulations 1979, S.I. 1979 No. 654 (in force on 12th July 1979), amend the Road Transport (International Passenger Services) Regulations 1973, S.I. 1973 No. 806, to bring within the scope of the regulations services starting or finishing in a country which is not a member state of the EEC. They also make various other amendments in pursuance of certain Council Regulations (EEC).

2846   **Passenger vehicles—designation of experimental areas**

The Passenger Vehicles (Experimental Areas) Designation Order 1977 (Variation and Extension of Duration) Order 1979, S.I. 1979 No. 1167 (in force on 17th October 1979), deletes the experimental areas specified in the 1977 Order, Sch. paras. 2, 3, 5, 7, 1977 Halsbury's Abridgment para. 2341, and extends the duration of the order for a further two years.

2847   Road haulage workers—remuneration

See *Re R.H.M. Foods*, para. 1118.

2848   Taxi cab—fares for hiring—byelaws

The Hackney Carriage Fares (Amendment of Byelaws) Order 1979, S.I. 1979 No. 722 (in force on 4th July 1979), empowers a local authority to increase taxi fares which are fixed by byelaw, with a view to offsetting higher operating costs attributable to increases in the rates of excise duty on petrol and diesel oil and of value added tax. The power was exercisable by resolution at any time before 31st August 1979 or at the first meeting of the local authority on or after that date. A surcharge of not more than 10p in respect of each hiring is permitted. A notice relating to the surcharge must be displayed.

2849   —— —— London

The London Cab Order 1979, S.I. 1979 No. 706 (in force on 22nd July 1979), increases the existing fares payable for the hiring of a motor cab in the Metropolitan Police District and the City of London in respect of all journeys beginning and ending there. It also increases the extra charges payable for hirings at night, at weekends and on public holidays. If a cab is fitted with a taximeter which is not capable of recording the new fares automatically, a notice setting out the fares payable must be prominently displayed in the cab.

TRESPASS

Halsbury's Laws of England (3rd edn.), Vol. 38, paras. 1194–1282

2850   Trespass to land—drain—connection to private drain from neighbouring property—connection without permission

See *Cook v Minion*, para. 2496.

2851   —— proof of loss—measure of damages

See *Swordheath Properties Ltd v Tabet*, para. 900.

TRUSTS

Halsbury's Laws of England (3rd edn.), Vol. 38, paras. 1346–1833

2852   Articles

Increasing Trustees' Remuneration, F. Graham Glover (the nature and extent of the court's inherent jurisdiction to order the payment of remuneration to trustees): 129 NLJ 501.

Protective Trust: Anachronism or Useful Device?, A. A. Preece (analysis of the scope of the protective trust, as defined in the Trustee Act 1925, s. 33 (1), in financial and tax planning): [1979] LS Gaz 874.

Evidence in Support of Secret Trust, F. Graham Glover (law in the light of *Re Snowdon* [1979] 2 All ER 172, para. 3094): 129 NLJ 1080.

Taxation and Breaches of Trust, J. B. Morcom (an examination of the view of Lord Lindley MR in *Perrins v Bellamy* [1899] 1 Ch 797 that "the main duty of a trustee is to commit judicious breaches of trust"): 129 NLJ 848.

Trustees' Power to Compromise, F. Graham Glover (on whether the bank has the power to compromise an action in the light of s. 15 of the Trustees Act 1925): 129 NLJ 805.

2853   Breach of trust—liability of solicitor's partner

See *Re Bell's Indenture; Bell v Hickley*, para. 2692.

2854   Constructive trust—acquiescence—expenditure on property of another—whether trust created

See *Pascoe v Turner*, para. 1127.

2855   Express trust—creation—moneys paid into segregated account

Canada
A travel agent became insolvent and its clients presented a petition for a declaration that their advance payments for package tours which had been deposited in a "trust account" by the travel agent were held in trust for them. *Held*, the mere fact that the travel agent kept the moneys in a segregated account did not make them trust moneys. There were no specific trust arrangements and the moneys were therefore available to the travel agent's general creditors.

RE H. B. HAINA & ASSOCIATES INC (1978) 86 DLR (2d) 262 (Supreme Court of British Columbia).

2856   Public trustee—fees

The Public Trustee (Fees) (Amendment) Order 1979, S.I. 1979 No. 189 (in force on 1st April 1979), amends the Public Trustee (Fees) Order 1977, 1977 Halsbury's Abridgment para. 2919. It increases the standard rate of the administration fee for estates and trusts accepted before 1st April 1977 and the rate of the income collection fee.

2857   Secret trust—intention of testatrix that beneficiary distribute residuary estate among relatives—whether sufficient evidence of secret trust

See *Re Snowden (Deceased)*, para. 3094.

2858   Superannuation and other trust funds—fees

The Superannuation and other Trust Funds (Fees) Regulations 1979, S.I. 1979 No. 1557 (in force on 1st January 1980), increase the fees payable to the Registrar of Friendly Societies in respect of the registration of amendment of rules of funds and other matters.

2859   Trustee—powers—power to compromise

Under will trusts successive life interests were given to the testator's daughters, then to his grandson. A dispute arose as to whether certain valuable chattels belonged to the daughters absolutely or to the will trusts. The daughters suggested a compromise under the Trustee Act 1925, s. 15 whereby they would retain half the chattels, the other half going to the trusts with the daughters surrendering their life interests in the property, thereby accelerating the grandson's life interest. He opposed the compromise, claiming that without the surrender of the interests the compromise would not reflect the strength of the trustee's claim to the disputed chattels and the surrender of the interests would constitute a variation of the trusts which was outside the powers conferred by s. 15. At first instance the court held that it had jurisdiction to approve the compromise under s. 15. The grandson appealed. *Held*, dismissing the appeal, it could not be argued that the surrender of an interest varied a trust where it merely eliminated the interest, yet left the trusts intact. In deciding whether a compromise was beneficial the trustee was entitled to weigh the prospect of a successful claim against the value of the recovered assets plus the advantages to the continuing beneficiaries from the acceleration of their interests.

RE EARL OF STRAFFORD, ROYAL BANK OF SCOTLAND LTD V BYNG [1979] 1 All ER 513 (Court of Appeal: BUCKLEY, LAWTON and GOFF LJJ).

UNFAIR DISMISSAL

Halsbury's Laws of England (4th edn.), Vol. 16, paras. 615–639:15

2860   Articles

Compensation for Stress in Unfair Dismissal, Andrew Hillier (employees' rights to compensation under the Employment Protection Act 1975): 128 NLJ 1212.

Dismissal and Normal Retiring Age, A. N. Khan (Trade Union and Labour Relations Act 1974, Sch. 1, para. 10 (b) (now Employment Protection (Consolidation) Act 1978, s. 64(1)) in the light of *Nothman v Barnet London Borough Council* [1979] 1 All ER 142, HL, 1978 Halsbury's Abridgment para. 2961): 123 Sol Jo 330.

Dismissal for Activities Outside Working Hours, David Newell (an examination of the fairness of dismissal when it relates to an activity not directly connected with the employment and outside working hours): 123 Sol Jo 511.

2861   Capability or qualifications—health—employee also refusing to accept change in job content—sufficiency of reason for dismissal.

The appellant was employed, according to the terms of her contract of employment, as a copy-typist/general clerical duties clerk. Redundancies were made in the clerical department and as a result she was asked to operate the duplicating machine in addition to her existing duties. She agreed but only worked on the duplicator for a short time claiming that the vapour given off by the fluid caused headaches. Her employers accepted the reaction was genuine and took her off the machine. There were however, no other jobs available in the clerical department and she was offered a job in the accounts department which she refused. She was subsequently dismissed. In an application for unfair dismissal she claimed that there was no contractual authority for her employers to require her to operate the duplicating machine. *Held*, the operation of the machine fell within the ambit of general clerical duties as outlined in her contract. She had, in any case, agreed to work on the duplicator. She had been fairly dismissed on the grounds that she could not operate the machine due to an adverse medical condition and her employers had acted fairly in offering her the only other job available. In a small company where the job description was wide, it was necessary for the employees to understand the need for flexibility.

GLITZ v WATFORD ELECTRIC CO LTD [1979] IRLR 89 (Employment Appeal Tribunal: ARNOLD J presiding).

2862   —— —— express term providing for termination of employment if employee ill—offer of alternative employment

Scotland

An employee commenced employment of a physically demanding nature under a special contract which included a clause ensuring that should he be absent through frequent sickness he would be deemed medically unsuitable and his contract would be terminated. Over a period of three months the employee was absent on a number of occasions, twice for a period of two to three weeks on account of injury. The employee was dismissed on grounds of medical unfitness for work. He appealed against findings that his dismissal had been reasonable by both an industrial tribunal and the Employment Appeal Tribunal. *Held*, although the employers did not consult the employee as to the nature of his injuries and as to his fitness for future employment, and further had failed to offer alternative work, the employee had failed to meet the terms of his contract by being absent so frequently on medical grounds, and had indicated his incapacity for alternative work by removing himself from his place of employment. The appeal would therefore be dismissed.

LEONARD v FERGUS AND HAYNES CIVIL ENGINEERING LTD 1979 SLT (Notes) 38 (Court of Session).

2863   Compensation — assessment — calculation of compensatory award — reduction for contributory conduct of employee

An employee was dismissed and paid ten weeks' wages in lieu of notice. He complained to an industrial tribunal, which found that although his dismissal was unfair his own conduct had contributed to it to the extent of 50 per cent. Accordingly, in awarding compensation the payment in lieu of notice was deducted from the net amount of the compensatory award and the result reduced by half. The employers appealed. *Held*, the appeal on the merits would be dismissed but the amount of the compensatory award would be adjusted since the consequence of the tribunal's method of compensation was to penalise an employer where the dismissal was contributed to by the employee's own conduct. Rather, credit for payment in lieu of notice should be given after the net amount of compensation had been reduced to take account of the employee's own contribution. The award would be reduced accordingly.

CLEMENT-CLARKE INTERNATIONAL LTD v MANLEY [1979] ICR 74 (Employment Appeal Tribunal: KILNER BROWN J presiding).

2864   In the course of an appeal against a reduction of compensation for unfair dismissal, the Court of Appeal stated that, in such a case, an industrial tribunal was required to make three findings: (i) that there was culpable or blameworthy conduct on the part of the employee; (ii) that the conduct related to the complaint (for example of unfair dismissal); (iii) that it was just and equitable to reduce the assessment as a result.

In the case before the court, the compensation had been reduced on the ground that the claimant had contributed to his loss by refusing a reasonable offer of alternative employment. The tribunal had erred in law because the offer was not made as the result of a redundancy but was an attempt to vary his employment within the terms of his contract. Although the employer was entitled to make such variation without his consent, the court found, STEPHENSON LJ dissenting, that the tribunal's error of law was so grave that it vitiated their decision.

NELSON v BBC (No. 2) [1979] IRLR 346 (Court of Appeal: STEPHENSON, GOFF and BRANDON LJJ).

For earlier proceedings see *Nelson v BBC* [1977] IRLR 148, CA, 1977 Halsbury's Abridgment para. 3019.

2865   An employee was offered a job on the understanding that he joined the appropriate trade union. He joined and became employed but due to a disagreement over industrial action he withheld his subscriptions, resulting in fellow employees refusing to work with him and his eventual dismissal. He claimed compensation for unfair dismissal. An industrial tribunal found that by virtue of the Trade Union and Labour Relations Act 1974, Sch 1, para. 15 they had to disregard the pressure on an employer to dismiss an employee when considering whether dismissal was fair and they held the employee to be unfairly dismissed. A basic award of compensation was made but no compensatory award on the grounds that the employee was wholly to blame for his dismissal. The employee appealed against the lack of a compensatory award. *Held*, it was open for the tribunal to consider the employee's contribution to his own dismissal and in exceptional cases could deduct 100 per cent from the compensatory award. The tribunal was justified in doing so for the employee knew he would be unable to work without being a member of the trade union and his conduct was the sole cause of his dismissal.

SULEMANJI v TOUGHENED GLASS LTD [1979] ICR 799 (Employment Appeal Tribunal: SLYNN J presiding).

1974 Act, Sch. 1, para. 15 now Employment Protection (Consolidation) Act 1978, s. 63.

2866   An industrial tribunal found that an employee had been unfairly dismissed but had contributed to his own dismissal so as to reduce the compensatory award by twenty-five per cent in accordance with the Employment Protection (Consolidation) Act 1978, s. 74 (6). In calculating the award, the tribunal assessed the net loss of wages from the date of dismissal until the commencement of a new job. From this sum the payment made in lieu of notice was deducted and then the sum further reduced by twenty-five per cent. On appeal, the company contended that the industrial tribunal had erred in its method of computation, stating that the percentage deduction should have been made from the net loss of wages before the deduction of the payment in lieu, thereby reducing the total award by a substantial amount. *Held*, the industrial tribunal had not erred. In determining an award the tribunal had first to compute the loss attributable to the action taken by the employer and finally, where part of the loss was due to the employee's conduct, a percentage reduction could be made. The appeal would be dismissed.

PARKER AND FARR LTD v SHELVEY [1979] ICR 896 (Employment Appeal Tribunal: BRISTOW J presiding).

2867 —— —— **effect of receiving sickness benefit**

An employee's compensation for unfair dismissal included a sum for loss of wages in the period between her dismissal and the date on which she obtained new employment. During that period the employee had been in receipt of sickness benefit. The employers contended that there was entitlement to sickness benefit only during a period of unemployment and that the amount of the benefit should be deducted from the compensatory award. *Held*, for the purposes of the Social Security Act 1975, s. 17 (1) (c), it did not matter that a person who suffered from an incapacity for work had a current contract of employment. If the employee had been ill but had been paid wages under a continuing contract of employment she would have been entitled to both wages and sickness benefit. There was no ground on which to reduce the compensatory award by the amount of the sickness benefit.

SUN AND SAND LTD (SABLE & SOLEIL) LTD v FITZJOHN [1979] LS Gaz R 101 (Employment Appeal Tribunal: ARNOLD J presiding).

2868 —— —— **loss of future earnings—award for period of unemployment**

An industrial tribunal awarded compensation for unfair dismissal to an employee who refused to join a trade union in contravention of a closed shop agreement made after the commencement of his employment, because he had not been warned of the consequences of his refusal. He appealed against the award for loss of future earnings, which was based on a three month period of unemployment, because he had been unemployed for a longer period. *Held*, there was a maximum period for which such compensation could be awarded. In respect of a person who remained unemployed the period was that from the date of dismissal to the estimated date of re-employment. As the tribunal had correctly based their award on loss to the employee the award would be upheld.

EDWARDS v PETBOW LTD (1978) 13 ITR 431 (Employment Appeal Tribunal: PHILLIPS J presiding).

2869 —— —— **loss of pension rights**

On 3rd December 1973, an employee joined his employer's pension scheme which specified a period of five years before a pension could be drawn. He was unfairly dismissed on 30th November 1977. An industrial tribunal found that his employment would have ended in any case on 31st January 1978. Consequently, of the compensation awarded him, £17 was attributable to loss of pension rights representing two months of his own contributions; his past contributions were refunded under the scheme. The employee appealed against the sum awarded on the ground that he had not been compensated for the loss of the benefit of his employer's contributions during the period of his employment. *Held*, since the employee would not have qualified for a pension under the scheme even if he had not been unfairly dismissed, the tribunal had held correctly that the employee's rights were limited to those to which he was contractually entitled. The appeal would be dismissed.

MANNING v R & H WALE (EXPORT) LTD [1979] ICR 433 (Employment Appeal Tribunal: ARNOLD J presiding).

2870 —— —— —— unreasonable refusal to accept re-instatement

A dismissed employee had been offered re-instatement on terms that a tribunal found to be reasonable, but he had refused to accept the offer. The tribunal held that he had been unfairly dismissed but that, as his refusal of re-instatement had been unreasonable, he had suffered no loss after dismissal, for which his employer was responsible, and a basic award only would be made. The tribunal made no award for loss of pension rights, and under pension arrangements the employee was able to recover only his own contributions and not those made by the employer on his behalf. He appealed, claiming that he should have received a compensatory award in respect of the employer's pension contributions. *Held*, as the employee's refusal of re-instatement had been unreasonable no compensatory award would be made in respect of the employer's contributions. The appeal would therefore be dismissed.

Sweetlove v Redbridge and Waltham Forest Area Health Authority [1979] ICR 477 (Employment Appeal Tribunal: Slynn J presiding).

2871 —— duty to mitigate loss—effect of free-lance earnings on assessment

An industrial tribunal found that the two claimants before it had been unfairly dismissed, and made a compensatory assessment of loss of earnings in respect of each claimant. The employers appealed against the assessment, contending firstly that the tribunal had erred in finding no failure to mitigate loss by registering as unemployed, and secondly that the tribunal had been wrong in not deducting from the award two sums of money earned after dismissal by the claimant. *Held*, the assessment made by the tribunal was a fair one, based on a sensible investigation of the facts. On the first point of appeal, having taken into account the claimant's occupation as an editor, the tribunal judged it unlikely that he would regain employment through registration; the second claimant had registered briefly before finding another job. The tribunal's decision was therefore an acceptable one. On the second point the claimant was entitled to earnings by free-lance work under his contract with the former employers, and therefore an estimate of all likely earnings during the possible period of unemployment had been included when an assessment was made. The appeal would therefore be dismissed.

Penthouse Publications Ltd v Radnor (1978) 13 ITR 528 (Employment Appeal Tribunal: Phillips J presiding).

2872 —— —— opportunity to be considered for vacancies

An employee was awarded compensation by an industrial tribunal when it was found that he had been unfairly dismissed on grounds of redundancy. Of the compensation awarded him, £50 was to take account of the employer's delay in giving him a written reference. The compensation, however, made no allowance for loss of earnings because his former employer had offered to consider him for two new vacancies during the period covered by payment in lieu of notice, and the employee had not applied for either of the jobs. The tribunal held that the employee had failed to mitigate the loss flowing from his dismissal as required by the Employment Protection Act 1975, s. 76 (4). The employee appealed against the decision not to award him compensation for loss of earnings. The employer cross-appealed against the award of £50. *Held*, (i) the duty on an employee to mitigate his loss required him to act reasonably; although there was no duty to take any job that might be offered, the employee had to be reasonable about an offer of employment and take employment that was reasonably and properly offered to him; (ii) A loss consequent upon a failure to give a written reference was not an expense reasonably incurred as a result of a dismissal nor was it the loss of any benefit which an employee might reasonably be expected to have had but for the dismissal, within s. 76 (3) of the 1975 Act. Further, there was no duty upon an employer to give a dismissed employee a written reference, and the award of £50 was inconsistent with the finding that the employee had failed to mitigate his loss. Accordingly, the employee's appeal would be dismissed, and the cross-appeal would be allowed.

GALLEAR V J. F. WATSON & SON LTD [1979] IRLR 306 (Employment Appeal Tribunal: TALBOT J presiding).

1975 Act, s. 76 (3), (4) now Employment Protection (Consolidation) Act 1978, s. 74 (3), (4).

2873   —— —— reduction of award on failure to mitigate loss

The employee, a chef, was dismissed in November 1977, remaining unemployed until April 1978 and during that period he applied for several jobs. His complaint of unfair dismissal succeeded before an industrial tribunal but it was found that had he tried harder he could have found a job earlier, and thus had failed to mitigate his loss. The tribunal arrived at the compensation award by assessing his total of earnings and then deducted 40 per cent for failure to mitigate his loss. The employee appealed against the compensation award. *Held*, the industrial tribunal, when assessing the amount of a deduction for failure to mitigate loss, should not reduce the whole award by a percentage, but rather decide on a date by which the employee should have found employment, and assess his loss up to that date. The appeal would be allowed and the case remitted to the tribunal.

PEARA V ENDERLIN LTD [1979] ICR 804 (Employment Appeal Tribunal: TALBOT J presiding).

2874   —— increase of limit

The Unfair Dismissal (Increase of Compensation Limit) Order 1979, S.I. 1979 No. 1723 (in force on 1st February 1980), increases from £5,750 to £6,250 the limit on the amount of compensation which can be awarded by an industrial tribunal in claims for unfair dismissal as the compensatory award or as compensation for failure to comply fully with the terms of an order for reinstatement or re-engagement. The Unfair Dismissal (Increase of Compensation Limit) Order 1978, 1978 Halsbury's Abridgment para. 2926 is revoked.

2875   —— loss of pension rights—calculation of loss

An employee was found to have been unfairly dismissed and, in assessing his compensatory award, an industrial tribunal took into account the loss of pension rights. Under the particular pension scheme operated, the employer did not make fixed contributions in respect of individual employees, but paid the gross sum required over and above the employees' contributions to provide the benefits payable under the scheme. Another feature of the scheme was that the contributions made by an employee in the early years were in excess of what was actually required to purchase the pension to which he was at that time entitled. In later years however, the rights bought were not covered by the employee's own contributions. The dismissed employee was given a refund of his contributions but an industrial tribunal also gave him a sum in respect of loss of future pension rights. On appeal by the employer, *held*, when the employee was dismissed he had lost a valuable benefit, the right to pay contributions when he was older which would have been less than actually required by his pension. He was entitled to compensation for loss of that benefit. Although no specific sum had been allocated by the employer to the credit of any individual, the employer had paid an annual sum amounting to 14 per cent of the total salaries of the employees to the scheme and this percentage would be regarded as a notional payment in respect of the dismissed employee in calculating the award. Further, the employee was entitled to a sum in respect of the fact that he might not have the advantage of such a beneficial pension scheme in any future employment and that he may have voluntarily terminated his employment in the future and received an accelerated lump sum payment. The industrial tribunal's assessment would be upheld.

WILLMENT BROS LTD V OLIVER [1970] IRLR 393 (Employment Appeal Tribunal: SLYNN J presiding).

2876   —— qualifying period—temporary cessation of work

See *Wessex National Ltd v Long*, para. 1038.

2877   —— right to compensation—existence of contract of employment

See *Barthorpe v Exeter Diocesan Board of Finance*, para. 1042.

2878   Complaint to industrial tribunal—jurisdiction—dismissal on grounds of pregnancy—whether need for twenty-six weeks continuous employment

See *Singer v Millward Ladsky and Co*, para. 2929.

2879   —— right to bring complaint prior to termination of employment—notice of termination given by employee

An employee gave notice of the termination of his employment on the grounds that the conduct of his employers amounted to a constructive dismissal, and presented a complaint of unfair dismissal before an industrial tribunal. The tribunal held that it had no jurisdiction to hear the complaint prior to the termination of the employment, since the Trade Union and Labour Relations Act 1974, Sch. 1, para. 21 (4A) (as added by the Employment Protection Act 1975, Sch. 16, Pt. III, para. 21) applied only to cases where the notice had been given by the employer. The employee appealed. *Held*, the meaning of "notice" in para. 21 (4A) was not restricted to notice by the employer, and accordingly the tribunal had jurisdiction to hear a complaint by an employee after he had given notice but prior to the termination of the employment. The appeal would be allowed.

Presley v Llanelli Borough Council [1979] ICR 419 (Employment Appeal Tribunal: Talbot J presiding).

1974 Act, Sch. 1, para. 21 (4A) now Employment Protection (Consolidation) Act 1978, s. 67 (4).

2880   —— time limit—date of dismissal—discovery of documents

An employee was told that he was to be retired on health grounds but that he could appeal against this decision on production of a fitness certificate issued by his own doctor. He was dismissed on 14th January 1977 and his appeal was dismissed by the medical board on 27th May. An industrial tribunal decided that his claim that he had been unfairly dismissed, which was received by the Central Council of Industrial Tribunals on 29th June, had been presented in time and that he should have been given copies of both the medical report and the board's findings. The employers appealed. *Held*, where an employee who was retired on health grounds failed on his appeal, the effective date of termination of his contract returned to the date when he was originally informed of his dismissal, since the effect of the appeal was to confirm the original decision. Accordingly the employee had been dismissed on 14th January and his claim that he had been unfairly dismissed had been presented out of time. The tribunal had also erred in holding that the employee should have been given access to the medical report, because an applicant should never be permitted to see confidential documents.

Crown Agents for Overseas Governments and Administration v Lawal [1978] IRLR 542 (Employment Appeal Tribunal: Kilner Brown J presiding).

2881   Conduct—breach of company rules—claim for reinstatement

A gatekeeper was found asleep whilst on duty and was dismissed. He was invited to give an explanation of his conduct only after the decision to dismiss him had been communicated to him. A right of appeal against the decision lay with the company's disciplinary committee. An industrial tribunal found that his dismissal was unfair but refused to allow reinstatement on the basis that it would not be "expedient" to do so. The company appealed against the finding of unfair dismissal and the gatekeeper cross-appealed against the refusal to allow reinstatement. *Held*, the company had acted unreasonably in dismissing the gatekeeper without giving him an opportunity to explain his conduct before the decision to dismiss was taken. The fact that he was allowed to appeal against the dismissal did not dispense with the requirement of inviting an explanation. The industrial tribunal had erred however in refusing to make a reinstatement order on the basis of "expediency". The factors to be taken into account, in deciding whether or not to make a reinstatement order, were clearly set out in the Employment Protection Act 1975, s. 71. The finding of unfair dismissal would stand and the case would be returned to the tribunal for their consideration as to whether reinstatement should be made.

QUALCAST (WOLVERHAMPTON) LTD V ROSS [1979] IRLR 98 (Employment Appeal Tribunal: ARNOLD J presiding).

1975 Act, s. 71 now Employment Protection (Consolidation) Act 1978, s. 70.

2882 —— breach of disciplinary rules—sufficiency of breach as reason for dismissal

Employers, who were investigating the running of one of their betting shops where they suspected fraudulent practices were being carried on, discovered that two employees had at one time placed bets on behalf of other people. One had placed bets for two old age pensioners and the other for her brother. This practice was expressly forbidden by the employers' disciplinary rules and conditions of employment and the employees were dismissed. An industrial tribunal found the dismissals unfair. On appeal by the employers, *held*, express contractual terms of a disciplinary code did not exclude an industrial tribunal's discretion to consider whether an employer had acted reasonably in dismissing employees. In the present case the employers' attitude had been too extreme and the tribunal's conclusion had been correct.

LADBROKE RACING LTD V ARNOTT [1979] IRLR 192 (Employment Appeal Tribunal: LORD MCDONALD MC presiding).

2883 —— clocking in another employee—sufficiency of reason for dismissal

An employee clocked in a fellow worker half an hour before he appeared for work. This was detected by television recording apparatus but when he was challenged the employee denied it and accused another person of making false statements against him. He was summarily dismissed. The company's induction booklet stated that if a person clocked another in he was liable to instant dismissal. In an application for compensation for unfair dismissal, the employee contended that the offence had never been specifically defined as one which would result in instant dismissal and that it was reasonable to suppose that a first offence would not necessarily lead to dismissal. *Held*, there was no rule of law that a warning had to precede instant dismissal. The Appeal Tribunal was satisfied that the offence and the conduct of the employee were sufficient reasons for dismissal and the employers had acted reasonably. The dismissal was fair.

ELLIOT BROTHERS (LONDON) LTD V COLVERD [1979] IRLR 92 (Employment Appeal Tribunal: TALBOT J presiding).

2884 —— criminal offence—possession of cannabis

An advisory drama teacher was convicted by magistrates of possession and cultivation of cannabis. He was dismissed from his employment as a result and complained to the industrial tribunal, which found his dismissal unfair. On appeal, *held*, there was no rule that dismissal for a criminal offence was automatically fair or unfair. Each case was dependent upon its facts. The teacher was mainly concerned with the training of teachers, not of children, and was of previous good character. The tribunal had not erred in law in finding his dismissal unfair in all the circumstances.

NORFOLK COUNTY COUNCIL V BERNARD [1979] IRLR 220 (Employment Appeal Tribunal: TALBOT J presiding).

2885   —— —— theft—summary dismissal—reasonableness

Three roof insulators were summarily dismissed after having been charged by the police with theft of property from a house in which they were working. The employer's labour officer, when informed of the charges, did not attempt to find out the identity of the men or the nature of the allegations against them. The employer, however, dismissed the men on his advice. The three men claimed that they had been unfairly dismissed. An industrial tribunal found that the employer did not, in the circumstances, have reasonable grounds for supposing that the men had committed the offence, and therefore no ground for dismissing them. The employer appealed. *Held*, in order to show that a dismissal for suspected dishonesty was fair, an employer had to show that he believed that the employee had committed the offence, that he had reasonable grounds for holding that belief, and that he had formed the belief on those grounds following upon as much investigation as was reasonable in the circumstances. Here, the employer had made no further inquiries whatsoever and the mere fact of a charge of theft being preferred was not sufficient grounds. Further, the employer should have given independent consideration to the position of each employee and should not have made "blanket" dismissals. The dismissals were, accordingly, unfair. The appeal would be dismissed.

SCOTTISH SPECIAL HOUSING ASSOCIATION v COOKE [1979] IRLR 264 (Employment Appeal Tribunal: LORD MCDONALD MC presiding). *British Home Stores Ltd v Burchell* [1978] IRLR 397, 1978 Halsbury's Abridgment para. 2938 applied. *Carr v Alexander Russell Ltd* [1976] IRLR 220, 1976 Halsbury's Abridgment para. 2725 distinguished.

2886   —— —— —— whether employee entitled to put his case

During police investigations into widespread thefts from the respondent employers the appellant was accused of stealing certains goods. The police informed the employers and, in accordance with the terms of his contract of employment, the appellant was dismissed. Although the appellant was aware of the reasons for the dismissal he made no attempt to offer an explanation or to invoke the grievance procedure. He appealed against an industrial tribunal's finding that the dismissal was fair, contending that there was an established principle that an employee should be given an opportunity to offer an explanation. *Held*, there was no requirement that an employee should be given an opportunity to explain his conduct in a situation when such an opportunity would make no difference to the employer's decision to dismiss. The employers had acted reasonably on receiving the police information by implementing the contractual terms which stated that theft of company property would result in dismissal. The appellant had made no attempt to explain his conduct at the appropriate time or to implement the grievance procedure. His appeal would be dismissed.

PARKER v CLIFFORD DUNN LTD [1979] IRLR 56 (Employment Appeal Tribunal: ARNOLD J presiding).

2887   —— dishonesty—false claims of hours worked—summary dismissal

A bus driver who was believed to have finished a shift early was watched twice by inspectors without his knowledge and was seen to leave early on both occasions. They filed a complaint and he was dismissed immediately on the grounds that he had left the premises without permission and recorded hours which he had not worked. An industrial tribunal rejected his claim that he had been unfairly dismissed. On appeal, *held*, false claims of hours worked were serious offences of dishonesty which would entitle an employer to dismiss employees summarily. The industrial tribunal had therefore been correct in deciding that the driver had been fairly dismissed although the employer's rule relating to instant dismissal did not state that dismissal would take effect automatically for offences of dishonesty.

STEWART v WESTERN SMT CO LTD [1978] IRLR 553 (Employment Appeal Tribunal: SLYNN J presiding).

2888   —— —— theft from employer—summary dismissal—reasonableness

An employee was summarily dismissed when a quantity of copper belonging to his
employer was found in his garden by the police. He was charged with theft and
subsequently convicted. The employee claimed that he had been unfairly
dismissed. An industrial tribunal held that his dismissal was unfair because the
employer had not asked him for an explanation for his conduct. They further held
that the explanation which he would have given (that it was common practice for
employees to take scrap copper and known to the site agent) would have meant that
he would not have been dismissed. The employer appealed. *Held*, where an
employee reasonably appeared to have been caught red-handed, dismissal without
further investigation might be appropriate depending on the circumstances of the
case. As the employee had been found in possession of stolen goods belonging to the
employer, the failure of the employer to demand an explanation before dismissing
him was not such as to render the dismissal unfair. Further, the explanation that the
employee would have given for his conduct had he had the opportunity would not
have prevented his dismissal. On the evidence, no reasonable tribunal could have
reached the conclusion that the employee reasonably believed that he was entitled to
use his employer's property in this way. The appeal would accordingly be allowed.

SCOTTISH SPECIAL HOUSING ASSOCIATION v LINNEN [1979] IRLR 265 (Employment Appeal Tribunal: LORD McDONALD MC presiding).

2889   —— internal appeal—dismissal confirmed on new grounds—admissibility of second reason

A large sum of money was found to be missing at an employer's area headquarters,
but there was no sign that the office had been broken into. The employer concluded
that either the area manager or his assistant had taken the money, because only they
knew the safe combination, and dismissed both men. The manager utilised an
internal appeal procedure but the employer confirmed his dismissal on the ground
that he had not acted responsibly in his exercise of control over the money and was
in breach of trust. An industrial tribunal found that his dismissal was fair on both
grounds. On appeal, *held*, where it could not be ascertained which of two employees
had committed a theft neither could be fairly dismissed and therefore the tribunal
had erred in their finding that the manager had been fairly dismissed on that
ground. However, the employer was able to rely on the reasons given later because
the manager's internal appeal had amounted to a rehearing. It was clearly possible
to dismiss an employee for a variety of reasons provided there was a reason which
was sufficient to justify a dismissal. The manager's breach of trust had clearly been
such a reason and therefore the dismissal had been fair.

MONIE v CORAL RACING LTD [1979] ICR 254 (Employment Appeal Tribunal:
KILNER BROWN J presiding).

2890   —— refusal to reimburse employers for stock deficiency—employers' failure to give written reasons for dismissal—reasonableness of dismissal

A steward at a club was required by his contract of employment to make up any cash
or stock deficiencies. When a deficiency of £1,300 occurred, the club asked the
steward to sign a letter instructing him to make good the deficit and warning him
that he would be liable to instant dismissal in the event of future stock deficiencies.
The steward refused to sign the letter and was dismissed. He asked for the reasons
for his dismissal to be set down in writing in accordance with the Employment
Protection Act 1975, s. 70, which was not complied with within the statutory
fourteen days. An industrial tribunal held that his conduct in refusing to sign the
letter was a repudiation of a material term in his contract and justified his dismissal.
They failed to discuss the complaint under s. 70. On appeal, *held*, the industrial
tribunal had failed to decide whether the refusal to sign was a sufficient reason for
dismissal in the circumstances, and that part of the case would be remitted to a
different tribunal for consideration. The tribunal had also erred in not considering
the complaint under s. 70. However, mere failure to comply with a request for

written reasons did not amount to an unreasonable refusal. The refusal itself had to be unreasonable and there had been no refusal in this case, merely a breakdown in communications between the club and its solicitors. That part of the appeal would accordingly be dismissed.

LOWSON V PERCY MAIN AND DISTRICT SOCIAL CLUB AND INSTITUTE LTD [1979] IRLR 227 (Employment Appeal Tribunal: BRISTOW J presiding).

1975 Act, s. 70 now Employment Protection (Consolidation) Act 1978, s. 53.

2891 Constructive dismissal—abolition of standby duties for full time firemen—whether change in contract by notice a consensual variation

The terms and conditions of firemen's employment drawn up by the National Joint Council of Local Authorities' Fire Brigades, which represented both the employers and the Fire Brigades Union, permitted full time firemen to volunteer for standby duties on the same basis as retained firemen. Those terms were incorporated into the contracts of firemen who chose to undertake such dutes. In 1974 the union recommended the abolition of retained duties in order to facilitate negotiations for a better basic rate of pay and the firemen who protested were ultimately expelled from the union. The union policy was accepted in principle by the National Joint Council in 1975. The defendant employers requested those of their men affected to vary their contracts by excluding the retained element. Two of the dissidents regarded the change as a dismissal and claimed compensation for unfair dismissal. An industrial tribunal considered that there had been a consensual variation of the contract and dismissed the claim. On appeal, *held,* where an employee continued work after an important part of his contract had been terminated with notice, this would not normally amount to a consensual variation but to re-engagement under a new contract. However, the employee would retain his right to claim compensation for unfair dismissal in respect of the old contract. The claim would in this case be dismissed, because the employers had been obliged to carry out National Joint Council policy and had treated the employees as fairly as possible in the circumstances.

LAND AND WILSON V WEST YORKSHIRE METROPOLITAN COUNTY COUNCIL [1979] ICR 452 (Employment Appeal Tribunal: KILNER BROWN J presiding). *Marriott v Oxford and District Co-operative Society Ltd (No. 2)* [1970] 1 QB 186 distinguished.

2892 —— circumstances entitling employee to terminate employment—breach of mutual trust and confidence

The employee, who had worked for his employers for eighteen years, had an argument with an assistant manager. During the course of the argument there was a certain amount of provocative observation on both sides culminating in the assistant manager's comment "you can't do your bloody job anyway". This was not his true opinion but the employee reacted by resigning. On a question of whether the behaviour of the employer had constituted such a breach of contract that the employee was entitled to treat himself as discharged, *held,* there was an implied term in a contract that an employer would not conduct himself in a manner calculated to destroy or seriously damage the relationship of mutual trust and confidence between the parties. The statement of the assistant manager, particularly when it was not his true opinion, amounted to a breach of this implied term. The employee had been constructively dismissed.

COURTAULDS NORTHERN TEXTILES LTD V ANDREW [1979] IRLR 84 (Employment Appeal Tribunal: ARNOLD J presiding).

2893 —— —— contractual term of liability for cash deficiencies

A petrol pump forecourt attendant did not have a contract in writing, although it had been agreed on her engagement that she would be responsible for a proportion of any cash shortages arising whilst she was on duty. A series of cash deficiences arose at the petrol station and the employers concluded they were due to dishonesty. They deducted a proportion of the loss from the attendants' wages, believing themselves entitled to do so under the contract of employment. The attendant claimed this was in breach of contract and that she was entitled to resign and claim that she had been constructively dismissed. *Held*, it was necessary to imply a term in the contract limiting the expressed absolute liability. It was not reasonable that the contract would operate expressly so that the attendant would be liable for all deficiences no matter what the cause. No employee would have been willing to be engaged as an attendant if all losses, no matter how occasioned, were to be paid for. The employers had repudiated the contract and the attendant had been unfairly dismissed.

BRISTOL GARAGE (BRIGHTON) LTD v LOWEN [1979] IRLR 86 (Employment Appeal Tribunal: ARNOLD J presiding).

2894   —— —— employer's failure to make overtime payments

It was agreed that the manageress of an off-licence could claim overtime for the hours she worked in excess of her basic thirty-two-hour week over the Christmas period. She worked eighty-eight hours' overtime during the period. The manageress was not paid for the overtime when her next weekly wage became due. She received promises of payment from her employer's personnel department, but they were not fulfilled. On 24th February, she was paid for forty of the eighty-eight overtime hours. She telephoned the secretary at her employer's head office and was informed that she would only receive the forty hours' overtime. This was then confirmed by the area manager. The manageress finally spoke to the assistant area manager who told her that he would look into the matter and ring her back. She replied that if she did not hear from him by the following day, she would resign. He did not telephone her the next day, and so she handed in her notice. The manageress claimed that she had been constructively dismissed, and that the dismissal had been unfair. An industrial tribunal dismissed her application. The manageress appealed. *Held*, when the manageress was told that she was not going to be paid the forty-eight hours' overtime that was due to her, the employer had committed a breach going to the very root of the contract of employment. The subsequent promise by the assistant area manager to look into the matter did not affect the fact of this fundamental breach. When that promise was not fulfilled, the manageress had been entitled to accept the repudiation of the contract by the employer and to treat it as at an end. The appeal would be allowed.

STOKES v HAMPSTEAD WINE CO LTD [1979] IRLR 298 (Employment Appeal Tribunal: TALBOT J presiding).

2895   —— —— failure of employer to deal with victimisation by fellow employees

An employee was being ostracised by her fellow employees. The situation became so intolerable that she resigned, and an industrial tribunal upheld her claim that she had been constructively dismissed. On appeal, *held*, the employers had been in breach of a contractual term to render reasonable support to the respondent employee, to ensure that she could carry out her duties without disruption and harassment from her fellow workers. The onus of proof was on the employers to show that there were no reasonable steps that could have been taken to comply with this obligation and the employer had failed to discharge this onus of proof. The appeal would be dismissed.

WIGAN BOROUGH COUNCIL v DAVIES [1979] IRLR 127 (Employment Appeal Tribunal: ARNOLD J presiding).

2896   —— —— failure to pay salary on due date—whether fundamental breach

A senior consultant with a firm of management consultants which relied heavily on income from overseas was told that his salary for April 1977 was to be paid out of money due from an Argentinian company. He had had some difficulty when he tried to present his February salary cheque and when payment of the April cheque was delayed because the Argentinian credit had not arrived, he elected to treat it as conduct on the part of his employer entitling him to resign. He appealed against an industrial tribunal's rejection of his claim that he had been unfairly dismissed. *Held*, an employee would not always be entitled to treat his employer's failure to pay his salary on the due date as a breach which entitled him to resign. The consultant had known that his employer was eager to pay his salary as soon as the Argentinian credit arrived and had raised no objection when he first learned that the payment would be delayed due to circumstances beyond the employer's control. The employers had not evinced any intention not to be bound by an essential term of the contract and therefore the breach had not been so serious as to go to the root of the contract. Accordingly the consultant had not been entitled to resign.

ADAMS v CHARLES ZUB ASSOCIATES LTD [1978] IRLR 551 (Employment Appeal Tribunal: SLYNN J presiding).

2897   —— —— **fundamental breach of contract by employer**

An industrial tribunal found that an employee had been constructively dismissed after she had terminated her employment, following her employer's refusal to provide her with a junior to assist her in her work as a hairdresser, which was an implied condition of her contract of employment. The employee refused to avail herself of the employer's grievance procedure. The employer appealed against both the finding of the tribunal and the assessment of compensation. *Held*, the employer was in fundamental breach of a condition of the contract, as the breach went to the root of the contract. There was no duty on the employee to use the grievance procedure, as the fundamental breach entitled her to treat the contract as at an end. Further, there would be no reduction in the award made to the employee, as the tribunal had already taken into account the employee's failure to mitigate any loss when assessing the award. As there was no obligation on the employee to use the grievance procedure, the tribunal had been right in not taking her failure to do so into consideration when assessing compensation.

SELIGMAN AND LATZ LTD v MCHUGH [1979] IRLR 130 (Employment Appeal Tribunal: TALBOT J presiding).

2898   —— —— **requirements in excess of contractual terms**

The employee became the warden of a council-run estate for old people which provided communal facilities and a communication system linking the flatlets to the warden's residence. The employee knew that she was expected to be on call for five days each week but thought she was allowed to leave her post provided all her duties were covered. Her working week was thirty-seven hours in accordance with a collective agreement with the council. The employee was dissatisfied with her conditions of employment and wrote a letter of complaint to the housing department which remained unanswered. The employee raised the matter with a housing visitor who led her to understand that she was to stay within earshot of the intercommunication system five days a week. The employee attempted to comply with this requirement but became ill. The matter was raised again with the same result culminating in the employee immediately terminating her employment. The industrial tribunal found that the council by insisting that the employee remained on the premises for five days a week had repudiated the contract and the employee was by virtue of the Trade Union and Labour Relations Act 1974, Sch. 1, para. 5 (2) (c) to be treated as having been dismissed. *Held*, the council had repudiated the contract and the employee had therefore been constructively dismissed. It was for the council to prove the reason for dismissal and since no reason had been given the tribunal had not erred in law in failing to consider under Sch. 1, para. 6 (8) of the Act whether the council had acted reasonably in dismissing the employee.

DERBY CITY COUNCIL v MARSHALL [1979] ICR 731 (Employment Appeal Tribunal: BRISTOW J presiding).

1974 Act, Sch. 1 paras. 5 (2) and 6 (8) now Employment Protection (Consolidation) Act 1978, ss. 55 (2) and 57 (3).

2899   —— —— **test to be applied**

The employee, who worked in the information office of a railway station, became involved in a heated argument with members of the public. This resulted in a disciplinary hearing and the employee was dismissed. He exercised the right of appeal contained in his contract of employment and, two months after his purported dismissal, the dismissal was replaced by transfer to another job. When he reported for the new job the employee discovered that he would not get the shift and Sunday working allowances which he had previously received. As this involved a substantial drop in his earnings he resigned. An industrial tribunal held that the employee had never been dismissed and that the circumstances of his resignation did not constitute constructive dismissal. On the employee's appeal *held*, the industrial tribunal had reached the correct conclusion. As the employee had exercised the right of appeal contained in his contract of employment that contract was still in existence, and he could not have been dismissed. The circumstances did not constitute constructive dismissal as the new position offered to the appellant was in the same grade as his previous job and there was nothing in the employers' behaviour to indicate that they intended to break the contract of employment.

HIGH v BRITISH RAILWAYS BOARD [1979] IRLR 52 (Employment Appeal Tribunal: TALBOT J presiding).

2900   An employee worked in a garage. His employment included a variety of unskilled duties of a general nature, but he devoted a quarter of his time to car hire reception work. The employee liked reception work, but his employer was not entirely satisfied with the way in which he performed this aspect of his duties. The employer informed him that he would no longer be required to work at the car hire reception. The employee objected. He resigned and claimed that the employer's refusal to allow him to continue performing his car hire reception duties amounted to constructive dismissal. A Scottish industrial tribunal found that the employer was in significant breach of contract, entitling the employee to terminate his employment without notice. The employer appealed. *Held*, the tribunal had erred in law as they had clearly applied a test of reasonableness, rather than the proper test, a contractual one. The employee was not employed as a car hire receptionist and the employer was not contractually bound to retain him on reception duties. It could not be held that an alteration of his general duties amounted either to a material breach going to the root of the contract of employment or an indication that the employer no longer intended to be bound by an essential term of the contract. The appeal would be allowed.

PETER CARNIE & SON LTD v PATON [1979] IRLR 260 (Employment Appeal Tribunal: LORD McDONALD MC presiding). *Western Excavating (ECC) Ltd v Sharp* [1978] 1 All ER 713, CA, 1977 Halsbury's Abridgment para. 2960 applied.

2901   **Contract of employment**

See EMPLOYMENT.

2902   **Dismissal procedure—consideration of individual case**

Due to a reorganisation by their employers the appellants were required to extend their working week by eleven hours. The employers and the staff association had entered into an agreement to that effect, but the appellants felt that their individual situations had not been properly considered and refused to go along with the new arrangement. An industrial tribunal found that their subsequent dismissals were fair as the employers had consulted the staff association over the proposed changes. On appeal, *held*, the industrial tribunal had erred in holding that the dismissals were fair because there had been consultation with the staff association. The proper approach was to examine the contract of employment and see whether the employer was unilaterally enforcing a change in the original contract. Proper handling of such a unilateral variation of the contract involved consideration of the position of individual employees. The case would be remitted to a different tribunal for consideration on these grounds.

MARTIN v AUTOMOBILE PROPRIETARY LTD [1979] IRLR 64 (Employment Appeal Tribunal: KILNER BROWN J presiding).

2903   —— **employee absent from disciplinary hearing—whether breach of natural justice—procedure for order of re-engagement**

An employee was dismissed for failing to obey an order from his foreman. At the disciplinary hearing the employee was represented by two shop stewards, but he was not present when the foreman gave his version of what had happened, nor at the appeal hearing which confirmed his dismissal. An industrial tribunal decided he had been unfairly dismissed on the ground that there had been a breach of natural justice because he had not been present when important evidence was given. It made an order for re-engagement on terms to be agreed between the parties. The employers appealed. *Held*, it was not necessary for an employee to be personally present for the rules of natural justice to be complied with and in this case the employee had been adequately represented by his shop stewards. The tribunal had also erred in failing to follow precisely the procedure laid down in Employment Protection (Consolidation) Act 1978, s. 68 (1) relating to the making of an order of re-engagement and in not setting out the terms of re-engagement. There was insufficient evidence for the appeal tribunal to decide whether the dismissal had been unfair and therefore the case would be remitted to a differently constituted tribunal.

PIRELLI GENERAL CABLE WORKS LTD v MURRAY [1979] IRLR 190 (Employment Appeal Tribunal: BRISTOW J presiding).

2904   —— **failure to comply with procedure—breach of natural justice**

Two employees engaged in a fight at their employer's premises. Both alleged that the other had begun the fight and each was interviewed separately by the personnel officer, following which one employee was dismissed. He appealed against the decision and was interviewed by the financial controller, contrary to the company's procedure which provided for a director to hear such appeals. Further, neither the other party nor the witnesses to the incident were present, and copies of statements of the latter were not made available to the employee. He was thus ignorant of the case against him and unable to challenge it. The decision was confirmed and the employee applied for compensation for unfair dismissal to an industrial tribunal, which found that although prima facie he had been involved in conduct justifying dismissal it was unfair, on the grounds that it had not been equitably dealt with. The company appealed. *Held*, in a case of this kind natural justice required that a man should know in one way or another what was being said against him in order properly to put forward his own case. Accordingly, in the light of the facts found by the tribunal, coupled with the less significant reason that the company had departed from its own procedure, the tribunal had been entitled to conclude that the dismissal was unfair. The appeal would be dismissed.

BENTLEY ENGINEERING CO LTD v MISTRY [1979] ICR 47 (Employment Appeal Tribunal: SLYNN J presiding).

2905   —— —— **lack of consultation with trade union**

An employee was dismissed for misconduct. The employers did not follow the disciplinary procedure agreed between them and the trade union, in that they did not inform an official of the union of their intention to dismiss the employee. An industrial tribunal held the dismissal had been fair. On appeal, *held*, the employers' failure to follow the procedure was unreasonable. Under the terms of the procedure the employers were exempt from informing the union before dismissal only where to do so would have been impossible. There was no evidence that it had been impossible in this case. Furthermore there was a possibility that had an official been notified of the employers' intentions he might have persuaded the employers to impose a less severe punishment. The appeal would be allowed.

BAILEY v BP OIL (KENT REFINERY) LTD [1979] IRLR 150 (Employment Appeal Tribunal: ARNOLD J presiding).

2906   —— —— **refusal of right of representation**

Five salesmen were dismissed when their employers discovered that they had been falsifying their expenses claims. At a subsequent disciplinary hearing their employers refused to allow them to be represented by either a trade union official or a solicitor, contrary to their agreed procedure. An industrial tribunal upheld the salesmen's claim that they had been unfairly dismissed because their employers had been unreasonable in refusing to allow representation at the disciplinary hearing. The employers appealed, and argued that their conduct of the disciplinary hearing was irrelevant because it took place after the effective date of dismissal. *Held*, an employee who had been accused of serious criminal conduct was entitled to representation at any disciplinary hearing and the industrial tribunal had therefore been correct in its conclusion that the employer had acted unreasonably. It did not matter that the hearing had been conducted after the effective date of dismissal, because had the dismissals been rescinded there would have been continuity of employment.

RANK XEROX (UK) LTD v GOODCHILD [1979] IRLR 185 (Employment Appeal Tribunal: TALBOT J presiding).

2907   —— —— result of non-compliance

A driver and another man were dismissed for theft from their employers, and the managing director investigated the matter. A shop steward admitted that he had been technically involved in the theft, that he had not participated in it, but was aware of it and would get a share of the proceeds. He was interviewed without a full-time union official to represent him and the company's disciplinary procedure was not followed. He contended that he had been unfairly dismissed in that had the proper procedure been followed the company would have taken the shop steward's particular circumstances, the nature of his involvement and his good record into account and a lesser penalty than dismissal would have been imposed. *Held*, where the proper procedures had not been carried out, the proper course was to decide whether, on a balance of probabilities, the result would have been the same if they had been carried out. Further, whether, in view of the information the employers would have received had the procedures been carried out, their decision would have been reversed. Neither of these tests had been satisfied and the shop steward had been unfairly dismissed.

BRITISH LABOUR PUMP CO LTD v BYRNE [1979] IRLR 94 (Employment Appeal Tribunal: SLYNN J presiding).

2908   —— whether employer under duty to provide procedure

In a case concerning a complaint of unfair dismissal by a housemistress at a girls' public school, the Employment Appeal Tribunal stated that there was no principle of law or statutory requirement that an employer had to provide a grievance procedure, so that when a dispute between an employer and an employee arose the matter could be taken to a higher and impartial authority for investigation. The Code of Practice had been designed for industry and large enterprises and was net necessarily appropriate in the context of an independent school with a staff of forty. The housemistress was responsible to the headmistress and it was not unfair for the former to answer directly to the latter or to the board of governors.

ROYAL NAVAL SCHOOL v HUGHES [1979] IRLR 383 (Employment Appeal Tribunal: BRISTOW J presiding).

2909   Employment

See EMPLOYMENT

2910   Excluded employment—age limit—normal retiring age

An employee's contract of employment stated that both the pensionable age and normal retiring age were sixty-five. In 1973 his employers changed their pension scheme so that the employees were to be pensioned at sixty-two, and the employee consented to this in writing. Details of the scheme were laid out in a booklet which gave employees the right to ask to remain in their employment until they were sixty-five. The employee claimed that right, but was told that he was to retire at sixty-two. He claimed that he had been unfairly dismissed. *Held*, the concept of normal retiring age was not synonymous with pensionable age and therefore an agreement about pensions could not alter an employee's contractual terms unless it was expressly stated to do so. The contract in this case had not been changed but had it been, he would have been entitled to extend his retirement age to sixty-five according to the terms laid down in the scheme.

STEPNEY CAST STONE CO LTD V MACARTHUR [1979] IRLR 181 (Employment Appeal Tribunal: TALBOT J presiding).

2911   The minimum age of retirement in the Civil Service was between sixty and sixty-five years and, although retention beyond sixty was discretionary, it was intended that employees should stay until they were sixty-five or had achieved twenty years' service. Owing to cuts in public expenditure, economies were made and an employee was given twelve months' notice of retirement, at which time he would have completed nineteen years' service and be aged sixty-one. He applied for compensation for unfair dismissal but this was refused by a tribunal and on appeal, *held*, he was excluded from bringing a complaint because he had attained the age of sixty which, as it was permissible not to extend the period of employment of an employee over the age of sixty, was the normal retiring age.

HOWARD V DEPARTMENT FOR NATIONAL SAVINGS [1979] ICR 584 (Employment Appeal Tribunal: SLYNN J presiding).

2912 —— —— —— **effect of collective agreement**

When the Post Office changed from being a government department to a public corporation in 1969, the employees were assured that their job security and superannuation benefits would not be adversely affected. In 1975 the Post Office agreed with the relevant trade unions that sixty should be the normal retiring age for employees. The appellants assumed that the assurances meant they would be entitled to work after the age of sixty because some employees had been allowed to do so previously. An industrial tribunal refused to allow their claim that they had been unfairly dismissed when they were retired at sixty. On appeal, *held*, although some employees had been allowed to carry on working in the past the normal retiring age had always been sixty and the assurances made in 1969 could not give the employees a right which they had not had before. This retiring age had been reinforced by a union agreement made in the interests of good industrial relations and accordingly the appellants' claim that they had been unfairly dismissed would fail.

NELSON AND WOOLLETT V POST OFFICE [1978] IRLR 548 (Employment Appeal Tribunal: KILNER BROWN J presiding).

2913 —— **employment for less than twenty-one hours per week— construction of contract**

In July 1975 the employee started work as a cleaner under a contract which did not specify her hours of employment. Initially she worked for a few hours each afternoon, but later worked mornings as well and was employed for about thirty hours per week until April 1976 when, for a short period, she worked a fourteen hour week. She then reverted to a thirty hour week until November 1976 when she was absent for several weeks because of illness. On her return to work she was employed for fourteen hours per week until her dismissal in January 1977. On the employee's claim for unfair dismissal the industrial tribunal held that as she had not been employed under a contract which normally involved employment for twenty-one hours per week she did not fulfil the minimum qualifying period of twenty-six weeks continuous employment under the Trade Union and Labour Relations Act 1974, Sch. 1, para. 10 (a). The employee contended that, by virtue of the Employment Protection Act 1975, Sch. 16, Part II, para. 14 and Sch. 17, para. 17 she was entitled to preserve her continuity of employment by the Contracts of Employment Act 1972, Sch. 1, para. 4 A (1). This provision had come into force after her dismissal but before the tribunal hearing. *Held*, the employee could not rely on para. 4 A (1) as it had come into force after her dismissal. Where a contract of employment did not specify the number of hours to be worked, an industrial tribunal was entitled to look at the hours actually worked to determine whether the contract normally involved working for more than twenty-one hours per week.   In the last twenty-six weeks of her employment the employee had normally worked more than a twenty-one hour week, and had therefore satisfied the requirement of the 1974 Act, Sch. 1, para. 10 (a).

LARKIN v CAMBOS ENTERPRISES (STRETFORD) LTD [1978] ICR 1247 (Employment Appeal Tribunal: SLYNN J presiding).

The relevant enactments are now contained in Employment Protection (Consolidation) Act 1978.

2914   —— —— work done by teacher outside normal contractual hours

The employee was a part-time teacher.   Under her contract of employment she was obliged to work approximately twenty hours per week, including four hours of free time to be spent on preparation and marking.   She found the latter hours insufficient and did additional school work outside duty hours.   Her complaint of unfair dismissal was dismissed by an industrial tribunal as she was employed for less than twenty-one hours weekly within the meaning of the Trade Union and Labour Relations Act 1974, Sch. 1, para. 9 (1) (f).   The Employment Appeal Tribunal allowed her appeal on the ground that there was an implied term in her contract whereby she was to do as much work outside the school hours specified in her contract as was necessary for the proper performance of her teaching duties in school hours.   On appeal, *held*, such a term could not be implied into the contract of a part-time teacher.   It was too vague and unpredictable to be given efficacy and would have been impossible for her employers to supervise or measure for the purpose of payment.   There was time allocated for preparation and marking and any work she chose to do outside those hours was done voluntarily outside her contractual obligations.   The time thus spent could not be counted as part of her contractual hours of work.   The appeal would be allowed and the decision of the industrial tribunal restored.

LAKE v ESSEX COUNTY COUNCIL [1979] ICR 577 (Court of Appeal: LORD DENNING MR, LAWTON and GEOFFREY LANE LJJ).   Decision of Employment Appeal Tribunal [1978] ICR 657, 1977 Halsbury's Abridgment para. 2978, reversed.

1974 Act, Sch. 1, para. 9 (1) (f), as amended, has been consolidated in Employment Protection (Consolidation) Act 1978.   The statutory period is now sixteen weeks.

2915   —— employment for less than twenty-six weeks—employee seeking re-engagement

The employee, who was not a registered seaman, applied for a vacancy on a ship.   The company obtained his registration and offered him the post by letter in June 1976.   The employee accepted and signed the crew agreement which provided for a voyage not exceeding three months and incorporating national agreements.   A new crew agreement was signed in November but the employee signed off a few days later having been paid for his voyage leave calculated with reference to his service at sea and his national insurance contributions also having been deducted.   In April 1977 the employee sought further employment with the company on the basis that his voyage leave was at an end.   The company stated that his employment with them had terminated in November 1976 and the employee claimed compensation for unfair dismissal.   The tribunal dismissed the claim on the grounds that his employment had ceased in November 1976 and he had therefore not been in twenty-six weeks continuous employment as required for jurisdiction to hear the complaint under the Trade Union and Labour Relations Act 1974, Sch. 1, para. 10.   Furthermore the complaint was out of time because three months had elapsed since the termination of employment.   On appeal, *held*, as the employee was a registered seaman his terms of employment were subject to the national scheme and crew agreement and there was nothing amounting to a service contract.   Although his voyage leave was calculated with reference to his length of service he was free after signing off to take other employment; accordingly, employment ceased when he left the ship.   The employee neither satisfied the qualifying period for claiming compensation for unfair dismissal nor made his claim within three months of termination of employment. The appeal would be dismissed.

DUFF v EVAN THOMAS RADCLIFFE & CO LTD [1979] ICR 720 (Employment Appeal Tribunal: SLYNN J presiding).

The qualifying period for a complaint of unfair dismissal is now fifty-two weeks: Unfair Dismissal (Variation of Qualifying Period) Order 1979, para. 2917.

1974 Act, Sch. 1, para. 10 now Employment Protection (Consolidation) Act 1978, s. 64 (1).

2916 —— —— method of calculation of period

An employee commenced his employment on Tuesday 30th August 1977 and was dismissed on Wednesday 15th February 1978. He claimed that he had been unfairly dismissed. On the question of whether he had been employed for twenty-six weeks, *held*, under Contracts of Employment Act 1972, Sch. 1, para. 4, any week during the whole or part of which an employee's relations with his employer were governed by a contract involving employment for sixteen hours or more had to be counted in computing a period of employment. As the employee was entitled to have his week's statutory notice included in that period he had been employed for the requisite period.

COOKSON AND ZINN LTD v MORGAN [1979] ICR 425 (Employment Appeal Tribunal: SLYNN J presiding).

1972 Act, Sch 1, now Employment Protection (Consolidation) Act 1978, Sch. 13.

The qualifying period for a complaint of unfair dismissal is now fifty-two weeks: Unfair Dismissal (Variation of Qualifying Period) Order 1979, para. 2917.

2917 —— variation of qualifying period

The Unfair Dismissal (Variation of Qualifying Period) Order 1979, S.I. 1979 No. 959 (in force on 1st October 1979), increases the qualifying period of twenty-six weeks, for unfair dismissal complaints to an industrial tribunal, to fifty-two weeks where the effective date of termination falls on or after 1st October 1979.

2918 —— weekly hours—effect of change in legislation

See *Active Elderly Housing Association v Sparrow*, para. 1033.

2919 Fixed term contract—decision not to renew—professional footballer

On the advice of the club's new and experienced team manager, a footballer was not re-engaged at the termination of his contract. The employee appealed against his dismissal to an industrial tribunal, but the tribunal found the dismissal fair. The employee then appealed against its finding on the grounds that, (i) he had received no complaints about his play prior to the arrival of the new manager, and (ii) that two recent injuries had resulted in a temporary lowering of his normal standard, which the club had not taken into account. *Held*, the appeal failed on both counts, since it had to be the aim of a football club to try to rise through the league table and the new manager had been employed with that end in view. It was his responsibility to structure the team according to the style of play he had calculated as being most conducive to its success. In this case the employee lacked the necessary skills for the form of game advocated by the manager and was consequently not re-engaged. No criticism was being made of his standard of play and therefore any disability owing to injury was irrelevant. The appeal would therefore be dismissed.

GRAY v GRIMSBY TOWN FOOTBALL CLUB LTD [1979] ICR 364 (Employment Appeal Tribunal: SLYNN J presiding).

2920 Industrial action—dismissal in connection with a lock-out— whether "relevant employees"

A company requested thirty-four employees to sign an undertaking to work at the normal incentive pace, believing that they were deliberately working slowly. If they failed to sign the undertaking they would be suspended. The following day the employees did not work but held a meeting to discuss the matter resulting in all but seven signing the undertaking. The seven were treated as being suspended and although they came to the factory they were not allowed to work. A week later a further warning was given, stating that should the undertaking remain unsigned they would be dismissed. The seven employees did not sign the undertaking and were dismissed. On a claim for compensation for unfair dismissal, an industrial tribunal found that the company had conducted a lock-out as defined by the Contracts of Employment Act 1972, Sch. 1, para 11 (1). They held that the only employees directly interested in the dispute and thus the "relevant employees" for the purposes of the Trade Union and Labour Relations Act 1974, Sch. 1, para. 7 were the seven employees, and since they were all dismissed the tribunal had no jurisdiction to hear the complaint by virtue of para. 7 (2) (a). On appeal, *held*, the dispute was one between the company and employees as to the terms and conditions of employment and was therefore a "trade dispute" within s. 29 (1) of the 1974 Act, and since the suspensions had occurred when the employees presented themselves for work it fell within the definition of a lock-out in Sch. 1, para. 11 (1). On the true construction of Sch. 1, para. 7 the "relevant employees" were not confined to those actually locked out but included those employees directly interested in the trade dispute. The lock-out occurred when the thirty-four employees were suspended and since they had not all been dismissed the tribunal had jurisdiction in accordance with para. 7 (2) to determine whether the employees had been unfairly dismissed.

FISHER v YORK TRAILER CO LTD [1979] ICR 834 (Employment Appeal Tribunal: SLYNN J presiding).

Sch. 1, para. 11 (1) of the 1972 Act now Employment Protection (Consolidation) Act 1978, Sch. 13, para. 24 and Sch. 1, para. 7 of the 1974 Act now Employment Protection (Consolidation) Act 1978, s. 62.

2921   —— dismissal of striking employees—employee on leave during strike—whether employee taking part in strike

Industrial tribunal decision:

DIXON v WILSON WALTON ENGINEERING LTD [1979] ICR 438 (entire work force dismissed after industrial action on oil rig; employee on shore leave with no knowledge of strike; dismissal unfair under Employment Protection (Consolidation) Act 1978, s. 62 (1) (b); employee was not taking part in strike as no element of active assent or activity on his part; "taking part in" involves measure of individual responsibility and not merely associated, vicarious or artificial responsibility; s. 62 (1) (b) purely objective and should not be interpreted in light of employer's belief at time of dismissal).

2922   —— participation   in   strike—dismissal   of   employees— re-engagement of one employee—whether dismissal unfair

An employee was dismissed, with others, while taking part in a strike at his employer's abattoir. An offer of re-engagement was subsequently made to one of the other dismissed strikers. The employee complained that his dismissal had been unfair. An industrial tribunal construed the Trade Union and Labour Relations Act, Sch. 1, para. 7 (3), as amended, as requiring the tribunal to consider whether the employer had shown that he acted reasonably in treating his reason for not re-engaging an employee dismissed while on strike, when another dismissed striker was re-engaged, as a sufficient reason for dismissal. On this basis, the tribunal concluded that the employer had acted reasonably in dismissing the employee because of his conduct in refusing to work. The employee appealed. *Held*, upon the correct construction of para. 7 (3), the tribunal had to determine whether the employer had acted reasonably in treating the reason given as a sufficient reason for not offering re-engagement (not as a sufficient reason for dismissal). The question was not whether the initial dismissal was justified, but whether the employer acted reasonably in not re-engaging the employee and thereby in making a distinction between him and the man who was taken back. The case would be remitted to the tribunal for reconsideration.

EDWARDS V CARDIFF CITY COUNCIL [1979] IRLR 303 (Employment Appeal Tribunal: SLYNN J presiding).

1974 Act, Sch. 1, para. 7 (3) now Employment Protection (Consolidation) Act 1978, s. 62 (3).

2923 Industrial tribunal—jurisdiction—complaint of unlawful discrimination on ground of race—power to amend application to include unfair dismissal

See *Home Office v Bose*, para. 1078.

2924 —— —— complaint presented prior to termination of employment

See *Presley v Llanelli Borough Council*, para. 2879.

2925 —— —— power to adjourn hearing

See *Carter v Credit Change Ltd*, para. 1075; *Bastick v James Lane (Turf Accountants) Ltd*, para. 1076.

2926 —— matters to be considered—length of notice of dismissal

An employee was given three months' notice of dismissal on the grounds of redundancy, following local government reorganisation. He complained to an industrial tribunal that his dismissal had been unfair. The tribunal found that although the borough council were entitled to dismiss him for reasons of redundancy, he should have received six months' notice and accordingly the dismissal had been unfair. On appeal by the council, *held*, the tribunal had misdirected itself in applying a two-stage test, whether the council had acted reasonably in dismissing for redundancy, and whether it had acted reasonably in the way in which the decision was carried out. The second part of the test was not in accordance with the Employment Protection (Consolidation) Act 1978, s. 57 (3), which provided that the test was whether the employer had acted reasonably in dismissing the employee. Accordingly the appeal would be allowed.

HINKLEY AND BOSWORTH BOROUGH COUNCIL V AINSCOUGH [1979] ICR 590 (Employment Appeal Tribunal: PHILLIPS J presiding).

2927 —— procedure—duty to hear evidence of both sides

An employee was dismissed on the grounds of collaborating with an ex-employee in using the firm's premises for carrying out work not connected with the firm and of a competitive nature. The employee lied about his activities when questioned by his employer. On appeal, the industrial tribunal decided that he had been unfairly dismissed, due to insufficiency of reason, without hearing the employee's evidence. Later, when hearing his evidence for compensation, the tribunal acknowledged that the employee had lied to his employers. The employers appealed against the decision. *Held*, the industrial tribunal had misdirected itself by failing to hear evidence from both sides at the outset; the employee was guilty of disloyalty and breach of trust to the firm in using their premises for his own purposes, and then denying that he had done so. The appeal would be allowed.

GOLDEN CROSS HIRE CO LTD V LOVELL [1979] IRLR 267 (Employment Appeal Tribunal: TALBOT J presiding).

2928 Interim relief—validity of certificate

An employee, contending that he had been dismissed for taking part in union activities, sought interim relief under the Employment Protection (Consolidation) Act 1978, s. 77 (1). His notice of application stated that he considered that he had been dismissed because he had organised a trade union at his place of work. An official of the union to which he belonged sent a letter to the tribunal purporting to be a certificate supporting the employee's application as required by s. 77 (2) (b). However, the letter omitted to state that there appeared to be reasonable grounds for supposing that the reason for dismissal was the one alleged in the complaint, as further required by the section. An industrial tribunal held that the certificate did not comply with the requirements of the statute and accordingly that it had no jurisdiction to hear the application. The employee appealed. *Held*, although it was important that such certificates should be given in the correct form, too great a concentration on technicality was to be avoided. In the instant case, as the union official had intended to link his letter with the employee's application of the same date, there had been a substantial compliance with the section. Accordingly the appeal would be allowed.

BRADLEY V EDWARD RYDE & SONS [1979] ICR 488 (Employment Appeal Tribunal: SLYNN J presiding).

2929   Pregnancy—reasonableness of dismissal—necessity for twenty-six weeks continuous employment to bring complaint

Industrial tribunal decision:

SINGER V MILLWARD LADSKY AND CO [1979] IRLR 217 (after four months employment employee contended she had been unfairly dismissed on the grounds of pregnancy; employers contended that industrial tribunal had no jurisdiction to hear the complaint as employee did not have twenty-six weeks' continuous employment; tribunal upheld employers' submission; notwithstanding that in certain circumstances dismissal on grounds of pregnancy was unlawful, the only exception to the service requirement was where dismissal was for an inadmissible reason within the Employment Protection (Consolidation) Act 1978, s. 58 and the definition of an inadmissible reason related only to membership of a trade union).

2930   Reason for dismissal

See capability or qualifications, conduct, pregnancy, redundancy, some other substantial reason, trade union membership or activities.

2931   Redundancy

See EMPLOYMENT for cases on redundancy unconnected with unfair dismissal.

2932   —— failure to warn employee that redundancy imminent

An employee who was dismissed for redundancy was not considered for alternative employment in another department because of his poor work record. An industrial tribunal dismissed the employee's claim that he had been unfairly dismissed. On appeal, *held*, the employers had failed to give the employee a proper warning that dismissal for redundancy was probable if there was no improvement in her work. The lack of warning constituted a sufficient degree of unfairness to make the dismissal unfair.

MAGRO V PERFORMING RIGHTS SOCIETY LTD (1978) 13 ITR 198 (Employment Appeal Tribunal: ARNOLD J presiding).

2933   —— offer of alternative employment—no offer made—whether reasonable

A company which reorganised its business making one of its senior agents redundant, failed to offer him the position of site agent on the grounds that it was a demotion and that they believed he wished to find another job with a different company. The agent claimed that the company had acted unreasonably and had unfairly dismissed him. *Held*, the company had acted without due care in not offering the agent the post, the demotion being a question for him to consider. Further, he had been with the company for five years and there was no reason to suppose he wished to change employers. The company had acted unreasonably and had unfairly dismissed him.

AVONMOUTH CONSTRUCTION CO LTD V SHIPWAY [1979] IRLR 14 (Employment Appeal Tribunal: BRISTOW J presiding).

2934   —— **selection of redundant employees**

The respondent company was forced to make redundancies and they drew up a random list of people and presented it to the union. The appellant was not on the list. The union suggested that redundancies be made on a voluntary basis or on a basis of last in, first out. The company drew up a second list on the latter basis and the appellant, being on this list, was made redundant. An industrial tribunal dismissed his claim for compensation for unfair dismissal. On appeal, *held*, the tribunal had erred in failing to consider whether the respondents had adequately considered the alternative measures of voluntary redundancy or short time for everyone. However no difference would have been made to the outcome as the principle of last out, first in was the only way that the necessary reduction in the workforce could take place. The dismissal was not, therefore, unfair.

HASSALL v FUSION WELDING AND CONSTRUCTION (BIRKENHEAD) CO LTD [1979] IRLR 12 (Employment Appeal Tribunal: SLYNN J presiding).

2935   —— —— **agreed procedure—last in, first out**

The appellant company needed to dismiss one of its employees on the grounds of redundancy and agreed with the union that the selection for redundancy should be on the basis of last in, first out. The defendant complained about his selection under this system. He contended that it should have been another employee who, although employed for longer than the defendant, had left the company for several weeks. The company had subsequently invited him to return and had agreed that his employment would be regarded as continuous so, for the purposes of selection for redundancy, his period of continuous service was regarded as longer than the defendant's. An industrial tribunal held that the dismissal was unfair and the employers appealed. *Held*, for the purposes of selection for redundancy under the last in, first out system the relevant period was continuous service not cumulative periods of service. If employers and an employee entered into an agreement which was contrary to the usual industrial practice, the terms of such agreement should be made known to other members of staff who were likely to be involved. As the defendant had been unaware of the agreement, and as the circumstances of the present case were not sufficiently special to justify a departure from the usual procedure, the defendant's selection had been unfair.

INTERNATIONAL PAINT CO LTD v CAMERON [1979] IRLR 62 (Employment Appeal Tribunal: LORD MCDONALD MC presiding).

2936   —— —— **basis of selection—reasonableness**

Industrial tribunal decision:

GRIEG v SIR ALFRED MCALPINE AND SON (NORTHERN) LTD [1979] IRLR 372 (selection of employees for redundancy made on basis of managerial skill and judgment; applicant made redundant, claimed unfair dismissal; tribunal stated that if criteria for selection anything other than last in, first out, employer had to show criteria adopted were reasonable and were objectively and rationally applied to individual; criteria of performance, attendance record and service adopted by employer were reasonable but had failed to establish that it had decided claimant not suitable for retainment after thorough and objective assessment; dismissal therefore unfair).

2937   —— —— **diminution in work requirements**

The employee, a research bio-chemist, was shortly before his dismissal regraded to a higher grade. His dismissal arose after staffing requirements by the funding authorities were changed and one lower grade researcher only was needed. An industrial tribunal found that in the circumstances the employee had been fairly dismissed on the ground of redundancy or, alternatively, he had been dismissed for some other substantial reason within the Trade Union and Labour Relations Act 1964, Sch. 1, para. 6 (1) (b). The employee appealed. *Held*, the industrial tribunal had erred in holding that the dismissal had been on the ground of redundancy since it was not possible to say that there had been a diminution in the kind of work that the employee was doing. Alternatively the employers did not satisfy their duty under para. 6 (8) as they had not satisfied the tribunal that they had acted reasonably in all the circumstances. The appeal would be allowed.

PILLINGER v MANCHESTER AREA HEALTH AUTHORITY [1979] IRLR 430 (Employment Appeal Tribunal: SLYNN J presiding).

Trade Union and Labour Relations Act 1964, Sch. 1, paras. 6 (1) and 6 (8) now Employment Protection (Consolidation) Act 1978, s. 57.

2938   —— whether the redundancy situation existed

See *O'Hare v Rotaprint Ltd*, para. 1095.

2939   Sex discrimination

See SEX DISCRIMINATION.

2940   Some other substantial reason—breach of company rules—salesman dealing in other manufacturers' goods

A salesman was summarily dismissed from his job for persistently dealing in other manufacturers' goods, despite an express prohibition and a number of verbal warnings. An industrial tribunal found his dismissal fair. On his appeal, *held*, there was no need to show that there had been a serious loss to the employer's business. It would place an unreasonable burden upon employers if they were expected to establish prejudice or loss before they could dismiss an employee behaving in an unacceptable fashion. The tribunal had been entitled to conclude that in the circumstances the dismissal had been fair and the appeal would be dismissed.

MCCALL v CASTLETON CRAFTS [1979] IRLR 218 (Employment Appeal Tribunal: LORD MCDONALD MC presiding).

2941   —— deliberate omission to reveal history of mental illness during application for job

When applying for a job as a district agent for an insurance company, the applicant deliberately omitted to tell his future employers that he had a long and serious history of mental illness, despite specific questions asked during a medical examination. Upon discovering this his employers terminated his employment because it was not their practice to employ anyone who had suffered from mental illness as a district agent, as the job entailed visiting people in their homes. An industrial tribunal found that the employee had been dismissed for "some other substantial reason" within the meaning of the Trade Union and Labour Relations Act 1974, Sch. 1, para. 6 (1) (b), and that the dismissal was fair. On appeal, *held*, upholding the tribunal's decision, in view of his past illness it was reasonable to maintain that he was not suitable to be a district agent and the employers' refusal to offer him alternative employment was justified, considering his deliberate omission to tell them about his previous illness.

O'BRIEN v PRUDENTIAL ASSURANCE CO LTD [1979] IRLR 140 (Employment Appeal Tribunal: SLYNN J presiding).

1974 Act, Sch. 1, para. 6(1) now Employment Protection (Consolidation) Act 1978, s. 57(1).

2942   —— employee's refusal to accept change in place of work

A sales engineer was appointed to, and worked solely in, the export field. He became ill and was unable to specify when he would be fit to work abroad again. His employers therefore required him to work at home, but he refused and was consequently dismissed. On an interpretation of his contract of employment in a claim for unfair dismissal, *held*, whilst his conditions of employment stated that his duties would be "as required", he had always worked in the export field and was always treated as an export sales engineer. His dismissal upon his refusal to work at home was accordingly unfair.

DEELEY v BRITISH RAIL ENGINEERING LTD [1979] IRLR 5 (Employment Appeal Tribunal: BRISTOW J presiding).

2943   —— **expiry of fixed term contract—other matters to be taken into consideration**

The appellant was employed on a temporary basis as a needlework teacher. A vacancy subsequently arose in the same school for a teacher of needlework who was also qualified to teach modern languages or religious education. The appellant, who had the appropriate qualifications, applied for the job, but was not called for interview. When her contract of temporary employment expired it was not renewed and the appellant complained that she had been unfairly dismissed. The industrial tribunal found that the employers had genuinely overlooked the fact that the appellant was suitably qualified and therefore it could not be said that they had acted unreasonably within the meaning of the Trade Union and Labour Relations Act 1974, Sch. 1. para. 6 (8). On appeal, *held*, the expiry of a fixed term contract could be sufficient justification for dismissal, but it was necessary to consider whether the employers had acted reasonably in the circumstances of the case. As the appellant had notified her employers that she had the necessary qualifications, she should have been considered for the job. By overlooking her qualifications the employers had failed to give her application proper consideration and the dismissal had been unfair.

     BEARD v ST JOSEPH'S SCHOOL GOVERNORS [1978] ICR 1234 (Employment Appeal Tribunal: SLYNN J presiding).

     1974 Act, Sch. 1, para. 6 (8) now Employment Protection (Consolidation) Act 1978, s. 57.

2944   —— **failure to return to work after strike ended—prevention by illness—contributory fault**

A plumber who failed to answer a call to return to work after a strike, because he was ill, was summarily dismissed. He did not inform his employers of his illness until after he had received a letter of dismissal. In an appeal against a finding of unfair dismissal by the employers, the plumber cross-appealed against a sixty per-cent reduction in compensation due to his own contribution to his dismissal in failing to inform them of his illness, *held*, both appeals would be dismissed. The employers had acted unreasonably in not giving the plumber an opportunity to explain and they could have ascertained the reason for his non-attendance before sending out the letter. Further, the tribunal had the discretion to set the contribution figure and their decision would not be interfered with.

     JOHN CRAWFORD & CO (PLUMBERS) LTD v DONNELLY [1979] IRLR 9 (Employment Appeal Tribunal: LORD McDONALD MC presiding).

2945   —— **part-time employee dismissed consequent to employer's policy to eliminate part-time employment**

A part-time consultant surgeon was dismissed under an Area Health Authority's rationalisation policy, which aimed at eliminating part-time consultancies. An industrial tribunal held that the dismissal was either on the grounds of redundancy or for "some other substantial reason" under the Trade Union and Labour Relations Act 1974, Sch. 1, para. 6 (1) (b), and that the dismissal was fair. On appeal, *held*, the dismissal was not for redundancy as the work for which the employee had been responsible, was still being done. Furthermore the authority had failed to show that it was for "some other substantial reason", as it had not been demonstrated what importance or advantage the rationalisation policy was to the authority. The appeal would be allowed.

     BANERJEE v CITY AND EAST LONDON AREA HEALTH AUTHORITY [1979] IRLR 147 (Employment Appeal Tribunal: ARNOLD J presiding).

     1974 Act, Sch. 1, para. 6(1) now Employment Protection (Consolidation) Act 1978, s. 57(1).

2946   —— **poor performance of employee**

An employee who suffered from a bad back was not able to meet the level of output expected of her by her employers. The employers gave her six weeks to improve her output but when she failed to improve she was given notice of termination of

employment.   She complained she had been unfairly dismissed.   An industrial
tribunal found that the dismissal was unfair and that a reasonable employer would
have given three months' notice.   On appeal by the employers, *held*, when applying
the test laid down in Trade Union and Labour Relations Act 1974, Sch. 1, para. 6
(8) an industrial tribunal was not able to import gradations of reasonableness.   The
employers' actions were either reasonable or unreasonable.   In the circumstances
the employers had acted reasonably although it might have been more fair to give
the employee a longer period of notice.

BRITISH MAN-MADE STAPLE FIBRES LTD V ROBINSON (1978) 13 ITR 241
(Employment Appeal Tribunal: BRISTOW J presiding).

The 1974 Act, Sch. 1, para. 6 (8) now Employment Protection (Consolidation)
Act 1978, s. 57.

2947   —— refusal to work hours requested

A radiographer's contract of employment stated that he was required to work "such
overtime as is necessary to ensure continuity of service".   He repeatedly refused
requests to work overtime and after such a refusal during an emergency, he was
dismissed.   In a claim for compensation for unfair dismissal, *held*, the contract
showed an obligation to work overtime and the request was reasonable in the
circumstances.   He had previously been warned about his reluctance to work
overtime and as a prior warning could be implied it had not been necessary to warn
him on this occasion; nor was the dismissal unfair merely because he was not given
an opportunity to explain his refusal.   His claim would be dismissed.

MARTIN V SOLUS SCHALL [1979] IRLR 7 (Employment Appeal Tribunal: LORD
MCDONALD MC presiding).

**2948   —— reorganisation of business—reasonableness of dismissal—
whether need for consultation**

A trade union dismissed one of its group secretaries who refused to accept various
proposed changes in the organisation of and wages structure in the local branches.
He claimed that he had been unfairly dismissed and that he should have been
consulted about the changes.   An industrial tribunal rejected his claim on the ground
that his failure to accept the reorganisation amounted to some other substantial
reason for dismissal within the Trade Union and Labour Relations Act 1974, Sch. 1,
para. 6 (1) (b) and stated that consultation was unnecessary in such a case.   The
decision was reversed by the Employment Appeal Tribunal and on appeal, *held*, the
industrial tribunal's decision would be restored.   The 1974 Act para. 6 (8) required
the tribunal to look at all the circumstances of the case and whether what the
employer did was fair and reasonable in the circumstances.   There was no
requirement that there always had to be consultation.   Consultation was only one
factor to take into consideration in looking at the circumstances of the case.   The
industrial tribunal had addressed themselves correctly to the words of the statute and
had concluded that the employer had acted reasonably.   Therefore the appeal would
be allowed.

HOLLISTER V NATIONAL FARMERS UNION [1979] ICR 542 (Court of Appeal: LORD
DENNING MR, EVELEIGH LJ and SIR STANLEY REES).   Decision of Employment
Appeal Tribunal [1978] ICR 712, 1978 Halsbury's Abridgment para. 2997 reversed.

1974 Act Sch. 1, paras. 6 (1), 6 (8) now Employment Protection (Consolidation)
Act 1978, s. 57 (1)–(3).

**2949   Trade union membership or activities—appropriate time for
activities—meaning—whether employer's consent may be
implied**

An employee, who had been appointed as a shop steward by an independent trade
union, was informed at a meeting with his employers that they were unable to accept
his status as shop steward.   When the employee called a meeting of maintenance
men in working hours to inform them of the position, the employers made no
comment.   As a result of the meeting, the maintenance men stopped working for

one hour. The employee was dismissed. The employee successfully claimed that his dismissal was unfair because he had been dismissed for an inadmissible reason, under the Trade Union and Labour Relations Act 1974, Sch. 1, para. 6 (6), in that he had taken part in the activities of a trade union at an appropriate time. The tribunal, however, failed to identify the exact reason for his dismissal. On appeal by the employers, *held*, the tribunal had not identified the reason for the dismissal, and it was therefore open to the court to find that the reason was calling the men to the meeting. The action amounted to his participation in union activities, but the activities were only at an "appropriate time", within the meaning of the 1974 Act, Sch. 1, para. 6 (4A), if the employer's consent had been obtained. Such consent did not necessarily have to be express, but consent could not be deduced from silence. In the circumstances, there was no warrant for inferring the requisite consent, and the activities did not therefore take place at an appropriate time. The dismissal was not unfair, and the appeal would be allowed.

MARLEY TILE CO LTD v SHAW [1980] ICR 72 (Court of Appeal; STEPHENSON, GOFF and EVELEIGH LJJ). Decision of Employment Appeal Tribunal [1978] ICR 828, 1978 Halsbury's Abridgment para. 2988 reversed.

1974 Act, Sch. 1, para. 6 (4A), (6) now Employment Protection (Consolidation) Act 1978, s. 58 (2), (5).

2950 —— dismissal in pursuance of closed shop agreement—existence of agreement

Employers agreed that their employees were to be members of one of four trade unions, and that an employee who refused to join or was expelled from one of those unions would be liable to be dismissed. An employee who was not a member was dismissed and claimed that the dismissal had been unfair. On appeal against the decision of an industrial tribunal that the dismissal had been fair, *held*, under the terms of the agreement, mere failure to belong to one of the four unions was insufficient to justify dismissal. The onus was on the employers to show that they had complied with the detailed provisions of the agreement, and the case would be remitted to a differently constituted tribunal to decide whether they had done so.

CURRY v HARLOW DISTRICT COUNCIL [1979] IRLR 269 (Employment Appeal Tribunal: ARNOLD J presiding).

2951 Voluntary aided school—dismissal of teacher—conditions of tenure—whether consent of county council required

See *Jones v Lee*, para. 1011.

VALUE ADDED TAX

Halsbury's Laws of England (4th edn.), Vol. 12, paras. 846–1053

2952 Article

VAT Treatment of Interests In, and Rights Over Land and Licences to Occupy Land, H. H. Mainprice: [1979] BTR 229.

2953 Appeal—appeal against assessment—distress levied by commissioners—effect on appeal made out of time

Value added tax tribunal decision:

DAVIES v CUSTOMS AND EXCISE COMRS (1979) MAN/79/9 (unreported) (assessment for tax made in November 1978; time for appeal lapsed after thirty days; notice of appeal lodged in January 1979; meanwhile commissioners recovered tax due by levying distress; claimant applied for extension of time for appeal; commissioners contended that levying of distress was final and precluded any subsequent right of appeal against assessment; tax assessed had to be paid as a condition of appeal therefore no reason why it could not be recovered by distress, which itself did not extinguish the jurisdiction of the tribunal to allow an extension of time to hear an appeal).

2954 —— appeal to tribunal—exercise of discretion by tribunal—factors to be considered

The taxpayer, a restaurant, failed to make any return for the relevant period and in November 1975 was assessed to tax under the Finance Act 1972, s. 31 (1). In December 1975, the joint owner returned from abroad. In September 1976, the taxpayer appealed against the assessment and the hearing was fixed for 17th March 1977. On 1st March 1977, the tribunal notified the taxpayer's accountant that it could not entertain the appeal under s. 40 because the requirements of s. 40 (2) had not been complied with since the return required to be made under s. 30 (2) had not been made nor the tax shown paid. The taxpayer then applied for the appeal to be entertained without payment of tax on the ground of hardship and for an extension of time for service of the application. No return had been made when the matter came before the tribunal, which was therefore bound by the Value Added Tax Tribunals Rules 1972 either to adjourn the proceedings or to dismiss the appeal. An adjournment was refused and the appeal dismissed. On appeal by the taxpayer, *held*, the tribunal had exercised its discretion correctly. From 1975 the owner had been aware that the taxpayer's VAT affairs required urgent attention and from 1st March 1977 both he and the accountant had known of the facts relating to the absence of the return which had to be filed under s. 30 (2). He had had adequate time to make the return and the appeal would be dismissed.

ABEDIN V CUSTOMS AND EXCISE COMRS [1979] STC 426 (Queen's Bench Division: NEILL J). *Ottley v Morris (Inspector of Taxes)* [1978] STC 594, 1978 Halsbury's Abridgment para. 1554 applied.

2955 —— —— failure to make necessary tax returns—whether dismissal of appeal mandatory

Value added tax tribunal decision:

HODGES V CUSTOMS AND EXCISE COMRS (1979) LON/78/32 (unreported) (commissioners contended that where appellant failed to make required returns before hearing of appeal against assessment, it was mandatory upon tribunal to dismiss appeal; tribunal rejected contention, tribunal also had power to issue directions as to conduct of appeal and to extend time within which any party to appeal was required to do something; vital witness ill so unable to obtain information to complete missing returns, therefore hearing postponed).

2956 —— —— jurisdiction

See *Customs and Excise Comrs v C and A Modes*, para. 2993.

2957 —— hearing—absence of party—application for adjournment

Value added tax tribunal decision:

RAJ MAHAL RESTAURANT V CUSTOMS AND EXCISE COMRS (1979) BIR/78/214 (unreported) (restaurant appealed against assessment for VAT; both partners of restaurant unable to attend due to illness; restaurant requested an adjournment; commissioners had already consented to an extension of time being granted for restaurant's appeal and to adjournment of two earlier hearings; further adjournment only granted provided that restaurant deposited a substantial sum with commissioners by a certain date; failing that deposit, date fixed for hearing of appeal).

2958 —— —— —— appellant in liquidation

Value added tax tribunal decision:

EASTHOLME CONSTRUCTION CO LTD (IN LIQUIDATION) V CUSTOMS AND EXCISE COMRS (1979) MAN/78/129 (unreported) (company appealed against assessment; nobody appeared at hearing on behalf of company; commissioners contended tribunal should proceed in appellant's absence under Value Added Tax Tribunals Rules 1972, r. 26 (2); after service of notice of appeal, order made for compulsory liquidation of company and liquidator appointed; assets of company, including right to prosecute appeal, had vested in liquidator and thus in his absence court could proceed under r. 26 (2); prior to winding up order company had applied for direction that appeal be heard without payment or deposit of tax assessed on grounds of hardship; where right to appeal vested in liquidator, requisite hardship was that of the liquidator in respect of his vicarious responsibility for general body of creditors; creditors would suffer hardship if liquidator required to pay or deposit tax due; appeal could be entertained; no evidence to displace assessment and appeal dismissed).

2959 —— **time for service of notice—discretion of tribunal to extend time—factors to be considered**

Value added tax tribunal decisions:
PRICE V CUSTOMS AND EXCISE COMRS [1978] VATTR 115 (appellant assessed to VAT on 25th October 1977; notice of appeal against assessment received at tribunal centre on 24th January 1978; more than thirty days had elapsed between date of assessment and receipt of notice of appeal; appellant applied for extension of time for service of notice; tribunal had discretion to extend time for service; had to consider where balance of prejudice lay if application to be granted; commissioners would not be prejudiced by grant of extension; extension granted).

2960 TRIPPETT V CUSTOMS AND EXCISE COMRS [1978] VATTR 260 (commissioners notified appellant of decision on 20th April 1976; on 17th April 1978, notice of appeal received accompanied by notice of application for extension of time to serve notice of appeal; in exercise of its discretion to extend time for service, tribunal should consider whether any prejudice which could not be compensated by imposition of conditions would result to either party from grant of extension; no such prejudice would arise in this case and extension would be granted).

2961 RANDLES V CUSTOMS AND EXCISE COMRS (1979) MAN/78/218 (unreported) (commissioners notified applicant of decision on 19th January 1977; forms regarding application for an extension of time to appeal sent to applicant on 14th September 1978; forms not received at tribunal office until 22nd November 1978, despite reminders; tribunal found no grounds to warrant such a serious delay; application dismissed).

2962 **Assessment—assessment based on aggregate—burden of proof**

Value added tax tribunal decision:
WICKHAM RIDING SCHOOL AND STUD V CUSTOMS AND EXCISE COMRS (1979) LON/79/14 (unreported) (riding school assessed to value added tax in aggregate amount for period of two years; reason given for assessment was tax not accounted for all income declared at final accounts; riding school appealed on ground that assessment was raised on figure that did not represent income of business; book-keeper and accountants of riding school did not give evidence; evidence submitted did not account for discrepancy between income returned on final accounts and lesser amount of income disclosed on tax returns; riding school had not discharged burden of proof to show that amount of assessment was incorrect; appeal would be dismissed).

2963 —— **assessment based on court's decision relating to another matter—review of assessment by tribunal**

Value added tax tribunal decision:
ANGLO BENGAL RESTAURANT V CUSTOMS AND EXCISE COMRS (1979) MAN/78/179 (unreported) (owners of restaurant admitted suppression of takings in restaurant; notwithstanding their conviction by the courts they appealed to a tribunal against assessment of tax, in respect of the period in which the charges related, on the grounds that the assessment was based on incorrect hypotheses; simply because the restaurateurs had been convicted of fraud did not mean that the quantum of their fraud would be accepted as the basis of their liability for value added tax; the

assessment may have included a quasi-penal element; the assessment had been based on the assumption that only standard rate sales were suppressed and not zero-rated sales; there was no justification for that assumption and accordingly the assessment would be re-calculated).

2964   —— driving school—status of instructors

Value added tax tribunal decision:
NEW WAY SCHOOL OF MOTORING LTD v CUSTOMS AND EXCISE COMRS [1979] VATTR 57 (driving school appealed against assessment based on fact that it acted as principal, and not as booking agents in respect of the supply of lessons to pupils; necessary to consider degree of control exercised by school, ownership of cars; chance of profit and risk of loss; on interpretation of contracts of employment, instructors did not give tuition as persons in business on their own account but on behalf of the school; the driving school would be assessed accordingly).

2965   —— exercise of commissioners' judgment

Value added tax tribunal decision:
S. GASCOIGNE & SONS LTD v CUSTOMS AND EXCISE COMRS (1979) BIR/77/265 (unreported) (company carried on retail business at three separate premises; commissioners concluded that amount of output tax declared had been understated, after visiting main office only and making inquiries; company appealed against assessment; commissioners had based their calculations on a relatively small sample of items and had failed to visit other branches and interview the person responsible for sales and purchases; assessment was not made to the best of the commissioners' judgment; appeal would be allowed).

2966   —— failure to specify accounting periods—effect

Value added tax tribunal decisions:
BEAMAN v CUSTOMS AND EXCISE COMRS (1979) BIR/78/80 (unreported) (commissioners found discrepancies between outputs declared on taxpayer's value added tax returns compared with sales figures in annual accounts for years ending March 31st 1974, 1975 and 1976; taxpayer's returns incomplete in respect of 1974 and 1975; commissioners made assessment under Finance Act 1972, s. 31 (1) in respect of whole period, based on estimate taken from annual accounts; taxpayer appealed, contending that commissioners could specify period of time for assessment only where it was impossible to split assessment up into three-monthly periods; further contended that assessment was wholly or in part out of time; assessment was valid; on the facts it would have been impossible to make assessment relating to each accounting period separately; assessment was not out of time; commissioners had received copies of annual accounts in August 1977 and made assessment in November 1977, within one year period prescribed by s. 31 (1) (b)).

2967   BELL v CUSTOMS AND EXCISE COMRS [1979] VATTR 115 (assessment made in respect of VAT underdeclared for period 1st August 1975 to 30th April 1978; notice of assessment merely stated that correct amount of VAT due for period no. 61 ending on 30th April 1978 had not been declared or assessed; thus did not on its face cover more than one prescribed accounting period; appeal against assessment; there was authority for proposition that assessment did not have to relate to single prescribed accounting period; however, assessment was not valid for period 1975 to 1978 since to be valid it had to specify the period to which it related; since assessment only specified period no. 61, it was valid for that period but not rest of period 1975 to 1978; *S. J. Grange Ltd v Customs and Excise Comrs* [1979] 2 All ER 91, CA, 1978 Halsbury's Abridgment para. 3055 applied).

2968   HEYFORDIAN TRAVEL LTD v CUSTOMS AND EXCISE COMRS [1979] VATTR 139 (a coach hire company appealed against an assessment for value added tax in respect of the purchase of Range Rover vehicles and the supply of packaged holidays; they claimed they had been told the supply of the vehicles was deductible as input tax in

1973 and that the packaged tours were zero-rated in 1975; the commissioners claimed to have corrected this in August 1977 by informing the company book-keeper of the liability to tax; the first assessment was issued in October 1977, but was not split into precise accounting periods; a second assessment was issued for the same period which related to a larger sum; company argued that both assessments were invalid because the first was not split and the second related to the same period; if they were valid they had been made out of time because the commissioners had known all the relevant facts more than a year before making the assessment; first assessment was valid; period to which it referred was clear and it was often impossible to say which liabilities arose in each accounting period; second assessment invalid and should be withdrawn because it related to same period and was not made on the basis of new information; on the evidence the commissioners had not had all relevant information until August 1977 and the assessments were not made out of time).

2969   —— further assessment in same tax period—validity—new information

See *Heyfordian Travel Ltd v Customs and Excise Comrs*, para. 2968.

2970   —— —— —— whether duplication of assessment

Value added tax tribunal decision:

JUDD (trading as C J PLANT HIRE) V CUSTOMS AND EXCISE COMRS (1979) LON/79/9 (unreported) (appeal against assessment to VAT in respect of supply of excavator; assessment was for period 47; previous assessment contained figure representing under-assessment for periods 31–56, including an amount due for period 47; appellant contended commissioners had no power to raise more than one assessment in respect of one period unless after they had revised first assessment further evidence came to light; component relating to period 47 comprised in earlier assessment did not cover supply of excavator as appellant had been given extension of time to obtain proof of export of excavator; as this was not forthcoming an assessment had been issued in respect of it; hence there was no duplication of assessment; assessment upheld; *Jeudwine v Customs and Excise Comrs* [1977] VATTR 115, 1977 Halsbury's Abridgment para. 3034 distinguished).

2971   Collection by receiver—receiver appointed under debenture—whether money payable to debenture holder

See *Re John Willment (Ashford) Ltd.*, para. 357.

2972   Exempt supply—betting, gaming and lotteries—charge for provision of entertainment—taxpayer's burden of proof

A working men's club held bingo sessions for its members; additional entertainment was provided on certain nights and for this members made such payments as the club committee thought fit. A dispute arose as to whether the payments should properly have been included in the club's value added tax returns. The club maintained that they were exempt under the Finance Act 1972, Sch. 5, group 4, item 1 as being for the provision of facilities for the placing of bets or playing of games of chance, the commissioners that they were composite payments and thus had to be apportioned. The club appealed under the 1972 Act, s. 40. A value added tax tribunal held that the payments were additional to other payments made for the provision of facilities for the placing of bets etc. and were not therefore exempt. The club appealed further, contending both that the tribunal had failed to ask itself what the club supplied in consideration of the payments and that it had misdirected itself in considering the onus of proof when it should have been determining the sum due as tax whatever the state of the evidence. *Held*, the tribunal had erred in not asking itself what consideration the club gave in return for the payments and had additionally failed to make the findings of fact necessary to the determination of that question. Accordingly, the case would be remitted to a differently constituted tribunal for a rehearing.

The court considered it incumbent on taxpayers appealing under s. 40 to shoulder the onus of proving that the assessment was wrong; if the taxpayer did not have to do that then there was no basis on which the tribunal could find any error in the assessment.

TYNEWYDD LABOUR WORKING MEN'S CLUB AND INSTITUTE LTD v CUSTOMS AND EXCISE COMRS [1979] STC 570 (Queen's Bench Division: FORBES J). Decision of value added tax tribunal (unreported), 1978 Halsbury's Abridgment para. 3021 set aside pending a rehearing.

2973 —— —— shooting gallery in amusement park—whether game of chance

Value added tax tribunal decision:

GRANTHAM v CUSTOMS AND EXCISE COMRS (1979) MAN/79/102 (unreported) (claimant, proprietor of shooting gallery in amusement park, appealed against assessment on the ground that supply of service of amusement was exempt supply as being a game of chance, target at shooting gallery was white circular bull's-eye enclosed within black inner; in order to win prize competitor required to shoot out, with four shots, the white bull's-eye leaving no part of it showing within the black inner; expert evidence showed that immaculate marksmanship, which resulted in every shot being in the white bull's-eye, could not necessarily shoot it out completely as required; it was therefore, on its special facts, a game of chance and skill combined and thus exempt supply).

2974 —— finance

The Value Added Tax (Finance) Order 1979, S.I. 1979 No. 243 (in force on 2nd April 1979), varies item 2 of Group 5 of Schedule 5 to the Finance Act 1972, by extending the exemption to include certain additional supplies associated with instalment credit finance, the total charges for which do not exceed £10.

2975 —— land—hire of market stall site—whether grant of licence

Value added tax tribunal decision:

TAMESIDE METROPOLITAN BOROUGH COUNCIL v CUSTOMS AND EXCISE COMRS [1979] VATTR 93 (1979) MAN/78/243 (unreported) (commissioners claimed that hire of market stall sites for one day only was not grant of licence to occupy land; hire of site was licence to occupy land and no minimum time limit imposed by legislation, therefore hire, even for only one day, was exempt supply).

2976 —— —— lease by members' club—whether increased subscriptions represented members' contribution to purchase of lease

A golf club sold a lease of land to the defendants, a club which had as its object the provision of holidays and recreational facilities for its members. The defendants sublet individual sites on the land to the members, as a result of which members' subscriptions were increased by £25 per annum. The whole of the subscription was taxed at the standard rate as being the consideration for the supply of holiday and recreational facilities. The club appealed, contending that (i) the increase of £25 was outside the scope of value added tax. It was used to pay off the loan incurred to buy the lease and as such was a contribution or levy towards the permanent capital of the club and analagous to the subscription for shares in a company limited by shares; (ii) for the purposes of value added tax, the £25 was an exempt supply, paid in respect of the grant of an interest in land under the Finance Act 1972, s. 13 (1), Sch. 5, Group 1, item 1. Held, (i) no special rights to share in the capital assets of the club were conferred by the payment and the analogy to subscriptions for shares was incorrect. The additional payment was not outside the scope of value added tax; (ii) the additional £25 was treated as part of the members' subscriptions and was not paid by way of increased rent or additional licence in respect of user of the land. The consideration for the increase in subscription was the continued supply of the club's facilities. The payments were not exempt and were taxable at the standard rate.

CUSTOMS AND EXCISE COMRS v LITTLE SPAIN CLUB LTD [1979] STC 170 (Queen's Bench Division: NEILL J).

2977 —— payment partly for taxable supply of services and partly for exempt supply

Value added tax tribunal decision:

DYRHAM PARK COUNTRY CLUB v CUSTOMS AND EXCISE COMRS [1978] VATTR 244 (company responsible for running golf club; commissioners held payments for bonds issued by club were part of consideration for facilities supplied by club; therefore required to account for tax on payments at standard rate; bonds issued by club to new members, entitled them to use golfing and social facilities, also to £350 in event of company winding up; club claimed subscriptions for bonds exempt from tax because under Finance Act 1972, Sch. 5, group 5 bonds securities, either within item 1 or item 4; commissioners argued bonds not securities as not negotiable or marketable; furthermore subscriptions for bonds in reality entrance fees for supply of facilities provided by club; tribunal held although bonds not negotiable, they were securities within item 4; but also conferred on members rights to facilities offered by club; subscriptions paid for bonds should be apportioned between the two, proportion in relation to latter being subject to standard rate).

2978 —— trade unions and professional bodies—bookmakers' association

Value added tax tribunal decision:

BOOKMAKERS PROTECTION ASSOCIATION (SOUTHERN AREA) LTD v CUSTOMS AND EXCISE COMRS (1979) LON/79/129 (unreported) (appellant appealed against assessment on ground that supply of services to members was made by association, the prime purpose of which was the advancement of particular branch of knowledge or professional expertise; test was subjective; main activities of appellant were giving members advice and help with day-to-day business and not advancement of knowledge; bookmaking not a profession and association not concerned with fostering members' expertise as bookmakers; appeal therefore dismissed).

2979 Finance (No. 2) Act 1979

See para. 2247.

2980 Higher rate goods—boat—whether designed for recreation

Value added tax tribunal decision:

CALLISON v CUSTOMS AND EXCISE COMRS (1979) EDN/78/34 (unreported) (appeal against assessment to higher rate of value added tax on sale of yacht; question was whether yacht designed for recreation or pleasure or for work; tribunal obliged to look at the actual design, not intention of designer; although yacht suitable for several types of work, she had been designed as a pleasure craft).

2981 —— domestic appliances—whether operated by electricity

Value added tax tribunal decision:

MORCO PRODUCTS LTD v CUSTOMS AND EXCISE COMRS (1979) MAN/78/270 (unreported) (manufacturers assessed to higher-rate VAT on supplies of hairdryers under Finance (No. 2) Act 1975, Sch. 7, Group 1, item 1; appeal against assessment on ground that hairdryers did not fall within Group 1, item 1 as they were not operated by electricity; over 99 per cent of energy required to operate hairdryer obtained from gas, compared to less than 1 per cent obtained from electric battery to operate fan inside hairdryer; device could be described as operated by electricity if an essential functioning part of it was powered by electricity; fan was essential functioning part of device; thus appliance operated by electricity and liable to higher-rate tax).

2982   Imposition of VAT

The Value Added Tax (General) (Amendment) Regulations 1979, S.I. 1979 No. 1614 (in force on 1st January 1980) amend the Value Added Tax (General) Regulations 1977, 1977 Halsbury's Abridgment para. 3052, by converting reg. 30 (9) (b) to a convenient metric equivalent.

2983   —— reliefs and rate of tax

The Value Added Tax (General) Order 1979, S.I. 1979 No. 657 (in force on 18th June 1979), substitutes a new note (7) of the Finance Act 1972, Sch. 4, Group 9, and continues the exclusion from zero-rating of certain insurance services relating to certain types of boats, aircraft and hovercraft. The order also substitutes a new Group 17 of Sch. 4 of the Act and continues the exclusion from zero-rating for children's clothing, of certain articles made wholly or partly of fur skin. The order is consequential upon the repeal of the Finance (No. 2) Act 1975, Sch. 7.

2984   Input tax—deduction—agency business—whether business carried on during accounting periods

Value added tax tribunal decision:

Boros v Customs and Excise Comrs (1979) LON/78/400 (unreported) (commissioners reclaimed input tax paid to building agent during relevant accounting periods on the ground that he was not trading during these periods; agent claimed that he continued to carry on agency business, although no outputs made due to slump in building work; agent had placed advertisements in trade journal, telephoned his contacts in the trade and travelled extensively looking for business for his agency; on the balance of probability, agent had never ceased to carry on his agency business; an adjournment would be granted for a limited period).

2985   —— —— building materials

The taxpayer constructed a block of flats which had concrete floors. It was necessary to insulate the floors against sound in order to comply with building regulations. The taxpayer provided sound insulation by bonding rubber-backed carpets to the floors. This was a new process, and not a conventional method of providing such insulation. The local authority passed the flats fit for occupation when the carpets were laid. The taxpayer claimed that the value added tax paid on the carpets was deductible as input tax. The commissioners decided that the tax could not be deducted because the carpets were not materials of a kind ordinarily installed by builders as fixtures, within the Input Tax (Exceptions) (No. 1) Order 1972, para. 3. On appeal by the taxpayer, a tribunal found that the carpets were building "materials" within the meaning of para. 3, because they were used as such. The commissioners appealed. *Held*, the word "materials" in para. 3 was to be construed as meaning conventional building materials. Rubber-backed carpets did not fall within the term "materials", even when fulfilling an insulating role. Accordingly, the appeal would be allowed.

Customs and Excise Comrs v Westbury Developments (Worthing) Ltd [1979] STC 665 (Queen's Bench Division: Neill J).

1972 Order now consolidated in the Value Added Tax (Special Provisions) Order 1977, 1977 Halsbury's Abridgment para. 3053.

2986   —— —— business entertainment

Value added tax tribunal decision:

Shaklee International and Shaklee UK Service Corpn v Customs and Excise Comrs (1978) LON/78/210 (unreported) (appellant firm was direct selling organisation; sold goods wholesale to main distributors who sold wholesale to distributors who carried out entire retail sales for appellants; appellants organised meetings and training sessions for distributors and provided meals and accommodation; appellants contended they were entitled to deductions in input tax under Value Added Tax (Special Provisions) Order 1977, para. 9 as meetings were for business purposes only and did not amount to business entertainment; proper training was essential to operation of appellants' business and provision of meals and accommodation was to facilitate such training; appeal allowed as training was exclusively for business purposes and was not business entertainment.)

2987   —— —— "delivery charge" on motor vehicle

Value added tax tribunal decision:

WIMPEY CONSTRUCTION UK LTD v CUSTOMS AND EXCISE COMRS (1979) LON/79/59 (unreported) (applicant supplied with motor cars by dealer at factory price plus a "delivery charge" and deducted, as input tax, tax payable on that "delivery charge"; commissioners contended that supply of cars included related supplies such as delivery and was not deductible; evidence showed that "delivery charge" was not merely charge to customer for obtaining car and delivering it to the appropriate address, but was sum stipulated by dealer to cover a number of matters and was part of the consideration for the supply of the car to the customer; input tax not therefore deductible in respect of it).

2988   —— —— motor cars

The Value Added Tax (Cars) (Amendment) Order 1979, S.I. 1979 No. 819, (in force 16th July 1979), varies the 1977 Order, 1977 Halsbury's Abridgment para. 3061, by allowing input tax to be deducted on the purchase of new cars by certain organisations for the sole purpose of ultimate leasing to disabled persons in receipt of a mobility allowance.

2989   —— —— motor vehicles

Value added tax tribunal decision:

KNAPP v CUSTOMS AND EXCISE COMRS (1979) LON/79/55 (unreported) (businessman appealed against an assessment of value added tax in respect of a Toyota Hiace motor vehicle which had been acquired for business purposes; vehicles which are subject to tax are those adapted solely or mainly to carry passengers or those which have side windows; the Hiace had side windows and would be subject to tax if it could not be brought within the exception for vehicles constructed for a special purpose; the only purpose for which the Hiace was adapted was that of carrying goods which was not a special purpose; accordingly the appeal would fail).

2990   —— —— petrol used by agents of company

Value added tax tribunal decision:

S AND U STORES LTD v CUSTOMS AND EXCISE COMRS (1978) BIR/76/89 (unreported) (clothing company used self-employed agents to collect payment from company's customers; agents, many part-time, paid for petrol themselves and were given allowance by company to cover expenses; cost of petrol often exceeded allowance; company sought to deduct input tax in respect of supplies of petrol, contending petrol was supplied to it, through agency of agents, for purpose of a business carried on by it; commissioners contended supply was to agents for purpose of business carried on by them to enable them to supply services to company; commissioners' contention upheld; agents were independent contractors carrying on business on own account and petrol was supplied to them for purpose of their business; company not entitled to deduct input tax). *Berbrooke Fashions v Customs and Excise Comrs* [1977] VATTR 168, 1977 Halsbury's Abridgment para. 3062 followed.

2991   —— —— power boat

Value added tax tribunal decision:

20TH CENTURY CLEANING AND MAINTENANCE CO LTD v CUSTOMS AND EXCISE COMRS (1979) LON/79/89 (unreported) (company maintained and raced a power boat; contended it was entitled to deduct input tax in respect of boat's purchase and maintenance; managing director alleged it was purchased and raced for business purposes but could not specify examples of business arising out of racing activities; boat found to have been purchased and raced for business purposes and therefore input tax was deductible).

2992 ———— **purchase tax charged on goods—goods held for purpose of hiring**

Value added tax tribunal decision:

HUMM ELECTRICAL CO LTD v CUSTOMS AND EXCISE COMRS (1979) LON/78/448 (unreported) (appellant company purchased television sets before April 1973, in respect of which they paid purchase tax; hired these out to customers, but in 1975 terminated hire agreements and sold sets to another company; they were liable to value added tax on the sales; contended that they ought to have some allowance for purchase tax paid on the televisions; relief against double charge limited to goods which were unused in April 1973 and were held by taxable person for sale or under hire-purchase agreement; no provision made relating to goods held for purpose of hiring, therefore liable to value added tax).

2993 ——— ——— ——— **meaning of charged**

In April 1973, the taxpayers, clothing retailers, claimed relief under the Finance Act 1973, s. 4, on the ground that purchase tax had been charged on goods they held in stock when VAT was introduced, and accordingly they should be permitted to deduct it as input tax. The claim was rejected by the commissioners on the ground that there was no satisfactory evidence that purchase tax had been charged on the goods in question. The taxpayers appealed to a VAT tribunal, which on 12th March 1978 held that it had jurisdiction to hear the appeal under the Finance Act 1972, s. 40 (1) (d), being an appeal against a decision of the commissioners with respect to the amount of any input tax which might be deducted, and on 7th June 1978 allowed the appeal. On appeal by the commissioners by notice of motion dated 3rd July 1978, *held*, the notice of motion was out of time in respect of an appeal against the decision of 12th March. However, the time for appealing would be extended under RSC Ord. 3, r. 5, since after the decision on jurisdiction the parties had agreed to go straight on with the substance of the appeal.

The tribunal was correct in deciding that it had jurisdiction to hear the appeal by virtue of s. 40 (1) (d), since on its true construction s. 40 (1) (d) expressly granted a right of appeal to a tribunal against a decision of the commissioners that they were not satisfied that purchase tax was charged.

Purchase tax had been charged on the goods in question since tax was "charged" within s. 4 when goods were delivered under a transaction chargeable to purchase tax although the supplier did not intend to account for and pay purchase tax. The appeal would be dismissed.

CUSTOMS AND EXCISE COMRS v C AND A MODES [1979] STC 433 (Queen's Bench Division: DRAKE J). Decision of value added tax tribunal [1978] VATTR 61 affirmed.

2994 ——— ——— **supply for purposes of business**

Value added tax tribunal decision:

SMALLEY AND MACK, TRADING AS M AND S INTERNATIONAL v CUSTOMS AND EXCISE COMRS (1979) MAN/78/137, MAN/78/226 (unreported) (appellant partnership firm dealt in imports and exports; partner purchased heavy clothing suitable for business trips to Far East; telephones installed for mainly business purposes were in names of companies that partner had previously been associated with; value added tax paid on acquisition of clothing could not be claimed as input tax as no evidence before tribunal that it was acquired as partnership asset; input tax could be claimed in relation to telephones as application had been made to change names of accounts and delay was not caused by appellant).

2995   —— —— —— **apportionment where supply partly for business purposes**

See *National Water Council v Customs and Excise Comrs*, para. 3024.

2996   —— —— —— **supply of racehorse for promotional campaigns**

The business of a company included the publication of records, tapes and books marketed under the name of "Galaxy Records". One of the directors was a bloodstock dealer who arranged for the alteration of the objects clause in the memorandum of association to include buying, selling, breeding and racing horses. In July 1977 the same director arranged for a new company "Galaxy Tape" to be incorporated and take over the business assets and undertaking of the original taxpayer company. Shortly afterwards six young racehorses were purchased and supplied to the taxpayer company, each of them having names containing the word "Galaxy". It was intended that by 1978 the horses having reached the appropriate age would race and thus promote the name "Galaxy". In their value added tax return the taxpayer company deducted as input tax under the Finance Act 1972, s. 3 (1) the value added tax incurred on the supply of racehorses to it. The commissioners claimed that the value added tax paid on the supply of the racehorses was not deductible because the supply was not, within the meaning of s. 3 (1), a supply for the purpose of a business carried on or to be carried on by the taxpayer company. The taxpayer company appealed to a value added tax tribunal against the assessment. The tribunal found that it had been decided prior to the purchase of the horses that the business assets of the company should be transferred to Galaxy Tape and it was concluded that there had never been any real intention that the taxpayer company should carry on the bloodstock business. The supply of horses was merely a preliminary step towards the carrying on of the business by Galaxy Tape and was therefore not a supply for the purpose of a business carried on or to be carried on by the taxpayer company within s. 3 (1). The taxpayer company appealed. *Held,* there were no grounds for interfering with the tribunal's decision since in asking whether it was ever intended that the taxpayer company should carry on the bloodstock business it had asked the right question in the circumstances. In the light of the finding that it had been decided before the purchase of the horses that the business assets were to be transferred to Galaxy Tape, it was open for the tribunal to decide the way it did. The appeal would be dismissed.

ASHTREE HOLDINGS LTD v CUSTOMS AND EXCISE COMRS [1979] STC 818 (Queen's Bench Division: NEIL J).

2997   Value added tax tribunal decision:

TALLISHIRE LTD v CUSTOMS AND EXCISE COMRS (1979) MAN/79/42 (unreported) (company called "Tallishire Ltd" who built housing estates claimed goods and services supplied to it in respect of racehorse owned by company was tax deductible as being for purpose of business; company used "shire" as key word for advertising campaigns, for example stationery carried picture of shire horse; racehorse called "Tallishire Beverly" bought in furtherance of advertising promotion; company's contention rejected; horse did not promote company's products, houses; class of members of public purchasing houses limited and not necessarily racegoers; business had no connection with racing; "Tallishire" not descriptive of company's business nor key name of company).

2998   **Liability to tax—partnership—existence of partnership**

See *Peter v Customs and Excise Comrs*, para. 2011.

2999   —— **sums representing tax not received by appellant**

Value added tax tribunal decision:

ALDON ENGINEERING (YORKS) LTD v CUSTOMS AND EXCISE COMRS (1979) MAN/78/235 (unreported) (an insurance company paid the appellant in respect of his repair of a dumper but refused to pay value added tax; company claimed the insured should pay; appellant contested the assessment because he had not received the tax from the company or the insured; tribunal was obliged to uphold the assessment because the appellant was a taxable person who had made a taxable supply).

3000   Metrication—fuel and power—temperature and pressure

The Value Added Tax (Fuel and Power) (Metrication) Order 1979, S.I. 1979 No. 1646 (in force on 1st January 1980) converts to a convenient metric equivalent the standard temperature and pressure used to determine whether an agent for lubrication is liquid and eligible for zero-rating.

3001   —— motor cars—weight limit

The Value Added Tax (Cars) (Amendment) (No. 2) Order 1979, S.I. 1979 No. 1648 (in force on 1st January 1980), further amends the Value Added Tax (Cars) Order 1977, 1977 Halsbury's Abridgment, para. 3061. The Order converts to a convenient metric equivalent the weight limit above which vehicles are excluded from the provisions of the 1977 Order.

3002   Recovery of tax—amount of tax shown on invoice—taxpayer's attempt to reclaim tax

Value added tax tribunal decision:

TEMPLE GOTHARD & CO v CUSTOMS AND EXCISE COMRS (1978) LON 78/238 (unreported) (accountants issued invoices for accountancy services rendered to several companies which were subsequently put into hands of a receiver; accountants had paid VAT on invoices; accountants sent receiver credit notes purporting to cover balance of fees due from each company; VAT shown on credit notes added to total of VAT on input claimed by appellants; commissioners considered VAT had been improperly reclaimed and issued assessment to re-impose it; tax accrued when services were supplied which occurred before issue of credit notes; object of credit notes was to recover VAT already paid on invoices; accountants' appeal dismissed).

3003   Refund—church committee building scheme—whether supplies received in course of business

Value added tax tribunal decision:

TRINITY METHODIST CHURCH, ROYTON (BUILDING COMMITTEE) v CUSTOMS AND EXCISE COMRS (1979) MAN/78/159 (unreported) (appellant committee established as project organisation by Methodist Church to enlarge church hall by addition of community recreation centre; construction effected by self-help project under aegis of Manpower Services Commission; appellant sought recovery of tax paid on supply of material, had to establish project was carried out in course of business; building of centre was isolated and no continuity found that was necessary for business; further appellant not separate entity but only project committee of Church; Church did not make taxable supplies only gratuitous supplies of facilities; not carrying on business for value added tax purposes).

3004   —— "do-it-yourself" housebuilders' scheme—reconstruction of existing building

Value added tax tribunal decision:

OWEN v CUSTOMS AND EXCISE COMRS (1979) LON/78/345 (unreported) (owner extensively rebuilt derelict property and built new building alongside, attached to derelict property, for use as dwelling-house by himself and family; tribunal held not construction of new dwelling, but enlargement of existing dwelling; therefore no refund of tax).

3005   **Registration—discretionary registration—project organisation**

Value added tax tribunal decision:

CANDO 70 v CUSTOMS AND EXCISE COMRS [1978] VATTR 211 (appellants unincorporated body established as project organisation by Baptist Church to convert church into social, educational and recreational centre; appellants sought discretionary registration under Finance Act 1972, Sch. 1, para. 11 (a), on basis of Public Notice SHP 1 issued by commissioners allowing registration of project organisations established as separate entities by voluntary bodies for purpose of construction projects; application refused; appellants were not separate entity but only building or projects committee of Church; hence Church itself was doing work, and Church did not make taxable supplies but only gratuitous supplies of facilities; thus neither Church nor appellants entitled to be registered; scheme set out in Public Notice SHP 1 was concessionary and extra-statutory and tribunal had no jurisdiction to interfere in relation to it).

3006   —— **group of companies—conditions**

Value added tax tribunal decision:

MANNIN SHIPPING LTD v CUSTOMS AND EXCISE COMRS [1979] VATTR 83 (family company registered as representative member of group of companies; shares of all the companies held mainly by members of the family; commissioners sought to cancel registration; under Act of Tynwald corresponding to Finance Act 1972, s. 21 (3), two or more bodies corporate eligible to be treated as members of a group if (i) one of them controls each of the others; (ii) one person, whether body corporate or individual, controls all of them; or (iii) two or more individuals carrying on a business in partnership control all of them; on analysis of shareholding in companies, none of conditions fulfilled; hence companies not entitled to be treated as members of a group and registration liable to cancellation).

3007   —— —— **"control" of trust company**

Value added tax tribunal decision:

BRITISH AIRWAYS BOARD v CUSTOMS AND EXCISE COMRS; AIRWAYS PENSION FUND TRUSTEES LTD v CUSTOMS AND EXCISE COMRS (1979) LON/79/107, 108 (unreported) (trust company contended that it was entitled to registration under Finance Act 1972, s. 21 as member of group of which British Airways Board was representative member, because Board controlled trust company; contention rejected; "control" limited to meaning given in s. 21 (3) and as Board was not holding company of trust company for purposes of Company's Act 1948 it did not apply in above case, nor was Board empowered by statute to "control" trust company as trust deed merely confirmed by Act of Parliament).

3008   —— **liability to be registered—accountability for tax during pre-registration period**

Value added tax tribunal decision:

DUKE (trading as RICHARD DUKE AND SON) v CUSTOMS AND EXCISE COMRS (1979) MAN/78/236 (unreported) (road haulage contractor registered for value added tax purposes on 13th November 1975; turnover of business was already at a level which rendered registration obligatory; contractor accordingly registered with effect from 21st April 1975; contractor failed to collect tax from some customers during pre-registration period; contractor unaware of liability to pay tax that had not been collected; appealed against assessment for period from 21st April to 13th November; contractor was accountable for tax on any taxable supply during pre-registration period subject to two limitations; liability did not extend to receipts after 13th November for supplies prior to that date; as some invoices recording input tax had not been retained during the pre-registration period, some compensating input tax could be allowed against the additional output tax).

3009   Relief—second-hand goods—cars

Value added tax tribunal decision:

WATSON V CUSTOMS AND EXCISE COMRS (1979) LON/78/115 (unreported) (taxpayer purchased cars in Holland for small sums and imported them into United Kingdom; he complied with requisite customs formalities and paid all due duty and fees, including value added tax; he then renovated cars and sold them; commenced trading on 19th January 1977; lived from week to week on proceeds of cars sold; all sales made for cash; no records kept of sales as taxpayer had difficulty in reading and writing; appealed against assessment; claimed allowances for expenditure on seat belts, petrol and spares and for cost of importing cars; as taxpayer worked from week to week, registration should take effect from 21st April 1977; allowance made for cost of seat belts, petrol and spares; no allowance made for cost of importation; taxpayer kept no records and no relief therefore available under Value Added Tax (Cars) Order 1972, reg. 7).

3010   Return—failure to make return—penalty

An information was preferred against the defendants on 9th March 1977 alleging that they had failed to furnish a value added tax return for a specified period, contrary to the Finance Act 1972, s. 38 (7). The information was heard on 18th April 1977 and the defendants pleaded guilty. The justices considered that failure to furnish a return continued until the date the information was preferred, and hence the daily penalty should cease on 9th March 1977. On appeal by the commissioners, *held*, s. 38 (7) provided that the defendant would be liable to a penalty for each day on which the failure continued. Giving the words their ordinary meaning, the daily penalty should be taken up to the date of the hearing. Unless terminated earlier on proof of compliance with the relevant regulations, the period of penalty ended with the hearing. The appeal would be allowed and the matter remitted to the justices for reconsideration of the sentence.

GRICE V NEEDS AND HALE [1979] STC 641 (Queen's Bench Division: LORD WIDGERY CJ and LLOYD J).

3011   Supply of goods and services—condition of making taxable supplies—power of commissioners to require security

Value added tax tribunal decision:

EVANS V CUSTOMS AND EXCISE COMRS (1979) CAR/79/124 (unreported) (as condition of supplying goods and services under taxable supply, commissioners, in exercise of powers under Finance Act 1972, s. 32 (2), required appellant to give security, in form of bond, of £10,000 with bank as surety; appellant, scrap metal dealer, exercised right of appeal under s. 40 (1) (i); appellant had been involved in four scrap metal companies all of which owed valued added tax to commissioners; also involved in legal proceedings against bank in connection with personal guarantee of loan to one of companies; difficult therefore to get bank as surety; effect of commissioner's requirement of security would be to put him out of business; penalty bond unreasonable mode of security; appellant now employed accountant to complete tax returns; evidence of good faith, therefore security not requisite for protection of revenue; appeal allowed).

3012   —— club, association or society—members' subscriptions and interest-free loans made to the club—whether supply for consideration in money

Value added tax tribunal decision

EXETER GOLF AND COUNTRY CLUB LTD V CUSTOMS AND EXCISE COMRS [1979] VATTR 70 (golf club required members to pay annual subscriptions and also annual interest-free loan; in return membership and the right to use the club facilities were conferred on members; commissioners contended consideration given for supply of membership etc. should be deemed to include interest on loans and that club should therefore be assessed to tax on supplies on that higher basis; club contended consideration consisted purely of money actually paid; club's contention upheld; consideration consisted only of actual cash payments paid to club).

3013   ——contract for supply imposing several obligations on tax-payer—whether each obligation to be treated as a separate supply

The taxpayers operated a stud farm which provided facilities for the keep and food of animals brought to stud. The invoices sent to customers distinguished between charges for stud services and those for keep and food, the latter being treated as zero-rated by the taxpayers on their value added tax returns. The Customs and Excise Commissioners claimed that since the feeding and stud services constituted a single supply the taxpayers were not entitled to the exemption, but the value added tax tribunal held the distinction to be valid and that the taxpayers' returns were therefore correct. The Commissioners appealed. *Held*, the supply of stud services and the keep of animals was one transaction, constituting one single supply: it was irrelevant that the taxpayers had apportioned the charges on the invoices. The appeal would be allowed.

CUSTOMS AND EXCISE COMRS v BUSHBY [1979] STC 8 (Queen's Bench Division: NEILL J). *Customs and Excise Comrs v Scott* [1978] STC 191, 1978 Halsbury's Abridgment para. 3059 applied.

3014   ——customer obtaining goods by fraud—whether supplier liable to tax

Value added tax tribunal decision:

HARRY B. LITHERLAND & CO LTD v CUSTOMS AND EXCISE COMRS [1978] VATTR 226 (appellant, a supplier of electrical goods, agreed to supply number of televisions to a regular customer; customer disappeared without paying for televisions and was subsequently convicted of obtaining property by deception; appellant appealed against assessment to VAT charged on the supply of the televisions; contended that contract of sale was voidable by reason of customer's fraud and that contract had been avoided by his communication to police; appellant had repudiated contract by informing police as soon as he discovered fraud; as there was no contract there could be no supply of goods under it; appellant not liable for VAT).

3015   —— gifts—business gifts incentive scheme

Value added tax tribunal decision:

GUS MERCHANDISE CORPN LTD v CUSTOMS AND EXCISE COMRS [1978] VATTR 28 (retail trader supplied goods costing less than £10 each to members of the public as inducements to become agents and to existing agents as inducements to become more active; trader advised by VAT officers that no tax chargeable on such supplies as treated as gifts under Finance Act 1972, Sch. 3, para. 6; trader operated retailers' special schemes and accounted for tax by reference to gross takings; did not account for tax on supplies made under incentive schemes; trader's books investigated by officers having knowledge of incentive scheme without challenging omission; assessment made on supplies under incentive schemes; trader appealed; goods supplied to members of the public not supplied under legally enforceable contracts were gifts and no tax chargeable; goods supplied to existing agents under legally enforceable contracts were not gifts and tax was chargeable; goods did not form part of retail stock and fell outside retailers' special schemes; tax chargeable had to be accounted for in addition to tax calculated by reference to gross takings; notwithstanding representations by officers and failure to challenge omission, no estoppel lay against commissioners).

3016   —— goods and services supplied for a consideration—meaning of consideration

The taxpayer company was a member of a group of companies, and by an agreement with the principal company of the group on 25th May 1973, it provided management services to other members of the group, to which it made no charges and consequently incurred losses. The taxpayer company was to surrender these losses to the other profit-making companies in exchange for group relief payments, pursuant to the Income and Corporation Taxes Act 1970, s. 258. To satisfy the auditors it was necessary for the taxpayer company and the principal company to enter into an agreement on 1st August 1974, incorporating the agreement of 25th May 1973 and guaranteeing the group relief payments in exchange for the surrender of the losses. The taxpayer company was assessed for value added tax on the basis that under the agreement it had supplied services for a consideration to the other companies. The taxpayer company appealed contending (i) the 1974 agreement was not entered into by the parties with the intention of affecting their legal relations, but merely to reassure their auditors; (ii) the 1974 agreement was not enforceable because the taxpayer company had provided no consideration. The provision of management services was not consideration because there was already a binding obligation on the taxpayer company to provide those services under the 1973 agreement; (iii) the procuring of group relief payments by the principal company was not consideration within the meaning of the Finance Act 1972, ss. 5 (2) and 10 (3). The value added tax tribunal allowed the appeal. The Crown appealed. *Held*, the services were supplied for a consideration and were thus liable to value added tax because (i) having regard to the fact that the agreement was a formal one entered into on professional advice, it was an agreement which was intended to be legally binding and have legal effect; (ii) if the obligation on the taxpayer company to provide the management services was binding from 1973 the Crown could have contended that the services were rendered for a consideration from that date: either the 1974 agreement did not impose an additional obligation so that the services after the date of that agreement were still supplied under the 1973 agreement for the consideration expressed in that agreement, or the services were supplied under the 1974 agreement for the consideration stated therein; (iii) the principal company's promise to procure group relief payments was a real and valuable consideration within the Finance Act 1972, s. 10 (3). The appeal would be allowed.

CUSTOMS AND EXCISE COMRS v TILLING MANAGEMENT SERVICES LTD [1979] STC 365 (Queen's Bench Division: NEILL J). Decision of value added tax tribunal (1977) LON/77/5 (unreported), 1977 Halsbury's Abridgment para. 3082 reversed.

3017 Value added tax tribunal decision:

PIPPA-DEE PARTIES LTD v CUSTOMS AND EXCISE COMRS (1979) MAN/79/43 (unreported) (appellant company conducted its business by its regional organisers selling goods at private house parties, the hostesses at those parties being entitled to a cash commission based on value of orders placed; hostesses had option to use commission to purchase appellant's goods at substantial discount; appellant contended value added tax payable only upon cash commission and not on open market value of goods; consideration was to be given its normal meaning in English law; if hostess chose to exercise her option, ordinary transaction of sale and purchase took place, sole consideration for supply of goods being the amount of the cash commission; tax chargeable therefore only on amount of money hostesses paid for goods and not their open market value).

3018 —— —— **whether consideration given**

Value added tax tribunal decision:

WARWICK MASONIC ROOMS LTD v CUSTOMS AND EXCISE COMRS (1979) BIR/79/33 (unreported) (company allowed various persons to park on its ground over a period of years; no payment was ever sought, but donations were sometimes made to the company's building fund; commissioners contended tax was payable on those sums as provision of car-parking was provision of a service; grant of parking facility held to be other than for consideration and there was thus no supply under Finance Act 1972, s. 5 (2) before 1978, or under that Act as amended by Finance Act 1977 after that date).

3019　—— nature of supply

Value added tax tribunal decision:

CHURCHWAY CRAFTS LTD v CUSTOMS AND EXCISE COMRS (1979) LON/78/143 (unreported) (appellant company allowed its agents to employ hostesses to effect retail sales of goods to the public on behalf of the company; hostesses held parties in their private houses, in consideration of which they were allowed a percentage of total party sales either in cash or goods; this percentage was assessed as a taxable supply of goods; company's contention that it sold goods to the hostesses who then became retailers, rejected; hostesses' percentage represented her commission on sales as an agent and tax was due on it).

3020　—— programme for stamp fair

Value added tax tribunal decision:

JARMAIN v CUSTOMS AND EXCISE COMRS [1979] VATTR 41 (stamp dealer who organised stamp fairs appealed against an assessment for value added tax in respect of money paid by visitors to fairs on entrance; alleged money received as payment for programme and therefore zero-rated; commissioners contended money paid as admission charge; question for tribunal was what was the supply for which payment was made; production cost of programme one quarter of price charged and a proportion was chargeable to tax).

3021　—— second-hand cars—whether hearse a motor car

Value added tax tribunal decision:

DAVIES v CUSTOMS AND EXCISE COMRS (1979) CAR/79/65 (unreported) (second-hand car dealer sold eight funeral hearses acquired second-hand in the course of business; appealed against assessment on ground that hearse was motor vehicle within meaning of Value Added Tax (Cars) Order 1977; hearse was vehicle constructed for special purpose, to carry coffin (either empty or containing corpse) accommodation for carrying persons provided only for driver and pall-bearers, who were incidental to purpose for which hearse constructed; hearse therefore within exception to definition of motor car by 1977 Order, art 2 (e); tax payable by reference to price for which dealer sold hearses and not difference between price for which he bought and sold them).

3022　—— supply by retailer

The Value Added Tax (Supplies by Retailers) (Amendment) Regulations 1979, S.I. 1979 No. 224 (in force on 2nd April 1979), make minor amendments to the Value Added Tax (Supplies by Retailers) Regulations 1972, regs. 1 (2) and 2 (2), to make clear that notice includes a leaflet and that the Commissioners of Customs and Excise may vary the terms of any method discribed in a notice published by them without republishing the whole of any notice previously issued.

3023　—— supply in the course of business—horse-breeding

Value added tax tribunal decision:

PRENN v CUSTOMS AND EXCISE COMRS (1979) LON/78/406 (unreported) (claimant both a horse-breeder and a horse-racer; commissioners cancelled his registration for value added tax purposes on grounds that his activities as a breeder were an adjunct to his activities as an owner of racehorses and did not amount to a business for tax purposes; breeding was a long term business and was regularly conducted on sound and recognisable business principles with the intention of making a profit; the breeding and racing activities were carried on entirely separately with separate accounts and bank accounts; claimant entitled therefore to be registered for tax purposes and to claim repayment of input tax in respect of sales of nominations to stallions and the supplies of horses from the breeding stables to racing activities).

3024 —— —— **meaning of business**

Under the Water Act 1973, the National Water Council was required to perform administrative, advisory and other services for ministers, regional water authorities and outside organisations. It claimed for value added tax purposes that all services supplied by it were supplied "in the course of a business" within the Finance Act 1972, s. 2 (2), and that it was entitled to charge output tax on them and under s. 3 (1) to deduct input tax on goods and services supplied to it. It also contended that even if it was only carrying on a business to a limited extent, it was entitled to deduct input tax on all supplies made to it in the course of such business activities. The commissioners rejected the claim and their decision was upheld by a value added tax tribunal. On appeal by the Council, *held*, the word "business" was not restricted to activities which were carried on commercially or with the object of making a profit. A service supplied in the performance of a statutory duty could be supplied in the course of a business. Whether it did so depended on to whom the supply was made, the contract or arrangement under which it was made and whether the service was supplied regularly and on a wide scale. Once relevant business had been shown to exist in relation to a particular service, there was a presumption that all supplies of that service were made in the course of a business. However, it was apparent from certain provisions of the Water Act that the Council's advisory and administrative functions performed exclusively for ministers or public bodies were to be excepted from the scope of its business activities. Under s. 3 (1), input tax could be apportioned where goods or services were supplied partly for business purposes and partly for other purposes. The appeal would be allowed in part and the case remitted to the tribunal.

NATIONAL WATER COUNCIL v CUSTOMS AND EXCISE COMRS [1979] STC 157 (Queen's Bench Division: NEILL J). *Customs and Excise Commissioners v Morrison's Academy Boarding Houses Association* [1978] STC 1, 1977 Halsbury's Abridgment para. 3084 applied. Decision of value added tax tribunal (1976) LON/76/9 (unreported), 1976 Halsbury's Abridgment para. 2777 reversed in part.

3025 As directed under a trust set up for the purpose of advancing public education, trustees raised substantial sums of money by appealing to the public for funds that did not involve any taxable supplies. They then incorporated a company, acquired a lease of a building for a term of twenty-five years and, having erected a theatre in the building, assigned the lease to the company as provided by the trust deed. A value added tax tribunal, allowing the trustees' appeal from the decision of the commissioners, held that the assignment of the lease was a supply in the course of a business within the Finance Act 1972, s. 2 (a). The commissioners appealed. *Held*, the complete absence of any monetary consideration from the company and the lack of any commercial element in the activities of the trustees meant that those activities were not business activities. Accordingly, the assignment of the lease to the company did not constitute a supply in the course of a business. The appeal would be allowed.

CUSTOMS AND EXCISE COMRS v ROYAL EXCHANGE THEATRE TRUST [1979] STC 728 (Queen's Bench Division: NEILL J). Dicta of Lord Emslie in *Customs and Excise Comrs v Morrison's Academy Boarding Houses Association* [1978] STC 1 at 6, 1977 Halsbury's Abridgment para. 3084 followed.

3026 —— —— —— **performance of statutory duty**

See *St. Helen's Metropolitan Borough Council v Customs and Excise Comrs*, para. 3046.

3027 —— —— —— **propagation of religion or religious philosophy**

The taxpayer, an American body incorporated with the object of propagating the religious faith scientology, had premises in England where it ran courses for persons interested in scientology and sold books and other materials connected with scientology. The Commissioners of Customs and Excise assessed the taxpayer to value added tax under the Finance Act 1972, s. 2 on payments received in respect of the courses and the sale of books and other materials, on the basis that the taxpayer was supplying goods and services in the course of a business carried on in the United

Kingdom. The assessment was upheld by a value added tax tribunal, which found that the combined activities of the taxpayer constituted the business of propagating scientology as a commodity, carried on in the United Kingdom, and that the relevant supplies were made as a commercial and economic activity, being part of that business. The taxpayer appealed. *Held*, the tribunal had not erred in law in finding that the propagation of scientology was carried on by the taxpayer as a business: there was no reason why the propagation of a religion or religious philosophy should not be regarded as a business for the purposes of s. 2 (2) (b), and the tribunal was entitled to consider the activities of the taxpayer as a whole in reaching its decision. Accordingly, the tribunal was justified in finding that the relevant supplies were made in the course of a business. The appeal would be dismissed.

CHURCH OF SCIENTOLOGY OF CALIFORNIA v CUSTOMS AND EXCISE COMRS [1979] STC 297 (Queen's Bench Division: NEILL J). *Customs and Excise Comrs v Morrison's Academy Boarding House Association* [1978] STC 1, 1977 Halsbury's Abridgment para. 3084 applied. Decision of value added tax tribunal [1977] VATTR 278, 1977 Halsbury's Abridgment para. 3039 affirmed.

3028   —— —— private use of company cars by directors

Value added tax tribunal decision:

MITCHELL HAZELHURST LTD v CUSTOMS AND EXCISE COMRS (1979) LON/79/61 (unreported) (appeal against assessment to value added tax on private use by company directors of cars owned by the company; directors made payments to company in respect of the use of the cars; such payments were intended to reduce their personal liability to tax by reducing their taxable income; the tribunal upheld the commissioners' claim that, by allowing directors to make personal use of the cars, the company was making a taxable supply; there was no reason to regard the supply of the cars as part of the directors' remuneration).

3029   —— —— services supplied as holder of office

HM Customs and Excise and the Law Society have agreed a statement setting out the views of HM Customs and Excise on s. 45 (4) of the Finance Act 1972, as substituted by the Finance Act 1977, s. 14, Sch. 6, para. 13. In determining whether an office-holder is liable to value added tax by virtue of his office, HM Customs and Excise look at the nature of the office and the duties involved; if professional skills are exercised the office is regarded as performed "in the course of" the holder's profession. However, the words "or furtherance" may bring offices where professional skills are not exercised within the charge to tax under s. 45 (4). The statement includes a definition of "office" for this purpose and sets out criteria whereby a partnership would not be regarded as supplying a service even though an individual partner might perform the duties of an office. Among offices liable to the charge to tax are: commissioners for oaths, under-sheriffs, receivers appointed by the Court of Protection, members of legal aid committees, clerks to the General Commissioners of Income Tax and certain part-time judicial appointments. The following offices are not regarded as liable to value added tax: deputy High Court judges, recorders, deputy circuit judges, deputy metropolitan magistrates, deputy provincial stipendiary magistrates, deputy court and district registrars, deputy masters and registrars of the Supreme Court, deputy assistants to Chancery registrars, coroners, deputy coroners and assistant deputy coroners.

LS Gaz, 21st November 1979, page 1151.

3030   —— —— supply of clothing to Olympic competitors

Value added tax tribunal decision:

BRITISH OLYMPIC ASSOCIATION v CUSTOMS AND EXCISE COMRS [1979] VATTR 122 (association formed to encourage interest in Olympic Games; subscriptions received from and facilities supplied to members; money raised by appeals to finance and clothe British competitors; association contended tax paid by it on supplies of such clothing deductible as input tax; whether supplies obtained for purpose of business carried on by association; under Finance Act 1972, s. 45 (1)(b) business includes provision by club or association of facilities available to its members; deemed business did not extend to supplies of clothing for competitors since competitors not members; nor was it carrying on business in general sense of the term; hence input tax not deductible).

1972 Act, s. 45, now as substituted by Finance Act 1977, Sch. 6.

3031   —— —— supply of vehicles to salesmen

Value added tax tribunal decision:

WILLIAM PETO & CO LTD v CUSTOMS AND EXCISE COMRS (1979) MAN/78/66 (unreported) (company provided cars for salesmen which they were entitled to use for private purposes; company charged salesmen £13 per month for private use of cars; company assessed to VAT on supply of cars; appeal to tribunal; privilege of using cars for private purposes was granted in furtherance of good industrial relations and was therefore done in course of business carried on by company; charge for private use irrelevant; also under Finance Act 1972, Sch. 2, para. 1, vehicles were acquired by company in course of business and applied by it to personal use of salesmen, thus deemed to be supplied by company in course of business; hence supply in course of business and VAT payable; *RHM Bakeries (Northern) Ltd v Customs and Excise Comrs* (1978) Times, 5th July, 1978 Halsbury's Abridgment para. 3058 applied).

3032   —— supply of stolen goods—nature of supply

A second-hand car dealer stole cars and then sold them by auction after changing their number plates, engines and chassis numbers. The commissioners appealed against a decision that, although the dealing was in the course of the car dealer's business, he had not transferred a proper title in the stolen cars, and no supply had therefore taken place for the purposes of value added tax assessment, within the meaning of the Finance Act 1972. *Held*, in s. 5 (2) of the 1972 Act, "supply" bore a wide meaning and was not limited to one which also constituted a sale. A supply occurred where possession passed pursuant to an agreement. "Possession" meant in this context control over the goods in the sense of having the immediate facility for their use; it was irrelevant that the agreement was in fact void or that the dealer was unable to transfer title. It was clear that a taxable supply had taken place, and the appeal would, accordingly, be allowed.

CUSTOMS AND EXCISE COMRS v OLIVER [1980] STC 73 (Queen's Bench Division: GRIFFITHS J).

3033   —— time of supply

Value added tax tribunal decision:

GEORGE HAMSHAW (GOLF SERVICES) LTD v CUSTOMS AND EXCISE COMRS [1979] VATTR 51 (golf club issued members with tax invoice in respect of subscriptions at the beginning of each year; when the club went into liquidation members were given credit notes for that proportion of the subscription relating to the remainder of the year; the club appealed against an assessment for value added tax in respect of the sums represented by the credit notes; services for which the tax was charged should be taken to have been performed at the time of issue of the tax invoice; credit notes invalid and sum not deductible from assessment).

3034   —— value of supply—gaming machines

Value added tax tribunal decision:

TOWNVILLE (WHELDALE) MINERS SPORTS AND RECREATION CLUB AND INSTITUTE v CUSTOMS AND EXCISE COMRS (1978) MAN/78/212 (unreported) (club steward jammed club's fruit machines so they paid out each time played; club assessed to VAT on full hypothetical takings of machines notwithstanding fraud; club owners contended tax chargeable only on actual takings since under Finance (No. 2) Act 1975, s. 21 (2) value of supplies determined as if consideration reduced by amount of winnings; therefore impossible to ascertain sum on which tax chargeable until known what machine paid out; commissioners contended time of supply under Finance Act 1972, s. 7 (3), was when services performed i.e. when each game over, consideration being coin inserted by each player; under s. 10 (2) value of supply was such amount as with addition of tax chargeable was equal to consideration; thus sum on which tax chargeable ascertainable at time machine played; commissioners' contention upheld; s. 21 (2) merely a mitigating section which reduced value of supply as provided by s. 10 (2); tax chargeable on full amount including that improperly abstracted).

3035   Value added tax tribunal—application for costs

Value added tax tribunal decision:
JOCELYN FEILDING FINE ART LTD v CUSTOMS AND EXCISE COMRS (1978) LON/78/81 (unreported) (application for costs in respect of successful appeal against assessment of value added tax; company represented by its managing director who alone was concerned with the day-to-day running of the company; claim for certain sum as proportion of average daily earnings of company; not possible to quantify loss of earnings but salary of director was recoverable as costs; also cost which would have been incurred had an independent adviser represented the company). *Re Nosren's Patent* [1969] 1 All ER 775 and *Re Eastwood (deceased), Lloyds Bank Ltd v Eastwood* [1974] 3 All ER 603, CA, 1974 Halsbury's Abridgment para. 2627 applied.
For the substantive proceedings see 1978 Halsbury's Abridgment para. 3052.

3036   —— jurisdiction—review of commissioners' discretion

Numismatists appealed against an assessment to VAT in respect of items which had been disallowed under the Value Added Tax (Works of Art, Antiques and Scientific Collections) Order 1972. The items had been disallowed as the commissioners were not satisfied that proper records had been kept in respect of them and thus the items did not qualify for the margin scheme set out in the order. The tribunal found that it had express jurisdiction over the assessment and had power to go into all matters relating to the appeal de novo, including re-examining the records. The commissioners' appeal was allowed on the ground that the commissioners had an unfettered discretion to determine whether the records were sufficient which the tribunal could not review. On appeal by the numismatists, *held*, the tribunal had jurisdiction to go into all matters relating to an appeal against assessment de novo and to substitute its own opinion for that of the commissioners. Accordingly the appeal would be allowed.
CUSTOMS AND EXCISE COMRS v J H CORBITT (NUMISMATISTS) LTD [1979] STC 504 (Court of Appeal: LORD DENNING MR, EVELEIGH LJ and SIR STANLEY REES). Decision of Neill J [1978] STC 531, 1978 Halsbury's Abridgment para. 3072 reversed.

3037   Zero rating—aids for the disabled

The Value Added Tax (Aids for the Disabled) Order 1979, S.I. 1979 No. 245 (in force on 2nd April 1979), zero-rates the supply to the Royal Institute for the Blind, the National Listening Library and other similar charities, of apparatus designed or adapted for the reproduction of speech recorded on magnetic tape and of those magnetic tape recordings.

3038   —— building work—construction or alteration of building

Value added tax tribunal decisions:
CHIGSHIRE LTD v CUSTOMS AND EXCISE COMRS (1979) MAN/78/115 (unreported) (company claimed that stone cladding, fixing manufactured material resembling stonework, to exterior walls of house was zero-rated by virtue of Finance Act 1972, Sch. 4, Group 8, item 2 as alteration work; stone cladding was of decorative nature only or in nature of repairs and was not of structural nature: not therefore supplied in course of alteration of buildings).

3039   NORTHLANDS SECURITIES DEVELOPMENTS LTD v CUSTOMS AND EXCISE COMRS (1979) LON/78/225 (unreported) (appellants contended that alteration of single flats into two penthouse maisonettes constituted the construction of a building and was therefore zero rated; distinction was to be drawn between the mere extension or improvement of a building and the construction of a building; there was no construction of a building where there was merely reconstruction and enlargement of rooms previously in existence).

3040   PAROCHIAL CHURCH COUNCIL OF ALL SAINTS CHURCH, WELLINGTON v CUSTOMS AND EXCISE COMRS (1979) MAN/79/34 (unreported) (during course of inspection of church, windows on upper level found to be in state of disrepair; glass removed and replaced with stained glass from lower windows, which in turn was replaced by plain glass and a sheet of protective glass; appellant contended that work on lower windows was zero-rated, being alteration to church rather than repair, and further, protective glass provided form of double glazing; however, tests applied should be whether alteration of a structural nature rather than merely visual, whether work carried out substantial in relation to building as a whole, and whether alteration permanent and irreversible; as alterations did not fulfil any of criteria demanded for work to be zero-rated, appeal would be dismissed).

3041 ———————— **repair or maintenance**

The foundations of some houses were damaged by subsidence and the taxpayers, who were builders, were employed to underpin them. As the original foundations were defective and could not be repaired, the taxpayers constructed additional foundations, leaving the originals unaltered. They were assessed to value added tax under the Finance Act 1972, Sch. 4, group 8, note 2, on the basis that although there had been a supply of services in the course of alteration of buildings, the work was maintenance and thus excluded from the zero-rating provisions of group 8. A value added tax tribunal upheld the assessment on the ground that the work done was "maintenance", basing their decision on a definition of the word given by a tribunal in a previous case. On appeal by the taxpayers, the commissioners contended that the appeal did not raise a point of law, since the tribunal's decision turned on the meaning of "maintenance", which was an ordinary English word. *Held*, where a tribunal purported to define the meaning of an ordinary English word for the purpose of applying a statute and gave an incomplete or unsatisfactory definition, such a misinterpretation involved an error of law and accordingly there was a right of appeal.

Where alteration to a building resulted in the building becoming substantially different in character, the work was not work of repair or maintenance, since "repair" was limited to putting an existing building into good order or restoring its condition and "maintenance" to keeping a building in good repair. Whether the character of a building was changed was a question of degree. The tribunal had erred in law in failing to ask themselves whether such a change had taken place. In view of the fact that the original foundations were defective, the character of the houses in question had been altered by the work and accordingly the work was not repair or maintenance and fell to be zero-rated. The appeal would be allowed.

ACT CONSTRUCTION LTD v CUSTOMS AND EXCISE COMRS [1979] STC 358 (Queen's Bench Division: DRAKE J). *Sotheby v Grundy* [1947] 2 All ER 761 and *Brew Brothers Ltd v Snax (Ross) Ltd* [1970] 1 All ER 587 applied. Decision of value added tax tribunal (1978) LON/78/144 (unreported), 1978 Halsbury's Abridgment para. 3078 reversed.

3042   The owners of a cinema employed builders to convert it into a bingo hall. The question arose whether the work carried out by the builders was a zero-rated supply by virtue of the Finance Act 1972, Sch. 4, group 8, item 2, being a supply in the course of the construction, alteration or demolition of a building, or whether it was a work of repair or maintenance and thus fell outside those provisions. A value added tax tribunal examined the disputed items individually and decided that some of them should be standard rated as works of repair or maintenance and the rest should be zero-rated under Sch. 4, group 8, item 2; although some of the latter items, consisting of redecoration and remedial work, would be regarded individually as repair or maintenance, each had in the context in which it appeared to be regarded as part of the alteration of the building. The commissioners appealed against the finding and the owners cross-appealed, contending that the tribunal was wrong to treat the items as a number of different supplies, as the work should have been treated as a single supply. *Held*, (i) the tribunal had not erred in looking at each item separately, since there was a real issue as to whether certain services fell outside the scope of Sch. 4, group 8, item 2. The cross-appeal would be dismissed. (ii) The tribunal had erred in its construction of Sch. 4, group 8, where "alteration" meant structural alteration to a building. The tribunal should first have looked to see what services were supplied in the course of the construction or structural alteration of the building, which would be zero-rated unless they included any work of repair or maintenance. Also zero-rated would be any consequential work flowing directly from the work of construction or alteration. The appeal would be allowed and the disputed items remitted to the tribunal for reconsideration.

CUSTOMS AND EXCISE COMRS v MORRISON DUNBAR LTD [1979] STC 406 (Queen's Bench Division: NEILL J).

3043   Value added tax tribunal decisions:

HORNBY ROAD INVESTMENTS LTD AND CO-OPERATIVE INSURANCE SOCIETY LTD v CUSTOMS AND EXCISE COMRS [1979] VATTR 1 (contractors built office block for appellant company; five years after completion of building cracks appeared in walls and had to be remedied; appellant company assessed to VAT on supplies for remedial works as being works of repair or maintenance; appellant company contended supplies were zero-rated as being made in the course of construction of the building, since subsequent cracks were due to bad original construction; a building could not continue in the course of construction indefinitely and consequently remedial work was not undertaken in course of construction of building; remedial measures could aptly be described as a work of repair; assessment upheld).

3044   L AND B LENDA LTD v CUSTOMS AND EXCISE COMRS (1979) CAR/78/402 (unreported) (commissioners contended work done by a builder in replacing timbers affected by dry rot and rewiring was a work of repair assessable at the standard rate of value added tax; builder appealed; work done on dry rot was a work of repair but much of the wiring was completely new; that part of the assessment which related to new installations was zero-rated).

3045   —— **charities—donated medical equipment**

The Value Added Tax (Donated Medical Equipment) Order 1979, S.I. 1979 No. 242 (in force on 2nd April 1979), varies item 3 of Group 16 of Schedule 4 to the Finance Act 1972, by extending the zero-rate relief to similar supplies of eligible equipment for donation to designated Regional and Area Health Authorities in England and Wales, Health Boards in Scotland and Health and Social Services Boards in Northern Ireland.

3046   —— **civil engineering work—alteration**

Value added tax tribunal decision:

ST. HELEN'S METROPOLITAN BOROUGH COUNCIL v CUSTOMS AND EXCISE COMRS (1979) MAN/78/147 (unreported) (council procured contractors to make carriage crossings over pavements to enable householders to drive vehicles from the road onto their properties; set charge made for facilities; council assessed to VAT on ground that it was making supplies of services to householders for consideration in the course of a business carried on by it; on appeal against assessment, council contended making of a crossing was an alteration of a civil engineering work, namely the highway, and therefore should be zero-rated under Finance Act 1972, Sch. 4, Group 8, items 2, 3; also that council was not acting in the course of any business carried on by it but carrying out a duty to provide and maintain highways imposed by Highways Act 1971; business could exist notwithstanding that crossings provided by statutory authority; giving word a wide construction, council was acting in the course of a business; construction of crossings did not amount to alteration of the highway since only change was to pavement; hence supplies taxable at standard rate; *National Water Council v Customs and Excise Comrs* [1979] STC 157, para. 3024 applied).

3047   —— exports—necessity for documentary proof of export

Taxpayer made wholesale export sales over the counter to overseas customers. Each customer was given an appropriate export form, a tax invoice and a stamped, addressed envelope. He was instructed to complete the form, have it stamped by a Customs and Excise officer on export and post it back to the taxpayer. Most of the customers failed to return the form. The taxpayer was assessed to value added tax in respect of the supply of goods to those customers. The taxpayer appealed, contending that the supply should be zero-rated under the Finance Act 1972, s. 12 and the Value Added Tax (General) Regulations 1975, reg. 44. The Value Added Tax Notice 703, para. 10, issued by the commissioners under s. 12 and reg. 44, stated that exported goods could be zero-rated only if prescribed proof of export was obtained within one month of the supply. The tribunal was satisfied that some of the goods supplied had been exported and that the taxpayer had done everything possible to comply with the conditions relating to proof of export. The appeal was dismissed, however, as the taxpayer could not produce proof of export because of the customers' failure to return the forms, and the conditions of para. 10 had not, therefore, been complied with. The taxpayer further appealed, contending that the conditions imposed by para. 10 were unreasonable and therefore void. *Held*, the requirement that the goods be exported within one month of supply was not unreasonable. However, the condition which required that only the stipulated method of proof was acceptable as proof of export was unreasonable for such proof was virtually impossible for the taxpayer to secure, as it depended on action by the customer who was outside the taxpayer's control. The goods which the tribunal found to have been exported should be zero-rated. The appeal would be allowed to that extent.

HENRY MOSS OF LONDON LTD v CUSTOMS AND EXCISE COMRS [1979] STC 657 (Queen's Bench Division: FORBES J).

3048   Value added tax tribunal decisions:

HELGOR FURS LTD v CUSTOMS AND EXCISE COMRS (1979) LON/78/339 (unreported) (company purported to export furs to Japanese visitor by means of "over the counter" scheme; no proof of export, as purchaser had been unable to get furs certified on departure from UK because furs too bulky to be carried as hand baggage; as no proof of export, zero-rating could not be applied to furs; tribunal expressed view that export of goods unacceptable to airlines as hand baggage, not suitable for "over the counter" scheme).

3049   SADRI (TRADING AS HUTOSH COMMERCIAL) v CUSTOMS AND EXCISE COMRS (1978) LON/78/265 (unreported) (appellant exported contact lenses to India; assessed to VAT on grounds that insufficient evidence of exportation produced in order to qualify for zero-rating; appellant contended that as she had proof of export, goods should be zero-rated within Finance Act 1972, s. 12 (6); commissioners contended goods could only be zero-rated if conditions in regulations made and notices given by commissioners under s. 12 (7) were complied with, and in any event, matter was entirely within their discretion; tribunal had jurisdiction to decide whether tax chargeable on supplies; tribunal satisfied that goods exported; however, s. 12 (6), (7), should be read together so that appellant was required to fulfil conditions imposed by commissioners; assessment upheld).

3050   —— food

Value added tax tribunal decision:

MACKLIN SERVICES (VENDING) WEST LTD v CUSTOMS AND EXCISE COMRS [1979]

VATTR 31 (unreported) (applicants owned hot drinks vending machines in various places only some of which were accessible to the public; the question arose as to whether the supply of drinks from the machines was a catering supply taxable at standard rate of value added tax; to be part of catering supply food and drink had to be consumed on the same premises as that on which it was supplied; none of the machines were on the public highway and so were all on premises; as a purchaser did not have to leave the premises to consume his drink there was a supply in the course of catering).

3051   —— international services

The Value Added Tax (International Services) Order 1979, S.I. 1979 No. 244 (in force on 2nd April 1979), amends the Finance Act 1972, Sch. 4, Group 9. The Order zero-rates under item 6 (a) the study of taxable insurance and re-insurance services other than those exempted by Sch. 5, Group 2. It removes, in part, the restrictions contained in note (5) and revokes note (7), thus zero-rating certain international services.

3052   The Value Added Tax (International Services) (No. 2) Order 1979, S.I. 1979 No. 1554 (in force on 1st January 1980), removes from eligibility to zero-rating the supply of any certificate of deposit, which is now exempt, whether made to a person in the United Kingdom or overseas.

3053   —— —— agent of overseas principals

Value added tax tribunal decision:
    JOHNSON v CUSTOMS AND EXCISE COMRS (1979) LON/78/449 (unreported) (woman who organised educational holidays in Britain for foreign students alleged the supply was zero-rated because she was acting as agent of principals resident overseas; two types of holiday arranged; for one she prepared details of what certain facilities would cost; holidays booked by overseas organisations according to requirements of students who booked with them; for others she sent brochures to organisations; some of latter holidays were booked by students personally; only those holidays were not zero-rated; in all other cases she acted as agent and alter ego of foreign organisations).

3054   —— —— services relating to land

HM Customs and Excise have made a statement outlining their views on the interpretation of the phrase "services relating to land" in the Finance Act 1972, Sch. 4, Group 9, Item 1, and Sch. 2A, para. 3. They have said that they regard the phrase as affecting only those services provided by lawyers which relate directly to the sale, disposal, transfer or surrender of an interest in or right over land or a building attached to the land. Accordingly, a solicitor's services in connection with a conveyancing transaction, whether the property be freehold or leasehold, are regarded as services relating to land; on the other hand, where a solicitor acts for a client in the take-over of a company, one of whose assets might be freehold land, the services are regarded as relating to the taking-over of the company and are not regarded as "services relating to land". A number of specific examples are given, illustrating the attitude of HM Customs and Excise.
    LS Gaz, 21st November 1979, page 1152.

3055   —— —— supply to overseas resident of services not used in United Kingdom

A company, formed to provide management development services to industry, ran a management course in Britain, specially tailored for Nigerian executives. The course was organised on a "package deal" basis and included accommodation, air travel etc. The company were assessed for tax in respect of a supply of services. A value added tax tribunal held that the supply was zero-rated under the Finance Act 1972, Sch. 4, Group 9, item 6, because the course was supplied to overseas residents only and was not "used" in the United Kingdom, as the information imparted on the course was usable only in Nigeria. *Held*, the course was "used" by the executives in the United Kingdom, when they attended lectures and other parts of the course, and it was irrelevant that the information imparted could only be used in Nigeria. The provision of the course was not therefore a zero-rated supply. Furthermore, as the course was marketed as a single supply, it was not a supply of a variety of services and could not therefore be apportioned under s. 10 (4) of the Act; instead the whole supply was taxable.

CUSTOMS AND EXCISE COMRS v G AND B PRACTICAL MANAGEMENT DEVELOPMENT LTD [1979] STC 280 (Queen's Bench Division: NEILL J). Decision of VAT tribunal [1977] VATTR 128, 1977 Halsbury's Abridgment para. 3107 reversed.

3056   —— —— work carried out on goods

Value added tax tribunal decision:

BANSTEAD MANOR STUD LTD V CUSTOMS AND EXCISE COMRS (1979) LON/78/412 (unreported) (appellants owned stud farm; mare imported from abroad to be covered and got in foal by a particular stallion owned by a syndicate; commissioners conceded that covering of mare was "work carried out on goods" for that purpose imported into the United Kingdom and was thus zero-rated under Finance Act 1972, Sch. 4, Group 9, item 10; appellants contended supply of keep and other services provided by stud should also be regarded as supplies of work carried out on goods; supply of stud services and keep normally standard-rated; however, purpose for which mare was imported and kept at stud farm was to become in foal to the stallion; major part of "work carried out on goods" was provided by stallion and his owners, but work could not have been carried out apart from stud services; accordingly latter fell within definition of "work carried out on goods").

3057   —— medical goods and services

The Value Added Tax (Medical Goods and Services) Order 1979, S.I. 1979 No. 246 (in force on 2nd April 1979), varies the Finance Act 1972, Schedules 4 and 5 (Groups 14 and 7 respectively). This takes account of changes in the registers of qualified medical practitioners introduced by the Medical Act 1978, 1978 Halsbury's Abridgment para. 1864. This Order extends to medical practitioners on the new register the value added tax relief in both Groups 14 and 7. It also extends the exemption under Group 7 of the Exemption Schedule to include the provision of a deputising service for doctors and, in addition exempts the supply of medical services by persons whose names appear in the statutory registers and roles referred to in the Group, where such professional services are supplied through a third party.

3058   —— —— adaptation of house for disabled person—supply of building materials

Value added tax tribunal decision:

WALSH V CUSTOMS AND EXCISE COMRS (1979) BEL/79/2 (unreported) (claimant, ninety-six per cent disabled, built extension to his house, designed to suit requirements of severely disabled person; work carried out by tradesman using materials provided by claimant from builders' merchants; sought to recover value added tax paid on supply of these materials on ground that extension was medical or surgical appliance for domestic use and therefore zero-rated; building materials not regarded as appliances; further, zero-rating restricted to appliances designed solely for relief of severe abnormality, and did not therefore include building materials; tax payable therefore at standard rate).

WAR AND ARMED CONFLICT

Halsbury's Laws of England (3rd edn.), Vol. 39, paras. 18–240

3059   Pensions—personal injuries due to war service

See PENSIONS.

3060   —— **personal injuries of civilians**

See PENSIONS.

WATER SUPPLY

Halsbury's Laws of England (3rd edn.), Vol. 39, paras. 241–652

3061   **National Water Council—supply of statutory services—whether supply in course of business for VAT purposes**

See *National Water Council v Customs and Excise Commissioners*, para. 3024.

3062   **Statutory water undertakers—duty to provide domestic supply to new dwellings—contribution to cost of construction—"necessary mains".**

A firm of developers had built seven hundred dwellings on a site where there was no existing mains water supply. They requested the local statutory water authority under the Water Act 1945, s. 37 (1), as amended, to provide a domestic water supply to the houses. The only distribution main which carried sufficient water and was not fully committed was some distance from the site. The water authority in response to the developers' request laid a pipe from the main to the site and demanded a contribution to the cost of laying it which the developers paid without prejudice to their contention that the amount claimed was not exigible. The developers contended that, although they had to pay for the necessary mains on the site, they were by s. 37 (1) required to pay only the cost of an off-site main from the boundary of the site to the nearest place off site where a distribution main existed even if it was over committed and unable to provide adequate supplies to the site. If it were necessary to supplement the supply the water authority should bear the cost. *Held*, (i) the starting point for any new main necessary for the connection of the proposed development did not have to be the nearest point to the proposed development at which there was an existing main. The point at which the new main had to start was where the new main could in the circumstances be fed with sufficient water to meet the particular purposes for which it was required. (ii) What was a "necessary main" was a question of fact according to sound water engineering point of view. The main in question was a "necessary main" within s. 37 (1) and the water authority was entitled to recover the appropriate amounts from the developers. (iii) The principle that the cost of improvements to the existing distribution system cannot be laid to the charge of the developers applied only to improvements executed on sections of the system short of the point at which any new main necessary for the connection of the proposed new development took its departure.

ROYCO HOMES LTD v SOUTHERN WATER AUTHORITY [1979] 3 All ER 813 (House of Lords: LORD WILBERFORCE, VISCOUNT DILHORNE, LORD SALMON, LORD RUSSELL OF KILLOWEN and LORD KEITH OF KINKEL). Decision of Forbes J [1978] 2 All ER 821, 1978 Halsbury's Abridgment para. 3096 affirmed. *Cherwell District Council v Thames Water Authority* [1975] 1 All ER 763 distinguished.

3063   **Water charges—equalisation**

The Water Charges Equalisation Order 1979, S.I. 1979 No. 1754 (in force on 28th December 1979) relates to the calendar year 1980. It directs specified statutory water undertakers to pay to the National Water Council a specified equalisation levy. It also directs the National Water Council to pay out the aggregate of those levies in the form of equalisation payments to specified undertakers, to the limit of specified amounts.

3064   **Water meters—European Community**

See para. 3075.

WATERS AND WATERCOURSES

Halsbury's Laws of England (3rd edn.), Vol. 39, paras. 653–1128

3065 Drainage works—collapse of bridge—liability of drainage board—Lands Tribunal decision

WARNER v KINGSTON BROOK INTERNAL DRAINAGE BOARD (1979) 37 P & CR 221: R C Walmsley FRICS (bridge stood over brook on claimant's land, providing access to farmstead for 150 years; in 1947 new bridge built on same foundations and extended in 1969; in 1971 drainage board carried out works to brook upstream of bridge; in 1977 in flood conditions, bridge collapsed; caused by scouring of material immediately below foundations; bridge replaced by claimants; drainage board liable for any injury sustained by reason of exercise of their powers under Land Drainage Act 1976, s. 17; claimants claimed compensation of amount being full cost of new bridge; board contended, inter alia, foundations inadequate of which they had no knowledge, damages should be assessed on diminution value of claimant's interest in farm or, if assessed on cost of reinstatement, deductions should be made for betterment arising from stronger bridge; foundations regarded as sound for 150 years and in 1947, 1969; not rebutted by board at time of works; reason for scouring was effect of board's works; damage to bridge was "injury" within meaning of the 1976 Act; no evidence as to quantum of diminution; extent of injury was full cost of bridge because this was only way of recreating access to farmstead).

3066 Public right of navigation—extent of right to moor and fix moorings

Scotland

A company laid down semi-permanent moorings for small craft on the seabed in Fairlie Bay. Some of the moorings laid by the company belonged to the owners of vessels, others belonged to the company and were hired out to vessels. The Crown Estate Commissioners brought an action claiming that the Crown had sole and exclusive right of property in the seabed at Fairlie Bay, had sole and exclusive right to permit the laying of fixed moorings in the seabed and for an interdict against the company from laying or maintaining fixed moorings. The company conceded that the Crown had a proprietary right in the seabed, but maintained that this proprietary right was subject to the right of the public to use the seabed for the purposes of navigation and that the moorings were needed to facilitate that purpose. *Held*, the Crown's proprietary right in the seabed was limited in that the Crown could not permit any use of the seabed which interfered with the rights of the public, but the public right of navigation did not include the right to lay on or fix to the seabed semi-permanent moorings without the consent of the Crown. Neither did it include the right to moor or anchor, except in the course of passage, without the consent of the Crown.

CROWN ESTATE COMRS v FAIRLIE YACHT SLIP LTD 1976 SC 161 (Outer House).

3067 Water charges—collection by local authorities on behalf of water authorities

The Water Authorities (Collection of Charges) Order 1979, S.I. 1979 No. 228 (in force on 31st March 1979), makes provision for the collection and recovery on behalf of water authorities, by local authorities who are rating authorities, of charges made by water authorities for the supply of water and for sewerage and environmental services during the year beginning on 1st April 1979.

WEIGHTS AND MEASURES

Halsbury's Laws of England (3rd edn.), Vol. 39, paras. 1129–1272

3068   Article

The History of the Mile, Alan Wharman (brief examination of the old laws relating to weights and measures): 129 NLJ 51.

3069   Alcohol tables—EEC requirements

The Alcohol Tables Regulations 1979, S.I. 1979 No. 132 (in force on 1st April 1979), implement Council Directive (EEC) 76/766 relating to alcohol tables. They provide definitions of "alcoholic strength by volume" and "alcoholic strength by mass" and symbols to be used in accordance with the Directive. The Regulations further provide that on and after 1st January 1980 figures for alcoholic strength by volume and alcoholic strength by mass are to be derived from tables to be drawn up in accordance with the formula shown in the Annex to the Directive.

3070   Egg-grading machines

The Weights and Measures (Egg-Grading Machines) (Revocation) Regulations 1979, S.I. 1979 No. 729 (in force on 1st August 1979), revoke the Weights and Measures (Egg-Grading Machines) Regulations 1964 which prescribed those machines grading eggs into one or more of the catagories Large, Standard, Medium or Small. The Eggs (Marketing Standards) Regulations 1973, as amended, make the grading of eggs into these catagories unlawful, as they have been replaced by the grades provided for in Council Regulation (EEC) 2772/75, which also stipulates that eggs are to be checked by means of random sampling.

3071   Food—pricing—price per unit of measurement

See para. 1223.

3072   Local standards—periods of validity

The Weights and Measures (Local Standards: Periods of Validity) Regulations 1979, S.I. 1979 No. 1436 (in force on 10th December 1979), prescribe the periods of validity of certificates of fitness of local standards of weights and measures authorities. The periods replace those in the Weights and Measures Act 1963, s. 4 (5) which ceased to have effect on 4th October, 1979 by virtue of the Weights and Measures Act 1979, s. 24 (3) (c), Sch. 5, para. 1, para. 3089. The periods of validity in respect of certificates for standards of length over three metres or ten feet and standards of capacity of over 500 millilitres or one pint are reduced from ten to five years. The periods of validity in respect of certificates for standards of weight and other standards of length and capacity remain unchanged at five and ten years respectively.

3073   Measuring equipment—measurement of liquid fuel

The Measuring Equipment (Liquid Fuel delivered from Road Tankers) Regulations 1979, S.I. 1979 No. 1720 (regs. 4, 8 (1) in force on 1st July 1983, remainder on 1st July 1980), prescribe measuring equipment used for trade for measuring bulk supplies of liquid fuel dispensed from road tankers in quantities in excess of 100 litres (mainly petrol to filling stations and central heating fuel oil to houses and other premises). The Regulations do not apply to equipment for use only for measuring liquefied petroleum gas and heated oil, or for refuelling ships and aircraft. A three year introductory period is allowed before testing and stamping become obligatory, with a further three year period before pattern approval becomes obligatory.

3074   The Working Standards and Testing Equipment (Testing and Adjustment) (Amendment) Regulations 1979, S.I. 1979 No. 1719 (in force on 1st January 1980), amend the Working Standards and Testing Equipment (Testing and Adjustment) Regulations 1970, which prescribe the methods of testing and adjusting, and the limits of error for, the working standards and testing equipment used by inspectors.

The Regulations prescribe appropriate requirements in respect of meters for use in testing measuring equipment used for the measurement of liquid fuel dispensed from road tankers.

3075   Measuring instruments—EEC requirements

The Measuring Instruments (EEC Requirements) (Amendment) Regulations 1979, S.I. 1979 No. 80 (in force on 21st February 1979), apply the Measuring Instruments (EEC Requirements) Regulations 1975, 1975 Halsbury's Abridgment para. 3515, as amended, to cold-water meters to which Council Directive (EEC) 75/33, 1975 Halsbury's Abridgment para. 3501 applies.

3076   The Measuring Instruments (EEC Requirements) (Amendment No. 2) Regulations 1979, S.I. 1979 No. 847 (in force on 20th August 1979) amend the 1975 Regulations, S.I. 1975 No. 1173, 1975 Halsbury's Abridgment para. 3515. The Regulations also apply the 1975 Regulations to measuring systems for liquid other than water and components of such systems, to which EEC Directive 77/313 applies.

3077   The Measuring Instruments (EEC Requirements) (Amendment No. 3) Regulations, S.I. 1979 No. 1459 apply the 1975 Regulations, 1975 Halsbury's Abridgment para. 3515 to non-automatic weighing machines to which Council Directive (EEC) 73/360 applies.

3078   —— —— fees

The Measuring Instruments (EEC Requirements) (Fees) Regulations 1979, S.I. 1979 No. 1342 (in force on 26th November 1979), revoke and replace the Measuring Instruments (EEC Requirements) (Fees) Regulations 1978, 1978 Halsbury's Abridgment, para. 3106 and the Alcoholmeters and Alcohol Hydrometers (EEC Requirements) (Fees) Regulations 1977, 1977 Halsbury's Abridgment para. 3121. The regulations increase certain of the fees payable in connection with services provided by the Department of Trade in respect of EEC pattern approval of certain measuring instruments.

3079   —— liquid fuel

The Measuring Instruments (Liquid Fuel and Lubricants) Regulations 1979, S.I. 1979 No. 1605 (regulation 3 (2) in force on 1st January 1980, remainder in force on 1st March 1980), replace the Measuring Instruments (Liquid Fuel and Lubricants) Regulations 1963, as amended. They make provision as to the principles of construction, marking of equipment, inspection, testing, passing fit for use for trade and stamping of such equipment (and obliteration of stamps on such equipment) and the prescribed limits of error.

3080   —— intoxicating liquor

The Measuring Instruments (Intoxicating Liquor) (Amendment) Regulations 1979, S.I. 1979 No. 41 (in force on 12th February 1979), amend the Measuring Instruments (Intoxicating Liquor) Regulations 1965. The principal effect of the amendments is that measuring instruments for beer and cider are no longer permitted to be fitted with sight glasses or other devices for showing that the measuring chamber is properly charged or discharged as an alternative to being fitted with devices which prevent liquid being discharged from the chamber before it is full. The provision does not apply until 1st January 1982 in relation to instruments fitted with such sight glasses and stamped as fit for use for trade before 12th February 1979.

3081   **Milk**

The Weights and Measures Act 1963 (Milk) Order 1979, S.I. 1979 No. 1752 (in force on 1st January 1980), implements the requirements of Council Directive (EEC) 75/106, as amended, as to the prescribed range of quantities for pre-packed liquid cows' milk and, with other requirements, supersedes the Weights and Measures Act 1963, Sch. 4, Part V. Milk is exempted from Sch. 4, Part XI. The Order also revokes the Weights and Measures (Exemption) (Milk) Order 1966 and the Weights and Measures (Pre-packed Milk in Vending Machines) Order 1976, 1976 Halsbury's Abridgment para. 2820, but re-enacts similar provisions.

The Order specifies that milk which is not pre-packed is to be sold only by capacity measurement or net weight and that milk in quantities of more than 50 millilitres may be pre-packed only in certain prescribed quantities by capacity measure. Further, prepacked milk may be sold in vending machines only if those machines display certain information (including the quantity of milk in each item).

3082   **Packaged goods**

The Weights and Measures (Packaged Goods) Regulations 1979, S.I. 1979 No. 1613 (in force on 1st January 1980), make provision for implementing the system of quantity control (the average system) applicable to the packaging of goods sold by weight or volume as provided for in the Weights and Measures Act 1979, Part 1. The regulations make general provision in connection with the duties to be complied with by packers and importers of packaged goods and provision (in accordance with certain Council Directives (EEC)) with respect to the EEC mark placed on packages as laid down by the Act.

3083   **Solid fuel**

The Weights and Measures Act 1963 (Solid Fuel) Order 1979, S.I. 1979 No. 1753 (in force on 1st January 1980), amends the Weights and Measures Act 1963, Sch. 6 so as to add to the quantities in which solid fuel may be made in a container for sale, or for delivery after sale, multiples of 50 kilograms.

3084   —— **carriage by rail**

The Weights and Measures (Solid Fuel) (Carriage by Rail) (Amendment) Order 1979, S.I. 1979 No. 955 (in force on 1st September 1979), amend the Weights and Measures (Solid Fuel) (Carriage by Rail) Order 1966, S.I. 1966 No. 238. The Order brings within the 1966 Order rail vehicles in the specified circumstances, not only, as previously, steel rail vehicles of a capacity of not less than 24 tons.

The Order also provides a simplified form of train bill where the vehicles comprised in the train are permanently coupled in such a manner that the train is weighed while in motion.

3085   **Taximeters—fees—EEC requirements**

See para. 2318.

3086   **Units of measurement—metrication—agriculture**

See para. 77.

3087   **Weighing and measuring equipment**

The Weights and Measures (Amendment) Regulations 1979, S.I. 1979 No. 1612, (in force on 1st January 1980), further amend the Weights and Measures Regulations 1963 by excluding certain weighing equipment and liquid capacity measures from the application of those Regulations.

3088   —— testing—fees

The Weights and Measures (Testing and Adjustment Fees) Regulations 1979, S.I. 1979 No. 1359 (in force on 1st January 1980), revoke and replace the 1976 Regulations, 1976 Halsbury's Abridgment para. 2823. The Regulations prescribe the increased fees to be paid for the testing of weighing or measuring equipment with a view to its being passed as fit for use for trade and stamped. The fees are payable whether or not the equipment is passed. They also prescribe the increased fees to be paid for the adjustment of weights or measures when a local authority provides an adjusting service.

3089   Weights and Measures Act 1979

The Weights and Measures Act 1979 makes new provisions relating to packaged goods and amends the Weights and Measures Act 1963. The Act received the royal assent on 4th April 1979 and the majority of it comes into force on 1st January 1980. Sections 6, 7 and Sch. 3 came into force on 2nd October 1979, S.I. 1979 No. 1228; Sch. 5, para. 1 and s. 20 so far as it relates to it, came into force on 4th October 1979. Section 19 will come into force on a day to be appointed.

Section 1 prescribes the duties to be performed by packers and importers of packages in operating the "average" system. Packages must be marked with the quantity contained in them, the packager's or importer's name and address or an identification mark enabling his name and address to be readily ascertained and, if required, a mark allocated to him under s. 7 (4) of this Act enabling the place where the package was made up to be easily ascertained. Non-compliance with s.1 is an offence and further specified action may be taken by inspectors in consequence: s. 2, Sch. 1. Section 3 prescribes the maximum penalties for offences under s. 2: an offence under s. 2 (4) (fraudulently purporting to comply with statutory duties) is punishable by six months' imprisonment and a fine of £1,000, other offences by a £1,000 fine. Proceedings may only be instituted by local weights and measures authorities or chief officers of police, and the time limits for prosecutions contained in the Weights and Measures Act 1963, s. 51 (2), (4) apply: s. 3 (2). Section 3 (4), (7) list defences to proceedings under this Act. Local weights and measures authorities must enforce these provisions in their areas: s. 4. In this connection, inspectors have the powers given them by virtue of Sch. 2. Section 4 specifically implements EEC Directives on packages which qualify for application of the EEC mark, and makes unauthorised use of that mark, or use of a mark so similar as to be likely to deceive, an offence.

Section 6 establishes a National Metrological Co-ordinating Unit of between five and fifteen persons appointed by the Secretary of State. Schedule 3 applies to the Unit. Section 7 lists its functions and duties, s. 8 empowers it to require information from local weights and measures authorities or to require those authorities to arrange for inspectors to perform specified functions and report to the Unit, s. 9 makes it incumbent on the Unit to make an annual report to the Secretary of State, s. 10 deals with accounts and audit and s. 11 empowers the latter to extend or transfer the Unit's functions and to abolish it altogether. Sections 12–15 make miscellaneous and supplemental provisions.

Sections 16–20 amend the Weights and Measures Act 1963. Section 16 and Sch. 4 amend the 1963 Act, s. 11, relating to the weighing or measuring equipment for use for trade, s. 17 and Sch. 4 amend s. 12, concerning approval of patterns of equipment for use for trade, s. 18 increases the penalties due under s. 52 of the 1963 Act, s. 19 amends Sch. 4, Pt VI of that Act (rate of beer and cider) and s. 20 and Sch. 5 make other amendments.

Sections 21–24 make general provisions. Section 21 and Sch. 6 modify the Act in its application to Northern Ireland, s. 22 deals with expenses, s. 23 repeals s. 6 of the Weights and Measures Act 1859 concerning the provision of scales by the owners of markets, and s. 24 deals with citation, interpretation and commencement.

WILLS

Halsbury's Laws of England (3rd edn.), Vol. 39, paras. 1273–1720

3090   Articles

Gift by Will to Friends, F. Graham Glover (in the light of *Re Barlow's Will Trusts* [1979] 1 All ER 296, para. 3092): 129 NLJ 742.

Revocation of Wills on Divorce, G. M. Bates (a review of the proposals for reform in this area): 129 NLJ 556.

Revocation of Wills on Marriage, G. M. Bates (a review of suggestions for reform in the law relating to this area): 129 NLJ 536.

3091   Construction—incorporation of trust by codicil—execution of codicil prior to signing of trust instrument

Canada

A testatrix sought, by means of a codicil to her will, to bequeath certain property to a trust. The trust instrument was not signed until two days after the signing of the codicil. *Held*, in order for the testatrix validly to have incorporated the document into her will, it should have been in existence at the date of the signing of the codicil. To allow otherwise would permit alteration of the will without compliance with the required formalities. As the trust document had not been signed at the time the codicil was executed, it had not been in existence at that time and thus had not been incorporated into the will.

RE CURRIE (1979) 21 OR (2d) 709 (Supreme Court of Ontario).

3092   —— meaning of "friends" and "family"

In her will, the testatrix made specific bequests and left the residue on trust for sale subject to "any member of my family and any friends of mine who may wish to do so" being allowed to purchase her paintings at less than their current market value. The executor sought the court's determination of the questions (i) whether the direction was void for uncertainty, and (ii) who were to be treated as being members of the testatrix' family. *Held*, (i) the direction to allow "friends" to purchase the paintings did not require all members of the class to be established before it took effect, since any uncertainty as to some of the persons who may have been intended to take did not affect the quantum of the gift to those who definitely qualified. The direction would be valid if it could be said that one claimant qualified, and thus was not void for uncertainty. Qualification as a friend depended on the length of the relationship with the testatrix, whether it was a purely social relationship and whether they met frequently. (ii) "Family" meant those related by blood to the testatrix. Since all members of the class did not have to be established before the gift took effect, the rule of construction limiting gifts to relations to the statutory next of kin did not apply. Thus anyone who proved a blood relationship with the testatrix was entitled to purchase the paintings.

RE BARLOW'S WILL TRUSTS [1979] 1 All ER 296 (Chancery Division: BROWNE-WILKINSON J). *Re Allen, Faith v Allen* [1953] 2 All ER 898, CA applied.

For a discussion of this case, see Finding out who one's friends are, Justinian, Financial Times, 12th March 1979.

3093   —— residuary gift on trusts—trusts accomplished—entitlement to residue

A testator bequeathed all rents from his leasehold properties in Nigeria for the maintenance of his second wife and for their daughter until she finished university. The residue of the estate was left to the second wife on trust for the above purposes. The testator died in 1965, his residuary estate including a house in London. His daughter graduated in 1975, her mother having died in 1970. The testator's son by his first marriage sought to determine whether the specified purpose having come to an end, his father's residuary estate in England was an absolute gift to the second wife and the daughter, or was held on intestacy. At first instance it was held that although the specified purposes could no longer be carried out, the court would readily continue such a residuary gift as being effective rather than leave it to pass on intestacy. The expression of purpose indicated an intention to make an absolute gift, but did not restrict the gift to those purposes only. The testator's overriding intention had been to provide for his immediate dependants. The residuary estate would be divided equally between the daughter and mother's personal representatives. On appeal, *held*, the gift of residue was not limited to specific purposes or uses, but was a gift on trust for the benefit of the second wife and their daughter absolutely and as joint tenants (there being no words of severance in the will). The mother had predeceased her daughter and as no evidence of the severance of the joint tenancy during her lifetime had been proved, the daughter was entitled to the whole of the residual estate as the only surviving tenant.

RE OSOBA, OSOBA v OSOBA [1979] 2 All ER 393 (Court of Appeal: BUCKLEY, GOFF and EVELEIGH LJJ). *Re Sanderson's Trusts* (1857) 3 K & J 497, *Presant v Goodwin* (1860) 1 Sw & Tr 544 and *Barlow v Grant* (1684) 1 Vern 255 applied. Decision of Megarry V-C [1978] 1 WLR 791, 1978 Halsbury's Abridgment para. 3118 affirmed in part.

3094   —— whether residuary estate held on secret trust by beneficiary— intention of testatrix that beneficiary distribute residue among relatives

A testatrix left the residue of her estate to her brother, and the evidence from discussions with her solicitor indicated that she intended the brother to distribute the residue among her nieces and nephews. The brother died six days after the testatrix, leaving all his estate to his son. One of the executors of the testatrix's will sought the determination of the court as to whether the residue should go to the brother's son absolutely or be distributed among the nieces and nephews on the ground that the brother had taken the residue subject to a secret trust. *Held*, from the evidence, the arrangement between the testatrix and her brother imposed merely a normal or family obligation on the brother, and not a secret trust, since there was no evidence that the testatrix intended the sanction of the court to enforce it if the brother failed to carry out her wishes. The brother therefore took the residue free from any trust, and it passed to the son absolutely.

RE SNOWDEN, SMITH v SLOWAGE [1979] 2 All ER 172 (Chancery Division: MEGARRY V-C).

3095   Family provision—application for financial provision for maintenance

See EXECUTORS AND ADMINISTRATORS.

3096   Gift to unincorporated association—validity

Premises, which had been the headquarters of the old Chertsey Constituency Labour Party (CLP), were being used, following the redistribution of constituency boundaries in 1970, as the headquarters of the new Chertsey CLP, and were under the management of a local property committee until the ownership of the property could be settled. The property was situated in what had been, prior to local government reorganisation, the Chertsey UDC area and was held on trust for the old Chertsey CLP. The question arose as to the validity of a testator's will which appointed the trustees of the headquarters property as executors and which devised the testator's estate to the Labour Party property committee for the benefit of the Chertsey headquarters of the new Chertsey CLP, providing that such headquarters remained in what was the Chertsey UDC area; if not the gift was to go to the national Labour Party absolutely. There was no body in existence known as the "Labour Party property committee" although it was generally agreed that the testator must have intended to refer to the local property committee. *Held*, the bequest was not a valid gift and the testator's estate thus devolved as on intestacy. The testator had not intended his estate to be held on the trusts applicable to the headquarters property because by the proviso in the will the testator contemplated that the property might not continue to be the headquarters. Therefore the testator's estate was not an addition to the property held on trust and would not follow its devolution. The bequest could not be construed as a gift to the members of the CLP because it did not fall within the second category of valid gifts to unincorporated associations outlined in *Neville Estates Ltd v Madden,* as the rules of the party placed restrictions on the members' freedom to dispose of property donated to the party. Furthermore under these rules upon a dissolution of the CLP any property would be held on resulting trust for the donors of the property, thus the testator's property would devolve as on intestacy. The bequest could not be construed as a gift to the members of the national Labour Party due to the gift over stipulated in the will whereby the estate could only pass to members of the national Labour Party if the headquarters did not remain in the Chertsey UDC area. Because the bequest was a gift to the Labour Party property committee, who were to hold the property on trust for the Chertsey headquarters of the CLP, the bequest was not a gift to the members of the CLP, but imposed a trust which, being non-charitable, failed because it infringed the rule against perpetuities.

RE GRANT'S WILL TRUSTS [1979] 3 All ER 359 (Chancery Division: VINELOTT J). Dictum of Cross J in *Neville Estates Ltd v Madden* [1961] 3 All ER 769 at 778–779 applied.

3097 Power of appointment—construction—persons entitled—date of commencement of absolute entitlement

Northern Ireland
The testator was the donee of a power of appointment of a residuary estate to 'such child or remoter issue' born within twenty-one years of the date of his own death, to take a vested interest in the estate not later than that date. In default or appointment the estate would devolve upon the testator's next-of-kin. On the death of the testator his will appointed the property to his daughter for life, with remainder to her issue. Should she be without issue, the property would go to his wife, if still living. If she should be dead the remainder would go to named charities. The daughter was without issue and in 1974 questions arose as to her absolute entitlement to the estate with reference to the possible interest of the named charities. The question was resolved in favour of the daughter only since the appointments to the testator's wife and the charities were void as in excess of the power. A further question now arose as to the actual date of the daughter's absolute entitlement. The two dates put forward were, the date of her father's death, and twenty-one years from that date. *Held,* the testator had had power to appoint the estate to 'such child or remoter issue' as should be born within twenty-one years of the testator's death, and that being so, since the daughter could have had a child after the death of her father, and that child could have been alive twenty-one years later, the child would have become absolutely entitled to the estate. Thus, the daughter could not become so entitled until twenty-one years from the date of the testator's death.

RE LOWRY (DECEASED); NORTHERN BANK EXECUTOR AND TRUSTEE COMPANY LTD v STONE [1978] NI 17 (Northern Ireland Chancery Division).

3098 Royal Commission on Legal Services—recommendations—drafting for reward

See para. 1720.

INDEX

ABORTION
failure properly to perform contract to carry out, 471

ACCIDENT
cost of full police report, 2315
failure to stop and report, 2252

ACCOMMODATION
agreement to provide, whether a licence or lease, 1666–1668
provision by local authority, charges, 2589

ACCUMULATIONS
whether discretionary power to accumulate within restrictions, 1390

ACCUSED
right to know accusation and to interpreter, 1463

ACTION
dismissal of—
abuse of process of court, 136
application for, 2128
preservation of subject-matter of cause of, 520
setting down for trial after expiry of period fixed, 2161
striking out of, appeal against, 2164

ACTUAL BODILY HARM
assault occasioning, appeal against sentence, 2385–2389

ADMINISTRATIVE LAW
certiorari. *See* CERTIORARI.
judicial control of administrative action, abuse of discretion, 1945
natural justice. *See* NATURAL JUSTICE.
Parliamentary Commissioner. *See* PARLIAMEN-TARY COMMISSIONER
Tribunal, vaccine damage tribunals, 23

ADMINISTRATOR OF BULGARIAN PROPERTY
proceedings against, 726

ADMINISTRATOR OF GERMAN ENEMY PROPERTY
proceedings against, 726

ADMINISTRATOR OF HUNGARIAN PROPERTY
proceedings against, 726

ADMINISTRATOR OF ITALIAN PROPERTY
proceedings against, 726

ADMINISTRATOR OF JAPANESE PROPERTY
proceedings against, 726

ADMINISTRATOR OF ROUMANIAN PROPERTY
proceedings against, 726

ADMIRALTY
actions—
commencement, procedure, 2102
in rem, form of writ, 2159
liability, limitation of, 27

ADOPTION
application by parent and step-parent, 1854
order, making of, 545
paramountcy of child's welfare, 1854
proceedings, domestic courts, 1856
rules—
county court, 1855
magistrates' court, 1856

ADULT EDUCATION
State bursaries, residents of Wales, 1003

ADVANCE CORPORATION TAX
rate of, 2247
supplement on repayment of, 1536
unpaid, interest on, 1536

ADVERTISING
barristers, by, 1720

ADVISORY, CONCILIATION AND ARBITRATION SERVICE
proceedings against, 726
statutory duties, inquiries deferred pending judicial proceedings, 2833

AERODROME
definition of, 172

AEROPLANES. *See also* AIRCRAFT
documents to be carried in, 166
emergency lighting in, 166
noise certificate, 169

AFFIDAVIT
person making, address of, 2156

AFFILIATION ORDER
enforcement, 31

AGENCY
agreement, alleged, revocation of, where breach committed, 427
business, whether carried on during accounting periods for VAT, 2984
creation, whether party to contract principal or agent, 42
termination of, appointment of receiver and winding up order, 385

AGENT
authority—
apparent, reliance by third party on representation by principal, 34
contract for sale of goods, 2332
negligence of, liability of principal, 44
overseas principals, of, VAT, 3053
right to set loss of profit against freight charges, 2547

BEES
importation restrictions, 106, 107

BEET SEEDS
regulations, 96

BENEFITS IN KIND
beneficial loans, tax liability, 1508

BERKSHIRE
West, structure and local plans, 2768

BERMUDA
constitution, 313, 314
ships registered in, 2540, 2554

BERTH
safety requirements, 2516

BICYCLES
lighting regulations, 2319

BIGAMY
appeal against sentence, 2459

BILL OF EXCHANGE
assignment, priority of previous charge, 245
date of maturity, 250
dishonour—
indorsement, transfer of liability, 246
partial failure of consideration, 247
plaintiff obtaining judgment, 1598
formal requirements, 250
incorrect company name on face, 365

BILL OF LADING
cargo destroyed, whether risk passed to buyer, 2327

BINDING OVER
power to attach conditions, 1295

BINGO CLUBS
entertainment charge, whether VAT payable, 2972
number of, 311
requirement to submit accounts, 244

BIRDS
importation of, 125
wild. See WILD BIRDS

BIRMINGHAM
airport—
navigation services provided at, 178
special rules, 165
derelict land clearance area, 2750

BIRTH
registration—
fees order, 2238
New Hebrides, 2239

BLASPHEMOUS LIBEL
intent, 583

BLOOD TEST
evidence of paternity, 32

BOARD OF TRADE
proceedings against, 726

BOAT
food hygiene in, 1321
input tax, 2991
insurance services relating to, VAT, 2983
whether designed for recreation for VAT, 2980

BONDED GOODS
customs warehouse, in, 743
excise warehouse, in, 744

BOOK DEBTS
assignment of, registration of, 2157

BOOKMAKERS
association, VAT, 2978

BORROWING
control order, 1895

BORSTAL TRAINING
concurrent sentence, power to recommend period of training, 2481
sentence subsequent to sentence of detention for other offences, 2482

BOUNDARY COMMISSION
revision of electoral arrangements, 1763

BOURNEMOUTH AERODROME
navigation services provided at, 178

BOVINE ANIMALS
contact with, 2634

BRAIN
damage, quantum of damages, 813–817

BREACH OF CONFIDENCE
action for—
application for dismissal, 2128
whether assertion sufficient to found, 2128
injunction to prevent, 1587

BREAD
prices, 1317

BREATH TEST. See DRIVING OFFENCES

BRIBERY
Crown official, of, appeal against sentence, 2479

BRIDGE
collapse of, liability for, 3065

BRITISH AEROSPACE
loans to, 2789

BRITISH AIRPORT AUTHORITY
power to ban minicabs, 2177

BRITISH BROADCASTING CORPORATION
broadcasting licence, 2727

BRITISH GAS CORPORATION
rating of, 2204

BRITISH NATIONALITY
fees regulations, 254

COMMISSIONERS OF INLAND REVENUE
proceedings against, 726

COMMON AGRICULTURAL POLICY
agricultural levy relief—
    beef, frozen, 51
    veal, frozen, 51
agricultural producer, definition, 57
beef, imports from non-member states, 1207
butter subsidy, 59
common organisation of markets—
    community legislation, supremacy of, 62
    principle of non-discrimination, 61
eggs, marketing standards, 63
European Monetary System, impact of, 64
meat—
    imports from non-member states, customs
        duties, 65
    protection of Community arrangements, 66
pigmeat—
    common price system, 67
    effect of common organisation of market, 62
sugar, common organisation of the market, 70,
    1171
transitional period—
    accession compensatory amounts, 71
    products not subject to common organisation
        of market, 72, 73
veal, imports from non-member states, 1207
wine—
    monetary compensation amounts, 1169
    regulations, 74, 75

COMMON LAW
Act amending or repealing, proceedings begun
    before in force, 2713

COMMONWEALTH DEVELOPMENT COR-
PORATION
members of, 316

COMMUNITY COUNCIL
copy of electoral register for, 1016

COMMUNITY SERVICE ORDER
power of Court to revoke, 561
whether can be accompanied by fine, 2484

COMPANIES
accountancy and disclosure, EEC requirements,
    356
accounts—
    negligent error in, liability for, 347
    regulations, 346
articles of association, provisions for remuneration
    of directors, 349
books, production of, application by Director of
    Public Prosecutions, 372
cars, private use by directors, VAT, 3028
contract for supply of goods, retention of equitable
    title to goods until payment made, 1137
debenture. See DEBENTURE
directors. See DIRECTOR
formed by persons exempt from taxation, 371
forms regulations, 367–369
infringement of patent by, personal liability of
    director, 2028
investigation of affairs, disclosure of information
    to Secretary of State, 192

COMPANIES—continued
legislation, commencement of, 352
loan to purchase holding company's shares, 379
private, number of, 359
public, number of, 359
records, use of computers, 374
register of members—
    rectification of entry of unauthorised issue of
        shares, 373
    use of computers, 374
registration of charges, nature of transaction, 376
resolution, special, notice specifying intention to
    propose, 377
shares. See SHARES
winding up. See WINDING UP

COMPANIES COURT
applications and orders heard by registrar, 2113
exercise of functions by chief clerk, 2113
jurisdiction, order for possession, 354
proceedings in chambers, business by post, 2114

COMPENSATION
compulsory acquisition of land, for. See COM-
    PULSORY ACQUISITION OF LAND
compulsory purchase, deduction for corporation
    tax, 1515, 1516
damage caused by laying sewer, 2497
oil pollution, 2571
pneumoconiosis, 2650

COMPTROLLER-GENERAL OF PATENTS
annual report, 2020

COMPULSORY ACQUISITION OF LAND
compensation—
    assessment—
        agricultural holding, 396
        Lands Tribunal Decisions. See LANDS TRI-
            BUNAL DECISIONS
        leasehold interest with uncertain freeholder,
            406
        market value, exclusion of purchasers want-
            ing land for special purposes, 982
        potential use of land, scheme underlying
            acquisition, 408
    disturbance—
        assessment, Lands Tribunal decision, 410
        whether interest charges recoverable, 411
        increase in operating costs following move
            to new premises, 412
        loss of agreed gross amount of profit, 1515,
            . 1516
    for injury, time limit for claim, 415
    notice of claim, particulars required, 421
    statement of rights of appeal not included in
        certificate of alternative development,
        409
compulsory purchase order—
    application for, cross-examination on affidavit,
        417
    confirmation by confirming authority, 416
    service of notice of order, failure to serve on
        joint owner, 417
entry on to land, entry before completion, rate of
    interest after entry, 418–420
notice to treat, withdrawal, 421
planning blight notice, 422

OBSCENE PUBLICATIONS—*continued*
duty of Metropolitan Police Commissioner, 2084
when articles seized by police to be brought before magistrate, 622

OCCUPATIONAL PENSION SCHEMES
approval for tax relief, 1546
public service regulations, 2054

OCCUPATIONAL PENSIONS BOARD
determinations by, 726

OCCUPIER
duty owed to visitor, 1979

OFFENSIVE WEAPON
article acquired immediately before use as, 627
possession, appeal against sentence, 2372

OFFICE
holder of, services supplied as, VAT, 3029

OFFICE BREAKING
appeal against sentence, 2451

OFFICE DEVELOPMENT
control, 2754

OFFICE OF POPULATION CENSUSES AND SURVEYS
establishment of, 726
proceedings against, 726

OFFSHORE INSTALLATION
construction of, sums borrowed for, 2808
life-saving appliances, 1847

OIL AND PLANT FIBRE SEEDS
regulations, 99

OIL BURNERS
portable domestic, paraffin used in, 1373–1376

OIL LAMPS
safety regulations, 459

OIL POLLUTION
compulsory insurance, 2572
convention countries, 2568–2570
international compensation fund, 2571

OIL REFINERY
liability of owners in nuisance, 1372

OLYMPIC GAMES
supply of clothing to competitors, 3030

OPENCAST COAL
rate of interest on compensation, 1848

OPTICIANS
enrolment order, 1833
registration order, 1833

OSLO AND PARIS COMMISSIONS
immunities and privileges, 1346

OVERSEAS PENSIONS
increase, 2055

OVERSEAS SERVICE
pensions supplement, 2056

OVERSEAS TERRITORIES
Internationally Protected Persons Act extended to certain, 1354
State immunity extended to certain, 1360

OXFORDSHIRE
structure and local plans, 2764

PACKAGED GOODS
legislation, 3089
weights and measures regulations, 3082

PAKISTAN
pensions increase, 2055

PAPER
import of, 753, 754

PAPERBOARD
import of, 753, 754

PARAFFIN
maximum retail prices, 1373–1376

PARALYSIS
quantum of damages, 818–820

PARAPLEGIA
quantum of damages, 818

PARENT
duty to prevent child from possession of dangerous tool, 1961
responsibility for negligence of children, 1985

PARISH COUNCIL
copy of electoral register for, 1016
elections, 1018

PARKING
multi-storey car parks, rating assessment, 2218, 2219
off-street parking, appeals procedure, 2310

PARLIAMENT
official reports as evidence, 1253

PARLIAMENTARY COMMISSIONER
Cabinet papers, access to, 18
delay in issuing documentation, 1235
direct access to, 18
investigation, matters excluded from, 22
jurisdiction, 18, 19
maladministration—
  remedies, 20
  report, 21
pension regulations, 2057
Select Committee on, 18

PARLIAMENTARY ELECTION
effect of simultaneous polling in local elections, 1018

PARLIAMENTARY PROCEEDINGS
sub judice rule, 2006

PUBLIC WORKS LOAN BOARD
proceedings against 726

PURCHASE TAX
charged on goods, VAT, 2992

QUADRIPLEGIA
quantum of damages, 819

QUEEN'S BENCH DIVISION
applications against immigration decisions, 2146
judgment, upon default of defence, 2147
Masters' summonses, return dates, 2148
orders, time for drawing up, 2149
personal injury actions—
agreed experts' reports, 2150
expert reports, order for disclosure, 1720

RABIES
importation control, 121

RACEHORSES
supply for promotional campaigns, VAT, 2996,
2997

RACIAL DISCRIMINATION
complaint in employment—
amendment to include unfair dismissal, 1078
production of documents, 912
when production of confidential reports ordered, 912
training of overseas applicants as barristers, 2195

RAILWAYS
carriage by rail. *See* CARRIAGE BY RAIL

RAPE
appeal against sentence, 2393, 2394
attempted, appeal against sentence, 2395

RATE REBATE
scheme regulations, 2206, 2207

RATE SUPPORT GRANTS
needs element, 1771
payment of, 1770

RATEABLE OCCUPATION
actual and exclusive occupation, 2209
occupation by spouse, 2210

RATEABLE VALUE
assessment—
aircraft maintenance hangars, etc., 2211
auction hall used as fruit and vegetable market,
2214
building found to have structural defects, 2212
clinic, 2216
ground floor offices in High Street, 2213
launderette, 2220
mansion, 2215
multi-storey car parks, 2218, 2219
property unoccupied and under reconstruction,
2217

RATEABLE VALUE—*continued*
assessment—*continued*
proposal for reduction, 2221
gas hereditaments, 1370
valuation list. *See* VALUATION LIST

RATES
distress for—
appeal against, 922
application for warrant of commitment, 922
levying of, 921
no summons received, 922

RATING
assessment—
appeal against, jurisdiction of Lands Tribunal,
2202
increase of, 2202
surcharge, unused commercial building, 2222
unoccupied property—
service of completion notice, 2223
unused commercial property, 2224–2226
valuation list. *See* VALUATION LIST

RATING AUTHORITIES
collection of water charges by, 3067

RATS
work in places infested by, 2634

RECEIVER
appointment—
by court, 938
by way of equitable execution, 938
effect upon authority of company's agent, 385
tenant in common of proceeds of sale of land,
938
under debenture, 357
fund for payment, whether receivership extends
to capital, 2237

RECEIVING ORDER
jurisdiction to make, 220
restriction on making, 208

RECOGNISANCE
forfeiture, culpability of surety, 1793

RECORDS
expenditure incurred in producing master copy
of, 1510

RECTIFICATION
solicitor's error, 1891

REDUNDANCY
alternative employment, no offer made, 2933
cessation of business, 1095
coal industry workers, concessionary coal, 1841
continuity of employment, employer's right to
recover rebate, 1098
diminution in work requirements, 2937
diminution of business, 1095
duty to consult trade union—
failure to provide details, 1099
special circumstances preventing compliance,
1100

SECRETARY OF STATE FOR SOCIAL SERVICES
transfer of functions from, 726

SECRETARY OF STATE FOR TRADE
transfer of functions to, 455

SECRETARY OF STATE FOR TRANSPORT
transfer of functions from, 456

SECRETARY OF STATE FOR WALES
transfer of functions to, 726

SECURITIES. *See also* SHARES
dealers in, licence holders, 2722
exchanges and conversions, 1926
purchase cum dividend, tax liability on interest, 1537
transactions, circumstances in which tax advantage counteracted, 1572
transfer to or from nominees, prescribed forms, 2725

SECURITY
person, of, meaning of "security", 1461

SEED POTATOES
fees regulations, 95

SEEDS
national lists, 100

SENTENCE
appeal against—
arson, 2444–2453
assault—
occasioning actual bodily harm, 2385–2389
with intent to rob, 2390, 2391
attempt to take a motor vehicle without authority 2441, 2443
bankrupt obtaining credit, 2435
bigamy, 2459
breach of suspended sentence, 2426
buggery, 2458
burglary, 2397, 2404–2411, 2419, 2451
aggravated, 2397, 2412
cannabis—
importation, 2462–2465
possession, 2466–2469
causing death by—
dangerous driving, 2470–2473
reckless driving, 2474
conspiracy to—
defraud, 2438
rob, 2403
criminal damage, 2420, 2451, 2454–2456
cruelty to persons under sixteen, 2389
damaging property, 2372, 2443
demanding money on a forged instrument, 2424
driving with excess alcohol in blood, 2473, 2475–2477
drug offences, 2461–2469
false—
accounting, 2421, 2439
imprisonment, 2397
forgery, 2436, 2457
furnishing false information, 2425

SENTENCE—*continued*
appeal against—*continued*
going equipped for theft, 2390
grievous bodily harm, 2378–2381
gross indecency, 2458
handling stolen goods, 2427–2429
importuning for immoral purposes, 2460
incest, 2396
indecent assault, 2396, 2458
kidnapping, 2397
making false statements to defraud Inland Revenue, 2431
malicious wounding, 2384
manslaughter, 2374–2377
matters to be considered, 2478, 2479
neglect of child, 2398
obtaining—
pecuniary advantage by deception, 2432–2434
property by deception, 2434–2437, 2439
office breaking, 2451
perjury, 2373
possession—
article with intent to damage property, 2452
firearm with intent to endanger life, 2392
imitation firearm, 2399
offensive weapon, 2372
rape, 2393, 2394
attempted, 2395
receiving stolen goods, 2430
robbery, 2399–2402
shoplifting, 2422, 2423
shortening shotgun, 2397
taking a conveyance without authority, 2397, 2402, 2434, 2440–2442
theft, 2411, 2413–2425, 2434, 2437, 2439, 2441, 2442
theft, attempted, 2426
trespassing with a firearm, 2397
unlawful wounding, 2383
uttering—
false document, 2425
forged document, 2424
wounding with intent, 2382, 2383
committal for—
offences triable either way, when proceedings commenced, 1775
young offender, validity of committal, 1776
extended, appeal against, matters to be considered, 2478
practice in magistrates' courts, 2489
suspended—
activation of, 2490
breach of, appeal against sentence, 2426

SENTENCING PRACTICE IN MAGISTRATES' COURTS
Home Office report, 2489

SERVICE AGREEMENT
payment for release from, whether chargeable gain, 274

SERVICE ELECTOR
requirement for, 1016

SINGAPORE
income taxed and trading losses sustained in, 1545
reciprocal enforcement of maintenance orders, 435, 436

SKULL INJURY
quantum of damages, 838

SLAUGHTERERS
registration of, 93

SLAUGHTERHOUSES
European convention on, 1336

SMELL
loss of sense of, quantum of damages, 830

SOCIAL SECURITY
adjudications governing, 726
benefits—
addition to, calculation of, 2622
availability, potential claimant not informed of, 21
claims for, 2611, 2612
computation of earnings, 2596
determination of claims and questions, 2621
EEC member states, in, documentation for claiming, delay in issuing, 1235
failure to bring availability to claimants' attention, 21
overlapping, 2596, 2597
overpaid, repayment of, 2600
payments of, 2611, 2613
persons abroad, 2598, 2599
reform of scheme, 2601
supplementary, reform of, 2601
uprating orders, 2605–2607
contributions—
amending regulations, 2614, 2615
earnings limits, 2616
exemptions, 2617
re-rating, 2618–2620
earnings factor—
regulations, 2622
revaluation, 2623
EEC. See EUROPEAN ECONOMIC COMMUNITY
legislation—
changes effected by, 2664
commencement, 2664–2667
transitional provisions, 2668
reciprocal agreements, 2653–2655
retirement pension. See RETIREMENT PENSION

SOLICITOR
absence from hearing, 2687
advertising by—
form to be allowed, 2688
recommendations of Royal Commission, 1720
advice given by counsel to, liability for, 2703
attestation of will, duty of care, 2698
audience, rights of, 1720
client dissatisfaction, 2701
disciplinary proceedings, Royal Commission's recommendations, 1720
documents disclosed to taxing master, professional privilege, 2704
duty of, 2130
duty of, care, attestation of will, 2698

SOLICITOR—continued

failure to give sound advice to vendor of house, 2691
investment of clients' money, whether acting in professional capacity, 2700
liability of partner, 2692
lodgment of notes of evidence, 2130
sale of land, refusal to pay purchase price to vendor, 2707
undertakings, liability on, whether acting as client's agent, 2702
unpaid bill of costs, duty to inform client of his rights, 2695
unpaid fees, lien over client's documents, 2696

SOLID FUEL
carriage by rail, 3084
weights and measures order, 3083

SOUND OF MULL
wreck protection, 2577

SOUTH AFRICA
double taxation relief, capital transfer tax, 1379

SOUTHERN RHODESIA
Commonwealth forces stationed in, 329
constitution, 330
consultations for constitutional settlement, 331, 332
exchange control—
directions revocation, 1907
exemption, 1908
expiry of orders, consequential provisions, 333
export of goods, removal of prohibition, 768
exports to, 1915
liability of Crown for acts of illegal regime in, 443
renamed Zimbabwe, 328
sanctions, 336
temporary provisions, 330

SOVEREIGN IMMUNITY
action in personam, doctrine of precedent, 1358
restrictive immunity, 1356
state trading activities, breadth of doctrine, 1357

SPAIN
fishery limits, 1301
fishing boats registered in, 1314

SPEAKER OF THE HOUSE OF COMMONS
pensions regulations, 2069
salaries order, 449

SPECIAL COMMISSIONERS
appeal to, procedure, 1499

SPECIAL CONSTABLE
pensions regulations, 2070

SPECIAL SCHOOLS
clothing expenses of children attending, 996

SPECIFIC PERFORMANCE
damages at common law on discharge of order, 2708

TEAR-GAS CAPSULES
prohibition of sale, 464

TELEGRAPHIC LINES
damage to, strict liability, 2731, 2732

TELEGRAPHY
interception of telephone conversations, police powers, 2093

TELEPHONE
monitoring of conversations, power of police to order, 2093

TELEVISION
coverage of election campaign, 1014
information as to sale and hire, 2737
licence, charges for, 2734, 2735
whether election candidates' consent required for coverage, 1014

TENANCY
estoppel, by, denial of landlords title, 1670
insufficient notice to terminate, 1697
protected, rooms sublet to students, 1699
statutory. *See* STATUTORY TENANCY

TENANT
contribution to maintenance costs by, waiver by landlord, 1683
disturbance, liability of landlord, 1690
harassment by landlord, 1697

TENANT IN POSSESSION
claim to acquire freehold, 1725

TENANTS IN COMMON
of proceeds of sale of land, appointment of receiver, 938

TERRORISM
suppression of, Cyprus, 1286

TETRAPLEGIA
quantum of damages, 820

TEXTILE PRODUCTS
determination of composition, 2812

THEFT
appeal against sentence, 2411, 2413–2425, 2434, 2437, 2439, 2441, 2442
appropriation, requirements of, 640
attempted—
appeal against sentence, 2426
intent necessary for offence, 641
going equipped for, appeal against sentence, 2390
intangible property, confidential information, 642
property abandoned where owner not liable to discover, it 643
unfair dismissal, 2885, 2886, 2888

THERMAL INSULATION
scheme, 1442

TIME
application made by post, when made, 2292

TOBACCO
products—
excise duty on—
administration, 761
enactments relating to, consolidation of, 780
metrication, 779

TOOLS
cost of upkeep of, 1568

TORT
action in, whether representative action should be permitted, 2152
conspiracy between husband and wife, 1646
representative action in, by shareholder, 2152

TRACTORS
agricultural or forestry, 2298
approval of, 103, 104

TRADE
Department of. *See* DEPARTMENT OF TRADE
interference with, injunction to prevent unlawful act, 525
speculation in stocks and shares, 1573

TRADE DESCRIPTION
false—
act or default of some other person, 2810
weight deficiency of coal due to moisture loss, 2811

TRADE DISPUTE. *See also* INDUSTRIAL ACTION
action in furtherance of—
interlocutory injunction to restrain—
action in contemplation of furtherance of dispute, 2829
balance of convenience, 2830
circumstances governing grant of injunction, 2828, 2831
legitimate trade object, 2832
claimant to unemployment benefit directly interested in, 2673, 2674
injunction to restrain action in furtherance of, 2829, 2830

TRADE LITERATURE
reproduction of leaflet for sale with product, 535

TRADE MARK
descriptive word, whether capable of distinguishing the goods, 2824
goods imported under, valuation, 772
non-use by registered proprietor, 2822, 2823
registration—
application for rectification of register, 2822, 2823
opposition, likelihood of confusion, 2825, 2826
use with alterations not substantially affecting its identity, 2823

TRADE NAME
distinctiveness of, 2820
passing-off—
application for interlocutory injunction, 2814
conversion of second-hand cars, 525
interlocutory injunction, 525, 2817, 2818, 2820
likelihood of confusion, 2814, 2815, 2817, 2818, 2820

WOMEN'S AUXILIARY FORCES
  allowance paid to disabled ex-members, 2076

WORK
  health and safety at. *See* HEALTH AND SAFETY

WORKMEN'S COMPENSATION
  supplementation scheme, 2685

WORLD HEALTH ORGANISATION
  immunities and privileges, 1347

WOUNDING
  malicious, appeal against sentence, 2384
  unlawful, appeal against sentence, 2383
  with intent, appeal against sentence, 2382, 2383

WRECK
  protection, restricted areas, 2575–2577

WRESTLING
  licensing of premises prohibiting women from
    taking part, 2505

WRIST INJURY
  quantum of damages, 839, 878, 879, 891

WRIT
  issue of, fee payable, 2166
  new forms of, 2159
  revision, 2159

YEMEN ARAB REPUBLIC
  oil pollution convention, 2568, 2573

YOUNG OFFENDER
  committal for sentence, validity, 1776

YOUNG PERSONS
  committal to prison, 1865

ZIMBABWE
  constitution for, 328
  constitution of—
    elections and appointments, 344
    provision for, 343
  establishment of, 342

WORDS AND PHRASES

accident (Road Traffic Act 1972, s. 8 (2))..2267
activity (Landlord and Tenant Act 1954, s. 23 (2))..1679
actual occupation (Land Registration Act 1925, s. 70 (1) (g))..1934
agriculture (common agricultural policy)..57
agriculture (Rent (Agriculture) Act 1976, s. 1)..53
all material times (Rent (Agriculture) Act 1976, Sch 9, para. 3)..54
alteration (Finance Act 1972, Sch. 4, group 8, item 2)..3042
annual payments ... due under a covenant (Finance Act 1965, Sch. 7, para 12 (c))..275
application (Bankruptcy Rules 1952, s. 139 (2))..209
appropriate time (Trade Union and Labour Relations Act 1974, Sch. 1, para. 6 (4A))..2949
as if (Leasehold Reform Act 1967, s. 3 (3))..1724
at the time of stealing (Theft Act 1968, s. 8 (1))..636
back-to-back houses (Housing Act 1957, s. 5 (1))..1431
business (Finance Act 1972, s. 2 (2))..3024, 3027
charged (Finance Act 1973, s. 4)...2993
clean (bill of lading)..2327
companies of which a third party has control (Contracts of Employment Act 1972, Sch. 1, para. 10 (2))..1034
competition (Lotteries and Amusements Act 1976, s. 14)..242
conditional discharge (Insolvency Act 1976, s. 7 (4))..213
conduct ... all the circumstances of the case (Matrimonial Causes Act 1973, s. 25)..942
conduct likely to cause a breach of the peace..658
control (Finance Act 1972, s. 21)..3007
control (Town and Country Planning Act 1971, s. 30 (1) (a))..2784
criminal cause or matter (Supreme Court of Judicature (Consolidation) Act 1925, s. 31 (1)).. 655
debt on a security (Finance Act 1965, Sch. 7, para. 11)..284
directly interested in the trade dispute (National Insurance Act 1965, s. 22 (1))..2673
eligible person (Agriculture (Miscellaneous Provisions) Act 1976, s. 18 (2))..47
emoluments (Income and Corporation Taxes Act 1970, s. 183 (1))..1567
explosive substance (Explosive Substances Act 1883, s. 4 (1))..1276
express agreement (Copyright Act 1911, s. 24 (1))..540
family (Rent Act 1968, Sch. 1, para. 3)..1709
fishing..1311
heard (Bankruptcy Rules 1952, r. 179)..208
ill-treatment (Mental Health Act 1959, s. 126)..1840
industrial building (Capital Allowances Act 1968, s. 7 (1) (e))..1509
in public (Copyright Act 1956, s. 2 (5))..530
indivisible load (Motor Vehicles (Construction and Use) Regulations 1973)..2309
interest in possession (Finance Act 1975, Sch. 5, para. 6 (2))..1384
judicial or other proceedings (Recognition of Divorces and Legal Separations Act 1971)..429
jurisdiction (European Convention on Human Rights, art. 1)..1446
keeps ... (Patents Act 1977, s. 60 (1) (a))..2023
known to the court (Inheritance (Provision for Family and Dependants) Act 1975, s. 1)..1266
let as a separate dwelling (Rent Act 1977, s. 1)..1699
liability of the Crown arising otherwise than in respect of His Majesty's Government in the United Kingdom (Crown Proceedings Act 1947, s. 40 (2) (b))..443
liable under the Act (Redundancy Payments Act 1965, s. 30 (1) (a))..1098
living on earnings of prostitution (Sexual Offences Act 1956, s. 30 (1))..633
lottery (Lotteries and Amusements Act 1976, s. 1)..242
made and published to the parties (R.S.C. Ord. 73, r. 5)..2525
materials (Input Tax (Exceptions) (No. 1) Order 1972, para. 3)..2985
money or money's worth (Land Charges Act 1925, s. 13 (2), now Land Charges Act 1972, s. 4 (6))...1657

881

Butt.
£29.50